Principles of Mechanics

Principles of Mechanics

Editor
Richard M. Renneboog, M.Sc.

SALEM PRESS
A Division of EBSCO Information Services, Inc.
Ipswich, Massachusetts

GREY HOUSE PUBLISHING

Publisher's Cataloging-In-Publication Data
(Prepared by Parlew Associates, LLC)

Names: Renneboog, Richard M., editor.
Title: Principles of mechanics / editor, Richard M. Renneboog, M.Sc.
Description: Ipswich, MA : Salem Press, a division of EBSCO Information Services, Inc. ; Amenia,
    NY : Grey House Publishing, 2023. | Series: [Principles of science]. | Includes bibliographic
    references and index. | Includes b&w photos and illustrations.
Identifiers: ISBN 9781637004227 (hardback)
Subjects: LCSH: Mechanics — Encyclopedias. | Engineering — Encyclopedias. | BISAC:
    TECHNOLOGY & ENGINEERING / Mechanical. | TECHNOLOGY & ENGINEERING /
    Reference. | SCIENCE / Mechanics / General.
Classification: LCC TA349.5 R46 2023 | DDC 620.100 3—dc23

FIRST PRINTING
PRINTED IN THE UNITED STATES OF AMERICA

CONTENTS

PUBLISHER'S NOTE

Mechanics is the next volume in *Salem's Principles of Science* series, which includes *Aeronautics*, *Microbiology*, *Energy*, *Marine Science*, *Geology*, *Information Technology*, and *Fire Science*.

This new resource explores the physical world and how it functions, introducing readers to the basic principles of classical mechanics.

Beginning with a comprehensive Introduction to the subject of mechanics written by volume editor Richard M. Renneboog, M.Sc, the entries in this title explore the mechanical functions, and the theories behind them, of concepts ranging from primitive stone weapons to space rockets, covering several important contributors to the field of classical mechanics as well. At its simplest level, mechanics involves understanding the principles by which the physical world functions and applying those principles to develop new uses.

Following the Introduction, *Principles of Mechanics* includes 130+ entries that follow an alphabetical arrangement, making topics easy to locate.

Entries begin by specifying related Fields of Study, followed by an Abstract and then a list of Key Concepts summarizing important points; all entries end with a helpful Further Reading section.

This work also includes helpful appendices, including:

- Bibliography;
- Glossary;
- Organizations;
- Subject Index

Salem Press extends appreciation to all involved in the development and production of this work. Names and affiliations of contributors to this work follow the Editor's Introduction.

Principles of Mechanics, as well as all Salem Press reference books, is available in print and as an e-book. Please visit www.salempress.com for more information.

INTRODUCTION

The field of mechanics can be thought of as applied physics in many ways, as it deals with understanding how the physical world and the things in it function, the principles behind those functions, and the application of those principles. This is what has produced essentially all of the modern world. But even the most advanced technology of today had its beginning thousands of years ago with ancient philosophers such as Archimedes, Hero of Alexandria, and Ctesibius of Alexandria. In actuality, the practice and science of mechanics as a human endeavor undoubtedly began many millennia before these men appeared. Although it is impossible to know the exact time or place, the exact incident is readily identifiable as the first time an individual understood how something had been made in nature and then applied that understanding to make something else. Perhaps it was the realization that rubbing a piece of wood with another one made it feel hot, and then using that understanding to make fire. Or perhaps it was seeing a piece of driftwood rubbing against a sharp rock and recognizing that the action had changed the shape of the wood, leading to creating a sharp stick by rubbing wood with a sharp stone.

To give it a somewhat finer definition, mechanics is the science of understanding the principles by which the physical world functions and applying those principles to the development of new uses and applications.

By examining a small selection of advances, we see that this describes every aspect of progress in mechanics right up to the present day. A sharp, pointy stick can be used to dig up edible roots, obtain meat, and fight an enemy. Making a pointed stick with a sharp rock—maybe a broken piece of obsidian or flint—to make a hand weapon can lead to the creation of a sharp, pointed rock with keen edges, the stone knife, and other stone cutting tools.

But what about rocks that aren't sharp, but round? They make good hammers for pounding those roots that were dug up with pointed sticks, for crushing seeds, and for bashing an enemy in a fight. They're also good for throwing at birds, small animals, and other humans. Once released from the hand, a thrown stone or rock becomes a projectile, an entirely different concept than the stone as a hammer.

Now let's take that pointed stick and throw it as if it were a stone. Thus, the spear is discovered. But what about the arm that throws the stone or the spear? Look at it as it goes through the motion of throwing and it will be readily seen that the forearm is essential to the performance of the projectile, and that humans with longer forearms were generally more effective in the use of spears. So, if longer forearms are more effective, then how can I make my forearms longer? How can I move my hand—the part that holds the thing I want to throw—farther way from the part where my arm bends, my elbow? If I tie the stone to a cord, I can move it as far away from my elbow as I wish, and I can swing it around in a circular motion so that if I let go of it at the right moment, the stone will go a lot farther than it would if I just threw it. It hits a lot harder, too. Now, if I can find a way to swing it around and let it fly without letting the cord fly away as well, I will have in effect succeeded in making my forearm longer in practice. I will have invented the sling, perhaps the very first projectile weapon based on mechanical principles.

The sling makes throwing a stone or other object much more effective, and even deadly. Hoplites, or citizen-soldiers, in the armies of ancient Greece used slings to hurl small round balls of lead at opposing forces, and there are few people who do not know the story of David and Goliath. But my arm is not strong enough to throw a spear anywhere near as far as I can sling a stone, because the spear is too large and heavy. Even my smallest spear cannot be thrown well, because my arm is simply not strong enough. No matter how I try it does not fly true; it wobbles and tumbles through the air. Trying to throw it with a cord doesn't work at all, but what if I use a stick with a "hand" at the end like my forearm? Now my small spear flies straight and true through the air, faster and farther than it ever could before. Thus is born the "throwing stick," or atlatl, as it is called.

As you can see, this progression can go on and on as humans use the basic mechanical principles of throwing a stone to make new and more effective methods to do just that. The sling, the atlatl, soon the bow and arrow, then the crossbow, the trebuchet, the catapult, the cannon, the musket, the rifle—all just more effective and powerful means of "throwing a stone."

The same type of progression is applicable to other mechanical actions as well. These, however, first require humans to recognize certain fundamental things that cannot be defined by any terms other than themselves. These are the so-called "simple machines"—the lever, the inclined plane, the wheel and axle, the pulley, the screw and the wedge. These six simple machines are the fundamental tools through which the principles of mechanics function. They facilitate the performance of work of all kinds and the construction of ever more complex machines.

By examining any complex machine, one can identify the individual simple machines that compose its overall structure. The Ferris wheel at a local fair, or the Eye of London cantilevered observation wheel in England, are just very large versions of the wheel and axle, and may require the incorporation of an inclined plane either as a ramp or a series of steps in a stairway for access. Every part of these large versions of the wheel and axle is held together by various screws and bolts, each one of which is an inclined plane wrapped around a cylinder in a helical manner. The plow, also held together by bolts, is a combination of a wedge that lifts the soil as it cuts through it, and an inclined plane that is curved rather than actually planar, that turns the lifted soil over for tillage. These are all still relatively simple machines, but the number of components in a machine increases greatly as they become more complex. A large steam engine, for example, like the behemoth housed in the Ford Museum in Michigan, consists of more than a quarter of a million individual mechanical parts, all working in unison.

In essence, mechanics has been and continues to be a progression of advances of applied thought. Each step builds upon the steps that came before it. To paraphrase Sir Isaac Newton, it is by standing on the shoulders of giants, or building on the works of others, that one can envision the new horizon of what is possible. A selection of those visionaries is included in this and other volumes in the *Principles of Science and Technology* series of reference works. The inventors discussed simply observed how something worked and thought of a better way to carry out that particular function. The probability that any of them purposefully set out to revolutionize the entire world with their invention is small. John Deere, for example, did not invent the plow; he made changes to existing plows without any design and changed the face of agriculture. He merely saw the problem inherent in the existing plows where he lived—wrought iron parts that became clogged when heavy, clay-like soil stuck to them and that wore out quickly—and saw a way to alleviate this by using steel instead of iron. In the same way, Jethro Tull saw the inefficiencies in the broadcast method of seeding—wasted and lost seeds planted haphazardly at irregular depths—and thought of a way to plant seeds in parallel rows at a consistent depth. John Kay saw the way the width of cloth formed on weaving looms was limited by the length of the weaver's arms when passing the shuttle through the loom, and he thought of a way for the weaver to pass the shuttle across any width of loom.

Others in the history of mechanics sought to understand and quantify physical principles mathematically. Newton, for example, concluded that there must be a force that draws one object to another. The actual role of the falling apple is open to debate with regard to where it landed (it probably never fell onto his head), but his own writings state that he did observe an apple fall from the tree to the ground, which led to his conclusions about gravity. Unlike classical Greek philosophers, who never experimented, believing thought and logic were the only requirements, Newton was a consummate scientist who believed conclusions must be justified by practical investigation to confirm their validity. In his practice, he revealed the relationship between mass and gravity, as well as his three laws of motion. Archimedes, D'Alembert, Euler and others followed similar procedures of observation and experimentation to identify the physical laws and principles for which they are known.

The history of mechanics is as rich as the field of mechanics itself. This volume focuses on a broad cross-section of both, with a number of explanatory articles. In this way, the door is opened for readers to explore the vastness of the subject and perhaps find their way to the idea that leads them to inventions and discoveries of their own. Each article includes a section of key concepts and definitions, as well as a section listing reference sources. Every effort has been made to ensure that the material is up to date and correct within the limits of current knowledge.

As this volume's Editor, I sincerely hope you will find it helpful in building your understanding of the physical world in which we all live.

—*Richard M. Renneboog*

Contributors

Amy Ackerberg-Hastings
University of Maryland, University College

Michael P. Auerbach
Marblehead, MA

Ellen Bailey
Independent Scholar

John H. Barnhill
Independent Scholar

Bezaleel S. Benjamin
University of Kansas

Alvin K. Benson
Utah Valley University

David M. Best
Northern Arizona University

Tyler Biscontini
Independent Scholar

Jeffrey Bowman
Independent Scholar

Howard Bromberg
University of Michigan

Lindsay K. Brownell
Somerville, MA

Eric Bullard
Independent Scholar

Jeffrey L. Buller
Georgia Southern University

Cait Caffrey
Northeast Editing, Inc.

J. Campbell
Independent Scholar

Daniel Castaldy
Framingham State University

Michael J. Caulfield
Gannon University

Diana C. Coe
Independent Scholar

Anne Collins
Independent Scholar

Nancy W. Comstoc
College Misericordia

Rafael de la Llave
Georgia Institute of Technology

David Driver
San Diego, CA

John J. Dykla
Loyola University

Said Elghobashi
University of California, Irvine

Reza Fazeli
ANU College of Engineering & Computer Science, Australia

David G. Fisher
Lycoming College

George J. Flynn
SUNY-Plattasburgh

Angel G. Fuentes
Chandler-Gilbert Community College

Joanta Green
Renewable Energy Systems in Southeast Asia

Gina Hagler
Rare Math

Angela Harmon
Independent Scholar

Sally Hibbin
Independent Scholar

J. D. Ho
Independent Scholar

James R. Hofmann
California State University, Fullerton

John R. Holmes
Franciscan University at Steubenville

Stephen Huber
LeTourneau University

J. Donald Hughes
University of Denver

Patrick Norman Hunt
Stanford University

Linda Hutchison
San Diego, CA

April D. Ingram
Kelowna, British Columbia

Micah L. Issitt
St. Louis, MO

Jamey D. Jacob
Oklahoma State University

John C. Johnson
University of Iowa

Douglas R. Jordan
Independent Scholar

Bassam Kassab
Santa Clara Valley Water District

Firman D. King
Independent Scholar

Narayanan M. Komerath
Georgia Institute of Technology

Bill Kte'pi
Independent Scholar

Donald L. Kunz
Air Force Institute of Technology

Lisa A. Lambert
Chatham College

Jack Lasky
Northeast Editing, Inc.

Kirk S. Lawrence
St. Joseph's College

Michele LeBlanc
New York University School of Medicine

M. Lee
Independent Scholar

Thomas A. Lehman
Independent Scholar

Josué Njock Libii
Purdue University

James Livingston
Northern Michigan University

M. A. K. Lodhi
Texas Tech University

L. L. Lundin
Independent Scholar

R. C. Lutz
Santa Barbara University of the Pacific

Fai Ma
University of California, Berkeley

Nancy Farm Männikkö
Centers for Disease Control & Prevention

James F. Marchman III
Virginia Tech

Michael Mazzei
Ladder Capital

Linda L. McDonald
University of Melbourne

Russell McKenna
University of Aberdeen, Scotland

William J. McKinney
Independent Scholar

Robert G. Melton
Pennsylvania State University, University Park

Julia M. Meyers
Duquesne University

Steve Miller
Independent Scholar

Elizabeth Mohn
Northeast Editing, Inc.

James A. Nickel
Texas A&M University

Robert J. Paradowski
Rochester Institute of Technology

Mary Parker
Allston, MA

George R. Plitnik
Frostburg State University

William O. Rasmussen
University of Arizona

Richard M. Renneboog
Independent Scholar

Joseph J. Romano
University of Pennsylvania

Casey M. Schwarz
University of Central Florida

Abhijit Sen
Suri Vidyasagar College

Richard Sheposh
Northeast Editing, Inc.

Daniel Showalter
Eastern Mennonite University

R. Baird Shuman
University of Illinois, Urbana-Champaign

Sanford S. Singer
University of Dayton

Peter D. Skiff
Bard College

Billy R. Smith
Anne Arundel Community College

Roger Smith
Portland, OR

R. Smith Reynolds
Independent Scholar

Judith L. Steininger
Milwaukee School of Engineering

Frederick M. Surowiec
Independent Scholar

Daniel Taylor
Bethel College

Dereje Teklemariam
Ethiopian Civil Service University

Garrett L. Van Wicklen
University of Delaware

Kenrick Vezina
Lowell, MA

Andrew J. Waskey
Dalton State College

Shawncey Webb
Taylor University

Edwin G. Wiggins
Webb Institute

Richard J. Wurtz
Independent Scholar

Scott Zimmer
Alliant International University

ACCELERATION

Fields of Study: Physics; Engineering; Mechanics; Mathematics

ABSTRACT

Acceleration is the rate of velocity change of a moving object, whether in a straight line or a curved or circular motion. This change of velocity is measured in meters per second, expressed as m/s². Acceleration occurs any time there is a change in speed or direction. It includes slowing down (negative acceleration) as well as speeding up. Because it involves both speed and direction, acceleration is a vector quantity.

KEY CONCEPTS

acceleration: the increase in velocity over a period of time; going faster

air resistance: opposition to motion due to air molecules experienced by an object passing through the air; also called drag with respect to flying machines

centripetal: acceleration or experienced force directed toward the focal point of curving motion or the center of a circle

deceleration: also called negative acceleration, the decrease of velocity over a period of time, the opposite of acceleration

tangent: a straight line external to a curve that touches the curve at one point only

OVERVIEW

Galileo Galilei (1564-1642), an Italian physicist, experimented with the velocity of objects by rolling them down an inclined plane. Velocity is the rate of change in an object's position. Galileo observed that the objects gained speed as they rolled. He conducted a long-term study of the distances objects rolled and the time it took them to roll this distance. He eventually was able to show that each distance was in proportion to the time squared. For example, a ball that reaches a speed of 5 meters per second in 10 seconds has an acceleration rate of 0.5 m/s². He wrote the mathematical equation to describe how the velocity of the objects increased as they rolled— the first accurate explanation of accelerated motion.

Although the first descriptions of velocity came from Galileo, Sir Isaac Newton (1642-1727), an English physicist, took the next step and explained that some force must act upon an object to increase its velocity. For the rolling objects (or falling apples), the force was gravity. Newton's First Law of Motion states that unless an external force acts upon them, objects at rest remain at rest and objects in motion at a constant velocity continue in their direction at the same velocity.

Newton's Second Law of Motion applies to acceleration. It states that the sum of all forces (F) acting on an object is equal to the mass (m) of the object multiplied by the acceleration (a) of the object, or F = ma. That means that acceleration occurs when a force affects an object or mass, and the greater the mass, the greater the force needed to cause acceleration. In other words, more force is required when moving heavier objects the same distance as lighter ones. For example, a person can kick a hollow plastic ball a considerable distance without much effort but would need substantial strength to push a rock of similar size the same distance.

Acceleration changes either the speed or the direction of an object. A car that pulls onto a street is accelerating as long as it is gaining speed; once the speed levels off and becomes constant, it is no longer accelerating. However, if it rounds a curve that changes its direction, it is then accelerating, even if the speed remains constant. Negative acceleration, or deceleration, occurs when the car slows down.

LINEAR ACCELERATION

The term linear acceleration refers to a change in velocity without a change in direction—the object travels in a straight line. When an object moves in one direction for a given time, such as a car driving on a straight highway, it is accelerating only if its speed varies. For example, if the car is traveling at 26 m/s west (about 94 kph) and speeds up to 31 m/s west (about 112 kph), it is accelerating.

But it is also accelerating if it slows to 14 m/s west (about 31 mph) when a deer crosses the road. Linear acceleration is expressed as a positive number if the car is speeding up and as a negative number if it is slowing down. Negative acceleration is generally called deceleration rather than negative acceleration.

CENTRIPETAL ACCELERATION

When an object rotates, or moves in a circular pattern, it changes velocity even though its speed does not change. Since velocity is a vector quantity, having both speed and direction, the velocity linear velocity vector of the circular motion is tangent to the circle and, because acceleration is always perpendicular to the velocity, the direction of the acceleration is toward the center of the circle. Thus, it is called centripetal acceleration.

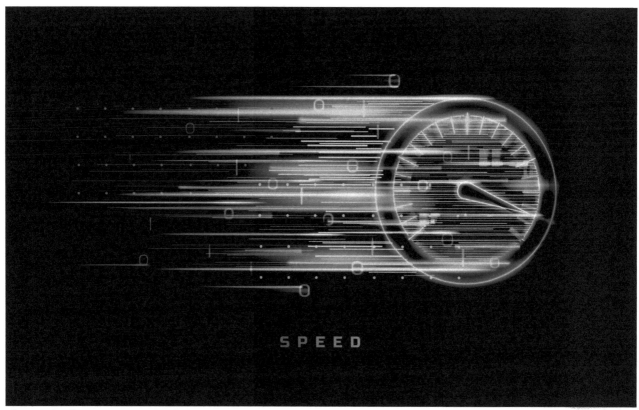

Photo via iStock/Sensvector. [Used under license.]

The force providing the acceleration can be the tension in a string, if the object is a tethered ball, or gravity if it is a moon orbiting a planet. The formula for calculating such circular acceleration is $a = v^2/r$, where r is the radius of the circular motion.

G FORCE

G force is measured in relation to the gravitational pull present on Earth's surface. Normal gravity is 1 G, or 9.8 m/s^2. Forces above 1 G cause the sensation of carrying greater weight. High G forces can be caused by sudden acceleration. Serious injury or even death is possible if a person is exposed to a force higher than 100 G for more than a few seconds.

In relation to acceleration, G force is the intensified gravitational pull on an object or body during increased velocity. The force can be strengthened further if the acceleration takes place in a circular pattern. For example, people riding in an airplane experience a mildly increased G force at takeoff, but a jet pilot flying in a tight circular pattern at a high speed will feel a pull as much as 10 times greater than normal gravity. Part of the thrill of roller coasters is the increased G forces produced by speed and sudden curves. The greatest force scientists have produced involves centrifuges, which spin at high speed, reaching G forces of several hundred thousand. In one experiment, scientists created a tiny vortex that accelerated to a G force of more than 1 million.

RESISTANCE

When an object is dropped, the force of gravity causes it to accelerate rapidly as it falls. However, as it falls, friction from the particles in the air reduces the acceleration. There is a point at which the force of resistance and the force of gravity balance out; after that, the object's acceleration is zero, and it simply falls at what is called terminal velocity. Although it is true that falling objects of unlike mass accelerate at the same rate, those with large surface areas, such as parachutes, encounter more air resistance and reach terminal velocity more quickly.

—Nancy W. Comstock

Further Reading

Burnett, Betty. "Acceleration." *The Laws of Motion: Understanding Uniform and Accelerated Motion*. Rosen Publishing, 2005.

Halliday, David, Robert Resnick, and Jearl Walker. *Fundamentals of Physics, Volume 1*. 12th ed., John Wiley & Sons, 2021.

Kudek, Jozef. "Circular Motion & Gravity." *Introductory General Physics*. Old Dominion University, 2013, ww2.odu.edu/~jdudek/Phys111N_materials/4_circular_motion_gravity.pdf. Accessed 10 Dec. 2014.

Ling, Samuel J., Jeff Sanny, and William Moebs. *University Physics, Volume 1*. Samurai Media Limited, 2017.

"Smallest Whirlpools Can Pack Stunningly Strong Force." *Science Daily*, 4 Sept. 2003, www.sciencedaily.com/releases/2003/09/030904075438.htm. Accessed 10 Dec. 2014.

See also: Angular forces; Angular momentum; Ballistic weapons; Celestial mechanics; Centrifugation; Circular motion; Classical or applied mechanics; Coriolis effect; Dynamics (mechanics); Force (physics); Friction; Linear motion; Moment of inertia; Momentum (physics); Motion; Newton, Isaac; Newton's laws; Pendulums; Speed; Vectors

ACOUSTICS

Fields of Study: Physics; Mechanics; Mathematics

ABSTRACT

Acoustics is the science dealing with the production, transmission, and effects of vibration in material media. If the medium is air and the vibration frequency is between 18 and 18,000 hertz (Hz), the vibration is termed "sound." Sound is used in a broader context to describe sounds in solids and underwater and structure-borne sounds.

KEY CONCEPTS

cocktail party effect: the ability to focus on and hear clearly a conversation taking place among other conversations in a generally noisy atmosphere

masking: a phenomenon in which the brain selectively hears what it expects to hear in the midst of noise

noise: generally, any undesired sound and discordant frequency combinations

piezoelectric: a material that emits an electrical signal when subject to impact

sound: the perception and interpretation of vibrations reaching the ear as they travel through a conductive fluid medium such as air or water

ultrasonic: vibrations having a frequency of 25,000 Hertz and greater

BASIC PRINCIPLES

Acoustics is the science dealing with the production, transmission, and effects of vibration in material media. If the medium is air and the vibration frequency is between 18 and 18,000 hertz (Hz), the vibration is termed "sound." Sound is used in a broader context to describe sounds in solids and underwater and structure-borne sounds. Because mechanical vibrations, whether natural or human induced, have accompanied humans through the long course of human evolution, acoustics is the most interdisciplinary science. For humans, hearing is a very important sense, and the ability to vocalize greatly facilitates communication and social interaction. Sound can have profound psychological effects; music may soothe or relax a troubled mind, and noise can induce anxiety and hypertension.

The words "acoustics" and "phonics" evolved from ancient Greek roots for hearing and speaking, respectively. Thus, acoustics began with human communication, making it one of the oldest if not the most basic of sciences. Because acoustics is ubiquitous in human endeavors, it is the broadest and most interdisciplinary of sciences; its most profound contributions have occurred when it is commingled with an independent field. The interdisciplinary nature of acoustics has often consigned it to a subsidiary role as a minor subdivision of mechanics, hydrodynamics, or electrical engineering. Certainly, the various technical aspects of acoustics could be parceled out to larger and better established divisions of science, but then acoustics would lose its unique strengths and its source of dynamic creativity. The main difference between acoustics and more self-sufficient branches of science is that acoustics depends on physical laws developed in and borrowed from other fields. Therefore, the primary task of acoustics is to take these divergent principles and integrate them into a coherent whole in order to understand, measure, and control vibration phenomena.

The Acoustical Society of America subdivides acoustics into fifteen main areas, the most important of which are ultrasonics, which examines high-frequency waves not audible to humans; psychological acoustics, which studies how sound is perceived in the brain; physiological acoustics, which looks at human and animal hearing mechanisms; speech acoustics, which focuses on the human vocal apparatus and oral communication; musical acoustics, which involves the physics of musical instruments; underwater sound, which examines the production and propagation of sound in liquids; and noise, which concentrates on the control and suppression of unwanted sound. Two other important areas of applied acoustics are architectural acoustics (the acoustical design of concert halls and sound reinforcement systems) and audio engineering (recording and reproducing sound).

CORE CONCEPTS

Ultrasonics. Dog whistles, which can be heard by dogs but generally not by humans, can generate ultrasonic frequencies of about 25 kilohertz (kHz). Two types of transducers, magnetostrictive and piezoelec-

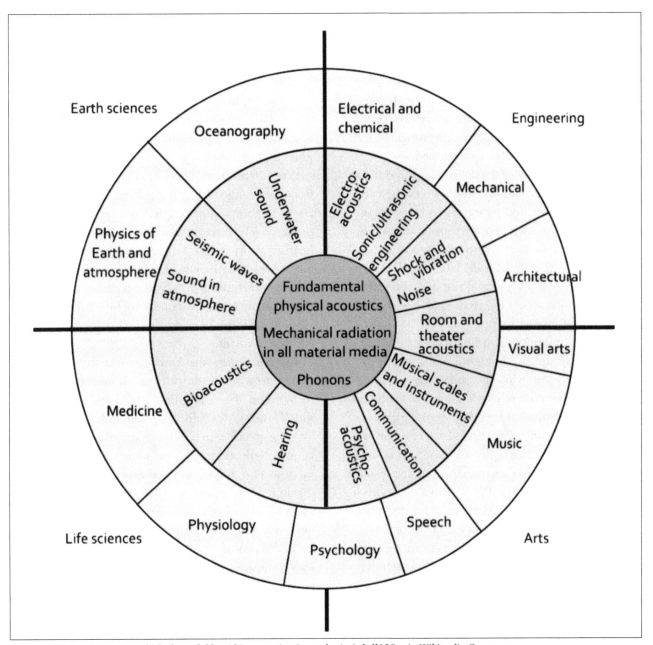

Lindsay's Wheel of Acoustics, which shows fields within acoustics. Image by Amitchell125, via Wikimedia Commons.

tric, are used to generate higher frequencies and greater power. Magnetostrictive devices convert magnetic energy into ultrasound by subjecting ferric material (iron or nickel) to a strong oscillating magnetic field. The field causes the material to alternately expand and contract, thus creating sound waves of the same frequency as that of the field. The resulting sound waves have frequencies between 20 Hz and 50 kHz and several thousand watts of power. Such transducers operate at the mechanical resonance frequency where the energy transfer is most efficient.

Piezoelectric transducers convert electric energy into ultrasound by applying an oscillating electric field to a piezoelectric crystal (such as quartz). These transducers, which work in liquids or air, can generate frequencies in the megahertz region with considerable power. In addition to natural crystals, ceramic piezoelectric materials, which can be fabricated into any desired shape, have been developed.

Physiological and psychological acoustics. Physiological acoustics studies auditory responses of the ear and its associated neural pathways, and psychological acoustics is the subjective perception of sounds through human auditory physiology. Mechanical, electrical, optical, radiological, or biochemical techniques are used to study neural responses to various aural stimuli. Because these techniques are typically invasive, experiments are performed on animals with auditory systems that are similar to the human system. In contrast, psychological acoustic studies are noninvasive and typically use human subjects.

A primary objective of psychological acoustics is to define the psychological correlates to the physical parameters of sound waves. Sound waves in air may be characterized by three physical parameters: frequency, intensity, and their spectrum. When a sound wave impinges on the ear, the pressure variations in the air are transformed by the middle ear to mechanical vibrations in the inner ear. The cochlea then decomposes the sound into its constituent frequencies and transforms these into neural action potentials, which travel to the brain where the sound is evidenced. Frequency is perceived as pitch, the intensity level as loudness, and the spectrum determines the timbre, or tone quality, of a note.

Another psychoacoustic effect is masking. When a person listens to a noisy version of recorded music, the noise virtually disappears if the music is being enjoyed. This ability of the brain to selectively listen has had important applications in digitally recorded music. When the sounds are digitally compressed, such as in MP3 (MPEG-1 audio layer 3) systems, the brain compensates for the loss of information; thus one experiences higher fidelity sound than the stored content would imply. Also, the brain creates information when the incoming signal is masked or nonexistent, producing a psychoacoustic phantom effect. This phantom effect is particularly prevalent when heightened perceptions are imperative, as when danger is lurking.

Psychoacoustic studies have determined that the frequency range of hearing is from 20 to about 20,000 Hz for young people, and the upper limit progressively decreases with age. The rate at which hearing acuity declines depends on several factors, not the least of which is lifetime exposure to loud sounds, which progressively deteriorate the hair cells of the cochlea. Moderate hearing loss can be compensated for by a hearing aid; severe loss requires a cochlear implant.

Speech acoustics. Also known as acoustic phonetics, speech acoustics deals with speech production and recognition. The scientific study of speech began with Thomas Alva Edison's phonograph, which allowed a speech signal to be recorded and stored for later analysis. Replaying the same short speech segment several times using consecutive filters passing through a limited range of frequencies creates a spectrogram, which visualizes the spectral properties of vowels and consonants. During the first half of the twentieth century, Bell Telephone Laboratories dedicated considerable time and resources to the systematic understanding of all aspects of speech, including vocal tract resonances, voice quality, and prosodic features of speech. For the first time, electric circuit theory was applied to speech acoustics, and analogue electric circuits were used to investigate synthetic speech.

Musical acoustics. A conjunction of music, craftsmanship, auditory science, and vibration physics, musical acoustics analyzes musical instruments to better understand how the instruments are crafted, the physical principles of their tone production, and why each instrument has a unique timbre. Musical instruments are studied by analyzing their tones and then creating computer models to synthesize these sounds. When the sounds can be recreated with minimal software complications, a synthesizer featuring realistic orchestral tones may be constructed. The second method of study is to assemble an instrument or modify an existing instrument to perform nondestructive (or on occasion destructive) testing so that the effects of various modifications may be gauged.

Underwater sound. Also known as hydroacoustics, this field uses frequencies between 10 Hz and 1 megahertz (MHz). The deployment of submarines in World War I provided the impetus for the rapid development of underwater listening devices (hydrophones) and sonar (sound navigation ranging), the acoustic equivalent of radar. Pulses of sound are emitted and the echoes are processed to extract information about submerged objects. When the speed of underwater sound is known, the reflection time for a pulse determines the distance to an object. If the object is moving, its speed of approach or recession is deduced from the frequency shift of the reflection, or the Doppler effect. Returning pulses have a higher frequency when the object approaches and lower frequency when it moves away.

Noise. Physically, noise may be defined as an intermittent or random oscillation with multiple frequency components, but psychologically, noise is any unwanted sound. Noise can adversely affect human health and well-being by inducing stress, interfering with sleep, increasing heart rate, raising blood pressure, modifying hormone secretion, and even inducing depression. The physical effects of noise are no less severe. The vibrations in irregular road surfaces caused by large rapid vehicles can cause adjacent buildings to vibrate to an extent that is intolerable to the buildings' inhabitants, even without structural damage. Machinery noise in industry is a serious problem because continuous ex-

posure to loud sounds will induce hearing loss. In apartment buildings, noise transmitted through walls is always problematic; the goal is to obtain adequate sound insulation using lightweight construction materials.

Traffic noise, both external and internal, is ubiquitous in modern life. The first line of defense is to reduce noise at its source by improving engine enclosures, mufflers, and tires. The next method, used primarily when interstate highways are adjacent to residential areas, is to block the noise by the construction of concrete barriers or the planting of sound-absorbing vegetation. Internal automobile noise has been greatly abated by designing more aerodynamically efficient vehicles to reduce air turbulence, using better sound isolation materials, and improving vibration isolation.

Aircraft noise, particularly in the vicinity of airports, is a serious problem exacerbated by the fact that as modern airplanes have become more powerful, the noise they generate has risen concomitantly. The noise radiated by jet engines is reduced by two structural modifications. Acoustic linings are placed around the moving parts to absorb the high frequencies caused by jet whine and turbulence, but this modification is limited by size and weight constraints. The second modification is to reduce the number of rotor blades and stator vanes, but this is somewhat inhibited by the desired power output. Special noise problems occur when aircraft travel at supersonic speeds (faster than the speed of sound), as this propagates a large pressure wave toward the ground that is experienced as an explosion. The unexpected sonic boom startles people, breaks windows, and damages houses. Sonic booms have been known to destroy rock structures in national parks. Because of these concerns, commercial aircraft are prohibited from flying at supersonic speeds over land areas.

Construction equipment (such as earthmoving machines) creates high noise levels both internally and externally. When the cabs of these machines are not closed, the only feasible manner of protecting operators' hearing is by using earplugs. By carefully designing an enclosed cabin, structural vibration can be reduced and sound leaks made less significant, thus quieting the operator's environment. Although manufacturers are attempting to reduce the external noise, it is a daunting task because the rubber tractor treads occasionally used to replace metal are not as durable.

APPLICATIONS PAST AND PRESENT

Ultrasonics. High-intensity ultrasonic applications include ultrasonic cleaning, mixing, welding, drilling, and various chemical processes. Ultrasonic cleaners use waves in the 150 to 400 kHz range on items (such as jewelry, watches, lenses, and surgical instruments) placed in an appropriate solution. Ultrasonic cleaners have proven to be particularly effective in cleaning surgical devices because they loosen contaminants by aggressive agitation irrespective of an instrument's size or shape, and disassembly is not required. Ultrasonic waves are effective in cleaning most metals and alloys, as well as wood, plastic, rubber, and cloth. Ultrasonic waves are used to emulsify two nonmiscible liquids, such as oil and water, by forming the liquids into finely dispersed particles that then remain in homogeneous suspension. Many paints, cosmetics, and foods are emulsions formed by this process.

Although aluminum can be soldered using modified conventional means, it is nonetheless difficult to achieve good results. However, two surfaces subjected to intense ultrasonic vibration will bond—without the application of heat—in a strong and precise weld. Ultrasonic drilling is effective where conventional drilling is problematic, for instance, drilling square holes in glass. The drill bit, a transducer having the required shape and size, is used with an abrasive slurry that chips away the material when the suspended powder oscillates. Some of the chemical applications of ultrasonics are in the atomization of liquids, in electroplating, and as a catalyst in chemical reactions.

Low-intensity ultrasonic waves are used for nondestructive probing to locate flaws in materials for which complete reliability is mandatory, such as those used in spacecraft components and nuclear reactor vessels. When an ultrasonic transducer emits a pulse of energy into the test object, flaws reflect the wave and are detected. Because objects subjected to stress emit ultrasonic waves, these signals may be used to interpret the condition of the material as it is increasingly stressed. Another application is ultrasonic emission testing, which records the ultrasound emitted by porous rock when natural gas is pumped into cavities formed by the rock to determine the maximum pressure these natural holding tanks can withstand.

Low-intensity ultrasonics is used for medical diagnostics in two different applications. First, ultrasonic waves penetrate body tissues but are reflected by moving internal organs, such as the heart. The frequency of waves reflected from a moving structure is Doppler-shifted, thus causing beats with the original wave, which can be heard. This procedure is particularly useful for performing fetal examinations on a pregnant woman; because sound waves are not electromagnetic, they will not harm the fetus. The second application is to create a sonogram image of the body's interior. A complete cross-sectional image may be produced by superimposing the images scanned by successive ultrasonic waves passing through different regions. This procedure, unlike an X-ray, displays all the tissues in the cross section and also avoids any danger posed by the radiation involved in X-ray imaging.

Physiological and psychological acoustics. Because the ear is a nonlinear system, it produces beat tones that are the sum and difference of two frequencies. For example, if two sinusoidal frequencies of 100 and 150 Hz simultaneously arrive at the ear, the brain will, in addition to these two tones, create tones of 250 and 50 Hz (sum and difference, respectively). Thus, although a small speaker cannot reproduce the fundamental frequencies of bass tones, the difference between the harmonics of that pitch will re-create the missing fundamental in the listener's brain.

Another psychoacoustic effect is masking. When a person listens to a noisy version of recorded music, the noise virtually disappears if the individual is enjoying the music. This ability of the brain to selectively listen has had important applications in digitally recorded music. When sounds are digitally compressed, as in MP3 systems, the brain compensates for the loss of information, thus creating a higher fidelity sound than that conveyed by the stored content alone.

As twentieth-century technology evolved, environmental noise increased concomitantly; lifetime exposure to loud sounds, commercial and recreational, has created an epidemic of hearing loss, most noticeable in the elderly because the effects are cumulative. Wearing a hearing aid, fitted adjacent to or inside the ear canal, is an effectual means of counteracting this handicap. The device consists of one or several microphones, which create electric signals that are amplified and transduced into sound waves redirected back into the ear. More sophisticated hearing aids incorporate an integrated circuit to control volume, either manually or automatically, or to switch to volume contours designed for various listening environments, such conversations on the telephone or where excessive background noise is present.

Speech acoustics. With the advent of the computer age, speech synthesis moved to digital processing, either by bandwidth compression of stored speech or by using a speech synthesizer. The synthesizer reads a text and then produces the appropriate phonemes on demand from their basic acoustic parameters, such as the vibration frequency of the vocal cords and the frequencies and amplitudes of the vowel formants. This method of generating speech is considerably more efficient in terms of data storage than archiving a dictionary of prerecorded phrases.

Another important, and probably the most difficult, area of speech acoustics is the machine recognition of spoken language. When machine recognition programs are sufficiently advanced, the computer will be able to listen to a sentence in any reasonable dialect and produce a printed text of the utterance. Two basic recognition strategies exist, one dealing with words spoken in isolation and the other with continuous speech. In both cases, it is desirable to teach the computer to recognize the speech of different people through a training program. Because recognition of continuous speech is considerably more difficult than the identification of isolated words, very sophisticated pattern-matching models must be employed. One example of a machine recognition system is a word-driven dictation system that uses sophisticated software to process input speech. This system is somewhat adaptable to different voices and is able to recognize 30,000 words at a rate of 30 words per minute. The ideal machine recognition system would translate a spoken input language into another language in real time with correct grammar. Although some progress is being made, such a device has remained in the realm of speculative fantasy.

Musical acoustics. The importance of musical acoustics to manufacturers of quality instruments is apparent. During the last decades of the twentieth century, fundamental research led, for example, to vastly improved French horns, organ pipes, orchestral strings, and the creation of an entirely new family of violins.

Underwater sound. Applications for underwater acoustics include devices for underwater communication by acoustic means, remote control devices, underwater navigation and positioning systems, acoustic thermometers to measure ocean temperature, and echo sounders to locate schools of fish or other biota. Low-frequency devices can be used to explore the seabed for seismic research.

Although primitive measuring devices were developed in the 1920s, it was during the 1930s that sonar systems began incorporating piezoelectric transducers to increase their accuracy. These improved systems and their increasingly more sophisticated progeny became essential for the submarine warfare of World War II. After the war, theoretical advances in underwater acoustics coupled with computer technology have raised sonar systems to ever more sophisticated levels.

Noise. One system for abating unwanted sound is active noise control. The first successful application of active noise control was noise-canceling headphones, which reduce unwanted sound by using microphones placed in proximity to the ear to record the incoming noise. Electronic circuitry then generates a signal, exactly opposite to the incoming sound, which is reproduced in the earphones, thus canceling the noise by destructive interference. This system enables listeners to enjoy music without having to use excessive volume levels to mask outside noise and allows people to sleep in noisy vehicles such as airplanes. Because active noise suppression is more effective with low frequencies, most commercial systems rely on soundproofing the earphone to attenuate high frequencies. To effectively cancel high frequencies, the microphone and emitter would have to be situated adjacent to the user's eardrum, but this is not technically feasible. Active noise control is also being considered as a means of controlling low-frequency airport noise, but because of its complexity and expense, this is not yet commercially feasible.

IMPACT ON INDUSTRY

Acoustics is the focus of research at numerous governmental agencies and academic institutions, as well as some private industries. Acoustics also plays an important role in many industries, often as part of product design (hearing aids and musical instruments) or as an element in a service (noise control consulting).

Industry and business. Many businesses (such as the manufacturers of hearing aids, ultrasound medical devices, and musical instruments) use acoustics in their products or services and therefore employ experts in acoustics. Businesses are also involved in many aspects of acoustic research, particularly controlling noise and facilitating communication. Raytheon BBN Technologies in Cambridge, Massachusetts, has developed low-data-rate Noise Robust Vocoders (electronic speech synthesizers) that generate comprehensible speech at data rates considerably below other state-of-the-art devices. Acoustic Research Laboratories in Sydney, Australia, designs and manufactures specialized equipment for measuring environmental noise and vibration, in addition to providing contract research and development services.

Government agencies and military. Acoustics is studied in many government laboratories in the United States, including the US Naval Research Laboratory (NRL), the Air Force Research Laboratory (AFRL), the Los Alamos National Laboratory, and the Lawrence Livermore National Laboratory. Research at the NRL and the AFRL is primarily in the applied acoustics area, and Los Alamos and Lawrence Livermore are oriented toward physical acoustics. The NRL emphasizes fundamental multidisciplinary research focused on creating and applying new materials and technologies to maritime applications. In particular, the applied acoustics division, using ongoing basic scientific research, develops improved signal processing systems for detecting and tracking underwater targets. The AFRL is heavily invested in research on auditory localization (spatial hearing), virtual auditory display technologies, and speech intelligibility in noisy environments. The effects of high-intensity noise on humans, as well as methods of attenuation, constitute a significant area of investigation at this facility. Another important area of research is the problem of providing intelligible voice communication in extremely noisy situations, such as those encountered by military or emergency personnel using low data rate narrowband radios, which compromise signal quality.

Academic research and teaching. Research in acoustics is conducted at many colleges and universities in the United States, usually through physics or engineering departments, but, in the case of physiological and psychological acoustics, in groups that draw from multiple departments, including psychology, neurology, and linguistics. The Speech Research Laboratory at Indiana University investigates speech perception and processing through a broad interdisciplinary research program. The Speech Research Lab, a collaboration between the University of Delaware and the A. I. duPont Hospital for Children, creates speech synthesizers for the vocally impaired. A human speaker records a data bank of words and phrases that can be concatenated on demand to produce natural-sounding speech.

Academic research in acoustics is also being conducted in laboratories in Europe and other parts of the world. The Laboratoire d'Acoustique at the Université de Maine in Le Mans, France, specializes in research in vibration in materials, transducers, and musical instruments. The Andreyev Acoustics Institute of the Russian Acoustical Society brings together researchers from Russian universities, agencies, and businesses to conduct fundamental and applied research in ocean acoustics, ultrasonics, signal processing, noise and vibration, electroacoustics, and bioacoustics. The Speech and Acoustics Laboratory at the Nara Institute of Science and Technology in Nara, Japan, studies diverse aspects of human-machine communication through speech-oriented multimodal interaction. The Acoustics Research Centre, part of the Na-

tional Institute of Creative Arts and Industries in New Zealand, is concerned with the impact of noise on humans. A section of this group, Acoustic Testing Service, provides commercial testing of building materials for their noise attenuation properties.

Academic positions dedicated to acoustics are few, as are the numbers of qualified applicants. Most graduates of acoustics programs find employment in research-based industries in which acoustical aspects of products are important, and others work for government laboratories.

INTERESTING FACTS ABOUT ACOUSTICS

Scientists have created an acoustic refrigerator, which uses a standing sound wave in a resonator to provide the motive power for operation. Oscillating gas particles increase the local temperature, causing heat to be transferred to the container walls, where it is expelled to the environment, cooling the interior.

A cochlear implant, an electronic device surgically implanted in the inner ear, provides a hearing ability to those with damaged cochlea or those with congenital deafness. Because the implants use only about two dozen electrodes to replace 16,000 hair cells, speech sounds, although intelligible, have a robotic quality.

MP3 files contain audio that is digitally encoded using an algorithm that compresses the data by a factor of about eleven but yields a reasonably faithful reproduction. The quality of sound reproduced depends on the data sampling rate, the quality of the encoder, and the complexity of the signal.

Sound cannot travel through a vacuum, but it can travel four times faster through water than through air.

The "cocktail party effect" refers to a person's ability to direct attention to one conversation at a time despite the many conversations taking place in the room.

Continued exposure to noise over 85 decibels (dB) will gradually cause hearing loss. The noise level on a quiet residential street is 40 dB, a vacuum cleaner 60-85 dB, a leaf blower 110 dB, an ambulance siren 120 dB, a rifle shot 160 dB, and a rocket launching from its pad 180 dB.

SOCIAL CONTEXT AND FUTURE PROSPECTS
Acoustics affects virtually every aspect of modern life; its contributions to societal needs are incalculable. Ultrasonic waves clean objects, are routinely employed to probe matter, and are used in medical diagnosis. Cochlear implants restore people's ability to hear, and active noise control helps provide quieter listening environments. New concert halls are routinely designed with excellent acoustical properties, and vastly improved or entirely new musical instruments have made their debut. Infrasound from earthquakes is used to study the composition of Earth's mantle, and sonar is essential to locate submarines and aquatic life. Sound waves are used to explore the effects of structural vibrations. Automatic speech recognition devices and hearing aid technology are constantly improving.

Many societal problems related to acoustics remain to be tackled. The technological advances that made modern life possible have also resulted in more people with hearing loss. Environmental noise is ubiquitous and increasing despite efforts to design quieter machinery and pains taken to contain unwanted sound or to isolate it from people. Also, although medical technology has been able to help many hearing- and speech-impaired people, other individuals still lack appropriate treatments. For example, although voice generators exist, there is considerable room for improvement.

—*Steve Miller*

Further Reading
Everest, F. Alton, and Ken C. Pohlmann. *Master Handbook of Acoustics*. 5th ed., McGraw-Hill, 2009.
Fellah, Zine El Abiddine, and Erick Ogam. *Acoustics of Materials*. BoD-Books on Demand, 2019.
Garrett, Steven L. *Understanding Acoustics: An Experimentalist's View of Sound and Vibration*. 2nd ed., Springer Nature, 2020.
Kistovich, Anatoly, Konstantin Pokazeev, and Tatiana Chaplina. *Ocean Acoustics*. Springer Nature, 2020.
Rossing, Thomas, and Neville Fletcher. *Principles of Vibration and Sound*. 2nd ed., Springer-Verlag, 2004.
Rumsey, Francis, and Tim McCormick. *Sound and Recording: An Introduction*. 5th ed., Elsevier/Focal Press, 2004.
Saxena, Vimal, Michel Krief, and Ludmila Adam. *Handbook of Borehole Acoustics and Rock Physics for Reservoir Characterization*. Elsevier, 2018.
Strong, William J., and George R. Plitnik. *Music, Speech, Audio*. 3rd ed., Brigham Young University Academic, 2007.

See also: Amplitude; Earthquake engineering; Harmonic oscillator; Materials science; Vibration

AERODYNAMICS

Fields of Study: Physics; Engineering; Mechanics; Mathematics

ABSTRACT
Aerodynamics is a branch of fluid dynamics. It studies the movement of bodies through gases such as air or the movement of these gases around stationary bodies; it is crucial in understanding the movement and safe operation of ground vehicles and aircraft and to the building and maintenance of skyscrapers.

KEY CONCEPTS
airfoil: the wing or other devices (e.g., the tail) used in enabling heavier-than-air aircraft to fly

angle of attack: the angle that an airfoil makes with the air flowing past it; changing this angle will increase or decrease an aircraft's lift force

Bernoulli principle: the discovery that the pressure of a fluid decreases as its speed increases, an important principle enabling the flight of heavier-than-air aircraft

boundary layer: a thin layer of gas (such as the air) immediately adjacent to an aircraft or some other body moving through a fluid

drag: the aerodynamic force that counters lift, slowing aircraft and diminishing ability to remain in flight

hypersonic flight: flight at very high airspeeds, usually at Mach 5 or above

lift: the force produced by the motion of an airfoil, which gives an aircraft the ability to leave the ground and holds it up during flight

Mach number: the number obtained by dividing an aircraft's airspeed by the speed of sound, under the conditions of the flight in progress

sonic boom: the bang or booming sound heard after a supersonic aircraft passes, caused by shock waves produced by the aircraft

subsonic flight: flight in which aircraft speeds are below that of sound (Mach 1)

supersonic flight: flight in which airspeeds are above Mach 1 but not at hypersonic speeds

thrust: the force provided by propeller-driven engines or jet engines of an aircraft; it enables forward aircraft motion

OVERVIEW

Without a knowledge of aerodynamic principles, heavier-than-air flight would not be possible. The Italian Renaissance architect, artist, and engineer Leonardo da Vinci studied birds in flight in the late fifteenth century and conceived of devices such as birdlike wings and helicopter-like machines that would enable human beings to fly. All of his proposed inventions failed, however, because he had no knowledge of aerodynamics. In fact, aerodynamics did not develop enough to enable heavier-than-air flight until the early twentieth century, when Wilbur and Orville Wright used aerodynamics principles to design the first manned aircraft, a biplane with two fixed wings.

In the case of heavier-than-air aircraft, before the vehicle can climb into the air in controlled flight, the force of gravity must be conquered. Three main forces are involved. The first is thrust (or thrust force). Thrust force is caused by the propeller-driven or jet-powered engines of an aircraft. It enables an aircraft to move forward as long as the aircraft's design allows the applied thrust to exceed the force (called "drag") caused by the viscosity of the air through which the aircraft moves. Drag diminishes the speed of any moving vehicle because of air resistance. The thrust-to-drag ratio can be greatly increased by streamlining the aircraft, or shaping it so that the drag experienced is minimized.

A knowledge of the forces of thrust and drag are enough to design a very fast-moving ground vehicle such as a race car, but the key to achieving flight is the third of the aerodynamic forces: lift. A thorough understanding of lift is necessary to conceptualize and actualize aircraft. Lift enables aircraft to rise into the air and move upward, at a right angle to the forward motion of the aircraft. It is supplied by the aircraft's airfoils (mostly by wings but also via tail assemblies). Airfoils are designed with a rounded leading (front) edge and a sharp trailing (rear) edge, so that the angle at which they meet the air causes air to flow much more rapidly past the upper airfoil surface than past its lower surface. This makes the air pressure above the airfoil lower than the air pressure below it, producing the amount of lift needed to raise an aircraft into flight. This asymmetrical airflow is produced by the curved shape of the airfoil (its camber) and its design, which allows it to meet approaching air at an angle (the angle of attack). In addition, the airflow from above and below an airfoil must merge smoothly as the air leaves its trailing edge, producing what is known as the "Kutta condition."

The importance of the angle of attack of airfoils is shown by pilot use and misuse of the angle during flight. An aircraft's angle of attack can be changed by altering its position in space. Up to 15 degrees, increasing the angle of attack enhances the lift produced by aircraft airfoils, enabling faster climbing rates, though slowing airspeed. Once the angle of attack becomes too steep, air eddies form atop the airfoil and cause large decreases in lift, which make the aircraft drop toward the ground in a stall. When a pilot's misjudgment produces a stall, the aircraft will crash unless the pilot quickly decreases the angle of attack to a safe value.

To produce appropriate lift, an airfoil must move through the air above a minimum speed that is associated with the aircraft to which it is attached. However, during landing and takeoff, safety concerns make it desirable to fly as slowly as possible. Because of these conflicting demands, aircraft have special assemblies (or parts) called high-lift devices. Two important high-lift devices are flaps and slats. A flap is the hinged portion of the back of each airfoil. In flight, it fits smoothly, in

A NASA wake turbulence study at Wallops Island in 1990. A vortex is created by passage of an aircraft wing, revealed by smoke. Vortices are one of the many phenomena associated with the study of aerodynamics. Photo via Wikimedia Commons. [Public domain.]

line with the airfoil. However, an aircraft's flaps may be lowered on takeoff or landing. The aircraft's camber increases when this is done. Lowered flaps furnish the extra lift needed on takeoff or a slower aircraft ground speed upon landing. The slats in aircraft airfoils are hinged sections that are located at the front tip of each airfoil. Slat design causes them to automatically move forward when an aircraft slows down, increasing the craft's lift by adding to the camber of each airfoil.

To create an operational aircraft design, the airplane's aerodynamics are analyzed to ensure that its overall composition, including fuselage, airfoils, and high-lifting devices will allow the aircraft to fly well and do so at a cost that makes its use economically feasible. The aircraft's body (or fuselage) is streamlined as much as possible, and the airfoil ability of the aircraft's wings and tail are modified as needed by changing their size, shape, and high-lift device content to optimum dimensions. Optimization is facilitated by studying scaled-down aircraft models in wind tunnels and via computer simulations.

Another aerodynamic concept aircraft manufacturers must consider is the boundary layer of air surrounding an aircraft. The boundary layer is the portion of the air closest to the aircraft's surface. This is the region where the very strongest effects of turbulence caused by air resistance occur. Minimization of this turbulence is essential for both the optimization of passenger comfort and aircraft longevity. Tools used to minimize air turbulence in the boundary layer include streamlining the aircraft and making all aircraft surfaces as smooth as possible.

Aircraft are designed somewhat differently for operation at subsonic, supersonic, and hypersonic airspeeds. These airspeeds are, respectively, below the speed of sound, between the speed of sound and twice that airspeed, and about five times the speed of sound or faster. Hypersonic aircraft are largely space vehicles. Subsonic aircraft are propeller-driven airplanes, and supersonic aircraft are jet planes.

The speed of sound varies with the density of the air through which it travels. Near Earth's surface, sound moves more slowly than high in the atmosphere where the air is thinner. Aircraft designers use the ratio of the airspeed attained to the speed of sound to more accurately designate aircraft speed. This ratio, created by Austrian engineer Ernst Mach is called the Mach number of an aircraft. All subsonic flight (below the speed of sound) therefore occurs at speeds under Mach 1. Aircraft flying at subsonic speeds are in a milieu where the air is an incompressible fluid of unchanging density. The aerodynamics of flight for these vessels is relatively simple. At Mach 1 and above, additional problems associated with flight and aircraft design occur. Air density, air pressure, and air temperature begin to have effects and complicate aerodynamic issues. To counter these effects, supersonic aircraft fly at much higher altitudes than subsonic aircraft. The main advantage of high-altitude flight is the much lower air density that the aircraft encounters. However, any high-altitude flight requires additional design changes such as pressurization of the aircraft cabin.

The increase of airspeed from just below Mach 1 to just above it is called breaking the sound barrier, a term originated by World War II pilots. Breaking this barrier causes variable shock waves that throw aircraft about and require additional aircraft modifications to minimize in-flight positional instability. Fortunately supersonic jets travel well above Mach 1 and do not have this turbulence problem because the shock waves that are associated with their flight speeds are more constant and therefore more manageable.

Another interesting aerodynamic property of aircraft relates to the air-pressure disturbances they create because of airflow around airfoils and fuselages. These pressure disturbances move away from the aircraft at the speed of sound. Therefore, aircraft in subsonic flight create pressure disturbances that precede them, and people on the ground hear these aircraft approaching and getting louder. In contrast, an aircraft in supersonic flight produces pressure disturbances that most often become sonic booms (or bangs) heard only after they pass by. These air-pressure disturbances can damage and even destroy aircraft that are not designed to withstand them. The effects of air-pressure disturbances are factored into aircraft design. In the early days of supersonic aircraft, the absence of alterations in aircraft design to accommodate the effects of air-pressure disturbances and shock waves led to numerous crashes.

APPLICATIONS

Aerodynamics can be applied to understanding the fabrication, the movement, and the safe operation of ground vehicles and aircraft and the construction of durable skyscrapers. A basic understanding of aerodynamics was necessary before flight was possible. The first heavier-than-air manned aircraft, developed by Wilbur and Orville Wright in 1903, was flown four times for a maximum flight time of one minute before it was destroyed in a crash. This biplane, which had paired airfoils joined by braces, was much slower than desired. However, it formed the basis for the much faster, more advanced biplane versions designed to better employ aerodynamic principles that were widely used for the next twenty years.

In the early 1920s, single-wing aircraft (or monoplanes) began to replace the biplanes. All modern aircraft, from propeller-driven to jet airplanes, are monoplanes. The main initial modifications of monoplanes were alterations of airfoil size, shape, and camber and the streamlining of their engines and fuselages.

The site where airfoils are attached varies greatly. One of the most common designs, low-wing aircraft, have twin airfoils located at the fuselage low point. Whether in a propeller-driven or jet aircraft, this arrangement is preferred because it engenders the fastest version of an aircraft whose speed is determined solely by airfoil position. It also gives pilots and passengers the greatest safety margin in crashes. However, airfoils may be put anywhere on the fuselage. For example, in seaplanes, where high speed is not the main determinant of aircraft function, the airfoils may consist of a single parasol wing connected to the fuselage top by braces.

Another important variant among aircraft has been the number and type of engines used to power them. Most aircraft flown before the 1960s were propeller driven, and their thrust derived from one to eight engines. In single-engine aircraft, the propeller-driven engines are put in the front of the vehicle's fuselage. In multiengine aircraft, up to four propeller-driven engines are located in each airfoil. Usually, four engines power even large aircraft, and eight engines are reserved for huge aircraft such as the largest bombers. These propeller-driven aircraft gradually began to be replaced by aircraft with jet engines, and by the early 1960s, jet engines had become very common. By the end of the twentieth century, almost all new aircraft except for small personal models used jet engines for the sake of speed. The fastest propeller-driven aircraft cannot exceed 650 miles per hour. Jet aircraft can exceed Mach 1, and rocket-propelled aircraft can approach or reach hypersonic speed (Mach 5). The increasingly powerful engines are necessitated by the horsepower needed to propel an aircraft at higher speeds. For example, if it takes 5,000 horsepower to fly a given aircraft at 500 miles per hour, attaining 600 and 1,000 miles per hour will require 20,000 and 70,000 horsepower, respectively.

Once the propulsion system has been designed to produce the desired thrust, aircraft manufacturers apply appropriate aerodynamic principles to airfoil design, streamlining, and high-lift devices to optimize performance. Airfoil shape is often deemed the most important of these factors. Besides the familiar straight wing, airfoils take the shape of gull wings, which extend upward at a steep angle and then bend at a chosen point to become parallel to the ground. Sometimes the airfoils are raked backward and combine camber with streamlining to maximize lift force. In some very fast supersonic jets and many hypersonic aircraft, airfoils are triangular delta wings, deemed superior for streamlining purposes. Tail airfoil assemblies also vary widely. Often one fuselage makes up the entire body of an aircraft. In some aircraft—for example, Lockheed's Lightning and some of the newest jet aircraft—portions of the fuselage behind the airfoils have been split for added stability. However, this is quite uncommon, perhaps because it leads to complications in sound aerodynamic aircraft design.

Manufacturers also strive to make every aircraft as light as possible in order to minimize the amount of fuel needed to fly the aircraft for a given length of time. Although the weight factor is not strictly an aerodynamic concern, it is very important to streamlining and all the other aspects of aircraft design because it determines the structural materials that can be used for airfoils, fuselages, and high-lift devices.

Another interesting aspect of aerodynamics is the development of vertical takeoff and landing (VTOL) aircraft. Interest in this type of aircraft has developed for a number of reasons, especially the overcrowding of modern airports. Some VTOL aircraft have been designed that have engines or airfoils that can tilt away from the horizontal and provide the needed thrust direction for vertical takeoff and landing. Once the aircraft have taken off, their engines or airfoils move to the appropriate position for horizontal flight. VTOL aircraft pose several aerodynamic problems associated with streamlining, airfoil design, and fuselage design, all of which have not been well enough solved to make VTOL aircraft ready for common, widespread use.

CONTEXT

The first reported air flight was made by the Greek Archytas of Tarentum in the fourth century BCE. He is supposed to have flown a gas-powered model of a bird for fifty feet. Modern interest in aerodynamics is said to have begun with Italian Leonardo da Vinci's fifteenth-century study of bird flight. However, its first solid conceptualization had to await Sir Isaac Newton's seventeenth-century theory of air resistance, which explained the behavior of forces between objects and fluids. Also crucial in the development of aerodynamics was the work of Newton's Swiss contemporary Daniel Bernoulli. Bernoulli showed that the pressure of a fluid decreases as its speed increases.

It was not until the middle of the nineteenth century when Otto Lilienthal and others in Europe developed gliders that the first valuable application of aerodynamic principles was made. Aerodynamicists such as American Samuel Langley produced small models of functional aircraft in the latter half of the nineteenth century, but it was not until 1903 that the first manned aircraft was flown. This was Wilbur and Orville Wright's propeller-driven aircraft, a biplane with two fixed wings.

The use of aircraft in World Wars I and II led to many advances in aerodynamics, including a switch first to single-wing propeller-driven aircraft and then to jet aircraft. In order for this to happen, the theory and practice of aerodynamics had to develop further. For example, with the advent in the 1940s of the jet aircraft, aerodynamicists and aircraft engineers had to explore the technology needed to conquer supersonic flight. The first supersonic flight was made by Charles E. "Chuck" Yeager in a Bell X-1 jet aircraft in 1947.

Among the advances developed to engender faster and better supersonic aircraft were their streamlined, daggerlike fuselage noses and variable-sweep airfoils, which could be adjusted to straight or swept-back positions in flight. By the late 1960s, these devices often enhanced or replaced earlier modes of streamlining and the use of wing camber and high-lift devices. The result was better lift force utilization, higher safe airspeeds, and safer landings. By the mid-1980s, design advances in large jet aircraft made the supersonic airliner widely available and led to efforts to build aerospace aircraft that could take off from any of the world's conventional airports, travel at hypersonic speeds, enter orbits around the earth, and then return to land at any chosen conventional airport.

Several aerodynamic issues demand attention. Among these is the minimization of sonic booms, which startle and annoy people on the ground and can cause damage (such as broken windows) to buildings in a supersonic aircraft's flight path. Aerodynamicists also seek to devise ways to quiet or better muffle jet engines to reduce noise levels at and around airports. Furthermore, the development of aircraft that are more economical to fly would make air travel more accessible to the average individual. Finally, because of airport crowding, practical vertical takeoff and landing aircraft may one day need to be developed.

—*Sanford S. Singer*

Further Reading

Badick, Joseph R., and Brian A. Johnson. *Flight Theory and Aerodynamics: A Practical Guide for Operational Safety.* 4th ed., John Wiley & Sons, 2021.

Dillmann, Andreas, and Alexander Orellano. *The Aerodynamics of Heavy Vehicles III. Trucks, Buses and Trains.* Springer, 2015.

Discetti, Stefano, and Andrea Ianiro. *Experimental Aerodynamics.* CRC Press, 2017.

Günel, Mehmet Halis, and Huseyn Emre Ilgin. *Tall Buildings: Structural Systems and Aerodynamic Form.* Routledge, 2014.

Hansen, Martin O. L. *Aerodynamics of Wind Turbines.* 3rd ed., Routledge, 2015.

Larsen, Allan. *Aerodynamics of Large Bridges.* Routledge, 2017.

Millikan, Clark B. *Aerodynamics of the Airplane.* Courier Dover Publications, 2018.

Noerstrud, Helge. *Sport Aerodynamics.* Springer Science & Business Media, 2009.

Schuetz, Thomas Christian. *Aerodynamics of Road Vehicles.* 5th ed., SAE International, 2015.

See also: Aeronautical engineering; Aerospace design; Ailerons, flaps, and airplane wings; Airfoils; Airplane propellers; Bernoulli, Daniel; Bernoulli's principle; Civil engineering; Computer-aided engineering; Fluid mechanics and aerodynamics; Projectiles; Structural engineering

AERONAUTICAL ENGINEERING

Fields of Study: Physics; Aeronautical engineering; Mechanical engineering; Mathematics

ABSTRACT

Aeronautical engineering is the study, design, and manufacture of aircraft and spacecraft. Aeronautical engineering is responsible for the development of and advancements in aviation and spaceflight.

KEY CONCEPTS

bomber: an aircraft designed for the delivery of bombs, water, and other ordinance to be dropped on a target

crewed flight: air travel requiring the presence of a pilot and other personnel to maintain the aircraft's flight

fighter: an aircraft designed for engaging other aircraft in aerial combat

SST: acronym for supersonic transport

supersonic: at speeds greater than the speed of sound

tanker: an aircraft designed to transport fuel for mid-air refueling

ENGINEERING

In the first century of crewed flight, which began in December, 1903, the application of the new science of aerodynamics was translated into flying machines by people who understood engineering and prob-

Orville and Wilbur Wright flew the Wright Flyer in 1903 at Kitty Hawk, North Carolina. Photo via Wikimedia Commons. [Public domain.]

lem solving. The industry that grew from this small beginning made amazing strides in the first century of air travel. It is an industry built around visionary engineers and pilots.

Aeronautical engineering had its true beginning before Orville and Wilbur Wright but the two brothers were pioneers in the techniques, processes, and system testing that were at the heart of the engineering design and development of aircraft and spacecraft. The conceptualization of an aircraft begins with the identification of something useful to be accomplished by an air machine. The process begins with sketches of an air vehicle to fulfill the performance expectations for the aircraft. In the first two decades of aircraft design and operations, many concepts were proposed, but by the end of World War I, the basics of successful aircraft design were established. Future refinements would come through better tools, materials, and concepts. At the beginning of the second century of crewed flight, the process involves digitally created drawings that are sent to machines that make the basic parts, which are then assembled, tested, and prepared for flight test.

Twentieth-century aircraft engineering refinements moved at a speed unseen in any previous period of the industrial world. The motivation and excitement of flying higher, faster, and with larger payloads seemed to drive innovation and to demand engineering solutions. By the end of World War II, the aviation industry was fully established as a significant contributor to the economic and military strength of the United States. European aerospace also produced leaders in this field. Companies were built on the talents of engineers and the skills of craftsman. Engineering disciplines expanded, and in the late 1950s, aeronautical engineering became aerospace engineering. In most aircraft manufacturing firms, the engineering department was second in size only to the production groups.

Typically, in the middle of the twentieth century, modern aerospace companies spread their products between commercial enterprises and government contracts. The bread-and-butter contracts came from the federal government until the end of the Cold War. Commercial applications of engineering ideas were spun off from aircraft and missiles that had been developed for the military. However, by 1990, the industry was in decline. Following the Gulf War in 1991, the downsizing of the air arms of the military accelerated. The demand for large numbers of new and different military aircraft came under such scrutiny that few of the new programs survived. On the commercial side of the industry, the engineering of new and better transports and aircraft destined for the air carrier markets stopped in favor of building on existing concepts to build bigger aircraft with bigger engines. Airspeed, comfort, and passenger loading ceased to be major requirements and took a back seat to economically viable air transport.

RESEARCH AND DEVELOPMENT

There are three significant eras in the expansion of the aerospace industry. These coincide with technology improvements as well as political changes that affected the industry. The first period started with the Wright brothers' successful efforts at powered flight and ended with the advent of the jet engine. The next period began when jet engines were being put into all new aircraft designs, and this period saw rapid advances in aircraft performance. The last period began with the introduction of digital computer controls for the aircraft. This development made it possible to design and build incredibly safe and reliable aerospace systems.

Out of World War II came large bombers and cargo aircraft. When jet engines were added to these aircraft they held promise for faster and higher, hence more efficient and comfortable, air transportation for the public. The first such jet transport built for the British Overseas Airway Corporation (BOAC, which became British Airways) was the Comet. However, the understanding of structural issues arising from rapid changes in pressure on certain parts of the aircraft, along with manufacturing techniques from the 1940s, resulted in an unsafe aircraft. After two exploded in flight due to structural failure and one burst during ground pressure testing, the world of aeronautical engineering became aware of fatigue failures and the need to design fail-safe structures. At the time, the US Air Force had Boeing designing and building a jet tanker using technology like that applied to its highly successful swept-wing B-47 jet bomber program. What came out of that work was the most successful aircraft transport design in history. The Boeing 707 model was the forerunner of all of today's large jet transports.

THE INDUSTRY

After World War II, the growth in the aviation industry, both commercial and military, saw a proliferation of new prime contractors who were building and selling aircraft. A prime contractor was defined as the company that was responsible for the concept, design, development, and final introduction of the new aircraft into operational use. In short, a prime contractor was responsible for all aspects of the life cycle of the aircraft. The prime would have subcontractors, perhaps hundreds, with which it did business.

At the start of the 1970s, and at the height of the Vietnam War, there were many primes in the aerospace business. The biggest and most successful were Boeing Aircraft, Douglas Aircraft, McDonnell Aircraft, Lockheed Aircraft, Republic Aircraft, General

Dynamics, Grumman Aircraft, North American Aviation (North American Rockwell), Northrop Aviation, LTV Aerospace (part of LTV, which used to be Chance Vought), Northrop Aircraft, Bell Airplane and Bell Helicopter, Sikorsky Helicopter, and a handful of general aviation companies, including Cessna, Beech, Piper, and others. At the end of the twentieth century there were only three major aerospace companies left, with all others being absorbed into the remaining companies or having gone out of business. Boeing took over McDonnell Douglas, which used to be McDonnell Aircraft and Douglas Aircraft. Lockheed Martin absorbed General Dynamics Aircraft Division and Martin Marietta. Northrop and Grumman joined, adding pieces of LTV and others. In addition, Raytheon Corporation, which was a small missiles and electronics outfit in the 1960s, took over Beech Aircraft and other subsidiary companies. Cessna and Piper nearly went out of business during the 1970s and 1980s, due to changes in liability laws. Chance Vought became Ling Temco Vought in the mid-1960s and changed its name to LTV Corporation in the 1970s. It was one of the first prime contractors that attempted product diversification, with markets in steel, appliances, missiles, and aircraft; the corporation went bankrupt in 1986.

FUTURE DEVELOPMENTS

Compared to the days of the Wright Flyer and the Curtiss JN-4, aircraft which were very difficult to control and which carried very small payloads, the F-22 automated advanced fighter and the Boeing 777 automated, large twin-engine transport are engineering marvels. At the beginning of the twenty-first century, there are several different paths that may provide the next major step forward in aeronautical engineering.

In June, 1963, President John F. Kennedy, speaking at the commencement of the fifth class to graduate from the US Air Force Academy, announced that the federal government would seek to develop the world's first supersonic passenger transport (SST). This never happened, for two reasons. The first was the economic issue. Such an aircraft, designed using late 1950s and early 1960s technology, would be very expensive. Airlines could not justify the costs to operate them. The second issue was environmental. Warnings and concerns about the pollution or damage to the upper atmosphere from turbojet engines and problems with sonic booms, which are caused by the shock waves from a supersonic aircraft, led to a premature end of the SST. Europe, in a cooperative move between British and French aircraft firms, did pursue a smaller version of the SST, called the Concorde. It operated successfully starting in January, 1976, although it was under a limitation forbidding it from flying supersonically over the United States. Technology improved during the twenty-two years the Concorde was operating, and by the late 1990s, the National Aeronautics and Space Administration (NASA) attempted to resurrect the SST concept. By then, the problems of jet exhaust and its impact upon the upper atmosphere had been nearly resolved. Ways to reduce the pressure from the sonic booms were being planned. The program ended in 1999 when, for the second time, the economic issues surrounding operational costs of a large SST overrode advances in the aerospace engineering field.

The next hope for large transport aircraft lies in engineering a craft that will cruise just under Mach 1. Most large aircraft can cruise efficiently at Mach .75 to .9 (the percent of the speed of sound) but if they could fly efficiently at 95 percent of the speed of sound this would mean a 5 to 20 percent increase in true airspeed (35 to 155 miles per hour). A speed increase of that magnitude would shorten the flight time from New York to Paris by approximately an hour and fifteen minutes. The potential savings in fuel, the increase in the number of aircraft that could fly the same route, and other factors make this an appealing possibility. It is not an easy engineering task, but then, most of the history of aviation has faced such challenging engineering tasks.

The ultimate flight would be one that takes the passenger into low-Earth orbit and flies across both continents and oceans. That aircraft will probably come about once the space program has fully established the safety and reliability of such travel. Aeronautical engineering and the companies that have come to the forefront in both engineering and applied sciences for aerospace purposes will be able to achieve these ideas.

—*R. Smith Reynolds*

Further Reading

Jandusay, D. E. P. *165 Solved Problems in Aeronautical Engineering: Explained. Solved. Final Answer Boxed.* Book Publishing House Gate 5, 2020.

Lopez, Francisco Gallardo, and Jens Strahmann. *Fundamentals of Aerospace Engineering (Beginner's Guide).* CreateSpace Independent Publishing Platform, 2016.

Mikel, Russell, editor. *Aerospace and Aeronautical Engineering.* Wilford Press, 2017.

Soler, Manuel. *Fundamentals of Aerospace Engineering: An Introductory Course to Aeronautical Engineering.* CreateSpace Independent Publishing Platform, 2017.

Spagner, Natalie. *A Researcher's Guide to Aerospace Engineering.* Clanrye International, 2019.

Ziegler, Margaret. *Aeronautical Engineering.* Wilford Press, 2016.

See also: Aerodynamics; Ailerons, flaps, and airplane wings; Computer-aided engineering

AEROSPACE DESIGN

Fields of Study: Physics; Mechanics; Mathematics

ABSTRACT

Aerospace design is crucial to the development and manufacturing of aircraft and spacecraft. Since the introduction of aircraft in the nineteenth century, aerospace design has led to the production of countless flight vehicles, including spacecraft used for space exploration. Aerospace design involves a design process, which may take several years to complete. The phases of this process typically are system/mission requirements, conceptual design, preliminary design, and critical design. With spacecraft, the design generally includes major components such as the mission payload and the platform. The design of the space shuttle is one good example.

KEY CONCEPTS

attitude control: the process of obtaining and sustaining the proper orientation in space

mission payload: the extra equipment carried by a craft for a specific mission; for a launch vehicle, payload usually refers to scientific instruments, satellites, probes, and spacecraft attached to the launcher

platform: all parts of a spacecraft that are not part of the payload; also known as the bus

telemetry: the process of transmitting measurement data via radio to operators on the ground; telemetry is used to improve spaceflight performance and accuracy; it provides important information about standard operational health and status of a craft as well as mission-specific payload data

thermal control: the system aboard a spacecraft that controls the temperature of various components to ensure safety and accuracy during a mission

tracking and commanding: tracking takes account of a craft's position in relation to the ground base with transponders, radar, or other systems; commanding refers to the ground station sending signals to a craft to change settings such as ascent and orbit paths

LEARNING TO FLY

The term "aerospace" refers to Earth's atmosphere and the space beyond. Aerospace design or aerospace engineering is the branch of science and technology that focuses on creating and manufacturing effective aircraft and spacecraft. Aerospace design is divided into two subfields: aeronautic design and astronautical design. Aeronautic design refers to the creation of machines that fly in Earth's atmosphere. Astronautical design deals with designing and developing spacecraft and their launch vehicles, generally powered by highly powerful rockets. The aerospace industry caters to military, industrial, and commercial consumers.

The history of aerospace design begins with the history of aviation. The first powered lighter-than-air craft existed as early as the 1850s. Jules Henri Giffard (1825-82) invented a steam-powered airship in 1852. Ferdinand von Zeppelin (1838-1917) introduced rigid airships in 1900; they came to be known as "zeppelins" and later as "blimps." Brothers Orville (1871-1948) and Wilbur Wright (1867-1912) designed a heavier-than-air, piloted airplane that is generally credited as the first of its kind to execute a successful powered flight, in 1903. Air flight designs continued to progress throughout the twentieth century, paving the way for the development of rotary winged aircraft such as helicopters, which use revolving wings or blades to lift into the air. Powerful air flight engines that fuel modern aircraft did not emerge until the mid-twentieth century.

At the same time that engine design was advancing, aerospace engineers also began developing machinery that would take humans to the upper atmosphere and into space. Konstantin Tsiolkovsky (1857-1935), known as the Russian father of rocketry, was a pioneer of astronautics with his insightful studies in space travel and rocket science. American engineer Robert Goddard launched the first liquid-fueled rocket in 1926. Goddard continually improved his rocket design over the years. His calculations contributed to the development of other rocket-powered devices such as ballistic missiles. Tsiolkovsky and German scientist Hermann Oberth (1894-1989) independently made similar breakthroughs in the same time period.

During World War I and World War II, aerospace design saw rampant progress as military engineers pursued higher-performance aircraft design. In particular, advances in rocket research during World War II laid the foundation for astronautics. Continued advances in aerospace design were spurred by the Cold War and the space race between the United States and the Soviet Union. The competition to reach outer space led to the launch of the first spacecraft, Sputnik I, by the Soviet Union in 1957. The United States established the National Aeronautics and Space Association (NASA) in 1958. Aerospace engineers designed a wide range of spacecraft to explore space, incorporating new technologies and capabilities as they became available. For example, in 1969, an American-made spacecraft successfully sent astronauts to the moon, which marked the first time humans landed on the moon. Many other spacecraft have been used to carry out missions elsewhere in the solar system. Artificial satellites have proven critical to twenty-first-century communications systems and become widespread with a variety of designs and functions.

DESIGN PROCESS

The design process of a spacecraft generally occurs in the following phases: system/mission requirements, conceptual design, preliminary design, and critical design. Some of these phases can take years to complete. In the system/mission requirements phase, the requirements of the spacecraft are addressed. The type of mission the spacecraft will be used for helps determine these requirements, as specific tasks may dictate certain design elements. For example, a deep space probe would require a significantly different design than a weather monitoring satellite.

The conceptual design phase deals with several possible system concepts that could fulfill the requirements of the mission. These concepts are first conceived and then analyzed. After the most suitable concept is chosen, costs and risks are examined and schedules are made.

The preliminary design phase involves several tasks. Variations of the selected concept are identified, examined, and improved. Specifications for each subsystem and component level are identified. The projected performance of the systems and subsystems is analyzed. Documents are composed, and an initial parts list is put together. This phase may run for several years depending on the novelty and complexity of the mission.

Last, the critical design phase, or detailed design phase, takes place. During this phase, the detailed characteristics of the structural design of the spacecraft are established. Equipment, payload, the crew, and provisions are all considered. Plumbing, wiring, and other secondary structures are reviewed. Various tests involving design verification are performed, including tests of electronic circuit models and software models. Design and performance margin estimates are improved. Test and evaluation plans are settled. Like the preliminary design phase, the critical design phase may take several years to complete.

Once the design process has been completed, the spacecraft can finally be built. It is then tested before being delivered for use.

TYPICAL COMPONENTS

Most spacecraft share two key components: the mission payload and the platform, or the bus. The mission payload includes all of the equipment that is specific to the mission, such as scientific instruments and probes, rather than general operation. The platform comprises all other parts of the spacecraft, used to deliver the payload. It consists of several subsystems, including the structures subsystem, thermal control subsystem, electrical power subsystem, attitude control subsystem, and telemetry, tracking, and commanding (TT&C) subsystem.

The structures subsystem serves various functions such as enclosing, supporting, and protecting the other subsystems, as well as sustaining stresses and loads. It also provides a connection to the launch vehicle. Two main types of structure subsystems exist: open truss and body mounted. The open-truss type typically has the shape of a box or cylinder, while the body-mounted type does not have a definite shape. The choice of structural materials is an important consideration in aerospace design. Light, durable, and heat-resistant materials, such as aluminum, titanium, and some plastics, are typically used.

The thermal control subsystem regulates the temperature of the spacecraft's components. This helps guarantee that the components function properly throughout the mission. Different components require different temperatures. Thermal control systems may be active or passive. Active thermal control involves the use of electrical heaters, cooling systems, and louvers. Passive thermal control includes the use of heat sinks, thermal coatings and insulations, and phase-change materials (PCM). With passive thermal control, electrical power is not needed and there are no moving parts or fluids.

The electrical power subsystem provides the power the spacecraft needs for the duration of the mission, which can last for years. In most cases, the subsystem includes the following components: a source of energy; a device that converts the energy into electricity; a device that stores the electrical energy; and a system that conditions, charges, discharges, distributes, and regulates the electrical energy. The source of energy is generally solar radiation, nuclear power, or chemical reactions.

The attitude control subsystem deals with the process and hardware necessary for obtaining and sustaining the proper orientation in space, or attitude. It has several functions, including maintaining an orbit (station keeping), adjusting an orbit, and stabilization. That subsystem typically includes navigation sensors, a guidance section, and a control section. As with thermal control, the attitude control may be either active or passive. Active attitude control uses continuous decision making and hardware that are closed loop. This includes the use of thrusters, electromagnets, and reaction wheels. Passive attitude control uses open-loop environmental torques to sustain attitude, such as gravity gradient and solar sails.

The telemetry, tracking, and commanding (TT&C) subsystem involves communication with operators on the ground. Telemetry uses a radio link to transmit measurement data to those operators. It is typically used for improving spacecraft performance and for monitoring the health of the spacecraft, including the payload. Tracking and commanding deals with the spacecraft's position. Tracking is used to report the spacecraft's position to the ground station, while commanding is used to change the spacecraft's position. Some common tracking methods are the use of a beacon or a transponder, Doppler tracking, optical tracking, interferometer tracking, and radar tracking and ranging. Commanding is achieved through coded instructions that the ground station sends to the aircraft.

PRACTICAL EXAMPLE

A good example of aerospace design is that of the space shuttle, officially called the Space Transportation System (STS). In 1969, US president Richard Nixon established the Space Task Group to study the United States' future in space exploration. Among other things, the group envisioned a reusable spaceflight vehicle. It was not long before NASA, along with industry contractors, began the design process of such a vehicle. The process involved numerous studies, including design, engineering, cost, and risk studies. Some of the studies focused on the concepts of an orbiter, dual solid-propellant rocket motors, a reusable piloted booster, and a disposable liquid-propellant tank.

In 1972, the design of the space shuttle was moved forward. It would feature an orbiter, three main engines, two solid rocket boosters (SRBs), and an exter-

The Space Shuttle Discovery in liftoff, 2007. Photo via Wikimedia Commons. [Public domain.]

nal tank (ET). The orbiter would house the crew, the SRBs would provide the shuttle's lift at the beginning of its flight, and the ET would hold fuel for the main engines. All of the components would be reusable, except for the ET, which would be jettisoned after launch. Refinements continued to be made as the project continued and systems were tested.

The first orbiter spacecraft, named *Enterprise*, was completed in 1976 and underwent several flight tests. However, *Enterprise* was merely a test vehicle and was not used for any actual space missions. In 1981, the first space shuttle mission took place. *Columbia* lifted off from the Kennedy Space Center and became the first orbiter in space. Over the next several decades, several shuttles successfully performed many space missions.

—*Michael Mazzei*

Further Reading

"Aerospace Design Lab." *Stanford University*, Department of Aeronautics and Astronautics, 28 July 2013. Accessed 9 June 2015.

Garino, Brian W., and Jeffrey D. Lanphear. "Spacecraft Design, Structure, and Operations." *AU-18 Space Primer*. Air University, 2009. Accessed 9 June 2015.

Lucas, Jim. "What Is Aerospace Engineering?" *Live Science*, 4 Sept. 2014. Accessed 9 June 2015.

Market Trends. "Top 4 Aerospace Engineering Software in 2021." *Analytics Insight*, 17 Sept. 2021, www.analyticsinsight.net/top-4-aerospace-engineering-software-in-2021/. Accessed 12 June 2022.

"Part I. Historical Context." *Space Transportation System*. Historic American Engineering Record (Denver), National Park Service, US Department of the Interior, Nov. 2012.

"Space Shuttle History." *Human Space Flight*. NASA, 27 Feb. 2008. Web. 9 June 2015.

"Spacecraft Design, Structure, and Operations." *AU Space Primer*. Air University, 2003. Accessed 9 June 2015.

See also: Aerodynamics; Ballistic weapons; Bernoulli's principle; Celestial mechanics; Dynamics (mechanics); Fluid mechanics and aerodynamics; Force (physics); Friction; Kinetic energy; Materials science; Mechanical engineering; Newton's laws; Projectiles; Propulsion technologies; Vacuum

AILERONS, FLAPS, AND AIRPLANE WINGS

Fields of Study: Physics; Aeronautical engineering; Mechanical engineering; Chemical engineering; Mathematics

ABSTRACT

Ailerons and flaps are hinged sections on the trailing edges of wings. Both ailerons and flaps can be deflected to change local wing camber and to increase or decrease local lift. Ailerons are used to control the airplane in roll, while flaps allow flight at lower speeds for landing and takeoff.

KEY CONCEPTS

aileron: a small secondary structure at the outer end of a wing, used to alter the lift of a wing for control the roll and pitch of the aircraft in motion

camber: the curvature of the cross-sectional shape of a wing

flap: a secondary structure of a wing near the fuselage, used to increase or decrease the lift of the wing for speed control during takeoffs and landings

AILERONS

Early experimenters with gliders turned their vehicles by shifting their bodies so their weight was to the left or right of their wing's lifting center. This action made the glider roll or bank to help it turn. Wilbur and Orville Wright improved on this effect by twisting or warping their wood and fabric wing with ropes and pulleys so that one wingtip was at a higher angle of attack than the other and the difference in lift on the two wingtips helped it roll. This design gave their airplane much greater maneuverability than early European designs, which tried to turn using only a rudder. This wing-warping control system was the essential element in the Wright patent on the first successful airplane.

Glenn H. Curtiss, another American aviation pioneer, patented a different way to control an airplane in roll, using ailerons, originally small, separate wings that were placed between the upper and lower wings of his biplane near the wingtips. The pilot could change the angle between these small wings and the flow to increase the lift on one wing and decrease that of the other. The Wrights claimed that this was a violation of their patent, and the case spent many years in the courts until the US government stepped in to resolve the dispute.

Today's ailerons are built into the trailing edge of wings near the wingtips, and they work by changing the wing's camber, or curvature, instead of its angle of attack. The ailerons deflect either up or down opposite to each other to increase the lift near one wingtip while lowering lift on the other wingtip. This makes the wing roll, with one wing moving up and the other down. Usually, the aileron deflecting up produces more drag than the one moving down, which helps the airplane turn. In most turns, the aileron movements are coordinated with the movement of the rudder to create a turn which is balanced so that the airplane passengers feel only a downward force and no sideward force. A coordinated turn not only feels better but also is more aerodynamically efficient.

If the pilot wants to roll the airplane without turning, the rudder must also be used to oppose the turning motion caused by aileron drag; this is called a cross-control maneuver. A similar cross-control use of rudder and ailerons can make the airplane rotate to the left or right in a sideslip motion without rolling.

FLAPS

Flaps often resemble ailerons except that they are placed on the wing near the fuselage rather than near the wingtips. Flaps normally are only deflected downward since they are used to increase temporarily the wing's lift on landing and sometimes on takeoff. This maneuver allows flight at lower speeds and landing and takeoff in shorter distances.

Photo via iStock/LuisPortugal. [Used under license.]

Early aircraft did not need flaps because they flew at low speeds and could land in much shorter distances than today's planes; however, as airplanes became more streamlined and could cruise at higher speeds and altitudes, they needed higher speeds for takeoff and landing. Designers added flaps to give additional lift and drag and to reduce landing speeds. The famous DC-3 airliner was one of the first commercial planes to use flaps to combine good cruise performance with reasonable landing and takeoff distances.

There are many types of flaps, from simple plates that deflect down from the bottom of the wing to very sophisticated combinations of little wings that extend down and behind a wing. The split flap was used on the DC-3 and many World War II airplanes. Fowler flaps are more common today, but many smaller aircraft use simple hinges on the rear part of their wings to deflect a plain flap. The Fowler flap increases the wing camber while increasing the wing area. The space that opens between the deployed Fowler flap and the wing allows an airflow that helps control the pressures over the flap and delay wing stall.

Many airliners designed in the mid-to-late twentieth century used complex flap systems that worked like the Fowler flap but had two or more flap elements that opened out below and behind the wing. These flap systems were very carefully designed temporarily to give very high lift at low speeds on sleek, modern wings that were shaped for flight near the speed of sound. They allowed airplanes that cruise at 500 to 600 miles per hour to land at low speeds and come to a stop on relatively short runways.

Today's commercial transport designs do not need these complex flap systems and tend to use simpler Fowler flaps, which are lighter and easier to build and maintain. This shift is partly because of improvements in wing and airfoil design and partly because most major airports now have longer runways.

FLAPERONS AND SLATS

Occasionally, an airplane design needs extra flap area to get lower landing speeds and the ailerons are also used as flaps. This kind of aileron is called a flaperon, and it requires a more complex hookup to the aircraft controls than a standard aileron and flap system.

Some aircraft have flaps on the front of their wings that can also be deflected downward to increase the wing camber. These leading-edge flaps, or slats, help control the flow over the wing at high angles of attack and allow the wing to go to a higher angle of attack before it stalls.

—*James F. Marchman III*

Further Reading

Kundu, Ajay Kumar, Mark A. Price, and David Riordan. *Conceptual Aircraft Design: An Industrial Approach.* Wiley, 2019.

National Aeronautics and Space Administration. *Aircraft Wing Structural Detail Design (Wing, Aileron, Flaps, and Subsystems).* CreateSpace Independent Publishing Platform, 2018.

Sabry, Fouad. *Adaptive Compliant Wing: No More Flaps, the Aircraft Wing Shape is Now Morphing.* One Billion Knowledgeable, 2022.

See also: Aerodynamics; Airfoils

AIRFOILS

Fields of Study: Physics; Aeronautical engineering; Mechanical engineering; Mathematics

ABSTRACT

An airfoil is a two-dimensional, front-to-back cross-section or slice through a wing from its leading edge to its trailing edge across the wing's long axis. The shape of a wing's airfoil section or sections determines the amount of lift, drag, and pitching movement the wing will produce over a range of angles of attack and determines the wing's stall behavior.

KEY CONCEPTS

camber: the curvature of the cross-section of a wing

lift: the upward force experienced by a wing as determined by its airfoil camber and thickness

symmetrical: having equal dimensions on either side of a bisecting plane or axis

THE WING IN CROSS-SECTION

The shape revealed if a wing were to be sliced from its leading edge to its trailing edge is called the wing's airfoil section. Although airfoils come in many different shapes, all are designed to accomplish the same goal: forcing the air to move faster over the top of the wing than it does over the bottom. The higher-speed air on the top of the airfoil produces a lower pressure than the flow over the bottom, resulting in lift. The shape of the upper and lower surfaces of the airfoil and the angle that it makes with the oncoming airflow, or angle of attack, determines the way the flow will accelerate and decelerate around the airfoil and, thus, determines its ability to provide lift.

Flow around the airfoil also causes drag, and an airfoil should be designed to get as much lift as possible while at the same time minimizing drag. The shape of the airfoil then determines the balance of lift and drag at various angles of attack. An airplane designer tries to select an airfoil shape that will give the best possible lift-to-drag ratio at some desired optimum flight condition, such as cruise or climb, depending on the type of aircraft. The amount of pitching movement, or tendency for the airfoil to rotate nose up or down, is also a function of the airfoil's shape and the way lift is produced. Pitch must be evaluated along with the forces of lift and drag.

CAMBER AND THICKNESS

Early airfoil shapes were thin, essentially cloth stretched over a wood frame, a type of airfoil sometimes seen today in the wings of ultralight or hang glider-type aircraft. Usually, the frame for such an airfoil was curved, or cambered. The camber line, or mean line, of an airfoil is a curved line running halfway between its upper and lower surfaces. If the airfoil is symmetrical, in other words, if its upper surface is exactly the inverse of its lower surface, then the camber line is coincident with its chord line, a straight line from the leading edge to the trailing edge of the airfoil. A symmetrical airfoil is said to have zero camber. The amount of camber possessed by an airfoil is defined by the maximum distance between the chord and camber lines expressed as a percentage of the chord. In other words, an airfoil has 6 percent camber if the maximum distance between its chord and camber lines is 0.06 times its chord length.

Experimenters in the late 1800s tried wings built with airfoils with different amounts of camber and different positions of maximum. They found that the location of maximum camber affected both the amount of lift generated at given angles of attack and the airfoil's stall behavior and that too much camber can give high drag. Later researchers learned to create temporary increases in camber by using flaps.

Later aircraft used thicker airfoils with both upper and lower surfaces covered first with fabric and then with metal. The thicker airfoils allowed a stronger wing structure as well as a place to store fuel. They also proved able to provide good aerodynamic behavior over a wider range of angle of attack as well as better stall characteristics, but excessive thickness made for increased drag.

NACA AIRFOILS

In the 1920s, the National Advisory Committee for Aeronautics (NACA) began an exhaustive study of airfoil aerodynamics, examining in detail the effects of variations in camber and thickness distributions on the behavior of wings. This systematic study of variations in the amount and position of maximum camber and thickness resulted in the wind-tunnel

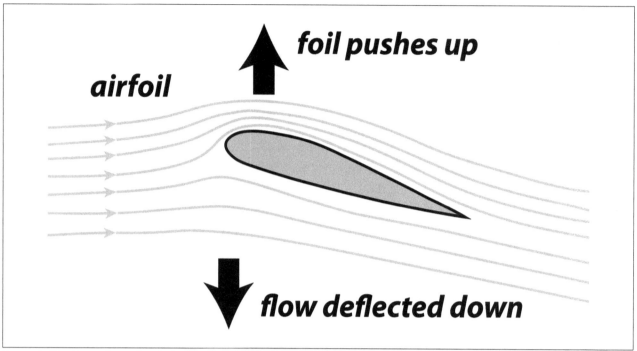

Image via iStock/gstraub.[Used under license.]

tests of hundreds of airfoil shapes. The NACA also developed a numbering system, or code, to describe the shapes. In the first series of tests, each of the numbers in a four-digit code was used in a prescribed set of equations to draw the airfoil shape. For example, the NACA 2412 airfoil had a maximum camber of 2 percent of its chord with the maximum camber point at 40 percent of the chord from the airfoil leading edge, and the maximum thickness was 12 percent of the chord.

Many other series of NACA airfoils were developed and tested. The 6-series airfoils were designed to provide very low drag over a set range of angle of attack by encouraging a low-friction laminar flow over part of the surface. Other series of airfoils were developed for use on propeller blades. The NACA's successor, the National Aeronautics and Space Administration (NASA), has continued to test and develop airfoils including a series of supercritical shapes that give lower drag near the speed of sound, as compared to older designs.

MODERN AIRFOIL DESIGN

Throughout the twentieth century, airfoil design was essentially a matter of creating a shape based on desired camber and thickness distributions, testing it in wind tunnels and then in flight. Today, airfoils can be selected from hundreds of past designs or custom-developed by specifying a desired distribution of pressure around the surface and using computers to solve for the shape that will give those pressures. Then wind-tunnel tests are done to validate the computer solution. The result is that every airplane can have a wing with a unique distribution of airfoil shapes along its span, all designed for optimum performance. The basic idea is the same as it has always been, to find the combination of camber and thickness that will give the best available mix of lift, drag, and pitching movement for the task at hand.

—*James F. Marchman III*

FURTHER READING

Cummings, Russell M., Scott A. Morton, William H. Mason, and David R. McDaniel. *Applied Computational Aerodynamics: A Modern Engineering Approach.* Cambridge UP, 2015.

Pope, Alan. *Basic Wing and Airfoil Theory.* Dover Publications, 2009.

See also: Ailerons, flaps, and airplane wings; Fluid dynamics

AIRPLANE PROPELLERS

Fields of Study: Physics; Aeronautical engineering; Mechanical engineering; Mathematics

ABSTRACT

Propellers are rotating airfoils driven by an engine to provide thrust to an aircraft. Propellers were a primary mode of thrust generation for all aircraft up to the development of the gas-turbine engine in the 1940s, and they remain in widespread use, especially on smaller commercial and general aviation aircraft.

KEY CONCEPTS

airfoil: the cross-sectional profile of an aerodynamic wing

angle of attack: the angle at which airflow encounters the leading edge of a wing or propeller relative to its chord line

drag: the resistance to motion through a fluid due to friction between the moving object and the fluid medium

pitch angle: the angle between a propeller's chord line and its plane of rotation

thrust: the force or pressure exerted on the body of an aircraft in the direction of its motion

HISTORY

Propellers have long been recognized as an efficient means of generating thrust. They were popularly used in aircraft design even before being used by Orville and Wilbur Wright to power the *Wright Flyer* in 1903. Leonardo da Vinci sketched propeller designs for helicopters in the 1500's. They have been commonly used as children's toys as well. Early propellers were based primarily on designs used for ships and windmills, but experiments soon found that long, thin airfoils provided better thrust than the shorter, thicker hydrofoil designs used in water.

NATURE AND USE

The function of a propeller is to create thrust to accelerate an aircraft forward. Although a wing creates lift to overcome an aircraft's weight, a propeller creates thrust to overcome its drag. This thrust keeps an aircraft moving. When the propeller's thrust is equal to the aircraft's drag, the aircraft travels at a constant speed. When thrust is greater than drag, the aircraft accelerates until drag is equal to the thrust. Likewise, when the propeller's thrust is less than the aircraft's drag, the vehicle decelerates until the drag and thrust are equal and the aircraft's velocity becomes constant. Thus, varying the propeller's thrust will change the aircraft's velocity.

In a helicopter, the propeller is turned upward, so that the thrust is generated vertically to overcome the weight of the aircraft. When a propeller is oriented primarily to overcome weight instead of drag, it is usually called a "rotor." The engine powering a propeller can be either a conventional piston (reciprocating) engine or a jet (gas turbine) engine. In the latter case, the propeller-and-engine combination is commonly referred to as a turboprop. Turboprops typically derive 95 percent of their thrust from the propeller, while the remainder comes from the jet-engine exhaust.

A propeller may be thought of as a severely twisted wing. In fact, the wings of many aircraft are twisted either to increase or decrease lift on certain portions of the wing by changing the local effective angle of attack. The propeller is twisted for a similar reason. Like an untwisted wing, a propeller could be designed without twist, as some of the first propellers were, but it would create less thrust than would a twisted propeller.

A propeller generates thrust in the same way that a wing generates lift. Instead of moving in a straight line, however, the propeller rotates about a hub that is turned by the engine shaft. A propeller traces out the shape of a helix as it travels around in flight. For this reason, propellers are often referred to as airscrews and are also analogous to the propeller screws found on a ship.

Both the rotating and forward movements of a propeller's airfoil influence how much thrust is developed. The velocity at each radial location of the propeller will be different, because the total velocity is the vector sum of the propeller radial velocity and the aircraft velocity. Because the propeller is rotating at a certain rotation rate, the propeller velocity at any distance from the axis of rotation is the rotational speed times the radial distance. Thus, the propeller velocity will be almost zero near the hub and a maximum near the tip. This difference in velocity requires that the cross-sections of the propeller's airfoil be twisted so that the chord line has a large angle of attack near the hub and a small angle of attack near the tip, in contrast to the airfoil of a wing that is nearly flat. The propeller's chord line increasingly points in the direction of the aircraft motion, as the propeller airfoil sections progress toward the hub.

The angle between the chord line of the propeller and the propeller's plane of rotation is called the "pitch angle." To determine the local angle of attack of a propeller, one uses the propeller's pitch angle at each blade section and subtracts the angle of attack of the incoming relative wind.

PROPELLER PLACEMENT

A propeller can be placed anywhere on an aircraft, either at the nose, tail, wings, or on a pod. In a trac-

tor configuration, the propeller is placed facing forward, usually on the nose, and pulls the aircraft. In a pusher configuration, the propeller is placed facing the rear of the aircraft and pushes the aircraft forward. One design has no real benefit over the other. The tractor configuration is more common, because it allows a better balance of the aircraft's center of gravity about the aerodynamic center of the wing with the engine placed near the nose. Pusher configurations are more common in canard aircraft for the same reason. In a tractor configuration, the slipstream from a propeller is often pushed over the wings, creating a faster flow over that part of the wing. This is sometimes used to generate more lift, but it is not commonly considered in aircraft design.

PROPELLER EFFICIENCY

The propeller efficiency is a measure of how effectively a propeller transforms the engine power into propulsive power. It is measured by dividing the power output by the power input. The power output is the thrust generated by the propeller multiplied by the aircraft velocity. The power input is the amount of shaft power generated by the engine, measured in horsepower or watts. A propeller that is 100 percent efficient means that all the power from the engine is transferred directly to the air. No propeller can achieve 100 percent efficiency, however, and is hindered by several factors. The propeller, as it rotates, adds energy to the air, and this energy is lost from the aircraft, because it remains with the air long after the aircraft has passed. Indeed, the most efficient propellers are the ones that take a large amount of air and increase the velocity of the air only slightly. Thus, all things being equal, larger-diameter propellers are more efficient than smaller ones. The drag forces that act on the aircraft also act on the propeller. These forces include pressure drag, such as separation of the flow over a propeller, and friction drag, in which viscous effects of the air retard propeller motion.

Typical propellers have efficiencies in the 70 to 90 percent range. Fixed-pitch propellers have the lowest efficiency and can drop below 70 percent if they are operating at a velocity for which they were not designed.

PROPELLER DESIGNS

The Wright brothers and Alexandre-Gustave Eiffel, among others, conducted early experiments on propellers. The Wright brothers were particularly concerned about maximum power output and thrust generation, because their early engines developed very little horsepower. They were able to design propeller blades with an efficiency of up to 70 percent, which was an extraordinary feat for the time. Eiffel, a French engineer and the builder of the Eiffel Tower in Paris, was also an ardent aerodynamicist who performed some of the first detailed wind-tunnel experiments on propellers. He was the first to show that propeller efficiency varied with the propeller's rotation rate, diameter, and aircraft velocity. This parameter is now called the advance ratio and is used in propeller design, optimization, and selection.

FIXED-PITCH PROPELLERS

Propellers can be used on aircraft in several different ways. In the fixed-pitch propeller, the propeller blade has a fixed angle of attack. Although the angle varies along the length of the propeller, the blade has a fixed orientation throughout its flight envelope, meaning that the propeller design has been optimized for a single speed. If the aircraft travels at another velocity, the propeller efficiency is reduced. Fixed-pitch propellers were used on all airplanes up to the 1930s, when variable-pitch propellers were introduced.

VARIABLE-PITCH PROPELLERS

The angle of attack of variable-pitch propellers can be changed by rotating the blade about the hub.

This allows pilots to adjust the propellers' relative angle of attack in flight to account for changes in the aircraft and wind velocity. A complex mechanism in the hub allows the pilot to change the propeller pitch in flight, thereby increasing overall performance. When variable-pitch propellers were introduced in the 1930s, propeller efficiency across the range of flight conditions was greatly increased. A major drawback, however, was that as the pitch was altered, the torque on the engine was also changed. This would, in turn, change the rotation speed of the engine, resulting in a lower engine-power output.

CONSTANT-SPEED PROPELLERS

Consequently, the constant-speed propeller was introduced in the 1940s. It is a variant of the variable-pitch propeller in which the propeller pitch is changed automatically to keep the engine speed constant and to maximize total power output. Variable-pitch and constant-speed propellers may be feathered in flight during an engine-out scenario to minimize the propeller drag.

To keep the propeller efficiency from dropping, the velocity of the propeller tip must be kept lower than the speed of sound, or Mach 1. If this velocity is exceeded, shock waves form at the tip of the propeller, and the efficiency drops dramatically as the available power is reduced by pressure losses. Shock waves can create other problems, such as severe noise, vibration, and structural damage to the propeller. Because the velocity at the tip is a function of the propeller radius, engine-shaft rotational speed, and aircraft speed, these three factors come into play when determining what size propeller should be used. During the tradeoff analysis of an aircraft design, as the speed of an aircraft increases, the diameter of the propeller decreases.

To generate the same thrust for a smaller-diameter propeller given the same engine speed, an aircraft designer may opt to go with a larger number of propellers. The propeller must be balanced, and two blades are the minimum used. However, any number of blades greater than two may be chosen, as long as the blades are evenly spaced to maintain balance. Increasing the number of propeller blades means that to achieve the same thrust, a smaller diameter can be used. This is sometimes done to avoid the sonic tip speeds that may be encountered with long propeller blades on fast aircraft. Two-, three-, four-, and five-bladed propellers have been commonly used on aircraft throughout the twentieth century.

To overcome the drawback of the sonic tip speed limitation of propellers on some commercial aircraft using turboprops, the use of unducted fan propellers has been proposed. The unducted fan propeller is a many-bladed propeller with short, curved blades that allow craft to overcome the sonic tip concerns that plague high-speed aircraft using traditional propeller designs.

—Jamey D. Jacob

Further Reading

Gudmondsson, Snorri. *General Aviation Aircraft Design: Applied Methods and Procedures.* Elsevier Science, 2021.

Hitchens, Frank. *Propeller Aerodynamics: The History, Aerodynamics and Operation of Aircraft Propellers.* Andrews UK Limited, 2015.

Kinney, Jeremy R. *Reinventing the Propeller: Aeronautical Specialty and the Triumph of the Modern Airplane.* Cambridge UP, 2017.

The Law Library. *Air Worthiness Standards-Propellers* (US FAA) (2018 Edition). CreateSpace Independent Publishing Platform, 2018.

National Aeronautics and Space Administration (NASA). *An Assessment of Propeller Aircraft Noise Reduction Technology.* CreateSpace Independent Publishing Platform, 2018.

Steinberger, Victoria. *Design of Zephyrus Human Powered Airplane Propellers.* Pennsylvania State University, 2018.

See also: Aeronautical engineering; Ailerons, flaps, and airplane wings; Propulsion technologies; Turbojets and turbofans; Turboprops

AMPLITUDE

Fields of Study: Physics; Mechanical engineering; Mathematics

ABSTRACT

Helicopters, often referred to as choppers, helos, whirlybirds, or copters, are any rotary-wing aircraft having powered, fixed rotors that provide lift and propulsion for the aircraft. The helicopter was the first operational vertical takeoff and landing (VTOL) aircraft and remains the most prevalent.

KEY CONCEPTS

crest: the highest point of a wave from its neutral value; the distance between the crest or trough of a wave and the wave's neutral value is called the amplitude

displacement: the upward or downward extent to which the amplitude differs from the neutral value of a wave

frequency: the number of complete wavelengths that occur within one unit of time, typically expressed as hertz (Hz; cycles per second)

loudness: the intensity of sound waves, which depends on the wave's amplitude; measurements of loudness or volume are expressed in decibels

oscillation: a variation between maximum and minimum values of displacement from a neutral value

peak amplitude: the value of the amplitude at its maximum displacement from the neutral value of the wave

peak-to-peak amplitude: the absolute value of the sum of the peak positive and peak negative amplitudes; the distance between the crest and the trough of a wave

root-mean-square amplitude: for sinusoidal wave systems, the square root of the sum of squared amplitude values divided by the number of amplitude values

trough: the lowest point of a wave from its neutral value

wavelength: in any wave system, the distance from one point in a wave to the equivalent point in the next wave, typically measured between successive peak values

PROPERTIES OF WAVES

A wave is any physical phenomenon that can be described as an oscillation, or an alternating upward (or positive) and downward (or negative) displacement that travels through a medium, such as water or air, or even through space. Waves in water and the vibrations of a guitar string are just two examples of waves. Visible light and all other wavelengths of light are electromagnetic wave phenomena. Sound is another physical phenomenon that can be described in terms of wave properties. An essential feature of wave systems is their specific wavelength. Wavelength describes the distance between two identical points in successive waves. Wavelengths are typically measured between successive peaks, or crests, of a wave system. Another property of waves is their frequency, or the number of times waves repeat in a single unit of time.

Wave properties can be clearly visualized in water. For example, if the crests of a series of waves approaching a shore are separated by a distance of 3 meters (10 feet) then the wavelength of those waves is 3 meters. If six waves pass the same point in a span of three seconds, then their frequency is two waves per second. Frequency is normally described in units of cycles per second called hertz (Hz). The neutral value of water waves is at the level of perfectly smooth, undisturbed water. The difference between this level and any part of a wave is the displacement. The maximum displacement either above or below the neutral level is the amplitude of the wave. As each wave approaches, half of the wave is above the neutral level and half is below the neutral level. The maximum upward displacement of the wave is the crest, and the maximum downward displacement of the wave is the trough. The terms

crest and *peak* amplitude are often considered synonyms.

SIMPLE HARMONIC OSCILLATIONS

The pendulum in a grandfather clock is one of the most common examples of a simple harmonic oscillator. The motion of a pendulum can be described in terms of wave functions. At rest, a pendulum hangs straight down, which is its neutral value. The distance that the pendulum is swung away from the neutral value is its displacement. The maximum displacement in either direction is the amplitude. The motion of the pendulum as it swings between its maximum displacement on either side demonstrates a sinusoidal relationship. Sinusoidal motion is a pattern of behavior that can be described by a sine wave function. Once the pendulum reaches its maximum displacement, its motion reverses and it falls toward the neutral position once again. The distance from the peak amplitude in one direction to the peak amplitude in the other direction is called the peak-to-peak amplitude.

A wave's amplitude is measured from the origin to the wave's crest, or half the wave height. Waves with higher amplitude are higher energy than waves with a lower amplitude. In terms of electricity, amplitude is the maximum or peak voltage of a current.

SOUND WAVES

Sound waves propagate or move through a medium such as air, water, rock and other solids when a force is exerted against the matter that makes up the medium, compressing the atoms or molecules together. This compression travels through the medium as the compressed molecules push against the molecules next to them. At the same time, the molecules of matter behind the compression are pulled farther apart. The compression is the positive part of the sound wave. The rarefied portion that follows is the negative part of the sound wave. The compression and rarefaction of the particles in the medium displace those particles from their neutral position. The loudness of the sound is determined by the extent that the particles are displaced. The greater the amplitude of a sound wave, the greater the loudness of the sound.

When the compression and the rarefaction stages have passed, the molecules return to their neutral position. The motion of the matter involved in a sound wave can therefore be described by the same sinusoidal wave functions as other waves. The displacement of the medium from its neutral position describes the amplitude of the sound wave. The number of sound waves per unit time defines the frequency of the sound (its pitch). The distance between equivalent points in successive sound waves defines the wavelength of the sound.

SINUSOIDAL MOTION AND AMPLITUDE

The amplitude of any wave is the maximum displacement of the wave from its neutral, or equilibrium, value. Smooth and cyclic wave functions can be described by a sine wave function, or sinusoidal

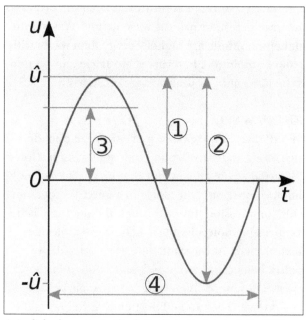

A sinodial voltage. 1=Amplitude (peak), 2=Peak-to-peak, 3=RMS, 4=Wave period. Image by Matthias Krüger, via Wikimedia Commons.

motion. In simple terms, sinusoidal motion follows the value of the sine of an angle about a fixed center, just like a point on a rotating wheel. Sine values cycle between a range of 1 and -1, beginning at an angle of 0 degrees, or 0 radians. A radian is the arc length along a circle that is equal to the length of the radius of the circle. An angle in radians is equal to the arc length divided by the radius, which is equal to approximately 57.3 degrees. As the point travels around the circle, it reaches an angle of 90 degrees (or $\pi/2$ radians) relative to its start point. As it travels further and again reaches the neutral level, the angle it makes with its starting point is 180 degrees (or π radians). At the lowest point the angle is 270 degrees (or $3\pi/2$ radians). The full circle is completed at the starting point, after moving through an angle of 360 degrees (or 2π radians) about the center of the circle.

A graph of the sine function exhibits the characteristic sideways S shape of a sine curve. In a sine wave, the amplitude is equal to the sine value of 90 degrees, which is 1, or 270 degrees, which is -1. Note that the trigonometric values of sine, cosine, and tangent have no units, as they are simply ratios and not measurements.

SINES AND COSINES

Both the sine and the cosine function are used to describe wave motion. They have the same behavior, but the value of the cosine is shifted 90 degrees ($\pi/2$ radians) from the value of the sine for the same angle. Whereas sine begins at 0, cosine begins at the peak amplitude of 1. The sine wave and the cosine wave are always on half of a cycle out of phase with each other because of this relationship. This feature is very important in mechanical operations such as the functioning of electric motors, electricity distribution networks, and especially in wireless and electronic communication systems. All systems that utilize vibrations can be described in terms of sine and cosine functions of the phase angle between them. Such systems generally are harmonic oscillators.

Harmonic oscillation from two or more sources has many applications with respect to waves. Their amplitudes are additive. When two waves of the same frequency and amplitude encounter each other and they are 180° out of phase with each other, their amplitudes add together and negate each other. At all other phase relations, the amplitudes add together to produce amplitudes that are greater or lesser than either one alone. This feature allows very accurate measurement of distances. For example, a wave signal can be transmitted to a target such as a distant satellite or the floor of the ocean or the atoms within a crystal structure. The signal will reflect from those targets in such a way that any difference in the phase relation of the outgoing signal and the returning signal can be determined and hence reveal the distance the signal has traveled. When sound waves are used, the process is called echo location, the principle that allows bats to fly safely in the dark, dolphins and whales to maneuver in the ocean waters and ships to find submarines and map the ocean floor, among other things. When electromagnetic signals are used, this is most familiar as radar and interferometry, and is how a global positioning system (GPS) determines distances from satellites in orbit about Earth.

WAVES IN REAL LIFE

Physical waves are seen every day in real life situations and their properties can be studied very easily. For example, on a windy day at the beach, waves may roll in regularly along a pier that rises 3 meters (10 feet) from the level seabed. The crest of each wave reaches the top of the pier, and the trough reaches only halfway to the top of the pier. It is easy to determine the peak amplitude of the waves. The piles of the pier mark a distance of 3 meters (10 feet) from the seabed to the top of the pier. The trough of each wave reaches one-half of that distance, or 1.5 meters (5 feet). The maximum difference between the crest and the trough of a wave, or the peak-to-peak amplitude of the waves, is therefore 1.5 meters (5 feet), corresponding to the distance from the top of the pier to the trough of the wave. The peak amplitude of the waves is equal to the difference in wave height from the neutral point to the crest, or one-half of the peak-to-peak amplitude, which in this case is 0.75 meters (2.5 feet). By counting the number of times the crest of the waves passes a specific point on the pier, it is easy to determine the frequency of the waves by dividing that number by the length of time in seconds that it took to count them. You may also notice that in the side view the waves demonstrate the classic sine wave shape.

Out in the open ocean or other large body of water, waves may add together to produce much larger waves, sometimes referred to as "rogue" waves. A rogue wave is a wave whose amplitude has been greatly augmented by other smaller waves until it is of a monstrous size compared to all the other waves in the water. In a very similar way, other systems exhibiting wave behavior can "go rogue" under the proper conditions. A classic example is that of a column of soldiers marching over a bridge. They are typically ordered to "break step" because the rhythm of marching in step generates and adds to an echoing vibration of the bridge itself, causing its amplitude to eventually become great enough to break the structural integrity of the bridge.

—*Richard M. Renneboog*

Further Reading

Augustine, Kingsley. *Sound and Wave Motion Calculations: A Physics Book for High Schools and Colleges*. Independently Published, 2018.

Buriyanyk, Michael. *Understanding Amplitudes: Basic Seismic Analysis for Rock Properties*. Society of Exploration Geophysicists, 2021.

De Mayo, Benjamin. *The Everyday Physics of Hearing and Vision*. Morgan & Claypool Publishers, 2014.

Fitzpatrick, Richard. *Oscillations and Waves: An Introduction.* 2nd ed., CRC Press, 2018.

Lasithan, L. G. *Mechanical Vibrations and Industrial Noise Control.* PHI Learning Pvt. Ltd, 2013.

Massel, Stanislaw Ryszard. *Ocean Surface Waves: Their Physics and Prediction.* 3rd ed., World Scientific, 2017.

McKeighan, Peter C., and Narayanaswami Ranganathan. *Fatigue Testing and Analysis Under Variable Amplitude Loading Conditions.* ASTM International, 2005.

See also: Acoustics; Angular forces; Angular momentum; Circular motion; Electromagnet technologies; Flywheels; Hertz, Heinrich Rudolf; Pendulums; Rotary engine; Tesla, Nikola; Vectors; Work and Energy

ANGULAR FORCES

Fields of Study: Physics; Mechanics; Mathematics

ABSTRACT

When an object moves in a circular path, as in a planetary orbit, it is subject to an angular force pulling it toward the center of the circle. This is called the centripetal force, and in the case of planetary orbits, it is gravity. Newton's laws for linear motion also describe circular motion and the forces at play.

KEY CONCEPTS

centrifugal force: a fictitious force that seems to push a body in circular motion away from the axis of rotation; in reality, objects in circular motion are subject to centripetal force

centripetal force: a force "toward the center" that, in combination with inertia, generates the curved path of an object in circular motion

cosine: a trigonometric function describing the relationship between sides of a right triangle; the cosine of an angle is equal to the length of the side adjacent to the angle divided by the length of the hypotenuse

inertia: the principle that an object at rest tends to stay at rest and an object in motion tends to stay in motion unless acted on by an outside force

perpendicular: being at a right angle relative to a given line or plane, as in the lines of the letter T

radian: a nondegree unit of angle measurement, based on the radius of a circle; there are 2π radians (equal to 360 degrees) in one complete circle or revolution

sine: a trigonometric function describing the relationship between sides of a right triangle; the sine of an angle is equal to the length of the side opposite the angle divided by the length of hypotenuse

vector: a quantity with both direction and magnitude

FORCES OF CIRCULAR MOTION

Whenever an object follows a curved path of motion, whether rotating about an internal axis or revolving around an external axis, an angular force is at play. Angular forces are forces that tend to produce circular motion. These forces act in a straight line, as all forces do. However, the result of their influence is a curved path of motion. This is in contrast to linear forces and linear motion, which follow straight lines.

The force that causes objects to follow a curved path is known as centripetal force. *Centripetal* comes from the Latin words for "center-seeking." Any curved motion can be thought of as tracing the circumference of an imaginary circle. The centripetal force always acts toward the center of this circle.

An object moving in a circular path is constantly caught in a tug-of-war between its inertia—that is, its tendency to move in a straight line at a constant speed—and the centripetal force. Centripetal describes a category of force and therefore may refer to a variety of forces, such as gravity (planetary orbits), tension (a ball on a string), or even friction (a car turning around a race track). At any given moment, an object in circular motion will tend to continue traveling in a straight line. The centripetal force acts to change this.

CENTRIPETAL VERSUS CENTRIFUGAL FORCE

The centripetal force (F_c) needed for an object to travel a circular path is described by the following equation, where m is the mass of the object in motion, v is its linear velocity, and r is the radius of the circular path it is following:

$$F_c = \frac{mv^2}{r}$$

The resultant path of a planet in orbit is dependent on the inertia of the planet and the gravitational force (FG) exerted on the planet by the sun. The angle of the resulting path falls between these two vectors.

Force is measured in newtons (N), an International System of Units (SI) derived unit. In SI base units, one newton is equal to one kilogram-meter per second squared (kg·m/s²). Be sure to use kilograms (not grams) for the mass when making calculations with this equation. Sometimes centrifugal force is incorrectly used in place of centripetal force. Centrifugal force is a fictitious or illusory force that seems to push outward from an object's axis of rotation. Imagine being the passenger in a car as it makes a sharp left turn and feeling pressed against the right-hand door. This "force" is not a real force, however. In the example of the turning car, the "force" being felt is that of the car pressing against the passengers to keep them from following their individual inertia and continuing forward in a straight line. When an object is set in circular motion and then released, such as a rock on a string that is spun around and then let go, it is not a "centrifugal force" that propels it outward. Rather, it is the lack of a centripetal force (the tension of the string) that suddenly allows the rock to travel unimpeded in a straight line.

FORCE VECTORS

Forces are vector quantities, meaning that they have both a magnitude and a direction. Vectors are typically indicated using arrows, with the length of the arrow corresponding to the magnitude of the force.

When two vectors are combined, their relative directions determine how they interact. Two forces of equal magnitude forces acting in opposite directions will cancel each other out. Two forces of equal magnitude acting in the same direction result in a doubled total, or net, force. When adding two forces, the angle formed between them determines their net magnitude and direction. Imagine hitting a baseball up and away from home plate. Ignoring drag, two forces are at play. First, the collision imparts the force of the bat's swing to the ball, pushing it in a straight line up and away toward some point above the horizon. Second, the force of Earth's gravity pulls the ball downward. The interaction of these forces gives the ball its curved trajectory.

UNIFORM CIRCULAR MOTION

In uniform circular motion, an object follows a perfectly circular path at a constant speed. At any given instant, centripetal force acts perpendicular to the linear momentum of the object in motion, forming a right angle between the two competing vectors. These two vectors can be thought of as two sides of a right triangle within the object's circular path of motion, with the apex of the triangle corresponding to a point along the circle's circumference. Therefore, trigonometric functions can be used to describe the relationship a given angle of rotation and the vectors at play in circular motion.

The two most commonly used trigonometric functions are sine (sin) and cosine (cos). The sine of a given angle (θ) in a right triangle is equal to the length of the side opposite that angle divided by the length of the triangle's hypotenuse (the longest side, opposite the right angle):

$$\sin\theta = \text{opposite} / \text{hypotenuse}$$

The cosine of the angle is equal to the length of the adjacent side divided by the length of the hypotenuse:

$$\cos\theta = \text{adjacent} / \text{hypotenuse}$$

The preferred unit of angular measure when dealing with circular motion is the radian (rad). Radians are based on the relationship between the radius of a circle and its circumference; there are 2π radians (corresponding to 360 degrees) in one complete revolution. Because circular motion traces the circumference of a circle, radians are also used to describe the angular distance an object travels—that is, how much of its circular path it completes.

Torque is a measure of rotational force acting on an object. Imagine the spoke of a wheel. A hand grips the wheel at some point along the spoke and applies a force perpendicular to the length of the spoke, causing the wheel to rotate around its central pivot point. The radius (r) is the length between that pivot point and the point where the force is applied. Torque (T) is the product of the radius, the force applied (F), and the sine of the angle between their directions (θ):

$$T = rF\sin\theta$$

Another use of these trigonometric functions is in finding the difference between two vectors. This has various applications, such as determining the change in velocity due to a glancing collision. In such a collision, the initial velocity vector and the final (postcollision) velocity vector form an angle at the point of impact, with the initial vector leading toward the impact and the final vector leading away. If the final vector were moved so that its starting point were the same as that of the initial vector, the difference between the two would be equal to a vector leading from the end point of the initial vector

to the end point of the final vector, forming the third side of a triangle. The law of cosines says that for a triangle with sides a, b, and c, the length c can be found when the angle C between lengths a and b (opposite side c) is known, according to the following equation:

$$c^2 = a^2 + b^2 - 2ab\cos C$$

Consider a car that is driving around a circular racetrack one kilometer (km) in circumference. It moves at a constant linear velocity of thirty meters per second (m/s) and has a mass of two thousand kilograms (kg). What is the magnitude of the centripetal force acting on the car?

The centripetal force is calculated as:

$$F_c = \frac{mv^2}{r}$$

Although the radius (r) of the racetrack is not given, it can be determined from the circumference. The equation for finding the circumference of a circle is as follows:

$$C = 2\pi r$$

Thus, the radius $r \approx 0.16$ km or 160 m.

Using this value for the radius, as well as the given values for linear velocity (v) and mass (m), the centripetal force (F_c) that the car experiences $= mv^2/r = 11{,}250$ newtons.

This is built into the formula for the cross product, or dot product, of two vectors. (The cross product is the product obtained when two vectors in a three-dimensional space are multiplied, resulting in a third vector perpendicular to both.) That is, the cross product of vectors X and Y is equal to the value $2|X||Y|\cos\theta$. Thus, if the angle (θ) between the initial velocity vector ($v\mathbf{i}$) and the final velocity vector ($v\mathbf{f}$) were known, the length of the difference vector ($v\mathbf{d}$) would be calculated as:

$$|v\mathbf{d}|^2 = (v\mathbf{f} - v\mathbf{i})^2$$

$$|v\mathbf{d}|^2 = (v\mathbf{f} - v\mathbf{i})(v\mathbf{f} - v\mathbf{i})$$

$$|v\mathbf{d}|^2 = (v\mathbf{f} \times v\mathbf{f}) - (v\mathbf{f} \times v\mathbf{i}) - (v\mathbf{f} \times v\mathbf{i}) + (v\mathbf{i} \times v\mathbf{i})$$

$$|v\mathbf{d}|^2 = |v\mathbf{f}|^2 + |v\mathbf{i}|^2 - 2|v\mathbf{f}||v\mathbf{i}|\cos\theta$$

Of course, objects do not always travel with uniform speed. Once an object in circular motion begins to speed up or slow down, the equations above no longer work. As long as the object continues to follow a circular path, the net force acting on the object will always equal the centripetal force, but its magnitude will vary depending on the acceleration of the object (remember, force equals mass times acceleration).

CIRCULAR MOTION IN EVERYDAY LIFE
It is not difficult to find examples of both rotation and revolution in everyday situations. Understanding torque and rotational motion is a vital part of engineering automobiles so that the wheels are given enough force to roll the car forward. Spin on an object moving through the air dramatically affects its aerodynamics and trajectory. In tennis, topspin is a vital technique that allows a player to make the ball drop much more sharply than it would under the influence of gravity alone. Putting "English" on the cue ball in a game of billiards, or throwing a breaking ball or a curve ball in a baseball game, or bending a soccer ball into the goal in a soccer (football) match are all examples of the same effect. Although these situations may seem more complicated than the more familiar linear motion of, for instance, billiard balls just bouncing around a pool table, it is important to remember that the physical principles underpinning linear and circular motion are the same.

—*Kenrick Vezina*

Further Reading

Davis, A. Douglas. *Classical Mechanics*. Elsevier, 2012.

Houk, T. William, James Poth, and John W. Snider. *University Physics: Arfken Griffing Kelly Priest*. Academic Press, 2013.

Ling, Samuel J., Jeff Sanny, and William Moebs. *University Physics Volume 1*. Samurai Media Limited, 2017.

Miller, Frederic P., Agnes F. Vandome, and John McBrewster, editors. *Centripetal Force: Osculating Circle, Uniform Circular Motion, Circular Motion, Cross Product, Triple Product, Banked Turn, Reactive Centrifugal Force, Non-uniform Circular Motion, Generalized Forces, Curvilinear Coordinates, Generalized Coordinates*. Alphascript Publishing, 2009.

Rau, A. R. P. *The Beauty of Physics: Patterns, Principles, and Perspectives*. Oxford UP, 2014.

See also: Acceleration; Billiards; Calculus; Celestial mechanics; Centrifugation; Circular motion; Coriolis effect; Dynamics (mechanics); Flywheels; Force (physics); Inertial guidance; Linear motion; Moment of inertia; Torque; Turbines

ANGULAR MOMENTUM

Fields of Study: Physics; Engineering; Mechanics; Mathematics

ABSTRACT
Angular momentum is the tendency of an object (or a system of objects rigidly held together in some way) to keep spinning or moving in a circle. Conservation of angular momentum is one of the most fundamental principles of physics, with a wide range of applications.

KEY CONCEPTS
angular acceleration: a change in angular velocity with time

angular velocity: equivalent to linear velocity, this is the change in the angular position of an object over time, measured in revolutions per unit time

inertia: the property of an object to resist change; an object at rest will remain at rest, while an object in motion will continue to move at a constant speed in the same direction, unless acted upon by some outside agent

mass: the amount of inertia of an object; a measure of the amount of matter or material in an object

quantized: any quantity that is said to be "quantized" can take on only certain values and no others; the quantity cannot vary continuously, but must discretely step from one accepted value to another

rotational inertia: the rotational equivalent of mass in linear motion, it depends not only on the mass but also on how that mass is distributed; rotational inertia is the product of a constant, the mass of the object, and the radius of the object squared

scalar: a quantity that can be described by a magnitude (amount) only; mass and time are both examples of scalar quantities

spectra: a plot of the intensity of light emitted from an atom or molecule as a function of wavelength (or energy)

torque: a twisting force that causes an object at rest to begin rotating or a rotating object to slow down and stop; it consists of a force applied perpendicular to some radius

vector: a quantity that requires both a magnitude (amount) and a direction to specify it; velocity and force are both examples of vector quantities

OVERVIEW

Sir Isaac Newton described the motion of objects in three basic laws. Newton's first law, the law of inertia, states that an object at rest will remain at rest, and an object in motion will continue to move in a straight line at a constant speed, unless acted upon by some external agent. The inertia of an object, or its resistance to change, is quantified by the mass of the object. An object's mass is simply a measure of the amount of matter or material in the object. (Mass is not to be confused with weight, which is the force that gravity exerts upon the mass. An object on

a planet having a higher or lower gravity has the same mass that it has on Earth, but its weight will be more or less than its weight on Earth.) The second of Newton's laws specifies the nature of the external agent. The push or pull that gets things moving (or slows them down and stops them) is called a "force." There are only two types of force; attraction and repulsion. When a force is exerted on an object, the object changes its motion. This change in the object's motion, speeding up or slowing down, is the acceleration of the object (the change in the velocity of the object over time). The more massive the object, the harder one must push on it to make it move; in other words, more force must be exerted. Also, for a given object, the harder one pushes, the faster the object accelerates or decelerates. Thus, the force depends directly on both the mass and the acceleration. A closer look at Newton's second law suggests a more complete definition of the inertia of an object. Mass does not completely describe the motional aspect of inertia; a new quantity, momentum, is a more complete description. The momentum of an object is the product of its mass and its velocity.

Momentum is a vector quantity (one requiring both a magnitude and a direction) and has a very important property in that it is conserved. In terms of momentum, Newton's second law can be expressed thus: The force is equal to the change in the momentum over time. Thus, if there are no external forces acting on an object or a system of objects, the momentum will not change; it will be constant, or conserved, in both magnitude and direction. Conservation of momentum is one of the most fundamental of physical concepts.

These laws also apply to objects in rotational motion. Rotational motion includes both an object spinning about an axis and an object (or a group of objects held rigidly together) moving in a circle. The rotational inertia of an object (sometimes also referred to as the "moment of inertia") is a little more complicated to define than the inertia for linear motion. It involves both the mass of the object and how that mass is distributed. For a mass moving in a circle, the rotational inertia is defined as the mass times the square of the radius of the circle. For a solid object spinning about an axis, the mass is distributed along a whole series of radii. Thus, it is necessary to find an effective average radius for the mass. This radius will be a fraction of the original radius and will depend on the shape of the object. (This effective radius is often referred to as the "radius of gyration.") For an object spinning about an axis, therefore, the rotational inertia will be some fraction times the mass times the radius squared, where the fraction depends on the shape of the object.

The basic quantities of rotational motion are defined analogously to the linear quantities. Thus, angular velocity is defined as the change in the angular position of an object per unit time. Angular velocity depends on the angle the object sweeps out or rotates through in some amount of time. The unit for angular velocity that is encountered in everyday usage is revolutions per minute (abbreviated rpm), although a more fundamental unit is radians per second; a radian is a unit of angular measurement such that one revolution (360 degrees) is equal to 2π radians. Similarly, angular acceleration is defined as the change in angular velocity per unit time.

Restating Newton's first two laws in terms of rotations thus yields the statement that an object at rest will remain at rest, while a rotating object will continue to rotate at a constant angular speed in the same direction (clockwise or counterclockwise), unless acted upon by an external agent. In rotations, this external agent is called a "torque." In order to create this twisting force, or torque, one must apply a force to the object. However, this force must be applied in a specific manner. First, the force must be applied some radial distance from the center of rotation. The farther out the force is applied, the greater the torque. Second, the force must be applied perpendic-

ular to the axis of rotation. Pushing along the axis of rotation merely makes the object slide linearly. In order to get a rotation (in this case, clockwise), the force F must be applied perpendicular to the axis of rotation. This is the basic principle by which all wrenches and screwdrivers function when tightening a nut or a bolt or when turning a screw.

The torque thus depends directly on both the radius and the perpendicular force. The result of the torque will be that the object begins to rotate (or to change its speed of rotation if it is already rotating). The amount of angular acceleration (or deceleration) the object experiences will depend on the amount of torque and the rotational inertia of the object. Thus, the amount of torque placed on an object will be directly related to its rotational inertia and its angular acceleration.

The rotational analog to linear momentum is angular momentum. It is defined in the same way as linear momentum. Angular momentum is the product of the rotational inertia times the angular velocity. Like linear momentum, angular momentum is a vector quantity. How can a rotation be described with a vector? Rotations are either clockwise or counterclockwise. In order to give the direction of rotation, and thus the angular momentum a vector, a right-hand rule is applied. If one curls the fingers of one's right hand in the direction of rotation, one's thumb will point in the direction of the vector. Thus the vector's direction will always lie perpendicular to the plane of the rotation.

Finally, as with linear momentum, it is possible to rewrite Newton's second law for a rotation. Applying a torque to an object will result in a change in angular momentum over time. The implications of this are the same as with linear momentum and force. If there are no external torques acting on an object, the angular momentum will not change; it will remain constant, or conserved, in both magnitude and direction. It is this last aspect, conservation of angular momentum, that has many applications.

The concept of conservation of angular momentum is one of the fundamental principles of much of modern atomic, nuclear, and elementary particle physics. Experimental evidence has led to the modern model of the atom with a small, dense, positively charged nuclear core surrounded by a large, structured, nebulous cloud of electrons. In a less refined model of the atom, the electrons were envisioned to be orbiting the nucleus along paths determined by specific energies. The angular momentum of the electrons had to be conserved, since they were envisioned as going in a circle. An early objection to this model was that in order for any object to go in a circle, it must experience a force toward the center of the circle and thus will have an acceleration. Accelerated charges radiate; thus, the electrons would continuously lose energy and spiral into the nucleus. Niels Bohr hypothesized that the electrons can only be found at certain radii from the nucleus. Since the angular momentum of the electron as it moves in a circle depends on the radius of the circle, Bohr expressed his hypothesis by saying that the angular momentum of the electrons must be "quantized"; not only is it conserved, but it can only take on certain discrete values. This quantization condition on the angular momentum was fundamental to working out the energies of the allowed orbitals and yielded the explanation of atomic spectra. When an electron moves from one orbital energy to another, energy must be absorbed or emitted, usually in the form of light. The light emitted is therefore characteristic of the atom.

In expanding this model to multielectron atoms, it was found that these electron orbitals could conform to several possible shapes at a given radius; thus, the angular momentum of these different shapes would also be slightly different. This further complicated the atomic spectra, because only certain transitions were allowed in order to conserve angular momentum. On further inspection, it was found that the spectral lines were sometimes actually composed of two or more lines very close together. The explanation for this fine structure seems to lie in the fact that the electrons have an intrinsic angular momentum. The only classical situation that corresponds to this is an object spinning about its axis, and so this intrinsic angular momentum is called "spin." The effect, however, is a purely quantum-mechanical one and does not really imply that the electrons are actually spinning. Very specific rules regarding the addition of these orbital and spin angular momenta in an atom govern the order in which the electrons fill the available energy levels. The order in which the orbitals are filled in turn determines the chemical properties of the atom and helps to explain the relationships seen in the periodic table of the elements. Conservation of these different types of angular momenta also plays a large role in the construction and properties of molecules.

It was subsequently discovered that several other fundamental particles, such as neutrons and protons, also exhibit this intrinsic angular momentum, or spin, to one degree or another. Further investigations of the implications of this intrinsic angular momentum in these elementary particles has led to an understanding of nuclear structure, electrical conduction in metals, the interactions of elementary particles, and the unusual properties of superfluidity and superconductivity.

APPLICATIONS

The most familiar application of conservation of angular momentum is seen in ice skating. Within a routine, an ice skater often performs a complicated maneuver, spinning with arms extended and then bringing the arms in to the body. As the arms are brought inward, rotational speed increases. This increase is the result of the decrease in rotational inertia caused by redistributing the body's mass over a much smaller radius. In order for angular momentum to be conserved, when the rotational inertia decreases, the angular velocity must increase. At the end of the spin, the skater's arms are thrown out wide in a dramatic gesture. The purpose of this movement is actually more physical than dramatic. By opening up the arms, the skater increases rotational inertia, thus decreasing angular velocity and making it easier to stop. Ballet dancers also use this technique, although they tend to be more subtle about it.

Conservation of angular momentum also includes conservation of the direction of angular momentum. The most obvious application of this is seen in a top. Trying to balance a top on its tip without spinning it borders on the impossible, but when the top is spinning, it balances readily. When the top is spinning, it has an angular momentum that points straight upward along the axis of the rotation. The direction of this angular momentum wants to be conserved; thus, when the top is pushed slightly to the side, it tends to right itself, so that its angular momentum returns to its original direction. The same principle is seen in riding a bicycle and in throwing a football. The spin imparted to a football helps it to travel straighter in order to conserve its angular momentum. The spin of the wheels on a bicycle acts as virtual training wheels, keeping the bicycle upright as long as it is moving. Tipping the bicycle to the side changes the direction of the angular-momentum vector of the wheels. In order to compensate for this, the bicycle needs to create another angular momentum to add to that of the wheels so that the total is the same direction as the original angular momentum. In order to do this, the bicycle goes in a circle. This is how it is possible to turn a bicycle without using one's hands.

One very useful application of the conservation of angular momentum is seen in a gyroscope. A gyroscope consists of a rotor, usually a solid, flat disk (called a "flywheel") on a shaft, which is mounted on frictionless bearings in a supporting frame. Once the rotor is spinning at a fairly high, constant rate, it will want to maintain its spin axis in order to conserve the direction of the angular momentum. If the bearings are truly frictionless and there are no other torques acting on the rotor, then the rotor will always stay aligned in the same direction, regardless of how the frame holding it is moved. This makes the gyroscope an excellent compass. Once it is set spinning in a preset direction, it will always return to that chosen direction. Gyroscopes and gyrocompasses are used in ship navigation and to guide the controls of airplane autopilots. Most important, they are used to maintain a spacecraft in a fixed orientation in space and can be used to help in automatic course corrections where a magnetic compass would be useless.

Conservation of angular momentum is seen in the solar system in a variety of ways. Earth orbits the Sun in an elliptical path. When it is closest to the Sun, at a point called "perihelion," it moves faster than when it is farthest away (a point called "aphelion"). This effect was observed by Johannes Kepler and is known as "Kepler's second law." The reason for this change in speed is simple conservation of angular momentum. When Earth is closest to the Sun, the radius of its orbit is smaller, and thus its rotational inertia is smallest. Conservation of angular momentum requires that as the rotational inertia decreases, the angular speed must increase. Space probes use this effect to change their direction and speed as they go out to explore the far reaches of the solar system; they slingshot themselves around the inner planets.

Conservation of angular momentum also played an important role in the formation of the Sun and the solar system. The current theory of the origin of the solar system postulates that the solar system began as a giant, swirling cloud of interstellar gas and dust called a "solar nebula." As a result of gravitational attraction between the particles of this nebula and some external influence, such as a collision with another nebula or the concussion from a nearby supernova, the nebula began collapsing. As it got smaller, conservation of angular momentum required it to spin faster. This increased angular velocity caused the shape of the nebula to change and flatten out, with the heaviest material near the center and lighter material moving outward toward the edge. As this solar nebula collapsed, it also began to get hotter, with the hottest region near the center, where the pressure from the outlying material was the greatest. This hot central core eventually formed a protosun, which continued to heat up until fusion began at its core and the Sun was born. The rest of the disk began to cool; small clumps of matter began to condense around the dust particles, and this accretion process eventually led to formation of the planets.

—*Linda L. McDonald*

Further Reading

Edmonds, A. R. *Angular Momentum in Quantum Mechanics*. Princeton UP, 2016.

Gordon, Opal. *A Comprehensive Guide to Angular Momentum*. Nova Science Publishers, 2019.

Marion, Jerry. *Physics in the Modern World*. Elsevier, 2012.

Mircescu, Alexander. *On the Conservation of Momentum, Angular Momentum, Energy, and Information*. BoD Third Party Titles, 2016.

Thompson, William J. *Angular Momentum: An Illustrated Guide to Rotational Symmetries for Physical Systems*. John Wiley & Sons, 2008.

See also: Angular forces; Biomechanics; Celestial mechanics; Centrifugation; Circular motion; Classical or applied mechanics; Coriolis effect; Electromagnetism; Flywheels; Helicopters; Inertial guidance; Linear motion; Magnetism; Momentum (physics); Newton's laws; Quantum mechanics; Solenoid; Torque; Vectors

ARCHIMEDES

Fields of Study: Physics; Engineering; Mechanics; Mathematics

ABSTRACT

Archimedes was a Greek mathematician and philosopher. He was born in Syracuse, Sicily, about 287 BCE, and died there in 212 BCE. Archimedes made his most important contributions to the field of geometry and founded the disciplines of statics and hydrostatics. He invented a screw device to move water from one level to another, approximated the value of pi (π), and developed the principle of mechanical advantage.

KEY CONCEPTS

mechanical advantage: the amount by which an applied force being used to perform work can be augmented through the use of mechanical devices

method of exhaustion: a means of determining the area of a planar surface with curved edges by inscribing within it successively smaller regular polygons (triangles, squares, etc.) whose areas can be accurately calculated, then summing those areas together

ARCHIMEDES'S EARLY LIFE

Few details are certain about the life of Archimedes. Syracuse generally is referred to as his birthplace, and his father Phidias was an astronomer and the author of a treatise on the diameters of the sun and moon. Some scholars have characterized Archimedes as an aristocrat who actively participated in the Syracusan court. He may have been related to King Hieron II, the ruler of Syracuse, whose son Gelon he tutored and to whom he dedicated one of his works. (Most of his books were first translated into English by Thomas L. Heath in *The Works of Archimedes*, 1897.)

Archimedes traveled to Egypt to study in Alexandria, where he befriended mathematicians Conon of Samos and Eratosthenes of Cyrene, both former students of the Greek mathematician Euclid. Judging from the prefaces to his works, Archimedes likely maintained friendly relations with several Alexandrian scholars and played an active role in Alexandria's mathematical traditions. He may have visited Spain before returning to Syracuse, and a return trip to Egypt is a possibility as well. This second visit would have been the occasion for his construction of dikes and bridges reported in some Arabian sources.

In Syracuse, Archimedes spent his time working on mathematical and mechanical problems. Although he was an ingenious inventor, his inventions were, according to Plutarch, mere diversions, the work of a geometer at play.

LIFE'S WORK

Archimedes's interests varied widely, encompassing statics, hydrostatics, optics, astronomy, and engineering, in addition to geometry and arithmetic. Many legendary stories circulate regarding his inventions, in particular. One such story poses his invention of a device called Archimedes's screw—a hollow cylinder containing a helical blade that could serve as a water pump when rotated; however, certain dates place the device before Archimedes's time. In another well-known story, Archimedes boasted to King Hieron that if he had a place on which to stand he could move the Earth. Hieron challenged him to make good on this boast by hauling ashore a fully loaded merchant ship. Using a compound pulley, Archimedes pulled the ship out of the harbor and onto the shore with modest effort. The compound pulley was likely Archimedes's invention (he is noted for his invention of block-and-tackle pulleys), but the story is probably a legend.

The most famous story of Archimedes is attributed to Roman writer and architect Vitruvius. King Hieron suspected that a golden wreath had been adulterated with silver, and he asked Archimedes to devise a way to test it. Archimedes pondered the problem, and one day, as he entered a full bath, he noticed that the deeper he descended into the tub the more water flowed over the edge. This suggested that the amount of overflowed water was equal in

Fig. 65. — Archimède.

Archimedes. Image via iStock/THEPALMER. [Used under license.]

volume to the portion of his body submerged in the bath. Archimedes is said to have leapt out of the tub and ran naked through the streets, shouting: "Eureka! Eureka!" Archimedes dipped into water lumps of gold and silver, each having the same weight as the wreath. He found that the wreath caused more water to overflow than the gold and less than the silver. From this experiment, he determined the amount of silver mixed with the gold in the wreath.

Archimedes's mathematical works can be divided into three groups: studies of figures bounded by curved lines and surfaces, works on statical and hydrostatical problems, and arithmetical works.

Archimedes used the method of exhaustion to find the areas of plane figures bounded by curved lines, as well as the volumes of solid figures bounded by curved surfaces. The term "exhaustion" is based on the idea that a circle, for example, would be exhausted by inscribed polygons with a growing number of sides. In *On the Sphere and the Cylinder*, Archimedes compares perimeters of inscribed and circumscribed polygons to prove that the volume of a sphere is two-thirds the volume of its circumscribed cylinder. He also proved that the surface of any sphere is four times the area of its greatest circle. Archimedes then applied the technique to spheroids, spirals, and parabolas. Archimedes's objective was to determine the volumes of conoidal and spheroidal segments cut off by planes, so he examined the area enclosed between the successive whorls of a spiral. Subsequent mathematicians and historians coined the term

Archimedes's spiral to describe a spiral in which a point rotates at a uniform rate from the central point, and along this same line another point starts at the central point, moves outward uniformly, and traces the spiral. Archimedes was also able to prove that the area of a parabolic segment is four-thirds the area of its greatest inscribed triangle—a theorem he was so fond of he gave it several different proofs. One such proof uses a method of exhaustion to approach a parabolic segment by a series of triangles. His most recently discovered work, *On the Method of Mechanical Theorems*, provides other examples of how Archimedes mathematically balanced geometrical figures as if they were on a weighing balance.

Archimedes also successfully applied geometry to statics and hydrostatics in order to search for the centers of gravity of several thin sheets of different shapes. Archimedes understood the center of gravity as the point at which an object can be supported so as to be in equilibrium with the pull of gravity. Earlier Greek mathematicians had made use of this principle to show that a small weight at a large distance from a fulcrum would balance a large weight near the fulcrum, but Archimedes worked this principle out in detail. In his proof, the weights are geometrical magnitudes acting perpendicularly to the balance beam, which itself is a weightless geometrical line. In this way, he reduced statics (i.e., the science related to weighing experiments) to a rigorous

discipline, comparable to what Euclid had done for geometry.

Archimedes also posed several principles of hydrostatics, the science of weight and pressure in relation to water, by proving that objects lighter than a fluid will, when placed in the fluid, sink only to the depth where the weight of the object is equal to the weight of the fluid displaced. Objects heavier than the fluid sink to the bottom. In other words, the weight of the fluid displaced by the object equals the force required to support it. This is the principle of buoyancy.

Although Archimedes's investigations were primarily in geometry and mechanics, he performed interesting studies in numerical calculation as well. *On the Measurement of the Circle* contains Archimedes's calculation of a value for the ratio of the circumference of a circle to its diameter (this figure was not called pi(π) until much later). By drawing polygons of more and more sides within and around a circle, Archimedes found that the ratio was between 223/71 and 220/71, the most accurate value of pi and the value that continues to be most widely known.

Toward the end of his life, Archimedes became involved in the worsening political situation in Syracuse and was said to have invented devices for warding off Roman enemies, such as large lenses to set fleets on fire and mechanical cranes to turn ships upside down. He devised so many war machines that the Romans would flee if so much as a piece of rope appeared above a wall. While these stories likely are a mixture of gross exaggeration and total fabrication, Archimedes indeed may have helped in the defense of his city. Amid the confusion of the sacking of Syracuse, Archimedes was killed by a Roman soldier, despite orders from Roman officials that he was to be spared. According to Archimedes's wishes, a cylinder circumscribing a sphere and an inscription of the ratio between their volumes was placed on his tomb, in remembrance of the accomplishment of which he was most proud.

ARCHIMEDES AND MECHANICAL ADVANTAGE

Ancient Greek mathematician Archimedes made his most important contributions to the field of geometry and also founded the disciplines of statics and hydrostatics. Archimedes applied his restless mind to the physical and intellectual challenges of his time. He invented a screw to move water from one level to another, approximated pi, and developed the principle of mechanical advantage, which explains the basic technology of the lever and Archimedes's own design of block-and-tackle pulleys.

While basic levers were in use throughout ancient Greece, Archimedes introduced theoretical ideas that concerned their use and advancement. A simple lever is used to lift heavy weights; it is a bar that sits on top of a pivot point known as a fulcrum. By moving the fulcrum farther from the force, the person using the lever can attain a mechanical advantage. This advantage, which Archimedes first conceptualized, is the quotient of the load and the effort required for its movement. The lever is still in use today, both as a simple machine and as a part of more sophisticated machinery.

Archimedes is recognized as the inventor of the block-and-tackle pulley, another simple machine that depends on the principle of mechanical advantage. The pulley is used to haul or lift heavy loads by changing the direction of the force that users administer. If one pulley is used, the only advantage is a change in the direction of the force; a user pulls on the pulley rope, and the attached load is lifted. In the case of two pulleys, the force is cut in half, as the distance that the rope must be pulled in order to lift the load is doubled. Additional pulleys can be added, further reducing the force required to lift the load and lengthening the distance that the rope must be pulled.

Archimedes also developed a screw device that can be used to raise water from one level to another.

Rather than using the point of the screw to dig into a surface, Archimedes's screw consists of a screw-shaped blade that revolves inside a cylindrical container. As the blade turns inside the cylinder, the liquid makes its way up the screw to a higher level. Originally, the device was used to irrigate crops in the Nile River delta, and many such screws are in use to this day.

IMPACT

Many scholars rank Archimedes as one of the greatest mathematicians who ever lived, and historians of mathematics agree that Archimedes's theorems raised Greek mathematics to a new level of understanding. He tackled problems of physical science and solved them and also developed the principle of mechanical advantage in ways that advanced existing technologies and led to the development of new inventions (such as the block-and-tackle pulley). His calculation of pi was the most accurate approximation yet; the method of exhaustion, by which Archimedes arrived at the value, points to the integral calculus of modern mathematics. His works were translated from Greek and Arabic into Latin during the twelfth century and played an important role in stimulating medieval natural philosophers. Knowledge of Archimedes's ideas spread during the Renaissance, and by the seventeenth century his insights had been almost completely absorbed into European thought and had deeply influenced modern science. Italian physicist Galileo Galilee, for example, was inspired by Archimedes and tried to do for analytical dynamics what Archimedes had done for statics.

—Robert J. Paradowski

Further Reading

Hasan, Heather. *Archimedes: The Father of Mathematics*. Rosen, 2006.
Kline, Morris. *Mathematical Thought from Ancient to Modern Times*. Oxford UP, 1990.

Netz, Reviel, and William Noel. *The Archimedes Codex: How a Medieval Prayer Book Is Revealing the True Genius of Antiquity's Greatest Scientist.* Hachette Books, 2007.

Rorres, Chris. *Archimedes in the 21st Century: Proceedings of a World Conference at the Courant Institute of Mathematical Sciences.* Birkhauser, 2017.

Stein, Sherman K. *Archimedes: What Did He Do Besides Cry Eureka?* Mathematical Association of America, 1999.

See also: Archimedes's principle; Aristotle isolates science as a discipline; Ballistic weapons; Discoveries of Archimedes; Load; Mechanical engineering; Projectiles

ARCHIMEDES'S PRINCIPLE

Fields of Study: Physics; Mechanics; Mathematics

ABSTRACT

Archimedes's Principle measures the buoyant force of an object immersed in fluid, which Archimedes found to be equal to the weight of the displaced water. This explains why objects sink or float, and has practical applications in shipbuilding, air and water travel, and hydraulic lifts.

KEY CONCEPTS

buoyancy: the upward force exerted by a fluid on a body immersed in that fluid

density: the mass of a substance per unit volume, measured in kilograms per cubic meter

displacement: in fluid mechanics, the process by which a body immersed in a fluid pushes the fluid out of the way and occupies the space in its stead. The volume of the displaced fluid is equal to the volume of the displacing body

mass: the amount of matter contained in an object

specific gravity: the ratio of the density of a substance to that of a standard reference substance; also known as relative density

volume: the amount of three-dimensional space enclosed within a given region or shape of specific dimensions

THE EUREKA MOMENT

It is said that while in the public bath one day, the ancient Greek philosopher Archimedes of Syracuse (ca. 287-212 BCE) realized the solution to a difficult problem. A king had given an artisan an amount of pure gold with which to make him a crown. Believing that the artisan had replaced some of the gold in the crown with an inferior metal and kept the extra for himself, the king asked Archimedes to determine if this was the case. Archimedes, however, could not think of a way to determine the purity of the gold without destroying the crown in the process. Simply weighing the crown and comparing it to the original weight of the pure gold would not work. Even if the crown was the same weight as the gold, it would have a different density than pure gold if it had been mixed with another metal. The artisan could simply have added more of a less dense material, or vice versa, to achieve the same weight.

According to popular legend, while pondering this problem, Archimedes visited a public bath to think it over. Once there, he noticed that the water level rose as he immersed himself in the bath and fell again as he stood to leave. Archimedes realized that his body was displacing the water when he was submerged. It is said that upon this realization, Archimedes leapt from the bath and ran through the streets naked, exclaiming, "Eureka!"

Further testing proved that when an object is submerged in water, the volume of the displaced water is equal to the volume of the object causing the displacement. Previously, Greek mathematicians had developed equations to calculate the volume of regular geometric objects, such as spheres and pyramids. However, they had no way to determine the volume of an object that could not be broken down into such shapes. Archimedes's discovery was significant because it allowed him to accurately measure the volume of an irregular object—in this case, the king's crown. Using this method, Archimedes could calculate the crown's density, because an object's density is equal to its weight divided by its volume. (Strictly speaking, density is in fact equal to mass divided by volume, while weight is equal to mass times the acceleration due to gravity. However, on Earth, an object's mass is more or less equivalent to its weight, because the average magnitude of acceleration due to gravity near Earth's surface—a quantity known as standard gravity—is defined as 1.) The density of the crown could then be compared to the density of pure gold. When Archimedes did this, he proved that the artisan had in fact cheated the king.

The discovery proved to be significant in another way as well: it allowed Archimedes to develop the principle that would bear his name. Archimedes's principle states that an object submerged in a fluid experiences an upward force equal to the weight of the fluid displaced by the object. This upward force is called buoyancy. If the weight of the submerged object is less than the weight of the displaced fluid, and thus less than the buoyant force, the object will rise to the top of the fluid; if its weight is greater, the object will sink; and if the weight is the same, the object will neither rise nor sink.

Because the volume of the object and the volume of the displaced fluid are the same, Archimedes's principle can be stated in another way: an object that is less dense than the surrounding fluid will float, while an object that is denser than the fluid will sink. This is related to the concept of specific gravity, also called relative density. An object's spe-

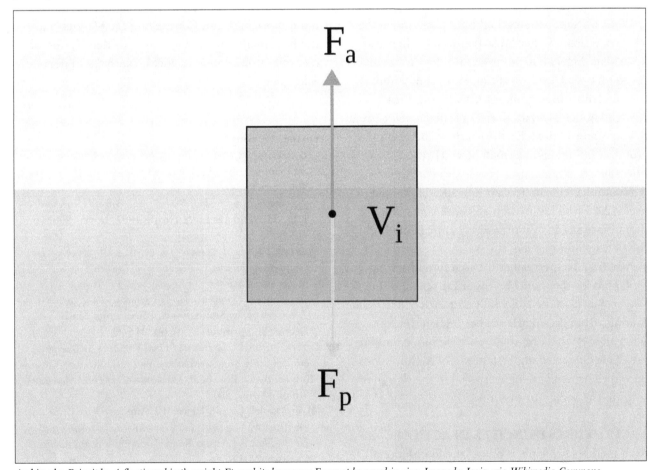

Archimedes Principle: A floating object's weight Fp and its buoyancy Fa must be equal in size. Image by Jooja, via Wikimedia Commons.

cific gravity is equal to the ratio of its density to the density of a standard reference substance, typically water. If the object's specific gravity is less than 1, it is less dense than the reference substance; if its specific gravity is greater than 1, its density is likewise greater.

THE BUOYANCY OF SHIPS

While it is true that Archimedes formalized the concept of buoyancy—a concept that shipbuilders had understood for many years—he did not expand on the idea or undertake additional research in that area. However, the concept later spread throughout the region when the Romans used it to build coin-operated water dispensers. Archimedes's method was used to check if the coins were genuine.

While ancient peoples might not have understood why wood floated, they knew that it did. They also knew that they had to be careful not to put too much cargo on board a ship and cause it to sink. Similarly, the ancient Chinese philosopher Zhuangzi (ca. 369-286 BCE) was aware that large ships need a great deal of water to float. He also understood that crumbs would float in a small bowl. He used such phenomena as a metaphor for knowledge and understanding. This understanding allowed people to use rocks for ballast in their ships, thus making them more stable by more closely approximating the density of water.

Additional experimentation in a formal setting took place in the model basins of Europe and the United States in the late 1800s and early 1900s. The findings from these early studies inform the computer models that eventually entered into common use. This enhanced understanding of Archimedes's buoyancy principle remains crucial to the design of ships in the twenty-first century.

ARCHIMEDES'S PRINCIPLE IN ACTION

Archimedes's principle is one of the foundational ideas in fluid mechanics. It allows engineers to de-sign ships that consider the motion of waves, enabling them to move faster and more efficiently even in rough waters. Archimedes's principle is also at the root of how submarines can ascend and descend in water. A submarine has floodable tanks that allow the operator to increase the vessel's mass by taking in water. This increases the submarine's density and makes it heavier than the water it displaces, causing it to sink to the desired depth.

Fish use a similar mechanism to alter their buoyancy. Many fish have an internal organ known as a swim bladder. They can expand or contract these bladders by retaining or expelling gas. When a fish's swim bladder expands, its body likewise expands to accommodate it, causing its overall volume to increase. As a result, the fish's density decreases, making it more buoyant. Contracting the bladder makes the fish smaller again, increasing its density and decreasing its buoyancy, so that it can swim in deeper water.

—*Gina Hagler*

Further Reading

Archimedes. *On Floating Bodies: Book I. The Works of Archimedes*. Edited by Thomas Little Heath. 1897. Dover, 2002, pp. 253-62.

_____. *On Floating Bodies: Book II. The Works of Archimedes*. Edited by Thomas Little Heath. 1897. Dover, 2002, pp. 263-300.

Costanti, Felice. "The Golden Crown: A Discussion." *The Genius of Archimedes: 23 Centuries of Influence on Mathematics, Science and Engineering; Proceedings of an International Conference Held at Syracuse, Italy, June 8-10, 2010*, edited by Stephanos A. Paipetis and Marco Ceccarelli, Springer, 2010, pp. 215-26.

Eckert, Michael. *The Dawn of Fluid Dynamics: A Discipline between Science and Technology*. Wiley, 2006.

Munson, Bruce Roy, et al. *Fundamentals of Fluid Mechanics*. 7th ed., Wiley, 2013.

Okoh, Daniel, Joseph Ugwuanyi, Ambrose Eze, Ernest Obetta, and Harrison Onah. *Archimedes' Principle and the Law of Flotation*. CreateSpace Independent Publishing Platform, 2017.

Starling, Frank. *Archimedes' Principle*. Genius Books, 2020.

Wysession, Michael, David Frank, and Sophia Yancopoulos. *Physical Science: Concepts in Action.* Prentice, 2004.

See also: Archimedes; Bernoulli, Daniel; Bernoulli's principle; Civil engineering; Discoveries of Archimedes; Fluid dynamics; Hydrodynamics; Materials science; Surface tension

ARISTOTLE ISOLATES SCIENCE AS A DISCIPLINE

Fields of Study: Physics; Engineering; Mechanics; Biology; Physiology; Mathematics; Philosophy

ABSTRACT

Aristotle (384-322 BCE) was the founder and head of the Lyceum, in Athens, Greece, about 325-323 BCE. Aristotle was the first philosopher to approach the study of nature in a systematic way, establishing science as a discipline and providing a starting place for natural philosophers into the Middle Ages.

KEY CONCEPTS

episteme: Aristotle's word for understanding the true character of a physical thing, only obtainable by studying the thing in such way that only one question about it can be answered at a time, which is the essence of scientific research

Forms: the rudimentary concept of matter being constructed as combinations of four basic anthropomorphic principles that define the character of any particular matter; these were later replaced by the four physical character principles earth, air, fire and water.

ARISTOTLE'S LIFE AND TIMES

Born in Stagira in northern Greece and the son of the physician to Amyntas II of Macedonia (r. ca. 393-370/369), Aristotle came to Athens when he was

Bust of Aristotle. Photo via iStock/Mo Semsem. [Used under license]

seventeen years old and studied at Plato's Academy for twenty years. When Plato died in 347 BCE, Aristotle left the academy and traveled for twelve years, visiting various centers of learning in Asia Minor and Macedonia. During this period of travel, he developed his interest in the natural sciences, to which he applied his method of inquiry. He returned to Athens in 335 BCE after a brief period of tutoring Alexander the Great (356-323 BCE), Amyntas's grandson, and established the Lyceum, a school that became a center of learning. He taught there until a year before his death.

The range of topics discussed and developed by Aristotle at the Lyceum is overwhelming: natural philosophy with its considerations of space, time, and motion; the heavenly bodies; life and psychic activities; ethical and political problems; animals and biological matters; and rhetoric and poetics. Further, he is sometimes credited with creating new fields of research, such as terrestrial dynamics and optics. He also taxonomized plants and animals and organized earlier Greeks' ideas about planetary astronomy in *Peri ouranou* (ca. 350 BCE; *On the Heavens*, 1939).

Perhaps the most significant aspect of Aristotle's work is his development of a "scientific" approach to these studies. This "scientific" approach recognizes the existence of independent disciplines, each employing its own principles and hypotheses. Such an approach also works out a methodology or procedure for each field of study, aiming at true and certain knowledge.

The Greek term that Aristotle used for "scientific knowledge" is *episteme* (επιϛτεμε), which can best be translated as "true knowledge" or the "most certain knowledge." This knowledge includes the awareness of an object, of its causes, and that it can be no other way. Medieval scholars translated the Greek *episteme* as the Latin *scientia*, which came into English as "science."

In recognizing independent fields of study, Aristotle showed a significant departure from Plato's philosophy. Plato had envisioned one single science. For him, true knowledge was the contemplation of the Forms: Virtue, Justice, Beauty, and Goodness. All other disciplines were subordinate to knowledge of the Forms. Aristotle, on the other hand, did not advocate a hierarchical structure of knowledge. Each study locates its own particular subject matter and defines its principles from which conclusions are to be drawn. Almost all his treatises begin with the same format: "Our task here concerns demonstrative science," that is, logic; or "Human conduct belongs to political science."

Aristotle's insistence on the division of sciences, each using special principles, is indicative of his re-

jection of any absolute master plan of knowledge. He does, however, recognize "common principles," or principles shared by more than one science. For example, the "equals from equals" principle of mathematics can be used in geometry to deduce a conclusion about a line. Aristotle warns the geometrician, however, that this can be done "if he assumes the truth not universally, but only of magnitudes." Aristotle never intends the same common principles to be universally applied in exactly the same way throughout all the sciences. If this were the case, there would not be "sciences," but rather "Science."

The second important feature of Aristotle's scientific approach concerns methodology. In the *Analytica posterioria* (335-323 BCE; *Posterior Analytics*, 1812), he develops the general technique that the particular disciplines are to employ in order to achieve scientific knowledge. First, an investigation must always begin with what is "better known" to humans. They must begin with observable data and facts, and not construct wild hypotheses. Second, human beings must proceed to a knowledge of the cause of the facts; mere observation is not enough. Observing something only indicates that something is the case; it does not explain why it is the case. Learning the cause tells people why, and this involves a logical demonstration. Third, the cause or reason of the fact must be of "that fact and no other." This criterion is the basis for a scientific law because it demands a universal connection between the subject and its attributes. The second and third criteria require a deductive system of demonstration that is expressed in the universal positive form of the syllogism that Aristotle developed in the *Analytica priora* (335-323 BCE; *Prior Analytics*, 1812). There is also what might be called an "inductive" approach to his method of science. Aristotle raises the question of how humans know the universal principles from which demonstration is to proceed. He answers that human knowledge of such principles begins with many sense perceptions of similar events. Human memory unifies these perceptions into a single experience. The human intellect or mind then understands the universal import of the experience. From many similar experiences, humans recognize a universal pattern.

Aristotle's method of science combines the theoretical and the practical. The theoretical aspect includes logical demonstrations and universal principles. The practical includes the necessary role of sense perception as it relates to particular objects. In the *Metaphysica* (335-323 BCE; *Metaphysics*, 1801), he warns that physicians do not cure men-in-general in a universal sense; rather they cure Socrates or Callias, a particular man. He adds that one who knows medical theory dealing with universals without experience with particulars will fail to effect a cure. Instead, he advises the use of procedures grounded in common sense that have proven their validity in practice.

One application of this method is in Aristotle's writings on biology. He makes theoretical interpretations based on his dissection of marine animals and empirical observations, although he does also rely on other writers' descriptions of some animals. Based on these researches, he arranges a "ladder of nature." Because he can see changes in the realm of plants and animals, he affirms the reality of nature and the value of its study. He is optimistic that he could use natural history to find causal explanations of physiology.

SIGNIFICANCE

For Aristotle, scientific knowledge included the observation of concrete data, the formulation of universal principles, and the construction of logical proofs. Greek "science" prior to Aristotle, largely a melange of philosophical and quasi-mythological assumptions, blossomed after his investigations into the specialized work of Theophrastus (ca. 372-287 BCE) in botany, Herophilus (ca. 335-280 BCE) in

medicine, and Aristarchus of Samos (ca. 310-230 BCE) in astronomy.

Aristotle also pioneered the notion that there are many, distinct disciplines of knowledge rather than a single, unified science; that there are multiple structuring principles for these disciplines rather than one, overarching set of concepts applicable to them all; that standards of scientific rigor vary among disciplines; and that there is no single, universal scientific method. At the same time, he believed in systematic, empirical investigation of natural phenomena, from which general theories might arise, as opposed to creating a theoretical structure and then fitting the data into it. His identification of many of the scientific disciplines and his methodology for studying them remain valid today.

—*Joseph J. Romano, updated by Amy Ackerberg-Hastings*

Further Reading

Barnes, Jonathan, editor. *The Cambridge Companion to Aristotle*. Cambridge UP, 1995.

Byrne, Patrick H. *Analysis and Science in Aristotle*. State U of New York P, 1997.

Ferejohn, Michael. *The Origins of Aristotelian Science*. Yale UP, 1991.

Hall, Edith. *Aristotle's Way: How Ancient Wisdom Can Change Your Life*. Penguin, 2019.

Lindberg, David C. *The Beginnings of Western Science*. U of Chicago P, 1992.

McKeon, Richard. *The Basic Works of Aristotle*. Reprint. Random House Publishing Group, 2009.

Sfendoni-Mentzou, Demetra, et al., editors. *Aristotle and Contemporary Science*. 2 vols. P. Lang, 2000-2001.

Shields, Christopher, editor. *The Oxford Handbook of Aristotle*. Oxford UP, 2015.

See also: Archimedes

ATOMS

Fields of Study: Chemistry; Physics; Biochemistry; Mathematics

ABSTRACT

The basic structure of atoms has been well defined by the development and elaboration of the modern theory of atomic structure. Atomic structure is fundamental to all fields of chemistry, but especially to fields that rely on the intrinsic properties of individual atoms, such as materials science and practices that pervade modern society.

KEY CONCEPTS

atomic mass: the total mass of the protons, neutrons, and electrons in an individual atom

atomic number: the number of protons in the nucleus of an atom, used to uniquely identify each element

electron: a fundamental subatomic particle with a single negative electrical charge, found in a large, diffuse cloud around the nucleus

element: a form of matter consisting only of atoms of the same atomic number

isotope: an atom of a specific element that contains the usual number of protons in its nucleus but a different number of neutrons

neutron: a fundamental subatomic particle in the atomic nucleus that is electrically neutral and about equal in mass to the mass of one proton

nucleus: the central core of an atom, consisting of specific numbers of protons and neutrons and accounting for at least 99.98 percent of the atomic mass

proton: a fundamental subatomic particle with a single positive electrical charge, found in the atomic nucleus

VISUALIZING THE ATOM

An atom is the smallest unit of elemental matter that retains and defines the specific properties of that material. The concept can be visualized by imagining a sample of a pure elemental material being repeatedly divided into ever-smaller portions. Eventually a point would be reached at which the material could no longer be subdivided without destroying its identity. The remaining ultimately indivisible portion is one atom of the element. Any further subdivision would require breaking the atom into its component protons, neutrons, and electrons, hence destroying its identity as an element.

HISTORICAL THEORIES OF ATOMIC STRUCTURE

In their attempts to comprehend the basic nature of the universe, early Greek philosophers, particularly Democritus (ca. 460-370 BCE), followed this kind of logical reasoning to the philosophical concept of the ατομος (*atomos*, indivisible), the fundamental thing from which all matter was made. Greek philosophy, however, was based on thought, not experimentation. Two thousand years later, in the Middle Ages, the practice of alchemy arose alongside the various practices of metallurgy, and alchemists sought means of transforming materials into other materials, typically through magic and arcane practices. The refinement and working of metals became a very important practical study and gave rise to the first truly scientific book of chemistry, *De re metallica* (*On the Nature of Metals*, 1556), by Georgius Agricola (1494-1555). Alchemy eventually gave way to more scientific study of matter through the use of weights and measures, enabling early scientists to recognize the relationships between different types of matter that formed the foundation on which the modern atomic theory has been constructed.

In the nineteenth century, scientists began to reject the philosophical *atomos* in favor of the physical atom as the basic building block of matter. John Dalton (1766-1844) conceived of the atom as though it were a billiard ball: a single, hard, uniform spherical object. He based this view on the behavior of gases, some of which he found he could describe mathematically in the same way he could describe the behavior of billiard balls with the billiard model. Other chemical behaviors required a mechanism to account for electrical charge, however, especially in to the case of ionic interactions.

In 1897, J. J. Thomson (1856-1940) discovered that when a polarized electricity source is discharged within a gas-filled tube, the rays emitted from the cathode (the negative electrode), known as cathode rays, obey the mathematics of a stream of charged particles. After calculating the likely mass of the particles, Thomson determined that they were even smaller than atoms, thus proving the existence of subatomic particles. He called these particles "corpuscles" at first, though they soon became known as electrons. Following this discovery, Thomson developed a new atomic model, one in which small, negatively charged particles—electrons—were embedded throughout a positively charged matrix, rather like the plums in a plum pudding. This came to be known as the plum-pudding model.

THE MODERN THEORY OF ATOMIC STRUCTURE

In 1909, Ernest Rutherford (1871-1937), aided by Hans Geiger (1882-1945) and Ernest Marsden (1889-1970), conducted the gold-foil experiment,

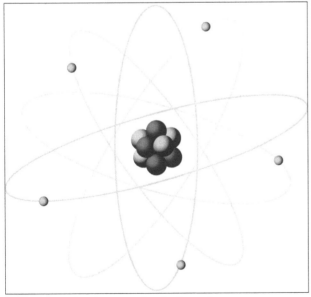

Image via iStock/jack0m. [Used under license.]

which demonstrated that atoms consist of a nucleus surrounded by what is essentially empty space. In this experiment, a beam of alpha particles (the nuclei of helium atoms) was directed at a piece of very thin gold foil, which was surrounded by a film strip that would detect alpha particles as they passed through the foil. Rutherford found that while the vast majority of the particles passed directly through the foil as though there was nothing there, some of the particles were deflected in all directions by the foil. This demonstrated that atoms consist of a very small, dense nucleus that can deflect alpha particles, surrounded by a thin, diffuse cloud that is not capable of affecting their movement. Rutherford continued experimenting with alpha particles, and in 1917 he discovered that the collision of an alpha particle with the nucleus of a nitrogen atom released a particle identical to a hydrogen nucleus—in other words, a proton.

Considerations of the energies associated with electrons in atoms led Niels Bohr (1885-1962) to postulate in 1913 that the electrons must be restricted to specific orbital paths around the nucleus, in accordance with the corresponding wavelengths calculated by Louis de Broglie (1892-1987). Measurement of the wavelengths of various emission and absorption spectra indicated that electrons in atoms can only have certain specific energy levels, which is consistent with the idea that electrons can only follow certain stable orbits around a nucleus.

Because of its electrical neutrality, the neutron remained an elusive theoretical construct until 1932, when an experiment by James Chadwick (1891-1974) demonstrated their existence. Chadwick used alpha particles to bombard a beryllium target, causing it to release radiation that would strike a paraffin target, which would in turn release protons from hydrogen nuclei into an ionization chamber. He determined that the radiation released from the beryllium was actually a neutral particle of approximately the same mass as a proton, and is now known to be a neutron.

These discoveries about the nature of the various subatomic particles formed the foundation of a new model of atomic structure, based on the principles of quantum mechanics. In this model, the energy levels of electrons can only change by discrete steps, or quanta, and thus electrons can occupy only specific regions of space about the nucleus, which came to be called atomic orbitals. These orbitals have specific shapes and orientations around the nucleus of the atom, and represent the probability that an electron will be found within that particular region of space abut the nucleus. Their orientations in turn determine how atoms interact to form chemical bonds. The physical orientation of those bonds determines the shapes and properties of both the atoms and the molecules that they form.

THE PERIODIC TABLE

The periodic table of the elements displays the relationships of the elements according to the quantum mechanical model of atomic structure. Chemists had tried to sequentially order the known elements by their common properties since the late eighteenth century. Dmitri Mendeleev (1834-1907) is credited with developing the first modern periodic table, which he published in 1869. Although much information was missing from that earliest version, he was nevertheless able to predict the existence of other as-yet-unknown elements with it. The periodic table of the elements contains all ninety-eight naturally occurring elements, as well as about twenty more that have been (or are claimed to have been) produced artificially. Each square in the table corresponds to a single element. In a standard periodic table, the internationally accepted symbol of the element is in the center of the square, with its atomic number at the top and its atomic mass at the bottom. Some periodic tables also include the normal oxidation states in which each element is found and its electron configuration according to the quantum mechanical model of atomic structure.

The identity of each atom is determined by the number of protons in its nucleus, meaning that all atoms with the same number of protons in their respective nuclei are atoms of the same element. However, the number of neutrons and electrons in an atom can change. Neutral atoms must have the exact same number of electrons orbiting the nucleus as there are protons within the nucleus; those atoms with more or fewer electrons than protons are ions, or atoms with a net electrical charge. Atoms with different numbers of neutrons in their nuclei are different isotopes of the same element. The atomic mass of an atom is the total mass of all protons, neutrons, and electrons in the atom; however, because electrons are so small and have such little mass, the atomic mass can be approximated by adding the number of neutrons and protons together. Atomic mass is measured in unified atomic mass units (u), one of which is approximately equal to the mass of a proton or neutron.

—*Richard M. Renneboog*

Further Reading

Agricola, Georgius. *De re metallica*. Translated by Herbert Clark Hoover and Lou Henry Hoover. Dover, 1950.

Gordin, Michael D. *A Well-Ordered Thing: Dmitri Mendeleev and the Shadow of the Periodic Table, Revised Edition*. Princeton UP, 2019.

Green, Dan. *The Periodic Table in Minutes*. Quercus, 2016.

Gribbin, John. *Science: A History, 1543-2001*. Lane, 2002.

Jackson, Tom. *The Periodic Table: A Visual Guide to the Elements*. White Lion Publishing, 2020.

Kragh, Helge. *Niels Bohr and the Quantum Atom: The Bohr Model of Atomic Structure, 1913-1925*. Oxford UP, 2012.

Scerri, Eric R. *The Periodic Table: Its Story and Its Significance*. 2nd ed., Oxford UP, 2019.

Whelan, Colm T. *Atomic Structure*. Morgan & Claypool Publishers, 2018.

See also: Classical or applied mechanics; Magnetism; Materials science; Nanotechnology; Photoelectric effect; Quantum mechanics; Superconductor; Thermodynamics

AUTOMATED PROCESSES AND SERVOMECHANISMS

Fields of Study: Physics; Mechanics; Mathematics

ABSTRACT

An automated process is a series of sequential steps to be carried out automatically. Servomechanisms are systems, devices, and subassemblies that control the mechanical actions of robots using feedback information from the overall system in operation.

KEY CONCEPTS

actuator: a device that functions to provide motion to a component for a particular purpose; operated hydraulically, pneumatically, or electrically

hydraulics: the application of pressurized liquids to perform work

industrialization: the replacement of manual and animal labor by machines

pneumatics: the application of pressurized air to perform work

BASIC PRINCIPLES

An automated process is any set of tasks that has been combined to be carried out in a sequential order automatically and on command. The tasks are not necessarily physical in nature, although this is the most common circumstance. The execution of the instructions in a computer program represents an automated process, as does the repeated execution of a series of specific welds in a robotic weld cell. The two are often inextricably linked, as the control of the physical process has been given to such digital devices as programmable logic controllers (PLCs) and computers in modern facilities.

Physical regulation and monitoring of mechanical devices such as industrial robots is normally achieved through the incorporation of servomechanisms. A servomechanism is a device that accepts information from the system itself and then uses that information to adjust the system to maintain specific operating conditions. A servomechanism that controls the opening and closing of a valve in a process stream, for example, may use the pressure of the process stream to regulate the degree to which the valve is opened.

Another essential component in the functioning of automated processes and servomechanisms is the feedback control systems that provide self-regulation and auto-adjustment of the overall system. Feedback control systems may be pneumatic, hydraulic, mechanical, or electrical in nature. Electrical feedback may be analog in form, although digital electronic feedback methods provide the most versatile method of output sensing for input feedback to digital electronic control systems.

BACKGROUND AND HISTORY

Automation begins with the first artificial construct made to carry out a repetitive task in the place of a person. One early clock mechanism, the water clock, used the automatic and repetitive dropping of a specific amount of water to measure the passage of time accurately. Water-, animal-, and wind-driven mills and threshing floors automated the repetitive action of processes that had been accomplished by humans. In many developing areas of the world, this repetitive human work remains a common practice.

With the mechanization that accompanied the Industrial Revolution, other means of automatically controlling machinery were developed, including self-regulating pressure valves on steam engines. Modern automation processes began in North America with the establishment of the assembly line as a standard industrial method by Henry Ford. In this method, each worker in his or her position along the assembly line performs a limited set of functions, using only the parts and tools appropriate to that task.

Servomechanism theory was further developed during World War II. The development of the transistor in 1951 enabled the development of electronic control and feedback devices, and hence digital electronics. The field grew rapidly, especially following the development of the microcomputer in 1969. By the twenty-first century, digital logic and machine control could be interfaced in an effective manner, enabling automated systems to function with an unprecedented degree of precision and dependability.

AUTOMATED PROCESSES

An automated process is a series of repeated, identical operations under the control of a master operation or program. While simple in concept, it is complex in practice and difficult in implementation and execution. The process control operation must be designed in a logical, step-by-step manner that will provide the desired outcome each time the process is cycled. The sequential order of operations must be set so that the outcome of any one step does not prevent or interfere with the successful outcome of any other step in the process. In addition, the physical parameters of the desired outcome must be established and made subject to a monitoring protocol that can then act to correct any variation in the outcome of the process.

A plain analogy is found in the writing and structuring of a simple computer programming function. The definition of the steps involved in the function must be exact and logical because the computer, like any other machine, can do only exactly what it is instructed to do. Once the order of instructions and the statement of variables and parameters have been finalized, they will be carried out in exactly the same manner each time the function is called in a program. The function is thus an automated process.

The same holds true for any physical process that has been automated. In a typical weld cell, for example, a set of individual parts are placed in a fixture that holds them in their proper relative orientations. Robotic welding machines may then act upon the setup to carry out a series of programmed welds to join the individual pieces into a single assembly. The series of welds is carried out in exactly the same manner each time the weld cell cycles. The robots that carry out the welds are guided under the control of a master program that defines the position of the welding tips, the motion that it must follow, and the duration of current flow in the welding process for each movement, along with many other variables that describe the overall action that will be followed. Any variation from this programmed pattern of movements and functions will result in an incorrect output.

The control of automated processes is carried out through various intermediate servomechanisms. A servomechanism uses input information from both the controlling program and the output of the process to carry out its function. Direct instruction from the controller defines the basic operation of the servomechanism. The output of the process generally includes monitoring functions that are compared to the desired output. They then provide an input signal to the servomechanism that informs how the operation must be adjusted to maintain the desired output. In the example of a robotic welder, the movement of the welding tip is performed through the action of an angular positioning device. The device may turn through a specific angle according to the voltage that is supplied to the mechanism. An input signal may be provided from a proximity sensor such that when the necessary part is not detected, the welding operation is interrupted and the movement of the mechanism ceases.

The variety of processes that may be automated is practically limitless given the interface of digital electronic control units. Similarly, servomechanisms may be designed to fit any needed parameter or to carry out any desired function.

APPLICATIONS AND PRODUCTS

The applications of process automation and servomechanisms are as varied as modern industry and its products. It is perhaps more productive to think of process automation as a method that can be applied to the performance of repetitive tasks than to dwell on specific applications and products. The commonality of the automation process can be illustrated by examining a number of individual applications, and the products that support them.

"Repetitive tasks" are those tasks that are to be carried out in the same way, in the same circumstances, and for the same purpose a great number of times. The ideal goal of automating such a process is to ensure that the results are consistent each time the process cycle is carried out. In the case of the robotic weld cell, the central tasks to be repeated are the formation of welded joints of specified dimensions at the same specific locations over many hundreds or thousands of times. This is a typical operation in the manufacturing of subassemblies in the automobile industry and in other industries in which large numbers of identical fabricated units are produced.

Automation of the process requires the identification of a set series of actions to be carried out by industrial robots. In turn, this requires the appropriate industrial robots be designed and constructed in such a way that the actual physical movements necessary for the task can be carried out. Each robot will incorporate a number of servomechanisms that drive the specific movements of parts of the robot according to the control instruction set. They will also incorporate any number of sensors and transducers that will provide input signal information for the self-regulation of the automated process. This input data may be delivered to the control program and compared to specified standards before it is fed back into the process, or it may be delivered directly into the process for immediate use.

Programmable logic controllers (PLCs), first specified by the General Motors Corporation in 1968, have become the standard devices for controlling automated machinery. The PLC is essentially a dedicated computer system that employs a limited-instruction-set programming language. The program of instructions for the automated process is stored in the PLC memory. Execution of the program sends the specified operating parameters to the corresponding machine in such a way that it carries out a set of operations that must otherwise be carried out under the control of a human operator.

A typical use of such methodology is in the various forms of computer numeric control (CNC) machining. CNC refers to the use of reduced-instruction-set computers to control the mechanical operation of machines. CNC lathes and mills are two common applications of the technology. In the traditional use of a lathe, a human operator adjusts all of the working parameters such as spindle rotation speed, feed rate, and depth of cut, through an order of operations that is designed to produce a finished piece to blueprint dimensions. The consistency of pieces produced over time in this manner tends to vary as operator fatigue and distractions affect human performance. In a CNC lathe, however, the order of operations and all of the operating parameters are specified in the control program and are thus carried out in exactly the same manner for each piece that is produced. Operator error and fatigue do not affect production, and the machinery produces the desired pieces at the same rate throughout the entire working period. Human intervention is required only to maintain the machinery and is not involved in the actual machining process.

Servomechanisms used in automated systems check and monitor system parameters and adjust operating conditions to maintain the desired system output. The principles upon which they operate can range from crude mechanical levers to sophisticated and highly accurate digital electronic-measurement devices. All employ the principle of feedback to control or regulate the corresponding process that is in operation.

In a simple example of a rudimentary application, units of a specific component moving along a production line may in turn move a lever as they pass by. The movement of the lever activates a switch that prevents a warning light from turning on. If the switch is not triggered, the warning light tells an operator that the component has been missed. The lever, switch, and warning light system constitute a crude servomechanism that carries out a specific function in maintaining the proper operation of the system.

In more advanced applications, the dimensions of the product from a machining operation may be tested by accurately calibrated measuring devices before releasing the object from the lathe, mill, or other device. The measurements taken are then compared to the desired measurements, as stored in the PLC memory. Oversize measurements may trigger an action of the machinery to refine the dimensions of the piece to bring it into specified tolerances, while undersize measurements may trigger the rejection of the piece and a warning to maintenance personnel to adjust the working parameters of the device before continued production.

Two of the most important applications of servomechanisms in industrial operations are control of position and control of rotational speed. Both commonly employ digital measurement. Positional control is generally achieved through the use of servomotors, also known as stepper motors. In these devices, the rotor turns to a specific angular position according to the voltage that is supplied to the motor. Modern electronics, using digital devices constructed with integrated circuits, allows extremely fine and precise control of electrical and electronic factors, such as voltage, amperage, and resistance. This, in turn, facilitates extremely precise positional control. Sequential positional control of different servomotors in a machine, such as an industrial ro-

bot, permits precise positioning of operating features. In other robotic applications, the same operating principle allows for extremely delicate microsurgery that would not be possible otherwise.

The control of rotational speed is achieved through the same basic principle as the stroboscope. A strobe light flashing on and off at a fixed rate can be used to measure the rate of rotation of an object. When the strobe rate and the rate of rotation are equal, a specific point on the rotating object will always appear at the same location. If the speeds are not matched, that point will appear to move in one direction or the other according to which rate is the faster rate. By attaching a rotating component to a representation of a digital scale, such as the Gray code, sensors can detect both the rate of rotation of the component and its position when it is functioning as part of a servomechanism. Comparison with a digital statement of the desired parameter can then be used by the controlling device to adjust the speed or position, or both, of the component accordingly.

SOCIAL CONTEXT AND FUTURE PROSPECTS

While the vision of a utopian society in which all menial labor is automated, leaving humans free to create new ideas in relative leisure, is still far from reality, the vision becomes more real each time another process is automated. Paradoxically, since the mid-twentieth century, knowledge and technology have changed so rapidly that what is new becomes obsolete almost as quickly as it is developed, seeming to increase rather than decrease the need for human labor.

New products and methods are continually being developed because of automated control. Similarly, existing automated processes can be reautomated using newer technology, newer materials, and modernized capabilities. Particular areas of growth in automated processes and servomechanisms are found in the biomedical fields. Automated processes greatly increase the number of tests and analyses that can be performed for genetic research and new drug development. Robotic devices become more essential to the success of delicate surgical procedures each day, partly because of the ability of integrated circuits to amplify or reduce electrical signals by factors of hundreds of thousands. Someday, surgeons may be able to perform the most delicate of operations remotely, as normal actions by the surgeon are translated into the miniscule movements of microscopic surgical equipment manipulated through robotics.

Concerns that automated processes will eliminate the role of human workers are unfounded. The nature of work has repeatedly changed to reflect the capabilities of the technology of the time. The introduction of electric streetlights, for example, did eliminate the job of lighting gas-fueled streetlamps, but it also created the need for workers to produce the electric lights and to ensure that they were functioning properly. The same sort of reasoning applies to the automation of processes today. Some tradi-

tional jobs will disappear, but new types of jobs will be created in their place through automation.

—*Richard M. Renneboog*

Further Reading

"History of CNC Machining." *Bantam Tools*, 12 Apr. 2019, medium.com/cnc-life/history-of-cnc-machining-part-1-2 a4b290d994d. Accessed 28 Nov. 2021.

James, Hubert M. *Theory of Servomechanisms*. McGraw, 1947.

Krar, Steve, Arthur Gill, and Peter Smid. *Technology of Machine Tools*. 8th ed., McGraw-Hill, 2020.

Mehta, B. R., and Y. Jaganmohan Reddy. *Industrial Process Automation Systems: Design and Implementation*. Butterworth-Heinemann, 2014.

Seal, Anthony M. *Practical Process Control*. Butterworth, 1998.

Seames, Warren S. *Computer Numerical Control Concepts and Programming*. 4th ed., Delmar, 2002.

Smith, Carlos A. *Automated Continuous Process Control*. Wiley, 2002.

See also: Computer-aided engineering; Mechanical engineering; Robotics

B

BALLISTIC WEAPONS

Fields of Study: Physics; Engineering; Mechanics; Mathematics

ABSTRACT

A ballistic weapon is a projectile weapon. That is, all ballistic weapons involve hurling or throwing an object over a distance. The word ballistic comes from the Greek word βαλειν (ballein), meaning "to throw." The bow and arrow, the automatic pistol, the cannon, and the intercontinental ballistic missile (ICBM) are all examples of ballistic weapons.

KEY CONCEPTS

ballistic: refers to the parabola-like trajectory of an object traveling by momentum through a constant gravitational field; with no atmosphere, the trajectory is a true parabola, but the presence of an atmosphere results in drag and foreshortens the leading edge of the parabola as the object loses velocity

catapult: a device that uses tension against one end of a strained lever to impart momentum to its payload and send it into a ballistic trajectory when the tension is released

guided missile: a missile whose flight can be controlled during its operation

missile: technically, any object that is set in motion on a ballistic trajectory without power; generally, a powered object or weapon that enters a ballistic trajectory using its own power

sling: typically, a patch of leather that can accommodate a stone or other small object, attached to two cords; twirling the loaded sling and releasing one of the cords flings the stone at high velocity

trebuchet: a device that uses the mass of a suspended counterweight acting upon a lever from which a payload is suspended to impart momentum to its payload when the mass is dropped

EARLY BALLISTIC WEAPONS

The first ballistic weapon was created the first time a person picked up a rock and threw it. Many thousands of years elapsed, however, between that first thrown rock and the emergence of formal ballistic weapons systems or the recognition of the science principles that could explain and improve their performance. Prehistoric hunters and warriors used trial and error to invent projectile weapons that allowed them to kill game or their enemies from a distance. Innovations such as slings meant rocks could be hurled with far more force than a rock from someone's unassisted hand. Using a sling, a hunter could easily kill smaller game animals, such as rabbits and squirrels.

A sling could also be a potent defensive weapon and, in the hands of a skilled user, was potentially deadly in battle. The best-known example of a sling being used in combat may be the biblical story of David and Goliath, but slings are mentioned in Greek and Roman histories of warfare as well as being shown in paintings on pottery and building walls as part of the standard equipment carried by a warrior.

Two other notable advances in ballistic weapons occurred during prehistoric times, the bow and arrow and the atlatl, or spear thrower. Both devices allowed the user to throw a pointed stick farther and with greater force and accuracy than could be achieved by the unaided human arm. The bow and

Photo via iStock/3D_generator. [Used under license.]

arrow later served as a model for more complex ballistic weapons, such as the Roman *ballista*, while the simple sling evolved into catapults such as the trebuchet and mangonel.

Catapults fall into three general types, those that take advantage of flexure in the arm of the catapult; those that are powered by the release of tension in a cord or rope; and those that use the dropping of a counterweight to generate projectile velocity. An ordinary bow and arrow combines all three sources of power: The archer flexes the bow and creates tension on the bowstring, and the archer's hand and body serve as counterweights to the arrow. One type of Roman ballista resembled a giant crossbow. The device fired large wooden bolts as much as a foot in diameter.

Trebuchets are the catapults most commonly portrayed in popular films and television programs. These devices had a bucket or sling in which to place objects such as rocks or containers of boiling oil and Greek fire (an early form of napalm) that were then hurled at opposing forces in battle or during a siege. Both the trebuchet and the ballista used a combination of tension and lever action to achieve their effectiveness, although the engineers building the devices had little theoretical understanding of the principles of physics underlying a catapult's operation. Mainly, they just knew how to make them work. For the Greeks, Romans, and other armies in the ancient world, knowledge of ballistas accumulated through trial and error. The builders of each machine determined the machine's range and accuracy through test firing it and taking measurements. Although theoretical concepts such as drag (the resistance an object encounters while moving through air or water) may have been unknown to the builders of Roman ballistas, empirical testing demonstrated that smooth round objects traveled farther than irregularly shaped ammunition.

THE MIDDLE AGES

In Europe, the art of constructing ballistas and similar machines, including the one-man crossbow, disappeared for centuries following the decline of the Roman Empire. The devices were reinvented during the Middle Ages, but were not accompanied by any immediate scientific interest in ballistic theories. The Roman Catholic Church, in fact, attempted to ban the use of the crossbow on the grounds that it was an inhumane and ungodly weapon that desecrated the sanctity of the symbol of the cross of Jesus Christ. Following the invention of gunpowder and firearms in the twelfth century, however, scholars gradually involved themselves in formulating scientific principles for use in explaining and improving ballistic weapons. Armor makers and gunsmiths recognized that gunpowder weapons required an understanding of both interior and exterior ballistics. Interior ballistics are the forces existing behind a projectile such as a bullet before it leaves the barrel of a gun, for example, the gas pressure created by burning gunpowder. Exterior ballistics include the behavior of the projectile as it passes through air, water, or space to reach its target.

Renaissance scholars, including Leonardo da Vinci, worked on ballistics problems but held erroneous beliefs concerning factors such as the effects of gravity. Leonardo da Vinci studied the trajectory of cannonballs but his conclusions regarding the relationships between force and velocity were later proven wrong. Despite the theoretical errors made by Leonardo da Vinci, Galileo, Pierre-Simon Laplace, and other early modern scientists, the

knowledge base in ballistics steadily expanded. During the mid-eighteenth century an English engineer, Benjamin Robins, developed a method for determining drag. Drag slows a projectile and thus leads to a reduction in force when the ballistic weapon hits its target.

The transition from catapults to cannons did not lead immediately to a change in the shape of hurled projectiles. In fact, early cannons and bombards fired the same ammunition as the trebuchets they would replace: rocks. Stonecutters shaped large stones into balls to fit into the barrels of cannons. The barrels themselves often bore a stronger resemblance to a funnel than to modern artillery pieces. Armor makers did not recognize the role the barrel of a weapon plays in accurate aiming of a projectile. Centuries passed before ammunition for ballistic weapons—cannon shells and rifle cartridges— achieved their familiar modern "bullet" shape. Gunsmiths also discovered that scoring the inside of a musket barrel with a spiral pattern, or rifling it, helped bullets fly farther and more accurately, and strike with greater force. Rifling meant the bullet spun as it left the barrel and so was less subject to tumbling in flight. Also, the angular momentum of the spinning bullet or projectile functions to maintain a true line of flight for the projectile. Early smooth-bore short-barreled muskets were remarkably inaccurate, deadly only at extremely close range. Long barreled rifles, in contrast, could be lethal at a distance as the extra barrel length tended to stabilize the bullet's motion as it leaves the barrel.

THE MODERN ERA AND ROCKETRY

Although the Chinese used gunpowder to propel small rockets as early as the tenth century, rockets remained primarily a curiosity for hundreds of years. Gunpowder proved to be an erratic source of propulsion, and the rockets themselves were difficult to aim. Early rockets were similar to today's "bottle rockets" but on a larger scale. The British army established rocketry units during the Napoleonic Wars, but found rockets to be effective in basically two areas: for use in signaling and to serve as a distraction. A rocket exploding in a line of oncoming infantry or cavalry could cause some confusion but inflicted little damage. There was, however, a real danger that a rocket intended to strike an enemy line would instead explode on the ground or fall on friendly troops instead.

Gunpowder's limitations as a propellant also restricted the effective range for heavy artillery, mortars, and cannons. Early black powder was a mixture of nitrates (often derived from manure piles), charcoal, and sulfur. The proportions of these ingredients varied depending on the manufacturer, as did the quality.

By the early years of the twentieth century, gunpowder evolved well beyond its crude black-powder origins, but it was the discovery of other fuels that provided the explosive force necessary for successful rocketry and long-range artillery. The large guns on battleships, for example, use an ammonium nitrate and fuel oil mix to propel mortar rounds many kilometers. Artillery can now strike at targets well out of sight of the operator of the weapon.

Rocket fuels also changed from ordinary gunpowder to more effective propellants, including ammonium nitrate. In the 1920s and 1930s, scientists such as Robert Goddard in the United States and Wernher von Braun in Germany experimented with different fuels and rocket designs. Working at a research facility at Peenemünde, German scientists and engineers achieved the first successes with rockets as ballistic weapons. German rockets terrorized Britons during World War II. The first German rockets, the V-1s, had a limited range and often missed their intended targets. Many reportedly fell short of the British coast.

The V-1's successor, the V-2, showed improvements in both range and accuracy. Not surprisingly, when the war ended with Germany's defeat, the governments of both the United States and the Union of Soviet Socialist Republics (USSR) hurried to capture and recruit German rocket scientists to work on missile programs. By the 1950s, both countries had developed intercontinental ballistic missiles (ICBMs) capable of carrying nuclear warheads. Today a bewildering array of ballistic weapons exists, ranging from small-caliber handguns to multiple-warhead missiles, as well as bows, crossbows, and rocks.

—*Nancy Farm Männikkö*

Further Reading

Breeze, John, Jowan G. Penn-Barwell, Damian Keene, David O'Reilly, Jayasankar Jayanathan, and Peter F. Mahoney. *Ballistic Trauma: A Practical Guide*. 4th ed., Springer, 2017.

Caelucci, Donald E., and Sidney S. Jacobson. *Ballistics: Theory and Design of Guns and Ammunition*. 3rd ed., CRC Press, 2018.

Cleckner, Ryan M. *Long Range Shooting Handbook: The Complete Beginner's Guide to Precision Rifle Shooting*. CreateSpace Independent Publishing Platform, 2016.

Dungan, T. D. *V-2: A Combat History of the First Ballistic Missile*. Westholme, 2005.

Landrus, Matt. *Leonardo Da Vinci's Giant Crossbow*. Springer Science & Business Media, 2010.

Manucey, Albert. *Artillery Through the Ages*. E-artnow, 2018.

Massaro, P. *Big Book of Ballistics*. Krause Publications, 2017.

Payne-Gallway, Ralph. *The Book of the Crossbow: With an Additional Section on Catapults and Other Siege Engines*. Courier Corporation, 2012.

Roy, Kaushik. *A Global History of Warfare and Technology: From Slings to Robots*. Springer Nature, 2022.

Saidian, Siyavush. *Ballistics: The Science of Weapons at Work*. Greenhaven Publishing LLC, 2017.

See also: Acceleration; Aerodynamics; Angular momentum; Classical or applied mechanics; Coriolis effect; Dynamics (mechanics); Engineering; Fluid mechanics and aerodynamics; Kinetic energy; Motion; Newton's laws; Potential energy; Projectiles; Vectors; Velocity

BERNOULLI, DANIEL

Fields of Study: Physics; Mechanics; Mathematics

ABSTRACT

Daniel Bernoulli was born February 8, 1700, in Groningen, Netherlands, and died 17 March, 1782, in Basel, Switzerland. Bernoulli is best known for his work in the field of fluid dynamics, particularly the Bernoulli equation. His book Hydrodynamica gave the field its original name. Bernoulli also worked in the fields of physics and acoustics.

KEY CONCEPTS

compressibility: the ability of air and all other gases to be compressed into a smaller volume than they would normally occupy

hydrodynamics: the science of the movement of fluids

incompressible: a gas that either cannot or does not become compressed under given conditions such as air in front of the wings of an aircraft

inviscid: a fluid having no resistance to objects moving through it

EARLY LIFE

Daniel Bernoulli was born into a family of prominent Swiss mathematicians in Groningen, Netherlands, on February 8, 1700. His father, Johann Bernoulli, was a professor of mathematics at the University of Groningen, and his uncle Jakob Bernoulli was the chair of mathematics at the University of Basel, Switzerland. In 1705, when Bernoulli was five years old, his father took over his uncle's position and the family moved back to Switzerland.

At the age of thirteen, Bernoulli was sent to the University of Basel to study philosophy and logic. He also excelled in mathematics and studied calculus under his older brother Nicolaus, their father having made significant discoveries in that disci-

pline. At the age of sixteen, Bernoulli earned a master's degree from Basel. Despite his skill and interest in mathematics, however, his father forbade him to pursue a career in the field. Johann Bernoulli tried at first to force his son to become a merchant, but Bernoulli refused. Johann then told his son to study to become a doctor. Bernoulli obliged, traveling to Italy to study medicine. He finished his studies in 1721. Unable to secure a teaching position, he continued to study medicine as well as mathematics.

While studying mathematics in Italy, Bernoulli wrote a treatise on probability and fluid motion. Published in Venice in 1724, *Exercitationes quaedam mathematicae* (*Certain Mathematical Exercises*) brought Bernoulli immediate recognition. He was offered a position as a professor of mathematics at the Saint Petersburg Academy of Sciences in Russia, where his brother Nicolaus also accepted an offer to teach mathematics. Before moving to Saint Petersburg in 1725, Bernoulli won first prize from the French Académie Royale des Sciences (Royal Academy of Sciences, now the French Academy of Sciences) for his essay on the best shape of

hourglass to use on ships. It was the first of ten prizes he would win from the Academy.

LIFE'S WORK

Bernoulli created the basis for his advances in mathematics, probability, and physics while teaching mathematics in Saint Petersburg. In addition to establishing him academically, his *Exercitationes* contained the origins of his exploration into fluid dynamics and probability. In 1726, he outlined the parallelogram of forces; the next year, he began regularly corresponding and collaborating with his friend Leonhard Euler, one of his father's pupils.

While trying to learn more about the flow of blood with Euler, Bernoulli developed a way of measuring blood pressure. This involved sticking a tube in an artery and measuring the height at which the blood filled the tube. The method became so popular that it was used throughout Europe for approximately the next 170 years. Bernoulli's method was later borrowed to measure airspeed.

Although Bernoulli found success in Russia, he was not happy there, and he left after eight years. Upon his return to Switzerland in 1733, he took a position at the University of Basel teaching botany, despite his lack of fondness for the subject. He continued working in other fields as well, such as mechanics and mathematics; in 1737, for example, he delivered a lecture on calculating the work done by the heart.

The next year, Bernoulli published his seminal *Hydrodynamica* (*Hydrodynamics*, 1738), establishing the field of hydrodynamics. This far-reaching work contained his famous fluid flow equation, called the Bernoulli equation, from which the Bernoulli principle was derived. The principle relates flow, speed,

Portrait of Daniel Bernoulli, c. 1725. Photo courtesy of Bammesk, via Wikimedia Commons.

pressure, and potential energy. *Hydrodynamica* laid the foundation for all later work in hydrodynamics and aerodynamics, referred to collectively as fluid dynamics. Bernoulli devised a number of experiments to demonstrate his theories. He also examined gas pressure, positing that it was composed of fast and randomly moving particles. His analysis confirmed Robert Boyle's 1660 gas law, which states that pressure multiplied by volume remains constant when the temperature does not change. This perspective paved the way for later studies, such as heat transfer.

THE BERNOULLI EQUATION(S)

The Bernoulli equation is not, in fact, one equation, but rather several equations created for specific situations. These equations apply an underlying system called Bernoulli's principle, which states that an increase in the speed, or flow, of a fluid results in a decrease in pressure and potential energy, and vice versa. Bernoulli's principle relates to the conservation of energy principle. Because the energy along a streamline—a set of curves tangent to the velocity vector of the flow at every point, describing how a particle would move if dropped into the flow—is constant, a loss in one form of energy must result in a gain in the other, and the converse is also true. In addition to the law of conservation, Bernoulli's principle also relates to Newton's second law of motion; as a particle moves from high to low pressure, it will accelerate.

The division of Bernoulli's principle into separate equations is caused by the difference in the behavior of air between compressible and incompressible flow, which are two flow models caused by changes in the nature of a fluid flow at different speeds. In many fluids and gases, the mass density can be assumed to be constant at low velocities, regardless of pressure changes; these are incompressible substances. Bernoulli worked only with incompressible gases and fluids, and his original equation works only for these. Flow is also assumed to be inviscid, meaning that there is no resistance to deformation. A low-viscosity fluid like water flows easily, while a high-viscosity one such as honey flows very slowly. The equation itself works by taking account of all forms of energy as pressures and ensuring that they are constant. Since the total is separated into components and must remain constant, the effects of pressure show as the variables are changed.

The compressibility of air becomes noticeable around Mach 0.3. Mach numbers are speed ratios in which the object's speed is divided by the speed of sound. There are several compressible models, each designed to handle a different set of conditions, such as high-speed subsonic flight or high-altitude hypersonic flight. In any formulation, the equations follow the logic of Bernoulli's original equation and, as such, are adaptations of his logic to new circumstances.

Bernoulli's equation has become fundamental to many fields that work with fluid flows, including marine architecture, hydraulic engineering, and aerodynamics. For example, by using Bernoulli's equation to find the pressure on the surface of an object, one can calculate the lift on an airplane's wing. Formulas based on Bernoulli's equation also allow for the calculation of airspeed in a device called a pitot tube, a fluid dynamic sensor that has been used on airplanes since their inception.

NEXT UP

Bernoulli also published a paper in 1738 that detailed the best shape for a ship's anchor. The paper won a prize from the Royal Academy. That same year, he published "Specimen theoriae novae de mensura sortis" ("Exposition of a New Theory on the Measurement of Risk"), in which he investigated the Saint Petersburg paradox as a base for risk analysis and utility investigation. The Saint Petersburg paradox is a probability theory based on the Saint Petersburg gambling game, in which a player flips a coin until the head side appears. The winnings are two guilders (or two dollars) if the head appears on the first toss, four if on the second, eight if on the third, and so on ad infinitum. The probability of winning decreases by half for each flip of the coin: a 50 percent chance the first time, 25 percent the second time, and so on. The paradox is how much a player would be willing to pay to play the game. Bernoulli proposed that the solution was not to calculate the expected winnings but instead to calculate by a utility function, determining how useful the winnings would be in comparison to the player's wealth.

In 1743, Bernoulli became a professor of physiology at the University of Basel. He used this opportunity to research subjects such as muscular contraction and the optic nerve. Seven years later, in 1750, he obtained the chair of experimental and speculative philosophy, now called theoretical physics. He was a very popular lecturer and continued to apply mathematics to physical phenomena.

Bernoulli was also elected a fellow of the Royal Society of London in 1750. Around this time, Euler and Bernoulli collaborated on the study of beam bending—that is, the sagging of a structure due to stress—and created a system later known as the Euler-Bernoulli beam equation. Their equation became the mathematical base for structural engineering projects such as the Eiffel Tower. Bernoulli also analyzed kinetic energy, which at the time was called *vis viva*, or living force. He posited that *vis viva* was conserved across the entire universe, anticipating the law of energy conservation, though he lacked the tools to prove it empirically.

As part of a scholarly dispute with Euler, Bernoulli investigated sound. He found that physical objects tend to vibrate at certain proper or natural frequencies. He named the lowest frequency the fundamental frequency and called the higher frequencies overtones. He also discovered that increases in frequency cause an increase in the number of nodes, or points, with no vibration. Bernoulli then built a mathematical framework around his findings, which were confirmed by Jean-Baptiste-Joseph Fourier's work on harmonics in the early 1800s.

Much of Bernoulli's later work involved the application of probability to disparate fields, including birth rate and inoculation. In one study in 1766, he used smallpox morbidity and mortality rates to illustrate the effectiveness of inoculation. In 1776, Bernoulli retired from teaching. He died in Basel, Switzerland, on March 17, 1782.

IMPACT

Bernoulli's contributions to mathematics influenced numerous later developments, leading to improvements ranging from better sound quality in MP3s to stealthier submarines. He is considered the father of fluid dynamics, and his work on fluid flows is an integral part of the science used in the design of travel vessels, including airplanes, cars, and ships. Bernoulli's fluid flow equation led to advances resulting in the modern practice of building ships based on model design, a process pioneered by naval architects such as William H. Froude (1810-79) and David Taylor (1864-1940), who then used fluid dynamics to predict the behavior of the full-size ship. Before these architects developed the idea of building ships in miniature first, the ships had to be built full scale before they could be tested.

Applied to aeronautics, Bernoulli's principle of fluid dynamics is essential in the development and functioning of airfoils. An airfoil is the part of a travel vessel, particularly an airplane's wing or propeller, that is designed to give the vessel speed in relation to the surrounding air pressure. The faster an airplane travels, the more lift it can achieve. Because Bernoulli's approach worked, his equations were expanded upon, and they became the basis for a set of equations governing pressure. Initially used for low speeds, Bernoulli's equations were extended to all velocity ranges, including modern hypersonic flight.

In addition to airplanes and submarines, Bernoulli's equations became important to the automobile industry, enabling the production of faster and more fuel-efficient cars. Additionally, his application of probability to physics provided better definitions to temperature and other such fundamental ideas, allowing for more accurate descriptions and further work in the various fields of physics. For example, the field of thermodynamics, which studies the flow of heat as a group of excited particles, uses Bernoulli's conjectures.

—Gina Hagler

Further Reading

Baigrie, Brian S. *The Renaissance and the Scientific Revolution: Biographical Portraits*. Scribner's, 2001.

Bernoulli, Daniel, and Johann Bernoulli. *Hydrodynamics and Hydraulics*. Translated by Thomas Carmody and Helmut Kobus. Dover, 2005.

Chakrabarti, Subrata K. *The Theory and Practice of Hydrodynamics and Vibration*. World Scientific, 2002.

Šejnin, Oskar B. *Portraits: Leonhard Euler, Daniel Bernoulli, Johann-Heinrich Lambert*. NG-Verl, 2009.

Vennard, John K. *Elementary Fluid Mechanics*. Read Books Ltd., 2011.

See also: Aerodynamics; Aeronautical engineering; Ailerons, flaps, and airplane wings; Airfoils; Airplane propellers; Bernoulli's principle; Calculus; Fluid dynamics; Fluid mechanics and aerodynamics; Helicopters; Hydraulics; Hydrodynamics; Plane rudders

BERNOULLI'S PRINCIPLE

Fields of Study: Physics; Engineering; Mechanics; Mathematics

ABSTRACT

Bernoulli's principle is a law of physical science that explains the relationship between a fluid's pressure and velocity. When the velocity of a fluid increases, its pressure decreases. Conversely, when the velocity of a fluid de-

creases, its pressure increases. The Bernoulli principle is an underlying concept in the science of flight.

KEY CONCEPTS

force: generally, the effect of pressure per unit area such as pounds per square inch

hydrodynamics: the physics of water in motion; fluid dynamics is the physics of fluids in motion

lift: the force produced by the motion of an airfoil, which gives an aircraft the ability to leave the ground and holds it up during flight

pressure: the force exerted by a mass against another mass

BACKGROUND

The Bernoulli principle was the work of Daniel Bernoulli, one of a family of Swiss scientists. Born in 1700, Bernoulli was the son of Johann Bernoulli, an accomplished mathematician. From an early stage, Bernoulli's relationship with his father was strained. The elder Bernoulli wanted his son to follow a profitable career path, but the younger was determined to pursue science. Eventually the younger Bernoulli got his way and quickly developed into an astute researcher.

In 1734, Bernoulli finished writing *Hydrodynamica*, his most famous work. Although it was not published until 1738, *Hydrodynamica* was a landmark accomplishment that led to the development of hydrodynamics, a new branch of physical science focused on the study of the motion of fluids. Unfortunately, the completion of *Hydrodynamica* also led to a further rift between Bernoulli and his father. Likely jealous of his son's success, the elder Bernoulli wrote a remarkably similar book called *Hydraulica* and allegedly predated it so that it appeared to have been written before *Hydrodynamica*. Regardless, *Hydrodynamica* eventually gained recognition as the leading early publication on hydrodynamics, most likely because the younger Bernoulli introduced a key principle within his historic work.

Bernoulli's principle is a law of physical science that explains the relationship between a fluid's pressure and velocity. The word "fluid" may refer to either a liquid or a gas. When the velocity of a fluid increases, its pressure decreases. Conversely, when the velocity of a fluid decreases, its pressure increases. Developed by Swiss scientist Daniel Bernoulli in the 1730s, this principle is readily observable in many real-world scenarios and has many practical applications. Most notably, the Bernoulli principle is an underlying concept in the science of flight. Moreover, the discovery of Bernoulli's principle was essential to the emergence of hydrodynamics, or the science of the motion of fluids, as a unique field of study.

THE PRINCIPLE

In *Hydrodynamica*, Bernoulli provided a comprehensive study of the pressure, velocity, and equilibrium of fluids. Chief among the breakthroughs his work yielded was the discovery of the relationship between the pressure and velocity of a fluid. While observing what happened when various fluids flowed through a tube, Bernoulli noticed that the fluids always sped up when they flowed through narrower portions of the tube. Intrigued, Bernoulli investigated the occurrence more thoroughly and realized that the velocity of the fluid was related to its pressure. Specifically, he found that as the pressure of a fluid increases, its velocity decreases. This phenomenon, which came to be known as Bernoulli's principle, results when a fluid's energy shifts from potential energy to kinetic energy as the velocity of its flow increases.

Bernoulli's principle is observable in many situations, most notably as it applies to the concept of flight. Indeed, Bernoulli's principle is a key aspect of air travel. Airplane wings are shaped so that, when the airplane is in motion, air moves more quickly across the top of the wing, which decreases pressure above the wing. In contrast, air moves more slowly across the bottom of the wing, which causes pressure

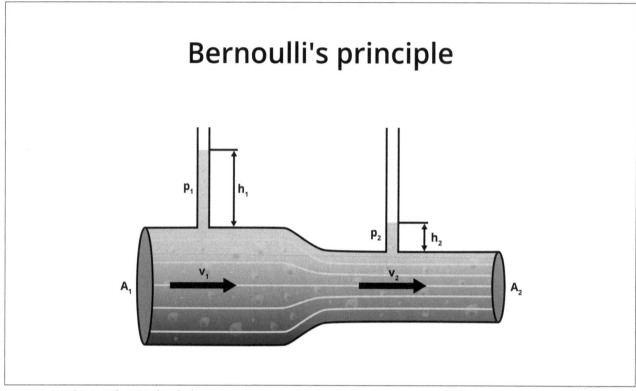

Image via iStock/petrroudny. [Used under license.]

below the wing to increase. Because the pressure below the wings is greater than the pressure above the wings, the upward force on the plane is stronger. This force, known as lift, helps the airplane rise off the ground and remain aloft when moving at speed. While this is the most well-known example of Bernoulli's principle at work, it is far from the only one.

Bernoulli's principle is observable on a smaller scale in backyards everywhere. When using a garden hose, one can increase the velocity of the water flowing through the hose simply by closing off part of the flow cross section where the water exits the hose. Restricting the flow forces the water to travel through a smaller area in the same amount of time that it would have taken the water to pass through an unrestricted portion of the hose. Therefore, as a result of the increase in the water's velocity, the pressure at the edges of the flow decreases.

Another demonstration of Bernoulli's principle in the real world is the potentially dangerous situation that can result if two ships sail side by side. The gap between the ships narrows in the middle because of the unique shape of the ships' hulls. When water passes through the narrowest portion of the gap, its velocity naturally increases. In turn, the water pressure between the ships decreases while the water pressure on the outside of each ship remains strong. As a result of the difference in water pressure, the ships are pushed toward each other. If navigators fail to account for the pressure difference, a serious collision could result.

IMPACT

Bernoulli's work in the field of fluid dynamics and his discovery of the principle that bears his name have had an undeniablye lasting influence. His efforts led to the creation of a whole new branch of science that has vastly improved understanding of the physical world. Moreover, application of the Bernoulli principle has led to technological advancements, including unlocking the secrets of flight.

—*Jack Lasky*

Further Reading

"Bernoulli, Daniel (1700-1782)." *Encyclopedia of Weather and Climate*, edited by Michael Allaby, Rev. ed., Vol. 1, Facts on File, 2002, pp. 66-68.

"Bernoulli's Principle." *Flight and Motion: The History and Science of Flying*. Vol. 2. Sharpe Reference, 2009, pp. 142-43.

Ling, Samuel J., Jeff Sanny, and William Moebs. *University Physics Volume 1*. Samurai Media Limited, 2017.

Masterson, Robert E. *Nuclear Reactor Thermal Hydraulics: An Introduction to Nuclear Heat Transfer and Fluid Flow*. CRC Press, 2019.

Pickover, Clifford. "Daniel Bernoulli." *Archimedes to Hawking: Laws of Science and the Great Minds Behind Them*, Oxford UP, 2008, pp. 124-34.

"Teaching from Space: The Bernoulli Principle." *PBS LearningMedia*. PBS & WGBH Educational Foundation, 2014, www.pbslearningmedia.org/resource/npe11.sci.phys.maf.bernoulli/teaching-from-space-the-bernoulli-principle/. Accessed 2 Dec. 2014.

See also: Aerodynamics; Aeronautical engineering; Aerospace design; Ailerons, flaps, and airplane wings; Airfoils; Airplane propellers; Bernoulli, Daniel; Clausius formulates the second law of thermodynamics; Fluid dynamics; Fluid mechanics and aerodynamics; Heat transfer; Hydraulics; Hydrodynamics; Plane rudders; Thermodynamics

BILLIARDS

Fields of Study: Physics; Mechanics; Mathematics

ABSTRACT

Playing billiards depends on an understanding of spin, momentum, and angles. Billiards is a cue sport game that involves the use of a rectangular table, billiard balls, and a stick called a "cue." Mathematics and physics are two important components of playing the game well.

KEY CONCEPTS

angle of incidence: the angle at which a billiard ball approaches and strikes a siderail of the billiard table, analogous to the approach of light rays to a reflective surface

angle of reflection: the angle at which a billiard ball rebounds from a siderail of a billiard table after striking it, analogous to the direction of light rays after striking a reflective surface

cue ball: a white billiard ball that is directed to strike other billiard balls using the principles of geometry, velocity, and momentum such that a struck ball goes into a pocket of the billiard table

cue stick: a precisely engineered straight, tapered, and polished cylindrical stick fitted with a felt pad at the tip, used to propel the cue ball

rebound: the action of a billiard ball striking a cushioned siderail of the billiard table and bouncing from it in a different direction

Billiards is a cue sport game that involves the use of a rectangular table, billiard balls, and a stick called a "cue." Mathematics and physics are two important components of playing the game well. Playing billiards depends on an understanding of spin, momentum, and angles. There are many different games within the cue sports that Americans typically call "billiards" or "pool." Billiard tables with pockets comprise games that are termed as "pool" or pocket billiards. The rectangular table has two long sides (twice the short side) and two short sides with six pockets—one at each corner, and one midway along the longer two sides of the table. The object of the game is to knock the billiard balls into the pockets using a cue ball (the lone white ball in the set). Gaspard Coriolis, known today for the Coriolis effect, wrote a work on the mathematics and physics of billiards in 1835. He stated that the curved path followed by the cue ball after striking another ball is always parabolic because of top or bottom spin. Further, the maximum side spin on a cue ball is achieved by striking it half a radius off-center with the tip of the cue.

The game of billiards is also a source for interesting mathematical problems, which are connected to dynamical systems, ergodic theory, geometry, physics, and optics. In mathematical billiards, the angle of incidence is the same as the angle of reflection for a point mass on a frictionless domain with a boundary. The dynamics depend on the starting position, angle, and geometry of the boundary and the table. Mathematicians investigate the motion and the path of the ball on a variety of differently shaped flat and curved tables, like triangular or elliptical boundaries or hyperbolic tables. In 1890, mathematician Charles Dodgson, better known as *Alice in Wonderland* author Lewis Carroll, published rules for circular billiards and may have also had a table built. In 2007, mathematician Alex Eskin won the Research Prize from the Clay Mathematics Institute for his work on rational billiards and geometric group theory.

EIGHT BALL

Eight ball is the pool game most commonly played in the United States, and it involves 16 billiard balls. To begin the game of Eight Ball, the numbered balls are placed in a triangular rack that sets the 8-ball in the middle position of the third row of balls with a single lead ball opposite the cue ball. The cue ball is placed on the midpoint of the line parallel to the short side at one-quarter of the long side known as the head spot. The point of the triangular-shaped

Photo via iStock/Nomadsoul1. [Used under license.]

racked set of billiard balls is placed on the opposite short end at one-quarter of the length of the long side from the other short side and is known as the foot spot. After one player "breaks" by hitting the cue ball from the head spot into the racked set of balls, the player then hits a set of balls into the pockets. A shot that does not cause a ball of his or her set to go into the pocket results in the next shot going to the other player.

BILLIARDS GEOMETRY AND PHYSICS

Shooting the balls into the pockets requires an understanding of angles and momentum, as well as placement of the cue so that the correct spin is achieved to place the cue ball where it can achieve the target ball going into a pocket. Coriolis investigated 90-degree and 30-degree rules of various shots and measured the largest deflection angle the cue ball can experience. Both skill and geometric understanding contribute to successful shots. Some shots require straight shooting; some shots need to be "banked" in by using the table sides. Players can use transformational geometry to approximate where on the table to hit the ball for it to return to a pocket. By measuring the angle from the ball to the side being used to bank off and reflecting the same angle with the cue stick, one can see the most viable spot to aim for so that the path of the caromed ball ends in a pocket. Using the diamonds found on the sides of most tables is one way of measuring these angles, and some systems for pool and billiards play use the diamonds. Using the diamond system for a different billiard game, Three Cushion Billiards is demonstrated on the 1959 Donald Duck Disney cartoon *Donald in Mathmagic Land*. The demonstration shows that it is possible to use subtraction to know where to aim the ball in relation to a diamond to make sure that all three balls are hit.

—*Linda Hutchison*

Further Reading

Alciatore, David G. *The Illustrated Principles of Pool and Billiards*. Dr. Dave Billiards Resources, 2004.

Koehler, Jack H. *The Science of Pocket Billiards*. 2nd ed., Sportology Publications, 2016.

Rozikov, Utkir A. *An Introduction to Mathematical Billiards*. World Scientific, 2018.

Tabachnikov, Serge. *Geometry and Billiards*. American Mathematical Society, 2005.

See also: Angular forces; Angular momentum; Atoms; Circular motion; Dynamics; Fluid dynamics; Force (physics); Friction; Heat transfer; Kinetic energy; Linear motion; Momentum (physics); Motion; Newton's laws; Rigid-body dynamics; Vectors; Velocity

BIOMECHANICS

Fields of Study: Physics; Aeronautical engineering; Mechanical engineering; Biomechanics; Physiology; Mathematics

ABSTRACT

Biomechanics is the study of the application of mechanical forces to a living organism. It investigates the effects of the relationship between the body and forces applied either from outside or within. Biomechanics integrates the study of anatomy and physiology with physics, mathematics, and engineering principles.

KEY CONCEPTS

digitized systems: systems that rely on digital or computer control and analysis

forensics: generally thought of as a study that occurs after a crime or a death, forensics simply has the sense of "examination after the fact" and applies to all fields and situations

kinesiology: the study of how human and animal bodies move

SUMMARY

Biomechanics is the study of the application of mechanical forces to a living organism. It investigates the effects of the relationship between the body and forces applied either from outside or within. In humans, biomechanists study the movements made by the body, how they are performed, and whether the forces produced by the muscles are optimal for the intended result or purpose. Biomechanics integrates the study of anatomy and physiology with physics, mathematics, and engineering principles. It may be considered a subdiscipline of kinesiology as well as a scientific branch of sports medicine.

DEFINITION AND BASIC PRINCIPLES

Biomechanics is a science that closely examines the forces acting on a living system, particularly the self-mobile systems of animals and people, and the effects that are produced by these forces. External forces can be quantified using sophisticated measuring tools and devices. Internal forces can be measured using implanted devices or from model calculations. Forces on a body can result in movement or biological changes to the anatomical tissue. Biomechanical research quantifies the movement of different body parts and the factors that may influence the movement, such as equipment, body alignment, or weight distribution. Research also studies the biological effects of the forces that may affect growth and development or lead to injury.

Two distinct branches of mechanics are statics and dynamics. Statics studies systems that are in a constant state of motion or constant state of rest, and dynamics studies systems that are in motion, subject to acceleration or deceleration. A moving body may be described using kinematics or kinetics. Kinematics studies and describes the motion of a body with respect to a specific pattern and speed, which translate into coordination of a display. Kinetics studies the forces associated with a motion, those causing it and resulting from it. Biomechanics combines kinet-

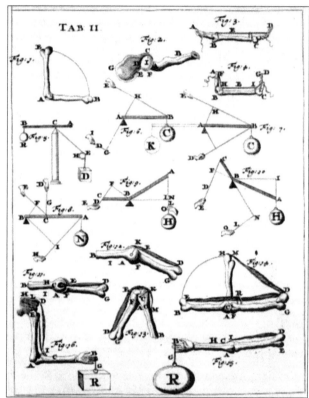

Page of one of the first works of biomechanics (De Motu Animalium of Giovanni Alfonso Borelli) in the 17th century. Image via Wikimedia Commons. [Public domain.]

ics and kinematics as they apply to the theory of mechanics and physiology to study the structure and function of living organisms.

BACKGROUND AND HISTORY

Biomechanics has a long history even though the actual term and field of study concerned with mechanical analysis of living organisms was not internationally accepted and recognized until the early 1970s. Definitions provided by early biomechanics specialists James G. Hay in 1971 and Herbert Hatze in 1974 are still accepted. Hatze stated, "Biomechanics is the science which studies structures and functions of biological systems using the knowledge and methods of mechanics."

Highlights throughout history have provided insight into the development of this scientific discipline. The ancient Greek philosopher Aristotle was the first to introduce the term "mechanics," writing about the movement of living beings around 322 BCE. He developed a theory of running techniques and suggested that people could run faster by swinging their arms. In the 1500s, Leonardo da Vinci proposed that the human body is subject to the law of mechanics, and he contributed significantly to the development of anatomy as a modern science. Italian scientist Giovanni Alfonso Borelli, a student of Galileo, is often considered the father of biomechanics. In the mid-1600s, he developed mathematical models to describe anatomy and human movement mechanically. In the late 1600s, English physician and mathematician Sir Isaac Newton formulated mechanical principles and Newtonian laws of motion (inertia, acceleration, and reaction) that became the foundation of biomechanics.

British physiologist A. V. Hill, the 1923 winner of the Nobel Prize in Physiology or Medicine, conducted research to formulate mechanical and structural theories for muscle action. In the 1930s, American anatomy professor Herbert Elftman was able to quantify the internal forces in muscles and joints and developed the force plate to quantify ground reaction. A significant breakthrough in the understanding of muscle action was made by British physiologist Andrew F. Huxley in 1953, when he described his filament theory to explain muscle shortening. Russian physiologist Nicolas Bernstein published a paper in 1967 describing theories for motor coordination and control following his work studying locomotion patterns of children and adults in the Soviet Union.

HOW IT WORKS

The study of human movement is multifaceted, and biomechanics applies mechanical principles to the study of the structure and function of living things. Biomechanics is considered a relatively new field of applied science, and the research being done is of considerable interest to many other disciplines, including zoology, orthopedics, dentistry, physical education, forensics, cardiology, and a host of other medical specialties. Biomechanical analysis for each particular application is very specific; however, the basic principles are the same.

Newton's laws of motion. The development of scientific models reduces all things to their basic level to provide an understanding of how things work. This also allows scientists to predict how things will behave in response to forces and stimuli and ultimately to influence this behavior. Newton's laws describe the conservation of energy and the state of equilibrium. Equilibrium results when the sum of forces is zero and no change occurs, and conservation of energy explains that energy cannot be created or destroyed, only converted from one form to another. Motion occurs in two ways, linear motion in a particular direction or rotational movement around an axis. Biomechanics explores and quantifies the movement and production of force used or required to produce a desired objective.

Seven Principles. Seven basic principles of biomechanics serve as the building blocks for analysis. These can be applied or modified to describe the reaction of forces to any living organism:

- The lower the center of mass, the larger the base of support; the closer the center of mass to the base of support and the greater the mass, the more stability increases;
- The production of maximum force requires the use of all possible joint movements that contribute to the task's objective;
- The production of maximum velocity requires the use of joints in order, from largest to smallest;
- The greater the applied impulse, the greater increase in velocity;
- Movement usually occurs in the direction opposite that of the applied force;

- Angular motion is produced by the application of force acting at some distance from an axis, that is, by torque;
- Angular momentum is constant when an athlete or object is free in the air.

Static and dynamic forces play key roles in the complex biochemical and biophysical processes that underlie cell function. The mechanical behavior of individual cells is of interest for many different biologic processes. Single-cell mechanics, including growth, cell division, active motion, and contractile mechanisms, can be quite dynamic and provide insight into mechanisms of stress and damage of structures. Cell mechanics can be involved in processes that lie at the root of many diseases and may provide opportunities as focal points for therapeutic interventions.

APPLICATIONS AND PRODUCTS

Biomechanics studies and quantifies the movement of all living things, from the cellular level to body systems and entire bodies, human and animal. There are many scientific and health disciplines, as well as industries that have applications developed from this knowledge. Research is ongoing in many areas to effectively develop treatment options for clinicians and better products and applications for industry.

Dentistry. Biomechanical principles are relevant in orthodontic and dental science to provide solutions to restore dental health, resolve jaw pain, and manage cosmetic and orthodontic issues. The design of dental implants must incorporate an analysis of load bearing and stress transfer while maintaining the integrity of surrounding tissue and comfortable function for the patient. This work has led to the development of new materials in dental practices such as reinforced composites rather than metal frameworks.

Forensics. The field of forensic biomechanical analysis has been used to determine mechanisms of injury after traumatic events such as explosions. This understanding of how parts of the body behave in these events can be used to develop mitigation strategies that will reduce injuries. Accident and injury reconstruction using biomechanics is an emerging field with industrial and legal applications.

Biomechanical modeling. Biomechanical modeling is a tremendous research field, and it has potential uses across many health care applications. Modeling has resulted in recommendations for prosthetic design and modifications of existing devices. Deformable breast models have demonstrated capabilities for breast cancer diagnosis and treatment. Tremendous growth is occurring in many medical fields that are exploring the biomechanical relationships between organs and supporting structures. These models can assist with planning surgical and treatment interventions and reconstruction and determining optimal loading and boundary constraints during clinical procedures. Increasingly, biomechanical modeling is used to deduce the appearance and movement of long extinct creatures such as dinosaurs and mammoths. This information informs various areas of art, especially the motion picture arts or cinema. Another aspect of biomechanical modeling is the transfer of that knowledge to entirely mechanical systems and robotics. Mechanisms of movement such as that of a centipede or a spider, for example, continue to be examined for the development of robots that must traverse rough or dangerous terrain. As well, assistive exoskeletons are designed to mimic the movement of the human body. Indeed, some robot designed enable the device to move with full articulation and dynamic balancing capabilities of a human, able to perform flips, rolls, and walk on unstable surfaces without falling. Other such robots have been designed to mimic the movement of dogs as they serve to carry various equipment.

Materials. Materials used for medical and surgical procedures in humans and animals are being evaluated and some are being changed as biomechanical science is demonstrating that different materials, procedures, and techniques may be better for reducing complications and improving long-term patient health. Evaluation of the physical relationship between the body and foreign implements can quantify the stresses and forces on the body, allowing for more accurate prediction of patient outcomes and determination of which treatments should be redesigned.

Predictability. Medical professionals are particularly interested in the predictive value that biomechanical profiling can provide for their patients. An example is the unpredictability of expansion and rupture of an abdominal aortic aneurysm. Major progress has been made in determining aortic wall stress using finite element analysis. Improvements in biomechanical computational methodology and advances in imaging and processing technology have provided increased predictive ability for this life-threatening event.

As the need for accurate and efficient evaluation grows, so does the research and development of effective biomechanical tools. Capturing real-time, real-world data, such as with gait analysis and range of motion features, provides immediate opportunities for applications. This real-time data can quantify an injury and over time provide information about the extent that the injury has improved. High-tech devices can translate real-world situations and two-dimensional images into a three-dimensional framework for analysis. Devices, imaging, and modeling tools and software are making tremendous strides and becoming the heart of a highly competitive industry aimed at simplifying the process of analysis and making it less invasive.

CAREERS IN BIOMECHANICS
Careers in biomechanics can be dynamic and take many paths. Graduates with accredited degrees may pursue careers in laboratories in universities or in private corporations researching and developing ways of improving and maximizing human performance. Beyond research, careers in biomechanics can involve working in a medical capacity in sport medicine and rehabilitation. Biomechanics experts may also seek careers in coaching, athlete development, and education.

Consulting and legal practices are increasingly seeking individuals with biomechanics expertise who are able to analyze injuries and reconstruct accidents involving vehicles, consumer products, and the environment. Biomechanical engineers commonly work in industry, developing new products and prototypes and evaluating their performance. Positions normally require a biomechanics degree in addition to mechanical engineering or biomedical engineering degrees.

Private corporations are employing individuals with biomechanical knowledge to perform employee fitness evaluations and to provide analyses of work environments and positions. Using these assessments, the biomechanics experts advise employers of any ergonomic changes or job modifications that will reduce the risk of workplace injury.

Individuals with a biomechanics background may choose to work in rehabilitation and prosthetic design. This is very challenging work, devising and modifying existing implements to maximize people's abilities and mobility. Most prosthetic devices are customized to meet the needs of the patient and to maximize the recipient's abilities. This is an ongoing process because over time the body and needs of a patient may change. This is particularly challenging in pediatrics, where adjustments become necessary as a child grows and develops.

SOCIAL CONTEXT AND FUTURE PROSPECTS
Biomechanics has gone from a narrow focus on athletic performance to become a broad-based science, driving multibillion dollar industries to satisfy the needs of consumers who have become more knowledgeable about the relationship between science,

health, and athletic performance. Funding for biomechanical research is increasingly available from national health promotion and injury prevention programs, governing bodies for sport, and business and industry. National athletic programs want to ensure that their athletes have the most advanced training methods, performance analysis methods, and equipment to maximize their athletes' performance at global competitions.

Much of the existing and developing technology is focused on increasingly automated and digitized systems to monitor and analyze movement and force. The physiological aspect of movement can be examined at a microscopic level, and instrumented athletic implements such as paddles or bicycle cranks allow real-time data to be collected during an event or performance. Force platforms are being reconfigured as starting blocks and diving platforms to measure reaction forces. These techniques for biomechanical performance analysis have led to revolutionary technique changes in many sports programs and rehabilitation methods.

Advances in biomechanical engineering have led to the development of innovations in equipment, playing surfaces, footwear, and clothing, allowing people to reduce injury and perform beyond previous expectations and records.

Computer modeling and virtual simulation training can provide athletes with realistic training opportunities, while their performance is analyzed and measured for improvement and injury prevention.

—*April D. Ingram*

Further Reading

"Bioengineers and Biomedical Engineers." *Occupational Outlook Handbook*, Bureau of Labor Statistics, US Department of Labor, 1 Feb. 2021, www.bls.gov/ooh/architecture-and-engineering/biomedical-engineers.htm. Accessed 31 Mar. 2021.

Bronzino, Joseph D., and Donald R. Peterson. *Biomechanics: Principles and Practices*. CRC Press, 2014. eBook Collection (EBSCOhost). 25 Feb. 2015.

Hamill, Joseph, and Kathleen Knutzen. *Biomechanical Basis of Human Movement*. 4th ed., Lippincott, 2015.

Hatze, H. "The Meaning of the Term 'Biomechanics.'" *Journal of Biomechanics*, vol. 7, no. 2, 1974, pp. 89-90.

Hay, James G. *The Biomechanics of Sports Techniques*. 4th ed., Prentice, 1993.

Kerr, Andrew. *Introductory Biomechanics*. Elsevier, 2010.

Peterson, Donald, and Joseph Bronzino. *Biomechanics: Principles and Applications*. CRC Press, 2008.

Watkins, James. *Introduction to Biomechanics of Sport and Exercise*. Elsevier, 2007.

See also: Angular forces; Biomedical engineering; Elasticity; Fluid dynamics; Force (physics); Kinematics; Load; Motion; Robotics; Work and energy

BIOMEDICAL ENGINEERING

Fields of Study: Physics; Mechanics; Mathematics

ABSTRACT

Biomedical engineering (BME) applies engineering design principles to the study of biology in order to improve health care. Products of BME include prosthetics, imaging equipment, regenerative medicine, medical implants, advances in drug production, and even telecommunications.

KEY CONCEPTS

bioinstrumentation: devices that are designed to interface directly with the human body, such as electronic glucose monitor systems for diabetics

biomechanics: the study of how (human) organisms function with regard to movement

gene manipulation: alteration of the genetic structure of an organism's DNA either by genetic engineering or by selective breeding methods

genetic engineering: commonly called gene modification, the direct manipulation of genetic material (specifically, deoxyribonucleic acid [DNA] and ribonucleic acid [RNA]) to impart or enhance gene-based characteristics

positron: identical to the electron, except that a positron bears a positive charge and the electron bears a negative charge

WHAT IS BIOMEDICAL ENGINEERING?

Biomedical engineering (BME) applies engineering design principles to the study of biology in order to improve health care. It developed from the overlap between engineering, biology, and medical research into its own branch of engineering. BME and related fields, such as biomedical research, remain distinct, as the case of the antibiotic penicillin shows. The accidental discovery that the Penicillium mold has antibacterial properties was a by-product of basic medical research, not BME. However, efforts to design and implement systems to mass-produce and distribute the drug were a textbook example of BME. Products of BME include prosthetics, imaging equipment, regenerative medicine, medical implants, advances in drug production, and even telecommunications.

Although many innovations in BME are high tech, not all are. Consider crutches, which assist people with mobility after a foot or leg injury. Modern crutches are designed to be strong, lightweight, and comfortable during extended use. They are informed by knowledge of human biology, especially biomechanics, to minimize strain on the patient's bones and muscles.

DEVELOPING THE TOOLS OF MEDICINE

Many BME projects involve instrumentation, the various devices used in medical care. Such devices include imaging tools such as magnetic resonance imaging (MRI) machines, positron emission tomography (PET) scanners, and X-ray machines. It also includes bioinstrumentation, devices specifically designed to connect to the human body. These either monitor health parameters or provide a therapeutic benefit. Implanted pacemakers, for example, use low-voltage electrical impulses to keep the heart

pumping in proper rhythm. Different bioMEMS can act as sensors, analyze blood or genes, or deliver drugs at a much smaller scale than traditional devices. Some bioMEMS are known as "labs-on-a-chip" because they incorporate the functions of a full-sized biology lab on a computer chip.

The development of smaller, highly portable, easy-to-use instrumentation is a keystone of telemedicine. With smartphone apps, bioMEMS, and cell-phone networks, it is increasingly possible to diagnose and treat patients far from hospitals and clinics. Telemedicine is especially helpful developing countries that lack a strong infrastructure.

ENGINEERING BIOLOGY

Another major area of BME involves the engineering of life itself. This includes regenerative medicine, in which organs and tissues are grown in a lab, often from a combination of synthetic and organic biomaterials, to replace damaged or diseased ones. It also includes genetic engineering, in which an or-

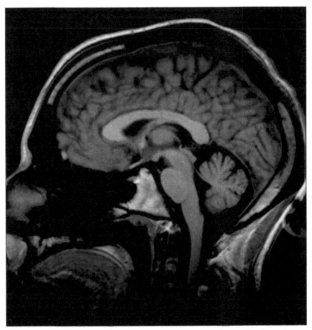

An MRI scan of a human head, an example of a biomedical engineering application of electrical engineering to diagnostic imaging. Photo by Chris Chan, via Wikimedia Commons.

ganism or cell's genes are manipulated toward a desired end. Genetic engineering of bacteria can produce useful drugs. Mice and other animals have been engineered to manifest traits such as cancer susceptibility to make them better study subjects. Genetic engineering could one day correct genetic conditions such as Huntington's disease in humans. Traditional breeding for desired traits among study organisms is also used in BME, though it is a slower, less powerful technique.

COMPUTERS IN BIOMEDICAL ENGINEERING

Computer use is widespread in BME design and device creation. Consider the design of a custom prosthetic. Computers scan the amputation site to ensure a secure fit, model the limb and a prosthetic to the correct proportions, and even print components of the prosthesis using a three-dimensional (3D) printer. Computer science techniques are also used to process the growing amount of patient data, searching out patterns of disease incidence.

Instrumentation is often built around computers. Medical imaging devices depend on embedded microcomputers and specialized software to process patient data and display it in a way that is useful to doctors. Smaller devices such as digital thermometers depend on microprocessors. An electrocardiograph (EKG) monitors a patient's heart rate and alerts the medical team if the patient goes into cardiac arrest. This is made possible through BME that combines biological knowledge (normal human heart rates) with sensors (electrodes that transmit electrical impulses from a patient's skin to a display) and computer science (processing the information, programming the device response). Advances in computer technology are driving advances in BME instrumentation. For instance, short-range wireless signals enable double amputees to walk by activating motorized joints and allowing the prostheses to communicate with one another.

—*Kenrick Vezina*

Further Reading

Badilescu, Simona, and Muthukumaran Packirisamy. *BioMEMS: Science and Engineering Perspectives*. CRC, 2011.

"Biomedical Engineers." *Occupational Outlook Handbook, 2016-2017 Edition*. Bureau of Labor Statistics, US Department of Labor, 17 Dec. 2015. Accessed 23 Jan. 2016.

Bronzino, Joseph D., and Donald R. Peterson. *Biomedical Engineering Fundamentals*. 4th ed., CRC Press, 2014.

Enderle, John Denis, and Joseph D. Brozino. *Introduction to Biomedical Engineering*. 3rd ed., Elsevier, 2012.

"Examples and Explanations of BME." *Biomedical Engineering Society*. Biomedical Engineering Society, 2012—14. Accessed 23 Jan. 2016.

Gzik, Marek, Zbigniew Paszenda, Ewa Pietka, Ewaryst Tacacz, and Krzysztof Milewski, editors. *Innovations in Biomedical Engineering*. Springer Nature, 2020.

"Milestones of Innovation." *American Institute for Medical and Biological Engineering*, 2016. Accessed 25 Jan. 2016.

Pavel, M., et al. "The Role of Technology and Engineering Models in Transforming Healthcare." *IEEE Reviews in Biomedical Engineering*. IEEE, 2013. Accessed 25 Jan. 2016.

Saltzman, W. Mark. *Biomedical Engineering: Bridging Medicine and Technology*. Cambridge UP, 2015.

———. "Lecture 1: What Is Biomedical Engineering?" *BENG 100: Frontiers of Biomedical Engineering*. Yale University, Spring 2008. Accessed 23 Jan. 2016.

See also: Biomechanics; Computer-aided engineering; Mechanical engineering; Mechatronics

C

CALCULATING SYSTEM EFFICIENCY

Fields of Study: Physics; Mechanics; Mathematics

ABSTRACT

Calculating system efficiency is a means of monitoring system functions and identifying aspects of a system that may be improved. The concept and methods are applicable in all fields, but especially in technology and engineering. Mechanical, electrical, and thermal efficiency are discussed.

KEY CONCEPTS

electrical efficiency: the ratio of the power applied to an electrical circuit to the power delivered by a particular device in the circuit

imperfect system: any system that functions with less than 100 percent efficiency

mechanical efficiency: the ratio of the power applied to a mechanical system relative to the power delivered by the system

system input: a force, such as voltage or torque, applied to a system

system output: the work that the system performs

thermal efficiency: the ratio of the work performed by a system relative to the heat energy that is supplied to the system

work: in mechanical systems, the result of a force operating through a distance

SYSTEMS AND WORK

A system consists of components that work together to perform a desired function. A system input is a force that causes the system to function and perform work. Work performed by the system is the system output. In a mechanical system, components might include pulleys, gears, drive belt, and other physical devices. These devices function together to perform work such as pumping water, lifting heavy weights, or propelling a vehicle. The system input for a mechanical system is also physical in nature. It can be the force supplied by muscles, the torque supplied by an attached engine, or the thrust produced by a jet engine, for example. The mechanical efficiency of such a system is affected by factors such as friction and slippage. Friction is the resistance of one component's motion relative to another. It always consumes some of the power within a system. Slippage occurs when not all of the power that could be delivered is actually delivered between components. An imperfect system is one in which the system input's power is not delivered with 100 percent efficiency to the system output. Since these factors are present in every mechanical system, no mechanical system can be 100 percent efficient. The mechanical efficiency of a system can be calculated by comparing the system output to the system input.

An electrical circuit is also a system designed to perform work. Electrical circuits function through the movement of electrical charge between two points. The factors that affect electrical efficiency are analogous to those that affect mechanical efficiency. The system input to an electrical system is the applied voltage, or electromotive force. This is also referred to as the electrical potential difference between two points in the circuit. This is typically delivered by a battery or a rectifier circuit for direct current (DC) applications. It is delivered by a generator for alternating current (AC) applications. The voltage for a small flashlight, for example, may be provided by three small dry-cell batteries. The batteries provide a constant electrical potential of 4.5 volts. In contrast, the voltage of a television set is typically provided by the alternating electrical potential of 110 volts of a standard North American wall socket. Electrical and electronic devices typically produce heat when they are in use. This can be thought of as the byproduct of the friction of electrons moving through the components of the circuitry. This is the resistance of the circuit and is the primary source of the heat generated by the circuit. A type of slippage exists in electrical systems. This slippage is the eddy currents and voltage losses that exist at junctions, such as solder joints, where different materials connect different components. As in mechanical systems, these factors combine to impair the overall efficiency of the system. The efficiency of any electrical system is typically very high and may be almost 100 percent for devices such as transformers, in which the system output is nearly equal to the system input.

Systems that rely on the transfer of heat from one part of the system to another are known as heat engines. Heat engines include steam engines and internal combustion engines. The efficiency with which such systems perform work relative to the heat that is transferred is the thermal efficiency of the system.

CALCULATING EFFICIENCY

System efficiency is calculated by comparing the system output to the system input and expressing the result as a percentage. For electrical systems, load power is the system output. Total power is the system input. Electrical efficiency is calculated as:

Efficiency = (Load power × 100%) / Total power

This same equation can be applied to each individual component of an electrical system as well as to the overall system or any part of the system. In such cases, it defines the electrical efficiency of that specific component or structure.

The thermal efficiency of a heat engine depends on the conversion of heat energy to work output. Since all heat engines absorb some of the heat that is produced without converting it to a work output, the thermal efficiency of a heat engine is never 100 percent. In an internal combustion engine, for example, combustion of the fuel produces heat. This heat causes the combustion gases to expand and push against the pistons, converting chemical energy into physical work. Not all of the heat produced is applied in this way, however. The material from which the engine is made absorbs a portion of the heat, which is then carried away by a coolant. Some of the heat is carried out as hot gases are exhausted. Such heat losses can be compared to slippage in mechanical systems, in which some of the input power is not delivered to the output as work but simply lost as waste. The thermal efficiency of such a system is calculated as:

Efficiency = [(Total heat − Lost heat) × 100%] / Work output.

The efficiency of simple machines can be calculated by finding the ratio of the work output divided by the work input and is typically converted to a percentage. It can also be calculated by measuring the actual mechanical advantage (actual *MA*) divided by the ideal mechanical advantage (ideal *MA*). The ideal mechanical advantage (*MA*) for each type of simple machine is calculated differently. Note that both heat and work require the same units (joules).

The efficiency of a mechanical system is perhaps also the simplest to calculate. It is the ratio of the actual work output to the work input expressed as a percentage. It is calculated as:

Efficiency = (Work output × 100%) / Work input

The mechanical efficiency can also be calculated as the ratio of the actual mechanical advantage to the ideal mechanical advantage expressed as a percentage, or:

Efficiency = (Actual mechanical advantage × 100%) / Ideal mechanical advantage

The actual mechanical advantage of a machine is the ratio comparing the output force to the input force, considering all the limitations on the efficiency of real-world machines. In contrast, the ideal mechanical advantage is the ratio comparing the output force to the input force, ignoring those limitations.

REAL-WORLD EFFICIENCY

Mechanical and electrical systems are central to all aspects of modern human endeavor. In any enterprise or economy, the systems that function most efficiently are also the systems that provide the highest return on investment. Efficiency is related to all aspects of production and quality control in industry and, indeed, in all aspects of modern life. The goal of efficiency, in any application, is to achieve the desired system output with the least waste of system input, no matter whether it is preparing a field for planting, manufacturing the most advanced microprocessor chip, or even engineering the acoustic characteristics of a concert hall for the best enjoyment of an artistic performance.

Consider a certain pulley system being used to lift a weight of 150 kilograms (330 pounds) to a height of 3 meters (9.8 feet) requires the user to exert a constant pulling force of 40 kilograms (88 pounds) through a distance of 21 meters (68.6 feet). What is the mechanical efficiency of the pulley system?

Since the newton is defined as the force required to accelerate a mass of 1 kg at a rate of 1 m/s² (1 N = 1 kg·m/s²), and the units will cancel out when expressed as a percentage, it is acceptable to use kilo-

grams instead of newtons as the units of force in such calculations.

The mechanical efficiency of a system is the work input to bring about a corresponding work output, expressed as a percentage. Work is calculated as the product of force and distance:

Work input = (40 kg × 21 m) = 840 kg·m and work output = (150 kg × 3 m) = 450 kg·m

The mechanical efficiency of the pulley system is therefore (450 kg·m × 100%) / 840 kg·m = 53.57%.

—Richard M. Renneboog

Further Reading

Baggini, Angelo, and Andreas Sumper. *Electrical Energy Efficiency: Technologies and Applications*. John Wiley & Sons, 2012.

Ling, James S., Jeff Sanny, and William Moebs. *University Physics, Volume 1*. Samurai Media Limited, 2017.

Martinez, Daniel M., Ben W. Ebenhack, and Travis P. Wagner. *Energy Efficiency: Concepts and Calculations*. Elsevier, 2019.

Pfeiffer, Friedrich. *Mechanical System Dynamics*. Springer Science & Business Media, 2008.

Senft, James R. *Mechanical Efficiency of Heat Engines*. Cambridge UP, 2007.

See also: Automated processes and servomechanisms; Computer-aided engineering; Conservation of energy; Dynamics (mechanics); Engineering; Heat transfer; Kinematics; Mechatronics; Mechanical engineering; Robotics; Work and energy; Work-energy theorem

Calculus

Fields of Study: Physics; Aeronautical engineering; Mechanical engineering; Biomechanics; Physiology; Mathematics

ABSTRACT

Calculus is the mathematics of functions and change. It is the bridge between the elementary mathematics of algebra, geometry, and trigonometry, and advanced mathematics. Knowledge of calculus is essential in fields such as chemistry, engineering, medicine, and physics. Calculus is employed to solve a large variety of optimization problems.

KEY CONCEPTS

derivation: the method of determining the equation describing the slope of a line tangent to a curve or of a function that is tangent to a function of higher order

function: a mathematical expression describing an actual relationship between two or more entities represented by mathematical variables

integration: the method of determining the area bounded by a curve or other function based on dividing that area into infinitesimal "slices" of area and summing them together

limit: the ultimate value of a particular function

DEFINITION AND BASIC PRINCIPLES

Calculus was developed from the study of functions and their properties, and is based on to two essential ideas: rate of change and total change. These concepts are linked by their common use of calculus's most important tool, the concept of the limit. It is the use of this tool that distinguishes calculus from elementary branches of mathematics such as algebra (devised by Arab mathematicians), geometry (formalized in classical Greece), and trigonometry (used in ancient Egypt). In elementary mathematics, one studies problems such as "What is the slope of a line?" or "What is the area of a parallelogram?" or "What is the average speed of a trip that covers three hundred miles in five and a half hours?" Elementary mathematics provides methods or formulas that can be applied to find the answer to these and many other problems. However, if the line becomes a curve, how is the slope calculated? What if the parallelogram becomes a shape with an irregularly curved boundary? What if one needs to know the speed at an instant, and not as an average over a longer time period?

Calculus answers these harder questions by using the limit concept. The limit is found by making an approximation to the answer and then refining that approximation by improving it more and more. If there is a pattern leading to a single value in those improved approximations, the result of that pattern is called the limit. Note that the limit may not exist in some cases. The limit process is used throughout calculus to provide answers to questions that elementary mathematics cannot handle.

The derivative of a function is the limit of average slope values within an interval as the length of the interval approaches zero. The integral calculates the total change in a function based on its rate of change function.

BACKGROUND AND HISTORY

Calculus is usually considered to have been developed in the seventeenth century, but its roots were formed much earlier. It is unfortunate that Eurocentric history has overlooked or discounted the much earlier mathematical work of Egyptian, Greek, Arab, Indian, and Chinese scholars who used advanced mathematical principles in some cases thousands of years before any European scholar formalized the practice as a mathematical discipline in European literature. Accordingly, it is accepted that in the sixteenth century, Pierre de Fermat did work that was very closely related to calculus's differentiation (the taking of derivatives) and integration. In the seventeenth century, René Descartes founded analytic geometry, a key tool for developing calculus. However, it is Sir Isaac Newton and Gottfried Wilhelm Leibniz who are given shared credit as the (independent) creators of calculus. Newton's work came first but was not published until 1736, nine years after his death. Leibniz's work came second but was published first, in 1684. Some accused him of plagiarizing Newton's work, although Leibniz arrived at his results by using different, more formal methods than Newton employed.

Both men found common rules for differentiation, but Leibniz's notation for both the derivative and the integral are still in use. In the eighteenth century, the work of Jean le Rond d'Alembert and Leonhard Euler on functions and limits helped place the methods of Newton and Leibniz on a firm foundation. In the nineteenth century, Augustin-Louis Cauchy used a definition of the limit to express calculus concepts in a form still familiar more than two hundred years later. German mathematician Bernhard Riemann defined the integral as the limit of a sum, the same definition learned by calculus students in the twenty-first century. At this point, calculus as it is taught in the first two years of college reached its finished form.

HOW IT WORKS

Calculus is used to solve a wide variety of problems using a common approach. First, one recognizes that the problem at hand cannot be solved using elementary mathematics alone. This recognition is followed by an acknowledgment: there are some things known about this situation, even if they do not provide a complete basis for solution. Those known properties are then used to approximate a solution to the problem. This approximation may not be very good, so it is refined by taking a succession of better and better approximations. Finally, the limit is discovered, and if the limit exists, it provides the exact answer to the original problem.

One speaks of taking the limit of a function f(x) as x approaches a particular value, for example, x = a. This means that the function is examined on an interval around, but not including x = a. Values of f(x) are taken on that interval as the varying x values get closer and closer to the target value of x = a. There is no requirement that f(a) exists, and many times it does not. Instead the pattern of functional values is examined as x approaches a. If those values continue to approach a single target value, it is that value that is said to be equal to the limit of f(x) as x

Image via iStock/Tomacco. [Used under license.]

approaches a. Otherwise, the limit is said not to exist. This method is used in both differential calculus and integral calculus.

Differential calculus. Differentiation is a term used to mean the process of finding the derivative of a function f(x). This new function, denoted f'(x), is said to be "derived" from f(x). If it exists, f'(x) provides the instantaneous rate of change of f(x) at x. For curves (any line other than a straight line), the calculation of this rate of change is not possible with elementary mathematics. Algebra is used to calculate that rate between two points on the graph, then those two points are brought closer and closer together until the limit determines the final value.

Shortcut methods were discovered that could speed up this limit process for functions of certain types, including products, quotients, powers, and trigonometric functions. Many of these methods go back as far as Newton and Leibniz. Using these formulas allows one to avoid the tedious limit calculations. For example, the derivative function of sine x is proven to be cosine x. If the slope of sine x is needed at x = 4, the answer is known to be cosine 4, and much time is saved.

Integral calculus. A natural question arises: If f′(x) can be derived from f(x), can this process be reversed? In other words, suppose an f(x) is given. Can a parent function F(x) be determined whose derivative is equal to f(x)? If so, the F(x) is called an antiderivative of f(x); the process of finding F(x) is called integration. In general, finding antiderivatives is a harder task than finding derivatives. One difficulty is that constant functions all have derivatives equal to zero, which means that without further information, it is impossible to determine which constant is the correct one. A bigger problem is that there are functions, such as sine (x^2), whose derivatives are reasonably easy to calculate but for which no elementary function serves as an antiderivative.

The definite integral can be thought of as an attempt to determine the amount of area between the graph of f(x) and the x-axis, usually between a left and right endpoint. This cannot typically be answered using elementary mathematics because the shape of the graph can vary widely. Riemann proposed approximating the area with rectangles and then improving the approximation by having the width of the rectangles used in the approximation get smaller and smaller. The limit of the total area of all rectangles would equal the area being sought. It is this notion that gives integral calculus its name: By summing the areas of many rectangles, the many small areas are integrated into one whole area.

As with derivatives, these limit calculations can be quite tedious. Methods have been discovered and proven that allow the limit process to be bypassed. The crowning achievement of the development of calculus is its fundamental theorem: The derivative of a definite integral with respect to its upper limit is the integrand evaluated at the upper limit; the value of a definite integral is the difference between the values of an antiderivative evaluated at the limits. If

one is looking for the definite integral of a continuous f(x) between x = a and x = b, one need only find any antiderivative F(x) and calculate F(b) minus F(a).

APPLICATIONS AND PRODUCTS

Optimization. A prominent application of the field of differential calculus is in the area of optimization, either maximization or minimization. Examples of optimization problems include: What is the surface area of a can that minimizes cost while containing a specified volume? What is the closest that a passing asteroid will come to Earth? What is the optimal height at which paintings should be hung in an art gallery? (This corresponds to maximizing the viewing angle of the patrons.) How shall a business minimize its costs or maximize its profits?

All of these can be answered by means of the derivative of the function in question. Fermat proved that if f(x) has a maximum or minimum value within some interval, and if the derivative function exists on that interval, then the derivative value must be zero. This is because the graph must be hitting either the top of a peak or the bottom of a valley and has a slope of zero at its highest or lowest points. The search for optimal values then becomes the process of finding the correct function modeling the situation in question, finding its derivative, setting that derivative equal to zero, and solving. Those solutions are the only candidates for optimal values. However, they are only candidates because derivatives can sometimes equal zero even if no optimal value exists. What is certain is that if the derivative value is not zero, the value is not optimal.

The procedure discussed here can be applied in two dimensions (where there is one input variable) or three dimensions (where there are two input variables).

Surface area and volume. If a three-dimensional (3D) object can be expressed as a curve that has been rotated about an axis, then the surface area and volume of the object can be calculated using integrals. For example, both Newton and Johannes Kepler studied the problem of calculating the volume of a wine barrel. If a function can be found that represents the curvature of the outside of the barrel, that curve can be rotated about an axis and pi (π) times the function squared can be integrated over the length of the barrel to find its volume.

Hydrostatic pressure and force. The pressure exerted on, for example, the bottom of a swimming pool of uniform depth is easily calculated. The force on a dam due to hydrostatic pressure is not so easily computed because the force of the water pushing against it varies according to depth. Calculus discovers the answer by integrating a function found as a product of the pressure at any depth of the water and the area of the dam at that depth. Because the depth varies, this function involves a variable representing that depth.

Arc length. Algebra is able to determine the length of a line segment. If that path is curved, whether in two or three dimensions, calculus is applied to determine its length. This is typically done by expressing the path in parametric form and integrating the function representing the length of the vector that is tangent to the path. The length of a path winding through 3D space, for example, can be determined by first expressing the path in the parametric form x = f(t), y = g(t), and z = h(t), in which f, g, and h are continuous functions defined for some interval of values of t. Then the square root of the sum of the squares of the three derivatives is integrated to find the length.

Kepler's laws. In the early seventeenth century, Johannes Kepler formulated his three laws of planetary motion based on his analysis of the observations kept by Tycho Brahe. Later, calculus was used to prove that these laws are correct. Kepler's laws state that any planet's orbit around the Sun is elliptical, with the Sun at one focus of the ellipse; that the line joining the sun to the planet sweeps out equal areas in equal times; and that the square of the period of revolution is proportional to the cube of the length of the major axis of the orbit.

Probability. Accurate counting methods can be sufficient to determine many probabilities of a discrete random variable. This would be a variable whose values could be, for example, counting numbers such as 1, 2, 3, and so on, but not numbers in between, such as 2.4571. If the random variable is continuous, so that it can take on any real number within an interval, then its probability density function must be integrated over the relevant interval to determine the probability. This can occur in two or three dimensions.

One common example is determining the likelihood that a customer's wait time is longer than a specified target, such as ten minutes. If the manager knows the average wait time that a customer experiences at an establishment is, for example, six minutes, then this time can be used to determine a probability density function. This function is integrated to determine the probability that a person's wait time will be longer than ten minutes, less than three minutes, between five and thirteen minutes, or within any range of times that is desired.

SOCIAL CONTEXT AND FUTURE PROSPECTS

A person preparing for a career involving the use of calculus will most likely graduate from a university with a degree in mathematics, physics, actuarial science, statistics, or engineering. In most cases, engineers and actuaries are able to join the profession after earning their bachelor's degree. For actuaries, passing one or more of the exams given by the Society of Actuaries or the Casualty Actuarial Society is also expected, which requires a thorough understanding of calculus.

In statistics, a master's degree is typically preferred, and to work as a physicist or mathematician, a doctorate is the standard. In terms of calculus-related coursework, in addition to the calculus sequence, students will almost always take a course in differential equations and perhaps one or two in advanced calculus or mathematical analysis.

Calculus itself is not an industry, but it forms the foundation of other industries. In this role, it continues to power research and development in diverse fields, including those that depend on physics. Physics derives its results by way of calculus techniques. These results in turn enable developments in small- and large-scale areas. An example of a small-scale application is the ongoing development of semiconductor chips in the field of electronics. Large-scale applications are in the solar and space physics critical for ongoing efforts to explore the solar system and beyond. These are just two examples of calculus-based fields that will continue to have significant impact in the twenty-first century.

—*Michael J. Caulfield*

Further Reading

"A-Index." *Occupational Outlook Handbook*, US Bureau of Labor Statistics, US Department of Labor, 20 Oct. 2021, www.bls.gov/ooh/a-z-index.htm. Accessed 28 Feb. 2022.

Banner, Adrian. *The Calculus Lifesaver: All the Tools You Need to Excel at Calculus*. Princeton UP, 2007.

Bardi, Jason Socrates. *The Calculus Wars: Newton, Leibniz, and the Greatest Mathematical Clash of All Time*. Thunder's Mouth Press, 2006.

Bittinger, Marvin L., et al. *Calculus and Its Applications*. 11th ed., Pearson Education, 2016.

Dunham, William. *The Calculus Gallery: Masterpieces from Newton to Lebesgue*. Princeton UP, 2005.

Hughes-Hallett, Deborah, Otto Bretscher, Adrian Iovita, and David Sloane. *Calculus*. 8th ed. Wiley, 2021.

Simmons, George F. *Calculus Gems: Brief Lives and Memorable Mathematics*. 1992. Mathematical Association of America, 2007.

See also: Acceleration; Acoustics; Aerodynamics; Amplitude; Angular forces; Angular momentum; Ballistic weapons; Celestial mechanics; Chaotic systems; Circular motion; Classical or applied mechanics; Differential equations; Electromagnetism; Euler paths; Euler's laws of motion; Fluid dynamics; Force (physics); Harmonic oscillator; Lagrange, Joseph-Louis; Laplace, Pierre-Simon; Leibnitz, Wilhelm Gottfried; Newton, Isaac; Linear motion; Pascal, Blaise; Poisson, Siméon Denis; Projectiles; Quantum mechanics; Vectors; Velocity

CARNOT, SADI

Fields of Study: Physics; Mechanics; Mathematics

ABSTRACT

Sadi Carnot was a French mathematician who is also referred to as the Father of Thermodynamics. He studied the transfer of heat when researching how to make a steam engine most efficient.

KEY CONCEPTS

entropy: the thermodynamic principle that represents the distribution of energy in a system, with entropy increasing as the system becomes less organized

heat engine: an engine whose functioning and efficiency is a function of temperature differences

thermodynamics: the science of the movement of heat energy

BIOGRAPHY

Nicolas Leonard Sadi Carnot was born in the Palais du Petit-Luxembourg, Paris, on June 1, 1796, the eldest son of Lazare Nicolas Marguerite Carnot (1753-1823), the Organizer of the Victory of the French Revolutionary Wars. His father was a member of the Directory, and a surviving member of the Committee of Public Safety. His younger brother, Lazare Hippolyte Carnot (1801-88), would become an important politician and preserved some of Sadi's notes among his papers. Lazare Carnot resigned from politics in 1807 in order to attend to the education of his sons.

Sadi was taught at home by his father, who had written on scientific and engineering problems. He had also studied the efficiency of water machines. The idea of work derived from falling water was Sadi's model for work on a heat engine caused by falling heat.

Sadi attended the Lycée Charlemagne in Paris in order to prepare for the entrance examination to the École Polytechnique, which he entered in 1812. In 1813, Sadi sought permission from Napoleon to join with other young students in defending France. In March 1814, he fought at Vincennes in the Battle of Paris. In October 1814, he graduated as a military engineer. His studies at the École Polytechnique placed him in the company of some of France's best scientists, including Siméon-Denis Poisson, Joseph Gay-Lussac, and André-Marie Ampère. Posted to the École du Genie at Metz as a student second lieuten-

Sadi Carnot, portrait, 1813. Image via Wikimedia Commons. [Public domain.]

ant, he wrote several scientific papers that are no longer extant. During the Hundred Days War, Lazare Carnot served as Napoleon's minister of the interior, but was exiled in October 1815, following the Restoration. This ended the special attention Sadi's superiors had previously given to him.

When his studies ended in 1816, Sadi began serving in the Metz engineering regiment as a second lieutenant. For several years, he moved from garrison to garrison inspecting fortifications, drafting plans, and writing reports that were thereafter neglected in bureaucratic files. In 1819, he was assigned to the general staff in Paris. He immediately gained a permanent leave of absence, which allowed him time to engage in studying physics. Between 1818 and 1824, Carnot spent many hours studying the steam engine, an improved version of which had been invented by James Watt (1736-1819). Hailed as the technology of the future, it was a very inefficient machine that lost most of its heat energy. Carnot sought to improve its efficiency by seeking to understand the nature of heat.

SCIENTIFIC STUDIES

In 1824, Carnot published *Réflexions sur la puissance motrice du feu et sur les machines propres a developer cette puissance* (*Reflections on the Motive Power of Fire*). In the title word *feu* (fire), Carnot meant heat, and by *puissance motrice* (motive power) he meant work. The book was his only scientific work. Published by Bachelier, the most important French scientific publisher of the time, it was well received, formally presented to the *Academie des Sciences*, and favorably reviewed by P. S. Girard in the *Revue encyclopedique*.

Réflexions showed that the efficiency of a heat engine—that is, an engine that changes heat into mechanical energy in order to do work—was dependent upon the difference between its hottest and coolest temperature. Using the formula $(T_1 - T_2)/T_2$, Carnot expressed the efficiency between the hottest temperature, T_1, and coolest temperature, T_2. The equation is considered to be the first statement of the theory of heat movement. Consequently, Carnot is considered the father of the science of thermodynamics. The equation was universal because it applied to any heat engine and any temperature. At the end of his *Réflexions*, Carnot included a definition of work. It was defined as weight that was lifted to some height. In modern physics, work is the force that is applied to a body through a distance against resistance.

French army reorganization in 1827 put Carnot back on active duty. This prevented him from engaging in more scientific studies until 1828, when he resigned. He then spent his time studying the relationship between temperature and pressure. His researches were cut short when he contracted scarlet fever. He had not yet recovered when a cholera epidemic swept across Paris, taking his life. He died in Paris on August, 24, 1832. His scientific papers and all of his possessions were burned, as was the practice in an effort to purge the disease with fire. Carnot's work in thermodynamics was generally ignored until 1848 when William Thomson (Lord Kelvin) was influenced by it as he studied heat for an absolute temperature scale, the Kelvin scale. The German physicist Rudolf Clausius later modified Carnot's work and spread his ideas as the second law of thermodynamics: Entropy occurs because heat cannot move from a colder substance to a hotter substance.

—*Andrew J. Waskey*

Further Reading

Bejan, Adrian. *Advanced Engineering Thermodynamics*. 4th ed., John Wiley & Sons, 2016.

Carnot, Sadi. *Reflection on the Motive Power of Fire*. Dover, 1960.

———. *Reflexions on the Motive Power of Fire: A Critical Edition with the Surviving Scientific Manuscripts*. Translated and edited by Robert Fox. Manchester UP, 1986.

Cropper, William H. *Great Physicists: The Life and Times of Leading Physicists from Galileo to Hawking*. Oxford UP, 2001.

Feidt, Michel, editor. *Carnot Cycle and Heat Engine Fundamentals and Applications*. MDPI, 2020.

Gillispie, Charles Coulston, and Raffaele Pisano. *Lazare and Sadi Carnot: A Scientific and Filial Relationship*. 2nd ed., Springer, 2014.

Jacoby, John. *The Most Efficient Engine: The New Carnot Cycle*. CreateSpace Independent Publishing Platform, 2014.

Mendoza, E., editor. *Reflections on the Motive Power of Fire by Sadi Carnot, and Other Papers on the Second Law of Thermodynamics by E. Clapeyron and R. Claussius*. Dover Publications, 1960.

See also: Clausius formulates the second law of thermodynamics; Conservation of energy; External combustion engine; Heat transfer; Mechanical engineering; Steam engine; Stirling, Robert; Thermodynamics; Work and energy; Work-energy theorem

CELESTIAL MECHANICS

Fields of Study: Physics; Mechanics; Mathematics

ABSTRACT

Celestial mechanics is a subfield of classical mechanics and a branch of astronomy that studies the motion of celestial objects and the forces affecting this movement. Several types of forces can affect the orbit of bodies in space. Gravity is the main cause of orbital motion. Other forces such as atmospheric interference, radiation pressure, and electromagnetic fields affect the movement of celestial bodies.

KEY CONCEPTS

classical mechanics: the study of the motion of bodies, rooted in Isaac Newton's physical and mathematical principles; also called Newtonian mechanics

eccentricity: the extent to which a celestial body's orbit deviates from a perfect circle

ellipse: a shape that resembles an elongated circle; mathematically speaking, a closed conic section

n-body problem: a mathematical model used to determine how gravity affects the motions and interactions of a group of celestial bodies

Newton's laws of motion: the three laws that describe how bodies respond to the application of force

perturbation: a change in the orbit of a celestial object caused by the gravitational force of another object

tidal evolution: the change in the rise and fall of an ocean caused by the gravitational force of a nearby celestial object

EXPLAINING THE MOTIONS OF THE HEAVENS

Ancient peoples viewed the stars, moon, and planets as objects of worship. They made up stories about them and believed in their power to affect conditions on Earth. Early observers were aware of the consistent motions of these objects; Mesopotamian, Egyptian, and Indus Valley civilizations understood them well enough to predict eclipses. However, few astronomical observers questioned the cause of this motion, although several Greek philosophers tried to calculate precise movements of the sun, moon, and planets.

The Greek Egyptian astronomer and mathematician Ptolemy (ca. 100-170) proposed that Earth was the center of the universe and all the other planets and stars orbited around it. This theory was known as "geocentrism." Ptolemy used mathematics to calculate and predict the movement of celestial bodies. His calculations told him that planets move in epicycles, or small circles, while simultaneously orbiting Earth. Ptolemy was not certain if this was true, but he simply could not calculate a better model of planetary motion.

Ptolemy's theories were widely accepted for many centuries before Polish mathematician Nicolaus Co-

pernicus (1473-1543) disproved them. Copernicus held that Earth orbited the sun; therefore, the sun was the center of the solar system. This theory was called "heliocentrism." Many scholars were slow to accept heliocentric views of the universe. However, Copernicus's mathematical calculations proved more accurate than Ptolemy's. This breakthrough led to what is sometimes called the "Copernican revolution."

Several other key astronomical breakthroughs occurred in the years following Copernicus's death. The celestial observations of Danish astronomer Tycho Brahe (1546-1601) greatly contributed to the accurate measurement of planet positions. Brahe's work influenced seventeenth-century German astronomer Johannes Kepler (1571-1630), considered by many to be the father of celestial mechanics. Kepler's laws of planetary motion state, among other things, that a planet's orbit is shaped like an ellipse.

English physicist Isaac Newton (1643-1727) refined Kepler's laws, working out the mathematics behind the movements of the planets. His *Philosophiae Naturalis Principia Mathematica* (1687; *The Mathematical Principles of Natural Philosophy*, 1729) laid the foundations for classical mechanics. In it, Newton put forth three fundamental principles, now commonly referred to as Newton's laws of motion, to explain how different forces affect the movement of any physical body. He also defined the law of universal gravitation, which played a key role in the development of celestial mechanics.

THE NATURE OF CELESTIAL MECHANICS

Classical mechanics laid the groundwork for celestial mechanics. Further progress was made by astronomers such as Félix Tisserand (1845-96), who compiled all known studies in the field into the compendium *Traité de mécanique céleste* (*Treatise on Celestial Mechanics*, 1889-96), and physicist Albert Einstein (1879-1955), whose theory of general relativity improved on Newton's description of gravity to allow

Image via iStock/pixelparticle. [Used under license.]

celestial movement to be calculated with greater accuracy. Celestial mechanics, also referred to as dynamic astronomy, calculates the motion and orbit of celestial bodies by measuring the effects of gravity and other forces.

Several basic problems make up the bulk of celestial mechanics equations. All of these problems rely on Newton's laws of classical mechanics. Most are variations on the n-body problem, which attempts to account for the overall motion of a group of n bodies that are each affected by the others' gravitational forces. When the gravitational forces of more than one body act on a single massive body, the result is a complex series of motions called perturbation. Perturbation also happens when air resistance and at-

mospheric pressure disturb a celestial body. Scientists must determine the orbital properties of a group of celestial bodies and how their forces will affect one another to predict their future orbital motions. Astronomers and physicists have only solved the n-body problem for situations in which n = 2 (two-body problem) and n = 3 (three-body problem). One well-known version of the three-body problem is the orbital relationship between Earth, the moon, and the sun.

CALCULATING THE N-BODY PROBLEM

Early mathematics did not account for the ways in which gravity affects the orbits of celestial objects. With the advent of Newton's law of universal gravitation, mathematicians could more accurately calculate the motions of two- and three-body systems. However, the unpredictability of perturbations makes solving the n-body problem difficult in cases involving three or more bodies.

The n-body problem involves a series of equations. The first calculates the number of celestial bodies being measured. Once this is established, the next step is to calculate each body's initial velocity, relative position and time, and mass. The motion of the bodies can be determined from the size and eccentricity of their orbits and their interactions according Newton's law of gravitation. However, numerical calculations of celestial motion offer only indefinite predictions of future orbits, given the chaotic nature of the universe. The motion of the eight planets of the solar system is an n-body problem that incites much debate. Scientists continually try to determine whether the current movement of the solar system is ultimately stable or will eventually change motion due to altered external forces.

IMPACT OF CELESTIAL MECHANICS

Understanding the motion of celestial bodies has allowed scientists to predict astronomical events such as eclipses. It has also contributed to the subfields of astrodynamics and lunar theory and led to a greater understanding of Earth's ocean tides. The moon's gravitational force is primarily responsible for Earth's tidal evolution. As the moon's orbit expanded over time, its effect on the tides dissipated, causing the Earth's rotation to slow and thus lengthening Earth's days.

Technological innovations have given scientists easier ways to calculate celestial motions. Dutch American astronomer Dirk Brouwer (1902-66) pioneered the use of digital computers to solve orbital problems. The digital calculations proved incredibly accurate, and Brouwer's methods were soon adopted worldwide. Computer-based problem solving en-

abled more accurate calculations of the orbits of artificial satellites, thus facilitating the development of satellite communications.

—*Cait Caffrey*

Further Reading

Bannikova, Eleria, and Massimo Capaccioli. *Foundations of Celestial Mechanics*. Springer International Publishing, 2022.

Coolman, Robert. "What Is Classical Mechanics?" *LiveScience*, 12 Sept. 2014. Accessed 6 May 2015.

Gurfil, Pini, and P. Kenneth Seidelmann. *Celestial Mechanics and Astrodynamics: Theory and Practice*. Springer, 2016.

Hockey, Thomas, et al., editors. *Biographical Encyclopedia of Astronomers*. 2nd ed., Springer, 2014.

Klioner, Sergei A. "Lecture Notes on Basic Celestial Mechanics." *Department of Astronomy/Lohrmann Observatory*. Technical University of Dresden, 2011. Accessed 14 May 2015.

Matzner, Richard A., editor. *Dictionary of Geophysics, Astrophysics, and Astronomy*. CRC Press, 2001.

Stern, David P. "How Orbital Motion Is Calculated." *From Stargazers to Starships*. Author, 6 Apr. 2014. Accessed 14 May 2015.

See also: Acceleration; Angular forces; Angular momentum; Circular motion; Classical or applied mechanics; Newton's laws

Centrifugation

Fields of Study: Physics; Chemistry; Engineering; Chemical methods

ABSTRACT

One mechanical technique useful for separating immiscible liquids or solids from liquids is centrifugation, the rapid spinning of solutions containing two or more components. By applying centrifugal force, these separations can be used for either analytical or preparative purposes.

KEY CONCEPTS

angular velocity: the rate of change of position of a body moving in a circle, commonly measured in rotations per minute

centrifugal force: the outward force exerted on an object moving in a circular path

centrifuge: a device that is used to spin materials at rates of up to 10,000 rpm, allowing them to separate by density

centripetal force: the inward force required to keep an object moving in a circular path

gravitation: the mutual attraction between all bodies in the universe, of which gravity, the force the earth exerts on all bodies on or near it, is an example

ultracentrifuge: a centrifuge that is used to spin materials at rates of 25,000 rpm and more, allowing separation of materials of similar density

OVERVIEW

Centrifugation is a mechanical technique useful for separating solids from liquids, liquids from gases, gases from other gases, and so on. A centrifuge is a device that relies on the power of centrifugal force to accomplish these types of separations.

Centrifugal force can be a confusing concept. Many texts define it as a "pseudoforce" that is "nonexistent" or "fictitious." Centrifugal force does exist, but only under certain conditions. To understand how this force is applied in centrifugation, it is necessary to consider another force, centripetal force.

Centripetal force is the inward force required to keep an object moving in a circular path. Imagine a turntable or flat disc, spinning about a central point. If an object is placed on the outer edge of this disc, gravity is the force that keeps it on the disc, but centripetal force is the force that allows it to move in a circle. If the object is too light, centripetal force may overcome the force of gravity, and the object will fly off of the spinning disc on a tangent to the point on the disc it has just departed.

If the spinning disc just described were large enough so that you could stand on the disc, the force you would feel pulling you toward the edge is centrifugal force. In other words, centripetal and centrifugal forces are mirror images; viewed from the outside, the force is termed "centripetal." Viewed from the inside, as the object upon which the force is acting, the force is called "centrifugal." One final example: Earth can be viewed as a large centrifuge. People are held on the face of the planet by the force of gravity. Without centrifugal forces acting to balance gravity, one would gradually be pulled in toward the center of the earth. Without gravity, one would be flung off into space. Most centrifuges are used to create forces many times the strength of gravity.

The amount of centrifugal (or centripetal) force a centrifuge can generate is defined by the following equation: $F_c = M\omega^2 R$ where F_c equals the centrifugal force, M is the amount of mass, ω is angular velocity, and R is the distance of an object to be spun from the axis of rotation of the centrifuge. This equation has many implications for the construction of a centrifugal device. For example, the amount of centrifugal force can be greatly increased by increasing the angular velocity. To go from an initial velocity of 1 rotation per minute to 10 rotations per minute actually increases the centrifugal force by a factor of 100. Some of the fastest centrifuges can make more than 1 million revolutions per minute, generating forces that are five million times as great as gravity. The limiting factor is the device itself. The force generated by a centrifuge affects the structure of the centrifuge itself; the fastest centrifuges tend to be very small and made of materials that can withstand great tensile stress.

A generic centrifuge will contain a rotor to which is attached a container or bowl that holds the material to be separated. Many different types of centrifuges exist, many of them highly specialized devices constructed for limited applications. Most centrifuges, however, are of one of two basic types: sedimenters or filters.

A sedimenting centrifuge uses a bowl with a solid wall that rotates on a horizontal or vertical axis. These devices separate material on the basis of weight or density. Most of the centrifuges used in chemical, biological, or medical laboratories are of this general type. In a standard "bench-top" centrifuge, multiple test-tube-shaped containers are mounted symmetrically around a vertical shaft, driven by an electric motor. These containers may be of the "swinging bucket" type, which are attached by joints that allow them to spin at right angles to the shaft while centrifugation is in progress. Other centrifuges will have containers that are fixed in place, often at an angle of about 37 degrees to the shaft. This reduces the amount of distance that the material must settle.

Another type of sedimenting centrifuge is the ultracentrifuge. In an ultracentrifuge, samples spin within a chamber in which the air has been replaced by a vacuum, a feature that reduces both air resistance and potential problems caused by the buildup of heat. Ultracentrifuges can generate angular velocities of more than 25,000 revolutions per minute.

Disk-type centrifuges are also used for sedimentation, but lack the tube or bottle-shaped containers found in the more common devices. This centrifuge contains multiple thin, cone-shaped disks that form a stack. The material to be separated moves between the disks, with the angle of the cones helping to separate the heavier material from light phases.

Filtering centrifuges feature a bowl with a perforated wall. The size of the holes in such a wall depends on the material to be filtered. This type of device is primarily used to separate liquids from solids very quickly. One common example of a filtering centrifuge is the drum of a household washing machine. During the spin cycle, the drum rotates rapidly, throwing off water drops that pass through the holes in the drum, while retaining the solid articles of clothing.

APPLICATIONS

The major application used for centrifugation in the physical sciences is, of course, the centrifuge. This device, in its many different forms, can perform many tasks useful for both preparation of materials and for analysis of the physical nature of some materials.

There are many preparative uses of centrifuges. Sedimentation centrifuges can be used to purify many different types of materials including food products, vaccines, and oils. For example, in the process of rendering, oils from different sources including seeds, fruits, or animal fats are separated from liquid and solid protein components to produce a good yield of

Laboratory centrifuge. Photo via WikimediaCommons. [Public domain.]

high-quality oil. Filtering centrifuges are used to clarify and collect sugar crystals from sugar cane syrup, and to wash and dry many other types of crystals or fibers. Disk-type centrifuges are used in the dairy industry. After whole milk is churned or homogenized, the fat-containing cream layer can be quickly drawn off through centrifugation, leaving behind the lower-fat skim milk.

In chemistry, gas centrifugation can be used to separate isotopes, which are forms of the same chemical element that differ slightly in their mass. This process works very much like the cream separator used by dairies. It was first successfully applied to isotopes of chlorine in 1936, and has also been used at times in the preparation of uranium. Natural uranium contains mostly uranium-238, but it is the lighter isotope, uranium-235, that undergoes fission. During the development of the atomic bomb, the United States government at one point considered investing millions of dollars in the construction of gas centrifuge plants devoted to the production of uranium-235. This idea was abandoned in favor of a different method, involving filtration. Still, a little less than 5 percent of the world's uranium is prepared in this manner.

One important analytical application of centrifugation is the determination of the molecular weights and concentrations of different molecules. This technique is especially important for protein chemistry, and it is also widely used for determining the density of nucleic acids, such as DNA (deoxyribonucleic acid), and for separating DNA molecules of different densities. In medicinal chemistry, centrifugation is used to isolate blood serum for analysis of cholesterol and triglycerides. The ultracentrifuge is the device of choice for this type of analysis. Two different methods for the determination of molecular weight are possible. In one method, called equilibrium density centrifugation, the unknown material is added to a heavy salt solution, usually cesium chloride.

As the centrifugation progresses over many hours, the salt forms a gradient within the sample tube, with the heaviest concentration of salt found farthest from the center of rotation. At some point in time, any added material will find a level at which its forward motion in the tube is balanced by its tendency to diffuse back into areas of lesser concentration. The point at which this material reaches its equilibrium point in a gradient is a function of its density and molecular weight. By comparing the distance traveled of an unknown material with distances traveled by materials of known molecular weights, the weight of the unknown can be determined.

A second method of determining the molecular weight of a molecule is called the rate of sedimentation method. In this method, a sample of the molecule whose molecular weight is to be determined is added to a solvent, and the solution is centrifuged at very high speeds. This will produce a very sharp boundary between the pure solvent and the sedimenting molecules. Over time, this boundary will move out, away from the center of rotation. The rate at which the boundary moves (that is, how quickly sedimentation occurs) can be measured and used in the calculation of the molecular weight of the molecule. This method also requires an ultracentrifuge, which must run for many hours.

The ultracentrifuge is also used for biomedical analysis when high precision measurements are required. After the sample has been 'spun down' the supernatant liquid is prepared with a reagent that reacts with the target material to produce a colored solution. The intensity of the color is measured using a spectrophotometer against a standard solution to determine the concentration of the target material in a specified amount of the solution.

Centrifuges are also important for other types of analyses. The centrifugal fast-scan analyzer uses a low-speed (350 revolutions per minute) centrifuge and a spectrophotometer to analyze up to sixteen samples at once. A spectrophotometer measures the amount of light of a given wavelength that is transmitted through, or absorbed by, a given substance. Analyzers of this type are often used to determine the concentration of an enzyme in a sample. Samples and reagents are placed in adjacent chambers in the arm of a centrifuge, and are then mixed by the rotational action of the device. The mixture flows into a special chamber at the end of the centrifuge arm. This chamber has a quartz window through which the light from a spectrophotometer can pass. With each spin of the centrifuge, the relative amount of the reagent can be measured by the spectrophotometer and stored in computer memory. These data are then used to calculate the rate of the reaction.

Another application of centrifugation is found in the centrifuge microscope. In this device, a stationary objective lens is pointed down at prisms located at the center of rotation of a small centrifuge. The samples to be observed are located in wells on slides mounted at right angles to the center of rotation. As the centrifuge spins, light from the samples is reflected back toward the prisms and up to the objective lens, producing a two-dimensional image. This device can be used to observe the movement of grains or crystals in fluids of different viscosities. In the biological sciences, the centrifuge microscope is used to examine the effects of centrifugal forces on living cells.

A very different application of centrifugation is seen in astronaut and pilot training. The force exerted on a person at the end of a centrifuge arm can be varied by the speed of the centrifuge. This allows pilots and astronauts to feel the forces equivalent to "high-g" gravitational forces experienced during rapid acceleration. This allows them to practice many actions and maneuvers during simulated flights before experiencing the real event. This also allows scientists to test how well and how long the human body can endure strong gravitational forces.

CONTEXT

Like so many natural phenomena, the understanding of centrifugal and centripetal forces is based on the laws of Sir Isaac Newton. In the eighteenth century, Newton described three fundamental principles that form the basis of classical mechanics. These laws have proved to be valid for all examples that involve masses greater than the size of the atom, and for speeds less than the speed of light.

Centrifugation applies Newton's second and third laws of motion. According to the second law, the acceleration of a particle (for example, in a centrifuge tube) is directly proportional to the force acting on a particle (the speed of the centrifuge), and is inversely proportional to the mass of the particle (that is, heavier particles require more force to cause them to spin). Newton's third law states that interacting particles exert equal and opposite effects on one another. In centrifugation, centripetal and centrifugal forces represent such an equal and opposite pair.

Simple applications of centrifugation do not require an understanding of the theoretical basis behind the process. Long before Newton, simple centrifuges were used to separate cream from milk and to reduce the sediment in wines. However, more sophisticated machines and more analytical uses did not develop until the twentieth century.

As an analytical tool, centrifugation is valuable, but perhaps not as informative as other processes including chromatography, electrophoresis, and spectroscopy. Aside from molecular-weight calculations, which are useful in many fields of chemistry, centrifugation's biggest contribution has been in the biochemical area. Applications of centrifugation have allowed the identification of new classes of molecules. For example, lipoproteins are lipid-protein complexes held together by weak physical forces. The different classes of lipoproteins were first identified when human blood was spun in an ultracentrifuge. This allowed the identification of high-density (low-fat) lipoproteins (HDLs), low-density (high-fat) lipoproteins (LDLs), and very-low-density lipoproteins (VLDLs). The relative amounts of these molecules in the blood are an important indicator of susceptibility to diseases such as arteriosclerosis.

Centrifugation is also essential for the study of DNA, the genetic material of all living things. Centrifugation is an important step in isolating DNA from the cells in which it is found.

Centrifugation is also used in estimating the size and chemical makeup of DNA from different sources.

The principles of centrifugation may one day be applied to the construction of revolving space stations or space colonies. As one's distance from Earth increases, the pull of gravity is lessened, resulting in "weightlessness." Artificial gravity can be created by the forces exerted on people or objects standing inside the outer ring of a spinning circle. Artificial gravity will allow people to live and work normally, free from possible physiological problems resulting from long-term exposure to the lack of gravity.

—*Lisa A. Lambert*

Further Reading

Graham, John. *Biological Centrifugation*. Garland Science, 2020.

Leung, Wallace Woon-Fong. *Centrifugal Separations in Biotechnology*. 2nd ed., Elsevier Science, 2020.

Naidoo, Shalinee. *Centrifugation Techniques*. Arcler Education Incorporated, 2017.

Price, C.A. *Centrifugation in Density Gradients*. Academic Press, 2014.

Sun, Xiaoming, Liang Luo, Yun Kuang, and Pengsong Li. *Nanoseparation Using Density Gradient Ultracentrifugation: Mechanism, Methods, and Applications*. Springer, 2018.

Taylor, R. N. *Geotechnical Centrifuge Technology*. CRC Press, 2018.

See also: Acceleration; Angular forces; Angular momentum; Circular motion; Fluid dynamics; Force (physics); Nanotechnology; Torque

CHAOTIC SYSTEMS

Fields of Study: Physics; Mechanics; Mathematics

ABSTRACT

Chaotic systems theory is a scientific field blending mathematics, statistics, and philosophy that was developed to study systems that are highly complex, unstable, and resistant to exact prediction. Chaotic systems include weather patterns, neural networks, some social systems, and a variety of chemical and quantum phenomena. The study of chaotic systems began in the nineteenth century and developed into a distinct field during the 1980s. Chaotic systems analysis has allowed scientists to develop better prediction tools to evaluate evolutionary systems, weather patterns, neural function and development, and economic systems. Applications from the field include a variety of highly complex evaluation tools, new models from computer and electrical engineering, and a range of consumer products.

KEY CONCEPTS

aperiodic: of irregular occurrence, not following a regular cycle of behavior

attractor: state to which a dynamic system will eventually gravitate—a state that is not dependent on the starting qualities of the system

butterfly effect: theory that small changes in the initial state of a system can lead to pronounced changes that affect the entire system

complex system: system in which the behavior of the entire system exhibits one or more properties that are not predictable, given a knowledge of the individual components and their behavior

dynamical system: complex system that changes over time according to a set of rules governing the transformation from one state to the next

nonlinear: of a system or phenomenon that does not follow an ordered, linear set of cause-and-effect relationships

randomness: state marked by no specific or predictable pattern or having a quality in which all possible behaviors are equally likely to occur

static system: system that is without movement or activity and in which all parts are organized in an ordered series of relationships

system: group interrelated by independent units that together make up a whole

unstable: state of a system marked by sensitivity to minor changes in a variety of variables that cause major changes in system behavior

DEFINITION AND BASIC PRINCIPLES

Chaotic systems analysis is a way of evaluating the behavior of complex systems. A system can be anything from a hurricane or a computer network to a single atom with its associated particles. Chaotic systems are systems that display complex nonlinear relationships between components and whose ultimate behavior is aperiodic and unstable.

Chaotic systems are not random but rather deterministic, meaning that they are governed by some overall equation or principle that determines the behavior of the system. Because chaotic systems are determined, it is theoretically possible to predict their behavior. However, because chaotic systems are unstable and have so many contributing factors, it is nearly impossible to predict the system's behavior. The ability to predict the long-term behavior of complex systems, such as the human body, the stock market, or weather patterns, has many potential applications and benefits for society.

The butterfly effect is a metaphor describing a system in which a minor change in the starting conditions can lead to major changes across the whole system. The beat of a butterfly's wing could therefore set in motion a chain of events that could change the universe in ways that have no seeming connection to a flying insect. This kind of sensitivity to initial conditions is one of the basic characteristics of chaotic systems.

BACKGROUND AND HISTORY

French mathematician Henri Poincaré and Scottish theoretical physicist James Clerk Maxwell are considered two of the founders of chaos theory and complexity studies. Maxwell and Poincaré both worked on problems that illustrated the sensitivity of complex systems in the late nineteenth century. In 1960, meteorologist Edward Lorenz coined the term "butterfly effect" to describe the unstable nature of weather patterns.

By the late 1960s, theoreticians in other disciplines began to investigate the potential of chaotic dynamics. Ecologist Robert May was among the first to apply chaotic dynamics to population ecology models, to considerable success. Mathematician Benoit Mandelbrot also made a significant contribution in the mid-1970s with his discovery and investigation of fractal geometry.

In 1975, University of Maryland scientist James A. Yorke coined the term "chaos" for this new branch of systems theory. The first conference on chaos theory was held in 1977 in Italy, by which time the potential of chaotic dynamics had gained adherents and followers from many different areas of science.

Over the next two decades, chaos theory continued to gain respect within the scientific community and the first practical applications of chaotic systems analysis began to appear. In the twenty-first century, chaotic systems have become a respected and popular branch of mathematics and system analysis.

CHARACTERISTICS OF CHAOTIC SYSTEMS

There are many kinds of chaotic systems. However, all chaotic systems share certain qualities: They are unstable, dynamic, and complex. Scientists studying complex systems generally focus on one of these qualities in detail. There are two ultimate goals for complex systems research: first, to predict the evolution of chaotic systems and second, to learn how to manipulate complex systems to achieve some desired result.

Instability. Chaotic systems are extremely sensitive to changes in their environment. Like the example of the butterfly, a seemingly insignificant change can become magnified into system-wide transformations. Because chaotic systems are unstable, they do not settle to equilibrium and can therefore continue developing and leading to unexpected changes. In the chaotic system of evolution, minor changes can lead to novel mutations within a species, which may eventually give rise to a new species. This kind of innovative transformation is what gives chaotic systems a reputation for being creative. Scientists often study complexity and chaos by creating simulations of chaotic systems and studying the way the systems react when perturbed by minor stimuli. For example, scientists may create a computer model of a hurricane and alter small variables, such as temperature, wind speed and other factors, to study the ultimate effect on the entire storm system.

Strange attractors. An attractor is a state toward which a system moves. The attractor is a point of equilibrium, where all the forces acting on a system have reached a balance and the system is in a state of rest. Because of their instability, chaotic systems are less likely to reach a stable equilibrium and instead proceed through a series of states, which scientists sometimes call a dynamic equilibrium. In a dynamic equilibrium, the system is constantly moving toward some attractor, but as it moves toward the first attractor, forces begin building that create a second attractor. The system then begins to shift from the first to the second attractor, which in turn leads to the formation of a new attractor, and the system shifts again. The forces pulling the system from one attractor to the next never balance each other completely, so the system never reaches absolute rest but continues changing.

Visual models of complex systems and their strange attractors display what mathematicians call fractal geometry. Fractals are patterns that, like chaotic systems, are nonlinear and dynamic. Fractal geometry occurs throughout nature, including in the formation of ice crystals and the branching of the circulatory system in the human body. Scientists study the mathematics behind fractals and strange attractors to find patterns that can be applied to complex systems in nature. The study of fractals has yielded applications for medicine, economics, and psychology.

Emergent properties. Chaotic systems also display emergent properties, which are system-wide behaviors that are not predictable from knowledge of the individual components. This occurs when simple behaviors among the components combine to create more complex behaviors. Common examples in nature include the behavior of ant colonies and other social insects.

Mathematical models of complex systems also yield emergent properties, indicating that this property is driven by the underlying principles that lead to the creation of complexity. Using these principals, scientists can create systems, such as computer networks, that also display emergent properties.

APPLICATIONS AND PRODUCTS

Medical technology. The human heart is a chaotic system, and the heartbeat is controlled by a set of nonlinear, complex variables. The heartbeat appears periodic only when examined through an imprecise measure such as a stethoscope. The actual signals that compose a heartbeat occur within a dynamic equilibrium.

Applying chaos dynamics to the study of the heart is allowing physicians to gain more accuracy in determining when a heart attack is imminent, by detecting minute changes in rhythm that signify the potential for the heart to veer away from its relative rhythm. When the rhythm fluctuates too far, physicians use a defibrillator to shock the heart back to its rhythm. A new defibrillator model developed by scientists in 2006 and 2007 uses a chaotic electric signal to force the heart back more effectively to its normal rhythmic pattern.

Consumer products. In the mid-1990s, the Korean company Goldstar manufactured a chaotic dishwasher that used two spinning arms operated with an element of randomness to their pattern. The chaotic jet patterns were intended to provide greater cleaning power while using less energy.

Chaotic engineering has also been used in the manufacture of washing machines, kitchen mixers, and a variety of other simple machines. Although most chaotic appliances have been more novelty than innovation, the principles behind chaotic mechanics have become common in the engineering of computers and other electrical networks.

Business and industry. The global financial market is a complex, chaotic system. When examined mathematically, fluctuations in the market appear aperiodic and have nonlinear qualities. Although the market seems to behave in random ways, many believe that applying methods created for the study of chaotic systems will allow economists to elucidate hidden developmental patterns. Knowledge of these patterns might help predict and control recessions and other major changes well before they occur.

The application of chaos theory to market analysis produced a subfield of economics known as fractal market analysis, wherein researchers conduct economic analyses by using models with fractal geometry. By looking for fractal patterns and assuming that the market, like other chaotic systems, is highly sensitive to small changes, economists have been able to build more accurate models of market evolution.

IMPACT ON INDUSTRY

The fact that chaos theory applies to so many fields means that there are numerous funding opportunities available. Many countries offer some government funding for studies into chaos theory and related fields.

In the United States, the National Science Foundation offers a grant for researchers studying theoretical biology, which has been awarded to several research teams studying chaotic systems. The National Science Foundation, National Institute of Standards and Technology, National Institutes of Health, and the Department of Defense have also provided some funding for research into chaotic dynamics.

Any product created using chaotic principles may be subject to regulation governing the industry in question. For instance, the chaotic defibrillator is subject to regulation from the Food and Drug Administration, which has oversight over any new medical technology. Other equipment, such as the chaotic dishwasher, will be subject to consumer safety regulations at the federal and regional levels.

CAREERS

Those seeking careers in chaotic systems analysis might begin by studying mathematics or physics at a university. Those with backgrounds in other fields such as biology, ecology, economics, sociology, and computer science might also choose to focus on chaotic systems during their graduate training.

There are a number of graduate programs offering training in chaotic dynamics. For instance, the Center for Interdisciplinary Research on Complex Systems at Northeastern University in Boston, Massachusetts, offers programs training students in many types of complex system analyses. The Center for Nonlinear Phenomena and Complex Systems at the Université Libre de Bruxelles offers programs in thermodynamics and statistical mechanics.

Careers in chaotic systems span a range of fields from engineering and computer network design to theoretical physics. Trained researchers can choose to contribute to academic analyses and other pertinent laboratory work or focus on creating applications for immediate consumer use.

SOCIAL CONTEXT AND FUTURE PROSPECTS

As chaotic systems analysis spread in the 1980s and 1990s, some scientists began theorizing that chaotic dynamics might be an essential part of the search for a grand unifying theory or theory of everything. The grand unifying theory is a concept that emerged in the early nineteenth century, when scientists began theorizing that there might be a single set of rules and patterns underpinning all phenomena in the universe.

The idea of a unified theory is controversial, but the search has attracted numerous theoreticians from mathematics, physics, theoretical biology, and philosophy. As research began to show that the basic principles of chaos theory could apply to a vast array of fields, some began theorizing that chaos theory was part of the emerging unifying theory. Because many systems meet the basic requirements to be considered complex chaotic systems, the study of chaos theory and complexity has room to expand. Scientists and engineers have only begun to explore the practical applications of chaotic systems, and theoreticians are still attempting to evaluate and study the basic principles behind chaotic system behavior.

—*Micah L. Issitt*

Further Reading

Argyris, John H., Gunter Faust, Maria Haase, and Rudolf Friedrich. *An Exploration of Dynamical Systems and Chaos: Completely Revised and Enlarged Second Edition.* Springer, 2015.

Ford, Kenneth W. *The Quantum World: Quantum Physics for Everyone.* Harvard UP, 2005.

Gleick, James L. *Chaos: Making a New Science.* Rev. ed., Penguin Books, 2008.

Gribbin, John. *Deep Simplicity: Bringing Order to Chaos and Complexity.* Random House, 2005.

Mandelbrot, Benoit, and Richard L. Hudson. *The Misbehavior of Markets: A Fractal View of Financial Turbulence.* Basic Books, 2006.

Skiadis, Christos H., and Ioannis Dimotikalis, editors. *Chaotic System: Theory and Applications.* World Scientific, 2010.

See also: Conservation of energy; Equilibrium; Stability

CIRCULAR MOTION

Fields of Study: Physics; Mechanics; Mathematics

ABSTRACT

Circular motion has captivated scientists and philosophers since antiquity. Although circular motion is described using distinct equations and terminology, these are all derived from Newton's laws of motion. In particular, the interplay between inertia and centripetal force accounts for everything from planetary motion to the feeling of being pressed against the side of a car during a sharp turn.

KEY CONCEPTS

angular momentum: the rotational momentum of an object around an axis, defined as the product of its moment of inertia and its angular velocity

centrifugal force: a perceived force that seems to act outward on a rotating object, pushing it away from the center of its circular path; commonly confused with centripetal force

centripetal force: the force that impels a rotating object inward, acting at a right angle to its momentum

Coriolis force: the effects of the spinning motion of a planet on objects at the planet's surface, such as deflection in large-scale wind patterns

inertia: the principle that an object remains at rest or continues moving in the same direction at the same speed unless an outside force acts on it

radian: abbreviated rad, the International System of Units standard unit of angular measure, the length of the corresponding arc in a unit circle; a full circle is composed of 2π radians

CIRCULAR MOTION AND NEWTON'S LAWS

Since antiquity, scientists and philosophers have recognized circular motion, particularly in the context of planetary orbits, as distinct from linear motion. This is somewhat misleading, however. While there are distinct equations to describe the properties of circular motion, these are all derived from the laws of motion codified by English physicist Isaac Newton (1642-1727). The same rules that govern the orbits that interested Renaissance astronomer and physicist Galileo Galilei (1564-1642) also govern a car turning around a race track or a tennis ball rotating with backspin. Angular momentum, just like linear momentum (often simply momentum), is conserved in a system. The total momentum of that system before and after any impact or exchange of energy is constant.

Objects moving in a circular path are subject to inertia, as described by Newton's first law. An object at rest will stay at rest, and an object in motion will continue moving in the same direction at the same speed, unless acted on by an outside force. In other words, objects "want" to move in a straight line. For an object to move in a curved path, a force must be acting on it. In circular motion, a centripetal force "pulls" or "pushes" the object toward the center of its circular path. Centripetal force simply describes the way a particular force acts. Gravity is the centripetal force in planetary orbits; the tug of a yo-yo string provides centripetal force during the around-the-world trick. The competing influences of inertia (straight-line tendency) and centripetal force (pull or push toward the center) result in the familiar arc of circular motion.

A bucket swinging by a rope in a circle from a fixed center (O) exhibits circular motion. The bucket accelerates in multiple directions simultaneously, including centrifugal acceleration (a_c) directed away from the center, centripetal acceleration (a_r) directed toward the center, and tangential acceleration (a_t) directed perpendicular to centrifugal and centripetal accelerations. These three accelerations sum to angular acceleration (α), which causes the circular motion of the bucket.

UNIFORM VERSUS NONUNIFORM CIRCULAR MOTION

Circular motion can be uniform or nonuniform. An object in uniform circular motion travels at the same speed throughout its path, with a constant rate of acceleration. It may seem strange at first to think that an object with constant speed is accelerating, but remember that acceleration is dependent on change in velocity, which in turn is dependent on speed and direction. If an object is maintaining a constant speed but constantly changing direction, it is still accelerating.

This constant acceleration is also predicted by Newton's laws. Because an object moving in a circular path must always be acted on by a centripetal force, it must always be accelerating. By definition, a mass must be accelerating if a nonzero net force is acting on it. With uniform circular motion, an object will always be accelerating toward the center of the circle.

Many of the most familiar forms of circular motion are uniform, or close enough to be treated as such. Examples include planetary orbits, the spin of a Ferris wheel, and the rotation of Earth on its axis. Even objects that vary in speed over time, such as a windmill varying with wind speed, often exhibit periods of roughly uniform motion.

Nonuniform circular motion, by contrast, involves an object moving in a circular path with varying speed and acceleration. A car accelerating into and out of a turn is one real-life example. Because the speed changes over time, so does the acceleration. In nonuniform circular motion, the vector of acceleration at any given moment may not be aimed at the center.

CENTRIFUGAL AND CENTRIPETAL FORCE

Anyone who has ever been a passenger in a car during a sharp turn can attest to the fact that there seems to be another force acting outward, away from the center of the arc. The same sensation can be felt during sharp turns in roller coasters and other amusement-park rides. This is commonly referred to as centrifugal force. However, it is not an actual force but a trick of perception.

Consider a passenger in a car driving in a straight line at a uniform speed. The car and the passenger are both moving forward at the same rate; the passenger perceives no force. When the car accelerates, the passenger feels as though he or she is being pressed backward into the seat. In fact, the seat, along with the rest of the car, is accelerating forward and pushing the person forward. The inertia of the passenger's body resists, creating the illusion of a backward force. Likewise, centrifugal force is a trick of perception caused by the inertia of an object in motion resisting inward acceleration caused by centripetal force.

CIRCULAR MOTION AROUND THE WORLD

Examples of circular motion abound. Many motors, whether in electric toothbrushes or cars, generate circular motion from an external energy source, such as electricity or fuel combustion. Merry-go- rounds spin children on playgrounds. Indeed, the entire planet is spinning, as are the solar system, the galaxy, and even, it seems, the entire universe.

Understanding circular motion not only helps understand motion at an everyday, human scale but also influences aspects of life at the planetary level. Understanding the motion of the moon has helped humans understand tides and navigate the seas. Understanding the interaction between Earth's rotation (faster at the equator than the poles) and its atmosphere explains the Coriolis effect, which causes winds that would normally travel across the planet in a straight line to bend clockwise in the Northern Hemisphere and counterclockwise in the Southern Hemisphere.

—*Kenrick Vezina*

Further Reading

Halliday, David, Robert Resnick, and Jearl Walker. *Fundamentals of Physics Extended*. 10th ed., Wiley Global Education, 2013.

Kumar, Sanjay. *Circular Motion*. Sanjay Kumar, 2020.

Ling, Samuel J., Jeff Sanny, and William Moebs. *University Physics Volume 1*. Samurai Media Limited, 2017.

Myers, Richard Leroy, and Rusty L. Myers. *The Basics of Physics*. Greenwood Publishing Group, 2006.

See also: Acceleration; Airplane propellers; Angular forces; Angular momentum; Ballistic weapons; Celestial mechanics; Centrifugation; Classical or applied mechanics; Conservation of energy; Coriolis effect; Dynamics (mechanics); Engineering; Euler's laws of motion; Flywheels; Force (physics); Inertial guidance; Kinematics; Kinetic energy; Newton's laws; Torque; Turbines

CIVIL ENGINEERING

Fields of Study: Physics; Mechanics; Mathematics

ABSTRACT

Civil engineering is the branch of engineering concerned with the design, construction, and maintenance of fixed structures and systems, such as large buildings, bridges, roads, and other transportation systems, and water supply and wastewater-treatment systems. Civil engineering is the second-oldest field of engineering, with the term "civil" initially used to differentiate it from the oldest field of engineering, military engineering. The major subdisciplines within civil engineering are structural, transportation, and environmental engineering. Other possible areas of specialization within civil engineering are geotechnical, hydraulic, construction, and coastal engineering.

KEY CONCEPTS

civil engineering: relating to the nonmilitary segment of society

flow: the movement driven only by gravity of fluids and fluid-like materials

hydroelectric: using the movement of water to drive electrical generators

static equilibrium: the state of an object such as a building that is not in motion or that is acted upon by no unbalanced forces

BASIC PRINCIPLES

Civil engineering is the second-oldest field of engineering, after military engineering. The term "civil engineering" came into use in the mid-eighteenth century and initially referred to any practice of engineering by civilians for nonmilitary purposes. Before this time, most large-scale construction projects, such as roads and bridges, were done by military engineers. Early civil engineering projects were in areas such as water supply, roads, bridges, and other large structures, the same type of engineering work that exemplifies civil engineering in modern times. Today, civil engineering encompasses a very broad field of engineering, ranging from subdisciplines such as structural engineering to environmental engineering, some of which have also become recognized as separate fields of engineering.

Civil engineering, like engineering in general, is a profession with a practical orientation, having an emphasis on building things and making things work. Civil engineers use their knowledge of the physical sciences, mathematics, and engineering sciences, along with empirical engineering correlations to design, construct, manage, and maintain structures, transportation infrastructure, and environmental treatment equipment and facilities.

Empirical engineering correlations are important in civil engineering, because usable theoretical equations are not available for all the necessary engineering calculations. These empirical correlations are equations, graphs, or nomographs, based on experimental measurements, that give relationships among variables of interest for a particular engineering application. For example, the Manning equation gives an experimental relationship among the flow rate in an open channel, the slope of the channel, the depth of water, and the size, shape, and material of the bottom and sides of the channel. Rivers, irrigation ditches, and concrete channels used to transport wastewater in a treatment plant are examples of open channels. Similar empirical relationships are used in transportation, structural, and other specialties within civil engineering.

CORE CONCEPTS

In addition to mathematics, chemistry, and physics, civil engineering makes extensive use of principles from several engineering science subjects: engineering mechanics (statics and strength of materials), soil mechanics, and fluid mechanics.

Engineering mechanics—statics. As implied by the term "statics," this area of engineering concerns objects that are not moving. The fundamental principle of statics is that any stationary object must be in static equilibrium. That is, any force on the object must be cancelled out by another force that is equal in magnitude and acting in the opposite direction. There can be no net force in any direction on a stationary object, because if there were, it would be moving in that direction. The object considered to be in static equilibrium could be an entire structure or it could be any part of a structure down to an individual member in a truss. Calculations for an object in static equilibrium are often done through the use of a free-body diagram, that is a sketch of the object, showing all the forces external to that object that are acting on it. The principle then used for calculations is that the sum of all the horizontal forces acting on the object must be zero and the sum of all the vertical forces acting on the object must be zero. Working with the forces as vectors helps to find the horizontal and vertical components of forces that are acting on the object from some direction other than horizontal or vertical.

Engineering mechanics—strength of materials. This subject is sometimes called mechanics of materials.

Tennessee Valley Authority civil engineers monitoring hydraulics of a Tellico Dam scale model. Photo via Wikimedia Commons. [Public domain.]

Whereas statics works only with forces external to the body that is in equilibrium, strength of materials uses the same principles and also considers internal forces in a structural member. This is done to determine the required material properties to ensure that the member can withstand the internal stresses that will be placed on it.

Soil mechanics. Knowledge of soil mechanics is needed to design the foundations for structures. Any structure resting on the Earth will be supported in some way by the soil beneath it. A properly designed foundation will provide adequate long-term support for the structure above it. Inadequate knowledge of soil mechanics or inadequate foundation design may lead to something such as the Leaning Tower of Pisa. Soil mechanics topics include physical properties of soil, compaction, distribution of stress within soil, and flow of water through soil.

Fluid mechanics. Fundamental principles of physics are used for some fluid mechanics calculations. Examples are conservation of mass (called the continuity equation in fluid mechanics) and conservation of energy (also called the energy equation or the first law of thermodynamics). Some fluid mechanics applications, however, make use of empirical (experi-

mental) equations or relationships. Calculations for flow through pipes or flow in open channels, for example, use empirical constants and equations.

Knowledge from engineering fields of practice. In addition to these engineering sciences, a civil engineer uses accumulated knowledge from the civil engineering areas of specialization. Some of the important fields of practice are hydrology, geotechnical engineering, structural engineering, transportation engineering, and environmental engineering. In each of these fields of practice, there are theoretical equations, empirical equations, graphs or nomographs, guidelines, and rules of thumb that civil engineers use for design and construction of projects related to structures, roads, stormwater management, or wastewater-treatment projects, for example.

Civil engineering tools. Several tools available for civil engineers to use in practice are engineering graphics, computer-aided drafting (CAD), surveying, and geographic information systems (GIS). Engineering graphics (engineering drawing) has been a mainstay in civil engineering since its inception, for preparation of and interpretation of plans and drawings. Most of this work has come to be done using computer-aided drafting. Surveying is a tool that has also long been a part of civil engineering. From laying out roads to laying out a building foundation or measuring the slope of a river or of a sewer line, surveying is a useful tool for many of the civil engineering fields. Civil engineers often work with maps, and geographic information systems, a much newer tool than engineering graphics or surveying, make this type of work more efficient.

Codes and design criteria. Much of the work done by civil engineers is either directly or indirectly for the public. Therefore, in most of civil engineering fields, work is governed by codes or design criteria specified by some state, local, or federal agency. For example, federal, state, and local governments have building codes, state departments of transportation specify design criteria for roads and highways, and wastewater-treatment processes and sewers must meet federal, state, and local design criteria.

APPLICATIONS PAST AND PRESENT

Structural engineering. Civil engineers design, build, and maintain many and varied structures. These include bridges, towers, large buildings (skyscrapers), tunnels, and sports arenas. Some of the civil engineering areas of knowledge needed for structural engineering are soil mechanics/geotechnical engineering, foundation engineering, engineering mechanics (statics and dynamics), and strength of materials.

When the Brooklyn Bridge was built over the East River in New York City (1870-83), its suspension span of 1,595 feet was the longest in the world. It remained the longest suspension bridge in North America until the Williamsburg Bridge was completed in New York City in 1903. The Brooklyn Bridge joined two independent cities, Brooklyn and Manhattan, and helped establish the New York City Metropolitan Area.

The Golden Gate Bridge, which crosses the mouth of San Francisco Bay with a main span of

4,200 feet, had nearly triple the central span of the Brooklyn Bridge. It was the world's longest suspension bridge from its date of completion in 1937 until 1964, when the Verrazano-Narrows Bridge opened in New York City with a central span that was 60 feet longer than that of the Golden Gate Bridge. The Humber Bridge, which crosses the Humber estuary in England and was completed in 1981, has a single suspended span of 4,625 feet and was the longest suspension bridge in the world until 1998, when the Akashi Kaikyo Bridge opened in Japan with a central span of 6,532 feet.

One of the best-known early towers illustrates the importance of good geotechnical engineering and foundation design. The Tower of Pisa, commonly known as the Leaning Tower of Pisa, in Italy started to lean to one side very noticeably, even during its construction (1173-1399). Its height of about 185 feet is not extremely tall in comparison with towers built later, but it was impressive when it was built. The reason for its extreme tilt (more than 5 meters off perpendicular) is that it was built on rather soft, sandy soil with a foundation that was not deep enough or spread out enough to support the structure. In spite of this, the Tower of Pisa has remained standing for more than six hundred years.

Another well-known tower, the Washington Monument, was completed in 1884. At 555 feet in height, it was the world's tallest tower until the Eiffel Tower, nearly 1,000 feet tall, was completed in 1889. The Washington Monument remains the world's tallest masonry structure. The Gateway Arch in St. Louis, Missouri, is the tallest monument in the United States, at 630 feet.

The twenty-one-story Flatiron Building, which opened in New York City in 1903, was one of the first skyscrapers. It is 285 feet tall and its most unusual feature is its triangular shape, which was well suited to the wedge-shaped piece of land on which it was built. The 102-floor Empire State Building, completed in 1931 in New York City with a height of

1,250 feet, outdid the Chrysler Building that was under construction at the same time by 204 feet, to earn the title of the world's tallest building at that time. The Sears Tower (now the Willis Tower) in Chicago is 1,450 feet tall and was the tallest building in the world when it was completed in 1974. Several taller buildings have been constructed since that time in Asia and the Middle East.

Some of the more interesting examples of tunnels go through mountains and under the sea. The Hoosac Tunnel, built from 1851 to 1874, connected New York State to New England with a 4.75-mile railway tunnel through the Hoosac Mountain in northwestern Massachusetts. It was the longest railroad tunnel in the United States for more than fifty years. Mount Blanc Tunnel, built from 1957 to 1965, is a 7.25-mile-long highway tunnel under Mount Blanc in the Alps to connect Italy and France. The Channel Tunnel, one of the most publicized modern tunnel projects, is a rather dramatic and symbolic tunnel. It goes a distance of 31 miles beneath the English Channel to connect Dover, England, and Calais, France.

Transportation engineering. Civil engineers also design, build, and maintain a wide variety of projects related to transportation, such as roads, railroads, and pipelines.

Many long, dramatic roads and highways have been built by civil engineers, ever since the Romans became the first builders of an extensive network of roads. The Appian Way is the best known of the many long, straight roads built by the Romans. The Appian Way project was started in 312 BCE by the Roman censor Appius Claudius. By 244 BCE, it extended about 360 miles from Rome to the port of Brundisium in southeastern Italy. The Pan-American Highway, often billed as the world's longest road, connects North America and South America. The original Pan-American Highway ran from Texas to Argentina with a length of more than 15,500 miles. It has since been extended to go from Prudhoe Bay, Alaska, to the southern tip of South America, with a total length of nearly 30,000 miles. The US Interstate Highway system has been the world's biggest earthmoving project. Started in 1956 by the Federal Highway Act, it contains sixty-two highways covering a total distance of 42,795 miles. This massive highway construction project transformed the American system of highways and had major cultural impacts.

The building of the US Transcontinental Railroad was a major engineering feat when the western portion of the 2,000-mile railroad across the United States was built in the 1860s. Logistics was a major part of the project, with the need to transport steel rails and wooden ties great distances. An even more formidable task was construction of the Trans-Siberian Railway, the world's longest railway. It was built from 1891 to 1904 and covers 5,900 miles across Russia, from Moscow in the west to Vladivostok in the east.

The first oil pipeline in the United States was a 5-mile-long, 2-inch-diameter pipe that carried 800 barrels of petroleum per day. Pipelines have become much larger and longer since then. The Trans-Alaska Pipeline, with 800 miles of 48-inch-diameter pipe, can carry 2.14 million barrels per day. At the peak of construction, 20,000 people worked twelve-hour days, seven days a week.

Water resources engineering. Another area of civil engineering practice is water resources engineering, with projects like canals, dams, dikes, and seawater barriers.

The oldest known canal, one that is still in operation, is the Grand Canal in China, constructed between 485 BCE and 283 CE The length of the Grand Canal is more than 1,000 miles, although its route has varied because of several instances of rerouting, remodeling, and rebuilding over the years. The 363-mile-long Erie Canal was built from 1817 to 1825 across the state of New York from Albany to Buffalo, thus overcoming the Appalachian Mountains as a barrier to trade between the eastern United States and the newly opened western United States. The economic impact of the Erie Canal was tremendous. It reduced the cost of shipping a tonne of cargo between Buffalo and New York City from about $100 per tonne (over the Appalachians) to $4 per tonne (through the canal).

The Panama Canal, constructed from 1881 to 1914 to connect the Atlantic and Pacific Oceans through the Isthmus of Panama, is only about 50 miles long, but its construction presented tremendous challenges because of the soil, the terrain, and the tropical illnesses that killed many workers. Upon its completion, however, the Panama Canal reduced the travel distance from New York City to San Francisco by about 9,000 miles.

When the Hoover Dam was built from 1931 to 1936 on the Colorado River at the Colorado-Arizona border, it was the world's largest dam, at a height of 726 feet and crest length of 1,224 feet. The technique of passing chilled water through pipes enclosed in the concrete to cool the newly poured concrete and speed its curing was developed for the construction of the Hoover Dam and is still in use. The Grand Coulee Dam, in the state of Washington, was the largest hydrolectric project in the world when it was built in the 1930s. It has an output of 10,080 megawatts. The Itaipu Dam, on the Parana River, along the border of Brazil and Paraguay, is also one of the largest hydroelectric dams in the world. It began operation in 1984 and is capable of producing 13,320 megawatts.

Dikes, dams, and similar structures have been used for centuries around the world for protection against flooding. The largest sea barrier in the world is a two-mile-long surge barrier in the Oosterschelde estuary of the Netherlands, constructed from 1958 to 1986. Called the Dutch Delta Plan, the purpose of this project was to reduce the danger of catastrophic flooding. The impetus that brought this project to fruition was a catastrophic flood in the area in 1953.

A major part of the barrier design consists of sixty-five huge concrete piers, weighing in at 18,000 tons each. These piers support tremendous 400-ton steel gates to create the sea barrier. The lifting and placement of these huge concrete piers exceeded the capabilities of any existing cranes, so a special U-shaped ship was built and equipped with gantry cranes. The project used computers to help in guidance and placement of the piers. A stabilizing foundation used for the concrete piers consists of foundation mattresses made up of layers of sand, fine gravel, and coarse gravel. Each foundation mattress is more than 1 foot thick and more than 650 feet by 140 feet, with a smaller mattress placed on top.

IMPACT ON INDUSTRY

In view of its status as the second-oldest engineering discipline and the essential nature of the type of work done by civil engineers, civil engineering is well established as an important field of engineering around the world. Civil engineering is the largest field of engineering in the United States.

Consulting engineering firms. This is the largest sector of employment for civil engineers. There are many consulting engineering firms around the world, ranging in size from small firms with a few employees to very large firms with thousands of employees. In 2010, the Engineering News Record identified the top six US design firms: AECOM Technology (Los Angeles); URS (San Francisco); Jacobs (Pasadena, California); Fluor (Irving, Texas); CH2M Hill (Englewood, Colorado); and Bechtel (San Francisco). Many consulting engineering firms have some electrical engineers and mechanical engineers, and some even specialize in those areas; however, a large proportion of engineering consulting firms are made up predominantly of civil engineers. About 60 percent of American civil engineers are employed by consulting engineering firms.

Construction firms. Although some consulting engineering firms design and construct their own projects, some companies specialize in constructing projects designed by another firm. These companies also use civil engineers. About 8 percent of American civil engineers are employed in the nonresident building construction sector.

Other industries. Some civil engineers are employed in industry, but less than 1 percent of American civil engineers are employed in an industry other than consulting firms and construction firms. The industry sectors that hire the most civil engineers are oil and gas extraction and pipeline companies.

Government agencies and military. Civil engineers work for many federal, state, and local government agencies. For example, the US Department of Transportation uses civil engineers to handle its many highway and other transportation projects. Many road or highway projects are handled at the state level, and each state department of transportation employs many civil engineers. The US Corps of Engineers and the Department of the Interior's Bureau of Reclamation employ many civil engineers for their many water resources projects. Many cities and counties have one or more civil engineers as city or county engineers, and many have civil engineers in their public works departments.

The military has about 7,200 civil engineers. On average, the armed services need about 350 more each year. Newly commissioned civil engineers usually assist senior engineering officers in planning and design. With experience, they may manage construction projects and, eventually, engineering offices. In time, they may advance to senior management or command positions in the engineering field. Duties and responsibilities may typically include the direct surveying of construction areas; the planning and of temporary facilities for emergency use; the management of master plans for purposes of facility updating for military bases; and the selection of contractors for facility construction.

Academic research and teaching. Because civil engineering is the largest field of engineering, almost every college of engineering has a civil engineering department, leading to a continuing demand for civil engineering faculty members to teach the next generation of civil engineers and to conduct sponsored research projects. This applies to universities not only in the United States but also around the world.

SOCIAL CONTEXT AND FUTURE PROSPECTS

Civil engineering projects typically involve basic infrastructure needs such as roads and highways, water supply, wastewater treatment, bridges, and public buildings. These projects may be new construction or repair, maintenance or upgrading of existing highways, structures, and treatment facilities. The buildup of such infrastructure since the beginning of the twentieth century has been extensive, leading to a continuing need for the repair, maintenance, and upgrading of existing structures. Also, governments tend to devote funding to infrastructure improvements to generate jobs and create economic activity during economic downturns. All of this leads to the projection for a continuing strong need for civil engineers.

SOME INTERESTING FACTS ABOUT CIVIL ENGINEERING

The Johnstown Flood in Pennsylvania, on May 31, 1889, which killed more than 2,200 people, was the result of the catastrophic failure of the South Fork Dam. The dam, built in 1852, held back Lake Conemaugh and was made of clay, boulders, and dirt. An improperly maintained spillway combined with heavy rains caused the collapse.

The I-35W bridge over the Mississippi River in Minneapolis, Minnesota, collapsed during rush-hour traffic on August 1, 2007, causing 13 deaths and 145 injuries. The collapse was blamed on undersized gusset plates, an increase in the concrete surface load, and the weight of construction supplies and equipment on the bridge.

On November 7, 1940, 42-mile-per-hour winds twisted the Tacoma Narrows Bridge over the Puget Sound in Washington state and caused its collapse. The bridge, with a central span of 2,800 feet, had been completed just four months earlier. Steel girders meant to support the bridge were blocking the wind, causing it to sway and eventually collapse.

Low-quality concrete and incorrectly placed rebar led to shear failure, collapsing the Highway 19 overpass in Laval, Quebec, on September 30, 2006.

The first design for the Gateway Arch in St. Louis, Missouri, had a fatal flaw that made it unstable at the required height. The final design used 886 tons of stainless steel, making it a very expensive structure.

On January 9, 1999, just three years after it was built, the Rainbow Bridge, a pedestrian bridge across the Qi River in Sichuan Province, collapsed, killing 40 people and injuring 14. Concrete used in the bridge was weak, parts of it were rusty, and parts had been improperly welded.

—*Michael P. Auerbach*

Further Reading

Arteaga, Robert R. *The Building of the Arch*. 10th ed., Jefferson National Parks Association, 2002.

Braham, Andrew, and Sadie Casillas. *Fundamentals of Sustainability in Civil Engineering*. 2nd ed., CRC Press/Taylor & Francis Group, 2020.

Davidson, Frank Paul, and Kathleen Lusk-Brooke, comps. *Building the World: An Encyclopedia of the Great Engineering Projects in History*. Greenwood, 2006.

Jayasree, P. K., K. Balan, and V. Rani. *Practical Civil Engineering*. CRC Press, 2021.

Labi, Samuel. *Introduction to Civil Engineering Systems: A Systems Perspective to the Development of Civil Engineering Facilities*. John Wiley & Sons, 2014.

Mosher, Daniel. *Civil Engineering Basics: Water, Wastewater, and Stormwater Conveyance*. CreateSpace Independent Publishing Platform, 2018.

Weingardt, Richard G. *Engineering Legends: Great American Civil Engineers: Thirty-Two Profiles of Inspiration and Achievement*. American Society of Civil Engineers, 2005.

See also: Aerodynamics; Angular forces; Archimedes; Circular motion; Classical or applied mechanics; Computer-aided engineering; Earthquake engineering; Engineering; Engineering tolerances; Force (physics); Friction; Hydraulic engineering; Load; Materials science; Newton's laws; Structural engineering; Transportation

CLASSICAL OR APPLIED MECHANICS

Fields of Study: Physics; Mechanics; Mathematics

ABSTRACT

An ancient branch of the physical sciences with roots at the foundations of Western scientific thought, mechanics has applications in a variety of modern scientific fields. Classical mechanics studies the physical laws and forces that govern the movements and interactions of objects; it covers the motion and behavior of all bodies, from celestial to biological and engineered. Applied mechanics is the branch of physics and engineering that studies the practical and engineering applications of principles of classical mechanics.

KEY CONCEPTS

acceleration: the increase in velocity over a period of time; going faster

angular velocity: the rate of change of position of a body moving in a circle, commonly measured in rotations per minute

force: a nonphysical manifestation that has the potential to interact with physical matter to cause either attraction or repulsion; generally, the effect of pressure per unit area such as pounds per square inch

function: a mathematical expression describing an actual relationship between two or more entities represented by mathematical variables

kinetic energy: the energy possessed by a mass by virtue of being in motion

momentum: a property of mass related to the movement of that mass, characterized by the tendency of a mass to remain in motion or motionless unless acted upon by a force, and defined as the product of mass and velocity

BASIC PRINCIPLES

English physicist and mathematician Isaac Newton is known as the father of mechanics for his formulation of the laws of motion, first published in his book *Philosophiae Mathematica Principia Naturalis* (1687). Newton's laws laid the foundation for the modern scientific understanding of motion using mathematical analysis. Newton also formulated one of the first scientific theories of gravitation, which became the foundation for the scientific understanding of planetary movement and Earth's orbit around the Sun.

Between the seventeenth century and the twentieth century, the principles of mechanics were reformulated by leading mathematicians, creating new approaches to mechanical analysis that are still used. French mathematician Joseph-Louis Lagrange presented the first important reformulation of Newtonian mechanics in the 1780s; fifty years later, Irish mathematician William Hamilton presented a reformulation of Lagrange's work that helped to connect classical mechanics with the movement of atoms and molecules. In the twentieth century, physicists developed quantum mechanics to study the motion and behavior of fundamental particles; this soon became the other major branch of mechanics, alongside classical mechanics.

In the twenty-first century, classical mechanics continues to provide the basis for the physical understanding of motion. It has been divided into numerous subfields, including celestial mechanics, which studies the motion of celestial bodies; continuum mechanics, which studies the behaviors of continuous materials; and statistical mechanics, which studies the thermodynamic and mechanical principles of individual molecules and atoms and how those principles translate into the observable behaviors of physical bodies.

CORE CONCEPTS

Newtonian mechanics. Newton's three laws of motion describe the fundamental forces acting upon bodies in motion and define the mathematical relationships between these fundamental forces and observed patterns of movement.

The first law states that an object does not change in its state of either rest or motion unless acted upon by an outside force. Therefore, if an object is at rest, it will remain at rest unless some external force compels it to move; similarly, a moving object will continue moving in the same direction and at the same speed unless its motion is changed by another force. The first law also defines the concept of inertia, which is defined as an object's tendency to resist changes in momentum or motion.

The second law defines the concept of force, describing it as equal to the change in an object's momentum of movement. Momentum can be understood as the product of an object's mass multiplied by its velocity, or speed of movement through space. In essence, the second law says that the acceleration of an object through space will be proportional to the force exerted on the object. A greater force will result in greater acceleration.

The third law is often summarized with the phrase "for every action, there is an equal and opposite reaction." In terms of mechanical movement, the law states that when two bodies exert force on one another, the reactions of both objects are equal in terms of intensity but opposite in terms of direction. Reaction engines, such as those that power the flight of jet aircraft and rockets, are based on this principle, using the opposing force created by the firing of jet thrusters to propel an object through space.

Measurement techniques. Research in classical mechanics relies on methods and tools used to measure the variables that contribute to patterns of movement. Physicists and engineers work together to develop measurement methods and equipment used to derive values for these parameters.

Velocity measurements are generally completed using laser or radar measurements, which gauge velocity by measuring the distance traveled by an object over time. Alternatively, high-speed cameras can be used to measure velocity.

Mass measurements can be conducted by using scales to gauge an object's weight, which can then be compared to the object's size and volume. The mass of gasses and liquids can be obtained using specialized equipment such as a thermal conductivity detector, which estimates the mass of a sample of gas by measuring thermal conductivity compared to a sample of gas with a known mass.

Force measurements are generally conducted using force gauges, which are devices that can translate the force placed on a target sensor into electric signals that provide a digital readout of the force applied.

Acceleration is measured using an accelerometer, an electrochemical device that works by translating the "squeezing" force applied to the device during acceleration into electric signals that can be used to measure the intensity of the movement. Accelerometers can be used to measure both the vibration of an object and its dynamic or directional acceleration.

Differential equations. Differential equations are mathematical formulations that relate to the differential of a quantity, that is, how quickly the quantity changes with respect to another quantity. Differential equations begin with a function, which is a mathematical process that can be used to yield a certain value. Solving a differential equation yields a different function that describes the relationship between the original function and one or more derivatives. A partial differential equation is a differential equation in which there is more than one independent variable used in the formulation of the equation.

The theory and mathematical processes behind differential equations are central to the study of physics and mechanics. Newton's second law of motion, for example, is based on mathematical formulations using differential equations. Differential equations also form the basis for the scientific understanding of fluid dynamics, which is an important topic in mechanics. A variety of naturally occurring processes, including atmospheric airflow, heat transfer between Earth and its atmosphere, and the movement of ocean currents, can be described and analyzed using differential equations.

Gravity and gravitational theory. Newton also contributed to mechanics the formulation of the laws of gravitation, which explain how gravity affects bodies in motion. Newton's law of universal gravitation describes the attraction between two bodies with mass as being both proportional to the product of the masses of the two bodies and inversely proportional to the square of the distance between them.

Newton's theory of universal gravitation was later replaced by Albert Einstein's theory of general relativity, which says that gravity is a result of a curvature in space-time that results from the mass of an object distorting space and time in the object's vicinity.

While the theoretical basis for the gravitational effect was altered by the introduction of Einstein's theory of general relativity, the equations that Newton derived to explain the gravitational attraction of bodies are still used in calculations of physical relationships. Accurate calculations of gravitational relationships are important to a number of scientific fields, including astrophysics and engineering.

Mechanical work and thermodynamics. In thermodynamics physics, work is defined as the product of a given force and the distance over which the force takes effect. The concept of work in physics is closely linked to the concept of energy and the equations of thermodynamics, which explain the relationship between matter and energy. Equations governing work in physics also must consider any countering forces that act against the direction of the initial force. For example, to model the distance a bullet will fly when fired from a gun, physicists need to know the initial force applied to the bullet, the gravitational drag on the bullet as the result of the mass of the earth, and the viscosity of the atmosphere through which the bullet is traveling.

Physicists and engineers use the basic equations governing the physical principle of work to calculate the movement of a variety of objects. Aerospace engineers, for example, calculate variables including force, gravity, torque, and displacement to map the trajectory of aircraft, satellites, and other objects propelled through space. Equations related to work are also used in the biological sciences to calculate and model physical movements, producing equations that relate the use of energy to the amount of physical activity that can be completed in a certain situation.

Continuum mechanics. Continuum mechanics is a subfield of classical and applied mechanics that deals with the behavior of bodies that are modeled as continuous materials, rather than discrete objects. Among the most important subfields of continuum mechanics are the fields of fluid mechanics and fluid dynamics, which study the behavior of liquids and gases, for example. A variety of specific measurement and analysis techniques have been developed for research into fluid and continuum mechanics, including wind tunnels, which allow researchers to model the behavior of airflow and wind currents, and laser Doppler velocimetry (LDV), which uses the reflection of laser beams to measure the speed of a moving liquid.

APPLICATIONS PAST AND PRESENT

Celestial mapping and exploration. The modern science of astronomy was built on the understanding of gravity and orbital motion planetary motion developed through classical mechanics research. Newton used his laws of motion and his concept of universal gravitation to complete some of the earliest mathematical models of planetary motion. Lagrange, one of the other major figures in the development of classical mechanics, also applied mechanical principles to orbital movement.

The orbital path of a planet can be represented by a mathematical formula relating the planet's mass to the mass of other astronomical bodies, such as stars, moons, and other planets, to calculate the gravitational pull acting on each body. Further mechanics formulations can be used to represent elliptical orbits and other variations in orbital path based on the gravitational interaction of multiple objects. The behavior of stars and planets as a result of gravitational fluctuations can also be used to study objects in distant solar systems. For example, scientists use variations in the movement of distant planets to detect which planets are surrounded by orbiting moons. Similarly, distant stars exhibit variations in movement when they are orbited by planets, and astronomers can use these minor variations in movement to map other solar systems.

In addition, classical mechanics is used extensively in engineering satellites and spacecraft for space exploration. The design of propulsion systems for rockets and shuttles is based directly on classical mechanics models of force, inertia, acceleration, and other factors that influence bodies in motion through the fluid of the atmosphere. Mechanics specialists also help to plot the trajectory of spacecraft to achieve orbit around Earth or other planets. For a spacecraft to achieve orbit around a planet or satellite, it is necessary to calculate precisely the angle of entry and approach that will be needed to compensate for gravitational pull and will allow the spacecraft to maintain orbital distance from a planet.

Sports engineering. The design of baseball bats, golf balls, hockey pucks, and footballs is based on engineering that utilizes principles of classical mechanics. For example, the path of a golf ball is determined by energy imparted from the club as it impacts the surface of the ball. As the ball makes its way through the air, its trajectory is determined by the angle of impact, the spin of the ball, and a variety of other factors, including wind speed and direction. The depressions on the surface of a golf ball are designed to reduce drag on the ball by altering the reducing turbulence on the leading edge and therefore increasing initial lift. Engineer William Taylor utilized equations from aerodynamics research to invent the dimpled surface design for modern golf balls. Classical dynamics equations can be used to model each aspect of a golf stroke, from the position of the player's body and angle of swing to the ultimate speed, path, and movement of the ball as it travels through the air.

Another example of applied mechanics in sports engineering is the design of shoes for various types of sporting activities. In recreational and professional running, for example, the soles of the shoes must be designed in such a way that they produce friction in contact with the ground surface, so that runners can push away from the ground to gain momentum. However, if the soles produce excess friction, runners will not be able to alternate steps quickly. Equations derived from mechanics research can be used to model the forces and countering forces involved in the impact of shoes against different types of surfaces. Using this data, engineers can attempt to mold the soles of shoes in such a way as to maximize initial friction while still allowing for rapid alternation of steps.

Hydraulic engineering. Hydraulics is a field of engineering that utilizes the principles of continuum or fluid dynamics for a variety of applications. Hydraulic engineers design methods of extracting energy from fluids by utilizing pressure and heat to produce potential energy, which can then be harvested to produce electric or mechanical energy. One example is the hydraulic pump, a machine that pressurizes and transports liquid through a system of tubes and reservoirs. The pressurized liquid can be used to complete mechanical work, such as turning a rotor or powering the movement of another object. In some applications, hydraulic pumps can be used to

power the generation of electricity by transitioning the mechanical energy in the pressurized liquid into electric energy through a generator.

Another application of hydraulic engineering is the design of hydroelectric dams or wave-power generators. Hydroelectric dams that do not have a naturally supplied reservoir behind them may use hydraulic pumps to fill a reservoir with water such that the water has potential energy based on the gravitational forces pulling it to the surface. The gravitational and potential energy of the water in the filled reservoir can then be used to rotate turbines connected to an electric generator. In this way, the rotation of Earth, represented by gravitational forces, can be used to generate electric power. Similarly, wave-power generators use hydraulic pumps and rotary generators to translate the kinetic energy in the movement of waves into electric currents. Wave power is an emerging area of research that has the potential to become a major avenue of future energy development.

Materials science. Materials science and engineering is the branch of classical mechanics research that studies the mechanical properties of various materials, especially with regard to the effects of motion and stress on material components. Thousands of practical applications have emerged from materials science, including the design and composition of automobile frames and bodies and refinements in the shape and structure of airplane wings. Materials-science specialists may study the way that different types of materials deform when subjected to pressure from airflow, for example. This data can be used to enhance the aerodynamic qualities of various vehicles or projectiles. Alternatively, physicists specializing in materials research may investigate the effects of increasing pressure on different materials, which can be used to refine designs used for submersible objects or pipes used in hydraulic engineering.

The design of "smart" materials provides a modern example of materials-science applications. Smart materials are materials that respond to certain external stimuli by undergoing a change in properties. For example, engineers and physicists are working on a variety of "self-healing" materials that automatically correct for minor damage caused by wear and mechanical stress. The design of self-healing materials generally involves utilizing polymers with chemical agents that can re-form chemical and physical bonds broken as a result of stress. While self-healing materials is a relatively new branch of research, there are thousands of potential applications in engineering, biomedical research, and commercial technology. Another example of smart-materials research is the development of thermoelectric technology, or materials that can convert changes in temperature into electric signals. The development of thermoelectric materials has the potential to majorly impact the energy industry, allowing engineers to create more efficient methods of harvesting energy from heat sources, such as solar or geothermal radiation.

SOCIAL CONTEXT AND FUTURE PROSPECTS
Classical and applied mechanics are fundamental to the modern scientific understanding of the world. In modern science, mechanics specialists rarely concentrate solely on classical mechanics, tending instead to specialize in one or more subfields. Because mechanics is applicable to a wide variety of scientific fields and engineering projects, research into basic mechanics still plays an important role in technological development and research.

Modern research in physics often falls into the category referred to as multiphysics, which is the application of methods or models from multiple disciplines to create models of complex phenomena. The theoretical and practical innovations of classical mechanics research are being combined with other forms of scientific inquiry and other models of physics to create innovative research techniques. The future of applied physics lies partially in the modern blending of theoretical models.

A relatively recent development in physics research involves the investigation of nonlinear dynamic systems, sometimes called chaotic systems. Such systems appear random in behavior but can be analyzed using complex models and equations that account for subtle variables in initial conditions and track how changes in these variables lead to overall system-wide behaviors. The principles of classical mechanics are essential to the modern understanding of chaotic-systems behavior and help scientists to devise methods used to model complex systems for enhanced predictability. Examples of chaotic systems found in nature include atmospheric gas flow, population dynamics of organisms, and the activity of the brain.

—*Gina Hagler*

Further Reading
Benacquista, Matthew J., and Joseph D. Romano. *Classical Mechanics*. Springer, 2018.

Finn, John Michael. *Classical Mechanics*. Jones, 2009.

Kibble, Tom W. B., and Frank H. Berkshire. *Classical Mechanics*. 5th ed., World Scientific, 2004.

Knauf, Andreas. *Mathematical Physics: Classical Mechanics*. Translated by Jochen Denzler. Springer, 2018.

McCall, Martin. *Classical Mechanics: From Newton to Einstein; A Modern Introduction*. Wiley, 2011.

Morin, David. *Introduction to Classical Mechanics: With Problems and Solutions*. Cambridge UP, 2008.

Youssef, George. *Applied Mechanics of Polymers: Properties, Processing, and Behavior*. Elsevier, 2021.

See also: Acceleration; Aerodynamics; Aeronautical engineering; Angular forces; Angular momentum; Automated processes and servomechanisms; Bernoulli's principle; Biomechanics; Biomedical engineering; Calculating system efficiency; Calculus; Celestial mechanics; Chaotic systems; Circular motion; Civil engineering; Computer-aided engineering; Differential equations; Dynamics (mechanics); Elasticity; Electromagnetism; Engineering; Euler's laws of motion; Fluid dynamics; Force (physics); Friction; Heat transfer; Hydraulic engineering; Kinematics; Kinetic energy; Lagrange, Joseph-Louis; Laplace, Pierre-Simon; Leibnitz, Gottfried Wilhelm; Magnetism; Mechanical engineering; Mechatronics; Moment of inertia; Momentum (physics); Motion; Nanotechnology; Newton's laws; Plasticity (physics); Projectiles; Quantum mechanics; Robotics; Structural engineering; Thermodynamics; Torque; Vacuum technology; Vectors; Velocity; Work and energy

CLAUSIUS FORMULATES THE SECOND LAW OF THERMODYNAMICS

Fields of Study: Physics; Biomechanics; Physiology; Mathematics

ABSTRACT

Rudolf Clausius's second law of thermodynamics states that entropy in a system tends to increase. Along with his insights into the first law of thermodynamics, Clausius's formulation of the second law established the foundation for modern thermodynamics. It also had profound effects upon the nineteenth-century imagination, because it predicted the "heat death" of the universe.

KEY CONCEPTS

heat engine: a device that converts the energy of heat into mechanical energy or motion

temperature reservoir: a contained mass of matter that can store heat, such as hot water that has condensed from steam and may then be used to regenerate steam without a large input of energy from an external source

thermodynamics: the study of the interaction of heat and energy with matter

THE LAWS OF THERMODYNAMICS

First law, Conservation of Energy. Energy is neither created nor destroyed; it simply changes from one form to another. Although energy can be changed into different forms, the total energy of an isolated system remains the same.

Second law, Entropy and Irreversibility. Energy available after a chemical reaction is less than that available at the beginning of the reaction; energy conversions are not completely efficient. Also, the natural tendency is for heat to flow from hot bodies to cold bodies and not the reverse.

Third law, Nernst Heat Theorem. It is impossible to reach a temperature of absolute zero; close to that temperature, matter exhibits no disorder; if one could reach absolute zero, all bodies would have the same entropy, or zero-point energy.

SUMMARY

While yet a young man, Rudolf Clausius developed the ability to think clearly, organize ideas, and see through the confusion that typically accompanies difficult problems. After entering the University of Berlin in 1840, Clausius decided to pursue a degree in physics and mathematics. In 1848, he earned his doctorate in physics from the University of Halle and became interested in the mechanical theory of heat. The 1840s were a time of great interest in thermodynamics, the study of the relationship between heat and other forms of energy. Around 1842, James Prescott Joule and Julius Robert von Mayer had discovered the first law of thermodynamics, or conservation of energy, which was confirmed by Hermann von Helmholtz in 1847. In 1850, Clausius published a paper in *Annalen der Physik* (*Annals of Physics*) that analyzed the relationship between heat, work, and other thermodynamic variables.

Prior to the appearance of Clausius's paper in 1850, the theory of heat, known as the caloric theory, was based on two fundamental premises: The heat in the universe is conserved, and the heat in a material depends on the state of that material. Pierre-Simon Laplace, Siméon-Denis Poisson, Sadi Carnot, and Émile Clapeyron had all developed thermodynamic concepts and relationships that were based upon the assumptions of the caloric theory. By reformulating the first law of thermodynamics using the concept of the internal energy of a system, Clausius showed in his 1850 paper that both assumptions of the caloric theory were incorrect. He stated additionally that the natural tendency is for heat to flow from hot bodies to cold bodies and not the reverse. This was the first published statement of what became known as the second law of thermodynamics. Although the idea seems rather obvious for heat flow that occurs through the process of conduction, the principle stated by Clausius goes much further, asserting that no process whatever can occur that is in conflict with the second law. His 1850 paper was monumental in the development of thermodynamics. It replaced the caloric theory of heat with the first and second laws of thermodynamics, laying the foundation for modern thermodynamics.

Rudolf Clausius. Photo via Wikimedia Commons. [Public domain.]

Between 1850 and 1865, Clausius published an additional eight papers that applied and clarified the second law of thermodynamics. One of his first applications was to the efficiency of a heat engine. A heat engine is any device that absorbs heat from a higher temperature source, or reservoir, converts part of that energy into useful work, and dumps the rest to a lower temperature reservoir. Steam engines are a prime example. In 1824, Carnot had derived an equation for the efficiency of a simple heat engine based strictly on the first law of thermodynamics. In the 1850s, Clausius determined the restrictions on the efficiency of a heat engine by also invoking the second law in the calculation of efficiency. He showed that the upper limit to the thermal efficiency of any heat engine is always less than one. He concluded that it is impossible to construct any device that will produce no effect other than the transfer of heat from a colder to a hotter body when it operates through a complete cycle. The consequence is that heat energy cannot be converted completely into mechanical energy by any heat engine.

Through his applications of the second law to heat engines and other thermodynamic systems, Clausius deduced that processes in nature are irreversible, always proceeding in a certain direction. This phenomenon is analogous to time only moving forward and not in reverse. Since it is impossible for a heat engine or any other system completely to convert the heat that it absorbs into mechanical work, the system cannot return to the same state in which it began. Clausius concluded that, since a system irrevocably lost some of its potential energy whenever it converted that energy from heat to work, the disorder of that system and its surroundings increased in the process. In a heat engine, for example, the particles that constitute the system are initially sorted into hotter and colder regions of space. This sorting, or ordering, is lost when the system performs work and thermal equilibrium is established.

Since the key word in the first law of thermodynamics was "energy," Clausius wanted to find a similar word to characterize the second law. He settled on the word "entropy," which originates from a Greek word meaning transformation and which he coined in a paper published in 1865. The word describes the increasing disorder endemic to natural processes. Clausius determined an equation that related entropy to heat and temperature. He then used entropy as a quantitative measure to determine the disorder or randomness of a system. In his 1865 paper, he restated the second law of thermodynamics in essentially the following form: the entropy of a system interacting with its surroundings always increases.

As revealed in the second law of thermodynamics, then, every event that occurs in the world results in a net increase in entropy. Although energy is conserved, useful energy is not, and an increase in entropy means a reduction in the ordered energy available for doing work in the future. The second law of thermodynamics is of utmost importance, since it imposes practical restrictions on the design and operation of numerous important systems, including gasoline and diesel engines in motorized vehicles, jet engines in airplanes, steam turbines in electric power plants, refrigerators, air conditioners, heat pumps, and the human body.

SIGNIFICANCE

Since energy conversion is an essential aspect of human technology and of all plant and animal life, thermodynamics is of fundamental importance in the world. The work of Clausius in formulating the second law of thermodynamics laid the framework for modern thermodynamics. The practical significance of his formulation of the second law was recognized on several occasions during his lifetime. He was elected to the Royal Society of London in 1868 and received the Huygens Medal in 1870, the Copley Medal in 1879, and the Poncelet Prize in 1883.

Baron Kelvin, who was also instrumental in the development of thermodynamics, pointed out that the principles of heat engines were first correctly established by applying Clausius's second law of thermodynamics and his statement of the first law of thermodynamics. The contributions of Clausius to thermodynamics also formed the basis for future interpretations of the second law of thermodynamics by Ludwig Eduard Boltzmann and others in terms of probability, which led to the development of the field of statistical mechanics.

Several scientific discoveries of the nineteenth century had philosophical implications that questioned the place of humanity in the universe. The scandal caused by Charles Darwin's theory of evolution, which seemed to question the biblical theory of Creation, is still well known today. Less remembered is the similar crisis caused by the second law of thermodynamics. Before Clausius's discovery, the universe could, in theory, be eternal. The second law of thermodynamics, however, suggested that the universe must someday end: It predicted what came to be referred to as the "heat death" of the universe.

The fields of modern thermodynamics and statistical mechanics, which evolved from the work of Clausius and other prominent scientists, provide immense insight into how the everyday world works, with applications to engineering, biology, meteorology, electronics, and many other disciplines. The operation of engines and the limits on their efficiencies, the operation of refrigerators and the limits on their coefficients of performance and energy efficiency ratings (EER), the function of semiconductors in solid-state circuits as a function of temperature, and the analytical aspects of the human body operating as a thermodynamic engine or fuel cell are all based upon Clausius's formulation of the second law of thermodynamics and his statement of the first law of thermodynamics. Energy-conversion research and the development of alternative energy resources, including solar energy systems, biomass systems, and nuclear power plants, are also dependent upon an understanding and application of Clausius's insights into thermodynamic processes and the fundamental laws that govern them.

—*Alvin K. Benson*

Further Reading

Attard, Phil. *Entropy Beyond the Second Law: Thermodynamics and Statistical Mechanics for Equilibrium, Non-equilibrium, Classical and Quantum Systems*. Institute of Physics Publishing, 2018.

Ben-Naim, Arieh. *Entropy Demystified: The Second Law Reduced to Plain Common Sense*. World Scientific, 2008.

———. *Discover Entropy and the Second Law of Thermodynamics: A Playful Way of Discovering a Law of Nature*. World Scientific, 2010.

Cardwell, D. S. L. *From Watt to Clausius: The Rise of Thermodynamics in the Early Industrial Age*. Cornell UP, 1971.

Chang, Raymond. *Physical Chemistry for the Biosciences*. University Science Books, 2005.

Sandler, Stanley I. *Chemical and Engineering Thermodynamics*. John Wiley & Sons, 1998.

Trefil, James, and Robert M. Hazen. *The Sciences: An Integrated Approach*. John Wiley & Sons, 2003.

See also: Chaotic systems; Heat transfer; Potential energy; Thermodynamics; Work and energy; Work-energy theorem

COMPUTER-AIDED ENGINEERING

Fields of Study: Physics; Mechanics; Mathematics

ABSTRACT

Computer-aided engineering (CAE), sometimes known as computer-assisted engineering, is a computational adjunct to computer-aided design (CAD). CAD programs are used to generate a detailed technical drawing or model that specifies the shape and dimensions of an object. CAE software is used to carry out computations of properties of the object in the CAD drawing. CAD and CAE applications are often part of the same program.

KEY CONCEPTS

additive machining: processes such as welding and three-dimensional (3D) printing that add material to a workpiece

blueprint: an engineering drawing form named for the specific blue-colored paper used for finished architectural drawings

multiphysics analysis: the process of analyzing the different physics principles involved in the engineering process and their effects and limiting characteristics regarding the particular engineering project

three-dimensional (3D) printing: a method of constructing objects from liquefied materials by extruding them in a set pattern that allows the object to be constructed layer by layer. The method is derived from the operating principle of ink-jet printers, and has been used with items ranging from small-scale plastic objects to welded metal objects to full-size concrete house foundations and other structures. The method is particularly suitable for producing prototypes and one-off items.

CAD, CAM, AND CAE

In 1957, Dr. Patrick Hanratty produced the first functional application of computer-controlled machine operation in the form of computer numerical control, or CNC. A programmable CNC controller uses a specified set of instructions based on data from the specifications in the appropriate technical drawing. CNC programming required a human user to compose the program, a step-by-step set of explicit instructions that direct the movement of machine parts in operation. This elementary step by Hanratty had the potential to be augmented and expanded, and as computer technology and software developed, the means was found to combine electronic drawing software with CNC controllers in such a way that specifications could be transferred directly from one to the other. The drawing software

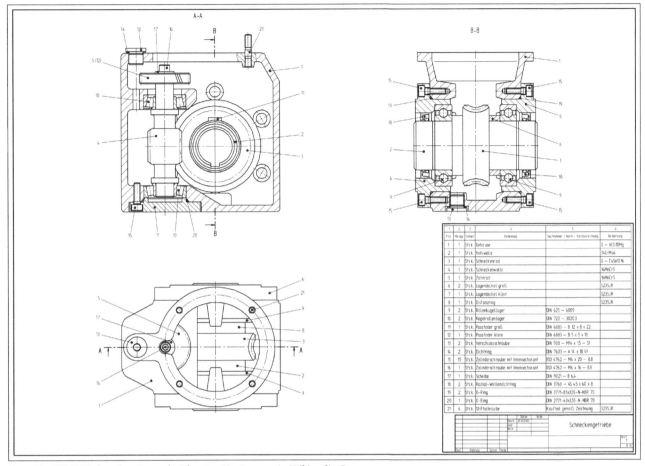

Example: 2D CAD drawing. Image by Thorsten Hartmann, via Wikimedia Commons.

is the basis of computer-aided design (CAD) and, by extension, of computer-aided engineering (CAE).

The technical drawing is the first major step in the engineering of an actual product, as it documents the specifications to which the object is to conform. This is where computer-assisted engineering plays its role. Underlying the actual creation of the object in the technical drawing are a great many property values and engineering factors that must be computed based on the desired performance of the object and the specifications assigned to it. These include physical factors such as load distributions, strain, compression, tension, deformation under load, and many others. CAE software uses the CAD data, along with direct user input—such as ma-

terial properties, thermal expansion rates, rotational speed, conductivity, and other properties that describe the object's response to the environment to which it will be exposed—to compute the object's expected behavior in operation. Computed values from the CAE software can, and often do, reveal weaknesses in the design of the object as its specifications were presented, which thus allows the designer to improve the design by adjusting various specifications.

ENGINEERING DESIGN

There are essentially four stages to the engineering process. The process begins with the definition of the particular engineering problem and a clear definition of what the engineered product is meant to achieve in order to solve the engineering problem. The second stage is the creative process, in which designers and engineers collaborate to ideate the form that the product might take. In the third stage of the process, the proposed product is subjected to critical analysis that may involve multiple product solutions and their evaluation, an area in which generative design software may be useful. This is the stage at which CAE software is used by engineers to evaluate the parameters and characteristics of the proposed product. The fourth and final stage of the process is prototype development and testing. In many cases, a prototype object can be produced by three-dimensional (3D) printing or another method of rapid prototyping. The working prototype constitutes the proof of concept for the solution to the engineering problem defined in the first stage of the engineering process.

There are many branches of engineering: chemical, electrical, mechanical, architectural, automotive, aeronautical, and civil, to name just a few. There are also many subbranches within each discipline. Chemical engineering, for example, includes biochemical engineering, and electrical engineering includes computer and software engineering. CAE is an applicable technology in all branches of engineering, though it is more prevalent in some than in others. CAE itself can be broken down into distinct application sectors. Mechanical CAE (MCAE), for example, is software used to simulate the performance or production methodology of a mechanical component, assembly, or product, and enable improvement of those entities. Circuit design and virtual testing carried out with electronic computer-aided design (ECAD) software with the appropriate simulation capabilities qualifies as electrical, or electronic, CAE (ECAE). Similarly, CAE software that simulates the design and operation of a chemical or biochemical production facility and computes numerical values for the different stages

of its operation corresponds to chemical CAE (CCAE). Accordingly, CAE software can be written specifically for a particular branch or subbranch of engineering without being generally applicable, although having specialized applications as modules within a general CAE software package is a more efficient approach.

A CLOSER LOOK AT MCAE AND CAE IN GENERAL

MCAE has the same basic purposes as all CAE programs: to simulate and improve the performance of concept designs, as well as of detailed designs; to confirm the performance of designs prior to prototyping and testing (a vitally important function, especially in architectural engineering); and to identify and address failure of a design as part of root cause analysis. Beyond this, specialized CAE software computes factors specific to its associated discipline. MCAE computes structural, kinematic and dynamic, vibrational, thermal, fluid, manufacturing, and multiphysics analyses of mechanical objects, each of which comprises a number of factors unique to the particular analysis. ECAE computes such factors as thermal response, gain fluctuation, hysteresis, magnetic susceptibility, and other factors affecting the performance of electronic circuitry. Other specific applied CAE software programs compute similar analyses corresponding to their particular fields of application. Not the least consideration, CAE software applications also compute cost analyses.

MCAE and other CAE software programs use preprocessor modules to carry out mathematical solutions of prepared simulation models that are termed solvers. A solver is a prewritten model that has been contrived specifically to be put through the solution process. The results of the solved simulations are then put through test modules called "postprocessors."

The performance of a design can be improved in a CAE program through automated functions. In a sensitivity study, for example, one component of a design such as a physical dimension or a material property is varied, and the effect of that variation on the performance of the design is monitored. This analysis measures how sensitive the performance of the design is to changes in a particular parameter. Thermal expansion, for example, changes the overall dimensions of an object in its working environment, and with the close tolerances allowed in engineered products, it is important to know just how a change in physical dimension would affect the performance of that product in real world applications. Sensitivity analysis allows the design engineer to adjust parameters to improve and optimize the performance of the design.

In an optimization study, improvement of the design with respect to a particular goal is an automated process. The desired goal of an optimization study generally is to improve the overall performance of a design by automatically varying individual design parameters and comparing performance with each variation. In a design-of-experiment study, the software changes several variables in the design and records the analysis of each change. This type of study provides designers with a more comprehensive view of the design's performance than can be achieved by sensitivity or optimization studies.

There are related software units that can be applied in conjunction with CAE software and may be a simulation capability embedded within CAD software. Alternatively, the module may be associated with CAD software to allow automatic exchange of geometry between CAD and CAE. In another arrangement, changes to design geometry are exchanged indirectly using import and export capabilities of two different programs.

CAE software simulations involve the creation and use of a number of digital artifacts that are tracked by simulation data management (SDM) software. SDM software tracks and manages simula-

tion changes throughout the design development process.

—*Richard M. Renneboog*

Further Reading

Bi, Zhuming, and Xiaoqin Wang. *Computer-Aided Design and Manufacturing*. Wiley, 2020.

Chang, Kuang-Hua. *e-Design: Computer-Aided Engineering Design*. Academic Press, 2016.

Filipovic, Nenad. *Computational Modeling in Bioengineering and Bioinformatics*. Academic Press, 2020.

Jackson, Chad. "What Is Mechanical Computer Aided Engineering (MCAE)?" *Lifecycle Insights*, 2021, www.lifecycleinsights.com/tech-guide/mcae/. Accessed 16 Dec. 2021.

Kyratsis, Panagiotis, Konstantinos G. Kakoulis, and Angelos P. Markopoulos, editors. *Advances in CAD/CAM/CAE Technologies*. MDPI, 2020.

Leondes, Cornelius T. *Computer-Aided Design, Engineering, and Manufacturing: Systems Techniques and Applications, Volume II, Computer-Integrated Manufacturing*. CRC Press, 2019.

Udroiu, Razvan, editor. *Computer-Aided Technologies: Applications in Engineering and Medicine*. IntechOpen, 2016.

Um, Dugan. *Solid Modeling and Applications: Rapid Prototyping, CAD and CAE Theory*. Springer, 2016.

See also: Aeronautical engineering; Aerospace design; Civil engineering

CONSERVATION OF ENERGY

Fields of Study: Physics; Mechanics; Mathematics

ABSTRACT

The motion of an object can be described by considering the various forms of energy the object has. In the absence of dissipative forces, the energy of a system can be neither created nor destroyed. This principle can be used to find the varying amount of kinetic energy of an object, which directly relates to the speed of that object.

KEY CONCEPTS

kinetic energy: energy due to any kind of motion, be it rotation, vibration, or translation

potential energy: energy that is stored in objects and has the potential to become other forms of energy, such as kinetic energy

total mechanical energy: the sum of all the kinetic and potential energies of an object in a closed system

CONSERVATION OF ENERGY AND MASS

To study the motion, or kinematics, of an object, one can apply Isaac Newton's (1642-1727) laws of motion and obtain results that match what happens in the real world. However, there is one small issue with this approach: it gets a lot more complicated when dealing with variable accelerations. When a car stops at a red light, it is not accelerating at that moment. When the light turns green, the driver applies a variable amount of pressure to the gas pedal. That variable amount of pressure produces a variable acceleration of the car. In these cases, applying Newton's laws of motion produce different results depending on the acceleration value used. Calculating energy is a simple approach to solving these kinds of problems. This is due to the fact that the total amount of energy an object has never changes. Physicists call this principle the conservation of energy.

Energy is conserved by all objects in the absence of friction or any other dissipative force. If a person rubs a finger on a table for a long period of time, his or her finger will get hotter and hotter. If the person hits the table with an open palm, his or her palm will also be warmer than before. This is because some of that person's energy was turned into heat, which is a form of energy. Heat then moves away from the person's hand in the form of infrared radiation and goes back into the environment. While it may seem like the energy was not conserved, it is still part of a larger overall system and did not disappear completely.

The law of conservation of energy states that the total energy in the universe is always the same, and therefore energy can be neither created nor destroyed. In other words, it is not possible to add energy to the universe or take some energy out of the universe. This law can be applied to any system in which one can assume no dissipating forces exist. In 1905, Albert Einstein (1879-1955) recognized in his theory of relativity that mass is itself a form of energy. Thus the law of conservation of energy also addresses the conservation of mass, in that the total amount of mass and energy in the universe is constant.

Inside the sun, mass is constantly being turned into energy. This is the energy that warms Earth. In a way, fossil fuels are a form of energy from the sun, if one considers the law of conservation of mass and energy. Eons ago, the sun converted mass into energy in the form of light and heat. When that light and heat reached Earth, plants, bacteria, and algae turned the sun's energy into mass in the form of food, which provided them with energy to live and grow. That energy was converted back into mass in the form of the newly grown plants, bacteria, and algae. Animals then ate those plants, bacteria, and algae as food, which they converted to energy. Over time, the remains of flora and fauna fossilized, becoming coal and oil. Humans use coal and oil as fuel to provide energy. Conservation of energy is all around, and it affects everyone in more ways than one might think.

DIFFERENT FORMS OF ENERGY

In order to understand conservation of energy, one must understand the different forms and properties of energy. Everything that is in motion has a form of energy called kinetic energy. In fact, the temperature of a room is defined as the average kinetic energy of the particles in the room. The air molecules in a room are in a constant state of motion. Not only are they moving around, they are also vibrating. If on average they are moving faster, then they have more kinetic energy, which makes the whole room warmer. If on average they move slower, then less kinetic energy leads to lower temperatures. The kinetic energy (K) of an object, in joules (J), is mathematically defined by the object's mass (m) and its velocity (v), as in the following equation:

$$K = \frac{1}{2}mv^2$$

But that is not the only form of energy objects can have. Objects tend to fall to Earth's surface due to the planet's gravitational attraction. Another simple way to say this is that the object has a store of energy that can potentially be used to perform work when it is above the surface of Earth. Thus, this energy is known as the gravitational potential energy (U_g), and it is determined by the object's height above the surface (h), its mass (m), and the strength of Earth's gravitational field (g). When a pencil is held, it has potential energy. As the pencil falls to the ground, it starts to lose some of that potential energy, which becomes kinetic energy. The pencil's velocity increases as it continues to fall. When it hits the ground, all of its potential energy has been turned into kinetic energy, and it lands at its highest possible speed. At that point, dissipative forces cause the energy to be lost to the surrounding environment. Mathematically speaking, the gravitational potential energy, in joules, is expressed as:

$$U_g = mgh$$

where g equals 9.8 meters per second per second, or meters per second squared (m/s^2), near the surface of Earth.

There are many other forms of stored or potential energy. There is stored energy in chemicals that are about to react in a chemical reaction. Some of this energy is released in the reaction as heat.

Another form of potential energy is found by the stretching and compression of a spring. If there is a mass (m) attached to a spring that has been fixed to a wall, and someone pulls on the mass without letting go, the mass now has potential energy. If the mass is released, it will begin to oscillate, gaining kinetic energy. At one point during this oscillation, the mass will compress the spring to the maximum possible amount and stop moving for a fraction of a second. When this happens, all the kinetic energy gained has been transformed back into potential energy. Then the spring will push back on the mass, allowing the stored energy to be transformed into kinetic energy. The entire process repeats itself for as long as the mass is allowed to oscillate. The potential energy stored in a spring is a function of the distance the spring is stretched or compressed (x) and the properties of the particular spring used, summarized as its unique spring constant (k). The spring constant is a measurement of how rigid the spring is and how it reacts to being stretched or compressed. In the International System of Units, it is measured in newtons per meter (N/m). Mathematically, the potential energy of a spring in joules, known as the elastic potential energy (U_e), is found using the following equation:

$$U_e = -\frac{1}{2}kx$$

Elastic potential energy only exists if a spring is part of the system in question. An object can have multiple forms of energy at once. A pendulum that is oscillating is moving, therefore it has kinetic energy, and is at a distance from the surface, so it has gravitational potential energy. When the pendulum is at its highest point, all of its energy is in the form of gravitational potential energy. When it is at its lowest point, it has zero potential energy (assuming it is at no distance above Earth's surface at that point) and the highest amount of kinetic energy it can have. In between, it has different amounts of potential and kinetic energies.

As described above, energy in a closed system is conserved. That means that all of the energy in the pendulum is always the same. Physicists have defined the total mechanical energy (E) as the sum of all the kinetic and potential energies of an object in a closed system:

$$E = K + U_g + U_e$$

When physicists say that the energy is conserved, they mean that mechanical energy is conserved. This means that there is no change in the total mechanical energy, or that the initial mechanical energy (E_i) equals the final mechanical energy (E_f):

$$E_i = E_f$$

Substituting the definitions of the different forms of energy into the mechanical energy conservation equation, the equation becomes:

$$K_i + U_{g,i} + U_{e,i} = K_f + U_{g,f} + U_{e,f}$$

Consider the example of a single-car roller coaster with a mass of 500 kilograms (kg) at the top of the track, waiting to begin its motion. After its initial descent, it travels up a smaller hill with an altitude of 10 meters (m). When at the top of this hill, it has a speed of 15 m/s. In order to calculate the final kinetic energy, the initial kinetic and potential energies must be found. There are no springs in this system, so there is no elastic potential energy. The first step is to use the information about the speed on the smaller hill to calculate the initial kinetic energy: Then use the same information to calculate the initial gravitational potential energy:

$$U_{g,I} = mgh_i$$

$$U_{g,I} = (500 \text{ kg}) (9.8 \text{ m/s}^2) (10 \text{ m})$$

$$U_{g,I} = 49,000 \text{ J}$$

Do the same thing for the final potential energy:

$$U_{g,f} = mgh_f$$

$$U_{g,f} = (500 \text{ kg}) (9.8 \text{ m/s}^2) (0 \text{ m})$$

$$U_{g,f} = 0 \text{ J}$$

Note that when the car is at the bottom of the hill, its height above the ground is 0 meters, so it has no final gravitational potential energy. Using the values for initial kinetic energy and initial and final gravitational potential energy, use the equation for the conservation of total mechanical energy to find the final kinetic energy:

$$K_i + U_{g,I} = K_f + U_{g,f}$$

$$56,250 \text{ J} + 49,000 \text{ J} = Kf + 0 \text{ J} \quad Kf = 105,250 \text{ J}$$

The final kinetic energy is 105,250 joules.

ENERGY PRODUCTION

By using energy to solve problems about motion, one can arrive at the same result without having to deal with variable forces and accelerations. This has wide implications and applications for the real world. When hydroelectric power plants produce energy, they do so by converting potential and kinetic energy into electrical energy. As water falls down from the top of a lake behind a dam through pipes called penstocks, it loses potential energy and gains kinetic energy. This allows the water to move faster and faster as it falls. It then hits the blades of a turbine and transfers its energy into the turbine, causing it to spin. The turbine turns a generator, which produces electrical energy.

Conservation of energy can also be seen in the production of energy by other means. Most of the electricity produced in the United States comes from the burning of coal. When coal is used to heat water to produce electricity, the power plant cannot produce more energy than is stored in the coal as chemical potential energy. The same can be said about gasoline cars. The kinetic energy obtained by the explosive reaction of gasoline in an engine cannot be greater than the chemical energy stored in that gasoline before the reaction. This means that no one will ever be able to attain infinite speeds by means of propulsion, as an ever-increasing need for kinetic energy comes from an ever-increasing amount of stored potential energy, and there is a limited, and not infinite, amount of energy in the universe. Nothing in the universe that has mass can propel itself at or faster than the speed of light.

—*Angel G. Fuentes*

Further Reading

Caneva, Kenneth L. *Helmholtz and the Conservation of Energy: Contexts of Creation and Reception*. MIT Press, 2021.

———. *Robert Mayer and the Conservation of Energy*. Princeton UP, 2015.

"Circus Physics: Conservation of Energy." *Circus*. PBS, 2010. Accessed 21 Apr. 2015.

"Conservation of Energy." Khan Academy, 2015. Accessed 21 Apr. 2015.

"Conservation of Energy: Physics." *Encyclopedia Britannica*, 23 Jan. 2014. Accessed 21 Apr. 2015.

Giambattista, Alan, and Betty McCarthy Richardson. *Physics*. 2nd ed., McGraw, 2010.

Ling, Samuel J., Jeff Sanny, and William Moebs. *University Physics Volume 1*. Samurai Publishing Company, 2017.

Moskowitz, Clara. "Fact or Fiction? Energy Can Neither Be Created nor Destroyed." *Scientific American*, 5 Aug. 2014. Accessed 21 Apr. 2015.

Young, Hugh D., and Francis Weston Sears. *Sears & Zemansky's College Physics*. 9th ed., Addison, 2012.

See also: Acceleration; Calculating system efficiency; Clausius formulates the second law of thermodynamics; External combustion engine; Flywheels; Force (physics); Friction; Harmonic oscillator; Heat transfer; Kirchhoff, Gustav Robert; Newton's laws; Pendulums; Quantum mechanics; Steam engine; Superconductor; Tesla, Nikola; Work-energy theorem

CORIOLIS EFFECT

Fields of Study: Physics; Mechanics; Mathematics

ABSTRACT

The Coriolis effect is an apparent acceleration of a moving object as seen in a rotating system. The acceleration is not a true change in velocity, but an illusion caused by the rotation of the system beneath the moving object.

KEY CONCEPTS

convection: the circular vertical movement of fluids due to differences in density as a result of temperature differences

unaccelerated: experiencing no effect from an external force

EXPECTATION VS. REALITY

An unconscious tendency to regard Earth as a fixed frame of reference generates an unrecognized expectation on the part of many people that objects free of forces will move with unchanging direction and speed. That is, they will be unaccelerated. This expectation is consistent with Sir Isaac Newton's First Law of Motion, which states that a body in motion will remain in motion, in a constant direction, with constant speed, unless acted on by an outside force.

Newton's First Law of Motion, however, applies only in frames of reference that are themselves not accelerating. These so-called inertial frames must be moving in a constant direction with constant speed. This condition is not met by rotating frames, such as Earth's surface, where every point in the frame (though traveling at a constant speed) is constantly changing direction as it completes a circular path around the axis of rotation.

The farther an object is from the axis of rotation, the faster it will travel on its circular path. An object on the equator, for example, completes a path of

40,000 kilometers in one day, while an object at 60° north latitude travels only half that distance in the same time. Thus, the object at 60° north latitude travels at half the speed of the object on the equator.

Wind and water that leave the equator headed due north carry their equatorial speed with them. As they move north, they pass over territory that is traveling eastward more slowly than they are. As a result, the wind and water move eastward relative to the ground or the seafloor. Conversely, wind and water starting at northern latitudes and moving due south will cross ground that is moving eastward faster than they are; they will move westward relative to the ground or seafloor. This deflection from the original direction of motion is the Coriolis effect.

SIGNIFICANCE FOR CLIMATE CHANGE

The Coriolis effect causes moving fluids to be deflected to their right in the Northern Hemisphere and to their left in the Southern Hemisphere.

Convection-driven currents carry warm water and air poleward from the equator and carry cool air and water from the polar regions toward the tropics. Both the tropical and the polar currents are deflected to the right, relative to their direction of motion, in the Northern Hemisphere and to the left, relative to their direction of motion, in the Southern Hemisphere. In regions where the currents converge, the deflections merge into circular rotations about the point of convergence. In the Northern Hemisphere, these rotations move counterclockwise; in the Southern Hemisphere, they move clockwise.

A low-pressure weather system in the Northern Hemisphere, for example, draws in air from the surrounding terrain in all directions. The wind flowing in from the north is deflected to the west. The wind from the west is deflected to the south, the wind from the south is deflected to the east, and the wind from the east is deflected to the north. In combination, the winds form a vortex rotating counterclock-

wise about the center of the low-pressure area. A high-pressure system, by contrast, repels winds, creating a clockwise vortex. In the Southern Hemisphere, these directions are reversed. Similar effects occur in ocean currents.

The magnitude of the deflection caused by the Coriolis effect is proportional to the distance from the point of deflection to the rotation axis. For that reason, the Coriolis effect is most prominent at the equator. It is also proportional to the speed of the currents involved. High winds associated with hurricanes readily display the effect, generating the characteristic circular wind pattern with a calm eye at the center.

The Coriolis effect establishes the circulation pattern of major storms, trade winds, jet streams, and large-scale ocean currents. All of these convection currents transport thermal energy from the warm tropics to the temperate and polar regions, moderating the global difference in temperatures. The Gulf Stream, for example, tends to keep Great Britain, Ireland, and the North Atlantic coast of Europe substantially warmer than other regions of the Northern Hemisphere that are located at the same latitude. Air currents also transport large amounts of water evaporated from tropical oceans to temperate and polar regions, where the water precipitates as rain and snow.

The rate at which convection currents transport mass and heat poleward from the tropics is a function of the temperature difference between the two regions. If climate change raises average temperatures in the tropics more than it raises them at the poles, it will create more energetic and powerful currents. If climate change raises polar temperatures more than it raises equatorial temperatures, it will dampen these currents. The resulting effects on the number, type, and destructive power of storms in either case would be complex and difficult to model.

—*Billy R. Smith Jr.*

Further Reading

Cossu, Remo, and Matthew G. Wells. "The Evolution of Submarine Channels under the Influence of Coriolis Forces: Experimental Observations of Flow Structures." *Terra Nova,* vol. 25, no. 1, 2013, pp. 65-71. Academic Search Complete. Accessed 19 Mar. 2015.

Goh, Gahyun, and Y. Noh. "Influence of Coriolis Force on the Formation of a Seasonal Thermocline." *Ocean Dynamics,* vol. 63, no. 9-10, 2013, pp. 1083-92. Energy & Power Source. Accessed 19 Mar. 2015.

Mayes, Julian, and Karel Hughes. *Understanding Weather: A Visual Approach*. Oxford UP, 2004.

Stommel, Henry, and Dennis Moore. *An Introduction to the Coriolis Force*. Columbia UP, 1989.

Walker, Gabrielle. *An Ocean of Air: Why the Wind Blows and Other Mysteries of the Atmosphere*. Harcourt, 2007.

Zhang, Lifeng, Antoine Allanore, Cong Wang, James Yurko, and Justin Crapps. *Materials Processing Fundamentals*. Springer, 2016.

See also: Acceleration; Angular forces; Bernoulli, Daniel; Bernoulli's principle; Circular motion; Force (physics); Torque

D

D'Alembert's Axioms of Motion

Fields of Study: Physics; Aeronautical engineering; Mechanical engineering; Biomechanics; Physiology; Mathematics

ABSTRACT
Drawing upon elements of Cartesian and Newtonian thought, d'Alembert formulated a set of laws describing the behavior of bodies in motion. The laws, all derived completely through mathematical calculation, combined to produce a general principle for solving problems in rational mechanics.

KEY CONCEPTS
analysis: any systematic method of determining the solution to a problem

experiment: an essential aspect of scientific study, in which one devises a specific test to determine a particular property or characteristic

force: a nonphysical manifestation that has the potential to interact with physical matter to cause either attraction or repulsion

geometry: literally means "earth measurement" and refers generally to the relationships between the dimensions and area of plane figures

SUMMARY OF EVENT
Jean le Rond d'Alembert (1717-83) is probably best known for his collaboration with Denis Diderot on the *Encyclopédie: Ou, Dictionnaire raisonné des sciences, des arts, et des métiers* (1751-72; partial translation *Selected Essays from the Encyclopedy*, 1772; complete translation *Encyclopedia*, 1965). His "*Discours préliminaire*" (preliminary discourse), which prefaced

the work, was known and admired throughout Europe, and he was responsible for many of the *Encyclopedia*'s technical articles. A favorite in the salons of Paris, d'Alembert was involved in all aspects of the intellectual life of his century. Beyond these pursuits, however, d'Alembert was a mathematician and scientist of considerable expertise who made significant contributions in the field of rational mechanics. In 1741, he was admitted as a member to the French Academy of Sciences. There, he met, discoursed with, and competed with men such as Alexis-Claude Clairaut and Daniel Bernoulli.

D'Alembert received his first instruction in mathematics at the Jansenist Collège des Quatres Nations. In his classes, he was introduced to the work of Cartesian thinkers such as Pierre Varignon, Charles Reyneau, and Nicolas Malebranche. Thus, his early education in mathematics was strongly influenced by the ideas of René Descartes. This background did not, however, prevent d'Alembert from recognizing the value of Sir Isaac Newton's work. He read Newton's *Philosophiae Naturalis Principia Mathematica* (1687; *The Mathematical Principles of Natural Philosophy*, 1729; best known as the *Principia*) shortly after 1739 and Colin Maclaurin's *A Treatise of Fluxions* (1742), which gave detailed explanations of Newton's methods, before publishing his own *Traité du dynamique* (1743; *Treatise on Dynamics*) and *Traité de l'équilibre et du movement des fluids* (1744; *Treatise on Equilibrium and the Movement of Fluids*). D'Alembert believed that mathematics was the key to solving all problems. He rejected the use of experiments and observation. He maintained that rational mechanics was a component of mathematics along with geometry and analysis. When d'Alembert set about writing his *Traité du Dynamique*, an enormous amount of work had already been done on the laws of motion. Much of existing theory was contradictory, however, because of the problems involved in defining terms such as force, motion, and mass. D'Alembert was convinced that a logical foundation applicable to all mechanics could be found through the use of mathematics. Although d'Alembert insisted that he had rejected the theories of Descartes that he had studied in his youth, his approach to mechanics still relied heavily on Descartes's method of deduction. D'Alembert wished to discover laws of mechanics that would be as logical and self-evident as the laws of geometry. Above all, he was determined to "save" mechanics from being an experimental science. D'Alembert, like his fellow scientists, was a great admirer of Newton, and Newton's *Principia* was for him the starting point in a study of mechanics. Thus, he developed his laws of mechanics using Newton's work as a model. In his first law, d'Alembert expressed his agreement with Newton's law of inertia, that is, that bodies do not change their state of rest or motion by themselves. They tend to remain in the same state; Newton would say, they remain in the same state until acted upon by a force. D'Alembert also was in accord with Newton's concept of hard bodies moving in a void.

D'Alembert, however, found Newton's second and third laws unacceptable, because they acknowledged force as real and relied upon experiments and observation. This may have been because "force" is very difficult to define in other than a cause-and-effect manner, not as an actual physical thing. The logical geometric basis that D'Alembert sought for the foundation of mechanics allowed no room for experiments and observations. Force was for d'Alembert a concept to be avoided because it did not lend itself to definition. He rejected not only innate force but all force. In contrast, Newton recognized force as having real existence. D'Alembert acknowledged that bodies would not move unless

some external cause acted upon them but defined causes only in terms of their effects. His third law was similar to Newton's third law. Newton had stated that two bodies must act on each other equally. D'Alembert proposed the concept of equilibrium, resulting from two bodies of equal mass moving in opposite directions at equal velocities.

Because of his rejection of force as a scientific concept, d'Alembert was closer in his theories to Malebranche, who viewed the laws of motion as entirely geometrical, than he was to Newton. D'Alembert's laws of motion dealt with idealized geometrical figures rather than real objects. These figures moved through space until they impacted, causing them either to stop or to slip past one another. Change of motion was necessitated by geometry; force was an unnecessary element and only brought into play disturbing metaphysical concepts.

From the last two laws of his axioms of motion, d'Alembert derived what is now known as d'Alembert's principle: The impact of two hard bodies either is direct or is transmitted by an intermediate inflexible object or constraint. He applied his principle the next year in his *Traité de l'Equilibre et du Mouvements des Fluides*, which was for the most part a criticism of Daniel Bernoulli's work on hydrodynamics. Although d'Alembert had used his principle successfully in his 1743 treatise, it failed to be very useful in fluid mechanics.

SIGNIFICANCE

During the eighteenth century, opinions about d'Alembert's contributions to science were many and varied. Some of his contemporaries credited him with having found a set of principles for rational mechanics; for some, his work verified Descartes's beliefs that the laws of mechanics could be deduced from matter and motion and that there was no force involved in movement. However, others criticized and rejected d'Alembert, because he refused to accept experimentation and simply eliminated concepts that he found resistant to mathematical expression. His most important contribution was d'Alembert's principle, which provided a general approach to solving mechanical problems. It was one of the first attempts to find simple and general rules for the movements of mechanical systems.

D'Alembert's laws of motion were accepted as the logical foundation of mechanics well into the nineteenth century. Ultimately, however, his refusal to discuss force proved to be a fatal flaw. Today, Newton's *Principia* is viewed as containing the basic laws of classical mechanics.

—*Shawncey Webb*

Further Reading

Boudri, J. C. *What Was Mechanical About Mechanics: The Concept of Force between Metaphysics and Mechanics from Newton to Lagrange.* Springer Science & Business Media, 2013.

Calero, Julian Simón. *Jean le Rond D'Alembert: A New Theory of the Resistance of Fluids.* Springer International Publishing, 2019.

Greenberg, John L. *The Problem of the Earth's Shape from Newton to Clairaut: The Rise of Mathematical Science in Eighteenth Century Paris and the Fall of "Normal" Science.* Cambridge UP, 1995. Chronicles the spread of Newtonian physics in France and discusses d'Alembert's treatises. Readers need some scientific background.

Grimsley, Ronald. *Jean d'Alembert, 1717-1783.* Clarendon Press, 1963.

Hankins, Thomas L. *Jean d'Alembert: Science and the Enlightenment.* Clarendon Press, 1970.

Shectman, Jonathan. *Groundbreaking Scientific Experiments, Investigations, and Discoveries of the Eighteenth Century.* Greenwood Press, 2003.

Yolton, John W., editor. *Philosophy, Religion, and Science in the Seventeenth and Eighteenth Centuries.* U of Rochester P, 1990.

See also: Acceleration; Angular forces; Angular momentum; Bernoulli, Daniel; Circular motion; Classical or applied mechanics; Equilibrium; Equivalence principle; Fluid dynamics; Force (physics); Friction; Laplace, Pierre-Simon; Moment of inertia; Momentum (physics); Motion; Newton, Isaac; Newton's laws; Thermodynamics; Velocity

DIESEL ENGINE

Fields of Study: Physics; Mechanical engineering; Mechanics; Mathematics

ABSTRACT

In February, 1892, German thermal engineer Rudolf Diesel developed and patented a prototype of an internal combustion engine that he believed could one day be operated on vegetable oils and other plentiful fuels rather than on petroleum.

KEY CONCEPTS

compression: the act of reducing the volume of a gas or other material without changing the amount of material by that action

exhaust port/valve: an opening and control system by which product gases are eliminated from combustion cylinders of an internal combustion engine after combustion of the air/fuel mixture

flywheel: a massive disk or gear that is set to spinning by a motor, thus allowing the flywheel's angular momentum and torque to maintain and stabilize the function of the motor

intake port/valve: an opening and control system through which fuel and air are admitted into the combustion cylinders of an internal combustion engine

sliding valve: a type of valve system in which an intake or exhaust port is sealed by a cover that slides into place, as compared to the type of valve system in which the ports are opened or closed by a matching device that moves in and out of the ports

EARLY YEARS

Rudolf Diesel spent his early years in Paris, where he lived with his parents, natives of Bavaria holding Bavarian citizenship. When the Franco-Prussian war erupted in 1870, the Diesel family, faced with the prospect of deportation from France, moved to London. Soon, young Rudolf was sent to Augsburg, Germany, his father's home town, to continue his schooling.

When he was old enough to begin his higher education, Diesel entered the Technische Hochschule, a university-level technical institute in Munich, where he showed a particular aptitude for engineering. Carl von Linde, a noted authority on refrigeration engineering who was associated with the Technische Hochschule, recognized Diesel's exceptional aptitudes while the youth was still a student and took a special interest in him. With von Linde's encourage-

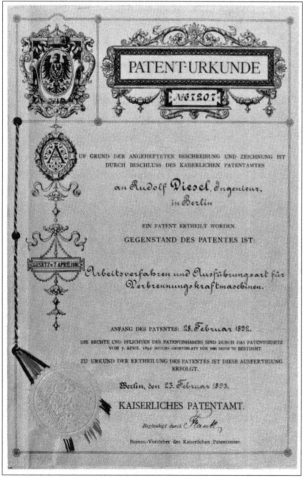

Rudolf Diesel's 1893 patent on a rational heat motor. Photo via Wikimedia Commons. [Public do-

ment, Diesel performed experiments that involved using ammonia to fuel an expansion engine. In 1880, von Linde employed Diesel in his corporation, stationing him in Paris. By 1890, Diesel moved to Berlin to take a new job with von Linde's company. It was there that he first conceived of developing an internal combustion engine different from those produced earlier by Nikolaus August Otto in Germany and Étienne Lenoir in France.

Diesel's ideas were not yet fully formed, so in February, 1892, he applied for a development patent on his engine. The German government issued the development patent, and the following year, Diesel published a more comprehensive explanation of the engine as he conceived it. This description, *Theorie und Konstruktion eines Rationellen Wäremotors* (*Theory and Construction of a Rational Heat Motor*), enabled Diesel to obtain a patent in 1893 for the compression-ignition engine that is now commonly referred to as the diesel engine.

The concept of compression ignition was articulated as early as 1824 by the French physicist Sadi Carnot, but no practical application of this technology appeared until 1876, when Otto built a working model of an engine in which the mixture of fuel and air was compressed in the cylinder before ignition. Fourteen years earlier, Alphonse Beau de Rochas had conceived theoretically of an engine built according to these principles, but he did not create any working models. Lenoir began building internal combustion engines in 1862 and produced about five hundred of them, all based upon concepts relating to the steam engine. Lenoir's engines used sliding valves to admit and dispel combustion gases. It took another fourteen years after Otto unveiled his model in 1876 before Diesel conceived of his engine in detail.

Otto and Eugen Langen—his partner in their joint venture, the *Gasmotorenfabrik*—built some five thousand engines before Diesel patented his engine. Their engines were more practical than Lenoir's in that they used flywheels to carry the pistons through their rest phases. Diesel's engine differed from those developed by Otto and Lenoir in that its power was achieved by compressing air in the cylinder. The air was compressed at a ratio of 52:1 to a pressure of about 765 hundred pounds per square inch and a temperature of about one thousand degrees Fahrenheit. Fuel was then ignited by pressure rather than by a spark and burnt before the piston descended. This action occurs so slowly that there is no significant increase in pressure resulting from the ignition. Previous engines had depended upon a spark to ignite the fuel in their cylinders. Diesel's model depended on heated, compressed air to achieve this ignition.

Whereas previous internal combustion engines had been powered by gasoline, Diesel's engine could operate on a variety of fuels. Indeed, his first working model was fueled by powdered coal, which was in plentiful supply but which quickly proved to be a less-than-ideal fuel for the engine. Diesel soon replaced powdered coal with alcohol and other liquid fuels.

As soon as the idea of Diesel's engine was protected by a patent, the inventor set about building working models. He received backing and encouragement from the *Maschinenfabrik* of Augsburg and the powerful Krupp enterprises. By 1897, he had produced several working models, the most promising of which was a four-stroke engine with a single perpendicular cylinder that served as the compression chamber. This early diesel engine delivered twenty-five horsepower.

Remarkably, Diesel's engine was sufficiently simple in its design that its commercial possibilities be-

First fully functional diesel engine, designed by Imanuel Lauster, built from scratch, and finished by October 1896. Photo by Olivier Cleynen, via Wikimedia Commons.

came evident quite quickly. The engine was pressed into service in a variety of ways that, by the turn of the century, brought Diesel remarkable wealth through royalties. For all of its promise and actual success, however, the engine was not without serious drawbacks. The early diesel engines were much larger and considerably heavier than the gasoline engines they were designed to replace. They also produced considerable air pollution, but comparable gasoline engines caused comparable amounts of pollution as well. Because of their size, the earliest diesel engines were most appropriate for use as stationery sources of power. Eventually, they were used to power large ships and locomotives. During World

War I, they provided power for Germany's fleet of submarines. It was not until the second quarter of the twentieth century, however, that diesel engines were commonly used to power trucks, which currently remains one of their major applications. Diesel engines have a much longer life than gasoline-powered engines, and they require considerably less upkeep than their gasoline-powered counterparts. They also can burn less expensive fuel, including easily replenishable vegetable oils.

SIGNIFICANCE

Diesel engines are the engines of choice for most trucks, locomotives, ships, buses, and stationary power plants. They are durable engines that, when Diesel first developed them, were too heavy and cumbersome to be practical for any but the largest vehicles. The power and cost-efficiency of the diesel engine made it possible for such vehicles to be put to work, however, and in some cases made it possible for them to exist at all.

Eventually, the weight of the diesel engine was reduced sufficiently to make practical its use in private passenger vehicles. Diesel-powered passenger automobiles have generally been more popular in Europe than in the United States, probably because the price of gasoline is much higher in Europe than it is in the United States, making diesel automobiles practical choices purely on economic grounds. Diesel envisioned his engine as running on vegetable oils and other renewable resources. The oil industry, however, created a new type of gasoline that could power a diesel engine so that it could still make profits from diesel-powered automobiles. During the early twenty-first century, a new interest in the use of biological fuels in diesel engines, commonly referred to as "biodiesel," began to gain strength, motivated by increasing gasoline prices.

—R. Baird Shuman

Further Reading

Bartlett, Melanie. *Adlard Coles Book of Diesel Engines*. 5th ed., Bloomsbury Publishing, 2018.

Cummins, C. Lyle, Jr. *Diesel's Engine: The Man, and the Evolution of the World's Most Efficient Internal Combustion Motor*. Octane Press, 2022.

Guo, Hingsheng, Hailin Li, Lino Guzzella, and Masahiro Shioji, editors. *Advances in Compression Ignition Natural Gas—Diesel Dual Fuel Engines*. Frontiers Media SA, 2021.

Kegl, Breda, Mark Kegl, and Stanislav Pehan. *Green Diesel Engines: Biodiesel Usage in Diesel Engines*. Springer Science & Business Media, 2013.

Wright, Gus. *Fundamentals of Medium/Heavy Duty Diesel Engines*. Jones & Bartlett Learning, 2021.

See also: Carnot, Sadi; Flywheels; Internal combustion engine; Jet engines; Rotary engine; Steam and steam turbines; Stirling, Robert; Turbines; Turbojets and turbofans; Turboprops

DIESEL, RUDOLF

Fields of Study: Physics; Mechanics; Mathematics

ABSTRACT

Rudolf Diesel was a German inventor and theorist. He studied the theories of French physicist Sadi Carnot, learning the principles of modern internal combustion. His studies convinced Diesel that he could build an engine four times as efficient as the steam engine by injecting fuel into an engine with air heated by compression to a temperature high enough to ignite the fuel. This is the principle of all Diesel engines in use today.

KEY CONCEPTS

cetane number: a classification of fuel oil combustibility relative to pure cetane (hexadecane, a C-16 hydrocarbon); analogous to the octane number for gasoline fuels relating gasoline combustibility to pure iso-octane (a C-8 hydrocarbon)

compression ignition: compressing a gas causes its temperature to increase; in a Diesel engine the temperature increase of air due to compression is high enough to ignite the fuel

four-stroke engine: an engine requiring four piston strokes for a single fuel combustion; one stroke draws in air, a second compresses the air, fuel is injected and ignited to drive the piston through the third stroke, and the fourth stroke pushes out the combustion gases; all four strokes are timed to the opening and closing of intake and exhaust valves

fractional distillate: petroleum (unrefined oil) is a complex mixture of different compounds; fractionation of the mixture by distillation separates the components according to their respective boiling points; each portion according to boiling point range is a fractional distillate

BACKGROUND

Rudolf Christian Karl Diesel was born March 18, 1858, in Paris. His father was a leather craftsman and his mother was a governess/language tutor. Diesel earned admission at age twelve to Paris's best school, the École Primaire Superieure. Classed as enemy aliens in France, Diesel's parents moved to London during the Franco-Prussian War of 1870, with Diesel himself moving to Augsburg, where he entered the Royal County Trade School. He then enrolled at the newly opened Industrial School of Augsburg. A scholarship enabled him to attend Munich's Technische Hochschule (Technical High School), where he studied engineering and graduated in 1879 with the highest examination scores on record. Also, at the Royal Bavarian he met and worked with Carl von Linde, inventor of refrigeration and gas separation.

Diesel worked for Sulzer Brothers at Winterthur, Switzerland, for two years before he returned to Paris as a refrigeration engineer and manager at Linde Refrigeration Enterprises. Working for Linde, Diesel filed patents in France and Germany in the 1880s.

Diesel married in 1883 and had three children. On September 30, 1913, while crossing the English Channel to consult with the British Admiralty, Diesel disappeared at sea, and his body was never recovered.

A portrait of Rudolf Christian Karl Diesel and an illustration of the engine he invented appeared on a German stamp to commemorate the 100th anniversary of his invention.

SCIENCE AND TECHNOLOGY

Diesel studied the theories of French physicist Sadi Carnot, learning the principles of modern internal combustion. His studies convinced Diesel that he could build an engine four times as efficient as the steam engine by injecting fuel into an engine with compressed air in a ratio up to 25 to 1. The com-

Rudolf Diesel. Photo via Wikimedia Commons. [Public domain.]

pression level would heat the air to almost 537°C (1,000°F), sufficient to ignite fuel without plugs or other ignition systems. He opened his first shop in 1885 in Paris to work on his engine. Work on the engine continued when he moved to the Berlin office of Linde Enterprises, working on thermodynamics and fuel efficiency.

The Diesel engine is a compression ignition engine with fuel ignition through sudden exposure to high temperature and pressure, rather than through a separate source such as a spark plug. Diesel worked on different designs for over a decade before receiving the 1892 patent for one running on the cheapest available fuel, powdered coal. He published *Theory and Construction of a Rational Heat-Engine to Replace the Steam Engine and Combustion Engines Known Today* in 1892, seven years after Karl Benz received the patent for the first automobile. The publication presented the core concepts of the diesel engine. He patented the engine in Germany in February 1892. After receiving the patent and financial assistance from the Krupp brothers and Augsburg-Nuremberg Company, he began building the prototype, which was ready to test in July 1893. The prototype used powdered coal injected by compressed air. Previously, Diesel had worked with compressed ammonia. The first prototype stood 10 feet (3 meters) tall, resembled steam engines of the era, and achieved compression of 80 atmospheres (8100 kPa), but required outside power. It demonstrated the feasibility of forced air ignition, but it exploded and almost killed Diesel. Hospitalized for months, he thereafter had health and vision problems.

Seven months later, on February 17, 1894, he ran a 13-horsepower single-piston engine for a minute. The engine used high compression of fuel to ignite it, eliminating the spark plug used in the internal combustion engine. He modified the second prototype over four years. By 1897, he had a working 25-horsepower, four-stroke, single-vertical-cylinder compression engine. This prototype had such a

strong enough resemblance to Herbert Akroyd Stuart's engine of 1890 that for some years they were in patent disagreements and arguments over whose came first. When Diesel prevailed, the engine came to carry his name. Diesel engines were relatively simple and as efficient as he had anticipated, but he allowed manufacture of only heavy stationary engines. He initially used coal dust because it was cheapest. By 1897, kerosene replaced powdered coal, and the engine presented at the 1900 Exposition Universelle ran on peanut oil.

AND THE REST IS HISTORY

After three additional years of development, production began, with the first engine at a US brewery. Licenses from firms in several countries made Diesel a millionaire. The first Diesels were unsuitable for automobiles, but popular for locomotives and ships. The Diesel engine propelled cars, trucks, motorcycles, boats, and locomotives. Packard used diesel motors in airplanes from 1927, and in 1928, Charles Lindbergh flew a Stinson SM1B with a Packard Diesel. Diesels powered aircraft that set nonstop flight records in the late 1920s and early 1930s. The ill-fated airship *Hindenburg* had four 16-cylinder Diesels, each capable of 850 horsepower for sustained cruising, and bursts of 1200 horsepower. The first Diesel automobile trip took place in 1930, 800 miles (1,280 kilometers) from Indianapolis to New York City. In 1931, Dave Evans drove a Cummins Diesel equipped car the entire Indianapolis 500 without a pit stop.

Diesel's engine runs on a specific fractional distillate of fuel oil, usually from petroleum. It also handles variants derived from other than petroleum, including biomass to liquid, gas to liquid, or biodiesel. Diesel oil is about 15 percent denser than regular gasoline distillate and simpler to refine. Until recently it was cheaper to purchase, although fluctuations in the market, as when cold weather increases demand for heating oil refined the same way as diesel, cause diesel to be more expensive. In 2022, price manipulation of refined petroleum products has seen significantly higher prices "at the pumps" for diesel fuel than for gasoline. Diesel-powered vehicles normally have better gas mileage than gasoline-powered vehicles because diesel has greater energy content and the diesel engine is more efficient. The difference is up to 40 percent better mileage than gasoline. At the same time however, diesel emits 15 percent more greenhouse gases than a comparable amount of gasoline, reducing the advantage. Diesel fuel also contains sulfur and, in the United States, a lower cetane number (which measures ignition quality), making for poorer cold weather performance.

Diesel's 1892 invention was a variant of the hot bulb engine. The modern diesel engine retains Diesel's compression ignition, but incorporates cold-fuel injection (pumps raise fuel to high pressures that activate fuel injectors), rather than compressed air, which heats the fuel slightly (thus hot-fuel injection). Hot fuel remains the preference for large marine engines and other low-speed, high-load conditions with poorer quality fuels. Many also incorporate "glow plugs" to provide a hot spot for fuel ignition on cold start-ups. Diesel engines became markedly cleaner in 2007 after manufacturers shut down production for two years to convert to lower sulfur diesel.

—*John H. Barnhill*

Further Reading

Bain, Don. "We Should Have Celebrated Rudolph Diesel's Birthday Yesterday." *Torque News*, 19 Mar. 2012, www.torquenews.com/397/we-should-have-celebrated-rudolph-diesel%e2%80%99s-birthday-yesterday.

Brunt, Douglas. *The Mysterious Case of Rudolf Diesel: Genius, Power, and Deception on the Eve of World War I*. Simon & Schuster, 2023.

Chalkley, A. P. *Diesel Engines for Land and Marine Work: With an Introductory Chapter by Dr. Rudolf Diesel*. BoD-Books on Demand, 2014.

"Obituary, Rudolf Diesel." *Power*, vol. 38, no. 18, 1913, p. 628.

"Rudolf Christian Karl Diesel Biography (1858-1913)." *Madehow.com*, www.madehow.com/inventorbios/11/Rudolf-Christian-Karl-Diesel.html.

"Rudolp [sic] Diesel and Diesel Oil." *Speedace.info*, speedace.info/diesel.htm.

Smil, Vaclav. *Two Prime Movers of Globalization: The History and Impact of Diesel Engines and Gas Turbines*. MIT Press, 2010.

See also: Carnot, Sadi; Diesel engine; Engineering; External combustion engine; Mechanical engineering; Rotary engine; Steam engine; Turbines

DIFFERENTIAL EQUATIONS

Fields of Study: Physics; Mechanics; Mathematics

ABSTRACT

Many laws of physics are best expressed by prescribing relationships between a function describing the phenomenon and its rate of change. Once these laws are supplemented by other conditions, such as the value of the functions at a specified time, it becomes possible to find out what happens.

KEY CONCEPTS

differential equation: a relationship between the derivatives of one or more functions and the functions themselves

general solution of a differential equation: a formula involving arbitrary constants such that, by assigning values to the constants, one gets all the solutions of the differential equation

order of the differential equation: the order of the derivative of highest order appearing in the differential equation

parameters: variables that do not enter in the differential equation but that correspond to magnitudes that can be set from the exterior

solution of a differential equation: a function or group of functions whose derivatives are related to the functions in the way prescribed by the differential equation

OVERVIEW

From the point of view of physics, perhaps the most important contribution of Sir Isaac Newton was the realization that many laws of nature are expressed by relations between functions and their derivatives. For example, in mechanics, if a body is moving under the gravitational influence of others, the position determines the force acting on it and, by Newton's law of motion, dividing this force by the mass of the body, one can determine the acceleration.

Since the acceleration is the second derivative of the position with respect to time, one finds that there should be a relationship between the position of a body and its second derivative with respect to time. Conversely, every motion described by functions satisfying the differential equation is possible for the system if one puts it in the appropriate initial state. Similar examples can be found in many physical sciences. For example, the rate of cooling of an object—the rate of change of its temperature—is very often proportional to the difference of temperatures between the body and its surrounding media.

Such relationships between functions and their derivatives are called "differential equations" because they rely on the difference between two states of the function. Given a differential equation, one may attempt to find all the possible functions that satisfy the equation. This is called "finding the general solution." If one succeeds in doing that, by reading out the formulas one may discover all possible motions that the system may experience. This may be useful if one wants to find some particular type of motion with desirable properties. For example, if one has an explicit general solution for the pendulum, one may inquire about whether there is a motion in which the pendulum rotates twice and stops.

Unfortunately, this procedure of finding explicit solutions is very difficult and, for some systems, even impossible. Many times one must settle for simpler problems. For example, one may prescribe the initial position and velocity of a space ship and ask where it will be one year from now. This is called the "initial value problem."

One important advantage of the differential equations method compared with other methods of encapsulating the laws of nature is that it allows its user to obtain approximate solutions systematically. One can, for example, use numerical methods, or one can systematically find out what the corrections are, starting from a simpler model. This is usually called a "perturbation analysis."

Perhaps the biggest triumph of the method of perturbation analysis is in solar system studies. If the planets had very small masses, the solar system could be understood using explicit formulas and one could derive Kepler's laws. In the time of Newton, it was known that these laws did not fit the observations exactly. Newton and others, notably Pierre-Simon de Laplace, found that most of these observations could be accounted for by the fact that the planets are massive. Even if they could not find exact formulas for the motions of the planets, they could find formulas that, even if approximate, were of comparable or better accuracy than the experimental observations of the time. As the techniques to obtain data were refined, it became necessary to work harder at improving the accuracy of the approximate formulas.

It was believed for a long time that this procedure of deriving more and more approximate solutions could be carried out to any degree of approximation. Nevertheless, in the last decades of the nineteenth century, Henri Poincaré started a systematic study of perturbation methods and discovered that some of them have intrinsic limitations. He also proposed a new way of studying differential equations, now called "the geometric approach." The basic idea is that many of the questions one asks about differential equations are really geometric questions.

For example, when one asks about an orbit going from Earth to the Moon and back, one is really asking about a line passing through regions in space. Even if one were to succeed in finding explicit formulas for the motions, it would be necessary to analyze the formulas to verify whether such orbits are possible. It then becomes natural to devise methods of reasoning that work with geometric objects using geometric arguments without making use of the crutch of deriving explicit formulas, whose geometric interpretation has to be worked out afterward.

One result along this line—derived before Poincaré—is the continuity with respect to initial conditions. For many differential equations, it is possible to show that any initial condition determines uniquely where one will be one unit of time later. Moreover, if one makes a small error in the initial condition, the corresponding error in the position one unit of time later is also small. This propagated error can be made as small as one wishes by ensuring that the error in the initial conditions is small.

For many differential equations whose defining functions admit derivatives of high order, one can get considerably more precise results. The results derived from the geometric program have had an enormous influence not only in applications but also in mathematics. Many new disciplines (such as topology) were created to serve as tools for the study of differential equations and then took on a life of their own. One important development has been the availability of digital computers. It is possible to write algorithms that produce very approximate solutions of the ordinary differential equations. In fact, one of the first problems that was tackled by computers was the production of "artillery tables," which solve differential equations that model the motion of

an artillery shell in the atmosphere subject to gravitation and friction.

The influence of computers has been very profound. For concrete applications in which the goal is to compute an actual orbit whose initial conditions are known, they are now the tool of choice. Perhaps more important, through judicious simulation of key cases, it is possible to develop intuitions that help solve the problem and lead to the understanding of new phenomena. Graphical representations that are easy to grasp have been developed, and the intuitions obtained through these graphical simulations are particularly helpful when used together with the mathematical results coming from the geometric approach. There are already several commercially available programs for the visual exploration of differential equations.

APPLICATIONS

Differential equations arose from the needs of classical mechanics, but they are fundamental tools for almost all branches of physical sciences and, more tentatively, for biology and economics.

In application to mechanics, the success has been spectacular. Almost all features of the solar system have been accounted for (notable facts that still lack a convincing explanation are the rings of Saturn and the fact that the Moon always faces Earth and that Mercury rotates exactly three times around its axis every two revolutions around the sun). It is also possible in a routine way to compute the motion of artificial satellites and of the Moon in such a way that the effects of all planets are included so as to get a precision of about a meter for the position of the Moon over a century. More important, it is possible to find orbits that are immune to disturbances or that use them to get several effects.

Differential equations gave rise to many mechanical inventions that dominated the science and technology until the beginning of the twentieth century. When mechanical devices were replaced by electric and electronic ones, differential equations remained the method of choice. By using very simple rules, it is easy to derive differential equations that model circuits.

The difference of voltage across a capacitor is proportional to the charge that it stores; the derivative with respect to time of this charge is the current flowing to the capacitor. The difference of voltage across a resistor is proportional to the current flowing through it (Ohm's law). For an electronic device such as a diode, the voltage as function of the current is a complicated nonlinear function. The voltage attributable to self-induction is proportional to the rate of change of the current. For some more complicated devices, such as transistors or vacuum tubes, the current flowing across a pair of legs is a function of the voltage applied to them as well as the voltage of a third leg. Such equations are at the basis of all electronic applications. For example, it is possible to understand how to build circuits that will keep oscillating with a fixed frequency. Such circuits are found in many useful devices, such as radio transmitters and receptors, television sets and computers.

Another important application of differential equations is in the kinetics of chemical reactions. The rate of change of the concentration of chemicals in a reactor tank is proportional to the number of reactions that take place. Those, in turn, are proportional to the number of collisions of appropriate molecules, which in turn depends in a simple way on the concentrations.

By using differential equations, it is possible to predict conditions in which the end product will be a useful material rather than a useless waste. It is also possible to predict regimes which stay safely away from dangerous behaviors such as explosions.

Besides the direct applications of differential equations to physics, many problems in mathematics—frequently arising from physics—can be reduced to differential equations. A particularly important one is the use of the method of separation of variables in partial differential equations. Other problems that frequently lead to differential equations are variational problems in which one tries to determine functions which are optional in a certain sense.

CONTEXT

Differential equations appeared with calculus in the hands of Newton as a tool for mechanics, and quickly developed into the method of choice for modeling physical systems. A drastic revolution took place at the end of the nineteenth century, when several mathematicians realized that it was advantageous to think of differential equations in geometric terms. This geometric program remained dormant for a long time. In the West, it was used mainly by mechanical engineers and those who studied celestial mechanics, whereas in the East it was developed mainly by electrical engineers. In the 1960s, it again caught the attention of mathematicians who, in the meantime, had developed many disciplines—such as topology—that had made precise many intuitions. Important leaders in this revival were the mathematicians Stephen Smale, Jack K. Hale, and J. Moser in the West and A. N. Kolmogorov, V. I. Arnold, and Y. Sinai in the East.

One important tool that made progress quicker and easier was the increasing availability of computers. The graphic displays made it easy to obtain a geometric intuition of phenomena and to test conjectures. Computers were also the only means of obtaining quantitative predictions that were useful in applied problems.

From the late 1970s, the fact that differential equations could solve physical problems that had been unsolved for a long time was increasingly recognized by physicists. A notable turning point was the realization by M. Feigenbaun that renormalization group methods could produce quantitative results for chaotic systems. From that time on, the field has experienced an explosive growth, and one can now find scientists in many disciplines (mathematics, physics, engineering, and even biology) making important contributions by using differential equations.

Besides the specialized journals devoted specifically to differential equations, one can now find important results in many journals devoted to chemistry, physics, or biology.

—*Rafael de la Llave*

Further Reading

Logan, J. David. *A First Course in Differential Equations*. 3rd ed., Springer International Publishing, 2016.

Polyanin, Andrei D., and Valentin F. Zaitsev. *Handbook of Ordinary Differential Equations*. 3rd ed., Taylor & Francis, 2016.

Shah, Nita H. *Ordinary and Partial Differential Equations: Theory and Applications*. 2nd ed., PHI Learning Pvt Ltd, 2015.

Strang, Gilbert. *Differential Equations and Linear Algebra*. Wellesley-Cambridge Press, 2015.

Teschl, Gerald. *Ordinary Differential Equations and Dynamical Systems*. American Mathematical Society, 2012.

See also: Aerodynamics; Angular forces; Angular momentum; Atoms; Bernoulli's principle; Celestial mechanics; Chaotic systems; Circular motion; Classical or applied mechanics; Electromagnetism; Fluid dynamics; Fluid mechanics and aerodynamics; Heat transfer; Magnetism; Momentum (physics); Motion; Newton's laws; Thermodynamics

DISCOVERIES OF ARCHIMEDES

Fields of Study: Physics; Engineering; Mechanics; Mathematics

ABSTRACT

Archimedes's theoretical and practical discoveries led to innovations in mathematical theory as well as technological inventions.

KEY CONCEPTS

ballistic weapon: any weapon that is projected through the air to follow a parabolic trajectory to its target or to the ground

fulcrum: a stationary point upon which a lever pivots

lever: a component that transmits force from one location to another by pivoting on a fulcrum

projectile: any object that is projected through the air by some means towards a target

pulley: a disc with a concave groove about its circumference that allows a rope or other type of line to roll it when mounted on a central axle

siege weapon: a structure designed to aide an attacking force to breach the walls of a castle or city

ARCHIMEDES

By far the best-known scientist of the third century BCE was Archimedes of Syracuse, a man revered in his own age for his skill as an inventor and since recognized as one of the greatest Greek mathematicians, ranking with Pythagoras (ca. 580-500 BCE) and Euclid.

Although tradition holds that Archimedes was born in Syracuse, virtually nothing is known of the scientist's early life. No one thought of writing a biography of Archimedes during his era, and posterity has had to depend on legend, Roman historical accounts, and the inventor's own works to piece together his life story. He may well have been of aristocratic descent, for the young Archimedes spent several years in study at Alexandria in Egypt, where he was introduced to the best mathematical and mechanical researchers. While there, he seems to have become such a close associate and admirer of the astronomers Conon of Samos (ca. 245 BCE) and Eratosthenes of Cyrene (ca. 285-205 BCE) that in later years he deferred to their judgment on the publication of his own mathematical treatises.

Following his stay in Egypt, Archimedes spent most of his remaining life in Syracuse, where he enjoyed the patronage of King Hieron II. It is around this monarch that many of the legendary episodes of Archimedes's life cluster, especially his development of a system of pulleys for drawing newly constructed ships into the water, his construction of military machinery, and his discovery of the fraudulent alloy in Hieron's crown.

Contemporaries and later generations of ancient writers praised Archimedes more for his colorful technical ingenuity than for his significant mathematical formulations. His discovery of the "law" of hydrostatics, or water displacement, and his application of this theory to determine the actual gold content of Hieron's crown may be true, but the exact methodology, if indeed he pursued any, is not at all clear in the ancient accounts. Similar vagueness surrounds the development of the cochlias (κοχλιας), or Archimedean screw, a device by which water could be raised from a lower level to a higher level by means of a screw rotating inside a tube. Supposedly, Archimedes developed this invention in Egypt, but he may well have taken an existing mechanism and improved it. Other pieces of apparatus he either invented or constructed include a water organ and a model planetarium, the latter being the sole item of booty that the conqueror of Syracuse, Marcus Claudius Marcellus, took back to Rome.

The great historians of the Roman Republican period, such as Polybius (ca. 200-118 BCE), Livy (59 BCE-17 CE), and Plutarch (ca. 46-after 12 CE), give accounts of Archimedes's genius in inventing military weapons. In his life of Marcellus in *Bioi paralleloi* (ca. 105-115 BCE; *Parallel Lives*, 1579), Plutarch emphasized Archimedes's dramatic role in the defense of Syracuse. In constructing military weapons, Archimedes seems to have put to use all the laws of physics at his disposal. His knowledge of levers and pulleys was applied to the construction of ballistic weapons, cranes, grappling hooks, and other devices, so that the Roman siege of Syracuse was stalemated for two years, from 213 to 211 BCE.

Even the improbable use of large mirrors for directing sharply focused rays of sunlight in order to ignite the Roman fleet is credited to Archimedes. Doubtless, he was the mind behind the defense of Syracuse, and the Romans respected his ability. Although Marcellus wished to capture Archimedes alive, the scientist was killed by a Roman legionnaire when the city of Syracuse fell.

SIGNIFICANCE

Archimedes preferred to be remembered for his theoretical achievements rather than his discoveries in mechanics. In the third century BCE, Greek mathematical thought had advanced as far as it could in terms of geometric models of reasoning without algebraic notation, and the mathematical work of Archimedes appears as the culmination of Hellenistic mathematics. His work on plane curves represented an extension of Euclid's geometry, and it predicted integral calculus. Archimedes's studies included conic sections, the ratio of the volume of a cylinder to its inscribed square, and some understanding of pure numbers as opposed to the then prevalent notion of infinity. Through his sand-reckoner, Archimedes supposedly could express any integer up to 8×10^{16}. In his own lifetime, Archimedes's works were forwarded to Alexandria, where they were studied and dispersed. Two major Greek collections of Archimedes's works made by the mathematical schools of Constantinople were later passed on to Sicily and Italy, and then to northern Europe, where they were translated into Latin and widely published after the sixth century CE.

Because none of the Greek collections is complete, Arabic collections and associated commentaries have been used to tabulate the works attributed to Archimedes. Through these legacies, modern scholars have been able to study Archimedes's work, and some modern scholars consider him to be the greatest mathematician of antiquity.

—*Richard J. Wurtz, updated by Jeffrey L. Buller*

Further Reading

Geymonat, Mario. *The Great Archimedes*. Baylor UP, 2010.

Hirshfeld, Alan. *Eureka Man: The Life and Legacy of Archimedes*. Bloomsbury Publishing USA, 2009.

Netz, Reviel, and William Noel. *The Archimedes Codex: How a Medieval Prayer Book Is Revealing the True Genius of Antiquity's Greatest Scientist*. Hachette Books, 2007.

Paipetis, S. A., and Marco Ceccarelli, editors. *The Genius of Archimedes-23 Centuries of Influence on Mathematics, Science and Engineering: Proceedings of an International Conference held at Syracuse, Italy, June 8-10, 2010*. Springer Science & Business Media, 2010.

See also: Archimedes; Archimedes's principle; Ballistic weapons; Calculus; Civil engineering; Displacement; Engineering; Euclid; Euclidean geometry; Hydraulic engineering; Hydraulics; Hydrodynamics; Mechanical engineering; Pascal, Blaise; Projectiles; Solid mechanics; Structural engineering

DISPLACEMENT

Fields of Study: Physics; Mechanics; Mathematics

ABSTRACT

Displacement is an object's net change in a position in a given direction. This is an important concept to understand because it is frequently used in physics to compute average linear or angular velocity, strain, and spring constants. Displacement is computed for linear positions, as well as angular positions.

KEY CONCEPTS

Cartesian grid: the standard grid pattern demarking the x, y, and z coordinates in two or three mutually orthogonal dimensions

scalar quantities: quantities that have magnitude or absolute value, but are not associated with a direction (e.g., 23 kilometers per hour)

vector quantities: quantities that have both a magnitude or absolute value and are associated with a direction (e.g., 23 kilometers per hour northwest)

DISTANCE VS. DISPLACEMENT

Distance is a more familiar concept than displacement and students often learn about distance before displacement. The two measures are related, and in specific situations can be equal, but their distinction is important to understand because most often they are different in value and definitely different in meaning. Distance, as in the distance between two points, is a scalar quantity having magnitude but not a direction. In another context, such the distance traveled to get from point A to point B, takes the initial and final position into account, and everywhere traveled between the initial and final position and does not distinguish directions. Displacement, on the other hand, is a vector that typically states the linear distance between two points and their direction relative to the starting and ending points of that linear distance.

For example, a person may go on a shopping trip from home to any number of stores in a town and end up at a store 20 kilometers away on the north side of town. The distance of that trip would include every straight run and detour taken to get to the desired stores for a total distance of 58 kilometers. One would state this as the person travelled 58 kilometers just to go 20. The final displacement, however, would be 20 kilometers north.

OVERVIEW

It is not clear when the concept of displacement was first used. However, Hooke's Law, discovered in 1660, states that the displacement of a spring is directly proportional to the force being made on the spring. In this case, the displacement is the difference in the length of the spring and can be positive or negative (the direction component of the displacement vector of the spring).

In a single dimension such as in a spring, the displacement from point x1 to point x2 is denoted $\Delta x(x1, x2)$ and $\Delta x(x1, x2) = x2 - x1$. Note that it is the final position minus the initial position. For this reason, the displacement from A to B is the opposite of the displacement from B to A. In two or three dimensions, displacement is specific to a direction. Suppose an object followed a line between two points on a Cartesian grid, with A at (4,2) and B at (2,1). The distance from A to B is 4 units. $\Delta x(A,B) = 4 - 1 = 3$ and $\Delta y(A,B) = 2 - 1 = 1$. The distance from B to A would also be 4 units. However, $\Delta x(B,A) = 1 - 4 = -3$ and $\Delta y(B,A) = 1 - 2 = -1$. The displacement values would be the same, but in opposite directions.

Linear displacement is an important concept as it is used to define other values, often-used values such as average linear velocity, $v = \Delta x/\Delta t$. Like displacement, average linear velocity can be positive or negative and is specific to the direction of the displacement. Angular movements also use displacement to describe the change in position of an object, as well as the corresponding average angular velocity. Strain, an important mechanical characteristics of materials, is the object's displacement over its original length, or $\Delta = \Delta L/L$. Mechanical work is defined as the product of the force made on the object and its displacement, $W = F\Delta x$.

—*Michele LeBlanc*

Further Reading

Arfken, George B., and Hans J. Weber. *Mathematical Methods for Physicists: A Comprehensive Guide*. Elsevier, 2012.

Durrant, Alan. *Vectors in Physics and Engineering*. Routledge, 2019.

Hewitt, Paul G. *Conceptual Physics*. 12th ed., Pearson, 2014.

Hsu, Tom. *Physics: A First Course*. 2nd ed., CPO, 2012.

Lavers, Christopher. *Reeds Introductions: Physics Wave Concepts for Marine Engineering*. Bloomsbury Publishing, 2017.

Ling, Samuel J., Jeff Sanny, and William Moebs. *University Physics, Volume 1*. Samurai Madia Limited, 2017.

See also: Acceleration; Amplitude; Angular momentum; Circular motion; Classical or applied mechanics; Dynamics; Elasticity; Equilibrium; Euclidean geometry; Har-monic oscillator; Linear motion; Motion; Pendulums; Springs; Vectors; Velocity; Vibration

DYNAMICS (MECHANICS)

Fields of Study: Physics; Mechanics; Mathematics

ABSTRACT

Dynamics is the branch of mechanics that deals with the motion of bodies under the action of forces. This includes both kinematics, which is the study of motion of objects without concern about the causes of motion, and kinetics, which is concerned with studying the effects of forces of motion. Dynamics is important both in the study of mechanics and in engineering, where forces must be considered in design and function. Several forces, such as drag and thrust, act on objects. To move, an object must overcome various forces, including frictional forces and inertia.

KEY CONCEPTS

air resistance: opposition to motion due to air molecules experienced by an object passing through the air; also called drag with respect to flying machines

biomechanics: the study of how (human) organisms function regarding movement

friction: a force that arises between two bodies in contact, resisting the movement between them

momentum: the product of the mass of a body and its velocity; the rate of change of momentum of a body is equal to the force acting on it

sunspot: a dark circular area observed on the surface of the Sun, determined to be a relatively cool region formed by the Sun's magnetic activity

weight: the apparent quality of mass under the influence of a gravitational field

BACKGROUND

The works of Galileo Galilei and Sir Isaac Newton are integral to understanding physics. They were not the first to study physics and develop theories about dynamics, but they studied earlier observations and theories and tested old ideas based on new discoveries. The works of ancient Greek philosophers such as Aristotle, for example, formed the basis of much scientific research.

Galileo made his own crude telescope based on descriptions of a new invention in 1609. His observations led to an early understanding of dynamics. He discovered sunspots and realized that the Sun was rotating, which meant Earth might also rotate. He discovered four moons around Jupiter. This discovery lent further weight to the idea that the planets orbit the Sun, because many believed that if Earth was in orbit around the Sun, the Moon would be left behind. Yet, something held the moons of Jupiter in orbit. With his telescope, Galileo proved the heliocentric model of the universe.

Galileo is popularly credited with the Leaning Tower of Pisa experiment, which involved dropping two objects of different weights from the tower, though it is likely he did not conduct this experiment himself. He did conduct a series of actual experiments using inclined planes, which helped him study the effects of gravity on objects. He showed that the acceleration of falling objects of very different weights is due to gravity rather than the weight of the object. He developed the concept of inertia, which is an object's resistance to a change in its state of motion. Galileo corrected Aristotle's ideas about motion—objects at rest remained at rest unless a force acted on them, but objects in motion did not continue to move unless a force continued to act on them. Galileo realized that Aristotle had not considered the frictional force between the moving object and the surface on which it traveled. The frictional force opposes the force that pushes an object. Any change in the frictional force—such as oiling the surface—changes the effects of the force of movement. Galileo's law of inertia states that if frictional forces could be eliminated, an object pushed at constant speed on an infinite frictionless surface would continue moving at the same speed forever, even if the motion force ceases, unless another force acts on it. Although frictional forces cannot be eliminated, they can be reduced to near zero.

Newton was born in 1643, the year after Galileo's death. He studied mathematics and physics, and in 1666 developed the theories of gravitation. He later developed his three laws of motion:

- *First Law.* Every object persists in its state of rest or uniform motion in a straight line unless it is compelled to change that state by forces impressed on it.
- *Second Law.* Force is equal to the change of momentum (mV) per change in time. For a constant mass, force equals mass times acceleration: F = ma.
- *Third Law.* For every action, there is an equal and opposite reaction, or the mutual actions of any two bodies are always equal and oppositely directed.

The first law is essentially the definition of inertia. An object on which no net force is acting will maintain a constant velocity, which is zero if it is not moving. Examples include a ball falling through the atmosphere or the movement of a kite due to a change in the wind. The second law explains how an external force changes an object's velocity. The change of velocity is determined by the object's mass. According to the third law, when one object exerts force on another, it is subject to an equal force exerted by the second object.

OVERVIEW

The general principles of dynamics are based on the laws of motion, which have an impact on the design and operation of machines. Many of the issues to be considered are action-at-a-distance forces, including gravitational force, electrical force, and magnetic force, and contact forces, which include frictional force, applied force, and air resistance. An applied force is a force applied to an object; it can be applied by another object or, for example, a person. Gravity force (weight) is applied by a large object, such as a planet or moon. Normal force is the support force a stable object exerts on another object. (The surface of a desk, for example, exerts upward force on items resting on it.) Air resistance acts on an object traveling through the air and usually acts against the object's motion. Tension force is the force in a cable, rope, string, or wire when forces on opposite ends are applied, pulling it tight. Spring force is force on an object attached to a spring that is compressed or stretched.

Aircraft and spacecraft designers and operators must consider the dynamics of flight and a number of forces. Four forces of flight that must be addressed are lift, drag, weight, and thrust.

Planes fly because their wings are designed to affect the air as it moves over the wing. The wings make the air over the top move faster, which decreases the pressure of the air. This creates lift, or an upward force due to the relatively higher pressure of the air moving more slowly across the underside of the wing. Drag is a backward force on an airplane, caused by friction with and compression of the air through which the airplane is moving. Weight is the downward force, and thrust is a forward force of the airplane's propulsion system. Other forces, such as frictional force, may be reduced, such as by the use of wheels on the ground.

An airplane's wings have flaps, called ailerons, on the back edge. The pilot can raise and lower the ailerons. This affects the amount of lift provided by the wings by changing the resistance on the wings. When the pilot raises the aileron on one wing and lowers it on the other, the plane rolls so the side with the raised aileron goes down and the side with the lowered aileron goes up.

—*J. Campbell*

Further Reading

"Galileo: The Telescope & the Laws of Dynamics." *University of Rochester Department of Physics and Astronomy*, www.pas.rochester.edu/~blackman/ast104/galileo12.html. Accessed 30 Jan. 2017.

Hall, Nancy, editor. "Newton's Laws of Motion." *NASA Glenn Research Center*, 5 May 2015, www.grc.nasa.gov/www/k-12/airplane/newton.html. Accessed 30 Jan. 2017.

Housner, George W., and Donald E. Hudson. *Applied Mechanics Dynamics*. 2nd ed., Division of Engineering California Institute of Technology, 1991, authors.library.caltech.edu/25023/1/Housner-HudsonDyn80.pdf. Accessed 30 Jan. 2017.

Karnopp, Dean. *Vehicle Dynamics, Stability, and Control*. 2nd ed., CRC Press, 2016.

Kurdila, Andrew J., and Pinhas Ben-Tzvi. *Dynamics and Control of Robotic Systems*. John Wiley & Sons, 2019.

"Laws of Motion: Galileo and Newton." *New Mexico State University*, astronomy.nmsu.edu/aklypin/WebSite/NewtonI.pdf. Accessed 30 Jan. 2017.

"Newton's Laws, Vectors, and Reference Frames." *Massachusetts Institute of Technology Open Courseware*, ocw.mit.edu/courses/mechanical-engineering/2-003sc-engineering-dynamics-fall-2011/newton2019s-laws-vectors-and-reference-frames. Accessed 30 Jan. 2017.

"Nova: Galileo's Inclined Plane." *PBS Learning Media*, pbslearningmedia.org/resource/phy03.sci.phys.mfw.galileoplane/galileos-inclined-plane. Accessed 30 Jan. 2017.

Shaw, Robert J., editor. "Dynamics of Flight." *NASA*, 12 June 2014, www.grc.nasa.gov/www/k-12/UEET/StudentSite/dynamicsofflight.html. Accessed 30 Jan. 2017.

"Types of Forces." *The Physics Classroom*, www.physicsclassroom.com/class/newtlaws/Lesson-2/Types-of-Forces. Accessed 30 Jan. 2017.

See also: Acceleration; Aerodynamics; Aeronautical engineering; Aerospace design; Ailerons, flaps, and airplane wings; Airfoils; Airplane propellers; Angular forces; Angular momentum; Archimedes; Aristotle isolates science as a discipline; Automated processes and servomechanisms; Bernoulli's principle; Biomechanics; Celestial mechanics; Centrifugation; Classical or applied mechanics; D'Alembert's axioms of motion; Discoveries of Archimedes; Engineering; Fluid mechanics and aerodynamics; Flywheels; Force; Galileo; Hertz, Heinrich Rudolf; Hooke, Robert; Kinematics; Kinetic energy; Linear motion; Mechatronics; Moment of inertia; Momentum (physics); Motion; Newton's laws; Plane rudders; Projectiles; Propul-sion technologies; Rigid-body dynamics; Robotics; Solid mechanics; Springs; Stability; Stabilizers; Steam energy and technology; Structural engineering; Torque; Tur-bines; Young, Thomas

E

EARTHQUAKE ENGINEERING

Fields of Study: Physics; Mechanics; Mathematics

ABSTRACT

Earthquake engineering studies the effects of ground movement on buildings, bridges, underground pipes, and dams to determine ways to build future structures or reinforce existing ones so that they can withstand tremors. Earthquake damage and injury are aggravated by the fact that neither the time nor the location of major tremors can be precisely predicted by earth scientists. Damage to human-made structures may be lessened, however, using proper construction techniques.

KEY CONCEPTS

epicenter: the central aboveground location of an earth tremor; that is, the point of the surface directly above the hypocenter

failure: in engineering terms, the fracturing or giving way of an object under stress

fault: a fracture or fracture zone in rock, along which the two sides have been displaced vertically or horizontally relative to each other

hypocenter: the central underground location of an earth tremor; also called the focus

natural frequency: the frequency at which an object or substance will vibrate when struck or shaken

natural period: the length of time of a single vibration of an object or substance when vibrating at its natural frequency

shear: a stress that forces two contiguous parts of an object in a direction parallel to their plane of contact, as opposed to a stretching, compressing, or twisting force; also called shear stress

unreinforced masonry (URM): materials not constructed with reinforced steel (e.g., bricks, hollow clay tile, adobe, concrete blocks, and stone)

EARTHQUAKES AND SOIL CONDITIONS

Earthquake engineering attempts to minimize the effects of earthquakes on large structures. Engineers study earthquake motion and its effects on structures, concentrating on the materials and construction techniques used, and recommend design concepts and methods that best permit the structures to withstand the forces.

One might logically expect that the structures nearest an earthquake fault would suffer the most damage from the earthquake. Actually, structural damage seems to bear little direct relation to the faults or to their distance from the structure. It is true that buildings near the fault are subject to rapid horizontal or vertical motion and that if the fault runs immediately beneath a structure (which is more likely in the case of a road or pipe than a building) and displaces more than a few inches, the structure could easily fail. The degree of damage, however, has more to do with the nature of the local soil between the bedrock and the surface. If the soil is non-cohesive and sand-like, vibrations may cause it to compact and settle over a wide area. Compaction of the soil raises the pressure of underground water, which then flows upward and saturates the ground. This "liquefaction" of the soil causes it to flow like a fluid so that sand may become quicksand. Surface structures, and even upper layers of soil, may settle unevenly or drop suddenly.

Sinkholes and landslides are possible effects.

NATURAL FREQUENCY

Ground vibration and most ground motion are caused by seismic waves. These waves are created at the earthquake's focus, where tectonic plates suddenly move along an underground fault. The waves radiate upward to the surface, causing the ground to vibrate. Wave vibrations are measured in terms of frequency—the number of waves that pass a given point per second.

Much earthquake damage depends on what is known as natural frequency. When any object is struck or vibrated by waves, it vibrates at its own frequency, regardless of the frequency of the incoming waves. All solid objects, including buildings, dams, and even the soil and bedrock of an area, have different natural frequencies. If the waves affecting the object happen to be vibrating at the object's frequency, the object's vibrations intensify dramatically—sometimes enough to shake the object apart. For this reason, an earthquake does the most damage when the predominant frequency of the ground corresponds to the natural frequency of the structures.

At one time it was thought that earthquake motion would be greater in soft ground and less in hard ground, but the truth is not that simple. Nineteenth-century seismographers discovered that the natural frequency of local ground depends on the ground's particular characteristics and may vary widely from one location to another. The predominant frequency of softer ground is comparatively low, and the maximum velocity and displacement of the ground are greater. In harder ground, the predominant frequency is higher, but the acceleration of the ground is greater. When the ground is of multi-ple layers of different compositions, the predominant frequency is quite complex.

FREE- AND FORCED-VIBRATION TESTS

In order to determine the effect of vibrations on a building, an engineer must do the obvious: shake it. Whereas the effects on a very simple structure such as a pipe or a four-walled shack may be computed theoretically, real-life structures are composed of widely diverse materials. By inducing vibrations in a structure and measuring them with a seismograph, one can easily determine properties such as the structure's natural frequency and its damping (the rate at which vibrations cease when the external force is removed).

The simplest type of test is the free vibration, and the oldest of these is the pull-back test. A cable is attached to the top of the test structure at one end and

Shake-table crash testing of a regular building model (left) and a base-isolated building model (right) at University of California San Diego. Photo by Shustuv, via Wikimedia Commons.

to the ground or the bottom of an adjacent structure at the other. The cable is pulled taut and suddenly released, causing the structure to vibrate freely. Other tests cause vibrations by striking the structure with falling weights or large pendulums or even by launching small rockets from the structure's top.

Forced-vibration tests subject test structures to an ongoing vibration, thereby giving more complete and accurate measurements of natural frequencies. In the steady-state sinusoidal excitation test, a motor-driven rotating weight is attached to the structure, subjecting it to a constant, unidirectional force of a fixed frequency. The building's movements are recorded, and the motor's speed is then changed to a new frequency. Measurements are taken for a wide range of different frequencies and forces. Surprisingly, the natural frequencies for large multistory buildings are so low that a 150-pound person rocking back and forth will generate measurable inertia in the structure, thereby providing an adequate substitute for relatively complex equipment.

Another useful device is the vibration table: a spring-mounted platform several meters long on each side. Although designed to hold and test model structures, some tables are large enough to hold full-scale structural components—or even small structures themselves. Useful forced vibrations are also provided by underground explosions, high winds, the microtremors that are always present in the ground, and even large earthquakes themselves.

EARTHQUAKE-RESISTANT DESIGN

Structures can be designed to withstand some of the stresses put upon them by large ground vibrations. They must be able to resist bending, twisting, compression, tension, and shock. Two approaches are used in earthquake-resistant design. The first is to run dynamic tests to analyze the effects of given ground motions on test structures, determine the stresses on structural elements, and proportion the members and their connections to restrain these

loads. This approach may be difficult if no record exists of a strong earthquake on the desired type of ground or if the research is done on simplified, idealized structures.

The other approach is to base the designs on the performance of past structures. Unfortunately, new buildings are often built with modern materials and techniques for which no corollary exists in older ones. It follows that earthquake-resistant design is easier to do for simple structures such as roads, shell structures, and one-story buildings than for complex skyscrapers and suspension bridges.

BASIC CONFIGURATION OF A STRUCTURE

The first concern in examining a structure is its basic configuration. Buildings with an irregular floor plan, such as an "L" or "I" shape, are more likely to twist and warp than are simple rectangles and squares. Warping also tends to occur when doors and windows are nonuniform in size and arrangement. Walls can fail as a result of shear stress, out-of-plane bending, or both. They may also collapse because of the failure of the connections between the walls and the ceiling or floor. In the case of bearing walls, which support the structure, failure may in turn allow the collapse of the roof and upper floors. Nonstructural walls and partitions can be damaged by drift, which occurs when a building's roof or the floor of a given story slides farther in one direction than the floor below it does. This relative displacement between consecutive stories can also damage plastering, veneer, and windowpanes.

Lateral (sideways) cross-bracing reduces drift, as do the walls that run parallel to the drift. Another way to avoid drift damage is to let the nonstructural walls "float." In this method, walls are attached only to the floor so that when the building moves laterally, the wall moves with the floor and slides freely against the ceiling. (Alternatively, floating walls may be affixed only to the ceiling.) Windows may be held in frames by nonrigid materials that allow the frames to move and twist without breaking the panes. The stiffness and durability of a wall can be improved by reinforcement. For reinforcement, steel or wooden beams are usually embedded in the wall, but other materials are used as well. If the exterior walls form a rectangular enclosure, they may be prevented from separating at the top corners by a continuous collar, or ring beam.

STRUCTURAL ELEMENTS

Frame buildings are those in which the structure is supported by internal beams and columns. These elements provide resistance against lateral forces. Frames can still fail if the columns are forced to bend too far or if the rigid joints fail. Unlike bearing walls, frame-building walls are generally nonstructural; the strength of the frame, however, can be greatly enhanced if the walls are attached to, or built integrally into, the frame. This method is called "in-filled frame" construction. Roofs and upper floors can fail when their supports fail, as mentioned earlier, or when they are subjected to lateral stress. An effective way to avoid such failure is to reduce the weight of the roof, building it with light materials.

Another danger to walls is an earthquake-induced motion known as pounding, or hammering, which can occur when two adjacent walls vibrate against each other, damaging their common corners. The collision of two walls because of lateral movement or the toppling of either is also called pounding. Columns and other structural elements may pound each other if they are close enough; in fact, the elements pounding each other may even be adjacent buildings. If the natural vibrations of the two structures are similar enough, the structures may be tied together and thus forced to vibrate identically so that pounding is prevented. Because such closeness in vibration is rare, the best way to avoid pounding is simply to build the structures too far apart for it to occur.

Shell structures are those with only one or two exterior surfaces, such as hemispheres, flat-roofed cyl-

inders, and dome-topped cylinders. Such shapes are very efficient, for curved walls and roofs possess inherent strength. For this reason, they are sometimes used in low-cost buildings, without reinforced walls. When failure does occur, it is at doors and other openings or near the wall's attachment to the ground or roof, where stress is the greatest.

Much earthquake damage could be prevented if the stresses on a structure as a whole could be reduced. One of the more practical methods of stress reduction uses very rigid, hollow columns in the basement to support the ground floor. Inside these columns are flexible columns that hold the rest of the building. This engineering technique succeeds in reducing stress, but the flexible columns increase the motion of the upper stories. More exotic methods to reduce stress involve separating the foundation columns from the ground by placing them on rollers or rubber pads. Castles in feudal Japan, one of the most earthquake-prone areas in the world, were constructed in a similar manner. Each story rested on crossmembers that were firred to the floor below in such a way that each floor could slide back and forth during the oscillations produced by an earthquake, leaving the entire structure essentially unaffected afterwards. Structures with several of these lines of defense are much less likely to collapse; should a vital section of cross-bracing, bearing wall, or partition fail, the building can still withstand an aftershock. Overall, the earthquake resistance of a structure depends on the type of construction, geometry, mass distribution, and stiffness properties. Furthermore, any building can be weakened by improper maintenance or modification.

ALTERNATIVES TO UNREINFORCED MASONRY

Buildings using unreinforced masonry (URM) or having URM veneers have a poor history in past earthquakes. Because URM walls are neither reinforced nor structurally tied to the roof and floors, they move excessively during an earthquake and often collapse. Similarly, ground floors with open fronts and little crosswise bracing move and twist excessively, damaging the building. URM chimneys may fall to the ground or through the roof. Buildings with URM bearing walls are now forbidden by California building codes, but URM is still common in many less developed areas of the world. There are several low-cost earthquake-resistant alternatives to such construction.

Adobe walls may be reinforced with locally available bamboo, asphalt, wire mesh, or split cane. Low-cost buildings should be only one or two stories tall and should have a uniform arrangement of walls, partitions, and openings to obtain a uniform stress distribution. The floor plan should be square or rectangular or, alternatively, have a shell shape such as a dome or cylinder. Roofs and upper floors should be made of lightweight materials—wood, cane, or even plastic, rather than mud or tile—whenever possible, and heavy structural elements should never be attached to nonstructural walls.

The Center for Planning and Development Research at the University of California at Berkeley noted certain features of modern wood-frame houses that make them especially susceptible to damage from strong ground motion. In addition to URM walls or foundations, such houses may have insufficient bracing of crawl spaces, unanchored water or gas heaters, and a lack of positive connections between the wooden frame and the underlying foundations. Porches, decks, and other protruding features may be poorly braced. Most of these deficiencies can be corrected.

PROTECTION AGAINST INJURY AND PROPERTY DAMAGE

Earthquakes are arguably the most destructive natural disaster on the planet. No other force has the potential to devastate so large an area in a very short time. Not only can it not be predicted, but there is also even less advance warning for the earthquake than for other types of disaster. A hurricane can be seen coming and tracked by radar and a volcano typically gives many warning signs before it erupts. An earthquake simply happens.

Yet the magnitude of the earthquake is not solely responsible for the destruction. Property damage and injury to humans also depend on the type and quality of construction, soil conditions, the nature of the ground motion, and distance from the epicenter. The tremor which struck Anchorage, Alaska, in 1964 measured 8.3 on the Richter scale and killed eleven people; by comparison, the earthquake that hit San Fernando, California, in 1971 measured only 6.6—less than a tenth of the force of the Anchorage quake—and fifty-nine people died. Most of the San Fernando deaths occurred in one building: a hospital that collapsed. It seems likely that the hospital had not been adequately constructed to withstand the stresses to which it was suddenly subjected. The higher damage toll resulted from the soil characteristics in San Fernando and an underground fault that had previously been unmapped.

The only protection earthquake-zone residents have against property damage is that given by the engineers who design and build their homes, workplaces, railway structures, dams, harbor facilities, and nuclear power plants and by the public officials who regulate them. Now that engineers can learn how ground movement affects engineered structures and can design new structures accordingly, many of the earthquake-prone regions have building codes mandating earthquake-resistant construction. In some communities, programs exist to determine which buildings are unsafe and how they may be made resistant. Unfortunately, not all quake regions have such rules and programs in place, because of apathy, high cost, or other reasons. The high costs of recovery after major quakes, however, provide a compelling rationale for better preparation.

—Shawn V. Wilson

Further Reading

Consortium of Universities for Research in Earthquake Engineering. *Earthquake Engineering*. Department of Building Inspection, City & County of San Francisco. 2006.

Estrada, Hector, and Luke S. Lee. *Introduction to Earthquake Engineering*. CRC Press, Taylor & Francis Group, 2017.

Federal Emergency Management Agency. *Designing for Earthquakes: A Manual for Architects*. FEMA 454, 2006.

Filatrault, André. *Elements of Earthquake Engineering and Structural Dynamics*. Presses Inter Polytechnique, 2013.

Pecker, Alain. *Advanced Earthquake Engineering Analysis*. Springer Science & Business Media, 2008.

Villaverde, Roberto. *Fundamental Concepts of Earthquake Engineering*. CRC Press, 2009.

See also: Amplitude; Civil engineering; Dynamics; Elasticity; Force (physics); Friction; Harmonic oscillator; Kinetic energy; Momentum (physics); Potential energy; Springs; Structural engineering; Vibration

Elasticity

Fields of Study: Physics; Mechanics; Mathematics

ABSTRACT

All materials, from rubber to steel, including nonhomogenous materials such as concrete and brittle materials such as cast iron and glass, have the property that if the material is subjected to a stress, it undergoes a deformation. This behavior is termed "elasticity." If the material were inelastic—and thus unable to deform—it would fracture instantaneously. Elasticity is therefore the capacity of a material to undergo deformation while absorbing the stress that is applied to it.

KEY CONCEPTS

anisotropic: a material that shows different elastic properties in different directions

isotropic: a material that shows identical elastic properties in all directions

linear elasticity: the behavior of a material when stress is linearly proportional to strain

modulus of elasticity: the ratio of applied stress to resulting linear strain, also known as Young's modulus

nonlinear elasticity: the behavior of a material when stress is not linearly proportional to strain

orthotropic: a material that shows the same elastic properties in two directions at right angles to each other

plasticity: a state in which there is an increase in the deformation of the material without a corresponding increase in applied stress

Poisson's ratio: the ratio of the strain in the transverse direction to the linear strain

set: a permanent change in the dimension of the material as a result of stressing it beyond the elastic limit, or yield point

yield point: the stress at which the material passes from elastic behavior into plasticity

OVERVIEW

In order to understand elasticity, it is necessary first to define the relationship between stress and strain in a material. Stress is the force applied to a material per unit area of cross section; it is typically measured in Newtons per square millimeter or pounds per square inch. Strain is the deformation of the member per unit length of the member, in the direction of the deformation. It has no units, though units such as millimeter per millimeter or inch per inch are often used. If the stress in the member is plotted against the corresponding strain, the nature of the resulting graph defines the elasticity of the member. For any material, this graph can fall into one or more of three distinct types of behavior: linear elasticity, nonlinear elasticity, and plasticity.

Consider a test specimen in the shape of either a flat bar or a round bar, with dumbbell-shaped ends, gripped in the jaws of a testing machine that can apply a force in tension to the specimen. By dividing the force by the cross-sectional area of the specimen, the stress in the specimen can be calculated at any time. At the same time, an extensometer, attached to the specimen, measures the extension between two predetermined gauge points, the distance between which is the original length of the specimen. The extension at any time divided by the original length then gives the strain in the specimen. The applied stress and the corresponding strain can be plotted on the vertical and horizontal axis of a graph, defining the behavior of the material. For a material such as steel, initially the stress/strain graph is a straight line, and this behavior is termed "linearly elastic." The slope of this line gives a quantity called the "modulus of elasticity" of the material, also called "Young's modulus"; it is typically denoted E. This value is a constant for a material; for steel, the value is 204 kilonewtons per square millimeter.

If the test is continued, a point (the "elastic limit" or "yield point") is reached at which the behavior of the material changes suddenly from linear elasticity to plasticity. In plasticity, the material "flows," with a sustained increase in strain, but without any corresponding increase in the stress applied to the specimen. The stress/strain graph is hence a horizontal straight line, showing no increase in the stress but a continuous increase in the strain. The difference between these two types of behavior is critical to the design of structures. In the linear-elastic zone of the stress/strain graph, if the specimen is "unloaded"—thereby removing the stress—the material recovers all of its deformation, restoring the specimen to its original gauge length. Once the material has suffered plasticity, however, the removal of the load causes the specimen to return along a line parallel to the linear-elastic line, thereby leaving the specimen with a permanent deformation, or "set." The specimen now has been permanently deformed.

If the test is continued past the zone of plasticity, a certain "strain hardening" occurs in the material,

as a result of which the specimen is now capable of carrying additional stress, though not at the same slope as given by the linear-elastic line. The load, and hence the stress, then reaches a maximum, a neck begins to form, leading to a sharply reduced cross-sectional area, and the specimen fractures.

In addition to linear elasticity and plasticity, there is yet another type of behavior in some types of plastic materials, termed "nonlinear" elasticity. A material that does not behave in linear-elastic fashion but is yet capable of recovering all of its deformation without permanent set exhibits nonlinear elasticity. Such a specimen, under test, would have the stress/strain graph as a curve, thereby showing the characteristics of both linear elasticity as well as plasticity by curving over. The stress is now not linearly proportional to the strain even at the outset. If the load is removed, however, the material does return along the same curve to the origin, thereby permitting the specimen to recover all of its deformation without set. Since there is no straight-line portion of the graph, the modulus of elasticity, which is still a very valuable quantity for design purposes, is assumed to be the tangent to the curve, usually at the origin.

If the material is tested in one direction, say in tension, its elastic behavior in the directions at right angles is determined by a quantity called the "Poisson's ratio." The tensile strain in the longitudinal direction causing elongation of the member is accompanied by a compressive strain causing shortening of the member in the transverse direction. The ratio of the induced transverse strain to the applied longitudinal strain is the Poisson's ratio; for steel, it is 0.3.

The transition of a material from elastic behavior to a state of plasticity can also be a function of temperature. Within a normal range of temperatures, which vary for different materials, the material may show a specific pattern of behavior as described above. However, at cryogenic temperatures, most materials tend to show brittle fracture without much elasticity. On the other hand, at high temperatures, many materials, including steel, show plasticity before a change occurs in the state of the material from solid to liquid.

In homogenous materials, such as steel or aluminum, the elastic properties of the material are the same in all directions. This is not, however, true of many nonhomogenous materials such as wood or fiber-reinforced composites. For this purpose, materials are classified as belonging to one of three types—isotropic, orthotropic, and anisotropic.

A material that shows the same elastic properties, such as the modulus of elasticity, in all directions through the material is isotropic. The orientation of the material within the component is not important. If the material shows varying elastic properties in different directions, it is anisotropic. In wood, for example, the elastic properties differ if measured along the grain or across the grain. Another example of anisotropy occurs in composites with fiber-reinforced polyesters or epoxies, in which the glass reinforcement is in the form of a cloth. The woven-cloth reinforcement has differing properties along the warp and the weft directions of the cloth. If a material shows identical elastic properties in two directions at right angles to each other but shows differing properties in all other directions, it is orthotropic. Such composites can be made by layering the reinforcement to achieve true orthotropy.

APPLICATIONS

The property of elasticity is possessed by all materials in some degree. An understanding of this property has been indispensable in construction, transportation, industrial design, and mechanical equipment, to name only a few fields. The capacity of material to strain under stress, thereby permitting it to absorb applied loads without brittle fracture, has made possible the design of large structures such as high-rise buildings, long-span bridges, and arch dams. The design of bicycles, au-

tomobiles, and airplanes is also possible because of the elasticity of the materials being used. In industrial design and mechanical engineering, the plasticity of a material can be vital to the design of components such as curved members. In all fields in which plastics composites are used, the nonlinear but elastic behavior of the materials is an important design consideration. Each of these three types of material behavior—linear elasticity, plasticity, and nonlinear elasticity—has different applications.

Consider the linear-elastic behavior of steel. When stressed below the yield point, the deformation is completely recoverable, without permanent set. Consider a long-span steel suspension bridge, with high-tension steel cables supporting the deck through steel hangers. The cables pass over twin towers and are anchored in massive concrete foundations set in rock. When the full load of traffic comes on the deck—for example, during rush hour—the cables elongate in tension, as do the steel hangers, and the deck deflects, all as a result of the strains to which the materials are being subjected. When the live load is removed from the deck—in the very early hours of the morning, for example—the deck must recover its deflection and the hangers and the cables must recover their elongations to return the bridge to its original position. It is only the linear-elastic behavior of the material that accomplishes this; otherwise, each subsequent application of the load would cause more and more permanent set, eventually rendering the bridge unusable. The same type of behavior is also vital to the performance of a multistory high-rise building such as the Sears Tower in Chicago, which is subject to high wind forces. The wind loads cause the building to sway at the top because of the linear-elastic deformations of the columns. No permanent set occurs, however, and thus the structure is able to recover its deflections and return to the vertical when the winds die down.

Plasticity, however, also has great applications in industrial design. The property of some metals to flow without brittle fracture permits the cold rolling of sections to curved shapes. Consider a flat steel bar that has to be bent at an angle of 90 degrees. The inside, or compression, surface is stressed past the elastic limit and suffers a permanent compressive set or shortening. The outside, or tensile, surface is also stressed beyond the elastic limit and suffers a permanent tensile set or elongation. Both of these deformations, which are nonrecoverable, permit the bar to bend into a 90-degree angle. Since the stress is zero, when the load is removed, the permanent set has not impaired the ability of the bar to carry its full design load.

The applications of nonlinear elasticity are apparent in anisotropic glass or carbon-fiber composites, which are used in fishing poles, rocket motors, and "stealth" aircraft. These are all applications in which a high-strength/lightweight material is desired. The fiber reinforcement, which can be in the form of cut fibers, longitudinal filament roving, mat, or cloth, is embedded in a matrix of a high-strength resin, such as an epoxy, to form a composite. The materials now show nonlinear elasticity, considerably complicating the design. Yet the materials also display "memory," permitting the component to recover completely without permanent set when the load is removed. In this case, the anisotropic nature of the materials can itself be used for the efficient design of the component. Consider a rocket motor cylindrical shell structure that is built using a filament-winding process. The glass or carbon-fiber filament, impregnated with a high-strength resin, is wound on a rotating mandrel to form the surface. When the resin has cured, the mandrel drum is collapsed and drawn out to leave the finished composite cylindrical shell structure. The elastic properties of the material are now quite different in the radial, or bursting, direction of the shell, where maximum strength is required, as compared to the longitudinal direction of the cylinder. A knowledge of the differing elastic properties in the two directions then permits efficient design of the component.

CONTEXT

In the seventeenth century, Robert Hooke, an English physicist and mathematician, discovered that within the elastic limit, strain is proportional to stress; this is called "Hooke's law." In the early years of the nineteenth century, English physicist Thomas Young established a coefficient to express this constant relationship for a specific material; this is the modulus of elasticity, also sometimes called "Young's modulus." Yet nature has used elasticity for millions of years in the evolution of structural systems that are visible all around. Consider the structure of a tall tree, anchored through its root system in the ground and reaching for light to perform its leaf functions of photosynthesis, "inhaling" carbon dioxide and "exhaling" oxygen into the atmosphere. Such a tall tree is subject to high winds, in just the same way as a high-rise building; for survival, such a tree must be able to recover its sway though the elastic behavior of the wood. The same principle of recovery of deformations on removal of the load applies to all forms of life that need to have a predetermined shape that does not acquire a permanent set on the application of a load. In its bones, muscles, ligaments, tendons, membranes—even down to its cellular structure—a living organism subjected to stress will deform to absorb that stress and then recover itself when unloaded. Whether the biological structure is linear elastic or nonlinear elastic, the results are the same. Biological structures also use plasticity during the growth phase, when the acquisition of permanent deformations and the deposition of new material enables an organism to enlarge in size. Essentially, the property of elasticity possessed by all materials has permitted the rich development of life in its various forms.

The development of new high-tensile materials and composites for use in the aerospace industry has always been coupled, though not always successfully, with the need to raise the modulus of elasticity in an effort to reduce deformations as much as possible. A structure itself may be perfectly safe with the deformations it is undergoing, but large deformations may be unacceptable. Consider the attachment of nonstructural finish construction, such as a plaster ceiling, to the underside of a concrete slab forming the floor of a building. The large deflection of the floor may not result in damage to the slab, but the plaster ceiling will certainly crack. The deflections of the floor hence need to be restricted, and the higher the modulus of elasticity, the more economical the design.

—*Bezaleel S. Benjamin*

Further Reading

Bertram, Albrecht. *Elasticity and Plasticity of Large Deformations, Including Gradient Materials*. 4th ed., Springer International Publishing, 2021.

Dixit, P. M., and U.S. Dixit. *Plasticity: Fundamentals and Applications*. CRC Press, 2018.

Goodier, J. N. and P. G. Hodge. *Elasticity and Plasticity: The Mathematical Theory of Elasticity and the Mathematical Theory of Plasticity*. Courier Dover Publications, 2016.

Jahed, Hamid, and Ali A. Roostaei, editors. *Cyclic Plasticity of Metals: Modeling Fundamentals and Applications*. Elsevier, 2021.

Lubliner, Jacob. *Plasticity Theory*. Courier Corporation, 2013.

Petruszczak, S. *Fundamentals of Plasticity in Geomechanics*. Reprint. CRC Press, 2020.

See also: Aeronautical engineering; Aerospace design; Civil engineering; Classical or applied mechanics; Computer-aided engineering; Engineering; Engineering tolerances; Flywheels; Force; Load; Materials science; Mechanical engineering; Plasticity (physics); Poisson, Siméon Denis; Rigid-body dynamics; Solid mechanics; Springs; Structural engineering; Surface tension; Young, Thomas

ELECTROMAGNET TECHNOLOGIES

Fields of Study: Physics; Mechanics; Mathematics

ABSTRACT

Electromagnetic technology is fundamental to the maintenance and progress of modern society. Electromagnetism is one of the essential characteristics of the physical nature of matter, and it is fair to say that everything, including life itself, is dependent upon it. The ability to harness electromagnetism has led to the production of most modern technology.

KEY CONCEPTS

Curie temperature: the temperature at which a ferromagnetic material is made to lose its magnetic properties

induction: the generation of an electric current in a conductor by the action of a moving magnetic field

LC oscillation: alternation between stored electric and magnetic field energies in circuits containing both an inductance (L) and a capacitance (C)

magnetic damping: the use of opposing magnetic fields to damp the motion of a magnetic oscillator

sinusoidal: varying continuously between maximum and minimum values of equal magnitude at a specific frequency, in the manner of a sine wave

toroid: a doughnut-shaped circular core about which is wrapped a continuous wire coil carrying an electrical current

DEFINITION AND BASIC PRINCIPLES

Magnetism is a fundamental field effect produced by the movement of an electrical charge, whether that charge is within individual atoms such as iron or is the movement of large quantities of electrons through an electrical conductor. The electrical field effect is intimately related to that of magnetism. The two can exist independently of each other, but when the electrical field is generated by the movement of a charge, the electrical field is always accompanied by a magnetic field. Together they are referred to as an electromagnetic field. The precise mathematical relationship between electric and magnetic fields allows electricity to be used to generate magnetic fields of specific strengths, commonly through the use of conductor coils, in which the flow of electricity follows a circular path. The method is well understood and is the basic operating principle of both electric motors and electric generators.

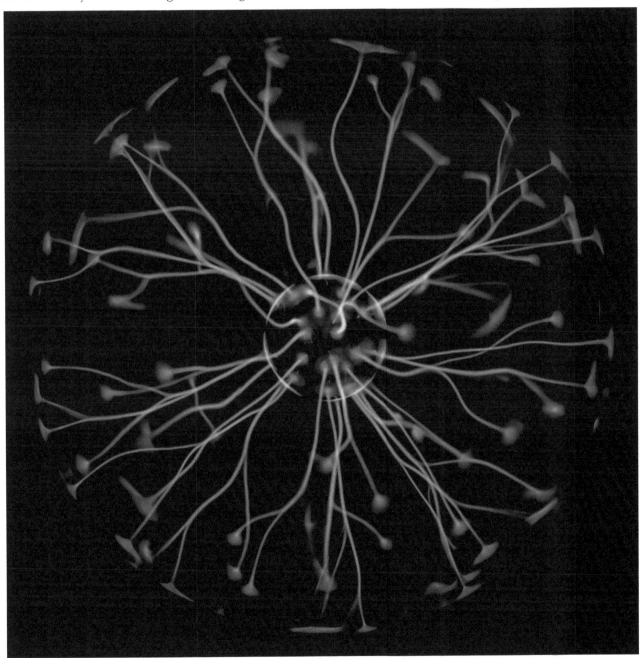

Electromagnetic interactions are responsible for the glowing filaments in this plasma globe. Photo by Colin, via Wikimedia Commons.

When used with magnetically susceptible materials, this method transmits magnetic effects that work for a variety of purposes. Bulk material handling can be carried out in this way. On a much smaller scale, the same method permits the manipulation of data bits on magnetic recording tape and hard-disk drives. This fine degree of control is made possible through the combination of digital technology and the relationship between electric and magnetic fields.

BACKGROUND AND HISTORY

The relationship between electric current and magnetic fields was first observed by Danish physicist and chemist Hans Christian Oersted (1777-1851), who noted, in 1820, how a compass placed near an electrified coil of wires responded to those wires. When electricity was made to flow through the coil, these wires changed the direction in which the compass pointed. From this Oersted reasoned that a magnetic field must exist around an electrified coil.

In 1821, English chemist and physicist Michael Faraday (1791-1867) found that he could make an electromagnetic field interact with a permanent magnetic field, inducing motion in one or the other of the magnetized objects. By controlling the electrical current in the electromagnet, the permanent magnet can be made to spin about. This became the operating principle of the electric motor. In 1831, Faraday found that moving a permanent magnetic field through a coil of wire caused an electrical current to flow in the wire, the principle by which electric generators function. In 1824, English physicist and inventor William Sturgeon (1783-1850) discovered that an electromagnet constructed around a core of solid magnetic material produced a much stronger magnetic field than either one alone could produce.

Since these initial discoveries, the study of electromagnetism has refined the details of the mathematical relationship between electricity and magnetism as it is known today. Research continues to refine understandings of the phenomena, enabling its use in new and valuable ways.

ELECTROMAGNETIC PRINCIPLES

The basic principles of electromagnetism are the same today as they have always been, because electromagnetism is a fundamental property of matter. The movement of an electrical charge through a conducting medium induces a magnetic field around the conductor. On an atomic scale, this occurs as a function of the electronic and nuclear structure of the atoms, in which the movement of an electron in a specific atomic orbital is similar in principle to the movement of an electron through a conducting material. On larger scales, magnetism is induced by the movement of electrons through the material as an electrical current.

Although much is known about the relationship of electricity and magnetism, a definitive understanding has so far escaped rigorous analysis by physicists and mathematicians. The relationship is apparently related to the wave-particle duality described by quantum mechanics, in which electrons are deemed to have the properties of both electromagnetic waves and physical particles. The allowed energy levels of electrons within any quantum shell are determined by two quantum values, one of which is designated the magnetic quantum number. This fundamental relationship is also reflected in the electromagnetic spectrum, a continuum of electromagnetic wave phenomena that includes all forms of light, radio waves, microwaves, X-rays, and so on. Whereas the electromagnetic spectrum is well described by the mathematics of wave mechanics, there remains no clear comprehension of what it actually is, and the best theoretical analysis of it is that it is a field effect consisting of both an electric component and a magnetic component. This, however, is more than sufficient to facilitate the physical manipulation and use of electromagnetism in many forms.

Ampere's circuit law states that the magnetic field intensity around a closed circuit is determined by the sum of the currents at each point around that circuit. This defines a strict relationship between electrical current and the magnetic field that is produced around the conductor by that current. Because electrical current is a physical quantity that can be precisely controlled on scales that currently range from single electrons to large currents, the corresponding magnetic fields can be equally precisely controlled.

Electrical current exists in two forms: direct current and alternating current. In direct current, the movement of electrons in a conductor occurs in one direction only at a constant rate that is determined by the potential difference across the circuit and the resistance of the components that make up that circuit. The flow of direct current through a linear conductor generates a similarly constant magnetic field around that conductor.

In alternating current, the movement of electrons alternates direction at a set sinusoidal wave frequency. In North America this frequency is 60 hertz, which means that electrons reverse the direction of their movement in the conductor 120 times each second, effectively oscillating back and forth through the wires. Because of this, the vector direction of the magnetic field around those conductors also reverses at the same rate. This oscillation requires that the phase of the cycle be factored into design and operating principles of electric motors and other machines that use alternating current.

Both forms of electrical current can be used to induce a strong magnetic field in a magnetic material that has been surrounded by electrical conductors. The classic example of this effect is to wrap a large steel nail with insulated copper wire connected to the terminals of a battery so that as electrical current flows through the coil, the nail becomes magnetic. The same principle applies on all scales in which electromagnets are utilized to perform a function.

APPLICATIONS AND PRODUCTS

The applications of electromagnetic technology are as varied and widespread as the nature of electromagnetic phenomena. Every possible variation of electromagnetism provides an opportunity for the development of some useful application.

Electrical power generation. The movement of a magnetic field across a conductor induces an electrical current flow in that conductor. This is the operating principle of every electrical generator. A variety of methods are used to convert the mechanical energy of motion into electrical energy, typically in generating stations.

Hydroelectric power uses the force provided by falling water to drive the magnetic rotors of generators. Other plants use the combustion of fuels to generate steam that is then used to drive electrical generators. Nuclear power plants use nuclear fission for the same purpose. Still other power generation projects use renewable resources such as wind and ocean tides to operate electrical generators.

Solar energy can be used in two ways to generate electricity. In regions with a high amount of sunlight, reflectors can be used to focus that energy on a point to produce steam or some other gaseous material under pressure; this material can then drive an electrical generator. Alternatively, and more commonly, semiconductor solar panels are used to capture the electromagnetic property of sunlight and drive electrons through the system to generate electrical current.

Material handling. Electromagnetism has long been used on a fairly crude scale for the handling and manipulation of materials. A common site in metal recycling yards is a crane using a large electromagnet to pick up and move quantities of magnetically susceptible materials, such as scrap iron and steel, from one location to another. Such electromagnets are powerful enough to lift a ton or more of material at a time. In more refined applications, smaller electromagnets operating on exactly the same principle are often incorporated into automated processes under robotic control to manipulate and move individual metal parts within a production process.

Machine operational control. Electromagnetic technology is often used for the control of operating machinery. Operation is achieved normally through the use of solenoids and solenoid-operated relays. A solenoid is an electromagnet coil that acts on a movable core, such that when current flows in the coil, the core responds to the magnetic field by shifting its position as though to leave the coil. This motion can be used to close a switch or to apply pressure according to the magnetic field strength in the coil.

When the solenoid and switch are enclosed together in a discrete unit, the structure is known as a relay and is used to control the function of electrical circuitry and to operate valves in hydraulic or pneumatic systems. In these applications also, the extremely fine control of electrical current facilitates the design and application of a large variety of solenoids. These solenoids range in size from the very small (used in micromachinery) and those used in typical video equipment and CD players, to very large ones (used to stabilize and operate components of large, heavy machinery).

A second use of electromagnetic technology in machine control utilizes the opposition of magnetic fields to effect braking force for such precision machines as high-speed trains. Normal frictional braking in such situations would have serious negative effects on the interacting components, resulting in warping, scarring, material transfer welding, and other damage. Electromagnetic braking forces avoid any actual contact between components and can be adjusted continuously by control of the electrical current being applied.

Magnetic media. The single most important aspect of electromagnetic technology is also the smallest and most rigidly controlled application of all. Mag-

netic media have been known for many years, beginning with the magnetic wire and progressing to magnetic recording tape. In these applications, a substrate material in tape form, typically a ribbon of an unreactive plastic film, is given a coating that contains fine granules of a magnetically susceptible material such as iron oxide or chromium dioxide. Exposure of the material to a magnetic field imparts the corresponding directionality and magnitude of that magnetic field to the individual granules in the coating. As the medium moves past an electromagnetic "read-write head" at a constant speed, the variation of the magnetic properties over time is embedded into the medium. When played back through the system, the read-write head senses the variation in magnetic patterns in the medium and translates that into an electronic signal that is converted into the corresponding audio and video information. This is the analogue methodology used in the operation of audio and videotape recording.

With the development of digital technology, electromagnetic control of read-write heads has come to mean the ability to record and retrieve data as single bits. This was realized with the development of hard drive and floppy disk-drive technologies. In these applications, an extremely fine read-write head records a magnetic signal into the magnetic medium of a spinning disk at a strictly defined location. The signal consists of a series of minute magnetic fields whose vector orientations correspond to the 1s and 0s of binary code; one orientation for 1, the opposite orientation for 0. Also recorded are identifying codes that allow the read-write head to locate the position of specific data on the disk when requested. The electrical control of the read-write head is such that it can record and relocate a single digit on the disk. Given that hard disks typically spin at 3,000 rpm (revolutions per minute) and that the recovery of specific data is usually achieved in a matter of milliseconds, one can readily grasp the finesse with which the system is constructed.

Floppy disk technology has never been the equal of hard disk technology, instead providing only a means by which to make data readily portable. Other technologies, particularly USB (universal serial bus) flash drives, have long since replaced the floppy drive as the portable data medium, but the hard disk drive remains the staple data storage device of modern computers. New technology in magnetic media and electromagnetic methods continues to increase the amount of data that can be stored using hard disk technology. In the space of twenty years this has progressed from merely a few hundred megabytes (10^6 bytes) of storage to systems that easily store 1 terabyte (10^{12} bytes) or more of data on a single floppy disk. Progress continues to be made in this field, with current research suggesting that a new read-write head design employing an electromagnetic "spin-valve" methodology will allow hard disk systems to store as much as 10 terabytes of data per square inch of disk space.

IMPACT ON INDUSTRY

It is extremely difficult to imagine modern industry without electromagnetic technologies in place. Electric power generation and electric power utilization, both of which depend upon electromagnetism, are the two primary paths by which electromagnetism affects not only industry but also modern society as a whole. The generation of alternating current electricity, whether by hydroelectric, combustion, nuclear, or other means, energizes an electrical grid that spans much of North America. This, in turn, provides homes, businesses, and industry with power to carry out their daily activities, to the extent that the system is essentially taken for granted and grinds to an immediate halt when some part of the system fails. There is a grave danger to society in this combination of complacency and dependency, and efforts are expended both in recovering from any failure and in preventing failures from occurring.

That modern society is entirely dependent upon a continuous supply of electrical energy is an unavoidable conclusion of even the most cursory of examinations. The ability to use electricity at will is a fundamental requirement of many of the mainstays of modern industry. Aluminum, for example, is the most abundant metal known, and its use is essentially ubiquitous today, yet its ready availability depends on electricity. This metal, as well as magnesium, cannot be refined by heat methods used to refine other metals because of their propensity to undergo oxidation in catastrophic ways. Without electricity, these materials would become unavailable.

Paradoxically, the role of electromagnetism in modern electronic technology, although it has been very large, has not been as essential to the development of that technology as might be expected. It is a historical fact that the development of portable storage and hard disk drives greatly facilitated development and spawned whole new industries in the process. Nevertheless, it is also true that portable storage, however inefficient in comparison, was already available in the form of tape drives and nonmagnetic media, such as punch cards. It is possible that other methods, such as optical media (CDs and DVDs) or electronic media (USB flash drives), could have developed without magnetic media.

One area of electromagnetic technology that would be easy to overlook in the context of industry is that of analytical devices used for testing and research applications. Because light is an electromagnetic phenomenon, any device that uses light in specific ways for measurement represents a branch of electromagnetic technology. Foremost of these are the spectrophotometers that are routinely used in medical and technical analysis. These play an important role in a broad variety of fields. Forensic analysis utilizes spectrophotometry to identify and compare materials. Medical analytics uses this technology in much the same way to quantify components in body fluids and other substances. Industrial processes often use some form of spectrophotometric process to monitor system functions and obtain feedback data to be used in automated process control.

In basic research environments, electromagnetic technologies are essential components, providing instrumentation such as the mass spectrometer and the photoelectron spectrometer, both of which function strictly on the principle of electric and magnetic fields. Nuclear magnetic resonance and electron spin resonance also are governed by those same prinspin resonance also are governed by those same principles. In the former case, these principles have been developed into the diagnostic procedure known as magnetic resonance imaging (MRI). Similar methods have application in materials testing, quality control, and nondestructive structural testing.

CAREERS AND COURSEWORK

Because electromagnetic technology is so pervasive in modern society and industry, students are faced with an extremely broad set of career options. It is not an overstatement to say that almost all possible careers rely on or are affected in some way by electromagnetic technology. Thus, those persons who have even a basic awareness of these principles will be somewhat better prepared than those who do not.

Students should expect to take courses in mathematics, physics, and electronics as a foundation for understanding electromagnetic technology. Basic programs will focus on the practical applications of electromagnetism, and some students will find a rewarding career simply working on electric motors and generators. Others may focus on the applications of electromagnetic technology as they apply to basic computer technology. More advanced careers, however, will require students to undertake more advanced studies that will include materials science,

digital electronics, controls and feedback theory, servomechanism controls, and hydraulics and pneumatics, as well as advanced levels of physics and applied mathematics. Those who seek to understand the electromagnetic nature of matter will specialize in the study of quantum mechanics and quantum theory and of high-energy physics.

SOCIAL CONTEXT AND FUTURE PROSPECTS

Electromagnetic technologies and modern society are inextricably linked, particularly in the area of communications. Despite modern telecommunications swiftly becoming entirely digital in nature, the transmission of digital telecommunications signals is still carried out through the use of electromagnetic carriers. These can be essentially any frequency, although regulations control what range of the electromagnetic spectrum can be used for what purpose. Cellular telephones, for example, use the microwave region of the spectrum only, while other devices are restricted to operate in only the infrared region or in the visible light region of the electromagnetic spectrum.

One cannot overlook the development of electromagnetic technologies that will come about through the development of new materials and methods. These will apply to many sectors of society, including transportation and the military. In development are high-speed trains that use the repulsion between electrically generated magnetic fields to levitate the vehicle so that there is no physical contact between the machine and the track. Electromagnetic technologies will work to control the acceleration, speed, deceleration, and other motions of the machinery. High-speed transit by such machines has the potential to drastically change the transportation industry.

In future military applications, electromagnetic technologies will play a role that is as important as its present role. Communications and intelligence, as well as analytical reconnaissance, will benefit from the development of new and existing electromagnetic technologies. Weaponry, also, may become an important field of military electromagnetic technology, as experimentation continues toward the development of such things as cloaking or invisibility devices and electromagnetically powered rail guns.

—Richard M. Renneboog

Further Reading

Batygin, Yutiy, Marina Barbashova, and Oleh Sabokar. *Electromagnetic Metal Forming for Advanced Processing Technologies*. Springer, 2018.

Crocco, Lorenzo, and Panos Kosmas, editors. *Electromagnetic Technologies for Medical Diagnostics: Fundamental Issues, Clinical Applications and Perspectives*. MDPI, 2019.

Funaro, Daniele. *Electromagnetism and the Structure of Matter*. World Scientific, 2008.

Gómez-López, Vicente M., and Rajeev Bhat, editors. *Electromagnetic Technologies in Food Science*. John Wiley & Sons, 2021.

Han, G. C., et al. "A Differential Dual Spin Valve with High Pinning Stability." *Applied Physics Letters*, vol. 96, 2010.

Prakash, Punit, and Govindarajan Srimathveeravalli, editors. *Principles and Technologies for Electromagnetic Energy Based Therapies*. Academic Press, 2021.

See also: Automated processes and servomechanisms; Electromagnetism; Force (physics); Gauss's law; Lenz's law; Magnetism; Solenoid; Tesla, Nikola

ELECTROMAGNETISM

Fields of Study: Physics; Mechanics; Mathematics

ABSTRACT

Electromagnetism is the theoretical framework that describes the dynamical effects that a collection of electric charges (at rest or in relative motion) has on other charges. The consequences of this theory include descriptions of a diverse range of phenomena, including the prediction of electromagnetic waves of which visible light is an example.

KEY CONCEPTS

charge: the intrinsic property of matter that is responsible for all electromagnetic phenomena

current: movement of one kind of charge relative to another

electric field: the influence that a distribution of charges has on the space around it such that the force experienced by a small test charge q is given by the value of that charge times the electric field, which results from the charge distribution

electromagnetic wave: time-varying electric and magnetic fields propagating through space (or through a medium); light is an example of an electromagnetic wave

electromotive force (emf): the potential difference between two points (or terminals) of a device that is used as a source of electrical energy

electrostatic: refers to situations where electric charges are at rest

flux: the value of the electric (or magnetic) field multiplied by the surface area that it crosses

frequency: the number of cycles or oscillations occurring during a unit of time; a standard unit of frequency is the hertz, which stands for one cycle per second

magnetic field: the influence that a distribution of electric currents has on the space around it

magnetostatic: refers to magnetic fields that result from constant electric currents

OVERVIEW

Electromagnetism is a study of the effects that a distribution of electric charges has on its surroundings, including its interactions with other electric charges. Representing one of the great syntheses of science, electromagnetism brings together previously separate electric, magnetic, and optical sciences into a single theoretical framework through a set of unifying underlying principles.

It is well known that electric charges come in two varieties, where "like" charges (charges of the same

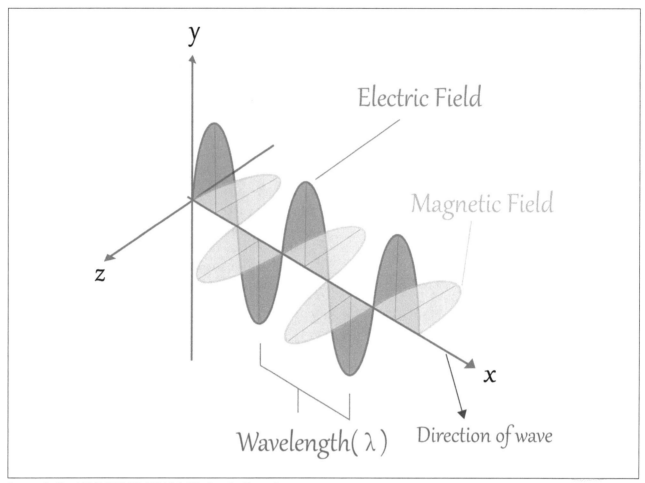

Image via iStock/KAMURAN A?BABA. [Used under license.]

kind) repel each other and "unlike" charges (charges of different kinds) attract each other. The two types of electric charges are conveniently labeled as positive and negative, a label that allows electric charges to be described by a conservation principle known as conservation of charge. This principle states that a net charge can be neither created nor destroyed. Rather, the net charge prior to a reaction must be equal to the net charge after the reaction.

An essential concept that distinguishes electromagnetism from other disciplines of study such as Newtonian mechanics is the concept of the field. Whereas Newtonian mechanics views forces in terms of action at a distance (i.e., the Moon is attracted by the distant Earth), with electromagnetism action is viewed locally. For example, if an electric field exists at a position P in space, then an electric charge q located at that position experiences an electric force, resulting from its own charge and from the electric field at position P.

Analogously, the Moon experiences a gravitational force because of its mass, and the gravitational field at its location results from Earth.

Coulomb's law states that two point charges experience an electrostatic force between them, which is proportional to the magnitude of each charge and inversely proportional to the square of the distance between them. In terms of the electric field concept, this can be viewed as the value of one of the charges times the influence that the other charge has on the space at the location of the first charge. This influence that a charge has on the space around it is known as its electric field, which, for a point charge, is proportional to the charge and inversely proportional to the square of the distance from it. The electric field for a charge distribution is often illustrated in terms of diagrams containing electric field lines. These electric field lines are merely convenient schematic representations, much as lines drawn to signify the flow of water in a stream are a schematic representation of the actual flow of the water. By convention, these electric field lines caused by charges at rest always begin on positive charges and always end on negative charges.

Likewise, the magnetic field is the influence that moving electrical currents have on the space around them such that other moving electric charges interact with the magnetic field, thus experiencing a resulting force. The magnetic field can also be schematically represented by magnetic field lines. Nevertheless, magnetic field lines do not begin or end on magnetic charges.

Rather, in contradistinction to electric field lines, magnetic field lines always form closed loops.

This results from the fact that, unlike electric charges, there seem to be no individually observed magnetic charges (known as magnetic monopoles). This can be demonstrated by a bar magnet, which always has a north and south pole. If the magnet is cut in half, then two smaller magnets are created, each with a north and a south pole. The poles cannot be isolated. Yet, it should be noted that there is no reason, on theoretical grounds, to support the nonexistence of magnetic monopoles.

There are a variety of individuals who made significant contributions to what ultimately became known as electromagnetism. These contributions, important in their own right, were subsequently gathered (and, in one case, modified) by James

Clerk Maxwell (1831-79) and are known as the Maxwell equations. The four basic principles making up this collection of equations include Gauss's law for electricity, Gauss's law for magnetism, Faraday's law of induction, and Ampere's law (as modified by Maxwell).

Gauss's law is a reformulation of Coulomb's law. It simply relates the electric field in a geometric way to the electric charges that are present. This is done by comparing the electric flux through an imaginary closed surface (a surface with no edge such as a sphere or a cube) to the charges present inside that surface. For example, consider an imaginary sphere around a point charge located at its center. Gauss's law simply relates the flux through this surface to the charge contained within the sphere. The greater the charge enclosed by the sphere, the greater the flux through the sphere. Gauss's law for the magnetic field states that the magnetic flux through any closed surface is zero, which is equivalent to the nonexistence of magnetic monopoles.

To illustrate Faraday's law of induction, consider sweeping a closed loop of wire through a magnetic field. The result of this motion is to induce a voltage that will cause an electric current to flow in the wire loop. This effect is one consequence of Faraday's law.

Deduced independently in England by Michael Faraday (1791-1867) and in the United States by Joseph Henry (1797-1878), Faraday's law recognizes that an induced voltage (known as an electromotive force, or emf) may be developed in a coil of wire by changing the magnetic flux passing through this coil. Here, the coil defines an open surface. For example, a wire loop in the shape of a circle bounds a circular area, which is an open surface. It has an edge. A closed surface as used in Gauss's law has no edge. Faraday's law relates the electromotive force generated in the wire loop to the time varying magnetic flux through an open surface bounded by the wire loop, that is, a voltage generated as a result of the effect of a magnetic field on a wire. In cases where the time varying magnetic flux is caused solely by a time-varying magnetic field, however, Faraday's law relates that time varying magnetic field to a resulting induced electric field; that is, a changing magnetic field induces an electric field.

If one were to hold an ordinary magnetic compass near a wire in which a steady direct current (DC) were flowing, then one would notice that the direction in which the compass pointed would not be north necessarily, but rather it would be affected by the current in the wire.

This effect is one consequence of Ampere's law, which plays the same role in magnetostatics that Gauss's law plays for electrostatics. As does Gauss's law, Ampere's law makes use of geometry, in this case to relate the magnetic field around an imaginary closed loop path to the electric current passing through that closed path. The greater the current through the loop, the stronger the resulting magnetic field.

Of the four principles, both Faraday's law and Ampere's law establish a connection between electric and magnetic phenomena. Gauss's law for the electric field is concerned only with electric charges. Likewise, Gauss's law for the magnetic field is concerned only with the lack of magnetic monopoles. Nevertheless, these four principles are incomplete; they do not explain electromagnetism thoroughly. Maxwell brought together the four principles and synthesized them into a coherent theory of electromagnetism. Vital to this synthesis was the important observation that Ampere's law did not fully describe the relationship between the magnetic field and sources responsible for it. Although Faraday's law describes the induced electric field caused by a time-varying magnetic flux, Ampere's law does not contain a comparable term allowing for an induced magnetic field caused by a time-varying electric flux.

This additional term, dubbed the "displacement current" (which is not a current, at least not in the usual sense), introduces a symmetry between Faraday's law and Ampere's law. Faraday's law predicts the existence of an induced electric field caused by a changing magnetic field and the modified Ampere's law (which is now referred to as the Ampere-Maxwell law) predicts that a changing electric field induces a magnetic field.

The recognition that time-varying electric and magnetic fields can induce each other continually led to the prediction of electromagnetic waves that propagate at the speed of light. In fact, light is merely the continual propagation of time-varying electric and magnetic fields that mutually induce each other. Furthermore, the value of the speed of light is determined by proportionality constants contained in Gauss's law and Ampere's law, which are defined solely in terms of static phenomena: The electric permittivity (the proportionality constant of Gauss's law, where charges are at rest) and magnetic permeability (the proportionality constant of Ampere's law, where electric current is constant). Hence, Maxwell's displacement current not only completed the unification of the sciences of electricity and magnetism contributed to by Faraday and Ampere and others but also brought the science of optics into this unification.

APPLICATIONS

Electromagnetic waves are a consequence of combining Faraday's law with the Ampere-Maxwell law. From Faraday's law, a time-varying magnetic field induces an electric field, and from the Ampere-Maxwell law, a time-varying electric field induces a magnetic field.

The mathematical combination of these two laws results in a classical wave equation for the electric field and for the magnetic field. The solutions of these equations are electromagnetic waves composed of electric and magnetic fields that are continually inducing each other with a propagation velocity of the speed of light. The prediction of electromagnetic waves was subsequently confirmed by Heinrich Hertz (1857-94), who generated and detected radio waves in the laboratory and confirmed that they propagate at the free space speed of visible light.

Visible light is an example of propagating electromagnetic waves. These, as well as other electromagnetic waves, are characterized by a frequency. Just as the frequency of a sound wave determines its pitch, the frequency of a monochromatic (single frequency) light beam characterizes its color. For example, a typical beam of light from a helium-neon laser has a frequency of 4.74×10^{14} hertz. This light is characteristically seen as red. The electric field associated with light waves interacts with the cone cells in the retina of the human eye, with the frequency of this electric field wave producing the sensation of color. Nevertheless, visible light is a small portion of the electromagnetic spectrum. Other forms of electromagnetic waves are radio, infrared, ultraviolet, X-rays, and even γ-rays, with each of these types of waves having characteristic applications.

In particular, consider the radio part of the electromagnetic spectrum. An application is radio and television communications. Radio waves can be generated by oscillating electric charges (as, for example, electrons in a transmitting antenna). The radio waves can carry information either by modulating (changing) the amplitude (AM radio) or the frequency (FM radio) of the wave. A receiver with appropriate antenna and electrical circuitry can detect and amplify the electromagnetic signal, decode the information carried on the signal, and display the information. Television viewing is a result of encoded information that rides on a carrier electromagnetic wave as it propagates from the transmission tower to the television set.

Radio astronomy is the study of the universe in the radio part of the electromagnetic spectrum. Quasars (quasi-stellar radio sources) are perhaps the most distant structures in the universe, and they are prodigious radio emitters. The mechanism that produces such strong radio emissions from quasars is still not well understood. Furthermore, the Sun and even the planet Jupiter emit electromagnetic energy in the radio part of the spectrum.

Electrical energy generated by the electric utilities is a classic example of electromagnetic induction, as described by Faraday's law. In nearly all cases, an electrical power plant uses either thermodynamic or mechanical energy sources to turn a shaft. A series of connected wire loops is mounted on that shaft. Sweeping these wire loops through a static magnetic field induces an emf in the wires and, therefore, produces an electrical current in the loops. This is how electrical power is generated for most cities. Another, simple example is the electromagnet. This is a device that generates a sizable magnetic field with the application of a modest electrical current. Consider a piece of iron shaped into a solid cylinder. Insulated electrical wire is then wrapped several times around the iron cylinder and connected to a battery or DC generator. A small current flowing through the wire loops produces a modest magnetic field. Yet, this magnetic field tends to induce a substantially stronger resulting magnetic field by aligning most of the little magnetic fields contained in the ferromagnetic iron. As a result, a substantially larger magnetic field is generated. Resultant magnetic fields with orders of magnitude greater than the magnetic fields as a result of the current alone can be generated this way.

The principle of the transformer is based upon electromagnetic induction, as described by Faraday's law and Ampere's law. Transformers are devices that transfer and convert an alternating voltage from a "primary" circuit to another "secondary" circuit by taking advantage of magnetic induction. A wire wrapped into a series of loops carrying a current (primary circuit) generates a magnetic field that affects charges in another coil of wire (secondary circuit) not physically connected to the first set of loops. If the magnetic field varies with time (as is the case with an alternating current—AC), then the secondary loops of wire experience an AC voltage generated in them as a result of the changing magnetic field generated by the primary circuit. The actual induced voltage is governed by the ratio of the number of loops in the secondary to the primary coils. In this way, it is relatively simple to step up voltages for transmission of electrical energy over long distances and to step down the voltage for local distribution to houses and the like for consumer use.

CONTEXT

At present, there appear to be four fundamental forces of nature: gravitation, electromagnetism, the strong nuclear force, and the weak nuclear force. Classical electromagnetism is the theoretical framework that describes phenomena specifically caused by the electromagnetic force within the classical domain of validity, which extends to, but does not include, atomic dimensions. In this regard, electromagnetism is one of the essential "core" areas of physics that includes classical mechanics, thermodynamics, statistical mechanics, electrodynamics, and quantum mechanics. Furthermore, it is the basis of electrical engineering.

All electrical applications are fundamentally governed by the principles of electromagnetism.

Electromagnetism as a field theory is a complete and successful theory within its domain of validity. Moreover, electromagnetism is the archetypal field theory upon which the inspirations for other field theories are often based. That domain of validity, however, does not include atomic-level phenomena, where the electromagnetic interaction is most dominant. The theory that generalizes electromagnetism to include atomic and subatomic-level phenomena involving only the electromagnetic interaction is quantum electrodynamics, or QED for short.

QED is also a field theory not without a sizable inspiration from classical electromagnetism and re-

duces to classical electromagnetism at macroscopic dimensions. Today, QED is arguably the most accurate and successful theory ever constructed. At present, QED predicts results that agree with experiments to as many as eleven significant figures. As pointed out by Richard P. Feynman, that is analogous to predicting the distance from Los Angeles to New York City to within the thickness of one human hair. Most attempts at grand unification theories (GUTs) employ the field theoretical approach exemplified by classical electromagnetism. Indeed, electromagnetism is, perhaps, the first major successful unification theory where electricity, magnetism, and optics were brought under the umbrella of Maxwell's equations.

Nevertheless, as a field theory, electromagnetism is plagued by a difficulty characterized by field theories in general. In the case of electromagnetism, one source particle for the electric field is the electron. The electron is a point particle. At present, it does not appear to have any spatial structure. According to the mathematics underlying the theory, an infinite self-energy is required to contain a finite amount of charge within an infinitesimal value. Hence, electrons would appear to have an infinite self-energy, an intolerable situation from the point of view of the theoretical physicist but of little impact to the practicing electrical engineer. In spite of this difficulty, electromagnetism has undoubtedly been one of the most remarkably successful theories in the history of science.

—*Stephen Huber*

Further Reading

Barrett, Terence William. *Topological Foundations of Electromagnetism*. 2nd ed., World Scientific, 2022.

Bettini, Alessandro. *A Course in Classical Physics 3-Electromagnetism* Springer, 2016.

Flewitt, Andrew J. *Electromagnetism for Engineers* John Wiley & Sons, 2022.

Franklin, Jerrold. *Classical Electromagnetism*. 2nd ed., Courier Dover Publications, 2017.

Shankar, R. *Fundamentals of Physics II: Electromagnetism, Optics, and Quantum Mechanics*. Yale UP, 2020.

Sibley, Martin J. *Introduction to Electromagnetism: From Coulomb to Maxwell*. 2nd ed., CRC Press, 2021.

Wald, Robert. *Advanced Classical Electromagnetism*. Princeton UP, 2022.

See also: Atoms; Classical or applied mechanics; Gauss's law; Hertz, Heinrich Rudolf; Lenz's law; Magnetism; Quantum mechanics; Solenoid; Work and energy

ENGINEERING

Fields of Study: Physics; Mechanics; Mathematics

ABSTRACT

Engineering is the application of scientific and mathematical principles for practical purposes. Engineering is subdivided into many disciplines; all create new products and make existing products or systems work more efficiently, faster, safer, or at less cost. The products of engineering are ubiquitous and range from the familiar, such as microwave ovens and sound systems in movie theaters, to the complex, such as rocket propulsion systems and genetic engineering.

KEY CONCEPTS

analogue: technology for recording a wave in its original form

design: series of scientifically rigorous steps engineers use to create a product or system

digital: technology for sampling analogue waves and turning them into numbers; these numbers are turned into voltage

energy: capacity to do work; can be chemical, electrical, heat, kinetic, nuclear, potential, radiant, radiation, or thermal in nature

feasibility study: process of evaluating a proposed design to determine its production difficulty in terms of personnel, materials, and cost

force: anything that produces or prevents motion; a force can be precisely measured

power: time rate of doing work

prototype: original full-scale working model of a product or system

quantum mechanics: science of understanding how a particle can act like both a particle and a wave

specifications: exact requirements engineers must comply with to create products or services

work: product of a displacement and the component of the force in the direction of the displacement

DEFINITION AND BASIC PRINCIPLES

Engineering is a broad field in which practitioners attempt to solve problems. Engineers work within strict parameters set by the physical universe. Engineers first observe and experiment with various phenomena, then express their findings in mathematical and chemical formulas. The generalizations that describe the physical universe are called laws or principles and include gravity, the speed of light, the speed of sound, the basic building or subatomic particles of matter, the chemical construction of compounds, and the thermodynamic relationship that to produce energy requires energy. The fundamental composition of the universe is divided into matter and energy. The potential exists to convert matter into energy and vice versa. The physical universe sets the rules for engineers, whether the project is designing a booster rocket to lift thousands of tons into outer space or creating a probe for surgery on an infant's heart.

Engineering is a rigorous, demanding discipline because all work must be done with regard to the laws of the physical universe. Products and systems must withstand rigorous independent trials. A team in Utah, for example, must be able to replicate the work of a team in Ukraine. Engineers develop projects using the scientific method, which has four parts: observing, generalizing, theorizing, and testing.

BACKGROUND AND HISTORY

The first prehistoric man to use a branch as a lever might be called an engineer although he never knew about fulcrums. The people who designed and built the pyramids of Giza (2500 BCE) were engineers. The term "engineer" derives from the medieval Latin word *ingeniator*, a person with "ingenium," connoting curiosity and brilliance. Leonardo da Vinci, who used mathematics and scientific principles in everything from his paintings to his designs for military fortifications, was called the *ingegnere generale* (general engineer). Galileo is credited with seeking a systematic explanation for phenomena and adopting a scientific approach to problem solving. In 1600, William Gilbert, considered the first electrical engineer, published *De magnete, magneticisque corporibus et de magno magnete tellure* (*A New Natural Philosophy of the Magnet, Magnetic Bodies, and the Great Terrestrial Magnet*, 1893; better known as *De magnete*) and coined the term "electricity." Until the Industrial Revolution of the eighteenth and nineteenth centuries, engineering was done using trial and error. The British are credited with developing mechanical engineering, including the first steam engine prototype developed by Thomas Savery in 1698 and first practical steam engine developed by James Watt in the 1760s.

Military situations often propel civilian advancements, as illustrated by World War II. The need for advances in flight, transportation, communication, mass production, and distribution fostered growth in the fields of aerospace, telecommunication, computers, automation, artificial intelligence, and robotics. In the twenty-first century, biomedical engineering spurred advances in medicine with developments such as synthetic body parts and genetic testing.

A SPECIALIZED PROFESSION

Engineering is made up of specialties and subspecialties. Scientific discoveries and new problems constantly create opportunities for additional subspecialties. Nevertheless, all engineers work the same way. When presented with a problem to solve, they research the issue, design and develop a solution, and test and evaluate it. For example, to create tiles for the underbelly of the space shuttle, engineers begin by researching the conditions under which the tiles must function. They examine the total area covered by the tiles, their individual size and weight, and temperature and frictional variations that affect the stability and longevity of the tiles. They decide how the tiles will be secured and interact with the materials adjacent to them. They also must consider budgets and deadlines.

Collaboration. Engineering is collaborative. For example, if a laboratory requires a better centrifuge, the laboratory needs designers with knowledge in materials, wiring, and metal casting. If the metal used is unusual or scarce, mining engineers need to determine the feasibility of providing the metal. At the assembly factory, an industrial engineer alters the assembly line to create the centrifuge. Through this collaborative process, the improved centrifuge enables a biomedical engineer to produce a lifesaving drug.

Communication. The collaborative nature of engineering means everyone relies on proven scientific knowledge and symbols clearly communicated among engineers and customers. The increasingly complex group activity of engineering and the need to communicate it to a variety of audiences has resulted in the emergence of the field of technical communications, which specializes in the creation of written, spoken, and graphic materials that are clear, unambiguous, and technically accurate.

Design and development. Design and development are often initially at odds with each other. For example, in an architectural team assigned with creating the tallest building in the world, the design engineer is likely to be very concerned with the aesthetics of the building in a desire to please the client and the city's urban planners. However, the development engineer may not approve the design, no matter how beautiful, because the forces of nature (such as wind shear on a mile-high building) might not allow for facets of the design. The aesthetics of design and the practical concerns of development typically generate a certain level of tension. The ultimate engineering challenge is to develop materials or methods that withstand these forces of nature or otherwise circumvent them, allowing designs, products, and processes that previously were impossible.

Testing. With computers, designs that at one time took days to draw can be created in hours. Similarly, computers allow a prototype (or trial product) to be quickly produced. Advances in computer simulation make it easier to conduct tests. Testing can be done multiple times and under a broad range of harsh conditions. For example, computer simulation is used to test the composite materials that are increas-

ingly used in place of wood in building infrastructures. These composites are useful for a variety of reasons, including fire retardation. If used as beams in a multistory building, they must be able to withstand tremendous bending and heat forces. Testing also examines the materials' compatibility with the ground conditions at the building site, including the potential for earthquakes or other disasters.

Financial considerations. Financial parameters often vie with human cost, as in biomedical advancements. If a new drug or stent material is rushed into production without proper testing to maximize the profit of the developing company, patients may suffer. Experimenting with new concrete materials without determining the proper drying time might lower the cost of their development, but buildings or bridges could collapse. Dollars and humanity are always in the forefront of any engineering project.

Photo via iStock/metamorworks. [Used under license.]

APPLICATIONS AND PRODUCTS

The collaborative nature of engineering requires the cooperation of engineers with various types of knowledge to solve any single problem. Each branch of engineering has specialized knowledge and expertise.

Aerospace. The field of aerospace engineering is divided into aeronautical engineering, which deals with aircraft that remain in the Earth's atmosphere, and astronautical engineering, which deals with spacecraft. Aircraft and spacecraft must endure extreme changes in temperature and atmospheric pressure and withstand massive structural loads. Weight and cost considerations are paramount, as is reliability. Engineers have developed new composite materials to reduce the weight of aircraft and enhance fuel efficiency and have altered spacecraft design to help control the friction generated when spacecraft leave and reenter the Earth's atmosphere. These developments have influenced earthbound transportation from cars to bullet trains.

Architectural. The field of architectural engineering applies the principles of engineering to the design and construction of buildings. Architectural engineers address the electrical, mechanical, and structural aspects of a building's design as well as its appearance and how it fits in its environment. Areas of concern to architectural engineers include plumbing, lighting, acoustics, energy conservation, and heating, ventilation, and air conditioning (HVAC). Architectural engineers must also make sure that buildings they design meet all regulations regarding accessibility and safety in addition to being fully functional.

Bioengineering. The field of bioengineering involves using the principles of engineering in biology, medicine, environmental studies, and agriculture. Bioengineering is often used to refer to biomedical engineering, which involves the development of artificial limbs and organs, including ceramic knees and hips, pacemakers, stents, artificial eye lenses, skin grafts, cochlear implants, and artificial hands. However, bioengineering also has many other applications, including the creation of genetically modified plants that are resistant to pests, drugs that prevent organ rejection after a transplant operation, and chemical coatings for a stent placed in a heart blood vessel that will make the implantation less stressful for the body. Bioengineers must concern themselves with not only the biological and mechanical functionality of their creations but also financial and social issues such as ethical concerns.

Chemical. Everything in the universe is made up of chemicals. Engineers in the field of chemical engineering develop a wide range of materials, including fertilizers to increase crop production, the building materials for a submarine, and fabric for everything from clothing to tents. They may also be involved in finding, mining, processing, and distributing fuels and other materials. Chemical engineers also work on processes, such as improving water quality or developing less-polluting, readily available, inexpensive fuels.

Civil. Some of the largest engineering projects are in the field of civil engineering, which involves the design, construction, and maintenance of infrastructure such as roads, tunnels, bridges, canals, dams, airports, and sewage and water systems. Examples include the interstate highway system, the Hoover Dam, and the Brooklyn Bridge. Completion of civil engineering projects often results in major shifts in population distribution and changes in how people live. For example, the highway system allowed fresh produce to be shipped to northern states in the wintertime, improving the diets of those who lived there. Originally, the term "civil engineer" was used to distinguish between engineers who worked on public projects and "military engineers" who worked on military projects such as topographical maps and the building of forts. The subspecialties of civil engineering include construction engineering, irrigation engineering, transportation engineering, soils and foundation engineering, geodetic engineering, hydraulic engineering, and coastal and ocean engineering

Computer. The field of computer engineering has two main focuses, the design and development of hardware and of the accompanying software. Computer hardware refers to the circuits and architecture of the computer, and software refers to the computer programs that run the computer. The hardware does only what the software instructs it to do, and the software is limited by the hardware. Computer engineers may research, design, develop, test, and install hardware such as computer chips, circuit boards, systems, modems, keyboards, printers, or computers embedded in various electronic products, such as the tracking devices used to monitor parolees. They may also create, maintain, test, and install software for mainframes, personal computers, electronic devices, and smartphones. Computer programs range from simple to complex and from familiar to unfamiliar. Smartphone applications are extremely numerous, as are applications for personal computers. Software is used to track airplanes and other transportation, to browse the web, to provide security for financial transactions and corporations, and to direct unmanned missiles to a precisely defined target. Computers can operate from a remote location. For example, anaerobic manure digesters are used to convert cattle manure to biogas that can be converted to energy, a biosolid that can be used as bedding or soil amendment, and a nonodorous liquid stream that can be used as fertilizer. These digesters can be placed on numerous cattle farms in different states and operated and controlled by computers miles away.

Electrical. Electrical engineering studies the uses of electricity and the equipment to generate and distribute electricity to homes and businesses. Without electrical engineering, digital video disc (DVD) players, cell phones, televisions, home appliances, and many life-saving medical devices would not exist.

Computers could not turn on. The global positioning system (GPS) in cars would be useless, and starting a car would require using a hand crank. This field of engineering is increasingly is involved in investigating different ways to produce electricity, including alternative fuels such as biomass and solar and wind power.

Environmental. The growth in the population of the world has been accompanied by increases in consumption and the production of waste. Environmental engineering is concerned with the reduction of existing pollution in the air, in the water, and on land, and the prevention of future harm to the environment. Issues addressed include pollution from manufacturing and other sources, the transportation of clean water, and the disposal of nonbiodegradable materials and hazardous and nuclear waste. Because pollution of the air, land, and water crosses national borders, environmental engineers need a broad, global perspective.

Industrial. Managing production and delivery of any product is the expertise of industrial engineers. They observe the people, machines, information, and technology involved in the process from start to finish, looking for any areas that can be improved. Increasingly, they use computer simulations and robotics. Their goals are to increase efficiency, reduce costs, and ensure worker safety. For example, worker safety can be improved through ergonomics and the use of less-stressful, easier-to-manipulate tools. The expertise of industrial engineers can have a major impact on the profitability of companies.

Manufacturing. Manufacturing engineering examines the equipment, tools, machines, and processes involved in manufacturing. It also examines how manufacturing systems are integrated. Its goals are to increase product quality, safety, output, and profitability by making sure that materials and labor are used optimally and waste—whether of time, labor, or materials—is minimized. For example, engineers may improve machinery that folds disposable diapers or that machines the gears for a truck, or they may reconfigure the product's packaging to better protect it or facilitate shipping. Increasingly, robots are used to do hazardous, messy, or highly repetitive work, such as painting or capping bottles.

Mechanical. The field of mechanical engineering is the oldest and largest specialty. Mechanical engineers create the machines that drive technology and industry and design tools used by other engineers. These machines and tools must be built to specifications regarding usage, maintenance, cost, and delivery. Mechanical engineers create both power-generating machinery such as turbines and power-using machinery such as elevators by taking advantage of the compressibility properties of fluids and gases.

Nuclear. Nuclear engineering requires expertise in the production, handling, utilization, and disposal of nuclear materials, which have inherent dangers as well as extensive potential. Nuclear materials are used in medicine for radiation treatments and diagnostic testing. They also function as a source of energy in nuclear power plants. Because of the danger of nuclear materials being used for weapons, nuclear engineering is subject to many governmental regulations designed to improve security.

IMPACT ON INDUSTRY

The US economy and national security are closely linked to engineering. For example, engineering is vital for developing ways to reduce the cost of energy, decrease American reliance on foreign sources of energy, and conserve existing natural resources. Because of its importance, engineering is supported and highly regulated by government agencies, universities, and corporations. However, some experts question whether the United States is educating enough engineers, especially in comparison with China and India. The number of engineering degrees awarded each year in the United States is not believed to be keeping pace with the demand for new engineers.

Government research. The US government has a vested interest in the commerce, safety, and military preparedness of the nation. It both funds and regulates development through subcontractors, laws, guidelines, and educational initiatives. For example, the Americans with Disabilities Act of 1990 made it mandatory that public buildings be accessible for all American citizens. Its passage spurred innovations in engineering such as kneeling buses, which make it possible for those in wheelchairs to board a bus. The US Department of Defense (DOD) is the largest contractor and the largest provider of funds for engineering research. For example, it issued 80,000 specifications for the creation of a synthetic jet fuel. The Federal Drug Administration (FDA) concentrates its efforts on supplier control and testing of products and materials. Funding for research in engineering is also provided by the National Science Foundation. The government has also sponsored educational initiatives in science, technology, engineering, and mathematics, an example of which is the America Competes Act of 2007.

Academic research. Universities, often in collaboration with governmental agencies, conduct research in engineering. Also, universities have entered into partnerships with private industry as investors have sought to capitalize on commercial possibilities presented by research, as in the case of stem cell research in medicine. Universities are also charged with providing rigorous, up-to-date education for engineers. Numerous accrediting agencies, including the Accreditation Board for Engineering and Technology, ensure that graduates from engineering programs have received an adequate and appropriate education. Attending an institution without accreditation is not advisable.

Industry and business. Engineering has a role in virtually every company in every industry, including nonprofits in the arts, if only because these companies use computers in their offices. Consequently, some fields of engineering are sensitive to swings in the economy. In a financial downturn, no one develops office buildings, so engineers working in architecture and construction are downsized. When towns and cities experience a drop in tax income, projects involving roads, sewers, and environmental cleanup are delayed or canceled, and civil, mechanical, and environmental engineers lose their jobs. However, some economic problems can actually spur developments in engineering. For example, higher energy costs have led engineers to create sod roofs for factories, which keep the building warmer in winter and cooler in summer, and to develop lighter, stronger materials to use in airplanes.

CAREERS

To pursue a career in engineering, one must obtain a degree from an accredited college in any of the major fields of engineering. A bachelor's degree is sufficient for some positions, but by law, each engineering project must be approved by a licensed professional engineer (PE). To gain P.E. registration, an engineer must pass the comprehensive test administered by the National Society of Professional Engineers and work for a specified time period. In addition, each state has its own requirements for being licensed, including an exam specific to the state. An engineer with a bachelor's degree may work as an engineer with or without P.E. registration, obtain a master's degree or doctorate to work in a specialized area of engineering or pursue an academic career, or obtain an MBA in order to work as a manager of engineers and products.

SOCIAL CONTEXT AND FUTURE PROSPECTS

Engineering can both prolong life through biomedical advances such as neonatal machinery and destroy life through unmanned military equipment and nuclear weaponry. An ever-increasing number of people and their concentration in urban areas means that ways must be sought to provide more food safely and to ensure an adequate supply of clean, safe drinking water. These needs will create projects involving genetically engineered crops, urban agriculture, desalination facilities, and the restoration of contaminated rivers and streams. The never-ending quest for energy will remain a fertile area for research and development. Heated political debates about taxing certain fuels and subsidizing others are part of the impetus behind solar, wind, and biomass development and renewed discussions about nuclear power.

The lack of minorities, including women, Hispanics, African Americans, and Native Americans, in engineering is being addressed through education initiatives. Women's enrollment in engineering schools has hovered around 20 percent since about 2000. African Americans make up about 13 percent of the US population yet only about 3,000 of them earn bachelor's degrees in engineering each year. About 4,500 Hispanics, who represent about 15 percent of the US population, earn bachelor's degrees in engineering each year.

—*Judith L. Steininger*

Further Reading

Addis, Bill. *Building: Three Thousand Years of Design Engineering and Construction.* Phaidon Press, 2007.

Baura, Gail D. *Engineering Ethics: An Industrial Perspective.* Boston: Elsevier Academic Press, 2006.

Dieiter, George E., and Linda C. Schmidt. *Engineering Design.* 4th ed., McGraw-Hill Higher Education, 2009.

Nemerow, Nelson L., et al., editors. *Environmental Engineering: Environmental Health and Safety for Municipal Infrastructure, Land Use and Planning, and Industry.* John Wiley & Sons, 2009.

Petroski, Henry. *Success Through Failure: The Paradox of Design.* 2006. Reprint. Princeton UP, 2008.

Yount, Lisa. *Biotechnology and Genetic Engineering.* 3rd ed., Facts On File, 2008.

See also: Aeronautical engineering; Aerospace design; Biomechanics; Biomedical engineering; Civil engineering; Computer-aided engineering; Earthquake engineering; Engineering tolerances; Hydraulic engineering; Mechanical engineering; Structural engineering

ENGINEERING TOLERANCES

Fields of Study: Physics; Mechanics; Mathematics

ABSTRACT

Technical drawings, including those created using computer-aided design (CAD) software, depict objects that will be manufactured, typically to function with many other pieces in an overall assembly. All parts of the finished assembly must fit together closely, with little or no variation from their design specifications. The very small amount that sizes can be allowed to vary is the tolerance of the dimensions.

KEY CONCEPTS

kerf: the extra width of a cut made with a saw due to the slight sideways cant of the sawteeth

precision: the degree to which a manufactured piece conforms to its design specifications

tolerance: the allowable difference in the dimensions of a manufactured piece from the dimensions specified in the design of the piece

CUMULATIVE ERROR

How precisely can a particular physical dimension be determined? In practice, students in technical programs are taught that measurements using a graduated scale that is read by eye, such as that on a steel rule in a metalworking class or the side of a dispensing burette in a chemistry laboratory, can only be determined with accuracy to one-tenth of the smallest division on the scale. On a scale graduated in one-millimeter divisions, for example, a trained technician may determine a measurement on one part of an assembly to be 10.3 millimeters with an uncertainty of 0.05 millimeter. That is to say, the true value of the measurement is somewhere between 10.25 and 10.35 millimeters. For several such measurements of pieces in the assembly, these small variances accumulate for the overall dimension of an object made up of several parts. If the object is made

of eleven such parts, the overall dimension of the object would nominally be 113.3 millimeters, but its actual dimension would be between 112.75 and 113.85 millimeters, a range of 1.1 millimeters. This is cumulative error. There is an upper and a lower limit of variance that can be tolerated in the assembly if it is to function properly in the purpose for which it was designed. Therefore, there are corresponding upper and lower limits on the variances of each part of the assembly. Those limits are the tolerance, the maximum and minimum amounts of variance from design specifications that can be tolerated.

The components of machines and structures are designed to very fine tolerances in order to fit together closely. The most familiar example is probably the piston and cylinder arrangement of internal combustion engines and compressors. The cylinders of a particular engine are machined to a specific diameter, and the associated piston must be machined to a diameter to match. The diameter of the piston cannot be even the slightest bit larger than the diameter of the cylinder, or it will not fit inside the cylinder. Nor can it be an exact match in size, or friction would quickly destroy both piston and cylinder. Therefore, the diameter of the piston must be smaller than the diameter of the cylinder. But how much smaller? The purpose of the piston is to compress the gases inside the cylinder, and if the diameter of the piston is much less than the diameter of the cylinder, the hot, compressed gases could escape between the rim of the piston and the wall of the cylinder and would eventually destroy both. Clearly, the tolerance of the fit between piston and cylinder must be small.

The piston and cylinder example demonstrates one level of tolerance, in that inconsistencies in the piston diameters that are within design tolerance can be compensated for by the use of metal spring rings and polymer O-rings to provide the necessary gas leakage seals. High-precision devices, however, demand much smaller tolerances, which become increasingly important as the physical size of the component pieces becomes smaller.

GEOMETRIC DIMENSIONING AND TOLERANCING

Technical drawings are used to depict accurately the design specifications of an object to be manufactured or constructed. Each view of the object or structure is accompanied by the appropriate dimensions and the tolerance range of those dimensions. A tolerance range sets the acceptable boundaries of deviation for the manufacture of the subject of the drawing. Materials and the components the materials are used to make will always have certain innate inconsistencies. Even the purest of materials will not have a perfectly homogeneous internal structure. Steel, for example, has internal microzones in which the iron atoms and the atoms of whatever other elements are in the steel alloy have crystallized in different patterns. Those zones have different strength properties and may be of a size that represents a flaw in the material itself, a potential point of failure in the manufactured product. Accordingly, the material itself is manufactured within a range of tolerances.

The macroscopic nature of the material being used is also a consideration of the production method. The specified material must be able to accept the tolerance range to which it is to be produced. A material that can only be machined to a tolerance of 0.1 millimeter, for example, would not be suitable for a design tolerance of 0.001 millimeter, a tolerance range that is readily achievable with twenty-first-century computer numerical control (CNC) and computer-aided manufacturing (CAM) machines. The engineering of a product thus includes all such relevant considerations in its inception and design. The technical drawing of the object therefore also includes the standards designations of the materials, as well as the drawing details.

ENGINEERING TOLERANCES IN HISTORICAL PERSPECTIVE

There is a definite relationship between tolerance and precision in engineering. In ancient times, stonework, woodwork, and metalwork were the epitome of engineering. All of the craft professions relied on the fitting together of materials formed to exacting specifications. In a Roman arch, for example, the keystone at the top of the arch had to be carefully shaped to the correct size and geometric dimensions in order to provide the necessary shape and strength in the arch. This was the handiwork of a master mason. In some ancient cities of Central and South America, the precision fit of huge blocks of stone in some structures continues to amaze. In Japan, an island nation subject to regular earthquakes and tremors, there are wooden buildings that have easily survived those environmental effects for many centuries. The key to their survival is a system of precision-made sliding beams that underlies each story of the structure. This allows each story to oscillate independently of the others, rather than the entire structure shaking back and forth as a single unit. Master woodworkers were responsible for their formation. Environmental effects and the passage of time have acted to obliterate much of the detailed work in most metal objects, but the surviving work of ancient goldsmiths often reveals a high degree of intricate metalwork.

Since the Industrial Revolution, metalworking has been the most important of these various craft professions and has passed through a number of stages in terms of tolerances and precision. The use of powered machinery is at the forefront of those technological changes. Though known since ancient times for use in woodwork, powered lathes for metalwork enabled the production of threaded bolts and nuts. Originally, these objects could only be made by a master machinist who could cut the threads on a bolt and those inside a nut to match. These were not interchangeable with other bolts and nuts. The development of standard bolt sizes and thread gauges became possible with the development of precision metal lathes that could be set to reproduce a specific thread gauge. Similarly, metallurgy produced steel alloys of sufficient hardness that taps and dies could be made to cut standard threads on softer steel and other metals.

Interchangeable parts are the basis of the assembly line method of production. The methodology was popularized in the early twentieth century by industrialist Henry Ford and adapted to the rapid production of the Ford Model T automobile. Threaded parts for these and other conveyances previously had required the work of a master machinist or metalsmith to produce a replacement part to match, but the use of interchangeable parts allowed anyone at all to provide the replacement. Interchangeable parts also requires that each part, whether the smallest of threaded nuts or the largest of structural beams in a superstructure, be made to the same geometric dimensions and tolerances.

—*Richard M. Renneboog*

Further Reading

Childs, P. R. N. *Mechanical Design: Theory and Applications*. 3rd ed., Butterworth-Heinemann, 2021.

Jensen, Cecil H., and Ed Espin. *Interpreting Engineering Drawings*. 7th Canadian ed., Nelson Education, 2015.

Leach, Richard, and Stuart T. Smith, editors. *Basics of Precision Engineering*. CRC Press, 2018.

Osakue, Edward E. *Introductory Engineering Graphics*. Momentum Press, 2018.

Plantenberg, Kirstie. *Engineering Graphics Essentials*. 5th ed., SDC Publications, 2016.

Winchester, Simon. *The Perfectionists: How Precision Engineers Created the Modern World*. HarperCollins, 2018.

See also: Aeronautical engineering; Aerospace design; Biomedical engineering; Civil engineering; Computer-aided engineering; Engineering; Mechanical engineering; Nanotechnology; Structural engineering

EQUILIBRIUM

Fields of Study: Physics; Mechanics; Mathematics

ABSTRACT

Equilibrium is a condition in which a body is at rest or, if it was previously in motion, moves with constant velocity along a straight line. It refers to the condition of the dynamic system in which there is no net change in any component of the system.

KEY CONCEPTS

couple: a system of two equal and opposite parallel forces, spaced a finite distance apart

equilibrant: a single force or couple that when applied to the system causes the body to be in equilibrium

fixed end: the end of a member that is not permitted either sliding movement or rotation

force: an action or reaction that attempts to cause the body to move along its own line of action

friction: a force that arises between two bodies in contact, resisting the movement between them

pinned end: the end of a member that is permitted rotation about one or more axes

resultant: a single force or couple that can represent the applied forces and couples in their action on the body

roller end: the end of a member that is permitted sliding movement in one or more directions

OVERVIEW

Sir Isaac Newton's first law of motion states that if an object is at rest, it will remain at rest, or if it is in motion, it will remain in motion at a constant velocity and in a straight line, unless some unbalanced force changes its condition. This unchanged condition of the object is called "equilibrium."

In other words, if a single, unopposed force acts on a body, it causes the body to move. If the force acts through the center of gravity of the body, the movement takes place in a straight line along the line of action of the force. This is called "translation." If, however, the force acts on the body, but not through its center of gravity, it not only causes the body to move but also causes the body to rotate. In either of these states, the body is not in equilibrium. Yet consider two forces acting on the body at the same time. If they are both equal in magnitude, act along the same straight line, but are in opposite directions, the body then cannot move, and equilibrium is maintained. The forces cause internal stress and strain within the body, but no movement. It can thus be seen that equilibrium exists when there is balance. An unbalanced system of forces upsets the equilibrium of the body, causing either movement or rotation along or about three mutually orthogonal, coordinate axes, typically termed the x, y, and z axes.

As noted, a single force acting on the body can never keep it in equilibrium. It is easy, however, to see that more than one force can act on the body at the same time. A simple example is the case of gravity loads and wind loads acting on a tall building. In this case, the two forces act on the body at an angle to each other. How, then, could equilibrium be maintained? To answer this, it is first necessary to determine the outcome of the original force system. This can be done graphically, by completing the parallelogram of forces and determining the diagonal of the parallelogram. The diagonal, or "resultant," is the direction in which the body will actually move under the action of the two forces. The same diagonal can also be obtained by placing one force at the tip of the other. The resultant is now the third side of the triangle. If equilibrium is to be maintained, an equilibrant has to be applied to the body. This is a force exactly equal to the resultant, also acting along the diagonal of the parallelogram, but in the opposite direction. The method can be expanded to any number of coplanar, concurrent

forces acting on the body, by completing the polygon of forces (or repetitively completing the triangles of forces). The resultant then is the last side of the polygon; the equilibrant is of the same magnitude of force, but in the opposite direction. When the body is in equilibrium, the polygon of forces is said to be "closed."

If two forces are not concurrent but parallel to each other, are equal in magnitude, and act in opposite directions, the body is acted upon by a couple. Since the forces are equal and opposite, there is no translation. The couple, though, rotates the body about the axis of the couple. The magnitude of the couple is determined by its moment, which is equal to one of the forces times the distance between them. In order to maintain equilibrium, therefore, the equilibrant would be a couple of exactly the same moment, but of opposite sense. A clockwise couple, for example, would need a counterclockwise equilibrant.

In the most general case, therefore, with any number of noncoplanar forces and moments acting on the body in three-dimensional space, the entire system can be reduced to resultants of forces along, and moments about, the three coordinate axes. When it can be categorically stated that the sum of all the forces about each of these three axes, together with the sum of all the moments about each of these three axes, is individually equal to zero, then the body will be in equilibrium.

Consider, once again, the forces applied to a tall building, such as vertical gravity forces caused by its own dead load and the weight of its occupants, together with horizontal wind forces acting on the height of the building. How, then, is equilibrium maintained? Newton's third law of motion states that for every action there is an equal and opposite reaction. It is this reaction that functions as the equilibrant and keeps the body in equilibrium. Consider the simple case of a rope, one end of which is attached to a wall and is being pulled by a person at the other end. The force is applied at only one end, but the rope is in equilibrium. The reason is that the wall generates a reaction that is exactly equal and opposite to the force that is being applied. If the applied force is reduced, the reaction decreases instantly; if the applied force is released, the reaction disappears. In the case of the tall building, the reactions of the soil in which the tall building is anchored provide the vertical and horizontal equilibrants that prevent the building from settling into the soil or sliding on it, thereby maintaining equilibrium.

These reactions can be, essentially, of three types. If the end of the member is supported so that it can slide across the face of the base support, such as in a roller-bearing support, then the force reaction is provided only at right angles to the face of the support. If, however, the member cannot move but is permitted rotation at the support, it is a pinned-end support. In such a support, force reactions can be developed, but no moment reactions develop that could prevent rotation of the member. Finally, if the member is anchored in such a way that the support can provide force and moment reactions about all three axes, then the support is a fully fixed end. Hybrid-end conditions such as partially fixed or partially pinned-end conditions are also possible. It is these reactions at the anchorage, whether for a tree, a tall building, or a bridge, that provide the force and moment equilibrants necessary to maintain equilibrium of the structure.

APPLICATIONS

It would be impossible to imagine life without conditions of equilibrium. From the simple act of walking to the structure of a tall building, it is only the state of equilibrium that permits safety. In the case of walking, the most common reaction or equilibrant is friction. This is the force that develops between two bodies in contact with each other that prevents sliding along the common surface. The coefficient of

friction is the ratio of the force developed along the surface as a proportion of the force applied between the bodies at the surface. As an example, the coefficient of friction of a rubber tire on asphalt is about 0.8. In comparison, the sliding coefficient of friction of steel on ice is about 0.014. It is easy to see that an automobile would have difficulty rolling down the street without the application of substantial power, because a large frictional reaction can be developed to prevent the wheels from spinning, whereas an ice skater, with steel skates, will slide easily without much friction on the ice. In both cases, however, the effect of wind resistance is also a reaction being developed on the body.

Equilibrium has many applications in the analysis and design of structural systems, because it assumes that an object is at rest. This implies that it is safe and failure has not occurred. Given such a condition, equilibrium permits a designer to determine the forces and moments that must exist, internally, within the structural system under the applied loads in order to maintain equilibrium. If equilibrium exists, then the resultant of all forces must be zero. This fact determines the value and directions of the equilibrants.

Consider a suspension bridge. The designer can determine the force in the cables under the applied loads on the bridge structure. This load will include the estimated weight of the bridge itself, together with the load from the lanes of traffic. The impact forces created by heavy trucks rolling down the bridge will also have been considered. If the bridge is to be in equilibrium, then the force in the cables has to be resisted by an equilibrant reaction that has to be provided by the anchorage of the cables in the surrounding rock. This equivalency gives the precise nature of the forces that the anchorage must provide to the bridge for safe design.

An excellent example of rotational equilibrium is the child's teeter-totter or see-saw in a playground. If a heavy child is seated close to the fulcrum, or point of rotation, the moment about the fulcrum can be balanced by a lighter child who is seated farther away from the fulcrum. The application of a small upward force by the child at one end will enable the plank to swing upward until the feet of the child at the other end reach the ground and provide a reaction to oppose it.

The application of equilibrium to the case of moving objects, such as cars, trains, or planes, is equally important. Consider an automobile in motion. It is subject to its own vertical gravity loads, which include the weight of its occupants and the luggage in the trunk. It is acted upon by the driving forces at the wheels, and this motion is resisted both by the friction at the road surface and by wind pressure. Under all these forces, if the automobile is moving at a constant velocity in a straight line, it is in equilibrium. If the driver presses on the gas pedal, however, the automobile accelerates, and equilibrium no longer exists. The acceleration will occur until the increased wind resistance and increased road friction equal the increase in the force that is being applied to the automobile, at which time the car will return to a constant velocity and, hence, to a state of equilibrium.

Finally, it is loss of equilibrium that results in failure, sometimes with disastrous consequences. A good example is foundation failure, which occurs in buildings when equilibrium cannot be maintained. If the soil is poor, with a low safe-bearing capacity, or if an incorrect choice of the type of foundation has been made, large forces (actions) are imposed on the soil. When the equilibrant reactions are not forthcoming, the foundation caves in, and failure occurs. In the case of cantilever-retaining walls, for example, sliding of the wall, caused by the horizontal pressure of the earth, has to be resisted by friction at the base. The heel of the wall is, therefore, kept long—more than two-thirds the length of the base—so that the weight of retained earth on the heel provides large vertical forces that produce cor-

respondingly large frictional equilibrants. The weight of the earth on the heel also prevents the wall from overturning, thereby maintaining equilibrium.

CONTEXT

Equilibrium has been intuitively understood by nature for many hundreds of millions of years, ever since the start of biological evolution. The anchorage systems developed by roots, such as buttress roots or stilt roots, to anchor tall trees are excellent examples of nature's attempts to maintain equilibrium for the safety of the organism. Anthropological humankind also understood the importance of maintaining equilibrium for the safety of shelters. Ancient humans also understood the need for a large base to prevent the overturning of structures, such as the pyramids. Even Galileo Galilei investigated the equilibrium of a cantilever. It was Isaac Newton who, with his laws of motion, set the framework for a more classical study of equilibrium. This study was prompted by the need to develop classical methods of analysis that would permit engineering design, as opposed to the intuitive design of structural systems. The foremost need was for the development of towers. City-states and governments had reached the conclusion that vertical height gave greater forewarning of attack, and the development of towers was a prime military objective. Unfortunately, this was not coupled with an understanding of the nature of soil; as a result, many of these towers leaned out of plumb. The study of dynamic equilibrium, with bodies in motion rather than at rest, took on added impetus with the Industrial Revolution and the development of the steam engine. This process continued with advances in the design of automobiles, airplanes, and space ships. Yet the principles on which equilibrium is based can never change. This is because they are, quite simply, based on fundamental laws of physics, and regardless of the applications to which the principles may be put, these laws are invariant and immutable. In an ever-changing world, it is, perhaps, comforting to know that these laws that govern the equilibrium of bodies, at rest or in motion, will forever be the same.

—*Bezaleel S. Benjamin*

Further Reading

Bryant, W. D. A. *General Equilibrium: Theory and Evidence.* World Scientific, 2010.

Cardenete, Manuel Alejandro, Ana-Isabel Guerra, and Ferran Sancho. *Applied General Equilibrium: An Introduction.* Springer Science & Business Media, 2012.

de Nevers, Noel. *Physical and Chemical Equilibrium for Chemical Engineers.* 2nd ed., John Wiley & Sons, 2012.

Mandy, David. *Producers, Consumers and Partial Equilibrium.* Academic Press, 2016.

Ottinger, Hans Christian. *Beyond Equilibrium Thermodynamics.* Wiley, 2005.

Sheppard, Sheri D., and Benson H. Tongue. *Statics: Analysis and Design of Systems in Equilibrium.* Wiley, 2006.

See also: Aerodynamics; Aeronautical engineering; Airfoils; Celestial mechanics; Chaotic systems; Classical or applied mechanics; Dynamics (mechanics); Flywheels; Heat transfer; Mechanical engineering; Newton's laws; Pendulums; Stability; Statics

EQUIVALENCE PRINCIPLE

Fields of Study: Physics; Mechanics; Mathematics

ABSTRACT

Experiments done in an accelerated frame of reference yield results that are equivalent to observations made in a gravitational field. This empirical fact, elevated to the status of a postulate, is one of the foundations of the general theory of relativity, Albert Einstein's theory of gravity.

KEY CONCEPTS

acceleration: the rate of change of velocity associated with a change in speed or direction of motion or both

frame of reference: a system of space-time coordinates used by an observer to measure the physical world

gravitational field: the region in which an object (a test particle) experiences acceleration caused by the masses and locations of other objects (sources of the field)

gravitational mass: the mass of a body defined as the quantity that determines its coupling to a gravitational field, either as a test particle or as a source

inertial frame: a frame of reference in which a body that has no force acting on it has no acceleration

inertial mass: the mass of a body defined as the measure of its opposition to acceleration by external forces

OVERVIEW

Albert Einstein's equivalence principle states that it is impossible to distinguish by means of any physical measurement between a uniform gravitational field and a uniform acceleration. This principle explains the identity of gravitational and inertial mass and is one of the foundations of Einstein's theory of gravitation, general relativity theory. Understanding the logical distinction between these masses requires an acquaintance with Sir Isaac Newton's law of gravitation and his laws of motion. The numerical identity of these two masses for any particular object is established by experiment.

Newtonian theory describes gravitation in terms of a force that acts on any particle in a gravitational field. This force is the product of a property of the particle, its gravitational mass, and the field at the particle's location. (The field is produced by the gravitational masses of all other particles and depends on their locations.) Newton's second law of motion asserts that the acceleration of any particle that is subject to a resultant force is inversely proportional to its inertial mass. Numerous experiments have verified that if the only forces acting on an object are gravitational, its acceleration is independent of its composition. This requires that the gravitational mass of each particle must be numerically equal (or proportional through a universal constant) to its inertial mass. In the Newtonian description of gravitation and motion, there is no explanation of this mysterious coincidence.

What is the experimental evidence that inertial masses and gravitational masses are the same? The identity of inertial and gravitational mass implies that the times of fall from rest through a given height of two different weights will be equal. In spite of the authoritative statement of Aristotle to the contrary, precisely such an equality was proposed by Giambattista Benedetti in 1553, tested experimentally by Simon Stevin in 1586, and explored in detail through the study of balls rolling down inclined planes by Galileo, who was a professor at the University of Pisa from 1589 to 1592. Newton devoted the first paragraph of his *Philosophiae Naturalis Principia Mathematica* (1687; Newton's *Principia: The Mathematical Principles of Natural Philosophy*, 1846) to a careful statement of this result as a fundamental principle of mechanics. He also tested the result to a precision of 1 part in 1,000 in experiments involving periods of equal length and pendulums of different compositions. By the early twentieth century, the precision had been refined by a factor of 100, but this approach had reached the limits of its accuracy, which were imposed by factors such as the effects of air currents and difficulties in timing slowly moving objects.

In the late nineteenth century, Roland Eotvos first achieved substantial improvements in accuracy by conducting a new type of experiment based on a torsion balance, similar to that which had been used to determine the Newtonian gravitational constant. The experiments searched for and failed to detect a difference between the mass (inertial) on which centrifugal torques depend and the mass (gravitational) on which torques caused by the gravitational influ-

ence of Earth depend. In two series of experiments, which were performed in Budapest in 1889 and 1908, Eotvos and his colleagues confirmed the identification of these masses for numerous test bodies of various composition to the sensitivity of their apparatus, about 3 parts per billion.

To explain the identity of inertial and gravitational mass, Albert Einstein adopted the postulate that no experiment can inform an observer whether local phenomena are caused by the "fictitious forces" (e.g., centrifugal and Coriolis) present in an accelerated frame of reference or by the gravitational field as a result of distant objects. This principle of equivalence is fundamental to the identification of the gravitational field with a distortion of the geometry of space-time, so that bodies subject only to gravitation follow local geodesics (extremal paths) in space-time but no longer appear to move along straight lines over extended regions of space.

When Einstein first proposed that the equivalence principle was important to the foundation of gravitational theory, in 1907, he was apparently unaware of the experimental work of Eotvos and the more precise support it gave this principle. Although the equivalence principle by itself dictates only half of gravitational theory (curved space-time tells matter how to move), in Einstein's thought it was a natural leap to a unique formulation of the other half (matter tells space-time how to curve), the general theory of relativity, which he published in 1916. In the meantime, he had become acquainted, apparently in 1912, with the experiments done in Budapest, and referred to them in his later writings.

Ever since, experimentalists have sought ways to improve the accuracy of equivalence principle tests, or new means of testing. Major improvements were achieved by Robert H. Dicke and his colleagues (1 part in 100 billion) at Princeton University in 1962 and Vladimir Braginsky and his colleagues (1 part in a trillion) at Moscow State University in 1970. They replaced Earth's gravitational field and the centrifugal effect of its rotation on its axis with the gravitational field of the Sun and the centrifugal effect of Earth's revolution in orbit around the Sun. This allowed the elimination of sources of noise and error associated with the earlier need to rotate bodily the apparatus in order to exchange the roles of two test objects with different compositions. This was now accomplished twice daily by the rotation of Earth on its axis.

Thus, both groups were able to exploit advances in torsion fiber technology, improved vacuum systems that minimized effects of air currents, automated temperature control of the experimental environment, and sophisticated electrical and optical monitoring techniques.

APPLICATIONS

Beyond its role as an explanation of the equality of inertial and gravitational masses, the equivalence principle predicts the outcome of other experiments that depend only upon the response of bodies to a given gravitational field, not how the field is generated by its sources. Of primary importance among these, for reasons of both history and precision, are experiments involving the gravitational redshift of light in both astrophysical and laboratory contexts.

Similarly interesting is the predicted rate change of a clock that experiences varying gravitational potentials, perhaps before being returned for comparison of total aging with its twin, which has remained at rest in a laboratory.

In his 1916 paper, Einstein proposed that observations of spectral lines from a region of very great gravitational potential, such as a white dwarf star, should show detectable shifts toward longer wavelengths. This has been roughly verified for numerous examples, beginning with observations reported in 1926 of the spectrum of the white dwarf companion to the bright star Sirius, the Dog Star, and ultimately extending to observations of ordinary stars such as the Sun using observational technology that

became available in the early 1960s. Unfortunately, the precise quantitative shift is also influenced by complicated astrophysical processes, so the contribution of the equivalence principle, though theoretically calculable, is in practice impossible to untangle from other contributions. This prediction of the equivalence principle is so well supported by the laboratory experiments, however, that the gravitational redshift from astronomical sources is an accepted working tool of the theoretical astrophysicist. An interesting application may be seen in studies made in the late 1960s that showed that it is not possible to explain the dominant part of the observed redshifts of quasars in terms of a gravitational redshift from sources whose structures could be stable over the periods of time for which some quasars of large redshift had been under continuous observation. This development helped to convince most astronomers that the dominant part of the redshift of quasars had to be interpreted as being caused by huge Doppler effects, implying cosmological recession velocities larger than those of any other discrete objects that have been observed.

If astronomical phenomena mix gravitational redshift effects with other ingredients in messy recipes, there is one type of laboratory application that can be used for a nearly clinically pure measurement of this manifestation of the equivalence principle. This is the precision measurement of shifts in spectral lines emitted and absorbed at different heights in Earth's gravitational field that are made possible by the phenomenon of recoilless emission of γ rays, an effect named for its discoverer, Rudolf Mössbauer. Photons emitted at the top of a tower are blueshifted to shorter wavelengths at the base of the tower, and photons emitted at the base are redshifted in the same proportion at the top. Just such an experiment was first reported by Robert V. Pound and Glen Rebka in 1960, who used the 23-meter tower of the physics building at Harvard University as a location in which to observe the

0.86-angstrom spectral line produced in the decay of the unstable isotope of iron known as iron-57. This first measurement yielded results within 10 percent of what was expected, and an improved experiment by Pound and Joseph Snider in 1963 yielded results within 1 percent.

If wavelengths of light are changed by vertical motion in a gravitational field, frequencies must change inversely so that the speed of light is invariant. The frequencies of radiation associated with transitions in electronic structure, however, are basic to the operation of atomic clocks, the devices used to define laboratory standards of time. Thus, the phenomenon of gravitational clock rate change is also an application of the equivalence principle. The analysis is complicated by the fact that at the speeds and altitudes of the commercial airliners that were used in the experiment performed by J. C. Hafele and Richard Keating in October of 1971, the effects predicted by the special theory of relativity as a result of relative velocity are of a magnitude comparable to that of the effects predicted by the equivalence principle as a result of variations in the gravitational potential between laboratory and flying clocks.

The special theory of relativity is so well established by numerous other experiments, however, that there is essentially no doubt of its correctness. Indeed, since November of 1983, international length and time standards have been related to each other so that the speed of light is defined as a constant (exactly 299,792,458 meters per second). Thus the effects of special relativity can be calculated with confidence and removed from measured "jet-lag" to yield effects of the equivalence principle. Comparisons of clocks flown eastward and westward around the earth with an identical clock left at rest in the laboratory showed agreement between observations of total aging differences as large as 273 nanoseconds and theoretical expectations to within the experimental error of 20 nanoseconds attributed to in-

accuracies in logs of flight data and variations within and among the cesium beam atomic clocks.

Comparison of twin hydrogen maser clocks, one carried to an altitude of more than 10,000 kilometers by a Scout D rocket launched from Wallops Island, Virginia, in the morning of June 18, 1976, and the other at rest on Merritt Island, Florida, yielded a continuous and much more precise confirmation of the equivalence principle's effect on clock rates. Clever use of a transponder within the payload allowed complete removal of the Doppler effect contribution in a continuous comparison of clock rates observed through radio signals between ground and rocket, leaving only the effects of special relativistic time dilation and the equivalence principle. After more than two years of analysis of data from this two-hour flight, Robert Vessot and his colleagues demonstrated that the agreement between theory and observation was within 70 parts per million throughout the parts of the trajectory for which reliable tracking had been possible.

CONTEXT

Einstein first stated the equivalence of uniform acceleration and a uniform gravitational field in 1907, but gravitational fields in nature are often of varying strength and direction. The presentation in the "Overview" assumed that the portion of the frame of reference in which an experiment verifies the equivalence principle is a sufficiently small region of space-time that the effects of gravitation may be "transformed away" throughout that portion by changing to a freely falling frame of reference. In a uniform freely falling frame, a man, a feather, and a block of iron all have the same weight: no weight at all. In a gravitational field of varying strength and direction, however, no such global freely falling frame is possible over larger regions of space-time. The relationship of various locally freely falling frames will depend upon the ways in which the sources of the gravitational field produce large-scale space-time curvature. Einstein's general theory of relativity, first published in 1916, is a unique theory of gravitation that extends the earlier "weak" form of the equivalence principle to a "strong equivalence principle." This demands that even extended objects with significant internal gravitational potential energy must respond in exactly the same way to external gravitational fields. In Newton's theory of gravity or any other theory consistent with the original form of the equivalence principle, balls of platinum and aluminum must fall in the same way in the earth's gravitational field. Only in Einstein's general theory of relativity, however, must Earth and the Moon fall in the same way in the Sun's gravitational field.

Analysis of possible deviations from the strong equivalence principle in a large set of alternatives to Einstein's theory of general relativity was first carried out by Kenneth Nordtvedt in 1967. For example, the predicted Nordtvedt effect amounted to an elongation in the Moon's orbit around the earth of as much as 1.3 meters, in the then viable Brans-Dicke theory of gravitation, along the direction toward the sun. Beginning with the American *Apollo 11* landing on July 21, 1969, and continuing with the *Apollo 14* and *15* missions and the unmanned Soviet *Luna 17* and *21* missions, retroreflectors were placed on the Moon. Subsequently, it became possible, through precise laser ranging between the prime foci of observatory telescopes and these reflectors, to measure the distances between well-defined points on Earth and the Moon to a precision on the order of 0.15 meter. The orbit of the Moon is subject to a very large number of perturbing influences, caused, for example, by other planets, which are well understood in principle.

Fortunately, the locations of the planets at this time could be determined sufficiently well from radar ranging and spacecraft data that their effects on the Moon's orbit could be removed from the laser ranging data to within the combined experimental uncertainties of 0.3 meter, leaving no evidence for

the Nordtvedt effect. This means that Earth and the Moon fall in the same way in the gravitational field of the sun to a precision of 1 part in 100 billion. Thus, the strong equivalence principle is supported experimentally with a precision comparable to the support given the weak equivalence principle by the best laboratory tests of identity of test body gravitational and inertial masses.

—John J. Dykla

Further Reading

Jones, Bernard J. T. *Precision Cosmology*. Cambridge UP, 2017.

Lebed. Andrei G., editor. *Breakdown of Einstein's Equivalence Principle*. World Scientific, 2022.

Ni, Wen-tou, editor. *One Hundred Years of General Relativity: From Genesis and Empirical Foundations to Gravitational Waves, Cosmology and Quantum Gravity-Volume 1*. World Scientific, 2017.

Will, Clifford M., and Nicolás Yunes. *Is Einstein Still Right?: Black Holes, Gravitational Waves, and the Quest to Verify Einstein's Greatest Creation*. Oxford UP, 2020.

Zhao, Bingcheng. *Look at the Mechanism Behind the Postulate of the Equivalence Principle: The Mechanism Behind the Extremely Important Postulate Has Been Revealed*. Amazon Digital Services LLC-Kdp Print Us, 2019.

See also: Acceleration; Angular forces; Angular momentum; Atoms; Celestial mechanics; Chaotic systems; Classical or applied mechanics; Kinetic energy; Motion; Newton's laws; Pendulums; Photoelectric effect; Quantum mechanics; Thermodynamics; Work-energy theorem

EUCLID

Fields of Study: Physics; Engineering; Mechanics; Mathematics

ABSTRACT

The Greek mathematician Euclid took the geometry known in his day and presented it in a logical system. His work on geometry became the standard textbook on the subject down to modern times.

KEY CONCEPTS

axiom: a self-evident statement that cannot be proven by manipulation of other statements

circle: a continuum of points that are a constant distance from one specific point

parallel: describing two lines, curves, or surfaces that extend in the same direction and are separated from each other by a constant distance

right angle: an angle of exactly 90 degrees formed by the intersection of two lines

square: an enclosed figure formed by the intersection of four lines forming four right angles on the interior of the figure

triangle: an enclosed figure formed by the intersection of three lines forming three angles on the interior of the figure

EUCLID WRITES ELEMENTS OF GEOMETRY

The Greek mathematician Euclid was born about 330 BCE in ancient Greece. He died in about 270 BCE in Alexandria, Egypt, and so is also known as Euclid of Alexandria. He is best known for his work in mathematics and geometry.

Some of what we think of today as Euclidean plane geometry certainly originated in Babylonian times, though no one knows quite how much. Euclid worked in Athens and Alexandria around 300 BCE. In addition to the codification of existing Babylonian mathematics, Euclid's great contribution was the extension to much more complex propositions by means of rigorous and innovative proofs. The earliest text of Euclid's treatise *Elements*, still in existence, was published seven hundred years later by Proclus (ca. 410-85 CE). Proclus himself had only secondhand access to the original.

Euclid's greatest achievement may have been in understanding that geometry—and mathematics generally—must rely on a set of axioms. Axioms are obvious rules that are accepted as the foundation for proofs of propositions. The smaller the number of axioms, the more powerful the resulting mathematical structure. Euclidean geometry relies on five axioms:

- A straight line can be constructed between any two points;
- A straight line can be extended continuously and indefinitely;
- A circle can be constructed with any center and radius;
- All right angles are equal to one another;
- Parallel lines never meet.

From these five unprovable basic assumptions sprang all subsequent Western mathematical and physical science until the advent of Albert Einstein's theories of special and general relativity in the early twentieth century.

Using these five axioms, Euclid was able to develop and prove many complex geometrical propositions, or theorems. For example, he proved the fa-

Euclid. Image via iStock/benoitb. [Used under license.]

mous Pythagorean theorem using only the five axioms and performing the construction with straight edge and compass alone. This theorem states that the hypotenuse of a right triangle is equal to the square root of the sum of the squares of the other two sides. (In algebraic notation, this would be represented as $x^2 = a^2 + b^2$, where x is the hypotenuse and a and b are the sides.) Euclid's proof has been taught to students for more than two thousand years. His geometry was also innovative in that it facilitates the analysis of all triangles, not just right triangles.

Euclid himself recognized that his fifth proposition was less intuitively obvious than the first four. Non-Euclidean geometries sprang up in the nineteenth century, challenging the universal application of the fifth postulate. In the era of space travel and deep exploration of the universe, it may turn out that the non-Euclidean geometries better describe reality when the gigantic distances of the universe are analyzed. Nevertheless, for ordinary use on Earth, Euclidean geometry and Newtonian mechanics continue to dominate nearly all scientific and engineering fields.

EARLY LIFE

Little is known about Euclid, and even the actual city of his birth is a mystery. Medieval authors often called him Euclid of Megara, but they were confusing him with an earlier philosopher, Eucleides of Megara, who was an associate of Socrates and Plato. It is virtually certain that Euclid came from Greece proper and probable that he received advanced education in the Academy, the school founded by Plato in Athens. By the time Euclid arrived there, Plato and the first generation of his students had already died, but the Academy was the foremost mathematical school of the time. The followers of Aristotle in the Lyceum included no great mathematicians. The majority of the geometers who instructed Euclid were adherents of the Academy.

Euclid traveled to Alexandria, where he was appointed to the faculty of the Museum, the great research institution that was being organized under the patronage of Ptolemy Soter (ruled 323-283 BCE). Ptolemy, a boyhood friend of Euclid and then a lieutenant of Alexander the Great, had seized Egypt soon after the conqueror's death, become the successor of the pharaohs, and managed to make his capital, Alexandria, an intellectual center of the Hellenistic Age that outshone Athens. Euclid presumably became the librarian, or head, of the Museum at some point in his life. He had many students, and although their names are not recorded, they carried on the tradition of his approach to mathematics. His influence can still be identified among those who followed in the closing years of the third century BCE. He was thus a member of the first generation of Alexandrian scholars, along with Demetrius of Phalerum and Strato of Lampsacus.

LIFE'S WORK

Euclid's reputation rests on his greatest work, the *Stoicheia* (first translated into English in the seventeenth century as *The Elements of Geometrie of the Most Auncient Philosopher Euclide of Megara*). This work consisted of thirteen books of his own and two spurious books added later by Hypsicles of Alexandria and others. This work is a systematic explication of geometry embracing and systematizing the achievements of earlier mathematicians. Books 1 and 2 discuss the straight line, triangles, and parallelograms; books 3 and 4 examine the circle and the inscription and circumscription of triangles and regular polygons; and books 5 and 6 explain the theory of proportion and areas. Books 7, 8, and 9 introduce the reader to arithmetic and the theory of rational numbers, while book 10 treats the difficult subject of irrational numbers. The remaining three books investigate elementary solid geometry and conclude with the five regular solids (tetrahedron, cube, octahedron, dodecahedron, and icosahedron). It should be noted that the *Elements* discusses several problems that later came to belong to the field of algebra, but Euclid treated them in geometric terms.

The genius of the *Elements* lies in the beauty and compelling logic of its arrangement and presentation, not in its new discoveries. Still, Euclid showed originality in his development of a new proof for the Pythagorean theorem, as well as his convincing demonstration of many principles that had been advanced less satisfactorily by others. The postulate that only one parallel to a line can be drawn through any point external to the line is Euclid's invention. He found this assumption necessary in his system but was unable to develop a formal proof for it. Modern mathematicians have maintained that no such proof is possible, so Euclid may be excused for not providing one.

Other extant Greek works by Euclid include *Ta dedomena* (*Data in Euclid's Elements of Geometry*), another work of elementary geometry; the *Optika* (*The Optics of Euclid*), which treats rays of light as straight lines, making its subject a branch of geometry; and *Phainomena* (*Euclid's Phaenomena*), which is an astronomical text based in part on a work of Autolycus of Pitane, a slightly older contemporary. Euclid also wrote on music and division, though surviving examples of his works in these subjects are rare.

In addition to the last two books of the *Elements*, there are works bearing Euclid's name that are not genuinely his. These include the *Katoptrica* (*Catoptrica*), a later work on optics, and *Eisagoge armonike* (*Introduction to Harmony*), which is actually by Cleonides, a student of Aristoxenus. None of Euclid's reputation, however, depends on these writings falsely attributed to him.

Two famous remarks are attributed to Euclid by ancient authors. On being asked by Ptolemy if there was any easier way to learn the subject than by struggling through the proofs in the *Elements*, Euclid replied that there is no "royal road" to geometry. When a student asked him if geometry would help

him get a job, Euclid ordered his slave to give the student a coin, "since he has to make a profit from what he learns." Despite this rejoinder, Euclid's usual temperament was described as gentle and benign, open, and attentive to his students.

IMPACT

Euclid left as his legacy the standard textbook in geometry. No other ancient work of science requires as little revision to make it current, although many modern scientists, including Nikolai Lobachevski, Bernhard Riemann, and Albert Einstein, have developed non-Euclidean systems in reaction to the *Elements*, thus doing it a kind of honor. The influence of Euclid on later scientists such as Archimedes, Apollonius of Perga, Galileo Galilei, Isaac Newton, and Christiaan Huygens was immense. Eratosthenes used Euclid's theorems to measure with surprising accuracy the size of the sphere of Earth, and Aristarchus attempted less successfully, but in fine Euclidean style, to establish the sizes and distances of the moon and the sun.

Other Hellenistic mathematicians, such as Hero of Alexandria, Pappus, Simplicius, and Proclus, produced commentaries on the *Elements*. Theon of Alexandria, father of the famous woman philosopher and mathematician Hypatia, introduced a new edition of the *Elements* in the fourth century CE. The sixth-century Italian philosopher Boethius is said to have translated the *Elements* into Latin, but that version is no longer extant. Many translations were made into Arabic by early medieval Muslim scholars, beginning with one made for Caliph Harun al-Rashid near 800 CE by al-Hajjaj ibn Yusuf ibn Matar. Athelhard of Bath made the first surviving Latin translation from an Arabic text in about 1120 CE. The first printed version, a Latin translation by the thirteenth-century scholar Johannes Campanus, appeared in 1482 in Venice. Bartolomeo Zamberti was the first to translate the *Elements* into Latin directly from the Greek, rather than Arabic, in 1505.

The first English translation, printed in 1570, was done by Sir Henry Billingsley, later the lord mayor of London. The total number of editions of Euclid's *Elements* has been estimated to be more than one thousand, making it one of the most translated and printed books in history and certainly the most successful textbook ever written.

—*J. Donald Hughes*

Further Reading

Bolton, David. *Euclid: Elements.* Lulu.com, 2019.

Euclid. *Euclid's "Elements."* Translated by Thomas Little Heath. Edited by Dana Densmore. Digireads.com Publishing, 2017.

Mlodinow, Leonard. *Euclid's Window: The Story of Geometry from Parallel Lines to Hyperspace.* Simon, 2002.

Reid, Constance. *A Long Way from Euclid.* Dover, 2004.

Stilwell, John. *Elements of Mathematics: From Euclid to Gödel.* Princeton UP, 2017.

Wardhaugh, Benjamin. *Encounters with Euclid: How an Ancient Greek Geometry Text Shaped the World.* Princeton UP, 2021.

See also: Archimedes; Archimedes's principle; Aristotle isolates science as a discipline; Civil engineering; Engineering; Euclidean geometry

EUCLIDEAN GEOMETRY

Fields of Study: Physics; Mechanics; Mathematics

ABSTRACT

Geometry is the branch of mathematics that investigates the relations between points, lines, planes, and solids. The system originated with the Greek mathematician Euclid and is normally formalized by axioms and derived results.

KEY CONCEPTS

axiom: a logically self-evident relationship that is assumed to hold between the fundamental elements of geometry

collinearity: the relationship that exists between points if they lie on the same straight line

concurrency: the relationship that exists between lines that all pass through the same point

congruency: the relationship that exists between two objects if they are alike in all aspects of size and shape

Euclidean Tools: the straightedge and the compass, the classical drawing tools used in making geometrical constructions

postulate: today, synonymous with "axiom"; originally, postulates were empirically self-evident relationships

theorem: a property or relationship that can be logically derived from an axiom and/or a previously established theorem

OVERVIEW

Investigating the relationships between points, lines, and planes constitutes the subject of geometry. These relationships are used in engineering and many areas of science. Geometry includes the development of proofs that things can be done and provides methods of construction using only the straightedge and compass. Geometry can be approached from two distinct points of view. One of these is intuitive, building on the observation and experiences of the investigator.

The second approach, the axiomatic approach, is more formal. The axiomatic approach, first formalized by Euclid of Alexandria (ca. 300 BCE), is based on a fundamental set of elements and their relationships. Demonstrations are developed to justify relationships that are dependent on the axioms and no other information.

The intuitive approach may require the definition of terms such as "congruent," leaving a formalization of the properties to theorems and demonstrations. In a well-formulated axiom system, the word "congruent" would probably be undefined, with its meanings made clear through axioms that characterize its properties. There are arguments for approaching a subject by each of these methods, but in practice both are frequently used. In either approach, the concept of discovering and developing other relationships on the basis of associations that have already been observed is critical. In developing any body of knowledge, this inductive step is important.

These inductive leaps, followed by their justification, provide growth to the field.

Some of the earliest-known observational facts included such statements as "Two lines in a plane intersect in a point" and "Two points determine a line." It was not recognized in the early history of geometry that these and many other observations have a dual in the sense that if one interchanges the words "point" and "line" and other relevant words such as "collinear" and "concurrent," a new and equally valid statement is derived. A characteristic of Euclidean geometry is that most theorems have a dual. In some cases, centuries elapsed before the dual was discovered. Recognizing this dualism is a relatively recent contribution to geometry. Observing properties such as dualism and attempting to organize the thought processes helped formalize the structure of an axiom system that is now known to have four components. These components are undefined terms whose meaning can be made clear only through axioms or postulates. For the purposes of this discussion, "axiom" and "postulate" are synonyms. They describe the relations between the undefined terms. A third element is derived or defined terms. These are introduced primarily to make the subsequent discussion easier and are given in terms of the previously given undefined terms. Finally, there are theorems and propositions, which can be demonstrated to follow logically from the axioms alone. Euclid provided the first axiom system for geometry. It has changed somewhat over the years. Today, there are other formulations, including that of David Hilbert (1862-1943), which seems to be

Detail from Raphael's The School of Athens *featuring a Greek mathematician—perhaps representing Euclid or Archimedes—using a compass to draw a geometric construction. Image via Wikimedia Commons. [Public domain.]*

free of inconsistencies. There is always the possibility that someone will replace one axiom system with another, equivalent one.

Among the geometrical relationships that have been recognized is the knowledge of the Pythagorean triple: 3, 4, 5. When these values are used as lengths for the sides of a triangle, a right triangle is formed. This triangle was used by early geometers, or "rope stretchers," to survey the fields in Egypt after the annual floods. These triples are called Pythagorean because they satisfy a theorem credited to Pythagoras (ca. 540 BCE), although there is sound evidence in the form of inscribed clay tablets demonstrating that the relationship was known and used at least 1,000 years before Pythagoras. This theorem states that the sum of the squares of the legs of a right triangle is equal to the square of the hypotenuse. For this statement to be complete, one needs to know that a right triangle has a right angle, that the legs are the sides forming the right angle, and that the hypotenuse is the longest side. Finding integral solutions to the Pythagorean theorem, of which there are many, is one of the challenges of geometry.

In organizing geometrical data, it is logical to start with the simplest concepts. Points and lines appear to be the best starting point. Two lines that intersect not only share a common point but also form angles. "Angle" is a derived term.

In building geometry intuitively and seeking the building blocks to develop an axiom system, it can be observed that a line can be drawn through two points. This can be restated as "Two points determine a line." This statement implies an element of uniqueness that leads to the concept of a line being straight, a property that is understood without being stated. If the element connecting the two points is not straight, it is called a curve. There are many possibilities of curves passing through two given points, contrary to the notion of uniqueness. Additional terms are needed for convenience. The "line segment," or the set of points on the line between the two points, is one such. Another is the "ray," a part of the line that starts at a point and extends in one direction from it.

Angles are best described in terms of the figure determined by two rays starting from a common point. The point is called the "vertex" of the angle and the rays, the "sides." It follows that two intersecting lines determine four angles that share the common vertex or point of intersection. When all four of these angles are congruent, the lines are said to be perpendicular and the angles are right angles. An angle divides the plane into two parts, as does a line. This poses the problem of identifying the inside and outside of the angle. Usually the smaller part is considered the inside, but it is possible that the angle selected may be the larger portion. For some purposes, angles can involve several rotations.

Intuition is important in developing an understanding of relations such as inside and outside, but it can pose problems when one tries to make precise statements.

Attempts to describe a plane, another fundamental element, are more difficult because of the care needed. One description can be based on an analogy between points and lines. Just as two intersecting lines determine a point, and have angles associated with them, two lines can also determine a plane. In order for the description to be complete, certain conditions must be established, as is illustrated by the following special cases.

First, two lines may intersect in a point (the dual of two points determining a line).

These two lines determine a point, and, on a little reflection, it can be seen that other lines can also pass through this common point, forming a "pencil" of lines. Some of these additional lines lie in the plane determined by the original lines, but some of them do not. This latter case can be illustrated by considering a piece of paper as a model of the plane and observing a line represented by a wire passing through the plane. Lines sharing only one point in a plane are inadequate for determining a plane.

Second, the two lines selected may be parallel. Two such lines lie in a plane, but consider what happens if one takes a family of parallel lines drawn on a piece of paper and then rolls the paper into a cylinder, keeping the lines parallel. The resulting surface obviously is not a plane even though the lines are still parallel.

Third, the two lines may be "skew"—that is, drawn in space so that they never intersect and are not parallel. No plane contains both lines.

To characterize the plane, something more than two intersecting or parallel lines is needed. Starting with two intersecting lines, as in the first case, and taking points other than the point of intersection on each of the two lines, one can construct another line. A plane can be thought of as being described by a line that must either intersect all three lines or intersect two of them and be parallel to the third. This leads to the well-known result that three points determine a plane and provides some insight into how they do so.

The three points used to describe a plane also form the vertices of a triangle, a fundamental plane figure of geometry. The triangle could be known as a "trilateral," since it is formed by the three side segments joining the points.

The properties of triangles provide one of the application areas of geometry. The rigidity of the triangle and the ways in which it can be constructed or shown to be congruent to another triangle prove to be very useful. Generally, three pieces of information are needed. One datum must be a length associated with the triangle. Among the well-known results are that a triangle is uniquely identified if the following are given: three sides, two sides and the included angle, two angles and a side, and two sides and the altitude drawn to one of them. If one is given two sides and the angle opposite one of them, the solution may not be unique; this is known as the ambiguous case.

The Pythagorean theorem is critical to the foundation of trigonometry, which is used in calculating the remaining parts of a triangle and providing identities used in problems of calculus and other applications.

Other geometrical areas of interest and use are found in the constructions. The challenge is to make the drawings with Euclidean tools: the straightedge for drawing lines and the compass for drawing circles. The more fundamental constructions include drawing a line through two points, duplicating a line segment, and constructing a circle with a given center and radius. From these, other constructions can be developed that are apparently more useful. These include duplicating an angle, constructing perpendicular and parallel lines, and bisecting angles and line segments.

In more advanced constructions, one finds problems of constructing triangles when the minimal required information is given, and of locating special points, lines, and circles associated with the triangle. Some of the special points are the centroid, the orthocenter, the incenter of the inscribed circle, and the circumcenter of the circumscribed circle. Useful lines of the triangle are the medians, the angle bisectors, the altitudes, and the perpendicular bisectors of the sides. There are other points and lines that can be described, and new ones are occasionally discovered.

Euclid's fifth postulate involved the property of parallelism. Some believed that this postulate was dependent on the other four. Many equivalent statements have been used in an attempt to demonstrate the expected dependence. One of the statements asserted that through a point not on a line, one and only one line could be drawn parallel to the given line. There are two ways of denying this postulate. One is to assume that there are no such things as parallel lines and the other is to assume that more than one parallel line can be drawn through the point. The initial approach was to try to show that assuming one of these contrary conditions and the other four postulates would lead to a contradiction. No contradictions were found, and ultimately models were created that showed that these assumptions produced self-consistent geometries now known as non-Euclidean geometries.

APPLICATIONS

Establishing the congruency of triangles has its counterpart in determining how a triangle can be constructed given selected parts. These and other construction problems represent one aspect of applications of geometry.

The center of gravity, or centroid, of a triangle plays an important role in many physical problems. Altitudes are also critical to some applications. Both are standard construction problems. Exploring properties of lines such as medians and altitudes associated with triangles can lead to generalizations that are potentially useful even though they are not necessarily obvious. Ceva's theorem (named for Giovanni Ceva, 1647?-1734) is one of these. It gives the necessary and sufficient condition for the lines drawn from the vertices of a triangle and intersecting the opposite sides to be concurrent. Medians used to find the centroid, as well as altitudes and angle bisectors, satisfy the conditions of this theorem, as do other, little-known lines.

The dual of Ceva's theorem, obtained by interchanging the roles of points and lines in Ceva's theorem and making one other simple change, gives Menelaus's theorem (named for Menelaus of Alexandria, ca. 100 CE), which addresses the points of intersection of a line that cuts the three sides of a triangle. This theorem provides the necessary and sufficient condition for three points on the sides or sides extended of a triangle to be collinear. It would seem that Ceva's theorem should have been discovered before Menelaus's theorem, since the lines involved have long been recognized as important lines of a triangle, but this was not the case.

The problem of finding the center of a circle can be readily solved by geometry. Instead of doing it geometrically, the methods of geometry are used to design a tool to do the job. The center is found by using angle bisectors. If the sides of the angle are tangent to the circle, the angle bisector will pass through the center of the circle. Relocating the angle bisector and finding the point of intersection of the two angle bisectors locates the center.

A slightly more complicated problem is that of finding the center of rotation to carry one object into a congruent image of it in the plane. This construction follows from an understanding of the geometry of rotation. To find the center, one needs two pairs of corresponding points. The point of intersection of the perpendicular bisectors to the line segments connecting the corresponding points will be the center of rotation. Should the congruent figures have corresponding parallel parts, the transformation in getting from one to the other is a translation. The translation, however, can be considered a rotation around a point at "infinity."

A protractor is a device for measuring the number of degrees in an angle. The size of the degree is arbitrary, but today it is accepted that a circle or round angle will be divided into 360 congruent parts called degrees. The construction of a protractor corresponds to inscribing a regular polygon with 360 congruent sides in a circle. The vertices of the polygon will mark off degrees on the circle. Using Euclidean tools, this subdivision cannot be done. It has long been known how to construct regular polygons of three, four, and five sides. Once one of these has been constructed, other polygons with twice the number of sides can be constructed. Carl Friedrich Gauss (1777-1855) proved that regular polygons of 17, 257, and 65,537 sides—and no other regular polygons that have a prime number of sides—can be constructed with Euclidean tools. Others have proved that arbitrary angles cannot be trisected—that is, divided into three congruent parts—with Euclidean tools. A consequence is that a regular polygon with 120 sides can be constructed, but the usual protractor requires a polygon with 360 sides. Fortunately, this curious selection of 360 degrees for a circle admits to a construction that can be resolved by methods that do not use Euclidean tools.

Another problem related to the circle is finding the ratio of the circumference to the diameter. This number, called pi (denoted by the Greek letter π), has an extensive history.

Through a study of similarities, it can be shown that the value does not depend on the size of the circle. Many approximations are known. The early Babylonians used the approximation (4/3) to the power of 4. Before the advent of the pocket calculator, many elementary mathematics books used 22/7 as a reasonable approximation. Today, the number

π is stored in many calculators, and one may find values with many more significant figures, such as 3.141592654. Procedures for determining the value of π are many, but one of the classical methods involved finding the perimeter of regular polygons. Values increasing to π were obtained by starting with a six-sided polygon inscribed in the circle and repeatedly doubling the number of sides. Similarly, a value always too large but approaching π was found by circumscribing a square about the circle and again repeatedly doubling the number of sides. The values obtained through these two approximations came closer and closer together. If the original had a radius of one unit, the diameter would be of length two and the value of π would be one-half the value of the perimeter or circumference.

Geometrical linkages provide another class of applications. The problem of converting rectilinear to circular motion is classical. The solution to this problem was critical in the design of steam engines. Another linkage problem is found in the pantograph, a drawing instrument that is used to trace images that are either larger or smaller than the original. Using computers as a drafting tool has eliminated the need for this application.

CONTEXT

The development of geometry as a formal system began with Euclid. Subsequent investigators have contributed to the field, and some observed errors and inconsistencies in Euclid's development. David Hilbert addressed these problems and formulated a system that is generally accepted to be error-free. Though different in organization, it is consistent with Euclid's formulation.

In trying to show that parallelism is a separate idea, elliptic and hyperbolic geometries have been discovered and developed. These geometries are called non-Euclidean. The elliptic geometries, in which there are no parallels, are called Riemannian geometries, named for Georg Friedrich Bernhard

Riemann (1826-66). Hyperbolic geometries can have more than one parallel to a given line through a given point. These geometries were developed by Janos Bolyai (1802-60) of Hungary and Nikolay Ivanovich Lobachevsky (1793-1856) of Russia. Both geometries have played a role in subjects such as relativity and astronomy, because of the concept of space curvature. In the "small," Euclidean geometry provides a good approximation of these other geometries. By modifying axioms, other geometries have been found, including some with interesting applications.

The work of René Descartes (1596-1650) changed the orientation used to study geometry from the synthetic approach to an analytical one. This was accomplished by means of the introduction of coordinate systems, which enhanced many applications and led to other subjects, such as differential geometry. By using coordinates to describe positions, a number of important relationships can be found, all contributing to the quantitative description of observed phenomena, which is so important in the physical sciences.

Euclidean geometry provides the structure from which trigonometry is developed.

From the properties of the angles of right triangles, given in part by the Pythagorean theorem that describes the relationship of the lengths of the sides, and the concept of congruent triangles, the trigonometric functions can be defined. These definitions provide the basis for calculating tables and establishing identities.

Problems involving collinearity of points and concurrency of lines can be addressed through Euclidean geometry and extended to three dimensions. Less obvious are the relationships needed to describe four- and higher-dimensional problems. Although a four-dimensional object cannot be seen in its entirety, one can, through geometry, discover many of its characteristics.

Computer graphics is an application that is gaining in popularity. In its early development, the process was relatively crude. Software has improved and will continue to do so. Some of the improvements take the form of constructions in the traditional mode that minimize the need for analytical solutions. Computer graphics has all but eliminated drafting and plays a major role in engineering design.

—*James A. Nickel*

Further Reading

Chen, Evan. *Euclidean Geometry in Mathematical Olympiads.* American Mathematical Society, 2021.

Euclid. *Euclid's "Elements."* Translated by Thomas Little Heath. Edited by Dana Densmore. Digireads.com Publishing, 2017.

Solomonovich, Mark. *Euclidean Geometry: A First Course.* Universe, 2010.

Stilwell, John. *Elements of Mathematics: From Euclid to Gödel.* Princeton UP, 2017.

Vaisman, Izu. *Foundations of Three-Dimensional Euclidean Geometry.* CRC Press, 2020.

Wardhaugh, Benjamin. *Encounters with Euclid: How an Ancient Greek Geometry Text Shaped the World.* Princeton UP, 2021.

See also: Computer-aided engineering; Engineering; Engineering tolerances; Structural engineering

EULER PATHS

Fields of Study: Physics; Mechanics; Geography; Civil Engineering; Mathematics

ABSTRACT

A graph consists of a set of vertices (points in space), and the edges that connect them. A Euler path through a graph travels along each edge exactly once. Because of their simplicity, Euler paths provide a good introduction to graph theory and its applications.

KEY CONCEPTS

Cartesian grid: the standard grid pattern that presents x, y, and z coordinates in two or three mutually orthogonal dimensions

graph: a pictorial representation of data presented on an appropriate grid

map: a graphic representation of areas such as countries enclosed by designated borders

mapping: identifying specific regions and their dimensions for the generation of maps, blueprints, technical drawings, and other relevant forms of data storage and representation

GRAPH THEORY

Graph theory is a relatively new but rapidly growing area of discrete mathematics. A graph consists of a set of vertices (points in space), and the edges that connect them. Although vertices in a graph do not need to be connected to an edge, every edge must begin and end at a vertex.

The origin of graph theory can be traced back almost three centuries with a problem posed around the concept of what is now known as a Euler path. A Euler path through a graph travels along each edge exactly once. Because of their simplicity, Euler paths provide a good introduction to graph theory and its applications.

OVERVIEW

In 1736, Leonhard Euler published an essay that attempted to solve the Seven Bridges of Königsberg problem. The problem is as follows: There are seven bridges in Königsberg that connect 4 different landmasses. Starting on land, is there a way to take a walk that crosses every bridge exactly once?

By creating an abstract graph of the Königsberg map, Euler was able to prove that such a walk was impossible. He represented each landmass with a vertex and each bridge with an edge connecting the respective vertices (landmasses). Euler then summed up the number of times an edge entered or exited a vertex and labeled this sum as the degree of the vertex. Using mathematical logic, he concluded that a Euler path through a graph exists if and only if either every vertex has an even degree or exactly two vertices have an odd degree. When every vertex has an even degree, it is possible to find a Euler path that begins and ends at the same vertex. This is known as a Euler circuit.

Euler paths and Euler circuits show up in a wide range of contemporary problems ranging from mapping deoxyribonucleic acid (DNA) patterns or social networks to planning snowplow routes through city streets. In some cases, such as a one-way street, a snowplow is permitted to travel along an edge only in a single direction. This results in a directed graph, or digraph. It is also useful in many cases to associate each edge with a weight, or cost. For example, in planning delivery routes

within a region, the weight of each edge might be the distance between the cities. Graph theory methods could then be used to find a Euler path of minimal weight.

Although graphs can help visualize complex systems, this does not always mean that an optimal solution can be found. In fact, it is just as likely that using a graph to describe a scenario allows one to realize that the problem is still an unsolved problem in mathematics. However, by connecting the real life problem with its corresponding problem in graph theory, it is possible to take advantage of several known algorithms that produce reasonably good outcomes.

—David Driver and Daniel Showalter

Further Reading

Agnarsson, Geir, and Raymond Greenlaw. *Graph Theory: Modeling, Applications, and Algorithms*. Pearson, 2007.

Aufmann, Richard, Joanne Lockwood, Richard Nation, and Daniel K. Clegg. *Mathematical Excursions*. 3rd ed., Brooks, 2013.

Epp, Susana S. *Discrete Mathematics and Applications*. Cengage, 2011.

Farlow, Stanley J. *Advanced Mathematics: A Transitional Reference*. John Wiley & Sons, 2019.

Marcus, Daniel A. *Graph Theory: A Problem Oriented Approach*. Mathematical Association of America, 2008.

See also: Biomedical engineering; Civil engineering; Computer-aided engineering; Engineering; Euler's laws of motion; Robotics; Structural engineering; Transportation; Vectors

Leonhard Euler. Image via iStock/ilbusca. [Used under license.]

EULER'S LAWS OF MOTION

Fields of Study: Physics; Mechanics; Mathematics

ABSTRACT

Newton's laws are generalizations, devised with reference to a singular point of mass that takes up zero hypothetical

space. Fifty years after they were published, Swiss physicist Leonhard Euler (1707-83) extended them by applying them to continuous bodies made up of these Newtonian point masses.

KEY CONCEPTS

angular momentum: the momentum of a rotating object, equal to the object's moment of inertia (its rotational inertia) times its angular velocity; also called rotational momentum

center of mass: the point in an object or system around which the mass of said object or system is evenly distributed

fixed reference frame: a frame of reference that is fixed to the environment and not to the subject being observed; sometimes specified as "Earth-fixed" or "space-fixed"

linear momentum: an object's mass times its velocity; often called simply "momentum," as the basic concept is defined in terms of an object moving in a straight line

Newton's laws of motion: three laws devised by physicist and mathematician Isaac Newton to describe the motion of objects in relation to the forces acting on them

rigid body: an idealization of a solid object that assumes that it cannot be deformed by the forces acting on it

torque: the tendency of a force to cause an object to rotate, defined mathematically as the rate of change of the object's angular momentum; also called moment of force

EXTENDING NEWTON'S LAWS OF MOTION

In 1686, English physicist and mathematician Isaac Newton (1643-1727) published his *Philosophiae Naturalis Principia Mathematica*. In it, he laid out three physical laws that govern interactions between objects and the forces acting on them. These laws are now known as Newton's laws of motion. The first law states that an object at rest tends to stay at rest, and an object in motion stays in motion, unless acted on by an outside force. The second law states that the net force applied to an object is equal to the resulting change in the object's momentum per unit time—that is, its mass times its acceleration. The third law states that every action produces an equal and opposite reaction. These laws form the foundation of classical mechanics and, by extension, of all of modern physics.

Fifty years after Isaac Newton published his laws of motion in the *Principia*, Swiss mathematician and physicist Leonhard Euler added to them with his own laws of motion. Euler's laws take Newton's laws, which apply only to a singular point of mass, and extend them to an entire rigid body and to rotational motion.

EULER'S FIRST LAW OF MOTION

Mathematically, Newton's second law is stated as F = ma where F is the net force applied to an object (specifically, a point mass), m is its mass, and a is its acceleration. Euler's first law extends this law to apply to an entire rigid body. A rigid body is a solid object that does not bend, twist, compress, or otherwise deform when acted on by an outside force. When assuming a rigid body, Euler's first law says, the total force acting on the body is equal to the sum of the forces acting on each individual particle in the body.

Euler's first law depends on the concept of center of mass. A point mass located at a body's center of mass and having the same mass as the body will follow the same trajectory as said body when acted on by the same force. For the human body, for example, the center of mass is typically located beneath the belly button. In practical terms, this means that Newton's first law (F = ma) can be rewritten for a rigid body as $\Sigma F = ma_{cm}$ where ΣF indicates the sum of all external forces acting on all particles of the body (as the symbol Σ represents summation) and acm is the acceleration of the body's center of mass.

LINEAR AND ANGULAR MOMENTUM

While the term "momentum" is usually used to mean linear momentum, there are in fact two types of momentum. Linear momentum is the momentum of an object moving in a straight line. For a point mass, it is defined as $p = mv$ where p is momentum, m is mass, and v is velocity.

In contrast, angular momentum is the momentum of an object that is rotating or traveling in a circle. Angular momentum (L) is defined as $L = I\omega$ where I is the moment of inertia and ω is the angular velocity. Moment of inertia, or rotational inertia, is the inertia of a rotating body. It represents an object's tendency to resist angular acceleration, just as an object tends to resist linear acceleration. Moment of inertia can be further broken down in terms of mass (m) and the distance of the object from the point of rotation (r), that is, the radius of the circular path the object is traveling:

$$I = r^2 m$$

Angular velocity, meanwhile, can be written in terms of the radius of the path of circular motion (r) and the object's tangential linear velocity (v) at a given instant:

$$\omega = v/r$$

Thus, in terms of radius, mass, and linear velocity, the equation for angular momentum is as follows:

$$L = (r^2 m)(v/r) = rmv$$

These equations apply to any type of circular motion. They work for spinning motion about an internal axis, such as the rotation of a planet. They also work for motion in a circular path around an external axis, such as the orbit of a planet around the sun.

EULER'S SECOND LAW OF MOTION

Euler's second law of motion extends Newton's laws to apply to rigid bodies in circular motion. It states that for an object rotating about a given point, whether that point is an external axis in a fixed reference frame or the object's own center of mass, the rate of change of angular momentum is equal to the sum of all external torques, or moments of force, acting about that point. Solving this equation involves differential calculus, specifically finding the derivative of L with respect to time (t). However, if the object is only moving in two dimensions (e.g., a flat, spinning disk), the equation can be rewritten in terms of the center of mass:

$$\Sigma M = rcm \times acmm + I\alpha.$$

Here, M is moment of force, rcm is the distance of the object's center of mass from the axis of rotation, acm is the tangential acceleration of the center of mass relative to the axis, and α is the object's angular acceleration. As before, m is the mass of the object, and I is its moment of inertia.

To illustrate the concept, consider a child riding the merry-go-round at a local playground. The merry-go-round is 3 meters (m) across, and the child, who has a mass of 30 kilograms (kg), is sitting on the outside edge. If the merry-go-round completes one full rotation every two seconds (s), calculate the child's angular momentum (L) in units of newton-meter-seconds (n·m·s). Note that one newton-meter-second is equal to one kilogram-square meter per second (kg·m²/s). Because the child is so small relative to the circular path of her motion, she can be treated as a point mass, so the simpler equations for circular motion can be used:

$$L = I\omega = r^2 m\omega$$

Here mass is given as 30 kg. She is sitting on the outside edge of the merry-go-round, so the circular path of her motion is the same as the circle formed by the ride. The radius of the ride is simply half the diameter:

$$r = d/2 = 1.5 \text{ m}$$

Angular velocity, which measures revolutions per second, is given in units of radians per second (rad/s). One full circle is made up of 2π radians. If the child completes one full circle every two seconds, her angular velocity in rad/s is

$$\omega = 2\pi/2s$$

$$\omega = \pi/s$$

Plug these values into the equation:

$$L = r^2 m\omega$$

$$L = (1.5 \text{ m})^2 \, (30 \text{ kg})(\pi/s)$$

$$L = (2.25 \text{ m}^2) \, (30 \text{ kg})(\pi/s)$$

$$L = 212.058 \text{ kg·m}^2/s = 212.0575 \text{ n·m·s}$$

So the child's angular momentum is approximately 212.058 newton-meter-seconds.

WHAT EULER'S LAWS MEAN

Euler's laws can be more difficult to calculate than the equations derived from Newton's laws. In particular, applying Euler's second law in three dimensions requires differential calculus. However, the fundamental idea behind Euler's math is easy to understand. Newton's laws assume a single, infinitely small point mass. Euler's laws assume rigid bodies made up of a continuous collection of these point masses all stuck together. This is a reasonable, if very basic, description of the actual composition of matter: countless tiny atoms bonded together, themselves consisting of subatomic particles linked by fundamental forces.

Euler's first law is used to calculate linear momentum (p) by multiplying mass (m) of an object by its velocity (v). Euler's second law is used to calculate angular momentum (L) by multiplying moment of inertia (I) by angular velocity (ω).

—*Kenrick Vezina*

Further Reading

Calinger, Ronald S. *Leonhard Euler: Mathematical Genius in the Enlightenment.* Princeton UP, 2019.

Coddington, Richard C. "Inertial Frame, Euler's First Law." *University of Illinois at Urbana-Champaign.* Department of Agricultural and Biological Engineering, 2015. Accessed 27 Aug. 2015.

Hall, Nancy. "Newton's Laws of Motion." *The Beginner's Guide to Aeronautics.* NASA, 5 May 2015. Accessed 27 Aug. 2015.

Henderson, Tom. *Motion in Two Dimensions.* N.p.: Physics Classroom, 2012. Digital file.

Musielak, Dora. *Leonhard Euler and the Foundations of Celestial Mechanics.* Springer Nature, 2022.

Negahban, Mehrdad. "Equations of Motion for a Rigid Body (Euler's Laws)." *University of Nebraska.* Department of Engineering Mechanics, 1999-2002. Accessed 27 Aug. 2015.

See also: Acceleration; Angular forces; Angular momentum; Circular motion; Classical or applied mechanics; D'Alembert's axioms of motion; Force (physics); Friction; Kinematics; Kinetic energy; Linear motion; Moment of inertia; Momentum (physics); Motion; Newton's laws; Potential energy; Rigid-body dynamics; Solid mechanics; Torque

EXTERNAL COMBUSTION ENGINE

Fields of Study: Physics; Mechanics; Mathematics

ABSTRACT

External combustion engines are characterized by an external combustion process followed by heat transfer into the working fluid within the engine, and are widely employed in the form of steam engines for electricity generation, as well as in Stirling engines for less centralized applications.

KEY CONCEPTS

Carnot limit: the upper limit for the efficiency of a heat engine; depends on the temperature difference between the working fluid and the surroundings; the higher this difference, the higher the theoretical maximum energetic efficiency

closed system: one in which the working fluid (steam) is condensed back to liquid water and returned for reuse rather than being vented away

heat exchanger: a structure that separates a heat source from a working fluid but allows heat to transfer from one to the other

open system: one in which the working fluid is not recaptured for reuse and must be replenished in order to maintain operation of the system; the opposite of a closed system

Rankine cycle: thermodynamic cycle employed in a steam engine involves four main stages: pumping of water, heat addition, work production, and heat removal

EXTERNAL HEAT SOURCE

An external combustion engine (EC engine) is a heat engine where, in contrast to an internal combustion engine (IC engine), the combustion takes place outside of the engine. Thus, the working fluid in the engine is externally heated through a heat exchanger or the wall of the engine. Most of the world's electricity generation occurs in fossil fuel or nuclear plants that raise steam to drive a turbine, that is, in an EC engine. Other examples of EC engines include the Stirling engine, which uses gas as the working fluid, or the Organic Rankine Cycle, which uses steam as the working fluid and is particularly well suited to electricity generation from low temperature heat.

Depending upon whether the working fluid operates in one or two phases, liquid or gas, or liquid and gas, the system may be referred to as single or dual phase. The EC engine may further be categorized depending upon whether the thermodynamic cycle is open or closed, and hence whether the working fluid is replenished or remains within the system: A steam engine using water is typically closed, as is a Stirling engine using gas. The upper limit for the efficiency of a heat engine is known as the Carnot limit, and depends on the temperature difference between the working fluid and the surroundings; the higher this difference, the higher the theoretical maximum energetic efficiency.

STEAM ENGINES

The most widespread type of EC engine is the steam engine, which is used the world over in centralized electricity generation plants, which are fueled by fossil fuels or nuclear power, and in some cases biomass. The history of the steam engine goes back thousands of years, but it wasn't until the Industrial Revolution in the eighteenth century that the engines found widespread application for providing motive power, after James Watt made significant improvements to a previous design, including the addition of a separate condenser. The thermodynamic cycle employed in a steam engine is the Rankine cycle, named after the Scottish polymath, Professor William Rankine, which involves four main stages: pumping of water, heat addition, work production, and heat removal. The components of the steam engine that carry out these stages are the pump, boiler, turbine, and cooling towers, if present, respectively. In cooling towers, the excess heat in the form of steam is condensed to water vapor, and this heat is transferred to water in the cooling cycle (not part of the closed-loop Rankine cycle) before being released to the environment. The steam can be exhausted directly to the environment, as in the case of a steam locomotive, but this is very inefficient because of the adverse effect on overall efficiency, due to the fact that the temperature difference between working fluid and environment is not maximized. In the case that cooling towers are present, the condensed hot water is pumped back to the boiler to be-

Model Stirling engine, with external heat from a spirit lamp (bottom right) applied to the outside of the glass displacer cylinder. Photo by Zephyris, via Wikimedia Commons.

gin the cycle again. In a small boiler for domestic use, the heat is either directly released, or used to preheat the boiler water as in condensing boilers.

Whether or not the removed heat is used, such as in centralized combined heat and power (CHP) applications with district heat networks, has a massive effect on the overall efficiency of the plant. While pure electrical efficiencies of about 40 percent may be achieved in coal-fired electricity-only plants, in CHP plants the overall efficiency is around 80 percent. The thermodynamic price paid for this higher

overall efficiency is a reduction in electrical efficiency, however, because some of the steam is extracted before passing through the turbine. Because this excess heat is generally not used for local heating, so that centralized electricity generation has average overall efficiencies lower than 50 percent on a global scale, this is an area in which there are large potential improvements in overall system efficiencies. In some European countries, particularly Scandinavian countries, the proportion of electricity generation from CHP plants is very high—in

Denmark over 50 percent, for example—such that the overall efficiency of the electricity system is also high.

STIRLING ENGINES

One of the best known and probably most widely employed EC engine other than the steam engine, the Stirling engine was invented in 1816 by Robert Stirling, who at that time demonstrated the first closed-cycle air engine. It was only in the latter half of the twentieth century that the term "Stirling engine" was universally applied to this kind of heat engine. In this device, the cyclical compression and heating, followed by expansion and cooling, of gas results in the conversion of heat energy to work output. The thermal efficiency of a typical Stirling engine for domestic applications ranges between 15 and 30 percent, but care needs to be taken in interpreting this value, given that a large proportion of the remaining energy input is available, and is therefore used in such an application, making the overall efficiency around 85 percent. A diesel or gasoline engine may have a higher overall electrical efficiency approaching 40 percent, but will not be much more efficient overall, perhaps reaching 90 percent. Hence, EC engines typically have a lower power to heat ratio, so are suited to CHP applications with substantial heat loads.

Due to the external combustion process, the Stirling engine is also very quiet in operation, which makes it useful for applications where this is an advantage, such as in small combined heat and power (CHP) applications for households, where the unit may sit in the kitchen or a utility room. It is also very versatile, because it can be applied in any application with an external heat source, and is very reliable compared to IC engines. The latter means that the Stirling engine has lower maintenance costs, but these are somewhat offset by the higher investment compared to IC engines for household CHP applications. Another application for Stirling engines is in concentrating solar power plants, whereby solar radiation is focused with a parabolic dish onto a point at the input to the heat engine. Hence, the solar radiation serves as a heat input for the Stirling engine, which can be used to generate electricity. This application is especially useful for decentralized power generation, in locations where access to the electricity network or other renewable energy sources might be limited.

ADVANTAGES AND DISADVANTAGES

On the other hand, there are several disadvantages of EC engines compared to IC engines. First, the latter are smaller and therefore lighter, due to the fact that the combustion, heat transfer, and work transfer all occur inside the same chamber. This size difference is only minor when comparing, for example, a Stirling engine with a gasoline engine; but when comparing a steam engine and an IC engine for the same application, such as providing motive power for a vehicle, the difference becomes much more significant. The large external boilers required for a steam engine mean that the whole engine requires a large amount of space, even for applications requiring only a small amount of power. Another disadvantage of EC engines is the relatively long time it takes for them to start, compared to IC engines that can be started almost instantly.

Steam engines are most suited to operation in the steady state, which is most efficient and therefore economical at their design point. Hence, large steam engines, such as those used in power plants, take a long time to run up and run down; operating them away from this optimal load makes them less efficient. In addition, one large disadvantage of steam engines is the very high pressures at which they operate, which poses a risk of explosion. Ways in which a boiler can fail include overpressurization, overheating due to insufficient water and/or flow rate, or steam leakage from the boiler and/or pipe work. Typically, steam engines have devices to account for these risks, including an emergency valve that allows a maximum pressure to build up inside the boiler. Furthermore, lead plugs may be employed in the boiler crown, so that if the pressure and temperature reaches an excessive level, these plugs melt and thus automatically allow some of the steam to be released and the pressure to dissipate.

—*Russell McKenna*

Further Reading

Beith, Robert, editor. *Small and Micro Combined Heat and Power (CHP) Systems. Advanced Design, Performance, Materials and Applications*. Woodhead Publishing, 2011.

Darlngton, Roy, and Keith Strong. *Stirling and Hot Air Engines: Designing and Building Experimental Model Stirling Engines*. Crowood Press, 2005.

Desmet, Bernard. *Thermodynamics of Heat Engines*. John Wiley & Sons, 2022.

Drbal, L., K. Westra, and P. Boston. *Power Plant Engineering*. Springer, 1996.

Eastop, T. D., and A. McConkey. *Applied Thermodynamics for Engineering Technologists*. 5th ed., Longman, 1993.

See also: Carnot, Sadi; Diesel engine; Heat transfer; Internal combustion engine; Jet engines; Rotary engine; Steam energy technology; Steam engine; Stirling, Robert; Work and energy

F

FLUID DYNAMICS

Fields of Study: Physics; Mechanics; Mathematics

ABSTRACT

Fluid dynamics is an interdisciplinary field concerned with the behavior of gases, air, and water in motion. An understanding of fluid dynamic principles is essential to the work done in aerodynamics. It informs the design of air and spacecraft. An understanding of fluid dynamic principles is also essential to the field of hydromechanics and the design of oceangoing vessels and submersibles. Knowledge of fluid dynamics is essential for understanding the motion of ocean currents and circulation. Any system with air, gases, or water in motion incorporates the principles of fluid dynamics.

KEY CONCEPTS

compressible fluids: fluids that can change volume by the application of external pressure, particularly gases

incompressible fluids: fluids that do not change volume with the application of external pressure, particularly liquids

laminar flow: flow in which there is no turbulence in the fluid as it flows, as all particles making up the fluid flow uniformly in parallel paths, or "lamina"

turbulence: nonlaminar flow, characterized by chaotic motion within the fluid, as the flowing motion of particles making up the fluid is disrupted and forced to flow in nonparallel paths, or "lamina"

viscosity: the temperature-dependent property relating the ability of different fluids to flow

DEFINITION AND BASIC PRINCIPLES

Fluid dynamics is the study of fluids in motion. Air, gases, water, and all other liquids are all considered to be fluids. When the fluid is air, this branch of science is called aerodynamics. When the fluid is water, it is called hydrodynamics.

The basic principles of fluid dynamics state that fluids are a state of matter in which a substance cannot maintain an independent shape. A fluid will take the shape of its container, forming an observable surface at the highest level of the fluid when it does not completely fill the container. Fluids flow in a continuum, with no breaks or gaps in the flow. They are said to flow in a streamline, with a series of particles following one another in an orderly fashion in parallel with other streamlines. Real fluids have some amount of internal friction, known as viscosity. Viscosity is the comparative temperature-dependent property that describes a fluid's ability to flow. Fluids with lower viscosity flow more readily than fluids with higher viscosity. Thus, molasses flows more slowly than water at room temperature.

Fluids are said to be compressible or incompressible. Water is an incompressible fluid because its density does not change when pressure is applied. Incompressible fluids are subject to the law of continuity, which states that fluid flows in a pipe are constant. This theory explains why the rate of flow increases when the cross-sectional area of a pipe is reduced and vice versa.

The viscosity of a fluid is an important consideration when calculating the total resistance on an object. The point where the fluid flows at the surface of an object is called the boundary layer. The fluid "sticks" to the object, not moving at all at the point of contact. The streamlines further from the surface are moving, but each is impeded by the streamline between it and the wall until the effect of the streamline closest to the wall is no longer a factor. The boundary layer is not obvious to the casual observer, but it is an important consideration in any calculations of fluid dynamics.

Most fluids are Newtonian fluids. Newtonian fluids have a stress-strain relationship that is linear. This means that a fluid will flow around an object in its path and "come together" on the other side without a delay in time. Non-Newtonian fluids do not have a linear stress-strain relationship. When they encounter shear stress, their recovery varies with the type of non-Newtonian fluid.

A main consideration in fluid dynamics is the amount of resistance encountered by an object moving through a fluid. Resistance, also known as drag, is made up of several components, all of which have one thing in common: they occur at the point where the object meets the fluid. The area can be quite large, as in the wetted surface of a ship, the portion of a ship that is below the waterline. For an airplane, the equivalent is the body of the plane as it moves through the air. The goal for those who work in the field of fluid dynamics is to understand the effects of fluid flows and minimize their effect on the object in question.

BACKGROUND AND HISTORY

Swiss mathematician Daniel Bernoulli (1700-1782) introduced the term "hydrodynamics" with the publication of his book *Hydrodynamica* in 1738. The name referred to water in motion and gave the field of fluid dynamics its first name, but it was not the first time water in action had been noted and studied. Leonardo da Vinci (1452-1519) made observations of water flows in a river and was the one who realized that water is an incompressible flow and that for an incompressible flow, V = constant. This law of continuity states that fluid flow in a pipe is

constant. In the late 1600s, French physicist Edme Mariotte (1620-84) and Dutch mathematician Christiaan Huygens (1629-95) contributed the velocity-squared law to the science of fluid dynamics. They did not work together, but they both reached the conclusion that resistance is proportional not to velocity itself but to the square of the velocity.

Sir Isaac Newton (1642-1727) put forth his three laws of motion in the 1700s. These laws play a fundamental part in many branches of science, including fluid dynamics. In addition to the term hydrodynamics, Bernoulli's contribution to fluid dynamics was the realization that pressure decreases as velocity increases. This understanding is essential to the understanding of lift.

Leonhard Euler (1707-83), the father of fluid dynamics, is considered by many to be the preeminent mathematician of the eighteenth century. He is the one who derived what is today known as the Bernoulli equation from the work of Daniel Bernoulli. Euler also developed equations for inviscid flows. These equations were based on his own work and are still used for compressible and incompressible fluids.

The Navier-Stokes equations result from the work of French engineer Claude-Louis Navier (1785-1836) and British physicist George Gabriel Stokes (1819-1903) in the mid-nineteenth century. They did not work together, but their equations apply to incompressible flows. The Navier-Stokes equations are still used. At the end of the nineteenth century, Scottish engineer William John Macquorn Rankine (1820-72) changed the understanding of the way fluids flow with his streamline theory, which states that water flows in a steady current of parallel flows unless disrupted. This theory caused a fundamental shift in the field of ship design because it changed the popular understanding of resistance in oceangoing vessels.

Laminar flow is measured today by use of the Reynolds number, developed by British engineer and physicist Osborne Reynolds (1842-1912) in

1883. When the number is low, viscous forces dominate. When the number is high, turbulent flows are dominant.

American naval architect David Watson Taylor designed and operated the first experimental model basin in the United States at the start of the twentieth century. His seminal work, *The Speed and Power of Ships* (1910), is still read. Taylor played a role in the use of bulbous bows on vessels of the navy. He also championed the use of airplanes that would be launched from naval craft underway in the ocean.

The principles of fluid dynamics took to the air in the eighteenth century with the work done by aviators such as the Montgolfier brothers and their hot-air balloons and French physicist Louis-Sébastien Lenormand's parachute. It was not until 1799, when English inventor Sir George Cayley (1771-1857) designed the first airplane with an understanding of the roles of lift, drag, and propulsion, that aerodynamics came under scrutiny. Cayley's work was soon followed by the work of American engineer Octave Chanute (1832-1910). In 1875, he designed several biplane gliders, and with the publication of his book *Progress in Flying Machines* (1894), he became internationally recognized as an aeronautics expert.

The Wright brothers are rightfully called the first aeronautical engineers because of the testing they did in their wind tunnel. By using balances to test a variety of different airfoil shapes, they were able to correctly predict the lift and drag of different wing shapes. This work enabled them to fly successfully at Kitty Hawk, North Carolina, on December 17, 1903.

German physicist Ludwig Prandtl (1875-1953) identified the boundary layer in 1904. His work led him to be known as the father of modern aerodynamics. Russian scientist Konstantin Tsiolkovsky (1857-1935) and American physicist Robert Goddard (1882-1945) followed, and Goddard's first successful liquid propellant rocket launch in 1926 earned him the title of the father of modern rocketry.

All of the principles that applied to hydrodynamics—the study of water in motion—applied to aerodynamics: the study of air in motion. Together these principles constitute the field of fluid dynamics.

MOTION THROUGH A FLUID

When an object moves through a fluid such as gas or water, it encounters resistance. How much resistance depends upon the amount of internal friction in the fluid (the viscosity) as well as the shape of the object. A torpedo, with its streamlined shape, will encounter less resistance than a two-by-four that is neither sanded nor varnished. A ship with a square bow will encounter more resistance than one with a bulbous bow and V shape. All of this is important because with greater resistance comes the need for greater power to cover a given distance. Since power requires a fuel source and a way to carry that fuel, a vessel that can travel with a lighter fuel load will be more efficient. Whether the design under consideration is for a submarine or submersible, a tractor-trailer, an automobile, an ocean liner, an airplane, a rocket, or a space shuttle, these basic considerations are of paramount importance in their design.

APPLICATIONS AND PRODUCTS

Fluid dynamics plays a part in the design of everything from automobiles to the space shuttle. Fluid dynamic principles are also used in medical research by bioengineers who want to know how a pacemaker will perform or what effect an implant or shunt will have on blood flow. Fire flows are also being studied to aid in the science of wildfire management. Until now the models have focused on heat transfer, but new studies are looking at fire systems and their fluid dynamic properties. Sophisticated models are used to predict fluid flows before model testing is done. This lowers the cost of new designs and allows the people involved to gain a thorough understanding of the tradeoff between size and power, given a certain design and level of resistance.

CAREERS

Fluid dynamics plays a part in a host of careers. Naval architects use fluid dynamic principles to design vessels. Aeronautical engineers use the principles to design aircraft. Astronautical engineers use fluid dynamic principles to design spacecraft. Weapons are constructed with and understanding of fluids in motion. Automotive engineers must understand fluid dynamics to design fuel-efficient cars. Architects must take the motion of air into their design of skyscrapers and other large buildings. Bioengineers use fluid dynamic principles to their advantage in the design of components that will interact with blood flow in the human body. Land-management professionals can use their understanding of fluid flows to develop plans for protecting the areas under their care from catastrophic loss due to fires. Civil engineers take the principles of fluid dynamics into consideration when designing bridges and highways, as the "flow" of traffic exhibits fluid dynamic behavior. Fluid dynamics also plays a role in sports: from pitchers who want to improve their curveballs to quarterbacks who are determined to increase the accuracy of their passes.

Students should take substantial coursework in more than one of the primary fields of study related to fluid dynamics (physics, mathematics, computer science, and engineering), because the fields that depend upon knowledge of fluid dynamic principles draw from multiple disciplines. In addition, anyone desiring to work in fluid dynamics should possess skills that go beyond the academic, including an aptitude for mechanical details and the ability to envision a problem in more than one dimension. A collaborative mindset is also an asset, as fluid dynamic applications tend to be created by teams.

SOCIAL CONTEXT AND FUTURE PROSPECTS

The science of fluid dynamics touches upon a number of career fields that range from sports to bioen-

gineering. Anything that moves through fluids or that is stationary within moving fluids such as air, water, or gases is subject to the principles of fluid dynamics. The more thorough the understanding, the more efficient vessel and other designs will be. This will result in the use of fewer resources in the form of power for inefficient designs and help create more efficient products.

—Gina Hagler

Further Reading

Çengel, Yunus A., and John M. Cimbala. *Fluid Mechanics: Fundamentals and Applications*. McGraw-Hill, 2010.

Darrigol, Olivier. *Worlds of Flow: A History of Hydrodynamics from the Bernoullis to Prandtl*. Oxford UP, 2005.

Davidson, P. A. *Incompressible Fluid Dynamics*. Oxford UP, 2022.

Eckert, Michael. *The Dawn of Fluid Dynamics: A Discipline Between Science and Technology*. Wiley-VCH, 2006.

Ferreiro, Larrie D. *Ships and Science: The Birth of Naval Architecture in the Scientific Revolution, 1600-1800*. MIT Press, 2007.

Ferziger, Joel H., Milovan Periæ, and Robert L. Street. *Computational Methods for Fluid Dynamics*. 4th ed., Springer, 2019.

Johnson, Richard W. *Handbook of Fluid Dynamics*. 2nd ed., CRC Press, 2016.

Nazarenko, Sergey. *Fluid Dynamics via Examples and Solutions*. CRC Press, 2015.

Rieutord, Michel. *Fluid Dynamics: An Introduction*. Springer International Publishing, 2016.

Visconti, Guido, and Paolo Ruggieri. *Fluid Dynamics: Fundamentals and Applications*. Springer International Publishing, 2021.

See also: Aerodynamics; Aeronautical engineering; Aerospace design; Airfoils; Bernoulli, Daniel; Bernoulli's principle; Calculus; Euler's laws of motion; Fluid mechanics and aerodynamics; Force (physics); Friction; Hydraulic engineering; Hydraulics; Hydrodynamics; Thermodynamics; Work and energy; Work-energy theorem

FLUID MECHANICS AND AERODYNAMICS

Fields of Study: Physics; Mechanics; Mathematics

ABSTRACT
Fluid mechanics and aerodynamics deal with the behavior of fluids in motion and at rest. How fluids influence objects, such as vehicles or animals, which pass through them is important in understanding the complex interactions involved in processes such as flight. Insights gained into fluid behavior possess valuable applications in fields as diverse as aerospace engineering, hydraulics, power plant design, and meteorology.

KEY CONCEPTS
airfoil: a structure that acts as a lifting body, such as certain wings that have evolved or been designed to maximize downwash and lift by their shape and angle of attack

angle of attack: the angle at which a body or structure, such as a wing, meets the airstream or fluid stream of whatever medium in which it is functioning

drag: the force with which a liquid medium, such as air or water, resists the motion of an object through it; can be classified as either parasitic or induced

flow: the motion of a fluid; more concrete, the behavior of a fluid substance, such as water or air, which deforms continuously, that is, changes its shape, in response to a shearing stress, no matter how small

lift: a force that acts to raise a wing, created by the formation of a pressure difference and by wing geometry, between air or another fluid moving at different speeds above and below the wing

streamlining: the designed or evolved reduction of drag by making a vehicle or animal's main body and other structures less turbulence-producing

thrust: any force that acts to move an object forward, such as an aircraft, regardless of mode of propulsion

viscosity: the internal friction of a fluid that acts as a force to inhibit flow; can be classified as either absolute or kinematic

OVERVIEW
The branch of classical physics that concerns itself with the study of the behavior of fluids both at rest and in motion is called fluid mechanics. To physicists, substances that are classified as fluids have specific and unique properties. These material properties are special characteristics of fluids, which among other things, constitute a separate state of matter distinct from other states such as solids and gases. These properties are reactions to known natural processes sometimes termed "physical laws." The primary property of fluids—and that which is their most distinguishing feature—is their ability to flow. While this statement may seem self-evident and redundant, a rigorous and comprehensive definition of the flow phenomenon proved to be a complex proposition that involved centuries of refinement by physicists. For example, fluid mechanics considers both gases and liquids to be fluids, as well as more solid-appearing substances such as glasses, whether artificial such as window glass or natural such as obsidian.

Specifically, fluids are understood to be substances that deform—that is, continuously change their shape or distort—under the application of a shear stress. Shear stress is an opposing force acting perpendicular to the surface or outer boundary of the original body of matter in question, regardless of whether the body is a solid or a fluid. An additional characteristic of a fluid is that it will deform to some degree from shear stress, no matter how small the amount of shear stress applied. Shear stress on a body, whether solid or fluid, can be expressed mathematically in terms of rates of angular deformation.

Fluids that behave in a regular, constant manner to shear stress and that experience a reaction that can be expressed by an equation employing a "constant of proportionality," are said to be "Newtonian fluids" in honor of Sir Isaac Newton, who initially formulated this equation regarding fluid friction. This constant is termed "absolute viscosity" or "dynamic viscosity." Many common fluids such as air and water belong to the class of Newtonian fluids, at least in their normally encountered states (average atmospheric temperatures and pressures). Nevertheless, a number of fluids exist that are non-Newtonian; among them are human blood, water-and-starch mixtures and many types of lubricating oils and suspensions. This results from the fact that such materials react to shear force in more complex ways: for example, changing their viscosity over time, either by decreasing or increasing.

The most important considerations involved in classical fluid mechanics equations are viscosity, pressure, compressibility, temperature, density and specific volume, and surface tension. Viscosity, the state of internal friction of any particular fluid, typically acts as a force to inhibit the ability of a substance to flow. Pressure, concerning fluids, can be regarded as a force per unit area or the effect of force acting on a particular surface of a fluid element. Compressibility is the ability of a given volume of a gas or liquid to be squeezed into a smaller unit area. Temperature can be regarded as the effect of heat or cold upon fluids (and, consequently, their viscosity). Density can be regarded as the amount of fluid per unit volume at a given temperature and pressure. Specific volume can be regarded as the reciprocal of the density. Surface tension is a property unique to fluids, where the fluid surface is in a state of stress and can sometimes support the weight of certain objects without permitting them to sink. Surface tension in fluids is dependent on temperature and on the composition and state of the substance upon which it is bounding.

Additional important factors concerning fluids involve properties of internal flow. The internal flow structure of a fluid is typically dichotomized along lines of whether a particular flow is laminar or turbulent. In laminar flow situations, a fluid, such as water, is observed to move in a relatively smooth, harmonious, and uniform manner. The fluid typically has a glassy, smooth appearance and is considered to be moving in layers. As the velocity of the fluid increases, the flow abruptly becomes very disturbed or turbulent. It reaches a critical threshold, where the dominant flow regime is chaotic in nature and the viscosity of the fluid, instead of being relatively uniform as in laminar flow, persists instead in flowing along in a state where viscosity wildly fluctuates.

Turbulent flow occurs in both common liquids and gases and is of great importance in understanding many applications of fluid mechanics theory, such as in aeronautics and meteorology.

A fluid's internal friction, shear stress, pressure, and types of flow structure are integrated theoretically in the concept of the "boundary layer," first formulated in Europe at the beginning of the twentieth century. The main elements of the concept postulate that in any flow of fluid molecules over an object, frictional effects are confined to a very thin layer (the boundary layer) found near the surface of an object; the fluid flow external to the boundary is relatively frictionless compared with the boundary layer; and a pressure variation from the main flow of the fluid is "impressed" upon the mainstream and affects the behavior of the boundary layer. The boundary layer interpretation assumes that no matter how smooth the surface of an object that a fluid flow is passing over or around, the molecules of the fluid in actual contact with the surface will remain static. A second, more external layer will be sandwiched between the outermost, normal, main fluid flow and the static flow at a reduced flow velocity. Finally, the third and outermost, "normal" fluid flow will be essentially unaffected in any way, sufficiently away from the boundary layer. In other words, a fluid velocity gradient is produced each time another object's surface comes into contact with a fluid flow. In a typical airstream, such as one produced on the surface of a moving aircraft, the velocity gradient produced is normally a small fraction of a centimeter thick.

As the velocity of a fluid flow increases across or around another surface, such as air over an aircraft airframe or water within the confines of a water pipe or narrow streambed, shear stresses of fluid molecule against fluid molecule increase at the boundary layer. If the fluid velocity increases still further, successive layers of fluid molecules will begin to build up over the boundary layer and a transitional point will be reached where flow is no longer laminar in the boundary layer but inclining more and more toward increased turbulent flow and increased friction. The outcome will eventually be the creation of highly turbulent flow, with rolling vortices and eddies of fluid indicative of chaotic viscosity and flow structure. Such flow structures are graphically familiar in the water patterns observed in rushing streams and brooks.

With regard to vehicles designed for travel in a fluid medium such as air or water, evident turbulent flow is typically symptomatic of design inadequacies regarding hull and control surfaces, which are inefficient and waste fuel because of increased friction.

Fluid mechanics theory has engendered a younger offshoot termed aerodynamics, a subbranch that deals with the physics of gases and their interactions with moving objects such as vehicles. Like classical fluid mechanics, aerodynamics utilizes the principles of Newtonian physics (various laws of motion) and the principles of thermodynamics (concepts of heat and work, properties of substances in relation to heat and work involved in various processes, and theoretical analysis and mathematical expression of such relationships) to solve problems by rigorously

describing phenomena and analyzing processes. Unlike pure fluid mechanics, aerodynamics deals with the realm of fluids restricted to gases (not both gases and liquids). Much of the work that has been done in the last century has been devoted, rather predictably, to the practical applications and problems involved in heavier-than-air manned flight, as the twentieth century has witnessed a rapid and explosive development of that field.

The basic flight equation regarding powered flight involves four basic factors: lift, weight, drag, and thrust. Successful, sustained, controlled flying involves the balance of these four forces. An aircraft, or any animal that has evolved successfully into a powered flyer, whether mammal, bird, or insect, uses these four forces in conjunction with some type of airfoil, a structure that acts as a lifting body, such as wings, which maximize downwash and lift by their shape and angle of attack. The angle of attack of the lifting body is simply the angle at which a body or structure such as a wing meets the airstream in which it is functioning. This angle is not synonymous with or necessarily parallel to the ground. Having a functional airfoil and having the airfoil oriented properly with respect to the angle of attack, a flying animal or machine must cope with the force of drag: the force with which the air resists the motion of an object through it.

Drag is a product of friction, as is lift; however, drag can be classified with regard to powered flying objects in two important, functional ways: It can be regarded as either parasitic or induced.

Induced drag is the useful and necessary drag found over the upper, curved surface of a properly designed (or evolved) airfoil or wing while it is in motion. Parasitic drag is the friction of the airflow over the main body of an animal or machine that is not contributing directly to lift (tail, head, or other protuberances). The difference in velocities and ratios of friction of airflows over the wing surface in such airfoils creates the lift necessary for flight. Lift is the utilized force that acts to raise a wing upward (and simultaneously the main body of a vehicle or animal) created by the formation of a pressure difference, which is produced by wing geometry between air moving at different speeds above and below the wing. Drag can be reduced to varying extents by streamlining or by the designed or evolved reduction of drag by making a vehicle or animal's main body and other structures less turbulence-producing. Thrust is the force that takes advantage of the airflow that acts to move an object, such as an aircraft, forward, regardless of mode of propulsion. The weight factor of the equation is the pull of gravity on the entire flying system that lift attempts to overcome.

APPLICATIONS

There are myriad useful applications that are direct and indirect products of the complementary fields of fluid mechanics and aerodynamics. Indeed, over the centuries, the intended and unintended processes, techniques, and industries that have been generated by this realm of scientific inquiry have become so pervasive as to become virtually synonymous with Western industrial society.

Essential, practical applications include power generation. The field of pure power generation—whether for electrical consumption for domestic or industrial use—owes a tremendous debt to the field of fluid mechanics by way of the many devices that are in constant, widespread, global use to generate power. Gravity- or tidal-fed hydroelectric turbines are mammoth installations using electromechanical devices that are direct spinoffs of fluid mechanic theory. The design of the intake ducts, outlets, piping, conduits, and the blades themselves are the concrete result of fluid mechanics. Along the same vein, the cooling systems of nuclear reactor-powered, electrical generating stations are likewise the progeny of fluid mechanics. They involve coolant systems and steam-driven electrical turbines. A portable, mo-

bile version of the nuclear-generating station also exists in hundreds of examples beneath Earth's oceans in the form of nuclear-powered submarines. The ubiquitous elevator, garage door lift, and countless smaller, similar devices utilizing hydraulic lifters also can be traced initially to fluid mechanics.

In fact, when closely analyzed, the internal combustion engine itself, whether fueled by diesel, alcohol or jet fuel, is a direct byproduct of conceptual paths generated by fluid mechanics.

Along raw power generating lines, one thinks of the rotor-powered wind turbine used increasingly in some areas for electricity production. The easiest paths to trace are those that originate from technology produced for flight itself from aerodynamic theory. One could list the vast industries manufacturing passenger, military, and research aircraft (both propeller and jet-driven, and rotary and fixed wing) and those servicing and being serviced by powered aircraft: tourism, air mail and product shipment, air ambulances, rescue and recovery aircraft, and so on. One of the least appreciated byproducts of aerodynamics and fluid mechanics is the great strides taken in weather and climate prediction and meteorology, which also owe their existence to the pioneering and ongoing mathematical modeling of weather systems and processes—physics of fluid masses on a grand scale.

CONTEXT

The genesis of fluid mechanics and aerodynamics can be effectively traced to the earliest recorded naturalists and inventors who used logic and empirical observation to try to understand phenomena they witnessed around them. Records from the first century show that the famous Roman naturalist and writer Pliny observed the effect of oil floating on water and speculated on the reasons for such behavior. Several centuries earlier, Hero of Alexandria, a Macedonian Greek living in Egypt, built a working model of a small, steam-driven engine. A Greek philosopher of the fifth century BCE, Empedocles, described the functioning of a mechanical water clock and made accurate conclusions about the air resistance of water pressure.

Despite the speculations and inventions of other ancients such as Archimedes and his original, practical device of a hydraulic lifting screw, it was not until the European Renaissance that a significant insight into fluid mechanics developed. Experimental equipment needed to be devised and basic concepts regarding the true nature of natural phenomenon and the states of matter had to be worked out. A solid step in this direction took place when the seventeenth-century Italian scientist Evangelista Torricelli invented a simple but effective barometer and worked out fairly accurately the amount of atmospheric pressure.

In the late seventeenth century, Sir Isaac Newton of England achieved a grand synthesis of empirical knowledge, mathematics, and logic to bring observable facts together in a manner that laid the cornerstone of modern scientific and mathematical thought. The modern science of physics, including that of fluid mechanics and aerodynamics, owes its existence to Newtonian physics. Other physicists refined and improved upon the experiments, observations, and theories of their contemporaries. The twentieth century saw further contributions, such as the German aerodynamicist, Ludwig Prandtl, author of the concept of the boundary layer, which has been such a cornerstone of modern physics theory and engineering.

—*Frederick M. Surowiec*

Further Reading

Alkemade, Fons. *A Century of Fluid Mechanics in The Netherlands*. Springer, 2019.

Ansari, Hasanraza. *Aerodynamics and Aircraft Performance*. Draft2digital, 2022.

Bertin, John J., and Russell M. Cummings. *Aerodynamics for Engineers: International Edition*. 6th ed., Pearson Education, 2013.

Katz, Joseph. *Automotive Aerodynamics*. John Wiley & Sons, 2016.

Liu, Peiqing. *A General Theory of Fluid Mechanics*. Springer Nature, 2021.

Vos, Roelof, and Saeed Farokhi. *Introduction to Transonic Aerodynamics*. Springer, 2015.

See also: Aerodynamics; Aeronautical engineering; Aerospace design; Ailerons, flaps, and airplane wings; Airfoils; Airplane propellers; Archimedes; Archimedes's principle; Bernoulli, Daniel; Bernoulli's principle; Biomechanics; Fluid dynamics; Friction; Hydraulic engineering; Hydraulics; Internal combustion engine; Jet engines; Newton's laws; Steam energy technology; Turbines

FLYWHEELS

Fields of Study: Physics; Mechanics; Mathematics

ABSTRACT

A flywheel is a heavy rotating wheel, the key component of a flywheel energy storage system, and a method of storing energy as rotational energy. They are used as alternatives to batteries or where energy use can be made more efficient by harnessing rotational energy from energy that is already being exerted.

KEY CONCEPTS

centrifugal force: an apparent force produced by the rotation of a mass about a central axis; it appears to act perpendicular to the axis of rotation in opposition to the centripetal force

centripetal force: a real force produced by the rotation of a mass about a central axis; it is formally the tension between the individual particles of the mass and the central axis proportional to the rate of rotation of the mass

drag: essentially, friction between moving surfaces and the surrounding air resulting in the generation of heat

gyroscopic force: a reactive force generated by a rotating mass to resist displacement from its original axis of rotation, consistent with conservation of angular momentum

magnetic bearing: a type of bearing that uses magnetic repulsion rather than physical contact to stabilize the rotation of an axle

rotational speed: simply, the rate at which a rotating mass travels about its central axis; for all particles in the mass the angular rotation speed is equal, but the physical distance traveled by individual particles about the axis increases directly with radius

tensile strength: the extent to which a material is able to resist forces acting in opposite directions without deformation and failure; a flywheel rotating at such a rate that the centrifugal force exceeds the centripetal force will fail and fly apart

A WHEEL THAT FLIES AROUND A CENTRAL AXIS

A flywheel is a mechanical device used to store rotational energy in an amount proportional to the square of its rotational speed. A flywheel energy storage system works because of the principle of conservation of energy. Rotational speed and stored energy are increased by applying torque to the flywheel, while the flywheel releases its energy by applying torque to a mechanical load. The common toy car that is dragged backwards and then released, propelled by the energy stored by the initial rotation of the wheels, is a familiar example of a simple flywheel system.

A component called a "flywheel" is an integral part of the electric ignition system of internal combustion engines. That application, however, is not intended to store energy for extended use. Rather, it is a large diameter heavy steel plate with a gear-tooth perimeter designed to engage the small spider gear of the electric starter motor, which drives it to turn the complete engine and initiate the firing sequence of the cylinders. The inertial mass of that flywheel serves to aid in smoothing the initial rotation by counteracting the force of the first few cylinder firings until all cylinders are operating, and to dampen the rundown of the engine when it is turned off. It does not store energy for further use.

Flywheels were a key component in James Watt's steam engine design, and some of the flywheels used in the first generation of those steam engines remain in use today. Although flywheel energy storage systems using mechanical energy to accelerate the flywheel are in development, current systems use electricity. Apart from the superconductors used to power magnetic bearings, if applicable, flywheels are not as affected by ambient temperature or temperature change as battery systems are, and have a much longer working life span.

DESIGN

Flywheel energy storage (FES) systems usually consist of a vacuum chamber (in order to reduce friction, or "drag"), a combination motor/generator that accelerates the flywheel and generates electricity, and a heavy steel rotor suspended on ball bearings inside the vacuum chamber. More sophisticated systems may use magnetic bearings to further reduce friction, though powering them may not be economically efficient. The advantage of a flywheel system is that it provides continuous energy, even when the output of the energy source is discontinuous or erratic. Energy is collected over a long period of time and released in a short spike, thus allowing the energy release to greatly exceed the ability of the energy source. Since 2001, FES systems have been able to provide continuous power with a discharge rate faster than batteries of equivalent storage capacity. Furthermore, flywheel maintenance is half as expensive as traditional battery system maintenance—even less than that when magnetic bearings are used. They are increasingly used as part of the integrated power design of large data centers. FES systems

Trevithick's 1802 steam locomotive used a flywheel to evenly distribute the power of its single cylinder. Photo by Birmingham Museums Trust, via Wikimedia Commons.

have also long been used in research and development laboratories where circuit breakers and other electrical equipment are tested.

APPLICATIONS

FES systems have numerous applications in transportation. Formula One race cars sometimes use flywheels to recover energy from the drive train during braking, which is then re-deployed during acceleration. While the purpose of this application is to improve acceleration, and the economic efficiency of the system is considered by different criteria in competitive motor sports than in the design of passenger vehicles, a similar system is used in electric vehicles to increase fuel efficiency or to provide faster acceleration than the power source would otherwise be able to provide. Flywheel systems have been proposed to replace chemical batteries in electric vehicles; a small number of vehicle designs before the current generation of electric and hybrid vehicles incorporated flywheels into their designs, including flywheel-powered Swiss buses in the 1950s.

Flywheels have also been used in rail systems, especially electric rail systems, to provide boosts to power or to provide power when there is an interruption in the electrical supply. Since 2010, the

London Midland train operator has operated two flywheel-powered railcars. New York's Long Island Rail Road (LIRR) has begun a pilot project to explore the possibility of using flywheels lineside to generate some of the electricity used by the LIRR's electric trains, to improve their acceleration and recover electricity during braking. Elsewhere in New York, Beacon Power opened a 20-megawatt flywheel energy storage plant in Stephentown, where power is purchased at off-peak hours and stored with fewer carbon emissions than traditional plants.

LIMITATIONS

The biggest limitations to flywheel systems are the rotor's tensile strength and the energy storage time. The tensile strength of the rotor determines how fast the rotor can rotate, and therefore the system's capacity; if it is exceeded, the flywheel can shatter in an explosion, the risk of which requires a containment vessel which increases the system's mass and cost. Because of the rotation of the planet, flywheels change orientation over time, which is resisted by the flywheel's gyroscopic forces exerted against the bearings. The resulting increase in friction results in a loss of energy of as much as 50 percent over two hours, when mechanical bearings are used, though careful design can reduce that amount by half. Magnetic bearings are much more efficient, losing only a few percent of their energy. Even so, until magnetic bearings are more cost-efficient, this limitation is one reason why flywheels are best used in applications where energy will not need to be stored for long periods of time, and why they are well-suited for public transit applications, where they are in near constant use.

—*Bill Kte'pi*

Further Reading

Alberg, Tom. *Flywheels: How Cities Are Creating Their Own Futures*. Columbia UP, 2021.

Bhandari, V. B. *Design of Machine Elements*. 3rd ed., Tata/McGraw-Hill, 2010.

Breeze, Paul. *Power System Energy Storage Technologies*. Academic Press, 2018.

Hebner, R. "Flywheel Batteries Come Around Again." *Spectrum*, vol. 39, no. 4, Apr. 2002.

Khan, B. H. *Non-Conventional Energy Resources*. Tata/McGraw-Hill, 2006.

Larminie, James, and John Lowry. *Electric Vehicle Technology Explained*. Wiley, 2003.

Leclercq, Ludovic, Benoit Robyns, and Jean-Michel Grave. "Control Based on Fuzzy Logic of a Flywheel Energy Storage System Associated with Wind and Diesel Generators." *Mathematics and Computers in Simulation*, vol. 63, no. 3-5, Nov. 2003.

National Aeronautics and Space Administration. *Metallic Rotor Sizing and Performance Model for Flywheel Systems*. NASA, 2019.

Rufer, Alfred. *Energy Storage Systems and Components*. CRC Press, 2018.

Sabry, Fouad. *Flywheel Energy Storage: Increasing or Decreasing Speed, to Add or Extract Power*. One Billion Knowledgeable, 2022.

See also: Acceleration; Aerospace design; Angular forces; Angular momentum; Centrifugation; Circular motion; Conservation of energy; Friction; Harmonic oscillator; Work and energy; Work-energy theorem

FORCE (PHYSICS)

Fields of Study: Physics; Mechanics; Mathematics

ABSTRACT

This article describes the principles of force, which is the product of an object's mass and its acceleration. Force of any kind functions in only one of two modes—as an attraction or as a repulsion. While force is invisible, its effects can be observed.

KEY CONCEPTS

acceleration: the rate of change of velocity associated with a change in speed or direction of motion or both; going faster

angular velocity: the rate of change of position of a body moving in a circle, commonly measured in rotations per minute

centrifugal force: the outward force exerted on an object moving in a circular path

centripetal force: the inward force required to keep an object moving in a circular path

deceleration: also called negative acceleration, the decrease of velocity over a period of time, the opposite of acceleration

displacement: the change of location of an object within a frame of reference as the result of an experienced force

frame of reference: a system of space-time coordinates used by an observer to measure the physical world

momentum: a property of mass related to the movement of that mass, characterized by the tendency of a mass to remain in motion or motionless unless acted upon by a force, and defined as the product of mass and velocity

FORCE AS WE KNOW IT

Force is not a physical entity; it is the product of an object's mass and its acceleration. Force of any kind functions in only one of two modes—as an attraction or as a repulsion, and both are experiences rather than actual physical entities, observable only as their effect. A billiard ball is a physical entity; the force that moves it when struck by the cue stick or another billiard ball is not, since only the effect of that force can be observed. In physics, force is characterized as any influence or interaction by one object on another object, which results in force being exerted on both objects, as well as changes in the motion and the velocity. Velocity is defined as the rate and direction at which a physical object changes position. When the velocity of an object is changing from one speed or direction to another, the word "acceleration" is used. For example, the action involved in pushing a door open or pulling it closed serves to provide the force that influences the door to change its velocity (to accelerate or decelerate) and its direction. Force is measured in units called Newtons, and the total amount of force (F) can be determined by multiplying an object's mass (m) by the amount of its acceleration (a), expressed by the equation $F = ma$.

Gravity is a naturally occurring force that exists in varying strengths throughout the universe as an intrinsic property of matter. On Earth, the gravitational pull effects objects on or surrounding the planet. For example, when a ball is bouncing, the force of gravity works to slow the ball down as it is going up, but when the ball begins to return to the ground, the force of gravity accelerates the downward motion of the ball.

BRIEF HISTORY

Sir Isaac Newton (1643-1727), an English physicist and mathematician, studied the motion of objects and found that all objects in motion are affected by certain laws. These laws, which he outlined in 1687, are referred to as Newton's three laws of motion.

Newton's first law of motion, also called the law of inertia, states that a resting object will tend to stay at rest because an object's motion cannot be initiated without an external force acting on it. An object that is already in motion, however, will tend to stay in motion and will continue to go in the same direction and at the same acceleration until a force is applied to it that then affects its direction and/or acceleration.

Newton's second law of motion deals with the size of an object, the force applied to it, and its resulting rate of acceleration. The second law shows that the greater the mass of the object, the greater the amount of force needed to accelerate the object. Put simply, objects that are heavier will require more force to move than objects that are lighter, and if the same amount of force is applied to two objects of different mass, the acceleration will be more noticeable in the object with a smaller mass than in the object with a larger mass.

Newton's third law of motion illustrates the statement that for every action there is an equal and opposite reaction. In other words, every time force is applied to an object from one direction, an equal amount of force will be dispersed onto the object in the opposite direction. This principle can be seen in the example of a rocket launch: When a rocket is launched, it is pushed through the air by the force of the explosion at the same time that it is being pushed back toward the earth by the force of gravity.

OVERVIEW

Hooke's law was named after seventeenth-century English scientist Robert Hooke (1635-1703), who discovered the law of elasticity in 1660 and the effect of force on solid matter. The law states that when a force is applied to a solid object, a deformation of the object or a displacement of its matter takes place. The size of the deformation or displacement is therefore directly proportional to the amount of force (or load) that is applied to the object. The resulting elasticity occurs when the force is removed and the object regains its original or natural shape, despite being stretched, compressed, bent, twisted, or squeezed. For example, when a wet sponge is squeezed and twisted in order to remove the water, the original shape of this solid object is deformed by the applied pressure or force. However, when the force is removed, such as when the sponge is no longer being squeezed, the sponge returns to its original state and shape. This is the concept of Hooke's theory of elasticity.

Additionally, two other concepts can also be used to describe types of force: stress and strain. Stress is defined as a force that is applied externally on the molecular units that make up the solid matter, while strain is defined as the deformity stress produces on the object on which the force is applied. This stress can be either proportional when the stress applied is relatively small, as in pressing a finger into putty, or

disproportional, like the force of a wind storm on a tree.

Force in and of itself cannot be seen, but the result of applied force can be observed. There are two categories of force. Contact force is when objects can be perceived as physically coming in contact with each other and includes frictional force, spring force, tension force, applied force, and air-resistance force. Action-at-a-distance force occurs when objects are not physically touching each other but are affected by each other through pushing or pulling. An example would be the gravitational forces on Earth. Other examples of action-at-a-distance force include electrical force and magnetic force.

—*L. L. Lundin*

Further Reading

Davies, Paul. *Information and the Nature of Reality: From Physics to Metaphysics*. Cambridge UP, 2014.

Finnis, Mike. *Interatomic Forces in Condensed Matter*. Oxford UP, 2010.

Freedman, Roger, Todd Ruskell, Philip R. Kesten, and David L. Tauck. *College Physics*. 2nd ed., W.H. Freeman, 2017.

Girifalco, Louis A. *The Universal Force: Gravity—Creator of Worlds*. Oxford UP, 2014.

Jammer, Max. *Concepts of Force: A Study in the Foundations of Dynamics*. Dover, 2005.

Kleppner, Daniel, and Robert J. Kolenkow. *An Introduction to Mechanics*. 2nd ed., Cambridge UP, 2014.

Ling, Samuel J., Jeff Sanny, and William Moebs. *University Physics, Volume 1*. Samurai Media Limited, 2017.

Pais, Abraham. *Inward Bound: Of Matter and Forces in the Physical World*. Oxford UP, 2002.

Stone, Anthony. *The Theory of Intermolecular Forces*. 2nd ed., Oxford UP, 2013.

Uicker, John J., Gordon R. Pennock, and Joseph E. Shigley. *Theory of Machines and Mechanisms*. 4th ed., Oxford UP, 2011.

See also: Acceleration; Aerodynamics; Angular forces; Angular momentum; Billiards; Centrifugation; Circular motion; Classical or applied mechanics; Coriolis effect; Displacement; Dynamics (mechanics); Elasticity; Friction;

Hooke, Robert; Kinetic energy; Moment of inertia; Momentum physics; Newton's laws; Potential energy; Quantum mechanics; Speed; Torque; Vectors; Work-energy theorem

Friction

Fields of Study: Physics; Mechanics; Mathematics

ABSTRACT
Friction is the "contact force," a force between two surfaces that are in contact that resists the sliding motion of one surface over the other. The friction force exerted by one object sliding over another object is always parallel to the contact surface between the two objects and always occurs in a direction opposite that of the motion.

KEY CONCEPTS
abrasion: the wearing away of surface material by friction

adhesion: the molecular attraction exerted between surfaces that are in contact

atomic forces: electronic forces that arise because of the interactions between electrons of nearby atoms

coefficient of friction: a dimensionless quantity, which depends on the types of materials involved, that characterizes the magnitude of the friction force between two surfaces of unit area

contact force: a force that occurs only when two objects are in direct contact

dissipative force: a force that, by its action, turns energy into heat

kinetic friction: the force that opposes one surface sliding over another when one surface is moving with respect to the other

normal force: a force in the direction normal, or perpendicular, to two surfaces in contact that pushes the two surfaces together

static friction: the force that resists one surface sliding over another when the two surfaces are not moving

OVERVIEW
Friction is the "contact force," a force between two surfaces that are in contact that resists the sliding motion of one surface over the other. The friction force exerted by one object sliding over another object is always parallel to the contact surface between the two objects and always occurs in a direction opposite that of the motion.

Friction is the force that resists the sliding of one surface over another. The force of friction is responsible for the wear experienced by mechanical devices using surfaces in contact and results in the heating of sliding surfaces.

The friction force is important in the common activities of everyday life. Friction produces the force between our feet and the floor, allowing us to walk; provides the force between automobile tires and the road, allowing cars to accelerate and to stop; and provides the force between an object and our hands, allowing us to pick things up, for example. A person walking normally along a sidewalk will generally slip when unexpectedly encountering a spot where friction is significantly reduced, such as an unseen icy patch.

When two objects are sliding, however, friction is a "dissipative force," a force that turns energy into heat. Under these circumstances, friction is frequently regarded as a nuisance, requiring the operator of mechanical devices to supply more energy to these devices than would otherwise be required to accomplish the desired objective. Most of the excess energy is transformed into heat by the friction force, though a small part of the excess energy actually abrades, or wears away, the surface of the weaker of the two materials. For example, some of the energy generated by burning gasoline in an automobile engine is dissipated by friction within the engine, transmission, and drive mechanism, rather than being used to accelerate the vehicle. Friction causes most mechanical objects to wear out as a result of abrasion (the loss of material as the surfaces in contact interact with each other) and because of the heating produced as one surface slides over another.

A complete theoretical description of friction has, thus far, eluded scientists, because the phenomenon involves the interaction forces between all the individual atoms or molecules on or near the two surfaces that are in contact. The modern theoretical understanding of friction attributes the friction force to the atomic forces of adhesion between atoms or molecules on the surfaces of the two materials. These forces are similar to the electronic bonding forces that hold the individual atoms together in liquids and solids. The more strongly the atoms on one surface attract those on the other surface, the greater the friction force between the two surfaces. However, detailed modeling of this adhesion force is possible only if a few atoms are interacting; such modeling cannot be done for the vast number of atoms that interact over the surface areas of real objects.

Because of the complexity of a complete theoretical description of friction, the friction force is usually approximated using "laws of friction" that are derived from experiment. These laws of friction, which were originally developed by the Italian scientist, engineer, and artist Leonardo da Vinci in the fifteenth century, are as follows: the friction force is proportional to the contact force that presses the two surfaces together; the friction force depends on the two types of material that are in contact; for objects in motion, the friction force is independent of the speed at which one surface is moving over the other surface; and the friction force is independent of the area of contact between the two surfaces.

There are two types of friction, "static friction" and "kinetic friction." Static friction occurs between two surfaces that are in contact but are not moving with respect to each other, for example, a book rest-

ing on top of a flat, horizontal table. If you push gently on one of the vertical sides of the book, the book will not move. Static friction provides the force that resists the motion of the book. However, there is a maximum force that the two surfaces in contact can exert. If you push hard enough to overcome this force, the book will begin to move.

The maximum force of static friction is modeled by physicists as the product of the "coefficient of static friction," a quantity that must be measured for each type of material sliding on another type of material, and the "normal force," which is a measure of how hard one surface is pushing on the other. In the case of the book on the table, the normal force is the weight of the book, which pushes it down onto the table. If the weight is increased by stacking a second book on top of the first one, the normal force increases, and the force that must be exerted on the side of the book to make it move also increases.

The coefficient of static friction between the book and the table can be measured by tilting the table, increasing the angle that the surface of the table makes with the horizontal until the book just starts to slide down the incline. The coefficient of static friction is equal to the numerical value of the tangent of the angle at which the table's surface is inclined relative to the horizontal when the book just begins to slide. This technique is used to measure the coefficient of static friction for many surface materials.

Kinetic friction occurs when one of the surfaces is moving with respect to the other one. Kinetic friction is modeled in the same way as static friction except that the coefficient of static friction is replaced by a coefficient of kinetic friction. For most materials, the coefficient of kinetic friction is less than the coefficient of static friction, so it requires a stronger push to start the book in sliding motion than it does to keep it sliding across the table at a constant speed.

The coefficient of kinetic friction can also be measured using an incline. If the angle of the incline is adjusted so that the object, once moving, slides down the incline at a constant speed, then the coefficient of kinetic friction is equal to the tangent of the angle of the incline relative to the horizontal.

Friction is one of a group of "drag forces," which resist the motion of one object in contact with another. Objects moving through gases or liquids experience similar dissipative forces, called "aerodynamic" drag or "fluid" drag.

APPLICATIONS

Most likely, the first practical application of friction may have been by prehistoric humans who used it to start fires. The friction force between two objects, such as sticks or stones that are rubbed together, can generate enough heat to ignite kindling material. This application of friction is still used today, as matches rubbed along a rough surface ignite the heat-sensitive chemical material on their surfaces.

In everyday life, friction is the force that allows us to lift objects without putting our hands underneath them. A cylindrical water glass can be lifted by gripping the hand around the glass. The fingers and palm pushing in on the sides of the glass produce a contact force, and static friction, which is parallel to the contact surface and opposite the direction of intended motion, exerts a force that is directed upward, keeping the glass from sliding downward as the glass is raised. However, if a lubricant such as water or oil is present on the outer surface of the glass or on the hand, the coefficient of static friction is reduced, and the glass may slip downward when the fingers and palm apply the same contact force.

Friction is the critical force involved in stopping most moving objects, whether by rubbing a foot along the pavement to stop a wagon or skateboard or by applying the brakes in a car. Two friction devices are used in stopping an automobile: the brakes and the tires. Automobile brakes work on the princi-

ple that the kinetic energy (the energy associated with motion) of the car can be transformed into heat energy by forcing one surface to slide over another. When the brakes in an automobile are activated, the stationary brake pads or brake shoes are brought into contact with a disk or a drum that rotates with each wheel. Kinetic friction between the brake pads or shoes and the rotating disks or drums transforms the kinetic energy of the vehicle into heat. Static friction between the tires and the road then slows the car as the wheels rotate more slowly. If the brakes are applied too strongly, the wheels may stop rotating, and the kinetic friction of the nonrotating tires sliding along the road surface will bring the vehicle to a more abrupt stop. In this case, the abrasion of the soft surface of the tires by the stronger surface of the road often results in a skid mark, as material wearing from the tires is deposited along the road.

The efficiency of braking depends on the magnitude of the coefficient of friction. A normal automobile on a dry road surface can come to a stop, from an initial speed of 100 kilometers per hour, in about 50 meters. However, if the road surface is wet, thus reducing the coefficient of friction between the tires and the road, the stopping distance increases to about 80 meters. Similarly, if the surfaces of the brakes get wet, for example by driving through a deep puddle, the braking effectiveness will be poor until the contact surfaces have dried. For a road surface covered with ice, which further decreases the coefficient of friction between the tires and the road, the stopping distance increases even farther. A train, which has steel wheels on a steel track, has a much lower coefficient of friction between its wheels and the track than that of automobile tires on the road. As a result, a train usually requires 135 to 165 meters to come to a stop from an initial speed of 100 kilometers per hour.

Much of the study of friction concentrates on methods to minimize or overcome friction, since the minimization of friction improves the "efficiency," a measure of the amount of useful work a device can do for a given amount of input energy. Lubrication is frequently used to reduce friction between two contact surfaces. Ice skates, for example, are designed to produce and trap a thin layer of water between the metal blade of the skate and the ice surface, allowing the skater to move on a thin layer of lubricant, reducing the frictional resistance from that of metal on ice.

One metal surface sliding on another metal surface can have a friction coefficient as high as 4 in a vacuum. In air, this friction coefficient is reduced to a value near 1. However, the introduction of a liquid lubricant can further reduce the friction coefficient. Values near 0.3 are measured using water as the lubricant; high-quality lubricating oils can reduce the friction coefficient to values near 0.1. Because lubricants can improve the efficiency of mechanical devices and minimize their wear, thus prolonging their useful lifetime, the development of better lubricants is an important area of engineering research.

In the adhesion model of friction, the action of lubricants is understood to reduce the atomic forces between the two surfaces. In this model, friction is attributed to the atomic forces between the atoms at the surfaces in contact. In solids, these atomic forces are generally quite high. The ability of liquids to flow is attributed to weaker atomic forces. Thus liquids, with their lower atomic forces, are believed to bond to both of the surfaces, and the atomic forces between these liquids is lower than between the two solid surfaces.

Friction can also be reduced by coating one of the surfaces with a solid material having a low coefficient of friction. Coatings of Teflon (polytetrafluoroethylene) or graphite (a pure form of carbon, ground to a fine powder) reduce the coefficient of friction between two surfaces. The coefficient of kinetic friction between Teflon and steel is 0.04, while that between steel and steel is 0.57. Thus, the application of a

Teflon coating to a steel surface will reduce the friction between the two surfaces by more than a factor of 10, increasing efficiency and reducing wear. Teflon coatings are frequently applied at points where two surfaces, metal or otherwise, would normally come into contact with each other.

The laws of friction are only approximately true, and small deviations from the third law—that the friction force is independent of the speed of motion of the two surfaces—give rise to "frictional oscillations," which have a variety of useful applications. Generally, for surfaces that are either not lubricated or are poorly lubricated, the coefficient of sliding friction decreases as the speed increases, resulting in an oscillatory motion, or vibration, by which the moving object speeds up, then slows down in a repeating fashion. This frictional oscillation produces the screech that is sometimes heard when chalk or fingernails are pushed across a blackboard. Frictional oscillation is also the mechanism by which bowed instruments, such as a violin, produce their harmonic tones. Frictional oscillations can also provide a warning that the lubricant has been lost from mechanical systems, and observant operators frequently have enough warning to shut down the system before it overheats or seizes.

CONTEXT

Prior to the recognition of the friction force, the understanding of mechanics—the science of how objects move—was impeded. Natural scientists in ancient Rome and Greece observed that when they ceased pushing on an object, it would quickly come to a stop. Based on this observation, they believed that an object in motion required the continual application of a force to remain in motion.

By the fifteenth century, Leonardo da Vinci had engaged in a study of friction in an effort to reduce its effects on mechanical systems. Experiments by Galileo Galilei and Isaac Newton recognized how friction had impeded earlier ideas about the motion of objects, and this resulted in a new formulation of the laws of motion. Newton's first law of motion states that an object in motion will remain in motion in a straight line at a constant speed until it is acted upon by an external force. The major reason why most moving objects eventually slow down is friction.

Early humans moved heavy objects on sleds or skids that they pulled across the ground. Because these sleds or skids have a high coefficient of friction with the ground, this method of moving objects dissipates, or wastes, a lot of energy. It is suspected that early humans developed lubricants, possibly wetting the ground surface with water, to reduce friction. A revolution occurred when it was recognized that the sled could be replaced with the wagon, a device that rolled, probably first along a runway of logs and, later, on its own wheels mounted on axles. The wagon greatly reduced the friction force that must be overcome to move objects and made it practical to transport heavy objects over large distances.

Friction was originally explained as a force that resulted from the imperfections of the surfaces of the two objects. It was imagined that one piece of rough wood had difficulty sliding over another piece of rough wood because the high points on one surface would get stuck in the low points of the second surface. However, in the twentieth century, as it became possible to prepare highly polished surfaces, it became clear that the friction force still persisted as the surfaces became flatter. In fact, two highly polished metal surfaces placed in contact in a vacuum will weld together, and the resistance to sliding will exceed that of rougher metal surfaces that do not experience welding. A detailed understanding of how polished metal surfaces weld in a vacuum has become important in the exploration of space, where metal is a common material used in construction of moving parts on spacecraft that operate in the high vacuum of space.

Developments in modeling the chemical bonding and atomic forces between atoms led to the modern understanding of friction as adhesion, or the atomic-scale attraction between the atoms or molecules in one surface and those in the other surface. Efforts to understand and control friction now focus on the detailed understanding of these atomic-scale forces.

The ultimate objective for certain mechanical devices is to eliminate friction entirely, thus eliminating wear and removing the energy penalty resulting from the production of heat. This objective can be achieved by keeping one surface suspended above the second, so that motion occurs without any contact between the surfaces. In the laboratory, this can be accomplished using air tracks or air tables, devices in which a continuous stream of high-pressure air is forced from small holes in the surface. The result is that an object placed on the surface is suspended on a thin cushion of air, never actually coming in contact with the track or table. This technology is used in the construction of "air-hockey" games, for example; however, it is not practical to use air tracks for large or heavy objects. Magnetic levitation, in which a moving object is suspended above its guide rails, is used instead and is the feature that enables high-speed "bullet trains" to function.

—George J. Flynn

Further Reading

Basu, Bikramjit, Mitjan Kalin, and B.V. Manoj Kumar. *Friction and Wear of Ceramics: Principles and Case Studies*. John Wiley & Sons, 2020.

Blau, Peter J. *Friction Science and Technology*. 2nd ed., CRC Press, 2019.

Chen, Gang Sheng. *Handbook of Friction-Vibration Interactions*. Elsevier, 2014.

Kumar, Sanjay. *Laws of Motion and Friction: Mechanics*. Independently Published, 2020.

Lewis, W. T. *Friction, Lubrication, and the Lubricants of Horology*. DigiCat, 2022.

Ludema, Kenneth C., and Layo Ajayi. *Friction, Wear, Lubrication: A Textbook in Tribology*. 2nd ed., CRC Press, 2018.

Popov, Valentin L. *Contact Mechanics and Friction: Physical Principles and Applications*. 2nd ed., Springer Berlin Heidelberg, 2018.

See also: Aerodynamics; Aeronautical engineering; Classical or applied mechanics; Dynamics (mechanics); Fluid dynamics; Fluid mechanics and aerodynamics; Kinematics; Nanotechnology; Vibration

G

GALILEO

Fields of Study: Physics; Engineering; Mechanics; Mathematics

ABSTRACT

Galileo was an Italian philosopher, astronomer, and mathematician. He was one of the first Europeans to experiment with and improve the rudimentary telescope and was one of the first to apply it to astronomy. He also created one of the earliest-known working microscopes. Deeply involved with observational physics and mechanics, he conducted experiments in gravity, light, sound, motion, and the pendulum, and he invented various objects, including pumps and the hydrostatic balance. History also credits him as one of the earliest advocates of heliocentrism.

KEY CONCEPTS

geocentrism: the view that the Sun, the planets, and the entire Universe revolve in orbit about Earth

heliocentric: orbits that have the Sun at their center

specific gravity: the mass of a pure material in a standard unit of volume, typically expressed as grams per cubic centimeter

water displacement: the principle by which an object of a particular mass will displace a volume of water equal to the object's mass, due to the fact that water has a specific gravity of 1 gram per cubic centimeter

GALILEO'S TELESCOPE

As author Fred Watson describes in his book *Stargazer* (2004), by mid-1609 Galileo had heard rumors about the new Dutch spyglass patented by Hans Lippershey called a "perspicillum" (from the Latin *perspicax*, "sharp-sighted"), although it is unlikely that Galileo saw a prototype. Being a mathematician, he deduced that the necessary magnification "was the result of the ratio of the focal length of the two lenses." Galileo soon found his own set of preexisting glass lenses and placed them at the right distance from each other in a lead tube. He used soft lead because it could be easily rolled and manipulated to hold the lenses securely. Galileo's telescope used one convex lens, called an objective, which gathers the light coming from the observed object, and one concave lens, the eyepiece; together, these lenses could magnify usually no more than three times. That year, Galileo steadily experimented by producing the shallow parabolic

Galileo. Image via iStock/ilbusca. [Used under license.]

curves needed on glass lenses. Improving on the grinding and polishing of his own lenses and experimenting with the shallow angles and variable distances between the lenses, Galileo soon improved this magnification to twenty times and ultimately to thirty times.

Whereas others had primarily used the telescope for land viewing during the day, Galileo applied the new instrument heavenward at night. Viewing the Moon, probably for the first time ever at such clarity, Galileo noticed its rough spherical surface, pitted with craters and likely chasms. He soon made other important discoveries about the phases of Venus, Jupiter's four largest moons, the Milky Way as a mass of stars, and other astronomical phenomena he quickly published in his *Sidereus nuncius* (*Starry Messenger*) in early 1610.

EARLY LIFE

Galileo was born in 1564 to minor gentry in Tuscany under the rule of the Medici family as the grand dukes of Florence. Galileo was the eldest of about six children. His mother was Giulia Ammannati, and his father, Vincenzo, was a prominent lute player, composer, and pioneer of music theory who had also dabbled in the applied mathematics of strings, having published treatises on vibrations of strings. As a musician and theorist, Galileo's father anticipated the harmonic theories of the Baroque, and his technical nature influenced his son's intellectual predilection for science. Galileo's first formal education was at the Camaldolese Monastery at Vallombrosa, south of Florence. His subsequent education was at the University of Pisa, where he had initially enrolled in medicine but was far more interested in mathematics.

LIFE'S WORK

In 1586, at the age of twenty-two, Galileo published a small treatise called *La Bilancetta* (*The Little Balance*), in which he added to discoveries of Archimedes about water displacement and specific gravity, weighing materials in air and water. By 1589, Galileo's burgeoning contacts brought him academic stature.

Cardinal Francesco Maria del Monte was a clerical courtier of the Florentine Medici and represented Medici interests in Rome to the Vatican. Cardinal del Monte, and especially his mathematician brother Guidobaldo del Monte, helped to secure academic positions for Galileo: first at his alma mater, the University of Pisa, where he was appointed chair of mathematics in 1589, and next at the University of Padua in 1592, where he also taught physics (mechanics) and astronomy. In 1590, following his experiments with motion, he published *De motu* (*On Motion*) at Padua. Galileo was also an apparent houseguest of Cardinal del Monte in Rome at Palazzo Madama on several occasions. Correspondence between the del Monte brothers and Galileo has survived, partly because the urbane cardinal saw himself as much a champion of science as a clergyman. By 1598, expanding on earlier instruments designed by Guidobaldo del Monte and others, Galileo had improved a geometric and military compass for surveyors and for army use. He published on his compass improvements in *Le Operazioni del compasso geometrico et militare* (*Operations of the Geometric and Military Compass*) in 1606. Following Archimedes, whom he much admired, he also invented a thermometer based on buoyancy and designed a related hydrostatic balance. Between 1600 and 1606, Galileo fathered three illegitimate children with Marina Gamba, whom he never married but who later married a Florentine man. Both of Galileo's daughters became nuns.

In the field of physics, Galileo experimented with motion, sound, inertia, and the speed of light. He posited a hypothesis on relativity, setting the stage for later improvements by Sir Isaac Newton and Albert Einstein. In astronomy, beginning in 1609—only a year or so after the likely invention of the telescope in northern Europe, although both Roger Bacon and before him Ibn al-Haytham had possibly pursued lens use for similar purposes—Galileo constructed a telescope and applied it first to land and then to the night sky. He observed and roughly mapped the surface of one side of the Moon, the phases of Venus, at least four moons of Jupiter, Saturn, the Milky Way, and other phenomena. Many of his astronomical discoveries were published in 1610 in his *Sidereus nuncius* (*Starry Messenger*). There is also evidence that he constructed one of the first microscopes. His study of sunspots was published in 1613. Another of Galileo's correspondents and acquaintances from around 1610 onward was Prince Federico Cesi (1585-1630), who in 1603 founded the Accademia Nazionale dei Lincei, an early scientific academy in Italy whose members were often accused of occultism and opposition to the doctrine of the Roman Catholic Church. Cesi was also a friend of both Cardinal del Monte and Giambattista della Porta, the latter of whom became one of the earliest members of the Lincei academy. At Cesi's palazzo, a Greek scientist named Giovanni Demisiani officially named the "telescope" (from the Greek τελε (*tele*), "far," and ςκοπειν (*skopein*), "to see") at a function in 1611 celebrating Galileo, who became an elected Lincei academy member on that occasion.

With initial patronage from the Barberini family in Rome, Galileo published *Il Saggiatore* (1623; *The Assayer*), a bold text about his philosophy of science wherein he asserted that mathematics was the optimum tool for measuring and expressing truths of nature through physics. Galileo's growing disputes with the Jesuits and Father Orazio Grassi, a capable Jesuit astronomer whom Galileo increasingly criticized in polemic writing, did not help his case for Copernican heliocentrism by greatly alienating the Jesuits. In 1632, Galileo published his polemical *Dialogo sopra i due massimi sistemi del mondo* (*Dialogue Concerning the Two Chief World Systems*), in which he compared Ptolemaic geocentrism with Copernican heliocentrism. Although he had been called to Rome in 1616 over his controversial views and prohibited from publicly advancing heliocentric arguments, Galileo still had friends in Rome. His 1632 work was his most strident, a clever literary construction about his views that in some way mocked Pope Urban VIII, who had earlier befriended and defended Galileo when he was still Cardinal Maffeo Barberini. By putting the pope's views in the mouth of the character Simplicio, a simpleton advocate of geocentrism, which he then vigorously attacked, Galileo made himself too visible to leave alone, a heretical loose cannon in the Church's eyes.

Arguably the most famous incident in his life was his 1633 call to Rome by the Inquisition to account for his "Copernican heresy" regarding heliocentrism. He defended his views vigorously but was publicly charged as a heretic and placed under house arrest near Florence for the rest of his life. The popular story of his stamping his foot and muttering "But it does move" is unprovable. Although his writings were banned, he continued to write on such topics as gravity, including such works as his 1638 *Discorsi e dimostrazioni matematiche intorno a due nuove scienze attenenti alla meccanica e i movimenti locali* (*Discourses and Mathematical Demonstrations about Two New Sciences Concerning Mechanics and Local Motion*). Although later legends are full of anecdotal information, there is no proof that he had actually conducted his experiments with falling objects from the Leaning Tower of Pisa. He did demonstrate the rate of falling objects in other experiments and was able to show the problems with prior Aristotelian ideas on falling bodies in his 1632 work and refined in his 1638 work onward.

Galileo died in 1642, blind and sick, at his house in Arcetri just outside Florence. He was buried in Florence's Basilica of Santa Croce, at first in a small and easily ignored corridor room but later in the main basilica by 1737. It took at least a century before some of his scientific writings were removed from the papal Index of prohibited books, and longer for others. To say the Church was an enemy of Galileo or vice versa, however, is simplistic, as he was far more tolerated—partly because he firmly maintained his Catholicism—than had been the heliocentrist Giordano Bruno, who was burned at the stake as a heretic in early 1600 in Rome. That Galileo's study of motion and the principle of inertia and his long-standing work on gravity had a lasting influence on Newton and later physicists such as Einstein is without question, earning him the deserved title of "father of modern science."

IMPACT

As an important early advocate of what was then called the "Copernican heresy" by the Church, now known as heliocentrism, Galileo was a notable figure of the Scientific Revolution, showing his resolute commitment to challenging dogma by braving the Inquisition's charge of theological error. His famous Pisan anecdotes and other experiments with gravity proved Aristotle wrong and were ultimately indispensable to Newton's formulations of the laws of gravity and inertia. Galileo's contributions to astronomy are derived not only from his improvements to the telescope but also its practical application to many later planetary studies.

Building on the work of Archimedes, Galileo's mathematical studies of the parabola and trajectory were important not only for military engineering but also for physics in general. His innovations and his many mechanical applications, pioneering of microscopes and thermometers and seminal studies of mathematical survey, motion, dynamics, and nautical technology, also blazed a trail others would follow. An early exemplar of the attitude of modern science, Galileo was usually willing to correct his previous errors and revise hypotheses and conclusions. His experimental observations and publications claimed and proved that the laws of nature can be stated mathematically, a notion that became a foundation of science. These are just some of the many reasons why Galileo is called the "father of modern science," a title acknowledged by no less than Albert Einstein and Stephen Hawking.

—*Patrick Norman Hunt*

Further Reading

Dreger, Alice. *Galileo's Middle Finger: Heretics, Activists, and One Scholar's Search for Justice*. Penguin Publishing Group, 2016.

Galilei, Galileo. *The Essential Galileo*. Edited by Maurice A. Finochiarro, Hackett Publishing Company, 2008.

Greco, Pietro. *Galileo Galilei: The Tuscan Artist*. Springer, 2018.

Heilbron, J. L. *Galileo*. Oxford UP, 2012.

Livio, Mario. *Galileo: And the Science Deniers*. Simon & Schuster, 2021.

See also: Archimedes; Aristotle isolates science as a discipline; Ballistic weapons; Celestial mechanics; Circular motion; Euclid; Euclidean geometry; Motion; Newton, Isaac; Newton's laws; Projectiles

GAUSS'S LAW

Fields of Study: Physics; Mechanics; Mathematics

ABSTRACT

Just as a magnet has a magnetic field, produced by the presence of a north magnetic pole and a south magnetic pole, an electric field is produced by the presence of two regions with different electrical potential. Gauss's law states that the electric flux is directly related to the net electric charge enclosed by a Gaussian surface. It is equal to the net electric charge divided by the permittivity of the medium.

KEY CONCEPTS

conservation of charge: the principle that the net electrical charge in an electric circuit does not change

Coulomb's law: a scientific law stating that the electric flux at any defined surface is the vector sum of the electric field strength at every point on that surface

electric flux: the measure of the strength of an electric field across an area with different electrical potentials

Faraday's law: the scientific law stating that when a magnetic field and a conductor move relative to each other, a voltage is induced in the conductor, the magnitude of which depends directly on the relative speed of the field and conductor

Gaussian surface: any closed or finite hypothetical surface

Maxwell's equations: a set of mathematical descriptions of electromagnetism, formulated by James Clerk Maxwell

permittivity: a measure of the ability of an electric field to penetrate a medium

ELECTRIC FIELDS AND ELECTRIC FLUX

Just as a magnet has a magnetic field, produced by the presence of a north magnetic pole and a south magnetic pole, an electric field is produced by the presence of two regions with different electrical potential. These regions are typically designated as positive and negative, like the positive and negative poles of a battery. For an electric field to exist, the two regions cannot be physically connected to each other, because this would cancel out their electrical potentials. An electrical potential exists because of the electric charge that is present at that location. When two points with different electric charges are connected to each other, charge moves from the area of higher charge to that of lower charge until both have equal charges. For example, lightning occurs when the electric field caused by charge separation between the ground and the clouds is short-circuited by negative ions from the clouds connecting with positive ions from the ground.

On a much smaller scale, an electric field can be generated by connecting two plates that can act as Gaussian surfaces to an electrical source but not to each other. The source, which may be either direct current (DC) or alternating current (AC), produces a different electrical potential on the two surfaces. In the case of a battery, one surface will be positive and the other negative, depending on which terminal it is connected to either plate. Because the surfaces are not in direct contact with each other, current cannot flow between them. Current is the movement of electric charge through a conducting medium. Certain mediums, such as air, are dielectric. This means that their molecules can be polarized by an electric field but do not normally conduct charge.

Current is usually thought of as electrons moving from atom to atom through a conducting material —that is, as negative charge flowing through a cir-

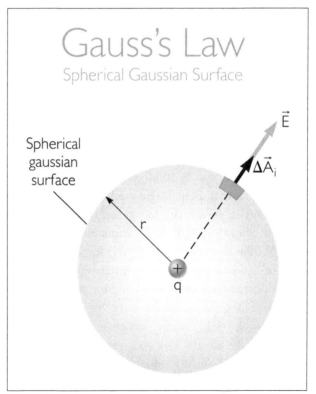

Image via iStock/DKN0049. [Used under license.]

cuit. Electric current can also be thought of as the movement of the location that can accept an electron in adjacent atoms. In either case, a dielectric field prevents the movement of charge from one surface to the other. As a result, one surface becomes enriched with electric charge, while the other is depleted. This lasts until the polarity of the field is reversed or neutralized. The law of conservation of charge states that the amount of charge gained by one surface must be equal to the charge lost by the other surface. Overall, the system is electrically neutral, even though a large difference in electrical potential may exist between the surfaces and an electric field exists between them.

Gauss's law states that the electric flux is directly related to the net electric charge enclosed by a Gaussian surface. It is equal to the net electric charge divided by the permittivity of the medium. This relationship is named for German theorist Karl Friedrich Gauss (1777-1855).

FLUX AND PERMITTIVITY

Electric flux (Φ_ε) is calculated as $\Phi_\varepsilon = q/\varepsilon_0$ where q is the net electric charge, given in coulombs (C), and ε_0 is the permittivity of the medium, given in farads per meter (F/m) or coulombs per volt-meter (C/V·m). The flux is usually given in volt-meters (V·m). Permittivity refers to a medium's ability to prevent penetration by an electric field. An electric field is less able to penetrate a medium with high permittivity than one with low permittivity.

Electric field strength, a vector quantity, can be thought of as the amount of electric force that is exerted on a positive test charge, either repelling it from a positive source or attracting it toward a negative one. The greater this force, the higher the electric flux of the field for any particular charge. Mathematically, the electric flux (Φ_ε) is the product of the electric field strength (E), the area affected (A), and the cosine of the angle between them (θ):

$$\Phi_\varepsilon = EA\cos\theta$$

Thus, the electric flux at any defined surface within the field can be visualized, according to Coulomb's law, as the sum of all the forces acting on each charge at each point on the surface.

Gauss's law relates electric flux to electric charge much as Faraday's law relates a magnetic field to magnetic flux. As Faraday noted, a conductor moving within a magnetic field experiences an induced voltage. That voltage is directly proportional to the rate of change of magnetic flux within the field. It also defines two areas of different electrical potential and therefore creates an electric field between those areas. By this relationship, electric and magnetic fields are shown to have a common nature as electromagnetic phenomena. Scottish physicist James Clerk Maxwell (1831-79) brought together the properties of electric and magnetic fields in a set of precise mathematical descriptions of electromagnetism, now known as Maxwell's equations.

CHARGE AND CAPACITANCE

Gauss's law is most commonly used in electronic components called capacitors. A capacitor consists of a dielectric material sandwiched between two conductors. The dielectric material can become polarized but will typically not conduct electric charge at any voltage below its particular threshold voltage. Above the threshold voltage, the electric potential between the conductors is sufficient to force electric charge to bridge the gap between them and create a short circuit. In normal use, a capacitor stores charge in the conductor with the higher electrical potential and loses charge from the conductor with lower potential, though current does not flow between them. In an electric circuit, this provides a buffer to compensate for slight fluctuations in current flow that would otherwise degrade the signal passing through the circuit.

Capacitors are designed to store a specific amount of charge when a circuit is operating. They are typically rated in units of microfarads (μF). One microfarad is one-millionth of a farad, and one farad is equal to one coulomb of charge per volt. One coulomb of charge is the amount of charge carried by an electric current of one ampere in one second, or 6.242×10^{18} electrons. Thus, one microfarad is equivalent to 6.242×10^{12} electrons when the potential difference between two conductors in a capacitor is just one volt. This is a significant amount of electric charge. Cattle prods and stun guns use capacitors to store electric charge from small batteries that produce a total voltage of as little as 9 volts. This amount of charge provides enough of an electric shock to incapacitate an adult when the capacitors are discharged.

—*Richard M. Renneboog*

Further Reading

Chakravorti, Sivaji. *Electric Field Analysis*. CRC Press, 2017.

Fleisch, Daniel. *A Student's Guide to Maxwell's Equations*. Cambridge UP, 2008.

Fitzpatrick, Richard. *Maxwell's Equations and the Principles of Electromagnetism*. Infinity Science, 2008.

Franklin, Jerrold. *Classical Electromagnetism*. 2nd ed., Courier Dover Publications, 2017.

Kelly, P. F. *Electricity and Magnetism*. CRC Press, 2015.

Ling, Samuel J., Jeff Sanny, and William Moebs. *University Physics Volume 2*. OpenStax, Rice University, 2016.

Mansfield, Michael, and Colm O'Sullivan. *Understanding Physics*. 2nd ed., Wiley, 2011.

Matsushita, Teruo. *Electricity and Magnetism: New Formulation by Introduction of Superconductivity*. Springer, 2014.

Robbins, Allan H., and Wilhelm C. Miller. *Circuit Analysis: Theory and Practice*. 5th ed., Delmar, 2013.

See also: Electromagnet technology; Electromagnetism; Lenz's law; Magnetism; Mechatronics; Photoelectric effect; Potential energy; Quantum mechanics; Tesla, Nikola; Work-energy theorem

Grimaldi Discovers Diffraction

Fields of Study: Physics; Optics; Mathematics

ABSTRACT

Francesco Maria Grimaldi showed that light passing through a small opening cannot be prevented from slightly spreading on the farther side. He termed this phenomenon "diffraction" and postulated that it was caused by light having a fluid nature analogous to a flowing stream of water.

KEY CONCEPTS

diffraction: the separation of a wave into smaller component waves as it passes around an obstruction or through an opening of an appropriate size

refraction: the change of direction of light when it passes from one medium to another having a different density; the magnitude of the change is termed the refractive index of the material

wave theory of light: the theory that light propagates through a medium as though it consists of waves, thus exhibiting the phenomena of refraction and diffraction; in the early twentieth-century experiments demonstrated that light also has the character of streams of particles, called "wave-particle duality"

SUMMARY

In about 1655, while serving as a mathematics instructor at the Jesuit University of Santa Lucia in Bologna, Francesco Maria Grimaldi began an elaborate set of optical experiments that occupied him for the remainder of his life. These experiments clearly demonstrated that light propagating through air does not simply travel in straight lines, but tends to bend slightly around objects. This new phenomenon Grimaldi termed "diffraction" (from the Latin, "a breaking up") because it indicated that light has a fluid nature allowing it to flow around objects like a stream of water divides around a slender obstacle in its path.

Prior to Grimaldi's experiments scientists assumed that light always propagates rectilinearly if it remains in the same medium, which gave credence to the prevailing view that light consists of small, rapidly moving particles. It was known since antiq-

uity that when light enters a different medium, for example, from air to water, it is bent, or refracted. Diffraction is a bending of light around objects or through openings in the same medium. Diffraction is exhibited by all types of waves—water, sound, and light—but had not been observed previously for light because the extremely small wavelengths ren-

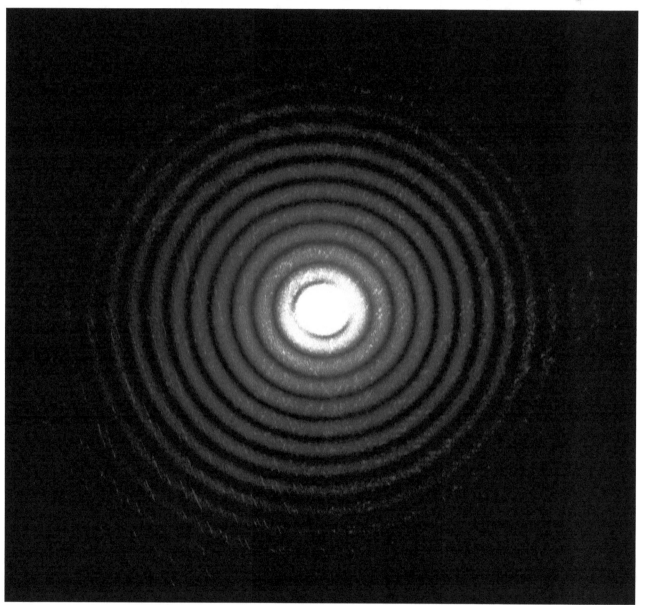

A diffraction pattern of a red laser beam projected onto a plate after passing through a small circular aperture in another plate. Photo by Wisky, via Wikimedia Commons.

der the effects difficult to perceive. Grimaldi's experiments on diffraction were of two different types: One type examined the shadows produced by opaque objects of different shapes; the other type examined light passing through circular apertures.

For the shadow experiments, Grimaldi allowed bright sunlight to enter a darkened room through a tiny hole (1/60 of an inch in diameter). This created a cone of light that Grimaldi projected on a white screen set obliquely to form an elliptical image of the sun. Between the hole and the screen he inserted a narrow opaque rod to create a shadow. Examining this shadow carefully, Grimaldi observed that its size was somewhat smaller than the linear projection of light rays predicted and, even more surprising, that the shadow's border was bounded by narrow fringes of color. He described these diffraction bands in some detail; there are usually three and they increase in intensity and width nearer to the shadow. The closest band consists of a central white region flanked by a narrow violet band near the shadow and a slender red band away from the shadow. Grimaldi cautioned that these color bands must be observed carefully to avoid mistaking the series for alternating stripes of light and dark.

Next, he examined the effect of varying the shape of the opaque object by replacing the rod with a step-shaped object with two rectangular corners. He meticulously recorded how the bands curved around the outer corner and continued to follow the shadow's edge. He also described that when the two series of bands from each edge of the inner corner approach they intersect perpendicularly to create regions of brighter color separated by darker areas.

Grimaldi also employed several L-shaped objects of different width to study the color bands produced. His diagrams show two sets of continuous tracks, parallel to the borders, which connect by bending around in a semicircle at the end of the L. He noted that the bands appear only in pairs, the number increasing with the width of the obstacle

and its distance from the screen. He also observed that at the corners of the L, an additional series of shorter and brighter colors emerged. He diagrammed these as five feather-shaped fringes radiating from the corner and crossing the paired tracks of light perpendicularly. Grimaldi compared this to the wash behind a moving ship.

Grimaldi's aperture experiment allowed the cone of light to pass through a second hole, about 1/10 inch in diameter, before being projected on a wall. The distances between the holes and between the wall and the second hole were equal at about 12 feet. Grimaldi observed that the circle of light cast on the opposite wall was slightly larger than predicted by rectilinear propagation theory, and the border displayed the same red and blue bands. He also mentioned that these diffraction effects are quite small and only observable if extremely small apertures are used.

Grimaldi also discovered that when sunlight entered a room through two small adjacent apertures, the region illuminated by the two beams was darker than when illuminated by either aperture separately. Although he did not understand that he was observing the now well-known principle of "interference of light waves," he regarded it as conclusive proof that light was not a material, particulate substance.

Grimaldi's carefully executed experiments convinced him that light had a liquid nature, a column of pulsating fluid that could produce color fringes when the luminous flow was agitated. The colors were inherent in the white light itself and not created by some outside agent. Although the diffraction effect so carefully measured and documented by Grimaldi is an unequivocal indicator that light consists of periodic waves, this notion seems not to have occurred to him.

Grimaldi detailed his experiments on diffraction, along with many other optical topics, in his comprehensive treatise *Physico-mathesis de lumine, coloribus, et iride*.

SIGNIFICANCE

Encouraged by Francesco Maria Grimaldi's work, Christiaan Huygens pursued the development of a wave theory of light. He envisioned waves propagating through an invisible all-pervasive medium and established a principle demonstrating how wave fronts progressed through this medium. Using his principle, he derived the well-known laws of reflection and refraction. A consequence of the wave theory is that when light passes obliquely from a less- dense to a more-dense medium, the speed of the wave must decrease to explain the observation that the light refracts to a smaller angle. Isaac Newton, who was also greatly influenced by Grimaldi's work, favored a particle theory of light in which refraction is explained by the particles increasing their speed when entering a denser medium. He objected to a wave theory because the predicted bending of light around corners was not observed. Grimaldi's diffraction results were explained as being due to refraction; he proposed that the density of a medium decreased near an obstacle, thus causing light to bend. Newton had observed wave interference for water waves and used it to explain anomalous tidal effects, but he did not apply this to optics. Such was the nature of Newton's fame that no one refuted him.

The issue was finally resolved in favor of the wave theory by English scientist Thomas Young (1773-1829), when, in 1802, he published experimental results documenting light interference and proving that Newton's experiments were easily explained by the wave theory. The final nail in the coffin lid of the particle theory was the experimental measurement of the speed of light underwater, accomplished in 1850 by the French physicist Léon Foucault (1819-68). His precise measurements proved that the speed of light under water was considerably less than its speed in air, as predicted by the wave theory.

—*George R. Plitnik*

Further Reading

Braat, Joseph, and Peter Török. *Imaging Optics.* Cambridge UP, 2019.

Darrigol, Olivier. *A History of Optics from Greek Antiquity to the Nineteenth Century.* Oxford UP, 2012.

Guenther, B. D. *Modern Optics Simplified.* Oxford UP, 2019.

Klem-Musatov, Kamill, Henning C. Heober, Tijmen Jan Moser, and Michael A. Pelissier, editors. *Classical and Modern Diffraction Theory.* SEG Books, 2016.

Ufimetsev, Pyotr Ya. *Fundamentals of the Physical Theory of Diffraction.* 2nd ed., John Wiley & Sons, 2014.

See also: Archimedes; Archimedes' principle; Galileo; Hertz, Heinrich Rudolf; Vibration

H

HARMONIC OSCILLATORS

Fields of Study: Physics; Mechanics; Mathematics

ABSTRACT

Harmonic oscillations are a fundamental feature of all mass-spring systems. They are modeled by the motion of pendulums. They can be mathematically described using the sine and cosine functions. Newton's laws of motion describe the physical behaviors of pendulums. Hooke's law describes the force that restores such systems to their equilibrium positions. Communication, power generation, motor control, and all digital electronic devices depend on harmonic oscillation to function.

KEY CONCEPTS

damped oscillator: an oscillator that is subject to friction or other braking forces

Hooke's law: the law stating that the deformation of an elastic object, such as a spring, is directly proportional to the force acting on the object, as long as the object's elastic limit is not exceeded

net force: the overall force acting on a system, calculated as the vector sum of all forces acting on and within the system

pendulum: a suspended mass that can undergo regular oscillations

resonance: the response of an elastic body to a force acting on the body at its natural frequency

spring constant: a characteristic factor of a particular spring that determines the expansion or contraction of the spring when displaced by a specific force

torque: a turning force acting radially about an axis or point

OSCILLATIONS

An oscillation is the variance of a physical property or its magnitude from one value to another and back again in a regular or cyclic manner. A harmonic oscillator is simply an object or system whose oscillation is caused by displacement that results in a restoring force. For example, imagine a marble sitting in the bottom of a circular bowl. The center of the bowl represents the marble's equilibrium point, because it is the lowest point to which the marble can roll. If the marble is held at the edge of the bowl, it has been displaced from its equilibrium point. When the marble is released, gravity acts as a restoring force, causing the marble to roll back down toward its equilibrium point. However, the marble will not stop at the bottom of the bowl. Instead, it will roll partway up the opposite side of the bowl, then back down to the bottom again and partway up the other side. This motion will repeat over and over until the marble eventually comes to rest at the bottom of the bowl. This repeated motion is oscillation, and the marble is a harmonic oscillator.

Oscillations can be described mathematically using sine and cosine waves. A sine wave begins at a value of zero (or some middle point represented by zero), increases to its maximum positive value, decreases below zero to its minimum negative value, and then increases to zero again. This is one cycle of the oscillation of a sine wave. The phrase "sine wave" describes a smooth, repetitive oscillation, such as the swing of a pendulum or the vibration of a guitar string. A cosine wave is similar to a sine wave, except that its cycle begins and ends at its maximum positive value rather than at zero. Thus, a cosine wave is also a type of sine wave. Electromagnetic waves are also sinusoidal in nature, as are waves rippling across a pond.

Oscillations are characterized by their amplitude, frequency, period, and sometimes wavelength. All oscillations have an equilibrium or neutral point in each cycle that is exactly midway between the extremes of their values. Displacement is the extent to which the value of the oscillating property varies from the neutral point at any given stage in its cycle. The amplitude of an oscillation is its maximum displacement from the neutral point. For example, the amplitude of a sine wave would be the distance of the maximum positive (or minimum negative) value from zero. The frequency of an oscillation is the number of cycles that occur in a given time. The period of the oscillation is the time required for one complete cycle. "Wavelength" is a term used to describe oscillations that travel in a linear fashion, such as electromagnetic waves. The wavelength is the distance traveled by the wave during one complete cycle of the oscillation.

STRINGS, SPRINGS, AND RESONANCE

A string on a musical instrument, such as a guitar or a piano, produces a sound when it vibrates. The frequency of the sound depends on the length of the vibrating string, and the intensity or loudness of the sound depends on the displacement of the string from its neutral position. The physical displacement of the string translates directly to the amplitude of the sound waves that are produced by the oscillation of the string as it vibrates. The sound fades and disappears as the string gradually ceases to vibrate and the amplitude decreases to zero. The frequency and the wavelength, of the sound remain the same, however, since these characteristics are not dependent on the amplitude or displacement of the oscillating string. In contrast, an ideal harmonic oscillator would produce the same values of frequency, wavelength, and amplitude over time.

A classic type of harmonic oscillator is the spring. Every spring has its own characteristic spring constant, which describes its stiffness and strength. The spring constant shows how much energy is required to displace the spring from equilibrium. It also shows how much restoring force the spring exerts to return to equilibrium. A coil spring can be either expanded or compressed. After either action, when the spring is released, it exerts a force that returns it to its neutral resting position, about which it then oscillates. This restoring force (F) is described by Hooke's law as the product of the spring's displacement (x) and its particular spring constant (k):

$$F = -kx$$

An oscillating spring and weight system shows the relationship among displacement (s), velocity (v), and acceleration (a). When the spring is fully compressed the velocity of the weight is zero and the acceleration will cause the spring to extend. When the spring is at a neutral displacement ($s = 0$) its velocity is maximum and the acceleration is zero, the spring will begin to decelerate. When the spring is fully extended the velocity of the weight is zero and the acceleration will cause the spring to compress.

The negative sign means that the restoring force is acting against the force that displaced the spring from its equilibrium position.

A spring does not have to be coiled in shape. Any structure that exerts a restoring force when displaced from its characteristic equilibrium shape can act as a spring system that obeys Hooke's law. The displacement can be lateral. It can also be caused by torque, as in some kinds of clocks or when a cable twists and untwists while supporting a suspended mass.

Hooke's law applies to all types of mass-spring systems. Every mass-spring system has its own characteristic resonance frequency (ω), which is related to its mass (m) and its particular spring constant (k), according to the following equation:

$$\omega = \sqrt{\frac{k}{m}}$$

When a system encounters another system or force oscillating at its resonance frequency, the first system resonates and vibrates at this frequency as well.

When resonant waveforms combine, their amplitudes also combine and increase, occasionally with disastrous results. Large groups of soldiers marching in lockstep are advised to break step when crossing a bridge so that they do not cause the bridge to resonate and collapse. On November 7, 1940, wind caused a bridge over the Tacoma Narrows strait in Washington State to oscillate at its resonance frequency. The amplitude of the vibration exceeded the limitations of the bridge's structural integrity, causing it to collapse. Similarly, Canadian truck drivers in the far north often take heavy loads over the "ice highway" on the frozen surfaces of lakes. More than one has been lost when the resonance frequency of the ice layer was met, causing the ice to break beneath the weight of the truck.

PENDULUMS

According to Isaac Newton's (1642-1727) second law of motion, a net force (F_{net}) acting on a body will cause the body to accelerate in the direction of the force. The acceleration (a) of the body will be directly proportional to the net force and inversely proportional to the mass (m) of the body:

$$F_{net} = ma$$

$$a = \frac{F_{net}}{m}$$

When an initial net force displaces a pendulum from its equilibrium position, it provides the pendulum with potential energy due to gravity. When the pendulum is released, gravity draws the pendulum back toward its equilibrium position, turning some of its potential energy into kinetic energy. As it passes through equilibrium, the pendulum has kinetic energy, but no potential energy relative to when it was released. The momentum that the pendulum has acquired due to its motion, in accord with Newton's first law, requires it to continue on its path until gravity, acting as a damping force, stops the motion at a certain distance and makes the pendulum once again fall back toward its equilibrium position. This oscillating motion continues until the kinetic energy and momentum of the pendulum have been lost to friction, air resistance, and other energy-consuming factors. The net force acting on the pendulum at any point is the vector sum of the force of gravity (its weight) and any frictional or other braking forces acting on it. The force of gravity imparts the motion, while braking forces detract from it.

The displacement of an oscillating string is described by the equation:

$$x = A\cos(\omega t)$$

where x is the displacement at time t, A is the initial displacement of the string, and ω is the frequency of the oscillation. Accordingly, the displacement of a string oscillating at a frequency ω of 440 hertz (Hz), or cycles per second (1/s), at a time of 100 milliseconds (ms) after release from an initial displacement of 5 millimeters (mm) is 3.6 is 3.6 millimeters.

A harmonic oscillator that is not subject to any braking forces is called a simple harmonic oscillator. An oscillator whose amplitude is decreased toward its equilibrium value by a braking force is called a damped oscillator. Almost all real physical oscillators are damped oscillators, because in the real world, braking forces are almost always present. To maintain the amplitude of a damped oscillation requires the constant input of energy into the system from an external source.

Torsional pendulums obey the same physical laws as linear pendulums. With a torsional pendulum, the displacement from the equilibrium position is brought about by torque about the central axis of the system. The restoring force of a torsional pendulum is not the force of gravity but the torque applied by the material that makes up the axis of the pendulum. A simple example of such a system is a metal wire or rod fixed to a weight. The radial length of the weight about the central axis determines the period and frequency at which the system can oscillate, while the radial displacement from its equilibrium position determines the spring force that acts on the system.

OSCILLATIONS IN OTHER SYSTEMS

Electromagnetic waves and electronic signals are oscillating systems that obey the same mathematical principles as pendulums and vibrating strings. Describing such waves requires more complex calculus involving sine and cosine functions than is required for the description of simple harmonic oscillators and pendulums. Electromagnetic waves are characterized by their frequency, period, and amplitude. These are also related to circular motion through the sine and cosine functions. Electromagnetic waves combine as the vector sum of their sinusoidal waveforms and resonate at specific frequency combinations to produce purely sinusoidal waveforms. This is an essential feature of "phase shift" in electrical power generation and motor control. Digital electronic devices also depend on harmonic oscillation. They use the specific vibrational frequency of quartz or other materials to control the timing of transistor switches.

—*Richard Renneboog*

Further Reading

Haraoubia, Brahim. *Nonlinear Electronics 1: Nonlinear Dipoles, Harmonic Oscillators and Switching Circuits.* Elsevier, 2018.

Kim, Young Suh. *Harmonic Oscillators and Two-by-Two Matrices in Symmetry Problems in Physics.* MDPI, 2018.

Ling, Samuel J., Jeff Sanny, and William Moebs. *University Physics, Volume 3.* Samurai Media Limited, 2017.

Shang, Yilun. *Harmonic Oscillators: Types, Functions and Applications.* Nova Science Publishers, 2019.

Sprott, Julien Clinton, William Graham Hoover, and Carol Griswold Hoover. *Elegant Simulations: From Simple Oscillators to Many-Body Systems.* World Scientific, 2022.

See also: Amplitude; Angular forces; Angular momentum; Displacement; Hooke, Robert; Kinetic energy; Momentum (physics); Pendulums; Potential energy; Torque; Vibration

HEAT TRANSFER

Fields of Study: Physics; Mechanics; Mathematics

ABSTRACT

Heat transfer is the movement of thermal energy from a region of high temperature to a region of lower temperature. While thermodynamics is used to determine the final thermal conditions between systems in equilibrium, heat transfer predicts actual temperatures of regions over time before equilibrium is reached.

KEY CONCEPTS

conduction: the transfer of heat through a solid or group of solids in contact in a direction where a temperature difference exists

convection: the transfer of heat between a moving fluid in contact with a solid surface at different temperatures

radiation: the transfer of heat by electromagnetic waves between surfaces at different temperatures

radiation shape factor: a parameter describing the percentage of thermal radiation leaving one surface and directly striking another surface; varies between value of zero and one

thermal conductivity: a property of a solid, liquid, or gas indicating how fast heat will conduct through it; the higher the conductivity, the faster heat will conduct

thermal insulation: a material with a low thermal conductivity or high thermal resistance used for energy conservation in buildings

thermal resistance: the ability of a material to resist heat transfer

OVERVIEW

Heat transfer is the movement of thermal energy from a region of high temperature to a region of low temperature. Specifically, it is the heat-transfer rate that is most often desired; that is, a prediction of how long it will take for thermal energy to transfer from one location to another. While thermodynamics is used to determine the final thermal conditions between systems in equilibrium, heat transfer predicts actual temperatures of regions over time before equilibrium is reached.

Heat is transferred by three mechanisms that are commonly known as "sensible" heat-transfer mechanisms. These include conduction heat transfer, convection heat transfer, and radiation heat transfer. Each of these mechanisms depends on a temperature difference at different positions in order for heat to be conveyed. A heat-transfer problem may include any two or all three of these mechanisms.

Conduction heat transfer is the transfer of heat through a solid or group of solids in contact where a temperature difference exists between one point and another. The rate of conduction heat transfer is directly related to the material's thermal conductivity, which is an intrinsic thermal property distinctive to each material. The greater a material's thermal conductivity, the faster heat will transfer through it. Pure metals such as copper and aluminum are materials with high thermal conductivities that transfer heat readily. Generally, materials that are good electrical conductors are also good thermal conductors. Conduction is also directly related to the magnitude of temperature difference and the solid's area perpendicular to the direction of temperature difference. The conduction rate will be inversely related to the thickness or distance between points of different temperature, so as a solid becomes thicker, it will take longer for heat to flow through it.

The most important law associated with conduction heat transfer is Fourier's conduction law, which states that the heat-transfer rate through a solid by conduction is directly proportional to the temperature difference between two locations, the solid's thermal conductivity, and the area perpendicular to the direction of temperature difference, and inversely proportional to the solid's thickness. This law assumes a steady-state temperature difference; that is, the temperatures at two distinct points in the solid are different but remain constant over a given time period. An example of steady-state conduction is the heat transfer across the wall of a home. During

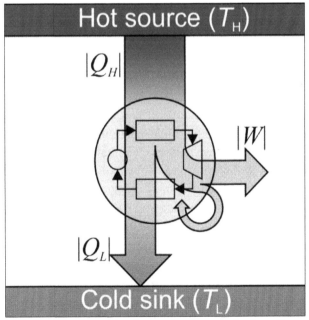

Schematic flow of energy in a heat engine. Image by Gonfer at English Wikipedia, via Wikimedia Commons.

a given period, the outdoor air temperature on one side of the wall may not change, and the heating or cooling system maintains the inside air temperature relatively constant. The conduction heat-transfer rate is directly proportional to the wall's height and length, the thermal conductivity of the wall materials, and the temperature difference between indoor and outdoor air, while it will be inversely related to the wall's thickness.

A common term associated with conduction heat transfer is a material's "thermal resistance." Thermal resistance, or R-value, is a material's ability to resist heat transfer. This is a particularly important concept related to the quality of thermal insulation materials, an important component of most buildings that is directly related to their energy use and efficiency. A material's thermal resistance is equal to its thickness in a direction of temperature difference divided by its thermal conductivity.

Materials with high thermal resistances are used as insulation, an important building component. Insulation's purpose is to reduce the expense and amount of fuel used to heat or cool a building's interior environment. Insulation's high thermal resistance is nearly always achieved by producing many small cells of still air or gas. Conduction depends on a solid's molecules coming into contact with one another to transport heat. Materials with pockets of still air deter this action and slow heat transfer, thus providing a good thermal insulation. Examples of good insulation are polystyrene board (with many small gas bubbles), fiberglass blankets, goose down, and sprayed foams.

Another important category of heat-transfer problem is that of time-dependent or transient conduction, in which temperatures at different points change over time. Transient conduction problems are more difficult to solve than steady-state problems. A well-known differential equation, the heat equation, relates transient temperatures, thermal and physical characteristics of the solid, and time.

An important parameter associated with transient conduction is a material's thermal diffusivity. Thermal diffusivity is equal to a material's thermal conductivity divided by the product of its density and specific heat; this product is known as the material's "thermal capacity." Specific heat is a property unique to each material that describes the amount of heat needed to raise a unit mass of material by one degree of temperature. A material with a high thermal diffusivity will have temperatures that change more quickly over time when exposed to heating or cooling than a material with a lower thermal diffusivity. A simple example of transient conduction can be observed by placing a potato in a pot of boiling water. The temperature of the potato will change quickly over the ensuing minutes, with the temperature on its surface warming sooner than the temperature at the potato's center. Using a knowledge of heat transfer, the time needed to cook the potato can be determined. This is the reason cooks typically cut potatoes into a number of smaller pieces in order to reduce the time required to cook them completely.

Convection heat transfer is the transfer of heat between a moving fluid (gas or liquid) in contact with its surroundings when the surroundings and the fluid are at different temperatures. When the fluid motion results from a fan or pump, the convection is known as "forced" convection. When a fluid increases in temperature, it becomes less dense, and it rises through the cooler, denser material of the surroundings. This fluid motion, without a fan or pump, results in convection known as "free" or "natural" convection. The convection heat-transfer rate can be determined using Newton's cooling law, which states that this rate is directly proportional to the product of the surface area in contact with the fluid and the temperature difference between them. The heat-transfer rate is also directly proportional to the convection coefficient, sometimes known as the "surface conductance" or "film coefficient," which relates a variety of factors, including fluid velocity, fluid viscosity, the surface roughness of the surroundings, and its general shape. A simple example of convection heat transfer can be experienced by placing one's face in front of a fan on a warm day to cool oneself. One can also look carefully at the striations that can be seen rising up in cold water when a hot spoon is inserted (be sure to use a clear glass container for this).

Radiation heat transfer is the heat exchanged between surfaces that emit electromagnetic waves proportional to their surface temperature when the surface temperature is above absolute zero. Thermal electromagnetic waves are but one type of electromagnetic wave, having wavelengths between 0.1 and 100 micrometers.

Unlike conduction and convection heat transfer, radiation heat transfer does not need a solid or liquid transfer medium; it can occur in a vacuum. The net rate of radiation heat transfer depends upon the difference in the amount of electromagnetic waves leaving and impinging on a surface. A simple example of radiation heat transfer can be observed in a restaurant where food on a buffet is heated by lamps. The lamps are warmest, the surrounding surfaces of the restaurant (walls and ceiling) are likely coolest, and the heated food should have a temperature in between them. The food, because it is warmer, radiates heat to the surroundings but gains radiant heat from the heat lamps above it to maintain its temperature.

When radiation waves collide with a surface, they are either reflected away from the surface, absorbed into the surface, or transmitted through the surface. These three surface characteristics are defined as the reflectivity, absorptivity, and transmissivity for each material's surface and are unique for each material's surface according to the surface color and texture and the wavelength of incoming radiation. A perfect absorbing surface has an absorptivity of one and is known as a "black body." Thermal radiation will have shorter wavelengths as the temperature of the emitting surface increases. To simplify the analysis of a surface's reaction to thermal radiation, the thermal-radiation wavelengths can be reduced to two main types: solar radiation (short wave) and earthwave radiation (radiation emitted from surfaces on Earth that are much cooler than the Sun's surface temperature). This can be illustrated by remembering that a person who wears a white shirt outdoors on a sunny day will remain cooler than a person who wears a black shirt. White surfaces reflect 92 percent of solar radiation, while black surfaces absorb 95 percent (and reflect only 5 percent) of incoming solar radiation.

An important parameter relating the orientation of one surface radiating heat to another is the shape or view factor. The shape factor, expressed as a decimal value between zero and one, reveals the percentage of waves emitted by one surface that directly hit another surface. Shape factors have many practical applications, among them determination of how far a radiant-type heater must be situated from its target, as in the case of the radiant heaters used to warm food in restaurants. Shape factors have been experimentally determined for several geometric configurations and are available from graphs published in heat-transfer textbooks. Radiation heat transfer does not have a single simple equation to quantify it.

APPLICATIONS

Heat transfer has a multitude of applications that affect everyday life. One of the most obvious is human thermal comfort. Nearly everyone assesses and comments on whether they are too hot, too cold, or comfortable. The following applications, although illustrating only one small segment of heat transfer, will focus on human thermal comfort.

An important influence on human thermal comfort in a home, school, or workplace is how the building is constructed and how the heating or cooling system is designed to maintain conditions in the space. There are many different heating and cooling systems used to condition air in enclosed spaces effectively so that occupants are comfortable. Since a large portion of the human body is typically exposed to the air while indoors, the two heat-transfer mechanisms influencing human thermal comfort the most are convection and radiation. Most heating and cooling systems distribute conditioned air from heating and cooling equipment to rooms using a fan to push air through ductwork. Ductwork, usually made of a metal with a high thermal conductivity, should be insulated so that heat does not quickly conduct through it into unconditioned spaces such as attics, basements, or crawlspaces; if it is not insulated, air emerging from the ductwork may no longer be warm or cold enough. Conditioned air emerges from ductwork through vent openings in the ceiling or floor and moves throughout the room. Occupants are cooled or heated by convection as the moving fluid (air) moves past body surfaces, assuming that the air and body surface temperatures are different.

Radiant floor-heating systems use radiation heat transfer to heat occupants. A heated fluid (liquid) is circulated through plastic tubing embedded in low-density concrete beneath the floor surface. Heat conducts through the tubing, concrete, and flooring material to heat the exposed floor surface and raise its temperature. As the floor surface temperature rises, it emits more thermal radiation. A portion of this radiation will be absorbed by and warm room occupants without heating air in the room. Heating air in large rooms frequently is ineffective, because warmed air becomes less dense and rises to near the ceiling, away from room occupants. Radiant floor heating is effective in large rooms because the heat is not used to heat air in the room; it is transferred directly from the floor to the occupants by radiation.

Thermal insulation to reduce heat transfer between the building envelope and outdoors is essential to maintain a cost-effective conditioning system and to achieve thermal comfort. Thermal insulations are materials with lower thermal conductivities that reduce conduction heat transfer. When a material has a lower thermal conductivity, its thermal resistance is increased. A properly insulated building slows the rate of heat gain or loss by conduction between indoors and outdoors, so that a given heating or cooling system can deliver heat or cooling as quickly or quicker than heat flows through the building boundaries to outdoors by conduction.

Lower conduction heat flow usually produces surface temperatures on interior surfaces that also reduce radiant heat transfer between the surfaces and humans. For example, if a building's walls are not insulated, during winter the interior wall surface temperature will be colder than insulated walls would be. A colder wall surface emits less thermal radiation, so the net exchange of radiation waves between uninsulated walls and humans will result in more radiant heat loss from humans. This is an example of why someone may feel cold in a room even though the air temperature is not cold.

A similar interesting example of radiation heat transfer explains why fruit such as oranges on trees in orchards might freeze even though the air temperature remains slightly above freezing. Air at temperatures near freezing circulating among the fruit cools it by convection to near freezing; on a clear, cold night, however, enough heat may radiate from the fruit to a cold sky so that the fruit freezes. Cloudy nights frequently result in warmer temperatures, because cloud cover tends to reflect thermal radiation from heated objects on the ground back toward the ground.

Thermally efficient windows use special films suspended between multiple glazings to reduce heat transfer by conduction and radiation between buildings and the outdoors. Films known as "low emissivity" coatings have a higher reflectivity to earthwave thermal radiation than untreated window glass. Normal window glass transmits nearly 85 percent of radiant heat, resulting in large amounts of heat loss from homes during cold weather. Double-glazed windows, which create a layer of still air or an inert gas such as argon between glazings, will decrease conduction heat transfer by 50 percent compared to single-glazed windows. Adding a suspended film with a low-emissivity coating to double-glazed windows will reflect radiation waves and hold heat in a building, reducing heat loss by approximately 60 percent compared to single-glazed windows. Thermally efficient windows will result in lower heating costs and a more comfortable interior environment.

Thermal comfort may sometimes be achieved by adjusting the velocity of air passing by one's body. In warm weather, fans are used to move air past bodies at higher velocity to provide cooling. During cold weather, air leaking through window and door frames can create uncomfortable drafts. Altering air velocity will effectively control convection heat transfer between humans and the surrounding air.

Increased convection heat loss from bodies outdoors under cold, windy conditions during winter is commonly expressed as "wind-chill" temperature. It often feels colder outdoors than the air temperature indicates because wind velocity increases convection heat transfer.

Clothing has long been designed to optimize thermal comfort. With the advent of synthetic clothing materials and production techniques, clothing can be designed to maintain body heat in cold weather without accumulating overwhelming weight. Cold-weather clothing utilizes the concept of creating many tiny pockets of still air to reduce heat transfer. This is achieved using lightweight, low-density materials such as goose down as opposed to a material basing its insulative value on bulk and thickness. For warm weather, fabrics have been developed that breathe and wick moisture away from body surfaces, thereby increasing heat transfer from the body surface. Athletic clothing is often made

with synthetic fibers that draw perspiration away from body surfaces, allowing athletes to remain dry.

CONTEXT

The science of heat transfer is a division of applied thermodynamics. Heat transfer is nearly always concerned with the rate at which heat flows, while thermodynamics focuses on the total amount of heat involved with a process. Heat transfer is based on the first and second laws of thermodynamics. The first law states that for a closed system, an increase in energy is equal to the sum of net heat gain and net gain in work. The second law dictates that heat will flow from a location of high temperature to a location of lower temperature.

Knowledge of heat transfer has developed largely since 1700. Early contributions were made by famous scientists such as Sir Isaac Newton, Jean-Baptiste Biot, and Joseph Fourier. These men were mathematicians as well as physicists and were involved with several branches of science. In 1701, Newton developed his cooling law, which is the basic equation for convection heat transfer. Biot worked on the analysis of conduction heat transfer in 1802. Fourier developed a mathematical description of conduction heat transfer in 1822, ultimately resulting in the formulation of Fourier's conduction law.

A multitude of European scientists during the nineteenth and early twentieth centuries expanded the science of heat transfer dramatically. Among these scientists were Osborne Reynolds, Leo Graetz, and Ernst Nusselt who were pioneers in developing analytical techniques for convection heat transfer. Josef Stefan and his student Ludwig Boltzmann made significant contributions to help explain radiation heat transfer. Between 1879 and 1884, Stefan and Boltzmann were responsible for establishing the relationship between energy radiating from a black-body surface and that surface's temperature.

The development of the US space program during the 1960s required important applications of heat transfer. More important, the space program helped to spawn computer technology and numerical techniques such as the finite-element method and the finite difference method, which were used to solve heat-transfer problems related to space flight.

Applications of heat transfer have influenced nearly every aspect of human life. These applications range from those necessary for human life to those that enhance human life. Thermal aspects of global climate and interaction with the Sun's radiant energy play an important role in sustaining life on Earth. Excessive weather-related phenomena such as heat, cold, rain, and drought as well as natural disasters such as tornadoes, hurricanes, volcanoes, and earthquakes are closely associated with heat transfer.

Heat transfer's impact extends to global pollution and influences ecology. Thermal inversions can adversely affect air quality in urban areas. Industrial and power generation facilities produce excessive heat that is usually dissipated by large amounts of water. Returning this warmer water to its source raises average water temperatures and often produces dramatic ecological changes.

Applications of heat transfer have made life much easier for humankind. Electrical power often involves conversion of heat to electrical energy. This has allowed air-conditioning and irrigation systems to transform unproductive areas into desirable locations. Heat transfer allows for food processing, sterilization, and packaging that not only provide a wide range of foods but also make them easy to prepare and safe to eat.

—*Garrett L. Van Wicklen*

Further Reading

Bacon, D. H. *Basic Heat Transfer*. Elsevier, 2013.

Barron, Tandall F., and Gregory F. Nellis. *Cryogenic Heat Transfer*. 2nd ed., CRC Press, 2017.

Han, Je-Chin. *Analytical Heat Transfer*. CRC Press, 2016.

Janna, William S. *Engineering Heat Transfer*. 3rd ed., CRC Press, 2018.

Jiji, Latif M. *Heat Conduction*. 3rd ed., Springer Berlin Heidelberg, 2009.

Kakac, Sadik, Yaman Yener, and Anchasa Pramuanjaroenkij. *Convective Heat Transfer*. 3rd ed., CRC Press, 2013.

Lienhard, John H. *A Heat Transfer Textbook*. 5th ed., Courier Dover Publications, 2019.

Sundén, Bengt. *Introduction to Heat Transfer*. WIT Press, 2012.

See also: Aerospace design; Biomechanics; Biomedical engineering; Clausius formulates the second law of thermodynamics; Equilibrium; Friction; Materials science; Steam energy technology; Stirling, Robert; Structural engineering; Thermodynamics; Work-energy theorem

HELICOPTERS

Fields of Study: Physics; Aeronautical engineering; Mechanical engineering; Biomechanics; Physiology; Mathematics

ABSTRACT

Helicopters, often referred to as choppers, helos, whirlybirds, or copters, are any rotary-wing aircraft having powered, fixed rotors that provide lift and propulsion for the aircraft. The helicopter was the first operational vertical takeoff and landing (VTOL) aircraft and remains the most prevalent.

KEY CONCEPTS

Coanda effect: the tendency of a jet of air to adhere to a curved surface and to entrain adjacent air thus creating a region of low pressure

fixed-wing aircraft: aircraft having the traditional structure of a fuselage and nonmoving wings on either side of the fuselage

rotary-wing aircraft: aircraft in which the function of wings and propellers has been replaced by the operation of spinning blades on a rotor

swashplate: a mechanical device on the rotor hub of a helicopter that translates control movements from the pilot's control stick into various pitch adjustments of the rotor blades

HELICOPTER CONFIGURATIONS

The helicopter is the principal type of vertical take-off and landing (VTOL) aircraft in service throughout the world. The name "helicopter" was coined by Viscomte Gustave de Ponton d'Amecourt, circa 1863. Helicopters can be distinguished from other rotary-wing aircraft by the fact that their rotors are fixed in position on the aircraft fuselage and simultaneously provide lift and propulsion. The vast majority of modern helicopters have either one or two rotors that provide lift and propulsive force.

Although helicopters can take off and land vertically, their maximum forward speed is much lower than that of fixed-wing aircraft. This limitation is due to the fact that the rotor or rotors must provide both propulsion and lift. Under high-speed flight conditions, the vibratory forces on the rotor blades become very large, thereby limiting the top speed of the helicopter. In order to increase the top speed, some helicopters, known as compound helicopters, have been equipped with auxiliary means of propulsion, such as propellers or jet engines.

Helicopters are built in a variety of configurations, including the single-rotor, the tandem, the coaxial, and the side-by-side helicopters. The single-rotor helicopter is the most common configuration currently in use. It can be identified by the single main rotor that provides thrust and propulsion, as well as pitch and roll control. A smaller tail rotor usually provides antitorque directional yaw control. However, other devices may be used instead of a tail rotor.

Another common configuration is the tandem helicopter. The tandem helicopter has two large rotors, one at the forward end of the helicopter and the other at the aft end. The two rotors rotate in opposite directions, thus eliminating the need for an antitorque device, such as a tail rotor. This configuration is particularly well-suited for the transport of heavy cargo, because the two rotors can accommodate large changes in the aircraft center of gravity due to the cargo load.

Less common configurations include side-by-side and coaxial helicopters. Like the tandem helicopters, side-by-side helicopters have two main rotors, but one is located on the right side of the aircraft, and the other is located on the left side. The rotors rotate in opposite directions, again eliminating the need for a tail rotor. A variant of the side-by-side helicopter is the synchropter, on which the two rotors are placed close together, so that the rotors intermesh. The synchropter has the advantage of being able to take off and land in more confined areas than either a side-by-side or tandem helicopter, because the close proximity of rotor masts reduces the area required for clearance around the rotors.

The coaxial helicopter has two counterrotating rotors that share a common mast. Because the rotors rotate in opposite directions, no tail rotor is needed for this configuration either. Coaxial helicopters also have the advantage of being able to land in more confined areas than any other configuration, because the swept area of the rotors is the smallest of all configurations.

HISTORY

Although the development of an operational helicopter is a relatively recent accomplishment, many of the concepts necessary for designing a practical helicopter have been known for a very long time. In fact, one could argue that a maple seed falling from a tree is nature's model for the helicopter. The Chinese top, which predates the Roman Empire, is perhaps humankind's first step toward modern helicopters. In addition, Leonardo da Vinci considered the possibility of vertical flight, and made sketches of his concept for such a vehicle.

The development of a practical helicopter was made possible by overcoming three major techno-

Photo via iStock/RobHowarth. [Used under license.]

logical barriers. The first barrier, and the easiest to overcome, was the design of a rotor system with rotor blades and a rotor hub that were strong but lightweight, with adequate aerodynamic efficiency. The second was to engineer a power plant with a sufficiently high ratio of power to weight, required in order to lift the aircraft off the ground. This barrier was overcome with the invention of the internal-combustion engine. The third technology barrier was to devise a method for controlling the helicopter in flight. The principles leading to controlled helicopter flight were developed gradually by helicopter pioneers.

Early helicopter pioneers tried a variety of power plants in their helicopter designs. During the latter half of the eighteenth century, Mikhail Vasilyevich Lomonosov in Russia, Launoy and Bienvenu in France, and Sir George Cayley in England provided

power to their helicopters by using different spring mechanisms. While spring-driven power plants have a good ratio of power to weight, they cannot provide sufficient sustained power for long flights.

In the nineteenth century, steam-powered helicopters were designed by Horatio Frederick Phillips in England, d'Amecourt and Alphonse Pénaud in France, Enrico Forlanini in Italy, and Thomas Edison in the United States. In contrast to spring power, steam power could provide sufficient sustained power, but its ratio of power to weight was very low.

Like that of the airplane, the concept of the helicopter did not become truly feasible until the invention of the internal combustion engine. Developments leading to a practical helicopter began to be achieved not long after Orville and Wilbur Wright flew their first airplane, but the availability of an adequate power plant brought problems of control to the fore. Paul Cornu and Charles Renard in France, Emile Berliner and Henry Berliner in the United States, and Igor Sikorsky and Boris Yuriev in Russia made significant contributions prior to 1920.

Renard introduced the flapping hinge, which improved rotor control; and Yuriev introduced the antitorque tail rotor for yaw control. In 1907, Cornu made the first piloted, free-flight, vertical takeoff, but the aircraft had to be stabilized manually by a ground crew. In the 1920s and early 1930s, George de Bothezat in the United States, Etienne Oemichen and Louis-Charles Breguet in France, Raoul Pescara in Spain, the Berliners in the United States, Louis Brennan in England, A. G. von Baumhauer in Holland, and Corradino D'Ascanio in Italy, M. B. Bleeker in the United States, and Yuriev in Russia all built prototype helicopters. Unfortunately, all of these designs either had controllability problems or were too complex to be practical. However, important contributions toward improved control were made by Bothezat, in differential collective pitch control; Pescara, in cyclic pitch control; von Baumhauer, in the area of the swashplate; and d'Ascanio, in servotab cyclic pitch control.

In 1936, German aircraft designer Heinrich Focke introduced the first practical helicopter, the Focke-Achgelis Fa-61, a side-by-side design in which all of the stability problems had been solved. In 1938, Hanna Reitsch flew the Fa-61 inside the Deutschland-Halle in Berlin, demonstrating its flying precision. In 1939, in the United States, Igor Sikorsky introduced the VS-300, a single-rotor helicopter, which may have been the world's first useful helicopter. Germany continued its development of the helicopter during World War II, and Anton Flettner's synchropter design, the FL-282 Kolibri, became the first production helicopter.

At about the same time, other individuals, including Arthur Young, Frank Piasecki, and Stanley Hiller in the United States, and Nikolai Kamov,

Mikhail Mil, and Ivan Bratukhin in the Soviet Union were developing their own independent helicopter designs.

MODERN HELICOPTERS

The basics of helicopter design have not changed greatly since the early days of helicopters in the 1940s. However, technological improvements have been incorporated that make the modern helicopter safer, easier, and more efficient to fly. One of the most significant advances in helicopter performance resulted from the introduction of the gas-turbine engine. The maximum power-to-weight ratio achievable with piston engines by the end of World War II was approximately 1 horsepower per pound. However, by the 1960, turbine engines had achieved power-to-weight ratios of 3 horsepower per pound, and by 2000 they had achieved weight ratios of up to 6 horsepower per pound.

Helicopter rotor systems have also undergone significant changes. In the early years, rotor blades were made exclusively of wood, one of the principal materials used for aircraft construction. In 1944, Hiller introduced metal rotor blades on the XH-44, but it was not until 1952 that metal blades were delivered on a production aircraft, the Sikorsky S-52.

The use of composite materials for rotor blade construction began in the early 1960s, and, by the 1970s, the Messerschmitt-Bölkow-Blohm company in Germany had built all-composite blades for the BO-105 helicopter. Virtually every modern helicopter is now equipped with composite blades. The rotor hub has also undergone changes in the way that the blades are attached. Many helicopter rotors are fully articulated. That is, each blade has physical hinges, which allow the blade to flap out of the plane of rotation and lag in the plane of rotation. A bearing also allows the blade to pitch. The concepts of a hingeless rotor that eliminates the flap and lag hinges and a bearingless rotor, which is basically a hingeless rotor without a pitch bearing, have found their way into the designs of many modern helicopters.

Technological improvements, such as vibration control devices in the rotor system and the fuselage, have improved the comfort level for passengers, as well as the performance of the flight crew due to reduced fatigue. Crash-worthy structural design, seats, and fuel systems have improved the safety of helicopters in emergency situations. Hydraulic control systems have replaced the mechanical control systems of early helicopters, and modern helicopters are often equipped with electronic flight control and stability augmentation systems to reduce pilot workload. Digital fly-by-wire and fly-by-light control systems, as well as glass cockpits, have been introduced in advanced production helicopters.

The late twentieth and early twenty-first centuries also saw an explosion in the development of unmanned aerial vehicles (UAVs), or drones, many of which used helicopter designs. Pioneered by militaries and operated with sophisticated remote-control systems, improved technology and miniaturization as well as declining costs soon led to consumer versions. Production models range from fairly large craft capable of various operations to handheld toys meant simply to fly a few feet in the air.

FLIGHT CONTROL

One of the first problems of helicopter flight control that must be solved is the question of how to keep the fuselage from rotating opposite the rotor. In order to spin the rotor, torque is applied by the engine to the rotor driveshaft. Therefore, the rotor has an angular momentum, which must be counteracted in some manner. If the angular momentum of the rotor is not equalized, the fuselage will begin to rotate in the opposite direction to the rotor rotation. Single-rotor helicopters equalize the angular momentum with countertorque devices, such as a tail rotor or a NOTAR (no tail rotor) system. The tail rotor is a smaller rotor mounted vertically at the end of a

tail boom that generates a lateral thrust. The NOTAR system also generates lateral thrust but does so using the slipstream of the rotor and air ejected from a slot in the tail boom to produce the Coanda effect. Helicopters with more than one rotor, such as the tandem, side-by-side, and coaxial types, equalize the angular momentum by employing equally sized rotors rotating in opposite directions.

In order to fly a helicopter, the pilot must be able to control the translation of the aircraft in the vertical, lateral (side-to-side), and longitudinal (forward-and-back) directions, as well as rotation in roll, pitch, and yaw. The pilot's controls include a collective lever beside the pilot seat, a cyclic stick between the pilot's knees, and foot pedals. It is interesting to note that in helicopters, the pilot sits in the right seat and the copilot sits in the left. In fixed-wing aircraft, the pilot sits in the left seat, and the copilot sits in the right. This seating arrangement is an artifact from one of Igor Sikorsky's early helicopters, which had such "backward" seating.

To explain helicopter control, consider a single-rotor helicopter. The main rotor of a single-rotor helicopter produces a thrust, which acts in a direction roughly normal to the rotor disk. Therefore, in order to control the helicopter, the pilot must be able to control the magnitude and direction of this thrust. The magnitude of the thrust is controlled by the collective lever, which equally increases or decreases the pitch angle of all rotor blades, thereby increasing or decreasing the thrust. In order to control the direction of the thrust, the pilot must be able to control the orientation of the rotor disk. One way to change the orientation of the rotor disk is to physically tilt the rotor hub.

For very small helicopters, hub tilt is a practical control method. However, for larger helicopters, the rotor acts like a large gyroscope, which makes tilting the hub extremely difficult. The alternative is to increase the thrust on one half of the disk, while simultaneously decreasing the thrust on the other half. This cyclic change in thrust causes the rotor disk to tilt and does so with much less effort than hub tilt.

In all but a few modern helicopters, the pilot's cyclic stick, acting through a swashplate, is used to change the cyclic pitch of the rotor blades. The swashplate consists of two parts: a nonrotating plate and a rotating plate. The nonrotating plate, which is connected to the pilot collective and cyclic pitch controls, slides up and down for collective-pitch changes and tilts for cyclic-pitch changes. The rotating plate sits on top of the nonrotating plate and spins with the rotor. Pitch links, attached to the rotating plate and the rotor blades, mechanically change the pitch angle of the blades. Yaw control is obtained through the foot pedals, which are connected to the collective pitch controls for the tail rotor.

MISSIONS

Because helicopters are able to take off and land vertically and hover in midair, they are ideal vehicles for a wide variety of missions. They do not require large runways or prepared landing areas, so they can take off and land in forest clearings, on the tops of buildings, and on ships at sea. As a result, they can be used in civil and military applications for which fixed-wing aircraft are unsuitable.

The transportation of passengers is one of the primary missions of helicopters. The largest civilian user of helicopter transportation is the petroleum industry. Helicopters regularly transport petroleum workers to and from offshore oil platforms, because they are much faster and more cost effective than boats. Many large corporations use helicopters to ferry their executives between sites. Commercial helicopter operators in scenic locations, such as the Grand Canyon and Hawaii, regularly carry passengers on sight-seeing tours, although increasingly stringent noise regulations have somewhat curtailed their business.

Commercial helicopter airlines have not been economically viable, despite the obvious advantages of ferrying passengers between airports and between airports and inner-city heliports. The US military services, particularly the Army and the Marines, make extensive use of helicopters for troop transport. Naval helicopters are often used for ship-to-shore and ship-to-ship transportation of personnel. In all services, helicopters are used for the insertion and extraction of special-operations forces at remote sites.

Cargo transportation is another important helicopter function. In the logging industry, helicopters may be used to transport logs from remote areas either directly to a mill or to rivers in which the logs are floated to a mill. Construction projects often use helicopters to transport heavy equipment, such as heating, ventilation, and air conditioning units, to the tops of tall buildings. The Statue of Freedom, atop the US Capitol Building, was removed by helicopter in 1993 for restoration and was later replaced in the same manner. Helicopters adapted as firefighting aircraft, such as with large buckets slung beneath them, are used to transport water from nearby lakes or flame-retardant chemicals to the site of a forest fire. On the military side, pilots often use helicopters to transport supplies and even small- and medium-sized vehicles from rear areas to troops in the field. Navies frequently use helicopters to transport supplies from shore to ships at sea and between ships at sea, due to the ability to land on ships smaller than aircraft carriers.

Many police departments, particularly in large cities, use helicopters for airborne patrol and surveillance. Because they operate at altitude, helicopters have a wider field of view than ground patrols. In cases of pursuit, it can be much easier for a helicopter to keep a fleeing suspect in view and safer for the ground units and the general public. In addition, when on patrol, a helicopter can often reach the crime scene more rapidly than can a ground unit. In a similar application, radio and television stations use helicopters for acquiring traffic reports and news gathering. News helicopters can often reach the scene of a news event more rapidly than can ground vehicles.

Another mission for which helicopters are particularly well-suited is search and rescue, including medical evacuation (medevac) using craft outfitted as air ambulances. Although this is primarily a military mission, police departments and the US National Park Service (NPS) also use helicopters to find and rescue hikers, campers, and others who find themselves in dangerous situations. The US Coast Guard is very active in search and rescue, patrolling the waters off the coast of the United States. A typical Coast Guard rescue mission would be to extract passengers from foundering sailing vessels. Combat search-and-rescue missions are flown primarily by the air forces and navies to locate and return aircrews of aircraft downed in combat. During the Vietnam War, the Jolly Green Giant (CH/HH-3E) helicopters were a welcome sight for many pilots who had been shot down while flying over North Vietnam.

Combat close air support and antiarmor are purely military missions that may be carried out by helicopter. Close air support involves using helicopters to support friendly ground troops by directing fire on enemy troops in the near vicinity. Helicopters used in antiarmor missions are equipped with ordnance that is capable of disabling or destroying tanks and other armored vehicles. The US Marines long made use of the versatile Bell AH-1 SuperCobra, while the US Army typically operated the similarly versatile Boeing AH-64 Apache for these missions.

Virtually all mission types traditionally carried out by manned helicopters have the potential to also be carried out by UAVs, or drones. While not all UAVs are helicopters, many do use rotor designs, and therefore have similar VTOL and hovering capabili-

ties to ordinary helicopters. Drones have particular value in situation that may be dangerous for a human pilot, such as combat or firefighting, or in which small size is important, such as surveillance. They have already been extensively employed by the US military for drone warfare, though this has often drawn controversy due to the possibility of targeting malfunctions and other ethical issues. Public use of helicopter drones has also increased dramatically in the twenty-first century, making formerly difficult and expensive tasks like aerial photography relatively easy, cheap, and unobtrusive. Scientists have embraced such technology for low-cost remote sensing missions. However, civilian use has also drawn controversy over the potential to breach privacy, as well as regarding license or permit issues and safety risks.

—Donald L. Kunz

Further Reading

Bichlmeier, Magnus. *Certifiable L1 Adaptive Control for Helicopters*. Cuvillier Verlag, 2016.

Croucher, Phil. *The Helicopter Pilot's Handbook*. CreateSpace Independent Publishing Platform, 2016.

"History of Helicopters." *American Helicopter Museum & Education Center*, 2016, americanhelicopter.museum/exhibits-and-resources/history-helicopters. Accessed 6 Dec. 2016.

Krasner, Helen. *The Helicopter Pilot's Companion: A Manual for helicopter Enthusiasts*. Crowood Press UK, 2008.

Padfield, Gareth D. *Helicopter Flight Dyanamics Including a Treatment of Tiltrotor Aircraft*. Wiley, 2018.

Ren, Beibei, Shuzhi Sam Ge, Chang Chen, and Cheng-Heng Fua. *Modeling, Control and Coordination of Helicopter Systems*. Springer New York, 2011.

Venkatesan, C. *Fundamentals of Helicopter Dynamics*. CRC Press, 2015.

Wagtendonk, Walter J. *Principles of Helicopter Flight*. Aviation Supplies & Academics Inc., 2015.

See also: Aerodynamics and flight; Aeronautical engineering; Airfoils; Propulsion technologies

Hertz, Heinrich Rudolf

Fields of Study: Physics; Mechanics; Mathematics

ABSTRACT

Heinrich Rudolf Hertz was born on February 22, 1857, in Hamburg, Germany, and died January 1, 1894, in Bonn, Germany. He is credited with being the first to send and receive radio waves. Hertz also proved that radio waves and all other electromagnetic waves behave in the same way as light waves.

KEY CONCEPTS

electromagnetism: the physical phenomenon that is the combined effect of an electric field and a magnetic field

half-wave tower: a radio transmitter tower whose height is exactly one-half of the wavelength of its transmitting frequency.

EARLY LIFE

Heinrich Rudolf Hertz was a nineteenth-century German physicist. He is remembered for sending and receiving the first radio waves. Using the mathematical equations and the theoretical framework developed by Scottish physicist James Clerk Maxwell, Hertz proved that electromagnetic waves and radio waves behave in the same way as light waves.

Heinrich was born in Hamburg, Germany to Gustav F. Hertz and Anna Elisabeth Hertz, formerly Anna Elisabeth Pfefferkorn. His father was a successful lawyer and later became a senator, and his mother was the daughter of a doctor. He had four younger siblings. His father was Jewish, but converted to Lutheranism when he married his Lutheran wife. The Hertz children were raised Lutheran.

Hertz began private school at age six. He was a bright student, and his mother and his teachers pushed him hard in his studies. In addition to science, he was gifted at languages and studied Sanskrit and Arabic.

After he left private school at age seventeen, Hertz studied at home for two years with the help of tutors and his mother. After one year of schooling at the Hamburg Gymnasium, he accepted an apprenticeship at a municipal engineering office in Frankfurt, where he attended lectures at the Frankfurt Physics Club. After his mandatory year of military service, Hertz still could not decide between engineering and natural sciences.

In a letter to his father Gustav written in late 1877, Hertz describes how he ultimately decided to give up a more lucrative career in engineering in favor of the natural sciences. In the letter, he explains that studying science was the only part of his work he looked forward to, and that he had lost interest in things like building and surveying. In 1878, Hertz enrolled at the University of Munich and studied physics and mathematics with German physicist and mathematician Johann Philipp Gustav von Jolly.

Heinrich Hertz. Photo via Wikimedia Commons. [Public domain.]

LIFE'S WORK

After beginning his studies in the natural sciences at the University of Berlin, Hertz fell under the guidance of German physicist Hermann von Helmholtz, who was researching electricity and electromagnetism at the time. Helmholtz convinced Hertz to begin working on the problem of the kinetic energy of electricity. His experiments and research were so detailed and impressive that Hertz was offered the job of assistant professor to Helmholtz, and in 1880, he began researching electromagnetism.

Eager to encourage his students to investigate one of the most important questions in physics of the day, Helmholtz challenged students at the Berlin Academy of Sciences to prove experimentally a theory posited in 1865 by Scottish physicist James Clerk Maxwell. Maxwell had demonstrated mathematically that electricity and magnetism travel at the speed of light. He believed that light itself was a form of electromagnetic wave but did not live to see his hypothesis proven experimentally. Helmholtz challenged Hertz to study the problem, but after considering the time and effort the research would require, Hertz declined. He did not think he was ready to tackle such an important problem, since it was likely to take at least three years of work.

After earning his doctorate in 1880, Hertz worked for Helmholtz for three years at the Berlin Physical Institute. In that time, he published over a dozen papers on several subjects, though most of his work focused on electricity. Hertz's career would likely have been very different if he had taken Helmholtz's advice and spent three years working on one big problem instead of numerous smaller ones.

After three years as an assistant, Hertz decided to advance his career by moving to a smaller academic community where he might make faster progress as a professional scientist. He accepted a professorship at the University of Kiel, where he quickly became one of the university's most popular lecturers. Because the university did not have an experimental physics laboratory, Hertz made do with a simple workshop at home. He wrote three important papers during his two years in Kiel, the last of which provided a solid foundation for his later work on electromagnetism. The paper offered a thorough analysis of Maxwell's work; Hertz gained a deep understanding of Maxwell's equations while researching the paper.

Eager to return to the laboratory, Hertz accepted a post at the Karlsruhe Physical Institute, which had extensive, state of the art facilities. Hertz's stay at Karlsruhe from 1885 to 1889 was the most productive of his career, and the place where he finally returned to the challenge set by his old mentor Helmholtz. Through frequent correspondence with his former professor, Hertz began to experiment in earnest.

With the help of some of his students, Hertz constructed a simple dipole antenna capable of producing ultra-high frequency (UHF) waves, and a receiver. The Hertz antenna receiver is also called the half-wave antenna, since its length is exactly half of a wavelength. With these instruments, Hertz was able to measure the speed of radio waves. As Maxwell predicted, their speed was equal to the speed of light.

Hertz's work was widely disseminated and embraced, but he did not live long enough to enjoy its rewards. He died of vasculitis, a blood vessel disorder, at the age of thirty-six, and was survived by his grieving mentor Helmholtz.

IMPACT

Hertz's desire to prove experimentally the mathematical theories of Maxwell led him to build the first primitive radio. He made Maxwell's elegant mathematical theories a laboratory reality, and his work shaped the direction of electromagnetism research. However, Hertz did not anticipate the commercial uses for his experiments.

Soon after the 1820 discovery of electromagnetism by Danish physicist Hans Christian Orsted, European scientists began developing their own theories to account for the phenomenon. Most of them were incorrect. In the earliest days of electromagnetic research, scientists had to start from scratch. They designed and built their own equipment and explained their theories based on their individual sets of scientific suppositions. After Hertz demonstrated the validity of Maxwell's work, scientists could rely on his equations backed with solid experimental data to guide them in improving their understanding of the nature of electricity and light.

Although he did not live long enough to witness the full implications of his work, Hertz's discoveries accelerated scientific research and helped lead to the development of the telegraph and the radio.

—*Mary Parker*

Further Reading

Amineh, Reza K. *Applications of Electromagnetic Waves*. MDPI, 2021.

Kimura, Wayne D. *Electromagnetic Waves and Lasers*. Morgan & Claypool Publishers, 2017.

Mulligan, Joseph F. *Heinrich Rudolf Hertz (1857-1894): A Collection of Articles and Addresses*. Routledge, 2018.

Norton, A. *Dynamic Fields and Waves*. CRC Press, 2019.

Stutzman, Warren L., and Gary A. Thiele. *Antenna Theory and Design*. 3rd ed., John Wiley & Sons, 2012.

See also: Acoustics; Amplitude; Electromagnetism; Grimaldi discovers diffraction; Lenz's law; Magnetism; Superconductors; Tesla, Nikola; Vibration

HOOKE, ROBERT

Fields of Study: Physics; Mechanics; Mathematics

ABSTRACT

Robert Hooke was born on July 18, 1635, in Freshwater, England, and died on March 3, 1703, in London, England. As curator of experiments for England's Royal Society, Robert Hooke proved to be one of the most influential experimentalists and inventors of the seventeenth century, contributing to a wide range of scientific fields.

KEY CONCEPTS

Hooke's law: the force (F) exerted by a spring is proportional to the length to which the spring is extended (x) and a coefficient characteristic of each individual spring (k), as $F = -kx$

microscope: a device similar to the telescope but used to examine objects at very close distances rather than far distances

universal gravitation: the concept and quantification of the gravity experienced as a force of attraction

EARLY LIFE

Robert Hooke was born in 1635 into the household of John Hooke, a minister, and his second wife, Cecelie. He was so sickly as a child that his parents did not expect him to survive, and frequent headaches later kept him from attending school. As a result, Hooke was schooled at home and largely left to pursue his own interests. These included drawing and studying the inner workings of machines, which he disassembled and used as guides for making his own devices; for instance, he constructed wooden clocks and a working model of a warship, complete with firing cannons.

Hooke's father died in 1648, and after collecting his inheritance, the thirteen-year-old Hooke moved to London. At first he intended to become the apprentice of Peter Lely, a celebrated painter of miniature portraits, but he soon changed his mind and entered Westminster School, a premier preparatory school. There, Hooke impressed the headmaster, Richard Busby, with his talent for language and geometry and his mechanical skills. With Busby's special tutelage and support, Hooke entered Christ Church College, Oxford, in 1653.

At Oxford, Hooke eventually joined a group of natural philosophers who viewed nature as a vast mechanism and sought to determine how it worked. Some members of this group, including Christopher Wren and Robert Boyle, became Hooke's lifelong friends and collaborators. In 1657, Boyle hired Hooke to construct laboratory equipment and help with experiments; Hooke's vacuum pump, a famous instrument of its day, permitted Boyle to explore the properties of air, part of the research that led to the discovery of Boyle's law (published in 1662). At the same time, Hooke began to explore his lasting interest in chronometers as he attempted to construct a timepiece that would remain accurate enough aboard a ship to use in determining longitudes.

LIFE'S WORK

Hooke's first solo publication was a 1661 pamphlet explaining capillary action. The work so impressed contemporary scientists that, with the help of Wren and Boyle, Hooke was hired as curator of experiments for the newly founded Royal Society, an organization of scientists and natural philosophers, in 1662. He was elected a full member the following year. His duties for the society were onerous; for the benefit of members, he was to perform several experiments of his own, as well as any that members themselves suggested at each weekly meeting. This he did with ingenuity and gusto, setting a high intellectual standard for the Royal Society. During the next twenty-six years, in hundreds of experiments, Hooke investigated the nature of light, air, gravity, magnetism, gunpowder, comets and other celestial phenomena, optics, chronometers (particularly the use of springs and pendulums), lightning, earthquakes, respiration, circulation, fossils, and medical treatments while also inventing carriages, the iris diaphragm, meteorological instruments, watches, and a wide variety of scientific tools. Hooke also took on a number of scientific posts, each with a considerable workload.

In 1664, John Cutler, a wealthy merchant, endowed a lecture series especially for Hooke in which he was to discuss the practical sciences and trades. The following year, Hooke became Gresham College's professor of geometry; the appointment included an apartment in the college's London premises, which remained his home from then on. Amid these manifold duties, Hooke published one of the masterpieces of seventeenth-century science literature, *Micrographia* (1665). It quickly became a bestseller and was admired for the wide range of topics discussed, including new theories of light and combustion, as well as for its beautiful drawings of the objects and creatures that Hooke had examined under his improved microscope. The book established the importance of the microscope as a scientific instrument and embodied Hooke's guiding principle, drawn from the ideas of Francis Bacon,

Robert Hooke, portrait c. 1680. Image via Wikimedia Commons. [Public domain.]

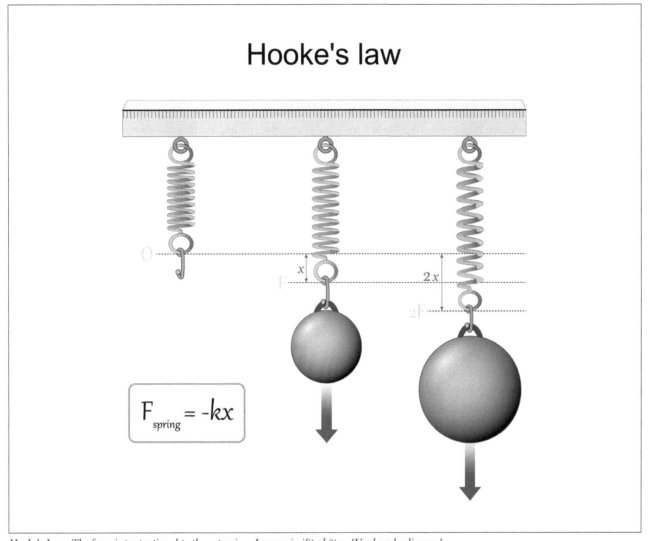

Hooke's Law: The force is proportional to the extension. Image via iStock/ttsz. [Used under license.]

that philosophers must base their understanding of the world on rigorous observation and experimentation; that is, theory must arise from demonstrable fact.

In subsequent publications, Hooke formulated the law of elasticity, later known as Hooke's law, which states that stress in springs is directly proportionate to strain; in other words, the force applied to and released by coiling and uncoiling a spring is directly proportionate to the amount of deformation undergone by that spring. Hooke also conducted an early analysis of harmonic motion, helped found the fields of meteorology and crystallography, proposed an explanation for celestial dynamics, and advanced broadly correct explanations for the origin of fossils and the evolution of species during environmental change.

ROBERT HOOKE PUBLISHES THE FIRST SCIENTIFIC BESTSELLER

As curator of experiments for England's Royal Society, Robert Hooke proved to be one of the most influential experimentalists and inventors of the seventeenth century, contributing to a wide range of scientific fields.

Robert Hooke's primary duty while serving as curator of experiments for the recently chartered Royal Society was to design and carry out experiments. Nevertheless, his colleagues also recognized his ability to observe, describe, and draw objects he studied with the rudimentary microscopes of his time, and he was asked to present drawings from his microscopic observations during the meetings of the membership. Throughout 1663 and the beginning of 1664, he shared drawings of objects ranging from a ribbon to a gnat. Impressed by the quality of his drawings, his colleagues urged him to publish his work in book form. Hooke completed his drawings by mid-1664; the work was published in January 1665.

Micrographia; or, *Some Physiological Descriptions of Minute Bodies Made by Magnifying Glasses with Observations and Inquiries Thereupon*, or simply *Micrographia*, was an instant success among Hooke's scientific colleagues and, later, with the public at large. The first major scientific text to be written in English, the book contains Hooke's descriptions of sixty diverse objects and phenomena, including mold, the head of a pin, and the sparks generated by a flint, and accompanying drawings rendered in minute detail. Perhaps the most impressive drawings are the microscopic views of insects; the book includes fold-out drawings of a flea and a louse that magnify each insect to about the size of a cat.

The book begins with a dedication to the reigning monarch, Charles II, followed by a dedication to the Royal Society. Hooke then presents a long preface that describes his methods in preparing his specimens as well as procedures for using the microscope itself—no simple task for even his scientific colleagues. Hooke's initial descriptions are those of mundane, common objects: a razor, snowflakes, cloth, and even gravel found in urine. He later goes on to describe his observations regarding air, stars,

and the moon. The first known use of the term cell as applied to the functional unit of life occurs almost in passing, as Hooke describes the honeycomb appearance of "pores" or "cells" found in a slice of cork.

Hooke's purpose was not only to provide entertainment for his scientific colleagues but also to enable members of the general public to enjoy the field that came to be known as science. In this he was partially successful, as many members of the public who had the opportunity to read his book became intrigued by the microscopic world. The book was not inexpensive, even for the time, costing thirty shillings and therefore somewhat limiting its readership. However, the significance of the work was far reaching, in that it inspired a new generation of microscopists.

LATER WORK

Following the Great Fire of London in 1666, Hooke helped to rebuild the devastated central city. He was appointed city surveyor in 1667 and became responsible for laying out the new streets, designing many new public buildings and overseeing their construction, enforcing building codes, and settling property disputes. He executed these many tasks in coordination with Wren, who had been appointed royal surveyor. This partnership broadened when Hooke became an assistant and virtual partner in Wren's architectural firm. Hooke assisted Wren in projects such as designing the new Saint Paul's Cathedral and also designed a number of private houses and public buildings on his own, including Bedlam Hospital, the Royal College of Physicians, and the towering monument memorializing the fire. In 1677, Hooke began a five-year term as secretary of the Royal Society, and he later served on its council while also caring for the society's library and its collection of rarities.

During the 1670s and 1680s, Hooke quarreled with fellow scientist Isaac Newton over the nature of light and the theory of universal gravitation. He held that light was composed of waves, while Newton insisted it was made up of tiny particles; both were later shown to be correct. Hooke also claimed to have first stated that gravity was centered in bodies and decreased in strength by the square of the distance between those bodies (the inverse-square law), but he could not demonstrate it mathematically; Newton did so in *Philosophiae Naturalis Principia Mathematica* (1687; *The Mathematical Principles of Natural Philosophy*, 1729) and ridiculed Hooke's claim to the discovery. These and other disputes, as well as failing health, led Hooke to become somewhat reclusive in his later life. He died at Gresham College in London in 1703.

IMPACT

During his lifetime, Hooke had an international reputation as the premier experimentalist in England, and his biographers have called him the first professional scientist in an era when most people interested in research were aristocratic dabblers. Despite his experimental genius and mechanical talent, however, Hooke's energies were scattered, and he seldom had the time or the mathematical skill to investigate topics fully. His insights were usually remarkably accurate and his suggested solutions to problems basically correct; however, he left it to others to supply proof. Accordingly, Hooke failed to receive credit for many ideas that others pursued and developed largely or solely on the basis of his work.

Hooke's rivalry with Newton further contributed to his decline in recognition. After Newton became president of the Royal Society in 1703, Hooke's influence quickly waned, and Newton's system of rigorous mathematical demonstration in scientific investigations became the intellectual standard, displacing Hooke's style of hypothesis and experimentation. Until a revival of interest in Hooke around the three hundredth anniversary of his death, he was known almost solely for Hooke's law.

Nevertheless, Hooke's scientific methods and ideas were pervasively influential during his lifetime, affecting the work even of such rivals as Newton.

—*Roger Smith*

Further Reading

Cooper, Michael. *"A More Beautiful City": Robert Hooke and the Rebuilding of London after the Great Fire*. Sutton, 2003.

Gribbin, John, and Mary Gribbin. *Out of the Shadow of a Giant: Hooke, Halley & the Birth of Science*. Yale UP, 2017.

Inwood, Stephen. *The Forgotten Genius: The Biography of Robert Hooke, 1635-1703*. MacAdam, 2005.

Jardine, Lisa. *The Curious Life of Robert Hooke: The Man Who Measured London*. Harper, 2005.

Sacco, Francesco G. *Real, Mechanical, Experimental: Robert Hooke's Natural Philosophy*. Springer Nature, 2020.

Sfetcu, Nicolae. *Isaac Newton vs. Robert Hooke on the Law of Universal Gravitation*. Multimedia Publishing, 2019.

See also: Aristotle isolates science as a discipline; Calculus; Dynamics (mechanics); Elasticity; Force (physics); Moment of inertia; Momentum; Newton, Isaac; Newton's laws; Pendulums; Springs; Thermodynamics; Vacuum; Vacuum technology

HYDRAULIC ENGINEERING

Fields of Study: Physics; Mechanics; Mathematics

ABSTRACT

Hydraulic engineering is a branch of civil engineering concerned with the properties, flow, control, and uses of water. Its applications are in the fields of water supply, sewerage evacuation, water recycling, flood management, irrigation, and the generation of electricity. Hydraulic engineering is an essential element in the design of many civil and environmental engineering projects and structures, such as water distribution systems, wastewater management systems, drainage systems, dams, hydraulic turbines, channels, canals, bridges, dikes, levees, weirs, tanks, pumps, and valves.

KEY CONCEPTS

hydraulic engineering: engineering relevant to the control of moving water

hydraulics: the application of pressurized liquids to perform work

incompressible fluids: fluids that do not change volume with the application of external pressure, particularly liquids

irrigation: the practice of moving water from one location with abundant water to another location where water is needed

DEFINITION AND BASIC PRINCIPLES

Hydraulic engineering is a branch of civil engineering that focuses on the flow of water and its role in civil engineering projects. The principles of hydraulic engineering are rooted in fluid mechanics. The conservation of mass principle (or the continuity principle) is the cornerstone of hydraulic analysis and design. It states that the mass going into a control volume within fixed boundaries is equal to the rate of increase of mass within the same control volume. For an incompressible fluid with fixed boundaries, such as water flowing through a pipe, the continuity equation is simplified to state that the inflow rate is equal to the outflow rate. For unsteady flow in a channel or a reservoir, the continuity principle states that the flow rate into a control volume minus the outflow rate is equal to the time rate of change of storage within the control volume.

Energy is always conserved, according to the first law of thermodynamics, which states that energy can neither be created nor be destroyed. Also, all forms of energy are equivalent. In fluid mechanics, there are mainly three forms of head (energy expressed in unit of length). First, the potential head is equal to the elevation of the water particle above an arbitrary datum. Second, the pressure head is proportional to the water pressure. Third, the kinetic head is proportional to the square of the velocity. Therefore, the conservation of energy principle states that the potential, pressure, and kinetic heads of water entering a control volume, plus the head gained from any pumps in the control volume, are equal to the potential, pressure, and kinetic heads of water exiting the control volume, plus the friction loss head and any head lost in the system, such as the head lost in a turbine to generate electricity.

Hydraulic engineering deals with water quantity (flow, velocity, and volume) and not water quality, which falls under sanitary and environmental engineering. However, hydraulic engineering is an essential element in designing sanitary engineering facilities such as wastewater-treatment plants.

Hydraulic engineering is often mistakenly thought to be petroleum engineering, which deals with the flow of natural gas and oil in pipelines, or the branch of mechanical engineering that deals with a vehicle's engine, gas pump, and hydraulic braking system. The only machines that are of concern to hydraulic engineers are hydraulic turbines and water pumps.

BACKGROUND AND HISTORY

Irrigation and water supply projects were built by ancient civilizations long before mathematicians defined the governing principles of fluid mechanics. In the Andes Mountains in Peru, remains of irrigation canals were found, radiocarbon dating from the fourth millennium BCE. The first dam for which there are reliable records was built before 4000 BCE on the Nile River in Memphis in ancient Egypt. Egyptians built dams and dikes to divert the Nile's floodwaters into irrigation canals. Mesopotamia (now Iraq and western Iran) has low rainfall and is supplied with surface water by two major rivers, the Tigris and the Euphrates, which are much smaller than the Nile but have more dramatic floods in the spring. Mesopotamian engineers, concerned about water storage and flood control as well as irrigation, built diversion dams and large weirs to create reservoirs and to supply canals that carried water for long distances. In the Indus Valley civilization (now Pakistan and northwestern India), sophisticated irrigation and storage systems were developed.

One of the most impressive dams of ancient times is near Marib, an ancient city in Yemen. The 1,600-foot-long dam was built of masonry strengthened by copper around 600 BCE. It holds back some of the annual floodwaters coming down the valley and diverts the rest of that water out of sluice gates and into a canal system. The same sort of diversion dam system was independently built in Arizona by the Hohokam civilization around the second or third century CE. In the Szechuan region of ancient China, the Dujiangyan irrigation system was built around 250 BCE and still supplies water in modern times. By the second century CE, the Chinese used chain pumps, which lifted water from lower to higher elevations, powered by hydraulic water-wheels, manual foot pedals, or rotating mechanical wheels pulled by oxen.

The Minoan civilization developed an aqueduct system in 1500 BCE to convey water in tubular conduits in the city of Knossos in Crete. Roman aqueducts were built to carry water from large distances to Rome and other cities in the empire. Of the 800 miles of aqueducts in Rome, only 29 miles were above ground. The Romans kept most of their aqueducts underground to protect their water from enemies and diseases spread by animals.

The Muslim agricultural revolution flourished during the Islamic golden age in various parts of Asia and Africa, as well as in Europe. Islamic hydraulic engineers built water management technological complexes, consisting of dams, canals, screw pumps, and *norias*, which are wheels that lift water from a river into an aqueduct.

The Swiss mathematician Daniel Bernoulli published *Hydrodynamica* (1738; *Hydrodynamics* by Daniel Bernoulli, 1968), applying the discoveries of Sir Isaac Newton and Gottfried Wilhelm Leibniz in mathematics and physics to fluid systems. In 1752, Leonhard Euler, Bernoulli's colleague, developed the more generalized form of the energy equation.

In 1843, Adhémar Jean Claude Barré de Saint-Venant developed the most general form of the differential equations describing the motion of fluids, known as the "Saint-Venant equations." They are sometimes called "Navier-Stokes equations" after Claude-Louis Navier and Sir George Gabriel Stokes, who were working on them around the same time.

The German scientist Ludwig Prandtl and his students studied the interactions between fluids and solids between 1900 and 1930, thus developing the boundary layer theory, which theoretically explains the drag or friction between pipe walls and a fluid.

Much like other branches of civil engineering, the field of hydraulic engineering benefited significantly from the development of computer-aided design (CAD) technology throughout the late twentieth and early twenty-first centuries. By 2021, CAD software such as Autodesk's Civil 3D enabled hydraulic engineers to design and model infrastructure such as dams and irrigation systems as well as to perform hydraulic analysis, among other tasks.

PRINCIPAL FACTORS OF HYDRAULIC ENGINEERING

Properties of water. Density and viscosity are important properties in fluid mechanics. The density of a fluid is its mass per unit volume. When the temperature or pressure of water changes significantly, its density variation remains negligible. Therefore, water is assumed to be incompressible. Viscosity, on the other hand, is the measure of a fluid's resistance to shear or deformation. Heavy oil is more viscous than water, whereas air is less viscous than water. The viscosity of water increases with reduced temperatures. For instance, the viscosity of water at its freezing point is six times its viscosity at its boiling temperature. Therefore, a flow of colder water assumes higher friction.

Hydrostatics. Hydrostatics is a subdiscipline of fluid mechanics that examines the pressures in water at rest and the forces on floating bodies or bodies submerged in water. When water is at rest, as in a tank or a large reservoir, it does not experience shear stresses; therefore, only normal pressure is present. When the pressure is uniform over the surface of a body in water, the total force applied on the body is a product of its surface area times the pressure. The direction of the force is perpendicular (normal) to the surface. Hydrostatic pressure forces can be mathematically determined on any shape. Buoyancy, for instance, is the upward vertical force applied on floating bodies (such as boats) or submerged ones (such as submarines). Hydraulic engineers use hydrostatics to compute the forces on submerged gates in reservoirs and detention basins.

Fluid kinematics. Water flowing at a steady rate in a constant-diameter pipe has a constant average velocity. The viscosity of water introduces shear stresses between particles that move at different velocities. The velocity of the particle adjacent to the wall of the pipe is zero. The velocity increases for particles away from the wall, and it reaches its maximum at the center of the pipe for a particular flow rate or pipe discharge. The velocity profile in a pipe has a parabolic shape. Hydraulic engineers use the average velocity of the velocity profile distribution, which is the flow rate over the cross-sectional area of the pipe.

Bernoulli's theorem. When friction is negligible and there are no hydraulic machines, the conservation of energy principle is reduced to Bernoulli's equation, which has many applications in pressurized flow and open-channel flow when it is safe to neglect the losses.

APPLICATIONS AND PRODUCTS

Water distribution systems. A water distribution network consists of pipes and several of the following components: reservoirs, pumps, elevated storage tanks, valves, and other appurtenances such as surge tanks or standpipes. Regardless of its size and complexity, a water distribution system serves the purpose of transferring water from one or more sources to customers. There are raw and treated water systems. A raw water network transmits water from a storage reservoir to treatment plants via large pipes, also called "transmission mains." The purpose of a treated water network is to move water from a water-treatment plant and distribute it to water retailers through transmission mains or directly to municipal and industrial customers through smaller distribution mains.

Some water distribution systems are branched, whereas others are looped. The latter type offers more reliability in case of a pipe failure. The hydraulic engineering problem is to compute the steady velocity or flow rate in each pipe and the pressure at each junction node by solving a large set of continuity equations and nonlinear energy equations that characterize the network. The steady solution of a branched network is easily obtained mathematically; however, the looped network initially offered challenges to engineers. In 1936, American structural engineer Hardy Cross developed a simplified method that tackled networks formed of only pipes. In the 1970s and 1980s, three other categories of numerical methods were developed to provide solutions for complex networks with pumps and valves. In 1996, engineer Habib A. Basha and his colleagues offered a perturbation solution to the nonlinear set of equations in a direct, mathematical fashion, thus eliminating the risk of divergent numerical solutions.

Hydraulic transients in pipes. Unsteady flow in pipe networks can be gradual; therefore, it can be modeled as a series of steady solutions in an extended period simulation, mostly useful for water-quality analysis. However, abrupt changes in a valve position, a sudden shutoff of a pump because of power failure, or a rapid change in demand could cause a hydraulic transient or a water hammer that travels back and forth in the system at high speed, causing large pressure fluctuations that could cause pipe rupture or collapse.

The solution of the quasi-linear partial differential equations that govern the hydraulic transient problem is more challenging than the steady network solution. The Russian scientist Nikolai Zhukovsky offered a simplified arithmetic solution in 1904. Many other methods—graphical, algebraic, wave-plane analysis, implicit, and linear methods, as well as the method of characteristics-were introduced between the 1950s and 1990s. In 1996, Basha and his colleagues published another paper solving the hydraulic transient problem in a direct, noniterative fashion, using the mathematical concept of perturbation.

Open-channel flow. Unlike pressure flow in full pipes, which is typical for water distribution systems, flow in channels, rivers, and partially full pipes is called "gravity flow." Pipes in wastewater evacuation and drainage systems usually flow partially full with a free water surface that is subject to atmospheric pressure. This is the case for human-built canals and channels (earth or concrete lined) and natural creeks and rivers.

The velocity in an open channel depends on the area of the cross section, the length of the wetted perimeter, the bed slope, and the roughness of the channel bed and sides. A roughness factor is estimated empirically and usually accounts for the material, the vegetation, and the meandering in the channel.

Open-channel flow can be characterized as steady or unsteady. It also can be uniform or varied flow, which could be gradually or rapidly varied flow. A famous example of rapidly varied flow is the hydraulic jump.

When high-energy water, gushing at a high velocity and a shallow depth, encounters a hump, an obstruction, or a channel with a milder slope, it cannot sustain its supercritical flow (characterized by a Froude number larger than 1). It dissipates most of its energy through a hydraulic jump, which is a highly turbulent transition to a calmer flow (subcritical flow with a Froude number less than 1) at a higher depth and a much lower velocity. One way to solve for the depths and velocities upstream and downstream of the hydraulic jump is by applying the conservation of momentum principle, the third principle of fluid mechanics and hydraulic engineering. The hydraulic jump is a very effective energy dissipater that is used in the designs of spillways.

Hydraulic structures. Many types of hydraulic structures are built in small or large civil engineering projects. The most notable by its size and cost is the dam. A dam is built over a creek or a river, forming a reservoir in a canyon. Water is released through an outlet structure into a pipeline for water supply or into the river or creek for groundwater recharge and environmental reasons (sustainability of the biological life in the river downstream). During a large flood, the reservoir fills up and water can flow into a side overflow spillway—which protects the integrity of the face of the dam from overtopping—and into the river.

The four major types of dams are gravity, arch, buttress, and earth. Dams are designed to hold the immense water pressure applied on their upstream face. The pressure increases as the water elevation in the reservoir rises.

Hydraulic machinery. Hydraulic turbines transform the drop in pressure (head) into electric power. Also, pumps take electric power and transform it into water head, thereby moving the flow in a pipe to a higher elevation.

There are two types of turbines, impulse and reaction. The reaction turbine is based on the steam-powered device that was developed in Egypt in the first century CE by Hero of Alexandria. A simple example of a reaction turbine is the rotating lawn sprinkler.

Pumps are classified into two main categories, centrifugal and axial flow. Pumps have many industrial, municipal, and household uses, such as boosting the flow in a water distribution system or pumping water from a groundwater well.

CAREERS

Undergraduate students majoring in civil or environmental engineering usually take several core courses in hydraulic engineering, including fluid mechanics, water resources, and fluid mechanics laboratory. Advanced studies in hydraulic engineering lead to a master of science or a doctoral degree. Students with a bachelor's degree in a science or another engineering specialty could pursue an advanced degree in hydraulic engineering, but they may need to take several undergraduate level courses before starting the graduate program.

Graduates with a bachelor's degree in civil engineering or advanced degrees in hydraulics can work for private design firms that compete to be chosen to work on the planning and design phases of large governmental hydraulic engineering projects. They can work for construction companies that bid on governmental projects to build structures and facilities that include hydraulic elements, or for water utility companies, whether private or public. Some common areas for hydraulic engineers to work in are stormwater management, sediment transport, and creation of canals for irrigation and transportation.

To teach or conduct research at a university or a research laboratory requires a doctoral degree in one of the branches of hydraulic engineering.

SOCIAL CONTEXT AND FUTURE PROSPECTS

In the twenty-first century, hydraulic engineering has become closely tied to environmental engineering. Reservoir operators plan and vary water releases to keep downstream creeks wet, thus protecting the biological life in the ecosystem. Hydraulic engineers can also be involved in coastal engineering, which includes fighting erosion through sediment delivery, and in flood management; their skills can also be applied to various other conservation projects involving rivers or oceans.

Clean energy is the way to ensure sustainability of the planet's resources. Hydroelectric power generation is a form of clean energy. Energy generated by ocean waves is a developing and promising field, although wave power technologies still face technical challenges.

—*Bassam Kassab*

Further Reading

Boulos, Paul F., Kevin E. Lansey, and Bryan W. Karney. *Comprehensive Water Distribution Systems Analysis Handbook for Engineers and Planners*. 2nd ed., MWH Soft Press, 2006.

Chow, Ven Te. *Open-Channel Hydraulics*. 1959. Blackburn, 2008.

Finnemore, E. John, and Joseph B. Franzini. *Fluid Mechanics with Engineering Applications*. 10th International ed., McGraw-Hill, 2009.

Julien, Pierre Y. "Our Hydraulic Engineering Profession." *Journal of Hydraulic Engineering*, vol. 143, no. 5, 2017.

Lindell, James E. *Handbook of Hydraulics*. 8th ed., McGraw Hill Professional, 2017.

Walski, Thomas M. *Advanced Water Distribution Modeling and Management*. Methods, 2003.

Yasmin, Nighat. *Introduction to AutoCAD 2022 for Civil Engineering Applications*. SDC Publications, 2021.

See also: Civil engineering; Conservation of energy; Engineering; Fluid dynamics; Force; Friction; Hydraulics; Hydrodynamics; Kinetic energy

HYDRAULICS

Fields of Study: Physics; Mechanics; Mathematics

ABSTRACT

Hydraulics is the study of the behavior of water and other liquids in motion and at rest. It deals primarily with the

properties and behavior of liquids at rest against or in motion relative to boundary surfaces and objects.

KEY CONCEPTS

density: the mass of a substance per unit volume, measured in kilograms per cubic meter

fluid: a liquid, vapor, or gas that fills the container that holds it; hydraulics limits its focus to liquids and those vapors and gases undergoing negligible changes in density

pressure: the measure of the force exerted by a fluid per unit area, measured in kilopascals

surface tension: the property of a liquid to adhere to capillary surfaces

viscosity: the measure of a fluid's resistance to shearing forces, that is, those forces that deform it, measured in kilograms per meters times seconds

OVERVIEW

Hydraulics is a branch of fluid mechanics that deals with the behavior of water and other liquids at rest against or in motion relative to boundary surfaces and objects. Hydraulic laws apply to gases as well, but only insofar as they are resistant to compression—that is, where density fluctuations are negligible. Such situations occur only where the velocity of the moving gas is significantly less than the speed of sound. Hydraulics is concerned only with the study of homogeneous and continuous bulk liquids at the macroscopic level and thus ignores molecular structure. The study of hydraulics and the physical laws that describe it is best understood in the examination of its two component parts: hydrostatics and hydrodynamics.

Hydrostatics is the most abstract of the two constituent parts of hydraulics, for it deals only with those liquids that are at rest and is thus a special case of the more general hydrodynamics. When liquids are at rest, there are no shearing or deforming forces, so that the primary phenomena of concern

are the pressures and forces exerted by the mass of the liquid upon its container. Since pressure is defined as a force per unit area, the forces exerted by a bulk liquid at rest can be determined mathematically by knowing the pressure of the liquid and the area of the surface containing the liquid. This is possible because only forces caused by gravity influence the liquid, making the pressure force uniform over horizontal cross sections of the liquid. The pressure of a liquid at rest acts equally in all directions; as a result, the forces on the boundary (container) are perpendicular to its surfaces. Pressure forces can be divided into two categories: forces on plane (flat) surfaces and forces on curved surfaces. Examples include liquid storage tanks, dams, underwater tunnels, and pressure-measuring devices.

Hydrostatic forces on plane surfaces can be characterized by the angle at which the surface of the liquid is penetrated by the boundary surface, the density and depth of the liquid, and the surface area of the plane boundary. By knowing these parameters, the scientist or engineer can easily determine the force caused by liquid pressure at any point on the plane surface. Such determinations are made mathematically by using formulas known as differential equations. Such formulas allow the scientist to calculate the effect of liquid pressure over the entire surface of the boundary by summing up the pressure effects on minute portions of the boundary surface known as "differential areas."

While the same parameters apply for the determination of pressure forces on curved surfaces, in general, such determinations are mathematically difficult, as the curved surface may be highly irregular, making the definition of differential areas rather unwieldy. In addition, forces act in parallel lines on plane surfaces; such is not the case for curved surfaces. Most commonly, however, the curved surface is either a cylinder or a sphere, such as a pipe, in which case the problem is quite tractable because of the regular and circular geometry of these surfaces.

For these surfaces, the force resulting from liquid pressure is calculated for either tension or compression, depending upon whether the liquid is on the inner or outer part of these closed surfaces, respectively.

Hydrodynamics is more complicated and general in its scope than hydrostatics, for it deals with the behavior and effects of liquids in motion. Hydrokinematics is a branch of hydrodynamics concerned with liquids in motion, but without regard for the forces responsible for setting the fluid into motion. Hydrodynamics proper, on the other hand, attempts to explain, describe, and predict liquid motion, the forces on both the liquid and its boundary surfaces, and any accompanying energy changes.

At its most basic level, hydrodynamic phenomena are characterized by two mathematical equations that describe two commonly understood physical principles: a "continuity equation," or mass conservation equation, which describes the condition of the liquid, and an equation of motion, which describes the conservation of momentum or energy in the moving liquid. As was the case with hydrostatics, these laws are described by differential equations. Scientists and engineers can make predictions of the behavior of hydraulic phenomena from these two physical principles. These phenomena include the various types of hydraulic flow that may occur in natural phenomena, such as coastlines, groundwater, rivers and streams, and floods; manmade structures such as irrigation canals; chemical processing facilities; mechanical devices such as hydraulic vehicle brakes; and in the construction of dams, dikes, and spillways.

Liquid flow is described mathematically as a liquid flow "field" by expressing the moving liquid's velocity, pressure, density, and temperature as a function of positions, or coordinates, in space and time. That is, the macroscopic physical properties of a liquid are described geometrically for ease in mathematical analysis. The principle of the conservation of

mass states that the net rate of mass increase into a fixed volume is equal to the net rate of mass flow into that same volume. This principle is quite intuitive, for it simply says that no more or less mass accumulates in a given volume than is actually flowing into that same volume. By knowing the volume and the density of the liquid, one can determine the mass of the liquid; knowing its velocity allows a determination of the flow of mass per unit time—the rate of mass increase. Any particle of mass that moves at a constant velocity has the property known as momentum; an object's momentum is equal to the product of its mass and its velocity. Liquids can be regarded as a continuous, many-particle system where all particles behave in the same way. Just as mass is conserved, so is momentum.

Waterwheels. Photo by Björn Appel, username Warden, via Wikimedia Commons.

Both the conservation of mass and momentum continuity relations ignore thermodynamic effects, which are described by the first law of thermodynamics. This law relates the temperature, heat, and internal energy of a moving liquid and thus considers the mechanical conditions and effects of its motion. Parameters such as elasticity and viscosity have profound influences upon the effects of a liquid's motion, especially in confined motion situations such as pipes and other conduits. For example, it requires far more energy to pump a given volume of crude oil through a pipe than it does distilled water, all other factors remaining equal, because crude oil is more viscous than water and thus resists the shearing stresses that move it.

In order to calculate the conservation of energy in a moving liquid, the scientist must balance the rate of increase of the internal energy of a fixed volume of liquid with the net rate of internal energy and work energy flow into the liquid. Such calculations require the scientist to gather large amounts of data regarding the temperature and flow rate of the liquid in question. In addition, scientists must conduct highly controlled experiments in order to disallow any extraneous sources of heat energy to enter the energy balance equation.

APPLICATIONS

Just as the theoretical side of hydraulics was divided into hydrostatics and hydrodynamics, its applications are divided also. Hydraulics applications abound in the fields of chemical, civil, and mechanical engineering in areas as diverse as the measurement of the most minute of flow rates and the construction of dams and hydroelectric facilities. Hydrostatic applications vary as widely as the plethora of structures that humans have placed under water.

The laws of hydrostatics apply to all the following structures and devices but are not limited to them: storage tanks, underwater gates, tunnels, walls and pipes, sheet piling and bulkheads for bridges and similar structures, and pressure measuring devices. Since the laws of hydrostatics deal only with pressure effects, only the circumstances of application change. Therefore, two examples will be discussed: pressure measuring devices and underwater gates.

The most common device used for the measurement of the pressure of a moving liquid is the manometer.

Manometers are an application of the laws of hydrostatics—that is, the physics of stationary liquids—to the phenomena of hydrodynamics. Manometers are essentially tubes, usually constructed of glass or strong plastic, which are attached to liquid reservoirs, pipes, or channels. The tubes are most commonly U-shaped and graded in either inches or millimeters.

Pressure is measured by noting the difference in liquid height between the two "legs" of the U. A manometer with one end open to the atmosphere to act as a reference is known as a barometer.

Liquids will flow only from higher pressures to lower pressures. Therefore, moving liquids act under what is known as a pressure difference or a "pressure gradient." In order to determine the pressure difference under which the liquid is moving, the scientist examines the manometer and notes the difference in the height of the liquid from the high-pressure end and the low-pressure end. If the two "legs" of the U-shaped tube have equal levels of liquid, there is no pressure difference and the liquid is not flowing. A lower level in a leg is indicative of a flowing liquid and also indicates the direction of flow. The pressure difference itself is determined by multiplying the difference in height between the two legs by the density of the liquid. Recall that the basic hydrostatic relation required the use of liquid height and density to calculate pressure.

Manometers are among the most common pressure-measuring devices and are often the first instruments used by chemical and civil engineering students.

Apart from the use of hydrostatics in measuring devices, the most common use of hydrostatics is in civil and chemical engineering in the design of structures used either to contain or restrain bodies of stationary liquids. One very common and practical application is in the calculation of the water pressure on the surfaces of pipes. Such calculations determine the stability of such structures, which in turn help to determine their safety. Since hydrostatics gives an indication that the pressure at any point on a surface is perpendicular to that surface, pressures on both the inside and the outside of pipes result in "tangential stresses," forces that could tear the pipe apart, endangering safety and wasting resources. By calculating or measuring the pressure of the liquid in and out of the pipe and determining the diameter of the pipe, the stress on the pipe becomes a function of the material of which the pipe is made.

The applications of hydrodynamics involve liquids in motion and run the range from understanding and determining the motion of liquids in pipes, to the flow of water in open channels such as rivers and streams, to the migration of pollutants in groundwater. The flow of liquids in pipes is the most common of all hydrodynamic applications and is one of the most basic calculations in the field of chemical engineering design.

There are two common parameters measured in the study of liquid flow in pipes: velocity and volumetric flow. Both of these measurements depend upon whether the flow of liquid is laminar or turbulent. Laminar flow is characterized by slow moving liquids where the water is often described as smooth and glasslike. Turbulent flow is most common in nature and is characterized by rushing currents, whirls, and eddies. In a series of now-classic 1883 experiments, Osborne Reynolds discovered a numerical way of determining such flows, which is known as the "Reynolds number," R. The quantity of R is found by multiplying the density of a moving liquid (in kilograms per cubic meter), its velocity (in meters per

second), and the length of the pipe, conduit, and the like (in meters) and dividing this quantity by the liquid's viscosity (in kilopascals). Reynolds numbers below 2,000 indicate laminar flow, while those greater than 4,000 indicate turbulent flow. The area from 2,000 to 4,000 is known as the transition region and is often assumed to be laminar.

There are only straightforward equations for the calculation of velocity and volumetric flow rate in laminar flow. In laminar flow, all fluid particles move in straight lines parallel to the pipe walls; as a result, flow rate is independent of the smoothness or roughness of the pipe walls.

In preliminary design work, at least, it is often assumed that the liquid is in a laminar flow regime. Both volumetric flow rate and liquid velocity depend upon the pressure drop along the length of the pipe, the radius of the pipe, the pipe's length, and the liquid's viscosity.

In turbulent flow, the liquid particles actually move in random and often unpredictable directions. As a result, the engineer must consider the characteristics of the moving liquid as well as those of the pipe itself. In such cases, the engineer uses a series of tables that relate the Reynolds number and the pipe roughness to determine a friction factor. The value of this factor determines how much energy is lost in turbulent liquid flow through pipes of varying roughness. Such charts have been compiled for a variety of commonly processed liquids. In such cases where the charts have not been prepared, experiments must be conducted in order to determine empirically the relationship between the Reynolds number and the pipe roughness for the particular situation.

Perhaps the most common use of turbulent flow information is in the study of flowing waters in nature, particularly the large rivers such as the Nile, the Amazon, and the Mississippi.

Understanding the flow characteristics of such bodies of water has a wide range of practical applications, from harnessing the energy of the flowing water for electrical purposes to using the water itself for irrigation. Natural flow has an additional problem not encountered in pipe flow: that of an irregular flow channel. The factors contributing to turbulent flow must be accounted for in such situations; however, in order to attain accuracy, the shape of the actual river bed must be accounted for as well. The liquid velocities in such situations are thus a product of viscosity, the river bed geometry, friction caused by irregularities in the river bed, and the surface tension of the liquid.

CONTEXT

Hydraulics, like many other engineering sciences, has a dual heritage. Both practical and theoretical developments helped to shape the growth of this discipline. Prior to any systematic studies of hydraulics, ancient civilizations such as the Chinese, Egyptians, and Mesopotamians used the properties of water to their practical advantage in such projects as irrigation and flood prevention. One example is the Sadd-el-Kafara dam, built between 2700 and 2600 BCE.

Constructed entirely of rock, the dam is 110 meters long and 14 meters high.

Archaeologists believe it to be the world's first large-scale dam for the purpose of flood protection.

Systematic theories regarding the behavior and effects of water are attributed to the Ancient Greeks, beginning with the philosopher Thales between 624 and 546 BCE.

Yet, it was not until the time of Archimedes (287-212 BCE) that the study of hydraulics took a shape resembling that of modern hydraulic science. Archimedes was, for the most part, a mathematician, so it should not be surprising that he analyzed the phenomena of hydrostatics, particularly flotation and buoyancy, in geometrical terms.

It was not until the sixteenth and seventeenth centuries, however, that the study of hydraulics gained a true scientific character—that is, the capacity for quantitative prediction and analysis. Until this time, hydraulics remained largely practical, steeped in an "artisan tradition,"

where empirical rules of thumb would be passed down from one generation of hydraulic builders to the next. This tradition saw its greatest achievements in the mammoth projects of the Roman Empire, which included water supply and sewage systems.

It was in the Renaissance period in Europe, and in the subsequent scientific revolution, that the Archimedean ideal of a mathematical study of hydraulics was reborn. This rebirth took shape in the studies of Galileo and his student, Evangelista Torricelli. While Galileo did little work on hydraulics, his scientific method, that of developing mathematical hypotheses to be tested experimentally, made a profound impact on Torricelli, who is heralded as the founder of modern hydraulic science. One example is his study of liquid jets—high-velocity streams of water from small orifices. Torricelli applied Galileo's analysis of projectile motion to this problem, confirming that liquid jets, like moving projectiles, could be described mathematically.

By the eighteenth century, the influence of Galileo and Torricelli had combined with the new physics of Sir Isaac Newton to produce the works of Johann Bernoulli and Leonhard Euler. In 1742, Bernoulli developed the streamline equation—the relation that describes the motion of fluids in pipes as a function of pressure and density. In 1749, Euler derived the continuity equations for both compressible and incompressible fluids.

In the nineteenth century, the complete joining of the ancient traditions of hydraulic engineering and the newly developed hydraulic sciences of hydrostatics and hydrodynamics was achieved, setting the study on course to the twentieth century. This period saw the Reynolds' studies of laminar and turbulent flow, as well as Henri-Philibert-Gaspard Darcy's

(1857) studies of the influence of pipe wall roughness, friction, and energy loss. In addition, engineering became known as a profession through both formal education, in the form of engineering schools in Europe and the United States and professional societies such as the American Society of Civil Engineers.

—*William J. McKinney*

Further Reading

Hager, Willi H. *Wastewater Hydraulics: Theory and Practice.* 2nd ed., Springer Berlin Heidelberg, 2010.

Hamill, Les. *Understanding Hydraulics.* 3rd ed., Bloomsbury Publishing, 2017.

Moore, Wade P., James E. Lindell, and Horace W. King. *Handbook of Hydraulics.* 8th ed., McGraw-Hill Education, 2017.

Vacca, Andrea, and Germano Franzoni. *Hydraulic Fluid Power: Fundamentals, Applications, and Circuit Design.* John Wiley & Sons, 2021.

Wass, Harold S., and Russell P. Fleming. *Sprinkler Hydraulics: A Guide to Fire System Hydraulic Calculations.* 3rd ed., Springer Nature, 2020.

Xu, Weilin. *Mesoscale Analysis of Hydraulics.* Springer Nature Singapore, 2020.

See also: Acceleration; Aeronautical engineering; Archimedes's principle; Automated processes and servomechanisms; Biomedical engineering; Biomechanics; Discoveries of Archimedes; Fluid dynamics; Hydraulic engineering; Hydrodynamics; Kinetic energy; Mechanical engineering; Statics; Steam energy technology; Steam engine

HYDRODYNAMICS

Fields of Study: Physics; Mechanics; Mathematics

ABSTRACT

Hydrodynamics is the branch of physics that describes the movement of idealized fluids. The mathematical techniques used for describing ideal fluid motion have been used successfully to describe not only the dynamics of many real fluids but also various forms of transport and dynamics in other fields.

KEY CONCEPTS

Bernoulli equation: a conservation-of-energy equation, used extensively in hydrodynamics analyses, that states that along the path of a small volume-element of ideal fluid, the sum of the kinetic, potential, and pressure energy terms is a constant

conservation of energy: in hydrodynamics, the principal that for an ideal fluid, the total energy associated with a small volume-element of fluid remains constant throughout its motion

conservation of mass: in hydrodynamics, the principal that the mass of ideal fluid entering a small body element equals the mass of fluid leaving the element

ideal fluid: a fluid assumed to have zero viscosity and to be incompressible

potential lines: a mathematical construction that defines regions of space where fluid movement has a potential to occur; a fluid element moves from a high potential line to a lower one

pressure: the force per unit area exerted by a fluid on a container; total pressure is the sum of a static pressure, as used in Archimedes's principle, and a dynamic pressure, caused by motion of the fluid

sink: the location where fluid is removed from a fluid system

source: the location where fluid is applied to a fluid system

streamline: during uniform flow, the line defined by the motion of a small fluid element; streamlines are perpendicular to potential lines

viscosity: the internal resistance to motion of a fluid caused by intermolecular forces

OVERVIEW

Hydrodynamics is the study of the motion of an ideal fluid flowing on or within a confining boundary. To simplify the description of movement and its analysis, the existence of an ideal fluid—an idealized material that has zero viscosity and that is incompressible—is assumed. In many cases, the dynamics of such a material are similar to the observed motions of water and other fluids.

Early researchers believed that an ideal fluid would behave much like a solid object. An ideal fluid flows in response to gravity from a region of high gravitational potential to a region of lower potential. This is similar to the motion of a solid object dropped from a height. In fact, it was observed that the velocity of a rock dropped from a specific height was the same as the velocity of water escaping through a hole in the bottom of an open container holding water to the same height as the rock was dropped; this observation was codified in Torricelli's law. An ideal fluid flowing from an opening at the bottom of an open container should, if directed by a flexible spout, be able to shoot to the height of the water in the container. The fact that real water, for example, does not reach that height is a consequence of the viscosity of water.

Another observation involved water flowing in a horizontal pipe with a varying diameter. From the principal of conservation of mass, it is known that the volumetric rate (cubic meters per second) at which water flows through any cross section of the pipe, regardless of diameter, is the same. The volumetric rate of flow is given by multiplying the cross-sectional area of the pipe by the average fluid velocity over the cross section. This product is constant for any cross section. The velocity of flow is then indirectly proportional to the cross-sectional area of the pipe. In a horizontal pipe, fluid flows faster through a small diameter than through a larger one. Leonardo da Vinci had earlier studied similar flow dynamics in streams and summed them up with his law of continuity, which expresses the same relationship.

A third finding that had a significant effect on the development of hydrodynamics was that when small

vertical open tubes were attached to a horizontal pipe that was conveying water, the height at which the water stood in the tubes was observed to be related to the diameter of the pipe. There was also a slight decrease in the height of water in the tubes over a length of pipe having a uniform diameter. It was proposed that this effect was caused by the water's internal friction, or viscosity. For regions of the pipe with a smaller diameter, the water stood lower in the tube. The height the water stood in the tube was interpreted as proportional to the pressure in the pipe at the point where the tube connected to the pipe. The pressure at the bottom of the tube equaled the height of the fluid in the tube multiplied by the weight density of the fluid.

By experiment, for water flowing in a horizontal pipe, vertical tubes attached to a smaller-diameter region of pipe showed the water pressure to be less than at a larger-diameter region of pipe. This was interpreted to mean that water flowing relatively faster through a smaller-diameter section of pipe has less pressure associated with it than when it is flowing slower through a larger-diameter region of pipe. This led Daniel Bernoulli to propose that the pressure of a fluid increases as its velocity decreases and, conversely, that pressure increases as velocity decreases. This understanding was extended to form Bernoulli's theorem, which states that the sum of the kinetic energy, potential energy, and pressure energy for a given volume-element of fluid is constant for all locations along the element's path. This relationship is used extensively in hydrodynamic analysis; with modifications for viscosity, the relationship can be used to understand the movement of any real fluid.

The objective of most hydrodynamics analysis is to determine the fluid "flow field," given certain boundary conditions, sources of fluid, sinks, and other specifics. Such a field can be visualized by thinking of the fluid as composed of numerous small volume-elements. The motion of each small volume-element is represented by a small arrow, the length of which is proportional to the flow velocity and the direction of which is the same as the fluid's motion. The velocity can be determined by measuring the distance traveled by a small volume-element in a specific time interval. The assemblage of all these motion arrows at a specific point in time gives an indication of the flow field. The average length of the arrows in a small region gives the average velocity of flow, and the average direction of flow is the average direction of all the arrows in the region. In hydrodynamics analyses, the flow field is assumed to be "stationary," or unchanging.

When an ideal fluid is moving uniformly, the motions of individual small volume-elements define lines through space that are called "streamlines." A three-dimensional (3D) collection of streamlines can be selected that define a bundle similar to the surface of a pipe. Such a collection of streamlines is known as a "stream-tube." The tube can have a varying diameter along its length. There are no volume-elements that move into or out of the side of a stream-tube; they enter and exit only at the ends of the tube. The rate of flow of fluid through a stream-tube is constant. The cross section of the stream-tube is an area. The volume per unit time rate of flow of fluid through the stream-tube equals the average velocity of the fluid crossing the cross-sectional area of the tube times the area of the tube. Constant flow rate within the tube requires that the average flow velocity at any cross section of the tube times the cross-sectional area be a constant. This means that when the cross-sectional area of the tube gets larger, the average flow velocity must become lower. The fluid pressure increases as the cross section gets larger.

The two-dimensional (2D) equivalents of stream-tubes are filaments. In performing a graphical analysis, the potential lines are first constructed; these are perpendicular to any fluid boundaries. The streamlines are then constructed perpendicular to the potential lines. The fluid is assumed to flow from

a higher potential to a lower one. The collection of streamlines and perpendicular potential lines defines a 2D "flow net."

In cases in which a fluid supply or loss is caused by a drain or some other point of exit, the flow net can be adjusted to show these situations. For a source—such as the end of a water hose—supplying fluid onto a smooth area, the idealized streamlines are radial out from the source location. The potential lines are concentric circles about the source. In the case of a sink, such as by a drain, the streamlines are directed radially inward to the sink location. The potential lines are, again, concentric circles. For impermeable boundaries, the streamlines are roughly parallel to the boundary with the potential lines perpendicular to the boundary.

While the 2D flow net is often used to predict the flow of water on a 2D surface, the equivalent 3D flow net is useful for 3D analyses. Numerous graphical and analytical techniques have been developed that utilize flow nets to analyze ideal fluid-flow problems.

Treating water as an ideal fluid has several logical consequences. One of these is the assumption that any rotation present in the fluid at the start of observation will continue and will not die out or increase. For example, if an ideal fluid is imagined to be circulating in a coffee cup, according to the ideal-fluid model, the circulation would not stop after time. The analysis of real fluids, however, must account for the effects of viscosity, which would cause such rotational motion to die out if it were not renewed by an outside force.

A major difference between ideal water and natural water, therefore, is that the ideal liquid is considered to have no internal viscosity and to experience no friction between itself and the edges of a pipe or a canal. For ideal water, the velocity of the fluid is considered to be uniform across the cross section of a pipe or a stream. For real water, however, there is friction that causes the water-flow velocity near the bounding structure to be very low (zero at the surface) and to increase to a maximum near the center of the cross section of the flow.

The inclusion of the effects of viscosity causes the real-world equations used to describe fluid motion to be considerably more complicated than those that describe the motion of an ideal fluid. Solutions to real-world equations are often achieved using numerical integration techniques on computers. Because of this complexity, and because ideal-fluid analysis often yields good approximations of fluid movement, ideal fluids are often assumed in order to obtain initial predictions for fluid movement in a given situation.

A common starting point in many fluid analyses is to suppose that the fluid being studied obeys Newton's laws. For water and air in typical environmental conditions, this is often not too far wrong, however there can be considerable deviation from Newton's laws in describing the dynamics of other fluids. These are called "non-Newtonian" fluids.

The mathematical and conceptual techniques used to quantify fluid flow developed shortly after Isaac Newton proposed his laws and after the introduction and early development of calculus. Calculus was well suited to describe some of the processes and effects observed in flowing water. Similarities between the flow of water, of heat, and of electromagnetic radiation caused the development of many analytical tools in these fields to be intertwined.

APPLICATIONS

Fluid motion is responsible for most of the transport and mixing that take place in the environment, in industrial processes, in living organisms, and in vehicles. Knowledge of fluid dynamics is responsible for the increased efficiency of energy recovery from fuels used in powering aircraft, ships, and automobiles. Fluid mechanics has been instrumental in the design of the shape of these structures and vehicles to reduce drag and help them move more effectively through the air or water. Fluid dynamics describes

the transport of pollutants in the air, surface, and subsurface as well as the transport of liquids on the surface and subsurface of the earth.

The Bernoulli equation, with a small correction for viscous losses, is used to design the extensive pipe networks employed in industrial facilities, water distribution in cities, and in irrigation. Successful analysis and prediction of the flow of water in open channels and on fields has as its basis a sound foundation in fluid dynamics. The siting and operation of power plants and other large facilities requires considerable flow analysis. Determination of the potential effects of a facility on regional air and water quality are required before construction can begin. These "environmental impact assessments" also examine groundwater and its location, motion, and sensitivity to pollution from surface spills and discharges from a facility. Analyses of the mixing of discharges from a facility in streams and lakes, as well as emissions into the airshed, require an understanding of fluid mechanics. After the fact, fluid analyses are critical in designing effective remediation and cleanup operations to stop further pollution.

The concepts and processes of hydrodynamics are also used in describing atmospheric processes and in attempting to predict the weather. The ocean plays a major role in these processes, with a slight change in temperature sometimes having far-reaching ramifications, as in the case of the Pacific Ocean phenomenon known as "El Niño." The ideas of fluid mechanics are used with those of heat transport in explaining the coupled ocean-atmosphere fluid system that controls the weather. The fluid mechanics of these processes share many common features and are often referred to as "geophysical fluid dynamics." The general ideas and concepts of fluid dynamics are also used to explain phenomena in outer space. Fluid mechanics is used in describing and analyzing the stars, the giant gaseous planets, and in other astrophysical problems. Back on Earth, fluid mechanics is used to analyze the shape and drift of the continents, volcanic activity, and the generation of the earth's magnetic field.

Improvements in the combustion of fossil fuels have reduced fuel consumption and pollutant generation. Fluid-mechanics research has contributed to this effort with large economic benefit. The technique of imparting a swirl to the air in jet-engine combustors, for example, improved the engines' fuel economy substantially. This technology migrated into the design of new high-efficiency home oil burners. Many other innovative engine designs have also been based on an understanding of fluid mechanics.

Small-scale physical models using water have often been used to predict how flow occurs in other areas of physics, such as electromagnetics. Wave movement in water is often used to represent the movement of light waves in optics. The effects of a smooth wave moving through double slits is readily apparent. This technique provides a convenient means to observe interference and diffraction by waves in one medium when analogous effects occur in another.

Fluid mechanics is also used in biology in many important applications. These range from a better understanding of normal biological processes to the development of therapeutic medical procedures. Among these are heart and heart-valve function and the design and evaluation of artificial replacements for these organs. Other medical areas in which an understanding of hydrodynamics is important include the measurement of cardiovascular flow and the measurement and modification of the characteristics of pulmonary flow. Additional work occurs in the microscopic realm at the level of cells, micropores, and microorganisms. In many of these instances, the fluids studied are non-Newtonian.

CONTEXT

While water-conveyance and water-storage structures have been used for centuries, it was not until the six-teenth century that mathematical techniques were developed to describe fluid flow quantitatively and to assist in the design of such structures. Leonardo da Vinci conducted studies in aerodynamics and hydraulics in the sixteenth century, while Evangelista Torricelli in the seventeenth century proposed the law governing the velocity of a fluid exiting from a tank drain.

Daniel Bernoulli introduced the term "hydrodynamics" in 1738 to cover the sciences of hydrostatics and hydraulics. He also laid the foundation for the theorem that bears his name, while he and his father Johann shared in the development of the concept of fluid pressure. Jean d'Alembert later developed the use of potential theory and complex variables in fluid analysis. Leonhard Euler integrated much of the previous work in hydrodynamics, formulated the equation of motion of an ideal fluid, and developed its mathematical theory.

In the nineteenth century, Sir George Stokes developed the equations of motion of a viscous fluid; he is sometimes regarded as having founded the modern theory of hydrodynamics. Stokes was followed by William Rankin, who developed the theory of sources and sinks, and Hermann von Helmholtz, who introduced the mathematical analysis of stream-lines, founded the theories of vortex motion and discontinuous motion, and made fundamental contributions to hydrodynamics. In 1879, Horace Lamb published *Hydrodynamics*, which has remained a major work of reference on the subject.

At the beginning of the twentieth century, various developments caused the unification of the fields of hydrodynamics and hydraulics into the science of fluid mechanics. Osborne Reynolds helped this process by promoting the use of models and the theoretical description of the flow of viscous fluids. He also studied and described the abrupt transition from laminar to turbulent flow. Ludwig Prandtl provided a means of linking hydraulics and hydrodynamics through the use of boundary-layer concepts.

Theodore von Karman furthered the unification of hydrodynamics and hydraulics by his work on vortex sheets, drag, and momentum.

The field of hydrodynamics has developed slowly. This has resulted not from a lack of research funding or an absence of military or commercial interest but rather from the extraordinary difficulty of the subject itself. Progress in the field has been difficult and seems likely to remain so. Many unsolved problems remain, and the ability to predict many flows is limited.

Throughout the development of hydrodynamics, many of the concepts, mathematical techniques, and forms of analysis have been used in other fields of physics, science, and engineering. Thus, despite its inherent difficulty, hydrodynamics continues to be a rich and fruitful topic of investigation.

—*William O. Rasmussen*

Further Reading

Arnold, Vladimir I., and Boris A. Khesin. *Topological Methods in Hydrodynamics*. Springer Science & Business Media, 2008.

Birk, Lothar. *Fundamentals of Ship Hydrodynamics: Fluid Mechanics, Ship Resistance and Propulsion*. John Wiley & Sons, 2019.

Chatzigeorgiou, Ioannis. *Analytical Methods in Marine Hydrodynamics*. Cambridge UP, 2018.

Guyon, Etienne, Jean-Piere Hulin, Luc Petit, and Catalin D. Mitescu. *Physical Hydrodynamics*. Oxford UP, 2015.

Hansen, Jesper Schmidt. *Nanoscale Hydrodynamics of Simple Systems*. Cambridge UP, 2022.

Raizer, Victor. *Optical Remote Sensing of Ocean Hydrodynamics*. CRC Press, 2019.

Renilson, Martin. *Submarine Hydrodynamics*. Springer, 2015.

Valle-Levinson, Arnoldo. *Introduction to Estuarine Hydrodynamics*. Cambridge UP, 2022.

See also: Aerodynamics; Ailerons, flaps, and airplane wings; Airfoils; Airplane propellers; Archimedes's principle; Bernoulli's principle; Biomedical engineering; Biomechanics; Calculus; Coriolis effect; Differential equations; Discoveries of Archimedes; Dynamics (mechanics); Fluid dynamics; Fluid mechanics and aerodynamics; Force (physics); Friction; Heat transfer; Hydraulic engineering; Hydraulics; Kinetic energy; Momentum (physics); Newton, Isaac; Newton's laws; Steam and steam turbines; Steam energy technology

I

Inertial Guidance

Fields of Study: Physics; Mechanics; Mathematics

ABSTRACT
Inertial guidance and navigation systems determine the positions of aircraft, spacecraft, missiles, ships, and other vehicles by using accelerometers and gyroscopes to integrate the accelerations and rotations they experience. They provide complete navigational solutions without the use of any external references.

KEY CONCEPTS

accelerometer: a device for measuring accelerations

fiber-optic gyro: a gyroscope employing a laser diode and a coil of fiber-optic material to detect rotational rates optically

gimbaled inertial systems: inertial guidance or navigation systems in which the inertial platform is suspended on gimbals and is kept in a fixed spatial orientation, not following the attitude changes of the vehicle

gyroscope (gyro): a device for measuring rotational motions

inertial platform: the rigid structure that holds the gyros and accelerometers of an inertial guidance system

positional gyro: a gyro that produces as its direct output the net angular displacement it has undergone about its sensing axis

rate gyro: a gyro that produces as its direct output the rate of angular displacement about its sensing axis

ring-laser gyro: a gyroscope employing a closed triangular or square laser cavity to detect rotational displacement optically

seismic mass (pendulous mass): the mass used by an accelerometer to detect accelerations, usually by measuring the force required to keep the seismic mass stationary with respect to the accelerometer housing

strapdown inertial systems: inertial guidance or navigation systems in which the inertial platform is rigidly fixed to the vehicle body and follows its attitude changes

OVERVIEW

Inertial guidance and navigation systems are used to determine the positions of the vehicles in which they are mounted. They do this without necessarily referring to any external landmark or signal but rather by sensing and tracking a vehicle's motions by using gyroscopes and accelerometers. Vehicles using such systems can navigate accurately in remote areas where no external references are available or in military situations where such references might be obscured or even falsified by enemy actions.

The "velocity" of an object is the rate at which its position changes, and the "acceleration" of an object is the rate at which its velocity changes. By continuously (or very frequently) measuring the acceleration an object experiences, it is possible to integrate these accelerations to determine the net change in velocity; similarly, it is possible to integrate a series of velocity estimates to determine the net change in the object's position. Thus if the initial position and velocity of an object are known, and its accelerations are measured, it is possible to know at all times its velocity and position.

Devices that measure acceleration are called "accelerometers." Usually, they consist of a housing and what is called a "seismic mass" or "pendulous mass" that can move back and forth within the housing in one direction only. Since the housing accelerates along with the vehicle, a force must be exerted on the seismic mass to keep it accelerating along with the housing. By Isaac Newton's second law of motion, this force will be directly proportional to the required acceleration.

The force itself can be measured readily. Some accelerometers simply employ springs, which exert a force proportional to their compression, which is then measured. Others use electrical or magnetic forces in a "feedback" loop to hold the mass in a constant position relative to the housing, and then determine the amount of force from the nical gyroscope, a rapidly rotating object with a high moment of inertia, hence high angular momentum. The seismic mass is attached to the gyroscope housing to unbalance it so that, when the housing is accelerated, the mass exerts a torque on it, causing the gyroscope's axis to change direction, or "precess." The rate of precession can then be related to the amount of acceleration.

If the vehicle moved only along a single straight line, a single accelerometer could be used to keep track of its position. For a vehicle such as an aircraft, however, which moves in three dimensions, at least three accelerometers are necessary. Sometimes more are employed for redundancy.

However, this does not completely solve the problem. Since the "attitude" (spatial orientation) of the vehicle can change, an accelerometer pointed toward its front might sometimes measure northward accelerations, and sometimes eastward, westward, or even southward. It is therefore also necessary to keep track of the orientation of the vehicle. This is done by means of gyroscopes, usually called "gyros" in this context.

The first inertial guidance systems used simple mechanical gyros—massive hoops of metal kept spinning around a single axis by an electric motor.

For this use, the gyros are carefully balanced, so that the vehicle acceleration exerts no torque on them. The "angular momentum" of the gyro, an expression of its rate and direction of rotation (multiplied by its "moment of inertia," which depends on its mass and shape), can only be changed by exerting a "torque" (an off-center force) on the gyro. This means that as the vehicle rotates, a torque must be exerted on the gyro to cause it to follow that motion. This torque can be measured and used to determine the rate at which the vehicle is turning.

A more modern variation of this is the "electrostatically suspended gyro (ESG)." The rotor in an ESG is a hollow sphere with electrically conductive areas on its surface. The sphere is kept suspended in a closely fitted cavity by electrostatic forces, so there is no contact of moving parts and, hence, very little friction. Electrical currents in the cavity wall induce currents in the conductive areas on the rotor, causing it to spin. The position and motion of the rotor are monitored optically. The low friction permits such gyros to be very accurate.

Two other modern gyros are the "ring-laser gyro (RLG)" and the "fiber-optic gyro (FOG)." These are not true gyroscopes but are called gyros because they are also used to detect rotations. They have no moving parts but instead use light beams, relying on what is called the "Sagnac effect" after French physicist Georges S. S. Sagnac, who demonstrated it in 1913. An exact analysis of either of these devices requires the use of Albert Einstein's general theory of relativity.

The Sagnac effect is that a light beam transmitted around a closed path is shifted in frequency if the path is rotated. In a fiber-optic gyro, the closed path is created by winding a fiber-optic conduit many times around a spool. A beam of light is split in two and transmitted around this fiber-optic coil in opposite directions, creating opposite frequency shifts. The beams are then recombined. If the coil is rotating, the two beams will have undergone slight frequency shifts in the opposite directions, resulting in a phase difference between them. This can be measured, thus determining the rate of rotation. Fiberoptic gyros are simple and extremely reliable, but they suffer accuracy limitations caused by scattering along the optical path, which makes phase-shift measurements difficult.

A ring-laser gyro is a gas laser built in the form of a triangle or square, with mirrors at the corners. An electrical current is passed through the gas (usually a mixture of helium and neon), causing it to act as a very low-power laser with no outlet. It thus becomes a "cavity resonator," not unlike a microwave oven, but at optical frequencies (with helium and neon, the beam is red). A standing-wave pattern is set up within the cavity; because of the Sagnac effect, this pattern tends to remain stationary even if the cavity rotates. The peaks and valleys of the pattern can be detected optically by placing a sensor at one of the mirrors; these extremes can then be counted to determine the angular displacement as the cavity rotates.

Ring-laser gyros are thus extremely accurate, but they too suffer from limitations. First, if the mirrors are imperfect, the standing-wave pattern will tend to "lock on" to them, and at low rotational rates, the pattern will turn with the cavity rather than remaining fixed in space. This results in extremely demanding specifications for the mirrors and normally requires that the gyro be kept constantly rotating. Usually, a vibrating device on the gyro is used for this purpose. Another potential problem is that gas in the laser must be maintained at a precise mixture and pressure. This can be difficult in spacecraft applications, where the seal on the laser cavity must be maintained reliably for long periods.

There are two fundamentally different methods for implementing an inertial guidance system, depending on how the "inertial platform" to which the accelerometers and gyros are fixed is mounted. Some (including the earliest) inertial guidance and navigation systems use gimbaled inertial platforms.

The platform is mounted on three motor-controlled gimbals so that it can be rotated in any direction. Output from the gyros is used as an input to the gimbals so as to result in no net rotation of the platform, which remains fixed in inertial space. Accelerometer outputs therefore can be directly integrated to produce true displacements. A potential drawback is that it is always possible to maneuver the system so that two of the gimbal axes become precisely aligned, leaving the platform with no third axis about which to turn. It is then unable to track rotations about that third axis. This is called "gimbal lock" or "dumping the platform" and is a favorite amusement of test pilots.

The alternative to this is a "strapdown inertial system," in which the inertial platform is rigidly attached to the body of the vehicle. Gyro outputs are used to determine how much the platform has rotated from its original position, and the accelerometer outputs are interpreted based on this. Strapdown systems are potentially simpler and more reliable than gimbaled systems, since they have no gimbals at all, but they have much larger computational requirements and usually have very demanding specifications on their gyros.

One interesting limitation of all inertial systems is that they cannot sense gravity directly. This is because inertial mass and gravitational mass are identical, so the force of gravity acts on the accelerometer housing and the seismic mass in the same way, producing no net force between them. This limitation means that high-precision guidance systems must consider the exact shape of Earth's gravitational field. The field varies with altitude, with latitude (since Earth is not a perfect sphere), and with local mass concentrations. It may be necessary for the inertial system to carry a complete map of the gravitational field so that it can be taken exactly into account.

Inertial guidance systems process their sensor data using a variation on the "Kalman filter," an optimal estimation algorithm named for Rudolf Kalman, to obtain the best possible position estimates.

APPLICATIONS

Inertial guidance and navigation systems are used on many civilian and military vehicles, including aircraft, ships, submarines, missiles, spacecraft, and some military land vehicles. Most large airliners employ inertial systems as their primary means of navigation. The systems are very accurate and reliable and do not require the use of external navigational aids such as radio beacons. This facilitates journeys over water and over polar regions where radio aids are not available. It also makes more direct routes feasible, since the aircraft does not have to fly from beacon to beacon. Typically, the inertial navigation system is integrated with a computer that provides several kinds of information to the crew and to other aircraft systems. The crew enters a series of "waypoints"—latitudes and longitudes along the intended route—into the navigation system, which determines the plane's position, and also such things as the heading to the next waypoint.

Inertial guidance systems provide all these advantages to military applications, as well as immunity from enemy interference. Enemy action can jam radio signals, destroy the stations that broadcast them, or even produce false signals. During World War II, faked radio beacons were used to confuse bombers, often causing them to miss their targets. In one extreme case, a German bomber pilot was so confused by British jamming that he landed in Scotland, erroneously believing he was safe in occupied France. Because they are entirely internal, inertial systems are immune to such enemy action.

Inertial systems provide another military advantage by being passive. These systems emit nothing, so they provide no extra information to the enemy. Some radar homing missiles, for example, use nothing but inertial guidance to fly to the vicinity of their targets. Only when the missiles are close enough for final homing is the radar activated. This strategy has several advantages. First, the enemy may be unaware that a missile is coming until it is too late. Second, when the radar system is carried on the missile itself, it need only be designed to work at short range and for a short time, so it can be made smaller and cheaper. Third, when the radar signal used by the missile for homing comes from a distant ship or aircraft, that signal is only needed for a short time, thus permitting the ship or aircraft to service more missiles over any given time period.

Missile systems that are intended to attack stationary targets on the ground may use inertial guidance alone to reach their targets. This is especially true of ballistic nuclear missiles, which must be designed to defeat all possible enemy countermeasures. Extreme accuracy is also required, since some of these are designed to destroy missile silos, which are protected against anything except very close nuclear explosions. Some military land vehicles, especially self-propelled artillery pieces, may also use inertial navigation systems.

All inertial systems must be initialized. This requires not only supplying an initial position and velocity but also—and to high accuracy—an initial orientation. For example, an aircraft may be parked at a surveyed location. The crew enters the known latitude, longitude, and altitude of that location into the inertial navigation system computer and allows it to remain stationary for a required period of time. The system then uses its accelerometers to determine the direction of the gravitational force, thus determining which way is up. Since the accelerometers cannot sense gravity, they actually determine the "acceleration" due to the upward force on the aircraft wheels, equal to and exactly countering the undetected force of gravity on the stationary aircraft. The gyros sense the only rotation they are undergoing, which is due to the rotation of Earth. In this way, they determine the direction of Earth's rotational axis, which is north. The system may take some time (usually several minutes or tens of minutes) to determine these two directions to the required accuracy. Once they have been determined, the orientation of the platform is known and the initialization is complete.

In other cases, one navigation system may be used to initialize another. An aircraft preparing to launch from an aircraft carrier is not stationary but may receive a continuous flow of data from the ship's inertial navigation system, which it compares to its own sensors. In this way, the relative alignment between the ship's inertial platform and the aircraft's inertial platform can be established and the initialization completed. If an aircraft is to launch an inertially guided missile, a similar exchange of data between the aircraft and missile is necessary, and the aircraft may need to perform turning maneuvers during the process to provide the inertial systems with rotational data to compare.

All inertial systems diverge over time, as errors from the sensors accumulate. This can be corrected, partially, by providing external information to the system. Most aircraft systems use an input from the aircraft's barometric altitude sensor to prevent the navigation system's estimate of the altitude from becoming unreasonable. In addition, many systems can be updated using manually entered data. For example, a pilot may fly over a known landmark and enter that landmark's location into the system. Since both the new data and the previous inertial navigation solution can have errors in them, a new position estimate is formed from both by combining them statistically.

Besides their general tendency to increase over time, errors in any inertial guidance system intended for use near Earth tend to oscillate with a period of about 84 minutes. This effect is called "Schuler oscillation" after its discoverer, Max Schuler. It reflects the fact that any system that can navigate accurately around a spherical planet must

be on the edge of instability, with a tendency to oscillate at a frequency determined by the radius and mass of the planet. Any errors in the system will stimulate oscillation at this frequency.

CONTEXT

Inertial guidance systems grew naturally out of the use of gyro compasses and artificial horizons. The gyro compass uses a single gyroscope to detect the direction of Earth's rotation. These became common on ships early in the twentieth century and have remained in use on ships and in aircraft. They have the advantages that they display true north, rather than magnetic north, and they are not affected by the metal in the vehicles, as a magnetic compass would be.

Aircraft have long carried artificial horizons (also called "attitude indicators" and several other names, depending on their exact functions), which use gyroscopes to provide an indication of the attitude of the aircraft. They are useful at night or in fog or clouds when the pilot cannot see the horizon clearly. They work much like an inertial navigation system, but without the accelerometers; they keep track of attitude, but not of position changes.

The addition of the accelerometers was a straightforward idea, and the principles of modern inertial systems were described by Schuler in 1923. During World War II, the German V-2 rockets used inertial guidance to strike their targets in England. After the war, the first really accurate inertial systems were developed by Charles S. Draper and others at the Massachusetts Institute of Technology. These quickly found their way into military and civilian applications.

In the 1980s and 1990s, an alternative navigation technology arose that has ultimately displaced inertial navigation for civilian purposes. This is a satellite-based system of beacons called the "Global Positioning System (GPS)." This system has global coverage, is extremely accurate, and requires only a simple and inexpensive receiver for use. It may replace inertial systems in civil aviation if questions regarding its control are resolved. At this writing, it belongs to the US military, which constructed it, and which retains the option to interrupt it if necessary in time of war. It is also conceivable that a future adversary could gain the capability to attack the satellites. These uncertainties continue to make the use of inertial guidance necessary in military systems.

—*Firman D. King*

Further Reading

Cicci, David A. *A Short Course in Inertial Navigation and Missile Guidance.* Independently Published, 2021.

Grewal, Mohinder S., Angus P. Andrews, and Chris G. Bartone. *Global Navigation Satellite Systems, Inertial Navigation, and Integration.* 3rd ed., John Wiley & Sons, 2015.

Jekeli, Christopher. *Inertial Navigation Systems with Geodetic Applications.* Walter de Gruyter, 2012.

Lawrence, Anthony. *Modern Inertial Technology: Navigation, Guidance, and Control.* 2nd ed., Springer Science & Business Media, 2012.

Maini, Anil K. *Handbook of Defence Electronics and Optronics: Fundamentals, Technologies, and Systems.* John Wiley & Sons, 2018.

Titterton, David, John L. Weston, and John Weston. *Strapdown Inertial Navigation Technology.* IET, 2004.

See also: Acceleration; Aeronautical engineering; Aerospace design; Angular forces; Angular momentum; Circular motion; Displacement; Dynamics (mechanics); Equilibrium; Linear motion; Mechatronics; Moment of inertia; Momentum; Motion; Newton's laws; Pendulums; Speed; Springs; Stability; Torque

INTERNAL COMBUSTION ENGINE

Fields of Study: Physics; Engineering; Mechanics; Mathematics

ABSTRACT

The technology of the internal combustion engine applies the reaction of an oxidizer (air) and a fuel in a combustion that produces the working fluids (in the form of expanding gases) to supply kinetic energy.

KEY CONCEPTS

crankshaft: in an internal combustion engine, a heavy structure with offset sections to which the pistons of the individual combustion cylinders are attached by connecting rods; the crankshaft rotates about a central axis so that the pistons move up and down within the cylinders as it rotates

exhaust: the elimination of combustion gases from the cylinders of an internal combustion engine at the completion of the combustion cycle of its operation

four-cycle engine: an engine that requires four complete revolutions of its crankshaft for the complete cycle of its operation, as compared to a two-cycle engine

intake: the introduction of fuel and air into the cylinders of an internal combustion engine prior to its combustion cycle

two-cycle engine: an engine that requires only two complete revolutions of its crankshaft for the complete cycle of its operation

ENGINES

Although electric vehicles are being widely promoted and so are becoming more common, for all practical purposes, the internal combustion engine is the primary type of engine in use in the vast majority of automobiles and trucks today—and that dominance of the transportation sector is likely to be little changed in future years. At the same time, commentators are raising more questions about whether the incorporation of electric motors would supersede the use of internal combustion engines, at least in automobiles, in the not-so-distant future. Advancements in battery technology, specifically regarding efficient lithium-ion batteries, combined with global efforts to fight climate change led to some arguments that it would not be long before carmakers would be shifting more to electric technology—or at least more of a hybrid between the two. As electric cars are simpler to make and maintain and drastically reduce carbon emissions as opposed to cars that use internal combustion engines, the call for electric cars may further increase. Yet others claim that with some companies working on methods for making the internal combustion engine more efficient, it will continue to remain in use for some time.

An internal combustion engine is one in which the working fluids are comprised of reactants of combustion—oxidizer and fuel—along with the products of combustion. The heat released by combustion of the oxidizer-fuel mixture causes the gaseous products of combustion to expand and exert force against the moving surfaces of the engine, whether a piston, turbine blade, or other device. The chief types of internal combustion engines are reciprocating and rotary (Wankel). Gas turbine types are also in use.

RECIPROCATING ENGINES

Reciprocating engines come in three general categories:

Continuous- and intermittent-combustion engines. A steady flow of fuel and oxidizer into the engine is the signature of the continuous-combustion engine. A stable flame is maintained; jet engines are typical. The intermittent-combustion engine applies periodic ignition of air and fuel; this is most often called a reciprocating engine; gasoline and diesel piston engines are the most common examples.

Spark ignition/compression ignition engines. Fuel and air are mixed prior to the intake stroke or just after inlet valve closure in the electric spark ignition, or Otto, engines. In compression ignition, or Diesel, versions, the diesel oil fuel is injected after the compression process; rather than a spark, the fuel is ignited by the high temperature of the compressed gas.

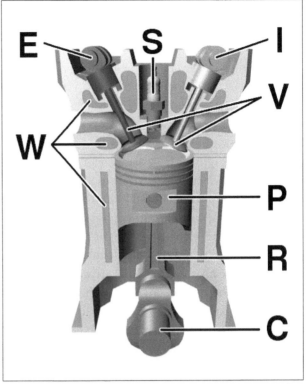

Diagram of a cylinder as found in an overhead cam 4-stroke gasoline engine: C – crankshaft E – exhaust camshaft I – inlet camshaft P – piston R – connecting rod S – spark plug V – valves. red: exhaust, blue: intake. W – cooling water jacket gray structure – engine block. Image by Wapcaplet, via Wikimedia Commons.

Otto-cycle engine: Four-stroke (4s) and two-stroke (2s) engines. The work cycle in a four-stroke engine takes two crankshaft revolutions, divided into intake, compression, expansion, and exhaust stages. This is sometimes called the Otto cycle, in honor of inventor Nikolaus Otto. One crankshaft revolution is sufficient for a complete two-stroke cycle, which has no intake or exhaust strokes. Gas exchange in these engines occurs when the piston is near the bottom center position, between the expansion and compression strokes.

ROTARY ENGINES

The rotary-piston engine (Wankel) rotary-piston engine, invented by Felix Wankel, generates power in the familiar four-stroke cycle of compression, ignition, and expansion of a gasoline-air mixture. However, the moving parts work in a continuous rotary motion, instead of a reciprocating movement.

The Wankel rotary engine delivers one power stroke for each full crankshaft rotation. Thus its displacement volume is used twice as often as in four-stroke engines. This allows the average Wankel to be engineered to roughly half the size and weight of a conventional engine. There are also far fewer components, usually about 40 percent of the number of moving parts a V-8 engine would have. There is a similar kind of advantage, although not as dramatic, over a four-cylinder engine. By reducing the number of components and the complexity of their interactions, engine manufacture costs are also reduced.

Ironically, the Wankel engine also embodies some manufacturing drawbacks, mainly the need for expensive materials and the requirement for higher-precision manufacturing techniques. For all that, the Wankel has tended toward low fuel economy and high emissions of incompletely combusted hydrocarbons. The high hydrocarbon emissions result from poor sealing between the rotor and housing. However, design and engineering improvements since 2003 have brought about production models of the Wankel type that meet contemporary fuel economy and emissions standards.

GAS TURBINE ENGINES

The gas turbine, or combustion turbine, engine is a rotary, continuous internal combustion engine wherein the fuel flows to a burner supplied with an excess of compressed air. The expanding combustion gases apply pressure to turbine blades; the turbine power is transferred via gearing to an output shaft.

The gas turbine engine embodies four main operations:

- *Compression*. Air enters the gas turbine and is compressed.

- *Heat exchange*. Heat is drawn from the exhaust gases and communicated to the compressed air.
- *Combustion*. Fuel is mixed with hot air and ignited. The pressure increases.
- *Expansion*. The hot exhaust gases drive the turbine, thus releasing their energy. The turbine turns the compressor and the output shaft.

The advantages of gas turbines include high rotational speed, yielding a very compact engine; rotating movement yields vibration-free operation; ability to operate on a wide variety of fuels; and continuous combustion yields reduced hydrocarbon and carbon monoxide emissions compared to internal combustion engines.

However, these advantages must be balanced against the following drawbacks when gas turbines are considered for automotive applications: quenching of the gases by the turbine and compressor yields high noise levels; low efficiency of the dynamic compressor and turbine at smaller scales yields relatively higher fuel consumption; to obtain the high rotating speeds needed to maximize efficiency, sophisticated and costly materials must be incorporated; and high cost materials must also be used to tolerate the higher temperature levels compared to other engine types.

COMPARISONS WITH EXTERNAL COMBUSTION ENGINES

An internal combustion engine is a heat engine; its thermal energy is derived from a chemical reaction within the working fluid. The working fluid itself is then exhausted to the environment, aiding excess heat rejection. In external combustion engines, heat is transferred to the working fluid through a solid wall and also expelled to the environment via another solid wall. Steam engines are in this class.

Internal combustion engines have two intrinsic advantages: Except for auxiliary cooling, they require no heat exchangers, thereby reducing weight, volume, cost, and complexity. With no requirement for high-temperature heat transfer through walls, the design of internal combustion engines permits the maximum temperature of the working fluid to exceed maximum allowable wall material temperature.

Intrinsic disadvantages include the fact that for all practical purposes the working fluids are limited to air and products of combustion. Nonfuel heat sources, such as waste heat, cannot be used to generate motive energy. Additionally, there is little flexibility in combustion conditions—they are largely set by engine requirements. This factor makes achieving low-emissions combustion more difficult.

—*Reza Fazeli*

Further Reading

"The Death of the Internal Combustion Engine." *The Economist*, 12 Aug. 2017, www.economist.com/news/ leaders/21726071-it-had-good-run-end-sight-machine-changed-world-death. Accessed 23 Aug. 2017.

Ehsani, Mehrdad, et al. *Modern Electric, Hybrid Electric, and Fuel Cell Vehicles, Fundamentals, Theory, and Design*. CRC Press, 2005.

Ferrari, Giancarlo, Angelo Onorati, and Gianluca D'Errico. *Internal Combustion Engines*. Societa Editrice Esculapio, 2022.

Fijalkowski, B. T. *Automotive Mechatronics: Operational and Practical Issues*. Vol. II. Springer, 2011.

Heywood, John. *Internal Combustion Engine Fundamentals 2E*. 2nd ed., McGraw Hill Professional, 2018.

Hiereth, Hermann, and Peter Prenninger. *Charging the Internal Combustion Engine (Powertrain)*. Springer, 2010.

Josephson, Paul R. *Motorized Obsessions: Life, Liberty, and the Small-Bore Engine*. Johns Hopkins UP, 2007.

Mayersohn, Norman. "The Internal Combustion Engine Is Not Dead Yet." *The New York Times*, 17 Aug. 2017, www.nytimes.com/2017/08/17/automobiles/wheels/ internal-combustion-engine.html. Accessed 23 Oct. 2017.

Smil, Vaclav. *Creating the Twentieth Century: Technical Innovations of 1867-1914 and Their Lasting Impact*. Oxford UP, 2005.

Van Basshuysen, Richard, Fred Schaefer, and TechTrans. *Internal Combustion Engine Handbook*. SAE International, 2016.

See also: Carnot, Sadi; Diesel engine; Engineering tolerances; External combustion engine; Jet engines; Mechatronics; Propulsion technologies; Rotary engine; Steam and steam turbines; Stirling, Robert; Transportation; Turbines; Turbojets and turbofans; Turboprops

J

Jet Engines

Fields of Study: Physics; Aeronautical engineering; Mechanical engineering; Thermodynamics

ABSTRACT

A jet engine is an internal combustion engine that converts the chemical energy of fuel into mechanical energy in the form of thrust by the high-speed exhaust gases leaving the engine nozzle. Fundamentally, a jet engine is a gas turbine. Gas turbines are used widely to generate electricity in power stations, to power boats, trains, military tanks, and to drive gas pipeline compressors. It is as a jet engine, however, that the gas turbine has had its greatest industrial impact.

KEY CONCEPTS

afterburner: a system that increases jet engine thrust by injecting additional fuel into the exhaust stream as it exits the combustion chamber, where the extra fuel is instantly ignited thus producing a large quantity of additional exhaust gas to augment thrust

axial compressor: a compressor in which air is driven through a tapering containment housing by a series of rotating blades that sweep a successively smaller diameter

centrifugal compressor: a compressor in which the rotating blades compress air by directing it outward radially from the central axis and forcing it against the containment housing

ideal gas law: the relationship of pressure (P), temperature (T), volume (V), mass in moles (n), and the universal gas constant, R, as $PV = nRT$

DESCRIPTION

A jet engine consists of several components: a compressor, a combustion chamber, a turbine, and an exhaust system. At the front of the jet engine is the compressor, driven by a shaft connected to the turbine. The compressor takes in air from the atmosphere and compresses it to produce high-pressure air. The air then enters the combustion chamber, where jet fuel is injected in fine droplets. Combustion occurs with ignition, and the hot gases exit the combustion chamber and enter the turbine, downstream of the combustion chamber. The hot gases leave the turbine through the exhaust system, exiting at high speed from the jet engine nozzle and propelling forward both the jet engine and the aircraft attached to it. The principle behind this propulsion is described by Newton's third law of motion, which states that for every action there is a reaction equal in magnitude and opposite in direction. Jet propulsion is the movement of a small mass of gas at a very high velocity, whereas in a propeller-driven airplane, the propeller moves a large mass of air at low velocity.

HISTORY

The first patent for the modern gas turbine was granted in 1930 in England to Sir Frank Whittle, whose design led to the W-l turbojet engine with a centrifugal compressor. Simultaneously yet independently, German engineer Hans P. von Ohain also obtained a patent for a turbojet engine less than five years after Whittle had received his patent. Von Ohain's engine also had a centrifugal compressor, whereas another German design, by Ernst Heinkel, had an axial compressor. A plane with von Ohain's

He-S3b engine made its test flight on August 27, 1939. Two years later, on April 12, 1941, a plane with Whittle's turbojet engine was tested.

By the 1940s, German turbojet engine prototypes had adopted the axial compressor, whereas British models all used the centrifugal compressor. By 1943, the two main turbojet engines were Germany's Junkers Jumo 004 and Britain's Rolls-Royce Welland. In the United States, General Electric Company engineers modified the Whittle engine and produced an American version called the I engine. In October, 1942, the I engine had its first test flight in the Bell P-59A.

During World War II, scientists from both Allied and Axis countries worked feverishly to design and test the jet engine. By 1946, several countries had successfully developed turbojet engines. In the United States, General Electric built the I-16 and the I-40. In England, Rolls-Royce built the Welland I, the Derwent I, and the Nene. In Germany, Junkers manufactured the Jumo 004-4.

By the 1950s, the turbojet had been applied to civilian aviation. Early passenger jets included the De Havilland Comet I, which first flew in 1952 but was withdrawn from service two years later because of fatal accidents. By 1954, the United States had successfully tested its Boeing 707 passenger jet, with regular flights commencing four years later. After adopting the jet engine, commercial aviation quickly developed into an international business, with most countries operating their own national airlines. International jet aircraft industries manufacture many types of planes: wide-body models that can carry hundreds of passengers; supersonic planes that can

A Pratt & Whitney F100 turbofan engine for the F-15 Eagle being tested in the hush house at Florida Air National Guard base. Photo via Wikimedia Commons. [Public domain.]

fly at Mach 2; aircraft that are capable of vertical takeoffs and landings (VTOL); and military jet aircraft that can take off and land on the relatively short deck of an aircraft carrier.

The gas-turbine engine that powers all jet aircraft is, however, basically the same engine that was designed by Sir Frank Whittle in 1930. It consists of a compressor, combustion chamber, turbine, and exhaust system. There are four major manufacturers of jet engines: Société Nationale de Construction de Moteurs Aeronautiques (SNECMA) in France, Rolls-Royce in the United Kingdom, and Pratt & Whitney and General Electric in the United States.

COMPONENTS

Compressor. The purpose of the compressor is to increase the pressure of the gas. In the compressor, atmospheric air is pressurized to typically ten to forty times the inlet pressure, and consequently the temperature of the air rises to between 200 and 550 degrees Celsius. The ideal gas law states the proportionality of the pressure and temperature of gases. The two basic types of compressors are the centrifugal-flow compressor and the axial-flow compressor.

The centrifugal-flow compressor, preferred for smaller engines, is a simpler device that uses an impeller, or rotor, to accelerate the intake air and a diffuser to raise the pressure of the air. The axial-flow compressor is favored for most engine designs, because it is capable of increasing the overall pressure ratio. The axial-flow compressor uses rotors fitted to many differently sized discs to accelerate the intake air and stationary blades, known as stators, to diffuse the air until its pressure rises to the correct value.

The type of compressor used in an engine affects the engine's exterior appearance: An engine with a centrifugal compressor usually has a larger front area than an engine with an axial compressor. An engine with an axial compressor is longer and has a smaller diameter than an engine with a centrifugal compressor.

Combustion chamber. In the combustion chamber, jet fuel, typically kerosene, is injected in fine droplets to allow for fast evaporation and subsequent mixing with the hot, compressed air. The compressed air is used for combustion, which occurs with ignition; the hot pressurized gases then reach temperatures of 1,800 to 2,000 degrees Celsius. To protect the combustion chamber walls from these high temperatures, some of the intake air, routed from the compressor, is used to cool the combustion chamber walls.

The three types of combustion chambers are the multiple chamber, annular chamber, and can-annular chamber. The multiple chamber, with individual chambers, or flame tubes, arranged radially, is used on engines with centrifugal compressors and early axial-flow compressor engines. The annular chamber has one annular flame tube with an inner and outer casing. The can-annular chamber combines characteristics of the multiple chamber and the annular chamber and has several flame tubes in one casing.

Turbine. In an aircraft engine, the sole function of the turbine, which is downstream of the combustion chamber, is to power the compressor. Similar to the compressor, the turbine has several large discs, though typically not as many as the compressor, fitted with many blades. Gases at temperatures between 850 and 17,000 Celsius exit the combustion chamber and enter the turbine. The hot gases impact the turbine blades, causing the discs carrying them to rotate at high speeds, averaging 10,000 revolutions per minute. The discs are mounted on a shaft that is connected at the other end to the compressor discs. The turbine blades are usually made of nickel alloys, because these materials are both strong and able to withstand the high temperatures within the turbine. The blades are fitted with many small holes through which cool air is forced to prevent the blades from melting.

Exhaust system. The jet engine's exhaust system is configured so as to maximize the thrust of the engine. The exhaust system consists of a nozzle and may also include a thrust reverser and an afterburner.

In a basic exhaust system, the hot gases leaving the turbine are discharged through a propelling nozzle at a velocity that provides thrust. In VTOL aircraft, the nozzle can be made to swivel vertically so the aircraft can move up and down.

The thrust reverser enables the aircraft to slow down and stop more quickly upon landing, allowing the aircraft to land on shorter runways without relying solely on braking devices. Thrust reversal quite simply reverses the direction of exhaust gases to decelerate the aircraft. The two main thrust reversal methods use either clamshell-type deflector doors or bucket-type deflector doors on a retractable ejector.

Afterburner. An afterburner is used in some aircraft, such as supersonic jets (SSTs) and military aircraft that need to reach high speeds in a short time. Unburned oxygen from the jet engine's exhaust system flows into an afterburner, where more fuel is injected into the hot gases to augment the thrust of the engine. The temperature of the exhaust gases increases, thereby increasing the gas velocity and the thrust of the engine. This additional thrust allows for acceleration to supersonic speeds or for faster takeoffs to accommodate combat situations or the shorter runways of aircraft carriers.

TYPES OF JET ENGINES

The basic types of jet engines are the turbojet, turbofan, turboprop, and turboshaft. Turbojet and turbofan engines are called reaction engines, because they derive their power from the reaction to the momentum of the exhaust gases. The turboprop and turboshaft engines, however, utilize the momentum of the exhaust gases to drive a power turbine that, in turn, drives either a propeller or an output shaft.

Turbojet. The turbojet was the first jet engine type to be invented and flown. In a turbojet, all of the intake air passes through the compressor and is burned in the combustion chamber. The hot gases pass through the turbine and are then expelled through the exhaust nozzle to provide the thrust required to propel the engine and the aircraft attached to it forward. Examples of the turbojet appear in both civilian and military aircraft, including the Olympus 593 in the Concorde SST.

Turbofan. By the end of the twentieth century, the turbofan had become the most popular choice for aircraft propulsion in both civilian and military aircraft. In a turbofan engine, a large fan is placed at the front of the compressor of the jet engine. The amount of intake air is increased up to ten times. Most of this cool intake air either bypasses the compressor, combustion chamber, and turbine and exits the fan nozzle separately, as in separate-flow turbofans, or gets mixed with the turbine exhaust and exits through a common nozzle, as in the mixed-flow turbofan.

Afterburners in turbofan engines are equipped with a mixer to mix the cooler bypass air with the hot exhaust gases, thus allowing an easier burning of the bypassed air. Turbofan engines are characterized by their bypass ratio, which is the mass flow rate, in pounds per second, of air going through the fan divided by the mass flow rate of air going through the compressor. Low-bypass engines have ratios of up to two; medium-bypass engines have ratios from two to four, and high-bypass engines have ratios from five to eight. Ultrahigh-bypass engines have bypass ratios from nine to fifteen or higher. The highest bypass ratios, although providing high propulsion efficiency, likewise involve large, heavy components.

The advantage of the turbofan is its greater thrust on the same amount of fuel, which results in more efficient propulsion, lower noise levels, and an improved fuel consumption. Turbofan jet engines power all modern commercial aircraft, such as the Boeing 747; business jets, such as the Gulfstream IV; and most military airplanes, such as the F-18. Future turbofans may combine various bypass features. For example, the variable-cycle engine (VCE) would have both high-bypass and low-bypass features. Such an engine would be designed for planes that travel at subsonic and supersonic speeds. The VCE would operate by a valve that would control the bypass stream, either increasing it for subsonic speeds or decreasing it for supersonic speeds.

Turboprop. A turboprop engine is a turbojet engine with an extra turbine, called a power turbine, that drives a propeller. In the turboprop engine, the jet exhaust has little or no thrust. Planes powered by turboprop engines typically fly at lower altitudes and reach speeds up to 400 miles per hour (640 kilometers per hour). An example of the turboprop engine is the Rolls-Royce DART in the British Aerospace 748 and the Fokker F-27.

Turboshaft. A turboshaft is a turboprop engine without the propeller. The power turbine is instead attached to a gearbox or to a shaft. One or more turboshaft engines are used on helicopters to power the rotors. The turboshaft engine has industrial applications, such as in power stations, and marine applications, such as in hovercrafts.

JET ENGINE POLLUTION

Because it is an internal combustion engine whose exhaust gases flow directly into the environment, a jet engine is a serious source of air pollution. Because of its high level of noise, it also causes noise pollution.

Air pollution. Air pollution results from the combustion process of the gas-turbine engine. Jet-engine emissions, including carbon dioxide, carbon monoxide, hydrocarbons, and nitrogen oxide gases, contribute to both the greenhouse effect and atmo-

spheric ozone depletion. They also endanger the health of people especially near airports.

Some regard aircraft transportation as more polluting than any other type of transportation, including the automobile. Generally, older aircraft are greater polluters than newer aircraft. The turbofan and bypass turbofan engines in particular use less fuel and therefore pollute less. A new MD-90 is about 50 percent more economical than a DC-9 or a DC-10, because the newer plane uses less fuel. Nevertheless, studies show that per passenger, an airplane uses twice as much fuel per passenger than does a car with three passengers, when the car drives the distance a jet travels in one hour (770 kilometers).

Airplane fuel consumption could be improved by eliminating various classes of cabins in commercial aircraft. Business- and first-class cabins seat fewer passengers, thereby reducing the overall fuel efficiency of the aircraft. If a reduction in carbon dioxide aviation emissions is to be realized, older aircraft must be replaced with newer ones that have more fuel-efficient engines. The most environmentally friendly aircraft include the B-777 and B-767. Carbon monoxide is contained in the combustion exhaust fumes. Both carbon monoxide and hydrocarbon emissions occur at the highest rates when airplanes idle their engines on runways, where often twenty planes are lined up waiting for takeoff. Airplanes pollute hundreds of times more when idling than when flying.

Nitrogen dioxide emissions contribute to acid-rain formation. The emission of hydrocarbons, especially hydrocarbon radicals, contributes to ozone formation. In terms of these emissions, the new high-bypass turbofan jet engines pollute much less than older turbofan and turbojet engines. Sulfur dioxide emissions also contribute to acid-rain formation. Nitrogen oxides have a possible role in ozone depletion, and its reduction can only be effected by less air traffic in general.

Noise pollution. Noise is measured on a logarithmic scale in decibels, a unit of audio power. The decibel range is normally from zero decibels to about 160 decibels, although the decibel scale is essentially unlimited. A normal conversation takes place at about 40 decibels, and a noise level of 90 decibels would make it impossible to hear a normal conversation. The noise from a nearby jet takeoff is about 110 decibels. The main source of jet-engine noise is the propulsion system and the resultant noises generated by both internal and external processes.

In early turbojet engines, the noise occurred behind the exhaust nozzles when the hot exhaust gases mixed with the cool atmospheric gas. The high-bypass turbofan engines alleviated this noise problem. Nevertheless, noise issues continue with the fan noise and core noise in high-bypass turbofan engines. Fan noise can be either broadband, discrete tone, or multiple tone, depending on whether the tip speed of the fan rotor blades is subsonic or supersonic. Core noise includes the noise from the rotation of the compressor, the noise from the turbulence generated in the combustion chamber, and the noise from the turbine.

Aircraft noise is regulated by federal rules that become increasingly stringent with time. Aircraft are classified as either stage one, for very noisy, 1960s-era jetliners; stage two, for moderately noisy, 1970s-era jetliners; or stage three, for more quiet, modern aircraft. Beginning in the year 2000, only stage-three aircraft may operate in the United States and Europe. Supersonic commercial aircraft, such as the Concorde, operate under different regulations and are only allowed to take off and land at certain airports because of the noise they make during take-off. In actuality, the Concorde was not allowed to fly over North American airspace at supersonic speeds, and after the fatal crash of a Concorde, the entire fleet was grounded after twenty-two years of service. An updated version of the aircraft is scheduled to fly only by Emirates Airline in the Middle East, beginning in 2022.

To reduce external noise, the exhaust stream velocity may be decreased by flying jets that have a turbofan engine with a bypass ratio of five or higher. Such engines reduce exhaust noise considerably. With lower levels of external noise, internal noises are more audible.

To reduce internal noise, the fan tip speed can be decreased, although this would result in the necessity of more compressor stages, therefore resulting in a heavier engine. More spacing between the rotor and stator would also lessen the noise, but the larger spaces would require a larger engine.

—*Said Elghobashi*

Further Reading

Crumpsty, Nicholas, and Andrew Heyes. *Jet Propulsion: A Simple Guide to the Aerodynamics and Thermodynamic Design and Performance of Jet Engines.* Cambridge UP, 2015.

Giffard, Hermione. *Making Jet Engines in World War II: Britain, Germany and the United States.* U of Chicago P, 2016.

Golley, John. *Jet: Frank Whittle and the Invention of the Jet Engine.* Datum Publishing Ltd., 2009.

Hunecke, Klaus. *Jet Engines: Fundamentals of Theory, Design and Operation.* Crowood Press, UK, 2010.

Rolls-Royce. *The Jet Engine.* 5th ed., Wiley, 2015.

See also: Aeronautical engineering; Fluid dynamics; Propulsion technologies; Turbojets and turbofans; Turboprops

K

KINEMATICS

Fields of Study: Physics; Mechanics; Mathematics

ABSTRACT

Kinematics is the branch of classical mechanics concerned with the motion of particles or objects without explicit consideration of the masses and forces involved. Kinematics focuses on the geometry of motion and the relationship between position, velocity, and acceleration vectors of particles as they move.

KEY CONCEPTS

acceleration: the rate of change of velocity associated with a change in speed or direction of motion or both; going faster

angular displacement: the measure of deviation from the vertical or equilibrium position

angular velocity: the rate of change of position of a body moving in a circle, commonly measured in rotations per minute

biomechanics: the study of how (human) organisms function with regard to movement

circular motion: motion of an object by translation on a circular, rather than linear, path

differential equation: a relationship between the derivatives of one or more functions and the functions themselves

dynamics: the science that deals with the motion of systems of bodies under the influence of forces; dynamics deals with the causes of motion

force: an action or reaction that attempts to cause the body to move along its own line of action

speed: the rate at which an object moves, regardless of the direction in which it moves

velocity: the rate of change of the position of a body, measured in terms of distance per unit time (e.g., meters per second) and associated with a specific direction

WHAT IS KINEMATICS?

Kinematics is the branch of classical mechanics concerned with the motion of particles or objects without explicit consideration of the masses and forces involved. Kinematics focuses on the geometry of motion and the relationship between position, velocity, and acceleration vectors of particles as they move. Kinematics is a subfield of classical mechanics, along with statics (the study of physical systems for which the forces are in equilibrium) and dynamics (the study of objects in motion under the influence of unequilibrated forces). In practice, kinematic equations appear in fields as diverse as astrophysics (e.g., to describe planetary orbits and the motion of other celestial bodies) and robotics (e.g., to describe the motion of an articulated arm on an assembly line).

MOTION OF A PARTICLE IN ONE DIMENSION

Kinematics focuses on the geometry of the motion of a particle, or point-like object, by investigating the relationship between position, velocity, and acceleration vectors of a particle without involving mass or force.

To describe mathematically the motion of a particle, it is first necessary to define a reference frame, or coordinate system, relative to which the motion of the particle is measured. For a particle moving in one dimension, a coordinate frame would be a number line.

The position, at time t, of a particle moving on a straight line can be described by its distance, x(t), from a fixed point on the coordinate number line identified as the origin (x = 0).

The velocity v(t) of the particle is the rate of change of its position with respect to time. Velocity is a vector quantity, which includes both the speed of the particle and its direction of motion. In one dimension, the speed of the particle is given by the absolute value of the velocity, $|v(t)|$. The direction of motion is given by the sign of v(t), with negative and positive values corresponding to motion to the left and right, respectively.

In general, the velocity is the first derivative, or rate of change, of the particle's position with respect to time:

$$v = \frac{dx}{dt}$$

In the special case of a particle moving at constant velocity v in one dimension, the position of the particle is given by $x(t) = vt + x_0$, where x_0 is the initial position of the particle at time t = 0.

The acceleration a(t) of a particle is the rate of change of its velocity vector with respect to time. Acceleration is also a vector quantity and includes both magnitude and direction. In one dimension, the absolute value $|a(t)|$ indicates the strength of the acceleration, or how quickly the velocity is changing. Note that the sign of a(t) is the direction of the acceleration, not of the particle itself. When the sign of the acceleration and velocity are opposite, the speed of the particle will decrease.

In general, the acceleration is the time rate of change of the particle's velocity:

$$a = \frac{dv}{dt}$$

Since velocity v = dx/dt, the acceleration is, equivalently, the second derivative of the particle's position with respect to time:

$$a = \frac{d_2 x}{dt^2}$$

In the special case of a particle moving with constant acceleration a in one dimension, the velocity of the particle is given by $v(t) = at + v0$, where v0 is the initial velocity of the particle at time t = 0, and the position of the particle is given by $x(t) = \frac{1}{2} at^2 + v_0 t + x_0$, where x_0 is the initial position of the particle.

MOTION OF A PARTICLE IN TWO OR THREE DIMENSIONS

The position of a particle moving in two dimensions is a vector quantity. The position vector p is given by its coordinates (x,y) with respect to a coordinate reference frame. Together, the coordinate functions, x(t) and y(t), give the position of the particle at time t.

The trajectory, or path, p(t) = (x(t), y(t)) of the particle is the curve in the plane defined parametrically by the coordinate functions.

Note that magnitude of the position vector, $p = |p| = \sqrt{(x^2 + y^2)}$ measures the distance from the particle to the origin.

As in one dimension, the velocity of a particle moving in two dimensions is the rate of change of its position with respect to time:

$$v(t) = \frac{d}{dt} p(t)$$

where the derivative is performed component wise. Thus, at time t, the velocity vector has x component v(t) = d/dt x(t) and y component v(t) = d/dt y(t).

Of key importance is the fact that the velocity vector v(t) = d/dt p(t) always points in the direction tangent to the trajectory p(t) of the particle, as the instantaneous velocity of the particle points in the direction the particle is moving at that instant.

The acceleration of a particle moving in two dimensions is the rate of change of its velocity vector with respect to time:

$$a(t) = \frac{d}{dt} v(t)$$

where the derivative is again performed component wise. Thus, at time t, the acceleration vector has x component $ax(t) = d/dt\ vx(t)$ and y component $ay(t) = d/dt\ vy(t)$.

Since velocity is, in turn, the time-derivative of position, the components of the acceleration vector are the second derivatives of the coordinate functions. That is, $ax(t) = d_2/dt^2 x(t)$ and $ay(t) = d_2/dt^2 y(t)$.

In three dimensions, the motion of a particle is described similarly, with the trajectory of the particle given parametrically by $p(t) = (x(t), y(t), zy(t))$ and the distance to the origin by $p = |p| = \sqrt{(x^2 + y^2 + z^2)}$. The velocity, v(t), and acceleration, a(t), vectors gain z components as well; namely, $vz(t) = d/dt\ z(t)$ and $az(t) = d_2/dt^2 z(t)$.

OTHER TYPES OF KINEMATIC MOTION

Kinematic considerations can be extended to particles that are rotating about an axis and the motion of a particle with respect to another particle.

A point on a rotating circle of fixed radius is also constrained to move in one dimension. The kinematic equations of a rotating particle have the same form as above, with the linear quantities x, v, and a replaced by their rotational counterparts, angular position θ, angular velocity ω, and angular acceleration α.

The position of a particle may be defined with respect to a point other than the origin. The relative position of a particle with position vector p with respect to the point q is simply the vector difference, p - q. For speeds much less than the speed of light c, the relative velocity and relative acceleration are the first and second time-derivatives of the relative position vector. However, at speeds approaching c, the relative motion of two particles is dictated by the laws of special relativity.

—Anne Collins

Further Reading

Angeles, Jorge. *Rational Kinematics*. Springer Science & Business Media, 2013.

Cohen, Michael. "Classical Mechanics: A Critical Introduction." *Physics & Astronomy*. The Trustees of the University of Pennsylvania, www.physics.upenn.edu/resources/online-textbook-mechanics. Accessed 14 Mar. 2016.

Goel, Anup. *Kinematics of Machinery*. Technical Publications, 2021.

"The Kinematic Equations." *The Physics Classroom*, www.physicsclassroom.com/class/1DKin/Lesson-6/Kinematic-Equations. Accessed 14 Mar. 2016.

Russell, Kevin, John Q. Shen, and Raj S. Sodhi. *Kinematics and Dynamics of Mechanical Systems, Second Edition: Implementation in MATLAB® and SimMechanics®*. CRC Press, 2018.

Waldren, Kenneth J., Gary L. Kinzel, and Sunil K. Agarwal. *Kinematics, Dynamics, and Design of Machinery*. 3rd ed., John Wiley & Sons, 2016.

"What Is a Projectile?" *The Physics Classroom*, www.physicsclassroom.com/class/vectors/Lesson-2/What-is-a-Projectile. Accessed 14 Mar. 2016.

Wittenburg, Jens. *Kinematics: Theory and Applications*. Springer, 2016.

See also: Acceleration; Aeronautical engineering; Aerospace design; Angular forces; Angular momentum; Automated processes and servomechanisms; Biomechanics; Calculus; Centrifugation; Circular motion; Classical or applied mechanics; Differential equations; Dynamics (mechanics); Engineering; Force; Friction; Linear motion; Mechanical engineering; Mechatronics; Moment of inertia; Momentum; Motion; Newton's laws; Pendulums; Potential energy; Projectiles; Rigid-body dynamics; Solid mechanics; Structural engineering; Torque; Vectors

KINETIC ENERGY

Fields of Study: Physics; Engineering; Mechanics; Mathematics

ABSTRACT

Kinetic energy is a property of a mass in motion and the ability of that moving mass to do work. Kinetic energy can take three forms: rotational, translational, and vibrational. Rotational kinetic energy comes from rotational motion, such as that produced from the spinning of Earth on its axis. Translational kinetic energy is generated when an object moves from one position to another, such as water flowing in a river or from a train traveling. Vibrational kinetic energy comes from vibration, such as the oscillation of a loudspeaker's cone.

KEY CONCEPTS

momentum: a property of mass related to the movement of that mass, characterized by the tendency of a mass to remain in motion or motionless unless acted upon by a force, and defined as the product of mass and velocity

rotation: refers to a physical mass revolving about an axis that passes through its center of mass

translation: refers to a physical mass moving from one point to another, either linearly or on a curved path

vibration: refers to a mass oscillating between two points with an appropriate frequency

SUMMARY

Kinetic energy occurs from motion and the object in motion's ability to do work. For example, rivers contain kinetic energy in currents, which can do work by turning a turbine in a dam to drive a generator that produces electricity.

The word "kinetic" is derived from the Greek word for "motion," κιν εςις (*kinesis*), and the word "energy" is the ability to do something ενεγγια (*energia*). Kinetic energy, then, occurs from motion and the object in motion's ability to do work. Kinetic energy can take three forms: rotational, translational, and vibrational. Rotational kinetic energy comes from its rotational motion, such as that produced from the spinning of Earth on its axis. Translational kinetic energy is generated when an object moves from one position to another, such as water flowing in a river or from a train traveling. Vibrational kinetic energy comes from vibration, such as the oscillation of a loudspeaker's cone.

HISTORY

From a historical perspective, Gottfried Leibniz (1646-1716) and Johann Bernoulli (1667-1748) depicted kinetic energy as a living force that was pro-

The cars of a roller coaster reach their maximum kinetic energy when at the bottom of the path. When they start rising, the kinetic energy begins to be converted to gravitational potential energy. The sum of kinetic and potential energy in the system remains constant, ignoring losses to friction. Photo by Brandon R., via Wikimedia Commons.

portional to mass times velocity squared. Gaspard-Gustave de Coriolis (1792-1843) first coined the term "work" and described the concept of kinetic energy in its contemporary form, equal to the expression $1/2 \, mv^2$. William Thomson (Lord Kelvin) (1824-1917) coined the term "kinetic energy" in 1856.

The total kinetic energy of an object is the sum of its translational and rotational forms. In classical physics, the amount of translational kinetic energy can generally be determined by the equation $KE = 1/2 \, mv^2$, with m as the mass of the object and v its speed at the center of the object. (This equation is for an object that is not also rotating, and when v is less than the speed of light.) As with work and potential energy, the quantity of kinetic energy is expressed in joules, with a joule expressed as $kg \cdot m^2/s^2$, where kg is a kilogram, m is a meter, and s is a second. Kinetic energy is a scalar quantity, having magnitude but not direction. Rotational kinetic energy is equal to one-half the product of the moment of inertia around the axis of rotation times the square of the angular velocity. In relativistic physics, kinetic energy is equal to the increase in mass caused by motion multiplied by the square of the speed of light. The kinetic energy of a system is the total kinetic energy of the objects within the system, and is also the capacity to do work on other systems or objects.

From a point of zero kinetic energy when an object is at rest, the level increases as work is done on it and the object accelerates, while the kinetic energy level decreases with deceleration. According to the Work-Energy Principle, the amount of work can be determined by subtracting the initial quantity of kinetic energy from its current quantity. The amount of kinetic energy is relational, subject to the frame of reference. For example, a car being observed by a person moving at the same speed would have zero kinetic energy.

Kinetic energy can be transferred to another object(s) or forms. For example, soccer players can supply kinetic energy from their swinging legs to move a ball a distance on the field or in the air, while the brakes of automobiles dissipate kinetic energy into heat through friction as they slow the vehicle. In the case of the soccer players' kicks, the energy is conserved in what is known as an elastic collision. In inelastic collisions, the total kinetic energy is not conserved as some is turned into other forms, such as the vibrating atoms in heat.

—*Kirk S. Lawrence*

Further Reading

Chen, Sophia, and Andrew Dean Foland. *Energy*. 3rd ed., Infobase Holdings Inc, 2021.

Ling, Samuel J., Jeff Sanny, and William Moebs. *University Physics Volume 1*. Samurai Media Limited, 2017.

Petersen, Kristen. *Understanding Kinetic Energy*. Cavendish Square Publishing LLC, 2014.

Raghuvanshi, G. S. *Engineering Physics*. PHI Learning Pvt Ltd, 2016.

Young, Hugh D. *College Physics*. Addison-Wesley, 2012.

See also: Acceleration; Ballistic weapons; Biomechanics; Celestial mechanics; Centrifugation; Circular motion; Classical or applied mechanics; Dynamics; Flywheels; Friction; Kinematics; Linear motion; Moment of inertia; Motion

KIRCHHOFF, GUSTAV ROBERT

Fields of Study: Physics; Mechanics; Mathematics

ABSTRACT

Gustav Robert Kirchhoff was born March 12, 1824, in Königsberg, Prussia, the present-day city of Kaliningrad, in Russia. He died on October 17, 1887, in Berlin, Germany. Kirchhoff developed a series of physical laws that synthesized knowledge in different fields of physics, including thermodynamics and optics. With Robert Bunsen, Kirchhoff carried out experiments that founded the field of spectroscopy.

KEY CONCEPTS

current: movement of one kind of charge relative to another

resistance: the opposition to the flow of electrical current through a material

spectroscopy: an analytical method in which light from a source is separated into its component wavelengths to reveal distinct wavelengths present due to emission or absent due to absorption

spectrum: a series of distinct wavelengths of electromagnetic radiation characteristic of a particular source

voltage: the difference in electrical potential between two separate points

EARLY LIFE

Gustav Robert Kirchhoff was born in Königsberg, then a city of the Kingdom of Prussia, on March 12, 1824. His father, Carl Friedrich Kirchhoff, was a Prussian law councilor and county judge. His mother, Johanna Henriette, was a homemaker. Kirchhoff was the youngest of three brothers.

Kirchhoff graduated from high school in 1842 and enrolled in the University of Königsberg, intending to study mathematics. At the university, Kirchhoff attended the lectures of noted mathematician Friedrich Julius Richelot, but he was particularly influenced by the physicist Franz Ernst Neumann, who encouraged Kirchhoff to study physics. Kirchhoff's mathematical talent served him well in the developing field of mathematical physics. Kirchhoff published his first scientific paper in 1845, while still a student. The paper articulates a series of laws for calculating the values (such as currents, voltages, and resistances) of electric currents. Kirchhoff discovered these laws while performing practical experiments in Neumann's laboratory. For theoretical background, Kirchhoff built on the work of German physicist Georg Simon Ohm. On the basis of this research, Kirchhoff received his doctorate from the University of Königsberg in 1847.

Kirchhoff's doctoral dissertation earned him a fellowship to study in another city. He initially planned to travel to Paris, France; however, because of political upheaval occurring in France, Kirchhoff instead settled in Berlin. In 1848, Kirchhoff passed his state doctoral exams, which permitted him to teach students in the German university system, and carried out further work on the effect of Ohm's law on currency and resistors in electric circuits.

LIFE'S WORK

In 1850, Kirchhoff was appointed extraordinary professor of experimental physics at the University of Breslau (now Wroclaw, Poland). He proved talented in conducting physical experiments. Based on

Gustav Robert Kirchoff. Photo via Wikimedia Commons. [Public domain.]

his experimental results, Kirchhoff modified the theory of elasticity, eliminating some erroneous assumptions made by the theory's founder, French physicist Siméon Denis Poisson. Kirchhoff's skill with experiments quickly earned him the admiration and lifelong friendship of German chemist Robert Bunsen. From 1851 to 1852, Bunsen was a professor at Breslau. After Bunsen accepted a professorship at the University of Heidelberg in 1852, he persuaded Heidelberg's faculty to offer Kirchhoff the position of professor of physics. Kirchhoff accepted gladly and moved to Heidelberg in 1854. In 1857, Kirchhoff married Clara Richelot, the daughter of his former mathematics professor, with whom he would have several children.

That same year, based on his theoretical calculations, Kirchhoff proposed that the speed of an electric impulse traveling across an ideal wire without resistance would be that of the speed of light. Turning toward the field that would later be called thermodynamics, in 1858, Kirchhoff developed his law of thermochemistry. This law states that the heat of a chemical reaction is determined by the difference in heat capacity (the amount of heat necessary to change the temperature of a substance) between products and reactants.

In 1858, Kirchhoff began a scientific collaboration with Bunsen that culminated in their development of spectroscopy. They built their own spectroscope, and in 1859, Kirchhoff and Bunsen compared the spectrum of sodium chloride vapors with the spectrum of sunlight. This led them to the discovery that spectral analysis of light emitted from a particular source could be used to determine the chemical composition of that source. They published their findings in 1860. That year, Kirchhoff and Bunsen discovered the element cesium by spectroanalysis of local mineral water. In 1861, they discovered rubidium by the same method.

A direct result of Kirchhoff and Bunsen's development of spectroanalysis was Kirchhoff's initial proposal of his law of thermal radiation in 1859. Reiterated in 1860 and reformulated in its final version in 1862, this law states that for anybody that emits and absorbs thermal electromagnetic radiation in thermal equilibrium, the ratio of its emission to its absorption is determined by the wavelength and temperature of its radiation. In 1862, Kirchhoff termed this ideal body a "blackbody"; the radiation that it emits and absorbs is "blackbody radiation."

For his analysis of the solar spectrum and the attendant discovery that when light passes through a gas, the spectral lines emitted by the gas absorb the same lines in the spectrum of the original light, leading to the appearance of dark lines in their place, Kirchhoff was awarded the prestigious Rumsford Medal in 1862. That year, Kirchhoff and Bunsen traveled to England upon the invitation of English chemist Henry Enfield Roscoe. Returning to Heidelberg, Kirchhoff focused on theoretical physics. A foot injury led Kirchhoff to concentrate further on theoretical areas of inquiry, as performing experiments became more difficult.

His wife, Clara, died in 1869, and Kirchhoff married Luise Brömmel, a nurse, three years later. In 1875, Kirchhoff accepted the position of professor of mathematical physics at the University of Berlin. While in Berlin, Kirchhoff developed what would be called the Kirchhoff equations. The series of equations describes mathematically the parameter of how a rigid body moves through the medium of an ideal fluid, a fluid that has no viscosity and cannot be compressed.

Kirchhoff continued to teach at the University of Berlin until 1886. He died in Berlin on the morning of October 17, 1887.

IMPACT

Kirchhoff's aptitude in theoretical physics led him to discover natural laws in many fields of physics, ranging from electromagnetism to spectroscopy to thermodynamics. He was able to synthesize and order many of the empirically based physical advances made previously and develop new laws from his own physical experiments. His collaboration with Robert Bunsen served as model of scientific teamwork, and his discoveries built a foundation from which the next generation of physicists examined both the smallest structure of matter and the composition of distant stellar bodies. Kirchhoff's combination of theoretical and experimental physics led to major advances and inspired further research in numerous fields.

The physical laws discovered and articulated by Kirchhoff have retained their validity and scientific importance. Kirchhoff's law of thermal radiation and his related three laws of spectroscopy proved invaluable for both the field of astrophysics and the development of quantum mechanics by German physicist Max Planck and others. These laws enabled, through spectroscopy, the first analysis of the chemical composition of celestial bodies. Kirchhoff's work on blackbodies and blackbody radiation influenced the work of future generations of astrophysicists. In electrical engineering, Kirchhoff's laws related to current and voltage have become important analytical tools and been incorporated into software applications. Kirchhoff's law of thermochemistry permits calculation of the heat generated by chemical reactions at different temperatures, an issue of importance in physical chemistry and with practical applications in industry.

—*R. C. Lutz*

Further Reading

Ball, David W. *The Basics of Spectroscopy*. SPIE, 2001.

Bartusiak, Marcia. "Deciphering the Solar Spectrum." *Archives of the Universe: 100 Discoveries That Transformed Our Understanding of the Cosmos*, edited by Marcia Bartusiak, Vintage, 2006, pp. 211-17.

Hentschel, Klaus, and Ning Yan Zhu, editors. *Gustav Robert Kirchhhoff's Treatise "On the Theory of Light Rays" (1882): English Translation, Analysis and Commentary*. World Scientific, 2016.

Huebener, Rudolf P., and Heinz Luebbig. *A Focus of Discoveries*. 2nd ed., World Scientific, 2012.

Kirchhoff, Gustav Robert. *Researches on the Solar Spectrum and the Spectra of the Chemical Elements*. Translated by H. E. Roscoe. Creative Media Partners LLC, 2022.

Maloberti, Franco, and Anthony C. Davies. *A Short History of Circuits and Systems*. CRC Press, 2022.

Sayood, Khalid. *Understanding Circuits*. Springer Nature, 2022.

See also: Classical or applied mechanics; Elasticity; Electromagnetism; Grimaldi discovers diffraction; Hertz, Heinrich Rudolf; Hooke, Robert; Magnetism; Newton's laws; Pascal, Blaise; Poisson, Siméon-Denis; Thermodynamics; Vibration

L

Lagrange, Joseph-Louis

Fields of Study: Physics; Engineering; Mechanics; Mathematics

ABSTRACT

One of the most brilliant mathematicians of the mid- to late eighteenth century, Lagrange accomplished astonishing syntheses of the mathematical innovations of his predecessors, especially in the systems underlying classic physics. Almost as remarkable for his winning personality as for his incisive intellect, Lagrange created the mathematical basis of modern mechanics.

KEY CONCEPTS

prime numbers: a number that is evenly divisible only by 1 and itself, such as 1, 3, 5, 7, 13 and a great many others

synthetic geometry: the method of solving mathematical problems through the use of geometric relationships such as inscribed polygons to construct or synthesize a solution

three-body problem: in celestial mechanics, refers to the gravitational and orbital relationship between the Earth, Moon, and Sun; generalized to any situation in which three individual entities rotate about a common central point

EARLY LIFE

Born January 25, 1736, in Turin, in what was then the kingdom of Sardinia of mixed French and Italian though predominantly French descent, Joseph-Louis Lagrange was the first son in an influential and wealthy family. His father, however, once a highly placed cabinet official, burned with the speculative fevers of the early eighteenth century and ended by losing everything. Typically, Lagrange took that in stride, remarking later that losing his inheritance forced him to find a profession; he chose wisely. Although early in his formal education he found mathematics boring, probably because it began with geometry, at age fourteen he chanced on an essay by the astronomer Edmond Halley, which changed his mind, and his life. In this essay, Halley, one of Isaac Newton's disciples, proclaimed the superiority of the new analytical methods of calculus to the old synthetic geometry. From that moment, Lagrange devoted as much time as he could to the new science, becoming a professor of mathematics at the Royal Artillery School in Turin before the age of eighteen.

From the beginning, Lagrange specialized in analysis, starting the trend toward specialization that has since characterized the study of mathematics. His concentration on analytical methods also liberated the discipline for the first time from its dependence on Greek geometry. In fact, of his major work, *Mécanique analytique (Analytical Mechanics)*, first conceived when he was nineteen but not published until 1788, he boasted that it contained not a single diagram. He then stated offhandedly that in the future the physics of mechanics might be approached as a geometry of four dimensions, the three familiar Cartesian coordinates combined with a time coordinate; in such a system, a moving particle could be defined in time and space simultaneously. This system of analyzing mechanics reemerged in 1916, when Albert Einstein employed it to explain his general theory of relativity.

From the ages of nineteen to twenty-three, Lagrange continued as a professor at Turin, producing a number of revolutionary studies in the calculus of variations, analysis of mechanics, theory of sound, celestial mechanics, and probability theory, for which he won a number of international prizes and honors. In 1766, he succeeded Leonhard Euler as court mathematician to Frederick the Great in the Berlin Academy, the most prestigious position of the time. There, freed from lecturing duties, he continued to produce epochal studies in celestial mechanics, number theory, Diophantine analysis, and numerical and literal equations. He also found it possible to marry a younger cousin; the marriage was successful, and Lagrange was later devastated when his wife died of a wasting disease. Characteristically, he tried to overcome his grief by losing himself in his work.

LIFE'S WORK

For most of Lagrange's life, overwork was a habit. Yet it enabled him to achieve much at an early age. At twenty-three, Lagrange wrote an article on the calculus of variations, in which he foreshadowed his later unifying theory on the whole of mechanics, both solids and fluids. This integrated general mechanics in much the same way that Newton's law of gravitation unified celestial motion. Lagrange's theory proceeds from the disarmingly simple observation that all physical force is identical, whether operating in the solid or liquid state, whether aural, visual, or mechanical. It thus integrates a diverse array of physical phenomena, simplifying their study. In the same work, Lagrange applied differential calculus to the theory of probability. He also surpassed Newton by absorbing the mathematical theory of sound into the theory of elastic physical particles, becoming the first to understand sound transmission as straight-line projection through adjacent particles. Furthermore, he put to rest a controversy over the proper mathematical description of a vibrating string, laying the basis of the more general theory of vibrations as a whole. At this early age, Lagrange al-

ready ranked with the giants of his age, Euler and the Bernoulli family.

The next problems Lagrange attacked at Turin were those involved in the libration of the Moon in celestial mechanics: Why does the Moon present the same surface to Earth at every point in its revolution? He deduced the answer to this special instance of the three-body problem, a classic in mechanics, from Newton's law of universal gravitation. For solving this problem, Lagrange won the Grand Prix award of the French Academy in 1764. The academy followed by proposing a four-body problem; Lagrange solved this, winning the prize again in 1766. The academy then proposed a six-body problem involving calculating the relative position of the Sun, Jupiter, and its four then-known satellites. This problem was not completely solvable by modern methods before the development of computers. Nevertheless, Lagrange developed methods of approximation that were superseded only in the twentieth century. After his move to Berlin, for further work on similar problems—the general three-body problem, the motion of the Moon, and cometary disturbances—Lagrange won further awards.

His career in Berlin lasted twenty years; during this career, he distinguished himself by unfailing courtesy, generosity to other mathematicians, and diplomacy in difficult situations—he was a stranger in a strange court, but he thrived. In addition to working on celestial mechanics there, he diverted himself by investigations into number theory, the humble matter of what his age considered higher arithmetic. Quadratic forms and Diophantine analysis—exponential equations—particularly interested him: He first solved the problem of determining for which square numbers x^2, $nx^2 + 1$ is also a square, when n is a nonsquare, for example, n = 3, x = 4. This problem was an ancient one; Lagrange's paper is a classic, couched in his elegant language and supported by his equally elegant reasoning. He followed this by offering the first successful proofs of some of Pierre de Fermat's theorems and the one of John Wilson that states that only prime numbers are factors of the sum of the factorial series of the next lowest number plus one—that is, p divides $(p-1)(p-2)...(3)(2)(1) + 1$ only if it is prime. His most famous proof in number theory shows that every positive integer can be represented as a sum of four integral squares—a theorem that has had extensive applications in many scientific fields. He later did great work—which proved preliminary—on quadratic equations in two unknowns.

Perhaps the most important work of the Berlin period, however, relates to Lagrange's work in modern algebra. In a memoir of 1767 and in later sequels, he investigated the theoretical bases for solving various algebraic equations. Though once again he fell short of providing definitive answers, his work became an invaluable source for the nineteenth century algebraists who succeeded in finding them. The essential principles—that both necessary and sufficient conditions be established before solution—eluded him, but his work contained the clue.

Eventually, Lagrange's propensity for work broke both his body and his spirit. By 1783, he had sunk into a profound depression, in the grip of which he found further work in mathematics impossible. When Frederick died in 1786 and Lagrange fell out of favor in Berlin, he willingly accepted a position with the French Academy. Still, a change of scene brought no renewal of his interest in mathematics. When his monumental *Mécanique Analytique* was published in 1788, Lagrange took no notice of it, leaving a copy unopened on his desk for more than two years. Instead, he turned his attention to various other sciences and the humanities.

It took the French Revolution to reawaken Lagrange's interest in mathematics. Although he could have fled, as many aristocratic scholars did, he did not. The atrocities of the Terror appalled Lagrange, and he had little sympathy with the destructive practices of revolutionary zealots. Yet when appointed to the faculties of the new schools—the École Normale and the École Polytechnique—intended to replace the abolished universities and academies, Lagrange took up his professional duties enthusiastically. Because he became aware of the difficulties his basically unprepared students had with the theoretical bases of calculus, he reformulated the theory to make it independent of concepts of infinitesimals and limits. His attempt was unsuccessful, but he prepared the foundation on which modern theories are built.

Part of his duties at the École Polytechnique required Lagrange to supervise the development of the metric system of weights and measures. Fortunately, he insisted that the base 10 be adopted. Radical reformers lobbied for base 12, alleging superior factorability; it is still occasionally proposed as more "rational," and for centuries it played an infernal role in the British monetary system. To suppress the reformers, Lagrange argued ironically for the advantages of a system with base 11, or any prime, since then all fractions would have the same denominator. A small amount of practice convinced the radicals that 10 was more functional.

Teaching and supervision alone, however, did not suffice to relieve Lagrange's besetting melancholy. He was saved from despair at the age of fifty-six, by the intervention of a young woman, the daughter (Renée-Françoise-Adélaide) of his friend the astronomer Pierre-Charles Lemonnier. She insisted on marrying him despite their disparity in age, and, contrary to all expectations, the marriage proved a brilliant success. For the following twenty years, Lagrange could not bear to have her out of his sight, and she proved to be a faithful companion, adept at drawing him out of his shell. At the end of his life, he worked on a second edition of his masterpiece, *Mécanique Analytique*, adding many profound insights. He was still improving it when death came, gradually and almost imperceptibly, on April 10, 1813, in Paris, France.

SIGNIFICANCE

Joseph-Louis Lagrange ranks with the outstanding mathematicians of all time; in his prime, he was widely recognized as the greatest living mathematician, and he is certainly the most significant figure between Leonhard Euler and Carl Friedrich Gauss. Beyond the quality of his work, he was noted equally for the brilliance of his demonstrations and for his accessibility and personal charm. He is particularly celebrated as one of the classic stylists of mathematical writing, almost the incarnation of mathematical elegance. His composition combines exceptional clarity of description and development with remarkable beauty of phrasing. His language is supple, never stilted or contorted; he somehow seems to ease the effort of strenuous thought. Lagrange once remarked that chemistry was as easy as algebra; in his writing, he is able to make things seem transparent, especially those which seemed particularly dense before reading him.

Perhaps because of this ease of expression, Lagrange is more important for the stimulus he provided for others than for his own original work. Time after time, his contemporaries and descendants found inspiration in him. He made his foundations so complete that others were able to apply them to other cases. In some instances, he was simply ahead of his time; his ideas have had to wait for the ground to be prepared. At any rate, Lagrange's work proved to be extraordinarily rich for those who labored after him.

Lagrange's most important contributions lie in mechanics and the calculus of variations. In fact, the latter is the centerpiece on which all of his achievements depend, the insight he used to integrate the theory of mechanics. This calculus derives from the ancient principle of least action or least time, which concerns the determination of the path a beam of light will follow when passing through or refracting off layers of varying densities.

Hero of Alexandria began the inquiry by determining that a beam reflected from a series of mirrors reaches its object by following the shortest possible route; that is, it is the minimum of a function. René Descartes elaborated on the theory by experimenting with the effects of various lenses on a ray of light, showing that refraction also produced minima. Lagrange then proceeded to demonstrate that the general postulates for matter and motion established by Newton, which did not seem to harmonize, also fit this scheme of minima. Thus, he used a principle of economy in nature—that physical mechanics also tended to minimal extremes—to unify the principles of particles in motion. This not only was revolutionary in his time but also gave rise to the further integrating work of William Rowan Hamilton and James Clerk Maxwell, and eventually blossomed in Einstein's general theory of relativity.

—James Livingston

Further Reading

Caddeo, Renzo, and Athanase Papadopoulos, editors. *Mathematical Geography in the Eighteenth Century: Euler, Lagrange and Lambert.* Springer Nature, 2022.

Canbolat, Hüseyin. *Lagrangian Mechanics.* IntechOpen, 2017.

Lagrange, Joseph Louis. *Lectures on Elementary Mathematics.* Translated by Thomas Joseph McCormack. 2nd ed., Open Court Publishing Company, 1901.

Lagrange, J. L. *Analytical Mechanics.* Translated by A. Boissonaide and V. N. Vagliente. Springer Science & Business Media, 2013.

Vanier, Jacques, and Cipriana Tomescu. *Universe Dynamics: The Least Action Principle and Lagrange's Equations.* CRC Press, 2019.

See also: Acoustics; Bernoulli, Daniel; Bernoulli's principle; Calculus; Celestial mechanics; Circular motion; Classical or applied mechanics; D'Alembert's axioms of motion; Differential equations; Dynamic systems theory; Euler paths; Euler's laws of motion; Gauss's law; Inertial guidance; Laplace, Pierre-Simon; Newton, Isaac; Newton's laws

LAPLACE, PIERRE-SIMON

Fields of Study: Physics; Mechanics; Mathematics

ABSTRACT

Pierre-Simon Laplace was born March 23, 1749, in Beaumont-en-Auge, France, and died March 5, 1827, in Paris, France. As a mathematician, he made groundbreaking mathematical contributions to probability theory and statistical analysis. Using Isaac Newton's theory of gravitation, he performed detailed mathematical analyses of the shape of the Earth and the orbits of comets, planets, and their moons.

KEY CONCEPTS

accretion: the gradual formation of a larger body by the accumulation due to gravity or other attractive force of smaller bodies into a single mass

accretion disc: a circular region of space in which there are numerous particles of various sizes in an essentially planar array orbiting about the center of the region

nebular hypothesis: the concept that stars and planets form by the accretion of particles within a spinning disc composed of particles in space

probability: the numerical likelihood that a specific event will occur in random events occurring within a set of defined conditions; for example, the occurrence of the 6 appearing on the roll of a standard cubic die

statistics: collections of specified data points used as the basis for probability calculations; for example, the outcomes of a number of rolls of a standard cubic die

EARLY LIFE

Pierre-Simon Laplace was born into a well-established and prosperous family of farmers and merchants in Beaumont-en-Auge, Normandy, France. Laplace's father encouraged him to pursue an ecclesiastical career, so he attended the Benedictine school in Beaumont-en-Auge between the ages of seven and sixteen. He developed an interest in mathematics during his studies at the University of Caen, which he began in 1766.

Laplace soon moved to Paris to pursue a career in mathematics; he would remain a resident of Paris and the surrounding area for the rest of his life. Soon after his arrival in Paris, he sought and won the patronage of Jean Le Rond d'Alembert, a mathematician, physicist, and philosopher with great influence among French intellectuals. D'Alembert found Laplace employment teaching mathematics to military cadets at the École Militaire, and it was in this position that Laplace wrote his first papers on mathematics and astronomy.

Some of Laplace's earliest mathematical interests involved the calculation of odds in games of chance.

Pierre Simon LaPlace. Image via iStock/traveler1116. [Used under license.]

Laplace played a major role in the early development of the systematic study of probability, carrying it beyond the rules of thumb of gambling and the preliminary conclusions of earlier mathematicians. He emphasized the relevance of probability to the analysis of statistics, particularly the importance of being able to calculate an appropriate average, or mean value, from a collection of observations. Furthermore, he argued that this mean value should be calculated in such a way as to minimize its difference from the actual value of the quantity being measured.

Statistical problems of this type inspired Laplace's initial interest in astronomy. He became intrigued by the process through which new astronomical data could be incorporated into calculations of probabilities for future observations. In particular, he concentrated on the application of Sir Isaac Newton's law of universal gravitation to the motions of the comets and planets.

LIFE'S WORK

In 1773, at the relatively young age of twenty-four, Laplace was elected to the French Academy of Sciences as a mathematician. This achievement was based upon the merits of thirteen papers he had presented to academy committees for review. As a member of the academy, he served on numerous research and evaluative committees that were commissioned by the French government. In 1788, he married Marie-Charlotte de Courty de Romanges, with whom he would have two children.

Following the French Revolution in 1789, Laplace became an influential designer and advocate of the metric system of scientific units. The academy was disbanded during the radical phase of the Revolution in 1793, but in 1796 Laplace became the president of the scientific class of the new Institut de France. The institute offered highly publicized prizes for essays in physics and mathematics, and Laplace exerted a powerful influence on French

physics through the attention he devoted to his choice of topics and his support for his preferred candidates. He also played an important part in the early organization of the École Polytechnique, the prestigious school of engineering founded in 1794. Although Laplace lived through turbulent political changes, he remained in positions of high scientific status through the Napoleonic era and into the Bourbon Restoration, when he was raised to the nobility as a marquis.

In 1812, Laplace published the first of two major works on probability theory, *Théorie analytique des probabilités* (*Analytic Theory of Probability*). The volume was the first comprehensive treatise devoted entirely to the subject of probability and provides a groundbreaking, though necessarily imperfect, characterization of the techniques, subject matter, and practical applications of the new field. Although the book relies on the traditional problems generated by games of chance such as lotteries, Laplace's work points toward the future by generalizing these methods and applying them to many other topics. For example, because the calculation of odds in games of chance so often requires the summation of long series of fractions, each term of which differs from the others according to a regular pattern, Laplace begins by reviewing some of the methods he discovered to approximate the sums of such series, particularly when very large numbers are involved.

Théorie analytique articulates what has since come to be called Bayes's theorem, after one of Laplace's early predecessors. This theorem describes how to use partial or incomplete information to calculate the conditional probability of an event in terms of its absolute or unconditional probability and the conditional probability of its cause. Laplace was one of the first to make extensive use of this theorem; it was particularly important to him because of its relevance to how calculations of probability should change in response to new knowledge.

Théorie analytique also includes Laplace's applications of his mathematical techniques to problems generated by the analysis of data from such diverse topics as census figures, insurance rates, instrumentation error, astronomy, geodesy, election prognostication, and jury selection.

Published in 1814, *Essai philosophique sur les probabilités* (*A Philosophical Essay on Probabilities*, 1902) became one of Laplace's most widely read works. In it, Laplace states and relies upon a definition of probability that has been a source of considerable philosophical debate. Given a situation in which specific equally possible cases are the results of various processes, such as rolling dice, and correspond to favorable or unfavorable events, Laplace defines the probability of an event as the fraction formed by dividing the number of cases that correspond to or cause that event by the total number of possible cases. When the cases in question are not equally possible, such as when the dice are loaded, the calculation must be altered to take this information into account.

In addition to probability theory, Laplace was interested in the application of Newton's law of universal gravitation to the solar system. Since Newton's publication of his theory in 1686, mathematicians and physicists had reformulated his results using increasingly sophisticated mathematics; by Laplace's time, the theory could be expressed using a type of mathematics known as partial differential equations. Laplace applied Newton's results to the orbits of the planets, moons, and comets. His most famous calculations include his demonstrations of the long-term periodic variations in the orbits of Jupiter and Saturn, which contributed to an increasing knowledge of the stability and internal motions of the solar system. He also applied gravitation theory to the tides, the shape of the Earth, and the rings of Saturn. His hypothesis that the solar system was formed by the condensation of a diffuse solar atmosphere became a starting point for more detailed subsequent theories. Newtonian gravitation theory became Laplace's model for precision and clarity in all other branches of physics, and he encouraged his colleagues to attempt similar analyses in optics, heat, electricity, and magnetism.

PIERRE-SIMON LAPLACE ADVANCES THE NEBULAR HYPOTHESIS

The nebular hypothesis proposes that solar systems form out of gas clouds, or nebulae. As these clouds rotate and cool, they slowly assume a disk-like shape. In the central region of a cloud, where gravity causes the density to be highest, particles begin to stick to one another; when the mass and density at the center are great enough, these particles form a star. Meanwhile, at the outskirts of the disk, particles agglomerate and form planets as well as celestial bodies such as moons and asteroids.

The nebular hypothesis was first suggested by Swedish scientist Emanuel Swedenborg in the first half of the eighteenth century, then reiterated by German philosopher Immanuel Kant in 1755. Pierre-Simon Laplace independently developed this idea and first articulated it in his work *Exposition du système du monde* (1796; *The System of the World*, 1809). Laplace had done a great deal of mathematical work on the laws of probability, using differential and integral calculus in new ways. These analyses formed the mathematical foundations of his nebular hypothesis.

The model proposed by Laplace had enormous influence on the development of scientific study of the solar system. A number of astronomers and physicists were critical of the hypothesis, arguing that it did not account for certain elements of planetary motion. However, it provided explanations for why planets revolve around the sun, move in the same direction, and rotate on their axes—explanations that were consistent with generally accepted elements of Newtonian mechanics. In light of these factors, scientists quickly accepted Laplace's theory. Some later individuals and groups objected to the hypothesis on religious grounds, as it contradicted the traditional religious views of the creation of the universe. Nevertheless, the nebular hypothesis became the standard model for understanding the development of the solar system through the entire nineteenth century.

Early in the twentieth century, new physical observations indicated that nearly all of the angular momentum of the solar system is concentrated in the planets. Laplace's system could not account for this, and the nebular hypothesis fell out of favor. However, Laplace's system was revived in the 1970s, supplemented by the solar nebular disk model proposed by Russian astronomer Victor Safronov, and once again came to be regarded as the standard model for understanding how the solar system formed. Developments in radio and optical telescope technology have resulted in the discovery of hundreds of planets around stars outside the Earth's solar system. These newly identified solar systems are generally considered to be consistent with the latest version of the nebular hypothesis.

Laplace died in Paris on March 5, 1827.

IMPACT

Laplace's cultural influence extended far beyond the relatively small circle of mathematicians who could appreciate the technical details of his work. He has become a symbol of some important aspects of the rapid scientific progress that took place during his career, resulting from his role in institutional changes in the scientific profession and the implications of his conclusions and methods. Aside from his work in probability and statistics, which had a direct influence on the work of later mathematicians, aspects of Laplace's work have contributed to general perceptions of the goals, limitations, and methods of science. Taking Newton's theory of gravitation as his model, Laplace believed that although human knowledge of nature is always limited, there are inevitable regularities that can be approximately ex-

pressed with ever-increasing accuracy. Laplace thus became a symbol of nineteenth-century scientific determinism, which is the view that uncertainty about the future is only the result of human ignorance of the natural laws that determine its every detail.

Similarly, Laplace's style of mathematical physics has become a primary example of a reductionist research strategy. Laplace believed that just as the gravitational effect of a large mass is determined by the sum of the forces exerted by all of its parts, so do all phenomena reduce to collections of individual interactions. His success in implementing this method contributed to its widespread perception as a necessary component of scientific investigation.

—*James R. Hofmann*

Further Reading

Chatterjee, Shoutir Kishore. *Statistical Thought: A Perspective and History*. Oxford UP, 2007.

Daston, Lorraine. *Classical Probability in the Enlightenment*. Princeton UP, 2021.

Gillispie, Charles Coulston. *Pierre-Simon Laplace, 1749-1827: A Life in Exact Science*. Princeton UP, 2018.

Hahan, Roger, and Roger Hahn. *Pierre-Simon Laplace, 1749-1827: A Determined Scientist*. Harvard UP, 2005.

Laplace, Pierre-Simon. *Pierre-Simon Laplace Philosophical Essay on Probabilities: Translated from the Fifth French Edition of 1825 with Notes by the Translator*. Translated by A. I. Dale. Springer New York, 2011.

Montemar, Claire. *Probability Theory and Examples*. Arcler Press, 2017.

See also: Calculus; Celestial mechanics; D'Alembert's axioms of motion; Motion; Quantum mechanics

LEIBNIZ, GOTTFRIED WILHELM

Fields of Study: Physics; Mechanics; Mathematics

ABSTRACT

Gottfried Wilhelm Leibniz was born July 1, 1646, in the city of Leipzig, and died November 14, 1716, in Hanover, both in what was then the Holy Roman Empire, but now Germany. Baron von Leibniz was a philosopher and mathematician. He developed both differential and integral calculus and is recognized today as the founder of symbolic logic. He also invented the stepped reckoner, an early calculator, and devised binary arithmetic.

KEY CONCEPTS

differential calculus: the study of mathematical relationships based on the differences of values between points that satisfy the relationship

integral calculus: the study of mathematical relationships based on determining the area bounded by a curve or other function based on dividing that area into infinitesimal "slices" of area and summing them together, or integrating them

GOTTFRIED WILHELM LEIBNIZ'S CONTRIBUTIONS TO CALCULUS AND THE PHILOSOPHY OF LOGIC

Leibniz is recognized as one of the leading intellectuals of the seventeenth and eighteenth centuries, having made major contributions to the development of mathematics and philosophy. His introduction to advanced mathematics came in 1672, when he began studying with Dutch mathematician and physicist Christiaan Huygens in Paris. It was during this time that Leibniz began working on infinite series, integrals, and derivatives, elements of what would later be called calculus.

During this same period, English physicist and mathematician Isaac Newton was independently developing the calculus system on his own. When Newton learned of Leibniz's efforts, he began a correspondence, which became tense when Newton came to believe that Leibniz had stolen some of his ideas. The Royal Society, after evaluating the case, recognized Newton for developing his system of calculus first; however, recent historians have verified that Leibniz developed his calculus independently of Newton. Over the ensuing decades, as mathemati-

Gottfried Leibniz. Image via iStock/ilbusca. [Used under license.]

cians struggled to expand upon basic calculus, it became clear that Leibniz had produced the more rigorous and fully realized version of the system.

In addition to his work on calculus, Leibniz is credited with refining the binary number system, which would later become the basis for all computing technology, and also made important advances in the field that would come to be known as symbolic logic. Though unpublished during his lifetime, his work anticipated that of English mathematician George Boole and strove toward a notational method for understanding basic propositions and claims. Leibniz's interest in computing and calculating engines led him to create and design numerous models for calculating machines. He is credited with inventing the pinwheel calculator, a small handheld calculator that performs addition and subtraction. While his stepped reckoner (another type of calculator) was not precise enough an instrument to work dependably, the operating mechanism, the Leibniz wheel, provided the model for similar machines in the centuries that followed.

As a philosopher, Leibniz was interested in a variety of fields, from metaphysics to logic. In his investigations of metaphysics, Leibniz theorized a system based on fundamental energetic particles he called monads, which he imagined as the fundamental constituents of all matter. He described the philosophy surrounding monads in his short work *Monadology* (1714). Leibniz also made significant contributions to physics; he was among the first to state the fundamental idea of the conservation of energy in mechanical systems—an important concept that was not formally developed or accepted until the mid-nineteenth century, long after Leibniz's initial essays on the subject.

EARLY LIFE

Gottfried Wilhelm Leibniz was born in 1646 in Leipzig, Saxony (then an electorate of the Holy Roman Empire, now in Germany), the son of Friedrich Leibniz and Katherina Schmuck. At the age of fifteen, he entered the University of Leipzig, where he studied such scientific writings as Francis Bacon's "*De Augmentis*" and the works of Galileo Galilee, Johannes Kepler, and René Descartes. One of his professors was Jacob Thomasius, one of the last of the scholastic group of philosophers. Hoping to earn a degree in law, Leibniz spent one term at the University of Jena, where he was introduced to the study of mathematics.

Upon submitting his doctoral dissertation, Leibniz was denied the degree due to his young age. He left Leipzig and never returned. He submitted his dissertation to the University of Altdorf in Nuremberg and was immediately awarded a degree. The rectors of the university were so pleased with his dissertation that they offered him a professorship, which he turned down.

Leibniz joined the Rosicrucian Society, an order of alchemists, and worked as secretary of the Nuremberg branch. At the time, alchemy and chemistry were considered one science. During this period, Leibniz met Johann Christian von Boineburg, a prominent statesman, and soon afterward went to Frankfurt to work for him. At Boineburg's suggestion, Leibniz wrote "*A New Method of Learning and Teaching Jurisprudence*" in 1667. He submitted the work to Johann Philipp von Schönborn, the elector (duke) of Mainz, who then hired Leibniz to reform the law code.

LIFE'S WORK

When Leibniz was twenty-three years old, Schönborn commissioned him to write a tract to influence the election of the Polish king. The tract was presented as an objective attempt to apply mathematical principles to politics, and Leibniz used a pseudonym to make it appear to have been written by a native Pole; by the time the tract was printed, however, it was too late to influence the election. In 1670, Leibniz edited and prefaced Marius Nizolius's *Antibarbarus* (1563) and wrote an attack against the Socinians, early Protestants who denied the divinity of Christ. He also wrote two treatises on dynamics, authored papers protesting France's designs for the rest of Europe, and began extensive international correspondences that would continue throughout his life. More than fifteen thousand of his letters have survived.

Leibniz wrote a memorandum suggesting that French king Louis XIV be persuaded to expel the Turks from Egypt and leave Germany alone, on the strength of which Schönborn sent Leibniz to Paris in 1672 to attempt to persuade the king. Like virtually all of Leibniz's diplomatic endeavors, the mission to Paris failed, but it did give him the opportunity to study with famed Dutch mathematician Christiaan Huygens, who was living in Paris at the time. Later that year, Leibniz's benefactor Boineburg died, making Leibniz's position in Mainz no longer secure.

In 1673, Leibniz traveled to London for another diplomatic mission. While there, he demonstrated a calculating machine of his own design to the Royal Society. Leibniz called his invention the "stepped reckoner" because it used a stepped-drum mechanism with teeth of varied lengths, later called the Leibniz wheel. The calculator, which performed addition, subtraction, multiplication, and division, was an improvement on that of French mathematician Blaise Pascal. Although some members of the Royal Society were critical of the machine, the invention earned Leibniz membership into the society. Leibniz gradually turned to other scientific pursuits, but the design of the Leibniz wheel was not improved for nearly two hundred years.

Leibniz developed infinitesimal calculus, the computational method concerned with infinitely small values, in 1675. This achievement was his greatest contribution to mathematics, and also the cause of a bitter dispute with English scientist Isaac Newton, who had developed calculus in 1665 but had not published his results. When Leibniz published papers on differential calculus (1684) and integral calculus (1686), Newton, who finally published in 1687, charged Leibniz with stealing his methods. The matter was submitted to the Royal Society, which finally decided in favor of Newton in 1713. The dispute resulted in a rift between English and German scientists. Both Leibniz and Newton erred in stating the principles of calculus, but today mathematicians use Leibniz's system of notation. It is now recognized that both men arrived at their results independently.

In 1676, John Frederick, Duke of Brunswick-Lüneburg appointed Leibniz as his librarian and historian, a position that required extensive traveling and writing. Leibniz was also involved in many other projects, advocating practical education and the founding of academies. He worked to develop mechanical devices such as clocks, windmills, lamps, carriages, and submarines. Leibniz also studied music theory and developed a language that he thought could be translated into music. Harmony in music, religion, philosophy, and politics was a major concern throughout his life.

At the age of thirty-three, Leibniz developed a binary system of arithmetic, using two as a base. English mathematician George Boole developed the system into Boolean algebra in the nineteenth century; today, the binary system is used to design electronic computer circuits. Around the same time, in 1679, John Frederick died and was succeeded by his brother, Ernst Augustus I. The new duke's wife and daughter, both named Sophie, became Leibniz's patrons. They were instrumental in helping Leibniz persuade Frederick I of Prussia to establish the Berlin Academy of Sciences in 1700.

In the years that followed, Leibniz worked as an engineer in the mines of Germany's Harz mountain range, where he invented a windmill-driven water pump and proposed the theory that the Earth was originally molten, making him one of the founders of the science of geology. At the same time, he was working on dynamics and his increasingly anti-Cartesian philosophy. Leibniz tried to develop a mechanical model of the universe, believing that it ran according to fixed laws rather than the whim of the supernatural, and developed the principle of sufficient reason, which holds that nothing occurs without a reason. In 1710, he published *Essais de Théodicée sur la bonté de Dieu, la liberté de l'homme et l'origine du mal* (*Theodicy: Essays on the Goodness of God, the Freedom of Man and the Origin of Evil*, 1952), or *Théodicée* for short, in an attempt to reconcile evil with what he concluded must be the best of all possible worlds; this idea led to Voltaire's satire of Leibniz in *Candide* (1759). However, he is perhaps best known for his philosophical doctrine of monads, which he believed to be immaterial entities of varying complexity and awareness that form a continuum from God down through the simplest creature and are related to each other through "preestablished harmony."

In 1712, Tsar Peter the Great of Russia appointed Leibniz imperial privy councilor, a post that kept him in Vienna until 1714. That year, Georg Ludwig, who had succeeded Ernst Augustus as duke of Brunswick-Lüneburg, was called to England to reign as George I. Leibniz asked him for a post but was refused. Banished to Hanover, Leibniz struggled for the next two years to complete a history of the House of Hanover for George I. He died on November 14, 1716, at the age of seventy.

IMPACT

Leibniz's work was not fully appreciated until over a century after his death. He made important contributions to mathematics, including formal notation, and to philosophy, such as the identity of indiscernibles—a principle holding that if entities are identical, they share all properties. His work regarding binary arithmetic has proved crucial to the language of modern computers. While Leibniz's early calculator, the stepped reckoner, was not precise enough an instrument to work dependably, the operating mechanism provided the model for similar machines in the centuries that followed. Leibniz has been ranked with Newton and Aristotle as one of the most original thinkers of the Western philosophical tradition. His contributions to philosophy include the theory of possible worlds, space-time frameworks, and the principle of sufficient reason.

—*Ellen Bailey*

Further Reading
Antognazza, Maria Rosa. *Leibniz: An Intellectual Biography*. Cambridge UP, 2011.
———. *Leibniz: A Very Short Introduction*. Oxford UP, 2016.
Caro, Herman D. *The Best of All Possible Worlds? Leibniz's Philosophical Optimism and Its Critics 1710-1755*. BRILL, 2020.
Jolley, Nicholas. *Leibniz*. Routledge, 2005.
Leibniz, Gottfried Wilhelm. *Theodicy: Essays on the Goodness of God, the Freedom of Man and the Origin of Evil*. Cosimo, 2009.
Rescher, Nicholas. *On Leibniz*. U of Pittsburgh P, 2003.
Strickland, Lloyd. *Leibniz's Monadology: A New Translation and Guide*. Edinburgh UP, 2014.

See also: Archimedes; Aristotle isolates science as a discipline; Calculus; Classical or applied mechanics; Differential equations; Euclid; Euclidean geometry; Geometry; Newton, Isaac; Newton's laws; Pascal, Blaise; Poisson, Siméon Denis; Quantum mechanics

LENZ'S LAW

Fields of Study: Physics; Mechanics; Mathematics

ABSTRACT

Coils react to any change in the magnetic environment around them. Induced currents are created in the coils to work against any change in magnetic field. Lenz's law states that in order to conserve energy, the induced current in a loop produces a magnetic field, which then opposes any changes in the existing magnetic field through the loop. By using coils and changing magnetic fields, humans have been producing electricity for decades.

KEY CONCEPTS

conservation of energy: the total amount of energy in a closed system is always the same, therefore energy can neither be created nor destroyed

current: the motion of charged particles as a function of time

electromagnetic field: a field created by the motion of charged particles

Faraday's law: a physical law that explains how changes in the strength of magnetic fields through coils induce a current in the coil to counteract the change in the magnetic field

inductance: the property by which a current is created in conductors to resist a change in the magnetic field through the conductor

right-hand rule: a technique used to find the direction of magnetic forces and induced currents by using the right hand; the direction of the current is expressed by the fingers, and the direction of the magnetic field is expressed by the extended thumb

INDUCED CURRENTS

Michael Faraday (1791-1867) was a British scientist who experimented extensively with currents. Although he had no formal training in physics, he was able to discover an important relation between electricity and magnetism. Faraday found that currents are induced by changing magnetic fields and currents create magnetic fields. The motion of charged particles creates electromagnetic fields. The two physical concepts are related. This is the basis of electric generators. By spinning coils around magnets or magnets around coils, electricity can be produced. Because Faraday did not have any formal training, he could not explain these effects with mathematics. It took many years and the work of Scottish physicist James C. Maxwell (1831-79) to discover the mathematical law that explains Faraday's discoveries. In order to correctly predict the behavior of induced currents, Maxwell had to include Lenz's law. The law states that the induced current in a loop produces a magnetic field, which then opposes any changes in the existing magnetic field through the loop.

THE MAGNETIC FIELD OF A CAR

When a motor vehicle stops at a traffic signal, a sensor is activated in order to detect the waiting vehicle. Many people assume that a pressure sensor is used, but if that were the case, smaller vehicles such as motorcycles would have a hard time activating the sensor. Instead, an inductive loop sensor is used,

and it is designed to detect changes in the magnetic field.

Cars and other motor vehicles are made of parts that contain ferromagnetic materials, which create magnetic fields. When a car stops at a red light, the magnetic field produced by the car induces a current in an inductive loop sensor. The size of the current created is relative to the magnetic field's strength and the inductance of the coil. This, in part, is analyzed by the electronics near the traffic light, which then trigger the light to change. These inductive loop sensors work on two basic laws of electromagnetism: Faraday's law and Lenz's law.

Faraday's law states that changes in the strength of magnetic fields through coils induce a current in the coil to counteract the change in the magnetic field. An inductive loop sensor is basically a loop of wire. The voltage induced (V_{ind}) in the inductive loop

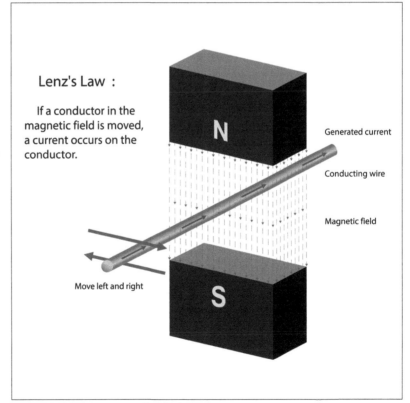

Image via iStock/Tsezer. [Used under license.]

or any other coil of wire is equal to the magnetic flux ($\Delta\Phi$) divided by the amount of time it takes for the field to change (t), expressed as

$$V_{ind} = -\frac{\Delta\Phi}{\Delta t}$$

The magnetic flux is a function of the magnetic field strength (B), the cross-sectional area of the loop exposed to the magnetic field (A), the number of turns in the loop (N), and the amount of time it takes for the field to change (t), or BA

$$V_{ind} = -N\left(\frac{\Delta(BA)}{\Delta t}\right)$$

In the example above, the area of the loop permeated by the magnetic field is constant. Therefore, the equation can be simplified to

$$V_{ind} = -N\left(A\frac{\Delta B}{\Delta t}\right)$$

In order to find the current through the loop, one must apply Ohm's law in combination with Faraday's law. Ohm's law states that the voltage (V) is the product of the current (I) and the resistance (R), or

$$V = IR$$

By substituting this into Faraday's law, the induced current in the inductive loop sensor can be obtained. Mathematically, this is expressed as

$$V_{ind} = -N\left(A\frac{\Delta B}{\Delta t}\right)$$

$$IR = -N\left(A\frac{\Delta B}{\Delta t}\right)$$

$$I_{ind} = -\left(\frac{NA}{R}\right)\left(\frac{\Delta B}{\Delta t}\right)$$

Lenz's law explains why a negative sign precedes the equation in Faraday's law. If the negative sign were not included, it would mean the induced current could create a magnetic field that enhances the existing magnetic field through the coil. In turn, this magnetic field would produce more current that would then produce even more magnetic field. The system would produce a feedback that would take the current into infinity. The law of conservation of energy states that in a closed system, the total amount of energy is always the same; energy in a closed system can neither be created nor destroyed. If an infinite current is induced, the implication is an infinite amount of energy, which is impossible. The negative sign in Faraday's law carries this second important property. It balances the magnetic field and makes the system conserve energy by keeping the induced currents opposing any change.

In order to correctly find the directions of the induced currents, a simple technique was devised. This technique, known as the right-hand rule, uses an individual's right hand. First, point the fingers of the right hand in the direction of the current. If it is a coil, curl the fingers so that they are pointing in the direction of the current. Next, extend the thumb, which will then be pointing in the direction of the induced magnetic field. This technique is also effective if the thumb of the right hand is first pointed in the direction of the induced magnetic field, with the fingers then naturally curling in the direction of the induced current.

Induction opposes the change in flux of a magnetic field (B). When a magnet passes through a coil, the change in magnetic field (B_{mag}) induces a current (I) in the coil according to the right-hand rule, with a magnetic field (B_{coil}) that moves in the opposite direction.

A SIMPLE ILLUSTRATION OF LENZ'S LAW

A coil of copper wire is being used by high school physics students in order to energize a light bulb. The students bring the north pole of a bar magnet closer to the coil of wire from the left side of the coil.

What is the direction of the induced current in the coil, clockwise or counterclockwise?

$$\Delta\Phi > 0$$

$$\Delta\Phi_{ind} < 0$$

I_{ind} is therefore counterclockwise.

Using Lenz's law, it is understood that a coil's induced current opposes any change in the magnetic environment around it. By bringing a magnet's north pole closer to the coil and from the left, the magnetic field is increasing in strength. Therefore, there are more magnetic field lines going through the coil to the right. The coil opposes this extra field, so it produces a field that is to the left. To find the direction of the current that produces the magnetic field, use the right-hand rule. Place the thumb of the right hand in the direction of the magnetic field, left. Now curl the fingers, and the direction of the fingers is the direction of the induced current, which in this case is counterclockwise.

GENERATING ELECTRICITY

Alternating current (AC) is produced by generators at power plants that use the principles described by Faraday's and Lenz's laws. These generators, whether powered by falling water, steam, or wind, consist of coils of wire and magnets. As the water, steam, or wind makes a turbine spin, the main shaft, which has magnets attached to it, also turns. When a magnet crosses in front of one of the coils, it increases the magnetic field through the coil. This induces a current in the coil, which creates a magnetic field to cancel the extra magnetic field through the coil. As the turbine keeps spinning, the magnet moves away from the coil. Then, the coil has less magnetic field through it, and an induced current is created on the coil to increase the magnetic field through the coil. In other words, coils resist change

and fight against any change in the magnetic field through them. If enough time passes, the coil gets used to the change and the induced currents disappear. But by that time, the shaft has spun more, and another magnet has moved in front of the coil.

—*Angel G. Fuentes*

Further Reading
Balaji, S. *Electromagnetics Made Easy*. Springer Nature, 2020.
Ford, Kenneth W. *Basic Physics*. World Scientific Publishing Company, 2016.
Ling, Samuel J., Jeff Sanny, and William Moebs. *University Physics, Volume 2*. Samurai Media Limited, 2017.
Navas, K. A., and T. A. Suhail. *Basic Electrical and Electronics Engineering: Conceptual Approach*. Rajath Publishers, 2011.
Norton, A., editor. *Dynamic Fields and Waves*. CRC Press, 2019.
Phillips, Peter. *Electrical Principles*. Cengage AU, 2019.
Rahman, Atowar. *Fundamentals of Magnetism and Spintronics*. Zorba Books, 2022.

See also: Automated processes and servomechanisms; Electromagnet technologies Electromagnetism; Gauss's law; Magnetism; Superconductor; Tesla, Nikola

LINEAR MOTION

Fields of Study: Physics; Mechanics; Mathematics

ABSTRACT
Kinematics is the study of the motion of objects, with a focus on linear motion. The motions of small objects, such as marbles, and large objects, such as planets, are all described by basic equations by which the position, velocity, and acceleration of objects can be calculated.

KEY CONCEPTS
acceleration: a vector quantity that describes the rate of change in velocity over time

dimension: a direction in which an object can move. In spatial physics, the three dimensions are traditionally represented by the symbols x, y, and z

displacement: the difference between the initial position of an object and its final position, regardless of the path taken

kinematics: the study of the motion of objects

magnitude: the size, or numerical measurement, of a vector

Newton's laws of motion: three laws, defined by Isaac Newton, that describe the motion and forces acting on large objects moving at speeds much smaller than the speed of light

SIMPLIFYING MOTION

Ancient civilizations in India and Asia, as well as the native cultures of North and South America, had traditional knowledge that described the motions of the planets and the structure of the universe quite accurately. However, for many centuries, the accepted model in Eurocentric cultures for the structure of the solar system stated that Earth was the center of the universe and that every celestial object moved around Earth in perfect circles. This model was established and backed up by many ancient Greek philosophers, including Aristotle (ca. 384-322 BCE). He posited that if Earth were moving, then dropped objects would be left behind in space. Because Aristotle did not see objects being left behind, he concluded that Earth must not be moving.

Many centuries later, Galileo Galilei (1564-1642) provided the key evidence that disproved this and many other Aristotelian views of the structure and motion of celestial bodies. Based on experimentation, Galileo posited that in the absence of friction, an object in motion will remain in motion. This was the beginning of a revolution in science. After Galileo's death, Sir Isaac Newton (1643-1727) improved on his work. He derived mathematical laws and equations to describe the motions of objects not only on Earth but also in space. We now know these laws

as Newton's laws of motion. Newton expanded on Galileo's experiments and defined his first law of motion, the law of inertia. This law states that any object at rest will remain at rest, and any object in motion will remain in the same state of motion, unless acted on by an external force. This can happen in any of the three spatial dimensions. Newton published his laws of motion and other such principles in his masterpiece *Philosophiae Naturalis Principia Mathematica* (1687), also known as the *Principia*.

THE MOTION OF OBJECTS

While Newton's first law of motion describes the state of motion of an object, it also describes how that state can be changed by external forces. An external force can change the speed of an object at rest, forcing it to move. An external force can also change the speed or direction of motion of an object already in motion.

In everyday usage, velocity and speed have similar meanings. In scientific contexts, however, their meanings differ. Physicists define velocity as the rate of change of position in a certain direction as a function of time. Velocity is a vector quantity because it describes both a magnitude and a direction of motion. Speed, on the other hand, is defined as the distance traveled by an object as a function of time, regardless of direction. Speed is not a vector quantity because it does not describe an object's direction of motion. In physics, an object that moves in a perfect circle with a constant speed has a variable velocity because its direction of motion around the circle is constantly changing.

Like speed, distance is not a function of the direction of motion and is therefore not a vector quantity. For example, if one walks five meters north or five meters south, the distance traveled is equal to five meters. Displacement, however, is a measurement of the change in position of an object as a function of the direction of motion. Like velocity, displacement is a vector quantity because it includes the direction of motion. A person who walks five meters to the north has a different displacement than a person who walks five meters to the south.

In terms of mathematical descriptions, speed and average velocity can be independently defined. Speed (v), not being a vector, is defined as the distance (d) an object moves divided by the time (t) it takes it to move that distance:

$$v = \frac{d}{t}$$

Average velocity (v) is also defined in terms of time, but instead of being a function of the distance traveled, it is a function of displacement (s), or change in position:

$$v = \frac{s}{t}$$

The velocity and displacement variables are bolded, meaning that they are vector quantities. Sometimes, instead of a bolded variable, a vector quantity is represented by a variable with a right-facing arrow above it.

Both velocity and speed are measured in units of meters per second (m/s). In order to calculate the velocity of an object, its change in position and the amount of time it takes to move must be given. For example, if a car starts moving east and takes 120 seconds (s) to travel 1,000 meters (m) to the next red light, then the average velocity of the car is calculated as follows:

$$v = \frac{s}{t}$$

$$v = \frac{1,000 \text{ m}}{120 \text{ s}}$$

$$v = 8.33 \text{ m/s east}$$

While the car was moving down the road, it could have gone faster or slower than this at any particular time, but on average it was moving at a velocity of 8.33 m/s east.

Average velocity is different from instantaneous velocity, which is the velocity of the car at every point in time. This is what a car's speedometer would display if the speedometer measured direction as well as speed. If a person records his or her car's velocity at every second, he or she would have a measurement that is closer to the car's instantaneous velocity (this is actually possible in modern vehicles that have a compass direction display as part of the dashboard display). If the person then averages all the values of the instantaneous velocity, the result will be the average velocity. This process is more complicated and requires very precise measurements of the instantaneous velocity at each point in time. It is much easier to calculate average velocity using the displacement and the time it took to move between the two points.

ACCELERATION

The rate of change of an object's position as a function of time is its velocity. Similarly, the rate of change of an object's velocity as a function of time is a vector quantity known as acceleration. Mathematically, acceleration (a) is a function of the change in velocity (Δv) and the time over which the change took place (t):

$$a = \frac{\Delta v}{t}$$

The change in velocity is simply the initial velocity (v_i) subtracted from the final velocity (v_f):

$$\Delta v = v_f - v_i.$$

Acceleration is measured in units of meters per second per second, or meters per second squared (m/s^2). Using the example of the car, imagine that the car is approaching a red light with an initial velocity of 8.33 m/s east. The car must come to a full stop at the red light, so its final velocity will be 0 m/s. It takes the car 1.5 seconds to come to a stop. To calculate the acceleration, first calculate the change in velocity:

$$\Delta v = v_f - vi$$

$$\Delta v = 0 \text{ m/s} - 8.33 \text{ m/s}$$

$$\Delta v = -8.33 \text{ m/s}.$$

The change in velocity of the car is negative because the car slowed down, so its final velocity was smaller than its initial velocity. Using the change in velocity, calculate the acceleration:

$$a = \frac{\Delta v}{t}$$

$$a = \frac{-8.33 \text{ m} / \text{s}}{1.5 \text{ s}}$$

$$a = -5.55 \text{ m/s}^2$$

Because the acceleration is a vector, the negative sign simply indicates the direction of the vector. The car was previously established to be moving east, so its acceleration when stopping at the red light can be given as 5.55 m/s² west—the opposite of the direction in which it was originally traveling. The word "deceleration" is not used in physics. Objects slow down not because they decelerate but because they accelerate in a negative sense, in the opposite direction of their motion. The car stops because it is moving east, yet accelerating west. A ball thrown vertically in the air will slow down on its way up because Earth's gravity is pulling on it, causing it to accelerate downward. Once the ball starts to fall back down, it will pick up speed because it is moving and accelerating in the same direction. As with velocity, this acceleration equation calculates the average acceleration, while instantaneous acceleration is the acceleration at every single point in time. In the example above, the person driving the car might press on the

brakes with a varying amount of force, causing the magnitude of the acceleration to be slightly different at each point in time.

KINEMATICS

Newton's ideas regarding kinematics revolutionized science, especially physics and astronomy. About four centuries after Newton published his *Principia*, humans used these basic laws, and others based on them, to land on the moon. The use of Newton's laws and many other kinematic equations is not just reserved for big leaps in human scientific knowledge. Every time someone calculates how long it will take to reach a destination based on a desired velocity, that person is putting kinematic equations to use. Such equations are also used by global positioning system (GPS)-enabled devices to estimate distance traveled and time of arrival.

—*Angel G. Fuentes*

Further Reading
Awrejcewicz. *Classical Mechanics: Kinematics and Statics*. Springer Science & Business Media, 2012.
Hurtado, John E. *A Kinematics and Kinetics Primer*. Lulu.com, 2014.
Myers, Richard Leroy, and Rusty L. Myers. *The Basics of Physics*. Greenwood Publishing Group, 2006.
Russell, Kevin. *Kinematics and Dynamics of Mechanical Systems: Implementation in MATLAB and SimMechanics*. CRC Press, 2016.
Spellman, Frank R. *Physics for Nonphysicists*. Government Institutes, 2009.

See also: Acceleration; Angular forces; Displacement; Kinematics; Kinetic energy; Newton's laws

LOAD

Fields of Study: Physics; Mechanics; Mathematics

ABSTRACT

Load in classical physics typically refers to "mechanical load"—the resistance acting against a mechanical system

or machine such as a pulley or a motor. This resistance is a force, measured in newtons. It is what must be overcome by the machine in order to move the target object. In most earthbound systems, the target object's weight—the downward force imparted to it by the planet's gravity—is a major component of the load.

KEY CONCEPTS

energy: a property of matter and objects that can be transferred and transformed but never created or destroyed, sometimes described as the ability to do work; measured in joules (J)

force: any interaction, such as a push or pull, that changes the motion of an object; measured in newtons (N)

mass: how much matter there is in an object; measured in kilograms or pounds; mass determines the effects of gravitation and inertia; unlike weight, which is dependent on gravitation, an object's mass remains constant throughout the universe

weight: the downward force imparted to an object by gravity acting on its mass; measured according to the International System of Units (SI) in newtons, though it is normally expressed in units of mass for everyday objects on Earth

MECHANICAL LOAD AS A FORCE

A load, colloquially, refers to some objects or other quantity that needs to be moved, manipulated, or otherwise worked with. In classical physics, load typically refers to mechanical load—that is, the resistance that a machine (such as a pulley or a motor) needs to overcome to do its job. This resistance acts as a force, an interaction that tends to change the motion of an object. When something or someone attempts to lift an object, for example, gravity creates a resistant force, the weight of the object.

Because load acts as a force, it is best quantified in terms of newtons (N), the standard unit of force. One newton is defined as the force needed to accelerate a mass of one kilogram at a rate of one meter per second over one second of time (kg· m/s²). This is roughly the force necessary to lift a medium-sized apple from the ground to chest height.

MACHINES, ENERGY, AND FORCE

Machines, at a basic level, transfer and transform energy. Energy is a fundamental property of matter that can be transferred or transformed but never destroyed. An automobile combustion engine, for example, transforms the chemical energy in gasoline into kinetic energy. Then it transfers this energy from the engine to the wheels. Energy is the capacity for doing work, and work is the application of a force over a distance (i.e., moving something). Machines transform the potential for work contained in energy (such as electrical energy from a power plant or chemical energy produced in the human body) into work by creating force.

When calculating mechanical load and the ability of machines to perform work, it is necessary to understand the forces in play. The net force is the sum of all the forces acting on the target object.

WEIGHT VERSUS MASS

Weight is the downward force applied to an object by gravity. As such, weight is often an important factor in the load of a machine, especially if the system is trying to lift something. Even when moving an object horizontally, however, the target object's weight will need to be compensated for by the machine.

On Earth, weight is often used interchangeably with mass, which is the amount of matter in an object and is not affected by gravity. Scales, for instance, measure weight but offer readings in terms of mass units—kilograms or pounds. What scales on Earth are actually measuring is the downward force of gravity, but mass units are much more familiar to people than units of force (newtons). On Earth, it does not matter much, because the force of gravity is essentially a constant.

Four pulley systems with an increasing number of pulleys require less force to lift the same load to the same height.

A SAMPLE PROBLEM

The maximum load that a given machine can handle can be calculated if one knows the force generated by the machine. Consider a simple single-pulley system attached to a weight. The pulley system does not move and serves only to alter the direction of the force applied. It is arranged vertically, so that a person can stand next to the weight and pull straight downward on one end of the rope running through the pulley. This produces an opposite, upward force on the weight at the other end of the rope. Assume a perfectly frictionless pulley. The person operating the pulley "weighs" seventy-five kilograms. What is the maximum load the person can lift? In other words, how much force can the person generate?

No matter how hard the person pulls, he or she will never be able to generate more force than his or her weight. So if the person jumps up and grabs the rope, letting his or her full weight act on it, the force applied to the rope will be equal to the person's weight. Use the formula for weight (W) as a force (F), where m is the mass and g is the acceleration due to gravity:

$$W = F = mg$$

Plug in the known values and solve, to determine that the maximum force is 735 N.

More advanced calculations of load and maximum load may be influenced by mechanical advantage (an amplification in force produced by many machines) or sources of resistance other than gravity (such as friction or water resistance). However, the key to determining load will always be in determining what force needs to be overcome in order to achieve the desired effect.

Once other planets and satellites come into play, however, the differences between weight and mass become apparent. Weight is actually a function of the mass of an object and the gravity acting on it. It changes when the gravity changes. So a person on Earth might step on a scale and see a weight of two hundred pounds (approximately ninety-one kilograms), but on the moon that person would weigh only around thirty-three pounds (fifteen kilograms).

The reality is, the downward force acting on this person is indeed different at the two locations. It is a function of gravity, and the moon's gravity is much smaller than Earth's. However, technically, the units are wrong. Kilograms and pounds are units of mass. Mass quantifies the amount of matter in an object, and mass remains constant throughout the universe regardless of gravitation; a ninety-one-kilogram person on Earth still contains ninety-one kilograms of matter on the moon.

FORCE, WEIGHT, AND ACCELERATION DUE TO GRAVITY

Weight is a force. Force (F), in classical physics, is equal to mass (m) multiplied by acceleration (a):

$$F = ma$$

Therefore, weight can be written as F_g, the force of gravity. Similarly, the acceleration in the above formula can be replaced with the acceleration due to gravity (g). To calculate an object's weight (W) in newtons using its mass, then, simply multiply the mass in kilograms times the acceleration due to gravity (g) acting on the object in meters per second squared:

$$W = F_g = mg$$

For example, acceleration due to gravity on Earth is 9.8 meters per second squared, so a two-hundred-pound (ninety-one-kilogram) person on Earth would have a weight of 891.8 N.

LOADS IN DAILY LIFE

Simple machines, and thus the loads they move, permeate every aspect of daily life. In industries like shipping, pulleys and inclined planes in the form of ramps often help lift large loads. Understanding the maximum load capacity of a given machine is vital to the safety of both the products being moved and the machine operator.

—Kenrick Vezina

Further Reading

Al Nageim, Hassan. *Structural Mechanics: Loads, Analysis, Design and Materials*. 6th ed., Prentice Hall, 2003.

O'Brien, Eugene, Andrzej Nowak, and Colin Caprani. *Bridge Traffic Loading from Research to Practice*. CRC Press, 2021.

Yazdi, Hassanali Mosalman. *Loading Structures*. U of Malaya P, 2013.

See also: Aeronautical engineering; Biomedical engineering; Civil engineering; Computer-aided engineering; Dynamics (mechanics); Earthquake engineering; Engineering; Engineering tolerances; Force (physics); Friction; Mechatronics; Mechanical engineering; Momentum (physics); Robotics; Springs; Structural engineering

M

MAGNETISM

Fields of Study: Physics; Mechanics; Mathematics

ABSTRACT

All materials experience some level of magnetization. Those materials that experience the strongest effect are called ferromagnetic. Magnetic fields have two opposing poles referred to as the north pole and the south pole. Opposite poles attract each other, and like poles repel each other.

KEY CONCEPTS

antiferromagnets: nonmagnetic components that are rendered highly magnetic by the application of an electric field

electromagnetism: magnetism produced by an electric current or field

igneous rock: rock formed as magma with Earth that has been extruded as lava and solidified

lodestone: the mineral hematite, an iron ore, that has been made magnetic by crystallizing in Earth's magnetic field

magnetization: imparting or receiving magnetic characteristic

INTRODUCTION

All matter is made up of tiny particles called atoms. Atoms contain electrons, which carry electric charges. The electrons spin around the core of the atom, which is called the nucleus. It is that spinning that creates an electric current. The electric current causes the electrons to act as tiny magnets. Magnets attract and repel other magnets and certain types of metals.

Most substances contain an equal number of electrons that spin in opposite directions, which cancels out a magnetic force. However, all materials experience some level of magnetization. Those materials that experience the strongest effect are called ferromagnetic.

Magnetic fields have two opposing poles referred to as the north pole and the south pole. Opposite poles attract each other, and like poles repel each other. Earth, which also has geomagnetic poles, can be considered a giant magnet. Its magnetic field is generated by electric currents that circulate deep within the core. The north and south poles of the Earth are not the same as its geomagnetic poles. Earth's geomagnetic poles shift with the activity of molten magma, which lies under Earth's crust. Magma is the molten (liquid) material from which all igneous rock is ultimately created. This igneous rock is the basis of Earth's crust and is the foundation of the rock formation cycle. Magma comes out of Earth in the form of lava. When it hardens and becomes rock, its particles are magnetized by Earth's magnetic field. The rock becomes a historic record of the position of Earth's geomagnetic poles at that given time.

Because Earth's magnetic field does not move quickly or often, it is a useful tool for navigation. People use magnetic compasses to pinpoint their direction. The magnetic needle of a compass is aligned with Earth's magnetic poles. The needle points toward the magnetic north pole.

BACKGROUND

The concept of magnetism has long been observed, but never clearly understood. Thales of Miletus, a Greek philosopher in the sixth century, BCE, noted the effects of magnetic stones. He wrote that the stones had a soul and could move iron. In 77 CE, Pliny the Elder wrote his *Naturalis Historia*. In it he named the stone *lithos magnes*, after the legend of the Greek shepherd Magnes. The nails in Magnes's shoes were attracted by the magnetic stones in the area in which he lived.

The first compass was created by the Chinese during the Qin Dynasty (221-206 BCE). It was designed on a square slab with markings for constellations and the four cardinal directions (north, south, east, and west). The magnetic needle was a spoon-shaped piece of lodestone. Lodestone is a magnetized fragment of the mineral magnetite, which has natural magnetic properties. The handle of the "spoon" always pointed south.

Englishman William Gilbert (1540-1603) was the first to discover that Earth is a magnet. He published an article called "De Magnete," in which he described the properties of magnetite. Further theories about Earth's magnetic field were proposed by Carl Friedrich Gauss (1777-1855), a German mathematician. Scottish scientist James Clerk Maxwell (1831-79) proved that electricity and magnetism represent two different aspects of the same force field.

MAGNETIC FORCES AT WORK

Magnetism is used in a variety of ways. Modern computers rely on ferromagnets to align the binary code that processes and stores information. In 2020, scientists from the University of Central Florida published findings of a project focused on pushing the limits of magnets to increase the speed of electronics. The team presented proof of successfully passing electrical currents through antiferromagnets on a very small scale. Antiferromagnets are much more powerful, but display no natural magnetism, requiring electricity to harness their power. The anti-ferromagnetic devices operate on a terahertz level. This means that calculations can be completed in a trillionth of a second. The research, funded by the De-

Lodestone, a natural magnet, attracting iron nails. Ancient humans discovered the property of magnetism from lodestone. Photo via Wikimedia Commons. [Public domain.]

partment of Defense in the United States, could have significant implications for guidance systems and communications. In April 2020, the findings were published in the journal *Science*, and summarized by *ScienceDaily*.

Scientists at the National Aeronautics and Space Administration's (NASA's) Goddard Space Flight Center noted data in 2020 regarding a weak spot in Earth's magnetic field. The weak spot, or dent, is called the South Atlantic Anomaly (SAA). It is located over South America and the southern Atlantic Ocean. Normally Earth's magnetic field protects the planet, repelling charged particles from the Sun. Over the SAA, however, these particles get closer to the Earth's surface and interfere with passing satellites. While the SAA was not yet impacting daily life on Earth, NASA scientists noted that it was expanding and splitting into two parts. The researchers continue to monitor the area in order to help prepare for further challenges to satellite data collection. Their findings were published by *ScienceDaily* in August 2020.

IMPACT

All matter, including humans, is exposed to magnetic fields at all times. In addition to Earth's natural magnetic field, humans have created artificial magnetic fields all over the globe. Power lines, transportation systems, medical equipment, and electrical appliances all exert some magnetic force. It has been unknown whether magnetic fields have a harmful effect on the human body.

Historically, alarm has been raised about the potentially dangerous effects of power lines on individuals who live in close proximity. The International Commission on Non-Ionizing Radiation Protection declared in 2020 that there was not enough evidence that residing near power lines increased the risk of cancer, as previously thought. Additionally in 2020, scientists at the global Utilities Threshold Initiative Consortium studied the human body's tolerance to magnetic forces. The threshold for a physiological response was well above what is encountered in everyday life.

—*Diana C. Coe*

Further Reading

Bellis, Mary. "The Compass and Other Magnetic Innovations." *ThoughtCo.*, 20 Nov. 2019, www.thoughtco.com/compass-and-other-magnetic-innovations-1991466. Accessed 27 Dec. 2020.

Lucas, Jim. "What Is Magnetism? Magnetic Fields & Magnetic Force." *Live Science*, 29 July 2015, www.livescience.com/38059-magnetism.html. Accessed 23 Dec. 2020.

"Magnetism." *DISCovering Science*, 1996, www.ucl.ac.uk/EarthSci/people/lidunka/GEOL2014/Geophysics9%20-Magnetism/Useful%20papers/Magnetism.htm#. Accessed 23 Dec. 2020.

NASA/Goddard Space Flight Center. "Researchers Track Slowly Splitting 'Dent' in Earth's Magnetic Field." *ScienceDaily*, 17 Aug. 2020, www.sciencedaily.com/releases/2020/08/200817144121.htm. Accessed 23 Dec. 2020.

Rutledge, Kim, et al. "Magnetism." *National Geographic*, 21 Jan. 2011, www.nationalgeographic.org/encyclopedia/magnetism/. Accessed 23 Dec. 2020.

Tennenhouse, Erica. "What Magnetic Fields Do to Your Brain and Body." *Discover*, 25 May 2018, www.discovermagazine.com/environment/what-magnetic-fields-do-to-your-brain-and-body. Accessed 23 Dec. 2020.

Towell, Gayle. "Magnetism: Definition, Types, Properties & How They Work (w/Examples)." *Sciencing*, 5 Dec. 2019, sciencing.com/magnetism-definition-types-properties-how-they-work-w-examples-13721191.html. Accessed 23 Dec. 2020.

University of Central Florida. "Magnet Research Takes Giant Leap." *ScienceDaily*, 10 Apr. 2020, www.sciencedaily.com/releases/2020/04/200410162413.htm. Accessed 23 Dec. 2020.

See also: Atoms; Electromagnetic technologies; Electromagnetism; Lenz's law; Materials science; Quantum mechanics; Superconductor

MATERIALS SCIENCE

Fields of Study: Physics; Chemistry; Aeronautical engineering; Mechanical engineering; Mathematics

ABSTRACT

Materials science examines the structure and properties of materials in order to create materials with useful and novel properties. Materials scientists use principles from chemistry, physics, various subfields of engineering, and applied mathematics. Depending on the material being studied and its intended applications, other fields, such as biology or even planetary science, may be relevant. Materials science has applications in every imaginable industry in which synthetic materials are used and is responsible for countless innovations in aeronautical engineering.

KEY CONCEPTS

accelerometer: a device that measures the change of stress on an internal component to determine the rate of acceleration or deceleration, and changes in the direction of motion

advanced: indicates a process or mechanism that functions beyond the current standard levels of performance

advanced polymer: a polymer that is typically of a complex molecular structure, produced by polymerization of similarly complex monomeric units, and having characteristic properties that greatly exceed those of simpler polymer systems

monomeric unit: refers to a small molecular species that is joined to an untold number of other such molecules to form the corresponding polymer; for example, polyethylene can be readily seen as the head-to-tail conjoining of multiple ethylene molecules; the monomeric unit retains its essential structure within the polymer

AN INTRODUCTION

Materials science examines the structure and properties of materials in order to create materials with useful and novel properties. To this end, materials scientists use principles from chemistry, physics, various subfields of engineering, and applied mathematics. Depending on the material being studied and its intended applications, other fields, such as biology or even planetary science, may be relevant. Materials science has applications in every imaginable industry in which synthetic materials are used and is responsible for countless innovations in aeronautical engineering, as well as lighter and stronger automotive parts, bacteria-resistant medical supplies, superior toothpastes, and plastic bags that keep fruit fresher.

BASIC PRINCIPLES

The advent of materials science occurred when humans first began to create tools and built structures.

Its importance is exemplified by the fact that many time periods, including the Bronze Age, the Iron Age, and the Silicon Age, are named for the materials that contributed greatly to human development during those periods. Similarly, the Industrial Revolution, while not named for a specific material, refers to a period of significant development in the means of creating materials and incorporating them into devices. For much of history, knowledge of what would now be considered materials science was passed from parent to child, leading to the use of terms such as "smith" and "cartwright" as family names in addition to job titles. Later, apprenticeship became the dominant form of education, eventually evolving into the higher education system of the twenty-first century. Materials science is a common major or academic department at larger or more science-oriented colleges and universities, and the fields of chemistry, physics, biology, and engineering also encompass elements of the science.

Materials science and materials engineering often overlap; however, science and engineering are distinct fields. Scientists attempt to understand phenomena, whereas engineers seek to apply scientific knowledge to problems. Although these definitions are not mutually exclusive, scientists and engineers approach their work differently: A scientist might design a device as a proof of concept, whereas an engineer would experiment with different designs to optimize the performance of a given device. Thus, materials scientists are primarily concerned with understanding why materials behave as they do and using that knowledge to devise new materials, while materials engineers focus on optimizing the application of these concepts and materials for particular uses.

CORE CONCEPTS

Metals. Metals, as materials, are composed of metallic elements that exist as positively charged ions embedded in a sea of electrons, known as "delocalized electrons" because they are not tightly bound to their source atoms. These bonds contrast with covalent and ionic bonds, in which electrons are localized between their source atom and the bonded atom. Metals conduct electricity and heat well. Metal materials may be pure metals or alloys, which are solid solutions composed of different metals. Brass (composed of copper and zinc) and bronze (copper and tin) are examples of alloys.

Ceramics. Ceramics are solids that are held together by covalent or ionic bonds. Because the nature (strength, length, orientation) of these bonds depends on the identity of the constituent compounds, the properties of these materials vary much more dramatically than those of metals. Ceramics may be semiconductors (conductors of electricity at high temperatures) or superconductors (perfect conductors of electricity) or may be piezoelectric (the application of pressure influences its mechanical properties and vice versa) and pyroelectric (the application of heat influences its electrical properties and vice versa).

Semiconductors. Semiconductors, the basis for modern electronics, conduct electricity at 'high' temperatures. The conductivity of semiconductors can be fine-tuned through a process called "doping," which is the intentional introduction of a given impurity into an otherwise perfectly ordered material. This introduced material has a different number of electrons than the host material, which affects how readily electricity flows through the material. Doping produces either n-type or p-type semiconductors, depending on whether the impurity has more or fewer electrons than the host atoms, respectively.

Polymers. Polymers are generally solids composed of chains of repeating units, or monomers. For example, silk is composed of repeating units of fifty-nine amino acids, and polyethylene is composed of repeating units of ethylene monomers. The properties of polymers can vary dramatically: Silk is a polymer, but amber and rubber are as well. This varia-

tion can be ascribed to the fact that both the identity of the monomer and its microstructure (how it is organized into a chain) determine how a polymer behaves. Examples of different microstructures include straight chains, chains with branches, comb polymers (many shorter chains descending from a central chain, forming a comb-like shape), and star polymers (numerous polymers all extending from the same central point, forming a star-like shape). Polymers also differ in chain length.

Plastics. Plastics are polymers that may retain whatever shape they are formed into, whereas nonplastic polymers, such as rubber, return to their original shape after the deforming force is removed. This property is known as plasticity. Plastics may also contain additives used as fillers or to fine-tune their properties. Like all polymers, plastics come in a wide variety of types, as defined by the constituent monomers and microstructure, and these types have different properties. Plastics are also categorized by how they respond to heating: Thermoplastics maintain their chemical structures when melted, while thermosetting plastics do not. Thus, thermoplastics can be molded repeatedly, whereas thermosets can only be molded once.

Composites. Composite materials contain numerous components with substantially different chemical and physical properties that retain these individual properties, but when combined produce a new material with very different properties. One example of a composite is concrete, which is composed of cement and an aggregate, such as sand or gravel. When combined to form concrete, neither the cement nor the aggregate undergoes physical or chemical changes, though the concrete so formed is very different from any of its individual components.

Biomaterials. Biomaterials are materials with biological applications and biological materials that can serve other uses. In the former case, materials are designed to be incorporated into living organisms and must therefore exhibit biocompatibility, which refs to a material's ability to be accepted by a biological system, without toxicity in the original material or any of the degradation products that might be produced by exposure to physiological conditions. In the latter case, biological materials are altered to serve human needs, such as when wood is pressurized to create a building material that is much more resistant to decay and deformation than the original material.

Nanomaterials. Nanomaterials are materials on the nanoscale, that is, on the order of 10^{-9} meters, or nanometers. These materials are particularly interesting because the properties of nanoscale components are at times dictated by quantum mechanics rather than classical (Newtonian) mechanics. An example of nanomaterials is quantum dots, which are semiconductor particles with diameters of 2 to 10 nanometers. The color that these particles emit can be adjusted by changing their size, with smaller particles emitting colors toward the blue end of the visible spectrum and larger particles emitting colors toward the red end of the visible spectrum. The rich crimson color found in older stained-glass windows is due to nanodots consisting of three atoms of gold within the glass.

APPLICATIONS PAST AND PRESENT

Aviation. There are few areas that surpass the aviation industry for the relevance of materials science. This is particularly true in regard to advanced composite materials, the precise combinations of specialized fabric materials and advanced polymer resins. In principle, the construction of an advanced composite is the same as embedding a mat of random glass fibers in an epoxy resin and waiting for the resin to harden. In practice, however, the process of preparing an advanced composite is very different; a painstaking process of fiber alignment in several layers, followed by impregnation with a thermosetting resin whose exact identity is often a proprietary secret, and completed by controlled heating of the raw

resin-fiber assembly on a mold using reduced pressure to extract contaminant residual gases with the entire workpiece perhaps subjected to increased external pressure. The advantages of advanced composites are their inherent high strength and relatively light weight. The wings of high-speed fighter aircraft, for example, are rock-hard structures of compressed carbon fiber/resin weighing and costing much less than any metal structure that would be needed to provide the same strength characteristics.

Medicine. The applications of materials science in medicine range from new drug delivery systems to improved prostheses and artificial organs. The discovery of new materials for use in medical equipment has led to improvements in durability, cost, and practicality. For example, dental fillings were made of gold for centuries. More recently, ceramic materials were used as cheaper alternatives, with the added advantage of being less noticeable due to their subtler, off-white color. However, ceramic fillings eventually degrade. To address this issue, researchers are working to develop new filling materials that are cheap, strong, biocompatible, and stable. One candidate material is titanium, which can be implanted into the jawbone itself in a biocompatible fashion. Materials science has similarly been key to the development of scaffolding used to grow tissue artificially. When tissues are grown in the laboratory, they require scaffolding for support, much like a vine requires a trellis. Materials scientists work to create biocompatible, effective scaffolding for this purpose.

Transportation. Materials scientists are responsible for scientific advancements that affect nearly every category of vehicle. The materials in the framework of these vehicles must be both lightweight for fuel efficiency and strong for safety. Furthermore, a wide range of materials is needed to produce everything from flame-retardant upholstery to heat-resistant engine parts. One example of a promising category of material for use in automobiles and other engine-propelled vehicles is piezoelectrics. Piezoelectric ceramics, which are ceramics that respond to physical deformation with an electrical response and electrical stimulation with a physical deformation. Lead zirconate titanate is an example of a piezoelectric ceramic. In cars, piezoelectrics are used as passive sensors (for instance, in accelerometers or airbag impact sensors) and generators (spark plugs) due to their ability to convert movement or impact into electricity. They also function as active sensors (such as fuel level sensors) and actuators (such as those used to position mirrors) thanks to their ability to respond to electricity mechanically.

Electronics. The electronics industry was born of the development of new materials that gave humans great control over the flow of electrons and the ability to create circuits, allowing scientists to build devices to serve their needs. One of the most important classes of materials in the electronics industry is semiconductors. Silicon is an example of a semiconductor, and its prevalence in electronics has given rise to terms such as "Silicon Valley" and "the silicon revolution." The purity of silicon in electronics applications is crucial; one area of continuing research focuses on the development of better methods for creating thin films of pure silicon based on an understanding of its structure and properties.

Food and drink. Packaging is crucial to keeping food fresh, especially considering how far most food must travel to reach the consumer's home. Containers for food such as produce must typically be transparent, allowing the buyer to check the contents for damage, and maintain the optimal levels of water vapor, oxygen, and carbon dioxide to maintain freshness and discourage rot or drying. For any food or drink container, it is crucial that the material not degrade or leach into the product, as such materials can harm human health. For example, bisphenol A (BPA) is present in some plastics but can disrupt the endocrine system when ingested over a period of time. Studies suggest that BPA is present in most

people in detectable quantities, which has raised particular concerns about pregnant women and the potential effects of fetal exposure to BPA. Companies have begun to phase out the use of BPA in food packaging both voluntarily and in response to new regulations. In response to such concerns, materials scientists are working to develop better materials and methods for packaging foodstuffs.

Energy. Materials science plays an important role in the attempt to meet ever-increasing energy demands across the globe as supplies of nonrenewable energy sources dwindle. For example, research into fuel cells, which turn fuel into electricity by means of a chemical reaction, relies on materials science to devise better anode, cathode, and electrolyte materials to improve the efficiency of these cells and best accommodate the specific fuels being used. Similarly, materials scientists are continually striving to create more efficient, sturdier, and more versatile photovoltaic systems, which convert solar energy into electricity, as well as to determine the materials that will create the cleanest, most efficient biofuels.

Sensors. Sensors are used in a wide range of fields to detect specific targets, which may include tumors, pollutants in wastewater, or physical imperfections in a crucial device component. Ideally, a sensor responds with high selectivity and specificity, meaning that it responds nearly every time it encounters the target and rarely responds to anything other than the target. The advantage of a sensor is that it responds to something that is difficult to detect, such as the presence of a contaminant in parts-per-million concentrations, in a way that is much easier to detect, such as by emitting light or changing color. One sensor design involves the use of self-assembled monolayers (that is, single layers of a material) on gold, glass, or another substrate to detect biologically relevant molecules. The binding of the target molecule improves the fluorescence of the self-assembled monolayer, and this change can be easily detected.

SOCIAL CONTEXT AND FUTURE PROSPECTS

Materials science will likely continue to contribute to significant advances in industry and science as a whole and particularly in the medical field. For example, much of the work in the fields of cancer detection and treatment involves the creation of biocompatible materials that can target tumors, such as tumor-targeting quantum dots that fluoresce after reaching their targets. Other materials are being designed to deliver chemotherapy drugs directly to tumors, minimizing the damage done to healthy cells and allowing the patient to maintain better overall health during the treatment. As these technologies mature, the identification and treatment of cancer will become more successful and less invasive. On a broader scale, materials science offers potential treatments for a wide range of human ailments, promising to improve the overall quality of life.

Another prominent example of the social significance of materials science is its relevance in addressing climate change. As the negative effects of human activity on the environment become increasingly clear, pressure is mounting to find more economical and efficient ways to use natural resources. To this end, materials science has sought to find ways to reduce dependence on nonrenewable resources and reuse "waste" material in an economically viable fashion. For example, a key area of research in materials science is the improvement of solar cells. Future solar cells will be more efficient, more versatile, and less expensive to make. Another popular research area is the use of waste material as a substitute for freshly generated material in various production and manufacturing processes. For example, materials scientists seek to incorporate agricultural waste, such as coconut husks and palm fronds, into new materials and use waste materials to generate energy to offset the energy consumed by processing raw agricultural products.

—*Richard M. Renneboog*

Further Reading

Ashby, M. F., Michael F. Ashby, Hugh Shercliff, and David Cebon. *Materials Engineering, Science, Processing and Design*. Elsevier Science, 2019.

Douglas, Elliot. *Introduction to Materials Science and Engineering*. Pearson, 2013.

Gordon, J. E. *The New Science of Strong Materials; or, Why You Don't Fall Through the Floor*. Princeton UP, 2006.

Hosford, William F. *Materials Science*. Cambridge UP, 2007.

Hummel, Rolf E. *Understanding Materials Science: History, Properties, Applications*. 2nd ed., Springer, 2004.

Irene, Eugene A. *Electronic Materials Science*. Wiley, 2005.

Lynch, Charles T. *Handbook of Materials Science. Volume I. General Properties*. CRC Press, 2019.

"Materials Science." *ACS*. American Chemical Society, n.d. Accessed 10 Sept. 2012.

Mercier, Jean P., Gerald Zambelli, and Wilfried Kurz. *Introduction to Materials Science*. Elsevier Science, 2012.

Sutton, Adrian P. *Concepts of Material Science*. Oxford UP, 2021.

See also: Aeronautical engineering

MECHANICAL ENGINEERING

Fields of Study: Physics; Engineering; Mechanics; Mathematics

ABSTRACT

Mechanical engineering is the field of technology that deals with engines, machines, tools, and other mechanical devices and systems. This broad field of innovation, design, and production deals with machines that generate and use power. In many universities, mechanical engineering is integrated with nuclear, materials, aerospace, and biomedical engineering. The tools used by scientists, engineers, and technicians in other disciplines are usually designed by mechanical engineers.

KEY CONCEPTS

additive machining: processes such as welding and three-dimensional (3D) printing that add material to a workpiece

benchmark: a current standard or minimum requirement that must be met for a particular product or process

carbon nanotube: one of several types of molecules consisting only of carbon atoms in hexagonal rings forming a closed tubular shape

reductive machining: processes such as grinding and milling that reduce the amount of material in a workpiece

system: collection of individual components interconnected in a way that performs a particular function

SUMMARY

Mechanical engineering is the field of technology that deals with engines, machines, tools, and other mechanical devices and systems. This broad field of innovation, design, and production deals with machines that generate and use power, such as electric generators, motors, internal combustion engines, and turbines for power plants, as well as heating, ventilation, air-conditioning, and refrigeration systems. In many universities, mechanical engineering is integrated with nuclear, materials, aerospace, and biomedical engineering. The tools used by scientists, engineers, and technicians in other disciplines are usually designed by mechanical engineers. Robotics, microelectromechanical systems, and the development of nanotechnology and bioengineering technology constitute a major part of modern research in mechanical engineering.

DEFINITION AND BASIC PRINCIPLES

Mechanical engineering is the field dealing with the development and detailed design of systems to perform desired tasks. Developed from the discipline of designing the engines, power generators, tools, and mechanisms needed for mass manufacturing, it has grown into the broadest field of engineering, encompassing or touching most of the disciplines of science and engineering. Mechanical engineers take

the laws of nature and apply them using rigorous mathematical principles to design mechanisms. The process of design implies innovation, implementation, and optimization to develop the most suitable solution to the specified problem, given its constraints and requirements. The field also includes studies of the various factors affecting the design and use of the mechanisms being considered.

At the root of mechanical engineering are the laws of physics and thermodynamics. Sir Isaac Newton's laws of motion and gravitation, the three laws of thermodynamics, and the laws of electromagnetism are fundamental to much of mechanical design.

Starting with the Industrial Revolution in the nineteenth century and going through the 1970s, mechanical engineering was generally focused on designing large machines and systems and automating production lines. Ever-stronger materials and larger structures were sought. In the 1990s and first part of the twenty-first century, mechanical engineering saw rapid expansion into the world of ever-smaller machines, first in the field of micro and then nano materials, probes and machines, down to manipulating individual atoms. In this regime, short-range forces assume a completely different relationship to mass. This led to a new science integrating electromagnetics and quantum physics with the laws of motion and thermodynamics. Mechanical engineering also expanded to include the field of system design, developing tools to reduce the uncertainties in designing increasingly more complex systems composed of larger numbers of interacting elements.

BACKGROUND AND HISTORY

The engineering of tools and machines has been associated with systematic processes since humans first learned to select sticks or stones to swing and throw. The associations with mathematics, scientific prediction, and optimization are clear from the many contraptions that humans developed to help them get work done. In the third century BCE, for example, the mathematician Archimedes of Syracuse was associated with the construction of catapults to hurl projectiles at invading armies, who must themselves have had some engineering skills, as they eventually invaded his city and murdered him. Tools and weapons designed in the Middle Ages, from Asia to Europe and Africa, show amazing sophistication. In the thirteenth century, Mesopotamian engineer Al-Jazari invented the camshaft and the cam-slider mechanism and used them in water clocks and water-raising machines. In Italy, Leonardo da Vinci designed many devices, from portable bridges to water-powered engines.

The invention of the steam engine at the start of the Industrial Revolution is credited with the scientific development of the field that is now called mechanical engineering. In 1847, the Institution of Mechanical Engineers was founded in Birmingham, England. In North America, the American Society of Civil Engineers was founded in 1852, followed by the American Society of Mechanical Engineers in 1880. Most developments came through hard trial and error. However, the parallel efforts to develop retrospective and introspective summaries of these trials resulted in a growing body of scientific knowledge to guide further development.

Nevertheless, until the late nineteenth century, engineering was considered to be a second-rate profession and was segregated from the "pure" sciences. Innovations were published through societies such as England's Royal Society only if the author was introduced and accepted by its prominent members, who were usually from rich landed nobility. Publications came from deep intellectual thinking by amateurs who supposedly did it for the pleasure and amusement; actual hands-on work and details were left to paid professionals, who were deemed to be of a lower class. Even in America, engineering schools were called trade schools and were separate from

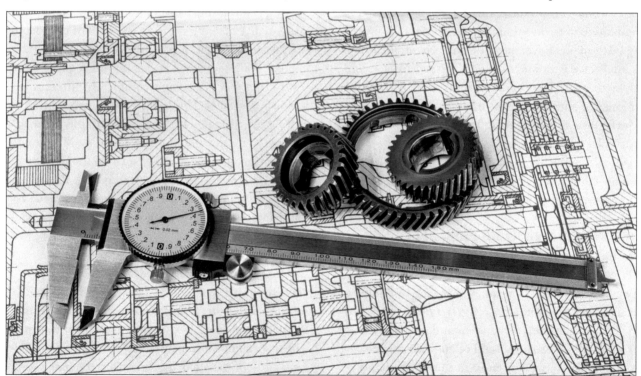

Photo via iStock/Ladislav Kubeš. [Used under license.]

the universities that catered to those desiring liberal arts educations focused on the classics and languages from the Eurocentric point of view.

Rigorous logical thinking based on the experience of hands-on applications, which characterizes mechanical engineering, started gaining currency with the rise of a culture that elevated the dignity of labor in North America. It gained a major boost with the urgency brought about by several wars. From the time of the American Civil War to World War I, weapons such as firearms, tanks, and armored ships saw significant advancements and were joined by airplanes and motorized vehicles that functioned as ambulances. During these conflicts, the individual heroism that had marked earlier wars was eclipsed by the technological superiority and scientific organization delivered by mechanical engineers.

Concomitantly, principles of mass production were applied intensively and generated immense wealth in Europe and the United States. Great universities were established by people who rose from the working classes and made money through technological enterprises. The Great Depression collapsed the established manufacturing entities and forced a sharp rise in innovation as a means of survival. New engineering products developed rapidly, showing the value of mechanical engineering. World War II and the subsequent Cold War integrated science and engineering inseparably. The space race of the 1960s through the 1980s brought large government investments in both military and civilian aerospace engineering projects. These spun off commercial revolutions in computers, computer networks, materials science, and robotics. Engineering disciplines and knowledge exploded worldwide, and there is little superficial difference between engineering curricula in most countries of the world.

The advent of the internet accelerated and completed this leveling of the knowledge field, setting up sharper impetus for innovation based on science and engineering. Competition in manufacturing advanced the field of robotics, so that cars made by robots in automated plants achieve superior quality more consistently than those built by skilled master craftsmen. Manufacturing based on robotics can respond more quickly to changing specifications and demand than human workers can.

Beginning in the 1990s, micro machines began to take on growing significance. Integrated microelectromechanical systems were developed using the techniques used in computer production. One by one, technology products once considered highly glamorous and hard to obtain—from calculators to smartphones—have been turned into mass-produced commodities available to most at an affordable cost. Other products—from personal computers and cameras to cars, rifles, music and television systems, and even jet airliners—are also heading for commoditization as a result of the integration of mechanical engineering with computers, robotics, and micro electromechanics.

HOW IT WORKS

The most common idea of a mechanical engineer is one who designs machines that serve new and useful functions in an innovative manner. Often these machines appear to be incredibly complex inside or extremely simple outside. The process of accomplishing these miraculous designs is systematic, and good mechanical engineers make it look easy.

System design. At the top level, system design starts with a rigorous analysis of the needs to be satisfied, the market for a product that satisfies those needs, the time available to do the design and manufacturing, and the resources that must be devoted. This step also includes an in-depth study of what has been done before. This leads to "requirements definition," where the actual requirements of the design are carefully specified. Experienced designers believe that this step already determines more than 80 percent of the eventual cost of the product.

Next comes an initial estimate of the eventual system characteristics, performed using simple, commonsense logic, applying the laws of nature and observations of human behavior. This step uses results from benchmarking what has been achieved before and extrapolating some technologies to the time when they must be used in the manufacturing of the design. Once these rudimentary concept parameters and their relationships are established, various analyses of more detailed implications become possible. A performance estimation then identifies basic limits and determines whether the design "closes," meeting all the needs and constraints specified at the beginning. Iterations on this process develop the best design. Innovations may be totally radical, which is relatively rare, or incremental in individual steps or aspects of the design based on new information, or on linking developments in different fields. In either case, extensive analysis is required before an innovation is built into a design. The design is then analyzed for ease and cost of manufacture. The "tooling," or specific setups and machines required for mass manufacture, are considered.

A cost evaluation includes the costs of maintenance through the life cycle of the product. The entire process is then iterated on to minimize this cost. The design is then passed on to build prototypes, thereby gaining more experience on the manufacturing techniques needed. The prototypes are tested extensively to see if they meet the performance required and predicted by the design.

When these improvements are completed and the manufacturing line is set up, the product goes into mass manufacture. The engineers must stay engaged in the actual performance of the product through its delivery to the end user, the customer, and in learning from the customer's experience in order to design improvements to the product as quickly as possible. In modern concurrent engineering practice, designers attempt to achieve as much as possible of the manufacturing process design and economic optimization during the actual product design cycle in order to shorten the time to reach market and the cost of the design cycle. The successful implementation of these processes requires both technical knowledge and experience on the part of the mechanical engineers. These come from individual rigorous fields of knowledge, some of which are listed below.

Engineering mechanics. The field of engineering mechanics integrates knowledge of statics, dynamics, elasticity, and strength of materials. These fields rigorously link mathematics, the laws of motion and gravitation, and material property relationships to derive general relations and analysis methods. Fundamental to all of engineering, these subfields are typically covered at the beginning of any course of study.

In statics, the concept of equilibrium from Newton's first law of motion is used to develop free-body diagrams showing various forces and reactions. These establish the conditions necessary for a structure to remain stable and describe relations between the loads in various elements.

In dynamics, Newton's second law of motion is used to obtain relations for the velocity and acceleration vectors for isolated bodies and systems of bodies and to develop the notions of angular momentum and moment of inertia.

The strength of materials is a general subject that derives relationships between material properties and loads using the concepts of elasticity and plasticity and the deflections of bodies under various types of loading. These analyses help the engineer predict the yield strength and the breaking strength of various structures if the material properties are known. Metals were the preferred choice of material for engineering for many decades, and methods to analyze structures made of them were highly refined, exploiting the isotropy of metal properties. Modern mechanical engineering requires materials the properties of which are much less uniform or exotic in other ways.

Graphics and kinematics. Engineers and architects use graphics to communicate their designs precisely and unambiguously. Initially, learning to draw on paper was a major part of learning engineering skills. However, students now learn the principles of graphics using computer-aided design (CAD) software and computer graphics concepts. The drawing files can also be transferred quickly into machines that fabricate a part in computer-aided manufacturing (CAM). Rapid prototyping methods such as stereolithography construct an object from digital data generated by computer graphics. The advent of three-dimensional (3D) printing added an entirely new method for the generation of prototypes and other items ranging from miniature replicas of large machines printed using plastics to entire houses printed using concrete. 3D printing is now even used to construct replacement body parts such as ears using the individual's own cells.

The other use of graphics is to visualize and perfect a mechanism. Kinematics develops a systematic method to calculate the motions of elements, including their dependence on the motion of other elements. This field is crucial to developing, for instance, gears, cams, pistons, levers, manipulator arms, and robots. Machines that achieve very complex motions are designed using the field of kinematics.

Robotics and control. The study of robotics starts with the complex equations that describe how the different parts satisfy the equations of motion with multiple degrees of freedom. Methods of solving large sets of algebraic equations quickly are critical in robotics. Robots are distinguished from mere manipulator arms by their ability to make decisions based on the input, rather than depend on a telepresence operator for commands. For instance, telepresence is adequate to operate a machine on the surface of the Moon, which is only a few seconds of round-trip signal travel time from Earth using electromagnetic signals. However, the round-trip time for a signal to Mars is several minutes, so a rover operating there cannot wait for commands from Earth regarding how to negotiate around an obstacle. A fully robotic rover is needed that can make decisions based on what its sensors tell it, just as a human present on the scene might do.

Entire manufacturing plants are operated using robotics and telepresence supervision. Complex maneuvers such as the rendezvous between two spacecraft, one of which may be spinning out of control, have been achieved in orbits in space, where the dynamics are difficult for a human to visualize. Flight control systems for aircraft have been implemented using robotics, including algorithms to land the aircraft safely and more precisely than human pilots can. These systems are developed using mathematical methods for solving differential equations rapidly, along with software to adjust parameters based on feedback. Artificial intelligence, or AI, is still in its infancy, but is rapidly developing. Tests conducted in 2023 have seen AI control piloting an F-14 jet fighter plane for fourteen hours or more. And AI has also been developed that can synthesize information it gleans from many sources, including the Internet, into written work that is almost indistinguishable from the work an actual human would produce.

Materials. The science of materials has advanced rapidly since the late twentieth century. Wood was once a material of choice for many engineering products, including bridges, aircraft wings, propellers, and train carriages. The fibrous nature of wood required considerable expertise from those choosing how to cut and lay sections of wood; being a natural product, its properties varied considerably from one specimen to another. Metals became much more convenient to use in design and fabrication because the energy to melt and shape metals cheaply became available. Various alloys were developed to tailor machinery for strength, flexibility, elasticity, corrosion resistance, and other desirable characteristics.

Detailed tables of properties for these alloys were included in mechanical engineering handbooks.

Materials used to manufacture mass-produced items have migrated to molded plastics made of hydrocarbon materialss derived from petroleum. The molds are shaped using such techniques as rapid prototyping and computer-generated data files from design software. Composite materials are tailored with fiber bundles arrayed along directions where high-tensile strength is needed and much less strength along directions where high loads are not likely, thus achieving large savings in mass and weight.

Fluid mechanics. The science of fluid mechanics is important to any machine or system that either contains or must move through water, air, or other gases or liquids (fluids). Fluid mechanics employs the laws of physics to derive conservation equations for specific packets of fluid (the Lagrangian approach) or for the flow through specified control volumes (Eulerian approach). These equations describe the physical laws of conservation of mass, momentum, and energy, relating forces and work to changes in flow properties. The properties of specific fluids are related through the thermal and caloric equations expressing their thermodynamic states. The speed of propagation of small disturbances, known as the speed of sound, is related to the dependence of pressure on density and hence on temperature. Various nondimensional groupings of flow and fluid properties—such as the Reynolds number, Mach number, and Froude number—are used to classify flow behavior. Increasingly, for many problems involving fluid flow through or around solid objects, calculations starting from the conservation equations are able to predict the loads and flow behavior reliably using the methods of computational fluid dynamics (CFD). However, the detailed prediction of turbulent flows remains beyond reach and is approximated through various turbulence models. Fluid-mechanic drag and the movements due to

flow-induced pressure remain very difficult to calculate to the accuracy needed to improve vehicle designs.

Methods for measuring the properties of fluids and flows in their different states are important tools for mechanical engineers. Typically, measurements and experimental data are used at the design stage, well before the computational predictions become reliable for refined versions of the product.

Thermodynamics. Thermodynamics is the science behind converting heat to work and estimating the best theoretical performance that a system can achieve under given constraints. The three basic laws of temperature are the zeroth law, which defines temperature and thermal equilibrium; the first law, which describes the exchange between heat, work, and internal energy; and the second law, which defines the concept of entropy. Although these laws were empirically derived and have no closed-form proof, they give results identical to those that come from the law of conservation of energy and to notions of entropy derived from statistical mechanics of elementary particles traced to quantum theory. No one has yet been able to demonstrate a true perpetual-motion machine, and it does not appear likely that anyone will. From the first law, various heat-engine cycles have been invented to obtain better performance suited to various constraints. Engineers working on power-generating engines, propulsion systems, heating systems, and air-conditioning and refrigeration systems try to select and optimize thermodynamic cycles and then use a figure of merit—a means of evaluating the performance of a device or system against the best theoretical performance that could be achieved—as a measure of the effectiveness of their design.

Heat transfer. Heat can be transferred through conduction, convection, or radiation, and all three modes are used in heat exchangers and insulators. Cooling towers for nuclear plants, heat exchangers for nuclear reactors, automobile and home air-conditioners, and the radiators for the International Space Station are all designed from basic principles of these modes of heat transfer. Some space vehicles are designed with heat shields that are ablative. The Thermos flask (which uses an evacuated space between two silvered glass walls) and windows with double and triple panes with coatings are examples of widely used products designed specifically to control heat transfer.

Machine design. Machine design is at the core of mechanical engineering, bringing together the various disciplines of graphics, solid and fluid mechanics, heat transfer, kinematics, and system design in an organized approach to designing devices to perform specific functions. This field teaches engineers how to translate the requirements for a machine into a design. It includes procedures for choosing materials and processes, determining loads and deflections, failure theories, finite element analysis, and the basics of how to use various machine elements such as shafts, keys, couplings, bearings, fasteners, gears, clutches, and brakes.

Metrology. The science of metrology concerns measuring systems. Engineers deal with improving the accuracy, precision, linearity, sensitivity, signal-to-noise ratio, and frequency response of measuring systems. The precision with which dimensions are measured has a huge impact on the quality of engineering products. Large systems such as airliners are assembled from components built on different continents. For these to fit together at final assembly, each component must be manufactured to exacting tolerances, yet requiring too much accuracy sharply increases the cost of production. Metrology helps in specifying the tolerances required and ensuring that products are made to such tolerances.

Acoustics and vibrations. These fields are similar in much of their terminology and analysis methods. They deal with wavelike motions in matter, their effects, and their control. Vibrations are rarely desirable, and their minimization is a goal of engineers in perfecting systems. Acoustics is important not only because minimizing noise is usually important, but also because engineers must be able to build machines to generate specific sounds, and because the audio signature is an important tool in diagnosing system status and behavior.

Production engineering. Production engineering deals with improving the planning and implementation of the production process, designing efficient and precise tools to produce goods, laying out efficient assembly sequences and facilities, and setting up the flow of materials and supplies into the production line, and the control of quality and throughput rate. Production engineering is key to implementing the manufacturing step that translates engineering designs into competitive products.

APPLICATIONS AND PRODUCTS

Conventional applications. Mechanical engineering is applied to the design, manufacture, and testing of almost every product used by humans and to the machines that help humans build those products. The products most commonly associated with mechanical engineering include all vehicles such as railway trains, buses, ships, cars, airplanes and spacecraft, cranes, engines, and electric or hydraulic motors of all kinds, heating, ventilation and air-conditioning systems, the machine tools used in mass manufacture, robots, agricultural tools, and the machinery in power plants. Several other fields of engineering such as aerospace, materials, nuclear, industrial, systems, naval architecture, computer, and biomedical developed and spun off at the interfaces of mechanical engineering with specialized applications. Although these fields have developed specialized theory and knowledge bases of their own, mechanical engineering continues to find application in the design and manufacture of their products.

Innovations in materials. Carbon nanotubes have been heralded as a future super-material with strength hundreds of times that of steel for the same mass. Composite materials incorporating carbon already find wide use in various applications where high temperatures must be encountered. Metal matrix composites find use in primary structures even for commercial aircraft. Several "smart structures" have been developed, where sensors and actuators are incorporated into a material that has special properties to respond to stress and strain. These enable structures that will twist in a desired direction when bent or become stiffer or more flexible as desired, depending on electrical signals sent through the material. Materials capable of handling very low (cryogenic) temperatures are at the leading edge of research applications. Magnetic materials with highly organized structure have been developed, promising permanent magnets with many times the attraction of natural magnets.

Sustainable systems. One very important growth area in mechanical engineering is in designing replacements for existing heating, ventilation, and air-conditioning systems, as well as power generators, that use environmentally benign materials and yet achieve high thermodynamic efficiencies, minimizing heat emission into the atmosphere. This effort demands a great deal of innovation and is at the leading edge of research, both in new ways of generating power and in reducing the need for power.

Medicine and biology. Biomechanics is an application of mechanical science in biomedical and biological sciences that helps in the fabrication of exoskeletons and prosthetics. Carbon nanotubes can be helpful in deoxyribonucleic acid (DNA) recognition, immunology, and antiviral resistance. Nanorobotics, a combination of nanotechnology, mechanics, and biomaterials, can be used to treat medical conditions such as cancer, cerebral aneurysm, and kidney stones. Computational fluid dynamics helps in the understanding of blood flows, human organ dynamics, and surgical simulations.

CAREERS

Mechanical engineers work in nearly every industry, in an innumerable variety of functions. The curriculum in engineering school accordingly focuses on giving the student a firm foundation in the basic knowledge that enables problem solving and continued learning through life. The core curriculum starts with basic mathematics, science, graphics and an introduction to design and goes on to engineering mechanics and the core subjects and specialized electives. In twenty-first-century engineering schools, students have the opportunity to work on individual research and design projects that are invaluable in providing the student with perspective and integrating their problem-solving skills. Courses include mechanical and aerospace engineering, computational engineering, robotics engineering, and engineering mechanics.

After obtaining a bachelor's degree, the mechanical engineer has a broad range of career choices. Traditional occupations include designing systems for energy, heating, ventilation, air-conditioning, pressure vessels and piping, automobiles, and railway equipment. Newer options include the design of bioengineering production systems, microelectromechanical systems, optical instrumentation, telecommunications equipment, and software.

SOCIAL CONTEXT AND FUTURE PROSPECTS

Mechanical engineering attracts large numbers of students and offers a broad array of career opportunities. Students in mechanical engineering schools have the opportunity to range across numerous disciplines and create their own specialties. With nano machines and biologically inspired self-assembling robots becoming realities, mechanical engineering has transformed from a field that generally focused on big industry to one that also emphasizes tiny and efficient machines. Energy-related studies are likely to become a major thrust of mechanical engineering curricula. It is possible that the future will unfold a postindustrial age where the mass-manufacture paradigm of the Industrial Revolution that forced the overcrowding of cities and caused extensive damage to the environment is replaced by a widely distributed industrial economy that enables small communities to be self-reliant for essential services and yet be useful contributors to the global economy. This will create innumerable opportunities for innovation and design.

—*Narayanan M. Komerath*

Further Reading

Bunnell, Brian, and Samer Najia. *Mechanical Engineering for Makers: A Hands-On Guide to Designing and Making Physical Things.* Make Community LLC, 2020.

Davies, Matthew A., and Tony L. Schmitz. *System Dynamics for Mechanical Engineers.* Springer, 2015.

Driss, Zied. *Mechanical Engineering Technologies and Applications.* Bentham Science Publishers, 2021.

Gallagher, Mary Beth. "MIT Mechanical Engineers Develop Solutions to Help Slow and Stop the Spread of COVID-19." *SciTechDaily,* 2 Dec. 2020, scitechdaily.com/mit-mechanical-engineers-develop-solutions-to-help-slow-and-stop-the-spread-of-covid-19. Accessed 15 June 2021.

Lienhard, John H., IV, and John H. Lienhard V. *A Heat Transfer Textbook.* 4th ed., Dover, 2011.

"Mechanical Engineering in Biology and Medicine." *Johns Hopkins University,* 2021, me.jhu.edu/research/mechanical-engineering-in-biology-and-medicine. Accessed 15 June 2021.

Pelesko, John A. *Self-Assembly: The Science of Things That Put Themselves Together.* Chapman, 2007.

Siciliano, Bruno, et al. *Robotics: Modelling, Planning and Control.* Springer-Verlag, 2010.

See also: Acoustics; Aeronautical engineering; Aerospace design; Automated processes and servomechanisms; Biomedical engineering; Centrifugation; Civil engineering; Classical or applied mechanics; Clausius formulates the second law of thermodynamics; Computer-aided engineering; Diesel engine; Dynamics (mechanics); Engineering; Engineering tolerances; External combustion engine; Fluid dynamics; Flywheels; Force (physics); Friction; Harmonic oscillator; Heat transfer; Hydraulic engineering; Internal combustion engine; Jet engines; Kinetic energy; Load; Materials science; Mechatronics; Nanotechnology; Pendulums; Robotics; Rotary engine; Solenoid; Solid mechanics; Springs; Structural engineering; Thermodynamics; Torque; Transportation; Tull, Jethro; Turbines; Work and energy

MECHATRONICS

Fields of Study: Physics; Mechanics; Mathematics

ABSTRACT

Mechatronics is a field of science that incorporates electrical and mechanical engineering, computer control, and information technology. The field is used to design functional and adaptable products and is concerned with traditional mechanical products that are controlled by electronic and computerized mechanisms. Mechatronics can be applied to a variety of fields.

KEY CONCEPTS

actuator: a device that functions to provide motion to a component for a particular purpose; operated hydraulically, pneumatically, or electrically

hydraulic system: a means of transferring mechanical power to various parts of a mechanical system by pumping oil at high pressure through a series of connecting hoses or pipes; used primarily to operate high-strength hydraulic rams and motors

pneumatic system: a means of transferring mechanical power to various parts of a mechanical system by pumping air at elevated pressure through a series of connecting hoses or pipes; used primarily to operate low-strength rams and actuators

solenoid: an electromagnetic device that uses the magnetic field generated inside a wire coil to drive the motion of a steel rod when an electrical current is passed through the coil; typically used as an actuating device

BACKGROUND AND OVERVIEW

Mechatronics is a field of science that incorporates electrical and mechanical engineering, computer control, and information technology. The field is used to design functional and adaptable products and is concerned with traditional mechanical products that are controlled by electronic and computerized mechanisms. A robot is an example of an item made using mechatronics. Its physical parts are produced using mechanical engineering, but its parts that power it and allow it to function are produced using electronic and computerized means. A robot itself is also an example of a mechatronic product because it contains both mechanical and electronic parts controlled by a computer. Mechatronics can be applied to a variety of fields.

Mechatronics can be used to describe the process in which machines are automated by way of computers and other electronic equipment. Prior to the 1970s, many everyday items such as machine tools, manufacturing equipment, and home appliances were made using and operating only on mechanical principles; they had few—if any—electronic elements. For example, cars of this era had mostly mechanical parts such as the engine, gearbox, and drive shaft. The lights, windshield wipers, and some auxiliary features such as blower motors and remote trunk latch solenoids were essentially the only electrical components in a car. As time passed, cars were made with both mechanical and electrical parts. Cars with electrical sensors warned drivers of potential problems that a car may have such as low tire pressure or low oil levels. Modern cars have features such as traction control, which is controlled by both mechanical elements such as the tires and electrical elements such as sensors. Antilock brakes, climate control, and memory-adjust seats also are examples of features made possible by mechatronics.

Near the early 1970s, Japanese engineer Tetsuro Mori coined the term mechatronic from the words mechanical and electronic to describe the functions

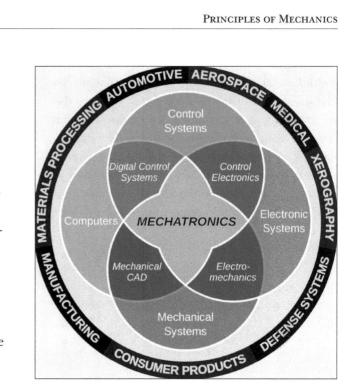

Aerial Euler diagram describes the fields that make up mechatronics. Image by Ahm2307, via Wikimedia Commons.

that the Yaskawa Electric Corp. used to manufacture mechanical factory equipment. The factory used both mechanical and electronic elements to produce electric motors that were controlled by computers. Yaskawa later registered the term, but it was not used regularly until electrical, electronic, and computerized systems were integrated into mechanical products.

The use of new technology, such as computer hardware and software, made controlling and operating machines much easier and less costly. This technology allowed factories to manufacture many new products that were both mechanical and electrical faster, more accurately, and less expensively since computers could be programmed to instruct machines.

Throughout the 1970s, mechatronic technology was used in the robotics field, such as to help robotic arms coordinate movements, and the automotive industry, such as to equip cars with electronic features. It was also used to advance servo technology, which controlled automatic door openers, vending machines, and more. In the following decade, the introduction of information technology allowed engineers to improve the performance of mechanical systems by installing microprocessors in the machinery. By the 1990s, advanced computer technology further influenced the field of mechatronics and expanded its reach into numerous fields.

TOPIC TODAY

As of the twenty-first century, mechatronics is used to make numerous items such as automobiles, home appliances, computer hard drives, medical devices, and automotive parts as well as the machinery used to produce these items, such as computerized assembly systems. Any machinery that requires the use of a senor is made using mechatronic technology. For example, a clothes dryer is programmed to stop when clothes are dry or windshield wipers slow down for drizzle or speed up for harder rain.

Mechatronics is used in an array of applications, including biomedical systems; computer-aided design; computer numerical control (CNC) and direct numerical control (DNC) of machinery; energy and power systems; data communication systems; industrial goods; machine automation; and vehicular systems. Mechatronics can be classified into ten technical areas: actuators and sensors; automotive systems; intelligent control; manufacturing; modeling and design; micro devices and optoelectronics (technology that uses electronics and light); motion control; robotics; system integration; and vibration and noise control. These areas depend on a blend of mechanical, computerized, and electronic systems for product development and production technology.

While the subject of mechatronics has been studied in Japan and Europe for several decades, the field has been slow to gain both industrial and academic acceptance in the United States. Before engineers were skilled in mechatronics, mechanical engineers focused on designing machines and products, while software and computer engineers worked on the control and programming elements of these machines. The introduction of mechatronics streamlined this process since engineers skilled in mechatronics can both construct machinery and write the control systems to operate it. They understand both the mechanical design and all of the electronic and computerized elements that allow the devices to operate.

Students interested in mechatronics can pursue degrees in mechanical engineering with a focus on electrical engineering and computer control. Some universities offer specialized mechatronics programs. Mechatronics is used to create an array of products in many different industries. Many manufacturing companies are requiring engineers to be trained in electronics, mechanics, computer control, and more. Individuals trained in mechatronics can also work in a variety of fields outside the manufacturing industry. They can oversee robots in factories where the machines assemble products such as vehicles. They can run greenhouses using controls that manage lighting, irrigation, and temperature to produce plants more effectively or construct wind farms.

Engineers skilled in mechatronics can help design systems that allow cars to drive themselves or drones to fly themselves. They can design high-tech security measures such as fingerprint sensors, voice-recognition programs, and retinal scans. They can design virtual reality interfaces for the gaming industry. The increased need for technological advances in the industrial and manufacturing sectors will continue to have an influence on the growing mechatronics field.

—Angela Harmon

Further Reading

"10 Surprising Things You Might Do with a Mechatronics Degree." *East Coast Polytechnic Institute Blog*, www.ecpi.edu/blog/10-surprising-things-you-might-do-with-mechatronics-degree. Accessed 19 Jan. 2017.

Bradley, David Allan, Derek Seward, David Dawson, and Stewart Burge. *Mechatronics and the Design of Intelligent Machines and Systems*. CRC Press, 2018.

Brown, Alan S. "Mechatronics and the Role of Engineers." *American Society of Mechanical Engineers*, Aug. 2011, www.asme.org/engineering-topics/articles/mechatronics/mechatronics-and-the-role-of-engineers. Accessed 19 Jan. 2017.

Doehring, James. "What Is Mechatronics Engineering?" *Wisegeek*, 20 Dec. 2016, www.wisegeek.com/what-is-mechatronics-engineering.htm. Accessed 19 Jan. 2017.

Jeffress, D. "What Does a Mechatronics Engineer Do?" *Wisegeek*, 12 Jan. 2017, www.wisegeek.com/what-does-a-mechatronics-engineer-do.htm#comments. Accessed 19 Jan. 2017.

Lyshevski, Sergey Edward. *Mechatronics and Control of Electromechanical Systems*. Taylor & Francis Limited, 2020.

"Mechatronics History." *Bright Hub Engineering*, 13 May 2010, www.brighthubengineering.com/manufacturing-technology/71180-the-history-of-mechatronics. Accessed 19 Jan. 2017.

Spiegel, Rob. "Mechatronics: Blended Engineering for the Robotic Future." *DesignNews*, 23 Nov. 2016, www.designnews.com/automation-motion-control/mechatronics-blended-engineering-robotic-future/199011163046152. Accessed 19 Jan. 2017.

"What Is Mechatronic Engineering?" *Brightside*, www.brightknowledge.org/knowledge-bank/engineering/features-and-resources/copy_of_what-is-mechatronic-engineering. Accessed 19 Jan. 2017.

"What Is Mechatronics?" *Institution of Mechanical Engineers*, www.imeche.org/get-involved/special-interest-groups/mechatronics-informatics-and-control-group/mechatronics-informatics-and-control-group-information-and-resources/what-is-mechatronics. Accessed 19 Jan. 2017.

"What Is Mechatronics?" *North Carolina State University*, www.engr.ncsu.edu/mechatronics/what-mech.php. Accessed 19 Jan. 2017.

Zhang, Dan and Bin Wei, editors. *Robotics and Mechatronics for Agriculture*. CRC Press, 2017.

See also: Acceleration; Acoustics; Aeronautical engineering; Aerospace design; Ailerons, flaps, and airplane wings; Automated processes and servomechanisms; Biomedical engineering; Calculating system efficiency; Computer-aided engineering; Dynamics (mechanics); Electromagnet technology; Electromagnetism; Engineering; Force (physics); Flywheels; Friction; Gauss's law; Harmonic oscillator; Inertial guidance; Kinematics; Lenz's law; Load; Magnetism; Momentum (physics); Motion; Newton's laws; Pendulums; Photoelectric effect; Robotics; Solenoid; Superconductor

MOMENT OF INERTIA

Fields of Study: Physics; Mechanics; Mathematics

ABSTRACT
Moment of inertia is a fundamental property in rotational mechanics that applies to any object that can be rotated. Put simply, moment of inertia is a determination of how difficult it is to change the rotational velocity of an object about its rotational axis. In rotational dynamics, moment of inertia plays essentially the same role that mass plays in linear dynamics, which deals with the motion of bodies in a straight line.

KEY CONCEPTS
flywheel: typically, a relatively massive circular object that functions to store and transfer rotational motion as it spins

inertia: the resistance of an object to any change in its state of motion

plane of the ecliptic: the geometric plane in which the planets orbit their star

polar axis: the line through a planet passing through its north and south poles, about which the planet rotates

rotational axis: a theoretical line passing through the point about which an object is rotating, always orthogonal to the direction of rotation

ROTATIONAL DYNAMICS AND LINEAR DYNAMICS
Moment of inertia is a fundamental property in rotational mechanics that applies to any object that

can be rotated. It is also sometimes known as mass moment of inertia or rotational inertia. Specifically, moment of inertia is a measure of an object's resistance to a change in its rotational state. Put simply, moment of inertia is a determination of how difficult it is to change the rotational velocity of an object about its rotational axis. As a physics concept, moment of inertia is one of the core principles of dynamics, a branch of mechanical science concerned with the motion of bodies under the action of various forces. In rotational dynamics, which deals with the motion of bodies in rotation, moment of inertia plays essentially the same role that mass plays in linear dynamics, which deals with the motion of bodies in a straight line. This means that moment of inertia is an important concept in determining the relationship between such factors as angular momentum and angular velocity, and torque and angular acceleration.

BACKGROUND

Moment of inertia is a concept that is broadly tied to a branch of physics called mechanics. Concerned primarily with the study of motion, this branch is further subdivided into two separate fields: statics and dynamics. Statics is the study of bodies in equilibrium, or a state of balance between opposing forces. Dynamics, meanwhile, is the study of bodies in motion. Within the discipline of dynamics, there are two additional subfields: kinematics and kinetics. While kinematics is concerned strictly with the geometry and time evolution of motion, kinetics is concerned with the relationship between motion and the various forces involved. It is with kinetics that moment of inertia is most closely associated.

The earliest significant studies in dynamics were first carried out by Italian scientist Galileo Galilei in the seventeenth century. Known mainly for his pioneering and often controversial contributions to astronomy and physics, Galileo conducted a series of experiments that ultimately led to the first major breakthroughs in the field of dynamics. In addition to discovering the laws of motion that govern projectiles and object in free fall, Galileo successfully outlined the law of inertia. Even more impressive was the fact that he did all this at a time when key branches of mathematics like differential and integral calculus were nonexistent and none of the modern instruments that allow for the exact measurement of time had yet been invented.

Later in the seventeenth century, English mathematician, astronomer, and physicist Isaac Newton further developed the scientific basis of dynamics when he created what are today known as Newton's laws of motion. These three laws represented a major scientific advance in that they provided a clear explanation of the experimental evidence previously gathered by scientists such as Galileo and showed that it was possible to make precise, accurate predictions about the behavior of objects in motion. Moreover, Newton's laws of motion served as the fundamental basis for the development of classical mechanics. As it pertains to moment of inertia, Newton's second law of motion, which states that the force acting on an object is equal to the mass of that object times its acceleration, is the most relevant of the three.

OVERVIEW

Moment of inertia is a measure of an object's resistance to changes in its rate of rotation. To fully understand what moment of inertia is and how it works, it is first necessary to know a number of key terms, including angular momentum, angular velocity, axis of rotation, torque, and angular acceleration.

Angular momentum is the quantity of rotation of a body and is the product of its moment of inertia and its angular velocity. Angular velocity is the rate of change in angular position in a rotating body. Axis of rotation is the straight line through all fixed points of a rotating body around which all other points of the body circle. Torque is a measure of the force that can cause an object to rotate about an axis. Angular acceleration is the rate of change in angular velocity. All of these factors play into moment of inertia in different ways.

The second key to understanding moment of inertia is recognizing the nature of its relationship to Newton's second law of motion. As written, Newton's second law applies specifically to linear dynamics. When applied to rotational dynamics, the moment of inertia takes the place of mass in the original law. As a result, the angular equivalent to Newton's second law states that the rate of change of angular momentum of a system is equal to the torque (or moment of inertia) applied to that system. In practice, this simply means that the farther away a mass moves from the axis of rotation, the more difficult it becomes to change the system's rotational velocity. This is true because momentum and the momentum vector, which is a quantity that is described by magnitude and direction, are both dependent on a mass's distance from the axis of rotation. As a mass moves away from the axis of rotation, its speed and momentum increase and its momentum vector begins changing more rapidly. This, in turn, makes it more difficult to turn the mass.

An object's moment of inertia is also affected by its size and shape. Where size is concerned, the bigger and heavier an object is, the higher its moment of inertia will be. At the same time, awkwardly shaped objects are also likely to have a higher moment of inertia. In either case, a higher moment of inertia means that larger or more awkwardly shaped objects will be more resistant to changes in their rate of rotation. Put another way, it can be accurately said that the more mass an object has farther away from the axis around which it rotates, the more work it will take to turn the object. As an example, if one were to attach a pair of weights at the center of a stick and an identical pair of weights at the end of

the same type of stick and attempted to rotate each stick from the center, it would be easier to rotate the first stick. This is because a greater portion of the mass of the second stick is located farther away from its axis of rotation, which means that its moment of inertia is higher.

—*Jack Lasky*

Further Reading

Gross, Dietmar, and Werner Hauger. *Engineering Mechanics 3: Dynamics*. Springer, 2011.

Holzner, Steven. "How to Calculate the Momentum of Inertia for Different Shapes and Solids." *Dummies.com*, www.dummies.com/education/science/physics/how-to-calculate-the-momentum-of-inertia-for-different-shapes-and-solids/. Accessed 26 June 2017.

Holzner, Steven, and Daniel Funch Wohns. "Moments of Inertia in Physics." *Dummies.com*, www.dummies.com/education/science/physics/moments-of-inertia-in-physics. Accessed 26 June 2017.

Ling, Samuel J, Jeff Sanny, and William Moebs. *University Physics Volume 1*. Samurai Media Limited, 2017.

"Moment of Inertia." *Isaac Physics*, isaacphysics.org/concepts/cp_moment_inertia. Accessed 26 June 2017.

"Moment of Inertia." *Shmoop*, www.shmoop.com/rotation/inertia.html. Accessed 26 June 2017.

Rhett, Allain. "Let's Explore the Physics of Rotational Motion with a Fidget Spinner." *Wired*, 23 May 2017, www.wired.com/2017/05/physics-of-a-fidget-spinner. Accessed 26 June 2017.

"Rotational Inertia." *Khan Academy*, www.khanacademy.org/science/physics/torque-angular-momentum/torque-tutorial/a/rotational-inertia. Accessed 26 June 2017.

Singh, D. K. *Strength of Materials*. 4th ed., Springer Nature, 2020.

"What Is Moment of Inertia?" *The Constructor*, theconstructor.org/structural-engg/moment-of-inertia-calculation-formula/2825/. Accessed 26 June 2017.

See also: Acceleration; Aeronautical engineering; Angular forces; Angular momentum; Celestial mechanics; Centrifugation; Circular motion; Flywheels; Force (physics); Friction; Materials science; Momentum; Motion; Newton's laws

Momentum (physics)

Fields of Study: Physics; Mechanics; Mathematics

ABSTRACT

Momentum is a measure of the motion of a physical object in terms of its mass and velocity. Mass is the amount of matter in a physical object, irrespective of its volume or any outside forces acting on it, while velocity is the rate at which an object changes position.

KEY CONCEPTS

angular momentum: the momentum of an object that is moving with circular motion, or rotating; an object can have both linear and angular momentum

linear momentum: the momentum of an object that is moving in a straight line, or translating; an object can have both linear and angular momentum

mass: the sum total of the masses of all atoms that comprise a body of matter whether gaseous, liquid, or solid

scalar quantities: quantities that have magnitude or absolute value, but are not associated with a direction (e.g., 23 kilometers per hour)

speed: the rate at which an object moves, regardless of the direction in which it moves

vector quantities: quantities that have both a magnitude or absolute value and are associated with a direction (e.g., 23 kilometers per hour northwest)

velocity: the rate of change of the position of a body, measured in terms of distance per unit time (e.g., meters per second)

MASS AND VELOCITY

In the field of physics, momentum is a measure of the motion of a physical object in terms of its mass and velocity. To adequately understand momentum, therefore, one must first understand mass and velocity. Mass is simply the amount of matter in a physi-cal object, irrespective of its volume or any outside forces acting on it, while velocity is the rate at which an object changes position. For example, if a person takes a step forward and then steps back to their original position, that person would be said to have zero velocity. However, if a person takes multiple steps to another location and does not return to the original starting point, that person has increased his or her velocity.

Momentum is related to Isaac Newton's first law of motion, which states, "Every body continues in its state of rest or of uniform motion in a straight line, except in so far as it may be compelled by impressed forces to change that state." In other words, an object at rest will remain at rest, and an object moving in a straight line will continue to move in that straight line, until a force such as friction, gravity, or collision with another object causes its velocity or direction to change. If no external force is applied and the object's mass and velocity remain the same, then its momentum will remain constant.

BACKGROUND

Momentum, sometimes called "linear momentum" or "translational momentum" to distinguish it from angular momentum, relates to the mechanics of how something moves. In simpler terms, it can be thought of as the force or speed of mass in motion. All objects have mass because all objects occupy space. If an object with mass moves from one location to another, even an infinitesimal distance, then that object has momentum. Thus, for an object to have momentum, it must have both mass and movement. A lighter object will have less momentum than a heavier object moving at the same speed, and a slow-moving object will have less momentum than an object of the same mass that is moving more quickly.

In a sense, momentum can be said to describe how difficult a moving object would be to stop. If a person were to throw two differently sized balls in the same direction at the same speed, the ball with the greater mass would hit its target with more force because its momentum would be greater, making it harder to stop. However, if the smaller object's velocity were sufficiently greater, the momentum of that smaller object would be greater than a larger object traveling at a fraction of its velocity. For example, a fired bullet would have greater momentum than a thrown ball because the difference between the two objects' masses is much smaller than the difference between their velocities.

OVERVIEW

The mathematical equation for momentum is written as $p = mv$, where p is momentum, m is mass, and v is velocity. Thus, the momentum of an object is directly proportional to both its mass and its velocity. The standard unit for momentum is kg·m/s, derived from the mass of the object in kilograms times its velocity in meters per second.

One of the most important laws in physics is the law of conservation of momentum, which states that an object cannot simply lose momentum. Rather, when two objects collide in an isolated system—that is, where no other outside forces can act on them—any momentum lost by one object is gained by the other object, and the sum total of their momenta remains the same. In other words, momentum is not lost, but simply transferred from one object to another. This law can be seen in action in sports such as tennis, baseball, or soccer, and especially in the game of billiards where the collision of one object (a racket, a bat, a player's foot, or a billiard ball) with another (the ball) imparts sufficient momentum to the second object to send it in another direction at speed.

Linear momentum is distinct from angular momentum, which measures the momentum of a spinning or rotating object. Angular momentum is still a function of mass and velocity, but it must account for the fact that the direction of a rotating object's momentum is always changing. In addition, the parts of a rotating object closest to the axis of rotation move more slowly than the parts farthest away because they have less distance to travel, so the total angular momentum of an object is actually the sum of the angular momenta of each of its constituent particles. Rather than calculate the angular momentum of each particle, one can determine an object's total angular momentum by multiplying its angular velocity (ω) by its moment of inertia (I), which is a measure of the torque, or twisting force, needed to change its angular velocity. Angular momentum is used to measure the momentum of objects in space, such as planets and stars, since these objects rotate around a more-or-less-fixed axis.

—*L. L. Lundin*

Further Reading

Andrews, David L., and Mohamed Babiker, editors. *The Angular Momentum of Light*. Cambridge UP, 2013.

Commins, Eugene D. *Quantum Mechanics: An Experimentalist's Approach*. Cambridge UP, 2014.

Edmonds, A. R. *Angular Momentum in Quantum Mechanics*. Princeton UP, 2016.

Kleppner, Daniel, and Robert Kolenkow. *An Introduction to Mechanics*. 2nd ed., Cambridge UP, 2014.

Ling, Samuel J., Jeff Sanny, and William Moebs. *University Physics Volume 3*. Samurai Media Limited, 2017.

Mircescu, Alexander. *On the Conservation of Momentum, Angular Momentum, Energy, and Information*. BoD Third Party Titles, 2016.

Murdoch, A. Ian. *Physical Foundations of Continuum Mechanics*. Cambridge UP, 2012.

Ohanian, Hans C., and Remo Ruffini. *Gravitation and Spacetime*. 3rd ed., Cambridge UP, 2013.

See also: Acceleration; Angular momentum; Calculus; Circular motion; Classical or applied mechanics; Displacement; Force (physics); Friction; Kinetic energy; Linear motion; Moment of inertia; Motion; Newton's laws; Torque; Vectors

MOTION

Fields of Study: Physics; Mechanics; Mathematics

ABSTRACT

Motion is the process of changing position over time. A push or pull on an object can cause the object to move. In other words, a force acting on an object can cause motion. Newton's three laws of motion explain how forces and motion are related. An object in motion has kinetic energy and travels at a particular velocity.

KEY CONCEPTS

circular motion: motion of an object by translation on a circular, rather than linear, path

linear motion: movement of an object in a straight line, or translation

rotational motion: the motion of an object that is spinning

speed: the rate at which an object moves, regardless of the direction in which it moves

velocity: the rate of change of the position of a body, measured in terms of distance per unit time (e.g., meters per second)

OBSERVING MOTION

When an object is at rest, it occupies a position in space. When a force acts on the object, the object may change its position. The act of changing position over time is called motion.

The only way to tell if an object is moving is to compare it to a reference point. A reference point is a different object that does not appear to be moving. On a city street, a street light could be a reference point. Anything that appears to be changing position in relation to the street light could be defined as having motion.

MOTION AND SCALE

On a city street, cars driving by or people walking on the sidewalk all have motion when compared to a reference point, such as a street light. But a parked car does not appear to have motion. In reality, a parked car does have motion, but not at the scale of the street. The particles in a parked car are constantly moving. So the car has motion at a very small scale. The car itself is located on Earth, which has motion within the solar system. So the car also has motion on a very large scale.

FORCES AND MOTION

A force is needed to cause the motion of an object. A force is an influence that pushes or pulls on an object. An object has many forces acting on it at any point in time. An object at rest has pairs of balanced forces acting on it. When forces are balanced, they have the same magnitude, but are acting in opposite directions. When one of the forces acting on an object increases in magnitude, that pair of forces becomes unbalanced. The force with greater magnitude causes motion when it pushes or pulls on the object.

NEWTON'S LAWS OF MOTION

Newton proposed three laws to explain motion. The first law states that an object will remain at rest or in straight-line motion until a force acts on it. This concept is called inertia. The second law of motion states that the velocity of an object will change when a force acts on it. Velocity describes the speed and direction of an object. The third law states that for every action, there is an equal and opposite reaction. For example, a force such as friction causes a change in the motion of an object that it opposes, such as tires on a car.

MOTION AND SPEED

An object in motion has velocity. The speed of an object is equal to the distance the object has traveled divided by the time it took the object to travel that distance; the velocity of an object is its speed and the direction in which its speed is taking it. In typical everyday usage speed is synonymous with velocity,

A motorcyclist doing a wheelie, representing motion. Photo by AngMoKio, via Wikimedia Commons.

even though the two are very different. Many different units may be used to measure speed. The speed of a very slow object, like a snail, might be measured in centimeters per hour. The speed of a fast object, like a rocket, might be measured in kilometers per second.

—*Catherine Podeszwa*

Further Reading

Kubitz, Alan A. *The Elusive Notion of Motion: The Genius of Kepler, Galileo, Newton, and Einstein.* Dog Ear Publishing, 2010.

Lambourne, Robert. *Describing Motion: The Physical World.* CRC Press, 2019.

Ling, Samual J, Jeff Sanny, and William Moebs. *University Physics Volume 1.* Samurai Media Limited, 2017.

"Newton's Laws of Motion." *The Beginner's Guide to Aeronautics.* National Aeronautics and Space Administration, 2014, www.grc.nasa.gov/WWW/k-12/airplane/newton.html/.

Zimba, Jason. *Force and Motion: An Illustrated Guide to Newton's Laws.* JHU Press, 2009.

See also: Acceleration; Biomechanics; Celestial mechanics; Circular motion; Classical or applied mechanics; Coriolis effect; Displacement; Flywheels; Harmonic oscillator; Kinematics; Levers; Linear motion; Moment of inertia; Momentum (physics); Newton's laws; Pendulums; Projectiles; Speed; Torque; Vectors, Velocity; Vibration

N

NANOTECHNOLOGY

Fields of Study: Physics; Chemistry; Engineering; Mechanics; Mathematics

ABSTRACT

Nanotechnology is dedicated to the study and manipulation of structures at the extremely small nano level. The technology focuses on how particles of a substance at a nanoscale behave differently than particles at a larger scale. Nanotechnology explores how those differences can benefit applications in a variety of fields.

KEY CONCEPTS

graphene: one of the fundamental forms of pure carbon, consisting of flat sheets of carbon atoms in hexagonal rings; graphene is the material of which graphite coal is formed

nanoparticles: particles whose dimensions are measured in nanometers, typically less than 100 nanometers in size

nanoscale: refers to particles and structures less than 100 nanometers in size

quantum mechanical tunneling: an electronic process occurring in atoms, by which electrons may become able to cross energy barriers into electronic regions where they would not otherwise be allowed

OVERVIEW

Nanotechnology is dedicated to the study and manipulation of structures at the extremely small nano level, in which objects are of a size measured in nanometers. The technology focuses on how particles of a substance at the nanometer scale behave differently than particles at a larger scale. Nanotechnology explores how those differences can benefit applications in a variety of fields. In medicine, nanomaterials can be used to deliver drugs to targeted areas of the body needing treatment. Environmental scientists can use nanoparticles to target and eliminate pollutants in the water and air. Microprocessors and consumer products also benefit from increased use of nanotechnology, as components and associated products become exponentially smaller.

DEFINITION AND BASIC PRINCIPLES

Nanotechnology is the science that deals with the study and manipulation of structures at the nano level. At the nano level, things are measured in nanometers (nm), or one billionth of a meter (10^{-9}). Nanoparticles can be produced using various techniques known as top-down nanofabrication, which starts with a larger quantity of material and removes portions to create the nanoscale material. Another method is bottom-up nanofabrication, in which individual atoms or molecules are assembled to create nanoparticles. One area of research involves developing bottom-up self-assembly techniques that would allow nanoparticles to recreate themselves when the necessary materials are placed in contact with one another.

Nanotechnology is based on the discovery that materials behave differently at the nanoscale, less than 100 nm in size, than they do at slightly larger scales. For instance, gold is classified as an inert material because it neither corrodes nor tarnishes; however, at the nano level, gold will oxidize in carbon monoxide. It will also appear as colors other than the yellow for which it is known. For example, the rich, deep red color seen in old stained glass windows is due to nanoparticles consisting of three atoms of gold.

Nanotechnology is not simply about working with materials such as gold at the nanoscale. It also involves taking advantage of the differences at this scale to create markers and other new structures that are of use in a wide variety of medical and other applications.

BACKGROUND AND HISTORY

In 1931, German scientists Ernst Ruska and Max Knoll built the first transmission electron micro-

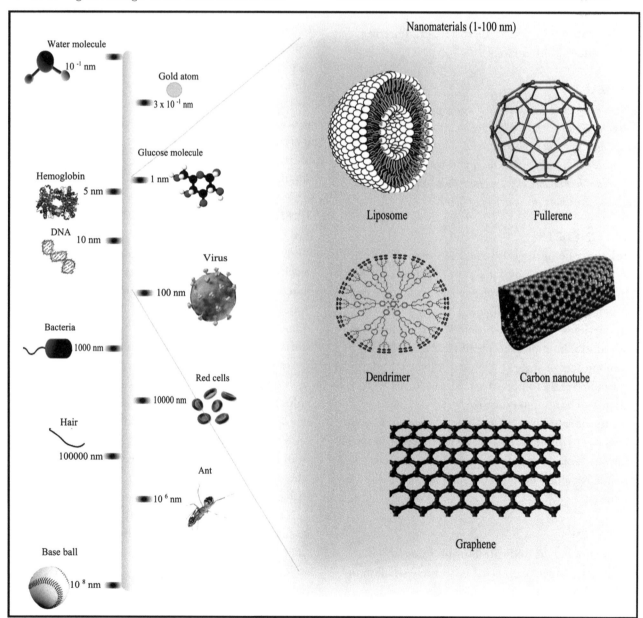

Comparison of nanotechnology sizes. Image by Sureshbup, via Wikimedia Commons.

scope (TEM). Capable of magnifying objects by a factor of up to one million, the TEM made it possible to see things at the molecular level. The TEM was used to study the proteins that make up the human body. It was also used to study metals. The TEM made it possible to view particles smaller than 200 nm by focusing a beam of electrons to pass through an object, rather than focusing light on an object, as is the case with traditional microscopes.

In 1959, the noted American theoretical physicist Richard Feynman brought nanoscale possibilities to the forefront with his talk "There's Plenty of Room at the Bottom," presented at the California Institute of Technology in 1959. In this talk, he asked the audience to consider what would happen if they could arrange individual atoms, and he included a discussion of the scaling issues that would arise. It is generally agreed that Feynman's reputation and influence brought increased attention to the possible uses of structures at the atomic level.

In the 1970s, scientists worked with nanoscale materials to create technology for space colonies. In 1974, Tokyo Science University professor Norio Taniguchi coined the term "nano-technology." As he defined it, nanotechnology would be a manufacturing process for materials built by atoms or molecules.

In the 1980s, the invention of the scanning tunneling microscope (STM) led to the discovery of fullerenes, or hollow carbon molecules, in 1986. The carbon nanotube was discovered a few years later. Ironically, such carbon molecules are formed naturally in carbonaceous smoke and have probably been in existence since the very first wood fire. In 1986, K. Eric Drexler's seminal work on nanotechnology, *Engines of Creation*, was published. In this work, Drexler used the term "nanotechnology" to describe a process that is now understood to be molecular nanotechnology. Drexler's book explores the positive and negative consequences of being able to manipulate the structure of matter. Included in his

book are ruminations on a time when all the works in the Library of Congress would fit on a sugar cube and when nanoscale robots and scrubbers could clear capillaries or whisk pollutants from the air. Debate continues as to whether Drexler's vision of a world with such nanotechnology is even attainable.

In 2000, the US National Nanotechnology Initiative was founded. Its mandate is to coordinate federal nanotechnology research and development. Great growth in the creation of improved products using nanoparticles has taken place since that time. The creation of smaller and smaller components—which reduces all aspects of manufacture, from the amount of materials needed to the cost of shipping the finished product—is driving the use of nanoscale materials in the manufacturing sector. Furthermore, the ability to target delivery of treatments to areas of the body needing those treatments is spurring research in the medical field.

The true promise of nanotechnology is not yet known, but this multidisciplinary science is widely viewed as one that will alter the landscape of fields from manufacturing to medicine.

HOW IT WORKS

Basic tools. Nanoscale materials can be created for specific purposes, but there exists also natural nanoscale material, like smoke from fire. To create nanoscale material and to be able to work with it requires specialized tools and technology. One essential piece of equipment is an electron microscope. Electron microscopy makes use of electrons, rather than light, to view objects. Because these microscopes have to get the electrons moving, and because they need several thousand volts of electricity, they are often quite large.

One type of electron microscope, the scanning electron microscope (SEM), requires a metallic sample. If the sample is not metallic, it is coated with gold. The SEM can give an accurate image with good resolution at sizes as small as a few nanometers.

For smaller objects or closer viewing, a TEM is more appropriate. With a TEM, the electrons pass through the object. To accomplish this, the sample has to be very thin, and preparing the sample is time consuming. The TEM also has greater power needs than the SEM, so SEM is used in most cases, and the TEM is reserved for times when a resolution of a few tenths of a nanometer is absolutely necessary.

The atomic force microscope (AFM) is a third type of electron microscope. Designed to give a clear image of the surface of a sample, this microscope uses a laser to scan across the surface. The result is an image that shows the surface of the object, making visible the object's "peaks and valleys."

Moving the actual atoms around is an important part of creating nanoscale materials for specific purposes. Another type of electron microscope, the STM, images the surface of a material in the same way as the AFM. The tip of the probe, which typically consists of a single atom, can also be used to pass an electrical current to the sample, which lessens the space between the probe and the sample. As the probe moves across the sample, the atoms nearest the charged atom move with it. In this way, individual atoms can be moved to a desired location by using a process known as quantum mechanical tunneling.

Molecular assemblers and nanorobots are two other potential tools. The assemblers would use specialized tips to form bonds with materials that would make specific types of materials easier to move. Nanorobots might someday move through a person's blood stream or through the atmosphere, equipped with nanoscale processors and other materials that enable them to perform specific functions.

Bottom-up nanofabrication. Bottom-up nanofabrication is one approach to nanomanufacturing. This process builds a specific nanostructure or material by combining components of atomic and molecular scale. Creating a structure this way is time consuming, so scientists are working to create nanoscale materials that will spontaneously join to assemble a desired structure without physical manipulation.

Top-down nanofabrication. Top-down nanofabrication is a process in which a larger amount of material is used at the start. The desired nanomaterial is created by removing, or carving away, the material that is not needed. This is less time consuming than bottom-up nanofabrication, but it produces considerable waste.

SPECIALIZED PROCESSES

To facilitate the manufacture of nanoscale materials, a number of specialized processes are used. These include nanoimprint lithography, in which nanoscale features are stamped or printed onto a surface; atomic layer epitaxy, in which a layer that is only one atom thick is deposited on a surface; and dip-pen lithography, in which the tip of an atomic force microscope writes on a surface after being dipped into a chemical.

APPLICATIONS AND PRODUCTS

Smart materials. Smart materials are materials that react in ways appropriate to the stimulus or situation they encounter. Combining smart materials with nanoscale materials would, for example, enable scientists to create drugs that would respond when encountering specific viruses or diseases. They could also be used to signal problems with other systems, such as nuclear power generators or pollution levels.

Sensors. The difference between a smart material and a sensor is that the smart material will generate a response to the situation encountered, while the sensor will generate an alarm or signal that there is something that requires attention. The capacity to incorporate sensors at a nanoscale greatly enhances the ability of engineers and manufacturers to create structures and products with a feedback loop that is not cumbersome. Nanoscale materials can easily be incorporated into the product.

Medical uses. The potential uses of nanoscale materials in the field of medicine are of particular interest to researchers. Theoretically, nanorobots, or nanobots, could be programmed to perform functions that would eliminate the possibility of infection at a wound site. They could also speed healing. Smart materials could be designed to dispense medication in appropriate doses when a virus or bacteria is encountered. Sensors could be used to alert physicians to the first stages of malignancy. There is great potential for nanomaterials to meet the needs of aging populations without intrusive surgeries requiring lengthy recovery and rehabilitation.

As an example of the potential medical benefits of nanotechnology, researches pursued several new uses for the technology in the early 2020s. According to a paper published in the journal *Frontiers in Bioengineering and biotechnology,* scientists studied the use of nanotechnology to stop the spread of tropical mosquitos that can carry diseases such as yellow fever, dengue, and the Zika virus. Another 2020 study published in the *Journal of Drug Delivery Science and Technology* touted the technology's success in helping patients heal from nerve injuries.

Energy. Nanomaterials also hold promise for energy applications. With nanostructures, components of heating and cooling systems could be tailored to control temperatures with greater efficiency. This could be accomplished by engineering the materials so that some types of atoms, such as oxygen, can pass through, while others, such as mold or moisture, cannot. With this level of control, living conditions could be designed to meet the specific needs of different categories of residents.

Extending the life of batteries and prolonging their charge has been the subject of decades of research. With nanoparticles, researchers at Rutgers University and Bell Labs have been able to better separate the chemical components of batteries, resulting in longer battery life. With further nanoscale research, it may be possible to alter the internal composition of batteries to achieve even greater performance.

Light-emitting diode (LED) technology uses 90 percent less energy than conventional, non-LED lighting. It also generates less heat than traditional metal-filament lightbulbs. Nanomanufacturing would make it possible to create a new generation of efficient LED lighting products.

Electronics. Moore's law states that transistor density on integrated circuits doubles about every two years. With the advent of nanotechnology, the rate of miniaturization has the potential to double at a much greater rate. This miniaturization will profoundly affect the computer industry. Computers will become lighter and smaller as nanoparticles are used to increase everything from screen resolution to battery life while reducing the size of essential internal components, such as capacitors.

SOCIAL CONTEXT AND FUTURE PROSPECTS

Whether nanotechnology will ultimately be good or bad for the human race remains to be seen, as it continues to be incorporated into more and more products and processes, both common and highly specialized. There is tremendous potential associated with the ability to manipulate individual atoms and molecules, to deliver medications to a disease site, and to build products such as cars that are lighter yet stronger than ever. Much research is devoted to using nanotechnology to improve fields such as pollution mitigation, energy efficiency, and cell and tissue engineering. However, there also exists the persistent worry that humans will lose control of this technology and face what Drexler called a "gray goo" scenario, in which self-replicating nanorobots run out of control and ultimately destroy the world.

Despite fears linked to cutting-edge technology, many experts, including nanotechnology pioneers, consider such doomsday scenarios involving robots to be highly unlikely or even impossible outside of science fiction. More worrisome, many argue, is the potential for nanotechnology to have other unintended negative consequences, including health impacts and ethical challenges. Some studies have shown that the extremely small nature of nanoparticles makes them susceptible to being breathed in or ingested by humans and other animals, potentially causing significant damage. Structures including carbon nanotubes of graphene have been linked to cancer. Furthermore, the range of possible applications for nanotechnology raises various ethical questions about how, when, and by whom such technology can and should be used, including issues of economic inequality and notions of "playing God." These risks, and the potential for other unknown negative impacts, have led to calls for careful regulation and oversight of nanotechnology, as there has been with nuclear technology, genetic engineering, and other powerful technologies. Further highlighting the importance of the field of nanotechnology, in 2020, the US Food and Drug Administration, responsible for overseeing a wide range of products across the many categories within its purview, released a report detailing the continued studies, partnerships, and regulation considerations the agency had conducted and committed to since 2007, the year in which it last reported on the subject.

Furthermore, in 2020, efforts to create a vaccine as quickly but safely as possible for the devastating coronavirus disease 2019 (COVID-19) pandemic brought the potential for the use of nanotechnology in the field of medicine to prominence once more. The two vaccines for the disease ultimately produced by the companies Moderna and Pfizer implemented messenger RNA (mRNA) technology, and lipid nanoparticles, which had been used as part of drug delivery in the past, were involved in protectively carrying the mRNA to the proper location within cells.

—*Gina Hagler*

Further Reading

Berlatsky, Noah. *Nanotechnology*. Greenhaven, 2014.

Binns, Chris. *Introduction to Nanoscience and Nanotechnology*. Wiley, 2010.

Biswas, Abhijit, et al. "Advances in Top-Down and Bottom-Up Surface Nanofabrication: Techniques, Applications & Future Prospects." *Advances in Colloid and Interface Science*, vol. 170, nos. 1-2, 2012, pp. 2-27.

Campo, Estefânia Vangelie Ramos, et al. "Recent Developments in Nanotechnology for Detection and Control of Aedes aegypti-Borne Diseases." *Frontiers in Bioengineering and Biotechnology*, vol. 20, 2020, doi:10.3389/fbioe.2020.00102. Accessed 15 Mar. 2022.

Demetzos, Costas. *Pharmaceutical Nanotechnology: Fundamentals and Practical Applications*. Adis, 2016.

Drexler, K. Eric. *Radical Abundance: How a Revolution in Nanotechnology Will Change Civilization*. PublicAffairs, 2013.

Khudyakov, Yury E., and Paul Pumpens. *Viral Nanotechnology*. CRC Press, 2016.

Kumar, Raj, et al. "Advances in Nanotechnology and Nanomaterials Based Strategies for Neural Tissue Engineering." *Journal of Drug Delivery Science and Technology*, vol. 57, 2020, doi:org/10.1016/j.jddst.2020.101617. Accessed 15 Mar. 2022.

Ramsden, Jeremy. *Nanotechnology*. Elsevier, 2016.

Ratner, Daniel, and Mark A. Ratner. *Nanotechnology and Homeland Security: New Weapons for New Wars*. Prentice, 2004.

Ratner, Mark A., and Daniel Ratner. *Nanotechnology: A Gentle Introduction to the Next Big Idea*. Prentice, 2003.

Rogers, Ben, Jesse Adams, and Sumita Pennathur. *Nanotechnology: The Whole Story*. CRC, 2013.

Rogers, Ben, Sumita Pennathur, and Jesse Adams. *Nanotechnology: Understanding Small Systems*. 2nd ed., CRC Press, 2011.

Stine, Keith J. *Carbohydrate Nanotechnology*. Wiley, 2016.

Tenchov, Rumiana. "Understanding the Nanotechnology in COVID-19 Vaccines." *CAS*, American Chemical Society, www.cas.org/blog/understanding-nanotechnology-covid-19-vaccines. Accessed 18 Mar. 2021.

See also: Atoms; Biomedical engineering; Materials science; Mechanical engineering; Photoelectric effect; Quantum mechanics; Robotics; Superconductor

NEWTON, ISAAC

Fields of Study: Physics; Mechanics; Mathematics

ABSTRACT

Isaac Newton was born December 25, 1642 (January 4, 1643) in Woolsthorpe Manor, near Colsterworth, Lincolnshire, England, and died March 31, 1727, in London, England. Newton's theory of gravitation and laws of mechanics described, for the first time, a natural world governed by immutable physical laws. In addition to creating a conceptual framework that underlay the practice of science until the twentieth century, Newton's understanding of the world in terms of natural laws profoundly affected the history of ideas and the practice of philosophy in the modern era.

KEY CONCEPTS

acceleration: the rate of change of velocity associated with a change in speed or direction of motion or both; going faster

classical mechanics: the study of the motion of bodies, rooted in Isaac Newton's physical and mathematical principles; also called Newtonian mechanics

diffraction: the separation of a wave into smaller component waves as it passes around an obstruction or through an opening of an appropriate size

gravitation: the mutual attraction between all bodies in the universe, of which gravity, the force the earth exerts on all bodies on or near it, is an example

inertia: the resistance of an object to any change in its state of motion

momentum: the product of the mass of a body and its velocity; the rate of change of momentum of a body is equal to the force acting on it

Newton's laws of motion: three laws devised by physicist and mathematician Isaac Newton to describe the motion of objects in relation to the forces acting on them

spectrum: a series of distinct wavelengths of electromagnetic radiation characteristic of a particular source

EARLY LIFE

Sir Isaac Newton was born on Christmas Day, 1642, to a farmer and his wife, at Woolsthorpe Manor, just south of Grantham in Lincolnshire. His father died shortly before Newton's birth, and when his mother remarried three years later and moved away to live with her new husband, Newton remained at Woolsthorpe to be reared by his grandparents.

Newton attended the grammar school in Grantham, and he demonstrated scientific aptitude at an early age, when he began to construct mechanical toys and models. Aside from a brief period when his mother tried to persuade him to follow in his fa-

Isaac Newton, portrait by Godfrey Kneller, 1702. Image via Wikimedia Commons. [Public domain.]

ther's footsteps and become a farmer, his education continued (it is said that Newton tended to read books rather than watch sheep, with disastrous results). He was accepted as an undergraduate at Trinity College, Cambridge, in 1661.

Although his mother provided a small allowance, Newton had to wait on tables at college to help finance his studies. Even at that time, his fellow students remarked that he was silent and withdrawn, and indeed, Newton throughout his life was something of a recluse, shunning society. He never married, and some historians believe that Newton had homosexual leanings. Whatever the truth of this speculation, it is certain that he preferred work, study, experimentation, and observation to social activity, sometimes to the detriment of his own health. After retreating to Grantham for a short time while Cambridge was threatened by plague, Newton returned to the university as a don in 1667 with an established reputation for mathematical brilliance.

LIFE'S WORK

It was not long at all before Newton proved his reputation for genius to be well deserved. Shortly after his graduation, Newton developed differential calculus, a mathematical method for calculating rates of change (such as acceleration) that had long evaded other scholars. As a result, in 1669, he was offered the Lucasian Chair of Mathematics at Cambridge, a position he held until 1701.

Newton's second major contribution of this period was in the field of optics. His experiments with light had led him to build a reflecting telescope, the first one of its kind that actually worked. After further refinements, he presented the device to the Royal Society, where he was asked to present a paper on his theory of light and colors. Shortly afterward, he was made a fellow of this august body, which contained all the prominent intellectuals of the day.

Newton's paper offered new insights into the nature of color. While experimenting with prisms,

Newton had discovered that white light is a mixture of all the colors of the rainbow and that the prism separates white light into its component parts. Newton's theory was controversial, provoking strong feelings at the Royal Society and initiating a lengthy dispute with Robert Hooke concerning the nature of light. Hooke criticized Newton with such vehemence that Newton presented no more theories on the nature of light until 1704, after Hooke's death.

For a scientist such as Newton, the seventeenth century was an interesting period in which to work. Scientific thought was still dominated by the Aristotelian worldview, which had held sway for more than two thousand years, but cracks in that outlook were beginning to appear. Galileo had shown that the planets traveled around the Sun, which was positioned at the center of the universe, while Johannes Kepler had observed that this motion was regular and elliptical in nature. The task confronting scientists, in keeping with the aim of explaining the universe mathematically from first principles, was to find some logical reason for this phenomenon.

Newton, among others, believed that there had to be a set of universal rules governing motion, equally applicable to planetary and earthbound activity. His researches finally led him to a mathematical proof that all motion is regulated by a law of attraction. Specifically, he proved that the force of attraction between two bodies of constant mass varies as the inverse of the square of the distance between those bodies (that is, $FA = k/D^2$, where FA is the force of attraction between the bodies, D is the distance between them, and k is a constant). From this beginning, he was able to explain why planets travel in ellipses around the Sun, why Earth's tides move as they do, and why tennis balls, for example, follow the trajectories that they do. The inverse square formula also led Newton toward a notion of gravity that neatly tied his mathematics together. When Newton published this work, it led to another major confrontation with Hooke, who claimed that he had reached the proof of the inverse square law before Newton; the argument between the two was lengthy and acrimonious.

In 1684, Edmond Halley, then a young astronomer, went to Cambridge to visit Newton, who was reputed to be doing work similar to Halley's. Halley found that Newton claimed that he had proved the inverse square law but had temporarily mislaid it. (Throughout his life, Newton worked on scraps of paper, keeping everything from first drafts to final copies, so this assertion has the ring of truth to it.) Halley was astounded: Here was a man who claimed to have solved the problem that was bothering many leading scientists of the day, and he had not yet made it public. When Halley returned, Newton had found the proof, and Halley persuaded him to publish his nine-page demonstration of the law. Still, Halley was not satisfied. Realizing that Newton had more to offer the world, he prodded him into publishing a book of his theories. The result was the *famous Philosophiae Naturalis Principia Mathematica* (1687; *The Mathematical Principles of Natural Philosophy*, 1729, best known as the *Principia*), which was published at Halley's expense. A year later, a second and third volume of the work reached the public.

The *Principia* was a highly technical and mathematical work that many of Newton's contemporaries had difficulty following, but its effect on the scientific community was profound. In it, Newton outlined his three laws of motion. The first states that every body continues in a state of rest or motion until it is acted on by a force. The second law states that the acceleration of a body is proportional to the force applied to it and inversely proportional to its mass. The third law, perhaps the most widely quoted, states that for every action there is an equal and opposite reaction. From these three fundamental laws, Newton went on to construct his theory of gravity—a force that acts at a distance between two or more bodies, causing an attraction between them that is in inverse proportion to the distance between them.

Newton's theories were a major challenge to the dominant worldview, constructing the world, as they did, purely from mechanics. His theories seemed revolutionary and initiated a great debate, which continued for the better part of a century after the *Principia* was published. When they were eventually accepted as a useful description of nature, Newtonian science formed the basis of modern thinking until the twentieth century, when Albert Einstein's theories turned the world upside-down again.

Writing the *Principia* dominated Newton's life to such an extent that he became completely obsessed with the project, often forgetting to eat or even to sleep while he continued working. Despite his reclusive tendencies, however, in 1687 Newton entered the public arena. Cambridge University and King James II, a Catholic, were in the midst of a battle over religion. The university had refused to grant a degree to a Benedictine monk, and the officials of the university, including Newton, were summoned to appear before the infamous Judge George Jeffreys to argue their case. Shortly afterward, Newton was elected the member of Parliament for Cambridge. Newton's entrance into politics was less than world-shattering, though; it is said that he spoke only once during his term of office, and that was to ask an usher to open a window.

In 1693, Newton suffered a mental breakdown about which little is known, and he withdrew into his previous solitary state. Two years later, he returned to public office when he was asked to take over the wardenship of the mint. There was to be a major reissue of coinage because of the increasingly pressing problem of clipped gold and silver coins. New coins needed to be minted with milled edges, and several prominent scientists were pressed into service to aid in the process. Newton discovered a hitherto unrecognized penchant for administration and proved himself a highly able bureaucrat, being promoted to master of the Mint in 1699. In 1701, he was reelected to Parliament and continued in the public eye for the remainder of his life.

Until his death in 1727, honors were heaped upon Newton, as befitted the most prominent scientist of his generation. In 1703, he was elected president of the Royal Society and was annually reelected to that post for the next twenty-five years. He moved to London and became more sociable but nevertheless earned a reputation for being cantankerous and ill-tempered. In 1704, Newton published *Opticks*, a tract about the theories of light that he had earlier expounded to the Royal Society. It was more accessible than the *Principia* and gained a wider audience. A year later, he was knighted by Queen Anne. Meanwhile, the *Principia* was proving to be a bestseller, as everyone wanted to read the theories that were pushing back the frontiers of contemporary science, and it went through second and third editions during Newton's lifetime.

Newton's work in the last years of his life was mainly religious, apart from another acrimonious dispute with the German philosopher Gottfried Wilhelm Leibniz over who had first invented differential calculus. Newton spent hours attempting to understand the messages hidden in the Book of Revelation, seeing this task as simply another aspect of the search for truth as revealed in God's works, both written and created. Thus, in the end, Newton proved himself to be a medieval thinker, despite his work laying the foundations of modern scientific thought.

SIGNIFICANCE

Newton made an outstanding contribution to the modernization of the Western scientific worldview. He followed in the footsteps of Nicolaus Copernicus, Galileo, Kepler, and others in asserting that the heavens and earth were a part of one solar system (not separated as they are in Aristotelian philosophy), with the Sun at the center. Newton further developed and refined the method of observation and

experiment that had already established itself in the seventeenth century, by carefully checking and rechecking his work and by creating experimental verifications of his various theories. Most important, he demonstrated that a comprehensive mechanical description of the world that explained matter and motion in terms of mathematics was actually possible. With the *Principia*, Newton effectively sounded the death knell of the old description of the universe and laid the basis for a modern approach. His was perhaps the greatest individual contribution to a rich and innovative period of scientific development.

NEWTON'S MAJOR WORKS

- 1687 *Philosophiae Naturalis Principia Mathematica* (*The Mathematical Principles of Natural Philosophy*, 1729)
- 1704 *Opticks*
- 1707 *Arithmetica Universalis* (*Universal Arithmetick*, 1720)
- 1711 *Analysis per Quantitatum Series, Fluxiones, ad Differentias: Cum Enumeratione Linearum Tertii Ordinis* (includes *De Analysi per Aquationes Infinitas; Fragmenta Epistolarum; De Quadratura Curvarum; Enumeratio Linearum Tertii Ordinis; and Methodus Differentialis*)
- 1728 *The Chronology of Ancient Kingdoms Amended*
- 1733 *Observations Upon the Prophecies of Daniel and the Apocalypse of St. John*
- 1736 *The Method of Fluxions and Infinite Series*

—*Sally Hibbin*

Further Reading

Aughton, Peter. *Newton's Apple: Isaac Newton and the English Scientific Revolution*. Weidenfeld, 2003.

Brewster, Sir David. *Memoirs of the Life, Writings, and Discoveries of Sir Isaac Newton*. Constable, 1855. Reprint. Johnson Reprint, 1965.

Christianson, Gale E. *Isaac Newton*. Oxford UP, 2005.

Cohen, I. Bernard, and George E. Smith, editors. *The Cambridge Companion to Newton*. Cambridge UP, 2002.

Fara, Patricia. *Newton: The Making of a Genius*. Columbia UP, 2002.

Gleick, James. *Isaac Newton*. Pantheon, 2003.

Losure, Mary. *Isaac the Alchemist: Secrets of Isaac Newton, Reveal'd*. Candlewick Press, 2017.

Manuel, Frank E. *A Portrait of Isaac Newton*. Harvard UP, 1968. Reprint. Da Capo, 1990.

Mount, Toni. *The World of Isaac Newton*. Amberley Publishing, 2020.

Newton, Sir Isaac. *Mathematical Principles of Natural Philosophy and His System of the World: Principia*. 2 vols. U of California P, 1934. Reprint. 1962.

Newton, Sir Isaac. *Opticks*. Dover, 1952.

Westfall, Richard S. *The Life of Isaac Newton*. Cambridge UP, 1980.

See also: Acceleration; Acoustics; Aristotle isolates science as a discipline; Calculus; Differential equations; Force (physics); Galileo; Hooke, Robert; Kinematics; Kinetic energy; Leibnitz, Gottfried Wilhelm; Linear motion; Momentum (physics); Motion; Newton's laws; Speed; Velocity

NEWTON'S LAWS

Fields of Study: Physics; Mechanics; Mathematics

ABSTRACT

The motion of any mechanical system (e.g., a single particle of mass, a complex flexible structure, or the solar system) is described by Newton's laws of motion. These laws define the inertia, momentum, and energy of objects.

KEY CONCEPTS

acceleration: the rate at which an object's velocity changes (in speed and/or direction)

energy: the amount of work done in moving an object to its current position (potential energy) or in getting an object to move with a particular speed (kinetic energy)

force: the amount of push or pull exerted against an object

mass: the amount of matter in an object

momentum: the mass of an object multiplied by its speed; momentum also has a direction, given by the direction of the velocity

velocity: the speed and direction of a moving object

OVERVIEW

Sir Isaac Newton's laws of motion describe how an object moves under the influence of one or more forces. In their exact form, these laws apply to particles of mass; that is, objects whose mass is concentrated at single points in space. It is relatively straightforward, however, to extend them to real objects with measurable dimensions. Although referred to as laws, they are really observations about the mechanical relations of objects within the realm of everyday experience. First published by Newton in *Philosophiae Naturalis Principia Mathematica* (1687; *Mathematical Principles of Natural Philosophy*, 1729), they formed the basis of all systematic study of motion that followed. Only when one considers extremely small or large masses, or extremely high speeds, do Newton's laws require modification (using the theories of quantum mechanics and relativity).

Newton's first law of motion states that an object's velocity (speed and direction) will be constant unless a force external to the object acts on the mass. (An example of an internal force would be the atomic forces holding the object together.) Therefore, an object will move along a straight path with constant speed unless an external force acts upon it. Indeed, the fundamental definition of force is derived from the first law: Force is a quantity that causes objects to change velocity. An object that is stationary will remain so in the absence of an external force; this is known as the principle of inertia. When more than one external force is present, it is the total (or net) force that acts on the object.

Applying an external force to a mass causes it to accelerate—its velocity will change either in speed or direction, or both. Newton's second law states that the relation between the force and the resulting acceleration is described by the equation F = ma, where ma is the object's mass (m) times its acceleration (a). The direction of the acceleration will be the same as that of the force. A comparison of the first two laws reveals that the second law is a more exact statement of the first: If there is no force, then the acceleration is zero, and the object maintains its velocity. If that initial velocity is zero, then it will remain zero.

Newton's third law of motion explains that mechanical forces always occur in pairs.

When one object exerts a force on a second, the second object exerts a force of equal magnitude on the first; this is sometimes called the reaction force. The reaction force will be in exactly the opposite direction of the force that acts on the second object. It is common to refer to this law as the "action-reaction principle," and to state it in the following terms: For every action, there is an opposite and equal reaction. An example of this phenomenon is observed by pushing on a massive object. The reaction force of the object is clearly felt by the pusher. If this experiment is conducted on a

Newton's laws of motion, combined with his law of gravity, allow the prediction of how planets, moons, and other objects orbit through the Solar System, and they are a vital part of planning space travel. During the 1968 Apollo 8 mission, astronaut Bill Anders took this photo, Earthrise; on their way back to Earth; Anders remarked, "I think Isaac Newton is doing most of the driving right now." Photo via Wikimedia Commons.

smooth surface, such as ice, both the object and the pusher will be accelerated from a condition of rest to some speed, each by the force exerted by the other. The forces and, hence, the accelerations will be in opposite directions.

Two useful quantities that help to describe motion are energy and momentum. In applying a force to a stationary object, causing it to begin moving, the force is doing work on the object. This work is manifested in the continued motion of the object, even after the force is removed (according to Newton's first law, the object's speed and direction will now remain constant unless another force acts); the object is said to possess kinetic energy (energy of motion). Alternatively, the work done by the force may be stored in a nonmoving form. For example, using a force to compress a spring results in energy being stored in the spring. This is called potential energy (energy of position). If one end of the compressed spring is kept stationary and the other end is allowed to push an object, then releasing the spring will result in a force acting on the mass, which then accelerates to some speed. The potential energy in the spring is thus converted to kinetic energy in the object. If the spring is attached to the object, then the spring will continue to extend, eventually starting to pull back on the object. At some point, the object will come to rest, as the spring reaches the limit of its extension. The kinetic energy of motion has now been converted back into potential energy and stored in the extended spring. In the absence of other forces, this alternating exchange of kinetic and potential energies will persist indefinitely as the mass oscillates back and forth.

A moving object is said to have momentum, a quantity whose magnitude is given by its speed times its mass and whose direction is the same as that of the object's motion. In terms of Newton's first law of motion, the momentum is constant unless an external force acts on the object. Newton's second law may be restated in terms of momentum: The rate at which an object's momentum changes is equal to the external force acting on the object. The greater the momentum, the stronger the force required to change it; for example, stopping a large truck moving at high speed requires a much greater force than stopping a small car moving at the same speed.

A real object—whose mass is distributed over measurable dimensions—is a collection of particles. The forces holding the collection together (atomic and molecular binding forces) are internal and do not affect the overall motion of the object. Newton's third law of motion indicates that, since every conceivable pair of particles within the object generates pairs of forces having equal magnitude and opposite direction, adding together all of these forces thus gives zero net force on the object as a whole.

In order to apply the second law of motion to such an object, it is necessary to use the concept of center of mass, which is the average location of all the mass in the object. For example, a uniform sphere has its center of mass located at the sphere's geometric center; a flat triangular plate has its center of mass at a point two-thirds the distance from each corner to the center of the opposite edge and halfway between the two flat sides. The net effect of all forces acting on the real object may be studied by adding all the forces in such a way as to consider that they are being exerted against the center of mass.

APPLICATIONS

Newton's laws of motion apply both to static (stationary) and dynamic (moving) systems. A system may consist of a single object or a complex arrangement of objects. The application of Newton's third law of motion to stationary systems constitutes the subject of statics, in which the set of forces acting among several objects, or among portions of a large object, is determined. The design of buildings and bridges, for example, depends upon the ability to predict the distribution of forces throughout the structure, and the concept of action and reaction forces plays a critical role.

A classic example of a dynamic system that illustrates all three laws of motion is that of a rocket being launched from Earth's surface. Prior to the launch, the rocket experiences only the force of gravity, pulling it downward onto the launch platform and the reaction force of the platform (the force of support), acting upward against the rocket. By the third law of motion, these forces have equal magnitude and opposite direction, giving a net force of zero on the rocket. Both the first and second laws then indicate that the rocket is not accelerating, since no net force acts on it. When the rocket engine ignites, though, a new force is introduced. The chemical reaction (burning fuel) in the engine's combustion chamber produces hot gases composed of highly energetic particles that collide with the chamber's walls; each collision exerts a small force against that particular side of the chamber. One end of the chamber is open to an exhaust nozzle, which allows the gases to escape to the outside. Inside the chamber, the large number of collisions per unit time is distributed randomly over the interior surface. On average, there are as many collisions on one side of the chamber as on the opposite side, resulting in no net force being exerted on the chamber as a whole, except on the chamber wall opposite the exhaust nozzle. Particles that collide here exert forces in the forward direction (away from the exhaust nozzle), but particles leaving through the nozzle do not exert any forces on the chamber. The result is a net force, called thrust, in the forward direction; the combustion chamber transmits this force to the structure of the rocket.

With the thrust acting upward and the gravitational force (weight) downward, the net force on the rocket is now the difference between the thrust and weight. According to Newton's second law, the rocket will accelerate upward at a value given by this net force divided by the rocket's mass. (Once the rocket begins to move, the platform no longer exerts a support force against it.) In order to continue producing sufficient amounts of thrust, the rocket must expel large quantities of gases, whose mass is simply the converted form of the original propellants. Therefore, the rocket is continually losing mass in the form of the exhaust gases. Most rocket engines are designed to produce a relatively constant level of thrust, and so, again by the second law, the rocket's acceleration will be increasing. Alternatively, one may view this entire process in terms of an exchange of energy. The combustion process releases energy, a considerable amount of which is lost as heat, but some of which is transformed into the kinetic energy of the rocket's motion and the potential energy of its position above Earth (produced by the thrust doing work on the rocket to move it against the pull of gravity).

A second example is that of a satellite in orbit around Earth. With its engines off, the satellite experiences only the force of gravity from Earth. From the first law of motion, it is necessary, then, that the satellite's velocity change in either speed, direction, or both quantities.

Giving a satellite exactly the right speed at a given distance from Earth will result in a circular orbit; under these conditions, gravity provides just the right acceleration to change only the satellite's direction, but not its speed. It thus maintains a constant speed at a fixed distance from Earth, with its direction of motion constantly changing to produce a circular path. For a somewhat different initial speed, the satellite describes an elliptical path, alternately closer, then farther from Earth. On a circular path, both the kinetic and potential energies are constant, since the satellite's speed and distance from Earth are unchanging. Yet, the elliptical path demonstrates an exchange of the two forms, with the potential energy increasing as the satellite moves farther from Earth (and the kinetic energy correspondingly decreasing), and the reverse occurs as the satellite moves closer to Earth.

A third example that illustrates the laws of motion is that of a wooden block that has been set sliding horizontally on a flat surface of ice. Here, the forces in the vertical direction are the block's weight (a downward force) and the reaction force of support from the ice, acting upward on the block. In the horizontal direction, the block experiences two forces, both directed opposite to the block's motion: air resistance, and friction between the block and the ice. Since the net force in the vertical direction is zero, the block will always have the same speed in the vertical direction, namely, zero. If it were not for the air resistance and friction with the ice, the block would (by the first law) continue with its original horizontal speed and direction indefinitely (or until it moved off the ice onto a rougher surface). Indeed, if the surface of the ice extended forever (and there were no horizontal forces), the block would never slow down. In reality, the air resistance and friction, which depend on the block's speed, decelerate it at a value given by the second law, namely, the total force of air resistance plus friction at any given moment, divided by the block's mass. As the speed decreases, the forces of air resistance and friction also decrease, until finally the block comes to rest with no horizontal forces acting upon it at all. In this example, the potential energy is constant (no work is done against gravity by lifting the block up off the ice), but the kinetic energy diminishes as the air resistance and friction do work against the block. This loss of energy takes the form of heat, which is dissipated into the surrounding air and the ice.

CONTEXT

Following their publication in 1687, Newton's laws of motion were to have a profound effect on how scientists viewed the mechanical world. Indeed, they represent the first case of a capability to predict the future behavior of a mechanical system, based only upon knowledge of its initial behavior (positions and velocities of its constituent masses) and application of the laws of motion. Two other accomplishments— his invention of the calculus and formulation of the law of universal gravitation—enhanced this predictive capability immeasurably. Despite their simple form, the laws of motion constitute the basis for the entire field of classical mechanics. Writing of Newton's great achievements, Edmond Halley, who encouraged him to publish his ideas in the *Principia*, penned "Nearer the gods no mortal may approach."

It was not until the end of the nineteenth century that physicists encountered phenomena that could not be predicted accurately by classical mechanics. Understanding the interaction of radiant energy with matter requires quantum mechanics, which recognizes the wavelike nature of matter on the atomic scale. In addition, Albert Einstein's theory of special relativity further modifies the Newtonian view by predicting changes in the length and mass of an object (properties that are absolute in classical mechanics) when it moves at some significant fraction of the speed of light. Yet another revision is required, by Einstein's theory of general relativity, if the motion occurs in close proximity to such massive objects as stars. Nevertheless, Newton's laws still maintain their accuracy and importance in the realm of human scales of mass, length, and speed; the new theories predict the same motions when applied to that domain.

The classical laws of motion continue to provide insights to mechanical and dynamical phenomena. Their application to some nonlinear systems has spawned the study of chaotic behavior, which deals with the sensitivity of a dynamical system to slight changes in its initial conditions. This has applications in such diverse systems as a simple pendulum with a nonlinear spring (that is, a spring whose force is not directly proportional to its compression or extension) connected at the hinge, and meteorological systems. In either example, minuscule changes in the initial conditions of motion can cause enormous changes in the system's behavior at a later time.

In many situations, the complexity of motion requires computer modeling to predict future behavior. Such matters as the long-term prediction of the solar system's motion or the analysis of systems with many interacting flexible components (for example, a robotic arm with several flexible structural members connected by hinged joints), are examples of problems for which the solutions are only approximate. Increasingly faster and higher-capacity computers will permit such systems to be studied more accurately and thoroughly, but here, as with much simpler cases, Newton's laws of motion will continue to hold the same importance as in the previous three centuries.

—*Robert G. Melton*

Further Reading

Alrasheed, Salma. Principles of Mechanics: Fundamental University Physics. Springer, 2019.

Kumar, Sanjay. Newton's Laws of Motion and Friction: Mechanics. Sanjay Kumar, 2020.

Ling, Samuel J., Jeff Sanny, and William Moebs. University Physics Volume 1. Samurai Media Limited, 2017.

Mahajan, Sanjoy A Student's Guide to Newton's Laws of Motion. Cambridge UP, 2020.

Zimba, Jason. Force and Motion: An Illustrated Guide to Newton's Laws. JHU Press, 2009.

See also: Acceleration; Angular forces; Angular momentum; Calculus; Celestial mechanics; Circular motion; Classical or applied mechanics; Differential equations; Displacement; Dynamics (mechanics); Engineering; Force (physics); Friction; Jet engines; Kinematics; Linear motion; Moment of inertia; Momentum (physics); Motion; Newton, Isaac; Pendulums; Projectiles; Propulsion technologies; Quantum mechanics; Speed; Vectors; Velocity

P

PASCAL, BLAISE

Fields of Study: Physics; Mechanics; Mathematics

ABSTRACT

Blaise Pascal was born June 19, 1623, in Clermont-Ferrand, France, and died August 19, 1662, in Paris, France. His primary interests were physics and mathematics. He is best remembered for the development of probability theory, and for important studies in geometry and mechanics.

KEY CONCEPTS

blacksmithing: the artisanal working of metal into a desired shape

equilibrium: the condition of a dynamic system consisting of two or more components in which there is no net change in any of its components

probability: the likelihood that a particular result will occur within a given set of circumstances

probability theory: the mathematical basis of determining the likelihood of a given outcome in a situation governed by random chance within a set of starting and boundary conditions, such as the rules by which a particular game of chance is played

EARLY LIFE

Blaise Pascal was the third child of Étienne Pascal, a government financial bureaucrat, and Antoinette Begon, who died when Pascal was about three. After his mother's death, Pascal and his family moved to Paris. Pascal's father decided to educate his children himself; he was associated with the intellectual circles of Paris and exposed Pascal to the best scientific and mathematical thinking of the time.

While still a teenager, the precocious Pascal attracted the attention of the court. He published his first mathematical treatise in 1640, and in 1642 he began working on a mechanical calculator to help in his father's work. Dissatisfied with the efforts of local craftspeople, he taught himself the mechanical skills necessary to create a calculating device. He also delved into blacksmithing to experiment with different materials for the gears. Pascal continued to improve his device for the next ten years, and in 1652, he sent a version of it to Queen Christina of Sweden.

In 1646, Pascal and his two older sisters came under the influence of Jansenism, a movement within the Catholic Church that stressed devotion, practical charity, and asceticism. While Pascal underwent a re-

Blaise Pascal. Image via iStock/Nastasic. [Used under license.]

ligious renewal, he did not give up his scientific and mathematical endeavors. His work at this time included experiments concerning the existence of an atmospheric vacuum, an often-debated area in seventeenth-century physics.

LIFE'S WORK

In 1647, Pascal entered into the first of the religious controversies that would preoccupy him for the rest of his life. He also continued his scientific work on the vacuum, recording his findings in his controversial book *Experiences nouvelles touchant le vide* (*New Experiments Concerning the Vacuum*, 1647). The following year, he wrote a mathematical essay on conic sections that was later commented on by German mathematicians Gottfried Leibniz and Ehrenfried Tschirnhaus, whose writings have proved important to modern work on Pascal's conics.

Throughout this period, Pascal was afflicted with serious illnesses. Nevertheless, he worked to disprove the mathematical assertions of Antoine Gombaud, Chevalier de Méré, specifically his claim that there was no solution to the problem of points—a conundrum that had been puzzled over since the Middle Ages. Corresponding with French mathematician Pierre de Fermat, Pascal developed the concept of the expected value, a principle stipulating that the value of future gains should be proportional to the chance of obtaining them. The idea of expected value proved crucial to the development of probability theory, as well as such sciences as economics, finance, and statistics.

Around 1653, Pascal began writing his *Traités de l'équilibre des liqueurs* (*Treatise on the Equilibrium of Liquids*), one of the first comprehensive works on hydrostatics, in which he described what came to be known as Pascal's law: the pressure applied to a fluid in equilibrium at a single point will be the same throughout the fluid. The following year, he wrote his *Traité du triangle arithmétique* (*Treatise on the Arithmetical Triangle*), in which he developed many uses

for what is called Pascal's triangle—a set of binomial coefficients arranged in a triangle. Both treatises were published posthumously, the first in 1663 and the second in 1665.

On the night of November 23, 1654, Pascal experienced an intense and mystical religious experience that changed the direction of his life. He traveled to Port-Royal Abbey in Paris, the center of Jansenism, for a two-week retreat in early 1655. There, he set out to reform his life in light of his religious reawakening. Jansenism was to dominate his life for the next few years. In 1653, Pope Innocent X had condemned the writings of Cornelius Otto Jansen, bishop of Ypres, upon which the Jansenist movement was based.

The great enemies of the Jansenists were the rationalistic Jesuits, and, in January of 1656, Pascal wrote the first of a series of anonymous letters now titled *Lettres provincials* (1656-57; *Provincial Letters*, 1657). Eighteen in all, these letters are masterpieces of satire, wit, analytic logic, and French prose style. Especially in the early letters, the fictitious writer of the work adopts a pose of objective, naive curiosity about the controversy between Jesuits and Jansenists. In reality, the letters are an impassioned defense of the principles of the Jansenist movement and a stinging attack on the Jesuits. The letters were enormously popular, and the local authorities went to great lengths to try to suppress them and discover their author. They have been admired ever since as masterpieces of French prose.

Pascal was not satisfied merely to defend a movement within the Catholic Church. He aimed to write a great defense of Christianity at a time when religious faith was increasingly under attack by skepticism and rationalism. In 1657, prompted in part by what he saw as the miraculous cure of his young niece, Pascal began to take notes for this work, which he once said would take ten years to write. Pascal never completed the work, or even a draft, but he did produce approximately one thousand notes, some only a few words and others pages long and substantially revised. The majority of these notes date from 1657 and 1658, after which time he fell into an extremely painful and debilitating illness that would largely incapacitate him until his death. The notes were first published in abbreviated form as *Pensées* (1670) and have become one of the classic texts of Western culture. Part of Pascal's enduring appeal is his very modern awareness of the difficulty of religious faith in a scientific and skeptical world.

For most of the last four years of his life, Pascal was seriously ill, but his health did not prevent him from working sporadically on a variety of projects. In 1658, he made further mathematical discoveries on the cycloid (a shape that resembles a circle) and publicly challenged the mathematicians of Europe to a contest. His concern for the poor led him to invent and launch a public transportation system in Paris in March 1662. Additionally, when his health permitted, he worked on the defense of Christianity that would become *Pensées*. After much suffering, Pascal died on August 19, 1662, at the age of thirty-nine.

BLAISE PASCAL DEVELOPS THE THEORY OF PROBABILITY

Mathematician and physicist Blaise Pascal invented an early form of the calculator, developed studies of conics and atmospheric pressure, and, with Pierre de Fermat, devised an early version of the theory of probability.

Before his religious awakening in 1654, French mathematician Blaise Pascal lived a worldly life and often frequented the salons of Paris, where intellectuals met to converse about current ideas. One of his friends, the writer and notorious gambler Antoine Gombaud, better known as Chevalier de Méré, sought Pascal's help in solving a gambling conundrum called the problem of points—a mathematical puzzle that had been discussed since the Middle Ages. Méré, an amateur mathematician himself, be-

lieved that there was no solution to the problem; in his view, it demonstrated that mathematics was a flawed science that could not be practically applied. Pascal was determined to prove Méré wrong.

The problem of points posits a scenario in which two players contribute to a prize pot and agree to play for the best out of a certain number of rounds. Each player has an equal chance of winning each round. Before the game is finished, however, it is interrupted by unforeseen circumstances. Because the players cannot complete the rounds, the question then becomes, how can they divide the stakes fairly, given that the winnings should depend on the number of rounds that each player wins?

At the time Méré posed this question, Pascal was corresponding with Pierre de Fermat, a lawyer and amateur mathematician. Fermat's approach was to look at the entire game as a whole and compute what the odds would be for each player to win. He created a table of possible outcomes, counted how many of those outcomes would result in a victory for each player, and apportioned the stakes in relation to the odds.

Pascal, on the other hand, focused on individual steps. For example, he imagined a situation in which the players had the opportunity to play one more round before being forced to stop. In this scenario, two futures are possible: one person wins or the other person wins. Pascal reasoned that in such a case, because both players have an equal opportunity to win, they should divide the stakes equally. He also demonstrated that the fair solution to a hypothetical situation in which fewer rounds remain to be played can be used to determine fair solutions to games with more rounds remaining.

The discussion between Fermat and Pascal gave birth to the concept of expected value. This basic principle dictates that the value of all future gain should be proportional to the chance of obtaining it. In contrast to Méré's assertion that higher mathematics has no practical impact on everyday life, expected value has proven to be central to the application of actuarial science, which includes probability, mathematics, statistics, finance, economics, and computer programming. In the insurance industry, for example, probability theory has been used to estimate how age and mortality rates could determine the payouts for those purchasing life insurance. Pascal's pioneering work in probability theory also influenced other scientists and mathematicians, including Christiaan Huygens (who wrote the first book on the topic), Abraham de Moivre, Pierre-Simon Laplace, and Gottfried Leibniz.

IMPACT

Pascal's many accomplishments span a number of different fields. He is considered an inventor, a superior mathematician, a major physicist from the early days of the science, a literary master of French prose, and a philosopher and religious thinker who wrote brilliantly about fundamental questions of the human condition. His work with Fermat led to the development of the modern field of probability theory, as they were the first to apply sufficient mathematical systematization to the questions arising from games of chance to arrive at satisfactory conclusions. One of the earliest programming languages used on the electronic computer, developed in the late 1960s and put into use in 1970, was named after Pascal in recognition of his achievements.

—*Daniel Taylor*

Further Reading

Caws, Mary Ann *Blaise Pascal: Miracles and Reason*. Reaktion Books, 2017.

Coleman, Francis X. J. *Neither Angel Nor Beast: The Life and Works of Blaise Pascal*. Routledge, 2013.

Groothius, Douglas. *On Pascal*. Thomson, 2003.

Hammond, Nicholas, ed. *The Cambridge Companion to Pascal*. Cambridge UP, 2003.

Pascal, Blaise *Delphi Collected Works of Blaise Pascal*. Delphi Classics, 2020.

Thakur, Rajesh. *Blaise Pascal*. Prabhat Prakashan, 2021.

See also: Archimedes; Aristotle isolates science as a discipline; Bernoulli, Daniel; Bernoulli's principle; Discoveries of Archimedes; Euclid; Euler's laws of motion; Galileo; Laplace, Pierre-Simon; Leibnitz, Gottfried Wilhelm; Newton, Isaac; Poisson, Siméon-Denis; Tesla, Nikola

PENDULUMS

Fields of Study: Physics; Mechanics; Mathematics

ABSTRACT

A pendulum is a classic example of an oscillatory system with a well-defined periodic motion caused by application of a restoring torque under conditions of mechanical energy conservation. In a free-hanging pendulum, the restoring torque is provided by gravity, while in a pendulum driven by a mechanical clockwork it is provided by spring tension via a regulating device to maintain a constant frequency.

KEY CONCEPTS

amplitude: the maximum angular displacement from the vertical or equilibrium position

angular displacement: the measure of deviation from the vertical or equilibrium position

damping force: a nonconservative influence that removes mechanical energy and diminishes oscillation amplitude, eventually bringing the pendulum to equilibrium

kinetic energy: an energy of motion that can be conservatively transformed to energy of position or be consumed as work done by nonconservative forces

moment of inertia: the property of a system that resists rotation under application of an external torque

natural frequency: the number of complete oscillations undergone per unit time; determined by pendulum length and mass

oscillation: a repetitive motion with a well-defined period and amplitude

period: the time to complete one oscillation; inverse of natural frequency

potential energy: the energy of position in a field of force that can be conservatively transformed to energy of motion

restoring torque: the application of a force at a distance from an axis about which a system can rotate, directed in such a way as to attempt to restore equilibrium

OVERVIEW

A simple pendulum can be formed by taking an inelastic string of a given length, attaching one end of the string to a small point mass, securing the other end to a rigid support, and allowing the string and mass to hang freely beneath the support. This pendulum's motion under displacement from equilibrium is a classic example of what is often referred to as a periodic, or oscillatory, motion in that the motion is repetitive in both its temporal and spatial characteristics. It retraces the same path as it swings and requires the same amount of time, called the period of the motion, to complete each cycle of oscillation. The motion of such a mechanical system is similar to that of a typical linear harmonic oscillator, namely a mass attached to a spring. Although the linear harmonic oscillator repeats a translational motion under conditions of conservation of energy, the simple pendulum repeats a rotational motion about its suspension point, also under conditions of conservation of energy.

To set up the initial conditions for pendulum release—an angular displacement from the vertical or equilibrium position—work must be done against gravity by an external agent. That work provides the pendulum with potential energy. By the work-energy principle, that potential energy is converted into kinetic energy as the pendulum gains angular velocity under influence of an angular acceleration provided by the pendulum's weight component, which is perpendicular to the tension acting along

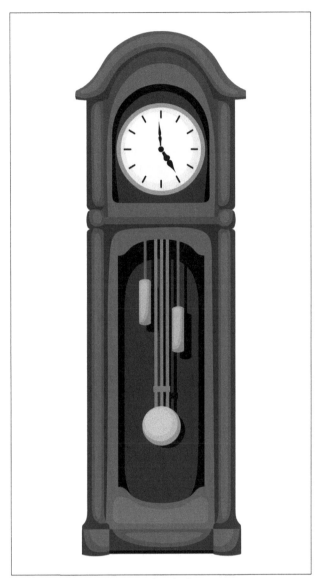

Image via iStock/Naddiya. [Used under license.]

the string. That weight component is not counterbalanced by any other force and acts through a perpendicular distance equal to the pendulum's length, thereby creating a torque that attempts to restore the pendulum to equilibrium. Starting from rest, as the pendulum swings, it decreases its potential energy, providing an equivalent increase in kinetic energy. (Because only potential energy changes are pertinent to determination of work, potential energy can be measured relative to any arbitrarily chosen reference value, in this case the system's equilibrium position, at which the reference value of potential energy is zero.)

As the pendulum swings through its equilibrium, its potential energy has vanished, having been conservatively transformed into kinetic energy. Therefore, the pendulum has maximum kinetic energy and maximum angular velocity as it passes through that point. As the pendulum continues past equilibrium and climbs uphill, it gains potential energy at the expense of kinetic energy, thereby increasing its angular displacement from the vertical and diminishing its angular velocity until it reaches an angle equal to that of the original angle of release. At this point, all the kinetic energy the pendulum possessed at equilibrium has been conservatively transformed back into potential energy. This constitutes half a cycle of oscillation. The pendulum achieves a maximum angle on the other side of vertical from that of original release with a momentarily vanishing angular velocity, but the restoring torque forces the pendulum to attempt to achieve equilibrium again. The pendulum once again passes through equilibrium with maximum angular velocity directed opposite of what it was when the pendulum first passed through equilibrium, having again conservatively transformed all potential energy to kinetic energy.

The swing continues until the pendulum returns to its original configuration, total potential energy at an angular displacement equal to the original angle of release, thereby completing one full oscillation. Because this configuration is identical to the initial condition of the pendulum, the oscillation begins again. As the system is conservative, oscillations continue ad infinitum, each oscillation taking place within the same amount of time—the period of the motion.

The period is observed to be independent of pendulum mass. Also, provided that the initial angle of release is relatively small (less than about fifteen de-

grees), that period is also observed to be independent of angle of release. What the period does depend on is the value of the acceleration due to gravity and the pendulum's length. If the angle of release is greater than fifteen degrees, the period has a measurable dependence on that initial angle.

This behavior is described by solving the equation of motion, a differential equation that indicates how the dynamics or energetics of pendulum motion varies with time or angular displacement. This behavior can be mathematically determined by generating the differential equation of the motion through two approaches, examining the nature of the restoring torque that seeks to return the pendulum toward equilibrium or looking at the nature of mechanical energy conservation, the conservative transformation from potential to kinetic to potential energy as the pendulum oscillates between maximum angular displacements on either side of equilibrium.

If the pendulum is displaced by an initial angle from the vertical, tension is directed along the line of the string that supports the pendulum weight and secures it to the point about which oscillations occur. The pendulum's weight is directed vertically down rather than totally along the line of the string. Therefore, the weight makes the same angle with the direction of the string as does the string with respect to the vertical.

The weight force can be resolved into two parts, one along the line of the string and the other perpendicular to it. The component parallel to the string is totally balanced by tension in the string. Therefore, no radial motion of the pendulum exists along the line of the string. The attached mass always remains at a distance equal to the string's length from the suspension point. However, the weight force component that is perpendicular to the line of the string points back toward the equilibrium position following the arc along which the pendulum swings. That force is the pendulum's weight multiplied by the sine of the angle the string makes with respect to the vertical. That angle will vary as the pendulum swings, ranging from plus to minus the original angle of release. That unbalanced force component acts through a perpendicular distance equal to the length of the string back to the point of suspension.

The differential equation of the motion can be obtained by equating this restoring torque, which is the product of the pendulum length and the unbalanced component of its weight, to the product of the pendulum's moment of inertia and its resulting angular acceleration. This is a differential equation in that the torque depends upon the angle the pendulum makes with the vertical, which is a function of time, and the pendulum's acceleration is the time rate of change of the time rate of change of that angle, hence the second derivative of angular position taken with respect to time.

The alternative approach is to determine the pendulum's total mechanical energy, which can be done by measuring the state of the motion at any instant. The initial condition, at which point all energy is potential, is principally convenient, and the value is determined by the pendulum's weight, length, and maximum angular displacement. At any other point than at the maximum angular displacement (where all the total mechanical energy is in the form of potential energy) or equilibrium position (where all the total mechanical energy is in the form of kinetic energy), the energy is partially potential and partially kinetic, with the sum of the kinetic and potential equal to that of the potential energy at initial release. This approach generates a differential equation of motion that can be solved for the time rate of change of the pendulum's angle measured with respect to the vertical; that is, the pendulum's angular velocity, which is the first derivative of the angle taken with respect to time. Once angular velocity is determined, the desired solution—the angular displacement as a function of time—can be found by integration.

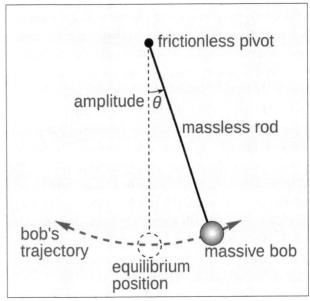

A simple gravity pendulum model assumes no friction or air resistance. Image via Wikimedia Commons. [Public domain.]

In either case, the solution is identical. In both cases, the mathematics is somewhat complicated by the fact that neither differential equation of motion is an ordinary linear differential equation with constant coefficients. The complete solution requires elliptic integrals or a numerical approach to approximate the solution. Nonlinearity in the dynamical equation arises because of the presence of the sine of the angle the pendulum makes with respect to the vertical. If the pendulum is restricted to small oscillations (under fifteen degrees), the exact equation can be approximated by replacing the angle's sine by the angle itself expressed in radians. In this case the equation of motion's form is that of an ordinary linear differential equation with constant coefficients and follows the same nature as the simple harmonic motion displayed by a linear oscillator.

APPLICATIONS

Before the advent of more sophisticated mechanical and electrical means, oscillatory systems such as the linear harmonic oscillator and simple pendulum were used to accurately measure time. In the real world, internal friction is always present, creating a damping force that produces a torque and results in nonconservative work. The effect of this damping influence is to remove mechanical energy from the system. With each successive swing, although the frequency is not altered, the pendulum's maximum angular displacement diminishes. Over time, the pendulum eventually comes to rest at its equilibrium position when the system's total mechanical energy has vanished. That energy can be replaced on each oscillatory cycle by a mechanical or electrical driving mechanism specifically tuned to supply energy to the oscillating system at the rate at which nonconservative work is being done, thereby maintaining the system's oscillatory motion.

Precise measurements of the oscillations of a pendulum permit accurate determination of the local value of the earth's gravitational acceleration. The acceleration due to gravity is directly proportional to the pendulum's length and inversely proportional to the square of the period of oscillation. Further, because the period of the motion is determined by both the gravitational acceleration and the pendulum's length, it is possible to design a pendulum that requires one second to complete a full oscillation. This device is a convenient means of keeping track of time. By watching this pendulum and counting the number of oscillations, it is possible to determine how much time has elapsed. On Earth, where the acceleration due to gravity has a value of 9.81 meters per second squared at sea level, a one-second pendulum would have a length of 24.85 centimeters. However, on the Moon, where the acceleration due to gravity is only about one-sixth as strong as on Earth, a one-second pendulum would be only 4.14 centimeters long.

Suppose, instead of a point-like mass, an extended object (one with significant physical extent, possibly even an asymmetrical shape) is suspended from the pendulum string. What has been created is often referred to as a physical, or compound, pendulum. With this device, the distribution of matter within the extended object must be taken into consideration, but conservation of mechanical energy is preserved. A detailed analysis of this motion yields the observation that there are two points relative to the physical pendulum's center of mass for which suspension of the object at those points yields precisely the same period of oscillation. The points are called centers of oscillation.

Another type of pendulum, a torsional pendulum, involves a twisting or torsional oscillation. Its behavior is similar to that of the simple pendulum in that (apart from internal frictional losses) the system oscillates between equal amplitudes of twist measured relative to the equilibrium, or relaxed, position. If a disk-shaped mass is suspended from a wire of arbitrary length and rotated away from its equilibrium condition in a horizontal plane perpendicular to the supporting wire, the twisted wire provides a restoring torque directly proportional to the amount of twist present when the torsional pendulum is released. The differential equation of the motion is identical to that for the simple pendulum under the small angle approximation, and the motion is strikingly similar to the simple linear harmonic motion of a spring-mass system set into oscillation. The constant of proportionality between the twist angle and restoring torque is referred to as the torsion constant. The disk's moment of inertia is determined by its mass and radius. The period and natural frequency of oscillation are determined by the square root of the ratio of the torsion constant to that moment of inertia.

A conical pendulum can be produced using a simple pendulum. Instead of oscillating in a plane containing the equilibrium position, the position of suspension, and the initial position from which the pendulum is released, the pendulum mass executes a circular motion in a plane perpendicular to the axis and the string traces out a cone shape. The pendulum is given an initial push perpendicular to the plane in which the simple pendulum would oscillate if released from rest. Although it is not intuitively obvious, the dynamics of the conical pendulum are exactly the same as the description of vehicles safely negotiating banked roadways at constant speed. In each case the speed around the circle is determined by the radius of the circular motion and the tangent of an angle; the angle the string makes with the vertical in the case of a conical pendulum and the angle of inclination in the case of a banked roadway.

Pendulums can be used to generate chaotic systems. Instead of using a string, attach a spring between the support and the pendulum mass. Because the spring is capable of linear oscillations, the length of the pendulum no longer remains constant. Regardless of how the chaotic pendulum is set into motion, it displays a complex mixture of oscillatory behavior attributable to a simple pendulum and linear expansion and contraction characteristic of the spring.

Another type of chaotic pendulum system can be made by constructing a pendulum that can undergo conical motion. Use a metallic ball for the pendulum mass, and place at least three strong flat magnets on a base just below the circular plane in which the conical pendulum mass will move. Set the pendulum in motion. Because of the magnetic influence, the pendulum will chaotically orbit between the magnets, displaying a much more complicated motion than an ordinary conical pendulum.

CONTEXT

In physics, a number of central themes pervade areas that at first thought would appear to have little in common. A variety of problems can be described by strikingly similar differential equations. In addition, many problems display similar driving mechanisms, such as an influence that attempts to restore the system toward equilibrium. The linear harmonic oscillator and pendulum are two such systems. Understanding the behavior of either system enables

the investigation of many other phenomena that are governed by equations of similar form or display oscillatory behaviors. Many other phenomena can be described in terms of pendulum-like characteristics.

Characteristics of pendulum motion were known for centuries before the development of Newtonian mechanics. That an ideal pendulum system repeats a motion characterized by energy conservation was understood before development of the calculus that is necessary to solve equations describing a pendulum's angular motion as a function of time. However, the pendulum's unique temporal period, which depends on its length but not its mass, was a property that could be used without being able to fully describe the motion.

Oscillatory motions like those of a pendulum are an important example of energy transfer mechanisms. In the simple pendulum, initial potential energy is transformed to kinetic energy, which reaches its maximum value as the pendulum swings through its equilibrium position, and then that kinetic energy is restored to potential energy as the pendulum achieves maximum angular displacement on the other side of equilibrium. The pendulum repeats the process in the reverse order and returns to its starting position. In the absence of nonconservative influences, this energy transfer mechanism completely conserves the available mechanical energy; it just transforms it from potential to kinetic to potential energy as the oscillations continue. Energy transfer is a central theme in physics and a useful technique in engineering applications.

Complex mechanical systems can be designed that make use of the simple pendulum's capability to oscillate and transfer energy. Two identical length simple pendulums suspended close to each other from a common support can be coupled by attaching a spring to where the pendulum strings attach to the pendulum masses. Each simple pendulum, if left unattached to the other, would oscillate with the same frequency. Connecting the two pendulums provides a more complicated means for energy transfer. If one pendulum is displaced from its equilibrium position and released from rest, initially only the displaced pendulum displays angular motion. However, energy is transferred through the connecting spring to the second pendulum. Both pendulums develop an oscillatory motion. At one point the first pendulum appears to stop, and only the second one undergoes angular motion. The process then repeats itself and returns to the originally observed motion. An analysis of this complicated system's behavior reveals that any motion that develops from the initial release is the superposition of two more simplified motions called normal modes. One normal mode is described by both pendulums moving in the same direction with equal amplitude. The other normal mode is described by both pendulums moving in opposite directions—toward each other—with equal amplitudes. The first normal mode is said to be in phase, the second normal mode is out of phase. Each normal mode is characterized by its own frequency. This type of approach is common for describing complicated wave phenomena and oscillatory systems.

—*David G. Fisher*

Further Reading

Aczel, Amir D. *Pendulum: Leon Foucault and the Triumph of Science.* Simon & Schuster, 2007.

Baker, Gregory L., and James A. Blackburn. *The Pendulum: A Case Study in Physics.* Oxford UP, 2008.

Beech, Martin. *The Pendulum Paradigm: Variations on a Theme and the Measure of Heaven and Earth.* Universal-Publishers, 2014.

Gitterman, M. *The Chaotic Pendulum.* World Scientific, 2010.

Matthews, Michael, Colin F. Gauls, and Arthur Stinner, editors. *The Pendulum: Scientific, Historical, Historical, Philosophical and Educational Perspectives.* Springer Science & Business Media, 2006.

Pook, L. P. *Understanding Pendulums: A Brief Introduction.* Springer Science & Business Media, 2011.

See also: Angular momentum; Automated processes and servomechanisms; Chaotic systems; Displacement; Dynamics (mechanics); Energy transmission; Equilibrium; Flywheels; Harmonic oscillator; Kinetic energy; Potential energy; Torque; Vibration

PHOTOELECTRIC EFFECT

Fields of Study: Physics; Mechanics; Mathematics

ABSTRACT

The photoelectric effect is the removal of electrons from a metal as a result of the absorption of light by electrons near the surface of the metal. Heinrich Hertz (1857-94) discovered the photoelectron effect. Albert Einstein carefully analyzed what was known about the photoelectric effect and in 1900, he found an explanation that fit the experimental facts perfectly, but it assumed that had no place in the physics he knew.

KEY CONCEPTS

diffraction of light: the bending of light's path when it passes a barrier; the bright and dark lines that result are caused by interference

electron: the fundamental negatively charged particle; a constituent of all atoms and solids and the carrier of electricity

electron-volt (eV): a convenient unit of energy for an electron, numerically equal to the voltage difference through which the electron moves

kinetic energy: the energy an object has because it is in motion

photon: the basic particle of light, which carries an energy given by the frequency of the light multiplied by Planck's constant

potential energy: the energy a body has because of its position or configuration; in this context, the energy that holds an electron inside a metal

work function: the potential energy of an electron that is held inside a metal; the minimum energy required to release the electron from the metal

OVERVIEW

The photoelectric effect is the removal of electrons from a metal as a result of the absorption of light by electrons near the surface of the metal. The experiment is simple in principle. Heinrich Hertz (1857-94) discovered it, but he was essentially looking for something else and did not pursue his observation. Phillip Lenard worked for Hertz and later found that an increase in the brightness of the light causes an increase in the number of electrons given off, but not in the energies of the individual electrons. This and related work brought him a Nobel Prize in 1905. Robert Millikan, a physicist at the University of Chicago, worked for several years to make satisfactory measurements. In 1923, he too won a Nobel Prize, in part for his experiments on the photoelectric effect.

Photoelectric experiments present serious experimental difficulties. Millikan knew that metals such as sodium and potassium, which would show the effect most clearly, were also the most reactive common metals, and therefore the most difficult with which to work. These metals are also very soft. The chief problem is that the light must fall on a clean metal surface, and the most reactive substances are by definition the ones for which it is hardest to produce a clean surface. They quickly undergo chemical reaction to form surface oxides with even tiny amounts of oxygen from the air. In general, metal surfaces always have molecules of gases such as oxygen bound to them, and for the reactive metals, the problem is severe. Millikan minimized the oxygen by doing his experiments inside a glass bulb from which he pumped as much air as possible, but this did not yield a clean surface for the reactive metals. He

solved the problem by placing a small knife inside the apparatus and manipulating it magnetically so as to shave the metal and expose a fresh surface.

In physics, it is always important to know the energies of the bodies being studied. To do this for the electrons leaving the metal surface, Millikan mounted a metal plate inside his glass bulb to collect electrons and connected it electrically to a variable voltage source outside the tube. Electrons moving toward such a collector plate will be attracted if the plate carries a positive voltage, and prevented from reaching the plate if the plate voltage is sufficiently negative. A stream of electrons reaching the plate is an electric current, and this current can be measured by placing an ammeter into the electric circuit. In experiments on the photoelectric effect, this current is called the "photocurrent." It can be

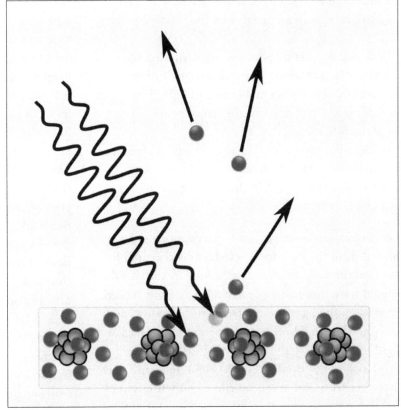

The emission of electrons from a metal plate caused by light quanta—photons. Image by Ponor, via Wikimedia Commons.

stopped by putting a small negative voltage on the plate. The negative voltage on the plate is caused by an excess of electrons on it. The stopping of the stream of electrons by the negative voltage on the metal plate happens because charges of like sign repel each other. The least voltage that reduces the current of electrons to zero for a particular metal is known as the "stopping voltage." This voltage also depends on the frequency of the light that is being absorbed by the electrons.

As the frequency of light becomes higher, the amount of energy the light imparts to the electrons increases. The metals with which Millikan worked are those that show a photoelectric effect readily—that is, they do so when illuminated with light of relatively low frequency. Because it is difficult to produce bright sources of light at high frequencies, Millikan gained a substantial advantage by learning how to produce clean surfaces on the reactive metals.

The results of early photoelectric experiments could not be explained by physicists with only a nineteenth-century understanding of light. From the perspective of that century, the major problems were the following:

- Electrons are emitted from the metal surface immediately after the light strikes the surface;
- No time is required for light energy to accumulate in the metal.

Light is a form of energy, and energy is being passed from the light to the electrons. According to classical physics, the electrons emitted by the metal should have more energy when a bright light is used than when the light is dim. This sensible expectation was found to be false; electrons produced under low light intensity have the same energy as electrons produced under bright light. A bright light produces more electrons, but it has no effect on their energies as long as the frequency is constant. The experimental evidence for this is that the stopping voltage does not depend on the brightness, or intensity, of the light.

For all of the metals that were studied in photoelectric experiments, there is a frequency below which no electrons are emitted by the metal, no matter how bright the light. This frequency, called the "threshold frequency," is different for each metal. This fundamental importance of frequency and the relative unimportance of the brightness of the light were completely at odds with nineteenth-century physics.

For all metals, the stopping voltage increases at the same rate as the frequency of the light increases.

Albert Einstein carefully analyzed what was known about the photoelectric effect. He was ready to use an idea developed by Max Planck, a physicist some twenty years older than himself, to explain the effect. Planck had studied the light given off by a glowing hot solid. The challenge was to find an equation to fit a well-known experimental relationship between the frequencies of the light and the brightness at each frequency. He sought unsuccessfully for an explanation based entirely on the physics of the late nineteenth century. In 1900, he found an explanation that fit the experimental facts perfectly, but it was assumed that had no place in the physics he knew. The assumption was that, for atoms vibrating in the hot solid, the energy of vibration is given by the frequency of vibration multiplied by a constant—that is, the energy of the vibration is tied to the frequency. The vibrations of the solid then set the vibrational frequencies of the light given off. For Planck, this assumption was only a mathematical device that enabled him to derive an equation that fit the experimental results. He did not attempt to attach any deep meaning to the relationship between energy and frequency. It did not seem correct to him, and he made a sustained effort to work out the same satisfying result without making the troublesome assumption. It could not be done.

In 1905, Einstein seized Planck's idea and built his explanation of the photoelectric effect around it. Whereas Planck reluctantly wrote that the energy of vibrating atoms was fixed by their vibrational frequency, Einstein said something far more radical—that light had to be understood as a stream of particles, each of which acted independently, and carried an energy proportional to the frequency of the light. By using the frequency of light, he was both accepting its wave nature and adding a particle nature to it. Some years later, the particles of light came to be called "photons." This premise led him to an amazingly simple explanation of the photoelectric effect. In addition to his recognition that the energy of a photon is set by its frequency, Einstein also recognized that one photon interacts with one electron to liberate it from the metal.

Physicists like to cast their arguments in terms of energies, because the total energy of any process is conserved, and the conservation plays an important part in understanding the process. Einstein wrote that the total energy of the photon goes into the photoelectric removal of an electron, and that this energy must be equal to the potential energy of the electron before it is removed, plus the kinetic energy it has after it leaves the metal. Stated differently, the light energy is spent in two ways: removing the electron from the metal (potential energy) and giving the electron energy of motion (kinetic energy) after it leaves the metal. All results of photoelectric experiments could be understood quite easily by those physicists who were willing to accept Einstein's insights. To see the details, consider again the four points made above:

The photoelectric effect begins immediately, because the first photons to arrive contain enough energy to remove electrons. The energy of the electrons does not depend on the brightness of the light, because the brightness is a consequence of the total number of photons falling on the metal surface, whereas it is the energy of individual photons that is taken up by individual electrons.

The threshold frequency represents exactly the energy required to remove an electron without giving it any additional kinetic energy. Any lesser amount of energy is not enough to remove the electron. The electron cannot store an insufficient amount of energy until a later time when more energy arrives. The energy carried by the photon is either adequate, or it cannot contribute to the removal of an electron.

That an increase in the frequency of the light should affect the rate of change of the stopping voltage in exactly the same way for all metals made it possible to find the value of the constant of proportionality between the frequency of light and the energy carried by each photon. This constant is called Planck's constant, and it is recognized as one of the fundamental quantities of the universe. To physicists, its prominence is comparable to that of the speed of light.

In the preceding discussion, it has been assumed that the light falling on a metal surface to cause the photoelectric effect has a frequency above the threshold frequency. However, only a small percentage of the photons in light of frequency above the threshold for a given metal will actually remove an electron from the metal surface. If the photoelectric efficiency were much higher, it would be much easier to generate electricity from light.

Values of the work function, defined above, vary from about 2.1 electron-volts (eV) for cesium to more than 5.5 eV for metals such as platinum that hold their electrons most tightly. For potassium and sodium, the values are 2.30 and 2.75 eV, respectively; these low values are convenient for experiments because visible light provides this much energy. This is the advantage that Millikan gained after overcoming the problems of working with the reactive metals sodium and potassium. The high values are those of photons well into the ultraviolet region.

APPLICATIONS

A simple photocell or light meter can be constructed from a photoelectric cell and a meter to measure the current. Such meters have limited use, because they are not very sensitive. One familiar use is in the light beam that detects when an elevator door should be closed. As long as the beam is blocked, the elevator door is in use. When the light is uninterrupted for a few seconds, the photoelectric current becomes a signal to close the door.

The audio portion of a motion picture can be stored on film by a method that uses the photoelectric effect. A continuous optical soundtrack extends along the edge of the film. It is a clear band of varying width. Light shining through the band will create a varying electrical signal as that light falls on a photoelectrically active metal surface. The signal is amplified to become the soundtrack.

The photon multiplier, or photomultiplier tube, is a prominent scientific device based on the photoelectric effect. Photons fall onto the surface of a suitable metal. Near this metal is another photoelectrically active metal surface that carries a voltage that is more positive than that on the first surface. The voltage causes electrons that are given off by the first surface to gain energy as they move toward the second surface, where each arriving electron can detach several electrons in the metal it strikes. These in turn are attracted to another nearby surface with a still more positive voltage on it, and still more electrons are released by impact with this surface. After this increasing stream of electrons has moved to several plates in turn, the current is great enough to provide a useful electrical signal. The most sensitive photomultipliers can detect photons arriving one at a time, in which case the device is sometimes called a "photon counter."

As described above, the photoelectric effect requires that light fall on a metal surface enclosed in a bulb from which as much air as possible has been removed. The same principle operates in some devices that have no evacuated space. Light-sensitive electrical resistors are devices with electrical resistance that decreases when light strikes the surface. The light is able to remove electrons from the atoms to which they are attached. They remain in the material, joining the electric current flowing through the resistor. Such light-sensitive resistors are commonly used to produce an electrical signal that depends on the brightness of light.

The scintillation counter is widely used to count the rate of radioactivity in solids and liquids. A high-energy particle from radioactive decay strikes a crystal in which the atoms give off light after they absorb energy from the radioactive particle. This light is detected and amplified in a photomultiplier.

CONTEXT

The nature of light has long been a central question in physics. Isaac Newton thought of light as a stream of particles. Early in the nineteenth century, Thomas Young showed that light could be diffracted, a convincing proof that it is a wave. Einstein's explanation of the photoelectric effect assumed that light had a particle nature that was just as important as its wave nature. However, the wave nature of light had been so firmly established that it made it difficult for physicists at first to accept Einstein's argument. In 1913, a young Danish physicist, Niels Bohr, assumed that the energy of photons is proportional to frequency in order to explain the puzzling frequencies of light given off by excited hydrogen atoms. In 1923, the American physicist Arthur Compton drew even more heavily on Einstein's work to explain the results of collisions between X-rays and electrons in solids. Compton wrote the particle view directly into his explanation. He also took account of the relativistic momentum of the X-ray photon; momentum is just as characteristic of particles as diffraction is of waves. Compton shared a Nobel Prize in 1927. That light is a stream of particles had been established. That it is also a wave is expressed in physicists' terms as the "wave-particle duality."

In 1923, even as waves came to be recognized as accounting for only part of the nature of light, Louis de Broglie suggested, based on good intuition rather than hard evidence, that the smallest particles, such as the electron, possessed wave properties. In a few years, this idea was shown to be correct by the diffraction of a beam of electrons. Thus light, regarded as a wave before the photoelectric effect was understood, had an equally fundamental particle aspect to it, and the electron, which was coming to be recognized as a fundamental electrically charged particle, was shown to have the fundamental property of a wave. These two deep insights into the behavior of light and electrons became the basis for the development of the theory of quantum mechanics, which is, along with the theory of relativity, the fullest expression of the revolution in physics that the twentieth century produced.

The photoelectric effect shows how light of sufficiently high frequency can affect bound electrons, that is, electrons that are held to the atoms of a solid. The principle that a photon of light delivers its entire energy to the electron that absorbs it has become a central idea in the physical sciences. The effect also provides a striking illustration of the unshakable importance of a simple explanation that fits the experimental facts. Max Planck put forth the idea that the energy of vibrating matter could be expressed as the product of the frequency of the associated light and a constant. For Planck, though, this idea was a mathematical convenience that enabled him to solve a conundrum known as the "black body problem." It did not take on deep physical meaning for him; indeed, he tried unsuccessfully to solve the problem without making this assumption. Einstein, aware of Planck's work, took the idea and applied it to the photoelectric effect, another vexing problem, with such good results that the idea won acceptance, though not immediately. Einstein's 1921 Nobel Prize was awarded chiefly for his explanation of the photoelectric effect. Today, he is remembered far more widely for his theory of relativity and for his derivation of the relationship between energy and mass that is the foundation of nuclear energy.

In the photoelectric effect, a photon releases an electron. The opposite effect is far better known; when a beam of electrons strikes the inside of a television picture tube or computer monitor, light is given off by a phosphorescent substance, or phosphor, that has gained energy as a result of being struck by electrons, and some of the energy is converted to light.

—*Thomas A. Lehman*

Further Reading

Dodd, John N. *Atoms and Light: Interactions*. Springer Science & Business Media, 2013.

Hentschel. Klaus. *Photons: The History and Mental Models of Light Quanta*. Translated by Ann M. Hentschel. Springer, 2018.

Hernandez, John. *Quantum Physics: A Simple Guide to Understanding the Principles of Physics (All the Major Ideas of Quantum Mechanics from Quanta to Entanglement in Simple Language)*. Zoe Lawson, 2022.

Ling, Samuel J., Jeff Sanny, and William Moebs. *University Physics, Volume 3*. Samurai Media Limited, 2017.

Ryvkin, Solomon M. *Photoelectric Effects in Semiconductors*. Springer US, 2012.

See also: Amplitude; Angular forces; Angular momentum; Atoms; Calculus; Classical or applied mechanics; Hertz, Heinrich Rudolf; Kinetic energy; Newton's laws; Potential energy; Quantum mechanics

PLANE RUDDERS

Fields of Study: Physics; Aeronautical engineering; Mechanical engineering

ABSTRACT

The rudder is a large, vertical, movable, flap-like device attached to the vertical stabilizer on most aircraft, or mov-

able vertical fins on a missile. The rudder is the primary device used to yaw, or steer the nose of the aircraft to the left or right, in a turn or to counteract the yaw resulting from aileron use in certain cross-control maneuvers.

KEY CONCEPTS

cross-control: use of both rudder and ailerons in the opposite sense of their regular use to control the approach of an airplane to a runway, producing a slip

lift: the upward pressure experienced by wings due to differential pressure between upper and lower surfaces of the wing as it moves through a fluid medium as determined by its airfoil camber and thickness

slip: a maneuver in which an aircraft is made to turn sideways slightly while maintaining the same direction of motion, thus presenting a greater surface area in the wind direction and acting to slow the aircraft somewhat

yaw: the tendency of an aircraft to turn horizontally about its center of mass as it moves through a fluid medium

FUNCTION OF A RUDDER

An aircraft's or a missile's rudder, a flap or a wing-shaped surface mounted at or near the craft's rear, serves a purpose similar to that of a rudder on a ship. When the rudder is deflected to one side or the other, it produces a force and a resulting moment, or yaw, about the vehicle's center of gravity. The force rotates the vehicle in the same direction as the deflection of the rudder.

Because rudders have been used for centuries to steer ships, early airplane designers naturally assumed that they could be used to steer airplanes. However, these designers often failed to anticipate the roll of the aircraft that resulted from the use of the rudder. When the rudder causes an airplane to yaw, it causes one wing to travel slightly more quickly through the air than the other and, hence,

to produce more lift, which subsequently causes the airplane to roll in the direction of the turn. This roll was a problem with early airplanes, which flew very close to the ground, and required the use of ailerons and similar devices to control the resulting roll. Through experimentation, early aviators learned that the most successful turns are coordinated turns, made using a combination of rudder and ailerons.

On wingless missiles, the rudder is the only device used to make the vehicle turn. A missile's rudder yaws the missile such that it flies at an angle to the airflow and develops a side-force on its body, or fuselage. This side-force produces the needed acceleration along the turn radius to carry the missile through the desired turn.

TURNS

Airplane turns are more complex and require more than the use of a rudder. As noted above, when the rudder is deflected, the fuselage yaws, and the wings develop different lift forces. The wing on the outside of the turn develops a larger lift than does the wing pointing into the turn. The difference in lift between the wings results in a roll of the fuselage, which tilts or rotates the lifting force of the wings into the direction of the turn. Because the lifting force of the wings is much greater than the forces on any other part of the airplane, it is the tilted lift that provides the force to turn the airplane. When the turn is properly coordinated, the combination of yaw caused by the rudder, roll caused by the ailerons, and the slight increase in thrust will produce just the right amount of lift to balance the weight of the aircraft, so that the aircraft can make the turn without losing altitude.

ENGINE LOSS

The rudder must also be used to keep the airplane from yawing or turning when a multiengine airplane loses one of its engines. When a multiengine plane

The rudder is controlled through rudder pedals on the bottom rear of the yoke in this photo of a Boeing 727 cockpit. Photo via Wikimedia Commons. [Public domain.]

encounters an engine-out situation, the rudder must be used to produce enough yaw to counteract the effect of having more thrust on one side of the airplane than on the other. For this reason, multiengine airplanes have much larger rudders than do single-engine airplanes.

LANDINGS

Another common use of the rudder is to cross-control an airplane, especially in its approach to landing. In an ideal landing, the atmospheric wind would be blowing straight down the runway. In the real world, the wind is often at an angle to the runway and, when landing or taking off, the pilot must adjust the flight of the plane to account for the

crosswind. On takeoff, this is done by allowing the plane to yaw into the wind as soon as it leaves the ground and by flying away in a straight line extending from the runway centerline with the airplane turned somewhat into the wind in a slightly sideways motion. The approach to landing can be made in the same manner, with the plane yawed into the wind; at some point, the pilot must align the fuselage with the runway before the wheels touch down, so the aircraft can be properly controlled on the ground. To do this, the pilot uses the rudder to yaw the airplane until it is parallel to the runway and uses the ailerons to keep the wings level. This use of rudder and aileron is the opposite of that used in a turn and is referred to as cross-control.

The rudder is controlled on most aircraft by cables or hydraulic lines connected to pedals on the floor of the cockpit. The pilot presses the right rudder pedal to move the rudder and, thus, the nose of the aircraft, to the right, or presses the left rudder to rotate left. Modern airliners and fighters use power-augmented hydraulic or electrical systems to connect the rudder pedals to the rudder, and the rudder is often connected to an automated control system, which will allow control of the airplane by a computer system.

—James F. Marchman III

Further Reading

Pamadi, Bandu N. *Performance, Stability, Dynamics, and Control of Airplanes.* American Institute of Aeronautics and Astronautics, 2004.

Williamson, Hank, editor. *Air Crash Investigations: Jammed Rudder Kills 132, The Crash of US Air Flight 427.* Lulu.com. 2011.

Wrigley, Sylvia. *Why Planes Crash Case Files: 2001-2003.* Fear of Landing, 2018.

See also: Aeronautical engineering; Ailerons, flaps, and airplane wings; Bernoulli, Daniel

Plasticity (physics)

Fields of Study: Physics; Mechanics; Mathematics

ABSTRACT

Plasticity is the ability of solid materials to deform or change shape permanently without breaking when subject to external forces. Plasticity differs from elasticity, which is the ability of a solid to change shape temporarily under stress before reverting to its original form.

KEY CONCEPTS

ductility: the extent to which a material is able to be stretched without fracturing in response to an applied force

elasticity: the extent to which a material is able to naturally revert to its original shape after being temporarily deformed by an applied force

strain: the response of a material to forces perpendicular to the stress in the material

stress: the response of a material to forces of compression and elongation (stretching)

BACKGROUND

In physics, plasticity is the ability of solid materials to deform or change shape permanently without breaking when subject to external forces. Plasticity differs from elasticity, which is the ability of a solid to change shape temporarily under stress before reverting to its original form. The plasticity of a material is affected by its ductility—the ability to stretch under stress—and its malleability—the ability to be shaped without breaking. Plasticity can be observed in metalworking when a piece of metal is heated and molded to form a new shape. Under very high temperatures, plasticity also occurs in glassworking and in geological processes such as the flow of molten rock within Earth.

Many solid materials undergo some physical change when subjected to stress. In physics, stress is the force per unit area applied to an object. The amount of stress can be measured by dividing the force exerted on an object by the cross-sectional area of the object. The ability of a material to return to its original shape after it has been deformed through stress is known as its elasticity. This property is best illustrated in the way a rubber band or coiled spring can be stretched but snaps back into shape when the force is removed. Denser objects such as metals also exhibit elasticity, however, considerably greater force is required to affect such objects and the results are far less noticeable. The energy used in the deformation of a material is completely recovered when the force is removed.

The measure of a material's elasticity is determined by a formula called Young's modulus, which in simple terms can be described as elasticity equals stress divided by strain. Strain is a measure of how much an object stretches or changes relative to its original length. If too much stress is applied to a material, it will break or rupture. A material's ultimate strength is the amount of stress it can withstand before it breaks. Metal and rock display high values of ultimate strength while a rubber band has a lower value.

OVERVIEW

If a material is subjected to an amount of stress great enough to permanently deform it but not great enough to break it, the material is said to have reached its elastic limit. The measure of force needed to deform a material permanently is called its yield strength. The property of material solids to deform permanently under stress is known as plasticity. Unlike elasticity, the energy expended in the plastic deformation of a material is dissipated in the process. In plastic deformation, there are no easily measured values that can be determined by a simple formula such as Young's modulus.

Nineteenth-century French engineer Henri Tresca, who is sometimes called the father of the science of plasticity, developed a standard to determine when plastic deformation would occur. This standard, called the Tresca criterion, is built on the principle that plasticity occurs when the maximum shear stress over all planes of a material reaches a critical value. Shear stress is a unit of external force that causes two contacting planes or layers to slide upon each other in opposite directions parallel to the plane of contact. A simple example of shear stress is using a pair of scissors to cut a thick material as the movement of the two blades of the scissors exert shear stress on the object.

In metals and other crystalline materials, plasticity occurs at the microscopic level because of dislocations or movement in the boundaries between the tightly packed grains of the material. In granular material, such as sand, plasticity occurs because of an irreversible rearrangement and crushing of individual particles. When a solid piece of metal is pounded into a new shape, it undergoes plastic deformation because of physical changes taking place within the material. In more fragile materials, such as rocks, plasticity usually occurs because of movement along microscopic cracks.

Since metals are more ductile materials, they can undergo significant plastic deformations without breaking or fracturing. Most metals exhibit increased plasticity when they are heated to a sufficient temperature. This allows them to become highly malleable and can more easily undergo plastic deformation by such processes as forging, rolling, and extrusion. Forging involves heating metal in a fire, and then pounding and shaping it with impact from a hammer or a hydraulic ram. Rolling is the process of shaping metal by forcing it through rotating rollers. Extrusion shapes heated metal by pushing it through a mold or die. Metals can also be heated to a melting point and poured into a mold. A process called cold working uses high pressure without heat to change the shape of a metal. The process is most often used on steel, aluminum, and copper.

Gold is the most ductile and plastic of metals and can be hammered or pounded into sheets only a few atoms thick while still maintaining its integrity. Gold leaf is thin enough to adhere to surfaces simply by pressing it to a surface with a fine paintbrush. Copper is also a very ductile metal and displays a high degree of plasticity. This aspect is one of the reasons copper is often used in wiring. Cast iron—a hard alloy made of iron, carbon, and silicon—is extremely brittle and cannot be plastically deformed. Even the most ductile metals will harden and become brittle if they undergo cold working, which is also known as work hardening. The effect can be reversed through a slow-heating process called annealing.

Finished glass displays essentially no plasticity, as any sufficient force will cause it to break. In the glassmaking process, however, silicon dioxide and several other substances are heated to the point of plasticity, molded into a shape, and hardened. Similar to glass, molten rock melted by the extreme pressures within the earth also display properties of plastic deformation.

—*Richard Sheposh*

Further Reading

Bell, Terence. "What Is Cold Working?" *The Balance*, 17 Mar. 2017, www.thebalance.com/what-is-cold-working-2340011. Accessed 22 June 2017.

Campbell, Allison, et al. "Elasticity vs. Plasticity." *Energy Education*, energyeducation.ca/encyclopedia/Elasticity_vs_plasticity. Accessed 22 June 2017.

Coleman, Lawrence B. "Elasticity and Plasticity." *University of California, Davis*, 14 June 1998, smartsite.ucdavis.edu/access/content/user/00002774/Sears-Coleman%20Text/Text/C11-15/12-4.html. Accessed 22 June 2017.

Dixit, P. M., and U.S. Dixit. *Plasticity: Fundamentals and Applications*. CRC Press, 2014.

Goodier, J. N., and P. G. Hodge, Jr. *Elasticity and Plasticity: The Mathematical Theory of Elasticity and The Mathematical Theory of Plasticity*. Courier Dover Publications, 2016.

Kachanov, L. M. *Fundamentals of the Theory of Plasticity*. Dover Publications, 2004.

Kelly, Piaras. "Introduction to Plasticity." *University of Auckland*, homepages.engineering.auckland.ac.nz/~pkel015/SolidMechanicsBooks/Part_II/08_Plasticity/08_Plasticity_01_Introduction.pdf. Accessed 22 June 2017.

Lubliner, Jacob. *Plasticity Theory*. 1990. Dover Publications, 2008.

Martinez, Tara. "Types of Metal Strength." *Monarch Metal Fabrication*, 24 Aug. 2016, www.monarchmetal.com/blog/types-of-metal-strength. Accessed 22 June 2017.

See also: Elasticity; Force (physics); Hydraulics; Materials science; Young, Thomas

Poisson, Siméon Denis

Fields of Study: Physics; Mechanics; Mathematics

ABSTRACT

Siméon Denis Poisson was born June 21, 1781, in Pithiviers, France, and died April 25, 1840, in Sceaux, France. Poisson made important contributions in the areas of statistics and physics. A student of French astronomer Pierre-Simon Laplace, he is one of seventy-two French scientists, engineers, and notables who have their names engraved on the Eiffel Tower in recognition of their work.

KEY CONCEPTS

celestial mechanics: the mathematical description of the motions of planets, stars, and other celestial objects due to their gravitational interactions

probability: the numerical likelihood that a specific event will occur in random events occurring within a set of defined conditions (e.g., the occurrence of the 6 appearing on the roll of a standard cubic die)

probability theory: the mathematical basis of determining the likelihood of a given outcome in a situation governed by random chance within a set of starting and boundary conditions, such as the rules by which a particular game of chance is played

statistics: collections of specified data points used as the basis for probability calculations (e.g., the outcomes of a number of rolls of a standard cubic die)

EARLY LIFE

Nineteenth-century French mathematician Siméon Denis Poisson made important contributions in the areas of statistics and physics. A student of French astronomer Pierre Laplace, Poisson is one of seventy-two French scientists, engineers and notables who have their names engraved on the Eiffel Tower in recognition of their work.

Siméon Denis Poisson was born in Pithiviers, France on June 21, 1781. His father, Siméon Poisson, was a soldier and neither he nor Poisson's mother was from a noble family. However, changes in French society that came about as a result of the French Revolution in 1789 would result in unprecedented educational opportunities for Poisson as a young man. Poisson was the first of the children in his family to survive beyond infancy. Because he was not of good health, his family put him in the care of a nurse to ensure his survival. His father taught him to read and write and wished for him to study medicine.

As a young man, Poisson was sent to Fontainebleau in Paris to apprentice with an uncle who was a surgeon. However, he found that he lacked the necessary hand coordination required for conducting surgery, and had little interest in being a physician.

In 1796, Poisson returned to Fontainebleau, this time to the École Centrale, where he quickly distinguished himself as a student of mathematics. At the urging of his teachers, he sat for the exam for École Polytechnique in Paris. Despite his lack of a formal education in mathematics, Poisson was named first in his class in 1798. His work in mathematics drew the attention of two men whose work was deeply respected: astronomer Pierre-Simon Laplace and mathematician Joseph-Louis Lagrange. Poisson's lack of fine motor skills was again an impediment, as it made drawing mathematical diagrams tedious and difficult. This was especially problematic for geometry. Nonetheless, Poisson had an interest in pure mathematics and was able to work around this limitation.

LIFE'S WORK

Poisson's greatest achievements lay in his work as a theoretical mathematician and educator. By 1802, Poisson was a deputy director at École Polytechnique. Upon his graduation in 1800, he was appointed to the position of teaching assistant. He was also published twice in the École Polytechnique's *Recueil des savants étrangers* (*Reports of Foreign Scientists*), a great honor for an eighteen-year-old student.

In 1802, Poisson became an assistant professor. He attained a professorship in 1806, when

Simeon Denis Poisson. Image via Wikimedia Commons. [Public domain.]

Jean-Baptiste Joseph Fourier vacated the position. In 1808, Poisson was appointed as an astronomer at the Bureau des Longitudes. He also had a treatise on celestial mechanics published. This work, *Sur les inégalités séculaires des moyens mouvements des planets* (*On the Motions of Planets*), examined the stability of planetary orbits. By 1811, Poisson had begun his work on the application of mathematics to electricity and magnetism, mechanics, and other areas of physics. He published *Traité de mécanique* (*Treatise of Mechanics*) in 1811. This work served as a standard reference on the subject for many years.

In 1812, Poisson became a member of the Institut de France, an academic society. He also published a memoir on his two-fluid theory of electricity. In this theory, Poisson posited that electricity was made up of two fluids that contained particles, which repelled like particles and attracted unlike particles. He calculated the reactive force as inversely proportional to the square of the distance between them.

Poisson developed his probability theory, which became known as the Poisson equation, in 1813. He was named examiner for the military school at Saint-Cyr in 1815. In 1816, he was named graduation examiner at the École Polytechnique. He married Nancy de Bardi in 1817 and was elected a fellow of the Royal Society of London in 1818.

Poisson became a fellow of the Royal Society of Edinburgh in 1820. That same year, he accepted a nomination to the Conseil Royal de L'Université. During this time, professional science and science education were falling into disregard in France because of political instability, and Poisson used his position to defend the role of science in everyday life and in the academy.

He published *Sur la libération de la lune*, another work on celestial mechanics, in 1821. In 1822, he was elected a foreign member of the Royal Swedish Academy of Sciences. In 1924, he published a paper on his two-fluid theory of magnetic potential, and in 1825 he published his views on the wave theory of light.

When his longtime mentor Lagrange died in 1827, Poisson replaced him as geometer of the Bureau des Longitudes, a scientific association dedicated to navigational standards. In the interest of advancing Lagrange's work as well as his own, Poisson undertook the task of writing a comprehensive mathematical text made up of various volumes. He would not live to complete this task, but his work did produce another publication on celestial mechanics, *Sur le mouvement de la terre autour de son centre de gravité* (*On the Movement of the Earth Around Its Center of Gravity*), released in 1827. In 1829, Poisson published *Sur l'attraction des spheroids* (*On the Attraction of Spheroids*).

In 1832, he received the prestigious Copley Medal for his contributions to science form the Royal Society of London. He published a memoir on the movement of the moon in 1833.

IMPACT

Poisson's passion for mathematics is summed up in a statement attributed to him by French mathematician and politician Dominique François Jean Arago: "Life is good for only two things, discovering mathematics and teaching mathematics." In all, Poisson published over three hundred works in pure mathematics, applied mathematics, mathematical physics, and rational mechanics. His contributions to the field of electricity and magnetism were fundamental to the creation of a new branch of mathematical physics. Poisson's work on attractive forces influenced British mathematical physicist George Green's work on electricity and magnetism. He is equally well remembered for his work in celestial mechanics. The Poisson distribution, dealing with the law of large numbers, is still used to predict the occurrence of such unlikely events as airplane crashes.

—*Gina Hagler*

Further Reading

Gekhtman, Michael, Michael Shapiro, and Alek Vainshtein. *Cluster Algebras and Poisson Geometry*. American Mathematical Society, 2010.

Karasev, M. V., Maria Shishkova, Elena Novikova, and Yu M. Vorobjev. *Quantum Algebras and Poisson Geometry in Mathematical Physics*. American Mathematical Society, 2005.

Mittag, Hans-Joachim, and Horst Rinne. *Statistical Methods of Quality Assurance*. 2nd ed., CRC Press, 2018.

Petale, M. D. *Probability Distribution: (Theory & Solved Examples)*. Mangesh Devidasrao Petale, 2019.

Poisson, Siméon-Denis. *A Treatise of Mechanics; Volume 2*. Creative Media Partners LLC, 2018.

See also: Calculus; Celestial mechanics; Euclidean geometry; Geometry; Lagrange, Joseph-Louis; Laplace, Pierre-Simon; Pascal, Blaise; Quantum mechanics; Thermodynamics

POTENTIAL ENERGY

Fields of Study: Physics; Mechanics; Mathematics

ABSTRACT

There are many kinds of potential energy present in an object at once. These forms of potential energy can come from varied sources. They all affect the object's behavior in different ways, depending on their properties. Some of these potential energies include electric, gravitational, and elastic energy. This article defines these and provides examples on each and their mathematical descriptions.

KEY CONCEPTS

displacement: difference in the position of an object from its initial position to its final position, regardless of the path it takes

electric potential energy: energy that is present in particles due to their charge and closeness to other charges

force field: the effect of a field force and a function of the relative position of the object from the force field source; the object and the source do not need to be in physical contact for this effect to occur

gravitational force: the pull that objects exert on each other due to their masses and the separation between their centers of mass

Hooke's law: the pull or push on objects attached to springs due to the relative stiffness of the spring and the amount of stretch or compression of the spring

joule: a derived unit of energy from base units of the International System of Units (SI), or metric system, equal to a kilogram times one meter per second squared

kinetic energy: energy due to any kind of motion, be it rotation, vibration, or translation

law of conservation of energy: the total amount of energy in a closed system is always the same; therefore, energy can neither be created nor destroyed

STORING ENERGY

Potential energy is defined as the energy that an object possesses due to its physical position. Using this energy to do work converts it into another type of energy, such as kinetic energy. Scottish physicist William John Macquorn Rankine (1820-72) proposed the term "potential energy" in 1853, based on the research of English physician and physicist Thomas Young (1773-1829). Building on previous work from other physicists and mathematicians, Young had mathematically defined energy as the product of an object's mass (m) and the square of its velocity (v). Though partially correct, this definition was later expanded and corrected by French Italian mathematician Joseph-Louis Lagrange (1736-1813), who included a factor of one-half before the mass and velocity. The energy Young and Lagrange described was in fact kinetic energy, but no such distinction was made at the time. As a result, Rankine used the word "potential" to distinguish it from what he called "actual, or sensible energy." The term "kinetic" was later applied by William Thomson, Lord Kelvin (1824-1907).

All forms of energy, whether kinetic, potential, or other, are measured in joules (J). Named after English physicist James Prescott Joule (1818-89), the joule is part of the International System of Units (SI). It is a derived unit, comprising one or more of the seven SI base units. One joule is equal to the energy required to apply a force of one newton (N)—or, because the newton is also an SI derived unit, one kilogram-meter per second squared (kg·m/s^2)—over a distance of one meter (m). Thus, in SI base units, $1 J = 1$ kg·m/s^2.

Among the most important aspects of potential energy is its ability to move objects from one point to another. Physicists define the difference between an object's starting and end points, regardless of the path taken, as the object's displacement. If a plane flies from New York to London, whether it travels east across the Atlantic Ocean or west across North

America, the Pacific Ocean, Asia, and Europe, in both cases the plane will have the same displacement, even though the distance traveled was different. When potential energy is used to displace an object by any amount, it is said that work was done on that object.

THE POTENTIAL OF FORCES

As the definition of energy was expanded over the years, different forms of potential energy were identified for different forces. A form of potential energy exists for every type of conservative force. A conservative force is one that conserves mechanical energy by turning potential energy into kinetic energy, or vice versa, rather than some other form of energy. Examples of conservative forces include gravitational force and the restoring force of a spring. Friction is an example of a nonconservative force, because it converts mechanical energy into heat.

When an object is held above Earth's surface, the gravitational force is acting on it in order to bring it back down. Gravitational force (F_g) is the attraction that objects exert on each other due to their masses. It is defined by the equation:

$$F_g = (Gm_1m_2)/r^2$$

where G is the universal gravitational constant, m_1 and m_2 are the masses of the objects, and r is the distance between their centers of mass. The center of mass is the weighted average position of the center of the particles that make up an object. The value of the universal gravitational constant is 6.67384×10^{11} m³/kg·s².

Like other types of force, the gravitational force is a distance or field force. This means that the objects do not need to be in contact for the force to take effect. Field forces are important because they produce force fields around the objects that create them. In this case, the field produced by the gravitational force is known as gravity, or the gravitational

In the case of a bow and arrow, when the archer does work on the bow, drawing the string back, some of the chemical energy of the archer's body is transformed into elastic potential energy in the bent limb of the bow. Photo by Penny Mayes, via Wikimedia Commons.

field. On Earth, it has a value of about 9.8 meters per second squared.

The spring force, or elastic force, is called a restoring force because when a spring attached to a mass is either extended or compressed, the spring force acts to restore the mass to its original or equilibrium position. The mass must be in contact with the spring for this force to act on it, so it is not a field force and hence cannot be described by a force field. In 1660, English physicist Robert Hooke (1635-1703) noticed that the stiffer the spring, the greater the restoring force. He quantified spring stiffness as the spring constant (k), which is measured in newtons per meter and is unique to each spring. In 1678, he described the linear relationship between the spring force and the distance of the mass on the spring from equilibrium (x) and defined the spring force (Fs) as the product of k and x. This definition, now known as Hooke's law, is represented as

$$Fs = -1/2kx$$

The negative sign in this equation represents the restoring nature of the force. It is acting in the opposite direction of the displacement.

GRAVITATIONAL AND ELASTIC POTENTIAL ENERGIES

One of the main types of potential energy is gravitational potential energy. An object in a gravitational field acquires gravitational potential energy by changing position. The gravitational potential energy (U_g) of an object within another object's gravitational field is defined by:

$$U_g = -(Gm_1m_2)/r$$

Again, G is the gravitational constant, m_1 and m_2 are the objects' masses, and r is the distance between their centers of mass. This general equation works in every situation. However, when an object is within Earth's gravitational field near the planet's surface, this equation can be simplified, because the force of Earth's gravity (g) is already known:

$$U_g = mgh$$

Here, m is the mass of the object being affected and h is its height above Earth's surface.

The potential energy associated with the spring or elastic force is called elastic potential energy (U_s). Like the spring force, it is also a function of the spring constant and the distance of the mass from its equilibrium position:

$$U_s = kx$$

ELECTRIC POTENTIAL ENERGY

Another form of potential energy is electric potential energy. Electric potential energy derives from the electrostatic force, which is a conservative force. The electrostatic force is what causes two opposite electric charges to attract one another and two like electric charges to repel. It was first described mathematically by French physicist Charles-Augustin de Coulomb (1736-1806) in 1785. Coulomb defined the electrostatic force (F_e) between two electrically charged particles as a function of the charge of each particle (q1 and q2), the distance between them (r), and the electric force constant (k_e):

$$F_e = (k_e q1 q2)/r$$

This equation is known as Coulomb's law. The electric force constant, also called Coulomb's constant, is about 8.988×10^9 newton-meters squared per coulomb squared ($N \cdot m^2/C^2$). The coulomb is the SI derived unit of electric charge, equal to one ampere-second ($A \cdot s$). The ampere, an SI base unit, is used to measure electric current.

Like the gravitational force, the electrostatic force is a field force. This force produces a field called the electric field. Just as an object's gravitational field is dependent on its mass, the magnitude of an electric field (E) is dependent on the charge that generates it. The value of E is defined as the force that would be applied to a charged test particle within the field. It is measured in newtons per coulomb (N/C). The equation for determining E at a given point is derived from Coulomb's law, where one of the two charged particles is treated as the particle generating the field (q) and the other is considered to be the test particle:

$$E = kq/r^2$$

The value of r remains the same. Here, it represents the distance of the test particle from that generating the field.

Because the electrostatic force is a conservative force, a charge within an electric field can acquire electric potential energy. Notably, both the gravitational and electrostatic forces are equal to a constant multiplied by the basic property of the objects that are responsible for the force, the product of which is then divided by the square of the distance between them. This can be applied to the equation for electric potential energy as well. Take the general equation for gravitational potential energy, remove the negative sign (which is simply a convention indicating that gravitational force is attractive), then replace the masses m_1 and m_2 with the charges q_1 and q_2 and the universal gravitational constant (G) with the electric force constant (k_e).

The available amount of electric potential energy affects everyone. The electricity that allows most appliances to function is temporarily stored in miniature devices and circuit elements. Some of these small elements are called capacitors. A capacitor can be most simply defined as two parallel plates separated by some distance, each having an equal but opposite electrical charge. Between the plates is some type of insulator, such as air, a vacuum, or a poor conductor. An electric field is produced between the plates. The electric potential (V) of a charge at a given point within the field is equal to the electric potential energy (U_e) of the charge divided by the charge itself (q):

$$V = U_e/q$$

Electric potential is different from electric potential energy. It is the available amount of electric potential energy that a charged particle can obtain, equal to electric potential energy per unit charge. It is measured in volts (V), an SI derived unit equal to one joule per coulomb (J/C).

However, electric potential is not meaningful on its own. In order to obtain a useful quantity, one must measure the change in electric potential between two points—or, in a capacitor, between the two plates. This quantity is called potential difference, better known as voltage, and is also measured in volts. Using the magnitude of the electric field (E) and the distance between the plates (d), the potential difference (V) between the plates can be calculated:

$$V = Ed$$

The ability of a capacitor to store charge is proportional to the potential difference between the plates. This ability, called capacitance, is measured in farads (F). One farad is equal to one coulomb of electric charge per volt (C/V).

Capacitors store electric potential energy in a manner analogous to how springs store elastic potential energy. If a mass attached to a spring is pulled so that the spring is extended, the mass is attracted to its equilibrium position but cannot return, resulting in potential energy being stored in the mass. Similarly, because the plates of a capacitor have opposite charges, they are attracted toward each other, but because there is no connection between the plates, they cannot. As with gravitational force, the equation for the electrical potential energy of a capacitor resembles that for the elastic potential energy of a mass on a spring. Simply replace the spring constant with the capacitance (C) and the distance from equilibrium with its potential difference (V) to obtain the electric potential energy (Ue):

$$U_E = -CV$$

Electric energy, like all other forms of energy, must obey the law of conservation of energy. No matter what processes take place within a system, the sum of the energy that system has at the start must be equal to the sum of its energy at the end. If one form of energy is expended, it must become a different form of energy. As an electron moves toward a proton, it loses electric potential energy but gains the same amount of kinetic energy, causing its speed to increase.

ENERGY AND THE FUTURE

Understanding potential energy is a problem that everyone faces. Electricity is everywhere, whether produced by natural or artificial means. Lightning is an example of how electrical energy is stored and released. Computers, cell phones, and televisions all have capacitors in them that store charges and electric potential energy. An understanding of potential energy is necessary for many other areas of science and technology as well. Aircraft and spacecraft must be able to overcome the gravitational influence of Earth. To maintain a constant flow of electricity to houses, electric companies must calculate how much electric energy to release during different times of the day. Solar energy systems must store energy obtained from solar cells during the day in batteries so it can be used at night. In these ways and many others, potential energy plays a major role in people's daily lives.

—*Angel G. Fuentes*

Further Reading

Giambattista, Alan, Betty McCarthy Richardson, and Robert C. Richardson. *Physics*. 2nd ed. McGraw, 2010.

Henderson, Tom. "Electric Field and the Movement of Charge." *Physics Classroom*. Physics Classroom, 1996-2015. Accessed 7 May 2015.

Khan, Sal. "Conservation of Energy." *Khan Academy*, n.d. Accessed 7 May 2015.

———. "Electric Potential Energy." *Khan Academy*, n.d. Accessed 7 May 2015.

Nave, Carl R. "Energy Stored on a Capacitor." *HyperPhysics*. Georgia State University, 2012. Accessed 7 May 2015.

Rankine, William John Macquorn. "On the General Law of the Transformation of Energy." *Miscellaneous Scientific Papers: By W. J. Macquorn Rankine, CE, LLD, FRS*, edited by W. J. Millar. 1881. Elibron, 2005, pp. 203-8.

Simanek, Donald E. "Conservation Laws." *A Brief Course in Classical Mechanics*. Lock Haven University, Jan. 2011. Accessed 7 May 2015.

Young, Hugh D. *Sears and Zemansky' College Physics*. 9th ed., Addison, 2012.

See also: Acceleration; Atoms; Gauss's law; Kirchhoff, Gustav Robert; Photoelectric effect; Quantum mechanics; Superconductor; Tesla, Nikola; Work and energy; Work-energy theorem

PROJECTILES

Fields of Study: Physics; Mechanics; Mathematics

ABSTRACT

Physical objects moving by inertia above the surface within a gravitational field are called projectiles. The study of their motion is called ballistics. The mathematics that describes ballistic motion applies to objects as small as a subatomic particle and as large as an intercontinental missile. The physical size of the projectile makes no difference. This enables the use of ballistics in many applications of physical science.

KEY CONCEPTS

acceleration: the rate at which the velocity of an object increases over time

ballistic trajectory: the motion described by a projectile traveling by inertia in a gravitational field

deceleration: the rate at which the velocity of an object decreases over time; not an actual term in physics, but used in the sense of negative acceleration

inertia: the resistance of an object to changes in its velocity

initial velocity: the velocity of an object at the start of some interval of time

parabolic: refers to a shape (a parabola) that can be described by an equation of the form $y = ax^2 + b$

range: the horizontal distance that a projectile can travel before striking the ground

terminal velocity: the velocity at which the acceleration due to gravity of an object falling freely through a fluid medium, such as air or water, is exactly balanced by the deceleration of the object due to resistance from that medium

vertex: the uppermost point in a ballistic trajectory

WHAT IS A PROJECTILE?

A projectile is any object that is propelled through the air by an initial force. After this initial force, the projectile's motion is affected only by the force of gravity. Examples of projectiles are numerous, including sand and stones thrown up by the spinning wheels of a car, a baseball struck by a bat, a bullet fired from a gun, a golf ball in flight, and a satellite launched into orbit. Even very small particles such as ions (electrically charged atoms) traveling through a vacuum chamber are considered projectiles.

After a projectile has been given an initial velocity by some outside force, it maintains its horizontal velocity due to inertia. After that, it only changes its vertical position and speed because of gravity. When the initial force stops acting on the object, such as when a football leaves the hand of the person throwing it, the object becomes a projectile. The subsequent path it follows is called a ballistic trajectory. That trajectory is determined by the angle and velocity of the object when it first becomes a projectile. It is also determined by the force of gravity acting on the object.

The velocity of a projective can be separated into its horizontal (v_x) and vertical (v_y) components, or combined as the projectiles total velocity (v). A cannon ball fired from a cannon at an upward angle (θ) will reach a maximum height at which point the vertical velocity will become zero and the total velocity will be equal to the horizontal velocity. Changes in magnitude of the horizontal and vertical components result in a change in the total velocity's magnitude and direction.

The ballistic trajectory of a projectile is parabolic in shape. Its motion has only two directions, vertical and horizontal, which operate independently of one another. Generally, a projectile will move in both these directions, although it may have no horizontal movement at all. For example, a ball that is thrown straight up in the air and comes down in exactly the same spot has moved vertically but not horizontally.

BALLISTICS

A normal parabola is a symmetrical curve. Its shape is described by the mathematical formula $y = ax^2 + bx + c$, where y represents the vertical displacement, x represents the horizontal displacement, and a represents the change in vertical position relative to horizontal position. The coefficients b and c simply change the position of the curve. The simplest form of this equation is $y = ax^2$, where b and c both equal 0.

A ballistic trajectory differs somewhat from a normal parabola. Technically, a parabola is a curve whose ends go on forever. A ballistic trajectory, however, has distinct start and end points, separated by a horizontal range. The highest point of a ballistic trajectory is called the vertex. This is the point at which the projectile's vertical velocity is zero, as it transitions from traveling upward to falling back down. Ideally, if the start point and the end point are at the same elevation, the vertex will be exactly halfway between the two.

The vertical velocity and the horizontal velocity of a projectile can be calculated separately, as neither affects the other. In an idealized model, as the projectile travels, its horizontal velocity will remain constant, while its vertical velocity will steadily decrease as it travels upward. This deceleration is due to the force of gravity acting on the projectile. When the vertical velocity reaches zero, the projectile can go no higher. It then begins to fall back to the ground, accelerating at the same rate that it decelerated previously. This rate is the acceleration due to gravity,

A projectile being fired from an artillery piece. Photo via Wikimedia Commons.[Public domain.]

which on Earth is approximately 9.81 meters per second per second (m/s²).

SAMPLE PROBLEM

Consider a person who is standing at the top of a 30-meter-high cliff and throws a rock straight out at a zero-degree angle. Suppose the rock is released from a point 2 meters above the edge of the cliff and travels with an initial horizontal velocity of 25 meters per second. Ignoring the effects of air resistance, how far will the rock travel horizontally before striking the ground 32 meters below? Recall that the acceleration due to gravity is 9.81 meters per second per second.

The simplest way to solve this problem is to calculate the amount of time it would take for the rock to

fall straight down from a height of 32 meters, then calculate how far the rock will travel horizontally during that time at a velocity of 25 meters per second. If air resistance is ignored, it can be assumed that the horizontal velocity will remain constant throughout the rock's flight time.

The initial vertical velocity of the rock is 0 m/s. Its final vertical velocity of the rock is not known, but it is known that the rock travels a distance of 32 m in free fall, accelerating at a rate of 9.81 m/s². The final velocity of an object in free fall can be calculated using the following equations, known as equations of motion:

$$v_f^2 = v_0^2 + 2as$$

$$v_f = v_0 + at$$

where v_0 is the initial velocity, v_f is the final velocity, a is acceleration, s is displacement (in this case, vertical displacement), and t is time. The variable v_0 can be eliminated, because the initial velocity is 0. Therefore,

$$v_f^2 = 2as$$

$$v_f = at$$

Solve the first equation for v_f, combine both equations into one, and solve for t:

$$v_f = \sqrt{2as}$$

$$at = \sqrt{2as}$$

$$t = \frac{\sqrt{2as}}{a}$$

$$t = \frac{\sqrt{2(9.81\,\mathrm{m/s^2})(32\mathrm{m})}}{9.81\,\mathrm{m/s^2}}$$

$$t = 2.554\,\mathrm{s}$$

Multiply t (2.554 s) by the horizontal velocity (25 m/s) to determine that the rock traveled a horizontal distance of about 63.85 meters.

However, this model of ballistic trajectory does not consider the medium that the projectile travels through. The medium creates resistance as objects pass through it, and the greater the density of the medium, the greater the resistance. A bullet from a high-powered rifle, for example, can travel several hundred meters through the air without losing much horizontal velocity. However, the same bullet fired into water will lose almost all of its horizontal velocity after just two or three meters. If the same person tried to throw that same rock while under water would have seen it travel only a meter before dropping directly to the bottom.

A parachutist jumping from an airplane experiences the same thing as he or she falls through the air. When the parachutist exits the airplane, the initial horizontal velocity will be the same as that of the airplane, and the initial vertical velocity will be zero. Air resistance will cause the parachutist's horizontal velocity to decrease until it is essentially zero and the parachutist is falling straight down. Meanwhile, the parachutist's vertical velocity will increase at a rate of 9.81 m/s² until the force of the air resistance is equal to the force of gravitational acceleration, at which point he or she can fall no faster. The speed at which this occurs is called terminal velocity and is typically reached long before the parachutist will deploy his or her parachute.

PRACTICAL BALLISTICS

The phenomenon of medium resistance means that in reality, the ballistic trajectory of a projectile will not have a perfectly parabolic shape. Resistance will cause the projectile's horizontal velocity to decrease continually over time, reducing its range. Also, the vertex will not be exactly halfway between the start point and the end point. It will be some distance closer to the end point, because the decrease in horizontal velocity means that the projectile will travel a shorter horizontal distance after passing its vertex. This is a very important consideration for pilots, parachutists, target shooters, baseball players, basketball players, and anyone else who relies on ballistic motion to achieve the goal of hitting a target with a projectile.

Another important consideration is the flight time of a projectile following a ballistic trajectory. Because the horizontal velocity is not affected by the force of gravity, the projectile will continue to travel horizontally until the force of gravity has brought it into contact with the ground. This means that if a ball is thrown straight ahead in such a way that its initial vertical velocity is zero, it will travel through the air for the same amount of time as if it had been simply dropped from the same height. This is because the ball is accelerating toward the ground at the same rate in both cases. This length of time is the flight time, and it is determined solely by the force of gravity acting on the projectile. The greater the horizontal velocity of the projectile, the farther it will travel during the flight time. A slow projectile and a fast projectile will both strike the ground at the same time, however, as long as they are both thrown from the same point at a zero-degree angle.

EQUATIONS OF MOTION

Like all of physics, the description of ballistic trajectories relies heavily on mathematics. It is a fairly simple exercise to watch a projectile travel through the air and relate its motion to mathematics. This can be as simple as watching a stream of water come from a garden hose or tossing a ball into the air. The equations that describe the movements of objects through a constant gravitational field are called "kinematic equations" or "equations of motion." They can be remembered using the acronym VAST, which stands for velocity (v), acceleration (a), displacement (s), and time (t). As demonstrated in the sample problem, these equations can be rearranged and combined in such a way that if just two of these quantities are known, they can be used to calculate the other two.

—*Richard M. Renneboog*

Further Reading

Crawford, F. *Stone Projectile Points of the Pacific Northwest: An Arrowhead Collector's Guide to Type Identification*. 2nd ed., CreateSpace Independent Publishing Platform, 2017.

Hranicky, Wm. Jack. *North American Projectile Points*. Author House, 2014.

Klimi, George. *Exterior Ballistics: A New Approach*. Xlibris Corporation, 2010.

Knecht, Heidi. *Projectile Technology*. Springer Science & Business Media, 2013.

Mody, Vishal. *High School Physics: Projectile Motion*. CreateSpace Independent Publishing Platform, 2015.

Syngellakis, S. *Projectile Impact: Modelling Techniques and Assessment of Target Material Performance*. WIT Press, 2014.

White, Colin. *Projectile Dynamics in Sport: Principles and Applications*. Routledge, 2010.

See also: Aerodynamics; Angular momentum; Ballistic weapons; Kinetic energy; Momentum (physics)

PROPULSION TECHNOLOGIES

Fields of Study: Physics; Aeronautical engineering; Mechanical engineering; Mathematics

ABSTRACT

Propulsion deals with the means by which aircraft, missiles, and spacecraft are propelled toward their destinations. Subjects of development include propellers and rotors driven by internal combustion engines or jet engines, rockets powered by solid- or liquid-fueled engines, spacecraft powered by ion engines, solar sails or nuclear reactors, and matter-antimatter engines. Propulsion system metrics include thrust, power, cycle efficiency, propulsion efficiency, specific impulse, and thrust-specific fuel consumption. Advances in this field have enabled humanity to travel across the world in a few hours, visit space and the moon, and send probes to distant planets.

KEY CONCEPTS

grain: a shaped charge of solid rocket fuel designed to undergo oxidation combustion at a predetermined rate to provide a desired amount of thrust

Law of Conservation of Energy: the total energy of a system remains constant as the sum of the energies of the individual components of the system throughout any change of the system

LOX/LH2 engine: an engine that uses liquid hydrogen as fuel and liquid oxygen as the oxidizer for the combustion reaction of the fuel

momentum: a characteristic expressed as the product of mass and velocity that is conserved in accord with the law of conservation of energy such that the total momentum of the components of a system remains constant throughout any change of the system

specific impulse: thrust developed per second per weight of propellant consumed under standard gravity

thrust: the force or pressure exerted on the body of an aircraft in the direction of its motion

DEFINITION AND BASIC PRINCIPLES

Propulsion is the science of making vehicles move. The propulsion system of a flight vehicle provides the force to accelerate the vehicle and to balance the other forces opposing the motion of the vehicle. Most modern propulsion systems add energy to a working fluid to change its momentum and thus develop force, called thrust, along the desired direction. A few systems use electromagnetic fields or radiation pressure to develop the force needed to accelerate the vehicle itself. The working fluid is usually a gas, and the process can be described by a thermodynamic heat engine cycle involving three basic steps: First, do work on the fluid to increase its pressure; second, add heat or other forms of energy at the highest possible pressure; and third, allow the fluid to expand, converting its potential energy directly to useful work, or to kinetic energy in an exhaust.

In the internal combustion engine, a high-energy fuel is placed in a small closed area and ignited under compression. This produces expanding gas, which drives a piston and a rotating shaft. The rotating shaft drives a transmission whose gears transfer the work to wheels, rotors, or propellers. Rocket and jet engines operate on the Brayton thermodynamic cycle. In this cycle, the gas mixture is compressed adiabatically (no heat added or lost during compression). Heat is added externally or by chemical reaction to the fluid, ideally at constant pressure. The expanding gases are exhausted, with a turbine extracting some work. The gas then expands out through a nozzle.

BACKGROUND AND HISTORY

Solid-fueled rockets developed in China in the thirteenth century achieved the first successful continuous propulsion of heavier-than-air flying machines. In 1903, Orville and Wilbur Wright used a spinning propeller driven by an internal combustion engine to accelerate air and develop the reaction force that propelled the first human-carrying heavier-than-air powered flight.

As propeller speeds approached the speed of sound in World War II, designers switched to the gas turbine or jet engine to achieve higher thrust and speeds. German Wernher von Braun developed the V2 rocket, originally known as the A4 for space travel, but in 1944, it began to be used as a long-range ballistic missile to attack France and England. The V2 traveled faster than the speed of sound, reached heights of 83 to 93 kilometers, and had a range of more than 320 kilometers. The Soviet Union's 43-tonne Sputnik rocket, powered by a LOX/RP2 engine generating 3.89 million Newtons of thrust, placed a 500-kilogram satellite in low Earth orbit on October 4, 1957.

The United States' three-stage, 111-meter-high Saturn V rocket weighed more than 2,280 tonnes and developed more than 33.36 million Newtons at launch. It could place more than 129,300 kilograms into a low-Earth orbit and 48,500 kilograms into lunar orbit, thus enabling the first human visit to the moon in July, 1969. The reusable space shuttle weighed 2,030 tonnes at launch, generated 34.75 million Newtons of thrust, and could place 24,400 kilograms into a low-Earth orbit. In January, 2006, the New Horizons spacecraft reached 57,600 kilometers per hour as it escaped from Earth's gravity. Meanwhile, air-breathing engines have grown in size and become more fuel efficient, propelling aircraft from hovering through supersonic speeds.

HOW IT WORKS

Rocket. The rocket is conceptually the simplest of all propulsion systems. All propellants are carried on board, gases are generated with high pressure, heat is added or released in a chamber, and the gases are exhausted through a nozzle. The momentum of the working fluid is increased, and the rate of increase of this momentum produces a force. The reaction to this force acts on the vehicle through the mounting structure of the rocket engine and propels it.

Jet propulsion. Although rockets certainly produce jets of gas, the term "jet engine" typically denotes an engine in which the working fluid is mostly atmospheric air, so that the only propellant carried on the vehicle is the fuel used to release heat. Typically, the mass of fuel used is only about 2 to 4 percent of the mass of air that is accelerated by the vehicle. Types of jet engines include the ramjet, the turbojet, the turbofan, and the turboshaft.

Propulsion system metrics. The thrust of a propulsion system is the force generated along the desired direction. Thrust for systems that exhaust a gas can come from two sources. Momentum thrust comes from the acceleration of the working fluid through the system. It is equal to the difference between the momentum per second of the exhaust and intake flows. Thrust can also be generated from the product of the area of the jet exhaust nozzle cross section and the difference between the static pressure at the nozzle exit and the outside pressure. This pressure thrust is absent for most aircraft in which the exhaust is not supersonic, but it is inevitable when operating in the vacuum of space. The total thrust is the sum of momentum thrust and pressure thrust. Dividing the total thrust by the exhaust mass flow rate of propellant gives the equivalent exhaust speed. All else being equal, designers prefer the highest specific impulse, though it must be noted

that there is an optimum specific impulse for each mission. LOX-LH2 rocket engines achieve specific impulse of more than 450 seconds, whereas most solid rocket motors cannot achieve 300 seconds. Ion engines exceed 1,000 seconds. Air-breathing engines achieve very high values of specific impulse because most of the working fluid does not have to be carried on-board.

The higher the specific impulse, the lower the mass ratio needed for a given mission. To lower the mass ratio, space missions are built up in several stages. As each stage exhausts its propellant, the propellant tank and its engines are discarded. When all the propellant is gone, only the payload remains. The relation connecting the mass ratio, the delta-v, and specific impulse, along with the effects of gravity and drag, is called the rocket equation.

Propulsion systems, especially for military applications, operate at the edge of their stable operation envelope. For instance, if the reaction rate in a solid propellant rocket grows with pressure at a greater than linear rate, the pressure will keep rising until the rocket blows up. A jet engine compressor will stall, and flames may shoot out the front if the blades go past the stalling angle of attack. Diagnosing and solving the problems of instability in these powerful systems has been a constant concern of developers since the first rocket exploded.

APPLICATIONS AND PRODUCTS

Many kinds of propulsion systems have been developed or proposed. The simplest rocket is a cold gas thruster, in which gas stored in tanks at high pressure is exhausted through a nozzle, accelerating (increasing momentum) in the process. All other types of rocket engines add heat or energy in some other form in a combustion (or thrust) chamber before exhausting the gas through a nozzle.

Solid-fueled rockets are simple and reliable, and can be stored for a long time, but once ignited, their thrust is difficult to control. An ignition source decomposes the propellant at its surface into gases whose reaction releases heat and creates high pressure in the thrust chamber. The surface recession rate is thus a measure of propellant gas generation. The thrust variation with time is built into the rocket grain geometry. The burning area exposed to the hot gases in the combustion chamber changes in a preset way with time. Solid rockets are used as boosters for space launch and for storable missiles that must be launched quickly on demand.

Liquid-fueled rockets typically use pumps to inject propellants into the combustion chamber, where the propellants vaporize, and a chemical reaction releases heat. Typical applications are the main engines of space launchers and engines used in space, where the highest specific impulse is needed.

Hybrid rockets use a solid propellant grain with a liquid propellant injected into the chamber to vary the thrust as desired. Electric resistojets use heat generated by currents flowing through resistances. Though simple, their specific impulse and thrust-to-weight ratio are too low for wide use. Ion rocket engines use electric fields or, in some cases, heat to ionize a gas and a magnetic field to accelerate the ions through the nozzle. These are preferred for long-duration space missions in which only a small level of thrust is needed but for an extended duration because the electric energy comes from solar photovoltaic panels. Nuclear-thermal rockets generate heat from nuclear fission and may be coupled with ion propulsion. Proposed matter-antimatter propulsion systems use the annihilation of antimatter to release heat, with extremely high specific impulse.

Pulsed detonation engines are being developed for some applications. A detonation is a supersonic shock wave generated by intense heat release. These engines use a cyclic process in which the propellants come into contact and detonate several times a second. Nuclear-detonation engines were once proposed, in which the vehicle would be accelerated by shock waves generated by nuclear explosions in space to reach extremely high velocities. However, international law prohibits nuclear explosions in space.

Ramjets and turbomachines. Ramjet engines are used at supersonic speeds and beyond, where the deceleration of the incoming flow is enough to generate very high pressures, adequate for an efficient heat engine. When the heat addition is done without slowing the fluid below the speed of sound, the engine is called a scramjet, or supersonic combustion ramjet. Ramjets cannot start by themselves from rest. Turbojets add a turbine to extract work from the flow leaving the combustor and drive a compressor to increase the pressure ratio. A power turbine may be used downstream of the main turbine. In a turbofan engine, the power turbine drives a fan that works on a larger mass flow rate of air bypassing the combustor. In a turboprop, the power is taken to a gearbox to reduce revolutions per minute, powering a propeller. In a turboshaft engine, the power is transferred through a transmission as in the case of a helicopter rotor, tank, ship, or electric generator. Many applications combine these concepts, such as a propfan, a turboramjet, or a rocket-ramjet that starts off as a solid-fueled rocket and becomes a ramjet when propellant consumption opens enough space to ingest air.

Gravity assist. A spacecraft can be accelerated by sending it close enough to another heavenly body (such as a planet) to be strongly affected by its gravity field. This swing-by maneuver sends the vehicle into a more energetic orbit with a new direction, enabling surprisingly small mass ratios for deep space missions.

Tethers. Orbital momentum can be exchanged using a tether between two spacecraft. This principle has been proposed to efficiently transfer payloads from Earth orbit to lunar or Martian orbits and even to exchange payloads with the lunar surface. An extreme version is a stationary tether linking a point on Earth's equator to a craft in geostationary Earth orbit, the tether running far beyond to a counter-mass. The electrostatic tether concept uses variations in the electric potential with orbital height to induce a current in a tether strung from a spacecraft. An electrodynamic tether uses the force that is exerted on a current-carrying tether by the magnetic field of the planet to propel the tether and the craft attached to it.

Solar and plasma sails. Solar sails use the radiation pressure from sunlight bounced off or absorbed by thin, large sails to propel a craft. Typically, this works best in the inner solar system where radiation is more intense. Other versions of propulsion sails, in which lasers focus radiation on sails that are far away from the Sun, have been proposed. In mini magnetospheric plasma propulsion (M2P2), a cloud of plasma (ionized gas) emitted into the field of a magnetic solenoid creates an electromagnetic bubble around 30 kilometers in diameter, which interacts with the solar wind of charged particles that travels at 300 to 800 kilometers per second. The result is a force perpendicular to the solar wind and the (controllable) magnetic field, similar to aerodynamic lift. This system has been proposed to conduct fast missions to the outer reaches of the solar system and back.

CAREERS

Propulsion technology spans aerospace, mechanical, electrical, nuclear, chemical, and materials science engineering. Aircraft, space launcher, and spacecraft manufacturers and the defense industry are major customers of propulsion systems. Workplaces in this industry are distributed over many regions in the United States and near many major airports and National Aeronautics and Space Administration centers. The large airlines operate engine testing facilities. Propulsion-related work outside the United States, France, Britain, and Germany is usually in companies run by or closely related to their respec-

tive governments. Because propulsion technologies are closely related to weapon-system development, many products and projects come under the International Traffic in Arms Regulations.

Machinery operating at thousands to hundreds of thousands of revolutions per minute requires extreme precision, accuracy, and material perfection. Manufacturing jobs in this field include specialist machinists and electronics experts. Because propulsion systems are limited by the pressure and temperature limits of structures that must also have minimal weight, the work usually involves advanced materials and manufacturing techniques. Instrumentation and diagnostic techniques for propulsion systems are constantly pushing the boundaries of technology and offer exciting opportunities using optical and acoustic techniques.

SOCIAL CONTEXT AND FUTURE PROSPECTS

Propulsion systems have enabled humanity to advance beyond the speed of ships, trains, balloons, and gliders to travel across the oceans safely, quickly, and comfortably and to venture beyond Earth's atmosphere. The result has been a radical transformation of global society since the early twentieth century. People travel overseas regularly, and on any given day, city centers on every continent host conventions with thousands of visitors from all over the world. Jet engine reliability has become so established that jetliners with only two engines routinely fly across the Atlantic and Pacific oceans. However, jet engines are not very energy-efficient, which makes them expensive to operate and detrimental to the environment. As such, addressing this problem is a major area of jet engine research in the twenty-first century.

Propulsion technologies are just beginning to grow in their capabilities. As of the early twenty-first century, specific impulse values were at best a couple of thousand seconds; however, concepts using radiation pressure, nuclear propulsion, and matter-antimatter promise values ranging into hundreds of thousands of seconds. Air-breathing propulsion systems promise specific impulse values of greater than 2,000 seconds, enabling single-stage trips by reusable craft to space and back. As electric propulsion systems with high specific impulse come down in system weight because of the use of specially tailored magnetic materials and superconductors, travel to the outer planets may become quite routine. Spacecraft with solar or magnetospheric sails, or tethers, may make travel and cargo transactions to the moon and inner planets routine as well. These technologies are at the core of human aspirations to travel far beyond their home planet.

—*Narayanan M. Komerath*

Further Reading

De Luca, Luigi T., Max Calabro, Toru Shimada, and Valery P. Sinditskii, editors. *Chemical Rocket Propulsion: A Comprehensive Survey of Energetic Materials*. Springer International Publishing, 2018.

Faeth, G. M. *Centennial of Powered Flight: A Retrospective of Aerospace Research*. American Institute of Aeronautics and Astronautics, 2003.

Gohardani, Amir S. *Distributed Propulsion Technology*. Nova Science Publishers Inc., 2014.

Hunley, J. D. *The Development of Propulsion Technology for U.S. Space-Launch Vehicles, 1926-1991*. Texas A&M University Press, 2013.

Kucinski, William. *So You Want to Design Engines: UAV Propulsion Systems*. SAE International, 2018.

Martin, Richard. "The Race for the Ultra-Efficient Jet Engine of the Future." *MIT Technology Review*, 23 Mar. 2016, www.technologyreview.com/s/601008/the-race-for-the-ultra-efficient-jet-engine-of-the-future/. Accessed 31 Aug. 2018.

Musielak, Dora. *Scramjet Propulsion: A Practical Introduction*. Wiley, 2022.

Norton, Bill. *STOL Progenitors: The Technology Path to a Large STOL Aircraft and the C-17A*. American Institute of Aeronautics and Astronautics, 2002.

Peebles, C. *Road to Mach 10: Lessons Learned from the X-43 A Flight Research Program*. American Institute of Aeronautics and Astronautics, 2008.

Sabry, Foud. *Plasma Propulsion: Can SpaceX Use Advanced Plasma Propulsion for Starship?* One Billion Knowledgeable, 2021.

Schaberg, Christopher. "The Jet Engine Is a Futuristic Technology Stuck in the Past." *The Atlantic*, 11 Feb. 2018, www.theatlantic.com/technology/archive/2018/02/engine-failure/552959/. Accessed 31 Aug. 2018.

See also: Advanced propulsion; Aerodynamics and flight; Aeronautical engineering; Fluid dynamics; Jet engines; Materials science

Q

QUANTUM MECHANICS

Fields of Study: Physics; Mechanics; Mathematics

ABSTRACT
Quantum physics deals with phenomena at the atomic level and smaller. In the past, physicists assumed that the forces and reactions that occurred at the observable level would hold true at the atomic and subatomic levels. However, in the early twentieth century, that notion was disproved, and the field of quantum physics was born.

KEY CONCEPTS

blackbody radiation: radiation emitted by a body solely as a result of its temperature, regardless of its composition or any previously absorbed radiation

line spectrum: the lines of color that represent the characteristic frequencies at which atoms emit electromagnetic radiation

Schrödinger equation: a wave equation that describes the quantum state of a particle or system and can be used to predict its most likely future behavior

uncertainty principle: the idea, proposed by Werner Heisenberg, that one can determine with high precision either the position of a particle at a given time or its momentum, but not both

wave-particle duality: the idea that a particle can behave as either a particle or a wave, depending on how and when it is being observed

BEYOND CLASSICAL MECHANICS

As the start of the twentieth century, scientists believed they were on the cusp of a theory that would unify all known forces and provide an understanding of the universe as a whole. With Isaac Newton's (1642-1727) three laws of motion accounting for the behavior of objects at rest and in motion and James Clerk Maxwell's (1831-79) work with electromagnetism having unified the fields of electricity and magnetism, physicists believed that only a few pieces of the puzzle remained. However, the field of physics was about to change dramatically.

In the nineteenth century, physicists had discovered that the line spectra of different atoms show radiation being emitted at certain frequencies that are characteristic of each element. However, they did not know why this is so. In 1913, Danish physicist Niels Bohr (1885-1962) proposed a new atomic model that offered a solution. He theorized that an atom's electrons could only travel around its nucleus in certain discrete orbitals. They could only move from one orbital to another by absorbing or emitting specific amounts of energy. This energy is the source of the atom's characteristic spectrum lines.

Fundamentally, quantum mechanics is based on the idea that at the smallest possible level, certain physical properties are quantized—that is, made up of individual, discrete units, rather than an unbroken continuum. (A quantum is the smallest possible unit of a physical property.) The idea was first proposed in general terms by Austrian physicist Ludwig Boltzmann (1844-1906) in 1877. It was later picked up by German physicist Max Planck (1858-1947), who, though suspicious of Boltzmann's idea and its implications, nevertheless applied it to his study of blackbody radiation.

THE QUANTIZATION OF ENERGY

Planck's law of blackbody radiation, proposed in 1900, defines the energy emitted by an oscillating particle in a blackbody as $E = nh\nu$, where n is a positive integer, h is a constant value known as Planck's constant, and ν is the frequency of the par-

ticle. In other words, E can only ever equal multiples of $h\nu$. Planck believed that this quantization of energy was merely a mathematical convenience and did not reflect reality. However, German-born physicist Albert Einstein (1879-1955) disagreed. In 1905, he published a paper on the photoelectric ef-

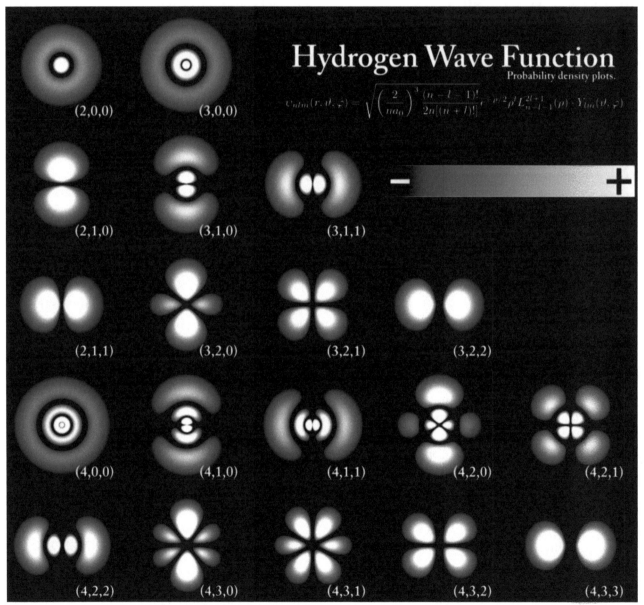

Wave functions of the electron in a hydrogen atom at different energy levels. Quantum mechanics cannot predict the exact location of a particle in space, only the probability of finding it at different locations. The brighter areas represent a higher probability of finding the electron. Image via Wikimedia Commons. [Public domain.]

fect—the emission of precise streams of electrons by certain metals when struck by certain wavelengths of light—in which he suggested that quantization is an inherent property of energy. Einstein argued that energy is in fact composed of individual "energy quanta," each with the energy $h\nu$. These quanta were later called photons.

Elements emit photons at very specific wavelengths. Hydrogen, for example, emits visible light at four distinct wavelengths. (It also emits at several other wavelengths outside the visible spectrum.) These emissions occur in discrete bursts, as opposed to continuous rays. Scientists observed that if they bombarded hydrogen atoms with photons of energies that corresponded to the emission wavelengths, the photons would be absorbed and later released. The energies of the photons were equal to the energy differences between the electron orbitals, which are specific to each element. Photons that are not of these energies simply bounce off.

The double-slit experimental design is used to show the wavelike behavior of particles. A screen with two slots is placed in front of a recording screen. Particles are shot at the slotted screen, pass through the slots, and hit the recording screen. Results from this experiment show that the particles move in a wavelike fashion. The path of individual particles cannot be accurately predicted, but the frequency of hits across the length of the recording screen indicate where particles are more likely to hit.

This phenomenon accounts for the different colors in "neon" signs. In a neon sign, electricity is run through a tube of gas, exciting the electrons and causing them to jump to higher energy levels. The electrons then emit the excess energy in the form of photons that correspond to specific wavelengths of visible light. Neon itself produces a reddish-orange light. Other gases, such as xenon, argon, and helium, are used to produce other colors.

WAVES OR PARTICLES?

In the 1920s, scientists were vexed by problems explaining the motion of electrons inside atoms. They did not seem to obey the laws of classical physics. Bohr's atomic model solved some of these problems, but it did not explain why electrons behave as they do. In 1924, French physicist Louis de Broglie (1892-1987) proposed a revolutionary idea that would lead to the development of modern quantum mechanics.

Scientists had long debated whether light was a particle or a wave. Einstein's 1905 paper on the photoelectric effect demonstrated that it is, in fact, both. Light can behave as either a wave or a particle, depending on the circumstances under which it is observed. This concept came to be known as wave-particle duality. In his doctoral thesis, de Broglie suggested that electrons can also behave as both waves and particles. This was confirmed by a 1927 experiment that showed electrons undergoing diffraction, a phenomenon characteristic of waves. It was later found that all matter exhibits wave-particle duality, not just electrons.

The behavior of any wave can be described by a wave equation. Austrian physicist Erwin Schrödinger (1887-1961) decided to find the wave equation of electrons. He published his result, now known as the Schrödinger equation, in 1926. The Schrödinger equation applies not just to electrons but to all isolated systems. Solving it results in a wave function, which is a mathematical function that describes the probability of finding a given particle in the system in a certain position at a certain time.

Another problem in the study of electrons was that the act of observing an electron involved exposing it to light. This caused the electron to interact with a photon, which could then alter the very qualities being observed. German theoretical physicist Werner Heisenberg (1901-76) discovered this problem while trying to observe an electron with a microscope. The short wavelengths of light required to accurately measure the electron's position exposed it to high-energy photons, which disturbed its momentum. The opposite was also true: any wavelength long enough to observe an electron's momentum without disturbing it would be too long to use for determining its position. This led Heisenberg to publish his uncertainty principle in 1927. The uncertainty principle essentially states that there are hard limits on what can be simultaneously known about any given quantum system. Heisenberg attributed this to the observer effect, wherein the act of observing a system causes that system to change in some way. However, it was later determined that while the observer effect often plays a role in the uncertainty principle, it is not its sole cause. Rather, uncertainty is an inherent property of all wavelike systems. And because all matter exhibits wave-particle duality, this could be extended to apply to all of reality, on the macro as well as the micro and quantum scales. Philosophically, this would require giving up the idea of a deterministic universe. Instead, reality would be considered to be probabilistic, describable only in terms of probability rather than as a certainty.

On the face of it, this idea sounds absurd. Indeed, the classic thought experiment of Schrödinger's cat, in which a cat in a box is considered to be simultaneously alive and dead until the box is opened, was intended to demonstrate this absurdity. The so- called Copenhagen interpretation of quantum mechanics, based on the work of Bohr and Heisenberg, left open the possibility of uncertainty on a macro scale but did not explicitly endorse it. Other physicists, including Einstein and Schrödinger, firmly opposed the idea. Since then, various other interpretations have also supported the probabilistic view.

QUANTUM MECHANICS AND THE UNIVERSE

Quantum mechanics remains an actively researched field. It has revealed that reality, at the smallest scales, occurs in discrete units, with mysterious gaps between the infinite set of possible positions. This contrasts to Newtonian physics; in quantum physics, even if everything is known about a system, at best, only a set of outcomes can be predicted. Until that outcome is decided, all of the possibilities exist in superposition.

Quantum physics is nonlocal, meaning that things can affect each other at long range with seemingly no contact. Particles can, and indeed must, jump between places without passing through the intervening space. Reality is a wave function, a set of possibilities and probabilities down to the deepest level. However, beyond the massive implications for ontology and the cutting edge of particle physics, it has pervasive practical uses.

For example, understanding quantum mechanics allowed for the invention of the transistor, needed to build miniaturized electronics, including computers. It has gone even farther now, with the realization of "quantum computers" and the incredible potential they hold. Quantum mechanics is also used by plants. They use quantum teleportation to transport electrons and allow the electrons to try out all the possible paths to choose the most efficient one. Quantum mechanics can be used in chemistry to better account for how reactions occur. Improvements in electronics have resulted from quantum mechanics. Examples include flash memories in universal serial bus (USB) drives. Even a simple light switch, where layers of oxidation would otherwise prevent transmission of current between the contacts, is subject to the reality of quantum mechanics.

—*Gina Hagler*

Further Reading

Berera, Arjun, and Luigi Del Debbio. *Quantum Mechanics.* Cambridge UP, 2021.

Hines, Edwin. *Quantum Physics for Beginners: Discover the Science of Quantum Mechanics and Learn the Most Important Concepts Concerning Black Holes, String Theory, and What*

We Perceive as Reality in a Simple Way. Dorling Kindersley, 2022.

Kramers, H. A. *Quantum Mechanics.* Translated by D. Ter Haar. Reprint. Courier Dover Publications, 2018.

Naber, Gregory L. *Quantum Mechanics: An Introduction to the Physical Background and Mathematical Structure.* Walter de Gruyter Gmbh & Co. KG, 2021.

Norsen, Travis. *Foundations of Quantum Mechanics: An Exploration of the Physical Meaning of Quantum Theory.* Springer, 2017.

Stephenson, Jason. *Quantum Physics for Beginners: Quantum Mechanics and Quantum Theory Explained.* Speedy Publishing LLC, 2015.

See also: Atoms; Calculus; Classical or applied mechanics; Conservation of energy; Differential equations; Grimaldi discovers diffraction; Kinetic energy; Newton's laws; Thermodynamics; Vectors (math and physics); Work and energy; Work-energy theorem

R

RIGID-BODY DYNAMICS

Fields of Study: Physics; Mechanics; Mathematics

ABSTRACT

Rigid-body dynamics is the science that deals with the motion of a rigid body under the influence of forces seeking to cause motion. A rigid body is a body with a definite shape that does not change under the influence of a force, so that the particles composing the body stay in fixed positions relative to one another.

KEY CONCEPTS

angular momentum: the product of a body's moment of inertia and its angular velocity; the rate of change of angular momentum is the torque acting on the body responsible for the rotational motion of the body about an axis

center of mass: a point in the body that moves (behaves) as though all the mass of the body were concentrated there and all external forces were applied there

dynamics: the science that deals with the motion of systems of bodies under the influence of forces; dynamics deals with the causes of motion

moment of inertia or rotational inertia: the capacity of a body to resist rotational acceleration; plays the same role for rotational motion that mass does for translational motion

momentum: the product of the mass of a body and its velocity; the rate of change of momentum of a body is equal to the force acting on it

rigid body: an aggregate of material particles in which the interaction of particles is such that the distance between any two particles remains constant with time in an ideal situation; in practice, slight variations in size and shape are accepted

OVERVIEW

When dealing with an extended body, or one that has size, the assumption is made that, in the simplest cases, it is a point particle and undergoes only translational motion. Real extended bodies, however, may undergo rotational and other types of motion. For example, if a baseball bat is flipped into the air, its motion as it turns is clearly more complicated than that of a nonspinning tossed ball, which moves similarly to a particle. Every part of the bat moves differently as it spins about its central axis, twirls about its center of mass and translates through the air on a ballistic trajectory, so it cannot be regarded as a particle that is tossed into the air; instead, it is regarded as a system of particles. A closer look reveals that there is one point in the bat that follows a simple parabolic path, just as a particle would if it were tossed into the air. In fact, that point moves as if the bat's total mass were concentrated there and the weight of the bat acted only there. This point is the center of mass of the bat. In general, the center of mass of a body (or a system of bodies) is the point that moves as though all the mass were concentrated there. The center of mass of a baseball bat lies along its central axis. It can be located by balancing the bat horizontally on an outstretched finger: The center of mass is on the bat's axis just above the finger on which the bat is balanced.

The concept of center of mass of a system of particles or a rigid body is important because it is directly related to the net force acting on the system as a whole. That is, the sum of all the forces acting on the system is equal to the total mass of the system times the acceleration of its center of mass. Thus the center of mass of a rigid body of mass M moves in the same way as a single particle of mass M would when acted on by the same net external force. Therefore, the translational motion of any body can be treated as the motion of a particle. This principle simplifies the analysis of the motion of a rigid body. Although the motion of various parts of the system may be complicated, often it is enough to know the motion of the center of mass. This principle can be extended to a rigid body's linear momentum (the product of its mass and velocity). The (linear) momentum of a rigid body equals the product of its total mass and the velocity of the body's center of mass. The rate of change of momentum is the net force acting on the body. In the absence of a force, the linear momentum remains conserved.

A concept similar to center of mass is center of gravity, which is the point upon which the force of gravity is considered to act. Of course, the force of gravity acts on all parts or particles of a body, but in order to determine the motion of a body as a whole, the entire weight of the body is assumed to act on the center of gravity. Strictly speaking, there is a conceptual difference between the center of gravity and the center of mass, but for practical purposes, they are generally the same point. A difference between the two would exist only if a body were so large that the acceleration due to gravity varied among its parts. The center of mass or center of gravity of an extended body can often be determined more easily through experimentation than by analysis, as was the case with the baseball bat, which was balanced on a finger to find its center of mass.

An ordinary object such as a baseball bat contains so many particles that it is best treated as a continuous distribution of matter. The particles then become differential mass elements of that rather solid body. The principal characteristic of a solid body is

its rigidity. Normally, its size and shape vary only slightly under stress, compression, pull, push, twist, changes in temperature, and other forces. This naturally gives rise to an idealization of a perfectly rigid body, whose size and shape are permanently fixed. Such a body may be characterized by the requirement that the distance between any two points of the body remains fixed under forces such as those just mentioned. A rigid body is a set of particles, but the constraints between the particles are so numerous and of such a special character that the study of rigid bodies has evolved into a subject of great importance for its applications.

A particle is defined as the simplest mechanical system that can be represented in the mathematical scheme of mechanics by a point. A particle is described when its position in space is given and when the values of certain parameters such as mass and electric charge are given. These parameters must have constant values because they describe the internal constitution of the particle. If these parameters vary with the time, the object is not a simple particle. The position of a particle can, of course, vary with time. The position of a single particle may be specified in space by giving its distances from each of three mutually perpendicular planes. These three numbers are called the "Cartesian coordinates" of the particle. The particles that are considered the "elementary particles" of physics are not particles in the strict sense of the word because they must be described by internal parameters that are not constant over time. The spin of a particle is such a parameter. The spin, representing an intrinsic angular momentum (tendency of rotation), has some, though not all, of the properties of angular momentum of a rigid body rotating about an axis through its center of mass.

A rigid body is a system of at least three particles, not lying in the same straight line, constrained to remain at fixed distances from one another. The number of coordinates needed to describe the configuration of a rigid body is six. The three noncollinear particles of a body have three coordinates each, but because of the constraint that they remain at fixed distances from one another, only six of the coordinates are free. Any other particle of the body also has three coordinates, but its distances from the first three particles are fixed, and so none of the additional coordinates is free. The six coordinates may be thought of as the three coordinates of any point in the body and the three coordinates needed to give the orientation of the body about that point.

The motion of a rigid body can be analyzed as the translational motion of its center of mass plus rotational motion about its center of mass. All points in the rigid body move in circles, and the centers of all these circles lie on a line called the axis of rotation. A rigid body rotating about an axis through its center of mass can be regarded as consisting of many particles located at various distances from the axis of rotation. If the mass of each particle is multiplied by the square of its respective distance from the axis of rotation and all these products are summed, the resulting quantity is designated by the moment of inertia or rotational inertia of the body, denoted by I. The moment of inertia plays the same role for rotational motion that mass does for translational motion. The rotational inertia of an object depends not only on its mass but also on how that mass is distributed with respect to the axis of rotation. When the mass is concentrated farther from the axis of rotation, the rotational inertia is greater. For rotational motion, the mass of a body cannot be considered as concentrated at its center of mass. If all the mass of an object is concentrated at a distance from the axis such that the product of the mass of the object and the square of this distance is the same as the moment of inertia of the object about this axis, this distance is called "radius of gyration," usually denoted by k.

Torque, responsible for a rotational motion of a body about an axis, is equal to the product of the moment of inertia and the angular acceleration. Angular acceleration is the rotational force analogous to linear acceleration. A body that rotates while its center of mass undergoes translational motion will have both translational and rotational kinetic energies. They are respectively half of the product of the mass of the body and the square of the velocity of the center of mass and half of the product of the moment of inertia and the square of the angular velocity. An example of this situation is a wheel rolling down a hill. The angular momentum is the product of the moment of inertia of the body about an axis and the angular velocity of the body about the same axis. The rate of change of the angular momentum is the torque acting on the body and causing the rotation. In the absence of any torque, the angular momentum remains conserved.

The law of conservation of angular momentum is a very important tool in understanding the dynamics of rigid bodies, including incredibly small systems in which the angular momentum is quantized. A physical quantity is said to be quantized if it can have only certain discrete values and all intermediate values are prohibited. There is an important difference between the classical (unquantized) and quantum properties of systems with respect to angular momentum. If a direction in space is defined (for example, by putting the bodies in a magnetic field that points in a fixed direction), there is not necessarily a connection between the angular momentum of a classical object and this direction. The classically spinning objects can have their angular momentum pointing in their original directions. The quantum mechanically spinning objects have their angular momentum oriented only in specific directions determined by the magnetic field and their original spinning directions. The dynamics of a rigid rotator in quantum mechanics is handled in an idealized situation, which does not exactly occur in nature. Some of the simple quantum rigid rotators are systems of two atoms of equal mass separated by a fixed distance (like a dumbbell) rotating as a whole about their midpoint fixed in space. There are many more quantum mechanical rigid systems besides those with a dumbbell-like shape. They can be treated with the coordinate system discussed earlier.

APPLICATIONS

The principle of rigid-body dynamics is the basis of many familiar and interesting devices in everyday life that involve both translational and rotational motions. For example, a simple rigid body such as a wrench translates and rotates in a constrained manner along a horizontal surface. Its center of mass will always be observed moving in a straight line, which is the direction of the force applied to the wrench. If its motion is considered in two dimensions as the action of two forces directed perpendicular to each other, its center of mass will move in a parabolic curve.

The path of a football projected at an angle into the air or that of a diver from the springboard into the water are also examples of both transitional and rotational motion. Knowing the center of mass of a body when it is in various positions could be of great use. If high jumpers clearing the bar can get into a position in which their center of mass lies outside their body, they can clear a bar that is higher than their actual, normal center of mass. They can achieve such positions by laying their body flat above the bar and parallel to it and first letting their arms and legs hang down, then lifting their arms and legs during the last stage in clearing the bar, a technique called the "Fosbury flop" after the high jumper who made it famous.

Another example can be found in rocket technology. A rocket designed to split apart is fired into the air to fall on a certain target. When the rocket reaches its highest point at a horizontal distance D from its starting point, it separates into two parts of equal mass. Part one falls vertically to the ground, but part two lands at a distance of 3D from the start-

ing point. Had the rocket not separated, the entire rocket would have fallen at a distance of 2D from the starting point. The path of the center of mass of the system continues to follow the parabolic path that is midway between the two distances. Therefore, while the first part lands at a distance of D, the second part will fall at a distance of 3D in order to land the center of mass at a distance of 2D.

Many interesting phenomena involving rigid-body dynamics can be understood based on how they conserve angular momentum. Figure skaters executing a spin rotate slowly when their arms are outstretched. When the skaters pull their arms in close to them, they suddenly spin much faster. This can be understood from the variation of the moment of inertia in the two positions. Recall that when the skaters pull their arms in, their moment of inertia is reduced. Because the angular momentum remains the same, if the moment of inertia decreases, the angular velocity increases because the angular momentum is the product of moment of inertia and the angular velocity. Similarly, as divers leave the springboard, the first push gives them an initial angular momentum about their center of mass. When they curl themselves into the tuck position, they rotate one or more times faster. They then stretch out again, increasing their moment of inertia and reducing their angular velocity to a smaller value before entering the water. The moment of inertia can reduce by as much as a factor of 3.5 from the upright to tuck position.

The law of conservation of angular momentum of a rigid body is really appreciated when applied to a gyroscope, an instrument that forms the basis of guidance systems for mariners and aircraft pilots. The rapidly spinning wheel is mounted on a set of bearings so that when the mount moves, no net torque acts to change the direction of the angular momentum. Thus, the axis of the wheel remains pointed in the same direction in space. The spacecraft *Voyager 2*, on a 1986 flyby mission to Uranus, was set into unwanted rotation by that wheel effect every time its tape recorder was turned on at high speed. The ground staff had to program the onboard computer to turn on counteracting thrust jets every time the tape recorder was turned on or off.

CONTEXT

The origin of the field of rigid-body dynamics is lost in antiquity. The first long-term written records of observations of celestial objects as rigid bodies were made by Mesopotamians around 4000 BCE, and Muslim scientists had begun work in this area during the medieval period. However, the modern, detailed understanding of dynamic phenomena began with Sir Isaac Newton in the eighteenth century. His calculus-based approach to solving the equations arising from laws of motion forms the foundation of modern mechanics, which made it possible to understand rigid-body dynamics at the most basic level and to exploit it more comprehensively.

The Newtonian mechanics for rigid bodies were historically developed for nonquantum and nonrelativistic systems, that is, for objects of large size and in ordinary motion (moving significantly slower than the speed of light). Conservation laws for rigid-body motion (and for all systems) hold beyond the limitations of Newtonian mechanics. They hold for bodies whose speed approaches that of light, where the theory of relativity reigns, and they remain true in the world of subatomic physics, where quantum mechanics reigns. No exception to the laws of conservation developed for "classical" rigid-body dynamics has ever been found when applied to those domains. The classical theory of rigid-body dynamics assumes even greater significance when applied to quantum mechanics. The quantum field theory of solids, for example, enables scientists to predict the thermal and mechanical properties of materials.

Stars produce nuclear energy in their cores at a very high rate. When this energy decreases, exhausting the nuclear fuel, the star may eventually begin to collapse, building up pressure in its interior. When this happens to the Sun, the collapse may reduce its radius from 700,000 kilometers during its full bloom to an incredibly small value of a few kilometers. At that stage, the Sun will become a neutron star—its material would be compressed to an incredibly dense gas of neutrons. During this shrinking, its angular momentum would not change. Because its moment of inertia would be greatly reduced, its angular speed would experience a corresponding increase from one revolution per month to as many as 600 to 800 revolutions per second.

The dynamics of a rigid body, in general, are determined by the linear momentum and angular momentum. The motion of the center of mass is determined by the momentum rate change, or the total force acting on the body. To discuss the rotational motion, it is convenient to refer to a set of principal axes. The rotational motion about a fixed axis is determined by the angular momentum rate change about the axis, or the total torque acting about the axis. The relation between the momentum and velocity of the center of mass is described by the mass of the body. The relation between the angular momentum and angular velocity is described by the moment of inertia.

—*A. K. Lodhi*

Further Reading

Aslanov, Vladimir S. *Rigid Body Dynamics for Space Applications* Butterworth-Heinemann, 2017.

Daqaq, Mohammed F. *Dynamics of Particles and Rigid Bodies: A Self-Learning Approach*. John Wiley & Sons, 2018.

Featherstone, Roy. *Rigid Body Dynamics Algorithms*. Springer US, 2016.

Hahn, Hubert. *Rigid Body Dynamics of Mechanisms:1 Theoretical Basis*. Springer Science & Business Media, 2013.

Sharma, A.K. *Dynamics of Rigid Bodies*. Discovery Publishing House, 2007.

Yehia, Hamad M. *Rigid Body Dynamics: A Lagrangian Approach*. Springer Nature, 2022.

See also: Acceleration; Aerodynamics; Aeronautical engineering; Aerospace design; Angular forces; Angular momentum; Ballistic weapons; Billiards; Calculus; Centrifugation; Circular motion; Classical or applied mechanics; Dynamics (mechanics); Flywheels; Force (physics); Kinematics; Kinetic energy; Linear motion; Mechanical engineering; Moment of inertia; Momentum (physics); Motion; Newton's laws; Pendulums; Propulsion technologies; Robotics; Solid mechanics; Steam energy technology; Structural engineering; Torque; Young, Thomas

ROBOTICS

Fields of Study: Physics; Mechanics; Mathematics

ABSTRACT

Robotics is an interdisciplinary scientific field concerned with the design, development, operation, and assessment of electromechanical devices used to perform tasks that would otherwise require human action. Robotics applications can be found in almost every arena of modern life. Among the most promising robot technologies are those that draw on biological models to solve problems.

KEY CONCEPTS

algorithm: a set of computer instructions that permit the interpretation of input data

proprioception: the ability of knowing where each part of your body is without having to think consciously where it is, as one knows where to put a finger to touch the nose, ears, mouth, other hand, etc., with one's eyes closed

proprioceptive sensors: a sensor and computing system that measure the internal system values of a robot, such as motor speed, wheel load, battery charge, and robot joint angles.

reflectance sensor: a sensor that detects the reflection of a light signal that it has emitted in order to compute distance

teleoperation: operation of a robotic device remotely by use of a wired or wireless communication connection

SUMMARY

Robotics is an interdisciplinary scientific field concerned with the design, development, operation, and assessment of electromechanical devices used to perform tasks that would otherwise require human action. Robotics applications can be found in almost every arena of modern life. Robots, for example, are widely used in industrial assembly lines to perform repetitive tasks. They have also been developed to help physicians perform difficult surgeries and are essential to the operation of many advanced military vehicles. Among the most promising robot technologies are those that draw on biological models to solve problems, such as robots whose limbs and joints are designed to mimic those of insects and other animals.

DEFINITION AND BASIC PRINCIPLES

Robotics is the science of robots—machines that can be programmed to carry out a variety of tasks independently, without direct human intervention. Although robots in science fiction tend to be androids or humanoids (robots with recognizable human forms), most real-life robots, especially those designed for industrial use, do not resemble humans physically beyond the articulation of certain programmed movements. Robots typically consist of at least three parts: a mechanical structure (most commonly a robotic arm) that enables the robot to physically affect either itself or its task environment; sensors that gather information about physical properties such as sound, temperature, motion, and pressure; and some kind of processing system that transforms data from the robot's sensors into instructions about what actions to perform. Some devices, such as the search-engine bots that mine the internet daily for data about links and online content, lack mechanical components. However, they are nevertheless often considered robotic because they can perform repeated tasks without supervision.

Many robotics applications also involve the use of artificial intelligence. This is a complex concept with a shifting definition, but in its most basic sense, a robot with artificial intelligence possesses features or capabilities that mimic human thought or behavior. For example, one aspect of artificial intelligence involves creating parallels to the human senses of vision, hearing, or touch. The friendly voices at the other ends of customer-service lines, for example, are increasingly likely to be robotic speech-recognition devices capable not merely of hearing callers' words but also of interpreting their meanings and directing the customers' calls intelligently.

More advanced artificial intelligence applications give robots the ability to assess their environmental conditions, make decisions, and independently develop efficient plans of action for their situations —and then modify these plans as circumstances change. Chess-playing robots do this each time they assess the state of the chessboard and make a new move. The ultimate goal of artificial intelligence research is to create machines whose responses to questions or problems are so humanlike as to be indistinguishable from those of human operators. This standard is the so-called Turing test, named after the British mathematician and computing pioneer Alan Turing.

BACKGROUND AND HISTORY

The word *robot* comes from a Czech word for "forced labor" that the Czech writer Karel Čapek used in his 1921 play *R.U.R.* about a man who invents a humanlike automatic machine to do his work. During the 1940s, as computing power began to grow,

Photo by Richard Greenhill and Hugo Elias, The Shadow Robotics Company, via Wikimedia Commons.

the influential science-fiction writer Isaac Asimov began applying "robotics" to the technology behind robots. The 1950s saw the development of the first machines that could properly be called robots. These prototypes took advantage of such new technologies as transistors (compact, solid-state devices that control electrical flow in electronic equipment) and integrated circuits (complex systems of electronic connections etched onto single chips) to enable more complicated mechanical actions. In 1959, an industrial robot was designed that could churn out ashtrays automatically. Over the ensuing decades, public fascination with robots expanded far beyond their actual capabilities. It was becoming clear that creating robots that could accomplish seemingly simple tasks—such as avoiding obstacles while walking—was a surprisingly complex problem.

During the late twentieth century, advances in computing, electronics, and mechanical engineering led to rapid progress in the science of robotics. These included the invention of microprocessors, single integrated circuits that perform all the functions of computers' central processing units; production of better sensors and actuators; and developments in artificial intelligence and machine learning, such as a more widespread use of neural networks. (Machine learning is the study of computer programs that improves their performance through experience.)

Cutting-edge robotics applications are being developed by an interdisciplinary research cohort of computer scientists, electrical engineers, neuroscientists, psychologists, and others, and combine a greater mechanical complexity with more subtle information processing systems than were once possible. Homes may not be populated with humanoid robots with whom one can hold conversations, but mechanical robots have become ubiquitous in industry. Also, unpiloted robotic vehicles and planes are essential in warfare, search-engine robots crawl the World Wide Web every day collecting and analyzing data about internet links and content, and robotic surgical tools are indispensable in health care. All this is evidence of the extraordinarily broad range of problems robotics addresses.

HOW IT WORKS

Sensing. To move within and react to the conditions of task environments, robots must gather as much information as possible about the physical features of their environments. They do so through a large array of sensors designed to monitor different physical properties. Simple touch sensors consist of electric circuits that are completed when levers receive enough pressure to press down on switches. Robotic dogs designed as toys, for example, may have touch sensors in their backs or heads to detect when they are being petted and signal them to respond accordingly. More complex tactile sensors can detect properties such as torque (rotation) or texture. Such sensors may be used, for example, to help an assembly-line robot's end effector control the grip and force it uses to turn an object it is screwing into place.

Light sensors consist of one or more photocells that react to visible light with decreases in electrical resistance. They may serve as primitive eyes, allowing unpiloted robotic vehicles, for example, to detect the bright white lines that demarcate parking spaces and maneuver between them. Reflectance sensors emit beams of infrared light, measuring the amounts of that light that reflect back from nearby surfaces. They can detect the presence of objects in front of robots and calculate the distances between the robots and the objects—allowing the robots either to follow or to avoid the objects. Temperature sensors rely on internal thermistors (resistors that react to high temperatures with decreases in electrical resistance). Robots used to rescue human beings trapped in fires may use temperature sensors to navigate away from areas of extreme heat. Similarly, altimeter sensors can detect changes in elevation, allowing robots to determine whether they are moving up or down slopes.

Other sensor types include magnetic sensors, sound sensors, accelerometers, and proprioceptive sensors that monitor the robots' internal systems and tell them where their own parts are located in space. After robots have collected information through their sensors, algorithms (mathematical processes based on predefined sets of rules) help them process that information intelligently and act on it. For example, a robot may use algorithms to help it determine its location, map its surroundings, and plan its next movements.

Motion and manipulation. Robots can be made to move around spaces and manipulate objects in many different ways. At the most basic level, a moving robot needs to have one or more mechanisms consisting of connected moving parts, known as links. Links can be connected by prismatic or sliding joints, in which one part slides along the other, or by rotary or articulated joints, in which both parts rotate around the same fixed axis. Combinations of prismatic and rotary joints enable robotic manipulators to perform a host of complex actions, including lifting, turning, sliding, squeezing, pushing, and grasping. Actuators are required to move jointed segments or robot wheels. Actuators may be electric or electromagnetic motors, hydraulic gears or pumps (powered by compressed liquid), or pneumatic gears or pumps powered by pressurized gas. To coordinate the robots' movements, the actuators are controlled by electric circuits.

Motion-description languages are a type of computer programming language designed to formalize robot motions. They consist of sets of symbols that can be combined and manipulated in different ways to identify whole series of predefined motions in which robots of specified types can engage. Motion-description languages were developed to simplify the process of manipulating robot movements by allowing different engineers to reuse common sets of symbols to describe actions or groups of actions, rather than having to formulate new algorithms to describe every individual task they want robots to perform.

Control and operation. A continuum of robotic control systems ranges from fully manual operation to fully autonomous operation. On the one hand, a human operator may be required to direct every movement a robot makes. For example, some bomb disposal robots are controlled by human operators working only a few feet away, using levers and buttons to guide the robots as they pick up and remove the bombs. On the other side of the spectrum are robots that operate with no human intervention at all, such as the KANTARO—a fully autonomous robot that slinks through sewer pipes inspecting them for damage and obstructions. Many robots have control mechanisms lying somewhere between these two extremes.

Robots can also be controlled from a distance. Teleoperated systems can be controlled by human operators situated either a few centimeters away, as in robotic surgeries, or millions of miles away, as in outer space applications. "Supervisory control" is a term given to teleoperation in which the robots themselves are capable of performing the vast majority of their tasks independently; human operators are present merely to monitor the robots' behavior and occasionally offer high-level instructions.

Artificial intelligence. Three commonly accepted paradigms, or patterns, are used in artificial intelligence robotics: hierarchical, reactive, and hybrid. The hierarchical paradigm, also known as a top-down approach, organizes robotic tasks in sequence. For example, a robot takes stock of its task environment, creates a detailed model of the world, uses that model to plan a list of tasks it must carry out to achieve a goal, and proceeds to act on each task in turn. The performance of hierarchical robots tends to be slow and disjointed since every time a change occurs in the environment, the robot pauses to reformulate its plan. For example, if such a robot is moving forward to reach a destination and an obstacle is placed in its way, it must pause, rebuild its model of the world, and begin lurching around the object.

In the reactive (or behavioral) paradigm, also known as a bottom-up approach, no planning occurs. Instead, robotic tasks are carried out spontaneously in reaction to a changing environment. If an obstacle is placed in front of such a robot, sensors can quickly incorporate information about the obstacle into the robot's actions and alter its path, causing it to swerve momentarily.

The hybrid paradigm is the one most commonly used in artificial intelligence applications being developed during the twenty-first century. It combines elements of both the reactive and the hierarchical models.

APPLICATIONS AND PRODUCTS

Industrial robots. In the twenty-first century, almost no factory operates without at least one robot—more likely several—playing some part in its manufacturing processes. Welding robots, for example, consist of mechanical arms with several degrees of movement and end effectors in the shape of welding guns or grippers. They are used to join metal surfaces together by heating and then hammering them, and produce faster, more reliable, and more uniform results than human welders. They are also less vulnerable to injury than human workers. Another common industrial application of robotics is silicon-wafer manufacturing, which must be performed within meticulously clean rooms so as not to contaminate the semiconductors with dirt or oil. Humans are far more prone than robots to carry contaminants on them.

Six major types of industrial robots are defined by their different mechanical designs. Articulated robots are those whose manipulators (arms) have at least three rotary joints. They are often used for vehicle assembly, die casting (pouring molten metal into molds), welding, and spray painting. Cartesian robots, also known as gantry robots, have manipulators with three prismatic joints. They are often used for picking objects up and placing them in different locations, or for manipulating machine tools. Cylindrical robots have manipulators that rotate in a cylindrical shape around a central vertical axis. Parallel robots have both prismatic and rotary joints on their manipulators. Spherical robots have manipulators that can move in three-dimensional spaces shaped like spheres. SCARA (Selective Compliant Assembly Robot Arm) robots have two arms connected to vertical axes with rotary joints. One of their arms has another joint that serves as a wrist.

SCARA robots are frequently used for palletizing (stacking goods on platforms for transportation or loading).

Service robots. Unlike industrial robots, service robots are designed to cater to the needs of individual people. Robopets, such as animatronic dogs, provide companionship and entertainment for their human owners. The Sony Corporation's AIBO (Artificial Intelligence roBOt) robopets use complex systems of sensors to detect human touch on their heads, backs, chins, and paws, and can recognize the faces and voices of their owners. They can also maintain their balance while walking and running in response to human commands. AIBOs also function as home-security devices, as they can be set to sound alarms when their motion or sound detectors are triggered. Consumer appliances, such as iRobot Corporation's robotic vacuum cleaner, the Roomba, and the robotic lawn mower, the RoboMower, developed by Friendly Robotics, use artificial intelligence approaches to maneuver around their task environments safely and effectively, while performing repetitive tasks to save their human users time. And no list would be complete without mentioning the lifelike robotic or animatronic dinosaurs and other creatures found in various amusement parks.

Even appliances that do not much resemble public notions of what robots should look like often contain robotic components. For example, digital video recorders (DVRs) such as TiVos contain sensors, microprocessors, and a basic form of artificial intelligence that enable them to seek out and record programs that conform to their owners' personal tastes. Cars can have robotic seats that can lift older people or passengers who are disabled inside. Many new cars can assist their owners with driving tasks such as parallel parking, or are even able to function without a human actually driving the vehicle, guided instead by global positioning system (GPS) and onboard traffic monitoring systems. In the 2010s, many companies actively explored technologies for autonomous cars (self-driving vehicles), with the goal of making mass-produced models available to the public that would function flawlessly on existing roads. As of the early 2020s, the technology company Google was testing a ride-sharing system called Waymo that used self-driving vehicles. Driverless features on passenger cars were limited to such things as autonomous cruise-control systems, but true self-driving passenger cars were considered to be just a matter of years away, and have in fact been tested on highways. Compare that with the autopilot feature found on almost all commercial aircraft. Autopilots accept input from sensors and use that that to operate the flight controls of the aircraft to maintain flight according to the aircraft's flight plan. The most advanced of such systems are capable of guiding the aircraft through its takeoff and landing procedures just as a human pilot would.

Many companies or organizations rely on humanoid robots to provide services to the public. The Smithsonian National Museum of American History, for example, has used an interactive robot named Minerva to guide visitors around the museum's exhibits, answering questions and providing information about individual exhibits. Other professional roles filled by robots include those of receptionists, floor cleaners, librarians, bartenders, and secretaries. At least one primary school in Japan even experimented with a robotic teacher developed by a scientist at the Tokyo University of Science. However, an important pitfall of humanoid robots is their susceptibility to the uncanny valley phenomenon. This is the theory that as a robot's appearance and behavior becomes more humanlike, people will respond to it more positively—but only up to a point. On a line graph plotting positive response against degree of human likeness, the response dips (the "uncanny valley") as the likeness approaches total realism but does not perfectly mimic it. In other words, while people will prefer a somewhat anthropomorphic robot to an industrial-looking one, a highly humanlike robot that is still identifiably a machine will cause people to feel revulsion and fear rather than empathy.

MEDICAL USES

Robotic surgery has become an increasingly important area of medical technology. In most robotic surgeries, a system known as a master-slave manipulator is used to control robot movements. Surgeons look down into electronic displays showing their patients' bodies and the robots' tool tips. The surgeons use controls attached to consoles to precisely guide the robots' manipulators within the patients' bodies. A major benefit of robotic surgeries is that they are less invasive—smaller incisions need to be made because robotic manipulators can be extremely narrow. These surgeries are also safer because robotic end effectors can compensate for small tremors or shakes in the surgeons' movements that could seriously damage their patients' tissues if the surgeons were making the incisions themselves. Teleoperated surgical robots can even allow surgeons to perform operations remotely, without the need to transport patients over long distances. Surgical robots such as the da Vinci system are used to conduct operations such as prostatectomy, cardiac surgery, bariatric surgery, and various forms of neurosurgery.

Humanoid robots are also widely used as artificial patients to help train medical students in diagnosis and procedures. These robots have changing vital signs such as heart rates, blood pressure, and pupil dilation. Many are designed to breathe realistically, express pain, urinate, and even speak about their conditions. With their help, physicians-in-training can practice drawing blood, performing cardiopulmonary resuscitation (CPR), and delivering babies without the risk of harm to real patients.

Other medical robots include robotic nurses that can monitor patients' vital signs and alert physicians to crises and smart wheelchairs that can automatically maneuver around obstacles. Scientists have developed nanorobots the size of bacteria that can be swallowed and sent to perform various tasks within human bodies, such as removing plaque from the insides of clogged arteries.

Robot exploration and rescue. One of the most intuitive applications of robotic technology is the concept of sending robots to places too remote or too dangerous for human beings to work in—such as outer space, great ocean depths, and disaster zones. The six successful crewed moon landings of the Apollo program carried out during the late 1960s and early 1970s are dwarfed in number by the uncrewed robot missions that have "set foot" not only on the moon but also on other celestial bodies, such as planets in the solar system. The wheeled robots Spirit and Opportunity, for example, began analyzing material samples on Mars and sending data and photographs back to Earth in 2004. Roboticists have also designed biomimetic robots inspired by frogs that take advantage of lower gravitational fields, such as those found on smaller planets, to hop nimbly over rocks and other obstacles. In 2020 the wheeled robot Perseverance landed on Mars, with the goal of finding signs of ancient life on the planet and returning samples of rock and soil to Earth.

Robots are also used to explore the ocean floor. The Benthic Rover, for example, drags itself along the seabed at depths up to 2.5 miles below the surface. It measures oxygen and food levels, takes soil samples, and sends live streaming video up to the scientists above. The rover is operated by supervisory control and requires very little intervention on the part of its human operators.

Rescue robots seek out, pick up, and safely carry injured humans trapped in fires, under rubble, or in dangerous battle zones. For example, the US Army's Bear (Battlefield Extraction-Assist Robot) is a bipedal robot that can climb stairs, wedge itself through narrow spaces, and clamber over bumpy terrain while carrying weights of up to three hundred pounds.

Military robots. Militaries have often been among the leading organizations pioneering robotics, as robots have the potential to complete many military tasks that might otherwise prove dangerous to humans. While many projects, such as bomb-removal robots, have proven highly useful and have been widely accepted, other military applications have proven more controversial. For example, many observers and activists have expressed concern over the proliferation of drones, particularly unpiloted aerial vehicles (UAVs) capable of enacting military strikes such as rocket or missile launches while going virtually undetected by radar. The US government has used such technology (including the Predator drone) to successfully destroy terrorist positions, including in remote territory that would otherwise be difficult and dangerous to access, but there have also been notable examples of misidentified targets and civilian collateral damage caused by drone strikes. Opponents of drones argue that the potential for mistakes or abuse of their capabilities is dangerous.

CAREERS IN ROBOTICS

Courses in advanced mathematics, physics, computer science, electrical engineering, and mechanical engineering make up the foundational requirements for those interested in pursuing careers as robotics engineers. Earning a bachelor of science degree in any of these fields would serve as an appropriate preparation for graduate work in a similar area. In most circumstances, either a master's degree or a doctorate is a necessary qualification for the most advanced future career opportunities in both academia and industry. However, an advanced degree is not generally required for a career as a robotics technician—someone who maintains and repairs robots rather than designs them.

Students should take substantial course work in more than one of the primary fields of study related to robotics (physics, mathematics, computer science, and engineering) because designing and testing robots requires skills drawn from multiple disciplines. In addition, anyone desiring to work in robotics should possess skills that go beyond the academic, including good physical coordination, manual dexterity, and an aptitude for mechanical details. A collaborative mindset is also an asset, as robotics work tends to be done by teams.

Careers in the field of robotics can take several different shapes. The manufacturing industry is the biggest employer of robotics engineers and technicians. Within this industry, robotics professionals might focus on developing, maintaining, or repairing production-line robots used in factory assembly. Other industries in which robotics engineers and technicians often find work include aviation, agriculture, nuclear energy, telecommunications, electronics, mining, health care and medicine, and education.

Many roboticists prefer employment within academic settings. Such professionals divide their time between teaching university classes on robotics and conducting their own research projects. Others find work in government agencies such as the National Aeronautics and Space Administration (NASA) and the Defense Advanced Research Projects Agency (DARPA), focusing on large-scale robotics applications in such areas as space exploration, warfare, and disaster management.

SOCIAL CONTEXT AND FUTURE PROSPECTS

In the twenty-first century, the presence of robots in factories all over the world is taken for granted. Meanwhile, robots are also increasingly entering daily life in the form of automated self-service kiosks at supermarkets; electronic lifeguards that detect when swimmers in pools are struggling; and cars whose robotic speech-recognition software enables them to respond to verbal commands. A science-fiction future in which ubiquitous robotic assistants perform domestic tasks such as cooking and cleaning may not be far away, but many technological

limitations must be overcome for that to become a reality. For example, it can be difficult for robots to process multipart spoken commands that have not been preprogrammed—a problem for researchers in the artificial intelligence field of natural language processing. However, the voice-activated personal assistant software in smartphone and computer operating systems, such as Apple's Siri, shows how such technology is rapidly evolving.

Robots that provide nursing care or companionship to the infirm are not merely becoming important parts of the health care industry but may also provide a solution to the problem increasingly faced by countries in the developed world—a growing aging population who need more caretakers than can be found among younger adults. Another area where robots can be particularly useful is in performing dangerous tasks that would otherwise put a human's life at risk. The use of robotics in the military remains a growing field—not only in the controversial use of combat drones, but also for tasks such as minesweeping. Robots are also more and more heavily used in space exploration, and robots have been used in other dangerous fields as well; during the coronavirus disease 2019 (COVID-19) pandemic declared in 2020, robots were used to disinfect contaminated areas, take the temperature of patients, and monitor mask-wearing and social distancing among citizens. The robotics company Boston Dynamics has developed prototypes of extremely human- and animal-like robots with arms and legs that can walk, jump, climb stairs, and even dance or perform parcour. Some of the company's robots are used by utility companies, construction sites, and police departments.

There are also concerns about the growing use of robots to perform tasks previously performed by humans, however. As robotics technology improves and becomes less expensive, companies may well turn to cheap, efficient robots to do jobs that are typically performed by immigrant human labor, particularly in such areas as agriculture and manufacturing. Meanwhile, some observers are concerned that the rise of industrial and professional service robots is already eliminating too many jobs held by American workers. Many of the jobs lost in the 2008 to 2009 recession within the struggling automotive industry never came back because costly human workers were replaced by cheaper robotic arms. However, the issue is more complicated than that. In certain situations, the addition of robots to a factory's workforce can actually create more jobs for humans. Some companies, for example, have been able to increase production and hire additional workers with the help of robot palletizers that make stacking and loading their products much faster.

Safety concerns can sometimes hinder the acceptance of new robotic technologies, even when they have proven to be less likely than humans to make dangerous mistakes. Robotic sheep shearers in Australia, for example, have met with great resistance from farmers because of the small risk that the machines may nick a major artery as they work, causing the accidental death of a sheep. And while fully autonomous vehicles, including self-driving cars, are seen by many automotive and technology companies alike as a major area of innovation, crashes and other accidents by several prototypes in the 2010s drew significant concerns from regulators and the general public. It is critical in the field of robotics to not only develop the technology necessary to make a design a reality, but to understand the cultural and economic landscape that will determine whether a robot is a success or failure.

—*M. Lee*

Further Reading

Faust, Russell A., editor. *Robotics in Surgery: History, Current and Future Applications*. Nova Science, 2007.

Floreano, Dario, and Claudio Mattuissi. *Bio-Inspired Artificial Intelligence: Theories, Methods, and Technologies*. MIT Press, 2008.

Gutkind, Lee. *Almost Human: Making Robots Think*. 2006. Reprint. Norton, 2009.

Jones, Joseph L. *Robot Programming: A Practical Guide to Behavior-Based Robotics*. McGraw-Hill, 2004.

"Our Friends Electric." *Economist*. Economist Newspaper, 7 Sept. 2013. Accessed 14 Nov. 2014.

Popovic, Marko B. *Biomechanics and Robotics*. CRC Press, 2013.

Niku, Saeed. *Introduction to Robotics: Analysis, Control, Applications*. 3rd ed., Wiley, 2020.

Samani, Hooman. Cognitive Robotics. CRC Press, 2016.

Siciliano, Bruno, et al. *Robotics: Modeling, Planning, and Control*. Springer, 2009.

Siciliano, Bruno, and Oussama Khatib, editors. *The Springer Handbook of Robotics*. Springer, 2016.

Springer, Paul J. *Military Robots and Drones: A Reference Handbook*. ABC-CLIO, 2013.

Tucker, Ian. "The Five: Robots Helping to Tackle Coronavirus." *The Guardian*, 31 May 2020, www.theguardian.com/technology/2020/may/31/the-five-robots-helping-to-tackle-coronavirus. Accessed 28 Feb. 2022.

Tucker, Sean. "Self-Driving Cars: Everything You Need to Know." *Kelley Blue Book*, 3 Aug. 2021, www.kbb.com/car-advice/self-driving-cars/. Accessed 28 Feb. 2022.

See also: Aeronautical engineering; Aerospace design; Ailerons, flaps, and airplane wings; Angular forces; Angular momentum; Automated processes and servomechanisms; Biomechanics; Computer-aided engineering; Dynamics (mechanics); Force (physics); Friction; Hydraulics; Inertial guidance; Kinematics; Load; Materials science; Mechatronics; Mechanical engineering; Motion; Newton's laws; Solenoid; Torque

ROTARY ENGINE

Fields of Study: Physics; Mechanics; Mathematics

ABSTRACT

A rotary engine is an internal combustion engine with cylinders. It is also called a Wankel engine, or Wankel rotary engine, for its creator, Dr. Felix Wankel. It has been popular at various times in sports cars because of the power it

can produce. The rotary engine delivers more power than a piston engine. Although it has fewer moving parts, and should be more reliable by design, the parts are prone to breakage and failure.

KEY CONCEPTS

abrasion: the wearing away of surface material by friction

compression: the act of reducing the volume of a gas or other material without changing the amount of material by that action

torque: the tendency of a force to cause an object to rotate, defined mathematically as the rate of change of the object's angular momentum; also called moment of force

OVERVIEW

Combustion engines combine air and fuel and burn them to produce pressure. In a piston engine, the pressure in the cylinders forces the pistons to move; the crankshaft converts this movement into rotational movement, which can be used to power a vehicle. Instead of pistons, a rotary engine uses a curved equilateral triangle-shaped rotor inside of a housing. As the rotor moves, the faces of the triangle create chambers within the housing. The gas and air mixture in these chambers ignites and then expands and contracts as the rotor moves, providing multiple effects at once: intake, compression, combustion, and exhaust. The combustion pressure in these chambers powers the movement of the vehicle. A rotary engine has multiple rotors; three or five are standard.

German engineer Felix Wankel developed the idea for the rotary engine in 1924, when he was seventeen years old. He set up a workshop and began refining the ideas for an engine that would rotate and simultaneously achieve the four important functions of a combustion engine. He developed his rotary valves and used these ideas during World War II (1939-45) when he worked for the German Aeronautical Re-

search Establishment developing aircraft engines. During the 1950s, he worked for a German car and motorcycle manufacturer, NSU Motorenwerke AG, where he finished developing the rotary-piston engine in 1954. It was tested three years later.

Bringing the engine to the market took many more years. Automakers competed to gain access to NSU's lightweight, smooth-running unit. Its simplicity in comparison to piston engines meant that it cost less to manufacture. It was not the only rotary engine being developed at the time, but the executives at Mazda were intrigued by Wankel's design. Mazda, which was working to become a global automaker, won the contract and began developing the rotary engine for use in vehicles. The company had to overcome some flaws, such as wear marks that quickly appeared within the rotary housing and seals on the three corners of the rotors that wore out quickly. Forty-seven engineers spent several years perfecting the design. The first dual-rotor rotary engine car, the Cosmo Sport, debuted in 1967. Mazda sports cars quickly drew fans worldwide. Other motor companies—including General Motors, Suzuki, and Toyota—also licensed the Wankel design, but Mazda sports cars became synonymous with the rotary engine.

Rotary engines have some significant drawbacks. The large combustion chamber burns more fuel, and vehicles tend to get low mileage per gallon. This produces significant carbon dioxide emissions. The engines are sometimes unreliable and produce low torque, or the engine's turning ability, which affects acceleration. During the early twenty-first century, however, Mazda developed a car powered by a hydrogen rotary engine. The company was also developing electric cars using rotary engines. The first model debuted in 2013.

—Josephine Campbell

Further Reading

"Chapter 1: Opening a New Frontier with the Rotary Engine." *Mazda*, www.mazda.com/en/innovation/stories/rotary/newfrontier/. Accessed 2 Oct. 2017.

"Chapter 3: Entering a New Era and Looking Further into the Future." *Mazda*, www.mazda.com/en/innovation/stories/rotary/newera/. Accessed 2 Oct. 2017.

"Engineering Explained: The Pros and Cons of Inline 5s, V10s and Rotary Engines." *Car Throttle*, 2014, www.carthrottle.com/post/engineering-explained-the-pros-and-cons-of-inline-5s-v10s-and-rotary-engines/. Accessed 2 Oct. 2017.

Fowler, Glenn. "Felix Wankel, Inventor, Is Dead; Creator of Rotary Engine Was 86." *New York Times*, 14 Oct. 1988, www.nytimes.com/1988/10/14/obituaries/felix-wankel-inventor-is-dead-creator-of-rotary-engine-was-86.html. Accessed 2 Oct. 2017.

Lewis, Owen (Quora). "Why Mazda's Rotary Automobile Engine Never Became Widely Popular." *Forbes*, 11 Apr. 2017, www.forbes.com/sites/quora/2017/04/11/why-mazdas-rotary-automobile-engine-never-became-widely-popular/#72f72ed43c79. Accessed 2 Oct. 2017.

Nice, Karim. "How Rotary Engines Work." *HowStuffWorks*, 29 Mar. 2001, auto.howstuffworks.com/rotary-engine.htm. Accessed 2 Oct. 2017.

"1902: Rotary Engine Inventor Felix Wankel Born." *History.com*, 2009, www.history.com/this-day-in-history/rotary-engine-inventor-felix-wankel-born. Accessed 2 Oct. 2017.

Rong, Blake Z. "12-Rotor Wankel Engine Will Melt Your Brain." *Autoweek*, 24 Feb. 2014, autoweek.com/article/car-life/12-rotor-wankel-engine-will-melt-your-brain. Accessed 2 Oct. 2017.

Russ, Carey. "The Wankel Engine History." *The Auto Channel*, 2004, www.theautochannel.com/news/2004/07/04/202357.html. Accessed 2 Oct. 2017.

Stecher, Nicolas. "Mazda's Confusing Plan to Resurrect the Famously Dirty Rotary Engine." *Wired*, 1 Dec. 2015, www.wired.com/2015/12/mazdas-confusing-plan-to-resurrect-the-famously-dirty-rotary-engine/. Accessed 28 Sept. 2017.

Webster, Larry. "How It Works: The Mazda Wankel Rotary Engine." *Popular Mechanics*, 1 Sept. 2011, www.popularmechanics.com/cars/a7103/how-it-works-the-mazda-rotary-engine-with-video/. Accessed 2 Oct. 2017.

See also: Carnot, Sadi; Diesel engine; Internal combustion engine; Mechanical engineering; Steam engine; Stirling, Robert

S

SOLENOID

Fields of Study: Physics; Mechanics; Mathematics

ABSTRACT

A solenoid is an electromagnetic device made up of a coiled conducting wire. An applied electrical current produces a strong magnetic field in a solenoid, according to Ampère's law. The fine electronic control of solenoids and electromagnets makes them suitable for a very broad range of applications.

KEY CONCEPTS

Ampère's law: the rule stating that the strength of a magnetic field about a current-carrying conductor is directly proportional to the magnitude of the current

electromagnet: a device that becomes magnetic due to the presence of an electric current

ferromagnetic: describing material that can be made permanently magnetic by the presence of a magnetic field, such as iron and other ferrous (ironlike) metals

inductance: the ability to generate a magnetic field when electrical current is flowing

permeability: the ability with which a magnetized material supports a magnetic field

right-hand rule: if a wire is grasped in the right hand with the thumb pointing in the direction of current flow, the fingers will point in the direction of the magnetic field around the wire

turns: the number of times that a conductor is wrapped around to form a helical coil

ELECTRICITY AND MAGNETISM

The magnetic field of a solenoid is directly dependent on the product of the turn density (N), permeability (μ), and current running through the solenoid (I). Because turn density is a ratio of the number of turns (n) per length of coil (L), the magnetic field of a solenoid will increase with an increase in the number of turns and will decrease as the length of the coil increases.

A solenoid combines the relationship between electricity and magnetism in a way that performs useful functions. In its simplest form, a solenoid consists just of a wire looped into the shape of a helical coil, like a spring. Electrical current flowing through the wire generates a magnetic field, which is what makes the solenoid so useful. Magnets made of a ferromagnetic material such as iron, nickel, or cobalt maintain their magnetism as permanent magnets. A solenoid, on the other hand, is an electromagnet. This means that it is magnetic due to an electric current and only as long as that current operates.

André-Marie Ampère (1775-1836) identified that an electrical current flowing in a conductor causes a magnetic field around the conductor. The right-hand rule can always be used to determine the direction of this magnetic field. According to Ampère's law, the strength of the magnetic field is directly proportional to the magnitude of the current. This is echoed in Faraday's law of magnetic induction, which states that a magnet moving past a conductor induces a voltage and current in the conductor and that the magnitude of these depends on changes in the magnetic field strength as it passes the conductor. The induced electrical current produces a magnetic field around the wire. Lenz's law states that this induced magnetic field opposes the original magnetic field. When the conductor, usually a wire, is wrapped into a helical coil, the magnetic fields about the individual turns of wire add together to form a single large magnetic field. This is a solenoid.

As electrical current flows through the wire of a solenoid, it generates a magnetic field according to Ampère's law. The magnetic field is produced at each point along the length of the coiled wire, just as it would be if the wire were straight. The helical shape causes the magnetic field around the adjacent coils of wire to align, forming a tube of concentrated magnetic flux lines within the coil. The flux lines surrounding the outside of the solenoid are also aligned in the opposite direction, but are widely dispersed. The magnetic field surrounding the outside

of an active solenoid is thus much weaker than the internal magnetic field, to the extent that it is negligible. A solenoid's internal magnetic field has much the same characteristics as a permanent bar magnet, but only when electric current is flowing through the wire. Often the wire is coiled around a metal core to increase the strength of the magnetic field produced.

ELECTROMAGNETS AND INDUCTORS
By itself, the coil of a solenoid produces a magnetic field that creates an induced voltage opposite the direction of current flow in the circuit. This is the basic principle of an electronic component called an inductor. These are readily identifiable on any circuit board as they typically are constructed by wrapping a length of fine wire around a small cardboard tube. The purpose of an inductor is to provide a buffer

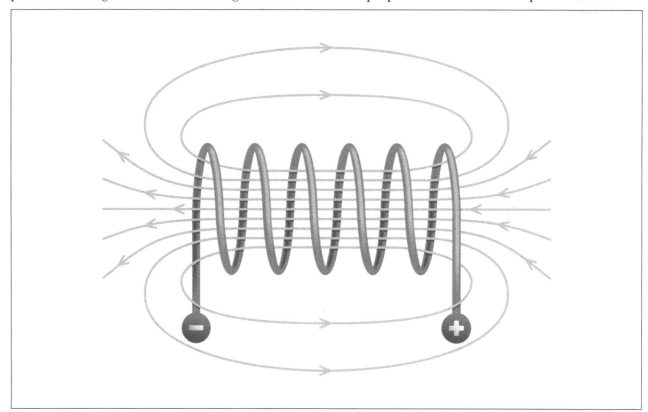

Magnetic field created inside a solenoid, described using field lines. Image via iStock/Dmitry Kovalchuk. [Used under license.]

against fluctuations in the voltage applied to the circuit so that the voltage remains constant. When an increase in voltage occurs, it increases the current flowing through the circuit, and this causes the inductor to produce a greater voltage in the opposite sense. Similarly, when applied voltage decreases, so does the counter voltage produced by the inductor. The inductance of an inductor depends on the number of turns of wire, the area of the inside of the coil, the length of the coil, and the permeability of the core material. Inductance is measured in henries (H), a standard unit named for Joseph Henry (1797-1878), according to the formula:

$$L = \frac{\mu N^2 A}{\ell}$$

where L is the inductance in henries, ϑ is the length of the solenoid in meters, N is the number of turns of coiled wire, A is the cross-sectional area of the solenoid coil in square meters ($A = \pi r2$), and μ is the permeability of the core material.

Inductors and inductance coils typically are constructed around a material that is not magnetizable, such as air, plastic, or cardboard. When the solenoid coil is wrapped instead about a core material that is magnetizable, such as an iron rod, an electromagnet is formed. While the material within the core may be permanently magnetized, its magnetic field strength is greatly enhanced by that of the solenoid while current is flowing.

The magnetic flux in the core of an electromagnet depends greatly on the magnetic permeability of the core material. Electricity and magnetism are related at the subatomic level through unpaired electrons in the atoms of the material. Ferromagnetic metals acquire greatly enhanced magnetic properties when acted upon by a solenoid and conduct magnetism much as they would conduct electricity.

The flow of electricity through a conductor is subject to electrical resistance. If the material's resis-

tance is completely eliminated, the material becomes a superconductor. In that state, an induced electric current will continue to flow indefinitely after the magnetic induction field is removed. Electrons moving through a superconducting medium move in pairs like a laser beam rather than individually moving through numerous collisions down the length of the conductor. Since there is no energy lost to collisions, there is no resistance to the movement of the electrons and no heat loss due to friction. Superconducting magnets can be based on the geometry of solenoids.

SOLENOIDS IN ACTION

The simplicity of a solenoid lends itself to a broad array of applications. Solenoids allow the creation of basic electromagnets and inductors. These devices can be controlled electronically with very high precision and are found in many places. One example is the starter motor of an internal combustion engine in a car or truck, which uses a solenoid to take a small current from the ignition switch and relay a stronger current from the battery to start the engine. Scrap yards also often make use of large electromagnetic hoists to move ferrous metals about efficiently. The current is turned on to activate the solenoid's magnetic field, allowing materials to be attached to the magnet. When they have been moved to the desired spot, the current is switched off and the materials are released.

Another common example of a solenoid is a simple electromagnetic lock or switch system. This can be produced using a solenoid and a rod that can be drawn into the core of the solenoid when current is flowing. Such a system is encountered whenever someone has to be remotely let in at an apartment building. A signal from a control panel typically closes a circuit that shunts electrical current into a solenoid. This causes it to generate a magnetic field and draw the lock pin into its open position. When the signal is released, the solenoid ceases to be active and allows a spring to pull the lock pin back into position. Basically all electromagnetic switch systems work this way. The security of such systems typically depends upon the manner in which the control circuit must be accessed, ranging from a simple push button to complex ID protocols.

Solenoids and their magnetic properties are also used in a number of very powerful analytical techniques. Among the most important is nuclear magnetic resonance (NMR) spectrometry. Chemists have used this method to analyze the structure of molecules since its development in the 1950s. The technique involves placing a homogeneous sample of a compound in solution into a strong magnetic field and detecting the energy levels that it absorbs when irradiated with a variable electromagnetic field. The energy and patterns of the absorption depend entirely on the three-dimensional structure of the molecule being examined, and provide very precise information about that structure.

The methodology of nuclear magnetic resonance was expanded with the development of superconducting magnets and magnetic resonance imaging (MRI) for medical diagnosis. The images are obtained by immersing the patient inside a strong magnetic field and plotting the patterns of energy absorption through irradiation by a variable electromagnetic field, just as in NMR spectrometry. The technique has been used routinely to examine living persons, ancient Egyptian mummies, and large zoo animals. Control of the stability and uniformity of the magnetic field is critical to these applications. Superconducting magnets made possible by solenoids help achieve this ability.

—*Richard M. Renneboog*

Further Reading

Haney, Robert M. *Solenoid Control, Testing, and Servicing: A Handy Reference for Engineers and Technicians.* McGraw-Hill Professional, 2013.

Kumar, L. Ashok, and M. Senthil Kumar. *Automation in Textile Machinery: Instrumentation and Control System Design Principles.* CRC Press, 2018.

Mitin, Vladimir V., and Dmitry I. Sementsov. *An Introduction to Applied Electromagnetics and Optics.* CRC Press, 2016.

Nayfeh, Munir H., and Morton K. Brussel. *Electricity and Magnetism.* Reprint. Courier Dover Publications, 2015.

Sclater, Neil. *Mechanisms and Mechanical Devices Sourcebook.* 5th ed., McGraw-Hill Professional, 2011.

Walsh, Ronald A. *Electromechanical Design Handbook.* 3rd ed., McGraw-Hill Professional, 2000.

See also: Automated processes and servomechanisms; Electromagnet technologies; Electromagnetism; Lenz's law; Tesla, Nikola

SOLID MECHANICS

Fields of Study: Physics; Mechanics; Mathematics

ABSTRACT

Solid mechanics is the study and testing of a solid material and structure as it reacts to outside influences such as force and temperature. Its practical applications include testing the load and stress limits of structures such as roofs and airplanes and structural materials such as pine and carbon composites. Solid mechanics uses applications that require an understanding of mathematics, computer algorithms, and the laws of physics.

KEY CONCEPTS

Hooke's law: the force (F) exerted by a spring is proportional to the length to which the spring is extended (x) and a coefficient characteristic of each individual spring (k), as $F = -kx$

law of the lever: for any lever that pivots against a fulcrum, a large mass M positioned to one side of the pivot point at a distance D can be balanced by a smaller mass m on the other side of the pivot point at a distance d such that $MD = md$

nanoparticles: particles whose dimensions are measured in nanometers, typically less than 100 nanometers in size

stress distribution: the load carried at various points along the length of a beam or other construction member

DEFINITION

Solid mechanics is the study and testing of a solid material and structure as it reacts to outside influences such as force and temperature. Its practical applications include testing the load and stress limits of structures such as roofs and airplanes and structural materials such as pine and carbon composites. Solid mechanics uses applications that require an understanding of mathematics, computer algorithms, and the laws of physics. Successfully predicting the reaction of a material to a variety of physical stresses addresses safety, economic, and practical concerns. The principles of solid mechanics are used across many branches of engineering.

BASIC PRINCIPLES

The theories and applications of solid mechanics have been practiced for centuries, with basic principles of engineering and mechanics first explained by the ancient Greeks. Greek mathematician Archimedes (ca. 287-212 BCE), for instance, developed the law of the lever, which explains mechanical force and stress. Fifteenth-century Italian artist and architect Leonardo da Vinci designed mechanisms made of beams and then identified stress distribution across a beam's section (deformation). Sixteenth-century Italian mathematician Galileo Galilei tested beams to their breaking point (failure). These discoveries and elucidations allowed early builders to know, among other things, the amount of stress materials could withstand before bending or breaking and subsequently compromising the structure being built. Today, advances in the study of solid mechan-

ics have made calculating either the mass of a planet or the properties of a nanoparticle solvable tasks.

The field of solid mechanics still tests solids for stress, deformation, and failure by using a combination of physical testing and mathematics to predict the interactions of matter and force. An additional distinction is now made, however, between statics (the study of objects that are motionless) and dynamics (those that are in motion). Additionally, if the shape of a solid is changed through stress or deformation and the solid returns to its original shape, it is considered elastic. If it remains changed, it is considered plastic.

Additionally, some materials show characteristics that are both solid and fluid, and these are studied in the related field of rheology. Rheology studies material that is primarily in a liquid state, but material that is plastic in nature is also studied. Solid mechanics and its sibling fluid mechanics are known together as "continuum mechanics," which studies the physical properties of both solids and fluids using mathematical objects and values. However, as solid matter studies delve deeper into micro- and nanotechnology, new mathematical models are constantly needed and being developed.

CORE CONCEPTS

The field of solid mechanics began as a branch of mathematics and did not become a branch of engineering until the mid-twentieth century. However, its principles and subspecialties have existed for centuries.

Early discoveries and applications of solid mechanics. Seventeenth-century English physicist and mathematician Isaac Newton developed three laws of motion that shaped the field of classical mechanics by explaining the relationship between forces applied to a material and the resulting motion caused by those forces. However, his laws did not take into consideration the motion of rigid bodies (solid material that does not change shape or size when force is applied) or of deformable bodies (solid material that undergoes a temporary or a permanent change in shape when force is applied). German mathematician Leonard Euler extended Newton's laws in 1750 by applying calculus equations in order to include rigid and deformable material in the laws of motion.

Robert Hooke, a late-seventeenth-century mechanician, studied the behavior of metal springs and made important progress in the subfield of elasticity. He discovered Hooke's law, which explains that force and deformation are related in a linear way: The amount of deformation of an object is in direct proportion to the deforming force, and when the force is removed, the object returns to its original shape and size.

In the nineteenth century, French mathematician Augustin Louis Cauchy developed the present-day mathematical theory of elasticity by studying the effect of pressure on a flat surface. Through this work he introduced the concepts of stress and strain into the theory of elasticity.

Force and stress. Solid mechanics is concerned with the study of material as it is affected by external force that may or may not cause it to undergo a change in its position or shape. Stress is the measure of the effect (such as twisting, bending, compressing, or stretching) that the external force has on an object or material. Force can bear on a solid in a "normal" (or perpendicular) direction, or it can bear "in shear." Shear stress occurs when force is applied at an angle, and materials that do not support shear stress are generally considered fluids. When shear stress causes an object to twist, the resulting condition is called torsion.

Deformation (strain), elasticity, and plasticity. Deformation, often referred to as strain, is the change in shape, size, or temperature of an object as a result of force being applied to it. Strain measures any internal or external change in the material and informs the mechanician how and where the solid object is changing as it accumulates stress. Applied force or

temperature can lead to temporary or permanent deformation of an object or can cause structural failure, which is the complete loss of the material's ability to support a load.

Elasticity is the ability of some materials to return to their original shape and size after external force or temperature is removed. Hooke's law explains the linear elasticity of most springs: Until a certain level of force is exhibited, the extension of the spring (its deformation) is in direct proportion to the load (or the force) applied to it. The muscles around the heart obey Hooke's law, as do spring-operated weighing machines. Structural analysts and engineers use mathematical equations to determine the linear elasticity of material in order to determine load capacity.

Plasticity, on the other hand, is a material's inability to return to its original size or shape once an applied force is removed. Plasticity is also referred to as nonlinear elasticity and is seen, for example, when metal is bent using force or high temperature.

Fracture, creep, and failure. Fractures are cracks in material when force or temperature is applied. Analytical solid mechanics uses mathematics and knowledge of stress and strain of a material to determine the level of force the material can withstand before fracturing. Fracturing occurs suddenly and often results in the failure of a material or object to perform as it was designed. Creep, on the other hand, is the gradual and permanent deformation of a material as a result of stress. It is time dependent, and the speed with which creep occurs is determined by the weight of the force or the temperature that is applied. Creep may or may not result in failure.

Mechanical engineering. Mechanical engineering and applied mathematics are two subfields of solid mechanics involved in the construction and efficiency of engines, turbines, and motorized vehicles. With modern levels of engine performance, extreme stress and strain are variables for consideration, and engineers must understand and predict potential areas of stress, fracture, creep, strain, and deformation for each piece of the equipment.

Materials science. Primary areas of research in materials science include energy storage and composite materials design. A relatively new solar energy technology is the development of thin-film photovoltaic cells, whereby any building surface that faces the sun can use strips of thin-film cells to convert solar energy into electricity. Material scientists and engineers also study the change in properties of materials whose dimensions approach nanometers (billionths of a meter).

Microelectronics and nanotechnology. The use of nanotechnology solid mechanics in microelectronics and nanotechnology involves creating custom-designed miniature electronic equipment for industry, manufacturing, academics, and the military, among other areas. "Packaging" microchips, microcircuits, and other devices, along with connecting them for better performance, involves consideration of material stress, strain, creep, and failure rates in order to keep up with the current demand for product and technological developments.

Nanotechnology, which merges sciences such as physics, chemistry, biology, and solid materials, involves the study and use of new nanoscale materials that are far lighter and stronger than old ones. These materials must be analyzed from a solid mechanics point of view for their use in, for example, medical devices and drugs, which has generated public concern. US government agencies such as the Occupational Safety and Health Administration (OSHA), the Food and Drug Administration (FDA), and the Environmental Protection Agency (EPA) have also voiced concern about the invasiveness and potential for unintended consequences of nanotechnology in medicine.

APPLICATIONS PAST AND PRESENT

Geomechanics. Geomechanics is the study of the behavior of Earth's soil and rock and how they react to fractures, strains, and stresses. Expertise in solid mechanics and knowledge of its related equipment and testing procedures is crucial to being better able to predict earthquakes, developing cleaner and safer methods of extracting oil from the ground, and to devising new technologies in building increasingly tall structures.

Cultural infrastructure. In the most basic sense, builders throughout history who attached a roof to a structure depended on solid mechanics. Materials science has its roots in the stonemasonry and ceiling management technology that advanced during the age of medieval cathedrals, especially with the addition of flying buttresses, which allowed ceilings of unprecedented height to be constructed. When steel was added to buildings in the nineteenth century, engineers and designers incorporated knowledge of statics, dynamics, and applied mathematics. Rectangular-shaped skyscrapers have been replaced by curving steel shapes with specially engineered glass in shell-type planes. Mechanicians and engineers employed solid mechanics' technology in order to be able to predict the thermal and wind stresses the glass could withstand as well as the potential effects of the building's strain as it expands and contracts with extreme temperatures or shifts in the wind.

Biomedical engineering or biomechanics. Biological organisms combine fluid dynamics and solid matter, as body fluids flow within a solid muscular, skeletal structure. Cells have cytoskeletons, and a cell shape, its "geometry," affects its life and death. Using nanotechnology, a cell's cytoskeleton can be stress-tested and mathematically analyzed. Biomedical engineering is profoundly affected by advances in solid mechanics. Prosthetic science, for example, has created metal "bones" that are made of carbon-fiber composites, which are lighter and more maneuverable than ever before.

Manufacturing engineering. Hermann Staudinger, a German chemist, proved the existence of macromolecules and subsequently won the 1953 Nobel Prize in Chemistry. Polymers are a kind of macromolecule composed of many similar units of molecules strung together. If one were to knit a scarf, for example, then knit another scarf onto the end of the first and a third onto the end of the second and so on, one would have an analogous design—a very long scarf made of single, shorter scarves. Solid mechanicians engineer new polymers and design the machines and other processes used to make them. Polymers have certain qualities that make them useful, such an ability to "stick" together. Naturally occurring cellulose polymers form wood by bonding together to make trees strong. Manufactured polymers have been used in plastics for many years in beverage bottles, garbage bags, and clothing such as raincoats. But new uses continually arise. Polyurethane, Teflon (polytetrafluoroethylene), and Dacron are well known for their uses in wood preservation, frying pan and other low friction coatings, and cloth, but all three materials are also used in the manufacture of artificial heart valves.

Manufacturing engineering is also concerned with formulating new metals and testing them for fracture and deformation as well as for thermal stress and strain. Engineers also predict a material's potential as a structural component and then determine the effective applications of the material. Polycrystalline substances that are used in solar cells and composites that are used in aerospace and military applications are solids that undergo the constant need for upgraded technology in order to allow them to perform efficiently and economically.

SOCIAL CONTEXT AND FUTURE PROSPECTS

Research into solid mechanics has changed a great many aspects of modern society. With the help of microelectronics, long-distance communication, once limited to landline phones in homes and offices or the postal service, now happens through cell phones, which take phone conversations almost anywhere. Email has replaced conventional mail as a so-

cial form and has permitted far more frequent and informal letter writing than ever before. Computers, run by the silicon-based microchip, have increased work time and efficiency in offices and schools.

Advances in tectonophysics and seismology are bringing us closer to realistic and reliable earthquake prediction, raising hopes of saving countless lives and dollars. The manufacture of composite materials has made airplanes lighter and armor stronger, which serves to better protect soldiers. Additionally, progress in materials science has given those who do survive battle but who have lost limbs access to better prosthetics than ever before. In the pharmaceutical field, new products include nanoparticles that deliver products more effectively to the body, thereby increasing survival rates in cancer patients. Cosmetics, where nanoparticles build better sunscreen and deliver lipids more effectively to thirsty skin, raise hopes for anti-aging products that will literally change the face of future elders. Nanoparticles are proving to be controversial, however, as their long-term effect on the body are unknown.

—*Daniel Castaldy*

Further Reading

Adhami, Reza, Peter M. Meenen III, and Dennis Hite. *Fundamental Concepts in Electrical and Computer Engineering with Practical Design Problems*. 2nd ed., Universal, 2005.

Arteaga, Robert R. *The Building of the Arch*. 10th ed., Jefferson National Parks Association, 2002.

Davidson, Frank Paul, and Kathleen Lusk-Brooke. *Building the World: An Encyclopedia of the Great Engineering Projects in History*. Greenwood, 2006.

Finn, John Michael. *Classical Mechanics*. Jones, 2009.

Goldfarb, Daniel. *Biophysics Demystified*. McGraw-Hill, 2010.

Lubliner, Jacob, and Panayiotis Papadopoulos. *Introduction to Solid Mechanics: An Integrated Approach*. 2nd ed., Springer, 2016.

Shurkin, Joel N. *Broken Genius: The Rise and Fall of William Shockley, Creator of the Electronic Age*. Macmillan, 2006.

See also: Aeronautical engineering; Ailerons, flaps, and airplane wings; Airfoils; Airplane propellers; Automated processes and servomechanisms; Biomedical engineering; Centrifugation; Civil engineering; Classical or applied mechanics; Diesel engine; Discoveries of Archimedes; Dynamics (mechanics); Earthquake engineering; Electromagnet technology; Engineering; External combustion engine; Flywheels; Friction; Heat transfer; Helicopters; Internal combustion engine; Jet engines; Materials science; Mechatronics; Mechanical engineering; Nanotechnology; Pendulums; Photoelectric effect; Plane rudders; Projectiles; Propulsion technologies; Quantum mechanics; Rigid-body dynamics; Robotics; Rotary engine; Springs; Stabilizers; Steam and steam turbines; Structural engineering; Superconductor; Tesla, Nikola; Thermodynamics; Transportation; Tull, Jethro; Turbines; Turbojets and turbofans; Turboprops; Vacuum technology

SPEED

Fields of Study: Physics; Mechanics; Mathematics

ABSTRACT

Speed is the rate of change in an object's position, measured in units of distance per unit of time. Speed is commonly expressed in miles per hour (mph) in the United States and kilometers per hour (km/h) throughout the rest of the world. Scientists usually express speed in terms of meters per second (m/s).

KEY CONCEPTS

relativistic speeds: speeds that are close to the speed of light and therefore are governed by relativity rather than Newton's laws

time dilation: the slowing of time for a moving object relative to an object that is not moving

SPEED VS. VELOCITY

Speed is the rate of change of an object's position, measured in units of distance per unit of time. Speed is commonly expressed in miles per hour (mph) in the United States and kilometers per hour

(km/h) throughout the rest of the world. Scientists usually express speed in terms of meters per second (m/s). The fastest possible speed is the speed of light in a vacuum, which is c = 299,792,458 meters per second (approximately 1,079,000,000 km/h or 670,600,000 mph).

There are two aspects of speed: average speed and instantaneous speed. Average speed is the distance that an object travels divided by the amount of time it was traveling. Instantaneous speed is the speed at which an object is traveling at any given instant in time. The equation for average speed is $s = d/t$, where s is speed, d is distance, and t is time.

Speed is closely related to velocity. Velocity is speed with the added component of direction. Speed is a scalar (meaning it is just a quantity), while velocity is a vector (meaning it is a quantity and a direction).

BACKGROUND

Galileo Galilei (1564-1642), an Italian physicist and mathematician, is sometimes credited with being the first to define speed mathematically as the distance traveled over a period of time. Galileo conducted numerous experiments on speed, most famously disproving the Aristotelian belief that, even in a vacuum, heavier objects fall faster than lighter ones.

Physicists in the ensuing centuries identified a number of benchmark speeds in the natural world. In the late seventeenth century, Sir Isaac Newton roughly estimated the speed of sound in air, and by the twentieth century the estimate became much more precise: sound travels at roughly 344 meters per second (769 mph) in dry air at around 21 degrees Celsius or 70 degrees Fahrenheit (the temperature and humidity of the medium affect the speed of sound). The speed of an object divided by the speed of sound is known as the object's Mach number; in other words, an object traveling at the speed of sound is traveling at Mach 1; twice the speed of sound is Mach 2; and so on. Before the twentieth century, the speed of sound had been broken by

Image via iStock/Ali Shahgholi. [Used under license.]

small objects, such as the tip of a whip or bullets fired from a gun. But self-propelled vehicles did not definitively reach supersonic (faster than sound) speeds until World War II, most famously in the case of the German V-2 ballistic missile.

Chuck Yeager, a captain in the United States Air Force, became the first human to travel at supersonic speed in horizontal flight in 1947.

The top speed in the universe is the speed of light in a vacuum; it has been measured to a very high degree of accuracy at close to 300 million meters per second, or roughly 186,000 miles per second. The symbol for the speed of light is c, a key part of many calculations in physics.

SPEED TODAY

The concept of speed has important applications on diverse levels of human experience, from the highly abstract, such as theoretical physics, to the very practical, such as traffic safety. In physics, understanding

the speed of light as a physical constant has been central to the current understanding how the universe works. In everyday life, advances in technology that allow humans to travel at ever greater speeds—whether in a chariot or an automobile or an airplane—have facilitated human movement around the world, making the world appear "smaller" all the time. Technological improvements also make these modes of transportation safer, but the increased speed also means that when there are accidents, the effects are more devastating.

In the early twentieth century, physicist Albert Einstein developed his special theory of relativity, which established among other things that the speed of light is constant for all frames of reference—in other words, traveling toward a light source does not make the light coming from it seem to move faster; similarly, the headlights on a moving car do not shine light at c plus the speed of the car—the light still travels at c. Understanding this has led to a number of seeming paradoxes in physics related to the behavior of space and time, or space-time as it is more properly called. One example is time dilation, which refers to the phenomenon of time moving more slowly on a moving object from the perspective of an object at rest; as an object approaches the speed of light, this phenomenon increases. Time dilation has been demonstrated a number of times in experiments where extremely accurate atomic clocks have been synchronized with one another and then sent into space or flown around the world and then found afterward to be out of sync by a few nanoseconds in a way that was predicted mathematically.

This is just one example of the significance of speed in high-level theoretical physics, although this does not really affect the average person's daily life in any way. In contrast, the ability to travel at elevated speeds in a car, train, or airplane has had a huge impact on people's daily lives. Just a few centuries ago, traveling great distances was a tremendous undertaking that took a long time and involved high risk. Traveling from Europe to America, or from coast to coast of the North American continent, could take weeks or months and involved exposure to the risk of accident, disease, or starvation. Today, those same trips are completely routine and take a matter of hours with substantially lower risks. The effect on people's lives and the global economy of this ability to travel at great speed cannot be overstated.

Having said that, it is also a physical reality that the faster an object is moving when it collides with another object, the greater is the force of impact that is exerted. Kinetic energy and momentum are transferred very suddenly. Thus, an automobile accident on the highway involving heavy vehicles traveling at 100 kilometers per hour or more is far more devastating than a wagon rollover at 30 kilometers per hour. Although automobile safety is constantly improving, and traffic fatalities decline almost every year, it remains the case that more than thirty thou-

sand Americans alone die every year in traffic accidents, not to mention other such incidents that occur in other countries, a reminder that in daily life, speed still carries risks as well as rewards.

—Douglas R. Jordan

Further Reading

Berman, Bob. *Zoom: How Everything Moves: From Atoms and Galaxies to Blizzards and Bees*. Little, 2014.

Collier, Peter. *A Most Incomprehensible Thing: Notes towards a Very Gentle Introduction to the Mathematics of Relativity*. 2nd ed. Incomprehensible, 2014.

Feynman, Richard, Robert Leighton, and Matthew Sands. *Six Easy Pieces: Essentials of Physics Explained by Its Most Brilliant Teacher*. 4th ed., Basic, 2011.

Lawrence, Martha, Richard Bullock, and Ziming Liu. *China's High-Speed Rail Development*. World Bank Publications, 2019.

Leslie-Pelecky, Diandra. *The Physics of NASCAR: The Science Behind the Speed*. Penguin, 2008.

Nalawade, Sharad. *The Speed of Time*. One Point Six Technology Pvt Ltd, 2012.

Yu, Daniel. *Speed: A Unified Field Theory in Physics: A Caveman Who Invented the Stone Wheel*. Fulton Books Incorporated, 2020.

See also: Acceleration; Acoustics; Aerodynamics; Aerospace design; Ballistic weapons; Celestial mechanics; Chaotic systems; Circular motion; Classical or applied mechanics; Coriolis effect; Dynamics (mechanics); Euler paths; Euler's laws of motion; Force (physics); Friction; Kinematics; Kinetic energy; Linear motion; Momentum (physics); Projectiles; Propulsion technologies; Steam engine; Transportation; Vectors; Velocity

SPRINGS

Fields of Study: Physics; Mechanics; Mathematics

ABSTRACT

Spring systems are related to Hooke's law, the conservation of energy, and harmonic oscillators. Hooke's law appears in all fields on physics and engineering because it can be

applied to most solid objects in addition to springs. Harmonic oscillators are important systems in classical mechanics; they are found in nature and used for devices.

KEY CONCEPTS

compression: the pushing forces applied to an object in order to diminish its size or volume

elongation: the lengthening of an object under stress

harmonic oscillations: the motion resulting from a system that when displaced from its equilibrium point exerts a restoring force that is proportional to the displacement

Hooke's law: the principle that states that the force necessary to compress or stretch a spring by a certain displacement is proportional to that displacement

kinetic energy: the energy associated with motion

potential energy: stored energy due to position or configuration

spring constant: a mathematical value that defines the stiffness of a spring

tension: the pulling force exerted longitudinally from the ends of a rope, wire, rod, or other object

HOOKE'S LAW

Elasticity is the ability of an object or material to return to its normal shape after experiencing elongation (lengthening) or compression (shortening) due to tension. An object is considered more elastic if it can be returned to its original shape more precisely. One example of an elastic object is the spring. When a spring is stretched or compressed, it exerts a restoring force that returns it to its beginning length. Hooke's law states that this restoring force (F) is proportional to the amount (x) by which it is stretched or compressed:

$$F = -kx$$

A spring will hold potential energy when it is compressed or stretched. As a spring passes through its neutral position, it reaches its maximum kinetic energy and its maximum velocity.

The spring constant (k) is a constant of proportionality that refers to the stiffness of the spring. The greater the value of k, the stiffer the spring. Force (F) has units of newtons (N), displacement (x) has units of meters (m), and therefore the spring constant (k) has units of newtons per meter (N/m). It is important to note that this equation gives magnitude only. To be more exact, one may establish the origin of the x-axis to be at the equilibrium length of a spring. If one stretches the spring in the positive x direction ($x > 0$), the spring exerts a force in the negative x direction with a magnitude of kx:

$$Fx = -kx$$

Likewise, if one compresses the spring in the negative x direction ($x < 0$), the spring exerts a force in the positive x direction with a magnitude of kx. The restoring force is opposite to the direction of the displacement. Hooke's law only works for small stretches and compressions, however. If a spring is stretched excessively far, then it will reach a point where it will become permanently deformed and will not return to its original shape.

Hooke's law can apply to forces other than those associated with springs. The force that holds atoms together can be modeled using Hooke's law. These forces are responsible for vibrations and oscillations, normal force, and wave motion.

ENERGY OF A SPRING

Hooke's law is also an example of the first law of thermodynamics. A spring conserves energy when it is compressed or stretched. The potential energy (U) of a spring when it has been displaced from its equilibrium by an amount x is:

$$U = 1/2kx^2.$$

A SIMPLE PROBLEM

Consider a spring that is compressed a distance of 3 centimeters by an applied force of 75 newtons. The spring constant can be determined by using Hooke's equation to solve for the spring constant (k). Plug in the values for force (F) and displacement (x), remembering to convert displacement from centimeters (cm) to meters (m) in order to have the proper dimensions in the answer:

$$F = kx$$

$$k = \frac{F}{x}$$

$$k = \frac{75\,\text{N}}{0.030\,\text{m}}$$

$$k = 2{,}500\,\text{N/m}$$

The spring constant is 2,500 N/m. By measuring the displacement of the spring from its original length by an applied force, one can determine the stiffness of the spring.

The potential energy of a spring at its equilibrium point is zero and always positively increases as it is displaced from its equilibrium point. This displacement can be due to either stretching or compression. The potential energy of the spring can be converted to kinetic energy (K), both measured in joules (J). Kinetic energy depends on an object's mass (m) and velocity (v):

$$U_{max} = K_{max}$$

$$\frac{1}{2}kx_{max}^2 = \frac{1}{2}mv_{max}^2$$

$$v_{max} = x_{max}\sqrt{\frac{k}{m}}$$

$$K = \frac{1}{2}mv^2$$

Consider a spring with one end attached to a support and the other end attached to a mass. Now one compresses the spring by a certain distance, then releases it on a frictionless surface. The total energy (E) of this system is the sum of the potential and kinetic energy:

$$E = U + K$$

The mass oscillates back and forth, and the energy changes from potential to kinetic energy. The maximum potential energy occurs when the spring is at maximum compression and extension at the endpoints of the oscillation. At the endpoints, the kinetic energy is zero. The maximum kinetic energy happens when the mass travels through the equilibrium position. One can find the maximum velocity (v_{max}) of the mass by setting the maximum potential energy (U_{max}) equal to the maximum kinetic energy (K_{max}) and solving for v_{max}:

$$U_{max} = K_{max}$$

$$\frac{1}{2}kx_{max}^2 = \frac{1}{2}mv_{max}^2$$

$$v_{max} = x_{max}\sqrt{\frac{k}{m}}$$

HARMONIC OSCILLATOR

A spring with a mass attached to one end demonstrates simple harmonic motion and is a classic example of a harmonic oscillator. Consider a mass on a spring that has been stretched or compressed, then let go. The mass will then exhibit harmonic oscillations, moving back and forth about its equilibrium position. The period (T) of a mass on a spring is:

$$T = 2\pi\sqrt{\frac{m}{k}}$$

Photo via iStock/nono57. [Used under license.]

The unit for the period is the second (s). The period is independent of the amplitude and gravitational acceleration and is the same for horizontal and vertical spring systems.

SPRINGS IN EVERYDAY USE

There are many different types of springs that come in various sizes and shapes that provide different functions. Large springs used in railroad cars are heavy and stiff and used to smooth the ride of the car. Small delicate spiral springs are used in mechanical watches. The fact that these small springs obey Hooke's law with a frequency determined by the mass and the spring stiffness allows for accurate mechanical watches and clocks to be manufactured.

—*Casey M. Schwarz*

Further Reading

Gans, Roger F. *Mechanical Systems: A Unified Approach to Vibrations and Controls*. Springer, 2014.

Hsu, Tai-Ran. *Applied Engineering Analysis*. John Wiley & Sons, 2018.

Josephs, Harold, and Ronald Huston. *Dynamics of Mechanical Systems*. CRC Press, 2002.

Kobelev, Vladimir. *Durability of Springs*. 2nd ed., Springer Nature, 2021.

Ling, Samuel J., Jeff Sanny, and William Moebs. *University Physics, Volume 1*. Samurai Media Limited, 2017.

Wilson, Jerry D., Anthony J. Buffa, and Bo Lou. *College Physics Essentials: Mechanics, Thermodynamics, Waves (Volume One)*. 8th ed., CRC Press, 2019.

See also: Amplitude; Calculus; Civil engineering; Conservation of energy; Earthquake engineering; Force (physics); Momentum; Harmonic oscillator; Hooke, Robert; Kinetic energy; Momentum (physics); Vibration

STABILITY

Fields of Study: Physics; Mechanics; Mathematics

ABSTRACT

A mechanical system is said to be statically stable if, when disturbed from its equilibrium condition, it experiences forces and/or torques (forces acting to cause rotation) that move it back in the direction of equilibrium. Equilibrium may be defined as that state of the system in which there exists no generalized forces that would cause the system to change.

KEY CONCEPTS

asymptotic stability: a condition in which a system will return to an equilibrium state and remain there

dynamic stability: a condition in which a system's motion falls within prescribed limits of position and velocity

equilibrium: a condition in which no generalized forces act that would cause the system to change

generalized force: a force and/or torque (force that causes a rotational motion)

state: the position and velocity of each mass in a system (the state completely specifies the system's physical condition)

static stability: a condition in which a system tends to move toward an equilibrium state after being disturbed from it

OVERVIEW

Stability of any physical system (e.g., mechanical, electrical, and thermal) has numerous definitions. It is possible, though, to divide them into two categories: static and dynamic stability. A mechanical system is said to be statically stable if, when disturbed from its equilibrium condition, it experiences forces and/or torques (forces acting so as to cause rotation) that move it back in the direction of equilibrium.

Equilibrium may be defined as that state of the system in which there exists no generalized forces that would cause the system to change.

Generalized force means a force or torque, or a combination of the two. A classic example of a statically stable system consists of a ball resting in a valley between two hills. Moving the ball a small distance from the bottom of the valley (the equilibrium point) and releasing it will result in a gravitational force pulling the ball back toward the bottom of the valley; hence, in this case, gravity behaves as a restoring force. Static stability does not guarantee when or if the system will ever return to equilibrium and remain there; however, in this example, displacing the ball and releasing it will result in oscillatory motion about the equilibrium point, with friction eventually dissipating the ball's energy and bringing it to rest at the bottom of the valley. (This system is visualized easily and will be used throughout the discussion to demonstrate the various concepts of stability.)

Balancing the ball initially at the top of a hill gives a statically unstable system. If the ball can be perfectly balanced there, the hilltop is an equilibrium point, but any small displacement of the ball will result in an unbalanced gravitational force that pulls it down and away from the initial equilibrium point, and thus gravity is not a restoring force in this case.

The only other static condition is called neutral stability, and is exemplified by a ball resting on a perfectly flat, horizontal surface. Displacing the ball from its initial position and releasing it results in no force that would change the ball's position. Indeed, the region of neutral stability formed by the flat surface is a continuum of equilibrium points.

A single system can have different modes or regions of stability, each with a different stability character: for example, a ball on a surface with several hills, valleys, and perfectly horizontal areas. With this added complexity, as well as the concept of dynamic stability (that of the system in motion), it is necessary to expand the definition of "state" to include the position *and* velocity (speed and direction) of the ball. A ball at rest in the bottom of a valley is thus in an equilibrium state, but so is a ball rolling at constant speed around the perimeter of a flat, circular, horizontal region (assumed to be frictionless) surrounded on all sides by a steep, sloping wall.

For certain initial states (positions and velocities), the ball can change to a region of different stability. Starting it with high speed on a horizontal surface (neutrally stable position) could result in the ball rolling over the next hill and into an adjacent valley (statically stable position).

A further characterization of a system's stability depends on the presence of friction. If friction exists in a region around a statically stable point, then it may be possible for the system, once disturbed from a static equilibrium point, to return to that point and remain there. This is referred to as asymptotic stability. Considering the ball in the valley, if only a small amount of friction is present, then the oscillations of the ball will decrease gradually in amplitude, and the ball will come to rest eventually at the equilibrium point.

The Soviet mathematician Aleksandr Mikhailovich Liapunov (frequently transliterated as Lyapunov) first gave a clear definition of dynamic stability for a system. In *Obshchaia Zadacha ob Ustoichivosti Dvizheniia* (1892; *The General Problem of the Stability of Motion*, 1966), he noted that some systems may be considered stable even though they do not return to equilibrium. A system is said to be "stable in the sense of Liapunov" if its state always remains within a certain set of states. For example, consider a ball rolling on a surface that is constantly changing shape. Even if some friction is present, the motion of the surface replenishes the energy of the ball and it will never come to rest. For certain restricted motions of the surface, this system is stable in the sense of Liapunov because the ball's position and velocity will always fall within certain limits: The

ball wanders about, never more than a given distance from its starting point and never obtaining sufficient speed to roll into regions progressively farther away from the origin.

Dynamic stability may be categorized further by its application to forced and unforced motion. Forced motion refers to the result of applying generalized forces to a system, while unforced motion is simply the result of displacing the system from equilibrium and releasing it. It is helpful to view a system in terms of input (the applied generalized force) and response (the resulting behavior). Linear systems are those for which the response is in some way directly proportional to the input. If a spring compresses by a given amount when squeezed by a certain force, and if doubling the force also doubles the amount of compression, then the spring is said to be linear.

If an object is suspended by a spring whose other end is attached to a fixed point above, then displacing the object from the spring's static equilibrium point and releasing it will result in oscillatory motion. In the case of a linear spring, the dynamic stability of this motion can be predicted easily, and, in fact, depends only upon the elasticity of the spring and the mass of the object.

Applying a periodic force to the mass (e.g., pushing on it and releasing it at a constant frequency) may change the system's stability. Making the frequency of the forcing action the same as the unforced frequency of the mass-spring oscillations results in resonant motion. Under this condition, energy is transferred into the system at the maximum possible rate.

Although the force may be relatively small, the amplitude of motion can grow to be quite large; in the extreme case of little or no friction, the amplitude will become so large that the system is destroyed or reaches the physical limits of its motion (e.g., the spring breaks because it is overextended, or the mass strikes the floor). Such a system is statically, but not dynamically, stable. When sufficient friction is present (e.g., the mass is rubbing against some surface as it oscillates), the system is stable in the sense of Liapunov for both unforced and forced motion.

If the spring is nonlinear, the question of stability is far more difficult to resolve. One may view the input as either the initial displacement (in the case of static stability considerations) or the applied force (for questions of dynamic stability). In either circumstance, since the response for nonlinear systems is not proportional to the input, one cannot generalize the results of one input to those of even a slightly different input; the motion may be stable in one case and unstable in the other.

Liapunov's direct method is a powerful means of determining if a nonlinear system is either stable in the sense of Liapunov or asymptotically stable. Essentially, this method states that if one can find a mathematical function of the system's state that is either constant or decreasing with time, then the system is stable in the sense of Liapunov. If one can find a function that always decreases with time, then the system is asymptotically stable.

Typically, the energy of the system (which is a function of the state, positions and speeds of the masses involved) behaves in one of these two fashions and, therefore, is a useful quantity for determining stability. The real power of Liapunov's direct method, though, is that any function of the state may be employed. For complex systems (having many masses, for example, or mass that is distributed in nonlinear flexible members), it may be impractical to express the total energy in terms of the system's state; however, a clever analyst may be successful in ascertaining a system's stability through the use of some other mathematical function of the state. For other types of physical systems, a suitable definition of "state" allows all the preceding definitions of stability to be applied. This is quite useful in electrical, thermal, hydraulic, or any other type of engineering system where the design must include

stability considerations. For example, in an electrical system, the state might be defined in terms of the voltages and their rates of change at certain key points in the circuit.

APPLICATIONS

Stability theory has many applications in the study of natural phenomena. In many cases, its use is connected with questions of energy transfer, since some removal of energy from a system guarantees that it is at least stable in the sense of Liapunov.

One of the more interesting examples of an interaction between nature and an artificial structure was that of the collapse of the 853-meter suspension bridge over Tacoma Narrows, Washington, on November 7, 1940. Prevailing winds blowing through the bridge's structure created a periodic force very nearly equal to the bridge's natural frequency of vibration. The resonant motion that ensued gave rise to large vibrational waves of the entire bridge, and it collapsed within a short time. An investigation afterward indicated that the designers had failed to analyze the structure for stability in the presence of such winds. The most common applications of stability theory are in automatic control systems.

These are used in much of modern technology to allow somewhat autonomous operation of powered equipment without the need for constant attention by people. A good example is the automatic cruise control found in many automobiles (used to maintain a constant speed). A sensor, usually connected to the speedometer, sends a signal to the controller indicating the automobile's speed. If that speed is less than what the driver has indicated to the controller as being the desired speed, then the controller opens the throttle, sending more fuel to the engine and thus increasing the speed. This change in fuel rate is proportional to the difference between the desired and actual speeds. Conversely, if the speed becomes too great, the controller partially closes the throttle to reduce the flow rate of the fuel, and thus, the speed. In this situation the fuel is viewed as the input to the system, and the speed as the response. The automatic controller continually monitors the difference between the desired and actual speeds; this is known as a feedback control system (with the sensor feeding the actual speed back to the controller).

Because of the time required for any system to respond completely to a given input, it is possible to have stability problems with feedback systems if they are not designed properly. For example, if the automobile's engine is sluggish in responding to an increase in the flow rate of the fuel, the controller might open the throttle even more. By then, however, the engine would be racing too fast, and the controller would reduce the flow rate. Again, because of sluggish response, the engine (and the automobile's speed) would fall below what was desired. The process would repeat at this point, with the speed alternately increasing, then decreasing, and so on, without ever reaching a steady value (equilibrium). From an operational viewpoint, this is unsatisfactory (and annoying to passengers); the system might be stable in the sense of Liapunov, but asymptotic stability is far more desirable. The designers therefore make the controller so that it adjusts the flow rate of the fuel while considering the time response of the engine (this is necessary even for a well-tuned engine). Generally, the engine response (with respect to fuel rate) is approximately linear, and the controller's design for stability is straightforward.

For other types of feedback systems, the response cannot be considered linear. An example is the use of a thermostat to control the air temperature in a room. When the temperature falls below what is desired, the thermostat switches on the heater and the air temperature begins to rise; however, the rate of heat flow into the room is constant when the heater is on, so the response is not proportional to the difference between desired and actual temperatures. As with the example of the speed controller, this system not only can, but also always does, exhibit some oscillatory behavior. For nonlinear systems, this is known as a limit cycle. Applying Liapunov's theory, it is seen that a limit cycle can be stable in the sense of Liapunov, or even asymptotically stable if energy is leaving the system faster than the control system is adding it.

CONTEXT

The notion of stability in mechanical motion has been understood and used with varying degrees of success since antiquity. It is known that the ancient Egyptians used a sequence of reservoirs, each draining into the other, to stabilize the workings of a rudimentary clock that depended on a constant flow rate of water into a container with a float that moved upward next to a set of time markings on the vessel. Sir Isaac Newton was among the first to employ the concept of static stability in analyzing mechanical systems in the late seventeenth century. Although the actual reason is much more complex than Newton believed, he theorized that the Moon keeps one face toward Earth because gravity attracts that side of the Moon (which has an irregular shape and mass distribution) with slightly more force than any other region. In that regard, the Moon's orientation is statically stable.

In the late nineteenth century, James Watt built the first successful steam engine, including an automatic speed controller. Although he did not apply stability theory rigorously in the design, through experimentation he was able to achieve dynamic stability of this control system and keep the engine running at nearly constant speed.

Modern control systems are able to take advantage of Liapunov's theory to predict stability, and thus give the designer great confidence in the success of the system's operation.

Liapunov's theory remains the single most powerful means of analyzing the stability of nonlinear systems, both natural and artificial.

—*Robert G. Melton*

Further Reading

al Mashhadany, Yousif, and Khalaf Geaed. *Classical Control Theory: Modeling of Physical Systems, Design and Analysis of Control Systems, Stability Theorems.* Lap Lambert Academic Publishing Gmbh KG, 2014.

Bacciotti, Andrea. *Stability and Control of Linear Systems.* Springer, 2018.

Bacciotti, Andrea, and Lionel Rosier. *Liapunov Functions and Stability in Control Theory.* 2nd ed., Springer Science & Business Media, 2005.

Doyle, John C., Bruce A. Francis, and Allen R. Tannenbaum. *Feedback Control Theory.* Reprint. Courier Corporation, 2013.

Gajic, Zoran, and Muhammad Tahir Javed Qureshi. *Liapunov Matrix Equation in System Stability and Control.* Reprint. Courier Corporation, 2008.

See also: Aeronautical engineering; Aerospace design; Biomedical engineering; Engineering; Equilibrium; Hydraulic engineering

STABILIZERS

Fields of Study: Physics; Aeronautical engineering; Mechanical engineering; Fluid dynamics; Mathematics

ABSTRACT

Small wings that are placed at positions forward or aft of an aircraft's wings to provide balance in pitch and yaw during flight. On a missile, stabilizers may also be known as fins. Without stabilizers, it would be very difficult or even impossible to control the orientation of an aircraft or missile in flight.

KEY CONCEPTS

canard: a small stabilizer wing system set ahead of the main wings of an airplane

center of gravity: the point within an aircraft, or any other body, about which the entire mass of that body is equally distributed

center of lift: the point at which the lift force appears to function against the weight of an airplane

stall: the loss of the ability of wings to provide lift due to ascending at an angle that causes the pressure difference between the upper and lower surfaces of a wing to decrease and equalize

PLAIN WINGS

Early attempts to achieve gliding flight used only wings, occasionally adding the shifting of weights beneath the wing to keep the wing balanced in its motion. At any given angle of attack, there is some point on the wing where the forces are in balance, but this position, sometimes known as the "center of lift" or "center of pressure," moves forward or aft as the wing's angle to the flow changes. The location of this point and its distance from the center of mass or gravity of the wing or vehicle will determine its pitching moment, that is, the tendency of its nose to move up and down, rotating around the center of gravity. It is considered desirable to have the center of lift behind the center of gravity for positive stability, that is, to create a natural tendency for the vehicle to return to level flight after any disturbance. For example, in a stable aircraft, a gust-induced increase in lift will cause the airplane to rotate nose downward and automatically reduce its lift in correction. Because of this, a stable airplane will always tend to rotate nose down in flight unless that rotation is counteracted by another force or moment. This correction is the purpose of the horizontal stabilizer.

HORIZONTAL STABILIZERS

The horizontal stabilizer is normally placed on the rear or tail of the fuselage, somewhat like the tail feathers of a bird. This placement requires the stabilizer to have a downward load or negative lift to counteract the nose-down moment of the wing. The common horizontal stabilizer is usually a small wing placed toward the rear of the fuselage and mounted at a negative angle of attack so that it will cause a downward force. The stabilizer is usually equipped with flaps known as elevators, which can be moved up and down to alter the force on the stabilizer, allowing the pilot to rotate the aircraft nose up or nose down in pitch. This allows control of the angle of attack of the wing and, hence, control of the lift produced by the wing. When larger control forces are needed, the whole stabilizer is designed to be moveable or to rotate about a pivot point, and it is then known as a stabilator or elevon.

Some airplane designers believe that the horizontal stabilizer should be in front of the wing, where it can correct the nose-down pitch of the stable wing with an upward force, thus increasing the lifting capability of the aircraft instead of decreasing it, as may happen with a tail-mounted stabilizer. The Wright brothers and other early aviators used this arrangement on their primitive designs but, like most others, eventually built airplanes with the horizontal stabilizers at the tail. When the horizontal stabilizer is in front of the wing, it is called a canard. There are special circumstances, such as transonic and supersonic flight, where canards may have advantages, but most analyses show that the best place for the horizontal stabilizer is near the tail of the aircraft.

VERTICAL STABILIZERS

The vertical stabilizer is almost always mounted above the tail of the airplane. It is designed to limit the rotation of the aircraft in yaw, operating as a sort of weathervane, much like the feathers at the aft end of an arrow. Attached to the vertical stabilizer or fin is the rudder, which acts as a flap on the winglike stabilizer to move left or right and create forces which will yaw the airplane when desired.

The vertical stabilizer on most single-engine airplanes is mounted on the fuselage at a slight angle to counteract the torque of the engine, which tends to make the fuselage try to roll in a direction opposite to the turning of the propeller. Some aircraft have two vertical stabilizers where larger control surfaces are needed or where at very high angles of attack, part of the stabilizer may be in the wake of the fuselage.

Vertical and horizontal stabilizers are placed on an airplane in many different arrangements, depending on the control needs of the design. Sometimes the horizontal stabilizer is mounted on the vertical stabilizer, either at its top in a T-tail arrangement or part of the way up in a cruciform design. Often the vertical/horizontal tail arrangement is dictated by the need to control the airplane in stall and to make sure that, in that situation, the vertical stabilizer and rudder are not in the wake of the horizontal stabilizer, where their usefulness would be very limited.

MISSILE STABILIZERS

The stabilizers on a missile are often simply referred to as fins. These small wings are mounted at the tail of the missile and are often fully moveable and do not have attached flaps. These moveable fins provide both balance or stability in flight and the control forces needed to maneuver.

—*James F. Marchman III*

Further Reading

Bibel, George, and Robert Hedges. *Plane Crash: The Forensics of Aviation Disasters*. Johns Hopkins UP, 2018.

Federal Aviation Administration (FAA). *Aircraft Weight and Balance Handbook (FAA-H-8083-1A)*. Skyhorse Publishing, 2011.

Yedavalli, Yeda K. *Flight Dynamics and Control of Aero and Space Vehicles*. Wiley, 2019.

Young, Trevor M. *Performance of the Jet Transport Airplane: Analysis Methods, Flight Operations, and Regulations*. Wiley, 2019.

See also: Aerodynamics and flight; Aeronautical engineering; Ailerons, flaps, and airplane wings; Airfoils; Fluid dynamics; Plane rudders

STATICS

Fields of Study: Physics; Mechanics; Mathematics

ABSTRACT
Statics is the branch of classical mechanics concerned with rigid objects or physical systems for which the acting forces and torques are in equilibrium. Statics is a subfield of classical mechanics, along with dynamics (the study of objects in motion under the influence of unequilibrated forces), and kinematics (the study of objects in motion without consideration of the masses and forces involved). Engineers apply the principles of statics to model the forces involved in mechanical systems, including the tension in trusses and cables when designing bridges and the stress on load-bearing beams in building construction.

KEY CONCEPTS
force: an action or reaction that attempts to cause the body to move along its own line of action

torque: the tendency of a force to cause an object to rotate, defined mathematically as the rate of change of the object's angular momentum; also called moment of force

vector quantities: quantities that have both a magnitude or absolute value and are associated with a direction (e.g., 23 kilometers per hour northwest)

weight: the apparent quality of mass under the influence of a gravitational field

STATIC EQUILIBRIUM
When a rigid object is in static equilibrium, all forces and torques acting on the object are balanced, resulting in no acceleration or rotation of the object. Mathematically, this means two things: The vector sum of all external forces acting on the object must be zero (translational equilibrium), and the vector sum of all external torques acting on the object must be zero (rotational equilibrium).

When a rigid object of mass m is acted on by a net force, the acceleration of the object is given by Newton's second law. A system in static equilibrium experiences no net force, so the object has zero acceleration.

When an object's acceleration is zero, only motion at a constant velocity is possible. Thus, an object in static equilibrium is either stationary (at rest), or else the center of mass of the object is moving at a constant velocity.

The net torque, or rotational force, on an object in static equilibrium is zero. This corresponds to zero angular acceleration, or no tendency for the object to rotate. Note that the study of statics assumes that all objects are rigid; that is, they do not deform when acted upon by the forces in question. The analysis of forces acting on deformable objects requires detailed knowledge of the material and is beyond the scope of statics.

FREE-BODY DIAGRAMS
Force is a vector quantity, which has both magnitude and direction. The net force acting on an object is the sum of the individual forces acting on the object. The net force is the vector sum of the forces involved, not the sum of the magnitudes of the forces.

An essential tool for analyzing the forces on an object in static equilibrium is a free-body diagram. An object in static equilibrium may be subject to a variety of forces, which might include push or pull, gravity, friction, tension, or torque. A free-body diagram of the system explicitly shows all the forces acting on the object. A visual representation of the system ensures that all forces are included and assists the component decomposition necessary to find the resultant vector sum of the applied forces.

Consider a mass suspended from a wire and the corresponding free-body diagram. The mass experiences a downward force, which is the weight of the mass due to gravity. At the same time, the wire exerts an upward force on the mass, which keeps it from falling. Since the mass is at rest, the upward force from the wire and the downward force due to gravity must have equal magnitudes but opposite directions. That is, in vector notation.

When forces are applied to an object in multiple directions, it is important to remember their vector nature. Consider two forces acting on an object, one horizontally with a magnitude of 4 newtons (N), and the other vertically with a magnitude of 3 N. The magnitude of the vector sum of the vertical and horizontal force vectors is the length of the hypotenuse of the right triangle they form. By the Pythagorean theorem, so the magnitude of the resultant force in this situation would be 5 N.

When a mass is suspended from two wires, the situation becomes more complicated. The force of gravity pulls the mass down, but neither wire is individually responsible for supporting the full weight. For such a system in static equilibrium the force due to gravity, or weight, induces a tension in each wire. This tension corresponds to the force applied to the mass by each wire. Since the mass is in static equilibrium, the net force acting on the mass by the two wires must be zero, so their vector sum vanishes. By symmetry, the two wires support the weight equally, and the tensions have equal magnitude, T. Each contributes an upward force of T/2 providing a net upward force of T to counter the downward force, due to gravity. In addition, each wire exerts a force in the horizontal direction. Since no other forces contribute a horizontal component to the vector sum, the horizontal components of the tension in the two wires are equal in magnitude but opposite in direction. Free-body diagrams are essential tools for the analysis of physical systems in static equilibrium. The techniques used to analyze the two-dimensional system of a mass suspended by two wires, which involve both trigonometric functions and complex number algebra, can be extended to forces acting in three dimensions and to physical systems involving multiple objects.

—*Anne Collins*

Further Reading

Colwell, Catharine H. "Static Equilibrium." *PhysicsLAB*. Catherine H. Colwell, dev.physicslab.org/document.aspx?doctype=3&filename=dynamics_staticequilibrium.xml. Accessed 9 Mar. 2016.
"Equilibrium and Statics." *The Physics Classroom*, www.physicsclassroom.com/class/vectors/Lesson-3/Equilibrium-and-Statics. Accessed 9 Mar. 2016.
"Static Equilibrium, Elasticity, and Torque." *Boundless*, www.boundless.com/physics/textbooks/boundless-physics-textbook/static-equilibrium-elasticity-and-torque-8. Accessed 9 Mar. 2016.

See also: Angular forces; Calculating system efficiency; Dynamics (mechanics); Engineering; Equilibrium; Force (physics); Geometry; Load; Mechanical engineering; Pendulums; Rigid-body dynamics; Torque; Vectors

STEAM AND STEAM TURBINES

Fields of Study: Physics; Mechanics; Mathematics

ABSTRACT

Fuels burned to heat water in a boiler produce pressurized steam that can be directed through the blades of a turbine to drive them around. Steam-driven turbines can be used to drive large-scale electrical generators and other machines.

KEY CONCEPTS

chemical energy: the energy contained within the bonds between atoms in a compound

nuclear energy: the energy contained within the bonds between the subatomic particles in the nucleus of an atom; when a nucleus undergoes fission and splits apart, it releases some of this energy which may then be captured by water molecules in a boiler system, eventually turning them to steam

BACKGROUND

Fossil fuels such as oil and coal contain chemical energy that is released when they are burned. Uranium contains nuclear energy that is partially released when radioactive atomic nuclei undergo nuclear fission. Either of these forms of energy can be converted into thermal energy (heat), and this thermal energy can be used to make steam in a boiler. A

steam turbine can be used to convert the thermal energy of steam into the mechanical energy of a rotating shaft. When the turbine shaft is used to drive an electric generator, electricity is produced. Although electric generators can be driven by diesel

he rotor of a modern steam turbine used in a power plant. Photo by Christian Kuhna, via Wikimedia Commons.

engines, gas turbines, and other devices, most electricity is generated using steam turbines.

PRINCIPLES OF TURBINE OPERATION

High-pressure, high-temperature steam enters a steam turbine through a throttle valve. Inside the turbine the steam flows through a series of nozzles and rotating blades. As it flows through a nozzle, the pressure and temperature of the steam decrease, and its speed increases. The fast-moving steam is directed against rotating blades, which work something like the blades on a pinwheel. The steam is deflected as it passes over the rotating blades, and in response the steam pushes against the blades and makes them rotate. As the steam flows over the rotating blades its speed decreases.

Large turbines are composed of many stages. Each stage has a ring of nozzles followed by a ring of rotating blades. The slow-moving steam leaving the rotating blades of one stage enters the nozzles of the next stage, where it speeds up again. This arrangement is called "pressure compounding." The energy of the steam is converted to mechanical work in small steps. Less of the steam's thermal energy is wasted or lost if it is converted in small steps.

The amount of power produced by a turbine depends on the amount of steam flowing through it and on the inlet and outlet steam pressures. Steam flow is constantly regulated by the throttle valve, but the steam pressures are fixed by the design of the system. Inlet steam pressure is determined by the operating pressure of the boiler that supplies it. Outlet pressure is determined by where the steam goes when it leaves the turbine. If the steam simply escapes into the atmosphere, the outlet pressure is atmosphere. If the outlet steam pressure is made lower than atmospheric pressure, the turbine produces more power. This is accomplished by having the steam leaving the turbine flow into a condenser. The decrease in volume as the exiting steam condenses creates a low pressure that acts to draw the steam through the turbine at a faster rate, almost as though it is being sucked out by a vacuum.

Cooling water passing through tubes inside the condenser removes heat from the steam flowing around the tubes and causes it to condense and become liquid water. Since water occupies a much smaller volume as a liquid than as steam, condensing creates a vacuum. When a turbine is connected to a condenser, the outlet steam pressure can be far below one atmosphere.

DETAILS OF TURBINE CONSTRUCTION

Inside the steel turbine casing, stationary partitions called "diaphragms" separate one turbine stage from the next. Each diaphragm has a hole at the center for the rotor shaft to pass through. Nozzle passages are cut through the diaphragms near their outer rims, and the steam is forced to pass through these nozzles to get to the next stage.

The rotor of a turbine is made up of solid steel disks that are firmly attached to a shaft. Rotating blades are mounted around the rims of the disks. Where the shaft extends from the casing at each end, it is supported by journal bearings and a thrust bearing. The journal bearings are stationary hollow cylinders of relatively soft metal that support the weight of the rotor. A thrust bearing consists of a small disk on the shaft of the turbine that is trapped between two stationary disks supported by the casing. If the rotor tries to move forward or back along its own axis, the rotating disk presses against one of the stationary disks. Thrust and journal bearings must be lubricated by a constant flow of oil that forms a thin film between the rotating and stationary parts of the bearing and prevents them from making direct contact. Without this film of oil, the bearing would wear out in a few seconds.

A seal must be provided where the shaft of the turbine passes through the casing. At one end of the casing the steam pressure inside is high. Outside the casing the air pressure is only one atmosphere. If there were no seal, steam would rush out through the space between the casing and the shaft. At the other end of the turbine, the pressure inside may be below atmospheric. Here air would rush in if there were no seal around the shaft.

ELECTRIC POWER GENERATION

Most electric power is produced by steam turbines driving electric generators. This is true whether the source of the steam is a nuclear reactor or a boiler burning fossil fuel. The turbines in power stations are extremely large. In nuclear plants the turbines may produce as much as 1,300 megawatts of power. Power stations are often located near rivers so that water from the river can be used as cooling water in the condensers that receive steam from the large turbines.

—*Edwin G. Wiggins*

Further Reading
Avallone, Eugene A., Theodore Baumeister III, and Ali M. Sadegh. "Steam Turbines." *Marks' Standard Handbook for Mechanical Engineers*. 11th ed., McGraw-Hill, 2007.
Bloch, Heinz P. *Steam Turbines: Design, Applications, and Rerating*. 2nd ed., McGraw-Hill, 2009.
Guyer, J. Paul. *An Introduction to Steam Turbine Design*. Guyer Partners, 2017.
Peng, William W. "Steam Turbines." *Fundamentals of Turbomachinery*. J. Wiley, 2008.
Richardson, Alexander. *The Evolution of the Parsons Steam Turbine*. Cambridge UP, 2014.
Swingle, Calvin F. *Steam Turbine Engines, Their Construction, Care and Operation: Full Instructions Regarding Correct Methods of Operating Steam Turbines, Adjusting Clearances, Etc. (Classic Reprint)*. LULU Press, 2018.
Tanuma, Tadashi. *Advances in Steam Turbines for Modern Power Plants*. Woodhead Publishing, 2017.
Termuehlen, Heinz. *One Hundred Years of Power Plant Development: Focus on Steam and Gas Turbines as Prime Movers*. ASME Press, 2001.

See also: Carnot, Sadi; External combustion engine; Fluid dynamics; Heat transfer; Internal combustion engine; Steam energy technology; Steam engine; Stirling, Robert; Thermodynamics; Turbines; Work-energy theorem

STEAM ENERGY TECHNOLOGY

Fields of Study: Physics; Mechanics; Mathematics

ABSTRACT

Steam energy technology is concerned with the conversion of the chemical energy in fuels into the mechanical energy of a rotating shaft. Steam energy is used to propel ships, drive electric generators, and power pumps. Components such as boilers, turbines, pumps, heat exchangers, and piping systems are involved. Most of the electric power in the United States is generated with steam. Steam is less popular for ship propulsion than in the past, but it is still used for nuclear-powered ships and for ships that transport liquefied natural gas. In combined cycle technology, the hot exhaust gas from a gas turbine is used to produce steam that is used to provide additional mechanical energy or to heat buildings.

KEY CONCEPTS
boiler: a device that uses heat from burning fuel to produce steam
condenser: a specialized heat exchanger that uses cooling water from a river or the sea to convert steam leaving a turbine back to water
fluid mechanics: the study of the flow of liquids and gases
heat transfer: the process of transmitting heat; heat travels through a solid by conduction, is transmitted from a solid surface to a liquid or gas by convection, and is transferred by radiation, which consists of electromagnetic waves
pump: a machine that adds mechanical energy to a liquid; the increased energy is indicated by an increase in pressure
reciprocating steam engine: a machine that uses steam to push pistons up and down in a cylinder; this motion can be used to drive a pump or a ship's propeller

reduction gear: a device that converts the high rotating speed of a turbine to the much lower rotating speed of an electric generator or ship's propeller

saturated steam: steam that is just at its boiling temperature; while water boils at 212 degrees Fahrenheit at atmospheric pressure, the boiling temperature rises at higher pressures

superheated steam: steam that has been heated above its boiling temperature; steam at atmospheric pressure and a temperature above 212 degrees Fahrenheit is superheated

superheater: part of a boiler that superheats steam; steam flows inside of superheater tubes while hot combustion gases flow around the outside of these tubes; heat is transferred from the combustion gas to the steam

thermodynamics: the study of energy conversion processes

turbine: a machine that converts the energy of high-pressure, high-temperature steam into mechanical energy to drive an electric generator or ship's propeller

DEFINITION AND BASIC PRINCIPLES

Modern steam energy technology may involve the production of superheated steam at relatively high pressure and the use of that steam to drive a mechanical device. It may also involve the production of saturated steam at relatively low pressure and the use of that steam to heat buildings or industrial processes.

Most of the electric power in the United States is produced by means of high-pressure, superheated steam driving a turbine. In turn, the turbine drives the electric generator that produces electricity for use in homes, businesses, and factories. This type of steam is also used to drive turbines aboard ships, and those turbines drive the ships' propellers. Because turbines operate best at several thousand revolutions per minute, and propellers operate best at a

few hundred revolutions per minute, a speed-reducing gear is used between turbine and propeller.

Many industrial processes in the chemical industry and elsewhere require large amounts of low-pressure saturated steam to heat the materials being processed. For instance, crude oil is made to boil in a distillation column as a way of separating volatile components such as gasoline from nonvolatile ones such as tar. Large buildings in cold climates may be heated by steam produced by a boiler in the basement.

In ancient times, energy was provided by human or animal strength. Steam energy technology was one of the first technologies that humankind used to produce greater force, higher speed, and greater endurance than living things could produce.

BACKGROUND AND HISTORY

Hero of Alexandria is credited with the invention of the first steam engine in about 200 BCE, although the device does not seem to have been put to practical use. The ancient Greek inventor Archimedes may have used steam cannons that converted about one-tenth of a cup of water into steam to propel hollow clay balls out of cannons during the siege of Syracuse. Records indicate that in 1543, Spanish naval officer Blasco de Garay attempted to propel a ship with paddle wheels driven by a steam engine. In the late 1600's, groundwater needed to be pumped out of English mines, and Thomas Savery patented a steam-powered pump on July 25, 1698. By 1767, fifty-seven steam engines were in use in mines near Newcastle, England, with a combined power of about 1,200 horsepower. James Watt was granted a patent for a much-improved engine in 1769. Watt coined the word "horsepower" to explain how much power his machine could generate to a potential customer. Robert Fulton launched his Hudson River steamboat in 1807. This vessel traveled from New York City to Albany, New York, a distance of 150 miles, in thirty-two hours. On April 27, 1865, a boiler on the steamboat *Sultana* exploded as it neared Mound City, Oklahoma, killing between 2,000 and 2,300 people. The steamboat, designed for 300 passengers, was loaded with Union soldiers who had just been released from Confederate prisoner-of-war camps. The Brush Electric Light Company in Philadelphia built the first electric generating station in the United States in 1881.

Sir Charles Algernon Parsons of England is regarded as the inventor of the modern steam turbine. He first built a small turbine and used it to drive an electric generator. In 1894, he built the first steam-turbine-powered watercraft. This vessel, the *Turbinia*, achieved the astounding speed of 34.5 knots (just under 40 miles per hour). George Westinghouse acquired the American rights to Parsons's invention in 1895. During the twentieth century, applications of steam energy technology expanded rapidly, and it became the dominant source of energy around the world. Molten rock, or magma, heats rainwater to create a superheated fluid used in geothermal power plants. The geothermal superheated fluid is converted to steam by crystallizer-reactor clarifier technology.

HOW IT WORKS

Steam is produced in a boiler, where fuel is burned and the heat released is transmitted to water, which boils to form saturated steam. The fuel can be almost anything that burns. Solid fuels include peat, wood, and coal, while liquid fuels range from residual fuel, which is so thick that it must be heated to about 100 degrees Celsius to make it flow easily, to kerosene and gasoline. Natural gas is also used as boiler fuel. Heat is produced as these fuels react with oxygen in the air. Boilers may operate at pressures from slightly above atmospheric pressure to about 240 atmospheres (about 3,500 pounds per square inch). Boilers at electric generating plants may produce about 4,550 kilograms of steam per hour. There are two basic boiler types: fire tube boilers, in which hot gases produced by combustion pass

through tubes surrounded by large quantities of water, and water tube boilers, where water-filled tubes are exposed to hot combustion gases. Fire tube boilers are suitable for low-pressure boilers, and water tube boilers are used for pressures above about 20 atmospheres (300 pounds per square inch).

Superheating steam. After steam is produced, it may pass through additional tubes that are exposed on the outside to hot combustion gases. This process, which is called superheating, raises the temperature of the steam above its boiling temperature. Superheating is done to increase the energy content of the steam without changing its pressure. The steam used in turbines is usually superheated to a temperature of 950 to 1,000 degrees Fahrenheit. Special steel alloys must be used in superheater tubes so that they can endure such high temperatures.

Combustion. Liquid fuels are sprayed into a cavity in the boiler called a furnace. Fuel is mixed with air and burned. In a water tube boiler, the hot gases produced by combustion flow first over the superheater tubes and then over tubes containing liquid water, where steam is produced.

Turbines. Superheated steam leaves the boiler and flows to the steam turbine. Here the steam is directed against blades mounted on disks that are attached to the rotating shaft. The shape of the blades deflects the steam, and the steam causes the blades to move in the opposite direction. The process is similar to what happens when someone blows on a pinwheel. In a typical steam turbine, there may be twenty or more disks attached to the shaft. Each disk has many blades arrayed around its rim.

Reduction gears. Often the desirable speed of a steam turbine is much greater than the speed of the device to which it is connected. For instance, a ship's turbine may rotate at several thousand revolutions per minute, while the propeller should rotate at about one hundred revolutions per minute. A reduction gear is used to convert the high speed of the turbine shaft to the low speed of the propeller. In a reduction gear, a small gear turning at high speed meshes with a large gear that turns at lower speed. Because there is a limit to the ratio of gear sizes, it is often necessary to perform the speed reduction in two steps.

Condensers. Leaving the turbine, the steam enters a condenser. This is a specialized heat exchanger that has cooling water flowing through thousands of tubes. The cooling water may come from a river or from the sea. As the steam comes into contact with the outsides of these tubes, it condenses back to liquid water and drops to the bottom of the condenser. Condensers often operate at 12 or 13 pounds per square inch below atmospheric pressure. This pressure is determined by the cooling water temperature. The lower the condenser pressure, the more energy the turbine is able to extract from the steam.

Pumping and air removal. Once the steam has been condensed, a series of pumps transfers the water back to the boiler where the process begins again. These pumps may be driven by electric motors or by small steam turbines. Because the condenser operates below atmospheric pressure, small amounts of air may leak into the water. Most of this air is removed by a vacuum pump, but some of the leaking air may dissolve in the condensing steam. This air is removed either by chemicals or by heating the water to its boiling point without boiling it after a pump has raised its pressure above atmospheric pressure.

Reciprocating engines. Early steam engines had pistons that moved up and down much as the pistons in an automobile engine do. These engines are known as reciprocating engines. The famous Liberty ships of World War II were powered by reciprocating engines. Turbines are much more efficient than reciprocating engines, so relatively few reciprocating engines remain in use.

APPLICATIONS AND PRODUCTS

Electric power generation. Most of the electricity used in the United States is generated in steam plants, powered by coal, oil-based fuels, natural gas, and nuclear power. Regardless of the type of fuel, these plants tend to be very large. In 2008, the United States had 29 coal-fired plants with capacities of more than 2,000 megawatts. In 2005, there were a total of 605 coal-fired plants in the United States with a combined generating capacity of 336,000 megawatts. In 2004, these plants produced more than 2 billion tons of carbon dioxide, about 8 percent of the world's total. In 2005, the states of Texas, Ohio, Indiana, and Pennsylvania had coal-fired generating capacities of more than 20,000 megawatts each, while Rhode Island and Vermont had no coal-fired plants.

In 2008, the United States had an oil-fired generating capacity of more than 57,000 megawatts, a natural-gas-fired generating capacity of almost 400,000 megawatts, and a nuclear generating capacity of just over 100,000 megawatts. All coal-fired plants and almost all nuclear plants use steam engineering technology. Most oil-fired plants and natural gas plants also use this technology.

A relatively new technology for electric power generation is a combined cycle plant. These use gas turbines driving electric generators for the majority of their power production. However, gas turbines alone have relatively low efficiencies (about 35 percent), because the exhaust gas contains a lot of unused heat energy. In a combined cycle plant, this hot exhaust gas is used to produce steam, and the steam drives a turbine that powers another electric generator. The efficiency of combined cycle plants is very attractive (50 percent or more).

Ship propulsion. For most of the twentieth century, steam was the dominant source of energy for ship propulsion. Early in the century, reciprocating engines were used, but turbine engines soon took over. The famous liner SS *United States* had four turbine engines producing a total of about 250,000 horsepower. This ship set and held the transatlantic speed record for nearly fifty years. In 1970, most of the ships in the US Navy were steam powered, and the world's merchant fleet was also primarily steam. Later, diesel and gas turbine propulsion became more popular than steam, but even in the early twenty-first century, most of the ships being built to carry liquefied natural gas to Europe and the United States were steam powered.

On ships propelled by steam, the electric generators are also driven by steam turbines. Some of the pumps on these ships are driven by small steam turbines, and steam is used as a heat source for boiling seawater to produce freshwater for human use and for replenishing the water in the steam system.

All nuclear-powered ships are powered by steam turbines. The nuclear reactor produces very hot water. This water exchanges heat with water at lower pressure in a steam generator, and the lower-pressure water turns to steam. This steam is then used to drive a turbine.

Proposals for the propulsion of liquefied natural gas ships have called for combined cycle systems much like those used for electric power generation. Such systems are much more efficient than conventional steam systems.

Nuclear power. Nuclear power is used extensively for electric power production, with more than 400 plants worldwide producing about 17 percent of the world's electricity. In France, about 75 percent of the electricity comes from nuclear plants. In 2008, about 104 nuclear power plants were operating in the United States. These plants produce nearly 20 percent of the country's electric energy. Because nuclear plants produce no carbon dioxide and no other airborne pollutants, the United States and other nations are looking to nuclear power to fulfill their future electric needs. There are several different types of nuclear power plants, but nearly all of them make use of steam energy technology. In these plants, the nuclear reactor replaces the boiler furnace as a heat source. Most of the rest of the plant closely resembles a conventional steam plant. Unlike conventional plants, nuclear plants use saturated steam rather than superheated steam because it is not feasible to superheat steam by means of a nuclear reactor.

Industrial processes. Many industrial processes, such as oil refineries, steel mills, chemical plants, and paper mills, require steam. In oil refineries, steam is used to heat various liquids and is also used in the cracking process that breaks large molecules into smaller ones. A byproduct of the cracking process is carbon monoxide. The blast furnace in a steel mill also produces large amounts of carbon monoxide. The carbon monoxide produced is used as fuel in a boiler to create steam. A paper mill uses roughly 10,000 pounds of steam per ton of paper produced. Much of this steam is generated using waste products such as tree bark as fuel. In the chemical industry, steam is used in the making of ethylene and the plastic styrene. It is also used to heat chemicals that would turn solid in their tanks at room temperature.

Steam heating. Consolidated Edison of New York (Con Edison), New York City's electric power utility, sells steam through 105 miles of pipes that run under Manhattan streets. At three of its electric generating plants, steam leaves the turbines at 195 degrees Celsius and at a pressure of about 8 times higher than atmospheric pressure. Instead of being condensed in the plant, steam flows through large pipes throughout Manhattan. About 100,000 buildings, including the United Nations building, Rockefeller Center, and the Metropolitan Museum of Art buy this steam and use it for heating. Altogether, Con Edison sells about 30 billion pounds of steam for heating each year. A church in lower Manhattan became one of the first steam customers in 1882, and it has been buying steam ever since. Other cities in the United States and Europe have similar systems, but New York's system is the largest.

IMPACT ON INDUSTRY

The components that make up a steam energy system—including boilers, turbines, reduction gears, pumps, and heat exchangers—are produced by large industrial corporations. Major boiler manufacturers include Babcock & Wilcox, Foster Wheeler, and Combustion Engineering. Steam turbines are manufactured by General Electric and Westinghouse, among others. Large reduction gears are a very specialized product with relatively few manufacturers. General Electric is one of the major sources.

On land, power plants are usually designed by architecture and engineering companies. KBR (Kellogg, Brown & Root), a company that resulted from the merger of Brown and Root with M. W. Kellogg, is a major company in this field. Fluor Corporation and Stone & Webster, part of the Shaw Group, are also large architecture and engineering companies. These companies perform design services and manage and supervise the construction of plants. Once built, the power plants are operated by electric utility companies such as Con Edison.

Ships are designed by naval architecture and marine engineering companies such as Gibbs & Cox, Alion, and Herbert Engineering. The final product of these companies is a set of drawings and specifications. The shipowner uses these to obtain bids from various shipyards. As the ship is built, the steam machinery is installed, and the shipyard runs the piping that connects everything together.

In the late 1800s, many boilers were poorly designed and constructed. Boiler explosions were common, and many people were killed every year in these explosions. The American Society of Mechanical Engineers (ASME) was originally founded to correct this problem by developing standards for safe boiler design and construction. This organization does not have legal authority to require boilers to be designed to its standards, but many government agencies that do have such authority have specified that boilers must comply with the ASME code. Insurance companies usually require ASME approval before writing insurance on a boiler. The US Coast Guard publishes rules regarding ships, and these rules invoke the ASME code. Individual state governments issue rules for boilers that operate within their jurisdictions, and these state rules also invoke the ASME code. Organizations called classification societies serve as arms of the ship insurance business. Their job is to verify that each insured ship is designed, built, and maintained in such a way that it represents a reasonable insurance risk. These organizations have rules that govern the design, construction, and maintenance of machinery on merchant ships, and these rules draw heavily on the ASME code.

CAREERS

Electric power plants are designed by architecture and engineering companies. Many of the people involved in designing the plants are mechanical engineers with either bachelor's or master's degrees in mechanical engineering. Students in mechanical engineering study advanced mathematics, thermodynamics, fluid mechanics, heat transfer, machine design, and other technical subjects. The design process also requires people with expertise in civil engineering and electrical engineering. The actual equipment—the boilers, turbines, pumps, and so on—are designed by companies that specialize in particular components, while the designers at architecture and engineering firms design the systems that connect these components and make them work together.

The people who manage these plants are usually employees of large public utilities that own the plants. They often have mechanical engineering degrees. In addition to an engineering degree, a manager may have a business degree. A college degree is not required for the people who actually operate and maintain these plants.

Designers of shipboard steam energy systems may have degrees in mechanical engineering or marine engineering. These two fields are closely related. The designers are typically employed by firms specializing in naval architecture and marine engineering.

Operating personnel on US Navy ships are, of course, naval officers and enlisted personnel. Officers on merchant ships must be licensed by the US Coast Guard as operating marine engineers. Many of the officers in the US Merchant Marine are graduates of state maritime academies or the US Merchant Marine Academy, but a college degree is not required to obtain a license. Some people obtain the knowledge required for a license by experience and specialized training. They gain this experience by serving in unlicensed positions such as oilers or qualified members of the engineering department on merchant ships.

SOCIAL CONTEXT AND FUTURE PROSPECTS

The demand for electricity continues to grow around the world. At the start of the twenty-first century, China's economy was growing very rapidly, and China's demand for electricity grows along with its economy. The United States has large reserves of coal. Increased use of this coal could reduce its dependence on foreign oil, but coal produces more emissions than any other fuel. In particular, coal produces large amounts of carbon dioxide. Research is ongoing on ways to recapture this carbon dioxide and prevent it from contributing to global warming. If this research is successful, there may be growth in the use of coal.

Supplies of oil and natural gas are finite, and renewable fuels are being sought. A significant advantage of steam energy technology is that boilers can burn all manner of fuels: solid, liquid, and gas. Increased use of solid fuels produced from agriculture may also cause growth in steam engineering technology. Because the combustion of fuels produces carbon dioxide, a major greenhouse gas, efforts are being made to reduce fuel usage. Wind and water power have a role here, but nuclear power, which produces no airborne emissions, appears poised for major growth. Since nearly all nuclear plants use steam, growth in nuclear power may cause growth in use of steam energy technology.

—*Edwin G. Wiggins*

Further Reading

Bloch, Heinz P., and Murari P. Singh. *Steam Turbines: Design, Applications, and Rerating*. 2nd ed., McGraw-Hill, 2009.

Eriksen, Vernon L. *Heat Recovery Steam Generator Technology*. Woodhead Publishing, 2017.

Gardner, Raymond, et al. *Introduction to Practical Marine Engineering*. Society of Naval Architects and Marine Engineers, 2002.

Kehlhofer, Rolf, et al. *Combined-Cycle Gas and Steam Turbine Power Plants*. 3rd ed., Penn Well, 2009.

Khartchenko, Nikolai V., and Vadym M. Kharchenko. *Advanced Energy Systems*. 2nd ed., CRC Press, 2013.

Woodruff, Everett B., Herbert B. Lammers, and Thomas F. Lammers. *Steam Plant Operation*. 10th ed., McGraw Hill Professional, 2016.

Yang, Zongming, Huabing Wen, Xinglin Yang, Viktor Gorbov, Vira Mitienkova, and Serhiy Serbin. *Marine Power Plant*. Springer Nature, 2021.

Yu, Junchong. *Marine Nuclear Power Technology*. Springer Nature, 2020.

Zabihian, Farshid. *Power Plant Engineering*. CRC Press, 2021.

See also: Archimedes; Atoms; Conservation of energy; Discoveries of Archimedes; Fluid dynamics; Heat transfer; Steam and steam turbines; Stirling, Robert; Thermodynamics; Turbines; Work and energy

STEAM ENGINE

Fields of Study: Physics; Engineering; Mechanics; Mathematics

ABSTRACT

A steam boiler converts the chemical energy in fuel into the thermal energy of steam. A steam engine converts this thermal energy into the mechanical energy of a rotating shaft.

This shaft can drive an electric generator, pump, or other machines.

KEY CONCEPTS

piston: a movable device contained within a cylinder such that its vertical movement can be used either to compress a gas within the cylinder or be depressed by expanding gases within the cylinder

BACKGROUND

The chemical energy that is contained within wood and fossil fuels such as oil and coal can be converted into thermal energy (heat) by burning the fuel. This thermal energy can be used to create steam in a boiler. A steam engine converts the thermal energy of steam into the mechanical energy of a rotating shaft, and this shaft can drive a pump, a ventilating fan, a ship's propeller, and many other devices.

HISTORY

Although there were attempts to use steam to drive mechanical devices as early as 60 CE by Hero of Alexandria, the first real steam engine was designed and built by Thomas Newcomen in 1712. That year Newcomen successfully used a steam engine to pump water from a coal mine near Dudley Castle, England. In 1765, as he walked across Glasgow Green in the city of Glasgow, Scotland, James Watt conceived the idea of connecting the steam engine to a separate condenser. The first full-size engines based on this concept were built in 1776: one at John Wilkinson's blast furnace near Broseley, England, and the other at Bloomfield coal mine near Tipton, England. Newcomen's design and Watt's early designs used steam at constant pressure. Over the course of his life, Watt invented many improvements to the steam engine, including rotary engines,

Union Pacific 844, a "FEF-3" 4-8-4 "Northern" type steam locomotive. Photo by Drew Jacksich, via Wikimedia Commons.

a device for measuring engine performance, and engines in which the steam expanded during the piston stroke. Expanding steam engines soon drove the earlier type off the market, because the fuel consumption associated with the boiler of an expanding steam engine is far less than that of a constant pressure engine. While modern steam engines operate at much higher pressure than Watt's, they are similar in design.

PRINCIPLES OF OPERATION

Early steam engines would be considered upside-down by modern standards. The piston was connected to a rod that emerged from the top of the engine, and steam was fed into the cylinder below the piston. A chain connected the piston rod to one end of a pivoted beam suspended above the engine, and the other end of the beam was connected to a pump that drew water up from the bottom of a mine. The weight of the pump rod was sufficient to pull the pump end of the pivoted beam downward, which caused the other end of the beam to rise and lift the piston upward. As the piston rose, steam at just above atmospheric pressure flowed from the boiler into the growing space below the piston. When the piston reached the top of its stroke, the valve between boiler and cylinder closed, and in Newcomen's engine water was sprayed into the cylinder. As the water absorbed heat from the steam, the steam condensed, which created a partial vacuum. This vacuum, combined with atmospheric pressure acting on the upper side of the piston, caused the piston to move downward. When the piston reached the bottom of its stroke, the steam valve opened again. The steam pressure balanced the atmospheric pressure on the other side of the piston, and the weight of the pump rod again raised the piston to the top of its stroke.

Watt recognized that spraying cold water directly into the cylinder not only condensed the steam but also cooled off the cylinder itself. On the next stroke some incoming steam was wasted in reheating the cylinder. The separate condenser in Watt's engine condensed the steam without chilling the cylinder. This resulted in a dramatic improvement in fuel consumption. Watt also closed off the upper side of the piston and provided a hole just big enough for the piston rod to pass out. Constant-pressure steam was admitted to the space above the piston, and this steam provided the pressure previously supplied by the atmosphere. Watt's original purpose here was to eliminate the cooling effect of the atmosphere, but he soon realized that there was another benefit. Instead of continuing to admit steam at constant pressure during the entire downward stroke, the steam valve could be closed and the steam could be allowed to expand. This further reduced fuel consumption and paved the way for modern expansion steam engines.

APPLICATIONS OF THE STEAM ENGINE

The first applications were to drive dewatering pumps in mines and to supply pressurized air for blast furnaces that produced cast iron. It was soon realized that rotary steam engines could be used to drive all kinds of machinery. Without the invention of the steam engine, the Industrial Revolution would not have occurred in the time and place that it did. Steam engines drove spinning and weaving machines in the textile industry. Ships and railroad locomotives powered by steam engines revolutionized transportation. There were steam-powered farm tractors, automobiles, and construction machines. Early electric generators were also driven by steam engines. Many of these applications are now powered by electric motors, gasoline and diesel engines, and steam turbines, but it was the steam engine that showed the way.

—*Edwin G. Wiggins*

Further Reading

Bray, Stan. *Making Simple Model Steam Engines*. Crowood, 2005.

Brown, Jonathan. *Steam on the Farm: A History of Agricultural Steam Engines 1800-1950*. Crowood Press, 2008.

Crump, Thomas. *A Brief History of the Age of Steam: The Power That Drove the Industrial Revolution*. Carroll & Graf, 2007.

Hayes, G. *Stationary Steam Engines*. Bloomsbury USA, 2011.

International Correspondence Schools. *Steam Engine Design and Mechanism*. Merchant Books, 2008.

Withuhn, William. *American Steam Locomotives: Design and Development*. Indiana UP, 2019.

See also: Calculating system efficiency; Diesel engine; External combustion engine; Flywheels; Heat transfer; Hydrodynamics; Internal combustion engine; Mechanical engineering; Steam and steam turbines; Steam energy and technology; Turbines

STIRLING, ROBERT

Fields of Study: Physics; Mechanics; Mathematics

ABSTRACT

A Church of Scotland minister, Stirling invented the Stirling hot-air engine, which he and his brother, civil engineer James Stirling, refined throughout their lives. Although never widely adopted, the Stirling engine is based on remarkable thermodynamic principles that promise great efficiency and energy conservation.

KEY CONCEPTS

boiler: a device that uses heat from burning fuel to produce steam

closed system: one in which the working fluid (steam) is condensed back to liquid water and returned for reuse rather than being vented away

compressible fluids: fluids that can change volume by the application of external pressure, particularly gases

heat engine: a device that converts the energy of heat into mechanical energy or motion

heat exchanger: a structure that separates a heat source from a working fluid but allows heat to transfer from one to the other

open system: one in which the working fluid is not recaptured for reuse and must be replenished in order to maintain operation of the system; the opposite of a closed system

EARLY LIFE

Robert Stirling was born in 1790 at Cloag Farm in the parish of Methven, Perthshire, in central Scotland. His father, Patrick Stirling, was a farmer. His mother was Agnis Stirling. The couple had eight children. Robert's grandfather, Michael Stirling, had invented a threshing machine in 1758. Robert at-

Robert Stirling. Photo via Wikimedia Commons. [Public domain.]

tended Edinburgh University from 1805 to 1808, studying a wide range of classical subjects. In November, 1809, he enrolled as a divinity student at Glasgow University. On November 15, 1814, he returned to Edinburgh to continue his divinity studies. The following year, he was licensed as a minister in the Presbyterian Established Church of Scotland. On September 19, 1816, he was ordained as a minister in second charge of the Laigh Kirk parish in the prosperous town of Kilmarnock.

On July 10, Stirling married Jane Rankin, daughter of the local wine merchant. Their first child, Patrick, was born on June 29, 1820. Patrick would become an inventor and engineer in his own right. Robert and Jane would go on to have four additional sons (three of whom became engineers, and one of whom became a minister) and two daughters.

LIFE'S WORK

Stirling came from a line of industrious farmers who diligently worked to improve their mechanical implements. Stirling apparently showed mechanical aptitude from youth and was carrying out practical experiments while studying for the ministry. On September 27, 1816, only eight days after his ordination, Stirling applied for his first patent, for a fuel-efficient air engine. This was the first version of what would become the famous Stirling hot-air engine. Stirling was motivated to develop it both to save fuel and to design a safe alternative to boiler engines, which were prone to explosions. It is also possible that he was inspired by the investigations into the transmission of heat by Edinburgh professor of mathematics John Leslie. (It is unclear how much Stirling knew of earlier proposals to obtain power from heated air such as the 1794 heated-air engine of Thomas Mead and the 1807 open-cycle engine of George Cayley.)

Stirling's engine represented an improved method of storing and exchanging heat. It essentially worked by the alternative expansion and contraction of enclosed air acting upon a piston. To emphasize its fuel efficiency, Stirling called the central component of his engine the "economiser," although it would soon take the name of a "regenerator." It was the economiser that stored and released heat as the air circulated. With the promising start of his engine design, Stirling was able to acquire laboratory facilities from Thomas Morton, an inventor and the town industrialist. It would be a very productive partnership. In his Morton workshop, Stirling built numerous optical and scientific instruments, including the object glass of telescopes, which he ingeniously constructed from the bottoms of tumbler glasses. In 1818, he constructed an engine based on his economiser design to pump water from a stone quarry. The engine worked well, generating about two horsepower, until the air vessel became overheated and was crushed by the pressure of the heated air. Morton and Stirling later founded a free school in Kilmarnock to educate orphans and neglected children.

In 1823, Stirling took up a post as minister of the Galston parish. Although Stirling was involved in a dispute over the power of the established Church of Scotland over the local presbytery, his work on improving his engine designs continued unabated. In 1824, Robert and his brother James, a mechanical engineer, tried to improve the efficiency of the economiser with the use of high-pressure air by using metal sheets to subdivide the air into multiple layers. They received a patent for this improved engine in 1827. Although the patent application listed four improvements to Robert's original design, the new hot-air engine was not a success. James built an engine at the local ironworks, but it failed to produce the more efficient use of heat that was expected.

In 1840, Robert Stirling received an honorary doctorate in divinity degree from the University of St. Andrews for his erudition in classical languages and devoted ministry. In that same year, the brothers received another patent, for a new version of their engine. The patent application again listed four improvements, including forming materials into rods, employing these rods for receiving and imparting heat, passing the air through extensive systems of surfaces, and applying cupped leathered collars around the piston rods. James Stirling built two new engines based on these improvements for the iron foundry he managed in Dundee. These engines operated on coal and proved more successful, one running continuously for a period of two years and nine months until an air vessel failed. The new engines were able to generate about forty-five horsepower. However, the cylinders were prone to burn out quickly, a problem the Stirling brothers never solved. Robert blamed the failure of the engines on the imperfections of the materials used in their construction, an unlikely explanation. He continued to express hope that his engine would become the mainstay in production of the new Bessemer iron.

STIRLING'S ENGINE

In simplest terms, Robert Stirling invented an engine that heats air to obtain power. The Stirling hot-air engine is a closed-cycle, external combustion engine. In other words, the working fuel is designed to stay within the engine. Although Stirling originally named the innovative design of his engine the "economiser" to emphasize its fuel economy, it soon came to be called a "regenerator" because it uses an internal heat exchanger to increase the engine's thermal efficiency. With this heat exchange, the engine can reuse heat that would otherwise be dissipated. Because it operates under low pressure, the hot-air engine does not cause steam burns and is unlikely to explode. Stirling hoped that his hot-air engine would be adopted by iron foundries, making the smelting process safer and cheaper. However, it never proved fully satisfactory for either iron or steel production.

Stirling's engine combines numerous parts in its operation. The heater burns fuel in an external combustion chamber. Almost any fuel source can be used. Because the fuel is burned continuously, the Stirling engine tends to operate smoothly. The heater is connected to a gas-filled cylinder. Two opposing pistons compress the gas as it is heated and push the gas through the engine's heat exchanger and cooler. The cycle is then started again as the gas enters the heater. The heat exchanger stores the thermal energy emitted as the gas is compressed. The energy is then recaptured by the system, as explained by Nicolas Léonard Sadi Carnot's thermodynamic theory.

As Robert and James Stirling had mixed results with the engine, it never achieved wide popularity. Steam engines, greatly improved by the 1850's, continued to power England's industrial revolution. Nevertheless, Stirling engines continued to be manufactured until the 1920's. After a period of nonuse, industrial interest in the Stirling engine was revived around World War II. Companies such as Dutch NV Philips experimented with a Stirling engine to generate radio power, and Ford Motor Company sought to use the engine in a fuel-efficient automobile. The Stirling engine's theoretical promise of almost complete efficiency without pollution continues to intrigue engineers. Even now, it is being proposed for hybrid-electric drive automobiles. However, the use of the Stirling engine remains to this day quite limited, confined mostly to specialized engines, cryogenic refrigerators, heat pumps, and small generators.

James Thomson, the brother of Lord Kelvin, claimed that Robert Stirling did not fully understand the principles of his own engine. Nevertheless, the regenerative principles demonstrated in Stirling's engine were successfully used by the inventor John Ericsson in his 1833 patented caloric engine; by Julius Jeffreys in his patented 1836 medical respirator; by industrialist brothers William and Frederick

Siemens in their 1856 patented regenerative steam engine, condenser, and furnaces; by Edward Cooper in his 1857 patented hot-blast furnaces; and by F. T. Botta and G. B. Normand in their 1855 and 1856 patented chimney regenerators for use in marine boilers. For the remainder of their lives, Robert and James Stirling took out no new patents on the hot-air engine and apparently worked on it only sporadically. In 1878, after fifty- five years as minister of the Galston parish and continual refining of his hot-air engine, Stirling died on June 6.

IMPACT

Robert Stirling lived the life of a distinguished country parson, becoming learned in biblical languages, arranging for charitable enterprises, succoring townspeople during a cholera epidemic, and pastoring his Church of Scotland flocks in the parishes of Laigh Kirk and Galston. During this life of religious duty, he and his brother James were working ambitiously on perfecting the design of the hot-air engine that had come to Robert as a youth.

Robert Stirling's idea for a hot-air engine had to some extent a charitable origin. He wanted to design an engine less susceptible to dangerous accidental explosions than the steam engine. With his mechanical mind, he focused on a design that centered on the efficient exchange of heat. How much of this design flowed from his understanding of thermodynamics is not certain, but the Stirling engine would in fact take advantage of scientific principles that were explained by the scientist Nicolas Léonard Sadi Carnot, who introduced the theory of the thermodynamic cycle. On April 21, 1847, William Thomson, better known as Lord Kelvin, the famed scientist who helped develop the laws of thermodynamics, delivered his first address to the Glasgow Philosophical Society on the subject of "Stirling's Air Engine." Thomson would also use the Stirling engine for demonstration purposes in his lectures at Edinburgh University.

The Stirling engine has intrigued engineers ever since, because of its theoretical possibilities for enormous efficiency and suggestion of a perpetual motion machine. However, no working Stirling engine has yet to come close to achieving this ideal. Although its use in industry remains limited, there are numerous researchers and Stirling engine societies convinced that its fundamental principles will one day provide a great breakthrough in the ability to generate clean, safe, and self-perpetuating power. Ingenious uses of these principles have been made over the last century. An engineer from Tyneside, England, John Malone, followed the Stirling model to invent a heat engine that used liquid at the critical point. Engineers at the Los Alamos National Laboratory have been experimenting with a Stirling engine that is powered by sound waves, and engineers from the National Aeronautics and Space Administration (NASA) have studied the use of Stirling engines with solar energy. Thus far, however, the Stirling hot-air engine remains more promise than reality.

—Howard Bromberg

Further Reading

Darlington, Ray, and Keith Strong. *Stirling and Hot-Air Engines.* Crowood Press, 2005.

Hills, Phillip. *The Star Drive: The True Story of a Genius, an Engine and Our Future.* Birlinn Limited, 2021.

Organ, Allan. *The Air Engine: Stirling Cycle Power for a Sustainable Future.* CRC Press, 2007.

Organ, Allan J. *Stirling Cycle Engines: Inner Workings and Design.* John Wiley & Sons, 2013.

Rizzo, James G. *Robert Stirling's Models of the "Air Engine."* Camden Miniature Steam Services, 2009.

Sier, Robert. *Hot Air Caloric and Stirling Engines.* L. A. Mair, 2000.

Sier, Robert. *John Fox Jennens Malone: The Liquid Stirling Engine.* L. A. Mair, 2008.

———. *Rev. Robert Stirling D.D.: A Biography of the Inventor of the Heat Economiser and Stirling Cycle Engine.* L. A. Mair, 1995.

Vineeth C. S. *Stirling Engines: A Beginners Guide.* Vineeth C. S., 2011.

See also: External combustion engine; Fluid dynamics; Heat transfer; Steam engine; Steam energy technology; Thermodynamics; Work-energy theorem

STRUCTURAL ENGINEERING

Fields of Study: Physics; Mechanics; Mathematics

ABSTRACT

Structural engineering is a science in which people work to design and construct buildings and structures that are strong, sturdy, safe, and long-lasting. Structural engineers must use knowledge from several different disciplines, such as physics and math, to do their job. To plan and build, structural engineers work with other engineers, architects, surveyors, and general contractors.

KEY CONCEPTS

architect: a structural engineering specialist who designs the inner and outer appearance of a building that is to be built

earthquake engineer:. a structural engineer who specializes in the design and construction of buildings to withstand the shocks and vibrations of earthquakes

transportation engineer: a structural engineer who specializes in the design and construction of roads, streets. and highways

water system engineer: a structural engineer who specializes in the design and construction of infrastructure for the delivery of freshwater, the removal of wastewater, and the redirection or control of water flows

ENGINEERING STRUCTURES

Structural engineering is a science in which people work to design and construct buildings and structures that are strong, sturdy, safe, and long-lasting. Structural engineers have to use knowledge from several different disciplines, such as physics and math, to do their job. To plan and build, structural engineers work with other engineers, architects, surveyors, and general contractors. They help design and build homes, office buildings, bridges, automobiles, and airplanes; however, engineers are often specialized to help ensure that they have the required knowledge for their projects. Because of this, structural engineers play a unique role in designing and building, and their job differs from that of an architect.

BACKGROUND

Structural engineering is a branch of civil engineering. Civil engineering deals with the built environment, or anything that people build or use as structures. Civil engineering is the oldest engineering discipline, as it encompasses any building that humans have carried out to create structures of their own. Although modern civil engineers use detailed mathematics and science, humans have been using their understanding of the world and its forces to build structures for countless years. Civil engineering has numerous disciplines. Transportation engineering is a branch of civil engineering that is responsible for designing safe and effective transportation systems. Water system engineering is a branch that deals with developing water systems that bring clean water to residents and dispose of wastewater. Material engineering focuses on developing the best possible materials to create the built environment. For example, material engineers could help develop the best possible concrete mixture for a particular structure. Earthquake engineering focuses on developing buildings and structures that stand up best to seismic activity. Structural engineering deals with creating structures that will stand up to outside forces and remain safe. The different branches of civil engineering overlap, and engineers from different disciplines work together to create a built environment that is safe and effective for humans.

OVERVIEW

Structural engineering is concerned with many of the same aspects as civil engineering but focuses mainly on creating structures that will withstand outside forces and function properly and safely. Structural engineering is a field that relies on the knowledge of many other fields. Civil engineering, in general, relies heavily on physics. Engineers must understand the laws of physics to be able to design structures that will remain safe and useful over time. They also have to use other types of mathematics, such as geometry, when designing structures. Structural engineers have to complete many equations while creating designs to ensure that structures will stay in place. Structural engineers also have to memorize and understand local and national building codes, which the engineers have to incorporate into their designs. Structural engineers should also have good communication skills. These engineers have to work with large teams and must fully understand what a client expects and wants from a building. Having good communication skills helps structural engineers meet expectations and complete the best possible products.

A structural engineer who is working on a project is just one member of a larger team. Modern building projects often include multiple structural engineers along with architects and general contractors. Structural engineers have different roles to play in the development, planning, and building of a structure. Often, structural engineers have specific titles reflecting the role they play. For example, a structural engineer of record oversees and manages the design of a structure to ensure that it will meet the requirements for the load-carrying structural system. This means that the engineer makes sure that the structure's overall design will be strong enough to withstand forces such as the structure's own weight, the weight of occupants or materials inside the structure, and forces from weather or seismic activity. Structural engineers have to determine the types of

forces that are most likely to affect a building and make decisions about its design to help it remain as strong as possible in the conditions it will most likely face. For example, those designing bridges in California must consider the strong seismic activity that bridges in that area could face. Structural engineers in New York may be able to focus less on seismic activity but must consider how the freezing and thawing of ice and water will affect bridges in that area.

Although structural engineers and architects both help plan structures, they have different jobs. The architect is often the main designer of a structure. He or she is concerned with the many elements of the structure such as ensuring that it is aesthetically pleasing and easy to use. The structural engineer does not think about the final appearance of the building as much as the way it will react to outside forces and continued use. Both the architect and the structural engineer want to create a well-liked, useful, safe structure, but the structural engineer has a narrower focus on the bones of the structure.

On larger construction projects, the structural engineer of record is the head structural engineer on the design team. This engineer may oversee a team of other structural engineers. A large project may have numerous structural engineers who develop plans, each one focusing on a specific part of the design. Each engineer will complete the calculations required to determine the best possible design for the various elements of the structure. The structural engineer of record reviews these designs and ensures that all the various elements work together to create a cohesive, sound structure.

The engineers working with the structural engineer of record are often called specialty structural engineers and each may work with a team to design specific elements of a structure such as the windows, columns, or roof. Specialty structural engineers might also collaborate with the construction teams that are working on the project. Specialty structural engineers have specific training in certain areas or specialties regarding a structure or its parts. This specialization helps these engineers create safer, well-designed structures. The specialty engineers often have to communicate with the structural engineers of record to ensure that all the pieces are working together and the overall design of the structure is sound. In the end, the structural engineer of record generally has the final say about a structure's design.

Structural engineers help plan all the different elements of structures. They are involved from the beginning of a project and help decide the type of construction that will take place. Structural engineers must fully understand the building code for a specific area and the International Building Code (IBC) to ensure that the structure meets all legal requirements and is structurally sound. When choosing the type of construction, the engineer will have to decide the size, scale, and design of a building. He or she will also have to either help choose a location for a building or create plans that work with a predetermined location. Structural engineers also help design specific elements of structures. For example, a structural engineer working on a building will decide where the columns, which hold up the building, should be placed and how large they should be. The engineer would also help decide the location of the walls. The forces on a building have to be distributed in a specific way to ensure that the building remains strong. A structural engineer also helps determine the distance between the floor and ceiling, the location of windows and doors, the framing for stairs and elevators, and other elements.

Structural engineers play an important role in the design and construction of a building but also work on renovating and repairing buildings. They may help design building renovations, such as constructing additional floors on an office building. Structural engineers also play an important role when a structure or building is damaged by a fire, flood, earthquake, or corrosion. They may inspect the structure and determine whether it is sound and safe. If the structure is unsafe, a structural engineer may suggest demolishing it or developing a plan to repair it.

—*Elizabeth Mohn*

Further Reading

Connor, Jerome J., and Susan Faraji. *Fundamentals of Structural Engineering*. Springer International Publishing, 2016.

El-Mogy, Mostafa "What Is Structural Engineering?" *Structural Engineer Basics*, 2019, structuralengineeringbasics.com/what-is-structural-engineering/. Accessed 20 Jan. 2020.

"Engineering Basics." *American Institute of Steel Construction*, www.aisc.org/why-steel/architect/guide-for-architects/engineering-basics/. Accessed 20 Jan. 2020.

Kelly, Wyatt. *Structural Engineering*. Larsen and Keller Education, 2019.

Mahamid, Mustafa, Edwin H. Gaylord. and Charles N. Gaylord. *Structural Engineering Handbook*. 5th ed., McGraw Hill Professionsl, 2020.

"The Role of the Specialty Structural Engineer." *Build Steel*, www.buildsteel.org/framing-products/structural/the-role-of-the-specialty-structural-engineer/. Accessed 20 Jan. 2020.

Schmidt, Jon A. "Structural Engineering." *Whole Building Design Guide*, 3 Nov. 2016, www.wbdg.org/design-disciplines/structural-engineering. Accessed 20 Jan. 2020.

"Structural Engineer of Record (SER)." *Schneider Structural Engineering*, 2020, cjseng.com/SSE/structural-engineer-of-record-ser.html. Accessed 20 Jan. 2020.

"What Do Structural Engineers Do?" *Schaefer*, 2017, schaefer-inc.com/what-do-structural-engineers-do. Accessed 20 Jan. 2020.

"What Is Civil Engineering?" *Columbia University in the City of New York*, civil.columbia.edu/about/what-civil-engineering. Accessed 20 Jan. 2020.

"What Is a Structural Engineer?" *Structural Engineers Association of California*, www.seaoc.org/page/whatisase. Accessed 20 Jan. 2020.

See also: Aerodynamics; Civil engineering; Earthquake engineering; Engineering; Force; Hydraulic engineering; Load; Materials science; Mechanical engineering; Rigid-body dynamics; Transportation

SUPERCONDUCTOR

Fields of Study: Physics; Mechanics; Mathematics

ABSTRACT

Superconductors have been known since 1911, but it is only recently that the property has been found to exist at temperatures up to 158°C (316°F). Superconducting materials have no electrical resistance, and an electrical current initiated in a superconducting circuit will flow indefinitely. Application of a critical magnetic field at a temperature below a superconductor's critical temperature will cause the material to exhibit normal conductivity rather than superconductivity. Superconductor technology has great potential for rapid transportation, energy transmission, and electromagnetic field generation.

KEY CONCEPTS

conductor: a material that has a low resistance to electric charges, allowing them to move through it easily

continuity: a clear path for electricity from point A to point B

current: the rate at which an electric charge, usually in the form of electrons, moves through a wire or other conductive material

eigensystem: the set of all eigenvectors of a matrix paired with their respective eigenvalues

electron: a negatively charged subatomic particle that is often bound to the positive charge of the nucleus but can also exist in a free state in an atom

quantum state: the condition of a physical system as defined by its associated quantum attributes

standard temperature and pressure (STP): standard reference conditions when dealing with gases, defined by the International Union of Pure and Applied Chemistry as a temperature of 273.15 kelvins (0 degrees Celsius or 32 degrees Fahrenheit) and pressure of 101.3 kilopascals (1 atmosphere); used in chemistry and physics to establish a standardized set of conditions for experimentation

wave function: a function that describes the quantum state of a system and represents the probability of finding the system in a given state at a given time

CONDUCTORS AND NONCONDUCTORS

The term *conductor* refers to the ability of a material to facilitate the transport of some property from one point to another. The medium of transport is matter in one form or another; matter can conduct heat, sound, and electrical current, primarily. An electrical current exists when electrons flow through a conductor from a point of higher electrical potential to a point of lower electrical potential. All conductors have a characteristic resistance to the flow of electrons through them. This typically results in the generation of heat, and more than one fire has been started by electrical conductors that have become overheated as the result of carrying more current than is safe.

Nonconductors, as the name suggests, do not conduct electrical current well, if they conduct it at all, and are generally referred to as insulators. Electrical components called resistors lie somewhere in between these two designations, because they are designed to carry an electrical current while providing a specific resistance to the flow of electrons.

A superconductor is a material that will conduct electrical current with absolutely no resistance to the flow of electrons through it. Metals are the most widely known conductors, having relatively low resistance to current flow. Recently, research has also identified several polymeric plastic materials that can carry an electrical current at least as well as metals.

Both metal and plastic conductors have the same weakness—namely that their ability to conduct electrical current is temperature-dependent. In general applications, typical conductors function best in con-

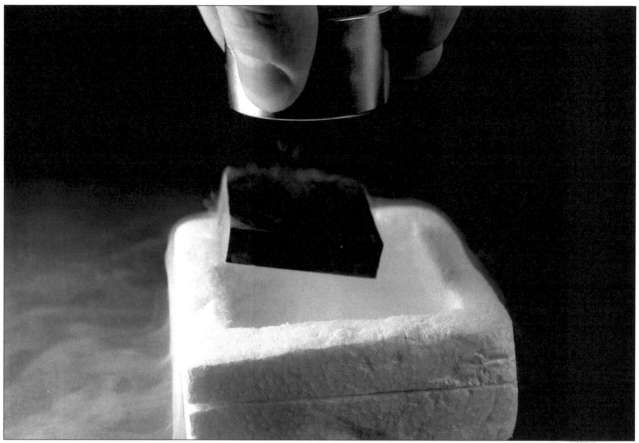

Superconductivity of magnets in liquid nitrogen. Photo via iStock/Lyagovy. [Used under license.]

ditions that are near standard temperature and pressure (STP). As the temperature of the material increases, however, its ability to conduct electrical current decreases. Reducing the temperature instead of raising it has its own kinds of problems, as the physical structure of the material changes to become more crystalline and brittle.

An ideal superconductor would exhibit none of these effects. Both metal and polymer conductors are able to transport electrical current because their respective atomic and molecular orbitals, as defined by their particular quantum state and wave function, are able to accept electrons from neighboring atoms. This requires the presence of unoccupied atomic or molecular orbitals that are similar to the occupied atomic or molecular orbitals with regard to energy.

As the temperature of a conductor decreases, the relative separation of the orbital energy levels decreases. Theoretically, at a sufficiently low temperature, the orbital energy separation becomes so low that there is effectively no barrier to the transfer of electrons between orbitals, and, at this point, the material is superconducting. This theory is the logical outcome of the band theory of solids, in which the various quantum states of the component atoms of a material essentially combine to define quantum states that span the entire material, rather than just individual atoms.

Quantum mechanics predicts the formation of Bose condensates by the same means, as the quantum states of a number of individual atoms combine to form what has been termed a *superatom*. Phonons are predicted to have the same behavior, since quantum vibrational states that span an entire mass of condensed matter are believed to have a role in superconductivity. In a superconductor, there is complete continuity across the quantum orbitals such that they form a complete eigensystem rather than a large collection of individual atomic eigensystems.

CURRENT RELATIONSHIPS

Electrical current in conventional conductors is described by a simple relationship called Ohm's law, which relates the current in an electrical circuit to the voltage that is applied to the circuit and the resistance that exists within the circuit. The relationship is given by the following formula: $E = I \times R$, where E is the voltage, I is the current and R is the resistance.

When the resistance is zero, as in a superconductor, this relationship breaks down, since it would suggest that the current could become infinitely high for any applied voltage, which in turn implies that the voltage source could supply an infinite number of electrons. Logically, this is an impossible condition, because the number of electrons that are available to flow through the circuit is finite.

AN EXAMPLE PROBLEM

The normal conductivity of a superconductor can be restored at any specific temperature by an applied magnetic field, according to the relationship:

$$B_C(T) = B_C(0)[1 - (T/T_C)^2]$$

where B_C is the critical magnetic field strength, T is the temperature, and T_C is the critical temperature for the material. For the element tantalum $T_C = 4.5K$ and $BC(0) = 83mT$ (milliTesla). $BC(T)$ the magnetic field strength required to convert superconducting tantalum to a normally conducting state, at a temperature of 2K can be calculated using the equation:

$$B_C (T) = B_C (0)[1 - (T/T_C)^2]$$

$$\text{as } (83mT)[1 - (2/4.5)^2] = 66.6mT$$

Fortunately, this can be interpreted in different ways. Certainly electrons will flow continuously through the circuit while the applied voltage exists, and because the circuit returns the electrons to the source as required by the conservation of charge, the supply of electrons could be thought of as infinite in a sense. Another way of interpreting the condition of zero resistance is this: The transfer of electronic charge is instantaneous, or in other words, requires zero time. In a practical sense, the relationship breakdown means that a current set in motion in a superconducting circuit will continue to flow essentially forever, in the absence of any resistance.

TYPES OF SUPERCONDUCTORS

Superconductors are generally designated as Type 1 or Type 2. Type 1 materials have normal conductivity and resistance, but at a sufficiently low temperature, they exhibit a sharp transition into the superconducting state. Typically the required temperatures are very low. Lead, for example, has the highest superconductivity transition temperature of the Type 1 materials, at just 7.88K (- 445°F). Aluminum becomes superconducting when the temperature is reduced to just 1.175K, while rhodium must be cooled to a mere 0.000375K to become superconducting.

Type 2 superconductors are, with very few exceptions, metallic compounds and alloys. These exotic materials exhibit superconductivity across a broad range of temperatures from near 0K to as high as 158°C (316°F).

APPLICATIONS

An important feature of superconductors is that they exhibit "perfect diamagnetism" and thus produce an equal and opposite magnetic field to an applied magnetic field. This can be demonstrated by attempting to place a permanent magnet atop a superconductor. The magnet will induce an equal and opposite magnetic field in the superconductor and will levitate. This effect is put to use in maglev (magnetic levitation) trains such as Japan's bullet trains that can run at very high speeds with essentially only the friction of the air to oppose their movement. Another application is lossless electrical energy transmission, which has been tested on a small scale and is expected to become a very important technology as new superconducting materials continue to be developed. Many types of industrial, analytical, and research devices use electromagnets as a vital component of their construction. Superconducting electromagnets often provide more stable and easily controlled alternatives to conventional electromagnets.

—*Richard M. Renneboog*

Further Reading

Buckel, Werner, and Reinhold Kleiner. *Superconductivity: An Introduction*. Translated by Rudolf Huebener. 3rd ed., John Wiley & Sons, 2016.

Ford, P. J., and G. A. Saunders. *The Rise of the Superconductors*. CRC Press, 2018.

Huebener, Rudolf P. *History and Theory of Superconductors: A Compact Introduction*. Springer Nature, 2021.

Inamuddin, editor. *Superconductors: Materials and Applications*. Materials Research Forum LLC, 2022.

Mohan, S. *Advances in High Temperature Superconductors and Their Applications*. MJP Publisher, 2019.

Poole, Charles P., Horacio A. Farach, Richard J. Creswick, and Ruslan Prozorov. *Superconductivity*. 2nd ed., Elsevier, 2010.

Tran, Lannie K. *Superconductivity, Magnetism and Magnets*. Nova Publishers, 2006.

See also: Atoms; Conservation of energy; Magnetism; Materials science; Quantum mechanics; Thermodynamics; Transportation

SURFACE TENSION

Fields of Study: Physics; Mechanics; Mathematics

ABSTRACT
Surface tension of a liquid is caused by the tendency of the liquid's molecules to be electromagnetically attracted to one another to such an extent that they can resist the application of external force at the boundary between the liquid and another substance. This resistance to external force is responsible for the ability of some liquids to support the weight of objects.

KEY CONCEPTS
molecular geometry: the bond angles and bond lengths between atoms in a molecule

molecular structure: the three-dimensional arrangement of atoms and bonds in a particular compound

polar: molecules that have an unequal distribution of electrical charge within their molecular structures but are nevertheless electrically neutral

water molecule: familiar as H_2O, the two hydrogen atoms and the oxygen form an angle of 109.5° between their bonds, which concentrates the positive charge character of the H atoms opposite the negative charge of the lone pairs of electrons on the O atom; this renders the molecule highly polar such that it can act much like a small magnet

WHY THERE IS SURFACE TENSION
Surface tension of a liquid is caused by the tendency of the liquid's molecules to be electromagnetically attracted to one another to such an extent that they can resist the application of external force at the boundary between the liquid and another substance. This effect causes the liquid to appear to be encased in a sort of outer skin, as when a water droplet rests upon a nonporous surface such as a pane of glass. This resistance to external force is

responsible for the ability of some liquids to support the weight of objects such as small insects (so-called water striders) and paper clips, as well as for the capillary action that can make liquids resist the pull of gravity.

Water molecules are attracted to one another because the structure of the molecule is polar—that is, one side of the molecule has a greater positive charge and the other side of the molecule has a greater negative charge. This is due to the arrangement of the two hydrogen atoms attached to the single oxygen molecule. When many water molecules are present, then, they tend to stick to one another as the negatively charged side of one molecule is attracted to the positively charged side of another water molecule. Within the mass of a body of water, each molecule is subject to attractive force from all directions, so the net effect is for the attractions to cancel each other out. At the outer surface where the water body comes into contact with air, however, the molecules are not subject to attractive force from the air molecules they touch, so they are more tightly attached to the water molecules next to them on the surface. This stronger horizontal attraction between water molecules at the surface of a body of water is responsible for surface tension.

BACKGROUND

The strength of the surface tension is measured in relation to the amount of surface in question, with the amount of surface given either as length or area. If length is specified, then surface tension is given as dynes per centimeter, meaning how many dynes of force would be required to break a liquid surface one centimeter long. If area is specified instead, then the units used are ergs per square centimeter. (Note that surface tension can also be measured in millinewtons per meter, mN/m, corresponding to the meter-kilogram-second system of SI measurement as compared to the centimeter-gram-second system.)

To illustrate, water has a surface tension of seventy-two dynes per centimeter at room temperature (about 70 degrees Fahrenheit or 20 degrees Celsius). Interestingly, surface tension decreases as the temperature of the water increases. This happens because the rising temperature causes the molecules to move around more, counteracting the effect of intermolecular attraction and making it easier to penetrate the surface. This is why hot water does a better job of cleaning—its lower surface tension permits it to move into smaller areas than would be possible with standard surface tension.

Surface tension is also responsible for the spherical shape of drops of water. When water is observed dripping from a faucet, initially it takes the familiar shape of a teardrop. Then, when it breaks free of the faucet and begins to fall, it quickly contracts into a spherical shape, as can be seen using high-speed photography. The reason for this is that the molecules of water inside it are all attracted to each other. This causes the water to assume the most compact shape it can—the shape with the smallest surface area—which is a sphere.

OVERVIEW

The larger a quantity of water's surface area at its boundary with air, the more energy is necessary to maintain the surface tension. Intuitively, this makes sense, because if one centimeter of water has a surface tension of 72 dynes per centimeter, two centimeters of water will have a surface tension of 144, three centimeters, 216; and so forth.

According to the second law of thermodynamics, systems naturally tend to move from high-energy states to low-energy states. This tendency manifests itself with regard to surface tension in the way in which quantities of water seek to minimize their own surface area, thereby reducing the energy required to maintain their surface tension.

Examples of this phenomenon abound in nature. For example, one may wonder why water emerging from a hose or showerhead does not remain in a continuous stream instead of breaking up into droplets. This happens because if the water were to remain in an unbroken stream, it would have a very large surface area with a correspondingly large amount of energy needed to maintain surface tension. Instead, small amounts of water separate from the stream as the force of their momentum overcomes the attractive force of the stream's surface tension. Then, as the water flies free of the stream, it assumes a spherical shape as discussed above.

Surface tension is relevant in many different contexts: industrial production, food preparation and packaging, cleaning, and so on. The active ingredients in cleaning products are chosen in part for their property of lowering the surface tension of water with which they are mixed, increasing the ability of the mixture to penetrate small spaces and porous surfaces. Food packaging often relies on the surface tension of the product it contains, as with toothpaste being dispensable from tubes because of its surface tension. Clothing companies seeking to produce waterproof materials for use as raincoats and tents must study the surface tension of water in order to create fabric surfaces that will preserve rather than penetrate the surfaces of droplets that land on the material, to keep it from soaking in. Even the chemical composition of paint is carefully adjusted to ensure that it has a surface tension that will allow the paint to spread easily while keeping a uniform thickness. Scientists are even beginning to develop synthetic "superhydrophobic materials,"

which have surfaces designed to change the angle of incidence for the moisture that lands on it, allowing the droplets to bounce and the material to remain dry.

—*Scott Zimmer*

Further Reading

Erbil, H. Y. *Surface Chemistry of Solid and Liquid Interfaces.* Blackwell, 2006.

Falkovich, G. *Fluid Mechanics: A Short Course for Physicists.* Cambridge UP, 2011.

Klein, Jürgen. *An Introduction to Surface Tension.* Nova Science Publishers, 2020.

Lambert, P. *Surface Tension in Microsystems: Engineering below the Capillary Length.* Springer, 2013.

Lambert, Pierre, and Massimo Mastrangeli, editors. *Microscale Surface Tension and Its Applications.* MDPI, 2019.

Lautrup, Benny. *Physics of Continuous Matter: Exotic and Everyday Phenomena in the Macroscopic World.* CRC Press, 2011.

Matubayasi, Norihiro. *Surface Tension and Related Thermodynamic Quantities of Aqueous Electrolyte Solutions.* Taylor, 2014.

Munson, Bruce R., T. H. Okiishi, Wade W. Huebsch, and Alric P. Rothmayer. *Fundamentals of Fluid Mechanics.* Wiley, 2013.

Robinson, James C., Diez J. L. Rodrigo, and Witold Sadowski. *Mathematical Aspects of Fluid Mechanics.* Cambridge UP, 2012.

Young, F. R. *Fizzics: The Science of Bubbles, Droplets, and Foams.* Johns Hopkins UP, 2011.

See also: Fluid dynamics; Fluid mechanics and aerodynamics; Hydraulic engineering; Hydrodynamics; Materials science

T

TESLA, NIKOLA

Fields of Study: Physics; Mechanics; Mathematics

ABSTRACT
Tesla spent his life researching new ideas in theoretical physics, electricity, and magnetism in the late nineteenth and early twentieth centuries. Although his brilliance was later obscured by mental illness, Tesla's work has garnered him recognition as the "inventor" of the twentieth century.

KEY CONCEPTS
fluorescent lamp: a lamp in which light is produced by electrical stimulation of a gas rather than by heating a tungsten metal filament to incandescence

polyphase: a system in which an electromagnetic field is composed of two or more sinusoidal emissions that are not in phase with each other

Tesla effect: the wireless transmission of electrical energy through the natural conductivity in the environment

EARLY LIFE
Nikola Tesla was one of five children born to the Reverend Milutin Tesla, a priest in the Serbian Orthodox Church Metropolitanate of Sremski Karlovci, and uka Mandiæ, herself a daughter of a Serbian Orthodox Church priest, in the village of Smiljan, Austro-Hungarian Empire (present-day Croatia). He was born at midnight between July 9 and 10, allegedly during an electrical storm.

As a child, Tesla was expected to become a minister like his father. His natural talents, however, caused Tesla to dream of pursuing a scientific career. He was born with a prodigious memory, could perform calculations in his head, and had the ability to visualize scenes, people, and objects vividly. This dream, however, seemed unreachable because of his father's expectations.

Unfortunately, though a fortunate happenstance for the present time, after graduating from the Realgymnasium in Austria, Tesla caught cholera and became gravely ill. Fearing that his son was dying, Milutin Tesla promised his son that he would allow him to attend engineering school if he would re-

Nikola Tesla. Photo via Wikimedia Commons. [Public domain.]

cover. Given Nikola Tesla's tremendous strength of will, it should not be a surprise that he survived, and he attended the Austrian Polytechnic School at Graz in 1875.

While at university, Tesla studied the uses of alternating current (AC), but a scholarship that had enabled him to attend classes was eventually terminated, a situation that Tesla exacerbated by a growing love of gambling. Tesla never officially returned to school beyond the first semester of his third year. In December of 1878, he left Graz.

By 1881, Tesla was working for a telegraph company in Budapest and finally able to begin his lifelong love of invention. He developed a type of telephone repeater or amplifier, a precursor to the modern loudspeaker. Although his work with Nebojša Petroviæ, a fellow inventor, resulted in several designs for a twin-turbine-powered engine, he wanted to work more definitively as an inventor and signed up with the Continental Edison Company in Paris, France. By the end of 1882, Tesla had conceived the earliest ancestors of what would become his most well-known invention, the induction motor, and began developing various devices using rotating magnetic fields.

LIFE'S WORK

On June 6, 1884, Tesla traveled to New York City with nothing in his pockets but a few cents and a letter of recommendation from his former manager Charles Batchelor addressed to American inventor Thomas Alva Edison. Impressed, Edison hired Tesla to work for the Edison Machine Works, beginning with simple electrical engineering and eventually becoming a troubleshooter for Edison's most complex engineering issues. Tesla's salary was a modest $18 per week; he was angered at Edison's dismissal of his value and promptly resigned when Edison would not offer him a raise.

After a brief stint digging ditches from 1886 to 1887, Tesla finally attracted the attention of wealthy inventor George Westinghouse and began the process of creating the initial brushless AC induction motor with his financial support. It was sufficiently ready in 1888 to demonstrate to the American Institute of Electrical Engineers (AIEE; later merged into the Institute of Electrical and Electronics Engineers, or IEEE). Tesla's design for a polyphase system transmitting electricity wirelessly further impressed Westinghouse, and he offered Tesla a position at the Pittsburgh laboratories at Westinghouse Electric and Manufacturing Company.

In 1891, while becoming a naturalized US citizen, Tesla demonstrated what came to be called the "Tesla effect," the wireless transmission of electrical energy based on electrical conductivity. He moved his scientific experiments to 35 S. Fifth Avenue in New York, and later to 46 E. Houston Street, much to the disgruntlement of his neighbors. Experimenting with sound resonances, Tesla accidentally discovered the vibrational frequency of his apartment building and several of the ones around it, causing them to violently shake on their foundations. Summoned by Tesla's terrified neighbors, the police encountered a calm Tesla surrounded by the crushed remains of his device; he had been forced to take a sledgehammer to his invention.

When he was thirty-six years old, Tesla's first patents for a polyphase power system were granted, encouraging him to further develop uses for alternating current. The 1893 World's Fair in Chicago showcased his wireless electric lights by allowing Tesla to illuminate the various buildings with his fluorescent lamps. His "Egg of Columbus," a sphere made of copper, stood on end as a demonstration of the rotating magnetic field principle. Despite his successes, however, Nikola Tesla's AC generator was made to directly compete with Edison's direct current (DC) motors for development funds. Because of this "War of Currents," Edison and Westinghouse suffered near financial ruin, forcing Tesla to tear apart his royalty contracts with Westinghouse.

By 1899, Tesla decided that his current quarters were inadequate to the task of housing his experiments with high voltage and high frequencies. He moved his research to Colorado Springs, Colorado, where he demonstrated the conductivity of Earth and generated ball lightning. He was still researching wireless technology, and he found that the resonant frequency of Earth was approximately 8 hertz.

Despite his many patents, Tesla was continually troubled by the lack of funding and ongoing harassment from Edison. On January 7, 1900, he was forced to sell his laboratory equipment and leave Colorado Springs. Still hopeful of a more successful future, Tesla built the Wardenclyffe laboratory and its famous transmitting tower in Shoreham, Long Island. The tower, copper-domed and 187 feet high, was intended to transmit both signals and power without wires to any destination. Unsure of the profitability of such an invention, however, financier J. P. Morgan pulled his monetary support. The unfinished tower would remain standing until 1917, when the US government decided that it was a national security risk and that the land it sat on would be more valuable without the tower.

Tesla's troubles continued to plague him. The rent on his two-room suite at the Waldorf-Astoria Hotel had been deferred because of a private agreement between Tesla and proprietor George Boldt, but mounting financial pressure forced Tesla to turn over his Wardenclyffe deed to pay the $20,000 he owed. Ironically, in 1917 Tesla established principles regarding frequency and power level for the first radio detection and ranging (radar) units and received AIEE's highest honor, the Edison Medal.

By 1943, Tesla was penniless and his life constricted by his ever-worsening phobias. His behavior, always marked by eccentricity, became bizarre. He became known for taking care of Central Park's pigeons, often taking injured ones home. He died of heart failure in Room 3327 of the New Yorker Hotel, but his reclusive nature made the exact day difficult to determine. One of the last times Tesla was seen alive, an assistant discovered Tesla standing in front of his open window in the middle of an electrical storm, feverish and claiming that he had made better lightning than God. It was later discovered that Tesla had died between the evening of January 5 and the morning of January 8, the constant effect of electricity upon his body having finally caused his heart to fail. Tesla never realized significant profits from the sale of his many patents, even though the ones describing AC electricity were extremely valuable. Nevertheless, his longtime feud with Guglielmo Marconi, who had successfully challenged Tesla's patent on the principles of radio and been awarded the Nobel Prize in Physics for radio in 1909, was ended with the US Supreme Court establishing Tesla as the inventor of radio, recognizing the validity of Tesla's US Patent number 645,576 (1893).

THE ROTATING MAGNETIC FIELD PRINCIPLE

A magnetic field, as defined by physics, is a field produced by moving electric charges that form currents, or waves. The charges exert a force on other moving charges. A magnetic field associates with every point in space a vector that may vary in time; hence, it is a vector field. A magnetic field affects the movement of magnetic dipoles and electric charges. It permeates space, surrounding all electrically charged objects, and exerts a magnetic force. Magnetic fields can be generated in a variety of ways, both through natural and artificial processes, and have an energy density proportional to the square of the field intensity. Stationary dipoles generate magnetic fields that are constant. Changing electric fields, one of the basic principles of electromagnetism, generate rotating magnetic fields.

Nikola Tesla discovered the rotating magnetic field as a precursor to his work on devices using alternating current (AC). Alternating current is so named because its magnitude and direction change frequently in a cyclical motion, rather than remaining constant like the electrical currents generated by the stationary fields created by direct current (DC) generators. The rotation of magnetic fields creates an electric impulse that is both efficient and cost-effective to transmit as a sine wave. Tesla adapted this principle in order to realize his vision of his induction motor and a polyphase system that not only can create electrical energy but also can transmit it efficiently and over vast distances by both cable conduction and, potentially, without wires using energy generated by the movement of the molten center of the Earth's core and conducted through the magnetic lines that make up the Earth's magnetic poles.

The AC induction motor continues to be used as the basis of consumer electronics and industrial machines. It formed the basis for the Industrial Revolution, since the polyphasic AC system is a highly adaptable method of powering everything from toasters to table lamps. Some examples of the many uses of AC are audio and radio signals. These devices emphasize the importance of data integrity, since inefficient transmission would reduce an audio or radio signal to incomprehensible babble.

REQUIEM FOR THE MAN WHO CREATED THE MODERN WORLD

Tesla's funeral was held at Manhattan's Cathedral of St. John the Divine on January 12, 1943, and the inventor's remains were cremated and enshrined in a golden sphere. Immediately thereafter, in spite of Tesla's status as a naturalized citizen, the government's Alien Property Custodian Office was directed by the Federal Bureau of Investigation (FBI) to impound Tesla's possessions in the hopes of recovering a so-called death-ray based on Tesla's experiments with controllable ball lightning and plasma. Although no such device was found, Tesla's papers were taken, and the War Department decided to classify his research as "top secret." Tesla's family and the Yugoslav embassy struggled to prevent the confiscation. Eventually, his nephew, Sava Kosanoviæ, was able to reclaim Tesla's cremated remains as well as some of Tesla's personal effects and placed them on permanent loan to the Nikola Tesla Museum in Belgrade, Serbia.

IMPACT

Tesla was one of those rare individuals whose contributions to society defy any attempt at summarization. He acquired more than seven hundred patents both in the United States and in Europe on a wide variety of topics. Some of the consequences of his work were the creation of the Nikola Tesla Award by the IEEE and the naming of the SI unit for measuring magnetic flux density (or magnetic induction), the tesla. He has been extensively recognized in his homeland, even though he is relatively unknown in the United States outside the field of electrical engineering.

It is hard to imagine what the world would be like if Tesla had not survived cholera in 1875. He was directly responsible for so many "fixtures" of modern life—such as AC electricity, radio, radar, and X-ray photography—that one cannot really comprehend how differently modern technology might have arisen. There have been a few monuments created to honor this brilliant man; his close friend Ivan Meštroviæ made a bust of him when the sculptor was in the United States. The artwork, finished in 1952, became the centerpiece of the Tesla exhibit in the Nikola Tesla Museum in Belgrade. Another statue was placed on the aptly named Nikola Tesla Street in Zagreb's city center on the 150th anniversary of Tesla's birth, with a duplicate erected at the Ruđer Boškoviæ Institute. Finally, in 1976, Niagara Falls commissioned a bronze statue of Tesla. It remains to be seen if Tesla's creative genius can fully overcome the obscurity to which his work has been condemned.

—Julia M. Meyers

Further Reading

Cheney, Margaret. *Tesla: Man Out of Time*. New York: Barnes & Noble Books, 1993.

Hourly History. *Nikola Tesla: A Life from Beginning to End*. Hourly History, 2017.

Hunt, Inez, and Wanetta W. Draper. *Lightning in His Hand: The Life Story of Nikola Tesla*. Sage Books, 1964.

Jonnes, Jill. *Empires of Light: Edison, Tesla, Westinghouse, and the Race to Electrify the World*. Random House, 2003.

Nikola Tesla Museum. *Nikola Tesla, 1856-1943: Lectures, Patents, Articles*. Kessinger, 2003.

Seifer, Marc. *Wizard: The Life and Times of Nikola Tesla*. Citadel, 2011.

Tesla, Nikola. *My Inventions—The Autobiography of Nikola Tesla*. Infinity, 2013.

———. *The Strange Life of Nikola Tesla*. Library of Alexandria, 2020.

See also: Acoustics; Conservation of energy; Electromagnetism; Gauss's law; Magnetism; Vibration

THERMODYNAMICS

Fields of Study: Physics; Mechanics; Mathematics

ABSTRACT

Adding heat can alter the temperature, pressure, entropy, and other properties of a system, thus becoming stored in the system or removed from the system, and it can cause the system to do work on the surroundings of the system. The laws of thermodynamics relate the heat to the stored energy and work done.

KEY CONCEPTS

adiabatic process: a process undergone by a system without addition or extraction of heat

coordinate: any of the quantities of temperature, pressure, volume, or entropy

entropy: the amount of heat transferred to or from a system (during a small interval of time) divided by the temperature at which it was transferred

heat capacity: the amount of heat an object can absorb divided by the temperature change in that absorption

internal energy: energy stored by a system, indicated by a change in temperature and volume

potential: any of the measures of stored energies measured as internal energy, enthalpy, Gibbs function, or Helmholtz function

pressure: the force per unit area exerted by the system on its surroundings

system: an amount of matter or radiation contained by a boundary

work: measured in joules; the pressure exerted on the surroundings (container) of a system multiplied by the change in volume of the system

OVERVIEW

Thermodynamics deals mainly with the energy content and production of systems. The "systems" are most often enclosed quantities of matter (solids, liquids, gases, plasmas, and mixtures of these components). In these cases, the laws of thermodynamics describe changes in properties of these systems as different forms of energy flow into or out of the system. The two principal kinds of energy of most concern are heat added to or taken from the system, and work done by the system on the confining environment. Theoretical thermodynamics can accommodate more abstract systems, such as confined (massless) radiation or fields or more subtle phases of matter, and even has extraordinary power in nonphysical systems, such as economic models (where economic analogies to thermodynamic terms and laws can be constructed).

The "properties" of a system can be virtually any measurable attribute, such as degree of magnetization or concentration of a dissolved chemical, but are usually illustrated by a basic discussion of a few typical measurables. There are two groups: the "coordinates" (pressure of the system on the environment, volume of a fixed mass of the system, temperature at points in the system, and entropy of the system) and the "potentials" for the system (internal energy, enthalpy, Gibbs function, and Helmholtz function). These potentials represent various forms in which energy is "stored" or "released" by the system as the coordinates change. For example, if a gas is compressed such that no heat is added from the environment, the temperature will rise, and the internal energy is said to rise to represent the energy stored in the gas. This example represents the main application of the "first law of thermodynamics," a thermodynamic version of the law of conservation of energy. Generalizing from mechanics, it includes energy dissipated by friction in considerations of energy balance (a bouncing ball eventually settles down and loses its energy of motion and position to heat energy). One advantage of thermodynamics is that it

accounts for energy conversions when more than one coordinate changes at a time (e.g., simultaneous change in pressure and temperature). The resulting change in the other properties (density, internal energy, and the like) can be computed from the thermodynamic laws.

The properties of a system are usually described in terms of a few basic familiar properties.

Temperature is defined as the reading on a standard thermometer, although the second law of thermodynamics allows a more abstract definition.

Pressure is defined as the mechanical force exerted by the system on its environment (or container) divided by the area over which this force acts. This definition allows the work done by the system on its environment to be computed as simply the product of the pressure and the volume change. This work only includes the mechanical energy delivered by changing the system, but it is of the most interest, since it represents the useful output of a system, while the heat added represents the expense of energy input. In some arrangements, such as refrigeration, the useful energy is the heat transferred and the expense is the work done (say by compression by a motor). In either case, the energy balance of heat, work, and (occasionally) other kinds of energy transfer is the focus of concern.

Heat, the major activating energy of systems, is described practically in terms of its effects on standard measuring systems. For example, one standard calorie is defined as the amount of heat required to raise the temperature of one gram of a standard substance (water) by 1 Kelvin. Another substance exposed to this same standard heat will have a temperature rise characteristic of its composition. The heat capacity of any substance is then its heat absorbed per degree of temperature rise. Experiments (originated by James Prescott Joule) can relate the standard calorie to the unit of energy used in mechanics. By experiment, 1 calorie equals about 4.2 joules. The more abstract use of the laws of thermodynam-

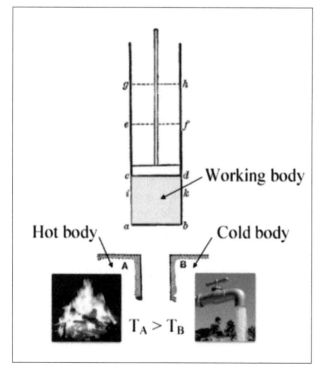

Annotated color version of the original 1824 Carnot heat engine showing the hot body (boiler), working body (system, steam), and cold body (water), the letters labeled according to the stopping points in Carnot cycle. Image via Wikimedia Commons. [Public domain.]

ics allows a more abstract definition of heat, and this definition is at the heart of the theoretical structure of the subject.

There are three central laws of thermodynamics. The first is the conservation of energy (often used to define the concept of internal energy). It asserts that the heat added to a system must reveal itself in the sum of work being done by that system and a rise in internal energy of the system. The system can respond to an input of heat in many ways under this rule, changing its coordinates to conserve energy. In an isochoric (constant volume) process, for example, no work is done by the system (since work done is defined through a change in volume), and all the heat goes into raising the internal energy. Energy relations in an isobaric (constant pressure) process are often theoretically revealing, since many chemical processes are isobaric, particularly if they occur on a tabletop where the atmospheric pressure is constant.

Adiabatic processes, where no heat is added, are the most useful, for they describe how the internal evolution of a system might proceed. This latter process becomes more interesting from the point of view of the second law of thermodynamics, the centerpiece of most discussions of the subject.

There are several statements of the second law of thermodynamics, which are all equivalent. The simplest statement asserts that heat cannot be entirely converted to work by a system. For example, a bouncing ball can eventually come to rest, thus converting all of its mechanical energy (or work) into heat; it heats up as it settles. Nevertheless, one does not expect to heat a resting ball and have it start bouncing; the heat cannot be entirely transformed into work. An equivalent statement asserts that heat will not flow spontaneously from a cold object to a hot object; an ice cube on a hot pavement is expected to warm, not cool. Another version asserts that when systems are out of equilibrium—that is, when parts of a system are at different temperatures—the temperature

changes to reduce the differences (toward equilibrium). In the case of the ice cube, one expects the pavement to cool a little while the ice cube heats up, not vice versa. The justification for asserting these laws can be either a statement about the observed properties of natural systems or a more abstract imposition of the second law as a condition of intelligibility of a system. In either case, the second law has fascinating and profound consequences.

A particularly convenient view of the second law of thermodynamics is provided by defining a new property of the system, a coordinate called entropy. Returning to the ice cube example, the entropy is defined by the amount of heat entering the cube (in a short instant) divided by the temperature (at that instant). If one claims that the second law requires the heat to flow from the pavement to the cube (not in reverse), then one notices that the entropy received by the cube is greater than that given up by the pavement. This is simply by definition, for the heat given and taken was the same (by the first law of thermodynamics), but the temperatures were different. The lower-temperature ice cube got more entropy (heat divided by temperature) than the hotter pavement gave up. In general, the second law of thermodynamics asserts that the entropy of a "universe" (system plus its surroundings) must always increase as the system tends toward equilibrium with its surroundings. This is a much-discussed aspect of the second law, as it provides an "arrow of time" for physical systems—that is, a natural direction of evolution—the reverse of which is prohibited. Quantitatively, the second law allows the prediction of the particular equilibrium state toward which chemical and other interactions will tend. This is immensely practical in studying such diverse systems as chemical reactions, heat flow in low-temperature solids, nuclear reactions, and even information flow in the analog nonthermodynamic systems of information theory.

Another abstract view of the first two laws of thermodynamics is that they prohibit certain processes in nature. Perpetual motion machines that deliver more work out than they take heat in, or that cycle work and heat without "running down," violate the laws of thermodynamics.

There are extensions of the basic arguments. Some natural systems, particularly biochemical ones, do seem to cycle from low- to high-entropy states, and this has led to an extension of the laws of thermodynamics to "nonequilibrium" systems, where self-organizing systems are permitted to tend toward ultimate equilibrium in surprising ways, sometimes lowering local entropy, as in the case of spontaneous organization ("de-evolution") of a genetic system from a state of molecular disorder to one of symmetric genetic material.

There are other forms of system energy considered besides internal energy, such as enthalpy, a combination of internal energy and the pressure and volume coordinates. Its use for isobaric (constant pressure) processes is similar to internal energy for adiabatic processes. The variants of internal energy called Helmholtz and Gibbs functions are similar, the latter being particularly useful in isothermal processes such as phase changes, where the system maintains its fixed temperature while using energy to change its physical structure, as when ice melts.

There is also a third law of thermodynamics, asserting that the rates of change in entropy will always diminish as the temperature of a system diminishes. This amplifies another of the consequences of the second law, which states that there must be a minimum (theoretical) temperature (0 Kelvin) for all equilibrium systems. The third law of thermodynamics is thus particularly useful in experimental low-temperature systems.

APPLICATIONS

Thermodynamics is very general in structure. It describes systems of a wide range of compositions and a very wide variety of properties. Examples of a system include the classical enclosed vapors of a steam engine, the mixtures of sand, lime, and chemicals that make up cement, and a volume of atmosphere that is the model for a storm at sea. Any knowledge of pairs (or more) of attributes of a system (such as the temperature and density of the elements mixed to make cement) allows the specification of all the other attributes (pressure, entropy, enthalpy, Gibbs function, and the like). Applying the laws of thermodynamics predicts how the variables of the system will evolve (toward equilibrium). Thus, the density (composition) and the "hardness" of the cement is calculable, or the speed and moisture content of the storm, or the "efficiency" of the steam engine.

Historically, the applications of thermodynamics are most visible in the study of engines, and particularly in the comparisons between the efficiency of steam engines and other types of such devices using chemical or electrical systems. The competition between steam, diesel, and electrical engines for railroads was an example of a thermodynamics-driven technology. Periodically, new kinds of engines are proposed for transportation or energy production, and their proposed merits must be analyzed. New combinations of processes for internal combustion (such as in the Wankel engine of the mid-twentieth century) or new working systems (such as the use of fuels such as methane, ethane, or hydrogen) are periodically proposed and require thermodynamic description.

Studies of weather patterns provide excellent opportunities for the thermodynamicist. A mass of wet air moving up a mountainside seems like an obvious "system," its pressure and temperature and the density of its moisture being some of its thermodynamic coordinates. The work done against gravity and the heat added by sunlight and the surrounding atmosphere raise its internal energy (and its other "potentials," such as Gibbs function), and the heat exhausted in the form of rain or snow represent calculable quantities in a model of the mass of air. In practice, the atmosphere is so complicated that the most advanced computers are required to keep track of all the details of a weather front, but the principles governing the computer's computations of detail are the simple principles of thermodynamics.

Low-temperature science and technology, from the early liquefaction of gases to the modern exploitation of the electrical peculiarities of very-low-temperature systems, have required extensive use of the principles of thermodynamics. In particular, the so-called superfluidity of helium at ultra-low temperatures (below 3 Kelvins) has provided both a theoretical challenge and a technical opportunity to investigate allied properties of matter—superconductivity (electrical conduction) and heat conduction at low temperatures.

Hydrodynamics (fluid flow), particularly highly frictional turbulent flow, can be organized by thermal principles, though much is still unknown about the transition from smooth to erratic (even chaotic) patterns of flow. Analogies to eddies and whirlpools in fluid flow can be mathematically constructed in other pictures, such as field-theoretical models of the flow of light or particles in the subatomic regime, and so algebraic models of radiation fields carry the models of thermodynamics into fundamental particle theory.

Practical thermodynamic engineering is more directly illustrative of the basic principles of thermodynamics. One can easily see the problems of the power output of electric or steam-generating plants as directly predictable from principle. Nonsteam engines and refrigerators are equally obvious candidates for analysis, as are ideas to generate work and energy in novel ways, such as solar energy, wind, and tidal power.

The characterization of forms or states of matter itself requires considerable study. The old classifications of matter—solid, liquid, and gas—have been augmented by another major class (plasma) and many subclasses. A plasma is an electrically charged gas, and has considerable utility in anything from lighting to energy generation. The subclasses of matter (phases) caused by different molecular crystalline patterns suggest ever more new kinds of matter, such as spin-glass and superfluid liquids.

Chemistry and biochemistry are perhaps the main arena of classical thermodynamics, for there the evolution and combination of diverse chemical systems are particularly sensitive to the energy balances of their successive states. Understanding the transfer of chemical energy across membrane boundaries is part of the explanation of muscle action, itself a user of chemical energy derived from nutrition and respiration (two fields of study prominent in the prehistory of thermodynamics). Rhythmic mechanisms in controlling the daily and monthly cycles of chemical changes in organisms yield secrets to application of nonequilibrium thermodynamic models.

Astrophysics and cosmology are perhaps the most dramatic arena of thermodynamic theory, for the evolution of stars and galaxies, the origins of the cosmic expansion, the explosions of stars, and the collapse of systems into black holes are dramatic cosmic examples of systems exchanging energy and matter with their surroundings—the central thematic topic of the theory. Like its companion subjects, mechanics and electrodynamics, thermodynamics is a central pillar of the kind of thinking known as physics.

CONTEXT

Modern thermodynamics arose in the middle of the nineteenth century, particularly from the work of Rudolf Clausius and Hermann Von Helmholtz. Before that time, there were many scattered investigations into phenomena of heat and temperature, but no clear theoretical central framework. In the eighteenth century, Sir Isaac Newton focused attention on thermodynamic problems (in addition to his better-known concerns), and experimental developments soon followed in measuring temperature and heat involved in chemical and digestive processes.

In the early nineteenth century, Nicolas-Leonard-Sadi Carnot formulated an early version of the heat-energy relations in his investigations into "the motive power of fire," or the nature of the power of steam engines. Carnot still thought of heat as a material, fluidlike substance (caloric) and did not have the advantage of the later notions of mechanical energy (developed by Helmholtz). Nevertheless, his consideration of the power and action of a steam engine (molded after his father Lazare-Nicolas-Marguerite Carnot's ideas of making more efficient waterwheels by minimizing the splash) contained the germs of the first and second laws of thermodynamics. His theoretical Carnot cycle would have lasting influence on the field.

Around the middle of the nineteenth century, Clausius combined the new notion of heat as a kind of motion with Carnot's theories on heat and Helmholtz's on energy. He produced the first modern statement of the first and second laws of thermodynamics. Physicists rapidly adapted the newest advances in mathematics to generalize and refine the theory. Engineers and mechanics began to investigate thermal devices and phenomena. For example, Rudolf Diesel, one of Clausius' students, developed the engine type that now bears his name. Also around the middle of the nineteenth century, Ludwig Boltzmann, James Clerk Maxwell, and Clausius developed a related discourse on heat (known as the kinetic theory), comparing notions of temperature, energy, and heat with the mechanical features of mixtures of atoms and molecules in motion. This later kinetic theory eventually grew into the science of statistical mechanics (particularly in the hands of Gibbs) by the early twentieth century.

Until the success of the theory of atomic-molecular motions of Albert Einstein and Jean-Baptiste Perrin with the atomic-molecular motions known as heat, most early-century thermal inquiries were conducted with the classical thermodynamics of Clausius and Helmholtz.

These investigations involved such diverse topics as the source of volcanoes, the cooling of Earth (too fast to allow geologists their evolutionary epochs), heating of the upper atmosphere, and chemical reactions requiring or delivering heat. The latter study led to a new field of physical chemistry sponsored by Wilhelm Ostwald, himself a skeptic about the new idea of atoms. Such investigations spawned interest in liquefying gases at low temperatures (Lord Rayleigh discovered argon in this manner) and the achievement of ever lower temperatures.

Walther Hermann Nernst was led to formulate the third law of thermodynamics during this quest early in the twentieth century.

In the twentieth century, thermodynamic theory became ever more mathematically sophisticated and general, while the practical applications multiplied still further. Fluid flow at low temperature and solid resistance to high pressure won Nobel Prizes for their investigators. Numerous chemists and biochemists adapted the laws for their use. By the late twentieth century, new areas of nonequilibrium thermodynamics were pioneered by Ilya Prigogine.

Engineering thermodynamics also kept pace with rapid industrialization and the new age of science. New internal combustion and electric engines and generators, and Linde and Carrier's systems of air-conditioning, were precursors to twentieth-century expansion of low- and high-temperature technology, energy production, polymer and biochemistry, weather studies, and space engineering.

In a sense, thermodynamics is incomplete, for its laws can be applied to ever subtler and more abstract systems. One can extend, for example, the number of independent coordinates (such as temperature and pressure) from two to three, or even to infinity, requiring perhaps new properties and potentials to be defined. It is clear that thermodynamics has even more development to come.

—Peter D. Skiff

Further Reading

Fermi, Enrico. *Thermodynamics*. 1936. Dover, 2012.

Kondepudi, Dilip, and Ilya Prigogine. *Modern Thermodynamics: From Heat Engines to Dissipative Structures*. 2nd ed., John Wiley & Sons. 2014.

Peliti, Luca, and Simone Pigolotti. *Stochastics Thermodynamics: An Introduction*. Princeton UP, 2021.

Steane, Andrew M. *Thermodynamics: A Complete Undergraduate Course*. Oxford UP, 2016.

"Thermodynamics." *Khan Academy*. Khan Academy, 2015. Accessed 3 Apr. 2015.

Zemansky, Mark Waldo, and Richard Dittman. *Heat and Thermodynamics*. 8th ed., McGraw-Hill, 2012.

See also: Atoms; Calculus; Carnot, Sadi; Differential equations; Equilibrium; Heat transfer; Kinetic energy; Potential energy; Quantum mechanics; Vibration; Work and energy; Work-energy theorem

TORQUE

Fields of Study: Physics; Mechanics; Mathematics

ABSTRACT

Torque is the rotational force applied to an object. The magnitude of torque depends on the rotational mass of the object and its distance from its axis, or point of rotation. Torque is relevant to many industrial and household machines.

KEY CONCEPTS

angular momentum: the rotational momentum of an object around an axis, defined as the product of its moment and its angular velocity

axis: the center around which an object rotates

cross product: an operation, broadly analogous to multiplication, performed on two vectors in a three-dimensional space that results in a third vector that is perpendicular to both; if both vectors have the same direction or if one of them has a value of zero, the cross product will be zero

fulcrum: the supporting point around which a lever pivots

mechanical advantage: a measurement of the increase in force achieved by applying a mechanical tool or device to an existing system

moment: a combination of a physical quantity and a distance with respect to a fixed axis; the physical quantities of an object as measured at some distance from that axis

vector: a quantity that has direction as well as magnitude

LINEAR AND ANGULAR MOMENTUM

All moving objects have momentum. An object's momentum is simply a measure of how much motion it has. The greater the momentum in a given direction, the more the object tends to continue moving in that direction. If an object is moving in a straight line, its linear momentum is equal to the product of its mass and its velocity.

Momentum and velocity are both vector quantities. Therefore, an object moving linearly has either a positive or negative velocity, depending on which way it is moving relative to its starting point. For example, if a car drives north at a velocity of 20 meters per second, north can be considered the positive direction. Then, if the car turns around and drives back to its starting point at the same speed, it will have a velocity of -20 meters per second.

However, most objects do not move only in straight lines. Many rotate around some kind of a fixed point, or axis. An object rotating around an axis has angular momentum. Angular momentum, like linear momentum, is the product of an object's mass and its velocity, but it is measured in different units. An object's angular mass, or moment of inertia, is how much it resists changing its angular velocity around its axis. Its angular velocity is the rate at which its angle around the axis changes. Thus, the angular momentum of an object is equal to the product of its moment of inertia and its angular velocity.

According to Isaac Newton's second law of motion, momentum stays constant if no outside force acts on a given system, as the rate of change in momentum is zero. However, once an external force interacts with a system, momentum can increase or decrease, depending on the direction and magnitude of the applied force. When the system involves rotation, that outside force is called torque.

TORQUE, FORCE, AND DISPLACEMENT VECTORS

Torque is the degree to which a force causes an object to rotate around an axis. It can also be thought of as an object's change in angular momentum, or a "twist" applied to a moving object. For example, a force applied to a door will cause the door to rotate around its hinges rather than moving in a straight line. The hinges serve as the door's axis. The rotational part of the applied force is the torque.

Mathematically, torque is calculated as $T = F \times r$ where T is torque, F is the rotational force, and r is the displacement vector, which measures the distance between the axis and the point of force application. (Vector quantities are often represented by bolded variables or with a direction arrow above them to distinguish them from scalar quantities, which have magnitude but no direction.) The unit of torque is the newton-meter (NNm), a compound unit of force and distance. By convention, torque is considered negative if the direction of rotation is clockwise and positive if it is counterclockwise.

Torque is important to many household tools and machines. Most of these are based on the six classical simple machines that use mechanical advantage to multiply force. Levers offer the best example of torque. A lever consists of a flat surface attached to a fulcrum. When no net torque is applied, the surface balances on the fulcrum. However, if more force is applied to one side than the other, it will produce a torque that causes the surface to rotate. The position of the fulcrum is key. As the distance from the fulcrum to the point of force application increases, the amount of force required to rotate the plane around the fulcrum decreases. This is because the lever applies a rotational torque that multiplies the force. For example, pushing on a door (a type of lever) very close to its hinges takes much more force than pushing farther away from the hinges. The longer the radius, the greater the torque applied. Similarly, another simple machine, the screw, can translate the rotational force of torque into an amplified linear force.

DIRECTION AND MAGNITUDE: CROSS PRODUCTS AND ANGLES

When multiplying vector quantities, direction and magnitude must be calculated separately. Because torque is the cross product of two vectors (F and r) in a three-dimensional space, its direction is perpendicular to both. For example, if the string of a yo-yo is pinned to a tabletop and a force is pushing the

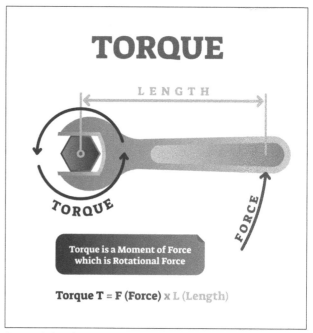

Image via iStock/VectorMine. [Used under license.]

yo-yo to rotate around the pin, the yo-yo's displacement vector points along the string and its force points along its spinning edge. The torque vector is thus perpendicular to both of them, pointing straight up in the air.

When calculating the magnitude of torque, the angle at which it is applied must be considered. By definition, the vector F in the torque equation represents only the part of the force perpendicular to the displacement vector r. The full equation for the magnitude of torque, not taking direction into account, is $T = Fr \sin \theta$ where θ is the angle between the vectors F and r. For example, if seventeen newtons of force are applied to a door at a point 1.5 meters from its hinges, and the angle of force application is sixty degrees from the flat of the door, then the magnitude of the torque would be calculated as follows: If the force is applied perpendicular to door, however, so that θ equals ninety degrees, then $\sin \theta$ is equal to 1 and can be disregarded.

CALCULATING TORQUE

Before calculating the torque of an object, the axis of rotation must be determined. For example, if the object is a lever, such as a seesaw, then the axis of rotation is the fulcrum. Next, the directions and magnitudes of the forces acting on the object must be identified. If two children are sitting on opposite sides of the seesaw, each child exerts a downward force on the lever that is a combination of the child's mass and the force of gravity. If the system in which the object exists is in equilibrium—for example, if the seesaw is perfectly balanced—then the net torque is be zero. If the system is not in equilibrium and an external force is acting on it to produce rotation, the torque can be calculated by using the equations above.

TORQUE IN DAILY LIFE

Torque is critical to many aspects of engineering and mechanical design, from static structures to complex machines. A car's engine, for example, produces torque from the combustion of gas. That torque turns the crankshafts, which then turn the wheels. The amount of torque ascribed to an engine reflects how quickly it can accelerate the car. That torque must overcome friction and air drag, among other forces, in order to move the car forward.

Torque can also be used to calculate an engine's power (P), or the amount of work it can perform over time, if the angular velocity (ω) of its output shaft is also known:

$$P = T\omega$$

This is especially useful for finding the power output of an electric motor.

For static structures, connecting elements (e.g., metal bolts that hold sheets of steel together) must be able to withstand the torque of potential outside forces, such as the weight of cars on the bridge or the strength of a storm's winds against the building.

—*Lindsay K. Brownell*

Further Reading

Ben Salem, Fatma. *Direct Torque Control Strategies of Electrical Machines*. BoD-Books on Demand, 2021.

Cooley, Brian. "CNET on Cars: Car Tech 101—Horsepower vs. Torque." *CNET*. CBS Interactive, 26 Feb. 2013. Accessed 7 Aug. 2015.

Khan, Salman. "Moments, Torque, and Angular Momentum." *Khan Academy*, 23 May 2008. Accessed 7 Aug. 2015.

Ling, Samuel J., Jeff Sanny, and William Moebs. *University Physics, Volume 1*. Samurai Media Limited, 2017.

Nappi, Virgil. *Physics and Math Formulas: Essential Physics and Math Formulas You Must Know: Torque*. Independently Published, 2021.

Nave, Carl R. "Torque." *HyperPhysics*. Georgia State University, 2012. Accessed 7 Aug. 2015.

Richmond, Michael. "Torque." *University Physics I*. Rochester Institute of Technology, 15 Feb. 2002. Accessed 7 Aug. 2015.

Roldán Cuenya, Beatriz. "Chapter 11: Torque and Angular Momentum." *Physics for Scientists and Engineers*

I. University of Central Florida, 2013. Accessed 7 Aug. 2015.

"Torque and Levers." *Siyavula Textbooks: Grade 11 Physical Science.* Rice University, 29 July 2011. Accessed 7 Aug. 2015.

See also: Acceleration; Aeronautical engineering; Aerospace design; Airplane propellers; Angular forces; Angular momentum; Circular motion; Coriolis effect; Dynamics; Flywheels; Force; Mechanical engineering; Rigid-body dynamics; Solid mechanics; Structural engineering

TRANSPORTATION

Fields of Study: Physics; Mechanics; Mathematics

ABSTRACT

Beginning from the time the internal combustion engine was invented, fossil fuels have been dominant sources of energy for the transportation sector. However, there is an emerging shift toward more energy-efficient modes to create multiplying effects in energy efficiency.

KEY CONCEPTS

biofuels: fuels produced or refined from biological matter, such as ethanol made from corn or biodiesel oil made from algae or vegetable oils

hybrid vehicle: a vehicle that has both an internal combustion engine and an electric motor available for propulsion

petroleum-based fuels: fuels ranging from methane to heavy oil that are refined from crude oil

ALTERNATIVE FUEL SOURCES FOR VEHICLES

Vehicles powered by battery-generated electricity are rapidly being introduced as alternatives to cars fueled by gasoline or diesel fuel. Moreover, a pure battery-powered electric vehicle is a more efficient alternative to a hydrogen-powered vehicle, as there is no need to convert energy into electricity (the electricity stored in the battery can power the electric motor). However, with current technology, the limited energy capacity of batteries renders most electric cars unable to compete with cars powered by internal combustion engines that use gasoline.

Hybrid vehicles use a propulsion system that combines an internal combustion engine with an electric motor and battery, providing the efficiency of electricity with the long-distance driving capacity of an internal combustion engine. A hybrid vehicle uses liquid fossil-based fuel as the main source of energy, but the engine is used to charge the battery through a generator. Propulsion can be provided by the electricity generated by the battery. When the battery is discharged, the engine starts mechanically, without intervention from the driver. The generator can also be fed by using the braking energy to recharge the battery. Such a propulsion design greatly contributes to overall fuel efficiency. Given that oil depletion is inevitable, the successful development and commercialization of hybrid vehicles appears, at least in the near term, to promise a certain modicum of sustainability in comparison to conventional gasoline-powered vehicles.

INDUSTRIAL DEVELOPMENT AND THE DEMAND FOR FUEL

Industrial development places huge demands on fossil fuels. In the twentieth century, the invention and commercial development of the internal combustion engine, notably for application to transportation, made possible the efficient mobility of people, freight, and information, which in turn stimulated the development of trade globally. With globalization, transportation has accounted for a mounting share of the total energy used for implementing, operating, and maintaining the international range and scope of human activities.

There is a strong correlation between energy consumption and level of economic development. In developed countries, transportation currently accounts for between 20 and 25 percent of the total energy being consumed. The utility conferred by additional mobility, notably the better exploitation of comparative advantages, has so far compensated for the growing amount of energy spent in supporting it. By the beginning of the twenty-first century, however, the transition had reached a stage where fossil fuels, prominently petroleum, were becoming dominant. Currently, out of the world's power production of nearly 15 terawatts a year, the contribution from fossil fuels is about 86 percent.

TRANSPORTATION AND ENERGY CONSUMPTION

A dominant trend that emerged in the 1950s concerns the growing contribution of transportation in the overall consumption of developed countries. During the period 1980-2000, world market consumption of all primary forms of energy grew by 40 percent. Transportation accounts for about 25 percent of global energy demand and for more than 62 percent of all the oil used annually. It should also be noted that the impacts of transport on energy utilization are many, including many that are necessary for the provision of transport facilities.

MODAL VARIATIONS IN ENERGY CONSUMPTION

Different modes of transportation involve different levels of consumption. Land transportation accounts for the majority of global energy consumption. In developing countries, road transportation alone is consuming, on average, 85 percent of the total energy used by the transport sector. Road transportation is almost the only mode responsible for additional energy demands over the last twenty-five years. However, trends within the land transportation sector are not uniform. Rail transport, for example, accounts for only 6 percent of worldwide transport energy demand.

Maritime transportation accounts for 90 percent of cross-border global trade on a volume basis. The nature of water transport and the economies of scale it offers make it the most energy-efficient mode of transportation; it uses only 7 percent of all the energy consumed by transport activities, a figure that compares favorably with its significant contribution to the overall mobility of goods.

Air transportation plays an integral role in the globalization of transportation networks. Generally, the aviation industry accounts for 8 percent of the transportation energy consumed. Air transport has high-energy consumption levels that are in line with its high speeds. Fuel is the second most important line item in the budget of the air transport industry, accounting for between 13 and 20 percent of total expenditures, or a daily consumption of about 1.2 million barrels of oil.

In addition to considering energy consumption for transport from the perspective of land, sea, and air modes of transport, one can consider energy consumption for passenger or freight transport. Passenger transportation accounts for 60 to 70 percent of energy consumption. Private automobiles and other personal vehicles are the dominant modes under this subcategory but have poor energy efficiency, although this performance has seen significant improvements since the 1970s mainly as a result of higher-energy prices, environmental regulations, and the demand for energy-efficient vehicles (hybrids and electric vehicles) that these conditions have encouraged. There is, however, a stronger correlation between rising income levels, automobile ownership, and distance traveled by a vehicle. For example, the United States has one of the highest levels of car ownership in the world, with one car for every two Americans. Almost 60 percent of all American households own two or more cars, and 19 percent own three or more cars.

Freight transportation constitutes rail and maritime shipping, which are the two most energy-efficient modes of transportation. Furthermore, coastal and inland waterways provide energy-efficient methods of transporting cargoes and passengers. Statistical evidence shows that a towboat with a typical 15 barges in tow is moving the equivalent of 225 railcar loads, which is the equivalent of about 870 truckloads. The justification for favoring coastal and inland navigation is based on the lower-energy utilization rates of shipping and the overall smaller externalities linked to water transportation. For instance, the US Marine Transportation System National Advisory Council has measured the distance that 1 ton of cargo can be moved with 3.785 liters of fuel. A towboat operating on an inland waterway can transport 1 ton of barge cargo 532 miles (857 kilometers). The same amount of fuel can be used to move 1 ton of rail cargo 209 miles (337 kilometers) or 1 ton of highway cargo 60 miles (98 kilometers).

PETROLEUM AND ALTERNATIVE FUELS

With the exception of railways using electric power, 95 percent of the world's transportation is dependent upon petroleum products. The growth in the demand for more transportation is the main reason for increasing petroleum demand; the use of petroleum for other economic operations has been relatively stable. There is some variation regarding the type and quality of petroleum-derived fuel in use; for example, air transportation requires a specialized fuel together with additives, whereas maritime transportation depends on low-quality bunker fuel. Assuming that all other variables remain constant, the lowest-cost energy source will always be sought.

The supremacy of petroleum-derived fuels is due to the relative simplicity of storing them as well as their energy efficiency when used in internal combustion engine vehicles. Other fossil fuels (such as natural gas, propane, and methanol) can be used as transportation fuels, but they require a more complicated energy storage system. However, the critical issue regarding large-scale uses of fuels other than petroleum is the high-capital investment required to establish or expand distribution facilities, which are already in place for conventional fossil fuels. Nonetheless, shrinking oil reserves, rising petroleum costs, and environmental concerns related to reducing harmful pollutants and greenhouse gas emissions are focusing attention on alternative fuel sources and technologies.

Biogas, for example, is a noncrude-oil category comprising ethanol, methanol, and biodiesel, which can be produced from the fermentation of certain crops (corn, sugarcane, sugar beets, wheat, and some nonfood crops such as jatropha) or waste from wood. The production of biogas, however, necessitates large harvesting areas that may compete with other land uses. It is estimated that one hectare of wheat produces less than or the equivalent of 264 gallons (1,000 liters) of transportation fuel per year, which is equivalent to the amount of fuel consumed by one passenger car traveling 6,213 miles (10,000 kilometers) annually. This limit is based on the capacity of plants to absorb solar energy and transform it into chemical energy through photosynthesis. The low productivity of biomass therefore cannot meet the transportation sector's energy demand. For instance, in 2007, the US government proposed a reduction in oil consumption by 20 percent and a shift to ethanol. The United States now produces about 26 billion liters of ethanol annually; the oil-reduction objective would require the production of nearly 30 billion gallons (115 billion liters) of ethanol by the year 2017, which amounts to the total annual US maize (corn) production. Furthermore, since the production of ethanol is an energy-intensive process, 1 thermal unit of ethanol requires the combustion of 0.76 unit of coal, natural gas, or petroleum.

Hydrogen is often mentioned as the future global energy resource. The steps in using hydrogen as a transportation fuel involve producing hydrogen by extracting it from hydrocarbons or by electrolysis of water; conserving or compressing hydrogen into liquid form; storing it on-board the vehicle using it as fuel; and using fuel cells to produce electric energy on demand from the hydrogen to propel a motor vehicle. From the perspective of efficiency, hydrogen fuel cells are twice as efficient as gasoline and generate almost no pollutants. However, hydrogen poses some significant challenges, ranging from the costly establishment of hydrogen plants to potentially dangerous explosions. First, a great amount of energy is required for the production, transfer, and storage processes involved with this fuel source. Second, hydrogen manufacturing requires electricity production. Third, a hydrogen-powered vehicle needs two to four times more energy for operation than does an electric car, rendering hydrogen-fueled vehicles cost-ineffective. Finally, hydrogen has a minimal energy density and requires very low-temperature and high-pressure storage tanks, adding weight and volume to a vehicle and thus increasing its need for fuel.

It therefore appears likely that transportation will shift toward more energy-efficient modes as well as integrated technologies to create multiplying effects in energy efficiency. While globalization has in large part been driven by cheaper and more efficient transportation systems running on fossil fuels, the new relationships between transport and energy are likely to streamline the global structure of production and distribution toward regionalization.

—*Dereje Teklemariam*

Further Reading

"Alternative and Advanced Fuels." *US Department of Energy*, www.afdc.energy.gov/afdc/fuels/biodiesel_publications.html.

Davis, S. C., S. W. Diegel, and R. G. Boundy. *Transportation Energy Data Book*. 30th ed., US Department of Energy, 2011, cta.ornl.gov/data/download30.shtml.

Greene, D. L. "Uncertainty, Loss, Aversion, and Markets for Energy Efficiency." *Energy Economics*, vol. 33, no. 4, July, 2011.

Greene, D. L., K. G. Duleep, and Girish Upreti. *Status and Outlook for the U.S. Non-automotive Fuel Cell Industry: Impact of Government Policies and Assessment of Future Opportunities*. ORNL/TM-2011/101. Oak Ridge National Laboratory, 2011.

Rodrigue, J-P., and C. Comtois. "Transportation and Energy." *The Geography of Transport Systems*, people.hofstra.edu/geotrans/eng/ch8en/conc8en/ch8c2en.html.

See also: Acceleration; Carnot, Sadi; Civil engineering; Diesel engine; External combustion engine; Helicopters; Internal combustion engine; Motion; Newton's laws; Propulsion technologies; Rotary engine; Structural engineering

TULL, JETHRO

Fields of Study: Physics; Mechanics; Mathematics

ABSTRACT

Tull, often hailed as the "father of British agriculture," paved the way for the late eighteenth-century agricultural revolution in England by inventing the seed drill, which resulted in increased crop yields (up to eightfold) and greater weed control over earlier hand-broadcasting methods.

KEY CONCEPTS

broadcasting: a technique of applying seed to a field by casting handfuls of seed using a sweeping motion of the arm; unfortunately, this method yields irregular and unreliable results

cultivation: the practice of preparing soil prior to planting and maintaining the soil after it has been prepared in order to produce grain and vegetable crops

drill: an agricultural implement used to insert or deliver seed to prepared soil in a regular and controllable manner

husbandry: an old term for the farming of plants and animals

plow: an agricultural implement used to lift and invert soil as it moves forward

EARLY LIFE

Jethro Tull was born in rural Berkshire, England, but his father, also named Jethro, and his mother, Diana Buckridge Tull, hoped he would train for public service rather than farming. He matriculated at St. John's College, Oxford, but finished without taking a degree, instead pursuing legal studies at Gray's Inn in London. When ill health interrupted his studies, he settled down to farm with his father on the family estate at Howberry. He also married Susannah Smith of Warwickshire, with whom he had a son, John, and a daughter, Susannah.

In the eighteenth century, the title "farmer" implied a gentleman who directed other men and women, not a laborer. As bailiff, or field supervisor, Tull was frustrated by the field hands' inability to plant seeds in a consistent, measured depth. In 1701, he invented a machine to do what his workers could not (or would not). Tull did not promote his invention, and it remained known only to his circle until circumstances forced him to move his family. In 1711, Tull's increasing illness (a weak heart) drove him to take a convalescence tour of the Continent, where he studied current European farming methods. Returning in 1714, he found the farm's revenue insufficient to cover the expenses of his three years in Europe. He sold the acreage and moved his family to a more modest farm near Hungerford, where he improved his machine and his methods, based on what he had seen in Europe.

LIFE'S WORK

Tull's seed drill might have remained a local innovation were it not for the enthusiasm of his Hungerford neighbors when he moved there in 1714. They encouraged him to publicize the success of his planting technique. Not conversant with the scientific community, however, Tull could think of no method of disseminating his ideas beyond publishing a book, which he could not afford to do. With his farm barely supporting his family, Tull decided to con-

tinue his legal studies, and he was admitted to the bar in 1724. About that time, he began writing a full account of his invention and his agricultural system. By 1731, he had finished his manuscript but could still not afford to publish a full-length book, so he had an eighty-one-page "specimen" published cheaply in Dublin under the title *The New Horse-Houghing Husbandry: Or, An Essay on the Principles of Tillage and Vegetation Wherein Is Shewn, a Method of Introducing a Sort of Vinyard-Culture into the Corn-Fields, in Order to Increase Their Product, and Diminish the Common Expence, by the Use of Instruments Lately Invented*. In two years, the sales of this pamphlet justified the publication of an expanded two-hundred-page volume under virtually the same title, and Tull's place in the history of agriculture was assured.

Jethro Tull. Image via Wikimedia Commons. [Public domain.]

Filling a feed-box of a seed drill, Canterbury Agricultural College farm, 1948. Photo by Ron C. Blackmore, via Wikimedia Commons.

In the interim, influential noblemen had become interested in what became playfully known as "Tullian" agriculture. Tull had criticized the fact that English farmers were still using the "Virgilian" methods described by the Roman poet Virgil (70-19 BCE) in his *Georgics* (37-29 BCE), popularized in his day by John Dryden's translation. Eighteenth-century wits noted the irony that the adjective applied to Virgil's near-contemporary Cicero (106-43 BCE) in earlier times had been "Tullian" (for Marcus Tullius Cicero). In 1729, the Scottish Lord Ducie (Matthew Ducie Moreton, 1663-1735) introduced what he called Tullian or "Anti-Virgilian" methods to Charles, Eighth Lord Cathcart (1686-1740), the

Parliamentarian in the House of Lords most active in agricultural concerns. On May 9, 1730, Lord Cathcart took a party of noble lords to meet with Tull and discuss his theories and results. Thus, when Tull's pamphlet appeared a year later, a great number of influential policy makers were prepared to read it with interest.

THE TULL SEED DRILL
Jethro Tull's first seed drill was constructed on the frame of a wheelbarrow. He removed the gudgeon—the metal cylinder mounted on the wheel's axle that allowed it to turn independently of the wheel—and replaced it with a larger cylinder

with holes drilled at intervals. This perforated cylinder was fitted into the trough of the wheelbarrow, into which a slot was cut opposite the gudgeon. As the cylinder turned, its holes would pick up one seed at a time from the trough and drop them into a tube. This was the basic design, but Tull did not stop there.

The rotating cylinder reminded Tull of the groove, tongue, and spring of the sounding board of a church organ he had worked on, so he replaced his crude perforated cylinder with a much more closely fitted one made from the foot pedal of an old organ. Having mechanized the placement of the seed, Tull realized that mechanization allows duplication. A wheelbarrow could only accommodate one row at a time; enlarging the frame could allow simultaneous deposit of multiple rows of seed. Doing so, however, would create a machine too heavy for one farmer to push.

English farmers of the time generally used oxen to plow their fields. Tull designed his second-generation, three-row (and later four-row) seed drill to be pulled by the lighter and smaller horse. However, the seed was only the middle part of the process. Ahead of his enlarged drill, Tull mounted three plowshares, which opened furrows immediately ahead of each seed depositor. Then, after the seed was dropped, a metal disk known as a coulter turned behind each row to place the soil back over the newly planted seed, spacing the rows widely enough to allow horse-drawn hoes to weed the fields once the crop germinated.

For the next two centuries, the only improvements on Tull's drill was simply increasing the number of rows: Tull's horse-drawn model remained basically unchanged until the 1930s, when they were attached to tractors. Twenty-first century seed drills move the seed by pneumatic tubes and inject them into the soil by air pressure. Nevertheless, other than the switch from Tull's gravity-feed (which remained in use to the end of the twentieth century),

modern seed drills still employ the principles Tull had perfected by the early 1700s.

CONTROVERSY IN THE AFTERMATH

Although the Tull seed drill soon became the standard implement for planting in Europe and its colonies, the complete adoption of Jethro Tull's agricultural method was delayed by controversy. The controversy was well founded, for one of Tull's theoretical assumptions was wrong. He opposed the use of animal waste as fertilizer, convinced, first, that the soil contained all of the nutrients grains needed and that it needed only to be pulverized to release the nutrients to the germinating seed; and second, that animal waste contained unwanted seeds that would compete with the grain seed. His first assumption was not completely accurate: Preparing the soil did release more of the nutrients, which explained the success of Tull's experiments, but he was not aware that the grains would eventually exhaust the nitrogen from the soil, which animal manure replaced. His second assumption, however, was correct, and the resultant weed control of Tull's method—weed seeds were no longer spread through animal dung—was an important factor in its success.

Weed control was not just a function of the elimination of fertilizer, however. The regular spacing that resulted from the use of the seed drill meant that weeds could be removed from the spaces between rows without harming the planted grain. In modern times, it is taken for granted that fields are planted in rows, but before Tull's seed drill planting was done by broadcast in a random fashion. The waste involved in this method—some landing on rocks or dry soil, some being eaten by birds—was considered unavoidable, which is the point of the familiar New Testament parable of the sower (Matthew 13:1-23, Mark 4:1-20, Luke 8:1-15). Tull's machine, however, placed each seed at an ideal, uniform depth and immediately covered it over with soil.

The seed drill was not the only Tull invention that would become standard throughout Europe by the end of the eighteenth century. Tull also improved plowing by inventing a plow that was essentially a horse-drawn hoe, with the blade elevated so that it uprooted grass and weeds, leaving them on the surface of cultivated land so that they could be gathered and destroyed (rather than reseeding). It is significant that the title of Tull's work emphasized the plowing and hoeing rather than the planting aspect of his method.

Tull never lived to see his agricultural methods become standard, as they were by the end of the century. His financial struggles continued to the end of his life, exacerbated by a profligate son John, who ended up in Fleet Prison, London, for debt, shortly after Tull died penniless in 1741.

IMPACT

Though the process of dropping grain individually through a tube pressed into the ground was known in ancient Babylon (as early as 1500 BCE), European farming had reverted to the broadcast method used by the ancient Romans and continued until Tull's day. Tull's innovation, therefore, lay not in the subsoil drilling but in the mechanical regularizing of the depth and distribution of seeds, as well as the simultaneous removal of weeds that would compete with the seed for nutrients, and covering over the seeds immediately after placement, to keep birds from eating them before they could germinate. By the end of the eighteenth century, agricultural authorities were still divided on whether the Tullian method worked, but influential authors such as John Randall in *The Semi-Virgilian Husbandry* (1764) and Francis Forbes in *The Modern Improvements in Agriculture* (1784) promoted it.

With the rise of industrial manufacturing in England, mass-production of the Tull seed drill became a key to its standardization, and James Smyth and Sons began producing modified Tull drills in 1800, continuing into the middle of the twentieth century. The invention of the subsoil plow in the 1830s improved Tull's drill and was seen to be an extension of his theory that tillage was more important than manuring; as late as 1859, Alexander Burnett's *Tillage a Substitute for Manure* presented the new soil aeration as an extension of *The Precepts and Practice of Jethro Tull*. Twentieth century planters continued Tull's basic design, though the emphasis in weed control shifted from hoeing to fertilizing. The increasing popularity of organic farming methods began to reverse that trend in the early twenty-first century, making plant culture in the United Kingdom, particularly in wheat, closer to the process Tull knew than it had been only fifty years earlier.

—*John R. Holmes*

Further Reading

Ambrosoli, Mauro. *The Wild and the Sown: Botany and Agriculture in Western Europe, 1350-1850.* Translated by Mary McCann Salvatorelli. Cambridge UP, 1997.

Bourde, André J. *The Influence of England on the French Agronomes, 1750-1789.* Cambridge UP, 1953.

Fussell, George E. *Jethro Tull: His Influence on Mechanized Agriculture.* Osprey, 1973.

MacDonald, William. *Makers of Modern Agriculture.* Macmillan, 1913.

Smith, D. J. *Discovering Horse-Drawn Farm Machinery.* 2nd rev. ed., Shire, 2008.

Thirsk, Joan. *England's Agricultural Regions and Agrarian History, 1500-1750.* Macmillan Education, 1987.

Thompson, Holland. *The Age of Invention: A Chronicle of Mechanical Conquest.* BiblioBazaar, 2007.

Tull, Jethro. *Horse-hoeing Husbandry, or, An Essay on the Principles of Vegetation and Tillage: Designed to Introduce a New Method of Culture, Whereby the Produce of Land Will be Increased, and the Usual Expence Lessened: Together with Accurate Descriptions and Cuts of the Instruments Employed in It.* 3rd ed., A. Millar, 1751.

See also: Engineering; Mechanical engineering; Tull, Jethro

TURBINES

Fields of Study: Physics; Mechanics; Mathematics

ABSTRACT

Turbines are an important component of many machines, large and small. They use rotational motion to convert energy from wind, water, or steam into electricity. They can also use fuel to power a diverse array of engines, such as those in cars, motorcycles, jets, rockets, and ships.

KEY CONCEPTS

force: the ability to produce motion, often calculated by multiplying the mass of an object by its acceleration

impulse turbine: a turbine set in motion by the velocity of a fluid hitting each blade

kinetic energy: the work capacity of an object in motion

potential energy: the stored work capacity of an object

power: the rate at which work is done

reaction turbine: a turbine set in motion by the pressure and flow of a fluid

torque: a twisting force that produces rotational motion

work: the energy transferred to an object by a force, calculated by multiplying the force applied to an object by the distance it has moved the object or the amount of resistance it has overcome

THE POWER OF ROTATIONAL MOTION

Turbines are an important component of many machines, large and small. They use rotational motion to convert energy from wind, water, or steam into electricity. They can also use fuel to power a diverse array of engines, such as those in cars, motorcycles, jets, rockets, and ships.

The word "turbine" comes from the Latin word turbo, which refers to something that spins. First used in the 1800s, the word described machines that harnessed energy from steam. Similar devices, such as waterwheels and windmills, have existed since ancient times, but the shift to the term "turbine" corresponded to major advances in technology.

In order for an object to move, something must transfer energy to it. Anything that uses energy to change an object's state of motion is called a force. If a force moves an object, it has done work. The rate at which work occurs is called power, calculated by multiplying force by speed. Greater force allows work to be done more quickly. Lifting a person straight up off the ground requires a large amount of force. A lever allows force to be applied over a greater distance, which means that less force is required at any given moment. A seesaw illustrates this principle. Two people on different ends of a seesaw can easily lift one another into the air, even if they cannot lift the other person's weight in their arms. Turbines use torque, a force that produces rotational motion around a central point. Using torque to accomplish a task is similar to using a lever.

Turbines vary greatly depending on their type and purpose, but all turbines have several basic components. Blades (also called vanes) catch the wind or water or respond to the pressure of water or steam. A child's toy, the pinwheel, demonstrates the way a wind turbine works. A rotor is the central part of a turbine to which the blades are attached. The rotor is connected to a shaft inside the turbine. There may be one or two shafts that spin to power a generator, which in turn creates electricity.

MAKING ENERGY MORE USABLE

A turbine is a way to transform energy from an unusable form (such as water, wind, or steam) to a usable form (electricity). Moving water and air have kinetic energy because they are in motion. If water is stored behind a dam, it has potential energy because it is being contained, but it has the potential to move. If the dam is removed, the water's potential energy becomes kinetic energy as the water flows again. When harnessed by a turbine, both water and air possess the ability to perform work. When water flows through turbines, it powers them with its kinetic energy. All types of turbines are essentially engines that use kinetic energy to cause rotational motion around a central axis. This movement can then power larger systems, such as geothermal or nuclear power plants, as well as water- or wind-powered systems.

The workings of turbines powered by wind and water are visible at wind farms or dams, but it is more difficult to see the workings of turbines powered by steam. As gases heat up, they expand, putting pressure on whatever is containing them. An empty milk jug placed outside on a hot day may pop its top when the air inside it expands too much. This same principle propels the blades of a turbine. Steam entering the turbine is under pressure because it is in an enclosed space, and that pressure forces the blades of the turbine to move.

Steam turbines are used in many types of power plants. In a geothermal power plant, hot water is drawn from underground reservoirs, such as hot springs or geysers, to power turbines that then create electricity. It is also possible to power turbines by concentrating solar energy to heat water and make steam. In a nuclear facility, steam created from nuclear reactions powers turbines to generate electricity.

Turbines may also increase the power of combustion engines that run on gasoline, as in a jet engine or a turbocharged automobile. A gas turbine, like a steam turbine, relies on the ability of gases to expand when heated. Gas turbines are used in jet engines and ships. In an airplane, the action of the turbine creates exhaust that propels the plane forward. In a ship, the turbine drives a propeller, which in turn moves the ship. In these cases, the turbine is not converting moving wind or water to electricity but rather using energy to increase power.

IMPULSE AND REACTION TURBINES

Turbines are designed with different environments and needs in mind. A turbine powered by wind is much different than one powered by water. Even among turbines designed for use with water, there is a great deal of variation because water itself varies in volume, speed, and force. When designing hydroturbines (water-powered turbines), engineers

A steam turbine with the case opened. Photo bySiemens Pressebild, via Wikimedia Commons.

consider the water's flow rate (volume per second) and its head (level or depth). High head is deep water, and low head is shallower water.

The two types of hydroturbine are impulse turbines and reaction turbines. Some turbines, called impulse-reaction turbines, are a mixture of these two types, which means they can adapt to a broad range of conditions.

An impulse is a force that acts for a short time to produce a particular change in momentum. Because of the way an impulse turbine is designed, force hits each blade in sequence, causing it to move. As the force hits each blade, the rotor assembly spins. An old-fashioned waterwheel demonstrates the physics behind impulse turbines: the water hits one blade at a time, turning the wheel. In a reaction turbine, the blades move in response to the steady application of force—that is, they react. Instead of water hitting each blade in sequence, it flows over the entire assembly, ideally with constant pressure.

An impulse turbine works best when hit at high velocity. Water hits each turbine blade with a lot of force and propels it. A reaction turbine does not require as much force to be set in motion. An impulse turbine would be suited to harnessing the energy from a small, fast-moving river, while a larger, deeper, slow-moving river would be better served by a reaction turbine. In real life, rivers can change seasonally or in response to storms, so many hydroturbines use combination impulse-reaction turbines in order to work with variable flow.

A wind turbine may be thought of as a reaction turbine because wind moves over the entire turbine, setting it in motion. The two types of wind turbine are vertical axis and horizontal axis. Horizontal-axis turbines resemble pinwheels and operate in much the same way. A vertical-axis turbine operates like a kitchen mixer; both the axis and the blades are oriented vertically, with the blades curving to catch the wind.

TURBINES AND THE FUTURE

Turbines facilitated the advent of the Industrial Revolution, and they continue to serve an important role in industry and technology. They are a part of almost every engine, from jets to cars. Turbines are also an important part of both alternative and fossil-fuel-based energy production. As a result, many innovators are working to streamline turbine operation and expand how turbines are used. For instance, in the wind industry, engineers are developing lightweight turbines that can hover high in the air to catch better air currents. They are also experimenting with adding a second rotor to traditional wind turbines in order to increase efficiency. In the water-power industry, turbines already generate power from rivers and tides and will be a part of generating power from tidal lagoons. In addition to industrial applications, engineers are developing hydroturbines for small-scale individual use, such as generating power for personal electronic devices.

—*J. D. Ho*

Further Reading

Breeze, Paul. *Power Generation Technologies*. Elsevier, 2014.

Chiras, Daniel D, Mick Sagrillo, and Ian Woofenden. *Power from the Wind*. New Society, 2009.

"Engineers Study the Benefits of Adding a Second, Smaller Rotor to Wind Turbines." *Phys.org*, 10 Mar. 2015. Accessed 14 Apr. 2015.

"How Do Wind Turbines Work?" *Office of Energy Efficiency & Renewable Energy*. US Department of Energy, n.d. Accessed 14 Apr. 2015.

Madrigal, Alexis C. "How to Make a Wind Turbine That Flies." *Atlantic*. Atlantic Monthly, 16 July 2012. Accessed 14 Apr. 2015.

Owano, Nancy. "Blue Freedom Uses Power of Flowing Water to Charge." *Phys.org Tech Xplore*, 26 Mar. 2015. Accessed 14 Apr. 2015.

Soares, Claire. *Gas Turbines: A Handbook of Air, Land and Sea Applications*. Butterworth, 2014.

"Types of Hydropower Turbines." *Office of Energy Efficiency & Renewable Energy*. US Department of Energy, n.d. Accessed 14 Apr. 2015.

Woodford, Chris, and Jon Woodcock. *Cool Stuff 2.0 and How It Works*. DK, 2007.

See also: Circular motion; Dynamics (mechanics); Energy transmission: Mechanical energy; Hydraulic engineering; Hydrodynamics; Jet engines; Steam energy technology; Torque; Work and energy

TURBOJETS AND TURBOFANS

Fields of Study: Physics; Aeronautical engineering; Mechanical engineering; Mathematics

ABSTRACT

Turbojets are jet engines that are turbocharged. Turbofans are turbojets onto the front end of which a large fan is added. Turbojets are used in most airplanes that are large and travel for long distances. They are also used in military applications such as bombers and special surveillance aircraft. Turbofans generate more thrust than turbojets. For this reason, they are used to power jumbo jets.

KEY CONCEPTS

combustion chamber: a structure as the second stage of a jet engine within which the fuel-air mixture is combusted, producing rapidly expanding hot exhaust gases

compression-ignition: an engine that uses the heat produced by the compression of air inside a combustion chamber as the ignition source for combustion of fuel

compressor: a rotating structure at the first stage of a jet engine that compresses air taken in

spark-ignition: an engine that uses an electrical spark inside a combustion chamber as the ignition source for combustion of fuel

thrust: the force or pressure exerted on the body of an aircraft in the direction of its motion

POWERFUL ENGINES

Propeller engines are suited for small airplanes that travel for short distances. Turbojets provide transport capabilities that propeller engines cannot. The McDonnell FH-1 Phantom was the first all-jet airplane ordered by the US Navy and the Navy's first airplane to fly 500 miles per hour. Its first flight took place on January 26, 1945. On July 21, 1946, an FH-1 Phantom became the first jet-propelled combat aircraft to operate from an American aircraft carrier. The Phantom weighed 4,552 kilograms, could accommodate one crew member, had a range of 1,119 kilometers, and was powered by two turbojets, the Westinghouse J30-WE-20, each of which could deliver 272 kilograms of thrust. A year later, the thrust delivered by turbojets had doubled. By the end of the 1950s, the turbojets could deliver thrusts that were twenty times that delivered by the J30-WE-20.

BASIC OPERATION OF A JET ENGINE

An appreciation of how a jet engine works requires understanding Bernoulli's principle, Sir Isaac Newton's third law of motion, and how these two ideas from physics come into play in the operation of a jet engine.

For ordinary commercial and pleasure flights, air is treated as an incompressible substance that has no viscosity, and the level flight is treated as steady. Under these circumstances, a principle of physics called Bernoulli's principle states that the sum of three forms of energy remains constant. These three forms are kinetic energy (energy associated with the motion of air), potential energy (that associated with weight and elevation above or below a reference level), and the energy associated with pressure. Air is a very light substance; it is conventional to neglect its potential energy because its contribution is typically very small compared to those of the other two forms of energy. Accordingly, when kinetic energy

Junkers Jumo 004, the first production turbojet in operational use. Photo by Nick-D, via Wikimedia Commons.

increases, pressure energy must decrease by the same amount, and vice versa.

Sir Isaac Newton formulated three laws of motion. Propulsion generated by a jet engine operates according to Newton's third law of motion. It states that for every action there is a reaction. The reaction is equal to the action in magnitude but opposite to it in direction. This law can be seen in operation in many ordinary ways. For instance, walking involves planting a foot and pushing backward (action). The ground provides the reaction by resisting against the foot in order to create the thrust that makes walking possible. When a surface is slip-

pery, this really means that its ability to provide a reaction is limited and that walking on that surface has become treacherous. As another example, if one inflates a small balloon but does not tie the open end shut before releasing the balloon, after release, the air inside the balloon will want to rush out of it. As it does so, a thrust will be created, helping the balloon sail forward for some time until most of the air has escaped. A jet airplane works a little bit like the inflated balloon. In a jet, a mechanism must be created to introduce air into the plane and release it in such a way that thrust is continuously created.

A jet engine utilizes jet propulsion, which is a kind of propulsion in which the force needed to move the body of the aircraft comes from discharging a jet of fluid from the body at high speed. As the fluid jet leaves the body, it produces a reaction force against the body and it is this force that propels the body forward, according to Newton's third law of motion.

Jet engines include turbojets, turboprops, ramjets, scramjets, and rockets. Rockets carry all they need with them to generate combustion. Therefore, they can operate in space because they do not need air to function. The other jet engines require air to operate properly. It is for this reason that they belong to a class called air-breathing propulsion, or simply air-breathing machines. They utilize the mechanical behavior of air in their operation.

The propulsion system of a jet engine consists of an inlet diffuser, a compressor, a fuel injection system, a combustion chamber (also called a combuster), a turbine, and an exhaust nozzle. A jet engine slows down incoming air as it enters the engine; that is, it causes a decrease in kinetic energy. Thus, the air pressure increases according to Bernoulli's principle.

The air goes through a series of compressor blades that look somewhat like fan blades. These blades help push the air forward, giving it new energy by doing work on them. This work increases the pressure energy of the air and thereby adds to the total energy. This high-pressure air enters the combustion chamber, where it is mixed with fuel, ignited, and burned. The hot gases resulting from this combustion want to expand and they leave the combustion chamber at very high speed and pressure. On their way out of the engine, the hot gases go through the blades of a turbine. They drive the turbine by pushing against its blades like a high wind blowing past a windmill. The turbine drives the compressor because the two units are connected to each other by a shaft. The movement of the compressor compresses the air that enters the engine. As the exhaust gases leave the engine, they exert a thrust that propels the airplane forward while the gases travel backward, again in accordance with Newton's third law of motion (action equals reaction). These exhaust gases leave the airplane in a fast-moving stream commonly called a jet. That is why this is called a jet engine.

DIFFERENT KINDS OF ENGINES

There are many different kinds of engines. They are classified a number of different ways. Classification hinges upon how the essential components are designed and the role they play. For example, if combustion takes place inside an enclosure, the engine is called an internal combustion engine. However, if it occurs in the open, the engine is called an external-combustion engine. Internal combustion engines are very common. They are used in planes and are designed to produce work at high efficiencies. The two main types of internal combustion engines are spark-ignition engines and compression-ignition engines. In spark-ignition engines, the fuel-air mixture is ignited using an electrical spark. In compression engines, there is no spark at all and ignition of the fuel-air mixture is achieved by increasing the temperature and pressure of the air inside the combustion chamber.

Propeller engines are well suited for low-speed flights, but they do not work as well for high-speed flights for two important reasons: as the forward speed of an aircraft increases, the thrust that propellers provide to move the craft forward decreases and the drag resistance associated with their operation increases. Jet engines do not have these limitations. They were introduced to provide power to aircraft that move at high speeds because they work better at these speeds. Ideally, internal combustion engines should have high efficiency, high output and rapid combustion, generate minimal pollution, and be very quiet. It is very challenging to design engines that would achieve all of these goals. In compression-ignition engines, volume requirements are higher but the combustion process is slower than in spark-ignition engines. Thus, the maximum speeds of compression-ignition engines are much lower than those of spark-ignition engines.

SUPERCHARGING AND TURBOCHARGING

Two effective techniques were found to increase the output of compression-ignition engines: supercharging and turbocharging. An engine is supercharged by supplying pressurized air to it. When the air at the inlet to an engine is pressurized, the mass flow rate of air into the engine increases. Typically, this is associated with an increase in the flow rate of fuel to the engine. These two factors lead to increases in power output and efficiency. Compressors need power to do their work. When a compressor is driven from the crankshaft of an engine, the arrangement is called a supercharger. However, when it is driven by the turbine, the arrangement is called a turbocharger, and the affected engine is said to be turbocharged. Thus, turbocharging is a particular form of supercharging in which a compressor is driven by an exhaust gas turbine. There are thermodynamic advantages to turbochargers over superchargers, principally because the former utilize exhaust gas energy during the so-called blow-down. Turbocharging also reduces the weight per unit output and increases fuel economy.

Work done by the turbine is just sufficient to drive the compressor. Hot gases enter the turbine where they are expanded to a pressure that allows the work done on the turbine to equal that done by the compressor. The pressure of the exhaust gases for the turbine is greater than that of the surrounding air, so the hot gases are expanded further in a nozzle so that their pressure will be lowered to that of the surroundings. The gases leave at high velocity, and thrust is generated by the change in momentum that the gases undergo.

CHARACTERISTICS AND PERFORMANCE OF TURBOJETS

Nine characteristics are used to describe a turbojet: its weight, its length, its diameter, the number of stages its compressor has, the number of stages its turbine has, the thrust it can deliver at takeoff, the best thrust it can deliver at cruising speeds, its speed range, and its specific fuel consumption. The specific fuel consumption of a turbojet is the amount (in weight) of fuel it consumes per unit weight of thrust delivered, per hour.

The characteristics of the latest models of turbojets are protected carefully by manufacturers because these machines are used for purposes of defense and surveillance. However, older models are available in museums of flight. For example, in the late 1950s, Pratt & Whitney designed the J-58 turbojet engine to be used by the US Navy. Its axial compressor had nine stages, its turbine had two stages, it had an afterburner, and it could provide a takeoff thrust of 14,742 kilograms. It weighed 2,721.6 kilograms and operated above 26 kilometers at speeds three times that of sound (Mach 3). The J-58 is currently in the museum of flight at Wright-Patterson Air Force Base.

TURBOFANS

The turbojet is very successful at increasing the speed of the air that enters the engine, which increases its kinetic energy, but another way to increase the total energy of the air is to increase the amount of air that enters the engine. A turbofan achieves this by mounting a large fan at the inlet to the engine. The design of the turbojet is modified accordingly. The addition of the fan creates two different paths that the incoming air can use to travel through the engine before leaving it. Some of the air follows the path that it would use in a conventional turbojet: from the inlet diffuser, it goes successively through the compressor, or compressors, the combustion chamber, the turbine, and the exit nozzle.

The remaining air bypasses the compressor altogether: it goes from the inlet diffuser, around the engine, and directly to the back of the plane. In doing so, it converts the pressure that it stored in the inlet diffuser directly into kinetic energy. Here, again, air leaves the engine traveling faster than when it entered it, and as this air leaves the fan, it exerts thrust on it. This mechanism provides a second thrust that is added to that due to the operation of a turbofan as a conventional turbojet. If one looks at modern jumbo jets at airports, their engines look like huge fans. Chances are very high that these engines are turbofans.

—*Josué Njock Libii*

FURTHER READING

Babu, V. *Fundamentals of Propulsion*. Springer International Publishing, 2021.

Barsoum, Michel, et al. "The MAX Phases: Unique New Carbide and Nitride Materials." *American Scientist,* 89, no. 4, July-Aug. 2001.

Decker, Reiner. *Powering the World's Airliners: Engine Developments from the Propeller to the Jet Age*. Pen & Sword Books, 2020.

El-Sayed, Ahmed F. *Fundamentals of Aircraft and Rocket Propulsion*. Springer London, 2016.

Hunecke, Klaus. *Jet Engines: Fundamentals of Theory, Design and Operation*. Crowood Press UK, 2010.

Linke-Diesinger, Andreas. *Systems of Commercial Turbofan Engines: An Introduction to Systems Functions*. Springer Berlin Heidelberg, 2010.

Richter, Hanz. *Advanced Control of Turbofan Engines*. Springer New York, 2014.

See also: Aeronautical engineering; Airplane propellers; Fluid dynamics; Jet engines; Propulsion technologies; Turboprops

TURBOPROPS

Fields of Study: Physics; Aeronautical engineering; Mechanical engineering; Mathematics

ABSTRACT

Also known as propjets or jetprops, a variation of the gas turbine engine that develops thrust with propellers instead of the exhaust duct. The turboprop is a very popular aviation engine designed to be fuel-efficient and to propel airplanes at moderately high speeds and altitudes.

KEY CONCEPTS

aerodynamic efficiency: the measure of the airfoil shape of a propeller blade to produce thrust relative to the forward speed of the aircraft

drag: the resistance to motion through a fluid due to friction between the moving object and the fluid medium

HISTORY

The idea for using a gas turbine engine to drive an airplane's propeller was first thought of by Sir Frank Whittle. His graduate thesis, written at the Royal Air Force (RAF) Staff College at Cranwell in 1928, predicted the use of turboprops even before the first gas turbine engine had been built. Turbojet engines were developed first and then adapted by adding more turbine blades, a reduction gearbox, and a propeller to become turboprops. The first flight of a turboprop airplane occurred in England on September 20, 1945. The engine was a Rolls-Royce RB50 Trent. It was installed in a modified Gloster Meteor aircraft. The first flight of the Vickers Viscount was made on December 6, 1948. The Viscount became the first turboprop-powered airplane to go into passenger service. The Tupolev Tu-95 was the former Soviet Union's primary nuclear bomber from the mid-1950s into the early 1990s. This Bear bomber set the speed record for a turboprop airplane by flying at 925 kilometers per hour at 11.6 kilometers. Many different models of turboprop engines and airplanes are still being manufactured, such as the Raytheon King Air and the Lockheed C-130.

THEORY OF OPERATION

Gas turbine engines consist of a compressor, a combustion chamber, and a turbine. These components are collectively referred to as a gas generator, a name arising from the purpose of the parts, which is to generate a stream of high-velocity gas. A turbojet generates all of its thrust from having high-pressure and high-velocity gases leaving the exhaust duct at the back of the engine. A turbojet only has enough turbine blades to extract energy to drive the compressor. A turboprop converts most of the exhaust pressure and velocity into rotational energy by adding extra turbine blades. The extra turbine blades extract energy to drive a reduction gearbox. This reduction gearbox is required so the large propeller will spin at a slower, more efficient speed. The reduction gearbox reduces the revolutions per minute (RPM) of the turbines, typically ten thousand to forty thousand RPM, down to two thousand. The turboprop engine's thrust produced by the exhaust is about 10 percent of the total thrust of the engine. The other 90 percent comes from the propeller. Turboprop and turboshaft engines are nearly identical except for their purpose. Turboprop engines drive propellers to provide forward thrust. Turboshaft engines drive helicopter transmission gearboxes which provide horsepower to drive rotor blades.

ADVANTAGES

The greatest advantage of the turboprop engine is its high fuel efficiency. It is more fuel-efficient than the two other types of gas turbine engines that propel airplanes: turbojets and turbofans. A turboprop acquires this efficiency from accelerating a large mass of air to only a slightly higher velocity. Turbojets accelerate a small mass of air to a much higher velocity. Less energy from fuel is required to affect mass than to affect velocity. Several advantages for

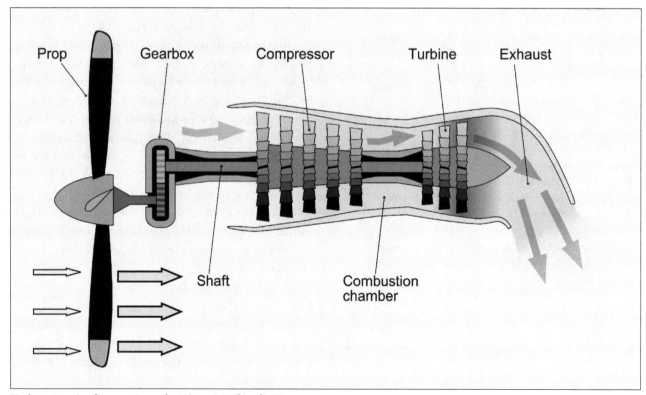

Turboprop engine diagram. Image by M0tty, via Wikimedia Commons.

using a turboprop engine to propel an airplane come from the propellers themselves. Turboprops have the shortest takeoffs of any airplane. This capability is provided by the variable pitch of the propeller blades. The use of variable-pitch blades is similar to the use of low gears in a car at slow speeds and the use of higher gears when reaching higher speeds. Unlike a car, this blade pitch is infinitely variable, so the propeller always has the perfect gear ratio. Turboprops can also put the propeller blades into reverse pitch. Although the blades continue to turn in the same direction of rotation, the pitch or angle of the blades change from blowing air backward to blowing air in a forward direction, thereby dramatically slowing the aircraft during landing. When the blade pitch is reversed, more fuel is sent to the engine to increase the amount of reversed airflow. This causes the engine to produce more noise during landing when the blades are reversed. This increase in noise and reversed airflow is similar to thrust reversers used during landing with turbojet and turbofan engines.

DISADVANTAGES

A turboprop airplane's greatest disadvantage is being limited in forward airspeed. This limit is imposed by the use of a propeller. By the time the airplane has reached Mach 0.6, which is 60 percent of the speed of sound, the propeller blades have lost much of their aerodynamic efficiency. This efficiency is lost because there is much greater drag on the blade tips at high forward speeds than at slow forward speeds. The combination of speed of the rotating blade with the forward speed of the airplane

produces speeds at the blade tips that are close to Mach 1.0. Aerodynamic drag when approaching Mach 1.0 becomes extremely high. To keep the propeller blade tips at slow enough speeds to be efficient, turboprops typically fly at speeds of less than Mach 0.6 (663 kilometers per hour at 7.62 kilometers altitude and temperature of -35 degrees Celsius). Since turbojets and turbofans do not have propellers, most commercial and corporate jets can easily fly at Mach 0.8 to 0.9. In the late 1990s, some smaller airlines started replacing their turboprop-powered airplanes with turbofan-powered airplanes, even though the fuel efficiency of turbofans is not quite as good. This replacement was for two major reasons: passengers feel more comfortable flying in "jets" than in "props," and more revenue-generating flights can be accomplished per day if the airplanes can travel faster.

—*John C. Johnson*

Further Reading

Cercerále, Jiri. *Whirl Flutter of Turboprop Aircraft Structures.* Elsevier Science, 2015.

Morales, João Paulo Zeitoun. *EMB-312 Tucano: Brazil's Turboprop Success Story.* Harpia Publishing, 2018.

Stroud, Nick. *The Vickers Viscount, The World's First Turboprop Airliner.* Pen & Sword Books Ltd., 2017.

Van Soest, Ton. *Business Jets and Turboprops Quick Reference Biz QR 2017.* Air Britain (Trading) Ltd., 2017.

Zichek, Jared A. *Goodyear GA-28A/B Convoy Fighter: The Naval VTOL Turboprop Tailsitter Project of 1950.* Retromechanix Productions, 2015.

See also: Aeronautical engineering; Airplane propellers; Fluid dynamics; Jet engines; Propulsion technologies; Turbojets and turbofans

V

VACUUM

Fields of Study: Physics; Mechanics; Mathematics

ABSTRACT

A perfect vacuum is defined as a space without any matter. However, experts believe a perfect vacuum state is impossible to achieve because of the quantum uncertainty principle. In practical terms, a vacuum is an area of space with so little matter that its atmospheric pressure is much less than what is normally experienced on Earth. The study of vacuums has proven very important in physics, quantum physics, engineering, and astronomy. Vacuums are also used in the creation of many modern conveniences.

KEY CONCEPTS

quantum mechanical tunneling: an electronic process occurring in atoms, by which electrons may become able to cross energy barriers into electronic regions where they would not otherwise be allowed

quantum mechanics: the mathematical system that describes the innermost workings of atoms and their subatomic particles

temporary particles: subatomic particles such as electrons and protons that seem to appear out of nothingness in a high vacuum

vacuum pump: a gas pumping system designed to extract air and other gases from an enclosed system

A SPACE FILLED WITH NOTHING

A perfect vacuum is defined as a space without any matter. However, experts believe a perfect vacuum state is impossible to achieve because of the quantum uncertainty principle. Instead, scientists measure degrees of vacuum by how few particles are found in a particular area and the amount of atmospheric pressure exerted in the area. Atmospheric pressure is a measurement of the strength of the pressure in an area when compared to the average amount of pressure commonly exerted on Earth.

According to these measurements, deep space is the closest example of a perfect vacuum found in nature. In practical terms, a vacuum is an area of space with so little matter that its atmospheric pressure is much less than what is normally experienced on Earth. The study of vacuums has proven very important in physics, quantum physics, engineering, and astronomy. Vacuums are also used in the creation of many modern conveniences.

THE STUDY OF VACUUMS

The original concept of a vacuum, a space occupied by nothing at all, is far from new. The ancient Greeks debated the possibility of the existence of a vacuum, but had trouble reconciling its existence with how they believed the world functioned. From their point of view, the concept that an area could both exist and be nothing was ridiculous. The idea was not commonly revisited until the philosopher Abu Muhammad Al-Farabi conducted experiments on vacuums using plungers in the late ninth and early tenth centuries. He agreed that vacuums were impossible, primarily because he believed air expanded to fill all empty space.

Researchers began experimenting with vacuums and atmospheric pressure during the seventeenth century, though most failed to realize that vacuums were behind the phenomena they observed. Scien-

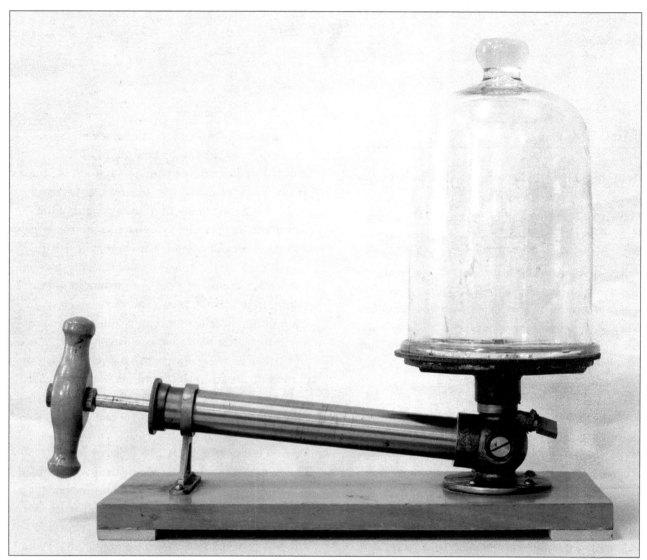

Pump to demonstrate vacuum. Photo by Hannes Grobe, via Wikimedia Commons.

tists studied airtight tubes filled with mercury and gas. They used a pump to remove gas (a form of matter) from the container. Removing the gaseous matter created a small vacuum. Because of the reduced pressure in the vacuum, the mercury rose higher in the tube.

Blaise Pascal was the first scientist to interpret these experiments correctly. He conducted more experiments that proved the mercury rose because of the reduced atmospheric pressure in the vacuum.

Still, many of the most prominent scientists of his time scorned his ideas. Even the famous philosopher René Descartes considered the idea that empty spaces could exist between atoms laughable. The pascal, a common unit of measurement for atmospheric pressure, was later named after Blaise Pascal in recognition of his contribution to science.

After Pascal's theories were dismissed, scientists and philosophers composed the theory of ether (also called æther) to account for perceived gaps in space.

It proposed that an invisible gas called ether filled all of outer space, allowing light and energy to move through it. However, this theory was comparatively short-lived. Einstein published his theory of relativity, which proposed that many of the grand functions of the universe were carried out through gravity. While Einstein's theories allowed for the existence of ether, they did not require it. Instead, they showed that the universe does not need to be consistently full of matter to function.

Paul Dirac and Werner Heisenberg, early proponents of quantum physics, also helped bring the scientific community's concepts of vacuums to their modern form. According to quantum physics, a true vacuum can never exist. While deep space is probably as close as possible to a true vacuum, the occasional atoms will still be found there. According to Heisenberg's famous uncertainty principle, the location of any particle is never truly certain. Because of this principle, temporary particles called virtual particles (most often virtual electrons and virtual positrons) will occasionally spring into existence out of nothingness and quickly disappear. This process is called vacuum fluctuation. Due to vacuum fluctuation, a space can never stay truly empty of particles.

Modern quantum mechanics defines vacuums as the state of having the lowest possible energy. Thus, degrees vacuums are measured in terms of how much atmospheric pressure is exerted in a given area. As a state gets closer to a perfect vacuum, less atmospheric pressure is exerted. As a state gets further from a perfect vacuum, more atmospheric pressure is exerted.

WHY STUDY VACUUMS?

Vacuums contribute to countless areas of modern life. As their name suggests, vacuum cleaners of all kinds use a pump to remove gas from a chamber, which causes air and debris to rush in and fill the partial vacuum created. In a vacuum cleaner, a filter traps and stores the debris. Water pumps utilize vacuums in a similar manner. Electric lights require a vacuum to function properly, and the semiconductors common to electronic devices are created using vacuums. Even many aircraft parts require being formed under vacuum, while others are designed to be vacuum powered. These parts continue to function properly during an electrical failure, improving the pilot's ability to safely land the aircraft.

Additionally, the study of vacuums leads to interesting observations about our universe. Studying how light moves in a vacuum, including what causes it to slow down, accelerate, or bend, is incredibly important for observing and mapping the known universe. Some scientists even think a better understanding of how quantum physics function in a vacuum, specifically the theoretical energy inherent in vacuums called zero point energy, will lead to a clearer understanding of why the universe is expanding.

Because most of outer space is an extreme vacuum, the study of vacuums is essential for any projects that involve humans or objects leaving Earth. Detailed knowledge of how physics and chemical reactions function in a vacuum is essential for navigating outer space. Experiments on Earth, along with data from accidents in space, showed scientists that humans exposed to extreme vacuums like those found in outer space lose consciousness in less than fifteen seconds and suffer fatal complications in just minutes. Studying how matter acts in a vacuum allows scientists and engineers to build spacecraft and space suits. These complex systems allow humans to survive in extreme vacuums for extended periods without harm.

—*Tyler Biscontini*

Further Reading

Bello, Igor. *Vacuum and Ultravacuum: Physics and Technology*. CRC Press, 2017.

Boi, Luciano. "A Scientific and Philosophical Concept, from Electrodynamics to String Theory and the

Geometry of the Microscopic World." *The Quantum Vacuum*. JHU Press, 2011.

Borichevsky, Steve. *Understanding Modern Vacuum Technology*. CreateSpace Independent Publishing Platform, 2017.

Gosline, Anna. "Survival in Space Unprotected Is Possible —Briefly." *Scientific American*. Scientific American, Inc. 14 Feb. 2008, www.scientificamerican.com/article/survival-in-space-unprotected-possible/. Accessed 23 Dec. 2014.

Matthews, Robert. "Nothing Like a Vacuum." *Calphysics.org*. Calphysics Institute, www.calphysics.org/haisch/matthews.html. Accessed 23 Dec. 2014.

"More About Vacuum Pumps." *ThomasNet.com*. Thomas Publishing Company, www.thomasnet.com/about/vacuum-pumps-65021602.html. Accessed 23 Dec. 2014.

"Supernova Study Might Change How Speed of Light in Vacuum Is Measured." *ZMEScience.com*. ZME Media, 25 June 2014, www.zmescience.com/space/supernova-speed-of-light-change053456/. Accessed 23 Dec. 2014.

See also: Acoustics; Aerospace design; Bernoulli's principle; Centrifugation; Materials science; Nanotechnology; Thermodynamics

Vacuum Technology

Fields of Study: Physics; Mechanics; Mathematics

ABSTRACT

Vacuum technology refers to any type of technology in which various processes are carried out in conditions lower than the atmospheric pressure. A pure vacuum is defined as any space that is completely empty of physical matter. For the purposes of manufacturing, however, a vacuum is used to describe differences in atmospheric pressure.

KEY CONCEPTS

mercury vapor pump: a specialized pump that uses diffusion of mercury vapor to decrease pressure further from the limit of a standard vacuum pump (10^{-3} atmospheres) to as low as 10^{-6} atmospheres

photoelectron spectroscopy: an analytical method that uses ultraviolet light to cause the ejection of electrons from within the atoms of a particular compound

pump: a device that moves fluids from one location to another

true vacuum: the condition in which the number of molecules or atoms of gases that exist within a defined space is effectively zero

vacuum pump: a pump designed to withdraw air and other gases from a sealed environment and expel it into the air, thus reducing the amount remaining within the sealed environment

VACUUMS

Vacuum technology refers to any type of technology in which various processes are carried out in conditions lower than the atmospheric pressure. A pure vacuum is defined as any space that is completely empty of physical matter. For instance, outer space (the zone between planets) consists of a partial vacuum. There is virtually no air or physical matter. In a true vacuum, not even sound can travel. For the purposes of manufacturing, however, a vacuum is used to describe differences in atmospheric pressure. Atmospheric pressure measures the weight of air and the resulting pressure exerted by it.

Earth has a layer of atmosphere that surrounds the planet. However, this layer has different amounts of air at various altitudes. Places located higher in the atmosphere have lower amounts of air than would be found at sea level. For instance, if someone were to fill a container with air on Mount Everest, it would contain a much lower percentage of air than if it had been filled at ground level. Therefore, there is low atmospheric pressure inside the container, which is to say that there is less air from above pushing down. If this container were not protected against changes in atmospheric pressure, when brought to ground level, it might be crushed by the changes in pressure. This is because air will naturally seek to fill the space where there is lower pressure. In the case of a sealed container such as a plastic bottle, the force from the higher air pressure outside will crush the bottle to fill the gap created by the lower air pressure inside the container.

Air particles create pressure on the walls of any space, such as a container. The fewer air particles in any given space, the less force that is exerted onto the walls of that container. Vacuum technology uses these principles to pump air from a chamber to create a lower atmospheric pressure. These principles have many real-world applications in industry, science, and technology.

BACKGROUND

Vacuum technology seeks to replicate a perfect vacuum. A perfect vacuum is one in which there are no air particles present. However, it is virtually impossible to create a perfect vacuum. The closest naturally occurring state to a perfect vacuum is found in outer space, where there are only a few trace hydrogen atoms per cubic meter. To simulate vacuum conditions on Earth, scientists have developed various types of vacuum chambers that are able to create different vacuum levels. These range from an extremely high vacuum (XHV), in which even trace gases are removed, to a low vacuum, like that used in vacuum cleaners. In between these extremes are several other forms of vacuums. Only a small number of specialized facilities in the world are capable of replicating XHV conditions, while low vacuums are a common piece of technology. The only practical uses for XHV conditions are for accelerator and storage ring facilities, to stimulate conditions in outer space, and, in some cases, to produce specialized forms of semiconductors.

Ultra-high vacuums (UHVs), which are slightly less powerful than XHVs, are primarily used by chemists, engineers, and physicists for scientific re-

search in such fields as X-ray photoelectron spectroscopy. To achieve this state, gases are forcibly pumped by such devices as UHV chambers, cryopumps, mercury vapor pumps, and helium compressors. These devices require special seals and gaskets that prevent even the slightest hint of air leakage. High vacuums (HVs) require less effort to create and are used for smelting and annealing processes that change the structure of metals to help make them stronger, harder, or more malleable. Ultracentrifuges, typically used in medical research, require the centrifugation chamber to be operated under UHV in order to prevent the working components from overheating due to friction with air.

Medium (or intermediate) vacuums have many applications. They are used in the production of steel, the manufacture of lightbulbs, the drying of plastics, and for freeze-drying food. Low (or rough) vacuums are used in the operation of vacuum cleaners and for industrial handling. Low vacuums are also created through some natural processes, such as human respiration.

An XHV is one in which a pump or chamber is able to replicate an environment that is 99.999 percent free of particles—only slightly less than a perfect vacuum and the closest rate achievable on Earth. UHVs and high vacuums are defined as those that establish environments between 99 and 99.999 percent of atmospheric pressure, while low and medium vacuums operate at levels at 99 percent or lower.

OVERVIEW

The applications of vacuum technology can be split into two categories: those that require vacuums to work, or alternately, those in which vacuums are used as part of the manufacturing process. In the first category are such devices as lamps, tubes, vacuums, pumps, accelerators, and actuators. Products that rely on vacuums during the manufacturing process include those in such industries as food packing, coating, degassing, composite materials, packaging, and electronics. About 40 percent of the sales of vacuum technology are used for the manufacture of semiconductors.

One of the most important mechanisms that rely on vacuums to work is a vacuum actuator. This device uses vacuum pressure to create and convert energy that is used to allow motion. Such devices are found in many systems in vehicles, including headlights, transmission shift controls, ventilation systems, and windshield wipers.

Outgassing is another form of vacuum technology. This process releases traces of gases trapped inside materials such as metals and composite materials. Using vacuum technology, all gas pockets are released by baking these materials under the pressure of a vacuum. This allows these materials to be boiled off by their vapor pressure and removed. They are then cooled to reduce the potential for natural outgassing that can occur when they are put into regular use. Outgassing is particularly useful for increasing the structural integrity of materials. This process is also used to create molds and to establish and preserve UHVs.

One of the most common uses for vacuums is for pumping. For instance, this technology can be used to suction materials from deep wells. This works by expanding the volume of a container and then lowering the pressure inside, thereby creating a type of artificial vacuum. This vacuum then fills with air as a result of the reduced pressure. This enables the creation of a suction force that pulls the materials up.

Vacuum technology also has a breadth of other uses. These may include removing gases for drying, dehydrating, or freeze-drying food. Similarly, vacuum technology can be used to remove atmospheric constituent parts to create lighting tubes and bulbs, for leak detection, to melt materials, for packaging, and for cooking *sous vide* (under vacuum). Vacuums also have applications for lifting or transporting ma-

terials by creating a pressure difference that functions as a type of suction.

—*Eric Bullard*

Further Reading

"Basic Principles of Vacuum Technology, Brief Overview." *Festo Group*, www.festo.com/net/SupportPortal/Files/286804/Basic_Vacuum_Technology_Principles.pdf. Accessed 20 Jan. 2017.

"The Everyday Applications of Vacuum Technologies." *Techiestuffs*, 10 June 2016, www.techiestuffs.com/the-everyday-applications-of-vacuum-technologies/. Accessed 20 Jan. 2017.

Gatzen, Hans H., et al. "Vacuum Technology." *Micro and Nano Fabrication*. Springer Berlin Heidelberg, 2015, pp. 7-63.

Hucknall, David J. *Vacuum Technology and Applications*. Butterworth-Heinemann, 1991.

Jorisch, Wolfgang, editor. *Vacuum Technology in the Chemical Industry*. Wiley, 2015.

Jousten, Karl. "Applications and Scope of Vacuum Technology." *Handbook of Vacuum Technology*. 2nd ed., Wiley, 2016, pp. 19-26.

Mandelis, Andreas. "Focus on Vacuum, Cryogenics, and Nanotechnology." *Physics Today*, vol. 68, no. 4, 2015, pp. 59-61.

O'Hanlon, John F. *A User's Guide to Vacuum Technology*. 3rd ed., Wiley, 2003.

Redhead, P.A. "Extreme High Vacuum." *National Research Council of Canada*, www.chem.elte.hu/departments/altkem/vakuumtechnika/CERN17.pdf. Accessed 20 Jan. 2017.

Roth, A. "Introduction: Fields of Application and Importance." *Vacuum Technology*. 3rd ed., North-Holland, 1998, pp. 6-10.

See also: Aerospace design; Automated processes and servomechanisms; Centrifugation; Fluid dynamics; Materials science

VECTORS

Fields of Study: Physics; Engineering; Mechanics; Mathematics

ABSTRACT

A vector is a quantity that has both magnitude and direction and adheres to the basic rules of algebra with respect to the operations of addition, subtraction, and multiplication. This quantity can be used to represent the displacement of a point through time and space.

KEY CONCEPTS

coordinate system: a grouping of magnitudes that are used to define the positions of points in space

initial point: the beginning point of a vector

origin: the reference point at which a coordinate system is centered

scalar: a quantity that has magnitude but not a direction, such as the nondimensional measurements of time or temperature

terminal point: the final or end point of a vector; it is the end at which the head or arrow of the vector is affixed

velocity: the rate of change of the position of a body, measured in terms of distance per unit time (e.g., meters per second)

OVERVIEW

A vector is defined as a quantity that has both magnitude and direction. Vectors are used to describe the position and motion of a body in space. An abstract concept (e.g., an airplane flying from Chicago to San Francisco, an automobile driving on a highway, a person walking down the street) possesses some amount of velocity which is pointed in a specific direction. In other words, each object has a vector associated with it that can define their respective positions and motion. Sometimes the object (which can be thought of as a point) is large, such as an airplane; perhaps it is small, such as a person walking, or perhaps it is infinitesimally small, as in the case of an electron moving around the nucleus of an atom.

The magnitude of the motion or displacement in each of the previous examples is described in terms of their respective velocities and directions, which

can be measured as an angle with respect to an arbitrary origin. This origin is part of a coordinate system that is used to describe the position of a point in space. Many different types of coordinate systems exist; some have very special purposes in solving advanced mathematical problems. Vectors can exist in any one of these different systems, and also in any dimension (from one-dimensional to infinitely dimensional, the latter being one with limitless coordinates). Although vectors can exist in any number of dimensions, they are usually discussed, and most clearly visualized, in two or three dimensions. Each of the earlier examples is operating in an assumed level plane, so these are thought of as lying in a two-dimensional plane. Of these examples, the airplane is capable of moving literally into a third dimension, which it does when it is climbing or descending along its flight path.

Coordinate systems allow one to establish a one-to-one correspondence between points in a plane or surface and a series of numbers that actually define the positions of the points. The coordinate system most commonly used is the Cartesian coordinate system. This system, which was devised by the French mathematician Rene Descartes (1596-1650), provides a means of referencing points in either two or three dimensions.

Suppose a person is in a room that has a linoleum tile floor along with four walls and a ceiling, all being perpendicular to one another. The walls and floor define a coordinate system, which is thought of as being orthogonal—that is, one in which all axes are mutually perpendicular to one another. If the person is standing in one corner of the room facing the openness of the room, the corner at the person's feet can be defined as the origin. The two lines along the floor where the walls adjacent to the person intersect the floor form the abscissa (or *x*-direction, which is to the right) and ordinate (or *y*-direction, which is to the left). Thus, one can use the *x*-axis and *y*-axis to measure distances from the origin. This relationship of having the *x*-axis to the right of the *y*-axis establishes a right-handed coordinate system (the more common one).

In measuring distances on the floor, let each linoleum tile represent one unit of distance. If there exists a point on the floor (2D space) which is three units away from the origin in the *x*-direction and four units away from the origin in the *y*-direction, then this point can be represented in terms of the point (*x,y*), in this case (3,4). A vector describing this point would extend from the origin (0,0) to the point (3,4). The length, or magnitude, of the vector is found by using the Pythagorean theorem; hence, the magnitude is the length of the hypotenuse of the triangle whose sides are 3 and 4 units each in length. The magnitude of the vector is thus 5 units. The direction of the vector is determined by finding the angle between the vector and the *x*-axis. For this vector, the angle is 53 degrees (arcsine of 4/5).

If the coordinate system is expanded to include the vertical direction by using the two walls, the number of dimensions is increased from two to three. In doing so, another axis will need to be incorporated, that of the vertical (*z*-axis). By doing so, a point in space can now be represented, such as defining the position of a light bulb suspended from the ceiling. The vector describing the position of the bulb has an initial point (in this case, located at the origin) and a terminus point (located at the bulb).

For a three-dimensional case, points in space can be described by using three numbers (*x,y,z*), which then gives the position of the point from the origin point.

Consider a room that is 5 meters in length, 5 meters in width, and 3.5 meters in height. If a light bulb were suspended in the center of the room 0.5 meter below the ceiling, then the coordinates of the bulb would be 2.5, 2.5, and 3, where the unit length along each axis is in terms of meters.

If the lightbulb has to be replaced, prior to doing so, it is placed in the corner; this is defined as the origin. The light bulb is then moved in a straight line to the fixture suspended from the ceiling. This line defining the movement (or displacement) of the bulb has now produced a 3D vector, because the bulb moved at a particular velocity and in a specific direction. If this movement were photographed using time-lapse photography and some type of strobe light, one could actually see the vector in space. (This record of the motion of an object in space can also be seen by following the condensation trail left by a jet plane when it flies at a high altitude.)

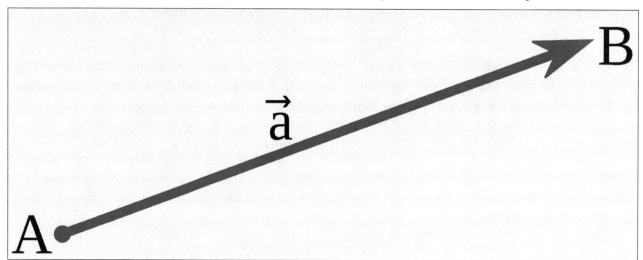

A vector from point A to B. Image by Nguyenthephuc, via Wikimedia Commons.

Vectors can be compared to one another in terms of their magnitudes and directions.

Two vectors are termed "equal" if both their magnitudes and directions are equal; this is true irrespective of the positions of their initial points. Also, one vector can be the exact opposite of another (sometimes referred to as an anti-vector) if the magnitudes of the two vectors are equal but their respective directions are exactly opposite (that is, the vectors are parallel to one another but point in opposite directions).

The operations of addition, subtraction, and multiplication can be extended to develop an algebra for vectors. These operations are necessary in order to aid in the description of how objects (or points) respond to motion in space. The end result of applying a series of forces to the object can be determined by an additive process. After the second force is applied following the first one, the object will come to rest (its new terminus point) in a position found by adding the two vectors.

The addition of two vectors produces their sum or resultant. For example, if vector PQ has an initial point P and a terminus Q and vector QR, which has Q as its initial point and terminus R, is added to vector PQ, then the resultant vector is vector PR, which has P as its initial point and R as its terminus. The sum is written as PR = PQ + QR. The resultant vector PR is the main diagonal of a parallelogram having vectors PQ and QR as sides. This summing process can be applied to more than two vectors. The procedure simply involves placing the initial point of one vector at the terminus of another until all the vectors are connected together.

The subtraction of vectors is performed in a similar manner. The difference of vectors BD and BE is written as BD - BE. This is the same as adding the negative of BE to BD [BD + (-BE)]. Therefore, the resultant BF is the one which, when added to BE, produces BD. Notice that if two vectors are equal, then their difference produces the null, or zero, vector. This has a magnitude of 0 but no direction is attached to it.

Vectors can be multiplied by a scalar, thus changing the value of the original vector. If a scalar c is multiplied times BA, then the result is cBA. If c is positive, then the magnitude of BA is increased by c times in the same direction as BA. If c is negative, then the direction of the product cBA is opposite that of BA. Should c be zero, then the product cBA produces the null vector.

Unit vectors have two primary properties. The first property is that a unit vector is a dimensionless value defined as having a length of unity. The second property is that a unit vector is parallel to (actually coincident with) one of the coordinate axes. Thus, for a 3D Cartesian coordinate system, there are three unit vectors, each parallel to one of the three axes, respectively. Standard nomenclature is used to represent the unit vector in the x-direction as Bib. The unit vector in the y-direction is Bjb, while the unit vector in the z-direction is Bkb.

Vectors that have more than one dimension can be broken down into various parts.

This process is termed "resolving a vector into its components." For a 2D vector in the x-y plane, the components of the vector can be determined in the x and y directions. This is done by projecting the vector onto each of the two axes. In actuality, this procedure can work for any n-dimensional vector in any coordinate system. Therefore, n components of the vector would be produced. A vector W can be resolved into two components: BWb_x Bb is the x-direction component and BWb_y Bjb is the component in the y-direction. Note that for 2D vectors, no reference is made to the third direction. Hence, a 2D vector in the x-y plane has no z component.

APPLICATIONS

In the physical world, vectors can be used to represent such quantities as velocity, displacement, force, acceleration, and magnetic or gravity fields, all of which have a magnitude and direction associated with them. In physics, if an object is affected by a force, then that object might move in response to the force. This motion can be described in terms of distance and rate.

Thus, a vector can be produced that would characterize the motion and describe the new position of the object.

Vectors are used in determining the paths of rockets when they are launched to place satellites into space. The velocity and acceleration of a rocket is expressed in terms of vectors, as well as the gravitational forces acting on the rocket to pull it back to Earth. Once a satellite is placed into orbit following the rocket launch, vectors are crucial in helping define the path and motion of the satellite. Scientists must be able to calculate the gravitational forces that are being exerted on the satellite in order to determine the proper orbit so it stays in orbit a maximum amount of time. Vectors are used to represent both the gravitational forces and the actual motion of the satellite around the earth. In this application, the coordinate systems are much more complicated than the simple Cartesian system. The fact that Earth is moving (both by rotation and revolution), the Moon is moving, and the satellite is in motion produces a very complex set of coordinates. Vectors, however, can serve as a means of describing the motion of each of these bodies in space.

Vectors are used by navigators to determine their future positions. In the case of a ship (which is essentially operating in a 2D system), the navigator considers the forces exerted on the ship by its engines, the wind, and any ocean currents. Each of these forces can be represented by a vector and their sum that will produce the resultant motion of the vessel. A similar set of calculations can be applied to an airplane, which must consider the effects of wind on the airplane.

CONTEXT

Vectors were developed in the late nineteenth century as another method to describe the mathematics associated with quaternions, a mathematical system that involves the combination of real and complex numbers. Vectors are an important means whereby physicists and mathematicians can describe the motion of a body in space. They provide a type of shorthand that simplifies the description of the magnitude and direction a body possesses. Because vectors can be written in general terms, they can be applied to any of the numerous coordinate systems scientists must use in describing motion.

Since vectors adhere to the basic algebraic operations of addition, subtraction, and multiplication, they can be used and understood in relatively simple terms. These characteristics allow them to reduce the complexity of many problems physicists and mathematicians encounter in the physical world and thus enable them to arrive at solutions to seemingly impossible problems. The need to describe motion which occurs in a very complex problem can be handled with vectors and their associated operations. Most are familiar with fixed coordinate systems (ones that do not have any apparent motion). Consider the need to describe the displacement in a series of coordinate systems, which are both moving through space and rotating at the same time, such as that experienced in satellite motion or in outer space with other solar systems. Vectors are crucial in allowing scientists to make an analysis of these types of motions.

—*David M. Best*

Further Reading

Durrant, Alan. *Vectors in Physics and Engineering*. Routledge, 2019.

Hayward, R. Baldwin. *The Algebra of Coplanar Vectors and Trigonometry*. Fb&c Limited, 2015.

Hoffman, Banesh. *About Vectors*. Courier Corporation, 2012.

Lepetic, Vladimir. *Classical Vector Algebra*. CRC Press, 2022.

Vince, John. *Vector Analysis for Computer Graphics*. Springer Nature, 2021.

Weinreich, Gabriel. *Geometrical Vectors*. U of Chicago P, 2020.

See also: Acceleration; Amplitude; Angular forces; Celestial mechanics; Circular motion; Electromagnetism; Kinematics; Magnetism; Moment of inertia; Momentum (physics); Motion; Projectiles; Speed; Torque

VECTORS (MATHEMATICS AND PHYSICS)

Fields of Study: Physics; Mathematics

ABSTRACT

There are some quantities, called "scalars," like time, distance, and work, which have only a magnitude. Quantities that require both a magnitude and a sense of direction for their complete specification are called "vectors." Vectors express magnitude and direction, and have applications in physics and many other areas.

KEY CONCEPTS

acceleration: the rate of change of velocity associated with a change in speed or direction of motion or both; going faster

Cartesian grid: the standard grid pattern demarking the x, y, and z coordinates in two or three mutually orthogonal dimensions

deceleration: also called negative acceleration, the decrease of velocity over a period of time, the opposite of acceleration

divergence theorem: the flux of a field passing through the surface of an enclosed space is equal to the divergence (change) of the field within the enclosed space

electric field: the influence that a distribution of charges has on the space around it such that the force experienced by a small test charge q is given by the value of that charge times the electric field, which results from the charge distribution

flux: the value of the electric (or magnetic) field multiplied by the surface area that it crosses

initial point: the beginning point of a vector

magnetic field: the influence that a distribution of electric currents has on the space around it

SUMMARY

There are some quantities, called "scalars," like time, distance, and work, which have only a magnitude. If one says the radius of a circle is 6 meters or the speed is 12 meters per second, it is adequate. When discussing velocity or force, however, then magnitude alone is not enough. If a particle has a velocity of five meters per second, this is not sufficient information because the direction of movement is unknown. Quantities that require both a magnitude and a sense of direction for their complete specification are called "vectors." Pilots use vectors to compensate for wind to navigate airplanes; sport analysts use vectors to model dynamics; and physicists use vectors to model the world.

Vectors express magnitude and direction, and have applications in physics and many other areas.

HISTORY AND DEVELOPMENT OF VECTORS

The term "vector" originates from *vectus*, a Latin word meaning "to carry." However, astronomy and physical applications motivated the concept of a vector as a magnitude and direction. Aristotle recognized force as a vector. Some historians question whether the parallel law for the vector addition of forces was also known to Aristotle, although they agree that Galileo stated it explicitly and it appears in the 1687 work *Principia Mathematica* by Isaac Newton. Aside from the physical applications, vectors were useful in planar and spherical trigonometry and geometry. Vector properties and sums continue to be taught in high schools in the twenty-first century.

The rigorous development of vectors into the field of vector calculus in the nineteenth century resulted in a debate over methods and approaches. The algebra of vectors was created by Hermann Grassmann and William Hamilton. Grassmann expanded the concept of a vector to an arbitrary number of dimensions in his book *The Calculus of Extension*, while Hamilton applied vector methods to problems in mechanics and geometry using the concept of a "quaternion." Hamilton spent the rest of his life advocating for quaternions. James Maxwell published his *Treatise on Electricity and Magnetism* in which he emphasized the importance of quaternions as mathematical methods of thinking, while at the same time critiquing them and discouraging scientists from using them. Extending Grassman's ideas, Josiah Gibbs laid the foundations of vector analysis and created a system that was more easily applied to physics than Hamilton's quaternions.

Oliver Heaviside independently created a vector analysis and advocated for vector methods and vector calculus. Mathematicians such as Peter Tait, who preferred quaternions, rejected the methods of Gibbs and Heaviside. However, their methods were eventually accepted and they are taught as part of the field of linear algebra. The quaternionic method of Hamilton remains extremely useful in the twenty-first century. Vector calculus is fundamental in understanding fluid dynamics, solid mechanics, electromagnetism, and in many other applications.

During the nineteenth century, mathematicians and physicists also developed the three fundamental theorems of vector calculus, often referred to in the twenty-first century as the "divergence theorem," "Green's theorem," and "Stokes's theorem." Mathematicians with diverse motivations all contributed to the development of the divergence theorem. Michael Ostrogradsky studied the theory of heat, Siméon Denis Poisson studied elastic bodies, Pierre Frederic Sarrus studied floating bodies, George Green studied electricity and magnetism, and Carl Friedrich Gauss studied magnetic attraction. The theorem is sometimes referred to as "Gauss's theorem." George Green, Augustin Cauchy, and Bernhard Riemann all contributed to Green's theorem, and Peter Tait and James Maxwell created vector versions of Stokes's theorem, which was originally explored by George Stokes, Lord Kelvin, and Hermann Hankel. Undergraduate college students often explore these theorems in a multivariable calculus class.

The concept of a space consisting of a collection of vectors, called a "vector space," became important in the twentieth century. The notion was axiomatized earlier by Jean-Gaston Darboux and defined by Giuseppe Peano, but their work was not appreciated at the time. However, the concept was rediscovered and became important in functional analysis because of the work by Stefan Banach, Hans Hahn, and Norbert Wiener, as well as in ring theory because of the work of Emmy Noether.

Vector spaces and their algebraic properties are regularly taught as a part of undergraduate linear algebra.

MATHEMATICS

A vector is defined as a quantity with magnitude and direction. It is represented as a directed line segment with the length proportional to the magnitude and the direction being that of the vector. If represented as an array, it is often represented as a row or column matrix. Vectors are usually represented as boldface capital letters, like A or with an arrow overhead.

The Triangle Law states that while adding, "if two vectors can be represented as the two sides of a triangle taken in order then the resultant is represented as the closing side of the triangle taken in the opposite order."

Any vector can be split up into components, meaning to divide it into parts having directions along the coordinate axes. When added, these components return the original vector. This process is called "resolution into components." Clearly, this resolution cannot be unique as it depends on the choice of coordinate axes. However, for a given vector and specified coordinate axes, the resolution is unique. When two vectors are added or subtracted, these components along a specific axis simply "add up" (like 2 + 2 = 4 or 7 - 2 = 5) but the original vectors do not, which follow the rule of vector addition that can be obtained by the Parallelogram Law of Vector Addition. Vector addition is commutative and associative in nature.

Multiplication for vectors can be of a few types:

1. For scalar multiplication (multiplication by a quantity that is not a vector), each component is multiplied by that scalar. Vector multiplication by a scalar is commutative, associative, and distributive in nature.

2. For the multiplication of two vectors, one can obtain both a scalar (dot product) or a vector (cross product). For a cross product the resultant lies in a plane perpendicular to the plane containing the two original vectors. Dot product is both commutative and distributive. But cross product is neither commutative nor associative in nature because the result is a vector and depends on the direction.

APPLICATIONS

Theoretical sciences have a wide spread of applications of vectors in nearly all fields:

Obtaining components. Occasionally, one needs a part (or component) of a vector for a given purpose. For example, suppose a rower intends to cross over to a point on the other side of a river that has a great current. The rower would be interested to know if any part of that current could help in any way to move in the desired direction. To find the component of the current's vector along any specified direction, take the dot product of that vector with a unit vector (vector of unit magnitude) along the specified direction. This method is of particular importance in studying of particle dynamics and force equilibria.

Evaluating volume, surface, and line integrals. In many problems of physics, it is often necessary to shift from either closed surface integral (over a closed surface that surrounds a volume) to volume integral (over the whole enclosed volume), or from closed line integral (over a loop) to surface integrals (over a surface). To accomplish these shifts, it is often very useful to apply two fundamental theorems of vector calculus, namely Gauss's divergence theorem and Stokes's theorem, respectively.

Particle mechanics. In the study of particle mechanics, vectors are used extensively. Velocity, acceleration, force, momentum, and torque all being vectors, a proper study of mechanics invariably involves extensive applications of vectors.

Vector fields. A field is a region over which the effect or influence of a force or system is felt. In physics, it is very common to study electric and magnetic fields, which apply vectors and vectorial techniques in their description.

—*Abhijit Sen*

Further Reading

Bernstein, Dennis S. *Scalar, Vector, and Matrix Mathematics: Theory, Facts, and Formulas-Revised and Expanded Edition*. Princeton UP, 2018.

Brand, Louis. *Vector and Tensor Analysis*. Courier Dover Publications, 2020.

Hausner, Melvin. *A Vector Space Approach to Geometry*. Courier Dover Publications, 2018.

Lepetic, Vladimir. *Classical Vector Algebra*. CRC Press, 2022.

Robinson, Glibert de B. *Vector Geometry*. Courier Corporation, 2013.

Stroud, K. A., and Dexter Booth. *Vector Analysis*. Industrial Press, 2005.

Thrall, Robert M., and Leonard Tornheim. *Vector Spaces and Matrices*. Courier Corporation, 2014.

See also: Acceleration; Calculus; Celestial mechanics; Circular motion; Classical or applied mechanics; Computer-aided engineering; Electromagnetism; Equilibrium; Fluid dynamics; Force (physics); Friction; Gauss's law; Inertial guidance; Linear motion; Magnetism; Momentum; Newton's laws; Pascal, Blaise; Poisson, Siméon Denis; Projectiles; Quantum mechanics; Torque; Velocity

VELOCITY

Fields of Study: Physics; Mechanics; Mathematics

ABSTRACT
Velocity is the speed of an object plus its direction of travel. Speed measures how fast an object covers distance, and is measured in units such as miles per hour or meters per second. In physics, the inclusion of direction when measuring velocity is crucial. Because speed is measured using just the one quantity, it is called a scalar; because velocity refers to the quantity (speed) and direction, it is called a vector.

KEY CONCEPTS

angular velocity: the rate of change of position of a body moving in a circle, commonly measured in rotations per minute

linear motion: movement of an object in a straight line, or translation

translation: refers to a physical mass moving from one point to another, either linearly or on a curved path

vector quantities: quantities that have both a magnitude or absolute value and are associated with a direction (e.g., 23 kilometers per hour northwest)

velocity: the rate of change of the position of a body, measured in terms of distance per unit time (e.g., meters per second) and associated with a specific direction

VECTORS AND SCALARS

Velocity is the speed of an object plus its direction of travel. Speed measures how fast an object covers distance, and is measured in units such as miles per hour or meters per second. An example of speed is 55 miles per hour, while an example of velocity is 55 miles per hour heading west. In everyday nonscientific contexts, the words "speed" and "velocity" are typically used synonymously, but in physics, the inclusion of direction when measuring velocity is a crucial distinction. Because speed is measured using just the one quantity, it is called a scalar; because velocity refers to the quantity (speed) and direction, it is called a vector.

More specifically, measuring speed considers distance—how far an object travels, or how much ground it covers—whereas velocity is concerned with displacement—how far the object moves from its original position. For example, if an object starts from one point and travels in a circle, returning to its starting point, then it traveled at some average speed, perhaps 5 meters per second, but its average velocity was zero, because its displacement was zero—its final location did not change. Similarly, if an object travels in a straight line 4 miles north and then turns left, traveling 3 miles west before stopping, the average speed would be measured based on how far it traveled straight plus how far it traveled to the left (7 miles total); thus, if it took an hour to travel that distance, the average speed was 7 miles per hour. On the other hand, the velocity would be measured based on the straight line from the starting point to the ending point—the hypotenuse of the right triangle created by the two directions of travel (5 miles); thus, the average velocity would be 5 miles per hour northwest.

BACKGROUND

Since ancient times, velocity has been a key part of developing many basic concepts in physics, such as momentum and kinetic energy.

Momentum was observed as an aspect of objects in motion from the time of ancient Greece. The Greek philosopher Aristotle (ca. 384-322 BCE) developed the first groundings of a theory of momentum,

As a change of direction occurs while the racing cars turn on the curved track, their velocity is not constant. Photo via Wikimedia Commons. [Public domain.]

which was critiqued and reworked some eight centuries later by the Byzantine philosopher John Philoponus (ca. 490-570 CE). Philoponus called his theory "impetus," which entails that an object will remain in motion until its energy is exhausted. This view was further developed in the Islamic world by the eleventh-century Persian scholar Avicenna. These ideas would eventually travel back to Europe and reach scientists such as Galileo Galilei, René Descartes, and Isaac Newton in the sixteenth and seventeenth centuries. By the eighteenth century the formal mathematical formulation of momentum was in use, today rendered as $p = mv$, where p is momentum, m is mass, and v is velocity.

Kinetic energy, or the energy that an object has by virtue of its motion, is defined as one-half its mass times its velocity squared ($1/2mv^2$). The formulation of kinetic energy was developed in 1829 by the French mathematician Gaspard-Gustave Coriolis (1792-1843). The term kinetic energy was not coined until some twenty years later by the British mathematician William Thomson (1824-1907), later known as Lord Kelvin.

VELOCITY TODAY

Velocity is a key concept in the study of physics; an understanding of velocity is fundamental to understanding kinetic energy, momentum, and other concepts on which much of modern engineering and transportation technology is based.

Kinetic energy is the energy of an object in motion. As the velocity and mass of the object increase, so too does the kinetic energy. For example, a roller coaster ride must be designed in such a way as to capitalize on the energy produced from the first hill to power the ride until the roller coaster makes it back to its starting position.

Momentum is the product of mass and velocity. Just as is the case for kinetic energy, as mass and velocity increase, so too does the momentum of an object. The concept of momentum is used in forensic investigations to determine fault and liability in situations such as automobile accidents. It is also used in billiards to determine how hard and where to hit the cue ball in order to make a shot.

—*Douglas R. Jordan*

Further Reading

Berman, Bob. *Zoom: How Everything Moves: From Atoms and Galaxies to Blizzards and Bees.* Little, 2014.

Collier, Peter. *A Most Incomprehensible Thing: Notes towards a Very Gentle Introduction to the Mathematics of Relativity.* Incomprehensible, 2014.

Einstein, Albert, and Leopold Infeld. *The Evolution of Physics: The Growth of Ideas from Early Concepts to Relativity and Quanta.* Simon, 1938.

Henderson, Tom. "Speed and Velocity." *Kinematics. Physics Classroom*, 2013. Accessed 10 Sept. 2014.

Ling, Samuel J., Jeff Sanny, and William Moebs. *University Physics, Volume 1.* Samurai Media Limited, 2017.

Shamos, Morris H. *Great Experiments in Physics: Firsthand Accounts from Galileo to Einstein.* Dover, 1987.

Walker, Jearl, Robert Resnick, and David Halliday. *Fundamentals of Physics.* 10th ed., Wiley, 2014.

See also: Acceleration; Circular motion; Euler's laws of motion; Inertial guidance; Linear motion; Motion; Newton's laws; Projectiles; Propulsion technologies; Speed; Steam engine; Transportation

VIBRATION

Fields of Study: Physics; Mechanics; Mathematics

ABSTRACT

The subject of vibration is the study of oscillatory motion. Vibration manifests itself in a great variety of ways in daily life, and an understanding of this subject is a prerequisite for the successful design of many systems.

KEY CONCEPTS

amplitude: the maximum displacement from equilibrium position in an oscillation

damping: the process by which vibration steadily diminishes in amplitude

degree of freedom: the number of independent coordinates required to specify a physical system

forced vibration: oscillatory motion driven by an external excitation

free vibration: oscillatory motion in the absence of external excitation

frequency: the number of oscillations per unit time

normal mode: a condition of vibration in which all components of a system reach maximum displacements simultaneously and pass their equilibrium positions simultaneously

period: the time required for one complete oscillation

resonance: a condition of large amplitude of vibration caused by the coincidence of natural and excitation frequencies

OVERVIEW

Physical systems possessing mass and elasticity are capable of relative motion. If the motion of such systems repeats itself after a given interval of time, the motion is known as "vibration." This periodic motion can be rather complex, and it may take a long time before the motion repeats itself. Yet vibration manifests itself in such a great variety of ways in daily life that an understanding of this subject is of primary importance.

Vibration can originate from many different sources. It may occur either in nature or in human-made devices. For example, sound is transmitted through the vibration of air particles. When these vibrating air particles impinge on the ear, they induce oscillations in the eardrum. A sensation is thereby produced in the auditory nerve that translates into hearing. In household products such as the washing machine, vibration is generated by an unbalance in the rotating and tumbling weight. The vibration is particularly noticeable during the spin cycle, in which the wet clothing rotates as a compact mass. In the extreme case, a washing machine can even rock its way across the floor. The vibration in an automobile is caused chiefly by surface roughness of the road over which it traverses. Thus, a properly designed suspension assembly is needed to provide a high-quality ride.

From the few examples cited above, it is clear that vibration is indeed of frequent occurrence.

Vibration phenomena, no matter how complex in appearance, can generally be characterized by a few common parameters. To prescribe some of these parameters, consider a simple spring-mass system. This prototype system consists of a mass of weight W suspended by means of a spring of stiffness k. The spring stiffness or spring constant k is specified as the force necessary to stretch or compress the spring by one unit of length. The mass is in equilibrium under the action of two equal and opposite forces: the weight W acting down and the spring force kd acting up. The quantity d is merely the static deflection of the spring caused by the hanging mass. The position in which the weight and the spring force balance each other is called the "equilibrium position" or "neutral position." It is convenient to measure any subsequent displacement of the mass from this position.

Suppose the mass is forced down an additional distance x from its neutral position of rest and then suddenly released. At the time of release, the spring force would be larger than the weight W by an amount kx, and the mass would start moving up. As long as the mass is below the neutral position, the

upward spring force is greater than the weight, and the mass will increase its upward speed. When the neutral position is reached, the mass will keep right on going because of its momentum, but the downward force will now be greater than the upward force, and this will tend to slow down the motion. Finally, the upward velocity will become zero when the mass reaches the upper extreme position, and the motion will thereafter be downward. The downward velocity will increase until the neutral position is reached again; it will then decrease and become zero when the mass reaches the lower extreme position. This is the position from which it started, and the mass has completed one cycle. The length of time it takes the mass to complete one cycle of motion is called the "period," and the number of cycles completed in one second is called the "frequency."

Car suspension: Designing vibration control is undertaken as part of acoustic, automotive or mechanical engineering. Photo via Wikimedia Commons. [Public domain.]

The vibration just described is called "free vibration" because it is performed under the action of forces inherent in the system itself, without the involvement of external forces of any kind. The force that tends to move the mass toward the neutral position is called a "restoring" force. It is evident that any freely vibrating system must possess both mass and some kind of restoring force. Most solids, when slightly deformed, generate a restoring force that opposes the deformation and is proportional to it. This restoring force, which arises from elasticity of the solids, is theoretically equivalent to the spring force in the prototype system.

Another type of force that is present to a greater or lesser degree in any practical vibrating system is friction. This friction force, which may be of a complex form, is called a "damping" force, and it always resists the motion of the vibrating mass. The amount of damping present in most practical systems, however, is so slight that quite often it may be neglected altogether. For this reason, the study of undamped vibration is considered adequate in many applications. If damping is absent in the spring-mass system, it will be found that the displacement of the mass at its upper extreme position is equal in magnitude to its displacement at the lower extreme position; this magnitude is called the "amplitude" of the motion. The frequency of free vibration of the undamped system is called its "natural" frequency. The natural frequency grows with increasing spring stiffness and with decreasing weight of the vibrating mass. If damping is present, it will be found that the amplitude of free vibration gradually decreases, and the frequency will be slightly lower than the natural frequency. The difference between these two frequencies is usually so small that the frequencies are, for all practical purposes, assumed to be equal.

Suppose that instead of simply being released at a displaced position, the mass is being shaken up and down by an external alternating force. The resulting vibration is called "forced" vibration, and the external force is referred to as an "excitation." When the frequency of excitation is varied, the amplitude of forced vibration of the hanging mass also changes. The largest amplitude of vibration will be attained when the frequency of excitation is approximately equal to the natural frequency of the system. This condition is termed "resonance," in which the amplitude of vibration can be disproportionately large. There are many examples of the occurrence of resonance in daily life. In an average car, it can nearly always be noticed that there are certain speeds at which certain parts of the car buzz or rattle: The gear lever may vibrate violently at one speed, a loose ashtray at another. Frequently, quite a small change in speed will stop the vibration. Another example, which the builder and architect will appreciate, is the way in which a scaffold plank will vibrate to a possibly dangerous extent if the person walking on it steps at the right frequency. Analogous to this is the resonant vibration of a bridge when walked upon, particularly a suspension bridge. It is usual, on this account, to give orders for soldiers to break step when marching across a bridge. Clearly, the alternating force in this case is supplied by the footfalls of the soldiers, and the resulting forced vibration is measured by the extent of the up-and-down motion of the bridge. It must be remembered that resonance occurs when the frequency of the alternating force is approximately equal to the natural frequency of a vibrating system. Therefore, in order to avoid disastrous effects resulting from very large amplitude of vibration at resonance, the natural frequency of a system must be determined and properly utilized in system design.

The spring-mass system used earlier as a prototype is of the simplest type insofar as only one coordinate, the displacement x of the mass from neutral position, is necessary to specify completely the associated vibration. Systems of this type are said to have a "single degree of freedom," and they have only one natural frequency. Many systems can vibrate in more than one manner and direction, and several coordinates may be needed to specify the vibration. The number of independent coordinates so required is referred to as the number of "degrees of freedom" of the system. The oscillations of strings, membranes, and plates are examples of vibrating systems possessing multiple degrees of freedom.

A system with several degrees of freedom also has multiple natural frequencies, at each of which resonance can occur. A typical example is a metal plate. The fact that it has a number of resonances can be heard when the plate is struck. The discordant nature of the sound emitted shows that a number of notes, each caused by some particular resonance, has been excited. This may be compared to the note from a tuning fork, which is designed so that one resonance predominates. The reason for the large number of resonances is that a plate, unlike a mass on a spring, can vibrate in a number of different ways. More or less complicated bending takes place, with the result that some parts of the plate move one way and others move in an opposite direction, while parts in between are motionless. If various parts of a system are oscillating in such a manner that they reach maximum displacements simultaneously and pass their equilibrium positions simultaneously, the corresponding state of motion is called a "normal mode" of vibration. In general, there are as many normal modes as the number of degrees of freedom. Moreover, it can be shown that free vibration of an undamped linear system is merely a suitable combination of the normal modes. Thus, a normal mode may be regarded as a constituent form of vibration of a system. Through the determination of the different natural frequencies and normal modes, the vibration of a vast majority of physical systems can be adequately characterized.

APPLICATIONS

Watching the daily ebb and flow of tides and listening to the steady hum of industrial machinery, one is constantly concerned and fascinated with vibratory motion. The swaying of a tree in the wind, the pitching and rolling of a ship at sea, and the turning of a generator in its journals all point to periodic variations of forces and displacements. Vibration of many different forms, some visible to the eyes or perceptible to the body, have challenged humankind from the beginning of time. Often, an understanding of vibration is a prerequisite for the advancement of science and technology.

In a majority of cases, vibration is a form of wasted energy and is undesirable. This is particularly true in machinery, in which vibration generates noise, breaks down parts, and transmits unwanted forces and movements to close-by objects. Physical systems are usually designed to reduce vibration and suppress resonances. This requires knowledge of the natural frequencies and normal modes of a system. In addition, the cause of vibration must be understood. Over the years, the vibration of many systems has been analyzed and subsequently controlled. In some cases, the vibration has even been utilized to advantage.

Most prime movers have problems with vibration because of the inherent unbalance in the engines. The unbalance, which may arise from faulty design or poor manufacturing precision, must be considered in the prediction of system performance. The wheels of some locomotives, for example, have been observed to rise by more than a centimeter off the track at high speeds as a result of imbalance. In turbines, vibration of blades and disks is often a cause of mechanical failure. Even when resonances are avoided, vibration in machines and structures can bring about material fatigue and excessive wear, resulting eventually in failure. In metal-cutting processes, vibration can cause chatter, which leads to a poor surface finish. Because of the popular use of electronic devices in recent years, the resistance of these devices to vibration has become a matter for concern. Common electronic equipment may include microcomputers, radars, and mobile telephones. It is reasonable to assume that all electronic equipment will be subjected to forced vibration at some point in its useful life. The vibration may arise from transportation of the equipment or from attachment to a machine or a moving vehicle. To order to design electronic equipment that will survive various types of forced vibration, it is necessary to conduct theoretical investigation and experimental testing of the equipment under different conditions of excitation.

When the first jet airplanes were constructed, standard instruments previously used on airplanes with piston engines and propellers were installed on the new airplanes without additional evaluation. As it turned out, these instruments failed to function properly on the jet airplanes and tended to stick. A subsequent investigation revealed that the problem was caused by the difference in the frequencies of excitation to which these instruments were subjected. The excitation produced by jet engines and piston-type engines simply had very different lower frequencies. To make the same instruments work in the first jet airplanes, small vibration absorbers had to be mounted on the instrument panels. Most modern electronic equipment is mounted on antivibration supports, which suppress vibration over a specified frequency range.

In earthquake-prone regions, a principal concern of the structural engineer is the vibration of buildings subjected to earthquake-induced motion at the base. It is found that ground motion induced by earthquake can be thought of as an external excitation proportional to the mass of the building. Thus, the earthquake force is increased if the building is made heavier. Extensive study of earthquake vibration has brought about new design codes for the construction of earthquake-resistant buildings.

Insulation against noise is another contemporary application of vibration. Noise is subjectively defined as unpleasant or unwanted sound. Technically, noise is simply a combination of many single-frequency sounds and thus is also transmitted through the vibration of air particles. Excessive noise interferes with work, sleep, and recreation. It has a lasting adverse effect on health and can decrease the efficiency of most human activities. Advanced techniques from vibration analysis are used in insulation design. Some notable designs include silencers for guns, new fiberglass packing for water pipes, and acoustic tiles for building walls. In fact, the control and insulation of noise in buildings now constitutes a discipline known as "architectural acoustics." Most residential buildings constructed in recent decades have some degree of acoustic insulation designed into them.

In spite of its detrimental effects, vibration can sometimes be used to advantage. For example, a sieve requires vibration to effect the separation of granular materials of different sizes, while a compactor requires vibration for effective consolidation of particles. Recently, the utilization of vibration has increased considerably in consumer and industrial applications. Vibration is exploited in oscillatory conveyers, hoppers, electric toothbrushes, pile driving, and electric massaging units. In a more scientific orientation, vibration is used in resonance testing of materials, machine and system diagnosis, and timekeeping. Vibration has also been found to improve the efficiency of certain chemical processes such as mixing and welding. By all indications, utilization of vibration will continue to grow. At the same time, new and more powerful avenues will be developed for suppression of unwanted vibration. Either for suppression or utilization, the study of vibration will remain one of the most important and applicable fields in classical physics and engineering mechanics.

CONTEXT

Vibration is one of the earliest fields of investigation undertaken by humankind. Interest in vibration began when the first musical instruments, probably whistles or drums, were discovered. An understanding of music and of consonance dates back at least to 3000 BCE in China, when the philosopher Foci wrote two monographs on the theory of music. The Greek mathematician Pythagoras is perhaps the first person to conduct scientific experiments on musical sounds. Pythagoras performed several experiments around 500 BCE on vibrating strings. Among other things, he observed that if two like strings of different lengths are subjected to the same force, the shorter one emits a higher note.

Although the concept of pitch was developed by the time of Pythagoras, its relation to the frequency of vibration of the sounding body was not understood. In fact, this relation remained unknown until the sixteenth century, when the Italian astronomer Galileo Galilei started to characterize vibration. In 1584, Galileo conceived the principle of the isochronous pendulum: the period of small oscillations of a simple pendulum is independent of its amplitude. This principle was later applied to the design of a clock by the Dutch mathematician Christiaan Huygens. Galileo also conducted experiments on forced vibration and resonance, and his work laid the foundation for subsequent studies in vibration. The publication of the laws of motion by Sir Isaac Newton in 1687 provided a theoretical basis on which vibration can be investigated analytically.

For about two hundred years after Newton, the study of vibration was mostly confined to pendulums and the motion of astronomical bodies and tides, and it was through the investigation of these problems of classical physics that a theory of vibration was first developed. Toward the end of the nineteenth century, there was rapid progress in the construction of high-speed machinery. Notable among these inventions were the locomotive and the steam turbine. Many new problems in vibration, mostly of engineering orientation, were introduced through the development of such machinery. Sophisticated methods for analyzing these new problems were then lacking. In 1877, the English physicist Lord Rayleigh published a treatise on the theory of sound. Among the numerous contributions contained in his book, Rayleigh expounded an efficient method for determining the lowest frequency of vibration of large classes of systems. The work of Lord Rayleigh revolutionized the study of vibration and is still considered a standard reference today.

Over the years, vibration as a subject has grown, and many related fields of study have sprung from it. Examples of such fields include nonlinear dynamics, random vibration, and computational mechanics. Many complex phenomena in vibration not previously understood can now be explained. Tremendous progress in both the theory and application of vibration have been made, and the end is not yet in sight. The study of vibration is one of the oldest fields of physical science, having matured slowly over thousands of years, and new techniques and uses of vibration continue to be developed for the better service of humankind.

—*Fai Ma*

Further Reading

Alexander, Stephon. *The Jazz of Physics: The Secret Link Between Music and the Structure of the Universe*. Basic Books, 2016.

Brennan, Michael J., and Bin Tang. *Virtual Experiments in Mechanical Vibrations: Structural Dynamics and Signal Processing*. John Wiley & Sons, 2022.

Garrett, Steven L. *Understanding Acoustics: An Experimentalist's View of Acoustics and Vibration*. Springer, 2017.

Gatti, Paolo Luciano. *Advanced Mechanical Vibrations: Physics, Mathematics and Applications*. CRC Press, 2020.

Lees, Arthur W. *Vibration Problems in Machines: Diagnosis and Resolution*. 2nd ed., CRC Press, 2020.

Maccari, Attilio. *Nonlinear Physics, from Vibration Control to Rogue Waves and Beyond*. Cambridge Scholars Publishing, 2023.

Pain, H. John, and Patricia Rankin. *Introduction to Vibrations and Waves*. John Wiley & Sons, 2015.

Watkins, William H. *Loudspeaker Physics and Forced Vibration*. Springer International Publishing, 2022.

See also: Acoustics: Aeronautical engineering; Atoms; Automated processes and servomechanisms; Centrifugation; Earthquake engineering; Equilibrium; Hooke, Robert; Materials science; Motion; Springs; Stabilizers

W

WORK AND ENERGY

Fields of Study: Physics; Engineering; Mechanics; Mathematics

ABSTRACT

The energy of a mass represents the capacity of the mass to do work. Energy is a positive, scalar quantity, although a change in energy can be either positive or negative. The total energy of a body can be calculated from its mass, m, and the specific energy, U (that is, the energy per unit mass): E = mU. Typical units of mechanical energy are foot-pounds and joules.

KEY CONCEPTS

kinetic energy: the energy possessed by a mass by virtue of being in motion

potential energy: the energy possessed by a mass due to its position relative to another mass

pressure energy: the energy possessed by a mass due to the pressure exerted on it by external factors

spring energy: the energy contained in a spring that has been either extended or depressed away from its normal position

SUMMARY

The energy of a mass represents the capacity of the mass to do work. Such energy can be stored and released. There are many forms that it can take, including mechanical, thermal, electrical, and magnetic. Energy is a positive, scalar quantity, although a change in energy can be either positive or negative. The total energy of a body can be calculated from its mass, m, and the specific energy, U (that is,

the energy per unit mass): $E = mU$. Typical units of mechanical energy are foot-pounds and joules. A joule is equivalent to the units of N·m and kg·m^2/s^2. In countries that use traditional English units, the British thermal unit (Btu) is used for thermal energy, whereas the kilocalorie (kcal) is still used in some applications in countries that use the International System of Units (SI units). Joule's constant, or the Joule equivalent (778.26 ft-lbf/Btu), is used to convert between English mechanical units and thermal energy units. Energy in Btu = energy in the ft-lbf/J.

LAW OF CONSERVATION OF ENERGY

The law of conservation of energy says that energy cannot be created or destroyed. However, energy can be converted into different forms. Therefore, the sum of all energy forms is constant.

$$E = (constant)(Work)$$

Work is the act of changing the energy of a particle, body, or system. For a mechanical system, external work is done by an external force, whereas internal work is done by an internal force. Work is a signed, scalar quantity. Typical units are inch-pounds, foot-pounds, and joules. Mechanical work is seldom expressed in British thermal units or kilocalories.

For a mechanical system, work is positive when a force acts in a direction of motion and helps a body move from one location to another. Work is negative when a force acts to oppose motion. Friction, for example, always opposes the direction of motion and can only do negative work. The work done on a body by more than one force can be found by super-position.

From a thermodynamic standpoint, work is positive if a particle or a body does work on its surroundings. Work is negative if the surroundings do work on the object. An example would be inflating a tire, which represents negative work to the tire. This is consistent with the law of conservation of energy, since the sum of the negative work and positive energy increase is zero (i.e., there is no net energy change in the system).

POTENTIAL ENERGY OF A MASS

Potential energy (gravitational energy) is a form of mechanical energy possessed by a body due to its relative position in a gravitational field. Potential energy is lost when the elevation of a body decreases. The lost potential energy usually is converted to kinetic energy or heat.

$$E_{potential} = mghE_{potential} = mgh/gc$$

In the absence of friction and other nonconservative forces, the change in potential energy of a body is equal to the work required to change the elevation of the body.

$$W = E_{potential}$$

KINETIC ENERGY OF A MASS

Kinetic energy is a form of mechanical energy associated with a moving or rotating body. The kinetic energy of a body moving with instantaneous linear velocity, v, is:

$$E_{kinetic} = (1/2)\ mv^2E_{kinetic} = mv^2/2\ gc$$

The work-energy principle states that the kinetic energy is equal to the work necessary to initially accelerate a stationary body or to bring a moving body to rest:

$$W = E_{kinetic}$$

A body can also have rotational kinetic energy.

$$E_{rotational} = (1/2)\ I\omega^2E_{rotational} = I\omega^2/2\ gc$$

SPRING ENERGY

A spring is an energy storage device, since the spring has the ability to perform work. In a perfect spring, the amount of energy stored is equal to the work required to compress the spring initially. The stored spring energy does not depend on the mass of the spring. Given a spring with spring constant (stiffness), k, the spring energy is as follows:

$$E_{spring} = (1/2)\ kx^2$$

PRESSURE ENERGY OF A MASS

Since work is done in increasing the pressure of a system, mechanical energy can be stored in pressure form. This is known as pressure energy, static energy, flow energy, flow work, and pV work (energy). For a system of pressurized mass, m, the flow energy is as follows:

$$E_{flow} = (mp/?) = mpvE_{flow} = (mp/gc?) = (mpv/gc)$$

INTERNAL ENERGY OF A MASS

The total internal energy, usually given the symbol U, of a body increases when the body's temperature increases. In the absence of any work done on or by the body, the change in internal energy is equal to the heat flow, Q, into the body. Q is positive if the heat flow is into the body and negative otherwise.

$$U_2 - U_1 = Q$$

The property of internal energy is encountered primarily in thermodynamics problems. Typical units are British thermal units, joules, and kilocalories.

WORK-ENERGY PRINCIPLE

As energy can be neither created nor destroyed, external work performed on a conservative system goes into changing the system's total energy. This is known as the work-energy principle (or principle of work and energy).

$$W = E = E2 - E1$$

The term "work-energy principle" is limited to use with mechanical energy problems, such as the conversion of work into kinetic or potential energy. When energy is limited to kinetic energy, the work-energy principle introduces some simplifications into many mechanical problems:

- It is not necessary to calculate or know the acceleration of a body to calculate the work performed on it.
- Forces that do not contribute to work—for example, are normal to the direction of motion—are eliminated.
- Only scalar quantities are involved.
- It is not necessary to individually analyze the particles of component parts in a complex system.

CONVERSION BETWEEN ENERGY FORMS
Conversion of one form of energy into another form of energy does not violate the law of conservation of energy. Most problems involving conversion of energy are really just special cases of the work-energy principle. An example is a falling body that is acted upon by a gravitational force. The conversion of potential energy into kinetic energy can be interpreted as equating the work done by the constant gravitational force to the change in kinetic energy.

POWER
Power is the amount of work done per unit time. It is a scalar quantity.

$$P = (W/t)$$

For a body acted upon by a force or torque, the instantaneous power can be calculated from the velocity.

$$P = F_v \text{ (linear systems)}$$

$$P = T\omega \text{ (rotational systems)}$$

Basic units of power are ft-lbf/sec and watts (J/s), although horsepower is also widely used. Some useful power conversion formulas include:

$$1 \text{hp} = 550 \text{ (ft-lbf/sec)} = 33{,}000 \text{ (ft-lbf/min)} = 0.7457 \text{ kW} = 0.7068 \text{ (Btu/sec)}$$

$$1 \text{ kW} = 737.6 \text{ (ft-lbf/sec)} = 44{,}250 \text{ (ft-lbf/min)} = 1.341 \text{ hp} = 0.9483 \text{ (Btu/sec)}$$

$$1 \text{ (Btu/sec)} = 778.26 \text{ (ft-lbf/sec)} = 46{,}680 \text{ (ft-lbf/min)} = 1.415 \text{ hp} \text{Efficiency}$$

For energy-using systems (such as cars, electrical motors, and televisions), the energy-use efficiency, η, of a system is the ratio of an ideal property to an actual property. The property used is commonly work, power, or, for thermodynamic problems, heat. When the rate of work is constant, either work or power can be used. Except in rare instances, the numerator and denominator of the ratio must have the same units:

$$\eta = (P_{ideal}/P_{actual}) \ (P_{actual} = P_{ideal})$$

For energy-producing systems (such as electrical generators, prime movers, and hydroelectric plants), the energy-production efficiency is $? = (P_{actual}/P_{ideal})$ $(P_{ideal} = P_{actual})$.

The efficiency of an ideal machine is 1.0 (100 percent). However, all real machines have efficiencies of less than 1.0.

—*Joanta Green*

Further Reading
Alrasheed, Salma. *Principles of Mechanics: Fundamental University Physics*. Springer, 2019.
Naskar, Anirban. *Work, Energy and Power-Thoughtful Physics*. Quantemporary, 2018.

Ross, John S. "Work, Power, Kinetic Energy." *Project PHYSNET*, Michigan State University, 23 Apr. 2002, www.physnet.org/modules/pdf_modules/m20.pdf.

Serway, Raymond A., and John W. Jewett. *Physics for Scientists and Engineers*. 8th ed.. Brooks/Cole Cengage Learning, 2010.

Smil, Vaclav. *Energy in Nature and Society: General Energetics of Complex Systems*. MIT Press, 2008.

Tipler, Paul. *Physics for Scientists and Engineers: Mechanics*. 3rd ed., W. H. Freeman, 2008.

See also: Bernouilli, Daniel; Bernoulli's principle; Calculating system efficiency; Classical or applied mechanics; Fluid dynamics; Friction; Load; Springs; Superconductor; Thermodynamics; Torque; Work-energy theorem

WORK-ENERGY THEOREM

Fields of Study: Physics; Mechanics; Mathematics

ABSTRACT

According to the work-energy theorem, the work done by all forces acting on an object equals the change in that object's kinetic energy. The theorem assists in calculating the work done by unknown forces, even if the amount of displacement or force is unknown. It is useful in analyzing how a rigid body should move under several forces.

KEY CONCEPTS

conservation of energy: the principle that energy in the universe can be neither created nor destroyed, only transformed and transferred

displacement: the absolute distance an object moves from its starting point, regardless of the path it travels

kinematics: a subfield of classical mechanics that studies the motion of objects without reference to the forces that cause this motion

kinetic energy: the energy contained in an object due to its motion

net force: the sum of all forces acting on an object

potential energy: the energy stored within an object or system due to its position or configuration relative to the forces acting on it

total mechanical energy: the sum of the kinetic energy and the potential energy an object possesses as a result of work done on it

work: the successful displacement of an object caused by the application of a force

WORK AND KINETIC ENERGY

The work-energy theorem describes the relationship between kinetic energy (the energy of an object in motion) and work (the displacement of an object by a force). It states that when work is performed on an object, the kinetic energy of that object will change. When the kinetic energy of an object changes, it moves. So, in simple terms, performing work on an object causes it to move.

Because the work-energy theorem is concerned only with masses and velocities, not with forces, it is considered part of the field of kinematics. Kinematics is a subfield within classical mechanics that studies the motion of objects without regard for the forces causing the motion. Classical mechanics, in turn, is the branch of physics concerned with the physical laws that govern both the motion of objects and the forces that move them. Isaac Newton (1642-1727) laid the foundations for modern classical mechanics with his three laws of motion, published in the late seventeenth century.

WORK, ENERGY, AND FORCE

Mathematically, the work-energy theorem is represented by the following equation, where W is the total work performed on an object, ΔK is the change in the object's kinetic energy, m is the mass of the object, and v_i and v_f are its initial and final velocities, respectively:

$$W = \Delta K = 1/2 \ mv_f^2 - 1/2mv_i^2$$

Thus, the total work done is equal to the total change in kinetic energy. In this sense, work can be thought of as the transfer of energy, if that transfer of energy results in displacement. Indeed, in the International System of Units (SI), the unit for both work and energy is the joule (J).

Consider a game of billiards. When the cue ball is in motion, it has kinetic energy. When it collides with another ball, it transfers some of its kinetic energy to the second ball. The force of the collision performs work on the second ball, causing it to move. This interaction underlines the relationship between energy, work, and force. In SI units, one joule represents the amount of work done or energy transferred when one newton (N) of force acts over a distance of one meter (m). In other words, if the cue ball exerts one newton of force on the second ball, causing it to be displaced by one meter, then one joule of energy has been transferred from the cue ball to the second ball, and one joule of work has been performed.

Forces in physics are interactions. According to Newton's second law, the net force (F; sum of the forces) acting on an object is equal to the object's mass (m) times its resulting acceleration (a):

$$F = ma$$

In turn, the work (W) done by that force is equal to the net force (F) applied times the resulting displacement (s) of the object:

$$W = Fs$$

Displacement is the absolute distance and direction an object has moved from its starting position, ignoring the path taken. Therefore, a car that drove in a perfect circle and stopped exactly where it started would have a displacement of zero, no matter how large the circle it traveled. Similarly, a car that drove ten miles east, made a U-turn, and drove back five miles west would only have a displacement of five miles east, even though it traveled fifteen miles total.

The equation for work reveals that in order for a force to have performed work on an object, the displacement of that object must have a nonzero value. In other words, the object has to have moved. If an applied force does not result in displacement, no work has been done.

CONSERVATION OF ENERGY

The law of conservation of energy states that in an isolated system, energy is conserved. An isolated system is one from which neither matter nor energy can escape. The universe is, in theory, the ultimate isolated system. Thus, according to this law, energy in the universe is never created or destroyed; it can only be transformed or transferred. The work-energy theorem is an extension of the law of conservation of energy, rewritten in a usable form.

Not all energy is kinetic energy. Energy can exist in a variety of forms. One such form is potential energy, which is energy that is stored in an object or system until it can be converted to another form of energy to do work. Potential energy itself comes in different forms, such as gravitational potential energy and chemical potential energy. The human body makes use of the chemical potential energy that exists in food due to its molecular configuration. When food is digested, it undergoes chemical reactions that break down its molecules and convert some of this chemical potential energy into the thermal energy of body heat and the kinetic energy of moving limbs and beating hearts. A combustion engine similarly converts the chemical potential energy of the fuel into the kinetic energy of the moving pistons that drive the engine.

The principle of conservation of energy is useful when examining any isolated system. Consider the billiards example again. The billiards table can be treated as an isolated system, because the balls stay on the table and any energy from the environment (heat from overhead lights, the kinetic energy in a gust of air) has such a small effect that it can be ignored. Therefore, when two balls collide, the total amount of energy in the system must remain the same before and after the impact. Kinetic energy is simply transferred from one ball to the other. A miniscule amount might be converted to thermal energy due to friction with the table.

Often, when considering some kinematic interaction, it is useful to know the total mechanical energy of the objects at play. The total mechanical energy of an object or system is simply the sum of its potential and kinetic energies. In the real world, total mechanical energy is not typically conserved, because friction must be considered. Consider a driver in a speeding car who suddenly slams on the brakes. As the car's tires stop rotating and start sliding across the surface of the pavement, they generate friction. Friction converts kinetic energy into thermal energy, which is not a form of mechanical energy. This energy then dissipates away from the tire tracks into the surrounding environment.

THE WORK-ENERGY THEOREM IN EVERYDAY LIFE

The work-energy theorem is useful whenever the effect of work on the motion of an object is of interest. For example, understanding how the chemical potential energy in a fuel source performs work when it is released and converted into kinetic energy is an essential part of engineering efficient combustion engines. The fuel has to contain enough energy to move the pistons without breaking them.

Countless other devices in modern life also convert potential energy into kinetic energy in order to perform work. Everyday examples include vacuum cleaners, clocks, and fans. By expressing the relationship between energy transfer (work) and the motion (kinetic energy) of these objects in easy-to-measure terms (mass and velocity), the work-energy theorem makes engineering these devices possible.

—*Kenrick Vezina*

Further Reading

Allain, Rhett. "What's the Difference between Work and Potential Energy?" *Wired*. Condé Nast, 1 July 2014. Accessed 22 Sept. 2015.

Boleman, Michael. "Experiment # 6: Work-Energy Theorem." *Mr. Boleman's Course Information*. University of South Alabama, n.d. Accessed 22 Sept. 2015.

Bouvet, Christophe. *Mechanics of Aeronautical Solids: Materials and Structures*. John Wiley & Sons, 2017.

"Energy, Kinetic Energy, Work, Dot Product, and Power." *MIT OpenCourseWare*. Massachusetts Institute of Technology, 13 Oct. 2004. Accessed 22 Sept. 2015.

Henderson, Tom. *Kinematics*. Physics Classroom, 2013. Digital file.

Nave, Carl R. "Work, Energy and Power." *HyperPhysics*. Georgia State University, 2012. Accessed 22 Sept. 2015.

Papachristou, Costas J. *Introduction to Mechanics of Particles and Systems*. Springer Nature, 2020.

Shankar, Ramamurti. "Lecture 5: Work-Energy Theorem and Law of Conservation of Energy." *Open Yale Courses*. Yale University, 2006. Accessed 22 Sept. 2015.

Simanek, Donald E. "Kinematics." *Brief Course in Classical Mechanics*. Lock Haven University, Feb. 2005. Accessed 22 Sept. 2015.

See also: Dynamics (mechanics); Energy transmission; Flywheels; Force (physics); Heat transfer; Kinetic energy; Potential energy; Rigid-body dynamics; Superconductor; Thermodynamics

Y

YOUNG, THOMAS

Fields of Study: Physics; Mechanics; Mathematics

ABSTRACT
British scientist Thomas Young was born June 13, 1773, in Milverton, England, and died May 10, 1829, in London, England. He is known for his contributions to the fields of physics, optics, and medicine. He proposed a wave theory of light, challenging the particle theory of earlier scientist Isaac Newton. The important characteristic of materials known as Young's modulus is named for him.

KEY CONCEPTS
rods and cones: two types of light receptor structures on the retina of the eye that are responsible for vision

wave-particle duality: the characteristic of light that allows it to act as a stream of particles and as electromagnetic waves

Young's modulus: a measure of the rigidity or stiffness of a material

EARLY LIFE
Thomas Young was born in 1773 in Milverton, England, to Thomas and Sarah Young. By the age of two, Young had learned to read. By the age of fourteen, he had mastered multiple languages, including Greek, Latin, French, Italian, Hebrew, Arabic, and Farsi.

Young completed his education quickly and soon began to prepare for a career in medicine. He enrolled at the University of Edinburgh but completed his studies at the prestigious University of Göttingen in the Holy Roman Empire (now Germany). In 1793, he lectured before the Royal Society on the eye and its muscular structure. On the basis of his paper "Observations on Vision," he was elected to the Royal Society at the age of twenty-one. He later became the society's secretary.

With the completion of his medical studies in 1796, Young continued his scholarly work at Emmanuel College, Cambridge. That year, he inherited the fortune of his granduncle, physician Richard Brocklesby, which allowed him to be financially independent. Thus, at a very young age, Young had

Thomas Young, portrait c. 1822 by Henry Perronet Briggs. Image via Wikimedia Commons. [Public domain.]

the freedom to pursue inquiries in whatever field interested him. He later moved to London and established a medical practice there.

LIFE'S WORK

While experimenting at Cambridge, Young became increasingly interested in optics and the perception of colors. Drawing on his earlier observations of the eye, Young advanced a theory on colors. He assumed there are three basic colors (red, green, and violet) and that the retina of the eye contains groups of receptors, later determined to be cone cells, that are sensitive to one of these three colors. For example, a red light stimulates a receptor sensitive to red colors, a violet light stimulates a receptor sensitive to violet colors, and so on. Young proposed that other colors are seen when different combinations of receptors are stimulated. For instance, a yellow color is seen when both violet and green receptors are stimulated at the same time.

Young published variations on this theory at several points in his career, eventually including elements of it in his article on chromatics for the *Encyclopedia Britannica*. Later, German scientist Hermann von Helmholtz developed Young's theory further, and it became known as the Young-Helmholtz theory. In the 1950s, new technology demonstrated conclusively that the Young-Helmholtz theory is largely correct and that the cone cells in the retina function according to Young's description.

From his initial forays into optics, Young began to experiment with the nature of light. Having previously investigated the transmission of sound, which he proposed traveled in waves, as well as the movement of waves in water, Young theorized that light travels in a similar manner. In 1802, he invented a simple experiment to prove this theory and demonstrated conclusively that light does indeed travel in waves. As he developed his wave theory of light, Young found that many English physicists were unreceptive to his findings because they contradicted

the particle theory of light developed by Isaac Newton more than a century earlier. However, French physicists Augustin-Jean Fresnel and François Arago tested Young's theory, and their experiments helped confirm that Young was correct in his findings.

On the basis of his experiments, in 1801, Young was appointed professor of natural philosophy, the field that later became known as physics, at the Royal Institution. Over the next two years, Young delivered lectures on nearly every subject then studied in physics. Young resigned his professorship in 1803, explaining that it was interfering with his medical duties. The following year, he married Eliza Maxwell.

Although he had resigned his professorship, Young continued to conduct experiments in physics. He made an important contribution to the theory of elasticity known as Young's modulus, a ratio used to measure the stiffness of elastic materials. In 1818, working with the Board of Longitude and the Royal Navy, he helped supervise the publication of a nautical almanac. In addition, Young made significant contributions to the field of medicine. Young was the first physician to describe astigmatism in the eye accurately. In recognition of his medical work, he was made a fellow at the College of Physicians in Cambridge. He was often invited to lecture on medical matters, and throughout his life, he practiced at St. George's Hospital in London.

Young applied himself to other areas of study as well. In 1799, French soldiers had discovered a stone buried outside the town of Rosetta, Egypt, on which was carved a proclamation in Greek, Egyptian hieroglyphics, and a third, unknown script that later became known as demotic. While Egyptian hieroglyphics were present on many monuments, scholars had been unable to decode what they meant. However, the Rosetta Stone placed a known language, Greek, alongside the hieroglyphics, allowing them to be translated. Young began to study the Rosetta Stone and discovered that the third language (demotic) was a mixture of phonetic and hieroglyphic signs. Thus, he was able to trace the demotic writing back to hieroglyphics and decode names and words from the ancient symbols.

Young spent his later years practicing medicine and contributing articles to the *Encyclopedia Britannica*. He died in London on May 10, 1829.

IMPACT

Young's work in the field of physics greatly influenced the development of scientific thought. His work on the wave theory of light not only served to displace the longstanding particle theory of Newton but also led to a variety of advances in the study of light. Early in the twentieth century, scientists determined that light behaves as both a wave and a particle, indicating that Newton and Young were both partially correct. This discovery, in turn, allowed scientists to make important contributions to the developing field of quantum physics. Young's research regarding how the eye recognizes and interprets different colors also proved to be influential, serving as the foundation for further study in that area.

Although Young is perhaps best known as a scientist, he was also a significant figure in the field of linguistics. He studied and compared the vocabulary and grammar of over four hundred languages, publishing his findings in a series of articles in the *Encyclopedia Britannica*. Finding similarities along a wide spectrum of languages, Young coined the term "Indo-European" to describe the family of European languages that includes Greek, Latin, Sanskrit, and many other modern languages. Young's articles and work on the Rosetta Stone were of great help to Egyptologist Jean-Francois Champollion, who ultimately translated the Egyptian hieroglyphics on the stone in the 1820s.

—*Jeffrey Bowman*

Further Reading

Atchison, David A., and W. Neil Charman. "Thomas Young's Contributions to Geometrical Optics." *Clinical and Experimental Optometry*, vol. 94, no. 4, 2011, pp. 333-40.

Davson, Hugh. *The Visual Process: The Eye*. Academic Press, 2014.

Heindl, R. A. *Young's Modulus of Elasticity at Several Temperatures for Some Refractories of Varying Silica Content (Classic Reprint)*. Fb&c Limited, 2018.

Rao, C. N., and A. Govindaraj. *Nanotubes and Nanowires*. 2nd ed., Royal Society of Chemistry, 2011.

Robinson, Andrew. *The Last Man Who Knew Everything: Thomas Young, the Anonymous Polymath Who Proved Newton Wrong, Explained How We See, Cured the Sick, and Deciphered the Rosetta Stone, among Other Feats of Genius*. Plume, 2007.

Tilley, Richard J. D. *Understanding Solids: The Science of Materials*. 2nd ed., John Wiley & Sons, 2013.

Wood, Alexander, and Frank Oldham. *Thomas Young: Natural Philosopher, 1773-1829*. 1954. Cambridge UP, 2011.

See also: Archimedes; Biomechanics; Biomedical engineering; Grimaldi discovers diffraction; Materials science; Newton, Isaac; Plasticity (physics)

BIBLIOGRAPHY

"10 Surprising Things You Might Do with a Mechatronics Degree." *East Coast Polytechnic Institute Blog*, www.ecpi.edu/blog/10-surprising-things-you-might-do-with-mechatronics-degree. Accessed 19 Jan. 2017.

"1902: Rotary Engine Inventor Felix Wankel Born." *History.com*, 2009, www.history.com/this-day-in-history/rotary-engine-inventor-felix-wankel-born. Accessed 2 Oct. 2017.

Aczel, Amir D. *Pendulum: Leon Foucault and the Triumph of Science*. Simon & Schuster, 2007.

Addis, Bill. *Building: Three Thousand Years of Design Engineering and Construction*. Phaidon Press, 2007.

Adhami, Reza, Peter M. Meenen III, and Dennis Hite. *Fundamental Concepts in Electrical and Computer Engineering with Practical Design Problems*. 2nd ed., Universal, 2005.

"Aerospace Design Lab." *Stanford University*, Department of Aeronautics and Astronautics, 28 July 2013. Accessed 9 June 2015.

Agnarsson, Geir, and Raymond Greenlaw. *Graph Theory: Modeling, Applications, and Algorithms*. Pearson, 2007.

Agricola, Georgius. *De re metallica*. Translated by Herbert Clark Hoover and Lou Henry Hoover. Dover, 1950.

"A–Index." *Occupational Outlook Handbook*, US Bureau of Labor Statistics, US Department of Labor, 20 Oct. 2021, www.bls.gov/ooh/a-z-index.htm. Accessed 28 Feb. 2022.

al Mashhadany, Yousif, and Khalaf Geaed. *Classical Control Theory: Modeling of Physical Systems, Design and Analysis of Control Systems, Stability Theorems*. Lap Lambert Academic Publishing Gmbh KG, 2014.

Al Nageim, Hassan. *Structural Mechanics: Loads, Analysis, Design and Materials*. 6th ed., Prentice Hall, 2003.

Alberg, Tom. *Flywheels: How Cities Are Creating Their Own Futures*. Columbia UP, 2021.

Alciatore, David G. *The Illustrated Principles of Pool and Billiards*. Dr. Dave Billiards Resources, 2004.

Alexander, Stephon. *The Jazz of Physics: The Secret Link Between Music and the Structure of the Universe*. Basic Books, 2016.

Alkemade, Fons. *A Century of Fluid Mechanics in The Netherlands*. Springer, 2019.

Allain, Rhett. "What's the Difference between Work and Potential Energy?" *Wired*. Condé Nast, 1 July 2014. Accessed 22 Sept. 2015.

Alrasheed, Salma. *Principles of Mechanics: Fundamental University Physics*. Springer, 2019.

"Alternative and Advanced Fuels." *US Department of Energy*, www.afdc.energy.gov/afdc/fuels/biodiesel_publications.html.

Ambrosoli, Mauro. *The Wild and the Sown: Botany and Agriculture in Western Europe, 1350–1850*. Translated by Mary McCann Salvatorelli. Cambridge UP, 1997.

Amineh, Reza K. *Applications of Electromagnetic Waves*. MDPI, 2021.

Andrews, David L., and Mohamed Babiker, editors. *The Angular Momentum of Light*. Cambridge UP, 2013.

Angeles, Jorge. *Rational Kinematics*. Springer Science & Business Media, 2013.

Ansari, Hasanraza. *Aerodynamics and Aircraft Performance*. Draft2digital, 2022.

Antognazza, Maria Rosa. *Leibniz: A Very Short Introduction*. Oxford UP, 2016.

———. *Leibniz: An Intellectual Biography*. Cambridge UP, 2011.

Archimedes. *On Floating Bodies: Book I. The Works of Archimedes*. Edited by Thomas Little Heath. 1897. Dover, 2002, pp. 253–62.

———. *On Floating Bodies: Book II. The Works of Archimedes*. Edited by Thomas Little Heath. 1897. Dover, 2002, pp. 263–300.

Arfken, George B., and Hans J. Weber. *Mathematical Methods for Physicists: A Comprehensive Guide*. Elsevier, 2012.

Argyris, John H., Gunter Faust, Maria Haase, and Rudolf Friedrich. *An Exploration of Dynamical Systems and Chaos: Completely Revised and Enlarged Second Edition*. Springer, 2015.

Arnold, Vladimir I., and Boris A. Khesin. *Topological Methods in Hydrodynamics*. Springer Science & Business Media, 2008.

Arteaga, Robert R. *The Building of the Arch*. 10th ed., Jefferson National Parks Association, 2002.

Ashby, M. F., Michael F. Ashby, Hugh Shercliff, and David Cebon. *Materials Engineering, Science, Processing and Design*. Elsevier Science, 2019.

Aslanov, Vladimir S. *Rigid Body Dynamics for Space Applications* Butterworth-Heinemann, 2017.

Atchison, David A., and W. Neil Charman. "Thomas Young's Contributions to Geometrical Optics." *Clinical and Experimental Optometry*, vol. 94, no. 4, 2011, pp. 333–40.

Attard, Phil. *Entropy Beyond the Second Law: Thermodynamics and Statistical Mechanics for Equilibrium, Non-equilibrium, Classical and Quantum Systems*. Institute of Physics Publishing, 2018.

Aufmann, Richard, Joanne Lockwood, Richard Nation, and Daniel K. Clegg. *Mathematical Excursions*. 3rd ed., Brooks, 2013.

Aughton, Peter. *Newton's Apple: Isaac Newton and the English Scientific Revolution*. Weidenfeld, 2003.

Augustine, Kingsley. *Sound and Wave Motion Calculations: A Physics Book for High Schools and Colleges*. Independently Published, 2018.

Avallone, Eugene A., Theodore Baumeister III, and Ali M. Sadegh. "Steam Turbines." *Marks' Standard Handbook for Mechanical Engineers*. 11th ed., McGraw-Hill, 2007.

Awrejcewicz. *Classical Mechanics: Kinematics and Statics*. Springer Science & Business Media, 2012.

Babu, V. *Fundamentals of Propulsion*. Springer International Publishing, 2021.

Bacciotti, Andrea. *Stability and Control of Linear Systems*. Springer, 2018.

Bacciotti, Andrea, and Lionel Rosier. *Liapunov Functions and Stability in Control Theory*. 2nd ed., Springer Science & Business Media, 2005.

Bacon, D. H. *Basic Heat Transfer*. Elsevier, 2013.

Badick, Joseph R., and Brian A. Johnson. *Flight Theory and Aerodynamics: A Practical Guide for Operational Safety*. 4th ed., John Wiley & Sons, 2021.

Badilescu, Simona, and Muthukumaran Packirisamy. *BioMEMS: Science and Engineering Perspectives*. CRC, 2011.

Baggini, Angelo, and Andreas Sumper. *Electrical Energy Efficiency: Technologies and Applications*. John Wiley & Sons, 2012.

Baigrie, Brian S. *The Renaissance and the Scientific Revolution: Biographical Portraits*. Scribner's, 2001.

Bain, Don. "We Should Have Celebrated Rudolph Diesel's Birthday Yesterday." *Torque News*, 19 Mar. 2012, www.torquenews.com/397/we-should-have-celebrated-rudolph-diesel%e2%80%99s-birthday-yesterday.

Baker, Gregory L., and James A. Blackburn. *The Pendulum: A Case Study in Physics*. Oxford UP, 2008.

Balaji, S. *Electromagnetics Made Easy*. Springer Nature, 2020.

Ball, David W. *The Basics of Spectroscopy*. SPIE, 2001.

Banner, Adrian. *The Calculus Lifesaver: All the Tools You Need to Excel at Calculus*. Princeton UP, 2007.

Bannikova, Eleria, and Massimo Capaccioli. *Foundations of Celestial Mechanics*. Springer International Publishing, 2022.

Bardi, Jason Socrates. *The Calculus Wars: Newton, Leibniz, and the Greatest Mathematical Clash of All Time*. Thunder's Mouth Press, 2006.

Barnes, Jonathan, editor. *The Cambridge Companion to Aristotle*. Cambridge UP, 1995.

Barrett, Terence William. *Topological Foundations of Electromagnetism*. 2nd ed., World Scientific, 2022.

Barron, Tandall F., and Gregory F. Nellis. *Cryogenic Heat Transfer*. 2nd ed., CRC Press, 2017.

Barsoum, Michel, et al. "The MAX Phases: Unique New Carbide and Nitride Materials." *American Scientist*, 89, no. 4, July-Aug. 2001.

Bartlett, Melanie. *Adlard Coles Book of Diesel Engines*. 5th ed., Bloomsbury Publishing, 2018.

Bartusiak, Marcia. "Deciphering the Solar Spectrum." *Archives of the Universe: 100 Discoveries That Transformed Our Understanding of the Cosmos*, edited by Marcia Bartusiak, Vintage, 2006, pp. 211–17.

"Basic Principles of Vacuum Technology, Brief Overview." *Festo Group*, www.festo.com/net/SupportPortal/Files/286804/Basic_Vacuum_Technology_Principles.pdf. Accessed 20 Jan. 2017.

Basu, Bikramjit, Mitjan Kalin, and B.V. Manoj Kumar. *Friction and Wear of Ceramics: Principles and Case Studies*. John Wiley & Sons, 2020.

Batygin, Yutiy, Marina Barbashova, and Oleh Sabokar. *Electromagnetic Metal Forming for Advanced Processing Technologies*. Springer, 2018.

Baura, Gail D. *Engineering Ethics: An Industrial Perspective*. Boston: Elsevier Academic Press, 2006.

Beech, Martin. *The Pendulum Paradigm: Variations on a Theme and the Measure of Heaven and Earth*. Universal-Publishers, 2014.

Beith, Robert, editor. *Small and Micro Combined Heat and Power (CHP) Systems. Advanced Design, Performance, Materials and Applications*. Woodhead Publishing, 2011.

Bejan, Adrian. *Advanced Engineering Thermodynamics*. 4th ed., John Wiley & Sons, 2016.

Bell, Terence. "What Is Cold Working?" *The Balance*, 17 Mar. 2017, www.thebalance.com/what-is-cold-working-2340011. Accessed 22 June 2017.

Bellis, Mary. "The Compass and Other Magnetic Innovations." *ThoughtCo.*, 20 Nov. 2019, www.thoughtco.com/compass-and-other-magnetic-innovations-1991466. Accessed 27 Dec. 2020.

Bello, Igor. *Vacuum and Ultravacuum: Physics and Technology*. CRC Press, 2017.

Ben Salem, Fatma. *Direct Torque Control Strategies of Electrical Machines*. BoD–Books on Demand, 2021.

Benacquista, Matthew J., and Joseph D. Romano. *Classical Mechanics*. Springer, 2018.

Ben-Naim, Arieh. *Discover Entropy and the Second Law of Thermodynamics: A Playful Way of Discovering a Law of Nature*. World Scientific, 2010.

———. *Entropy Demystified: The Second Law Reduced to Plain Common Sense*. World Scientific, 2008.

Berera, Arjun, and Luigi Del Debbio. *Quantum Mechanics*. Cambridge UP, 2021.

Berlatsky, Noah. *Nanotechnology*. Greenhaven, 2014.

Berman, Bob. *Zoom: How Everything Moves: From Atoms and Galaxies to Blizzards and Bees*. Little, 2014.

"Bernoulli, Daniel (1700-1782)." *Encyclopedia of Weather and Climate*, edited by Michael Allaby, Rev. ed., Vol. 1, Facts on File, 2002, pp. 66–68.

Bernoulli, Daniel, and Johann Bernoulli. *Hydrodynamics and Hydraulics*. Translated by Thomas Carmody and Helmut Kobus. Dover, 2005.

"Bernoulli's Principle." *Flight and Motion: The History and Science of Flying*. Vol. 2. Sharpe Reference, 2009, pp. 142–43.

Bernstein, Dennis S. *Scalar, Vector, and Matrix Mathematics: Theory, Facts, and Formulas—Revised and Expanded Edition*. Princeton UP, 2018.

Bertin, John J., and Russell M. Cummings. *Aerodynamics for Engineers: International Edition*. 6th ed., Pearson Education, 2013.

Bertram, Albrecht. *Elasticity and Plasticity of Large Deformations, Including Gradient Materials*. 4th ed., Springer International Publishing, 2021.

Bettini, Alessandro. *A Course in Classical Physics 3–Electromagnetism* Springer, 2016.

Bhandari, V. B. *Design of Machine Elements*. 3rd ed., Tata/McGraw-Hill, 2010.

Bi, Zhuming, and Xiaoqin Wang. *Computer-Aided Design and Manufacturing*. Wiley, 2020.

Bibel, George, and Robert Hedges. *Plane Crash: The Forensics of Aviation Disasters*. Johns Hopkins UP, 2018.

Bichlmeier, Magnus. *Certifiable L1 Adaptive Control for Helicopters*. Cuvillier Verlag, 2016.

Binns, Chris. *Introduction to Nanoscience and Nanotechnology*. Wiley, 2010.

"Bioengineers and Biomedical Engineers." *Occupational Outlook Handbook*, Bureau of Labor Statistics, US Department of Labor, 1 Feb. 2021, www.bls.gov/ooh/architecture-and-engineering/biomedical-engineers.htm. Accessed 31 Mar. 2021.

"Biomedical Engineers." *Occupational Outlook Handbook, 2016–2017 Edition*. Bureau of Labor Statistics, US Department of Labor, 17 Dec. 2015. Accessed 23 Jan. 2016.

Birk, Lothar. *Fundamentals of Ship Hydrodynamics: Fluid Mechanics, Ship Resistance and Propulsion*. John Wiley & Sons, 2019.

Biswas, Abhijit, et al. "Advances in Top-Down and Bottom-Up Surface Nanofabrication: Techniques, Applications & Future Prospects." *Advances in Colloid and Interface Science*, vol. 170, nos. 1–2, 2012, pp. 2–27.

Bittinger, Marvin L., et al. *Calculus and Its Applications*. 11th ed., Pearson Education, 2016.

Blau, Peter J. *Friction Science and Technology*. 2nd ed., CRC Press, 2019.

Bloch, Heinz P. *Steam Turbines: Design, Applications, and Rerating*. 2nd ed., McGraw-Hill, 2009.

Bloch, Heinz P., and Murari P. Singh. *Steam Turbines: Design, Applications, and Rerating*. 2nd ed., McGraw-Hill, 2009.

Boi, Luciano. "A Scientific and Philosophical Concept, from Electrodynamics to String Theory and the Geometry of the Microscopic World." *The Quantum Vacuum*. JHU Press, 2011.

Boleman, Michael. "Experiment # 6: Work-Energy Theorem." *Mr. Boleman's Course Information*. University of South Alabama, n.d. Accessed 22 Sept. 2015.

Bolton, David. *Euclid: Elements*. Lulu.com, 2019.

Borichevsky, Steve. *Understanding Modern Vacuum Technology*. CreateSpace Independent Publishing Platform, 2017.

Boudri, J. C. *What Was Mechanical About Mechanics: The Concept of Force between Metaphysics and Mechanics from Newton to Lagrange*. Springer Science & Business Media, 2013.

Boulos, Paul F., Kevin E. Lansey, and Bryan W. Karney. *Comprehensive Water Distribution Systems Analysis Handbook for Engineers and Planners*. 2nd ed., MWH Soft Press, 2006.

Bourde, André J. *The Influence of England on the French Agronomes, 1750–1789*. Cambridge UP, 1953.

Bouvet, Christophe. *Mechanics of Aeronautical Solids: Materials and Structures*. John Wiley & Sons, 2017.

Braat, Joseph, and Peter Török. *Imaging Optics*. Cambridge UP, 2019.

Bradley, David Allan, Derek Seward, David Dawson, and Stewart Burge. *Mechatronics and the Design of Intelligent Machines and Systems*. CRC Press, 2018.

Braham, Andrew, and Sadie Casillas. *Fundamentals of Sustainability in Civil Engineering*. 2nd ed., CRC Press/Taylor & Francis Group, 2020.

Brand, Louis. *Vector and Tensor Analysis*. Courier Dover Publications, 2020.

Bray, Stan. *Making Simple Model Steam Engines*. Crowood, 2005.

Breeze, John, Jowan G. Penn-Barwell, Damian Keene, David O'Reilly, Jayasankar Jayanathan, and Peter F. Mahoney. *Ballistic Trauma: A Practical Guide*. 4th ed., Springer, 2017.

Breeze, Paul. *Power Generation Technologies*. Elsevier, 2014.

———. *Power System Energy Storage Technologies*. Academic Press, 2018.

Brennan, Michael J., and Bin Tang. *Virtual Experiments in Mechanical Vibrations: Structural Dynamics and Signal Processing*. John Wiley & Sons, 2022.

Brewster, Sir David. *Memoirs of the Life, Writings, and Discoveries of Sir Isaac Newton*. Constable, 1855. Reprint. Johnson Reprint, 1965.

Bronzino, Joseph D., and Donald R. Peterson. *Biomedical Engineering Fundamentals*. 4th ed., CRC Press, 2014.

Brown, Alan S. "Mechatronics and the Role of Engineers." *American Society of Mechanical Engineers*, Aug. 2011, www.asme.org/engineering-topics/articles/mechatronics/mechatronics-and-the-role-of-engineers. Accessed 19 Jan. 2017.

Brown, Jonathan. *Steam on the Farm: A History of Agricultural Steam Engines 1800–1950*. Crowood Press, 2008.

Brunt, Douglas. *The Mysterious Case of Rudolf Diesel: Genius, Power, and Deception on the Eve of World War I*. Simon & Schuster, 2023.

Bryant, W. D. A. *General Equilibrium: Theory and Evidence*. World Scientific, 2010.

Buckel, Werner, and Reinhold Kleiner. *Superconductivity: An Introduction*. Translated by Rudolf Huebener. 3rd ed., John Wiley & Sons, 2016.

Bunnell, Brian, and Samer Najia. *Mechanical Engineering for Makers: A Hands-On Guide to Designing and Making Physical Things*. Make Community LLC, 2020.

Buriyanyk, Michael. *Understanding Amplitudes: Basic Seismic Analysis for Rock Properties*. Society of Exploration Geophysicists, 2021.

Burnett, Betty. "Acceleration." *The Laws of Motion: Understanding Uniform and Accelerated Motion*. Rosen Publishing, 2005.

Byrne, Patrick H. *Analysis and Science in Aristotle*. State U of New York P, 1997.

Caddeo, Renzo, and Athanase Papadopoulos, editors. *Mathematical Geography in the Eighteenth Century: Euler, Lagrange and Lambert*. Springer Nature, 2022.

Caelucci, Donald E., and Sidney S. Jacobson. *Ballistics: Theory and Design of Guns and Ammunition*. 3rd ed., CRC Press, 2018.

Calero, Julian Simón. *Jean le Rond D'Alembert: A New Theory of the Resistance of Fluids*. Springer International Publishing, 2019.

Calinger, Ronald S. *Leonhard Euler: Mathematical Genius in the Enlightenment*. Princeton UP, 2019.

Campbell, Allison, et al. "Elasticity vs. Plasticity." *Energy Education*, energyeducation.ca/encyclopedia/Elasticity_vs_plasticity. Accessed 22 June 2017.

Campo, Estefânia Vangelie Ramos, et al. "Recent Developments in Nanotechnology for Detection and Control of Aedes aegypti-Borne Diseases." *Frontiers in Bioengineering and Biotechnology*, vol. 20, 2020, doi:10.3389/fbioe.2020.00102. Accessed 15 Mar. 2022.

Canbolat, Hüseyin. *Lagrangian Mechanics*. IntechOpen, 2017.

Caneva, Kenneth L. *Helmholtz and the Conservation of Energy: Contexts of Creation and Reception*. MIT Press, 2021.

———. *Robert Mayer and the Conservation of Energy*. Princeton UP, 2015.

Cardenete, Manuel Alejandro, Ana-Isabel Guerra, and Ferran Sancho. *Applied General Equilibrium: An Introduction*. Springer Science & Business Media, 2012.

Cardwell, D. S. L. *From Watt to Clausius: The Rise of Thermodynamics in the Early Industrial Age*. Cornell UP, 1971.

Carnot, Sadi. *Reflection on the Motive Power of Fire*. Dover, 1960.

———. *Reflexions on the Motive Power of Fire: A Critical Edition with the Surviving Scientific Manuscripts*. Translated and edited by Robert Fox. Manchester UP, 1986.

Caro, Herman D. *The Best of All Possible Worlds? Leibniz's Philosophical Optimism and Its Critics 1710–1755*. BRILL, 2020.

Caws, Mary Ann. *Blaise Pascal: Miracles and Reason*. Reaktion Books, 2017.

Çengel, Yunus A., and John M. Cimbala. *Fluid Mechanics: Fundamentals and Applications*. McGraw-Hill, 2010.

Cercerále, Jiri. *Whirl Flutter of Turboprop Aircraft Structures*. Elsevier Science, 2015.

Chakrabarti, Subrata K. *The Theory and Practice of Hydrodynamics and Vibration*. World Scientific, 2002.

Chakravorti, Sivaji. *Electric Field Analysis*. CRC Press, 2017.

Chalkley, A. P. *Diesel Engines for Land and Marine Work: With an Introductory Chapter by Dr. Rudolf Diesel*. BoD–Books on Demand, 2014.

Chang, Kuang-Hua. *e-Design: Computer-Aided Engineering Design*. Academic Press, 2016.

Chang, Raymond. *Physical Chemistry for the Biosciences*. University Science Books, 2005.

"Chapter 1: Opening a New Frontier with the Rotary Engine." *Mazda*, www.mazda.com/en/innovation/stories/rotary/newfrontier/. Accessed 2 Oct. 2017.

"Chapter 3: Entering a New Era and Looking Further into the Future." *Mazda*, www.mazda.com/en/innovation/stories/rotary/newera/. Accessed 2 Oct. 2017.

Chatterjee, Shoutir Kishore. *Statistical Thought: A Perspective and History*. Oxford UP, 2007.

Chatzigeorgiou, Ioannis. *Analytical Methods in Marine Hydrodynamics*. Cambridge UP, 2018.

Chen, Evan. *Euclidean Geometry in Mathematical Olympiads*. American Mathematical Society, 2021.

Chen, Gang Sheng. *Handbook of Friction-Vibration Interactions*. Elsevier, 2014.

Chen, Sophia, and Andrew Dean Foland. *Energy*. 3rd ed., Infobase Holdings Inc, 2021.

Cheney, Margaret. *Tesla: Man Out of Time*. New York: Barnes & Noble Books, 1993.

Childs, P. R. N. *Mechanical Design: Theory and Applications*. 3rd ed., Butterworth-Heinemann, 2021.

Chiras, Daniel D, Mick Sagrillo, and Ian Woofenden. *Power from the Wind*. New Society, 2009.

Chow, Ven Te. *Open-Channel Hydraulics*. 1959. Blackburn, 2008.

Christianson, Gale E. *Isaac Newton*. Oxford UP, 2005.

Cicci, David A. *A Short Course in Inertial Navigation and Missile Guidance*. Independently Published, 2021.

"Circus Physics: Conservation of Energy." *Circus*. PBS, 2010. Accessed 21 Apr. 2015.

Cleckner, Ryan M. *Long Range Shooting Handbook: The Complete Beginner's Guide to Precision Rifle Shooting*. CreateSpace Independent Publishing Platform, 2016.

Coddington, Richard C. "Inertial Frame, Euler's First Law." *University of Illinois at Urbana-Champaign*. Department of Agricultural and Biological Engineering, 2015. Accessed 27 Aug. 2015.

Cohen, I. Bernard, and George E. Smith, editors. *The Cambridge Companion to Newton*. Cambridge UP, 2002.

Cohen, Michael. "Classical Mechanics: A Critical Introduction." *Physics & Astronomy*. The Trustees of the University of Pennsylvania, www.physics.upenn.edu/resources/online-textbook-mechanics. Accessed 14 Mar. 2016.

Coleman, Francis X. J. *Neither Angel Nor Beast: The Life and Works of Blaise Pascal*. Routledge, 2013.

Coleman, Lawrence B. "Elasticity and Plasticity." *University of California, Davis*, 14 June 1998, smartsite.ucdavis.edu/access/content/user/00002774/Sears-Coleman%20Text/Text/C11-15/12-4.html. Accessed 22 June 2017.

Collier, Peter. *A Most Incomprehensible Thing: Notes towards a Very Gentle Introduction to the Mathematics of Relativity*. 2nd ed. Incomprehensible, 2014.

Colwell, Catharine H. "Static Equilibrium." *PhysicsLAB*. Catherine H. Colwell, dev.physicslab.org/document.aspx?doctype=3&filename=dynamics_staticequilibrium.xml. Accessed 9 Mar. 2016.

Commins, Eugene D. *Quantum Mechanics: An Experimentalist's Approach*. Cambridge UP, 2014.

Connor, Jerome J., and Susan Faraji. *Fundamentals of Structural Engineering*. Springer International Publishing, 2016.

"Conservation of Energy." *Khan Academy*, 2015. Accessed 21 Apr. 2015.

"Conservation of Energy: Physics." *Encyclopedia Britannica*. Encyclopedia Britannica, 23 Jan. 2014. Accessed 21 Apr. 2015.

Consortium of Universities for Research in Earthquake Engineering. *Earthquake Engineering*. Department of Building Inspection, City & County of San Francisco. 2006.

Cooley, Brian. "CNET on Cars: Car Tech 101—Horsepower vs. Torque." *CNET*. CBS Interactive, 26 Feb. 2013. Accessed 7 Aug. 2015.

Coolman, Robert. "What Is Classical Mechanics?" *LiveScience*, 12 Sept. 2014. Accessed 6 May 2015.

Cooper, Michael. *"A More Beautiful City": Robert Hooke and the Rebuilding of London after the Great Fire*. Sutton, 2003.

Cossu, Remo, and Matthew G. Wells. "The Evolution of Submarine Channels under the Influence of Coriolis Forces: Experimental Observations of Flow Structures." *Terra Nova*, vol. 25, no. 1, 2013, pp. 65–71. Academic Search Complete. Accessed 19 Mar. 2015.

Costanti, Felice. "The Golden Crown: A Discussion." *The Genius of Archimedes: 23 Centuries of Influence on Mathematics, Science and Engineering; Proceedings of an International Conference Held at Syracuse, Italy, June 8–10, 2010*, edited by Stephanos A. Paipetis and Marco Ceccarelli, Springer, 2010, pp. 215–26.

Crawford, F. *Stone Projectile Points of the Pacific Northwest: An Arrowhead Collector's Guide to Type Identification*. 2nd ed., CreateSpace Independent Publishing Platform, 2017.

Crocco, Lorenzo, and Panos Kosmas, editors. *Electromagnetic Technologies for Medical Diagnostics:*

Fundamental Issues, Clinical Applications and Perspectives. MDPI, 2019.

Cropper, William H. *Great Physicists: The Life and Times of Leading Physicists from Galileo to Hawking.* Oxford UP, 2001.

Croucher, Phil. *The Helicopter Pilot's Handbook.* CreateSpace Independent Publishing Platform, 2016.

Crump, Thomas. *A Brief History of the Age of Steam: The Power That Drove the Industrial Revolution.* Carroll & Graf, 2007.

Crumpsty, Nicholas, and Andrew Heyes. *Jet Propulsion: A Simple Guide to the Aerodynamics and Thermodynamic Design and Performance of Jet Engines.* Cambridge UP, 2015.

Cummings, Russell M., Scott A. Morton, William H. Mason, and David R. McDaniel. *Applied Computational Aerodynamics: A Modern Engineering Approach.* Cambridge UP, 2015.

Cummins, C. Lyle, Jr. *Diesel's Engine: The Man, and the Evolution of the World's Most Efficient Internal Combustion Motor.* Octane Press, 2022.

Daqaq, Mohammed F. *Dynamics of Particles and Rigid Bodies: A Self-Learning Approach.* John Wiley & Sons, 2018.

Darlington, Roy, and Keith Strong. *Stirling and Hot Air Engines: Designing and Building Experimental Model Stirling Engines.* Crowood Press, 2005.

Darrigol, Olivier. *A History of Optics from Greek Antiquity to the Nineteenth Century.* Oxford UP, 2012.

———. *Worlds of Flow: A History of Hydrodynamics from the Bernoullis to Prandtl.* Oxford UP, 2005.

Daston, Lorraine. *Classical Probability in the Enlightenment.* Princeton UP, 2021.

Davidson, Frank Paul, and Kathleen Lusk-Brooke. *Building the World: An Encyclopedia of the Great Engineering Projects in History.* Greenwood, 2006.

Davidson, P. A. *Incompressible Fluid Dynamics.* Oxford UP, 2022.

Davies, Matthew A., and Tony L. Schmitz. *System Dynamics for Mechanical Engineers.* Springer, 2015.

Davies, Paul. *Information and the Nature of Reality: From Physics to Metaphysics.* Cambridge UP, 2014.

Davis, A. Douglas. *Classical Mechanics.* Elsevier, 2012.

Davis, S. C., S. W. Diegel, and R. G. Boundy. *Transportation Energy Data Book.* 30th ed., US Department of Energy, 2011, cta.ornl.gov/data/download30.shtml.

Davson, Hugh. *The Visual Process: The Eye.* Academic Press, 2014.

"The Death of the Internal Combustion Engine." *The Economist,* 12 Aug. 2017, www.economist.com/news/leaders/21726071-it-had-good-run-end-sight-machine-changed-world-death. Accessed 23 Aug. 2017.

De Luca, Luigi T., Max Calabro, Toru Shimada, and Valery P. Sinditskii, editors. *Chemical Rocket Propulsion: A Comprehensive Survey of Energetic Materials.* Springer International Publishing, 2018.

De Mayo, Benjamin. *The Everyday Physics of Hearing and Vision.* Morgan & Claypool Publishers, 2014.

de Nevers, Noel. *Physical and Chemical Equilibrium for Chemical Engineers.* 2nd ed., John Wiley & Sons, 2012.

Decker, Reiner. *Powering the World's Airliners: Engine Developments from the Propeller to the Jet Age.* Pen & Sword Books, 2020.

Demetzos, Costas. *Pharmaceutical Nanotechnology: Fundamentals and Practical Applications.* Adis, 2016.

Desmet, Bernard. *Thermodynamics of Heat Engines.* John Wiley & Sons, 2022.

Dieiter, George E., and Linda C. Schmidt. *Engineering Design.* 4th ed., McGraw-Hill Higher Education, 2009.

Dillmann, Andreas, and Alexander Orellano. *The Aerodynamics of Heavy Vehicles III. Trucks, Buses and Trains.* Springer, 2015.

Discetti, Stefano, and Andrea Ianiro. *Experimental Aerodynamics.* CRC Press, 2017.

Dixit, P. M., and U.S. Dixit. *Plasticity: Fundamentals and Applications.* CRC Press, 2018.

Dodd, John N. *Atoms and Light: Interactions.* Springer Science & Business Media, 2013.

Doehring, James. "What Is Mechatronics Engineering?" *Wisegeek,* 20 Dec. 2016, www.wisegeek.com/what-is-mechatronics-engineering.htm. Accessed 19 Jan. 2017.

Douglas, Elliot. *Introduction to Materials Science and Engineering.* Pearson, 2013.

Doyle, John C., Bruce A. Francis, and Allen R. Tannenbaum. *Feedback Control Theory.* Reprint. Courier Corporation, 2013.

Drbal, L., K. Westra, and P. Boston. *Power Plant Engineering.* Springer, 1996.

Dreger, Alice. *Galileo's Middle Finger: Heretics, Activists, and One Scholar's Search for Justice.* Penguin Publishing Group, 2016.

Drexler, K. Eric. *Radical Abundance: How a Revolution in Nanotechnology Will Change Civilization.* PublicAffairs, 2013.

Driss, Zied. *Mechanical Engineering Technologies and Applications.* Bentham Science Publishers, 2021.

Dungan, T. D. *V-2: A Combat History of the First Ballistic Missile.* Westholme, 2005.

Dunham, William. *The Calculus Gallery: Masterpieces from Newton to Lebesgue.* Princeton UP, 2005.

Durrant, Alan. *Vectors in Physics and Engineering*. Routledge, 2019.

Eastop, T. D., and A. McConkey. *Applied Thermodynamics for Engineering Technologists*. 5th ed., Longman, 1993.

Eckert, Michael. *The Dawn of Fluid Dynamics: A Discipline between Science and Technology*. Wiley, 2006.

Edmonds, A. R. *Angular Momentum in Quantum Mechanics*. Princeton UP, 2016.

Ehsani, Mehrdad, et al. *Modern Electric, Hybrid Electric, and Fuel Cell Vehicles, Fundamentals, Theory, and Design*. CRC Press, 2005.

Einstein, Albert, and Leopold Infeld. *The Evolution of Physics: The Growth of Ideas from Early Concepts to Relativity and Quanta*. Simon, 1938.

El-Mogy, Mostafa "What Is Structural Engineering?" *Structural Engineer Basics*, 2019, structuralengineeringbasics.com/what-is-structural-engineering. Accessed 20 Jan. 2020.

El-Sayed, Ahmed F. *Fundamentals of Aircraft and Rocket Propulsion*. Springer London, 2016.

Enderle, John Denis, and Joseph D. Brozino. *Introduction to Biomedical Engineering*. 3rd ed., Elsevier, 2012.

"Energy, Kinetic Energy, Work, Dot Product, and Power." *MIT OpenCourseWare*. Massachusetts Institute of Technology, 13 Oct. 2004. Accessed 22 Sept. 2015.

"Engineering Basics." *American Institute of Steel Construction*, www.aisc.org/why-steel/architect/guide-for-architects/engineering-basics. Accessed 20 Jan. 2020.

"Engineering Explained: The Pros and Cons of Inline 5s, V10s and Rotary Engines." *Car Throttle*, 2014, www.carthrottle.com/post/engineering-explained-the-pros-and-cons-of-inline-5s-v10s-and-rotary-engines. Accessed 2 Oct. 2017.

"Engineers Study the Benefits of Adding a Second, Smaller Rotor to Wind Turbines." *Phys.org*, 10 Mar. 2015. Accessed 14 Apr. 2015.

Epp, Susana S. *Discrete Mathematics and Applications*. Cengage, 2011.

"Equilibrium and Statics." *The Physics Classroom*, www.physicsclassroom.com/class/vectors/Lesson-3/Equilibrium-and-Statics. Accessed 9 Mar. 2016.

Erbil, H. Y. *Surface Chemistry of Solid and Liquid Interfaces*. Blackwell, 2006.

Eriksen, Vernon L. *Heat Recovery Steam Generator Technology*. Woodhead Publishing, 2017.

Estrada, Hector, and Luke S. Lee. *Introduction to Earthquake Engineering*. CRC Press, Taylor & Francis Group, 2017.

Euclid. *Euclid's "Elements."* Translated by Thomas Little Heath. Edited by Dana Densmore. Digireads.com Publishing, 2017.

Everest, F. Alton, and Ken C. Pohlmann. *Master Handbook of Acoustics*. 5th ed., McGraw-Hill, 2009.

"The Everyday Applications of Vacuum Technologies." *Techiestuffs*, 10 June 2016, www.techiestuffs.com/the-everyday-applications-of-vacuum-technologies. Accessed 20 Jan. 2017.

"Examples and Explanations of BME." *Biomedical Engineering Society*. Biomedical Engineering Society, 2012–14. Accessed 23 Jan. 2016.

Faeth, G. M. *Centennial of Powered Flight: A Retrospective of Aerospace Research*. American Institute of Aeronautics and Astronautics, 2003.

Falkovich, G. *Fluid Mechanics: A Short Course for Physicists*. Cambridge UP, 2011.

Fara, Patricia. *Newton: The Making of a Genius*. Columbia UP, 2002.

Farlow, Stanley J. *Advanced Mathematics: A Transitional Reference*. John Wiley & Sons, 2019.

Faust, Russell A., editor. *Robotics in Surgery: History, Current and Future Applications*. Nova Science, 2007.

Featherstone, Roy. *Rigid Body Dynamics Algorithms*. Springer US, 2016.

Federal Aviation Administration (FAA). *Aircraft Weight and Balance Handbook (FAA-H-8083-1A)*. Skyhorse Publishing, 2011.

Federal Emergency Management Agency. *Designing for Earthquakes: A Manual for Architects*. FEMA 454, 2006.

Feidt, Michel, editor. *Carnot Cycle and Heat Engine Fundamentals and Applications*. MDPI, 2020.

Fellah, Zine El Abiddine, and Erick Ogam. *Acoustics of Materials*. BoD–Books on Demand, 2019.

Ferejohn, Michael. *The Origins of Aristotelian Science*. Yale UP, 1991.

Fermi, Enrico. *Thermodynamics*. 1936. Dover, 2012.

Ferrari, Giancarlo, Angelo Onorati, and Gianluca D'Errico. *Internal Combustion Engines*. Societa Editrice Esculapio, 2022.

Ferreiro, Larrie D. *Ships and Science: The Birth of Naval Architecture in the Scientific Revolution, 1600–1800*. MIT Press, 2007.

Ferziger, Joel H., Milovan Peric, and Robert L. Street. *Computational Methods for Fluid Dynamics*. 4th ed., Springer, 2019.

Feynman, Richard, Robert Leighton, and Matthew Sands. *Six Easy Pieces: Essentials of Physics Explained by Its Most Brilliant Teacher*. 4th ed., Basic, 2011.

Fijalkowski, B. T. *Automotive Mechatronics: Operational and Practical Issues*. Vol. II. Springer, 2011.

Filatrault, André. *Elements of Earthquake Engineering and Structural Dynamics*. Presses Inter Polytechnique, 2013.

Filipovic, Nenad. *Computational Modeling in Bioengineering and Bioinformatics*. Academic Press, 2020.

Finn, John Michael. *Classical Mechanics*. Jones, 2009.

Finnemore, E. John, and Joseph B. Franzini. *Fluid Mechanics with Engineering Applications*. 10th International ed., McGraw-Hill, 2009.

Finnis, Mike. *Interatomic Forces in Condensed Matter*. Oxford UP, 2010.

Fitzpatrick, Richard. *Maxwell's Equations and the Principles of Electromagnetism*. Infinity Science, 2008.

———. *Oscillations and Waves: An Introduction*. 2nd ed., CRC Press, 2018.

Fleisch, Daniel. *A Student's Guide to Maxwell's Equations*. Cambridge UP, 2008.

Flewitt, Andrew J. *Electromagnetism for Engineers* John Wiley & Sons, 2022.

Floreano, Dario, and Claudio Mattuissi. *Bio-Inspired Artificial Intelligence: Theories, Methods, and Technologies*. MIT Press, 2008.

Ford, Kenneth W. *Basic Physics*. World Scientific Publishing Company, 2016.

———. *The Quantum World: Quantum Physics for Everyone*. Harvard UP, 2005.

Ford, P. J., and G. A. Saunders. *The Rise of the Superconductors*. CRC Press, 2018.

Fowler, Glenn. "Felix Wankel, Inventor, Is Dead; Creator of Rotary Engine Was 86." *New York Times*, 14 Oct. 1988, www.nytimes.com/1988/10/14/obituaries/felix-wankel-inventor-is-dead-creator-of-rotary-engine-was-86.html. Accessed 2 Oct. 2017.

Franklin, Jerrold. *Classical Electromagnetism*. 2nd ed., Courier Dover Publications, 2017.

Freedman, Roger, Todd Ruskell, Philip R. Kesten, and David L. Tauck. *College Physics*. 2nd ed., W.H. Freeman, 2017.

Funaro, Daniele. *Electromagnetism and the Structure of Matter*. World Scientific, 2008.

Fussell, George E. *Jethro Tull: His Influence on Mechanized Agriculture*. Osprey, 1973.

Gajic, Zoran, and Muhammad Tahir Javed Qureshi. *Liapunov Matrix Equation in System Stability and Control*. Reprint. Courier Corporation, 2008.

Galilei, Galileo. *The Essential Galileo*. Edited by Maurice A. Finochiarro, Hackett Publishing Company, 2008.

"Galileo: The Telescope & the Laws of Dynamics." *University of Rochester Department of Physics and Astronomy*, www.pas.rochester.edu/~blackman/ast104/galileo12.html. Accessed 30 Jan. 2017.

Gallagher, Mary Beth. "MIT Mechanical Engineers Develop Solutions to Help Slow and Stop the Spread of COVID-19." *SciTechDaily*, 2 Dec. 2020, scitechdaily.com/mit-mechanical-engineers-develop-solutions-to-help-slow-and-stop-the-spread-of-covid-19. Accessed 15 June 2021.

Gans, Roger F. *Mechanical Systems: A Unified Approach to Vibrations and Controls*. Springer, 2014.

Gardner, Raymond, et al. *Introduction to Practical Marine Engineering*. Society of Naval Architects and Marine Engineers, 2002.

Garino, Brian W., and Jeffrey D. Lanphear. "Spacecraft Design, Structure, and Operations." *AU-18 Space Primer*. Air University, 2009. Accessed 9 June 2015.

Garrett, Steven L. *Understanding Acoustics: An Experimentalist's View of Sound and Vibration*. 2nd ed., Springer Nature, 2020.

Gatti, Paolo Luciano. *Advanced Mechanical Vibrations: Physics, Mathematics and Applications*. CRC Press, 2020.

Gatzen, Hans H., et al. "Vacuum Technology." *Micro and Nano Fabrication*. Springer Berlin Heidelberg, 2015, pp. 7–63.

Gekhtman, Michael, Michael Shapiro, and Alek Vainshtein. *Cluster Algebras and Poisson Geometry*. American Mathematical Society, 2010.

Geymonat, Mario. *The Great Archimedes*. Baylor UP, 2010.

Giambattista, Alan, Betty McCarthy Richardson, and Robert C. Richardson. *Physics*. 2nd ed. McGraw, 2010.

Giffard, Hermione. *Making Jet Engines in World War II: Britain, Germany and the United States*. U of Chicago P, 2016.

Gillispie, Charles Coulston. *Pierre-Simon Laplace, 1749–1827: A Life in Exact Science*. Princeton UP, 2018.

Gillispie, Charles Coulston, and Raffaele Pisano. *Lazare and Sadi Carnot: A Scientific and Filial Relationship*. 2nd ed., Springer, 2014.

Girifalco, Louis A. *The Universal Force: Gravity—Creator of Worlds*. Oxford UP, 2014.

Gitterman, M. *The Chaotic Pendulum*. World Scientific, 2010.

Gleick, James L. *Chaos: Making a New Science*. Rev. ed., Penguin Books, 2008.

———. *Isaac Newton*. Pantheon, 2003.

Goel, Anup. *Kinematics of Machinery*. Technical Publications, 2021.

Goh, Gahyun, and Y. Noh. "Influence of Coriolis Force on the Formation of a Seasonal Thermocline." *Ocean*

Dynamics, vol. 63, no. 9-10, 2013, pp. 1083–92. Energy & Power Source. Accessed 19 Mar. 2015.

Gohardani, Amir S. *Distributed Propulsion Technology*. Nova Science Publishers Inc., 2014.

Goldfarb, Daniel. *Biophysics Demystified*. McGraw-Hill, 2010.

Golley, John. *Jet: Frank Whittle and the Invention of the Jet Engine*. Datum Publishing Ltd., 2009.

Gómez-López, Vicente M., and Rajeev Bhat, editors. *Electromagnetic Technologies in Food Science*. John Wiley & Sons, 2021.

Goodier, J. N., and P. G. Hodge, Jr. *Elasticity and Plasticity: The Mathematical Theory of Elasticity and The Mathematical Theory of Plasticity*. Courier Dover Publications, 2016.

Gordin, Michael D. *A Well-Ordered Thing: Dmitri Mendeleev and the Shadow of the Periodic Table, Revised Edition*. Princeton UP, 2019.

Gordon, J. E. *The New Science of Strong Materials; or, Why You Don't Fall Through the Floor*. Princeton UP, 2006.

Gordon, Opal. *A Comprehensive Guide to Angular Momentum*. Nova Science Publishers, 2019.

Gosline, Anna. "Survival in Space Unprotected Is Possible —Briefly." *Scientific American*. Scientific American, Inc. 14 Feb. 2008, www.scientificamerican.com/article/survival-in-space-unprotected-possible. Accessed 23 Dec. 2014.

Graham, John. *Biological Centrifugation*. Garland Science, 2020.

Greco, Pietro. *Galileo Galilei: The Tuscan Artist*. Springer, 2018.

Green, Dan. *The Periodic Table in Minutes*. Quercus, 2016.

Greenberg, John L. *The Problem of the Earth's Shape from Newton to Clairaut: The Rise of Mathematical Science in Eighteenth Century Paris and the Fall of "Normal" Science*. Cambridge UP, 1995.

Greene, D. L. "Uncertainty, Loss, Aversion, and Markets for Energy Efficiency." *Energy Economics*, vol. 33, no. 4, July, 2011.

Greene, D. L., K. G. Duleep, and Girish Upreti. *Status and Outlook for the U.S. Non-automotive Fuel Cell Industry: Impact of Government Policies and Assessment of Future Opportunities*. ORNL/TM-2011/101. Oak Ridge National Laboratory, 2011.

Grewal, Mohinder S., Angus P. Andrews, and Chris G. Bartone. *Global Navigation Satellite Systems, Inertial Navigation, and Integration*. 3rd ed., John Wiley & Sons, 2015.

Gribbin, John. *Deep Simplicity: Bringing Order to Chaos and Complexity*. Random House, 2005.

———. *Science: A History, 1543–2001*. Lane, 2002.

Gribbin, John, and Mary Gribbin. *Out of the Shadow of a Giant: Hooke, Halley & the Birth of Science*. Yale UP, 2017.

Grimsley, Ronald. *Jean d'Alembert, 1717–1783*. Clarendon Press, 1963.

Groothius, Douglas. *On Pascal*. Thomson, 2003.

Gross, Dietmar, and Werner Hauger. *Engineering Mechanics 3: Dynamics*. Springer, 2011.

Gudmondsson, Snorri. *General Aviation Aircraft Design: Applied Methods and Procedures*. Elsevier Science, 2021.

Guenther, B. D. *Modern Optics Simplified*. Oxford UP, 2019.

Günel, Mehmet Halis, and Huseyn Emre Ilgin. *Tall Buildings: Structural Systems and Aerodynamic Form*. Routledge, 2014.

Guo, Hingsheng, Hailin Li, Lino Guzzella, and Masahiro Shioji, editors. *Advances in Compression Ignition Natural Gas—Diesel Dual Fuel Engines*. Frontiers Media SA, 2021.

Gurfil, Pini, and P. Kenneth Seidelmann. *Celestial Mechanics and Astrodynamics: Theory and Practice*. Springer, 2016.

Gutkind, Lee. *Almost Human: Making Robots Think*. 2006. Reprint. Norton, 2009.

Guyer, J. Paul. *An Introduction to Steam Turbine Design*. Guyer Partners, 2017.

Guyon, Etienne, Jean-Piere Hulin, Luc Petit, and Catalin D. Mitescu. *Physical Hydrodynamics*. Oxford UP, 2015.

Gzik, Marek, Zbigniew Paszenda, Ewa Pietka, Ewaryst Tacacz, and Krzysztof Milewski, editors. *Innovations in Biomedical Engineering*. Springer Nature, 2020.

Hager, Willi H. *Wastewater Hydraulics: Theory and Practice*. 2nd ed., Springer Berlin Heidelberg, 2010.

Hahan, Roger, and Roger Hahn. *Pierre-Simon Laplace, 1749–1827: A Determined Scientist*. Harvard UP, 2005.

Hahn, Hubert. *Rigid Body Dynamics of Mechanisms:1 Theoretical Basis*. Springer Science & Business Media, 2013.

Hall, Edith. *Aristotle's Way: How Ancient Wisdom Can Change Your Life*. Penguin, 2019.

Hall, Nancy, editor. "Newton's Laws of Motion." *The Beginner's Guide to Aeronautics*. NASA, 5 May 2015. Accessed 27 Aug. 2015.

Halliday, David, Robert Resnick, and Jearl Walker. *Fundamentals of Physics, Volume 1*. 12th ed., John Wiley & Sons, 2021.

Hamill, Joseph, and Kathleen Knutzen. *Biomechanical Basis of Human Movement*. 4th ed., Lippincott, 2015.

Hamill, Les. *Understanding Hydraulics*. 3rd ed., Bloomsbury Publishing, 2017.

Hammond, Nicholas, ed. *The Cambridge Companion to Pascal*. Cambridge UP, 2003.

Han, G. C., et al. "A Differential Dual Spin Valve with High Pinning Stability." *Applied Physics Letters,* vol. 96, 2010.

Han, Je-Chin. *Analytical Heat Transfer*. CRC Press, 2016.

Hankins, Thomas L. *Jean d'Alembert: Science and the Enlightenment*. Clarendon Press, 1970.

Hansen, Jesper Schmidt. *Nanoscale Hydrodynamics of Simple Systems*. Cambridge UP, 2022.

Hansen, Martin O. L. *Aerodynamics of Wind Turbines*. 3rd ed., Routledge, 2015.

Haraoubia, Brahim. *Nonlinear Electronics 1: Nonlinear Dipoles, Harmonic Oscillators and Switching Circuits*. Elsevier, 2018.

Hasan, Heather. *Archimedes: The Father of Mathematics*. Rosen, 2006.

Hatze, H. "The Meaning of the Term 'Biomechanics.'" *Journal of Biomechanics*, vol. 7, no. 2, 1974, pp. 89–90.

Hausner, Melvin. *A Vector Space Approach to Geometry*. Courier Dover Publications, 2018.

Hay, James G. *The Biomechanics of Sports Techniques*. 4th ed., Prentice, 1993.

Hayes, G. *Stationary Steam Engines*. Bloomsbury USA, 2011.

Hayward, R. Baldwin. *The Algebra of Coplanar Vectors and Trigonometry*. Fb&c Limited, 2015.

Hebner, R. "Flywheel Batteries Come Around Again." *Spectrum*, vol. 39, no. 4, Apr. 2002.

Heilbron, J. L. *Galileo*. Oxford UP, 2012.

Heindl, R. A. *Young's Modulus of Elasticity at Several Temperatures for Some Refractories of Varying Silica Content (Classic Reprint)*. Fb&c Limited, 2018.

Henderson, Tom. "Electric Field and the Movement of Charge." *Physics Classroom*. Physics Classroom, 1996–2015. Accessed 7 May 2015.

———. *Kinematics*. Physics Classroom, 2013. Digital file.

———. *Motion in Two Dimensions*. N.p.: Physics Classroom, 2012. Digital file.

———. "Speed and Velocity." *Kinematics. Physics Classroom*, 2013. Accessed 10 Sept. 2014.

Hentschel. Klaus. *Photons: The History and Mental Models of Light Quanta*. Translated by Ann M. Hentschel. Springer, 2018.

Hentschel, Klaus, and Ning Yan Zhu, editors. *Gustav Robert Kirchhhoff's Treatise "On the Theory of Light Rays" (1882): English Translation, Analysis and Commentary*. World Scientific, 2016.

Hernandez, John. *Quantum Physics: A Simple Guide to Understanding the Principles of Physics (All the Major Ideas of Quantum Mechanics from Quanta to Entanglement in Simple Language)*. Zoe Lawson, 2022.

Hewitt, Paul G. *Conceptual Physics*. 12th ed., Pearson, 2014.

Heywood, John. *Internal Combustion Engine Fundamentals 2E*. 2nd ed., McGraw Hill Professional, 2018.

Hiereth, Hermann, and Peter Prenninger. *Charging the Internal Combustion Engine (Powertrain)*. Springer, 2010.

Hills, Phillip. *The Star Drive: The True Story of a Genius, an Engine and Our Future*. Birlinn Limited, 2021.

Hines, Edwin. *Quantum Physics for Beginners: Discover the Science of Quantum Mechanics and Learn the Most Important Concepts Concerning Black Holes, String Theory, and What We Perceive as Reality in a Simple Way*. Dorling Kindersley, 2022.

Hirshfeld, Alan. *Eureka Man: The Life and Legacy of Archimedes*. Bloomsbury Publishing USA, 2009.

"History of CNC Machining." *Bantam Tools*, 12 Apr. 2019, medium.com/cnc-life/history-of-cnc-machining-part-1-2 a4b290d994d. Accessed 28 Nov. 2021.

"History of Helicopters." *American Helicopter Museum & Education Center*, 2016, americanhelicopter.museum/ exhibits-and-resources/history-helicopters. Accessed 6 Dec. 2016.

Hitchens, Frank. *Propeller Aerodynamics: The History, Aerodynamics and Operation of Aircraft Propellers*. Andrews UK Limited, 2015.

Hockey, Thomas, et al., editors. *Biographical Encyclopedia of Astronomers*. 2nd ed., Springer, 2014.

Hoffman, Banesh. *About Vectors*. Courier Corporation, 2012.

Holzner, Steven. "How to Calculate the Momentum of Inertia for Different Shapes and Solids." *Dummies.com*, www.dummies.com/education/science/physics/how-to-calculate-the-momentum-of-inertia-for-different-shapes-and-solids. Accessed 26 June 2017.

Holzner, Steven, and Daniel Funch Wohns. "Moments of Inertia in Physics." *Dummies.com*, www.dummies.com/education/science/physics/moments-of-inertia-in-physics. Accessed 26 June 2017.

Hosford, William F. *Materials Science*. Cambridge UP, 2007.

Houk, T. William, James Poth, and John W. Snider. *University Physics: Arfken Griffing Kelly Priest*. Academic Press, 2013.

Hourly History. *Nikola Tesla: A Life from Beginning to End*. Hourly History, 2017.

Housner, George W., and Donald E. Hudson. *Applied Mechanics Dynamics*. 2nd ed., Division of Engineering California Institute of Technology, 1991, authors.library.caltech.edu/25023/1/Housner-HudsonDyn80.pdf. Accessed 30 Jan. 2017.

"How Do Wind Turbines Work?" *Office of Energy Efficiency & Renewable Energy*. US Department of Energy, n.d. Accessed 14 Apr. 2015.

Hranicky, Wm. Jack. *North American Projectile Points*. Author House, 2014.

Hsu, Tai-Ran. *Applied Engineering Analysis*. John Wiley & Sons, 2018.

Hsu, Tom. *Physics: A First Course*. 2nd ed., CPO, 2012.

Hucknall, David J. *Vacuum Technology and Applications*. Butterworth-Heinemann, 1991.

Huebener, Rudolf P. *History and Theory of Superconductors: A Compact Introduction*. Springer Nature, 2021.

Huebener, Rudolf P., and Heinz Luebbig. *A Focus of Discoveries*. 2nd ed., World Scientific, 2012.

Hughes-Hallett, Deborah, Otto Bretscher, Adrian Iovita, and David Sloane. *Calculus*. 8th ed. Wiley, 2021.

Hummel, Rolf E. *Understanding Materials Science: History, Properties, Applications*. 2nd ed., Springer, 2004.

Hunecke, Klaus. *Jet Engines: Fundamentals of Theory, Design and Operation*. Crowood Press, UK, 2010.

Hunley, J. D. *The Development of Propulsion Technology for U.S. Space-Launch Vehicles, 1926–1991*. Texas A&M University Press, 2013.

Hunt, Inez, and Wanetta W. Draper. *Lightning in His Hand: The Life Story of Nikola Tesla*. Sage Books, 1964.

Hurtado, John E. *A Kinematics and Kinetics Primer*. Lulu.com, 2014.

International Correspondence Schools. *Steam Engine Design and Mechanism*. Merchant Books, 2008.

Inwood, Stephen. *The Forgotten Genius: The Biography of Robert Hooke, 1635–1703*. MacAdam, 2005.

Irene, Eugene A. *Electronic Materials Science*. Wiley, 2005.

Jackson, Chad. "What Is Mechanical Computer Aided Engineering (MCAE)?" *Lifecycle Insights*, 2021, www.lifecycleinsights.com/tech-guide/mcae. Accessed 16 Dec. 2021.

Jackson, Tom. *The Periodic Table: A Visual Guide to the Elements*. White Lion Publishing, 2020.

Jacoby, John. *The Most Efficient Engine: The New Carnot Cycle*. CreateSpace Independent Publishing Platform, 2014.

Jahed, Hamid, and Ali A. Roostaei, editors. *Cyclic Plasticity of Metals: Modeling Fundamentals and Applications*. Elsevier, 2021.

James, Hubert M. *Theory of Servomechanisms*. McGraw, 1947.

Jammer, Max. *Concepts of Force: A Study in the Foundations of Dynamics*. Dover, 2005.

Jandusay, D. E. P. *165 Solved Problems in Aeronautical Engineering: Explained. Solved. Final Answer Boxed*. Book Publishing House Gate 5, 2020.

Janna, William S. *Engineering Heat Transfer*. 3rd ed., CRC Press, 2018.

Jardine, Lisa. *The Curious Life of Robert Hooke: The Man Who Measured London*. Harper, 2005.

Jayasree, P. K., K. Balan, and V. Rani. *Practical Civil Engineering*. CRC Press, 2021.

Jeffress, D. "What Does a Mechatronics Engineer Do?" *Wisegeek*, 12 Jan. 2017, www.wisegeek.com/what-does-a-mechatronics-engineer-do.htm#comments. Accessed 19 Jan. 2017.

Jekeli, Christopher. *Inertial Navigation Systems with Geodetic Applications*. Walter de Gruyter, 2012.

Jensen, Cecil H., and Ed Espin. *Interpreting Engineering Drawings*. 7th Canadian ed., Nelson Education, 2015.

Jiji, Latif M. *Heat Conduction*. 3rd ed., Springer Berlin Heidelberg, 2009.

Johnson, Richard W. *Handbook of Fluid Dynamics*. 2nd ed., CRC Press, 2016.

Jolley, Nicholas. *Leibniz*. Routledge, 2005.

Jones, Bernard J. T. *Precision Cosmology*. Cambridge UP, 2017.

Jones, Joseph L. *Robot Programming: A Practical Guide to Behavior-Based Robotics*. McGraw-Hill, 2004.

Jonnes, Jill. *Empires of Light: Edison, Tesla, Westinghouse, and the Race to Electrify the World*. Random House, 2003.

Jorisch, Wolfgang, editor. *Vacuum Technology in the Chemical Industry*. Wiley, 2015.

Josephs, Harold, and Ronald Huston. *Dynamics of Mechanical Systems*. CRC Press, 2002.

Josephson, Paul R. *Motorized Obsessions: Life, Liberty, and the Small-Bore Engine*. Johns Hopkins UP, 2007.

Jousten, Karl. "Applications and Scope of Vacuum Technology." *Handbook of Vacuum Technology*. 2nd ed., Wiley, 2016, pp. 19–26.

Julien, Pierre Y. "Our Hydraulic Engineering Profession." *Journal of Hydraulic Engineering*, vol. 143, no. 5, 2017.

Kachanov, L. M. *Fundamentals of the Theory of Plasticity*. Dover Publications, 2004.

Kakac, Sadik, Yaman Yener, and Anchasa Pramuanjaroenkij. *Convective Heat Transfer*. 3rd ed., CRC Press, 2013.

Karasev, M. V., Maria Shishkova, Elena Novikova, and Yu M. Vorobjev. *Quantum Algebras and Poisson Geometry in Mathematical Physics*. American Mathematical Society, 2005.

Karnopp, Dean. *Vehicle Dynamics, Stability, and Control*. 2nd ed., CRC Press, 2016.

Katz, Joseph. *Automotive Aerodynamics*. John Wiley & Sons, 2016.

Kegl, Breda, Mark Kegl, and Stanislav Pehan. *Green Diesel Engines: Biodiesel Usage in Diesel Engines*. Springer Science & Business Media, 2013.

Kehlhofer, Rolf, et al. *Combined-Cycle Gas and Steam Turbine Power Plants*. 3rd ed., Penn Well, 2009.

Kelly, P. F. *Electricity and Magnetism*. CRC Press, 2015.

Kelly, Piaras. "Introduction to Plasticity." *University of Auckland*, homepages.engineering.auckland.ac.nz/~pkel015/SolidMechanicsBooks/Part_II/08_Plasticity/08_Plasticity_01_Introduction.pdf. Accessed 22 June 2017.

Kelly, Wyatt. *Structural Engineering*. Larsen and Keller Education, 2019.

Kerr, Andrew. *Introductory Biomechanics*. Elsevier, 2010.

Khan, B. H. *Non-Conventional Energy Resources*. Tata/McGraw-Hill, 2006.

Khan, Sal. "Conservation of Energy." *Khan Academy*, n.d. Accessed 7 May 2015.

———. "Electric Potential Energy." *Khan Academy*, n.d. Accessed 7 May 2015.

———. "Moments, Torque, and Angular Momentum." *Khan Academy*, 23 May 2008. Accessed 7 Aug. 2015.

Khartchenko, Nikolai V., and Vadym M. Kharchenko. *Advanced Energy Systems*. 2nd ed., CRC Press, 2013.

Khudyakov, Yury E., and Paul Pumpens. *Viral Nanotechnology*. CRC Press, 2016.

Kibble, Tom W. B., and Frank H. Berkshire. *Classical Mechanics*. 5th ed., World Scientific, 2004.

Kim, Young Suh. *Harmonic Oscillators and Two-by-Two Matrices in Symmetry Problems in Physics*. MDPI, 2018.

Kimura, Wayne D. *Electromagnetic Waves and Lasers*. Morgan & Claypool Publishers, 2017.

"The Kinematic Equations." *The Physics Classroom*, www.physicsclassroom.com/class/1DKin/Lesson-6/Kinematic-Equations. Accessed 14 Mar. 2016.

Kinney, Jeremy R. *Reinventing the Propeller: Aeronautical Specialty and the Triumph of the Modern Airplane*. Cambridge UP, 2017.

Kirchhoff, Gustav Robert. *Researches on the Solar Spectrum and the Spectra of the Chemical Elements*. Translated by H. E. Roscoe. Creative Media Partners LLC, 2022.

Kistovich, Anatoly, Konstantin Pokazeev, and Tatiana Chaplina. *Ocean Acoustics*. Springer Nature, 2020.

Klein, Jürgen. *An Introduction to Surface Tension*. Nova Science Publishers, 2020.

Klem-Musatov, Kamill, Henning C. Heober, Tijmen Jan Moser, and Michael A. Pelissier, editors. *Classical and Modern Diffraction Theory*. SEG Books, 2016.

Kleppner, Daniel, and Robert J. Kolenkow. *An Introduction to Mechanics*. 2nd ed., Cambridge UP, 2014.

Klimi, George. *Exterior Ballistics: A New Approach*. Xlibris Corporation, 2010.

Kline, Morris. *Mathematical Thought from Ancient to Modern Times*. Oxford UP, 1990.

Klioner, Sergei A. "Lecture Notes on Basic Celestial Mechanics." *Department of Astronomy/Lohrmann Observatory*. Technical University of Dresden, 2011. Accessed 14 May 2015.

Knauf, Andreas. *Mathematical Physics: Classical Mechanics*. Translated by Jochen Denzler. Springer, 2018.

Knecht, Heidi. *Projectile Technology*. Springer Science & Business Media, 2013.

Kobelev, Vladimir. *Durability of Springs*. 2nd ed., Springer Nature, 2021.

Koehler, Jack H. *The Science of Pocket Billiards*. 2nd ed., Sportology Publications, 2016.

Kondepudi, Dilip, and Ilya Prigogine. *Modern Thermodynamics: From Heat Engines to Dissipative Structures*. 2nd ed., John Wiley & Sons. 2014.

Kragh, Helge. *Niels Bohr and the Quantum Atom: The Bohr Model of Atomic Structure, 1913–1925*. Oxford UP, 2012.

Kramers, H. A. *Quantum Mechanics*. Translated by D. Ter Haar. Reprint. Courier Dover Publications, 2018.

Krar, Steve, Arthur Gill, and Peter Smid. *Technology of Machine Tools*. 8th ed., McGraw-Hill, 2020.

Krasner, Helen. *The Helicopter Pilot's Companion: A Manual for helicopter Enthusiasts*. Crowood Press UK, 2008.

Kubitz, Alan A. *The Elusive Notion of Motion: The Genius of Kepler, Galileo, Newton, and Einstein*. Dog Ear Publishing, 2010.

Kucinski, William. *So You Want to Design Engines: UAV Propulsion Systems*. SAE International, 2018.

Kudek, Jozef. "Circular Motion & Gravity." *Introductory General Physics*. Old Dominion University, 2013, ww2.odu.edu/~jdudek/Phys111N_materials/4_circular_motion_gravity.pdf. Accessed 10 Dec. 2014.

Kumar, L. Ashok, and M. Senthil Kumar. *Automation in Textile Machinery: Instrumentation and Control System Design Principles*. CRC Press, 2018.

Kumar, Raj, et al. "Advances in Nanotechnology and Nanomaterials Based Strategies for Neural Tissue Engineering." *Journal of Drug Delivery Science and Technology*, vol. 57, 2020, doi:org/10.1016/j.jddst.2020.101617. Accessed 15 Mar. 2022.

Kumar, Sanjay. *Circular Motion*. Sanjay Kumar, 2020.

———. *Laws of Motion and Friction: Mechanics*. Independently Published, 2020.

———. *Newton's Laws of Motion and Friction: Mechanics*. Sanjay Kumar, 2020.

Kundu, Ajay Kumar, Mark A. Price, and David Riordan. *Conceptual Aircraft Design: An Industrial Approach*. Wiley, 2019.

Kurdila, Andrew J., and Pinhas Ben-Tzvi. *Dynamics and Control of Robotic Systems*. John Wiley & Sons, 2019.

Kyratsis, Panagiotis, Konstantinos G. Kakoulis, and Angelos P. Markopoulos, editors. *Advances in CAD/CAM/CAE Technologies*. MDPI, 2020.

Labi, Samuel. *Introduction to Civil Engineering Systems: A Systems Perspective to the Development of Civil Engineering Facilities*. John Wiley & Sons, 2014.

Lagrange, J. L. *Analytical Mechanics*. Translated by A. Boissonaide and V. N. Vagliente. Springer Science & Business Media, 2013.

Lagrange, Joseph Louis. *Lectures on Elementary Mathematics*. Translated by Thomas Joseph McCormack. 2nd ed., Open Court Publishing Company, 1901.

Lambert, P. *Surface Tension in Microsystems: Engineering below the Capillary Length*. Springer, 2013.

Lambert, Pierre, and Massimo Mastrangeli, editors. *Microscale Surface Tension and Its Applications*. MDPI, 2019.

Lambourne, Robert. *Describing Motion: The Physical World*. CRC Press, 2019.

Landrus, Matt. *Leonardo Da Vinci's Giant Crossbow*. Springer Science & Business Media, 2010.

Laplace, Pierre-Simon. *Pierre-Simon Laplace Philosophical Essay on Probabilities: Translated from the Fifth French Edition of 1825 with Notes by the Translator*. Translated by A. I. Dale. Springer New York, 2011.

Larminie, James, and John Lowry. *Electric Vehicle Technology Explained*. Wiley, 2003.

Larsen, Allan. *Aerodynamics of Large Bridges*. Routledge, 2017.

Lasithan, L. G. *Mechanical Vibrations and Industrial Noise Control*. PHI Learning Pvt. Ltd, 2013.

Lautrup, Benny. *Physics of Continuous Matter: Exotic and Everyday Phenomena in the Macroscopic World*. CRC Press, 2011.

Lavers, Christopher. *Reeds Introductions: Physics Wave Concepts for Marine Engineering*. Bloomsbury Publishing, 2017.

The Law Library. *Air Worthiness Standards–Propellers (US FAA) (FAA) (2018 Edition)*. CreateSpace Independent Publishing Platform, 2018.

Lawrence, Anthony. *Modern Inertial Technology: Navigation, Guidance, and Control*. 2nd ed., Springer Science & Business Media, 2012.

Lawrence, Martha, Richard Bullock, and Ziming Liu. *China's High-Speed Rail Development*. World Bank Publications, 2019.

"Laws of Motion: Galileo and Newton." *New Mexico State University*, astronomy.nmsu.edu/aklypin/WebSite/NewtonI.pdf. Accessed 30 Jan. 2017.

Leach, Richard, and Stuart T. Smith, editors. *Basics of Precision Engineering*. CRC Press, 2018.

Lebed. Andrei G., editor. *Breakdown of Einstein's Equivalence Principle*. World Scientific, 2022.

Leclercq, Ludovic, Benoit Robyns, and Jean-Michel Grave. "Control Based on Fuzzy Logic of a Flywheel Energy Storage System Associated with Wind and Diesel Generators." *Mathematics and Computers in Simulation*, vol. 63, no. 3-5, Nov. 2003.

Lees, Arthur W. *Vibration Problems in Machines: Diagnosis and Resolution*. 2nd ed., CRC Press, 2020.

Leibniz, Gottfried Wilhelm. *Theodicy: Essays on the Goodness of God, the Freedom of Man and the Origin of Evil*. Cosimo, 2009.

Leondes, Cornelius T. *Computer-Aided Design, Engineering, and Manufacturing: Systems Techniques and Applications, Volume II, Computer-Integrated Manufacturing*. CRC Press, 2019.

Lepetic, Vladimir. *Classical Vector Algebra*. CRC Press, 2022.

Leslie-Pelecky, Diandra. *The Physics of NASCAR: The Science Behind the Speed*. Penguin, 2008.

Leung, Wallace Woon-Fong. *Centrifugal Separations in Biotechnology*. 2nd ed., Elsevier Science, 2020.

Lewis, Owen (Quora). "Why Mazda's Rotary Automobile Engine Never Became Widely Popular." *Forbes*, 11 Apr. 2017, www.forbes.com/sites/quora/2017/04/11/why-mazdas-rotary-automobile-engine-never-became-widely-popular/#72f72ed43c79. Accessed 2 Oct. 2017.

Lewis, W. T. *Friction, Lubrication, and the Lubricants of Horology*. DigiCat, 2022.

Lienhard, John H. *A Heat Transfer Textbook*. 5th ed., Courier Dover Publications, 2019.

Lienhard, John H. IV, and John H. Lienhard V. *A Heat Transfer Textbook*. 4th ed., Dover, 2011.

Lindberg, David C. *The Beginnings of Western Science*. U of Chicago P, 1992.

Lindell, James E. *Handbook of Hydraulics*. 8th ed., McGraw Hill Professional, 2017.

Ling, James S., Jeff Sanny, and William Moebs. *University Physics, Volume 1*. Samurai Media Limited, 2017.

Ling, Samuel J., Jeff Sanny, and William Moebs. *University Physics Volume 2*. OpenStax, Rice University, 2016.

———. *University Physics Volume 3*. Samurai Media Limited, 2017.

Linke-Diesinger, Andreas. *Systems of Commercial Turbofan Engines: An Introduction to Systems Functions*. Springer Berlin Heidelberg, 2010.

Liu, Peiqing. *A General Theory of Fluid Mechanics*. Springer Nature, 2021.

Livio, Mario. *Galileo: And the Science Deniers*. Simon & Schuster, 2021.

Logan, J. David. *A First Course in Differential Equations*. 3rd ed., Springer International Publishing, 2016.

Lopez, Francisco Gallardo, and Jens Strahmann. *Fundamentals of Aerospace Engineering (Beginner's Guide)*. CreateSpace Independent Publishing Platform, 2016.

Losure, Mary. *Isaac the Alchemist: Secrets of Isaac Newton, Reveal'd*. Candlewick Press, 2017.

Lubliner, Jacob. *Plasticity Theory*. Courier Corporation, 2013.

Lubliner, Jacob, and Panayiotis Papadopoulos. *Introduction to Solid Mechanics: An Integrated Approach*. 2nd ed., Springer, 2016.

Lucas, Jim. "What Is Aerospace Engineering?" *Live Science*, 4 Sept. 2014. Accessed 9 June 2015.

———. "What Is Magnetism? Magnetic Fields & Magnetic Force." *Live Science*, 29 July 2015, www.livescience.com/38059-magnetism.html. Accessed 23 Dec. 2020.

Ludema, Kenneth C., and Layo Ajayi. *Friction, Wear, Lubrication: A Textbook in Tribology*. 2nd ed., CRC Press, 2018.

Lynch, Charles T. *Handbook of Materials Science. Volume I. General Properties*. CRC Press, 2019.

Lyshevski, Sergey Edward. *Mechatronics and Control of Electromechanical Systems*. Taylor & Francis Limited, 2020.

Maccari, Attilio. *Nonlinear Physics, from Vibration Control to Rogue Waves and Beyond*. Cambridge Scholars Publishing, 2023.

MacDonald, William. *Makers of Modern Agriculture*. Macmillan, 1913.

Madrigal, Alexis C. "How to Make a Wind Turbine That Flies." *Atlantic*. Atlantic Monthly, 16 July 2012. Accessed 14 Apr. 2015.

"Magnetism." *DISCovering Science*, 1996, www.ucl.ac.uk/EarthSci/people/lidunka/GEOL2014/Geophysics9%20-Magnetism/Useful%20papers/Magnetism.htm#. Accessed 23 Dec. 2020.

Mahajan, Sanjoy *A Student's Guide to Newton's Laws of Motion*. Cambridge UP, 2020.

Mahamid, Mustafa, Edwin H. Gaylord. and Charles N. Gaylord. *Structural Engineering Handbook*. 5th ed., McGraw Hill Professionsl, 2020.

Maini, Anil K. *Handbook of Defence Electronics and Optronics: Fundamentals, Technologies, and Systems*. John Wiley & Sons, 2018.

Maloberti, Franco, and Anthony C. Davies. *A Short History of Circuits and Systems*. CRC Press, 2022.

Mandelbrot, Benoit, and Richard L. Hudson. *The Misbehavior of Markets: A Fractal View of Financial Turbulence*. Basic Books, 2006.

Mandelis, Andreas. "Focus on Vacuum, Cryogenics, and Nanotechnology." *Physics Today*, vol. 68, no. 4, 2015, pp. 59–61.

Mandy, David. *Producers, Consumers and Partial Equilibrium*. Academic Press, 2016.

Mansfield, Michael, and Colm O'Sullivan. *Understanding Physics*. 2nd ed., Wiley, 2011.

Manucey, Albert. *Artillery Through the Ages*. E-artnow, 2018.

Manuel, Frank E. *A Portrait of Isaac Newton*. Harvard UP, 1968. Reprint. Da Capo, 1990.

Marcus, Daniel A. *Graph Theory: A Problem Oriented Approach*. Mathematical Association of America, 2008.

Marion, Jerry. *Physics in the Modern World*. Elsevier, 2012.

Market Trends. "Top 4 Aerospace Engineering Software in 2021." *Analytics Insight*, 17 Sept. 2021, www.analyticsinsight.net/top-4-aerospace-engineering-software-in-2021. Accessed 12 June 2022.

Martin, Richard. "The Race for the Ultra-Efficient Jet Engine of the Future." *MIT Technology Review*, 23 Mar. 2016, www.technologyreview.com/s/601008/the-race-for-the-ultra-efficient-jet-engine-of-the-future. Accessed 31 Aug. 2018.

Martinez, Daniel M., Ben W. Ebenhack, and Travis P. Wagner. *Energy Efficiency: Concepts and Calculations*. Elsevier, 2019.

Martinez, Tara. "Types of Metal Strength." *Monarch Metal Fabrication*, 24 Aug. 2016, www.monarchmetal.com/blog/types-of-metal-strength. Accessed 22 June 2017.

Massaro, P. *Big Book of Ballistics*. Krause Publications, 2017.

Massel, Stanislaw Ryszard. *Ocean Surface Waves: Their Physics and Prediction*. 3rd ed., World Scientific, 2017.

Masterson, Robert E. *Nuclear Reactor Thermal Hydraulics: An Introduction to Nuclear Heat Transfer and Fluid Flow*. CRC Press, 2019.

"Materials Science." *ACS*. American Chemical Society, n.d. Accessed 10 Sept. 2012.

Matsushita, Teruo. *Electricity and Magnetism: New Formulation by Introduction of Superconductivity*. Springer, 2014.

Matthews, Michael, Colin F. Gauls, and Arthur Stinner, editors. *The Pendulum: Scientific, Historical, Historical, Philosophical and Educational Perspectives*. Springer Science & Business Media, 2006.

Matthews, Robert. "Nothing Like a Vacuum." *Calphysics.org*. Calphysics Institute, www.calphysics.org/haisch/matthews.html. Accessed 23 Dec. 2014.

Matubayasi, Norihiro. *Surface Tension and Related Thermodynamic Quantities of Aqueous Electrolyte Solutions*. Taylor, 2014.

Matzner, Richard A., editor. *Dictionary of Geophysics, Astrophysics, and Astronomy*. CRC Press, 2001.

Mayersohn, Norman. "The Internal Combustion Engine Is Not Dead Yet." *The New York Times*, 17 Aug. 2017, www.nytimes.com/2017/08/17/automobiles/wheels/internal-combustion-engine.html. Accessed 23 Oct. 2017.

Mayes, Julian, and Karel Hughes. *Understanding Weather: A Visual Approach*. Oxford UP, 2004.

McCall, Martin. *Classical Mechanics: From Newton to Einstein; A Modern Introduction*. Wiley, 2011.

McKeighan, Peter C., and Narayanaswami Ranganathan. *Fatigue Testing and Analysis Under Variable Amplitude Loading Conditions*. ASTM International, 2005.

McKeon, Richard. *The Basic Works of Aristotle*. Reprint. Random House Publishing Group, 2009.

"Mechanical Engineering in Biology and Medicine." *Johns Hopkins University*, 2021, me.jhu.edu/research/mechanical-engineering-in-biology-and-medicine. Accessed 15 June 2021.

"Mechatronics History." *Bright Hub Engineering*, 13 May 2010, www.brighthubengineering.com/manufacturing-technology/71180-the-history-of-mechatronics. Accessed 19 Jan. 2017.

Mehta, B. R., and Y. Jaganmohan Reddy. *Industrial Process Automation Systems: Design and Implementation*. Butterworth-Heinemann, 2014.

Mendoza, E., editor. *Reflections on the Motive Power of Fire by Sadi Carnot, and Other Papers on the Second Law of Thermodynamics by E. Clapeyron and R. Claussius*. Dover Publications, 1960.

Mercier, Jean P., Gerald Zambelli, and Wilfried Kurz. *Introduction to Materials Science*. Elsevier Science, 2012.

Mikel, Russell, editor. *Aerospace and Aeronautical Engineering*. Wilford Press, 2017.

"Milestones of Innovation." *American Institute for Medical and Biological Engineering*, 2016. Accessed 25 Jan. 2016.

Miller, Frederic P., Agnes F. Vandome, and John McBrewster, editors. *Centripetal Force: Osculating Circle, Uniform Circular Motion, Circular Motion, Cross Product, Triple Product, Banked Turn, Reactive Centrifugal Force, Non-uniform Circular Motion, Generalized Forces, Curvilinear Coordinates, Generalized Coordinates*. Alphascript Publishing, 2009.

Millikan, Clark B. *Aerodynamics of the Airplane*. Courier Dover Publications, 2018.

Mircescu, Alexander. *On the Conservation of Momentum, Angular Momentum, Energy, and Information*. BoD Third Party Titles, 2016.

Mitin, Vladimir V., and Dmitry I. Sementsov. *An Introduction to Applied Electromagnetics and Optics*. CRC Press, 2016.

Mittag, Hans-Joachim, and Horst Rinne. *Statistical Methods of Quality Assurance*. 2nd ed., CRC Press, 2018.

Mlodinow, Leonard. *Euclid's Window: The Story of Geometry from Parallel Lines to Hyperspace*. Simon, 2002.

Mody, Vishal. *High School Physics: Projectile Motion*. CreateSpace Independent Publishing Platform, 2015.

Mohan, S. *Advances in High Temperature Superconductors and Their Applications*. MJP Publisher, 2019.

"Moment of Inertia." *Isaac Physics*, isaacphysics.org/concepts/cp_moment_inertia. Accessed 26 June 2017.

"Moment of Inertia." *Shmoop*, www.shmoop.com/rotation/inertia.html. Accessed 26 June 2017.

Montemar, Claire. *Probability Theory and Examples*. Arcler Press, 2017.

Moore, Wade P., James E. Lindell, and Horace W. King. *Handbook of Hydraulics*. 8th ed., McGraw-Hill Education, 2017.

Morales, João Paulo Zeitoun. *EMB-312 Tucano: Brazil's Turboprop Success Story*. Harpia Publishing, 2018.

"More About Vacuum Pumps." *ThomasNet.com*. Thomas Publishing Company, www.thomasnet.com/about/vacuum-pumps-65021602.html. Accessed 23 Dec. 2014.

Morin, David. *Introduction to Classical Mechanics: With Problems and Solutions*. Cambridge UP, 2008.

Mosher, Daniel. *Civil Engineering Basics: Water, Wastewater, and Stormwater Conveyance*. CreateSpace Independent Publishing Platform, 2018.

Moskowitz, Clara. "Fact or Fiction? Energy Can Neither Be Created nor Destroyed." *Scientific American*, 5 Aug. 2014. Accessed 21 Apr. 2015.

Mount, Toni. *The World of Isaac Newton*. Amberley Publishing, 2020.

Mulligan, Joseph F. *Heinrich Rudolf Hertz (1857–1894): A Collection of Articles and Addresses*. Routledge, 2018.

Munson, Bruce R., T. H. Okiishi, Wade W. Huebsch, and Alric P. Rothmayer. *Fundamentals of Fluid Mechanics*. 7th ed., Wiley, 2013.

Murdoch, A. Ian. *Physical Foundations of Continuum Mechanics*. Cambridge UP, 2012.

Musielak, Dora. *Leonhard Euler and the Foundations of Celestial Mechanics*. Springer Nature, 2022.

———. *Scramjet Propulsion: A Practical Introduction*. Wiley, 2022.

Myers, Richard Leroy, and Rusty L. Myers. *The Basics of Physics*. Greenwood Publishing Group, 2006.

Naber, Gregory L. *Quantum Mechanics: An Introduction to the Physical Background and Mathematical Structure*. Walter de Gruyter Gmbh & Co. KG, 2021.

Naidoo, Shalinee. *Centrifugation Techniques*. Arcler Education Incorporated, 2017.

Nalawade, Sharad. *The Speed of Time*. One Point Six Technology Pvt Ltd, 2012.

Nappi, Virgil. *Physics and Math Formulas: Essential Physics and Math Formulas You Must Know: Torque*. Independently Published, 2021.

NASA/Goddard Space Flight Center. "Researchers Track Slowly Splitting 'Dent' in Earth's Magnetic Field." *ScienceDaily*, 17 Aug. 2020, www.sciencedaily.com/releases/2020/08/200817144121.htm. Accessed 23 Dec. 2020.

Naskar, Anirban. *Work, Energy and Power—Thoughtful Physics*. Quantemporary, 2018.

National Aeronautics and Space Administration (NASA). *Aircraft Wing Structural Detail Design (Wing, Aileron, Flaps, and Subsystems)*. CreateSpace Independent Publishing Platform, 2018.

———. *An Assessment of Propeller Aircraft Noise Reduction Technology*. CreateSpace Independent Publishing Platform, 2018.

———. *Metallic Rotor Sizing and Performance Model for Flywheel Systems*. NASA, 2019.

Navas, K. A., and T. A. Suhail. *Basic Electrical and Electronics Engineering: Conceptual Approach*. Rajath Publishers, 2011.

Nave, Carl R. "Energy Stored on a Capacitor." *HyperPhysics*. Georgia State University, 2012. Accessed 7 May 2015.

———. "Torque." *HyperPhysics*. Georgia State University, 2012. Accessed 7 Aug. 2015.

———. "Work, Energy and Power." *HyperPhysics*. Georgia State University, 2012. Accessed 22 Sept. 2015.

Nayfeh, Munir H., and Morton K. Brussel. *Electricity and Magnetism*. Reprint. Courier Dover Publications, 2015.

Nazarenko, Sergey. *Fluid Dynamics via Examples and Solutions*. CRC Press, 2015.

Negahban, Mehrdad. "Equations of Motion for a Rigid Body (Euler's Laws)." *University of Nebraska*. Department of Engineering Mechanics, 1999–2002. Accessed 27 Aug. 2015.

Nemerow, Nelson L., et al., editors. *Environmental Engineering: Environmental Health and Safety for Municipal Infrastructure, Land Use and Planning, and Industry*. John Wiley & Sons, 2009.

Netz, Reviel, and William Noel. *The Archimedes Codex: How a Medieval Prayer Book Is Revealing the True Genius of Antiquity's Greatest Scientist*. Hachette Books, 2007.

Newton, Sir Isaac. *Mathematical Principles of Natural Philosophy and His System of the World: Principia*. 2 vols. U of California P, 1934. Reprint. 1962.

———. *Opticks*. Dover, 1952.

"Newton's Laws of Motion." *The Beginner's Guide to Aeronautics*. National Aeronautics and Space Administration, 2014, www.grc.nasa.gov/WWW/k-12/airplane/newton.html.

"Newton's Laws, Vectors, and Reference Frames." *Massachusetts Institute of Technology Open Courseware*, ocw.mit.edu/courses/mechanical-engineering/2-003sc-engineering-dynamics-fall-2011/newton2019s-laws-vectors-and-reference-frames. Accessed 30 Jan. 2017.

Ni, Wen-tou, editor. *One Hundred Years of General Relativity: From Genesis and Empirical Foundations to Gravitational Waves, Cosmology and Quantum Gravity–Volume 1*. World Scientific, 2017.

Nice, Karim. "How Rotary Engines Work." *HowStuffWorks*, 29 Mar. 2001, auto.howstuffworks.com/rotary-engine.htm. Accessed 2 Oct. 2017.

Nikola Tesla Museum. *Nikola Tesla, 1856–1943: Lectures, Patents, Articles*. Kessinger, 2003.

Niku, Saeed. *Introduction to Robotics: Analysis, Control, Applications*. 3rd ed., Wiley, 2020.

Noerstrud, Helge. *Sport Aerodynamics*. Springer Science & Business Media, 2009.

Norsen, Travis. *Foundations of Quantum Mechanics: An Exploration of the Physical Meaning of Quantum Theory*. Springer, 2017.

Norton, A. *Dynamic Fields and Waves*. CRC Press, 2019.

Norton, Bill. *STOL Progenitors: The Technology Path to a Large STOL Aircraft and the C-17A*. American Institute of Aeronautics and Astronautics, 2002.

"Nova: Galileo's Inclined Plane." *PBS Learning Media*, pbslearningmedia.org/resource/phy03.sci.phys.mfw.galileoplane/galileos-inclined-plane. Accessed 30 Jan. 2017.

O'Hanlon, John F. *A User's Guide to Vacuum Technology*. 3rd ed., Wiley, 2003.

"Obituary, Rudolf Diesel." *Power*, vol. 38, no. 18, 1913, p. 628.

O'Brien, Eugene, Andrzej Nowak, and Colin Caprani. *Bridge Traffic Loading from Research to Practice*. CRC Press, 2021.

Ohanian, Hans C., and Remo Ruffini. *Gravitation and Spacetime*. 3rd ed., Cambridge UP, 2013.

Okoh, Daniel, Joseph Ugwuanyi, Ambrose Eze, Ernest Obetta, and Harrison Onah. *Archimedes' Principle and the Law of Flotation*. CreateSpace Independent Publishing Platform, 2017.

Organ, Allan J. *The Air Engine: Stirling Cycle Power for a Sustainable Future*. CRC Press, 2007.

———. *Stirling Cycle Engines: Inner Workings and Design*. John Wiley & Sons, 2013.

Osakue, Edward E. *Introductory Engineering Graphics*. Momentum Press, 2018.

Ottinger, Hans Christian. *Beyond Equilibrium Thermodynamics*. Wiley, 2005.

"Our Friends Electric." *Economist*. Economist Newspaper, 7 Sept. 2013. Accessed 14 Nov. 2014.

Owano, Nancy. "Blue Freedom Uses Power of Flowing Water to Charge." *Phys.org Tech Xplore*, 26 Mar. 2015. Accessed 14 Apr. 2015.

Padfield, Gareth D. *Helicopter Flight Dyanamics Including a Treatment of Tiltrotor Aircraft*. Wiley, 2018.

Pain, H. John, and Patricia Rankin. *Introduction to Vibrations and Waves*. John Wiley & Sons, 2015.

Paipetis, S. A., and Marco Ceccarelli, editors. *The Genius of Archimedes–23 Centuries of Influence on Mathematics, Science and Engineering: Proceedings of an International Conference held at Syracuse, Italy, June 8–10, 2010*. Springer Science & Business Media, 2010.

Pais, Abraham. *Inward Bound: Of Matter and Forces in the Physical World*. Oxford UP, 2002.

Pamadi, Bandu N. *Performance, Stability, Dynamics, and Control of Airplanes*. American Institute of Aeronautics and Astronautics, 2004.

Papachristou, Costas J. *Introduction to Mechanics of Particles and Systems*. Springer Nature, 2020.

"Part I. Historical Context." *Space Transportation System*. Historic American Engineering Record (Denver), National Park Service, US Department of the Interior, Nov. 2012.

Pascal, Blaise *Delphi Collected Works of Blaise Pascal*. Delphi Classics, 2020.

Pavel, M., et al. "The Role of Technology and Engineering Models in Transforming Healthcare." *IEEE Reviews in Biomedical Engineering*. IEEE, 2013. Accessed 25 Jan. 2016.

Payne-Gallway, Ralph. *The Book of the Crossbow: With an Additional Section on Catapults and Other Siege Engines*. Courier Corporation, 2012.

Pecker, Alain. *Advanced Earthquake Engineering Analysis*. Springer Science & Business Media, 2008.

Peebles, C. *Road to Mach 10: Lessons Learned from the X-43A Flight Research Program*. American Institute of Aeronautics and Astronautics, 2008.

Pelesko, John A. *Self-Assembly: The Science of Things That Put Themselves Together*. Chapman, 2007.

Peliti, Luca, and Simone Pigolotti. *Stochastics Thermodynamics: An Introduction*. Princeton UP, 2021.

Peng, William W. "Steam Turbines." *Fundamentals of Turbomachinery*. J. Wiley, 2008.

Petale, M. D. *Probability Distribution: (Theory & Solved Examples)*. Mangesh Devidasrao Petale, 2019.

Petersen, Kristen. *Understanding Kinetic Energy*. Cavendish Square Publishing LLC, 2014.

Peterson, Donald, and Joseph Bronzino. *Biomechanics: Principles and Applications*. CRC Press, 2008.

Petroski, Henry. *Success Through Failure: The Paradox of Design*. 2006. Reprint. Princeton UP, 2008.

Petruszczak, S. *Fundamentals of Plasticity in Geomechanics*. Reprint. CRC Press, 2020.

Pfeiffer, Friedrich. *Mechanical System Dynamics*. Springer Science & Business Media, 2008.

Phillips, Peter. *Electrical Principles*. Cengage AU, 2019.

Pickover, Clifford. "Daniel Bernoulli." *Archimedes to Hawking: Laws of Science and the Great Minds Behind Them*, Oxford UP, 2008, pp. 124–34.

Plantenberg, Kirstie. *Engineering Graphics Essentials*. 5th ed., SDC Publications, 2016.

Poisson, Siméon-Denis. *A Treatise of Mechanics; Volume 2*. Creative Media Partners LLC, 2018.

Polyanin, Andrei D., and Valentin F. Zaitsev. *Handbook of Ordinary Differential Equations*. 3rd ed., Taylor & Francis, 2016.

Pook, L. P. *Understanding Pendulums: A Brief Introduction*. Springer Science & Business Media, 2011.

Poole, Charles P., Horacio A. Farach, Richard J. Creswick, and Ruslan Prozorov. *Superconductivity*. 2nd ed., Elsevier, 2010.

Pope, Alan. *Basic Wing and Airfoil Theory*. Dover Publications, 2009.

Popov, Valentin L. *Contact Mechanics and Friction: Physical Principles and Applications*. 2nd ed., Springer Berlin Heidelberg, 2018.

Popovic, Marko B. *Biomechanics and Robotics*. CRC Press, 2013.

Prakash, Punit, and Govindarajan Srimathveeravalli, editors. *Principles and Technologies for Electromagnetic Energy Based Therapies*. Academic Press, 2021.

Price, C.A. *Centrifugation in Density Gradients*. Academic Press, 2014.

Raghuvanshi, G. S. *Engineering Physics*. PHI Learning Pvt Ltd, 2016.

Rahman, Atowar. *Fundamentals of Magnetism and Spintronics*. Zorba Books, 2022.

Raizer, Victor. *Optical Remote Sensing of Ocean Hydrodynamics*. CRC Press, 2019.

Ramsden, Jeremy. *Nanotechnology*. Elsevier, 2016.

Rankine, William John Macquorn. "On the General Law of the Transformation of Energy." *Miscellaneous Scientific Papers: By W. J. Macquorn Rankine, CE, LLD, FRS*, edited by W. J. Millar. 1881. Elibron, 2005, pp. 203–8.

Rao, C. N., and A. Govindaraj. *Nanotubes and Nanowires*. 2nd ed., Royal Society of Chemistry, 2011.

Ratner, Daniel, and Mark A. Ratner. *Nanotechnology and Homeland Security: New Weapons for New Wars*. Prentice, 2004.

Ratner, Mark A., and Daniel Ratner. *Nanotechnology: A Gentle Introduction to the Next Big Idea*. Prentice, 2003.

Rau, A. R. P. *The Beauty of Physics: Patterns, Principles, and Perspectives*. Oxford UP, 2014.

Redhead, P. A. "Extreme High Vacuum." *National Research Council of Canada*, www.chem.elte.hu/departments/altkem/vakuumtechnika/CERN17.pdf. Accessed 20 Jan. 2017.

Reid, Constance. *A Long Way from Euclid*. Dover, 2004.

Ren, Beibei, Shuzhi Sam Ge, Chang Chen, and Cheng-Heng Fua. *Modeling, Control and Coordination of Helicopter Systems*. Springer New York, 2011.

Renilson, Martin. *Submarine Hydrodynamics*. Springer, 2015.

Rescher, Nicholas. *On Leibniz*. U of Pittsburgh P, 2003.

Rhett, Allain. "Let's Explore the Physics of Rotational Motion with a Fidget Spinner." *Wired*, 23 May 2017, www.wired.com/2017/05/physics-of-a-fidget-spinner. Accessed 26 June 2017.

Richardson, Alexander. *The Evolution of the Parsons Steam Turbine*. Cambridge UP, 2014.

Richmond, Michael. "Torque." *University Physics I*. Rochester Institute of Technology, 15 Feb. 2002. Accessed 7 Aug. 2015.

Richter, Hanz. *Advanced Control of Turbofan Engines*. Springer New York, 2014.

Rieutord, Michel. *Fluid Dynamics: An Introduction*. Springer International Publishing, 2016.

Rizzo, James G. *Robert Stirling's Models of the "Air Engine."* Camden Miniature Steam Services, 2009.

Robbins, Allan H., and Wilhelm C. Miller. *Circuit Analysis: Theory and Practice*. 5th ed., Delmar, 2013.

Robinson, Andrew. *The Last Man Who Knew Everything: Thomas Young, the Anonymous Polymath Who Proved Newton Wrong, Explained How We See, Cured the Sick, and Deciphered the Rosetta Stone, among Other Feats of Genius*. Plume, 2007.

Robinson, Gilbert de B. *Vector Geometry*. Courier Corporation, 2013.

Robinson, James C., Diez J. L. Rodrigo, and Witold Sadowski. *Mathematical Aspects of Fluid Mechanics*. Cambridge UP, 2012.

Rodrigue, J-P., and C. Comtois. "Transportation and Energy." *The Geography of Transport Systems*, people.hofstra.edu/geotrans/eng/ch8en/conc8en/ch8c2en.html.

Rogers, Ben, Jesse Adams, and Sumita Pennathur. *Nanotechnology: The Whole Story*. CRC, 2013.

Rogers, Ben, Sumita Pennathur, and Jesse Adams. *Nanotechnology: Understanding Small Systems*. 2nd ed., CRC Press, 2011.

Roldán Cuenya, Beatriz. "Chapter 11: Torque and Angular Momentum." *Physics for Scientists and Engineers I*. University of Central Florida, 2013. Accessed 7 Aug. 2015.

"The Role of the Specialty Structural Engineer." *Build Steel*, www.buildsteel.org/framing-products/structural/the-role-of-the-specialty-structural-engineer. Accessed 20 Jan. 2020.

Rolls-Royce. *The Jet Engine*. 5th ed., Wiley, 2015.

Rong, Blake Z. "12-Rotor Wankel Engine Will Melt Your Brain." *Autoweek*, 24 Feb. 2014, autoweek.com/article/car-life/12-rotor-wankel-engine-will-melt-your-brain. Accessed 2 Oct. 2017.

Rorres, Chris. *Archimedes in the 21st Century: Proceedings of a World Conference at the Courant Institute of Mathematical Sciences*. Birkhauser, 2017.

Ross, John S. "Work, Power, Kinetic Energy." *Project PHYSNET*, Michigan State University, 23 Apr. 2002, www.physnet.org/modules/pdf_modules/m20.pdf.

Rossing, Thomas, and Neville Fletcher. *Principles of Vibration and Sound*. 2nd ed., Springer-Verlag, 2004.

"Rotational Inertia." *Khan Academy*, www.khanacademy.org/ science/physics/torque-angular-momentum/torque-tutorial/a/rotational-inertia. Accessed 26 June 2017.

Roth, A. "Introduction: Fields of Application and Importance." *Vacuum Technology*. 3rd ed., North-Holland, 1998, pp. 6–10.

Roy, Kaushik. *A Global History of Warfare and Technology: From Slings to Robots*. Springer Nature, 2022.

Rozikov, Utkir A. *An Introduction to Mathematical Billiards*. World Scientific, 2018.

"Rudolf Christian Karl Diesel Biography (1858–1913)." *Madehow.com*, www.madehow.com/inventorbios/11/Rudolf-Christian-Karl-Diesel.html.

"Rudolp [sic] Diesel and Diesel Oil." *Speedace.info*, speedace.info/diesel.htm.

Rufer, Alfred. *Energy Storage Systems and Components*. CRC Press, 2018.

Rumsey, Francis, and Tim McCormick. *Sound and Recording: An Introduction*. 5th ed., Elsevier/Focal Press, 2004.

Russ, Carey. "The Wankel Engine History." *The Auto Channel*, 2004, www.theautochannel.com/news/2004/07/04/202357.html. Accessed 2 Oct. 2017.

Russell, Kevin. *Kinematics and Dynamics of Mechanical Systems: Implementation in MATLAB and SimMechanics*. CRC Press, 2016.

Russell, Kevin, John Q. Shen, and Raj S. Sodhi. *Kinematics and Dynamics of Mechanical Systems, Second Edition: Implementation in MATLAB(r) and SimMechanics(r)*. CRC Press, 2018.

Rutledge, Kim, et al. "Magnetism." *National Geographic*, 21 Jan. 2011, www.nationalgeographic.org/encyclopedia/magnetism. Accessed 23 Dec. 2020.

Ryvkin, Solomon M. *Photoelectric Effects in Semiconductors*. Springer US, 2012.

Sabry, Fouad. *Adaptive Compliant Wing: No More Flaps, the Aircraft Wing Shape is Now Morphing*. One Billion Knowledgeable, 2022.

———. *Flywheel Energy Storage: Increasing or Decreasing Speed, to Add or Extract Power*. One Billion Knowledgeable, 2022.

———. *Plasma Propulsion: Can SpaceX Use Advanced Plasma Propulsion for Starship?* One Billion Knowledgeable, 2021.

Sacco, Francesco G. *Real, Mechanical, Experimental: Robert Hooke's Natural Philosophy*. Springer Nature, 2020.

Saidian, Siyavush. *Ballistics: The Science of Weapons at Work*. Greenhaven Publishing LLC, 2017.

Saltzman, W. Mark. *Biomedical Engineering: Bridging Medicine and Technology*. Cambridge UP, 2015.

———. "Lecture 1–What Is Biomedical Engineering?" *BENG 100: Frontiers of Biomedical Engineering*. Yale University, Spring 2008. Accessed 23 Jan. 2016.

Samani, Hooman. Cognitive Robotics. CRC Press, 2016.

Sandler, Stanley I. *Chemical and Engineering Thermodynamics*. John Wiley & Sons, 1998.

Saxena, Vimal, Michel Krief, and Ludmila Adam. *Handbook of Borehole Acoustics and Rock Physics for Reservoir Characterization*. Elsevier, 2018.

Sayood, Khalid. *Understanding Circuits*. Springer Nature, 2022.

Scerri, Eric R. *The Periodic Table: Its Story and Its Significance*. 2nd ed., Oxford UP, 2019.

Schaberg, Christopher. "The Jet Engine Is a Futuristic Technology Stuck in the Past." *The Atlantic*, 11 Feb. 2018, www.theatlantic.com/technology/archive/2018/02/engine-failure/552959. Accessed 31 Aug. 2018.

Schmidt, Jon A. "Structural Engineering." *Whole Building Design Guide*, 3 Nov. 2016, www.wbdg.org/design-disciplines/structural-engineering. Accessed 20 Jan. 2020.

Schuetz, Thomas Christian. *Aerodynamics of Road Vehicles*. 5th ed., SAE International, 2015.

Sclater, Neil. *Mechanisms and Mechanical Devices Sourcebook*. 5th ed., McGraw-Hill Professional, 2011.

Seal, Anthony M. *Practical Process Control*. Butterworth, 1998.

Seames, Warren S. *Computer Numerical Control Concepts and Programming*. 4th ed., Delmar, 2002.

Seifer, Marc. *Wizard: The Life and Times of Nikola Tesla*. Citadel, 2011.

Šejnin, Oskar B. *Portraits: Leonhard Euler, Daniel Bernoulli, Johann-Heinrich Lambert*. NG-Verl, 2009.

Senft, James R. *Mechanical Efficiency of Heat Engines*. Cambridge UP, 2007.

Serway, Raymond A., and John W. Jewett. *Physics for Scientists and Engineers*. 8th ed.. Brooks/Cole Cengage Learning, 2010.

Sfendoni-Mentzou, Demetra, et al., editors. *Aristotle and Contemporary Science*. 2 vols. P. Lang, 2000–2001.

Sfetcu, Nicolae. *Isaac Newton vs. Robert Hooke on the Law of Universal Gravitation*. Multimedia Publishing, 2019.

Shah, Nita H. *Ordinary and Partial Differential Equations: Theory and Applications*. 2nd ed., PHI Learning Pvt Ltd, 2015.

Shamos, Morris H. *Great Experiments in Physics: Firsthand Accounts from Galileo to Einstein*. Dover, 1987.

Shang, Yilun. *Harmonic Oscillators: Types, Functions and Applications*. Nova Science Publishers, 2019.

Shankar, Ramamurti. *Fundamentals of Physics II: Electromagnetism, Optics, and Quantum Mechanics*. Yale UP, 2020.

———. "Lecture 5: Work-Energy Theorem and Law of Conservation of Energy." *Open Yale Courses*. Yale University, 2006. Accessed 22 Sept. 2015.

Sharma, A.K. *Dynamics of Rigid Bodies*. Discovery Publishing House, 2007.

Shaw, Robert J., editor. "Dynamics of Flight." *NASA*, 12 June 2014, www.grc.nasa.gov/www/k-12/UEET/StudentSite/dynamicsofflight.html. Accessed 30 Jan. 2017.

Shectman, Jonathan. *Groundbreaking Scientific Experiments, Investigations, and Discoveries of the Eighteenth Century*. Greenwood Press, 2003.

Sheppard, Sheri D., and Benson H. Tongue. *Statics: Analysis and Design of Systems in Equilibrium*. Wiley, 2006.

Shields, Christopher, editor. *The Oxford Handbook of Aristotle*. Oxford UP, 2015.

Shurkin, Joel N. *Broken Genius: The Rise and Fall of William Shockley, Creator of the Electronic Age*. Macmillan, 2006.

Sibley, Martin J. *Introduction to Electromagnetism: From Coulomb to Maxwell*. 2nd ed., CRC Press, 2021.

Siciliano, Bruno, and Oussama Khatib, editors. *The Springer Handbook of Robotics*. Springer, 2016.

Siciliano, Bruno, et al. *Robotics: Modelling, Planning and Control*. Springer-Verlag, 2010.

Sier, Robert. *Hot Air Caloric and Stirling Engines*. L. A. Mair, 2000.

———. *John Fox Jennens Malone: The Liquid Stirling Engine*. L. A. Mair, 2008.

———. *Rev. Robert Stirling D.D.: A Biography of the Inventor of the Heat Economiser and Stirling Cycle Engine*. L. A. Mair, 1995.

Simanek, Donald E. "Conservation Laws." *A Brief Course in Classical Mechanics*. Lock Haven University, Jan. 2011. Accessed 7 May 2015.

———. "Kinematics." *Brief Course in Classical Mechanics*. Lock Haven University, Feb. 2005. Accessed 22 Sept. 2015.

Simmons, George F. *Calculus Gems: Brief Lives and Memorable Mathematics*. 1992. Mathematical Association of America, 2007.

Singh, D. K. *Strength of Materials*. 4th ed., Springer Nature, 2020.

Skiadis, Christos H., and Ioannis Dimotikalis, editors. *Chaotic System: Theory and Applications*. World Scientific, 2010.

"Smallest Whirlpools Can Pack Stunningly Strong Force." *Science Daily*, 4 Sept. 2003, www.sciencedaily.com/releases/2003/09/030904075438.htm. Accessed 10 Dec. 2014.

Smil, Vaclav. *Creating the Twentieth Century: Technical Innovations of 1867–1914 and Their Lasting Impact*. Oxford UP, 2005.

———. *Energy in Nature and Society: General Energetics of Complex Systems*. MIT Press, 2008.

———. *Two Prime Movers of Globalization: The History and Impact of Diesel Engines and Gas Turbines*. MIT Press, 2010.

Smith, Carlos A. *Automated Continuous Process Control*. Wiley, 2002.

Smith, D. J. *Discovering Horse-Drawn Farm Machinery*. 2nd rev. ed., Shire, 2008.

Soares, Claire. *Gas Turbines: A Handbook of Air, Land and Sea Applications*. Butterworth, 2014.

Soler, Manuel. *Fundamentals of Aerospace Engineering: An Introductory Course to Aeronautical Engineering*. CreateSpace Independent Publishing Platform, 2017.

Solomonovich, Mark. *Euclidean Geometry: A First Course*. Universe, 2010.

"Space Shuttle History." *Human Space Flight*. NASA, 27 Feb. 2008. Web. 9 June 2015.

"Spacecraft Design, Structure, and Operations." *AU Space Primer*. Air University, 2003. Accessed 9 June 2015.

Spagner, Natalie. *A Researcher's Guide to Aerospace Engineering*. Clanrye International, 2019.

Spellman, Frank R. *Physics for Nonphysicists*. Government Institutes, 2009.

Spiegel, Rob. "Mechatronics: Blended Engineering for the Robotic Future." *DesignNews*, 23 Nov. 2016, www.designnews.com/automation-motion-control/mechatronics-blended-engineering-robotic-future/199011163046152. Accessed 19 Jan. 2017.

Springer, Paul J. *Military Robots and Drones: A Reference Handbook*. ABC-CLIO, 2013.

Sprott, Julien Clinton, William Graham Hoover, and Carol Griswold Hoover. *Elegant Simulations: From Simple Oscillators to Many-Body Systems*. World Scientific, 2022.

Starling, Frank. *Archimedes' Principle*. Genius Books, *2020*.

"Static Equilibrium, Elasticity, and Torque." *Boundless*, www.boundless.com/physics/textbooks/boundless-physics-textbook/static-equilibrium-elasticity-and-torque-8. Accessed 9 Mar. 2016.

Steane, Andrew M. *Thermodynamics: A Complete Undergraduate Course*. Oxford UP, 2016.

Stecher, Nicolas. "Mazda's Confusing Plan to Resurrect the Famously Dirty Rotary Engine." *Wired*, 1 Dec. 2015, www.wired.com/2015/12/mazdas-confusing-plan-to-resurrect-the-famously-dirty-rotary-engine. Accessed 28 Sept. 2017.

Stein, Sherman K. *Archimedes: What Did He Do Besides Cry Eureka?* Mathematical Association of America, 1999.

Steinberger, Victoria. *Design of Zephyrus Human Powered Airplane Propellers.* Pennsylvania State University, 2018.

Stephenson, Jason. *Quantum Physics for Beginners: Quantum Mechanics and Quantum Theory Explained.* Speedy Publishing LLC, 2015.

Stern, David P. "How Orbital Motion Is Calculated." *From Stargazers to Starships.* Author, 6 Apr. 2014. Accessed 14 May 2015.

Stilwell, John. *Elements of Mathematics: From Euclid to Gödel.* Princeton UP, 2017.

Stine, Keith J. *Carbohydrate Nanotechnology.* Wiley, 2016.

Stommel, Henry, and Dennis Moore. *An Introduction to the Coriolis Force.* Columbia UP, 1989.

Stone, Anthony. *The Theory of Intermolecular Forces.* 2nd ed., Oxford UP, 2013.

Strang, Gilbert. *Differential Equations and Linear Algebra.* Wellesley-Cambridge Press, 2015.

Strickland, Lloyd. *Leibniz's Monadology: A New Translation and Guide.* Edinburgh UP, 2014.

Strong, William J., and George R. Plitnik. *Music, Speech, Audio.* 3rd ed., Brigham Young University Academic, 2007.

Stroud, K. A., and Dexter Booth. *Vector Analysis.* Industrial Press, 2005.

Stroud, Nick. *The Vickers Viscount, The World's First Turboprop Airliner.* Pen & Sword Books Ltd., 2017.

"Structural Engineer of Record (SER)." *Schneider Structural Engineering,* 2020, cjseng.com/SSE/structural-engineer-of-record-ser.html. Accessed 20 Jan. 2020.

Stutzman, Warren L., and Gary A. Thiele. *Antenna Theory and Design.* 3rd ed., John Wiley & Sons, 2012.

Sun, Xiaoming, Liang Luo, Yun Kuang, and Pengsong Li. *Nanoseparation Using Density Gradient Ultracentrifugation: Mechanism, Methods, and Applications.* Springer, 2018.

Sundén, Bengt. *Introduction to Heat Transfer.* WIT Press, 2012.

"Supernova Study Might Change How Speed of Light in Vacuum Is Measured." *ZMEScience.com.* ZME Media, 25 June 2014, www.zmescience.com/space/supernova-speed-of-light-change053456. Accessed 23 Dec. 2014.

Sutton, Adrian P. *Concepts of Material Science.* Oxford UP, 2021.

Swingle, Calvin F. *Steam Turbine Engines, Their Construction, Care and Operation: Full Instructions Regarding Correct Methods of Operating Steam Turbines, Adjusting Clearances, Etc. (Classic Reprint).* LULU Press, 2018.

Syngellakis, S. *Projectile Impact: Modelling Techniques and Assessment of Target Material Performance.* WIT Press, 2014.

Tabachnikov, Serge. *Geometry and Billiards.* American Mathematical Society, 2005.

Tanuma, Tadashi. *Advances in Steam Turbines for Modern Power Plants.* Woodhead Publishing, 2017.

Tariq Altalhi, Inamuddin, Vikas Gupta, and Mohammad Luqman, editors. *Superconductors: Materials and Applications.* Materials Research Forum LLC, 2022.

Taylor, R. N. *Geotechnical Centrifuge Technology.* CRC Press, 2018.

"Teaching from Space: The Bernoulli Principle." *PBS LearningMedia.* PBS & WGBH Educational Foundation, 2014, www.pbslearningmedia.org/resource/npe11.sci.phys.maf.bernoulli/teaching-from-space-the-bernoulli-principle. Accessed 2 Dec. 2014.

Tenchov, Rumiana. "Understanding the Nanotechnology in COVID-19 Vaccines." *CAS,* American Chemical Society, www.cas.org/blog/understanding-nanotechnology-covid-19-vaccines. Accessed 18 Mar. 2021.

Tennenhouse, Erica. "What Magnetic Fields Do to Your Brain and Body." *Discover,* 25 May 2018, www.discovermagazine.com/environment/what-magnetic-fields-do-to-your-brain-and-body. Accessed 23 Dec. 2020.

Termuehlen, Heinz. *One Hundred Years of Power Plant Development: Focus on Steam and Gas Turbines as Prime Movers.* ASME Press, 2001.

Teschl, Gerald. *Ordinary Differential Equations and Dynamical Systems.* American Mathematical Society, 2012.

Tesla, Nikola. *My Inventions—The Autobiography of Nikola Tesla.* Infinity, 2013.

———. *The Strange Life of Nikola Tesla.* Library of Alexandria, 2020.

Thakur, Rajesh. *Blaise Pascal.* Prabhat Prakashan, 2021.

"Thermodynamics." *Khan Academy.* Khan Academy, 2015. Accessed 3 Apr. 2015.

Thirsk, Joan. *England's Agricultural Regions and Agrarian History, 1500–1750.* Macmillan Education, 1987.

Thompson, Holland. *The Age of Invention: A Chronicle of Mechanical Conquest.* BiblioBazaar, 2007.

Thompson, William J. *Angular Momentum: An Illustrated Guide to Rotational Symmetries for Physical Systems.* John Wiley & Sons, 2008.

Thrall, Robert M., and Leonard Tornheim. *Vector Spaces and Matrices.* Courier Corporation, 2014.

Tilley, Richard J. D. *Understanding Solids: The Science of Materials*. 2nd ed., John Wiley & Sons, 2013.

Tipler, Paul. *Physics for Scientists and Engineers: Mechanics*. 3rd ed., W. H. Freeman, 2008.

Titterton, David, John L. Weston, and John Weston. *Strapdown Inertial Navigation Technology*. IET, 2004.

"Torque and Levers." *Siyavula Textbooks: Grade 11 Physical Science*. Rice University, 29 July 2011. Accessed 7 Aug. 2015.

Towell, Gayle. "Magnetism: Definition, Types, Properties & How They Work (w/Examples)." *Sciencing*, 5 Dec. 2019, sciencing.com/magnetism-definition-types-properties-how-they-work-w-examples-13721191.html. Accessed 23 Dec. 2020.

Tran, Lannie K. *Superconductivity, Magnetism and Magnets*. Nova Publishers, 2006.

Trefil, James, and Robert M. Hazen. *The Sciences: An Integrated Approach*. John Wiley & Sons, 2003.

Tucker, Ian. "The Five: Robots Helping to Tackle Coronavirus." *The Guardian*, 31 May 2020, www.theguardian.com/technology/2020/may/31/the-five-robots-helping-to-tackle-coronavirus. Accessed 28 Feb. 2022.

Tucker, Sean. "Self-Driving Cars: Everything You Need to Know." *Kelley Blue Book*, 3 Aug. 2021, www.kbb.com/car-advice/self-driving-cars. Accessed 28 Feb. 2022.

Tull, Jethro. *Horse-hoeing Husbandry, or, An Essay on the Principles of Vegetation and Tillage: Designed to Introduce a New Method of Culture, Whereby the Produce of Land Will be Increased, and the Usual Expence Lessened: Together with Accurate Descriptions and Cuts of the Instruments Employed in It*. 3rd ed., A. Millar, 1751.

"Types of Forces." *The Physics Classroom*, www.physicsclassroom.com/class/newtlaws/Lesson-2/Types-of-Forces. Accessed 30 Jan. 2017.

"Types of Hydropower Turbines." *Office of Energy Efficiency & Renewable Energy*. US Department of Energy, n.d. Accessed 14 Apr. 2015.

Udroiu, Razvan, editor. *Computer-Aided Technologies: Applications in Engineering and Medicine*. IntechOpen, 2016.

Ufimetsev, Pyotr Ya. *Fundamentals of the Physical Theory of Diffraction*. 2nd ed., John Wiley & Sons, 2014.

Uicker, John J., Gordon R. Pennock, and Joseph E. Shigley. *Theory of Machines and Mechanisms*. 4th ed., Oxford UP, 2011.

Um, Dugan. *Solid Modeling and Applications: Rapid Prototyping, CAD and CAE Theory*. Springer, 2016.

University of Central Florida. "Magnet Research Takes Giant Leap." *ScienceDaily*, 10 Apr. 2020, www.sciencedaily.com/releases/2020/04/200410162413.htm. Accessed 23 Dec. 2020.

Vacca, Andrea, and Germano Franzoni. *Hydraulic Fluid Power: Fundamentals, Applications, and Circuit Design*. John Wiley & Sons, 2021.

Vaisman, Izu. *Foundations of Three-Dimensional Euclidean Geometry*. CRC Press, 2020.

Valle-Levinson, Arnoldo. *Introduction to Estuarine Hydrodynamics*. Cambridge UP, 2022.

Van Basshuysen, Richard, Fred Schaefer, and TechTrans. *Internal Combustion Engine Handbook*. SAE International, 2016.

Van Soest, Ton. *Business Jets and Turboprops Quick Reference Biz QR 2017*. Air Britain (Trading) Ltd., 2017.

Vanier, Jacques, and Cipriana Tomescu. *Universe Dynamics: The Least Action Principle and Lagrange's Equations*. CRC Press, 2019.

Venkatesan, C. *Fundamentals of Helicopter Dynamics*. CRC Press, 2015.

Vennard, John K. *Elementary Fluid Mechanics*. Read Books Ltd., 2011.

Villaverde, Roberto. *Fundamental Concepts of Earthquake Engineering*. CRC Press, 2009.

Vince, John. *Vector Analysis for Computer Graphics*. Springer Nature, 2021.

Vineeth C. S. *Stirling Engines: A Beginners Guide*. Vineeth C. S., 2011.

Visconti, Guido, and Paolo Ruggieri. *Fluid Dynamics: Fundamentals and Applications*. Springer International Publishing, 2021.

Vos, Roelof, and Saeed Farokhi. *Introduction to Transonic Aerodynamics*. Springer, 2015.

Wagtendonk, Walter J. *Principles of Helicopter Flight*. Aviation Supplies & Academics Inc., 2015.

Wald, Robert. *Advanced Classical Electromagnetism*. Princeton UP, 2022.

Waldren, Kenneth J., Gary L. Kinzel, and Sunil K. Agarwal. *Kinematics, Dynamics, and Design of Machinery*. 3rd ed., John Wiley & Sons, 2016.

Walker, Gabrielle. *An Ocean of Air: Why the Wind Blows and Other Mysteries of the Atmosphere*. Harcourt, 2007.

Walker, Jearl, Robert Resnick, and David Halliday. *Fundamentals of Physics*. 10th ed., Wiley, 2014.

Walsh, Ronald A. *Electromechanical Design Handbook*. 3rd ed., McGraw-Hill Professional, 2000.

Walski, Thomas M. *Advanced Water Distribution Modeling and Management*. Methods, 2003.

Wardhaugh, Benjamin. *Encounters with Euclid: How an Ancient Greek Geometry Text Shaped the World*. Princeton UP, 2021.

Wass, Harold S., and Russell P. Fleming. *Sprinkler Hydraulics: A Guide to Fire System Hydraulic Calculations*. 3rd ed., Springer Nature, 2020.

Watkins, James. *Introduction to Biomechanics of Sport and Exercise*. Elsevier, 2007.

Watkins, William H. *Loudspeaker Physics and Forced Vibration*. Springer International Publishing, 2022.

Webster, Larry. "How It Works: The Mazda Wankel Rotary Engine." *Popular Mechanics*, 1 Sept. 2011, www.popularmechanics.com/cars/a7103/how-it-works-the-mazda-rotary-engine-with-video. Accessed 2 Oct. 2017.

Weingardt, Richard G. *Engineering Legends: Great American Civil Engineers: Thirty-Two Profiles of Inspiration and Achievement*. American Society of Civil Engineers, 2005.

Weinreich, Gabriel. *Geometrical Vectors*. U of Chicago P, 2020.

Westfall, Richard S. *The Life of Isaac Newton*. Cambridge UP, 1980.

"What Do Structural Engineers Do?" *Schaefer*, 2017, schaefer-inc.com/what-do-structural-engineers-do. Accessed 20 Jan. 2020.

"What Is Civil Engineering?" *Columbia University in the City of New York*, civil.columbia.edu/about/what-civil-engineering. Accessed 20 Jan. 2020.

"What Is Mechatronic Engineering?" *Brightside*, www.brightknowledge.org/knowledge-bank/engineering/features-and-resources/copy_of_what-is-mechatronic-engineering. Accessed 19 Jan. 2017.

"What Is Mechatronics?" *Institution of Mechanical Engineers*, www.imeche.org/get-involved/special-interest-groups/mechatronics-informatics-and-control-group/mechatronics-informatics-and-control-group-information-and-resources/what-is-mechatronics. Accessed 19 Jan. 2017.

"What Is Mechatronics?" *North Carolina State University*, www.engr.ncsu.edu/mechatronics/what-mech.php. Accessed 19 Jan. 2017.

"What Is Moment of Inertia?" *The Constructor*, theconstructor.org/structural-engg/moment-of-inertia-calculation-formula/2825. Accessed 26 June 2017.

"What Is a Projectile?" *The Physics Classroom*, www.physicsclassroom.com/class/vectors/Lesson-2/What-is-a-Projectile. Accessed 14 Mar. 2016.

"What Is a Structural Engineer?" *Structural Engineers Association of California*, www.seaoc.org/page/whatisase. Accessed 20 Jan. 2020.

Whelan, Colm T. *Atomic Structure*. Morgan & Claypool Publishers, 2018.

White, Colin. *Projectile Dynamics in Sport: Principles and Applications*. Routledge, 2010.

Will, Clifford M., and Nicolás Yunes. *Is Einstein Still Right?: Black Holes, Gravitational Waves, and the Quest to Verify Einstein's Greatest Creation*. Oxford UP, 2020.

Williamson, Hank, editor. *Air Crash Investigations: Jammed Rudder Kills 132, The Crash of US Air Flight 427*. Lulu.com. 2011.

Wilson, Jerry D., Anthony J. Buffa, and Bo Lou. *College Physics Essentials: Mechanics, Thermodynamics, Waves (Volume One)*. 8th ed., CRC Press, 2019.

Winchester, Simon. *The Perfectionists: How Precision Engineers Created the Modern World*. HarperCollins, 2018.

Withuhn, William. *American Steam Locomotives: Design and Development*. Indiana UP, 2019.

Wittenburg, Jens. *Kinematics: Theory and Applications*. Springer, 2016.

Wood, Alexander, and Frank Oldham. *Thomas Young: Natural Philosopher, 1773–1829*. 1954. Cambridge UP, 2011.

Woodford, Chris, and Jon Woodcock. *Cool Stuff 2.0 and How It Works*. DK, 2007.

Woodruff, Everett B., Herbert B. Lammers, and Thomas F. Lammers. *Steam Plant Operation*. 10th ed., McGraw Hill Professional, 2016.

Wright, Gus. *Fundamentals of Medium/Heavy Duty Diesel Engines*. Jones & Bartlett Learning, 2021.

Wrigley, Sylvia. *Why Planes Crash Case Files: 2001–2003*. Fear of Landing, 2018.

Wysession, Michael, David Frank, and Sophia Yancopoulos. *Physical Science: Concepts in Action*. Prentice, 2004.

Xu, Weilin. *Mesoscale Analysis of Hydraulics*. Springer Nature Singapore, 2020.

Yang, Zongming, Huabing Wen, Xinglin Yang, Viktor Gorbov, Vira Mitienkova, and Serhiy Serbin. *Marine Power Plant*. Springer Nature, 2021.

Yasmin, Nighat. *Introduction to AutoCAD 2022 for Civil Engineering Applications*. SDC Publications, 2021.

Yazdi, Hassanali Mosalman. *Loading Structures*. U of Malaya P, 2013.

Yedavalli, Yeda K. *Flight Dynamics and Control of Aero and Space Vehicles*. Wiley, 2019.

Yehia, Hamad M. *Rigid Body Dynamics: A Lagrangian Approach*. Springer Nature, 2022.

Yolton, John W., editor. *Philosophy, Religion, and Science in the Seventeenth and Eighteenth Centuries*. U of Rochester P, 1990.

Young, F. R. *Fizzics: The Science of Bubbles, Droplets, and Foams*. Johns Hopkins UP, 2011.

Young, Hugh D. *College Physics*. Addison-Wesley, 2012.

Young, Hugh D., and Francis Weston Sears. *Sears & Zemansky's College Physics*. 9th ed., Addison, 2012.

Young, Trevor M. *Performance of the Jet Transport Airplane: Analysis Methods, Flight Operations, and Regulations*. Wiley, 2019.

Yount, Lisa. *Biotechnology and Genetic Engineering*. 3rd ed., Facts On File, 2008.

Youssef, George. *Applied Mechanics of Polymers: Properties, Processing, and Behavior*. Elsevier, 2021.

Yu, Daniel. *Speed: A Unified Field Theory in Physics: A* Caveman *Who Invented the Stone Wheel*. Fulton Books Incorporated, 2020.

Yu, Junchong. *Marine Nuclear Power Technology*. Springer Nature, 2020.

Zabihian, Farshid. *Power Plant Engineering*. CRC Press, 2021.

Zemansky, Mark Waldo, and Richard Dittman. *Heat and Thermodynamics*. 8th ed., McGraw-Hill, 2012.

Zhang, Dan and Bin Wei, editors. *Robotics and Mechatronics for Agriculture*. CRC Press, 2017.

Zhang, Lifeng, Antoine Allanore, Cong Wang, James Yurko, and Justin Crapps. *Materials Processing Fundamentals*. Springer, 2016.

Zhao, Bingcheng. *Look at the Mechanism Behind the Postulate of the Equivalence Principle: The Mechanism Behind the Extremely Important Postulate Has Been Revealed*. Amazon Digital Services LLC–Kdp Print Us, 2019.

Zichek, Jared A. *Goodyear GA-28A/B Convoy Fighter: The Naval VTOL Turboprop Tailsitter Project of 1950*. Retromechanix Productions, 2015.

Ziegler, Margaret. *Aeronautical Engineering*. Wilford Press, 2016.

Zimba, Jason. *Force and Motion: An Illustrated Guide to Newton's Laws*. JHU Press, 2009.

GLOSSARY

3D printing: a method of constructing objects from liquefied materials by extruding them in a set pattern that allows the object to be constructed layer by layer; the method is derived from the operating principle of ink-jet printers, and has been used with items ranging from small-scale plastic objects to welded metal objects to full-size concrete house foundations and other structures

abrasion: the wearing away of surface material by friction

acceleration: the rate of change of velocity associated with a change in speed or direction of motion or both; going faster; a vector quantity that describes the rate of change in velocity over time

accretion: the gradual formation of a larger body by the accumulation due to gravity or other attractive force of smaller bodies into a single mass

accretion disc: a circular region of space in which there are numerous particles of various sizes in an essentially planar array orbiting about the center of the region

actual mechanical advantage: the ratio comparing the output force of a machine to the input force, taking into account friction and other factors that limit the efficiency of real-world machines; a mechanical advantage of more than one indicates an amplification of force

actuator: a device that functions to provide motion to a component for a particular purpose; operated hydraulically, pneumatically, or electrically

additive machining: processes such as welding and 3D printing that add material to a workpiece

adhesion: the molecular attraction exerted between surfaces that are in contact

adiabatic process: a process undergone by a system without addition or extraction of heat

airfoil: the wing or other devices (for example, the tail) used in enabling heavier-than-air aircraft to fly

air resistance: opposition to motion due to air molecules experienced by an object passing through the air; also called drag with respect to flying machines

algorithm: a set of computer instructions that permit the interpretation of input data

Ampère's law: the rule stating that the strength of a magnetic field about a current-carrying conductor is directly proportional to the magnitude of the current

amplitude: the maximum angular displacement from the vertical or equilibrium position

analogue: technology for recording a wave in its original form

analysis: any systematic method of determining the solution to a problem

angle of attack: the angle that an airfoil makes with the air flowing past it; changing this angle will increase or decrease an aircraft's lift force

angle of incidence: the angle at which a billiard ball approaches and strikes a siderail of the billiard table, analogous to the approach of light rays to a reflective surface

angle of reflection: the angle at which a billiard ball rebounds from a siderail of a billiard table after striking it, analogous to the direction of light rays after striking a reflective surface

angular displacement: the measure of deviation from the vertical or equilibrium position

angular momentum: the momentum of an object that is moving with circular motion, or rotating; an object can have both linear and angular momentum

angular velocity: the rate of change of position of a body moving in a circle, commonly measured in rotations per minute

anisotropic: A material that shows different elastic properties in different directions

anti-ferromagnets: non-magnetic components that are rendered highly magnetic by the application of an electric field

aperiodic: Of irregular occurrence, not following a regular cycle of behavior

aqueduct: a conduit constructed for the delivery of water from water-rich sources at higher elevation to locations where the demand for water exceeds the supply

Archimedes screw: a device that uses a helical coil turning inside of a cylindrical tube to move water from one level to a higher level

architect: a structural engineering specialist who designs the inner and outer appearance of a building that is to be built

atmospheric pressure: pressure at sea level that air exerts that will counterbalance a mercury column 760 millimeters high

atomic forces: electronic forces that arise because of the interactions between electrons of nearby atoms

atomic mass: the total mass of the protons, neutrons, and electrons in an individual atom

atomic number: the number of protons in the nucleus of an atom, used to uniquely identify each element

attitude control: the process of obtaining and sustaining the proper orientation in space

attractor: state to which a dynamic system will eventually gravitate—a state that is not dependent on the starting qualities of the system

automata: mechanical representations of humans or animals operated by pneumatics or hydraulics

axiom: a self-evident statement that cannot be proven by manipulation of other statements; a logically self-evident relationship that is assumed to hold between the fundamental elements of geometry

axis: the center around which an object rotates

ballistic: refers to the parabola-like trajectory of an object travelling by momentum through a constant gravitational field; with no atmosphere, the trajectory is a true parabola, but the presence of an atmosphere results in drag and foreshortens the leading edge of the parabola as the object loses velocity

ballistic weapon: any weapon that is projected through the air to follow a parabolic trajectory to its target or to the ground

bar: atmosphere of pressure

benchmark: a current standard or minimum requirement that must be met for a particular product or process

Bernoulli equation: a conservation-of-energy equation, used extensively in hydrodynamics analyses, that states that along the path of a small volume-element of ideal fluid, the sum of the kinetic, potential, and pressure energy terms is a constant

Bernoulli's principle: the discovery that the pressure of a fluid decreases as its speed increases, an important principle enabling the flight of heavier-than-air aircraft

biofuels: fuels produced or refined from biological matter, such as ethanol made from corn or biodiesel oil made from algae or vegetable oils

bioinstrumentation: devices that are designed to interface directly with the human body, such as electronic glucose monitor systems for diabetics

biomechanics: the study of how (human) organisms function with regard to movement

blackbody radiation: radiation emitted by a body solely as a result of its temperature, regardless of its composition or any previously absorbed radiation

blacksmithing: the artisanal working of metal into a desired shape

blueprint: an engineering drawing form named for the specific blue-colored paper used for finished architectural drawings

boiler: device that uses heat from burning fuel to produce steam

bottom: the underside of a plow, designed to stabilize the plow in its function to prevent the plowshare from digging too deeply or driving upward out of the soil; also called the shoe or sole

boundary layer: a thin layer of gas (such as the air) immediately adjacent to an aircraft or some other body moving through a fluid

broadcasting: a technique of applying seed to a field by casting handfuls of seed using a sweeping motion of the arm; unfortunately, this method yields irregular and unreliable results

buoyancy: the upward force exerted by a fluid on a body immersed in that fluid

butterfly effect: theory that small changes in the initial state of a system can lead to pronounced changes that affect the entire system

CAD: computer-assisted design, or computer-assisted design and drafting (CADD)

cam: a circular disc designed having an eccentric profile that will perform a unique function such as raising and lowering a valve once with each revolution

carbon nanotube: one of several types of molecules consisting only of carbon atoms in hexagonal rings forming a closed tubular shape

Carnot limit: the upper limit for the efficiency of a heat engine; depends on the temperature difference between the working fluid and the surroundings; the higher this difference, the higher the theoretical maximum energetic efficiency

Cartesian grid: the standard grid pattern demarking the x, y and z coordinates in two or three mutually orthogonal dimensions

catapult: a device that uses tension against one end of a strained lever to impart momentum to its payload and send it into a ballistic trajectory when the tension is released

celestial mechanics: the mathematical description of the motions of planets, stars and other celestial objects due to their gravitational interactions

center of mass: a point in the body that moves (behaves) as though all the mass of the body were concentrated there and all external forces were applied there

centrifugal force: a fictitious force that seems to push a body in circular motion away from the axis of rotation; in reality, objects in circular motion are subject to centripetal force

centrifuge: a device that is used to spin materials at rates of up to 10,000 rpm, allowing them to separate by density

centripetal: acceleration or experienced force directed toward the focal point of curving motion or the center of a circle

centripetal force: a force "toward the center" that, in combination with inertia, generates the curved path of an object in circular motion; a perceived force that counteracts the outward-directed centrifugal force

cetane number: a classification of fuel oil combustibility relative to pure cetane (hexadecane, a C-16 hydrocarbon); analogous to the octane number for gasoline fuels relating gasoline combustibility to pure iso-octane (a C-8 hydrocarbon)

charge: the intrinsic property of matter that is responsible for all electromagnetic phenomena

chemical energy: the energy contained within the bonds between atoms in a compound

circle: a continuum of points that are a constant distance from one specific point

circular motion: motion of an object by translation on a circular, rather than linear, path

circumvallation: the surrounding of a besieged city with a wall or similar structure

civil engineering: relating to the non-military segment of society

classical mechanics: the study of the motion of bodies, rooted in Isaac Newton's physical and mathematical principles; also called Newtonian mechanics

closed system: one in which the working fluid (steam) is condensed back to liquid water and returned for reuse rather than being vented away

cocktail party effect: the ability to focus on and hear clearly a conversation taking place among other conversations in a generally noisy atmosphere

coefficient of friction: a dimensionless quantity, which depends on the types of materials involved, that characterizes the magnitude of the friction force between two surfaces of unit area

collinearity: the relationship that exists between points if they lie on the same straight line

complex system: System in which the behavior of the entire system exhibits one or more properties that are not predictable, given a knowledge of the individual components and their behavior

compressibility: the ability of air and all other gases to be compressed into a smaller volume than they would normally occupy

compressible fluids: fluids that can change volume by the application of external pressure, particularly gases

compression: the act of reducing the volume of a gas or other material without changing the amount of material by that action; the pushing forces applied to an object in order to diminish its size or volume

compression ignition: compressing a gas causes its temperature to increase; in a diesel engine the temperature increase of air due to compression is high enough to ignite the fuel

compressor: mechanical portion of a system that applies pressure on a gas reducing its volume and raising its temperature readying it to do work

concurrency: the relationship that exists between lines that all pass through the same point

condenser: specialized heat exchanger that uses cooling water from a river or the sea to convert steam leaving a turbine back to water

conductor: a material that has a low resistance to electric charges, allowing them to move through it easily

conduit: a channel connecting two points, designed to isolate what flows through the channel from what is outside of the channel

congruency: the relationship that exists between two objects if they are alike in all aspects of size and shape

conservation of charge: the principle that the net electrical charge in an electric circuit does not change

conservation of energy: generally, the principle that energy in the universe can be neither created nor destroyed, only transformed and transferred; in hydrodynamics, the principal that for an ideal fluid, the total energy associated with a small volume-element of fluid remains constant throughout its motion

conservation of mass: in hydrodynamics, the principal that the mass of ideal fluid entering a small body element equals the mass of fluid leaving the element

coordinate: any of the quantities of temperature, pressure, volume, or entropy

contact force: a force that occurs only when two objects are in direct contact

continuity: a clear path for electricity from point A to point B

convection: the circular vertical movement of fluids due to differences in density as a result of temperature differences

conveyor: a belt or belt-like structure that transports, or conveys, objects placed upon it as the belt operates through a continuous loop

coordinate system: a grouping of magnitudes that are used to define the positions of points in space

Coriolis force: the effects of the spinning motion of a planet on objects at the planet's surface, such as deflection in large-scale wind patterns

cosine: a trigonometric function describing the relationship between sides of a right triangle; the cosine of an angle is equal to the length of the side adjacent to the angle divided by the length of the hypotenuse

Coulomb's law: a scientific law stating that the electric flux at any defined surface is the vector sum of the electric field strength at every point on that surface

couple: a system of two equal and opposite parallel forces, spaced a finite distance apart

crankshaft: in an internal combustion engine, a heavy structure with offset sections to which the pistons of the individual combustion cylinders are attached by connecting rods; the crankshaft rotates about a central axis so that the pistons move up and down within the cylinders as it rotates

crest: the highest point of a wave from its neutral value; the distance between the crest or trough of a wave and the wave's neutral value is called the amplitude; the highest point in the height of a sinusoidal wave

cross product: an operation, broadly analogous to multiplication, performed on two vectors in a three-dimensional space that results in a third vector that is perpendicular to both; if both vectors have the same direction or if one of them has a value of zero, the cross product will be zero

cue ball: a white billiard ball that is directed to strike other billiard balls using the principles of geometry, velocity and momentum such that a struck ball goes into a pocket of the billiard table

cue stick: a precisely engineered straight, tapered and polished cylindrical stick fitted with a felt pad at the tip, used to propel the cue ball

cultivation: the practice of preparing soil prior to planting and maintaining the soil after it has been prepared in order to produce grain and vegetable crops

Curie temperature: the temperature at which a ferromagnetic material is made to lose its magnetic properties

current: the rate at which an electric charge, usually in the form of electrons, moves through a wire or other conductive material; the motion of charged particles as a function of time

damped oscillator: an oscillator that is subject to friction or other braking forces

damping: the process by which vibration steadily diminishes in amplitude

damping force: a nonconservative influence that removes mechanical energy and diminishes oscillation amplitude, eventually bringing the pendulum to equilibrium

deceleration: correctly termed negative acceleration, the decrease of velocity over a period of time, the opposite of acceleration

degree of freedom: The number of independent coordinates required to specify a physical system

denier: the number of threads per inch in a cotton fabric

density: the mass of a substance per unit volume, measured in kilograms per cubic meter

derivation: the method of determining the equation describing the slope of a line tangent to a curve or of a function that is tangent to a function of higher order

design: series of scientifically rigorous steps engineers use to create a product or system

dibbling: use of a tapered stick to poke a hole in the ground where a seed or seedling plant is to be placed

diekplous (διεκπλους): a military movement achieved when two forces of warships face each other in lines and ships from one force are able to break through the opposing line, enabling attack from the side instead of the front

differential calculus: the study of mathematical relationships based on the differences of values between points that satisfy the relationship

differential equation: a relationship between the derivatives of one or more functions and the functions themselves

diffraction: the separation of a wave into smaller component waves as it passes around an obstruction or through an opening of an appropriate size

digital: technology for sampling analogue waves and turning them into numbers; these numbers are turned into voltage

digitized systems: systems that rely on digital or computer control and analysis

dimension: a direction in which an object can move; in spatial physics, the three dimensions are traditionally represented by the symbols x, y, and z

displacement: the upward or downward extent to which the amplitude differs from the neutral value of a wave; the absolute distance an object moves from its starting point, regardless of the path it travels; the change of location of an object as the result of an experienced force; in fluid mechanics, the process by which a body immersed in a fluid pushes the fluid out of the way and occupies the space in its stead and in which the volume of the displaced fluid is equal to the volume of the displacing body

dissipative force: A force that, by its action, turns energy into heat

divergence theorem: the flux of a field passing through the surface of an enclosed space is equal to the divergence (change) of the field within the enclosed space

drag: the aerodynamic force that counters lift, slowing aircraft and diminishing ability to remain in flight

drill: an agricultural implement used to insert or deliver seed to prepared soil in a regular and controllable manner

ductility: the extent to which a material is able to be stretched without fracturing in response to an applied force

dynamical system: complex system that changes over time according to a set of rules governing the transformation from one state to the next

dynamics: the science that deals with the motion of systems of bodies under the influence of forces; dynamics deals with the causes of motion

earthquake engineer: a structural engineer who specializes in the design and construction of buildings to withstand the shocks and vibrations of earthquakes

eccentricity: the extent to which a celestial body's orbit deviates from a perfect circle

Edison "myth": the common perception that Thomas A. Edison actually invented many of the things that he claimed when in reality they were invented by others and Edison claimed their work as his own

efficiency: the measure of how effective a machine is at transforming or transferring energy, quantified as the ratio of the actual performance of the machine to an idealized, theoretical version of it; a perfect machine would have an efficiency value of one

eigensystem: the set of all eigenvectors of a matrix paired with their respective eigenvalues

elasticity: the extent to which a material is able to naturally revert to its original shape after being temporarily deformed by an applied force

electric field: the influence that a distribution of charges has on the space around it such that the force experienced by a small test charge q is given by the value of that charge times the electric field, which results from the charge distribution

electric flux: the measure of the strength of an electric field across an area with different electrical potentials

electric potential energy: energy that is present in particles due to their charge and closeness to other charges

electrical efficiency: the ratio of the power applied to an electrical circuit to the power delivered by a particular device in the circuit

electricity: the movement of electrical charge through a conductor

electrodynamics: the original name for what is now called electromagnetism

electromagnet: a device that becomes magnetic due to the presence of an electric current

electromagnetic field: a field created by the motion of charged particles

electromagnetic wave: time-varying electric and magnetic fields propagating through space (or through a medium); light is an example of an electromagnetic wave

electromagnetism: the physical phenomenon that is the combined effect of an electric field and a magnetic field; a magnetic field generated around a conductor by an electrical current flowing through the conductor, also an electrical current generated in a conductor that is passing through a magnetic field

electromotive force (emf): the potential difference between two points (or terminals) of a device that is used as a source of electrical energy

electron: a fundamental subatomic particle with a single negative electrical charge, found in a large, diffuse cloud around the nucleus; a negatively charged subatomic particle that is often bound to the positive charge of the nucleus but can also exist in a free state in an atom

electrostatic: refers to situations where electric charges are at rest

electrostatic charge: the accumulation of excess electrons on a material through friction with another material

electrostatic repulsion and attraction: charges of the same sign, whether positive or negative, repel each other, while charges of opposite sign are attracted to each other

element: a form of matter consisting only of atoms of the same atomic number

ellipse: a shape that resembles an elongated circle; mathematically speaking, a closed conic section

elongation: the lengthening of an object under stress

energy: capacity to do work; can be chemical, electrical, heat, kinetic, nuclear, potential, radiant, radiation, or thermal in nature

entropy: the amount of heat transferred to or from a system (during a small interval of time) divided by the temperature at which it was transferred; the thermodynamic principle that represents the distribution of energy in a system, with entropy increasing as the system becomes less organized

epicenter: the central aboveground location of an earth tremor; that is, the point of the surface directly above the hypocenter

episteme: Aristotle's word for understanding the true character of a physical thing, only obtainable by studying the thing in such way that only one question about it can be answered at a time, which is the essence of scientific research

equilibrant: a single force or couple that when applied to the system causes the body to be in equilibrium

equilibrium: the condition of a dynamic system consisting of two or more components in which there is no net change in any of its components

escalade: an attempt to scale the walls of a besieged city by its attackers

Euclidean tools: the straightedge and the compass, the classical drawing tools used in making geometrical constructions

Euler paths: in CNC milling of a workpiece, an approach to determining the desired result from the least amount of machine motions and operation interruptions

exhaust: the elimination of combustion gases from the cylinders of an internal combustion engine at the completion of the combustion cycle of its operation

exhaust port/valve: an opening and control system by which product gases are eliminated from combustion cylinders of an internal combustion engine after combustion of the air/fuel mixture

experiment: an essential aspect of scientific study, in which one devises a specific test to determine a particular property or characteristic

failure: in engineering terms, the fracturing or giving way of an object under stress

Faraday's law: the scientific law stating that when a magnetic field and a conductor move relative to each other, a voltage is induced in the conductor, the magnitude of which depends directly on the relative speed of the field and conductor

fault: a fracture or fracture zone in rock, along which the two sides have been displaced vertically or horizontally relative to each other

feasibility study: process of evaluating a proposed design to determine its production difficulty in terms of personnel, materials, and cost

ferromagnetic: describing material that can be made permanently magnetic by the presence of a magnetic field, such as iron and other ferrous (ironlike) metals

filter: portion of a system that cleans gas of impurities

fixed reference frame: a frame of reference that is fixed to the environment and not to the subject being observed; sometimes specified as "Earth-fixed" or "space-fixed"

flow: the motion of a fluid; the behavior of a fluid substance, such as water or air, which deforms continuously—that is, changes its shape—in response to a shearing stress, no matter how small; also the movement driven only by gravity of fluids and fluid-like materials

fluid: a liquid, vapor, or gas that fills the container that holds it; hydraulics limits its focus to liquids and those vapors and gases undergoing negligible changes in density

fluid mechanics: study of the flow of liquids and gases

fluid power: term used to describe the use of both liquids and gas for mechanical purposes

fluorescent lamp: a lamp in which light is produced by electrical stimulation of a gas rather than by heating a tungsten metal filament to incandescence

flux: the value of the electric (or magnetic) field multiplied by the surface area that it crosses

flying shuttle: a device used in weaving that automatically pulls the weft strands across the loom between the warp strands; allowed the weaver to greatly increase weaving speed and the production of cloth of any width

flywheel: a massive disk or gear that is set to spinning by a motor, thus allowing the flywheel's angular momentum and torque to maintain and stabilize the function of the motor

force: a non-physical manifestation that has the potential to interact with physical matter to cause either attraction or repulsion; generally, the effect of pressure per unit area such as pounds per square inch; an action or reaction that attempts to cause the body to move along its own line of action

force field: the effect of a field force and a function of the relative position of the object from the force field source; the object and the source do not need to be in physical contact for this effect to occur

forced vibration: oscillatory motion driven by an external excitation

forensics: generally thought of as a study that occurs after a crime or a death, forensics simply has the sense of "examination after the fact" and applies to all fields and situations

forms: the rudimentary concept of matter being constructed as combinations of four basic anthropomorphic principles that define the character of any particular matter; these were later replaced by the four physical character principles earth, air, fire and water

four-cycle engine: an engine that requires four complete revolutions of its crankshaft for the complete cycle of its operation, as compared to a two-cycle engine

four-stroke engine: an engine requiring four piston strokes for a single fuel combustion; one stroke draws in air, a second compresses the air, fuel is injected and ignited to drive the piston through the third stroke, and the fourth stroke pushes out the combustion gases; all four strokes are timed to the opening and closing of intake and exhaust valves

fractional distillate: petroleum (unrefined oil) is a complex mixture of different compounds; fractionation of the mixture by distillation separates the components according to their respective boiling points; each portion according to boiling point range is a fractional distillate

frame of reference: a system of space-time coordinates used by an observer to measure the physical world

free vibration: oscillatory motion in the absence of external excitation

frequency: the number of complete wavelengths that occur within one unit of time, typically expressed as hertz (Hz; cycles per second)

friction: a force that arises between two bodies in contact, resisting the movement between them

frictional resistance: the force created by the resistance to relative motion between solid surfaces; it is normally proportional to the roughness of the surfaces as well as the force squeezing the surfaces together

friction wheels: wheels that turn in contact with each other, one driving the rotation of the other in proportion to their respective circumferences; this is the basic operating principle of gears

fulcrum: a stationary point upon which a lever pivots

function: a mathematical expression describing an actual relationship between two or more entities represented by mathematical variables

Gaussian surface: any closed or finite hypothetical surface

gears: objects designed to rotate with each other such that the teeth machined into their circumferences are able to mesh enabling one to drive the other; the teeth are designed such that their surfaces roll against each other rather than just push, thus reducing wear

gene manipulation: alteration of the genetic structure of an organism's DNA either by genetic engineering or by selective breeding methods

general solution of a differential equation: a formula involving arbitrary constants such that, by assigning values to the constants, one gets all the solutions of the differential equation

genetic engineering: commonly called gene modification, the direct manipulation of genetic material (specifically, DNA and RNA) to impart or enhance gene-based characteristics

geocentrism: the view that the sun, the planets, and the entire universe revolve in orbit about Earth

geometry: literally means "earth measurement" and refers generally to the relationships between the dimensions and area of plane figures

glacis: a sloped structure at the base of the walls of a besieged city, designed to cause attackers to lose their footing as though they were walking on an icy path, making it very difficult to bring other attackers and siege machines close to the walls

graph: a pictorial representation of data presented on an appropriate grid

graphene: one of the fundamental forms of pure carbon, consisting of flat sheets of carbon atoms in hexagonal rings; graphene is the material of which graphite coal is formed

gravitation: the mutual attraction between all bodies in the universe, of which gravity, the force the earth exerts on all bodies on or near it, is an example

gravitational field: the region in which an object (a test particle) experiences acceleration caused by the masses and locations of other objects (sources of the field)

gravitational force: the pull that objects exert on each other due to their masses and the separation between their centers of mass

gravitational mass: the mass of a body defined as the quantity that determines its coupling to a gravitational field, either as a test particle or as a source

gravity: the attractive force of one body on another

guided missile: a missile whose flight can be controlled during its operation

gyroscopic force: a reactive force generated by a rotating mass to resist displacement from its original axis of rotation, consistent with conservation of angular momentum

half-wave tower: a radio transmitter tower whose height is exactly one-half of the wavelength of its transmitting frequency

hand-filing: the practice of shaping metal components from stock by the use of files to remove material from the workpiece

harmonic oscillations: the motion resulting from a system that when displaced from its equilibrium point exerts a restoring force that is proportional to the displacement

heat capacity: the amount of heat an object can absorb divided by the temperature change in that absorption

heat engine: a device that converts the energy of heat into mechanical energy or motion

heat exchanger: a structure that separates a heat source from a working fluid but allows heat to transfer from one to the other

heat transfer: process of transmitting heat; heat travels through a solid by conduction, is transmitted from a solid surface to a liquid or gas by convection, and is transferred by radiation, which consists of electromagnetic waves

heliocentric: orbits that have the sun at their center

high pressure steam: a relative term for steam engines operating at significantly higher pressures than low-pressure steam engines; an engine whose functioning and efficiency is a function of temperature differences

Hooke's law: the force (F) exerted by a spring is proportional to the length to which the spring is extended (x) and a coefficient characteristic of each individual spring (k), as $F = -kx$

husbandry: an old term for the farming of plants and animals

hybrid vehicle: a vehicle that has both an internal combustion engine and an electric motor available for propulsion

hydraulic engineering: engineering relevant to the control of moving water

hydraulic organ: an organ that uses pumped water to pressurize air within a chamber allowing the air to be directed to a series of pipes and emerge as musical sound

hydraulic system: a means of transferring mechanical power to various parts of a mechanical system by pumping oil at high pressure through a series of connecting hoses or pipes; used primarily to operate high-strength hydraulic rams and motors

hydraulics: the application of pressurized liquids to perform work

hydrodynamics: the physics of water in motion; fluid dynamics is the physics of fluids in motion

hydroelectric: using the movement of water to drive electrical generators

hypersonic flight: flight at very high airspeeds, usually at Mach 5 or above

hypocenter: the central underground location of an earth tremor; also called the focus natural frequency; the frequency at which an object or substance will vibrate when struck or shaken

ideal fluid: a fluid assumed to have zero viscosity and to be incompressible

ideal mechanical advantage: the ratio comparing the output force of a machine to the input force, ignoring friction and other factors that limit the efficiency of real-world machines; a mechanical advantage of more than one indicates an amplification of force

igneous rock: rock formed as magma with Earth that has been extruded as lava and solidified

imperfect system: any system that functions with less than 100 percent efficiency

impulse turbine: a turbine set in motion by the velocity of a fluid hitting each blade

inclined plane: a flat surface set at an angle relative to the horizontal plane

incompressible: a gas that either cannot or does not become compressed under given conditions such as air in front of the wings of an aircraft

incompressible fluids: fluids that do not change volume with the application of external pressure, particularly liquids

inductance: the property by which a current is created in conductors to resist a change in the magnetic field through the conductor; the ability to generate a magnetic field when electrical current is flowing

induction: the generation of an electric current in a conductor by the action of a moving magnetic field

industrialization: the replacement of manual and animal labor by machines

inertia: the principle that an object at rest tends to stay at rest and an object in motion tends to stay in motion unless acted on by an outside force; the resistance of an object to any change in its state of motion

inertial frame: a frame of reference in which a body that has no force acting on it has no acceleration

inertial mass: the mass of a body defined as the measure of its opposition to acceleration by external forces

initial point: the beginning point of a vector

initial velocity: the velocity of an object at the start of some interval of time

input: the force (or energy) that is "put in" to a machine; for example, the horizontal force of wind provides the input for a windmill

intake: the introduction of fuel and air into the cylinders of an internal combustion engine prior to its combustion cycle

intake port/valve: an opening and control system through which fuel and air are admitted into the combustion cylinders of an internal combustion engine

integral calculus: the study of mathematical relationships based on determining the area bounded by a curve or other function, based on the concept of dividing that area into infinitesimal "slices" of area and summing them together, or integrating them

integration: the method of determining the area bounded by a curve or other function based on dividing that area into infinitesimal "slices" of area and summing them together

internal energy: energy stored by a system, indicated by a change in temperature and volume

irrigation: the practice of moving water from one location with abundant water to another location where water is needed

isotope: an atom of a specific element that contains the usual number of protons in its nucleus but a different number of neutrons

inviscid: a fluid having no resistance to objects moving through it

isotropic: a material that shows identical elastic properties in all directions

jenny: in actuality a female mule; also a term once used to refer to a device that carries out a task

joule: a derived unit of energy from base units of the International System of Units (SI), or metric system, equal to a kilogram times one meter per second squared; equivalent to the work done by a force of one newton applied over a distance of one meter

kerf: the extra width of a cut made with a saw due to the slight sideways cant of the saw teeth

kinematics: a subfield of classical mechanics that studies the motion of objects without reference to the forces that cause this motion; the study of the motion of objects

kinesiology: the study of how human and animal bodies move

kinetic energy: energy due to any kind of motion, be it rotation, vibration, or translation; the work capacity of an object in motion

kinetic friction: the force that opposes one surface sliding over another when one surface is moving with respect to the other

laminar flow: flow in which there is no turbulence in the fluid as it flows, as all particles making up the fluid flow uniformly in parallel paths, or "lamina"

law of conservation of energy: the total amount of energy in a closed system is always the same; therefore, energy can neither be created nor destroyed

law of the lever: for any lever that pivots against a fulcrum, a large mass M positioned to one side of the pivot point at a distance D can be balanced by a smaller mass m on the other side of the pivot point at a distance d such that MD = md

LC oscillation: alternation between stored electric and magnetic field energies in circuits containing both an inductance (L) and a capacitance (C)

lever: a component that transmits force from one location to another by pivoting on a fulcrum

levers: systems in which a rigid linear surface, or an equivalent structure, is used to manipulate a mass and perform work at a distance by pivoting against a point acting as a fulcrum

lift: the force produced by the motion of an airfoil, which gives an aircraft the ability to leave the ground and holds it up during flight

limit: the ultimate value of a particular algebraic function

line spectrum: the lines of color that represent the characteristic frequencies at which atoms emit electromagnetic radiation

linear elasticity: the behavior of a material when stress is linearly proportional to strain

linear momentum: the momentum of an object that is moving in a straight line, or translating; an object can have both linear and angular momentum

linear motion: movement of an object in a straight line, or translation

locomotive: a steam-powered train engine

lodestone: the mineral hematite, an iron ore, that has been made magnetic by crystallizing in Earth's magnetic field

loudness: the intensity of sound waves, which depends on the wave's amplitude; measurements of loudness or volume are expressed in decibels

Luddites: workers violently opposed to the use of machines to replace their skilled labor, thought to be followers of an 18th-century weaver named Ned Ludd

Mach number: the number obtained by dividing an aircraft's airspeed by the speed of sound, under the conditions of the flight in progress

magnetic bearing: a type of bearing that uses magnetic repulsion rather than physical contact to stabilize the rotation of an axle

magnetic damping: the use of opposing magnetic fields to damp the motion of a magnetic oscillator

magnetic field: the influence that a distribution of electric currents has on the space around it

magnetism: an innate property of certain atoms due to the distribution of electrons within them

magnetization: imparting or receiving magnetic characteristic

magnetostatic: refers to magnetic fields that result from constant electric currents

magnitude: the size, or numerical measurement, of a vector

map: a graphic representation of areas such as countries enclosed by designated borders

mapping: identifying specific regions and their dimensions for the generation of maps, blueprints, technical drawings, and other relevant forms of data storage and representation

masking: a phenomenon in which the brain selectively hears what it expects to hear in the midst of noise

mass: the sum total of the masses of all atoms that comprise a body of matter whether gaseous, liquid or solid

mass-spring system: a system consisting of an elastic object connected to an object with mass

matter: anything that occupies space and has weight within a gravitational field

Maxwell's equations: a set of mathematical descriptions of electromagnetism, formulated by James Clerk Maxwell

mechanical advantage: the amount by which an applied force being used to perform work can be augmented through the use of mechanical devices

mechanical efficiency: the ratio of the power applied to a mechanical system relative to the power delivered by the system

mercury vapor pump: a specialized pump that uses diffusion of mercury vapor to decrease pressure further from the limit of a standard vacuum pump (10^{-3} atmospheres) to as low as 10^{-6} atmospheres

method of exhaustion: a means of determining the area of a planar surface with curved edges by inscribing within it successively smaller regular polygons (triangles, squares, etc.) whose areas can be accurately calculated, then summing those areas together

microscope: a device similar to the telescope but used to examine objects at very close distances rather than far distances

missile: technically, any object that is set in motion on a ballistic trajectory without power; generally, a powered object or weapon that enters a ballistic trajectory using its own power

mission payload: the extra equipment carried by a craft for a specific mission; for a launch vehicle, payload usually refers to scientific instruments, satellites, probes, and spacecraft attached to the launcher

modulus of elasticity: the ratio of applied stress to resulting linear strain, also known as Young's modulus

moldboard: the upright curved portion of a plow, designed to guide the soil to turn over as the plow passed through it

molecular geometry: the bong angles and bond lengths between atoms in a molecule

molecular structure: the three-dimensional arrangement of atoms and bonds in a particular compound

moment: a combination of a physical quantity and a distance with respect to a fixed axis; the physical quantities of an object as measured at some distance from that axis

moment of inertia: the property of a system that resists rotation under application of an external torque

moment of inertia or rotational inertia: the capacity of a body to resist rotational acceleration; plays the same role for rotational motion that mass does for translational motion

momentum: the product of the mass of a body and its velocity; the rate of change of momentum of a body is equal to the force acting on it

mule: a term often used to refer to a device designed to transport material that is to be used in a broader purpose

multiphysics analysis: the process of analyzing the different physics principles involved in the engineering process and their effects and limiting characteristics with regard to the particular engineering project

nanoparticles: particles whose dimensions are measured in nanometers, typically less than 100 nanometers in size

nanoscale: refers to particles and structures less than 100 nanometers in size

natural frequency: the number of complete oscillations undergone per unit time; determined by pendulum length and mass

natural period: the length of time of a single vibration of an object or substance when vibrating at its natural frequency

n-body problem: a mathematical model used to determine how gravity affects the motions and interactions of a group of celestial bodies

nebular hypothesis: the concept that stars and planets form by the accretion of particles within a spinning disc composed of particles in space

net force: the sum of all of the forces acting on an object; note that forces with equal magnitude but opposite directions negate each other; also, an object moves in the direction of the net force acting on it

neutron: a fundamental subatomic particle in the atomic nucleus that is electrically neutral and about equal in mass to the mass of one proton

newton: the International System of Units (SI) unit of force; one newton is equal to the force required to accelerate a one-kilogram mass at one meter per second per second

newton-meter: the International System of Units standard unit for torque; one newton-meter (N·m) is equal to the torque resulting at the axis from the force of 1 newton applied perpendicularly to an attached 1-meter-long moment arm (i.e., a lever)

Newton's laws of motion: three laws devised by physicist and mathematician Isaac Newton to describe the motion of objects in relation to the forces acting on them

node: the neutral point that separates the rising part of the wave from the lowering part of the wave

noise: generally, any undesired sound and discordant frequency combinations

nonlinear: of a system or phenomenon that does not follow an ordered, linear set of cause-and-effect relationships

nonlinear elasticity: the behavior of a material when stress is not linearly proportional to strain

normal force: a force in the direction normal, or perpendicular, to two surfaces in contact that pushes the two surfaces together

normal mode: a condition of vibration in which all components of a system reach maximum displacements simultaneously and pass their equilibrium positions simultaneously

nuclear energy: the energy contained within the bonds between the subatomic particles in the nucleus of an atom; when a nucleus undergoes fission and splits apart, it releases some of this energy which may then be captured by water molecules in a boiler system, eventually turning them to steam

nucleus: the central core of an atom, consisting of specific numbers of protons and neutrons and accounting for at least 9998 percent of the atomic mass

open system: one in which the working fluid is not recaptured for reuse and must be replenished in order to maintain operation of the system; the opposite of a closed system

order of the differential equation: the order of the derivative of highest order appearing in the differential equation

origin: the reference point at which a coordinate system is centered

orthotropic: a material that shows the same elastic properties in two directions at right angles to each other

oscillation: a variation between maximum and minimum values of displacement from a neutral value

output: the force (or energy) produced by a machine The machine transforms the input into the output; for instance, a windmill transforms the force of wind (input) into the circular motion of a millstone for grinding (output)

parabolic: refers to a shape (a parabola) that can be described by an equation of the form $y = ax^2 + b$

parallel: describing two lines, curves or surfaces that extend in the same direction and separated from each other by a constant distance

parameters: variables that do not enter in the differential equation but that correspond to magnitudes which can be set from the exterior

peak amplitude: the value of the amplitude at its maximum displacement from the neutral value of the wave

peak-to-peak amplitude: the absolute value of the sum of the peak positive and peak negative amplitudes; the distance between the crest and the trough of a wave

pendulum: a suspended mass that can undergo regular oscillations

period: the time to complete one oscillation; inverse of natural frequency

periplous (περιπλους): a military movement achieved when two forces of warships face each other in lines and ships from one force are able to go around the opposing line, enabling attack from the side instead of the front

permeability: the ability with which a magnetized material supports a magnetic field

permittivity: a measure of the ability of an electric field to penetrate a medium

perpendicular: being at a right angle relative to a given line or plane, as in the lines of the letter T

perturbation: a change in the orbit of a celestial object caused by the gravitational force of another object

petroleum-based fuels: fuels ranging from methane to heavy oil that are refined from crude oil

photoelectron spectroscopy: an analytical method that uses ultraviolet light to cause the ejection of electrons from within the atoms of a particular compound

piezoelectric: a material that emits an electrical signal when subject to impact

pinned end: the end of a member that is permitted rotation about one or more axes

piston: a movable device contained within a cylinder such that its vertical movement can be used either to compress a gas within the cylinder or be depressed by expanding gases within the cylinder

plane of the ecliptic: the geometric plane in which the planets orbit their star

plasticity: a state in which there is an increase in the deformation of the material without a corresponding increase in applied stress

platform: all parts of a spacecraft that are not part of the payload; also known as the bus

plow: an agricultural implement used to lift and invert soil as it moves forward

plowshare: the portion at the leading edge of a plow, designed to cut through the soil below the surface of the ground at the desired depth of tilth

pneumatic system: a means of transferring mechanical power to various parts of a mechanical system by pumping air at elevated pressure through a series of connecting hoses or pipes; used primarily to operate low-strength rams and actuators

pneumatics: the application of pressurized air to perform work

Poisson's ratio: The ratio of the strain in the transverse direction to the linear strain

polar: molecules that have an unequal distribution of electrical charge within their molecular structures but are nevertheless electrically neutral

polar axis: the line through a planet passing through its north and south poles, about which the planet rotates

polyphase: a system in which an electromagnetic field is composed of two or more sinusoidal emissions that are not in phase with each other

positron: identical to the electron, except that a positron bears a positive charge and the electron bears a negative charge

postulate: today, synonymous with "axiom"; originally, postulates were empirically self-evident relationships

potential: any of the measures of stored energies measured as internal energy, enthalpy, Gibbs function, or Helmholtz function

potential energy: energy that is stored in objects and has the potential to become other forms of energy, such as kinetic energy; the energy stored within an object or system due to its position or configuration relative to the forces acting on it

potential lines: a mathematical construction that defines regions of space where fluid movement has a potential to occur; a fluid element moves from a high potential line to a lower one

power: the rate of work (energy transfer) over time; the International System of Units unit of power is the watt (W), which equals one joule per second (J/s)

precision: the degree to which a manufactured piece conforms to its design specifications

pressure: the force per unit area exerted by a fluid on a container; total pressure is the sum of a static pressure, as used in Archimedes's principle, and a dynamic pressure, caused by motion of the fluid

pressure energy: the energy possessed by a mass due to the pressure exerted on it by external factors

prime numbers: any number that is evenly divisible only by 1 and itself, such as 1, 3, 5, 7, 13 and a great many others

probability: the numerical likelihood that a specific event will occur in random events occurring within a set of defined conditions; e.g., the occurrence of the 6 appearing on the roll of a standard cubic die

probability theory: the mathematical basis of determining the likelihood of a given outcome in a situation governed by random chance within a set of starting and boundary conditions such as the rules by which a particular game of chance is played

projectile: any object that is projected through the air by some means towards a target

proprioception: the ability of knowing where each part of your body is without having to think consciously where it is, as one knows where to put a finger to touch the nose, ears, mouth, other hand, etc., with one's eyes closed

proprioceptive sensors: a sensor and computing system that identifies the relative location and orientation of the other parts of the machine

proton: a fundamental subatomic particle with a single positive electrical charge, found in the atomic nucleus

prototype: Original full-scale working model of a product or system

pulley: a disc with a concave groove about its circumference that allows a rope or other type of line to roll it when mounted on a central axle

pulleys: systems consisting essentially of wheels aver which a rope, cable or chain can pass, rolling the wheel as it is pulled around to provide an enhanced ability to perform work

pump: a device that moves fluids from one location to another; a machine that adds mechanical energy to a liquid; also the increased energy is indicated by an increase in pressure

quantum mechanical tunneling: an electronic process occurring in atoms, by which electrons may become able to cross energy barriers into electronic regions where they would not otherwise be allowed

quantum mechanics: the mathematical system that describes the innermost workings of atoms and their subatomic particles; the science of understanding how a particle can act like both a particle and a wave

quantum state: the condition of a physical system as defined by its associated quantum attributes

radian: a nondegree unit of angle measurement, based on the radius of a circle; there are $2p$ radians, or $2p$ rad, (equal to 360 degrees) in one complete circle or revolution

randomness: State marked by no specific or predictable pattern or having a quality in which all possible behaviors are equally likely to occur

range: the horizontal distance that a projectile can travel before striking the ground

Rankine cycle: thermodynamic cycle employed in a steam engine involves four main stages: pumping of water, heat addition, work production, and heat removal

reaction turbine: a turbine set in motion by the pressure and flow of a fluid

rebound: the action of a billiard ball striking a cushioned siderail of the billiard table and bouncing from it in a different direction

receiver: container for holding gas under controlled temperature and pressure until it is needed

reciprocating steam engine: machine that uses steam to push pistons up and down in a cylinder This motion can be used to drive a pump or a ship's propeller

reduction gear: device that converts the high rotating speed of a turbine to the much lower rotating speed of an electric generator or ship's propeller

reductive machining: processes such as grinding and milling that reduce the amount of material in a workpiece

reflectance sensor: a sensor that detects the reflection of a light signal that it has emitted in order to compute distance

refraction: the change of direction of light when it passes from one medium to another having a different density; the magnitude of the change is termed the refractive index of the material

relativistic speeds: speeds that are close to the speed of light and therefore are governed by relativity rather than Newton's laws

resistance: the opposition to the flow of electrical current through a material

resonance: a condition of large amplitude of vibration caused by the coincidence of natural and excitation frequencies; the response of an elastic body to a force acting on the body at its natural frequency

restoring torque: the application of a force at a distance from an axis about which a system can rotate, directed in such a way as to attempt to restore equilibrium

resultant: a single force or couple that can represent the applied forces and couples in their action on the body

right angle: an angle of exactly 90 degrees formed by the intersection of two lines

right-hand rule: if a wire is grasped in the right hand with the thumb pointing in the direction of current flow, the fingers will point in the direction of the magnetic field around the wire

rigid body: an aggregate of material particles in which the interaction of particles is such that the distance between any two particles remains constant with time in an ideal situation; in practice, slight variations in size and shape are accepted

rods and cones: two types of light receptor structures on the retina of the eye that are responsible for vision

roller end: the end of a member that is permitted sliding movement in one or more directions

root-mean-square amplitude: for sinusoidal wave systems, the square root of the sum of squared amplitude values divided by the number of amplitude values

rotation: refers to a physical mass revolving about an axis that passes through its center of mass

rotational axis: a theoretical line passing through the point about which an object is rotating, always orthogonal to the direction of rotation

rotational motion: the motion of an object that is spinning

rotational speed: simply, the rate at which a rotating mass travels about its central axis; for all particles in the mass the angular rotation speed is equal, but the physical distance traveled by individual particles about the axis increases directly with radius

roving: a single strand of a woven fiber

safety brake: a device that automatically engages to prevent the elevator cab from falling freely when the support cables fail, either braking the descent or stopping it completely

saturated steam: steam that is just at its boiling temperature; while water boils at 212 degrees Fahrenheit at atmospheric pressure, the boiling temperature rises at higher pressures

scalar: a quantity that has magnitude but not a direction, such as the nondimensional measurements of time or temperature

scalar quantities: quantities that have magnitude or absolute value, but are not associated with a direction; e.g., 23 kilometers per hour

Schrödinger equation: a wave equation that describes the quantum state of a particle or system and can be used to predict its most likely future behavior

seed drill: a machine drawn behind horses or a tractor that lays seeds at a uniform depth in parallel rows

set: a permanent change in the dimension of the material as a result of stressing it beyond the elastic limit, or yield point

shear: a stress that forces two contiguous parts of an object in a direction parallel to their plane of contact, as opposed to a stretching, compressing, or twisting force; also called shear stress

shuttle: a device used in weaving to pull the weft strands across the loom between the warp strands; typically required the weaver to move the shuttle manually and so limited the width of material that could be woven

siege weapon: a structure designed to aide an attacking force to breach the walls of a castle or city

sine: a trigonometric function describing the relationship between sides of a right triangle; the sine of an angle is equal to the length of the side opposite the angle divided by the length of hypotenuse

sink: the location where fluid is removed from a fluid system

sinusoidal: varying continuously between maximum and minimum values of equal magnitude at a specific frequency, in the manner of a sine wave

sliding valve: a type of valve system in which an intake or exhaust port is sealed by a cover that slides into place, as compared to the type of valve system in which the ports are opened or closed by a matching device that moves in and out of the ports

sling: typically, a patch of leather that can accommodate a stone or other small object, attached to two cords; twirling the loaded sling and releasing one of the cords flings the stone at high velocity

slope: the ratio of the change in vertical distance to the change in horizontal distance

solenoid: an electromagnetic device that uses the magnetic field generated inside a wire coil to drive the motion of a steel rod when an electrical current is passed through the coil; typically used as an actuating device

solenoid valve: valve capable of converting electrical energy into mechanical energy, which in turn opens or closes the valve mechanically

solution of a differential equation: a function or group of functions whose derivatives are related to the functions in the way prescribed by the differential equation

sonic boom: the bang or booming sound heard after a supersonic aircraft passes, caused by shock waves produced by the aircraft

sound: the perception and interpretation of vibrations reaching the ear as they travel through a conductive fluid medium such as air or water

source: the location where fluid is applied to a fluid system

sowing: planting seeds or seedlings as the beginning of a crop

specific gravity: the ratio of the density of a substance to that of a standard reference substance; also known as relative density

specifications: the exact requirements engineers must comply with to create products or services

spectroscopy: an analytical method in which light from a source is separated into its component wavelengths to reveal distinct wavelengths present due to emission or absent due to absorption

spectrum: a series of distinct wavelengths of electromagnetic radiation characteristic of a particular source

speed: the rate at which an object moves, regardless of the direction in which it moves

spindle: a cylindrical device upon which raw fiber material was wound, enabling the fibers to be fed into a machine to be spun into yarn or thread

spit: a metal rod that is inserted through a large piece of meat or a bird such as a chicken, then set to turning in an oven or over a fire to roast the meat

spring constant: a characteristic factor of a particular spring that determines the expansion or contraction of the spring when displaced by a specific force

spring energy: the energy contained in a spring that has been either extended or depressed away from its normal position

square: an enclosed figure formed by the intersection of four lines forming four right angles on the interior of the figure

standard temperature and pressure: standard reference conditions when dealing with gases, defined by the International Union of Pure and Applied Chemistry as a temperature of 27315 kelvins (0 degrees Celsius or 32 degrees Fahrenheit) and pressure of 1013 kilopascals (1 atmosphere); used in chemistry and physics to establish a standardized set of conditions for experimentation

superheated steam: steam that has been heated above its boiling temperature Steam at atmospheric pressure and a temperature above 212 degrees Fahrenheit is superheated

superheater: part of a boiler that superheats steam; steam flows inside of superheater tubes while hot combustion gases flow around the outside of these tubes and heat is transferred from the combustion gas to the steam

surface tension: the property of a liquid to adhere to capillary surfaces

static equilibrium: the state of an object such as a building that is not in motion or that is acted upon by no unbalanced forces

static friction: the force that resists one surface sliding over another when the two surfaces are not moving

static system: system that is without movement or activity and in which all parts are organized in an ordered series of relationships

statistics: collections of specified data points used as the basis for probability calculations; e.g., the outcomes of a number of rolls of a standard cubic die

steam-winding engine: a small steam engine used to operate the lifts in coal mines in Trevithick's time

strain: the response of a material to forces perpendicular to the stress in the material

streamline: during uniform flow, the line defined by the motion of a small fluid element; streamlines are perpendicular to potential lines

streamlining: the designed or evolved reduction of drag by making a vehicle or animal's main body and other structures less turbulence-producing

stress: the response of a material to forces of compression and elongation (stretching)

stress distribution: the load carried at various points along the length of a beam or other construction member

subsonic flight: flight in which aircraft speeds are below that of sound (Mach 1)

sunspot: a dark circular area observed on the surface of the sun, determined to be a relatively cool region formed by the sun's magnetic activity

supersonic flight: flight in which airspeeds are above Mach 1 but not at hypersonic speeds

synthetic geometry: the method of solving mathematical problems through the use of geometric relationships such as inscribed polygons to construct or synthesize a solution

system: collection of individual components interconnected in a way that performs a particular function

system elements: the individual components that work together and make up an overall system used to complete a task

system input: a force, such as voltage or torque, applied to a system

system output: the work that the system performs

tangent: a straight line external to a curve that touches the curve at one point only

telemetry: the process of transmitting measurement data via radio to operators on the ground; used to improve spaceflight performance and accuracy by providing important information about standard operational health and status of a craft as well as mission-specific payload data

teleoperation: operation of a robotic device remotely by use of a wired or wireless communication connection

temperature reservoir: a contained mass of matter that can store heat, such as hot water that has condensed from steam and may then be used to regenerate steam without a large input of energy from an external source

temporary particles: subatomic particles such as electrons and protons that seem to appear out of nothingness in a high vacuum

tensile strength: the extent to which a material is able to resist forces acting in opposite directions without deformation and failure; a flywheel rotating at such a rate that the centrifugal force exceeds the centripetal force will fail and fly apart

tension: the pulling force exerted longitudinally from the ends of a rope, wire, rod, or other object

terminal point: the final or end point of a vector; it is the end at which the head or arrow of the vector is affixed

terminal velocity: the velocity at which the acceleration due to gravity of an object falling freely through a fluid medium, such as air or water, is exactly balanced by the deceleration of the object due to resistance from that medium

Tesla effect: the wireless transmission of electrical energy through the natural conductivity in the environment

theorem: a property or relationship that can be logically derived from an axiom and/or a previously established theorem

thermal control: the system aboard a spacecraft that controls the temperature of various components to ensure safety and accuracy during a mission

thermal efficiency: the ratio of the work performed by a system relative to the heat energy that is supplied to the system

thermodynamics: the study of the interaction of heat and energy with matter; the science of the movement of heat energy

three-body problem: in celestial mechanics, refers to the gravitational and orbital relationship between Earth, moon and sun; generalized to any situation in which three individual entities rotate about a common central point

thrust: the force provided by propeller-driven engines or jet engines of an aircraft; it enables forward aircraft motion

tidal evolution: the change in the rise and fall of an ocean caused by the gravitational force of a nearby celestial object

time dilation: the slowing of time for a moving object relative to an object that is not moving

tolerance: the allowable difference in the dimensions of a manufactured piece from the dimensions specified in the design of the piece

toroid: a doughnut-shaped circular core about which is wrapped a continuous wire coil carrying an electrical current

torque: the tendency of a force to cause an object to rotate, defined mathematically as the rate of change of the object's angular momentum; also called moment of force; a twisting force that produces rotational motion

total mechanical energy: the sum of all the kinetic and potential energies of an object in a closed system

tracking and commanding: tracking takes account of a craft's position in relation to the ground base with transponders, radar, or other systems while commanding refers to the ground station sending signals to a craft to change settings such as ascent and orbit paths

traction: the ability to move according to the amount of friction between the wheel and the rail of a railway, or between the soles of the feet and the ground, etc.

traction engine: an electrical motor that drives a wheel or wheels on a train engine thus using the traction between wheel and rail to move the train along the tracks

translation: refers to a physical mass moving from one point to another, either linearly or on a curved path

transportation engineer: a structural engineer who specializes in the design and construction of roads, streets and highways

treadmill: a wheel driven from within by the walking motion of a person or an animal, used as a means of transferring mechanical energy to do work

trebuchet: a device that uses the mass of a suspended counterweight acting upon a lever from which a payload is suspended to impart momentum to its payload when the mass is dropped

triangle: an enclosed figure formed by the intersection of three lines forming three angles on the interior of the figure

trough: the lowest point of a wave from its neutral value; the lowest point in the height of a sinusoidal wave

true vacuum: the condition in which the number of molecules or atoms of gases that exist within a defined space is effectively zero

turbine: machine that converts the energy of high-pressure, high-temperature steam into mechanical energy to drive an electric generator or ship's propeller

turbulence: nonlaminar flow, characterized by chaotic motion within the fluid, as the flowing motion of particles making up the fluid is disrupted and forced to flow in nonparallel paths, or "lamina"

turns: the number of times that a conductor is wrapped around to form a helical coil; the magnetic field of a solenoid is directly dependant on the product of the turn density (N), permeability (μ), and current running through the solenoid (I); because turn density is a ratio of the number of turns (n) per length of coil (L), the magnetic field of a solenoid will increase with an increase in the number of turns and will decrease as the length of the coil increases

turnspit: a mechanism that uses a driving force such as wind or a treadmill to drive the rotation of a spit for the roasting of meat, an early version of the modern rotisserie

two-cycle engine: an engine that requires only two complete revolutions of its crankshaft for the complete cycle of its operation

type 1 lever system: a lever system in which the fulcrum is positioned between the load and the operator (like a seesaw)

type 2 lever system: a lever system in which the load is positioned between the fulcrum and the operator (like a wheelbarrow)

type 3 lever system: the operator is in the middle between the fulcrum and the load

ultracentrifuge: a centrifuge that is used to spin materials at rates of 25,000 rpm and more, allowing separation of materials of similar density

ultrasonic: vibrations having a frequency of 25,000 Hertz and greater

unaccelerated: experiencing no effect from an external force

uncertainty principle: the idea, proposed by Werner Heisenberg, that one can determine with high precision either the position of a particle at a given time or its momentum, but not both

universal gravitation: the concept and quantification of the gravity experienced as a force of attraction

unreinforced masonry (URM): materials not constructed with reinforced steel (for example, bricks, hollow clay tile, adobe, concrete blocks, and stone)

unstable: state of a system marked by sensitivity to minor changes in a variety of variables that cause major changes in system behavior

vacuum pump: a gas pumping system designed to extract air and other gases from an enclosed system

valve: portion of a system designed to manipulate the gas quantity, distribution, and delivery regularly and precisely

vector: a quantity that has direction as well as magnitude

vector quantities: quantities that have both a magnitude or absolute value and are associated with a direction; e.g., 23 kilometers per hour northwest

velocity: the rate of change of the position of a body, measured in terms of distance per unit time (e.g., meters per second) and associated with a specific direction

vertex: the uppermost point in a ballistic trajectory

vibration: refers to a mass oscillating between two points with an appropriate frequency

viscosity: the internal friction of a fluid that acts as a force to inhibit flow; can be classified as either absolute or kinematic; the measure of a fluid's resistance to shearing forces, that is, those forces that deform it, measured in kilograms per meters times seconds; the temperature-dependent property relating the ability of different fluids to flow

voltage: the difference in electrical potential between two separate points

volume: the amount of three-dimensional space enclosed within a given region or shape of specific dimensions

warp: the threads placed lengthwise on a loom for weaving

water displacement: the principle by which an object of a particular mass will displace a volume of water equal to the object's mass, due to the fact that water has a specific gravity of 1 gram per cubic centimeter

water molecule: familiar as H_2O, the two hydrogen atoms and the oxygen form an angle of 1095° between their bonds, which concentrates the positive charge character of the H atoms opposite the negative charge of the lone pairs of electrons on the O atom, rendering the molecule highly polar such that it can act much like a small magnet

water organ: a mechanical device that forces water into a chamber to pressurize the air above, the pressurized air then being directed into a system of tubes to produce sound

water system engineer: a structural engineer who specializes in the design and construction of infrastructure for the delivery of freshwater, the removal of wastewater, and the redirection or control of water flows

wave function: a function that describes the quantum state of a system and represents the probability of finding the system in a given state at a given time

wave-particle duality: the characteristic of light that allows it to act as a stream of particles and as electromagnetic waves

wave theory of light: the theory that light propagates through a medium as though it consists of waves, thus exhibiting the phenomena of refraction and diffraction; in the early 20th century experiments demonstrated that light also has the character of streams of particles, termed wave-particle duality

wavelength: in any wave system, the distance from one point in a wave to the equivalent point in the next wave, typically measured between successive peak values

weft: the threads placed crosswise on a loom for weaving

weight: the apparent quality of mass under the influence of a gravitational field

work: measured in joules; the pressure exerted on the surroundings (container) of a system multiplied by the change in volume of the system; also, a force moving an object, or the energy transferred to an object by a force, calculated by multiplying the force applied to an object by the distance it has moved the object or the amount of resistance it has overcome

yield point: The stress at which the material passes from elastic behavior into plasticity

Young's modulus: a measure of the rigidity or stiffness of a material

Organizations

American Association of Engineering Societies
1801 Alexander Bell Dr.
Reston, VA 20191
info@aaes.org

American Association of Physicists in Medicine
1631 Prince St.
Alexandria, VA 22314-2818
571-298-1300
aapm.org

American Astronomical Society
1667 K Street NW
Suite 800
Washington, DC 20006
202-328-2010
aas@aas.org

American Indian Science and Engineering Society
6321 Riverside Plaza Lane NW
Unit A
Albuquerque, NM 87120
505-765-1052
aises.org

American Institute of Aeronautics and Astronautics
12700 Sunrise Valley Drive
Suite 200
Reston, VA 20191-5807
800-639-2422
aiaa.org

American Institute of Physics
1 Physics Ellipse
College Park, MD 20740
301-209-3100
aip.org

American Society for Engineering Education
1818 N Street NW
Suite 600
Washington, DC 2006
202-949-6726
www.asee.org

American Society of Civil Engineers
800-548-2723
asce.org

American Society of Mechanical Engineers
Two Park Avenue
New York, NY 10016-5990
800-843-2763
asme.org

American Vacuum Society
125 Maiden Lane, 15B
15th Floor
New York, NY 10038
212-248-0200
avs.org

Institute of Electrical and Electronics Engineers
445 and 501 Hoes Lane
Piscataway, NJ 08854-4141
732-981-0060
ieee.org

Institute of Industrial and Systems Engineers
3577 Parkway Lane
Suite 200
Norcross, GA 30092
770-449-0460
iise.org

Institute of Physics
37 Caledonian Road
London N1 9BU UK
education@iop.org

National Society of Black Physicists
3033 Wilson Boulevard
Suite 700
Arlington, VA 22201
703-647-4176
nsbp.org

National Society of Hispanic Physicists
hispanicphysicists.org

National Society of Professional Engineers
1420 King St.
Alexandria, VA 22314
888-285-6773
nspe.org

Society of Physics Students
1 Physics Ellipse
College Park, MD 20740

301-209-3007
spsnational.org

Society of Women Engineers
1630 East Randolph Street
Suite 3500
Chicago, IL 60601
312-596-5223
swe.org

Subject Index

The Principles of... Series

Principles of Science

SALEM PRESS   https://salempress.com   (800) 221-1592

The Principles of... Series

Principles of Health
Principles of Health: Allergies & Immune Disorders
Principles of Health: Anxiety & Stress
Principles of Health: Depression
Principles of Health: Diabetes
Principles of Health: Nursing
Principles of Health: Obesity
Principles of Health: Pain Management
Principles of Health: Prescription Drug Abuse

Principles of Business
Principles of Business: Accounting
Principles of Business: Economics
Principles of Business: Entrepreneurship
Principles of Business: Finance
Principles of Business: Globalization
Principles of Business: Leadership
Principles of Business: Management
Principles of Business: Marketing

Principles of Sociology
Principles of Sociology: Group Relationships & Behavior
Principles of Sociology: Personal Relationships & Behavior
Principles of Sociology: Societal Issues & Behavior